THE PIONEERS OF MASSACHUSETTS

A DESCRIPTIVE LIST
Drawn from Records of the
Colonies, Towns, and Churches, and
Other Contemporaneous Documents

Charles Henry Pope

PASTOR FIRST CHURCH, CHARLESTOWN, BOSTON,
COMPILER OF THE DORCHESTER POPE FAMILY, THE CHENEY GENEALOGY, ETC.

HERITAGE BOOKS
2007

HERITAGE BOOKS
AN IMPRINT OF HERITAGE BOOKS, INC.

Books, CDs, and more—Worldwide

For our listing of thousands of titles see our website
at
www.HeritageBooks.com

A Facsimile Reprint
Published 2007 by
HERITAGE BOOKS, INC.
Publishing Division
65 East Main Street
Westminster, Maryland 21157-5026

Originally published 1900

— Publisher's Notice —
In reprints such as this, it is often not possible to remove blemishes from the original. We feel the contents of this book warrant its reissue despite these blemishes and hope you will agree and read it with pleasure.

International Standard Book Number: 978-1-55613-398-5

INTRODUCTION.

The Pioneers of Massachusetts deserve high honor from the people of the United States of America. They composed and signed, in the cabin of the Mayflower, Nov. 11, 1620, the grand though simple "Compact," model of all our constitutions; they organized General Courts, patterns of our legislative bodies; courts of judicature and commissions for the settlement of minor cases,—"to end small causes,"—types of our municipal and justices' courts; they gathered congregational bodies of worshippers, embodiments and types of our best, fraternal, religious life; they crystalized the old Saxon town idea into systematic town meetings; they first subscribed to support schools for their children, then devised the scheme of bearing the burden by general taxation, making schools by the people, for the people. And they and their descendants went forth to settle other parts of the great land, and built the foundation of new states out of granite, quarried from Massachusetts ledges. Thus it is the "Commonwealth of Massachusetts" where the largest number of American families had their first home this side of the Atlantic; and to her records and relics come yearly the largest processions of pilgrims, seeking to obtain clues to the still earlier history of their ancestry. Love of family and desire to know and preserve the memory of worthy fore-fathers lead many inquirers into this field. The admirable organizations which keep alive the memory of the Mayflower passengers, which place fresh laurels on the graves of colonial worthies and warriors, which pay honor to the guardians of a country in the face of foreign oppression, the founders of our republican institutions—these societies have deepened the interest and greatly advanced the knowledge of our ancestors.

Thus an increasing amount of examination of old records is made; and the courteous town and church clerks, recorders of deeds and wills, custodians of filed documents in court houses and the office of the Secretary of the Commonwealth, have abundant opportunity for the display of that remarkable affability and helpfulness which characterize the officials of our state.

Numerous family histories and sketches of the founders have appeared, some of which are models of research and honesty; what a fine list that is which Munsell's Sons present in their American Genealogist! Other books are in preparation and much investigation and compilation is being done for simple, private satisfaction.

But the work of historical research is an art; records, ever so accessible, need skilled readers and interpreters. Apparatus is demanded for the work; charts are needed for the chart-makers.

John Farmer, M.A., having explored to the best of his ability a part of the early records, published in 1628 "A Genealogical Register of the First Settlers of New England," which had great value, and marked him as a benefactor of American students of history. Dr. James Savage constructed a treatise on somewhat different lines, and issued in

1858 his "Genealogical Dictionary of New England." In this four-volume work he undertook to present the chief points of interest in the life of every settler of each of the New England states from the settlement of Plymouth to the close of the century; and to trace out each family through four generations. How well he succeeded in this vast enterprise, how much information he amassed and presented may be told by any genealogist of experience. The scheme was Titanic; the service rendered was Herculean; the name of Dr. Savage deserves high renown. But full success in such a vast undertaking was at that date simply impossible; and searchers find at the close of each volume an alarming list of errata, discovered by the author while the printers were doing their work; and the rolling years have added astonishingly to the list. Had Dr. Savage lived he would have issued a corrected edition, no doubt.

But, meantime, by the liberality of the Athens of America and some lesser cities and towns, a good number of ancient town and church records have been copied with minute care and printed verbatim; the annals of both colonies have been made accessible in this way; and Suffolk county has set a fine example by its publication of almost a dozen volumes of deeds. The state has issued Bradford's History; the notarial records of Lechford and Aspinwall have been brought out; these three volumes illuminating the period of the Pioneers remarkably.

The Mass. Historical Society, the Historic-Genealogical Society, Essex Institute, and other organizations have fixed in type many documents which the tooth of time had begun to gnaw; and the task of the searcher has been wonderfully lightened. These printed books and papers, however, contain only a small minority of the records essential to the making of such a work as Farmer and Savage designed; but they make the difference between an impossible and a practicable undertaking.

The present writer conceived, quite a number of years since, the plan of making a revised edition of Dr. Savage's magnificent work. This scheme was revolved and discussed with gentlemen of wide acquaintance with the subject. At last this conclusion was reached: no man can to-day construct a trustworthy compendium of so many families and so many generations as Dr. Savage attempted. The problem must be separated into parts; *divide et impera.*

THE PRESENT WORK

narrows the field to the single state of Massachusetts, as bounded to-day; restricts the genealogy to the first settlers and their children only; and confines the study still further to those persons who came here early enough to be foundation-layers, first fellers of the primeval forests, first ploughers of the virgin soil, first makers of homes in the new counery, first worshippers in the log meetinghouses, first freeman and officers in the plantations and colonies. What were these but "pioneers," whose bravery, earnestness, fidelity, love, made them worthy to be enrolled by themselves, an honorable list of heroes and heroines. All who came after the year 1650 found Massachusetts a reality, a single state, practically, although under two fraternal colonial governments; all who came before that date helped essentially to make it. Although their jurisdiction extended over a wider field than the present state limits, there seems to the writer a propriety in restricting this volume in this way.

Later volumes by this or some other hand may present the Pioneers of Maine, New Hampshire, Rhode Island and Connecticut for that early period, with all the light now thrown on their monuments. This list is large enough for one volume, grand enough for the citizens of one state to call its very own.

The limit of the "pioneer" period is an open question. It might be fixed by the statement of Winthrop in his History.

"2 (4) 1641.
The parliament of England setting upon a general reformation, both of church and state . . . this caused all men to stay in England in expectation of a new world, so as few came to us."

Although "few" arrived after 1641, yet the records show occasional additions; and a man did not always buy or receive an allotment of land or join the church or do anything which was noted in public records for several years after his arrival. Accordingly the limit has been fixed at 1650, to include all who came before the beginning of that "reformation" which Winthrop counted so significant, and to allow for the full development of the state in its life here and its significance abroad.

The names here given are *all* which have been found in the journals and lists of the colonies, towns, churches and counties of the period, 1620-1650, inclusive, as well as those perpetuated in the passenger-lists of that time which have survived to our day. When once a name has been found within that period, it has been followed to the last day of the pioneer's life; in a few cases this has extended to the second or third decade of the following century. This has necessitated the scrutiny of the documents until 1720 for record of deaths and probate proceedings.

While the names, dates and facts here stated have been taken by the compiler from the original documents or from such copies of them as have been made and verified by the highest authority, references are often given to pages in the Historic-Genealogical Register or other publications where copies or abstracts of the same may be seen. This is particularly noteworthy in the case of the exceedingly valuable notes of English wills, made by Henry F. Waters, A.M., and the abstracts of Suffolk Co. wills by William B. Trask, A.M.

The original words and phrases are quoted generally. Only in very rare instances has the compiler ventured to introduce an opinion of his own, preferring to put the reader in possession of the materials out of which an individual opinion may be formed. If you had the books before you and could read the peculiar chirography; if you critically studied the words employed, and tested your impressions by comparing one document with another; if you brought years of practise in this sort of reading to bear on the documents,—you would write down in your book the very things which are here presented.

This volume represents the relative amount of matter which exists to-day about these people. Not that all is copied; far from it. But this is a characterizing list; this is sufficient to rank the pioneers for inspection. A full copy of every original line about them would not change materially the impression here given.

THE PURITAN PILGRIMS OF MASSACHUSETTS.

Governor William Bradford, who is the highest authority on the subject, tells us that the persons who came to Plymouth were called Puritans; that their English neighbors opprobriously & most injuriously imposed upon them that name of Puritans which it is said the Novatians out of prid did assume & take unto themselves." The colonists of Massachusetts Bay were chiefly Puritans, also; the most perfect understanding existing between the religious leaders of the two colonies in most respects.

The nucleus of the colony of Plymouth, every one knows, was the little band of men and women who met in apostolic fashion in a private house at Scrooby, Nottinghamshire, on the flat banks of the Idle; whence they removed in 1607-8 to Leyden, Holland, and then came toward the sunset, full of faith in a coming day. The germ of the colony of Massachusetts Bay was a company of business men who met at London, planning for a settlement wherein should dwell righteousness and profit. But Dorchester was founded by a church as definitely organized as that of Scrooby, and brought its two ministers, chosen in Plymouth, Eng., in 1629.

Rev. John Cotton, in 1629, accompanied some of his parishioners from their home in old Boston to Southampton, whence they were to sail for New England, and charged them to "take advice of them of Plymouth and do nothing to offend them." When Salem and Charlestown churches were organized the brethren of Plymouth church were consulted and similar statements of faith and polity adopted.

Bradford says: "Rev. Mr. Warham of the church in Dorchester expressed a desire to one of Plymouth Church in 1630, to be on friendly terms with that church and people, and he declared himself satisfied with their ecclesiastical government and proceedings."

Thomas Holland of Yarmouth was "still a member of a separated church in Old England" in 1641, when his babe was baptized at Barnstable. Michael Metcalf of Dedham left on record an account of the persecutions he had endured at Norwich, Eng., for his puritanic life. Governor John Winthrop wrote honeyed words of farewell to the Church of England, and straightway joined in founding a *separate church* under the Charlestown oak. Robert Massall was dismissed from Boston church "to the church of Christ at Dover in England" in 1646, and John Westgate to "the church of Pulham Mary in Norfolk, Eng.," in 1674; and Mrs. Lydia Banks, a resident of Salem from 1636 to 1642, was dismissed "to a church at London of which Mr. Nye is pastor," at her request, 6 (9) 1664. Mr. Johnson was received to the church of Charlestown 29 (5) 1660, "by dismission from a church of Christ at Canterbury in Old England." Mrs. Elizabeth Conant's child was baptized at Salem 12 (11) 1662, "upon ye letter from ye church at Corke testifying of her membership there."

These and many other evidences prove the identity of the people of both these colonies with the grand Puritan host of England, described so admirably by Macaulay in his Essay on Milton; who, whether remaining in the organization of the church of England or refusing to conform to ceremonies they believed anti-christian, were one in pure faith and life, one in resolute attempts to carry the doctrines of the Fatherhood of God and the Brotherhood of Man into all departments of religious and secular life. The term Bradford abhorred was really a good, discriminating title, and it has passed into history. It is not correct, therefore, to call the people of one of the colonies "Pilgrims" and those of the other "Puritans," for both were Puritans in the fact of a holy determination to avoid every impure, degrading fashion and to live by the standards of the Revealed Word of God; and both were Pilgrims in the fact of making a journey from a high religious motive.

These people, however, were not perfect, and they learned slowly the art of giving and taking liberty. The annals of that early period are full of strife; our ancestors brought over many an old notion of intolerance and persecution, which they were sufficiently "conforming" to practice; it took long years for Puritanism to escape from those toils; but by and by came the real fruits of the system. In some cases a person is said to have been "in court" when the whole cause was the harsh method employed by the government in attempting to guard what seemed to the rulers the essential elements of pure religion and good government. The *severe* legislation of the Puritans was simply imitation of English and continental methods. The cruelties of the Middle ages lingered in statute books on the other side of the Atlantic longer than they did here. Puritanism actually softened the laws, increased the protection of the weak; and it was here, where the Bible was widely opened and Jesus Christ was acknowledged absolute King, that political and religious liberty and fraternity first found complete expression.

One exceedingly valuable feature of this compilation is the presentation of the occupations, estates and social standing of the Pioneers. The summary of these, given on another page, is well worth studying.

The number who took to themselves the designation "gentleman," or had it attached to their names by the writers of passenger-lists, deeds, wills, church, town or court lists, is not very large; in some cases the title was used when a person had been in public office here, and was given by recorders, without reference to social standing in England. With very few exceptions, however, those noted as of "gentle" blood were entitled to use coats of arms and crests. Probably quite a number more had this dignity at home, but did not so appear on New England records. But the great majority of the pioneers were the plain, untitled *people*, bred to industry and economy, trained to professions, merchandise, trades, husbandry or service. Those who came of noble families were often apprenticed in childhood to learn some trade, or to do house work; and persons who were employed, even in positions of trust and dignity, bore the title "servant" like humble menials. They were educated beyond the average of English people of their time, and their habits were cleaner, more virtuous than the majority of their old associates. And thus they had the stuff and force as well as the faith and patience for the enterprise which made such drafts on body, mind and character as the laying of the foundations of a commonwealth.

The writer wishes to acknowledge very gratefully the privileges and aid extended to him by the clerks of the old towns and churches, registers of Probate, recorders of Deeds, and custodians of ancient books and documents. In addition to placing these treasures at his service without fees, they have shown great courtesy in arranging the most convenient desk-room, light, freedom from intrusion, and in giving assistance when desired. They have recognized the special character of the work, and united to secure its thorough and exact performance. Three summers in England have also given the writer a long list of names to whom similar acknowledgements are cheerfully rendered, for very courteous opening of ancient treasures and facilities extended; and in the city of Leyden, Holland, polite attentions and valuable privileges were also accorded.

It would be impossible to mention by name these many persons, to each of whom gratitude is felt deeply, and without whom the work could not have been accomplished.

SPECIAL DIRECTIONS FOR SEARCHERS.

1. Look for **many variations of surnames**; allow for phonetic spelling and carelessness The diphthong ea was usually pronounced a long; consonants were often doubled after **long** vowels; ph and f were interchanged recklessly; and other alterations were loosely made, such as Hayward, Heywood, Howard and Hawoorth. The indexing of such matter is therefore difficult; and one must sometimes look on several pages before discovering a desired name. Not only did public recorders vary the orthography, but a man sometimes spelled his own name in two or more ways.

2. **Always consult the index,** and there exercise the same liberal method.

3. Fail not to **guage the meaning of the Abbreviations** employed, since many lines of original record have sometimes been compressed into one, in this volume.

4. **The source** from which a particular word or statement has been drawn can be inferred in most cases from its nature; as proprietorship and town office from town records; church membership, dismission, etc., from those of the churches; purchase and sale of lands from county Records of Deeds; depositions, giving age, etc., from records or files of the Courts or Colonies; designations of trade, occupation or social position were usually given in deeds, but sometimes in records of admission to churches; wills and administrations of estates in Probate Records or those of the County or Colony. When an item was found in an unusual place, the source has been noted.

5. The **dates** are given **as** they were **recorded.** March 25 was New Year's Day in England and her colonies in the seventeenth century. It is at once a blunder and a crime to alter such dates to suit a calendar which our Forefathers did not use. Their "style" was just exactly "old style," not at all "new." From January 1 to March 25, during which some other nations used the new year number, they often wrote a double date; as "3 February, 1621-2"; but February was still "moneth 12," and even 24 March was in the old year, although the month, by anticipation of "day 25," was "moneth 1."

6. The Author will be grateful for information of any error discovered in this volume, and for facts of definite importance respecting the Pioneers recorded in either American or English documents of that period.

For list of Authorities, Table of Abbreviations, Roll of Pioneer Towns, Cross Index and Table of Occupations, Trades, and Social Position, see pp. 520 et. seq.

The Pioneers of Massachusetts.

ABBE, ABBEY, ABBEE, ABBY,
John, yeoman, Salem, propr. 1636. Ch. recorded: Rebecca, (m. 13 (3) 1667, Richard Kimball,) John b. and d. 1665, John b. 15 Dec. 1666, Thomas b. 5 (12) 1667, Joseph b. 18 Aug. [1672.] His wife Mary d. Sept. 9, 1672, and he m. Nov. 25, 1674, Mary Goldsmith.

Rem. to Wenham about 1642. He deeded land to son Samuel April 3, 1675; and gave property Aug. 3, 1683, to son John in trust, to care for himself and wife the rest of their lives, and to pay bequests to his other children, viz. Samuel, Sarah, Marah, Rebecca, Obediah and Thomas. [Es. Prob. 307, 451.]

ABBOT, ABBOTT, ABBETT, ABBITT,
Daniel, Cambridge, propr., frm. May 18, 1631. Rem. to Providence before 4 (4) 1639. [Col. Rec.]

Edward, Taunton, atba. 1643.

George, Rowley, propr. 1643. Son George b. about 1630. [Depos.] The Gen. Court referred his will to Salem Court 11 Nov. 1647. Inv. taken 30 Aug. 1649; house, land, etc.; some lands at Newbury; 30 books; household effects. We learn of his family from the folg.: his son Thomas A. of Rowley, made will 5 (7), prob. 27 (7) 1659; beq. to wife Dorothy, father-in-law Richard Swan, bros. George, Nehemiah and Thomas A. [Ipswich De.] George, of Andover, Nehemiah, of Ipsw. and Thomas, of Concord, sold, 25 Nov. 1659, land at Rowl. formerly belonging to their father George A., dec., subject to life of widow Dorothy A.

George, Sen. Andover, propr. 1643. He testified in Joseph Parker's suit in Mdx. Court, 17 (4) 1673, ae. about 60 years. He

ABBOT, etc., cont.
m. at Roxbury, Dec. 12, 1646, Hannah, dau. of William and Annis Chandler. Ch. John, Joseph b. March 11, 1649, d. 24 June, 1650, Hannah b. June 9, 1650, Joseph b. March 30, 1652, George b. June 7, 1655, William b. Nov. 18, 1657, Sarah b. Nov. 14, 1659, Benjamin b. Dec. 20, 1661, Timothy b. Nov. 17, 1663, Thomas b. May 6, 1666, Nathaniel b. July 4, 1671, Elizabeth b. Jan. 29, 1673-4.

Will dated 12 Dec. 1681, prob. at Ips. 28 March, 1682; beq. to wife Hannah; to eldest son John; other ch. to inherit at death of wife. Bros. Thomas and William Chandler overseers. [Compare with Genealogy and Es. Ant. 1, 35.]

John, accidentally shot at Concord in 1636 by Matthew Bridge. [W.] Probably the person who came, ae. 16, in the Hopewell in 1635, with Marie, ae. 16.

Robert, Watertown, propr., frm. Sept. 3, 1634. Rem. to Wethersfield, Conn.

ABDA, ABDY,
Matthew, ae. 15, came in the Abigail in July, 1635; settled at Boston; fisherman. Wife Tabitha, dau. of Robert Reynolds, d. in 1661. He m. 2, Alice Cox, May 24, 1662; ch. Mary b. May 24, 1648, Tabitha b. 24 Nov. 1652.

ABEL, ABELL,
Robert, Weymouth, frm. May 18, 1631; propr. 1643. Wife Joanna; ch. Abraham bur. 14 (9) 1639, Mary b. 11 (2) 1642. Rem. to Rehoboth; propr. 1643; lic. to keep an ordinary, 1656.

Inv. of his est. taken 9 Aug. 1663; admin. gr. to widow Joanna. House and lands

ABEL, etc., cont.
given to eldest son; a cow and calf to dau. Mary; the widow to have her thirds; rest to the other five children.

ACEY, ACY, ASEY,
William, Rowley, propr. 1643; town officer. Wife Margaret. He made an agreement 21 (2) 1675, with son John and dau. Mary, wife of Charles Brown, concerning his est.
Will dated 22 April, 1689, being very aged; prob. 30 Sept. 1690; gr. ch. John Brown, of Rowl., Nathaniel and Ebenezer B.; son John A.'s 3 daus. Elizabeth, Hannah and Margaret.

ADAMS,
Alexander, shipwright, Boston, bought house in 1645, adm. chh. 31 (3) 1646; frm. May 10, 1648. With wife Mary, dism. to Chh. of Dorchester for a season 23 (10) 1647. Ch. Mary b. 9 (11) 1645, Susanna, b. 14 (3) 1648, Martha bapt. 27 (5) 1650, John b. 26 Feb. 1652, Samuel b. 7 May, 1656, Susanna b. July 21, 1658, *Elizabeth* bapt. 25 (5) 1658, Elizabeth b. Oct. 1, 1660.
Admin. gr. Feb. 28, 1677-8 to his widow Mary.

Ferdinando, shoemaker, Dedham, propr. 1637, adm. chh. 25 (11) 1639; frm. May 13, 1640. Wife, Ann adm. chh. in 1639; ch. Abigail b. 45 (7) 1639, Bethia b. 10 (4) 1640, Nathaniel b. 16 (1) 1642. He went to England 3 (6) 1641, and his wife followed in 1642. [Chh. Rec.] He res. in St. Katharine's in 1653, when his agent sold lands in Dedham.

George, glover, Watertown, 1645, propr. at Nashaway or Lancaster in 1647; sold land in Wat. Nov. 4, 1664. Rem. to Cambridge.
Wife, Frances; ch. John b. 16 (8) 1645, Joseph b. March 6, 1657; other ch. George, and Mary.
He d. Oct. 10, 1696. Admin. on his est. was gr. to the widow Frances Oct. 28.

Henry, Sen., Braintree, had land grant at Mr. Wollaston 24 (12) 1639-40, 40 acres for 10 heads. Signed petition about meadows in 1646. [Arch. 45.]
He was bur. 8 (8) 1646. Nunc. will prob. 8 (4) 1647, on testimony of Benjamin Allbe and Richard Brackett. Inv. filed. Beq. to wife; to sons Peter, John, Joseph, Edward

ADAMS, cont.
and Samuel, and dau. Ursula. House and lands, etc. Books to be divided among his children. Money due to son Samuel for ground bought of him; part of his land to return to the town. John (probably this son), depos. at Cambridge 7 (8) 1656, ae. about 35 years. [Mdx. Files.] Samuel m. Mary Eaglesfield, q. v. [Henry, town clerk, lieut., owner of a mill afterwards at Medfield, who m. Elizabeth, dau. of Moses Paine, is believed to have been another son of Henry, Sen.; but the writer has found no proof of this nor any trace of the origin of the family, in any contemporaneous document.]

Jeremy, Cambridge, propr. 1633, frm. May 6, 1635.

John, Plymouth, came in the Fortune in 1621; frm. 1632. Wife Eleanor and son James recd. shares of cattle in 1627.
He d. in 1633; inv. of his est. taken Oct. 24, 1633. Ch. James, John and Susan. The widow m. 2, in June, 1634, Kenelm Winslow, who paid her son John his portion 26 Dec. 1651. She was bur. Dec. 5, 1681, ae. 83. [Reg. XXXIII, 410.]

John, Salem left his master Thorndike in 1636. [Court Rec.]

Nathaniel, dish-turner, Weymouth, frm. May 26, 1647; town officer. He rem. to Boston; bought house and land about 1651. Town officer; had large estate. Wife Sarah; ch. Abraham b. 16 (11) 1641. He deposed about 2 (2) 1661, ae. about 60 years, concerning a bargain made in 1657. [Mdx. Files.]
He made will 14 July, 1675; "aged;" prob. 1 (9) folg.; beq. to wife Sarah, sons Nathaniel, David, Abraham, Jonathan, Isaac (if yet alive and shall return to Boston); to David's ch. Sarah and David; to Mary Tinwell. The widow's will, dated Oct. 16, 1684, prob. 14 May, 1685. The son Nathaniel depos., 1681, ae. about 50 years.

Richard, ae. 29, with Susan, ae. 26, came in the Abigail June 26, 1635, cert. from Northampton, Eng. Settled at Salem. Frm. Sept. 2, 1635. Deputy, town officer. Bought land, 1646. Wife Elizabeth d. at Malden (9) 1656.

Richard, ae. 29, servant to Wm. Read of Batcome, Eng., tailor, came from Weymouth, Eng. before March 20, 1635, with wife Mary, ae. 26, and ch. Mary, ae. 1. Set-

ADAMS, cont.
tled at Weymouth. Com. for Gen. Court 6 (7) 1638. Excused from bearing arms on account of age 20 (4) 1665. [Mdx. Files.] Ch. Sarah b. 3 (5) 1637, Samuel b. 6 (4) 1639, Ruth b. 3 (4) 1642.

Robert, yeoman, tailor, Salem, propr. 1638; employed to "ring" the swine in 1646. Rem. to Newbury about 1649. Wife Eleanor d. June 12, 1677. He m. 2, Feb. 6, 1678, Sarah, widow of Henry Short. Ch. John, Joanna, (m. Launcelot Granger,) Abraham, Elizabeth, (m. Edward Phelps,) Mary, (m. Jeremiah Goodridge,) Isaac, Jacob b. and d. 1649, Hannah b. 25 June, 1650, (m. William Warham,) Jacob b. 13 Sept. 1651, Jacob b. April 14, 1654, Archelaus. Joanna, ae. 17, and Abraham, ae. 10, depos. in 1651.

He d. 12 Oct. 1682, ae. 81. Will dated 7 March, 1680, and 27 June, 1682, prob. 28 (9) folg.; beq. to wife Sarah, sons John, Isaac, Jacob, Abraham, and daus. Hannah A., Elizabeth Phelps, Joanna Granger, Mary Goodridge; to several of their ch. and to Mary, Abraham's wife. The widow d. 24 Oct. 1697.

Thomas, Cambridge, propr. 1639. Rem. to Braintree; propr. also at Weymouth, 1643. Rem. to Concord; sold house and land, lately called that of John A., 1 Jan. 1654. Rem. to Chelmsford. Wife Mary; ch. Jonathan and Pelatiah b. 6 (1) 1646, Timothy b. 15 (2) 1648, George b. 29 (3) 1650.

His will, dated March 28, 1688, prob. Oct. 7, 1690, beq. to wife Mary, sons Pelatiah, Jonathan, Timothy, Samuel, and dau. Cooper. Inv. taken 11 Aug. 1688.

William, ae. 15, came in the Elizabeth and Ann in May, 1635. Settled at Cambridge; planter; propr. 1636; frm. May 22, 1638. Rem. to Ipswich. Memb. grand jury, 1642. He made exchange of land about 1651, as his son Lieut. John testified March 29, 1692, being about 60 years old; mentioning his bro. William, and the latter's ch. William, Simon and John.

William, b. May 27, 1650, who was ord. minister at Dedham in 1673, is doubtless the grandson here mentioned. His diary is printed in Mass. Hist. Coll. 4-1.

ADDINGTON,
Isaac, surgeon, merchant, Boston, adm. chh. 13 (4) 1640, frm. 22 May, 1650. He m. Anne, dau. of elder Thomas Leverett; ch.

ADDINGTON, cont.
Isaac b. 22 (11) 1644, Anne b. 10 (1) 1646, (m. 1, Samuel Mosely, 2, Nehemiah Pearce,) Rebecca bapt. 11 (1) 1649, (m. Capt. Eleazer Davenport,) Sarah b. 12 (2) 1651, d. 2 (6) 1652, Sarah b. 11, bapt. 13 (12) 1652, (m. Col. Penn Townsend).

He d. in 1652. Admin. 10 (10) 1652. [Reg. IV, 17, and VIII, 128x.]

ADDIS,
Henry, brought suit in Es. Court in 1640.

William, Gloucester; town officer, 1641. Manson of Sci. Ch. Mary, Elizabeth, Sarah, all bapt. in 2d chh. June 20, 1651, and Dart, of B.

ADFORD, ADVARD,
Henry, Scituate, Marshfield, atba. 1643, propr. 1645. He m. 6 Oct. 1643, Tamson Manson, June 29, of Sci. Ch. Mary, Elizabeth, Sarah, all bapt. in 2d chh. 1651, and Experience bapt. April 18, 1652.

He d. in 1653.

AGAR, AGER, AGUR,
William, Salem, 1636; frm. May 18, 1643. He summoned proprs. to meetings; was recorder of births, etc. Wife Alice memb. chh. before 1636. Ch. Benjamin bapt. 12 (12) 1636, Jonathan bapt. 10 (9) 1639.

Will prob. Nov. 1654; wife Alice; ch. Joseph, Jonathan, Benjamin, Abigail Kibben.

AINSWORTH, EYNSWORTH,
Anchor, shipwright, Boston, of ship Indevor, bound for Malaga, made his bro.-in-law Henry Rashley attorney for sale of land in B. 8 (7) 1645. [A.]

Daniel, Roxbury, sold land in R. 15 (12) 1648; do, Nov. 4, 1664, wife Alice consenting.

Admin. of his est. was gr. 21 Feb. 1680, to William Garey and Robert Pepper; transferred to John Gore Feb. 18, 1684, at the death of the widow Alice, for the benefit of the next of kin. The widow d. 9 Jan. 1684.

AKERS,
Thomas, mariner, Charlestown; d. in Mr. Garrett's ship in 1650.

Admin. gr. in 1660 to widow Priscilla who m. 2, William Knapp of Watertown. Ch.

AKERS, cont.

Thomas, Sarah, (m. William Mulford, of East Hampton,) Rachel, b. about 1643; (she made Anthony Waters her attorney Aug. 22, 1659, to receive portion of the estate of her bro. Thomas, who went into the wars of Ireland more than 10 years before, and had not been heard of since). [Mdx. Files.]

ALBEE, ALBYE,

Benjamin, carpenter, miller, land-surveyor, Boston, 1639, Braintree, 1640; frm. May 18, 1642. Signed peitition about meadows in 1646. [Arch. 45.] Rem. to Meadfield; selectman. Rem. to Mendon; built the first mill there. Wife, Hannah; ch. James, [John.]

ALBESON, see Nicholas.

ALBON,

Alice, ae. 25, came in the Hopewell in Sept., 1635. Sister Olbon (lately Cole), now deceased, left ch. Reuben and Elizabeth, who were bapt. at Cambridge; Reuben was in the family of John Fessenden in 1658. [Mi.]

ALCOCK, ALLCOCK,

Annis, ae. 18, came in the Abigail in July, 1635.

Francis, ae. 26, came in the Bevis in May, 1638.

Mr. George, Roxbury, came with the first company, anno 1630. [E.] Frm. May 18, 1631; deputy, deacon. His first wife, a sister of Rev. Thomas Hooker, d. in 1630. [Du.] Wife, ——; ch. John b. in Eng. about Jan. 1, 1626, (a celebrated physician;) Samuel b. April 16, 1637.

He was bur. Dec. 30, 1640. Will prob. 28 (11) 1640. Wife, sons John and Samuel, bro. Thomas of Ded., Elizabeth Blandfield, Joseph Wise, John Plimton, bros. Edward Porter, Chandler, Mr. Hooker, and Carwithy.

Thomas, Boston, memb. chh. 1630-1; dism. 8 (7) 1639 to Dedham. His sister Elizabeth Whitehead of Lemington Priors wrote him 25 (8) 1647 concerning her sons, John and Thomas W. then with Francis Hall of New Haven, who formerly lived in Buckintun parish where her uncle Darbie lived [A.] Wife, Mary; ch. Mary bapt. 8 (10) 1635, Elizabeth bapt. 10 (10) 1637, (m. 6 (3) 1656, Joseph Soper,) Sarah bapt. 5 (11) 1634, Han-

ALCOCK, etc., cont.

nah bapt. 28 (3) 1642. By wife Margery he had John b. 2 (5) 1651.

He d. 14 (7) 1657. Admin. Jan. 30, 1657. [Reg. IX, 344.]

ALDEN,

John, cooper, hired at Southampton, came in the Mayflower, signed the Compact. Frm. and councilor 1633. Town and colonial officer. Settled at Duxbury. A partner in the Trading Co. [B.] He m. Priscilla, dau. of William Mullins; ch. Elizabeth, (m. 26 Dec. 1644, William Paybodie,) and John,—both named at the division of cattle in 1627,—Joseph, David, Jonathan, Sarah, (m. Alexander Standish,) Ruth, (m. Feb. 13, 1657, John Bass,) Mary, (m. Thomas Delano). He deposed 6 July, 1682, ae. about 83 years.

His heirs gave receipt June 13, 1688, to Jonathan, admin. for their portions of his est.; John, Joseph, David, Priscilla and Mary Alden; William Paybody, Alexander Standish in right of his dec. wife Sarah, John Bass in right of his wife Ruth A., dec. and Thomas Dillano. [Gen. Adv. I, 19.]

ALDERMAN,

"One Alderman of Bear Cove (Hingham) being about fifty years old, lost his way between Dorchester and Wessaguscus," 30 Sept. 1634, but escaped without serious effects. [W.]

John, Salem, 1636; town officer; frm. May 22, 1638; juryman, 1646. Wife Jane one of the first chh. membs. recorded.

Will dated 3 (5) prob. 3 (7) 1657; beq. to Mrs. Norrice; to Mr. Elliot and the Iudians to whom he preaches; to Mr. Thatcher, Mr. Whiting, Mr. Walton and Mr. Cobat; to John Horne; house and land to go to Ezra, son of Edward, and Nathaniel, son of Nicholas Clap, who shall pay certain sums to Israel, dau. of Major Mason; to John, Elizabeth and Jonathan Pickering; to good wife and Joshua Buffam; to Edward C., the two daus. of Prudence, and the two daus. of Nicholas C. all his household stuff; to bro. Marshall, Mrs. Felton, widow Denis and goody Curtice. Edward C. exec.

ALDOUS, ALDIS, ALDHOUSE, ALDYS, ALDUS,

Nathan, yeoman, Dedham, propr. 1638, adm. chh. 11 (12) 1639. Frm. May 13, 1640.

ALDOUS, etc., cont.
Part owner of a water-mill, 1642. Deacon, town officer. Signed as witness to the will and inv. of Richard Barber in 1644. Propr. at Cambridge in 1646. His wife was adm. chh. 11 (1) 1641. Mary adm. chh. 30 (5) 1641. He d. 15 (1); admin. gr. 28 April, 1676, to widow Mary and John Aldis their son.

ALDBURGH,
John, ae. 14, came in the Francis of Ipswich April 30, 1635, with Wm. Freeborn.

ALDRIDGE, OLDRIDGE,
George, tailor, Dorchester, with wife Katharine, memb. chh. about 1636; ch. Mary bapt. in 1637, Miriam bur. 27 (11) 1639, Experience d. 2 (12) 1641. Katharine deposed 18 (4) 1670, ae. about 60 years. [Mdx. Files.] Rem. to Braintree; sold land June 9, 1663. Will dated Mendon, Nov. 2, 1682, prob. 26 April, 1683; to wife, ch. Joseph, John, Jacob, Mary, Sarah Bartlett, Mercy Randall and Martha Dunbar.

Henry, Dedham, propr. Nov. 11, 1641, adm. chh. 8 (7) 1643; frm. May, 1645. Wife, Mary; ch. Mary b. 10 (1) 1643, Thomas bapt. 17 (7) 1643, Samuel b. 10 (1) 1644. He d. 23 (12) 1645. The widow m. 2, Samuel Judson, and 3, John Hayward.

Widow, her case before Plymouth Court 5 Nov. 1638.

ALEWORTH,
Francis, [Dorchester?] Frm. May 18, 1631. Chosen lieut. to Mr. Southcoate July 5, 1631. Had liberty to ret. to Eng. Oct. 3, 1632.

ALEXANDER,
James, servant to Theodore Atkinson, d. 19 (6) 1644.

John, Plymouth Colony, punished and banished 6 Aug. 1637.

ALFORD,
Mr. William, merchant, Salem, 1635; memb. chh., contracted to build ammunition house in 1637. Rem. to Boston; rec'd to chh. 9 (2) 1654. Town officer. Wife, Mary, memb. chh. Salem, 1636; ch. Nathaniel bapt. 21 (1) 1636-7, Samuel bapt. 17 (12) 1638, Joseph bapt. 26 (4) 1642, Jonathan bapt. at B. 5 (10) 1647, ae. about 6 days. Second wife Ann. Ch. John b. Nov. 29, 1658, Jon-

ALFORD, cont.
athan b. and d. 1663. His dau. Elizabeth m. Dec. 1, 1659, Nathaniel Hudson.

He was bur. Jan. 13, 1676. [S.] Will prob. Jan. 23, 1676-7; aged; beq. to dau. Mary, wife of Hezekiah Usher, and her ch. Peter, Hannah, Samuel and Mary Butler; to Hez. U. Jr. his wife Elizabeth, and John U.; to dau. Hudson, her dau. Elizabeth, and Hudson Leveritt; to the First chh. of B.; to Peter Lidgett and his wife; to dau. Bethiah, wife of his son Elisha.

ALLEN, ALLIN, ALLEYN, ALLINE,
Bozoun, mercer, with wife and two servants, came from Lynn, Eng. in 1638, and settled at Hingham. Captain, town officer, deputy. Rem. to Boston. [See will of his bro. William in Reg. XLVI, 331, and that of his bro. Thomas in LIII, 23.]
Wife, Anne; ch. Priscilla b. Aug. 1639, Ephraim and John b. Oct. 13, 1641, Ann b. Oct. 8, 1643, Deborah b. Nov. 10, 1645, d. Feb. 1660, Isaac b. April 6, 1651, Bozoin b. Feb. 13, 1652.
He d. 14 (7) 1652. His will, dated Sept. 9, 1652, mentions his wife; ch.; sisters Elizabeth Burcham and Joanna Peck, Mr. Hubbard, his pastor, and Matthew Hawks. The inv. contains the names of 286 persons with whom he had accounts. [Reg. V, 299 and VIII, 60.] His widow m. 13 (3) 1653 Joseph Jewett of Rowley. Marriage contract in Es. files XXII, 44.

Edward, gent., merchant, Dedham, 1636, memb. chh. 1638; frm. March 13, 1638-9. Deputy; d. at Court 8 (7) 1642. Upon his death-bed gave his est. to his kinsmen, Edward A. of Bo. and John Newton of Orentun, co. Suffolk, Eng. [Suff. De. 1, 34 and 233.]

Mrs. Elizabeth, Boston, adm. chh. 24 (1) 1639; dism. to Hartford 25 (5) 1641, having become the wife of Mr. Samuel Stone.

Francis, Sandwich, atba. 1643. Note also Francis, Roxbury, was bur. 1 Dec. 1692; will dated 10 Nov. 1692, produced in court May 19, 1693; beq. to wife Hannah and children John, Mary and Francis. Widow declined to admin.

George, ae. 24, [54?] with wife Katharine, ae. 30, ch. George, ae. 16, William, ae. 8, Matthew, ae. 6, and servant Edward Poole,

ALLEN, etc., cont.

ae. 26, came from Weymouth, Eng. before March 20, 1635. Settled at Weymouth; petitioned about the ferry in 1640. [L.] Propr. frm. 3 Sept. 1639. Rem. to Sandwich; town officer, juryman. Ch. John, (of Rehoboth, ae. 80, in 1689,) Robert ("revolted from the covenant of his father," [Sand. town rec.] d. at the house of his bro. John at Reh. [Plym. Col. Rec.], Ralph, (calls William bro.) George, William, Matthew, Henry, (sells land in 1684 to bro. G. wh. had come from father G. by will,) Samuel; the folg. are not specified of George, Sen. or Jun.; Caleb b. June 27, 1648, Hester b. Dec. 8, 1648, Ebenezer b. Feb. 10, 1649.

He was bur. May 2, 1648. Will prob. 7 June, 1648, beq. to wife Katharine, sons Matthew, Henry, Samuel, William, and five least ch. [Reg. IV, 284.]

George, bricklayer, mason, Boston, 1644; frm. May, 1645. [See George, above.] Wife Susan adm. chh. 15 (12) 1651; ch. Hannah b. 10 (1) 1644, Naomi b. 26 (10) 1646, Ruth b. 3 (8) 1648; Susanna b. May 11, 1652, Elnathan b. Dec. 26, 1653.

Henry, carpenter, house-wright, Boston, memb. chh. 23 (3) 1647, frm. May 10, 1648. Propr. at Weymouth but res. at Bo. Deacon.

He m. the widow of William Tifte, and adjusted the claim of her dau. Lydia and her husband, Abraham Deeble of Haddam, Conn., after her death, 8 (3) 1673. [Suff. De. VIII, 153.] He m. Judith ——, who joined him in a deed of land 5 Jan. 1677-8.

He d. Jan. 9, 1694-5. Inv. of his est. taken 24 Feb. 1695-6, presented by widow Judith. Division made 18 July, 1701, to her and the sons Joseph, Henry and John.

James, Dedham, propr. 1638, frm. May 26, 1647. He rem. to Medfield.

He m. 16 (1) 1638 Ann Guild; ch. John b. 4 (10) 1639, Martha and Mary b. 11 (10) 1641, Sarah b. 4 (3) 1644, James b. 28 (2) 1646, Nathaniel b. 29 (6) 1648.

Will dated 23 (7) 1676, in old age; son Nathaniel, son-in-law Joseph Clarke, dau. Sarah, wife of Domingo White of Lynn, dau. Martha, wife of William Saben of Rehoboth. Prob. Jan. 30, 1676-7.

Mr. John, Dorchester, 1634. Rem. to Springfield. Witness of the Indian deed in 1636; was paid £3 for thatching the planta-

ALLEN, etc., cont.

tion house in 1638. He m. 10 (9) 1651, Mrs. Hannah Smith.

Rev. John, bapt. at Colby, co. Norfolk, Eng. May 22, 1597; Caius Coll. Cambridge, Eng., 1612, A. B. 1615, A. M. 1619. He m. at Wrentham, Eng. Oct. 22, 1622, Margaret Morse. She d. 1 (3) 1653; He m. 8 (9) 1653 Katharine, widow, in turn, of Samuel Hagborne and Governor Thomas Dudley; ch. John bapt. Oct. 24, 1623, Benjamin b. 11 (6) 1654, Daniel b. 31 (5) 1656, Eliezer b. 26 (3) 1658. Mrs. Katharine Allin d. Aug. 29, 1671.

He settled at Dedham, N. E. in 1637; was ord. pastor in 1638 and continued in office until his death, Aug. 26, 1671. "He was a man of peace and truth;" author of A Paper marking the just limitations of colonial allegiance and imperial right, 1643; and other works. See introduction to and early portion of Dedham chh. rec.

Will dated 23 (6) 1670, prob. —— 1671; beq. to near kinsmen Samuel Fisher, Thomas Fisher and Robert Allin; cousin, the widow [Caine] living at Cambridge; cousin James Allin of Medfield; sons John, Benjamin, Daniel and Eleazer; daus. Dudley and Chickerin. Wife exec. The widow made nunc. will 28 (6) 1671. To sister Negus; to dau. Hunting and her dau. Katharine; to her son [Henry] Chickerin's 2 daus.; to dau. Wade's 2 daus. and sundry other persons.

John, husbandman, ae. 30, with wife Anne, ae. 30, cert. from Herrn-hill, Kent, Eng., came in the Abigail in June, 1635. Plymouthr, propr. 1637, sold land in 1642. Rem. to Scituate; frm. 1 June, 1647, town officer, juror.

Nunc. will prob. June 2, 1663. To wife Anna and "boy" Josias Lichfield.

Mr. John, mariner. Charlestown, 1639, adm. chh. 22 (3) 1641, frm. June 2, 1641. Captain of ship Speedwell in 1666. He deposed (10) 1667, ae. about 52 years. [Mdx. Files.] Part owner of mills at Char., at Kennebeck and Pascataquack. Wife, Sarah, adm. chh. 4 (9) 1643; second wife, Mary; third wife, Sarah, d. 27 (1) 1675. Ch. John b. 16 (8) 1640, bapt. 30 (3) 1641, Sarah b. and d. 1642, Mary b. 6 (12) 1643-4, (m. Nathan Rainsford,) Elizabeth, (m. Nathan Hayman,) Rebecca, (m. John Goodrich,) Samuel b. Nov. 29, 1656, Sarah b. and d. 1659, Thomas b. 1 (6) 1667.

ALLEN, etc., cont.
He d. in 1675; will dated 1 (12) 1672-3, ae. 57 years or thereabout; beq. to wife, Sarah and ch. Samuel, Thomas, Elizabeth and Rebecca.

Matthew, son of Richard A. of Braunton, Devon., Cambridge, propr. 1633; frm. March 4, 1634-5. Deputy, comr. of the United Colonies. Rem. to Conn. With wife Margaret conveyed lands to [his brother,] Thomas Allyn of Barnstaple, Eng. 17 (10) 1638. [L.] Thomas came later to Barnstable, N. E.; see below.

Nathan owned land in Dorchester in 1650.

Nicholas, see Ellen, Nicholas.

Robert, Salem, 1636, adm. chh. 15 (3) 1642. Propr. at Teffrey's Creek 1638. Wife Sarah witness in court in 1642. Ch. John and Sarah bapt. 22 (3) 1642, Mary bapt. 19 (9) 1648. Dismissed to chh. at Norwich [Eng.?] 12 (11) 1662.

Robert, Sandwich, served against the Narrangansetts in 1645. Rem. to Yarmouth; in court in 1651.

Samuel, sawyer, Boston, Braintree, frm. May 6, 1635. [See sons of George, above.] He m. 1, Anne, who d. 29 (7) 1641. He m. 2, Margaret, widow of Edward Lamb. Ch. Joseph b. May 15, 1650, Sarah b. in Br. 30 (1) 1639.
In his will dated Aug. 2, prob. Sept. 16, 1669, he mentions wife Margaret, eldest son Joseph, other sons Samuel and James, dau. Abigail under 21, sons-in-law Josiah Standish and Nathaniel Greenwood. He d. 5 (6) 1669.

Thomas, gent, Boston, drew on his friend Mr. Roger Delbridge, merchant, Barnstable, co. Devon, 23 Sept., 1639. [L.] Thomas, gent, Dorchester, gave bonds in a suit 10 (10) 1640.

Thomas, yeoman, Barnstable, N. E., sold to John Eells of Dorch. 8 July, 1641, a house and lands in Barnstable, co. Devon, Eng. and also gave an order for money upon his brother Richard A. of the same place, yeoman. [See wills of Richard and other relations in Reg. L, 504.] Frm. Plym. Col. 3 June, 1652. With wife Winnifred sold land at Watertown in 1655. Ch. Samuel b. 1 Feb.

ALLEN, etc., cont.
1643, John bapt. Sept. 27 1646, Mehetabel bapt. Aug. 20, 1648.
Will dated 28 Feb. 1675, prob. 5 March, 1679-80; beq. to son Samuel's eldest son Thomas; to dau.-in-law Sarah, William Clarke's wife; to Martha, Benjamin's wife; to dau.-in-law Rebecca, wife of Samuel Sprague; rest to sons Samuel and John and dau. Mehetabel. Son-in-law Samuel Annible one of the execs.

Rev. Thomas, came first to Boston; adm. chh.—a student—27 (11) 1638; dism. to chh. of Charlestown 9 (4) 1639, and ordained pastor of that chh. in Feb. 1639-40. He m. Anna, widow of Rev. John Harvard, and received from the Gen. Court 500 acres of land 6 June, 1639, in regard of Mr. Harvard's gift. He m. after 1656, Joanna, widow of Maj. Robert Sedgwick. He accomplished a good work in his pastorate, showing a commendable spirit and excellent abilities. See letter in Arch. 240. He returned to England about 1650. Was of Norwich in 1657, when he sold land at Char. by attorney. [Mdx. De. IV.] Ch. Thomas, Mary b. in Boston 31 (11) bapt. at Char. 13 (12) 1639-40, Sarah b. 8 (6) 1641, bur. 21 (2) 1642, Elizabeth b. and d. 1643, Mercy b. and d. 1646.

Timothy, Salem, called to court in 1645.

Walter, hatter, Newbury, 1641; rem. to Charlestown about 1652. Res. at Watertown 1662-1673; returned to Char. He m. 1, Rebecca ——; he m. 2, Nov. 29, 1678, Abigail Rogers. Ch. Abigail b. 1 Oct. 1641, Benjamin b. 15 April, 1647, Joseph b. 1659.
He d. July 8, 1681. Will prob. Aug. 1681, beq. to sons John, of Sudbury, Daniel and Joseph.

William, carpenter, Salem, appl. frm. oct. 19, 1630, adm. frm. May 18, 1631. Juryman, 1637. Town officer. Richard Brakenbury deposed to finding him at S. in 1628. He depos. 30 (9) 1664, ae. about 62 years; had lived in S. about 38 years. One of the grantees of Jeffreys Creek in 1640, but not a resident. Wife Elizabeth memb. chh. before 1636. Ch. certified by himself, [Es. Files,] Persis b. and d. 1630, Samuel b. 8 (11) 1631, by wife Alis; Elizabeth b. (7) 1634, by wife Elizabeth; in chh. record: Deborah bapt.

ALLEN, etc., cont.
23 (2) 1637, Bethiah bapt. 16 (11) 1639, Onesiphorus bapt. 3 (5) 1642, William bapt. 31 (3) 1646, Jonathan bapt. 29 (5) 1649.

He d. May 10, 1678. Will prob. 26 (4) 1679, beq. to wife Elizabeth and sons Samuel, Onesiphorus and William.

William, carpenter, Salisbury, propr. 1639. Wife Ann, dau. of Richard Goodale; ch. Abigail b. 4 (11) 1639, Hannah b. 17 (4) 1642, Mary b. 29 (5) 1644, Martha b. 1646, John b. 9 (8) 1648, William b. 2 (8) 1650, Benjamin b. 1652, Joseph b. 13 (8) 1653, Richard b. 8 (9) 1655, Ruth b. 19 (12) 1657, Jeremiah b. 17 (12) 1658. The wife Ann d. 31 May, 1678.

He d. June 18, 1686. Will dated 16 April, 1674, codicil 7 Nov. 1676, prob. 22 July, 1686, beq. to wife Ann; ch. John, William, Benjamin, Joseph, Richard, Jeremiah, Abigail, Wheeler, Hannah Ayers, Mary Hewes and Martha Hubbard. Mentions son George Hews and father and brother Goodale.

ALLERTON, ALDERTON,
Mr. Isaac, tailor, of London, adm. frm. of Leyden, Holland, Feb. 7, 1614, m. Nov. 4, 1611, Mary Morris of Newbury, Eng., who d. Feb. 25, 1620-1; he m. 2, about 1626, Fear, dau. of elder William Brewster, who d. in 1634; he m. 3, Joanna ——. He was a man of great enterprise, active in the affairs of the Pilgrim chh. and colony. Came in the Mayflower; signed the Compact; was Asst. 1633; agent for the Colony in Eng. etc. He deposed 24 (7) 1639, ae. about 53 years. [L.] Carried on trade at Machias and Kennebec in Maine, and at other coast points. Resided at Plymouth till about 21 (1) 1639, when he desired acommodations of Salem, near his son-in-law, at Marblehead. Adm. Chh. Sal. 21 (1) 1647. Rem to New Haven. He was a brother of Zarah, wife of Godbert Godbertson. Ch. Bartholomew, Remember, (m. Moses Maverick,) Mary, (m. Thomas Cushman,) Sarah; these came in the Mayflower and had shares of cattle in 1627; Isaac. Bartholomew ret. to Eng. [B.]

He d. at New Haven about Feb. 12, 1669. Son Isaac had the est., subject to the widow's life-interest. [Reg. VIII, 265, et als.]

John, a seaman, reputed as one of the Company; came in the Mayflower to Plym.; was to go back for the help of others, but died before the ship returned. [B.]

ALLESTREE,
Ralph, planter, Boston; placed his son Paule, apprentice, with Valentine Hill for 8 years, 29 (5) 1641. Paul was factor of the ship Hope of Rotterdam, of whose cargo Hill was part owner, 9 (6) 1649. [Lechford and Suff. Deeds, Vol. 1.]

ALLEY,
Hugh, came as a servant to Henry Collins in 1635. Settled at Lynn. He deposed in 1662, ae. about 53, relative to Mr. Humphrey's farm. Wife Mary; ch. Mary b. 6 (11) 1641, John b. 30 (9) 1646, Martha b. 31 (5) 1649, Sarah b. 15 (2) 1651, Hugh b. 15 (8) 1653, Solomon b. 2 (6) 1656, Hannah b. 1 (4) 1661, Jacob b. 5 (7) 1663.

Will dated 2 (11) 1673, prob. 2 (5) 1674, beq. to son John and his ch.; gr. ch. Eleazer Linsy; Martha Willis and her ch. Martha; rest to wife. Widow Mary admin.

Philip, Salem, called to court in 1645.

ALLIS, ALLISE, ALLYCE, ELLIS,
Richard, embarked June 22, 1632.

William, Boston, Braintree, 1639; frm. May 18, 1640; deacon. Had a lot for 3 heads, 24 (12) 1639-40. Wife Mary d. Aug. 10, 1677; he m. 2, June 25, 1678, Mary, dau. of John Bronson and widow of John Graves of Haddam, Conn.; ch. John b. 5 (1) 1641, Samuel b. 24 (12) 1646, Josiah d. 15 (8) 1651, William b. 20 (8) 1651, Mary b. 25 (8) 1653, William b. Jan. 10, 1656, Hannah, (m. William Scott). Rem. to Hadley and then to Hatfield; Lieut.; asst. of court, 1676.

Will prob. Sept. 24, 1678; beq. to wife, and to ch. John, Samuel, Hannah and Mary.

ALLISON,
James, Boston, 1650, owned a warehouse at Charlestown before 1657. Wife, Christian; ch. James b. 20 (8) 1650, John d. 2 (2) 1653. James bapt. 19 (4) 1653.

ALMOND, ALMY, ALMIE,
William, ae. 44, came in the Abigail in July, 1635, with [wife] Awdry, ae. 32, and ch. Annis, ae. 8 and Chri: ae. 3. He deposed 20 (4) 1654, ae. about 53 years. [Mdx. Files.] Settled at Saugus, (Lynn). In Gen. Court June 14, 1631. Land gr. at Sandwich 3 April, 1637. Rem. and sold Sand. lands 22 June 1642. See Atkinson.

ALSOPP,
Joseph, ae. 14, came in the Elizabeth and Ann in April, 1635.

Key, res. not stated; inventory taken 30 April, 1672. Daniel Stone and Wm. Kent signed admin. bond of widow Mary. [Suff. Prob.] The widow m. Capt. Wm. Turner.

ALXARSON,
Ann, ae. 20, and Mary, ae. 24, came as servants of John Baker in 1637.

AMMIDOWN, AMMIDON, AMMA-DOWNE, AMMEDOWNE, HANNA-DOWN,
Roger, Salem, 1640, rem. to Weymouth, then to Boston, 1643; later to Rehoboth. Wife, Sarah; ch. Sarah b. at Wey. 10 (6) 1640, Lydia b. 27 (2) 1643, bapt. at Bo. as from the chh. of Wey.

He was bur. Nov. 13, 1673. Division of the est. made 4 March folg.; widow Joannah; son Ebenezer, by his representative John Coblech of Swansey; dau. Hannah, wife of Jeremiah Wheaton; John Harrod of Patucksett, bro. of the widow, gave advice.

AMBLER,
Richard, Watertown. Wife, Sarah; ch. Sarah b. 4 (10) 1639, Abraham b. and d. in 1641, Abraham b. 22 (7) 1742. He sold his land to J. Norcross previous to 1644.

AMBROSE, AMBROSS,
Henry, house carpenter, Hampton, 1640; frm. May 18, 1642. Rem. to Salisbury; propr. 1649. Rem. to Charlestown; deposed in court in 1653, ae. 40. Rem. to Boston. Wife Susanna; ch. Ebenezer, Samuel bapt. July 25, 1641, Henry b. (4) 1649, Abigail b. at Boston Dec. 28, 1654, (m. William Osgood).

He d. in 1658. Inv. filed Nov. 19, 1658. The widow m. 2, Oct. 2, 1663, John Severance.

AMEE, AME,
John, ship-carpenter, Woburn; ch. Mary b. 3 (12) 1649. Rem. to Boston. Shipped as carpenter on the Mary, Capt. Trumbull, for Barbadoes in 1657. [Wy.] He testified, 18 (10) 1672, ae. about 55 years, that land in Woburn was in possession of his bro. Edward Johnson in 1646. [Mdx. Files.] He m. 18 (1) 1650 [1649?] Mary Johnson; ch. Mary b. 3 (12) 1649-50.

AMES, AIMES, AMEES, AYMES, AMYES, (see also EAMES,)
Joane, of Yarmouth, widow, ae. 50, passed exam. May 11, 1637, to go to N. E., with ch. Ruth, ae. 18, William and John. Came first to Salem; adm. chh. 1637; Ruth adm. 1644. Propr. 1639. Rem. to Cambridge. The Gen. Court gave 40 pounds to "Mrs. Ames, the widow of Doctor Ames, of famous memory, who is deceased," 15 Nov., 1637. [W.]

She was bur. Dec. 23, 1644. Dau. Ruth m. Edmund Angier.

John, Duxbury, atba. 1643. Town officer. Rem. to Bridgewater. He m. 20 Oct. 1645, Elizabeth Heyward.

He d. leaving est. to his brother's heirs. [Hist. Dux.]

William, Braintree, 1641, frm. May 26, 1647. Wife, Hannah; ch. Hannah b. 12 (3) 1641, Rebecca b. (8) 1642, John b. 24 (3) 1647, Sarah b. 1 (1) 1650, Deliverance (dau.) b. 6 (12) 1653.

He d. 1 (11) 1653. Adm. gr. to the widow March 6, 1654. She m. 2, 6 (2) 1660, John Heiden.

ANCHOR,
Thomas, Boston, mortg. house 27 (10) 1648.

ANDERSON,
Gowen, Roxbury, Frm. May 13, 1640. Bought house in Boston 29 (11) 1641. Wife Alice.

John, shipwright, Boston, sold one half of ship John and Sarah to Robert Allen of Norwich, Eng., merchant, 10 (5) 1648. [A.] Had liberty to wharf before his property in 1647. He m. 1, Jane ——; she d. 4 (3) 1654; he m. 2, Jan. 3, 1654-5, Mrs. Mary Hodges, sister of Nicholas Davison. Ch. Samuel d. 10 (5) 1654, Joanna b. Dec. 25, 1655, Anna b. May 5, 1657, d. March 12, 1660, Amy [Em], (m. 17 (5) 1655, John Brakenbury).

He d. at Char. Sept. 28, 1677. Will beq. to son Henry in Eng.; to heirs of son David, and 4 married daughters.

The widow's will signed Nov. 6, 1689, prob. March 11, 1692-3, beq. to daus. Mary, wife of Samuel Hayman of Char.; Emme, wife of Mr. Joseph, of the same, and the 7 children he had by my sister's daughter; to John Brakenbury and his sister Katharine

17

ANDERSON, cont.
Phelps; to my dau. Katharine Philips, wife to Maj. John P. of Char., and to his 4 ch.; to Joanna, dau. of my bro. George Miller, of Swanzey in Wales; to my sister Joanna Kent of Newbury; to cousin Daniel Davidson, her son, and his dau. Joanna; to my dau. Katharine, wife of Capt. Richard Sprague; to gr. ch. Abigail, wife of Mr. Cotton Mather; to the second chh. of Bo.; to Harvard College.

Robert before Gen. Court June, 1637.

ANDREW, ANDREWS, ANDROS, ANDROSSE,
Edward. His wife had a son John Dotteris, who came over as an apprentice in 1637, and was allowed to remain with her. [W.]

Mr. Henry, yeoman, planter, Taunton, frm. 4 Dec., 1638. Deputy, 1639. Attorney for Nathaniel Patten 2 (7) 1640. [L.]

Will, dated March 13, 1652; prob. 6 June, 1653; wife Mary; daus. Mary, (wife of William Hedges,) and her son John; Sarah and Abigail; son Henry. The widow's will Feb. 14, 1654, ae. 43 years, beq. to same persons. [Reg. V, 259, and LI, 453.]

The dau. Sarah m. 1 April, 1664, Israel Talbut.

Johanna, maid servant of George Burdon, adm. chh. Boston 3 (2) 1640.

John, cooper, Charlestown, 1637. Owned land at Mystic side; rem. to Boston. His wife Lucie d. 1 (7) 1653. He m. Hannah ——. Ch. John b. Nov. 21, 1656, Hannah b. Feb. 20, 1657-8, Susanna b. Aug. 12, 1659, Martha b. Dec. 5, 1660, Mary [Susanna?] bapt. with Hannah and Martha 2 (4) 1661; John bapt. 21 (7) 1663, James b. March 17, 1666, Samuel b. May 18, 1668, Mary bapt. 9 (2) 1671.

Admin. of his est. gr. to widow Hannah 18 Aug. 1679.

Mabel, single woman, adm. chh. Boston 4 (7) 1636.

Robert, Ipswich, propr., frm. May 6, 1635. Gave security April 2, 1641, to William Franklin of Boston, for the marriage portion of his dau. Alice, late wife of W. F., to be given her dau. Elizabeth. Refers to Phebe, present wife of W. F. Son Thomas, school master; daus. Abigail m. Daniel Hovey, Elizabeth m. Humphrey Griffin.

ANDREW, etc., cont.
He d. in 1643. Will dated April 2, 1641, prob. 22 (8) 1647, beq. to wife Elizabeth, sons John and Thomas, son-in-law Franklyn and his dau. Elizabeth; gr. son Daniel Hovey; to John, son of Humphrey Griffin and two other sons, all under 21 years; to kinsmen John, Thomas and Robert Burnam. His widow had lawsuit 31 (1) 1647, with Humphrey Griffin, husband of her dau. Elizabeth. [Es. Files.] John depos. 1692, ae. 70.

Samuel, ae. 37, with wife Jane, ae. 30, and daus. Jane, ae. 3, and Elizabeth, ae. 2, and Ellen Lougie, servant, ae. 20, came in the Increase, April 14, 1635. He was one of four "sent away" by Robert Cordell, goldsmith, Lombard St., London. Res. at Charlestown. "Having had the command of ships upon several voyages," he and Mr. Jonas Clarke were appointed 13 Oct. 1654, to take observations at the northerly bounds of Mass. plantation. [Arch. Col. 23.]

Inv. of his est. taken by Nicholas Davison and two other Charlestown men the last of Oct. 1659, shows merchandise; gives list of debts due from persons at Oyster Bay, L. I., Huntington, Hampstead, Stanford, Stratford, various Indians, etc. House, land given him by the town, etc. No clue as to family in the document.

Thomas, Watertown, before the Court Sept. 27, 1631. He joined Mrs. Rebecca Craddock in a petition in 1648. He rem. to Cambridge about 1645. Wife Rebecca; ch. Thomas b. Oct. 15, 1641, Daniel, Rebeccah b. 18 (2) 1646.

He d. about 1648. The widow m. 2, Nicholas Wyth. [Mi.]

Thomas, Dorchester, propr. Nov. 22, 1634; with wife memb. chh. His dau. Hannah Garnesy was dism. to chh. of Roxbury 22 (2) 1660; son Thomas bapt. 23 (4) 1639.

He d. May 20, 1673. Will dated 6 April, 1667, prob. 21 (6) 1673. Wife Ann, son Thomas, dau. Hannah Hopkins and her children. Widow Anne d. Jan. 13, 1684.

Thomas, Hingham, propr. 1635. [See Plaisto.] Son Joseph came with him; had adjacent lot; was town officer and deputy; d. 27 Sept. 1679, ae. 83 years.

Old Thomas Andrews d. Aug. 1643. [Hob.]

William, mariner, Cambridge, frm. Mar

ANDREW, etc., cont.

4, 1633-4. Godly parents brought him up till 17 years of age; was apprenticed at Ipswich, Eng. Came first to Charlestown. In his absence his wife rem. to Cambridge, which pleased him. [Rel.] Town officer. Sold house, all lands and rights in C. Sept. 25, 1637. Sold land again 2 (2) 1651. Wife Mary d. Jan. 19, 1639-40. He m. 2, (contract Aug. 11, 1640,) Reana James of Watertown.

He d. in 1652, leaving an only son Samuel, who was adm. chh. Dec. 10, 1658. The widow m. 2, Robert Daniels and 3, Edmund Frost.

William, carpenter, Hampsworth, Eng., came in the James Apr. 5, 1635. Salem, juryman, 1637; servant of Mr. Henry Coggan, before Gen. Court 4 (10) 1638. Assigned to Mr. Endecott 3 (7) 1639. Frm. May 13, 1640.

ANGIER, ANGER,

Mr. Edmund, (Edward) woolen draper, Cambridge, propr. 1636, frm. May 13, 1640. Town officer. Propr. Watertown in 1644. "He was a son of John Angier of Dedham, Eng., and was b. about 1612; his wife Ruth was dau. of that famous Light Dr. [William] Ames." [Mi.] [Reg. L, 400. etc.] [See letter concerning family connections in Mdx. Files No. 14] Wife Ruth d. July 3, 1656. He m. 2, June 12, 1657, Anna, dau. of Christopher Batt. She d. 3 Oct. 1688, in her 58th year. [Gt. St.] Ch. John b. 21 (6) 1645, bur. 2 (11) 1647, Ruth b. 28 (7) 1647, Ephraim, Samuel, John b. 22 April, bapt. May 15, 1649, d. Decem. 9, 1659, Edmund bapt. Sept. 25, 1659, Hannah bapt. Dec. 16, 1660, Mary bapt. May 10, 1663. [Mi]

He d. March 4, 1691-2, ae. 80. [Gr. St.] The inv. of his est. was filed in May, 1692, and admin. gr. to his son Samuel.

ANGLESEY,

Margaret, Dorchester, adm. chh. June 9, 1640.

ANNABALL, ANNIBALL, ANNABLE,

Anthony, came in 1623 with wife Jane and daus. Sarah and Hannah. Settled at Plymouth; planter; town officer; frm. 1632. Rem. to Scituate. He and wife Jane were membs. chh. at its organization Jan. 8, 1634. Ch. Deborah bapt. May 7, 1637, Samuel b.

ANNABALL, etc., cont.

Jan. 2, 1646, Esek (Ezekiel) bapt. April 29, 1649, Desire bapt. Oct. 16, 1653, Hannah, (m. March 1, 1645-6, Thomas Boreman,) Susanna, (m. May 13, 1652, William Hatch, Jr.), Sarah, (m. at Green's Harbour Nov. 23, 1638, Henry Ewell).

He rem. to Barnstable 22 Jan. 1638-9. His wife Jane was bur. Dec. 10, 1643. He m. 2, March, 1644-5, Ann Alcocke; she was bur. May 16, 1651. He m. 3, Hannah [Ann] Barker, who was bur. about March 16, 1657-8.

Will dated 24 Feb. 1672, prob. 4 June, 1674, beq. to wife Ann, son Samuel, dau. Desire and other daus. not specified.

John, tailor, Ipswich, came from Boston, Eng. in 1638, as a servant of John Whittingham; commoner at Ips. in 1641. Bought house and land in 1647. Ch. John, b. before 1651; ch. mentioned in Dorchester records: Anna A., who m. 19 (10) 1671, Consider Atherton, Elizabeth A. ae. 15, and Robert A. ae. 13, named among children to be catechised in 1676, and Sarah A. who d. June 28, 1674.

He d. before 7 Nov. 1664, when inv. of his est. was taken; his widow Anna m. Nicholas Clap of Dorchester before April 15, 1667, when they sold land in Ips.; deeded still other land in 1672 to son John.

ANTER,

Joan, maid servant of one Mr. Martin Holman of Biddiford, Eng., adm. chh. Boston 18 (12) 1643; dism. to Rowley 31 (1) 1644, and letters of dism. sent 8 (1) 1646, to her, "now wife of one Heseltine of the ch. of R."

ANTHONY,

John, came in the Hercules in April, 1634.

ANTROBUS,

Joan, ae. 65, cert. from St. Albons, Herts. Eng., came in the Planter April 1, 1635.

ANTRUM, ANTRAM, ANDRAM, ANTHROPP,

Thomas, weaver, came in the James April 5, 1635; settled at Salem; propr. 1636; bro. of Edmund Batter. [Town rec.] Frm. May 18, 1642. Town officer, juryman. Ch. — bapt. 8 (5) 1637, Obediah bapt. 7 (4) 1640.

ANTRUM, etc., cont.
Mary bapt. 16 (5) 1643, John bapt. 29 (1) 1646, Hannah, (m. Isaac Burnap).
Will dated 24 (11) 1662, prob. 3 (5) 1663; beq. to son Obediah A., dau. Hannah Burnape and her son Isaac B.; to Thomas Spooner and Hilliard Veren. Review of the est. (9) 1684, on petition of Edmund Batter.

APPLEGATE,
Thomas, planter, Weymouth. Lic. to keep a ferry 2 Sept. 1635. Wife Elizabeth in Court 6 Sept. 1636. Suit in Plymouth Court 1 June, 1641.

APPLETON,
Mr. Samuel, gent., son of Thomas and Mary A. of Little Waldingfield, co. Suffolk, Eng., bapt. Aug. 13, 1686. Rem. about 1628 to Reydon, Eng. Came about 1634 to Ipswich. One of the earliest town officers; frm. May 25, 1636; deputy, 1637. He sent power of attorney Aug. 8, 1639, for management of his lands and tenements at Monks Ely, Eng. to Isaac A., ar. and others of L. W. [L.] Is called my brother by Robert Ryece of Preston, Eng. in a letter to Gov. Winthrop 17 Jan. 1636. He is said by family historians to have m. 1, Judith Everard, and 2, Martha ——. Ch. b. at L. W.: Mary, Judith, (d. in 1629,) Martha, (m. Richard Jacobs,) John, Samuel, Sarah, (m. Samuel Phillips,) Judith b. 1634, (m. Samuel Rogers).
He d. at Rowley in June, 1670. Genealogies.

APY,
James, Lynn. Held property secured to Richard Russell, 1643. [A.]

ARRATT,
John, Boston, propr. 1635.

ARCHER, ARCHARD, ORCHARD,
Giles, Boston, d. before 1638; had built a house on lands of Thomas Matson. [Suff. De. IV, 170.]

Henry, planter, Ipswich, propr.; frm. June 2, 1641. A case of his was referred 4 (4) 1639 by Gen. Court to Ipswich Court. Sold land in Ips. in 1649; his wife released dower on it in 1660. He witnessed a bond given in Boston in favor of Francis Archer of Rotterdam 26 (6) 1650. He m. at Roxbury Dec. 4, 1639, Elizabeth, dau. of John Stow.

ARCHER, etc., cont.
Samuel, carpenter, Salem, appl. frm. Oct. 19, 1630; propr. 1636; town officer. One of the grantees at Manchester 13 May, 1640. With Wm. Allin made an ammunition house in 1639. He deposed in 1660, ae. 52 years, and in 1667, ae. about 58 years. Wife Susanna adm. chh. 30 (1) 1656; ch. John bapt. 7 (2) 1639, Bethiah bapt. 3 (5) 1642, Samuel m. at Andover 21 May, 1660, Hanna Osgood.
Est. settled at Salem 30 (4) 1668; report allowed 29 (4) 1669; wife Susanna and son Samuel.

ARMESBEY, see Ormsby.

ARMITAGE, HERMITAGE,
Godfrey, tailor, Lynn, frm. March 14, 1638-9. Rem. to Boston about 1644. Wife ——; ch. Samuel b. 7 (8) 1645, John bapt. 20 (6) 1648. Samuel bapt. 24 (12) 1649, ae. about 2 days, Samuel b. 14 (2) 1651.
Will dated 22 Dec. prob. 11 (12) 1674-5. Wife Mary, son Samuel, dau. Rebecca Tarbox, bro. Joseph.

Joseph, tailor, Lynn, bro. of Godfrey, frm. March 9, 1636-7; juryman, 1637. He deposed in 1661, ae. about 60. [Mdx. Files.] He kept an ordinary. Carried goods in his boat to Boston. [Es. Files 3, 97.]
He d. June 27, 1680. His wife Jann [Jane?] d. March 3, 1678. [Reg. XXXIII, 60.]

Thomas, came in the James from Bristol, Eng. May 23, 1635, with Mr. Richard Mather. Settled at Ipswich; frm. 7 Feb. 1636-7; constable, 1638.

ARMSTRONG,
Gregory, Plymouth; had liberty to dwell at Yarmouth 3 Sept. 1638.

ARNOLD, ARNALD, ARNOLL, ARNELL,
Edward, butcher, Boston, 1641.

George, Charlestown, sold land in the name of Edward Payne 19 (1) 1640-1.

Jasper, ae. 40, with Ann ae. 39, came in the Abigail in July, 1635.

John, Cambridge, propr. 1634. Rem. to Hartford.

ARNOLD, etc., cont.

John, plasterer, Boston, inhab. 1639, adm. chh. a singleman, 22 (2) 1643. Frm. May 16, 1643. Admin. gr. to his bro. Samuel A. of Marshfield May 18, 1661.

Joseph, Braintree. He m. 8 (4) 1648, Rebecca Curtis; ch. William b. 16 (1) 1649, Joseph b. 18 (8) 1652, John b. 2 (2) 1655, Ephraim b. 4 (11) 1664. Rebecca d. 14 Aug. 1693.

Samuel, Sandwich, atba. 1643. Rem. to Yarmouth. Rem. to Marshfield before 1661. Ch. Samuel b. May 9, 1649. Will dated Aug. 19, prob. Oct. 18, 1693, beq. to wife Elizabeth, sons Samuel and Seth, gr. ch. Elizabeth and Isaac Holmes; dau. Elizabeth's children. His divinity books in folio to son Samuel; a great Latin book to Mr. Rowland Cotton.

Thomas, came in the Plain Joan in May, 1635, ae. 30 [?]. Watertown, propr. 1636, frm. May 13, 1640. Presented by jury concerning baptism (8) 1651. [Mdx. Files.] He m. Phebe dau. of George Parkhurst, Sen.; they sold 30 (1) 1655 to her bro. George P. of Wat. land bought of her father G. P. and his wife Susanna 20 Dec. 1648. Ch. Ichabod b. 1 (1) 1640, Richard b. 22 (1) 1642, John b. 19 (12) 1647, Eleazor b. 17 (4) 1651. Rem. to Providence, R. I.; sold Wat. property in 1661.

William, Hingham, propr. 1635, Pautuxet, placed himself under the jurisdiction of Mass. about 28 (8) 1642. [Suff. De. 1, 33.]

ARRINGTON, see Errington.

ASH,

William, Gloucester, 1650, m. Millicent, widow of William Southmeade, and recd. deed of land in trust for the children (4) 1650.

ASHLEY,

Robert, Springfield, propr., taxed in 1638. Keeper of the ordinary in 1646. Town officer. Made marriage contract with widow Mary Horton Aug. 7, 1641. Ch. David b. June 2, 1642, Mary b. 6 (2) 1644, (m. Oct. 18, 1664, John Roote of Farmington,) Jonathan b. 25 (12) 1645, Sarah b. 23 (6) 1648, Joseph b. 6 (5) 1652.

ASHLEY, cont.

He d. Nov. 29, 1682. Will dated 9 Oct. 1679, prob. March 27, 1683; aged; beq. to wife Mary, sons David, Jonathan and Joseph; gr. son John; son John Root. [See Reg. XXXIII, 310.]

Thomas, fisherman, Charlestown, ae. about 26 years, servant of Thomas Rucke, deposed to list of goods July 19, 1639. [L.] Res. at Cape Ann (Gloucester) in 1639. [Es. Files.] Adm. inhab. Boston, 1658.

ASKEW,

John, Cambridge, had been a servant of Thomas Bendight of Yarmouth, Eng.; was transferred 14 (12) 1640, to Edward Winslow of Salisbury; law suit. [L.]

ASLETT,

John, Andover, propr. 1649. [Es. Files.] He m. at Newbury 8 Oct. 1648, Rebecca Ayres; ch. Rebecca b. 6 May, 1652, Mary b. 24 April, 1654, John b. 16 Feb. 1656, Sarah b. 14 Jan. 1658, Ruth b. 3 Aug. 1660, Sarah b. 14 Aug. 1662, Elizabeth b. 26 May, 1666, d. 15 March, 1667, Samuel d. 20 Dec. 1669.

He d. 6 June, 1671; will dated 15 (3) prob. 27 (4) 1671, beq. to wife Rebecca, son John, and all my daughters.

ASPINWALL, ASPENWALL, ASPINALL,

Peter, Dorchester, propr. 1645, frm. May, 1645. Rem. to Muddy River, Boston. Bought farm of 150 acres 14 (6) 1650, in co. with Robert Sharpe. Town officer. He deposed 4 (8) 1664, ae. about 52 years. [Mdx. Files.] He m. first Alice Sharpe who, as a maid servant to William Ting, was adm. chh. Boston 9 (8) 1642, and, as wife of P. A. Dorch. was dism. to that chh. 30 (1) 1645. He m. second 12 Feb. 1661-2 Remember, dau. of Peter Palfrey, who as a maid servant was adm. chh. of Roxbury 24 (9) 1661. Ch. rec. in Bo. and Rox.: Samuel b. Nov. 10, 1662, Peter b. June 14, 1664, Nathaniel b. June 5, 1666, Thomas bapt. 26 (11) 1667, Mehetabel bapt. 10 (10) 1669, Elizabeth b. 26 (9) 1671, Eleazer and Joseph bapt. 12 (8) 1673, Job bapt. 27 (12) 1675, Timothy bapt. 16 (2) 1682.

Will dated 29 Nov. 1687, prob. Jan. 28,

ASPINWALL, etc., cont.

1691-2. To wife Remember; eldest son Samuel and other ch. named above, except Job; Mary is added. Inv. shows farming and tanning outfit.

Mr. William, notary, Boston, appl. frm. Oct. 19, 1630, deacon, 1630, adm. frm. April 3, 1632; res. at Charlestown some time, [town rec.]; deputy, 1637. Wrote most of the Book of Possessions. His notarial record, long lost, has come to light in the Boston Athenæum Library, and is being printed by the Boston Record Commission; it is of great value to students of colonial history. He sympathized with the Hutchinson party, and drew up the famous petition, asking for lenient treatment; was sentenced to be banished, but apologized and was excused. Signed the compact of Rhode Island and Providence Plantation 7 (1) and joined in the purchase of land from Indians 24 (1) 1637-8. [Arch. 2, 1.] Was clerk of R. I., but left the plantation in 1639 and returned to Boston. He was a member of a company of adventurers, incorporated by the Gen. Court 7 March, 1643-4, and led an exploring party that went from Boston in 1644, in a pinnace, to discover the great lake by sailing up the Delaware river, where he had formerly been. They returned in a few months, having been opposed by the Dutch. [W.] The Gen. Court accused him 14 Oct. 1651, of charging the court and jury to make the landlord pay rent to the tenant; forbade his acting as clerk or recorder of any county court, and deposed him from the office of clerk of writs of Boston. He deposed before the Court in case of Thomas Geyner, 31 May, 1652. He gave his house and lands in Bo. to his son-in-law, Mr. John Angier of Bo. June 8, 1652.

Wife Elizabeth; ch. Edward b. 26 (7) 1630, d 10 (8) 1630, Hannah b. 25 (10) 1631, (m. John Angier,) Elizabeth b. 30 (7) 1633, Samuel b. 30 (7) 1635, Ethlan b. (1) 1636-7, Dorcas b. 14 (12) 1639.

He rem. to Chester, Eng., whence he wrote 13 (1) 1662 to some of the magistrates here, relative to the land which he had given to his son [Angier]. He wrote several books which were published in Eng. See sketch in introduction to Suffolk Deeds, Vol. X. We may note that Mr. Edward Aspinwall of Toxteth, Eng. was a patron of Richard Mather in 1611. [C. M.]

ASTWOOD,

James, yeoman, Roxbury, frm. May 22, 1639. Rem. to Boston about 1647. Had bond from Joseph Godfrey, Aug. 24, 1647, for money to be paid in Eng. 1 June, 1648. [A.] Wife Sarah; ch. James b. Nov. 29, 1638, John b. and d. in 1640, John b. March 7, 1641-2, Joseph bapt. Nov. 19, 1643, Joseph b. Nov. 10, 1644, Sarah b. Jan. 10, 1646, Mary b. Dec. 21, 1647.

Will Sept. 17, 1653; wife Sarah; sons James, John and Joseph; dau. Sarah; bro. John A. He desired to be bur. at the feet of Mr. Cotton. Wife declined to be exec. because she was going to England, and Wm. Parks was appointed. [Reg. VII, 337, VIII, 275, and IX, 40; Suff. De. III, 463.]

John, husbandman, ae. 26, came in the Hopewell in April, 1635. Frm. March 3, 1635-6. He rem. to Conn.

He d. at Abutley, Eng.; will dated 27 June, prob. 31 Aug. 1654; wife Sarah; son Samuel exec.; bros. William and Robert A.; mother. [Reg. XIV, 304, XXXV, 245, and XXXVIII, 421.]

ATHERSON,

John, ae. 24, came in the Susan and Ellen in Apr. 1635.

ATHERTON, ADERTON,

Humphrey, Dorchester, first mentioned in records March 18, 1637; frm. and deputy May 2. 1638. Magistrate, deputy governor, active in the affairs of the United Colonies, Major-General. [See many notices in historical works; epitaph in Reg. II, 382.] As birth records of certain children at Winwick, Eng. correspond with known facts about some of his children, it has been inferred that he came from that parish. Nathaniel Wales, Sen. calls him brother-in-law. Wife Mary; ch. Elizabeth, (bapt. at Winwick, Eng. Sept. 28, 1628,) (m. Timothy Mather,) John bapt. at W. Dec. 26, 1629, Isabel bapt. at W. Jan. 23, 1630, (m. Nathaniel Wales, Jr.) Jonathan, Consider, Mary, (m. Joseph Weeks,) Margaret (m. James Trowbridge,) Rest bapt. at Dorch. 26 (3) 1639, (m. Obediah Swift,) Increase bapt. 11 (2) 1641, Thankful bapt. 29 (2) 1644, (m. Thomas Bird, Jr.) Hope bapt. 30 (6) 1646, Watching bapt. 24 (6) 1651, Patience bapt. 21 (2) 1654, (m. Isaac Humphrey).

He d. Sept. 17, 1661. His will not being

ATHERTON, etc., cont.

left in legal form, admin. was gr. 27 Sept. 1661, to his eldest son Jonathan and to his sons-in-law, Timothy Mather, James Trowbridge and Obadiah Swift. Extensive estate.

ATKINS,

Henry, Plymouth, atba. 1643, frm. 6 June, 1654. Rem. to Barnstable; m. July 9, 1647, Elizabeth Wells. Ch. Mary b. March 13, 1647-8, d. June 15, 1649, Samuel b. Feb. 24, 1651, Isaac b. June 14, 1657.

ATKINSON, ADKINSON,

Theodore, came as servant to John Newgate, from Bury St. Edmunds; settled at Boston; feltmaker, hatter, merchant; adm. chh. 11 (11) 1634. Town officer. He m. first Abigail, sister of Ann, the wife of Thomas Matson, Sen. [Suff. De. VI, 333.] She was adm. chh. from Ipswich 15 (8) 1648. He m. 2, Mary Lyde, widow, dau. of Rev. John Wheelwright, deeded to her 21 Oct. 1667, as a portion before marriage certain lands in Boston. [Norf. co. Deeds II, 94.] Ch. Theodore b. 10 (2) 1644, Nathaniel b. 28 (9) 1645, Abigail b. 24 (6) 1647, Eleazer bapt. 3 (12) 1649, ae. about 8 days, Thomas bapt. 22 (8) 1654, Abigail b. 9 Dec. 1657, John b. June 13, 1672, Theodore b. Feb. 28, 1673, Elizabeth b. Nov. 28, 1692.

He d. in 1701, ae. 89. Admin. gr. 3 Oct. 1701, to his grandson Theodore A. of Portsmouth, N. H., feltmaker, the widow Mary having declined to admin.

Thomas, yeoman, Plymouth, frm. 1634, propr. 1636.

Thomas, Concord, frm. Dec. 7, 1636; wife Susan; ch. Susanna b. 28 (2) 1641, (m. 10 April, 1660, Caleb Brooks,) Hannah b. 5 (1) 1643, Rebecca, (m. John Haward Aug. 17, 1656).

He d. 18 (1) 1643. Admin. gr. to his widow 25 (9) 1646; "80 pounds to be rec'd from Eng." Major Willard petitioned the court with reference to the estate (paper undated;) Thomas Atkinson, late of Concord, came out of England about 25 years since; left an estate in Eng. Left widow (who married "Willi. Almie, the tyler,") and three daughters. Robert Tillison and Robert Atkinson in Eng. named. [Mdx. Files, 1659.] See letter from his brother Robert Adkinson of

ATKINSON, etc., cont.

Timby in the parish of Halifax, Eng.; March 29, 1652, other letters. Thomas went to N. E. 17 years ago this spring, Sold land before he went. Admin. gr. Oct. 4, 1659, to John Hayward and Susanna and Hannah A. on the est. of "Wm. Alline," who m. their mother. [Mdx. Files, 1671.]

ATWOOD, see Wood.

Elizabeth, Charlestown, adm. chh. 12 (6) 1663.

Herman, cordwainer, came from Sanderstead, co. Surrey, 15 miles from London; Boston, servant to our bro. Buttall, adm. chh. 24 (12) 1643. Deacon of second chh. He m. 11 (6) 1646 Ann Copp.

Admin. gr. 19 (9) 1651. Wife and two ch. [Reg. VIII, 57.] The widow m. Thomas Sexton.

Mr. John, gent., Plymouth, frm. 3 Jan. 1636. Assistant 6 March 1637-8. One of the referees in the settlement of the Plymouth partnership in 1641. [B.]

Will dated 20 Oct. 1643, prob. Feb. 27, 1643-4. Refers to his brethren. His widow Ann rem. to Boston; adm. chh. 8 (12) 1651. Her will dated April 27, 1650, was prob. June 1, 1654. Both wills beq. to bro. Robert and sister Mary Lee and their ch. Ann and Mary, and to nephew William Crow.

Philip, ae. 12, and Philip, ae. 13, are mentioned in the passenger lists of the Planter and the Susan and Ellen in 1635. Are these two persons or do both entries refer to the same as shipping in one vessel and sailing in the other?

Philip, Malden, town officer, deposed in 1660, ae. 40. [Mdx. Files.] He m. first Rachel, dau. of Joseph Bacheller, who d. Feb. 5, 1673-4; m. second Elizabeth Grover, April 7, 1675; she d. Oct. 1676, and he m. third Elizabeth ——; ch. Philip, Abigail b. Dec. 1662, (m. Andrew Mitchell,) Oliver, Rachel b. Aug. 1653, Mary b. (11) 1655, and Philip b. (7) 1658. The wife Elizabeth d. April 3, 1688.

Philip, father or son, d. at Bradford Feb. 1, 1700-1701.

AUDEY, ADY, ADDY,

Webb, (called also Ady Webb,) Plymouth, taxed, 1632; propr. 1636; in court, 1637.

AUDEY, etc., cont.
He d. 4 March, 1651. Nunc. will prob. March 19, 1651, beq. to Mr. Reyner, his minister, and to the poor. No family mentioned. [Reg. IV, 320.]

AUDLY, AUDELEY, see Odlin.
Edmund, Salem, suit in court in 1636. He was adminr. of the goods of Francis Dent of Salem, 1638-9.

AUSTIN, AUSTEN, ASTEN,
Francis, a pioneer at Dedham, 1636; his lot passed to Francis Chickering before (7) 1640.

Jonas, of Tenterden, Eng., with wife Constance and 4 ch. came in the Hercules in March, 1634. Settled at Cambridge; propr. 1635; sold land and rem. to Hingham; propr. 1636; sold land in H. 6 (12) 1650. Rem. to Taunton; juror, 1651. His wife Constant d. 22 April, 1667. He m. 2, Dec. 14, 1667, Frances, widow of John Hill of Dorchester; she d. Nov. 18, 1676. Ch. Esther b. 3 Jan. 1662, Mary b. 12 May, 1663, Sarah b. 4 Nov. 1665, Jonah b. 1667, John b. July 1, 1671.

He d. May 10, 1676. Inv. of his est. filed 2 Nov. 1676.

Richard, tailor, of Bishopstocke, Eng., ae. 40, with wife and 2 ch. came in the Bevis in May, 1638.

AVERILL, AVERIE, AVERITT, AVERY,
Christopher, Gloucester, town officer, 1646. His wife was in England in 1653. [Es. Files.]

James, Gloucester, propr. 1649. His wife Joan [Greenslade] was adm. to chh. of Boston, "singlewoman" 18 (4) 1643, m. Nov. 10, 1643, and dism. to Gloc. 17 (1) 1644, as wife of J. A. He was a witness to the will of John Bridgman in 1655. Ch. Hannah b. Nov. 12, 1644, James b. Jan. 16, 1646, Marie b. Feb. 19, 1648.

Matthew, Charlestown, propr. 1638; ret. to Eng.; will dated at Wapping, Parish of St. Mary, White Chapel, Eng. 22 April, 1642, prob. London April 13, 1643; recorded. [Mdx. De. II, 90.] Wife Anna and son John; kinsmen Wm. Baudrock, Jr., and Wm. Humphrey, Jr.

AVERILL, etc., cont.
The widow m. 2, Wm. Roberts; she and son John sold land in Char. and Eng. in 1656.

Rev. Joseph, a minister from Wiltshire, with wife and six small ch. wrecked upon Cape Ann Aug. 16, 1635. [R. M. and S.] His name is given to the outer rock of the Cape. Admin. of his est. Gen. Court Sept. 1, 1635.

Thomas, came in the Mary and John March 24, 1633. Res. at Salem; frm. Feb. 28, 1642. Blacksmith; propr. With wife Susanna sold land in 1657-8.

William, Ipswich, propr. 1637; kept the herd of goats in 1646.

Will signed 3 (4) 1652, prob. March 29, 1653, beq. to wife Abigail and seven children not mentioned by name.

William, blacksmith, Dedham, townsman 1(11) 1650; sergt. 1658. Wife Margaret; ch. Jonathan b. 26 (3) 1653, Hannah b. 27 (7) 1660, (m. 22 (3) 1677, Benjamin Dyer,) Ebenezer b. 24 (9) 1663, Rachel, (m. 22 (3) 1677, William Sumner). The wife Margaret d. 28 (7) 1678.

William, practitioner in physick, ae. about 61 years, Boston, made will 15 Oct. 1683, prob. 13 Mar. 1686-7; beq. to wife Mary and ch. William, Robert and Jonathan A. and Mary Tisdale; sons-in-law William Sumner and Benjamin Dyer. Owned housing and land at Dedham.

AWARD, see Hayward.

AWKLEY,
Miles, Boston. Wife Mary; ch. Elizabeth b. in 1635, Miles b. 1 (2) 1638.

AXE, AXEY, AXLEY,
James, Lynn; propr. in 1638; res. April 7, 1643. [Suff. De. 1, 41.] Constable, 1644; clerk of market, 1648. [Es. Files.]

He d. June 7, 1669; nunc. will, having grown aged; beq. to John Pearson; admin. gr. to wife Frances. She made will Oct. 18, 1670, which was prob. 2 (10) 1670; many bequests; Joseph Fiske admin.

AXTELL, AXDELL,
Thomas, Sudbury, propr.; bought land in 1643. Took oath of fidelity 9 (5) 1645. Wife Mary; ch. Lydia b. 1 (4) 1644, [Hannah,

AXTELL, etc. cont.
(m. June 18, 1659, Capt. Edward Wright,)] Mary, (m. Sept. 19, 1656, John Goodenow). He was bur. 8 (1) 1646; inv. taken 6 (3) 1646; he desired that his wife Mary should have the est. to bring up his children. The widow m. 16 (4) 1646, John Maynard. [Genealogy in Reg. LIII, 227.]

AYER, AYERS, AIR, AIRS, EIRES, EYRE, EYRES, see also Eire,
John, Sen., Salisbury, propr. 1640. Sold house and lands and rem. to Haverhill, where he was propr. and purchaser 1648-9. Town officer. Ch. John, Jr., Robert and Thomas also proprs. at Haverhill in 1650; see deed to Abra. Clement in 1692; Hannah b. Dec. 21, 1648, (m. Stephen Webster).

He d. March 31, 1657. Will dated 12 March, 1656, prob. at Hampton 6 (8) 1657; beq. to wife Hannah, sons John, Robert, Thomas, Obediah, Peter and Nathaniel; daus. Hannah, Rebecca and Mary. The widow Hannah, "aged," d. Oct. 8, 1688.

John, husbandman, Ipswich, 1643-1669; tenant of Mr. John Norton; bro. of Wm. Lampson and his wife and of Edward Chapman. Rem. about 1672 to Brookfield. Wife Susan; ch. [John, Samuel, Thomas, Joseph, Susanna, Edward;] Mark b. at Ipswich Dec. 14, 1661, Nathaniel b. July 6, 1664.

He was killed by the Indians at Squakeag Aug. 3, 1675; inv. filed in 1676, mentions 7 sons and 1 dau. The widow Susanna d. at Ipswich Feb. 8, 1682-3.

Samuel, of Norwich, Eng., apprentice, ae. 15, passed exam. May 11, 1637, to go to N.E. to his master John Baker.

BABER,
Francis, chandler, ae. 36, came from Weymouth, Eng. March 20, 1635. Settled at Scituate. Bought land of William Wills; suit in court, 1637.

BABB,
Mr. Thomas, attorney for Christopher Browning in Essex court 27 (10) 1636.

BABSON,
Isabel, widow, Salem, 1637; rem. to Gloucester. She was a midwife; testified in a case in 1657, ae. about 80 years. She d. 6 April, 1661.
Admin. gr. to her son James.

BABSON, etc., cont.
James, Gloucester, frm. May 23, 1666. presumably came with his mother before 1637; sold land in 1647. He deposed in 1663, ae. 30 years. He m. Nov. 16, 1647, Eleanor Hill; ch. James b. Sept. 29, 1648, Eleanor b. June 15, 1651, Philip b. Oct. 15, 1654, Sarah b. Feb. 15, 1656, d. Jan 19, 1676; Thomas b. May 21, 1658, John b. Nov. 27, 1660, Richard b. June 1, 1663, Elizabeth b. 8 (8) 1665, Ebenezer b. Feb. 8, 1668, Abigail b. May 13, 1670.

He d. Dec. 21, 1683; his wife d. March 14, 1714, ae. 84. Will dated 4 Dec. 1683. prob. 25 March, 1684, beq. to wife, son John and "other children;" son Philip exec.

BACHILER, BACHELER, BACHILLER, BATCHELDER, BATCHELOR,
Henry, of Dover, Eng., brewer, with wife Martha and four servants, came from Sandwich, Eng. before June 9, 1637. Settled at Ipswich; propr. before 1639.

The inv. of his est. was presented by John B. of Wenham and others, admins., 30 Sept. 1679.

John, Sen., Watertown, 1635. Rem. to Dedham. Town officer. Rem. to Reading; propr. 1650. He and his wife Rebecca recd. to Reading chh. from that of Ded. She d. March 17, 1661-2; he m. 2, Sarah ——. Ch. Samuel b. 8 (11) 1639, Jonathan and David b. 14 (10) 1643, Jonathan d. at Read. Dec. 4, 1653; Rebecca b. Oct. 30, 1660, John b. Feb. 23, 1663, Henry b. July 29, 1664, Sarah b. July 9, 1670, Samuel b. Jan. 23, 1661, Nathaniel b. March 17, 1674-5.

Will dated 2 July 1670, codicil 3 April, 1676, beq. to sons John and David and dau. Mary Cowdrey. Overseers Francis Skerry of Salem, Joseph Hills of Newbury, John Brown and Jonathan Poole of Reading.

John, tailor, Salem, 1638, frm. May 13, 1640. His wife memb. chh. 1639. Ch. John bapt. 20 (11) 1638, Mary bapt. 19 (7) 1640, Abigail bapt. 12 (12) 1642, adm. to full com. 12 (11) 1662, Hannah bapt. 23 (4) 1644, Hannah bapt. 25 (3) 1645, John bapt. 23 (4) 1650, Joseph bapt. 8 (3) 1653. He deposed in 1658, ae. about 47 years.

His wife d. 10 (9) and he d. 13 (9) 1675. Will dated in 1673, ae. 63 years; prob. Dec. 4, 1675, beq. to sons John and Joseph and dau. Hannah Corning; to gr. ch. John Cressey. Wife Elizabeth to be exec.

BACHILER, etc., cont.

Joseph, of Canterbury, Eng., tailor, with wife Elizabeth, one ch. and three servants came from Sandwich, Eng. before June 9, 1637. Brought cattle with him in partnership with Henry Paramor of Thanet; see accounts July 20, 1639. [L.] Settled at Salem, propr. 1637, frm. March 16, 1637-8, deputy 1643. Ch. Joseph bapt. 22 (6) 1647, Elizabeth adm. chh. 12 (11) 1662. He rem. to Wenham. ,
He d. (1) 1647.

Rev. Stephen, b. about 1561, matr. St. John's coll. Oxford, Nov. 17, 1581, B.A. Feb. 3, 1586-7, vicar of Wherwell, Hants, 26 Jan. 1587-8 to 1601; came in the William and Francis June 5, 1632, ae. 71, with wife Helen and others of his family. Settled at Saugus, (Lynn). Frm. May 6, 1635. Entered at once upon church life, drawing down the suspicions and oppositions of some in power for such independancy. Undertook a scheme for founding a plantation at Yarmouth, but the winter season and the poverty of his associates caused the brave attempt to fail. Rem. to Newbury; thence in 1638-9 joined in the settlement of Hampton, N. H., to which he is said to have given the name, and whose first minister he became.

After earnest service, mingled with injudicious (if not erring) conduct, which brought conflicts with his associates and the Mass. government, he rem. to Strawberry Bank, (Portsmouth,) whence he returned to England not far from 1647. Deeded land 8 (7) 1647, to his three grandsons, John and William Sanborne and Nathaniel Bachiler, Jr., all of Hampton. The place of his later residence and the date of his death are not known.

He m. first ——; he m. 2, Helen ——, who was ae. 48 in 1631, when he visited ch. at Flushing; she came hither and died; he m. 3. widow Mary ——, at Strawberry Bank, from whom he separated, leaving her here to a sad and unsavory life. Ch. Theodate, (m. Christopher Hussey,) Deborah, (m. Rev. John Wing,) Stephen, (ae. 16 on entering Oxford in 1610,) Ann, (ae. 20 in 1630; m. John Sandburn,) Nathaniel, (m. Hester Mercer; son Nathaniel came here and was an early citizen of Hampton. [See W.; Reg. XVII, XXXVII, XLV, XLVII and Genealogy.] frm. May 29, 1644. Sold land in 1653. First

William, victualer, Charlestown, 1634,

BACHILER, etc., cont.

wife Jane, second wife Rachel; ch. Seaborne bapt. 12 (1) 1634-5, Abigail bapt. 1 (5) 1637, (m. Richard Austin,) Rachel, (m. Philip Atwood,) Susanna, (m. John Lawrence,) Joseph b. 20 (6) 1644, Benjamin.
He d. Feb. 20, 1669, ae. 72. Will dated 12 (11) 1669-70, beq. to wife Rachel, daus. Atwood and Austin, son Joseph and Joseph and Benjamin Cromwell and Susanna Lawrence, gr. ch., living with him. The widow Rachel d. May 28, 1676, ae. 73.

BACON,

George, ae. 43 with ch. Samuel ae. 12, Susan ae. 10, John ae. 8 came in the Increase in April, 1635. (Name originally written Mason on the ship's roll, and re-written Bacon.) Settled at Hingham; propr. Sept. 1635. Ch. —— bapt Nov. 27, 1640.
He was bur. May 3, 1642. Admin. of the est. of George Bacon, sometime of Hingham, many years since deceased, was gr. 28 March, 1684, to Capts. John Smith and John Jacob, upon petition of his son Peter, who had maintained his aged mother till her death, and had purchased the rights of his bros. and sisters.

Michael, coming from Ireland, with Samuel Cooke and John Smyth, proposed as proprs. 23 (3) 1640, at Dedham. His wife who arrived in Ded. before him was adm. chh. 17 (7) 1641; she d. in 1647. His dau. Alice m. Thomas Bancroft. [His son] Michael of Woburn deposed 17 (4) 1668, ae. about 60 years. [Mdx. Files.]
He d. 18 (2) 1648. Will prob. 26 (2) 1649; sons Michael, Daniel and John; dau. Sarah; son-in-law Thomas Bancroft. [Reg. VII, 230.]

Nathaniel, tanner, Barnstable, atba. 1643, frm. 2 June, 1646; town officer. He joined the chh. May 3, 1648. He m. Dec. 4, 1642, Hannah Mayo, who was adm. ch. March 18, 1648; ch. Hannah b. Sept. 4, 1643, Nathaniel b. Feb. 5, 1645, Mary b. Aug. 12, 1648, Samuel b. Feb. 25, 1650, Elizabeth b. Jan. 28, 1653, Jeremiah b. May 8, 1657, Mercy b. Feb. 8, 1659, John b. June, 1661.
Admin. gr. and inv. rendered 29 Oct. 1673, to the widow Hannah. The dau. Elizabeth d. in 1676, and one of the heirs was Hannah, wife of George Shove.

Nicholas, rented land of Mr. John Cogan. [Court Rec. 1640.]

BACON, cont.

Rebecca, residence not stated, inventory of her goods taken by John Russell and Edward Collins 1 (8) 1638. [Suff. Prob.]

Thomas, witness to will of Ro. Hunt of Sudbury in 1640.

Mr. William, Salem, 1641. Res. at Dublin, Ireland, in 1639. His wife Rebecca was sister of Humphrey Potter, and dau. of Thomas Potter, sometime mayor of Coventry, co. Warwick. Humphrey Potter was killed in the massacre in Ireland and left one dau. Ann, who was taken to Coventry and thence brought to Salem, where she m. Anthony Needham. [Reg. XXXIX, 28.]

His will prob. 9 (9) 1653; wife Rebecca; minor son Isaac; Ann Potter. The widow's will was prob. 29 (9) 1655; her bro. Robert Buffum to assist her son Isaac as exec.; bros. Joseph Boys, Thomas Avery, and Nathaniel Felton; sisters Buffum, Boys, Avery, Sugthwick and Horn; cousins Ann P. and Richard Cheelcraft; freed her man Cornelius, and gave him a new suit of clothes. Left a fund for the poor in case son die before majority. A debt t obe paid to sister Judith in Eng.

BADCOCK, BABCOCK,

George, Dorchester, rem. to Milton.

Will dated 26 Sept. prob. 2 Feb. 1671. Est. to wife Mary, to bring up the children with; ch. Benjamin, Returne, George, Joseph and Enoch B.; Mary Ellen; Dorothy, Rachel and Leah B., Bro. Robert B. and neighbour Joseph Belcher overseers. Lands in Dorch. and Milton, and mill and lands at Dartmouth in Plymouth patent.

Robert, yeoman, captain, Dorchester, propr. before 1648, when he bought additional lands in every division; deed confirmed by Mrs. Ann Glover 26 (8) 1671. Town officer; captain. Ch. Samuel bapt. 7 (5) 1650, Jonathan bapt. 7 (1) 1651, James bapt. 12 (1) 1654, Abigail bapt. 27 (2) 1656, ae. about 3 months, Nathaniel b. 14 (1) 1657-8, bapt. 6 (4) 1658, Caleb bapt. 21 (8) 1660, ae about 2 months, Ebenezer bapt. 5 (5) 1663, ae. about 7 months, Hopestill bapt. 8 (9) 1663, Hannah bapt. 28 (3) 1665, ae. about 3 months, Elizabeth bapt. 14 (5) 1667, ae. about half a year, Thankful bapt. 27 (4) 1669.

Will dated 11 Nov. prob. 7 March, 1694, beq. to wife Joanna, son Nathaniel, gr. child Caleb, son-in-law Henry Vose.

BADGER,

Giles, Newbury, propr. 1638. Rem. to Wenham about 1655; ret. to Newb. [Wen. chh. rec.] He m. Elizabeth, dau. of Edmund Greenleaf, who survived him and m. 2, Feb. 16, 1648, Richard Browne. Ch. John b. June 30, 1643.

He d. July 10, 1647. Will dated 29 June, prob. 28 Sept. 1647, beq. to wife and child; father Greenleaf and others to divide est. when son is 18 years old.

Nathaniel, Newbury, in Ipswich court in 1642.

BAGLEY, see Bigelow,

BAGNALLY, BAGULEY, BAYNLY,

Thomas, Concord, before Gen. Court 1 (7) 1640.

He d. 18 (11) 1643; will prob. 13 (3) 1643. Beq. all to his partner Francis Barker. Inv. mentions carpenter's tools; debt due from Mr. Barnes of Braintree.

BAITON, BETON,

J., an early res. of Dorchester. Perhaps husband of Thomassin, memb. chh. before 1639.

BAKER.

Alexander, ae. 28, with wife Elizabeth, ae. 23, daus. Elizabeth, ae. 3, and Christian, ae. 1, came in the Elizabeth and Ann in April, 1635. Propr. at Gloucester before 1642. Settled at Boston; collar maker. Adm. to chh. with wife Elizabeth 4 (8) 1645. Frm. May 6, 1646. Ch. b. in B.: Alexander b. 15 (11) 1635, Samuel b. 16 ((11) 1637, John b. 20 (4) 1640, Joshua b. 30 (2) 1642, Hannah b. 29 (7) 1644,—all bapt. 5 (8) 1645; William b. 15 (3) 1647, Joseph bapt. 8 (2) 1649, ae. 2 days, Sarah bapt. 25 (3) 1651, Benjamin b. 16 March, 1652, bapt. 27 (1) 1653, Josiah b. 26 Feb. 1654. The dau. Christian m. 18 (5) 1654, Simon Roberts.

He d. 1685. Will dated 18 Feb. 1684, prob. 11 May, 1685. In his 79th year; 12 ch. living, viz. John, Joshua, William, Josiah, Elizabeth Watkins, Christian Roberts; gr. dau. Elizabeth Remington.

Ann. See Bayes.

Edward, Lynn, propr.; frm. March 14, 1638-9. One of the creditors of the Ironworks co. in 1654. [Suff. De., II, 266.] Of

BAKER, cont.
Boston, wife Jane; ch. Jonathan b. 20 Feb. 1657.

Francis, tailor, ae. 24, cert. from St. Albons, Herts. came in the Planter, April 2, 1635. Settled at Boston; wife Isabel; ch. Nathaniel b. 27 (1) 1642.

Francis, cooper, Yarmouth, adm. inhabitant 1 June, 1641. Ch. Samuel b. 1 May, 1648, Daniel b. Sept. 2, 1650.
Will dated 4 March, 1692, prob. Dec. 8, 1696, beq. to wife Isball; ch. John, Daniel and William B., Elizabeth Chase and Hannah Pearse; to Samuel, eldest son of son Nathaniel B.

John, Charlestown, 1629-30; No. 12 on first list of inhab. With wife Charity adm. chh. in 1630, frm. March 3, 1634. Ch. Charity bapt. 12 (2) 1635.
The Gen. Court allowed him 38 s. from Mr. Clerke 7 Sept. 1630, for damages in a bargain of cloth.

John, tailor, Charlestown, adm. chh. 31 (3) 1640, with wife Sarah; ch. Sarah bapt. 13 (7) 1640. Frm. June 2, 1641. "Sarah, dau. of John Baker, formerly my baylie,—the ch. b. in my house," rec'd a beq. from Mr. Robert Keayne, May 2, 1656.

John, husbandman, Boston, adm. chh. 26 (1), frm. May 18, 1642. Dism. to the chh. at Gorgeana 6 (7) 1646. [W.]

John, grocer, ae. 39, b. in Norwich, Eng. passed exam. to come to Charlestown, N. E. and there to reside, April 8, 1637, with wife Elizabeth, ae. 31. ch. Elizabeth, John and Thomas and servants Mary Alxarson, ae. 24, Ann Alxarson, ae. 20, Bridget Boulle, ae. 32, and Samuel Arres, ae. 14. Propr. at Watertown, and at Newbury, 1638. Rem. to Ipswich [L.] Propr. Bought a farm in Reading, adjoining Andover in 1661. Conveyed his estate to son Thomas, on condition that he should an annuity to himself, his wife and his dau. Elizabeth. The wife Elizabeth testified in 1666 regarding the will of her son Obediah Antrim; who beq. to his wife Martha and bros. John and Thomas B.

Launcelot, Boston. Wife Judith; ch. Elizabeth b. 13 (10) 1644.

Nathaniel, yeoman, Watertown, propr. before 1636. He deposed Sept. 21, 1677, ae. about 66 years, regarding Dexter's purchase of Nahant in 1632 or 1633. [Es. Files.] Hull propr. 1642, Hingham propr. and resident. Town officer. Deeded lands Jan. 15, 1672 to his dau. Mary and her husband, John Loring.
He d. June 3, 1682. Will dated 11 May, prob. 25 July, 1682. Wife Sarah; son-in-law John Loring and his ch. Joseph, Jacob, Marah, Rachel, Nathaniel, Isaac and David; to the six ch. of his bro. Nathaniel B., dec.
The widow d. at her dau.'s house 19. Aug., 1695.

Rev. Nicholas, came early to Hingham; propr.; frm. March 3, 1635-6, deputy. Rem. to Hull. Propr. Applied to Gen. Court 2 Aug. 1642, for liberty to plant at Seaconk, but does not seem to have gone. Was ordained minister at Scituate in 1660, and did a good work. He deposed to the will of John Allin June 2, 1663, ae. 53 years. His wife d. 23 April, 1661; he m. 2, Grace —. Ch. Samuel b. Oct. 2, 1638, Mary b. Dec. 1640, (m. Stephen Vinal,) Nicholas, Sarah, (m. Josiah Litchfield,) Deborah bapt. 6 June, 1652, (m. Israel Chittenden). The son John d. April 19, 1678, and his est. was admin. by his bro. Samuel 1 May folg.
He d. 22 Aug. 1678. He beq. to wife "in consideration of her extraordinary love and faithfulness in the discharge of her duty unto me and my children during the whole time of her lower station with me all that was hers before marriage with me, plate, clothing and books," with life use of house at Hull, lands, etc.; to sons Samuel and Nicholas and daus. Mary, Elizabeth, Sarah and Deborah; to wife's gr. ch. Mary Webb; to my gr. ch. Mercy B.; bro. Nathaniel B. one of the overseers of the will. Mistress Grace B. deposed. Her dau. Grace Dipple m. at Sci. 16 April, 1666, Joseph Webb of Boston.

Richard, Dorchester, propr. Nov. 4, 1639, frm. May 18, 1642. Signed inv. of John Pope in 1649. He m. Faith, dau. of Henry Withington; she d. Feb. 3, 1688-9. Ch. Mary bapt. 14 (12) 1640, Mary, (John?) b. 27 (2) 1643, John bapt. 30 (2) 1643, Sarah bapt. 22 (4) 1645, (m. 22 (12) 1664 James White,) John bapt. 28 (7) 1645, Thankful bapt. 19 (1) 1646, Elizabeth bapt. 27 (8) 1650, James bapt. 30 (2) 1654, Elizabeth bapt. 29 (5) 1656, Hannah b. 9 (11) bapt. 11 (11) 1662.

BAKER, cont.
He d. Oct. 25, 1689.
Will, dated 7 Oct., 1689. Sons John and James, son-in-law Samuel Robinson and my dau. his wife, James White, husband of dau. Sarah, dec., daus. Thankful, wife of William Griggs, Sarah Wiswell and Hannah B. [Reg. XXXIII, XLIII, XLIX.]

Robert, ship-carpenter, Salem, propr. 1637; d. from an accident in the building of a ship; the Court caused Richard Hollinsworth, the master builder, to pay 10 pounds to the wife and ch. of Baker in March, 1641. [W.]

Samuel, ae. 30, came in the Elizabeth and Ann in May, 1635.

Sarah, Ipswich, d. in 1651; admin. gr. 30 (7) 1651, to kinswoman Sarah Lumpkin.

Thomas, blacksmith, Roxbury, propr. frm. May 2, 1649. Wife —; ch. Elizabeth b. Oct. 2, 1641, Joseph b. Feb. 24, 1647, Sarah bapt. April 24, 1650, Mary bapt. June 2, 1652, Mary bapt. Sept. 5, 1653. He admin, June 8, 1676, on the est. of his son Thomas, slain by the Indians. [Reg. XXXIV, 201.]

He d. Jan. 28, 1683; "Old blind godly father Baker bur. 30 (11) 1683." Will, dated 27, Oct. 1683. prob. 27 Feb. 1683-4. Wife Elizabeth, son John, the ch. that were dau. Elizabeth's; ch. of dau. Sarah, wife of Jabez Jackson; ch. of dau. Maria, wife of Roger Adams; bro. Richard Baker. The widow Elizabeth d. 6 (6) 1685.

Walter, Salem, had letter of recommendation from Rev. Hugh Peter to Gov. Winthrop 25 (8) 1638.

William, sawyer, Plymouth, made bargain with Richard Church about work Jan. 7, 1632-3.]Ply. Col. Rec.[Had liberty to reside in the colony 5 Nov. 1638. Is probably William, carpenter, Boston, adm. inhabitant 28 (5) 1651. He m. 23 (7) 1651, Mary, dau. of Edmund Eddington. He m. 2, 22 (2) 1656, Pilgrim, dau. of John Eddy of Watertown. Ch. Mary b. and d. 1652, John b. 14 Dec. 1653, William b. 19 Oct. 1655, Nathaniel b. May 13, 1661.

William, husbandman, Charlestown, propr. 1633. With wife Joan was adm. chh. 31 (6) 1633. He was ae. 52 in 1651. Rem. to Watertown and later to Billerica. Ch. Sarah bapt. 20 (3) 1638, (m. Nathaniel Hutchinson), Mary bapt. 3 (6) 1640 (m. Samuel Petteford).

BAKER, cont.
Stephen bapt. 19 (12) 1641, Martha b. 21 (2) 1644, (m. Wm. Smith,) Bethia.

Will dated 19 (11) 1655, prob. 28 (10) 1658, beq. to wife Joan and children; ch. Sarah to remain at her dame Whitman's, Stephen and Mary at Thomas Gould's, Matthew [Martha?] at bro. James' and Bethia with bro. Russell of Woburn. The widow d. Sept. 26, 1669.

BALCH,
John, Salem, a very early settler, perhaps one of the Cape Ann Colony under Mr. Thomas Gardner in 1623. Resident before 1628. [Depos. of R. Brakenbury.] Adm. frm. May 13, 1631. Juryman in Gen. Court in 1630. Margery, [wife or dau.?] memb. chh. before 1636.

His will signed 15 May, prob. 28 (4) 1648, beq. to wife Annis (Agnes), sons Benjamin, John and Freeborn. The widow's est. went to son Benjamin for expenses of her last sickness. Admin. Nov. 25, 1657.

BALDEN, BALDUCKE,
John, Dedham. Wife Joanna, ch. John b. 21 (4) 1635. He d. about 1639, and his widow m. 2, John Gay, q. v.

BALDWIN, BALDIN,
George, Boston. Wife Anna; ch. John b. 25 (8) 1639, d. (6) 1643, Sarah bapt. 14 (3) 1648, ae. about 3 1-2 years, the mother being now wife of Richard Bradly.

Henry, Woburn, propr. He m. Nov. 1, 1649, Phebe Richardson; is she the P.R., widow, who d. Sept. 13, 1716? Ch. Susanna b. Aug. 30, 1650, d. Sept. 28, 1651, Susanna b. July 25, 1652, Phebe b. Sept. 7, 1654, John b. Oct. 28, 1656, Daniel b. March 15, 1659, Timothy b. May 27, 1661, Mary b. and d. 1663, Abigail b. Aug. 20, 1667, Ruth b. July 31, 1670, Benjamin b. Jan. 20, 1673.

John, ae. 13, with William, ae. 9, came in the Pied Cow, July, 1635. He may be the John Balden who covenanted in 1648 to work four years for Wm. Collier of Duxbury. Settled in Woburn. Rem. to Billerica. He m. May 15, 1655, Mary Richardson; ch. Mary b. and d. 1659, Mary b. April 11, 1663, John b. Sept. 25, 1665, Jonathan b. Jan. 28, 1667, Susanna b. 1670, d. 1675, Thomas b. March 26, 1672, Phebe b. and d. 1675, Su-

BALDWIN, etc., cont.
sanna b. April 14, 1677, Phebe b. Feb. 7, 1679.

He d. Sept. 25, 1687. Will prob. at Boston, before Gov. Andros, 28 March, 1688, beq. to present wife Mary; sons John, Jonathan and Thomas; daus. Mary Jeffs, and Susanna and Phebe B. Henry B. as witness.

Sylvester. His wife Sarah and son Richard allowed execs, according to the will before Court of Asst. at Boston 4 (7) 1638.

BALE, BALL,
Nathaniel, Concord, frm. May 22, 1650. Wife Mary; ch. John d. 27 (5) 1649, Nathaniel b. and d. in 1649, Nathaniel b. 3 July, 1663.

BALL, BALE,
Francis, Springfield, propr. 1643. Contracted to build a shop for a smith Sept. 4, 1646. Town officer. He m. 3 (8) 1644, Abigail Burt; ch. Jonathan b. 7 (8) 1645, Samuel b. 16 (1) 1647-8.

He was drowned in the Great River in Oct. 1648. The widow m. 2. 12 (2) 1649, Benjamin Mun; after his death she m. 3. Dec. 21, 1672, Thomas Stebbins, Jr. who d. Sept. 5, 1683. She deposed regarding land of Francis Ball, Feb. 9, 1690, ae. about 67 years. Made agreement with sons Jonathan and Samuel B. Sept. 30, 1684.

John, Watertown, frm. May 22, 1650. Rem. to Concord. Perhaps it was his wife Elizabeth who bore child Abigial at W. 26 (2) 1656.

He was buried 1 (8) 1655. Inv. filed.

Matthew, Dorchester, a witness in 1646.

Richard, Salisbury; propr. 1650.

BALLARD,
William, came in the Mary and John, March 26, 1634.

William, husbandman, ae. 32, with [wife] Mary, ae. 26, [ch.] Hester, ae. 2, and John, ae. 1, came in the James in July, 1635.

Mr. William appointed by the Gen. Court magistrate at Salem in 1638. Propr. at Sal. and also at Lynn. His children had lands assigned them at Reading in 1644.

BALLARD, cont.
Mr. William, of Lynn, failed to make a will, but told Nicholas Browne and Gerard Spencer, Jr., that he wished half his est. to go to his wife, and the rest to be divided amongst his children. Test 1 (1) [1639]. [Suf. Prob.] John deposed 29 (4) 1655, ae. about 21 years, regarding his bro. Jenckes, in whose service he was.

William, propr. at Newbury in 1645.

William, propr. at Andover, by wife Grace, had ch. John b. 17 Jan. 1653, Hannah b. 14 Aug. 1655, Lydia b. 13 April, 1657. He deposed in 1662, ae. about 45 years; [sic copia.]

He d. 10 July, 1698. Agreement signed 23 Oct. 1689, between his heirs William Blunt, Henry Holt, Samuel and Joseph Butterfield, John Spalden, Abigail, William and John Ballard and the widow Grace. She d. 27 April, 1694.

BALSTON,
Jonathan, Boston, adm. townsman 31 (1) 1645; was building a bark in 1649. Wife Mary, ch. John b. (8) 1645, Jonathan b. 2 March 1651, Prudence b. 28 May 1655, Lydia d. 6 (11) 1655, Elizabeth b. Sept. 18, 1660, Robert b. Dec. 3, 1662 and d. 3 Oct., 1663, Benjamin b. Feb. 8, 1663, Jonathan bapt. 28 (1) 1669, Mary (of sister Balston,) bapt. 10 (6) 1673.

Mr. William, Boston, juryman Nov. 9, 1630; frm. May 18, 1631; wife Elizabeth also memb. chh.; "d. soon." Town officer. Sold all his land and buildings to Thomas Connell Aug. 5, 1638. Banished for sympathy with Mrs. Hutchinson. His dau. Pittie b. (8) 1630, William bapt. 15 (2) 1633, Mary bapt. 14 (7) 1634, Mehetabel bapt. 24 (11) 1635, Meribah bapt. 9 (2) 1637.

BAMBRIDGE, BANBRIDGE, BAINBRICK, BANBRICKE. BANBROOKE.
Guy, housekeeper, Cambridge, propr. 1634, frm. March 4, 1634-5. He was bur. April 10, 1645. His widow Justice deposed 11 (5) 1664, ae. about 64 years. [Mdx. Files.] Dau. Jane m. Samuel, son of Bartholomew Green. [Mi.]

BANCROFT, BANCROFTE, BANCRAFT,
Edward, Plymouth, taxed in 1632; atba. 1643.

BANCROFT, etc., cont.

Roger, weaver, Cambridge, 1636, frm. May 18, 1642; town officer, propr.
He signed inv. of Frances Blosse in 1647. He d. Nov. 28, 1653. Will prob. 4 (2) 1654. All to wife Elizabeth save beqs. to Mr. Mitchell and elder Frost; wife exec. [Reg. XVI. 74]

Thomas, Dedham, townsman, 1648. Rem to Reading about 1653. He deposed in 1681, ae. about 58 years. He m. 31 (1) 1647, Alice, dau. of Michael Bacon; she d. 29 (1) 1648; ch. Thomas b. and d. 1648. He m. 2, 15 (5) 1648, Elizabeth Metcalf, who was adm. chh. 14 (10) 1651; and to that of R. from that of Ded. 22 (9) 1669; ch. Elizabeth b. and d. 1650, John b. 3 (12) 1651, Elizabeth b. at R. 7 (10) 1653.

He d. at Lynn, lieut., 19 Aug. 1691. Inv. of his est. filed 24 Nov. 1691 by son Ebenezer, shows land at Reading and Lynn, etc. Agreement for division was made between the widow Elizabeth, sons Thomas, John and Ebenezer, Joseph Brown, husband of the dau. Elizabeth, and Sarah B., the youngest dau., yet unmarried. His widow Elizabeth d. 1 May, 1711.

Widow had land assigned her in 1638 at Lynn.

BANES,

Martha, ae. 20, came in the Defense in July, 1635.

BANGS,

Edward, yeoman, Plymouth, came in 1623; had 4 lots; frm. 1633. Juror, commissioner; rem. to Eastham; town officer 1647. Ch. Bethia b. May 28, 1650, Mercy and Apphia b. Oct. 15, 1650. His wife Rebecca joined him in a deed in 1651. Dau. Rebecca m. Oct. 26, 1654, Jonathan Sparrow.
He made will 11 Oct. 1674,ae. 86 years; beq. to sons Jonathan, John and Joshua; to Jona.'s eldest son, Edward; to daus. Howes, Higgens, Hall, Merrick and Atwood; to the ch. of dau. Rebecca, dec.

BANKS, BANKES,

Mrs. Lydia, Salem, memb. chh. 1636. After being absent from the chh. 22 years she was dismissed, at her request, 6 (9) 1664, to a chh. in London of which Mr. Nye is pastor. [Salem chh. rec.] She wrote from Maidstone, Kent, Eng. Aug. 28, 1646, to her

BANKS, etc., cont.

bro. William Hathorne; spoke of bro. Read; mentioned W. H.'s sale of her land at the plains; of her cattle; of a trunk left at bro. Mores. [Es. Files XXXVI, 56.] Another letter, dated 18 April, 1648, refers to bro. Roger Moorie; to "my sister, your wife;" to "my bro. Read." She also wrote from London in 1673, to Daniel Epps, calling him her cousin; spoke of seeing him as a child in Holland, and at his mother's house in New Eng.; sent respects to his father Symonds, her cousin; refers to his aunt Lake. [E. and W.] [Reg. LI, 262.]

BANSHOTT,

Thomas, ae. 14, came in the Bevis in May, 1638.

BARBER, BABER, BARBOUR, BARBUR,

Edward, Dedham. He d. (5) 1644. [Chh. Rec.]

George, Dedham, townsman 2 (10) 1640, frm. May 26, 1647. Mr. Ralph Wheelocke, in his will, calls him brother-in-law. He rem. to Medfield; oldest sergeant authorized by Gen. Court to train men 19 Oct. 1652; captain; drew and attested many documents; signed Barbur. Wife Elizabeth, adm. chh. 27 (8) 1643; ch. Mary b. and d. 1643, Mary b. 31 (11) 1644, Samuel b. 6 (11) 1646, John b. 13 (1) 1649, Elizabeth b. 11 (2) 1651. Admin. of his est. gr. to his son Samuel 15 May, 1685; inv. taken April 23, 1685.

James, Dorchester, propr. about 1637.

Jeremy, beneficiary in will of Edward Skinner of Cambridge in 1641.

John, carpenter, Salem, propr. 1636; adm. chh. 3 (2) 1642. Wife adm. chh. 29 (10) 1640; ch. bapt. 27 (9) 1640. Faith B. who recd. beq. from Margaret Pease in 1642, was, perhaps, one of these persons.

Richard, Dedham, propr. 23 Nov. 1638. Adm. chh. (5) 1639; frm. May 13, 1640.
He d. 18 (4) 1644. His inv. taken 15 (5) 1644; will prob. 21 (5) 1646. No family mentioned. Henry Brock and his son John B. execs. [Reg. 111, 178.]

Thomas, ae. 21, came in the Christian March 16, 1634. [Thomas was at Windsor, Conn. in 1635.]

William, Dorchester. Rem. to Salem;

BARBER, etc., cont.
propr. 1639. Sold land in Dorchester Oct. 31, 1639; hailing from Ludgate Hill, London, he bought land in Watertown 31 (3) 1648. Res. in Boston in 1652. See draft of his son John "Baber" Oct. 28, 1651. [Suff. De. I, 258.] Had lawsuits in Es. court in 1641. Inv. of his est. mentions land at Dorch. Admin. gr. to widow Elizabeth 29 (4) 1677.

BARCROFTE,
John, embarked with [wife] Jane April 12, 1632. He gave bonds to the Court for her behavior Sept. 3, 1633.

BARDEN,
William, covenant servant of Thomas Boardman, transferred to John Barker, bricklayer, for 6½ years from 1 Dec. 1638, to learn the trade of bricklayer. Marshfield, atba. 1643. Rem. to Middleborough; widow Deborah admin. on his est. 22 March, 1692-3.

BARKER,
Edward, Boston. Wife Jane; ch. Elizabeth, "sonne," b. 17 July, 1650, Mary b. 15 Feb. 1652, John b. 15 Jan. 1653, Sarah b. 9 March, 1654, Thomas b. 23 Aug. 1657.

Will dated June 27, 1674, prob. 30 Oct. 1678. Wife Jane to have life use of all; division to be made to surviving ch. at her death.

James, tailor, Rowley, propr., frm. Oct. 7, 1640. Wife Grace was bur. 27 (12) 1665; he m. 2, May 22, 1666, Mary Wiat. Ch. Eunice b. 2 (4) 1642, bur. (3) 1645, Nathaniel b. 15 (8) 1644, Eunice b. 11 (12) 1645, Grace b. 1 (2) 1650, Tamar b. 15 (10) 1652, Stephen b. Sept. 1653.

He was bur. 7 Sept. 1678. Will dated 3 (7) prob. 24 (7) 1678. Says he was b. at Ragwell, co. Suffolk, Eng. Beq. to wife Mary good support and the fulfillment of marriage contract; to sons Barzillai, James and Nathaniel, dau. Eunice, her husband John Watson and their children; to dau. Grace B.; bro. George Kilborne.

Dorothy, Dorchester, memb. chh. before 1639.

John, bricklayer, Marshfield, propr. 5 Nov. 1638. Ferryman over Jones River. Took John Barden apprentice 10 Jan. 1638-8. Juror.

He d. by the casualty of the sea; inquest Dec. 14, 1652. Admin. gr. to his widow An-

BARKER, cont.
na Dec. 17, 1652. Division made 9 June, 1653, to daus. Anna, Deborah and Mary, to be paid at 21 years of age. The widow m. Abraham Blush, who settled with Wm. Barden, husband of Deborah, and John Pratt, husband of Ann, 27 Oct. 1666, and with Samuel Pratt, husband of Mary 2 (9) 1668, for their portions.

Robert, Plymouth, apprentice of John Thorp, carpenter, Jan. 20, 1632. [Plym. Col. Rec.] His time was to expire in April, 1637. Ferryman, town officer, keeper of an ordinary at Marshfield in 1646; frm. 6 June, 1654.

Will dated 18 Feb. 1689, prob. 16 March, 1691-2, beq. to ch. Francis and Robert B., Rebecca Snow and Abigail Rogers; gr. ch., children of dec. son Isaac, and others. John Barker and Desire his wife witnesses.

Richard, husbandman, Andover, bought stock and produce of Wm. Hughes in 1643. [Es. court rec.] Wife Joanna; ch. Ebenezer b. 22 March, 1651, Richard b. 10 April, 1654, Hannah b. 21 Oct. 1656, Stephen b. 6 July, 1659, Benjamin b. 28 Feb. 1663.

Will dated 7 April, 1688, prob. March 28, 1693, beq. to ch. John, William, Ebenezer, Richard, Stephen, Benjamin, Sarah and Hester, and to gr. daus. Priscilla, Hester and Sarah, ch. of dec. dau. Hannah.

Thomas, Rowley, propr. 1643.

He was bur. 30 Nov. 1650. Will prob. 25 (1) 1651, beq. to wife Mary; to sister Jane Lambert; to Thomas and Jane L. and their bros. and sisters; to the town and various individuals. The widow m. Mr. Ezekiel Rogers.

William, servant, in Court 6 Oct. 1635, witness from Marblehead in Essex Court in 1642.

BARLOW, BARLOE, BABLOOE,
Bartholomew, cooper, Boston, had suit in Salem court, 1645. Signed inv. of Wm. Joice in 1648. Bought house and land Jan. 20, 1653.

He d. 26 (7) 1657. Nunc. will prob. Oct. 15, 1657; whole est. to son Thomas. [Reg. IX, 229.]

George, before Gen. Court Sept. 19, 1637. Settled at Sandwich. Constable. He m. Jane, widow of Anthony Bessey, whose daus. were before Plym. Court 4 March, 1661-2 for ill-treating him.

BARLOW, etc., cont.

He made will Aug. 4, prob. Oct. 31, 1684; beq. to wife, sons John and Nathan; to Aaron and Moses B. The widow made will 6 Aug., prob. 5 Oct. 1693; beq. to sons John and Nathan B. and Nehemiah Bessie; to daus. Ann Hallett, Elizabeth Bodfish and Rebecca Hunter.

BARNARD, BERNARD,

John, ae. 30 with wife Phebe, ae. 27, and ch. Thomas King ae. 15, John Bernard, ae. 2, and Samuel Bernard, ae. 1, came in the Elizabeth of Ipswich April 30, 1634. Phebe and her ch. John and Samuel had beq. from her mother Anne, widow, successively, of Anthony Whiting of Dedham, Essex, clothier, and of Thomas Wilson of D., in her will prob. 13 Dec. 1638. [Reg. L, 390.] Settled at Watertown; propr. 1636; frm. Sept. 3, 1634. Ch. rec. at Wat., Mary b. 7 (9) 1639, Joseph b. 12 (9) 1642.

He was. bur. June 23, 1646. His widow d. Aug. 1, 1685. The inv. of her est. was taken 5 Oct. 1685, showed a good property.

John, ae. 36, with wife Mary, ae. 38, and Henry Haward, ae. 7, came in the Francis of Ipswich April 30, 1634. Settled at Cambridge; frm. March 4, 1634-5. Propr. 1634; sold some lands about 1639.

Methusalah, Masachell, Musachiel, of Batcombe, Eng., tailor, ae. 24, with wife Mary, ae. 28, sons John, ae. 3, Nathaniel, ae. 1, and his servant Richard Persons, salter, ae. 30, came from Weymouth, Eng., March 20, 1635. Settled at Weymouth. Ch. Mary b. 27 (7) 1635, Sarah b. 5 (2) 1637.

Richard, Watertown, town officer Nov 14, 1635.

Robert, husbandman, Salisbury, 1642; Andover 1644, and Nantucket 1663. Memb. chh. And. 1645. Wife Joanna d at Nan. March 21, 1705. Ch. Hannah, (m. John Stevens,) John b. at Salis. March 2, 1642, Stephen, Mary b. at And. April 8, 1658.

He d. at Nan. about 1682. Admin. of his est. was gr. to his son Robert B. Feb. 1, 1714-5, "after he had been dead more than 30 years."

Tobias, grad. Harv. Coll. in the first class, 1642.

Thomas, husbandman, Salisbury, 1642. Wife Ellen, Eleanor or Helena; ch. Thomas

BARNARD, etc., cont.

b. 10 (3) 1641, Nathaniel b. 15 (11) 1642, Martha b. Sept. 22, 1645, (m. Thomas Haynes, m. 2, Samuel Bucknam,) Mary, twin of Martha, (m. 1, Anthony Morse, m. 2, Philip Eastman,) Sarah b. Sept. 28, 1647, (m. William Hackett,) Hannah b. Nov. 24, 1649, (m. Benj. Stevens,) Ruth b. Oct. 16, 1651, (m. Joseph Peaseley,) John, Abigail b. Jan. 20, 1656, (m. Samuel Fellows).

He was killed by the Indians about 1677. Admin. of his est. was gr. to his widow Oct. 1677; division made in 1679 to nine ch. viz. Thomas B., Wm. Hackett, Thomas Haynes, Jos. Peaseley, Benj. Stevens, John B., widow Moyse, Abigail and Nathaniel B.

Mr. William, gent., Charlestown, 1639. Will composed in 1639; he drew exchange on his cousin, Mr. Thomas Free, merchant, Sept. 8, 1640. [L.] Wife Alice adm. chh. 1 (5) 1645.

BARNARDSTON,

Katharine, Salem, memb. chh. 1639.

BARNISTON,

Marmaduke, a servant, before Es. court 3 (8) 1637.

BARNES, BARRENS,

Mr. John, gent., merchant, yeoman, Plymouth, frm. 1633. Gave a bond Oct. 9, 1640. Bought house and land in Roxbury and sold it again June 17, 1656. Signed his name up to 1649, made his mark in 1651. He volunteered for the Pequot war in 1637. He m. Sept. 12, 1633, Mary Plummer; she d. June 2, 1651 or 1661. Ch. Lydia b. April 24, 1647, John d. Sept. 25, 1648, Mary m. Robert Marshall. He gave cattle to his ch. Jonathan, Mary, Hannah and Lydia 24 Aug. 1651.

Will, dated March 6, 1677-8, prob. 29 Oct. 1671; wife Jone, son Jonathan, gr. son, John Marshall, cousin, the wife of Henry Sampson; kinswoman, Ester Ricket. Refers to dau. Lydia, now deceased. [Reg. VII, 236.]

Joshua, planter, Plymouth, appr. to Mr. Paine for 5 years Sept. 4, 1632. Rem. to Yarmouth; com. for division of lands 5 March, 1638-9; prop. frm. 1 June, 1641.

Matthew, miller, Braintree, Boston. Ch. Sarah b. 29 (6) 1641. One of the com. to lay out lots at Concord, 1 Oct. 1645. One

BARNES, etc., cont.
of the owners of the tide mill in Boston in 1650. His wife Rebecca d. 19 (7) 1657. He m. 2, Elizabeth, widow of Thomas Hunt. She deposed in Mdx. Court 2 (1) 1655, ae. about 55 years. After Barne's death she had goods appraised at Boston which had been the property of her first husband, T. H. He d. [at Malden?] about 8 (4) 1667, when inventories of his est. and that Elizabeth inherited from her first husband were filed in Mdx. probate.

Richard, from Penton, Hants., came in the Jonathan in 1639. Brought suit 6 (2) 1652, against Thomas Blanchard for money beq. him by his mother Agnes Bent, who had m. Blanchard after the death of her husband Barnes. [Reg. XXXII, 407.]

Thomas, Salisbury, propr. 1639; may be the same as

Thomas, blacksmith, Salem. Wife Mary; ch. Benjamin b. 1 Oct. 1655, Mary b. 1658, d. 1660, Mary b. 19 (1) 1661.
He was drowned (10) 1663. Inv. filed 28 (4) 1664.

Thomas, farmer, weaver, Hingham, propr. 1637, frm. May, 1645. Ch. Thomas and John b. May 21, 1643, Elizabeth b. Dec. 8, 1644, Anna b. June, 1647, (m. Robert Breame,) James b. Apr. 8, 1649, Sarah b. and d. 1650, Peter b. June 6, 1652.
He d. 29 Nov. 1672, ae. 70 years. Will beq. to wife and ch. Widow Anna d. 5 April, 1691.

William, Gloucester, frm. June 2, 1641. His wife Sarah, of Boston, appl. for divorce and maintenance for herself and ch. 19 (8) 1647. [A.] Sarah, (the same?) m. John Tinker, and d. about 13 (10) 1648. [Reg. VII, 174.] Inv. of her estate, with list of debts on file. One of the 2 daughters Richard Cooke took to bring up; the other remained with John Tinker; 6, 13 s., 4 d. was apportioned to each.

William, house carpenter, Salisbury, propr. 1639. He deposed in 1680, ae. about 60 years. (Ipswich Deeds.) Ch. Mary, (m. John Hoyt,) Hannah b. 22 (11) 1643, (m. John Prowse,) Deborah b. April 1, 1646, (m. Samuel Davis,) Jonathan b. 1 (2) 1648, William d. 11 (4) 1648, Rachel b. 30 (2) 1649, (m. Thomas Sargent,) Sarah, (m. 1, Thomas

BARNES, etc., cont.
Rowell, 2, John Harvey,) Rebecca, (m. Moses Morrill.)
His will, dated at Almsbury, 7 April, 1696, prob. Sept. 28, 1698, beq. to daus. Mary Hoyt, Deborah Davis, Rachel Sargent, Sarah Harvey, Rebecca Morrill (and her son William Barnes Morrell,) to son-in-law John Prowse; Abigail Diamond; gr. ch. Sarah Hoyt; to James George, Sen.

BARNETT,
John, Watertown, propr. 1645.

BARNHOUSE,
Richard, gave bond Sept. 2, 1638, to Wm. Pester of Salem.

BARNEY, BARNY,
Jacob, Salem, frm. May 14, 1634; deputy 1635, 1647. He opposed the sentence of the Gen Court against those who petitioned for freer franchise. Anna, [his wife?] memb. chh. 1637. He m. 18 (5) 1657, Hannah Johnson. She d. 5 (4) 1659, and he m. 26 (2) 1660, Ann Witt. Ch. John bapt. 15 (10) 1639, Hannah b. 30 (3) 1659, Hannah b. 2 (1) 1660-1, Sarah b. 12 (7) 1662, Abigail b. 3 (8) 1663, John b. 1 (6) 1665, Jacob b. 21 (3) 1667, Ruth b. 27 (7) 1669.
He d. at Rehoboth. Will dated 30 July, 1690, aged; prob. Jan. 10, folg.; beq. to ch. John, Joseph, Israel, Jonathan, Samuel, Sarah Hampton, Ruth, Dorcas Throope, Abigail Marshall, and Hannah. Wife Ann.

Edward B., of Braddenham, Bucks, yeoman, beq. 9 Oct. 1643, to "son Jacob B., if he be living at time of my death and come over into England." [Reg. L, 534.]

BARNOPE, see Burnope,

BARRELL,
George, cooper, Boston, propr., 1638; adm. chh. 5 (7) 1641; frm. May 10, 1643. His wife Anne adm. chh. 25 (1) 1643.
He d. 11 (7) 1643. Will prob. 30 (8) 1643; wife Anne; ch. John, James and Anne. [Reg. II, 384, and VIII, 55.] [L.]

Thomas, residence not stated, frm. May, 1645.

William, d. in Boston 20 (6) 1639.

BARRENS, see Barnes.

BARRETT,
James, planter, Charlestown, 1643, rem. to Malden; ae. 50 in 1665. Wife Hannah (Fosdick) was ae. 50 in 1665. Ch. James b. 6 (2) 1644, Mary, (m. John Ross,) Hannah b. 21 (1) 1647, (m. John Scollay,) Stephen; John b. May 6, 1655, Sarah, (m. Simon Grover).

He d. Aug. 16, 1672. Will dated 8 (5) 1672, beq. to wife Hannah, eldest son James, daus. Hannah, Mary and Sarah, sons John and Stephen, and to gr. ch. John and Samuel Scolye and John Ross. The widow Hannah made will 9 April, prob. 20 June, 1681; beq. to gr. ch. Samuel and Thomas [Tingle;] to dau. Hannah Scolly's two ch.; to daus. Mary Ross and Sarah Grover and their ch.; to gr. ch. John Barrett. Bro. John Fosdecke exec.

John, Taunton, atba. 1643.

Stephen, Ipswich, placed by Vincent Potter 21 (4) 1639, with Wm. Foster, as an apprentice. [L.]

Stephen, brewer, Boston, made will 1 Aug., prob. 14 (7) 1671. Beq. to his dau. Elizabeth Jones; to her husband John and son John.

Thomas, Concord, landholder before 1650.

He d. 14 (4) 1652. Inv. of his estate filed 5 (8) 1652. Land, farming implements, household goods, house bought of Wm. Aline, etc. Mary, of Concord, who made will June 15, 1663, ae. about 73 years, and beq. to sons John and Humphrey B. may have been his wife.

Thomas, ae. 16, came in the Increase April 15, 1635.
Thomas of Chelmsford, propr. may be this man.

Will dated 1 (1) 1662, prob. 6 (8) 1668, beq. to wife Margaret, sons John, Thomas and Joseph.

BARRON, BARRONE,
Ellis, and Elliz, Watertown, frm. June 2, 1641; propr.; bought meadow in Cambridge in 1653. Wife Grace. Ellis, ae. about 20 in 1653. [Mdx. Files.] (m. 14 (10) 1658, Hannah Hawkins,) Mary, (m. Dec. 10, 1650, Daniel Warren;) Susanna, (m. 14 (10) 1653, Stephen Randall;) Hannah, (m. 17 (9) 1658, Simon Coolidge;) John, Sarah b. 25 (4) 1640, Moses b. (1) 1643. He m. 2, Han-

BARRON, etc., cont.
nah, widow of Timothy Hawkins, Sen., whose will, dated 18 Aug. 1683, prob. Oct. 6, 1685, mentions her son Timothy Hawkins and her dau. Hannah Barron's ch., gr. ch. Benjamin and Benoni Garfield.

He d. Oct. 30, 1676. His will prob. Dec. 19, 1676, beq. to wife, sons Elizeus, John and Moses, and the rest of his seven children; to gr. ch. Elizabeth B. The inventory mentions "barbaren instruments" and tools "to draw teeth," etc.

BARSHAM, BASHAM, BASSOM,
William, Watertown, 1630, juror, propr., frm. March 9, 1636-7. Wife Anniball; ch. John b. 8 (10) 1635, Anna b. 7 (11) 1637, Joshua b. 15 (1) 1640, Susanna b. 28 (11) 1641, Mary b. 23 (4) 1648, Rebecca b. 12 (10) 1657, Elizabeth b. July 29, 1658.

He d. 3 July, 1684. He made will 28 Aug. 1683, codicil dated 15 April, 1684, prob. 29 (6) 1684; beq. to sons John, Joshua and Nathaniel; daus. Hannah Spring, Susanna Capen, Sarah Browne, Mary Bright, Rebecca Winship and Elizabeth B.; gr. son William B., son of John.

BARSTOW, BAIRSTOW, BASTOW, BEARSTOW,
George, ae. 21 yrs. came in the Truelove Sept., 1635. Settled at Dedham; adm. propr. at request of his bro. Wm. 11 (6) 1637. Res. at Cambridge. Rem. to Scituate. Ch. Margaret bapt. Feb. 24, 1649, George bapt. after the father's death, June 12, 1653.

He d. at Camb. 18 (1) 1652. His will dated 10 (1) 1652, beq. to his wife and two children in equal portions. The widow Susan, dau. of Thomas Marritt, d. in 1654, leaving Margaret about 4 years old and son George about 2. Inv. taken 4 May, 1654; admin. gr. to Tho. Marritt.

John, Cambridge.
The inv. of his est. taken 2 (12) 1657, was filed by the widow, Lydia. She 2, Richard Standlake of Scituate; was appointed 7 June, 1674, guardian to her 2 sons, John and Jeremiah B., and authorized to receive for them the legacies left them by their uncle Michael B. of Wat., who also gave lands to her son Michael B.

Michael, Miles, Charlestown, with wife Marcia adm. chh. 5 (10) 1635; frm. May 3, 1635; propr. Rem. to Watertown about 1642,

BARSTOW, etc., cont.
deputy. Signed inv. of Henry Kemball in 1648.

His wife Grace d. July 20, 1671; he d. June 23, 1674. Will dated same day. Beq. to pastor, Mr. John Sherman; to the chh. of Wat. 16 pounds; to Elizabeth, wife of Wm. Randall of Sci.; to Hannah, widow of Wm. Barstow, now Prince; to Susan, wife of Wm. Perry of Marshf.; to Michael, John and Jeremiah, sons of John B., dec.; to 2 ch. of his bro. George B. dec. and 8 ch. of his bro. Wm. B. dec.; to deacons Thomas Hastings and Henry Bright. [Reg. VIII, 169.]

William, ae. 23 yrs. came in the Truelove in Sept., 1635. Before the Gen. Court June 7, 1636; Dedham, propr. 1636. Rem. to Scituate. Contracted to build a bridge and keep it in repair in 1664; refers to his son-in-law Moses Simons. He m. at Dedham 8 (5) 1638, Ann Hubbard; she was adm. chh. 16 (2) 1641. Ch. Joseph b. 6 (4) 1639, Mary b. 28 (10) 1641, Patience b. 3 (10) 1643; rec. at Sci.; Deborah bapt. Aug. 18, 1650, William b. Sept., 1652, Martha bapt. April 22, 1655.

He d. 1 Jan. 1668. [Dedham rec.] Admin. gr. to his widow Anna, [Plym. Court,] 2 March, 1668-9. Inv. filed April 5, 1669. She afterward m. [John] Prince (of Hingham).

BARTHOLOMEW, BARTELMEW,
Mr. Henry, Salem, 1635, frm. May 17, 1637; propr.; town officer; deputy. Wife Elizabeth; ch. Elizabeth bapt. 3 (8) 1641, Hannah bapt. 12 (12) 1642-3, John bapt. 10 (9) 1644, Abraham bapt. 22 (9) 1646, Eleazer bapt. 29 (5) 1649, Abigail bapt. 6 (8) 1650, William bapt. 2 (8) 1652, Eliza bapt. 2 (5) 1654, Henry bapt. 10 (3) 1657, Sarah b. 29 (11) bapt. 6 (12) 1658.

Admin. on his est. was gr. to his son Henry 20 Dec. 1692. Inv. shows a fourth part of a mill, land, etc.

Richard, Salem, 1637, adm. chh. 21 (4) 1640, frm. June 2, 1641.

Made will in letter to his bro. Henry when about to sail to London; prob. Essex Court 4 (6) 1646. To Henry's 2 ch.; to his bro. Williams 3 ch.; to his mother; to Mr. Gearing; to bros. Thomas and Abraham and sister Sarah; to Jacob Barney.

William, husbandman, Ipswich, merchant, propr., frm. March 4, 1634-5. Deputy;

BARTHOLOMEW, etc., cont.
register. Agent for Whittingham, Paine and Wade 14 (8) 1647. [A.] Bought land in Boston July 26, 1659. With wife Mary rec'd to Boston chh. 12 (1) 1662.

William, Dorchester, propr. 1636. When old and sick he was cared for by the town. his house and land going to them, and some goods to persons to whom he beq. He d. in 1652.

BARTLETT,
Richard, Sen., shoemaker, came to Newbury early. His family Bible is extant, in which he rec. the births of the following ch.: Joane b. Jan. 29, 1610, (m. Wm. Titcomb,) John b. 9 Nov. 1613, Thomas b. Jan. 22, 1615, Richard b. Oct. 31, 1621, Christopher b. 25 Feb. 1623, Anne b. Feb. 26, 1625); the sons John, Richard and Christopher came to Newbury. [Reg. XI, 192.]

He d. 25 May, 1647. Will (oral) prob. 29 Sept. 1647; John had already recd. his portion; he beq. to Christopher, Joane and her four daus., Richard and John. The latter had the "great Bible."

Robert, cooper, Plymouth, came in the Anne in 1623; frm. 1633; juryman and town officer. He m. Mary, dau. of Richard Warren; her marriage portion confirmed to him 7 March, 1636. Ch. Lydia b. June 8, 1647, Mercy b. March 10, 1650, (m. Dec. 25, 1668, John Ivey of Boston,) Rebecca, (m. Dec. 20, 1649, Wm. Harlow of Plymouth,) Sarah, (m. Dec. 23, 1656, Samuel Rider of Plymouth,) Mary, (m. Sept. 10, 1651, Richard Foster of Plymouth,) Elizabeth, (m. Dec. 26, 1661, Anthony Sprague of Plymouth).

He d. in 1676; will prob. 29 Oct. 1676; beq. whole est. to wife.

Robert, embarked June 22, 1632; before the Gen. Court 1638. He may be the Robert who was drowned in Watertown July 5, 1663. [Mdx. Files.] Another Robert was an early resident of Northampton.

Thomas, Watertown, servant to Mr. Pelham 1631. [Court Rec.] Frm. March 4, 1634-5. Propr. at Dedham 1636-1638, but not res. Town officer; app. lieut. by Gen. Court 10 (10) 1641. Wife Hannah; ch. Hannah bur. 26 (6) 1639, ae. 2 yrs., Mehitabel b. 15 (5) 1640, Hannah b. 6 (6) 1642, Bethsua b. 17 (2) 1647, Abiah b. May 28, 1651.

BARTLETT, cont.
He d. April 26, 1654, ae. about 60 yrs., his widow d. July 11, 1676. His will dated 22 April, 1653, beq. to daus. Mehitabel, Hannah, Bethsuah and Abiah, and to wife Hannah whom he made exec. [Reg. XVII, 158.] Inv. of the est. of the widow Hannah was taken 30 Sept. 1676.

William, before Gen. Court 4 (4) 1639.

BARTOLL,
John, planter, Marblehead, had lawsuits in 1640 and 1644. Sold a house and garden in Crewkerne, co. Somerset, legacie of his father John B., glover, 24 (5) 1641. Town officer, 1657. Wife Parnell; ch. Mary b. 1 Feb. 1642, William, ae. 32 in 1662, and John, ae. 42 in 1673, may have been children.
He was found drowned; inquest 1 Oct. 1664. Admin. Essex Court 29 (9) 1664.

BARTON,
Marmaduke, servant to Francis Weston of Salem, before Es. Court in 1638, and before Boston Court 14 June, 1642.

BASCOM, BASKECOMB,
Thomas, Dorchester, propr. Nov. 22, 1634. Rem. to Windsor, Conn.; thence to Northampton in 1656. Ch. b. at Windsor: Abigail bapt. 7 June ,1640, Thomas bapt. 20 Feb. 1641-2, Hephzibah bapt. 14 April or July, 1644. He was desired to assist his dau. Hannah, widow of John Broughton of North. in admin. of her husband's est. March 25, 1662.
His will, dated 8 July, 1679, beq. to son Thomas B.; daus. Hannah, wife of William Janes, and Hephzibah, wife of Robert Lyman. Inv. showed husbandry implements, mason's tools, house, lands, etc.

BASS,
Samuel, Boston, Braintree, deacon, frm. May 10, 1634, deputy 1643. Ch. Mary m. John Capen, Hannah m. 15 (9) 1651, Stephen Payne, Samuel d. of smallpox at Nantasket 9 Aug. 1690. Mrs. Ann, wife of deacon Samuel, d. 5 Sept. 1693, ae. 93. Deacon Samuel d. 30 Dec. 1694, ae. 94; father, gr. father and gr. gr. father of 162 persons before he died.

BASSETT,
Thomas, ae. 37, came in the Christian March 16, 1634. Rem. to Windsor, Conn.

William, specified as an Englishman, m. at Leyden, Holland, Aug. 13, 1611, Margaret Oldham; having previously had a wife named Cecil Light. [Ley. Rec.] Came to Plymouth in 1621. Frm. 1633. Res. at Duxbury; gunsmith; deputy. Res. at Sandwich in 1650. [Ply. Col. Rec.] Rem. to Bridgewater. Wife Elizabeth and ch. William and Elizabeth shared in the division of cattle in 1627. Sons Nathaniel B. and Peregrine White had deed of land from him in 1656. Dau. Elizabeth m. Nov. 8, 1648, Thomas Burgess of Sandwich.
He d. at Br. in 1667. Will dated 3 (2) prob. 5 June, 1667, beq. to wife Mary and sons William and Joseph.

William, ae. 9 years, came in 1635 with his step-father Hugh Burt, [q. v.] and settled at Lynn.
He d. March 31, 1703. Will dated Feb. 10, 1701, having arrived at a good old age, prob. May 22, 1703, beq. to wife; to ch. William, John, Elisha, Samuel, Elizabeth Bassett alias Richards, Sarah Elwell, Meriam Sandy, Mary Ruck, Rachel Silsbe, Rebecca B. and Hannah Lille.

BASSUNITHWITE,
Widow, propr. at Sudbury in 1640.

BASTAR, BASTARR,
Joseph, tailor, Boston, 1641. Wife Mary; ch. Mary b. in Cambridge 13 (3) 1643, Joseph b. Sept. 29, 1647, Benjamin b. April 4, 1652, Susanna b. 1 Sept. 1654, John b. 25 March, 1657, Anna b. July 26, 1650. Sold house and grounds June 15, 1657.
Admin. gr. 15 July, 1674, to widow Mary.

BATE, BATES, BAYTES,
Edward, Boston, servant to Thomas Leveritt, adm. chh. (9) 1633; rem. to Weymouth; frm. March 9, 1636-7, propr. 1643. Ruling elder, deputy. Ch. John bapt. 23 (11) 1641, ae. about 14 days, Prudence b. 11 (4) 1639, Increase b. 28 (10) 1641. He deposed to the will of Samuel Poole April 30, 1669, ae. about 63 yrs., and to that of Thos. Lawrence [q. v.] 16 (3) 1675, ae. about 61 yrs. The will of Thomas Lawrence of Hing. made in 1655, mentions elder Edward B. of Wey. as the brother of his wife Elizabeth.

BATE, etc., cont.

He made will 22 Oct. 1683, prob. 22 July, 1686. Wife; impotent dau. Jehoshabeath; gr. ch. John Bate; gr. ch. Patience; gr. ch. James Stewart; the rest of his grand children; son James Stewart and dau. Anna Stewart; son John Rogers; sons Increase and Edward Bates. Saw-mill and corn-mill mentioned.

Clement, was bapt. at Lydd, co. Kent, Eng., 22 Jan. 1595, son of James B., yeoman, and bro. of James B. of Dorchester. [Reg. LI, 268.] He was a tailor. He came in the Elizabeth April, 1635, ae. 40, with wife Ann, ae. 40, ch. James, ae. 14, Clement, ae. 12, Rachel, ae. 8, Joseph, ae. 5, and Benjamin, ae. 2. Res. in Hingham. Frm. March 3, 1635-6; propr. Ch. b. in Hingham, Samuel bapt. March 24, 1639; Clement, Jr. drowned in 1639, Rachel d. June, 1647. The wife Anna d. 1 Oct. 1669.

He d. "Sabb. day night," 17 Sept. 1671. [Hob.] Will, dated 12 Oct. 1669, prob. 2 (9) 1671, gave est. to his 4 sons, James, Joseph, Benjamin and Samuel.

George, thacker, Boston, had land grant in 1635 and 1637; adm. chh. 24 (11) 1635; frm. May 25, 1636; dism. to Exeter 6 (11) 1638, rec'd again 31 (3) 1640; his wife Anne rec'd from chh. Exeter 27 (9) 1642. Mary Preached, ae. 65 years, Joane Crowne, ae. 50 years, and Mary Crismas, ae. 23 years, deposed 31 Jan. 1675, that George Bates declared in the time of his sickness that all his estate belonged to William Lamb.

Mr. James, husbandman, ae. 53, with wife Alice, ae. 52, dau. Lydia, ae. 20, Marie, ae. 17, Margaret, ae. 12, James, ae. 9, came in the Elizabeth April 17, 1635. He was a son of James B. of Lydd, Kent, Eng.; bapt. 2 Dec. 1562. Settled at Dorchester; propr. Feb. 18, 1635-6; frm. Dec. 7, 1636; ruling elder of the chh., deputy, town officer.

His will prob. 17 (11) 1655, names wife Alice, sons Richard and James and dau. Margaret Gibson. The widow d. 14 (6) 1657.

"Mr. William,' Charlestown, had allotment of land in 1635. His land referred to in deeds in 1638 and later.

BATEMAN, BAYTMAN,

Thomas, Concord, frm. May 18, 1642. Wife Martha d. Aug. 3, 1665; ch. Hannah b. 28 (7) 1645, Samuel b. 7 (12) 1648, Elizabeth b. 6 March, 1658-9. He m. 2, at Concord, Jan. 27, 1668, Margaret Knight. He d. Feb. 6, 1669.

Will dated 29 (11) 1669, ae. 55 or thereabout; prob. 5 (2) 1670; beq. to wife; to daus. Sarah and Elizabeth, who are at brother [Hassalls;] to daus. Mathah [Martha] and Mary; to sons Thomas, Peter, John and "Elyester." Bros. Thomas Browne and William Buttrick and Richard Hassill overseers. The inv. contained schedule of what the widow brought at marriage. [The widow] Margery Batman m. Feb. 7, 1670, Nathaniel Ball.

The son Peter of Woburn died in 1676. The inv. of his est. mentions his indebtedness for the payment of five shillings a year to his mother-in-law, and that he left 8 bros. and sisters. Wm. Dean and Elizabeth and John Batman petitioned for the appointment of an administrator.

William, Charlestown, frm. May 18, 1631. He d. from exposure and sickness on an island in the harbor about Sept. 16, 1631. [Col. Rec.]

William, Charlestown, propr. 1638, frm. June 2, 1641.

BATT,

Christopher, of Sarum, tanner, ae. 37, with wife Ann, ae. 32, their sister Dorothie Batt, and five children under 10 years, came in the Bevis in May, 1638. Settled at Newbury. Frm. March 13, 1638-9. One of the incorporators of Salisbury, 6 (7) 1638; rem. thither about 1640. Deputy, commissioner, appointed to train the co. at S. 13 May, 1640. Rem. to Boston. Wife Ann deposed in 1673, ae. 72 years. Ch. b. at Salisbury, Eng.: Anne bapt. 1 Aug. 1630, (m. 12 June, 1657, Edmund Angier,) Jane bapt. Dec. 1631, (m. 3 April, 1661, Peter Toppan,) Christopher bapt. 22 Sept. 1633, Thomas bapt. 20 July, 1635, Elizabeth bapt. 1 Nov. 1636, (d. 6 July, 1652;) ch. b. in N. E.: Samuel, Timothy, John b. 4 (1) 1641, Paul and Barnabas b. 18 (12) 1642-3, Sarah, Abigail, Ebenezer.

He d. Aug. 10, 1661. Will prob. Sept. 19, beq. to wife and children. [Reg. X, 268.] The widow conveyed land to her son Thomas 12 June, 1667. She admin. 15 (4) 1671, on the est. of her son Barnabas, who d. in London. Her will, dated March 14, was prob.

BATT, cont.
May 21, 1678-9. [See Batt Ancestry and Genealogy in Reg. L and LI.]

Nicholas, of the Devises, linen weaver, came in the James April 5, 1635. Settled at Newbury. Frm. March 14, 1638-9,—"Nicholas Batter." Propr. at Lynn, 1638, "Battye." When his eldest dau. Anne was married, he promised to weave her cloth and to leave her his house and land as a double portion. [Depos. in Ips. De. II and IV.] Wife Lucy; ch. Anne, (m. June 13, 1653, John Webster,) Mary, (m. Nathaniel Elithorp,) Sarah b. June 12, 1640, (m. John Mighill). He d. Dec. 6, 1667. Will dated 18 June, 1674, being aged, prob. 26 March, 1678, beq. to wife Lucie; daus. Ann, Mary and Sarah; gr. ch. Nicholas, Sarah and John Webster, Nicholas and Sarah Mighill, and Mary Elithorp. The widow d. Jan. 26, 1678-9.

BATTEN,
Hugh, Dorchester. Inv. taken 19 (5) 1659. He m. Ursula, dau. of John Grenaway. Her will, dated 2 Feb. 1673, prob. 26 April, 1683, beq. lands to Moses Eyres, Jr., who had married Bethiah, dau. of her sister Millett, and to other "cousins."

BATTER,
Edmund came in the James April 5, 1635. Settled at Salem, maulter. Propr. 1635 with his bro. Mr. Andram. Town officer; deputy, 1637. He deposed 27 (4) 1673, ae. about 64 years. Called bro. in will of Richard Alwood of Salisbury, Eng. Wife Sarah memb. chh. before 1636, d. 20 (9) 1669. He m. 2, June 8, 1670, Mrs. Mary Gookin; ch. Edmund b. 8 Jan. 1673.
Will dated 11 Feb. 1684, prob. 14 Aug. 1685, beq. to wife and minor ch. Edmund, Mary, Elizabeth and Daniel; the eldest to enter college in 2 or 3 years if he is fitted. Present wife and father Gookin execs.

BATTLE, BATTELL, BATTELEY,
Thomas, Dedham, townsman, 1648; adm. chh. 22 (11) 1653; frm. May 3, 1654. Wife Mary adm. chh. 21 (11) 1648; ch. Mary b. 6 (3) 1650, John b. 1 (5) 1652, Sarah b. 8 (6) 1654, Jonathan b. 24 (5) 1658, Martha b. 19 (6) 1660.
The wife d. Aug. 6, 1691; he—the aged—d. Feb. 8, 1705-6. His will, dated 6 Feb. 1701-2, prob. 7 March, 1705-6, beq. to sons John and

BATTLE, etc., cont.
Jonathan; dau. Mary, wife of John Bryant, of Scituate; the children of dau. Sarah, wife of Silas Titus. Cousin Capt. Daniel Fisher one of the overseers of the will.

BAUNSH, Branch,
William, ae. 24, servant to Thomas Jones, came in the Confidence, April 11, 1638.

BAVER,
Mr. Thomas, Scituate, 1636. In Court 4 Sept., 1638. Rem to Hingham. Signed petition in 1645 for liberty to plant at Whitehead Neck [Arch.]

BAXTER,
Daniel, Salem, 1638. Wife Eliza; ch. Eliza b. (7) 1644, Susanna b. (7) 1646, Rebecca b. (11) ——, Priscilla b. June, 1652.

Gregory, Roxbury, frm. March 6, 1631-2. Ch. rec. in Rox.: Bethulia b. in June, 1632, Abigail b. in Sept., 1634, John b. Dec. 1, 1639.
He d. at Braintree 21 (4) 1659. Will prob. July 14, 1659; wife Margaret, son John, dau. Dearing and dau. the wife of Joseph Adams; gr. ch. Bethia Dearing and Joseph Adams. [Reg. IX, 136.] The widow d. 13 (12) 1661.

Nicholas, mariner, Boston. He was adm. chh. 25 (6) 1644. Wife Anne; dau. Mary b. (12) 1639, (m. Thomas Buttolph, Jr., Sept. 5, 1660).
He d. Jan. 10, 1691. Will dated April 4, 1680, "of great age;" prob. April 29, 1692. Beq. to dau. Mary Swett, son-in-law John Bull and his wife.

Richard, came in 1638 from Hingham, Eng., as a servant of Francis James. Settled at Hingham.

BAYES,
Thomas, carpenter, Dedham. Propr. 1638. He m. 26 (10) 1639, Ann Baker, a maid servant, who was adm. chh. 16 (4) 1639; ch. Ruth bapt. 16 (5) 1643, Thomas bapt. 22 (1) 1646. He gave power of attorney for collection of legacie from his grandfather —— Wiseman of Barrow Upton, co. Norfolk, 12 (10) 1646. [A.]

BAYLEY, BAILEY, BAILY, BAYLY,
Anne, Dorchester, memb. chh. before 1639.

Elizabeth, (parent not stated,) m. June 26, 1654, John Finney of Barnstable.

Guido, gardiner, Salem, propr. 1642. Sold house and land in 1652. Seems to be the man who res. at Bridgewater, juror, 1658-9. Wife Elizabeth; ch. Elizabeth b. at Sal. 27 July, 1642, Joseph b. 6 Nov. 1644. Admin. of the est. of G. B. of Br., Jr. was gr. April 1, 1690, to Ebenezer Hill.

Henry, Salem, 1638. In court in 1647 for refusing to watch.

James, Rowley, propr. 1642. He was 51 years old in 1663. Wife Lydia; ch. John b. 2 (12) 1642, Lydia b. (9) 1644, Jonathan b. Sept. 1646, Damaris b. 17 (11) 1648, James b. 15 (11) 1650, Thomas b. 1 (6) 1653, Samuel b. 10 (6) 1655.
He was bur. 10 Aug. 1677. Will prob. 25 Sept. folg. Beq. to wife; daus. Lydia Platts and Damaris Leaver; sons John and James.

John, Sen., weaver, Salisbury, propr. 1639; rem. in 1650 to Newbury. Sons John and Joseph came early and were citizens of prominence. His wife did not come over. [Court Rec.]
He d. 2 Nov. 1651. Will dated Oct. 28, 1651, prob. April 13, 1652, mentions wife, son Robert and daughters in England; beq. to son John and his sons John and Joseph, and the wife and ch. of Willi. Huntington, here. Calls John Emery, Sen. brother.

John, tailor, Salem, a witness in court in 1647. Sold a shop to William Payne of S., shoemaker, 8 (8) 1649.

Richard, ae. 15, came in the Bevis in May, 1635; was an apprentice of Christopher Stanley, tailor, and by him assigned to Isaac Cullimore, carpenter, 8 (6) 1639. [L.] Was of Lynn, a witness in court, in 1647. Settled at Newbury. Rem. to Rowley.
He was bur. Feb. 16, 1647. Will prob. 28 (1) 1648; wife Edna had a legacie from her bro. Wm. Halsteed; son Joseph, bro. James B., nephew John B. The widow m. 2, Ezekiel Northend, whom the Court made guardian of Joseph 2 May, 1649.

BAYLEY, etc., cont.
Robert, ae. 23, came in the Hopewell in Sept., 1635.

Robert, servant to John Bent of Penton, Eng., came in the Confidence April 11, 1638.

Thomas, Sen., Weymouth, frm. May 13, 1640. Town officer, 1645. Will dated 23 May, prob. 10 Oct. 1681, beq. to eldest son John, son Thomas, dau. Esther, wife of John King, and to each of his grand children.

BAYNLEY, see Bagnally.

BAZILL,
Ellen, maid servant to Atherton Haulgh, Boston, adm. chh. 9 (6) 1640.

BEACH, BEECH,
Richard, Watertown. Wife Mary; ch. John b. 6 (6) 1639, Mary b. 11 (10) 1641, Isaac b. July 5, 1646, Martha b. March 10, 1649, Abigail b. June 14, 1653, Joseph b. 15 (10) 1655, Richard b. 22 (8) 1657. The wife Mary d. about 1645, and he m. 2, Martha ——.
He d. Oct. 24, 1674.

BEACHAM, BEAUCHAMP, BURCHAM,
Edward, Salem, propr. 1636; memb. chh. 1639; frm. Feb. 28, 1642-3; propr. at Lynn 1638; clerk of writs, comr. Wife Mary adm. chh. Sal. 19 (7) 1640; ch. Samuel bapt. 31 (8) 1641, Mary bapt. 10 (7) 1643, Mary bapt. 27 (4) 1647, Eliza. bapt. 9 (5) 1648. Samuel d. 20 (9) 1662; the wife and dau. Mary d. (1) 1667-8.
His will, dated 29 March, 1668, prob. (4) 1684, beq. to dau. Elizabeth and son-in-law Zechariah Goodale.

Robert, carpenter, Ipswich, commoner 1641, propr. 1647. His petition to the Gen. Court denied 14 May, 1645. With wife Isabel sold land 2 Jan. 1651.

BEADLE, BEEDLE, BIDDLE,
Joseph, Plymouth, bought land of Isaac Robinson, 1635; in Court 5 Aug., 1636. He m. Oct. 28, 1636, Rachel Deane; volunteer for the Pequot war in 1637; Marshfield, atba. 1643.
Will, April 17, 1672; wife Rachel and dau. Martha Deane. [Reg. VII, 236.]

BEADSLEY,
William, frm. Dec. 7, 1636.

BEAL, BEALE, BEALS, BEALES, BIELL,
John, shoemaker, came in 1638, with wife, 5 sons, 3 daus. and 2 servants, from Hingham, Eng. to Hingham, N. E. [Hob.] Frm. March 13, 1638-9. Propr., deputy. Wife Nazareth, dau. of Edmund Hubbard, Sen., d. 23 Sept., 1658. He m. 2, March 10, 1659, Mary, widow of Nicholas Jacob. He is called uncle by David, son of Mr. Peter Hobart. Ch. Martha, (m. 1, William Falloway, 2, Samuel Dunham,) Mary, (m. James Whiton,) Sarah, (m. 1, Thomas Marsh, 2, Edmund Sheffield;) John, eldest son, Nathaniel, Jeremiah, Joshua, Caleb, Rebecca bapt. Feb., 1640-1, Jacob b. Oct. 13, 1642.

He was found dead in his yard April 1, 1688; 100 years old. [Statement of his son, Blake, the coroner, of Boston.] [S.] In his will, dated 27 Sept. 1687, he beq. to sons; to son-in-law Benjamin Dunnum and dau. Martha D.; to daus. Sarah Sheffield and Mary Witton; gr. ch. Nathaniel Beale and Martha Chubbock.

John, Jr., a brother of the above, Hingham, propr.; probably came before 1650.

Made will 26 Oct., 1657, prob. 28 July, 1658; about to go to Eng. Beq. to father Edmund B.; to cousins Mary, wife of James Whiton, Sarah, wife of Thomas Marsh, Jeremiah B., Rebecca, dau. of John Beales, Sen.; to Elizabeth, wife of John Lassell. Cousin Thomas Marsh, exec.

Robert, Sudbury, propr., 1640.

Thomas, Cambridge, propr., 1634; town officer. Sarah, ae. 28, came in the James in June, 1635, [probably wife of Thomas.] Adm. chh. Charlestown 30 (9) 1642. Membs. chh. Camb. 1658. [Mi.]

He d. in 1661, ae. 63. Will dated 24 Aug. prob. Oct. 27, 1661, beq. to wife Sarah, cousin Richard Post and sister Sarah Penn; to the president of the college and the pastor of the church, etc. His widow Sarah d. about 1679. Her will dated 29 June, 1677, prob. 1 (2) 1679, beq. to kinsmen Henry and Richard Frencham; to cousin Thomas Post and Elizabeth his dau.; to my sister Wing; to Daniel Gookin, Esq., his wife and children, and various friends; to the church, to be laid out in plate.

BEAL, etc., cont.
William, Plymouth, came in the Fortune in 1621.

William, miller, Marblehead, was grinding corn in the town in 1649 or 1650, as Moses Maverick deposed in 1653. Wife Martha d. April 6, 1675; he m. 2, Dec. 1676, Elizabeth Bert Jackson; she d. 5 Nov. 1683; he m. 3, March 5, 1683-4, Mary, widow of Samuel Hart, blacksmith, of Lynn. [Marb. and Lynn Rec.] Ch. Samuel b. 15 July, 1654, bapt. at Ipsw. by Mr. Cobbett, Martha b. 15 Sept. 1656, James b. 10 Dec. 1657, William b. 24 April, 1659, John b. 17 June, 1660, Moses b. 1662, d. 1663, Moses b. Aug. 8, 1664, Bridget b. 15 July, 1666, d. 5 Aug. 1683, Aaron b. 8 July, 1668, George b. 1 March, 1670, Anne b. Aug. 4, 1674, Elisabeth b. 10 Dec. 1677, —— b. 5 April, 1686.

His will dated 4 Jan. 1693-4, beq. to wife Mary, according to marriage agreement; to my eight children, Samuel, William, John, Aaron, Ebenezer, Martha, Elizabeth and Thomas.

BEAMAN, BEAUMONT, BEAMENT,
Gamaliel, ae. 12, came in the Elizabeth and Ann in May, 1635, Dorchester, propr. 1649. Resided at Lancaster in 1661, but ret. after a few years to Dorchester. His wife adm. chh. 1 (12) 1656; ch. Thomas, ae. 8 yrs., John, ae. 6 yrs., Gamaliel, ae. 4 yrs., and Mary, an infant, all bapt. 14 (4) 1657; Sarah b. 19 (11) 1658, Noah b. 3 (2) 1661.

John, ae. 23, came in the Elizabeth, April 15, 1635. Settled at Salem, propr. 1640.

John, Scituate, atba. 1643.

William, ae. 27, came in the Elizabeth April 15, 1635. Settled at Salem, 1637. Deposed in Court to R. Saltonstall's acct. 25 (5) 1644.

BEAMSLEY,
George, Boston. His lot at Muddy River ref. to in a deed in 1643.

William, yeoman, Boston, adm. chh.—laborer—5 (2) 1635. Ensign. Wife Anne; ch. Anne b. 13 (12) 1632, (m. Ezekiel Woodward,) Grace b. 20 (7) 1635, (m. Samuel Graves,) Mercie b. 9 (10) 1637, (m. 17 (8) 1656, Michael Willborne,) Samuel b. 31 (10) 1640, Samuel and Habbakuk bapt. 7 (12) 1640; Hannah b. (10) 1643, (m. Abraham Perkins,)

BEAMSLEY, cont.
Elizabeth, (m. Edward Page,) Mary, (m. 1, —— Robinson, 2, Thomas Dennis). His (second) wife Martha bore Abigail 8 (12) 1645. He d. Sept. 29, 1658. Will mentions wife Martha, ch. Anne Woodward, Grace Graves, Mercie Willborne, Hannah Beamsley, Edward Bushnell, Elizabeth Page, Mary Robison. Prob. 28 (8) 1658. [Reg. IX, 37.]

BEANE,
Thomas. Witness to deed of land in Lynn in 1649.

BEARE, BEARCE, BEARSE, BEIRCE, BEERE, BEERES, BEERS,
Anthony, Watertown, Roxbury, frm. May 6, 1657. Wife Elizabeth; ch. rec. at Wat.: Samuel b. 2 (3) 1647, Ephraim b. July 5, 1648, John b. Jan. 20, 1651, Hester b. Oct. 16, 1654, Samuel b. May 2, 1657, infant son d. at Rox. Sept. 16, 1657, Barnabas b. Sept. 6, 1658.

Augustine, ae. 20, came in the Confidence, Apr. 11, 1638. Joined the chh. at Barnstable Apr. 29, 1643. His wife —— joined Aug. 7, 1650. Ch. Mary b. 1640, Martha b. 1642, Priscilla bapt. March 11, 1643, Sarah bapt. March 29, 1646, Abigail bapt. Dec. 19, 1647, Hannah bapt. Nov. 18, 1649, Joseph b. Jan. 25, 1651, Hester bapt. Oct. 2, 1653, Lydia b. Sept. 1655, Rebecca b. Sept. 26, 1657, James b. July, 1660.

Philip, fisherman, Salem, rem. to Marblehead. In Court, 1640. He deposed in 1663, ae. 40 years.

Richard, Plymouth, Marshfield, in Court 5 Aug., 1638. Had land at Powder Point. Land on Duxbury side 6 March, 1638. atha. 1643. Town officer, propr.; frm. 5 June, 1651. Seems to be the R. B. who res. at Watertown in 1652. [Mdx. De. I.]

His will dated Jan. 1, prob. March 5, 1673, beq. to Moses Symons, Elizabeth and John French; Richard French, exec. [Plym. Prob.]

Richard, inn-keeper, Watertown, frm. Mar. 9, 1636-7. Town officer, Captain. He deposed 17 (10) 1662, that Thomas Mahew lived at Mistick, also Medford in 1636. [Mdx. Files.] Petitioned the governor, Oct. 24, 1665, for grant of land in consideration of services in the Pequot War, and other services, having been an inhab. of this jurisdiction ever since the first beginning thereof. Wife Elizabeth; ch. Sarah b. and d. in 1639, Mary b. 10 (1) 1642, Judith b. 26 (1) 1646, Jabez b. Oct. 4, 1651, Richard b. Oct. 22, 1659.

BEARE, etc., cont.

He was slain in battle Sept. 4, 1675. He made will Aug. 6, prob. Oct. 5, 1675; beq. to wife Elizabeth and children; dau. Sterns had recd. her portion. Agreement filed June, 1711, by the children and heirs of Capt. Richard Beers, viz.: Elnathan, Jabez, Richard, Mary Wheeler; Joseph and Mary Rice, heirs of Mary Rice; Judith Allen, Elizabeth and Samuel Ward, and David Stone. [Reg. XXXVIII, 325.]

BEARD,
Elizabeth, ae. 24, came in the Increase Apr. 15, 1635.

Richard, freed from his master before Boston Court 2 June, 1641.

Thomas, shoemaker, of St. Martins, [London?] a single man, ae. 30 yrs., arranged 23 March, 1628-9, with the Mass. Bay Co. to come to Salem. Came in the Mayflower in 1629 with materials for manufacture of boots and shoes; was to have 50 acres of land. Frm. May 10, 1643.

BEARSLEY,
Goodman, Concord, land adjoining S. Stretton's in 1648.

BEAUCHAMP, see Beacham.

BEAUMONT, see Beaman.

BEAVAN,
John, Plymouth. Agreement with John Winslow for 6 yrs. from June 24, 1633.

BECK, BECKS, BEX,
Alexander, laborer, husbandman, Boston; had XX s. damages from Joyce Bradwicke for breach of promise of marriage, April 1, 1633. He was adm. chh. 22 (4) 1634, frm. Sept. 3, 1634. Traded for tobacco at Barbadoes 4 (11) 1647. [A.] Conveyed lands to his only son Manasseh 31 March, 1668. His wife Mary d. 2 (3) 1639. He m. 2, Elizabeth Hinde. q. v. Ch. Ephraim b. 1 (4) 1640, Ephraim and Deliverance bapt. 7 (4) 1640,

BECK, cont.
Strange b. 31 (3) 1642, Manasseh b. 8 (8) 1645.
Will dated June 20, 1662, prob. 27 (8) 1674. Wife; son Manassa; Hanna Alcock.
Richard, Watertown, propr. 27 (7) 1645.

BEECHER,
Mr. Thomas, sea-captain, master of the ship Talbot, one of Winthrop's fleet. Settled at Charlestown; memb. chh. 1630-1; frm. Nov. 6, 1632; deputy, town officer; capt. of the Castle in 1635.
He d. before 29 (5) 1637, when inv. of his est. was made; filed at Boston.
Wife Christian, memb.chh. in 1630, formerly wife of Thomas Copper of Wapping, near London, who beq. to her est. at Harwich, Eng.; she m. 3, Nicholas Easton. [Wyman.]

BECKEELS,
Richard, Cambridge, cow-herd, 1639.

BECKWITH,
Thomas, Roxbury. Sold house Sept. 29, 1651.

BEDORTHA, BEDORDA, BURDONDON,
Rise or Reese, Springfield, leased land in 1644, propr. in 1646, town officer. He m. in 1646 Blanche Lewis; ch. a son b. 14 (3) 1646, John b. 13 (3) 1647, d. 30 (3) 1648, Joseph b. 15 (1) 1648-9, Samuel b. 1 (10) 1651, John b. 12 (4) 1654.
He was drowned March 18, 1682-3. Inv. pres. by widow Blanch March 27, 1683.

BECKLY, BEGGARLY,
Alice, wife of Richard, came to N. E. about 1630, and he rem. in England. She sought divorce from him 2 (4) 1636, and the court sent to Eng. for evidence. [W.] She had some connection, of family or service, with the minister, Mr. Skelton of Salem. Seems to be the Alice Daniel of later record, and the wife of John Greene of Providence. [See Es. Inst. Coll. XIII.]

BEEFER, BEEFORD,
, Richard, brought suit in Es. court in 1637. Propr. at Gloucester, 1647.

BELCHER, BELCHERE, BELSHAR,
Andrew, mariner, trader, vintner, painter, Cambridge; propr. Sudbury, 1639.

BELCHER, etc., cont.
Deposed 7 (2) 1658, ae. 44 years. [Mdx. Files.] He m. Oct. 1, 1639, Elizabeth, dau. of Nicholas Danforth. [Mi.] Ch. Elizabeth b. 17 (6) 1640, Jemina b. 5 (2) 1642, Martha b. 26 (5) 1644, Andrew b. 1 (11) 1646, Anna b. 1 (11) 1648-9.
The inv. of his estate was taken 25 Dec. 1673, and admin. gr. to widow Elizabeth. His widow d. June 26, 1680, ae. about 61. Her will dated 10 June, prob. 8 July, 1680, beq. to daus. Elizabeth Blower, Martha Remington and Hannah Ballard; to the daus. of dec. dau. Jemimah Scill; rest to son Andrew B.

Mr. Edward, (Edmund,) pipe-stave culler, soap-boiler, Boston; memb. chh. 1630; frm. May 18, 1631; water bailiff, 1649. Wife Christian. Edward, ae. 8, who came in 1635 was probably the son on whose account the above is called Senior in a deed of land May 1, 1661, and who m. 8 (11) 1655, Mary Wormwood, dau.-in-law to Edw. Belcher, Sen.
Will dated 17 Oct. 1671, prob. March 17, 1672-3, of Boston, N. E., late of Guilsburgh, co. of Northampton, Eng., gent.; confirmed a deed made to his dau.-in-law Mary Belcher in 1670; also ratified leases made to Richard Woodee in 1661 and 1670; to dau. Ann —— and her children; to his son Edward's two daus. Mary and Fayth.

Gregory, farmer, Braintree, 1637, propr.; frm. May 13, 1640. He leased the lings on whose est. she (Joanna) admin. Feb. tract including the Blue Hills of the town of Boston April 1, 1658. He deposed in June, 1665, ae. about 60 years. [Es. Files.] Ch. Samuel b. 24 (6) 1637, Mary b. 8 (5) 1639, Joseph b. 25 (10) 1641. With wife Katharine sold land in Br. 6 (4) 1667.
Admin. of his est. gr. 30 Jan. 1674, to widow Katharine, with whom the son Josiah was afterward joined. Her will, dated 3 Sept. 1679, prob. 20 July, 1680, beq. to sons Josiah, John and Moses B.; daus. Elizabeth Gilbert, and Mary, wife of Alexander Marsh, and gr. dau. Mary M.

Jeremiah, ae. 22, came in the Susan and Ellen in April, 1635; settled at Ipswich; merchant; frm. March 13, 1638-9; propr. He m. Mary Lockwood; deeded to her house and land for life 30 (7) 1652; deeded lands to sons Jeremiah and John B. 15 May, 1661. He deposed 21 (1) 1671, ae. 59 years.

BELDEN,
Henry, Woburn, 1640.

BELKNAP,
Abraham, Lynn, propr. 1638. He d. 1 (7) 1643. Inv. pres. by Mary B. 16 (12) 1643.

BELL,
John, Sandwich, atba. 1643.

Mr. Thomas, merchant, of London, came to Roxbury. Propr., frm. May 25, 1636. Ch. Sarah b. Oct. 4, 1640, John b. and d. in 1643, Mary bapt. 28 (7) 1645. He and his wife had letters of dism. gr. and sent into Eng. in the (7) 1654. Ret. to Roxbury.

He made will 29 Jan. 1671, prob. by his widow Susanna 3 May 1672. Beq. to Thomas Makins and one other ch. of his sister Makins in N. E.; all his property in Roxbury, N. E. to Mr. John Eliot and Capt. Isaac Johnson, in trust for the maintenance of a free school for poor men's children at Roxbury forever. [Reg. XXXVIII, 62.]

Thomas, Boston. Wife Anne; ch. John b. and d. 1638, Joan b. and d. 1640, Tabitha d. 27 (2) 1654, Thomas b. 3 (6) 1642, Hopestill (dau.) b. 2 (6) 1644, More-Mercy b. 14, bapt. 17 (11) 1646, Deborah b. 29 Nov. 1650, Joseph b. and d. 1653.

He d. 7 (4) 1655. His widow Anne admin. 4 (5) 1655; she m. 2, 7 (3) 1656, William Mullings, on whose est. she admin. Feb. 14, 1659; she m. 3, Sept. 21, 1659, John Laughton.

William, before Boston Court 2 (1) 1640-1.

BELLAMY,
Jeremiah, Nantasket or Hull, at its settlement, 20 May, 1642.

BELLFLOWER, BULFLOWER,
Henry, Salem, servant to Thomas West in 1642. [Es. Files.] Rem. to Reading before 1653. He deposed 21 (11) 1655, ae. about 25. [Mdx. Files.]

Benjamin, Salem; [was he a son of Henry?]
He d. Feb. 24, 1660. Admin. Essex Court; inv. by Robert Moulton and Henry Phety, 1661; "indebted to my father."

BELLINGHAM,
Mr. Richard, Esquire, gent., Governor, Boston. Adm. chh. 3 (6) 1634, with wife Elizabeth; went to Rowley in 1643, but rem. there only 2 or 3 yrs. Ret. to Boston. His wife d. about 1640 and he m. 9 (9) 1641, Penelope, sister of Mr. Herbert Pelham, performing the ceremony himself. [W.] Ch. Samuel, came with him, grad. Harv. Coll. 1642; ret. to Eng.; Hannah bapt. 14 (6) 1642, ae. about 7 days, James b. 2 (3), bapt. 10 (3) 1646, Sarah bapt. 30 (5) 1648, ae. about 2 days, Elizabeth bapt. 9 (10) 1649, ae. about 3 days, Ann bapt. 6 (5) 1652, Grace b. and d. 1654.

He d. Dec. 7, 1672, ae. 80. Will, dated 25 Nov. 1672, gave to his wife the farm where Nicholas Rice dwelleth; to his only son and to *his* dau. the farm where Lt. John Smith is tenant; the rents of the farms tenanted by John Belcher and goodman Townsend to go to the 4 daus. of Col. Wm. Goodrich; the estate at Winnisimmet to be in the hands of trustees, as the foundation of a religious establishment of peculiar type. [Reg. XIV, 23, and XXXVI, 391.] See numerous sketches.

Mr. William, bro. of preceding, res. at Ipswich; frm. Oct. 12, 1640. Made arrangements about cattle, etc. with Mr. Humphrey 17 (8) 1638. [L.]

Will prob. 24 (7) 1650, beq. to many friends. Rest to nephew Samuel, son of bro. Richard. Refers to deceased wife. See depositions accompanying the will in Essex files.

BELLOWS, BELLOWES, BELOUSE,
John, ae. 12, came in the Hopewell in April, 1635. Settled at Concord. Rem. to Marlborough. He m. May 9, 1655, Mary Wood. Ch. Mary b. April 26, 1657, Samuel b. 22 Jan. 1657, [9?] Abigail b. 6 May, 1661, Isaac b. Sept. 13, 1663, John b. May 13, 1666, Thomas b. Nov. 7, 1668, Eleazer b. April 13, 1671, Nathaniel b. April 3, 1676, Benjamin, "son of Mary B.," b. Jan. 18, 1676-7.

He d. Jan. 10, 1682. Will dated 19 June, prob. 2 Oct. 1683, beq. to wife Mary; to ch. Isaac, John, Thomas, Eleazer, Nathaniel, Mary, and Abigail. Dau. Abigail Lawrence had already recd. part of her portion.

BEMIS,
Joseph, planter, Watertown, 1640. [L.] Town officer. He deposed 23 (4) 1657, ae.

BEMIS, cont.
about 38, and Mary, ae. about 38. [Mdx. Files.] With wife Sarah sold land in 1654. Ch. Sarah b. 15 (11) 1642, Mary b. 10 (9) 1644, Joseph and Ephraim b. and d. 1647, Martha b. 24 (3) 1649, Joseph b. Dec. 20, 1651, Rebecca b. April 17, 1654, Ephraim b. Aug. 25, 1656, [John b. Aug. 1659?].
Will prob. Oct. 7, 1684, beq. to wife, dau. Martha, son Joseph and the other 5 children.

BENDALL,
Edward, merchant, planter, Boston, memb. chh. 1630-1, frm. May 14, 1634. He raised the ship Mary Rose and much of her cargo, in 1642. [W.] The Gen. Court declined to give him a patent on a diving tub 2 May, 1649. He was dism. to a chh. in London 12 (12) 1653. His wife Anne d. 25 (10) 1637; he m. Mary. She was rec'd from chh. of Roxbury 27 (9) 1642. Ch. Freegrace bapt. 5 (5) 1635, Freegrace b. 30 (7) 1636, Reforme b. 18 (8) 1639, Hopefor b. 7 (8) 1641, More Mercy bapt. 24 (7) 1643, ae. about 2 days, Ephraim b. 9 (4) 1648, Restore bapt. 30 (10) 1649, ae. about 17 days. His wife Mary was bur. (3) 1644.
He d. before 26 Jan. 1660, when his widow Jane gave letter of attorney to Capt. Samuel Scarlet for the sale of Boston property.

BENFIELD,
Alice, her parents having d. before they were settled in this country, she was placed in charge of Emanuel White and Katharine, his wife of Watertown for 15 yrs., 9 (10) 1636, being 3 yrs. old. [W.]

BENHAM,
John, Dorchester, frm. May 18, 1631. He m. in 1654, Sarah, widow of Richard Wilson.

BENJAMIN,
Mr. John, embarked June 22, 1632, came to Cambridge; frm. Nov. 6, 1632. Propr.; his house burned in 1636. [W.] Rem. to Watertown; town officer. Excused from training on acc. of age in 1634.
He d. June 14, 1645. Will prob. July 3, 1645. Son John had a double portion; wife to provide for the small children; eight in all. Bro. John Eddie and Thomas Marritt overseers. The sons John and Samuel gave testimony 5 (2) 1651 as to a fence put up in

BENJAMIN, cont.
their father's life-time. [Mdx. Files.] His dau. Marie made will May 16, prob. June 4, 1646. Beq. to pastor Knowles, aunt Wines and cousin Anne W.; to sister Abigail Stubbs; to bros. in general. [Reg. III, 177, 178.] The widow Abigail d. May 20, 1687, ae. 87.

Richard, embarked for N. E. June 22, 1632; settled at Watertown; propr. 1642. Wife Anna; dau. Anna b. 1 (7) 1643.

BENNETT, BENNITT, BENET,
Edward, Weymouth, frm. May 25, 1636. Recd. arms from Mr. Pynchon in 1636. Propr. 1643. Rem. to Rehoboth, propr. 1643, prop. frm. 4 June, 1645.

Edward, purser of the ship Mary Rose, which was was blown up accidentally in Boston harbor in 1648. [Suff. De I, 51.]

Francis, Boston. He deposed 26 (8) 1653, ae. about 30 years. [Es. Files.] Wife Alice; ch. Mary b. 15 (7) 1650, James b. Feb. 14 or 17, 1651-2, Elizabeth d. 17 (11) 1653, Elizabeth b. 20 Dec. 1654.
Admin. on his est. was gr. to widow Alice for herself and ch. 7 Feb. 1655; inv. having been taken 4 Dec. 1655. The widow m. 8 (6) 1656, Ralph Hutchinson.

George, Boston, 1647. Wife Faith, formerly Newell; ch. John bapt. 2 (11) 1647.
He was drowned 27 (1) 1652. Wife Adey, Audrey or Adeia; one ch.; another expected. The widow m. 2, Francis Brown, of Farmington, whose sale of land in B. was confirmed by Gen. Court 14 Oct. 1656.

James, Cambridge, 1636; Concord. Ch. Hannah b. 1 (4) 1640, Thomas b. 16 (8) 1640 (1641?).

John, Salem, Marblehead, propr. 1637. John Peach testified 23 June, 1684, that John Bennett came to N. E. in the same ship with him in 1630; that J. B.'s wife Margaret came some years after him, and lived with him many years in Marblehead. They had one dau. b. there named Mary and no other children; that she was the wife of Christopher Codner, dec., and afterward m. Richard Downing, by whom she had many children. That by Codner she had Joane, who m. Joseph Bubier. [Reg. XL, 65.] Ch. Marie b. 2 Sept. 1638. [Es. Files.]

BENNETT, etc., cont.

Richard, Salem, 1635. Rem. to Boston. His wife Sibel d. 13 (7) 1653. He m. 11 (5) 1655, Margaret Gurgefield, widow. Ch. Peter, Susanna b. 2 (12) 1650, Richard b. Sept. 3, d. 26 (11) 1653.

His will dated 21 June and 6 July, prob. 8 Sept. 1677, mentions wife Margaret, son Jonas Clarke and Susanna his wife; gr. ch. Susanna, dau. of his son Peter; cousin Anthony Bennett of Bass River; frees his negro man Jethro, and gives him a house lot. The son Peter was a legatee in the will of his mother's bro. Maj. Ralph Hooker of Barbadoes, dated 14 March, 1663, prob. 15 April, 1664. [Reg. XXXVIII, 323.]

Samuel, house carpenter, yeoman, ae. 24, came in the James in July, 1635. Settled at Lynn, propr. in 1638. Bought a windmill 22 (3) 1645. Had a law suit about an apprentice in 1641. [L.] Sold land in 1649; a deed of his in Es. files, vol. 38. Rem. to Boston in 1650. Wife Sarah joined him in a deed of Rumley Hall at Rumney Marsh Dec. 3, 1656. Made engagement for marriage of his son Samuel in 1664. [Suff. De. IV, 328]

William, Plymouth, taxed in 1632; suit with Dotey, 1633.

William, carpenter, Salem, 1636. Land at Jeffry's Creek, (Manchester). Suit in court, 1639. He deposed in 1676 that he dwelt and worked near Mr. Winthrop's salt house in Sal. about 1646. Wife Jane, ae. 16, came in the Elizabeth and Ann in April, 1635. Adm. chh. Salem 18 (4) 1643. Ch. Moses, Ann and Deliverance bapt. 2 (5) 1643, Mary bapt. 3 (7) 1654.

His nunc. will dated 20 Nov. 1682, prob. 27 June, 1683, beq. to wife Jane, sons Moses, Aaron and John; gr. ch. John Croe, and dau. Mary.

BENSLEY,

William, frm. May 25, 1636.

BENSON, BINSON,

John, ae. 30, came in the Confidence April 11, 1638, from Gonsham, Oxfordshire, Eng., with wife Mary and ch. John and Mary under 4 yrs. of age. Settled at Hingham. Petitioned with others in 1645 for liberty to plant and build at Whitehead Neck. Rem. to Hull; propr. 1657. Town officer, 1669. Ch. Martha bapt. Nov. 3, 1644.

BENSON, etc., cont.

He d. at Hingham 13 Jan. 1678. Will dated April 16, 1678, prob. 20 March, 1679, beq. to sons John, Joseph, daus. Combs, Hall, and children of dau. Shore, dec.; wife Marah. After her death 14 Dec. 1681, admin. was transferred to John and Joseph.

BENT, BENTE,

John, husbandman, ae. 35, came from Penton, Wayhill, Southampton, Eng. in the Confidence April 11, 1638, with wife Martha and ch. Robert, William, Peter, John and Ann, all under 12 yrs. of age. Deposition relative to his mother Anne, sister Agnes and bro.-in-law Thomas Blanchard. [Reg. XXXII, 409.] Res. in Sudbury; propr. 1639; frm. May 13, 1640. Selectman, 1640. Gave letter of attorney to his bro.-in-law Wm. Baker of New Sarum, Wilts., for collection of money, Aug. 26, 1640. [L.] See record of baptisms of J. B. and four of the above-named ch. and abstracts of the wills of his father, Robert, his grandfather, John, and gr. mo. Edith, in Reg. XLIX, 65. His dau. called "Ann" in ship's list was Agnes; she m. Edward Rice of S., and d. in 1713, ae. 83; other ch. Joseph b. May 16, 1641, Martha b. about 1643, (m. June 5, 1663, Samuel How or S.).

He d. Sept. 27, 1672. Will dated 14 Sept.; inv. taken 24 Sept. 1672; beq. to wife Martha, sons Peter, (eldest son,) Joseph and John, daus. Agnes Rice and Martha, wife of Samuel How; to Peter, son of son Peter, Hannah, dau. of son John, John, son of dau. Martha, and John, son of dau. Agnes.

Robert, Newbury, d. 30 Jan. 1647. Widow d. May 15, 1679. [Genealogy in Reg. XLVIII, 288.]

BENTLEY,

William, ae. 47, came in the Truelove in Sept. 1635; with him came John, ae. 17, and Alice, ae. 15. Mary, ae. 20, came in the Defense in July, 1635.

BERRY, BURY,

Anthony, Yarmouth, atba. 1643.

Christopher, Salem, defendant in law suit in 1640. Went to England same year. [Es. Court Rec.]

BERRY, etc., cont.

John, Boston, 1644. He was apprentice to Edward Keyley for 7 yrs. 30 (1) 1646.

Richard, Barnstable, atba. 1643. Before the Court 1649. He may be the Richard of Yarmouth, who d. 11 Sept. 1681; nunc. will proved by Mrs. Desire Gorum 17 Oct. folg. Left all to his wife for the bringing up of his small children. Widow Alice deposed.

Richard, Boston, "that was Thomas Hawkin's man," was cured from sickness by Thomas Oliver, and the town paid the bill 25 (11) 1646.

William, Newbury, commoner, 1641.

William, gent., Boston, gave bond 9 (8) 1647, to pay 20 li. within 2 mos. after his arrival in Eng. [A.]

BEESBEECH, BESBEACH, BESBIDGE, BISBY,

Elisha, Marshfield, 1646. Ch. Hopestill bapt. Sept. 7, 1645, John bapt. Dec. 21, 1645, Mary bapt. Sept. 10, 1648, Martha bapt. April 27, 1651, Elisha bapt. Oct. 29, 1654, Hannah bapt. Dec. 7, 1656.

His will dated 6 April, 1688, prob. June 4, 1690, beq. to sons Hopestill, John and Elisha, daus. Mary Beals, Martha Turner and Hannah Brooks and their children.

Thomas, of Sandwich, Eng., came in the Hercules in March, 1634. Settled at Cambridge; gent.; propr. 1636. Rem. to Scituate; frm. Feb. 7, 1636-7. Rec'd chh. 1637. Propr. at Barnstable 1638-9. Rem. to Duxbury 1639. Sold land in D., 1647, having rem. to Sudbury in 1645. Rem. to Marshfield, and sold land at S. 13 Oct. 1664. Ret. to Sudbury.

He d. March 9, 1673-4. Will dated 25 Nov. 1672, prob. 7 (2) 1674, (delivered by him to Edmund Browne to keep, as the latter attests;) beq. to gr. ch. and adopted son Thomas Beesbeech alias Browne, son of his dau. Mary, wife to William B. of Sudbury, lands in Hetcorne and Frittenden, co. Kent, Eng.; to dau. Mary; to dau. Alice, wife of John Bourne of Marshfield; to gr. ch. William, Edmund and Hopestill, sons of dau. Mary, and to her daus. Susanna, Elizabeth, Sarah and Mary, wife of John Rice; to Thomas and Sarah, ch. of dau. Alice Bourne; to

BEESBEECH, etc., cont.

Mary, dau. of Thos. Besbeech alias Browne; to Experience, son of Elizabeth, wife of Joseph Bent.

BESSEY,

Anthony, ae. 26, came in the James in July, 1635. Settled at Sandwich. Before the Court in 1638. Ch. David b. May 23, 1639.

Will Feb. 10, 1656; inv. May 21, admin. 3 June, 1657. Wife Jane, daus. Dorcas, Ann, Mary and Elizabeth; sons Nehemiah and David. If his mother send over anything as she has formerly done, it is to be divided among all. [Reg. V, 385.] The widow m. 2, George Barlow, who had her daus. Anna, Dorcas and Mary before the Court 4 March, 1661-2.

BEST, BEAST,

John, tailor, Sandwich, Eng., came in the Hercules in March, 1634; settled at Salem 1638.

Robert, Sudbury, took oath of fidelity in 1645.

Will, dated 21 June, 1654, prob. 2 (1) 1655. Beq. to Samuel, Nehemiah, Isaac, Elizabeth and Hannah, his nephews and nieces, children of his cousin Wm. Hunt of Concord. Other individuals. [Reg. XVII, 155.]

BESTHOPE,

John, Plymouth, summoned to Court 9 June, 1650. Ch. Hannah bapt. Jan. 26, 1639, Samuel bapt. Feb. 12, 1642, Hope bapt. March 16, 1644.

BETTS, BEET, BEETS, BEATH,

John, ae. 40, came in the Francis of Ipswich April 30, 1634. Settled at Cambridge; propr. 1635. Sold land about 1641. In Court in 1653. His wife Elizabeth deposed 21 June, 1653, ae. about 54. [Mdx. Files.]

He d. Feb. 21, 1662-3, ae. about 68. Admin. gr. to his widow; dea. John Bridge pres. inv. on her behalf. His widow Elizabeth d. Jan. 2, 1663-4. Will dated 16 (10) 1663, prob. March 14, 1663-4, beq. house to John Bridge, Sen.; to "sisters" Ann Steadman and Chesholm; to "brothers" Bridge, Cheever and Chesholm, and to many other individuals.

Richard, Ipswich, resident 1646.

BETTS, etc., cont.
Robert, Watertown, propr. 1636.

William, dish-turner, Scituate, adm. chh. Oct. 25, 1635. He m. Feb. 27, 1638, Alice, "goodman Ensygns maid in the Bey." Rem. to Barnstable; prop. frm. 1 June, 1641. Rem. to Dorchester. Sold house and lands 9 (1) 1651-2.

BETSCOMBE, BETSHAM,
Richard, haberdasher, from Bridport, Dorset, Eng., settled at Hingham. Propr. 1635; frm. March 9, 1636-7. Gave letter of attorney 25 (6) 1640, to his bros. Andrew, Robert, and Christopher to receive legacies due his daus. Mary and Martha from Philip Strong, late of the Devizes Wilts., gent. Ch. Anna bapt. Aug. 1639, Experience bapt. Oct. 24, 1641.
Mrs. Betscomb d. June 6, 1646.

BEWETT,
Hugh; he was banished by the Court of Assistants (9) 1640, for maintaining that he was free from original and actual sin, and other errors. [W.] [Court Rec.]

BEWLIE,
Grace, ae. 30, came in the Susan and Ellen in April, 1635.

BIBBLE, BIBBLES,
John, Boston; house-plot gr. him 4 (10) 1637. Brought a suit in Es. Court in 1639. His wife Sibil was in Shadwell in Stepney parish, Eng. Oct. 9, 1640. [L.] Lic. innkeeper at Hull 29 May, 1644. He rem. to Malden.
Will dated 21 July, prob. 21 Aug. 1653; beq. to son-in-law Robert Joanes of Hull; to dau. Anne; to their son John; to the children of Thomas Carter of Charlestown; to Charitie Whit of Boston; to Richard Adams of M., his wife and 5 children; rest to wife Sibell. The widow m. Miles Nutt and afterward John Doolittle. Will dated Dec. 25, 1683, prob. 1690. Beq. to Obediah Jenkins and wife Mary; to gr. ch. Robert, Zachary, Benjamin and Rebecca Jones; to gr. ch. Sarah Browne; to Mercy Jones; to Hannah Paddick, and her ch. John and Mary. Gr. son Ob. Jenkins exec. [Reg. IX, 306.]

BICKERSTAFFE,
John, before Gen. Court 4 (10) 1638.

BICKNELL, BICKWELL,
Zachary, ae. 45, with wife Agnes, ae. 27, son John, ae. 11, John Kitchin, his servant, ae. 23 yrs., came from Weymouth, Eng., before March 20, 1635. Settled at Weymouth.

He d. before 9 March, 1636-7, when the Court decreed that the sale of his house and land by Richard Rocket and his wife must be confirmed by Bicknell's son when he became of age.

BIDDLECOME,
Richard, servant to Walter Hayne, came in the Confidence in 1638.

BIDFIELD, BITFIELD,
Samuel, cooper, Boston, frm. June 2, 1641. One of the appraisers of the est. of Wm. Stevens of Newbury in 1653. [Es. Files.] Constable. He deposed in 1652, ae. about 60 years. [Arch. 38 B.]

He d. 10 Sept. 1660. Will, dated 12 (3) 1659, prob.: beq. to wife Elizabeth, son-in-law Samuel Plumer and his ch. Samuel, John, Ephraim and Mary P., dau. Stevens, (her ch.) John and Samuel S. The widow d. 30 (7) 1669. Her will, dated 13 (11) 1663, prob. Sept. 23, 1669, beq. to her sister Crowne and sister Margaret Parker; in case of their death to Ann Jeffreys ch. if they be not Quakers, and to cousin Katharine Dackes ch.; to be paid if sent for within 7 yrs.; to daus. Mary Plumer and Elizabeth Titcomb; to Samuel Plumer's and Wm. Titcomb's ch.; to John and Samuel Stevens and others. [Reg. XX, 239.]

BIDGOOD, BETGOOD,
Richard, merchant, of Romsey, Eng., came in the Confidence April 11, 1638. Late of London, clothworker, bought house and land in Boston and was adm. inhab. 29 (5) 1639. Rem. to Ipswich; commoner, 1641. Mrs. B. in court in 1652 for living apart from her husband. [Es. Files.]

BIGELOW, BIGULAH, BAGLEY,
John, blacksmith, Watertown, propr. 1642; bought house and land 1649; took oath of fidelity 1652. He m. 30 (8) 1642, Mary, dau. of John Warren; she d. Oct. 19, 1691,

BIGELOW, etc., cont.

and he m. Oct. 2, 1694, Sarah, dau. or widow of Joseph Bemis. Ch. John b. 27 (8) 1643, Jonathan b. 11 (10) 1646, Mary b. March 18, 1648, (m. June 3, 1674, Michael Flagg,) Daniel b. Dec. 1, 1650, Samuel b. Oct. 28, 1653, Joshua b. Nov. 5, 1655, Elizabeth b. June 18, 1657, (m. John Stearns, Jr.,) Sarah b. Sept. 29, 1659, (m. July 23, 1679, Isaac Learned,) James (known from parson Bailey's rec. of his marriage March 25, 1687;) Martha b. April 1, 1662, (m. —— Woods,) Abigail b. Feb. 4, 1663-4, (m. Dec. 10, 1684, Benjamin Harrington,) Hannah b. and d. in 1665, a son b. and d. in 1667.

He d. July 14, 1703, ae. (per dep.) 86. Will dated 4 Jan. 1702-3, prob. July 23, 1703, beq. to wife Sarah; sons John, Jonathan, Daniel, Samuel, Joshua, and James; daus. Mary Flegg, Elizabeth Sterne, (her children,) Sarah Larnard, Martha Wood, (her children,) and Abigail Harrington.

BIGGS,

John, Boston, memb. chh. 1630-1, frm. March 4, 1633-4. One of the first to plant at Agawam (Ipswich) April 1, 1633. [Col. Rec.] One of the richer inhabs. of Boston who contributed toward the free school 12 (6) 1636. Owner of marsh land, 1644. His wife Mary d. 10 (11) 1649.

He made will 19 (4) 1666, giving all to wife Mary, whom he appointed exec. Inv. taken 11 July, prob. 19 (8) 1666.

Rachel, widow, came in the Elizabeth April 17, 1635. Settled at Dorchester; memb. chh. and propr. in 1637.

Her will was prob. 30 (4) 1647; sons-in-law John Stow of Roxbury and Peter Masters in Eng. and their children; nephew Hopestill Foster; James Batte, Clement Batte and his dau. Rachel, and several other persons. [Reg. V, 300.] See wills of her sons John and Smalhope, of Cranbrooke, co. Kent, Eng. in Reg. XXIX, 256, XXXVIII, 61, and LII, 194.

Thomas, ae. 13, came in the Blessing in July in 1635.

BIGSBY, BIXBY,

Joseph, Ipswich, 1648, propr. 1649. Bought land of Joseph Jewett, and had deed from his execrs. He deposed in 1674, ae. 54 years. He m. in 1647 Sarah, widow of Luke Heard. Rem. to Boxford.

BIGSBY, etc., cont.

His will dated 11 Nov. 1699, being aged; prob. 6 March, 1703-4, beq. to sons Joseph, George and Jonathan; son Daniel had recd. his portion; to dau. Mary Ston and Abigail; provides for his wife's comfort.

Mary, widow, Boston, adm. chh. 20 (4) 1640. She d. 5 (11) 1654.

BILDCOME,

Richard, servant to Walter Hayne, came in the Confidence April 11, 1638, ae. 16.

BILL, BILLS,

James, yeoman, bought land at Pulling Point, Boston, of Wentworth Day, and sold it to Bernard Engle 10 (2) 1645; confirmed the sale with wife Mary July 6, 1666.

Will dated 31 Jan. 1687, prob. before Andros Feb. 22, 1687-8: three sons, James, Jr., Jonathan and Joseph;; daus. Mary Smith, Hannah Kent and Sarah Chevers. See Grover, John.

John, ae. 13, came in the Hopewell in 1635. Settled at Boston.
He d. (10) 1638.

Marie, ae. 11, came in the Planter in April, 1635.

Robert, husbandman, ae. 32, came in the Pied Cow in July, 1635. Settled at Charlestown; d. at the house of E. Carrington about 15 (10) 1635; his sister, formerly wife of Ephraim Davis, m. John Knowles, who admin. on his est. 4 Sept. 1638.

Inv. taken by Ralph Sprague and Robert Hale; goodmen Hazard and Kingman and James Clarke mentioned.

BILLING, BILLINGS, BILLINGE,

Nathaniel, Sen., Concord, frm. June 2, 1641.

He d. Aug. 24, 1673. Inv. of his est. taken 16 Sept. 1673, was presented by his sons Nathaniel and John B.

Roger, carpenter, propr., Dorchester, memb. chh. 9 (4) 1640; frm. May 10, 1648. The widow Ann Gill calls him brother in July, 1683. Wife Mary.

He d. Nov. 15, 1683, ae. 65 yrs. [Gr. st.] Will dated 2 Feb. 1680, and 13 Nov. 1683, prob. 13 Dec. 1683, beq. to wife; to Joseph, son of his dec. son Joseph; to son-in-law James Pennyman; dau. Mary, who m. Sam-

BILLING, etc., cont.
uel Belcher; Nathaniel Wales' dau. Elizabeth; John Pennyman, Nathaniel Wales' wife and Dea. Tomson's wife; dau. Mary Mels; sons Ebenezer and Roger Billing; cousin Alexander Marsh, and grandchildren.

BILLINGTON,
John, London, came in the Mayflower; signed the Compact. Wife Ellen; sons John and Francis. He was executed for murder in 1630.

Thomas, Lynn, workman at the Ironworks, a witness in Court in 1647.

BINKS,
Byron, in Court July 3, 1632.

BINFIELD,
John, residence not stated. He d. in 1637 leaving 2 children undisposed of; Mr. Craddock had his goods and one ch.; the other was to be disposed of by the country. [Col. Rec. June 6, 1637.]

BIRAM, BIROM,
Nicholas, Weymouth, son-in-law of Abraham Shaw of Dedham. Sold house and privileges in W. 2 (10) 1640. Bought house and lands 5 (8) 1647.

He d. April 13, 1688; will prob. June 13 folg.; ratified to his bro. John Shaw of Wey. certain land, and to each of his children what he had formerly given them. Rest to wife Susanna. [Gen. Adv. I, 20.]

BIRCH,
Thomas, Dorchester. He was paid 4 s. in 1651 for iron work done on the meeting house.

He d. 3 (8) 1657. In his will he provided for his ch. naming eldest son Joseph, dau. Mary and son Jeremiah, and referring to 2 other ch. The adminrs. asked the Court Jan. 31, 1664, that the whole est. might be made over to Joseph, now 21 yrs. old, he giving 30 li. apiece to his bros. and sisters at age. Jonathan, the youngest, chose Thomas Tilestone guardian. [Reg. XVI, 162.]

BIRCHALL, BURCHALL, BIRDSALL, BORDSALL,
Henry, Boston, frm. May 2, 1638. Propr. 14 (10) 1635. Rem. to Salem. Had care of meeting house in 1644. Bought land in 1649.
Admin. of his est 17 (9) 1651.

John, Dorchester, propr. 1648. Res. at Springfield in 1645; propr. Adm. inhab. Boston, 1655.

BIRCHER, BURCHARD,
Thomas, laboring man, ae. 40, with Mary, ae. 38, Elizabeth, ae. 13, Marie, ae. 12, Sarah, ae. 9, Susan, ae. 8, John, ae. 7, and Ann, ae. 18 mos., came in the Truelove in Sept. 1635. Residence here not stated. Frm. May 17, 1637.

BIRCHLER, BIRCHLEY,
John, Ipswich, defendant in Es. Court in 1647.

BIRD, BURD,
Jathniel, Ipswich, propr. 1639.

John, frm. May, 1645.

Simon, ae. 20, came in the Susan and Ellen in April, 1635. Settled at Boston, at Rumley Marsh; laborer; adm. chh. 24 (12) 1643; frm. May 29, 1644. Wife Mary adm. chh. 11 (4) 1643. Rem. to Billerica.

He d. in 1666. Will dated Jan. 4, 1665, prob. 2 (3) 1666, beq. to wife Mary; to cousins Mr. John Wilson, Jr., and Mary Danforth of Roxbury; to my landlady Buttolph; to Mary, dau. of Crispus Bruer of Lynne; to Mary, dau. of Jonathan Danforth, and to his pastor, Mr. Samuel Whiting, Jr. The widow's est. was admin. upon 6 (2) 1680.

Thomas, tanner, Dorchester, propr. 1640, memb. chh. in 1642.

He d. 8 (4) 1667, ae. 54. Will prob. July 17, 1667. Wife Anne one third of all for life; son Thomas to have 10 li. more than the other ch., deducting the 50 li. promised at his marriage, part of which is paid; sons John and James and dau. Sarah. Wife Anne d. 21 (6) 1673. Ch. Thomas b. 4 (3) 1640, John b. 11 (1) 1641, James bapt. (2) 1644, Sarah bapt. 12 (6) 1649, a son d. 26 (7) 1665.

Thomas, Scituate, propr. 1636. Town officer, juror, frm. 4 June, 1650.

BIRD, etc., cont.
His will dated Feb. 4, 1663, prob. Oct. 4, 1664, beq. to Gershom, son of Anthony Dodson, his house and lands after the death of himself and wife, he paying to the chh. of Marshfield 20 shillings a year forever; to A. D.'s son Jonathan and three daus.; to pastor Wm. Witherell; to kinsman Robert Marshall; to Wm. Brooks; to John, son of Elisha Bisbee; James Torrey, Sen., and Deborah Burden. Rest to wife Anne.

Thomas, Ipswich, propr. 1639.

Widow, Ipswich, commoner, 1641.

BISCOE, BISCO, BRISKOW, BISKOW, see Brisco,

Nathaniel, tanner, Watertown, a rich man; his barn burnt with corn, leather, etc. worth 200 li., in 1642. [W.] Wrote a pamphlet against supporting ministers by taxation. Sold lands in Wat. Oct. 2, 1651. Ret. to Eng. whence he wrote a letter which produced much excitement. [Mass. Hist. Coll. Vol. 1, 3d Series.] [W.] His wife was bur. 20 (9) 1642. Ch. Nathaniel, Mary, (m. Thomas Broughton,) John, Sarah, (m. William Bond).

BISHOP, BISHOPP, BUSHOP, BYSHOP,

Anne, Dorchester, memb. chh. before 1639.

Edward, Salem, 1646. Adm. chh. 6 (2) 1645. Ch. Hannah bapt. 12 (2) 1646, Edward bapt. 23 (2) 1648, Mary bapt. 12 (8) 1651, William (of bro. B.) bapt. 7 (6) 1666.

Edward, Rehoboth, innkeeper, aged, made will 10 May, 1711; beq. to wife Sarah, ch. Edward, Samuel, William, Jonathan, Joseph, David, John, Ebenezer, and Sarah Jordan; son-in-law Samuel Day.

James, Taunton, servant to Mr. Thomas Farrell, renewed his contract 11 June, 1639.

Job, Ipswich. He m. Elizabeth, dau. of Mr. George Phillips, q. v. She deposed in 1654, ae. about 40 years. [Es. Files.] Dau. Elizabeth d. at Boston 27 (12) 1651.

John, carpenter, miller, Newbury, 1637. Built a mill which he sold in 1644, and rem. to New Jersey. He m. Oct. 7, 1647, Rebecca, widow of Samuel Scullard; ch. John b. 19

BISHOP, etc., cont.
Sept. 1648, Rebecca b. 15 May, 1650, Hannah b. 10 Dec. 1653, Elizabeth b. and d. 1655, Jonathan b. 11 Jan. 1656, Noah b. 10 June, 1658, David b. 26 Aug. 1660.

Nathaniel, currier, Ipswich, propr. 1636-1639; rem. to Boston. Sold Ips. land 25 May, 1643; adm. chh. 24 (12) 1643; frm. May, 1645. He deposed to the will of Mary Drury 28 Nov. 1682, ae. 75 years. Wife Alice; ch. Sarah b. (rec. at Boston,) 20 (1) 1634, (m. 18 (7) 1654, Samuel Bucknell,) Ruth b. 14 (2) 1639, (m. 15 (2) 1656, John Peirce,) Joseph b. 14 (5) 1642, Benjamin b. 31 (3) 1644, (bapt. at Bo.,) John b. 31 (11) 1646, Samuel d. 7 (1) 1646, Hannah b. 11 (12) 1648, John bapt. 26 (11) 1650, Rebecca b. 8 (2) 1652. The widow Alice m. 22 Nov. 1659, John Lewis.

He made will 10 June, 1681, prob. 4 June, 1687, before Andros. Dau. Ruth, (wife of William Fuller, of Boston, victualler,) and her children, Ruth, wife of Philip Catland, Hannah, wife of William Smith, and Rebecca Peirce; dau. Rebecca, wife of Adam Holland.

Richard, Salem, propr. 1636; memb. chh. 1639. Constable 31 (10) 1644. [Es. Court.] Wife Dulsabel deposed in 1654, ae. about 50 years. She d. 24 (6) 1658; he m. 22 (5) 1660, Mary, widow of William Gault. [Contract in Es. Files XXIV, 64.] He admin. upon the est. of Richard King, June 2, 1635, in behalf of his wife. [Ess. Court Rec.]

Nunc. will prob. March 29, 1675. Widow Mary, son Thomas and his son Richard; gr. ch. Mary Durlan; son Nathaniel; a son at Long Island. Power of attorney filed from John Bishop of South Hampton, L. I.; contract of marriage made by Richard Bishop with Mary Gault 12 (5) 1660, filed. John Durlan, one of the adminrs. John Bligh deposed, calling him father Bishop. The widow Mary deposed, ae. about 64 yrs.

Richard, Plymouth. He hired Nathl. Souther Jan. 5, 1640-1. He m. 5 Dec. 1644, Alice, widow of George Clark.

Thomas, yeoman, Ipswich, propr. 1637. Sold land 20 (9) 1644, his wife consenting. His will dated Feb. 6, 1670, (endorsed by the witnesses Antipas Newman and Francis Wainwright,) prob. 28 March, 1671, beq. to wife Margaret, sons Samuel, John, Thom-

51

BISHOP, etc., cont.
as, Job and Nathaniel; to cousin Sarah B., now living with me; to bro. Paul B. of Kingston a hogshead of tobacco, to be sent over to him of the five that come to me from Virginia. Widow Margaret, exec. of the will of Thomas B., gave power of attorney 24 Nov. 1673, to her son Thomas. The inv. of her est. was pres. by Samuel B. 29 March, 1681.

Mr. Townsend, Salem, 1634; frm. Sept. 2, 1635. One of the commrs. of Salem Quarterly Court at its first session, 27 (4) 1636. Deputy, town officer. Ch. Leah bapt. 19 (4) 1637, John bapt. 31 (5) 1642.

BITFIELD, see Bidfield.

BITTLESTONE, BEETLESTONE, BIDDLESTON,
Thomas, Cambridge, propr. 1638. He d. Nov. 23, 1640. Will prob. in Gen. Court 7 (7) 1643. Wife Elizabeth, dau. Elizabeth; boy John Swan.

William, Cambridge, propr. 1638. He d. 5 (8) [1640.]

BITTON,
James, ae. 27, came in the Increase April 15, 1635.

BIXBY, see Bigsby.

BLACK, BLACKE,
John, with wife Susanna, adm. chh. Charlestown 4 (11) 1634-5, propr. 1635. Rem. to Salem, 1636; propr., juryman. One of the planters at Jeffreys Creek, 13 May, 1640. Ch. Lydia bapt. 25 (10) 1636, Lydia bapt. 3 (4) 1638, a dau. bapt. 27 (9) 1640, Persis, [a dau.?] m. 29 (9) 1655, Robert Follett. Admin. on his est. gr. (5) 1675.

Miles, Sandwich, creditor of Wm. Swift, 1642, atba. 1643.

Richard, residence not stated, frm. May, 1645.

BLACKBOURNE,
Mr. Walter, haberdasher, shop-keeper, planter, Roxbury, memb. chh. with wife Elizabeth about 1637. Rem. to Boston; frm. May 22, 1639. Sold land to William Cheney, and placed cows with him 30 (7) 1639. Ret.

BLACKBOURNE, cont.
to London, Eng.; made his wife his attorney for sale of house, etc. 22 (1) 1640; she sold to Francis Lisle 10 (6) 1641, and gave power of attorney to Thomas Fowle to collect and forward to her all dues. He was attorney for Elizabeth Sutton, jointly with Lisle, 23 (5) 1641. [L.]

BLACKETT,
Martha, maid-servant to our teacher, Mr. John Cotton, adm. chh. Boston, 20 (5) 1634.

BLACKLEACH, BLACKLEDGE, BLACKLIDGE,
John, Boston, sold land at Winnisimet Feb. 27, 1634. Frm. May 6, 1635. Rem. to Salem. Deputy 1636. An active worker for the improvement of the Indians. Wife Elizabeth memb. chh. 1638. They were dismissed from the chh. to that of Hartford, Conn. 5 Oct. 1661, having meantime rem. about 1646, and resided there. Ch. Exercise bapt. 24 (11) 1636, (m. Aug. 24, 1660, Richard Raser.) Joseph b. 8 (11), bapt. 3 (12) 1638, Elizabeth b. (10) 1641, Benoni bapt. 14 (3) 1643, Elizabeth b. 12 (6) 1644; all these given in by the parents. [Es. Files.] Ch. rec. at Boston: Solomon bapt. in Bo. 18 (8) 1646, Solomon bapt. 3 (7) 1648, ae. about 2 days, Mary bapt. 7 (7) 1651.

He d. at Wethersfield, Conn. Aug. 23, 1683. Will, dated at Boston 16 Aug. 1671. [Mass. Not. Rec. Book, IV, 91.] Beq. to wife Elizabeth, sons John, Benony, and Solomon, daus. Elizabeth and Marie. [Reg. XXXVI, 189.]

William, Boston, propr. adjoining Wm. Davies 9 (8) 1645.

BLACKLEY, BLAKELEY,
Edward, Roxbury.

He was bur,—a widower,—Nov. 3, 1637. His dau. Sarah was bur. May, 1638. The inv. of his est. was taken 25 (10) 1637, by John Stow, Isaac Heath, Joseph Weld, John Johnsone, Thomas Sams, William Parke and Sammwell Basse.

Thomas, ae. 20, came in the Hopewell in Aug. 1635.

Nunc. will on testimony of John and Martha Mellowes, 30 Jan. 1673; wife to have her thirds of the estate, money being best for

BLACKLEY, etc., cont.
her because she was aged. Inv. presented Jan 1, 1673, by wife Susanna.

BLACKMORE, BLAKEMORE,
John, Sandwich, propr. allowed to exercise inhabitants in arms in 1639; atba. 1643.

BLACKSTONE, BLAXTON, BLAXTONE,
Elizabeth, ae. 22, came in the Bevis in May, 1638.

Rev. William subscribed toward the expense of returning Thomas Morton to England in 1628. [Bradford's Letter Book, in Mass. Hist. Coll. 3.] A resident in Boston before the coming of the Dorchester or Charlestown settlers. Was appointed one of the attorneys of the Council for N. E. to put Mr. John Oldham in possession of his grant and to transfer the Council's grant to Thomas Lewis, gent., and Capt. Richard Bonython; the document, signed by Warwick and Gorges, was endorsed by the attorneys June 28, 1631. He invited the Winthrop party to come to the Boston peninsula from Charlestown in the fall of 1630; which they were glad to do. Special reserves of land were made for him, and the sum of 30 li. was raised for him by tax in 1634. He was adm. frm. May 18, 1631. He rem. to a section at the border of Mass. and R. I. colonies, "near Mr. Williams, but far from his opinions." [L., P. D.]

He m. in Bo. 4 July, 1659, Sarah Stephson (Stephenson), widow. Plymouth Court granted 55 acres of land to her son John S. in fulfillment of marriage contract made at this time. She d. June 15, 1673.

He d. in 1675. Inv. taken 28 May; admin. Plym. Court 27 Oct. 1675. Nathaniel Paine and Daniel Smith were app. guardians to his son John Blackstone. Library of 186 volumes beside 3 Bibles; household goods and tools of husbandry; 200 acres of ground. Memorandum by the recorder: "This estate was destroyed and carried away with the Indians."

BLACKWELL,
Jeremy, ae. 18, came in the Truelove in Sept. 1635. Had acct. with George Burcham of Lincoln, Eng., in 1641. [L.]

BLACKWELL, cont.
Michael, Sandwich, creditor of Wm. Swift in 1642; juror, 1648. Ch. Michael b. 1 June, 1648.

BLACKWOOD, BLAKEWOOD,
Rev. Christopher, planter, Scituate, bought the house and lands previously owned by Mr. John Lothrop, of Timothy Hatherly Nov. 23, 1640, and sold the same to Mr. Charles Chauncey 5 Oct. 1642. Is evidently the "Mr. Blackwood" who was invited to be the successor of Mr. Lothrop as pastor of the church, but who remained only a short time.

BLAGE, BLAGUE, BLAKE,
Henry, Plymouth, servant to Elizabeth Watson, widow, transferred to Thomas Watson and by him to John Rogers Nov. 8, 1638. May be supposed to be

Henry, brick-burner, Braintree, with wife Elizabeth memb. chh. Had accts. in 1639. [L.] Rem. to Boston; he and wife rec'd to chh. 3 (6) 1651. Ch. Philip b. at Br. 24 (1) 1643, Benjamin bapt. 18 (6) 1650, Elizabeth b. Oct. 28, 1652, Martha b. Nov. 2, 1655, Rebecca b. July 5, 1657, Joseph b. Sept. 2, 1660.

He d. July 28, 1662. Admin. gr. to the widow for herself and 7 children 12 (9) 1664. [Reg. XII, 48.]

BLAKE, BLACKE,
George, Gloucester, 1649, town officer. Rem. to Boxford. Wife Dorothy; ch. Rebecca b. Feb. 1641, Deborah b. 10 (9) ——, Prudence b. April 15, 1647, Elizabeth b. (3) 1650, Mary b. Feb. 14, 1652, Thomas b. June 9, 1658, Ruth b. Sept. 5, 1659.

Will dated 17 Jan. 1697-8, prob. 1698; beq. to daus. Rebecca Ham, Mary Curtis, and Ruth Shaw; gr. ch. Deborah Kimball, Deborah Perry, Moses Tyler, whose mothers are deceased; to gr. ch. John Eams, and to wife Dorothy. After the death of the widow admin. was gr. to John Eames; inv. taken 17 Feb. 1697-8.

Richard, servant, came in the Confidence April 11, 1638, ae. 16.

William, son of William, bapt. at Pitminster, Eng., July 10, 1594, m. there Sept. 27, 1617, Agnes Band, widow. Ch. bapt. at P.: John bapt. Aug. 30, 1618, Anne bapt.

BLAKE, etc., cont.
Aug. 30, 1618, (m. in Boston, Jacob Leager,) William bapt. Sept. 6, 1620, James bapt. April 27, 1624. Edward, (place and date of birth unknown).

He was one of the founders of Springfiela in 1636. [Reg. XIII, 297.] Rem. to Dorchester; earliest rec. there Jan. 3, 1637. He and his wife were membs. chh., and he was adm. frm. March 14, 1638-9. Town and county clerk, town officer.

He d. Oct. 25, 1663. Will, dated 3 Sept. 1661, prob. 28 Jan. 1663. Beq. 20 s. to the town for the repairing of the burying place. The remainder of his est. he gave one half to his wife and the other half to his 5 ch. The widow d. July 22, 1678. [See Increase Blake, his Ancestors and Descendants.]

BLANCHARD, BLANCHAR, BLANCHER,
Joseph, Boston, d. (10) 1637. [His son] William, tailor, Boston, made will 27 (7) 1652, and beq. to mother Ann, bro. John, sister Garlick's ch.; to his three ch.; to wife Hannah and her father James Everill. Widow Ann died [apparently at Woburn.] The inv. of her est. taken July 21, 1662, by Abraham and Jacob Barker, was presented by her son John B.

Thomas, yeoman, from Penton, Hants, Eng., came from London in the Jonathan in 1639; settled at Braintree. Bought lands in Boston and Charlestown of Mr. John Wilson. Rem. to Char. in 1651. He m. in Eng. ——, who died in Eng. He m. 2, widow Agnes (Bent) Barnes, who d. on the passage to N. E.; he m. 3, Mary ——.

He d. 21 (3) 1654. Will dated 16 (3), prob. 20 (4) 1654, beq. to wife Mary; ch. George, Thomas, Samuel, Nathaniel; gr. ch. Joseph; to the church of Malden. He provided that Benjamin Tompson should be fitted for the University if his parents consent. [Reg. XVII. 156, and XXXII, 411.] Widow admin. 3 (4) 1656.

BLAND,
Bridget, Charlestown, widow of Wm. Bland late of Oxford, glover, gave a letter of attorney for collection of legacies in Eng. 4 (9) 1646. [A.]

BLANDFORD,
John, came from Sutton Mansfield, co. Wilts, in the Confidence in 1638, as servant of Walter Hayne. Settled in Sudbury. Propr. 1639. He deposed to the will of Hugh Griffin in 1658, ae. about 50 years. Wife Mary; ch. Sarah b. 27 (11) 1642, Hannah b. 7 (1) 1644, Joan b. 6 (1) 1646, Lydia b. 28 (12) 1647, Stephen b. 3 Dec. 1649. Wife Mary d. 4 (10) 1641, and he m. 2, March 10, 1642, Dorothie, widow of —— Wright.

His will dated 21 Oct. 1687, prob. 23 Nov. folg., beq. to wife Dorothy, son Stephen, son (in-law) Jabesh Browne, son-in-law Edward Wright, dau. Maynard, and to Mary, Elizabeth and James Thackson.

BLANKET, BLANCHER, BLANCHARD,
John, Marblehead, 1643.

Widow, Marblehead, taxed in 1638. Was she the "Ann" who was memb. chh. Salem 30 (4) 1643?

William, Salem, Marblehead, 1643. Adm. chh. 14 (12) 1640.

BLANTON,
William, carpenter, Boston, 1639; adm. chh. 8 (8) 1642. Wife Phebe; dau. Phebe bapt. 21 (6) 1642, ae. about 5 days; Mary b. (5) 1645. Gen. Court allowed him to keep a cook's shop toward Roxbury in 1647.

He d. June 15, 1662. His will beq. to wife, Phebe, son William, daus. Phebe and Mary; to bros. Ralph and John Blantine, the latter of Upton upon Seavern in Worcestershire, Eng. Owned shares in the Iron works at Taunton.

BLASON,
Ann, ae. 27, came in the Susan and Ellen in April, 1635.

BLASDEL, BLESDALE,
Ralph, tailor, Salisbury, propr. 1639; lic. to sell wine, 1645. Wife Elizabeth; ch. [Henry,] Mary b. 5 (1) 1641, (m. 1, Joseph Stowers, m. 2, Wm. Sterling,) Sarah d. 17 (1) 1646, [Ralph.]

He d. before 1650. His widow d. (6) 1667. Admin. gr. to Joseph Stowers 8 Oct.

William, tailor, Boston, adm. inhab. in 1646.

BLEASE,
John, Cambridge, bur. 23 (2) 1646.

BLINMAN, BLINDMAN,
Rev. Richard, minister, from Wales. Came to Green's Harbor, Marshfield in 1640; rem. soon to Gloucester, of which he was one of the founders and pastor. He was prop. frm. Plym. Colony 1 March, 1640-1, but adm. frm. Mass. Colony Oct. 7, 1641. Rem. to New London, afterward to New Haven, Conn. Ret. to England via Newfoundland in 1659. [W.] His associates at Mars. and Gloc. were "Mr. Hugh Prychard, Mr. Obadiah Bruen, John Sadler, Hugh Cauken and Walter Tybbot." [Plym. Col. Rec.] Wife Mary; ch. Jeremiah b. July 20, 1642, Ezekiel b. Nov. 11, 1643, Azarikam b. 2 (11) 1646.

He d. at Bristol, Eng. Will dated Wed. April 13, 1687, prob. July 26, 1687; ae. 72 years and more; to be buried near his wife; beq. to sons-in-law Richard Bowes and dau. Margaret, his wife; Wadland and dau. Hannah his wife; Henry Acourt and dau. Margaret his wife; sons Jeremiah, Nathaniel and Azrikam (with his wife Elizabeth;) dau.-in-law Martha B. and her dau. Anne. [Reg. LIII, 234, and LIV, 39.]

BLISH, BLUSH,
Abraham, Barnstable, had accounts with John Cole in 1637; prop. for frm. 1 June, 1641; atba. 1643. Town officer. Ch. Sarah b. Dec. 2, 1644, Joseph bapt. April 9, 1648. His wife was bur. May 26, 1653, or May 16, 1651. He m. (date not given,) Hannah, widow of John Barker; ch. Abraham b. about 16 Oct. 1654. She was bur. about 16 March, 1658; he m. Jan. 4, 1658-9, Alice Derby, widow.

He d. 7 Sept. 1683.

He made will 17 April, 1682, prob. 5 March, 1683-4; beq. to wife Alice, sons Joseph and Abraham, dau. Sarah Orchyard and her 5 children.

BLISS, BLISE, BLYSSE,
George, Sandwich, propr. 1640.

Nathaniel, Springfield, propr. 1646. He m. 20 (9) 1646, Katharine Chapin; ch. Samuel b. 7 (9) 1647, Margaret b. 12 (9) 1649, Mary b. 23 (7) 1651, Nathaniel b. 27 (1) 1653. He was bur. 18 (9) 1654. His widow m. 31 (4) 1655, Thomas Gilbert; he d. 5 June,

BLISS, etc., cont.
1662, and she m. Samuel Marshfield. Mary, (m. 26 (9) 1646, Joseph Parsons,) Sarah, m. 20 (5) 1659, John Scott,) and Hester, (m. Dec. 26, 1661, Edward Foster,) may be ch. or Nathaniel. See Chapin.

Thomas, Boston, propr. at Mt. Wollaston 1639. Frm. May 18, 1642. Rem. to Rehoboth. Prop. frm. Plym. Colony 1645; town officer 1647. His will, 21 (6) 1647, names son Jonathan; eldest dau. wife of Thomas Williams; Mary, wife of Nathaniel Harmon, son-in-law Nicholas Ide, son Nathaniel. Nicholas Hyde petitioned Court 7 June, 1648, for a child's portion of the est. [Reg. IV, 282.]

BLINNFIELD,
Thomas, inv. of his est. taken about 1640 in Suff. Prob. records.

BLODGET, BLODGETT, BLOYETT,
Thomas, glover, ae. 30, with wife Susan, ae. 37, and ch. Daniel, ae. 4, and Samuel, ae. 1½, came in the Increase April 8, 1635. Settled at Cambridge. Propr. Frm. March 3, 1635-6. Wife Susan; ch. Daniel, Samuel, Susanna b. (4) 1637.

He d. 7 (6) 1639. His will prob. (Suff.) 25 (1) 1643, beq. to wife Susan, and the three ch. above named. [Reg. II, 186.]

BLOIS, BLOISE, BLOYS, BLOSSE,
Edmund, planter, Watertown, 1638; had grant of 40 acres of land. Frm. May 22, 1639. He deposed 2 (7) 1663, ae. about 75 years. [Mdx. Files.] His wife Mary, ae. 40, and ch. Richard, ae. 11, came in the Francis of Ipswich, April 30, 1634. The son Richard d. in 1665; inv. on file. His wife d. May 29, 1675; he. m. 2, Sept. 27, 1675, Ruth Parsons.

He d. about 1681. Will dated 5 Dec. 1676, prob. 5 April, 1681, beq. all to his wife.

Francis, Cambridge, frm. June 2, 1641. He was bur. 29 (7) 1646. Widow Frances; the inv. of her est. was taken 7 (10) 1647, by John Bridge and Roger Bancroft. [Suff. Prob. Reg. VII, 170.]

John, bur. in Cambridge April 23, 1646. [Genealogy, Reg. XLI, 298.]

BLOOD, BLOD, BLOT,
James, yeoman, sergeant, Concord, propr.; frm. June 2, 1641. One of the comrs.

BLOOD, etc., cont.
to lay out the Hough grant of 400 acres in 1650. Com. to end small causes at Chelmsford in 1660. He deposed 30 (1) 1660, ae. about 55 years, and requested a dispensation from training. [Mdx. Files.] Wife Ellen; ch. James, Mary, (m. Simon Davis). The wife d. Aug. 1, 1674.
He d. Sept. 17, 1683. Inv. taken Oct. 7, 1683; will dated June 18, 1680, prob. Dec. 18, 1683, beq. to son James B.; to dau. Mary Davis and her husband, Simon, with their ch. James and Ebenezer.
No evidence has been found by the writer to connect James with John and Robert.

John, Lynn, witness in court in 1647. Rem. to Concord. Admin. of his est. gr. 27 Sept. 1692 to his brother Robert B., Sen. [Court Rec.]

Robert, yeoman, planter, Lynn, before the court in 1647. Rem. to Concord. He sold, with John, May 1, 1649, the moietie of one tenement and half an oxe gang in Ruddington in the county of Nottingham, Eng., to William Crafts of Lynn. [Es. De. 1, 24.]
He m. 8 April, 1653, Elizabeth, dau. of Maj. Simon Willard; ch. Mary b. 4 March, 1655, Elizabeth b. 14 June, 1656, Sarah b. 1 Aug. 1658, Robert b. 20 Feb. 1659, Simon b. 5 July, 1662, d. April 2, 1692, Josiah b. 6 April, 1664, John b. 29 Oct. 1666, d. Oct. 24, 1689, Ellen b. 14 April, 1669, Samuel b. Oct. 1671, James b. 3 Nov. 1673, Ebenezer b. 15 Feb. 1676, Jonathan b. 1 (7) 1679.
He d. Oct. 22, 1701. Admin. gr. to widow Hannah and son Jonathan. Division made Nov. 10 folg. to the widow; sons Josiah, Samuel, James and Jonathan B.; sons-in-law John Buttrick, husband of Mary; Samuel Buttrick, husband of Elizabeth; Daniel Colburn, husband of Sarah, and Ebenezer B., 7 years old, son of the eldest son Robert B., Jr., dec.

BLOOMFIELD, BLOMFIELD,
John, Newbury, 1637.
He d. in 1639, and the Gen. Court, 3 March, 1639-40, app. his son Thomas to admin. and to have house and grounds; the lame dau. to have the over-plus of goods not disposed of; will and inv. to be recorded. The son Thomas was a propr. in 1638, and had family. Rem. to Woodbridge, N. J.

BLOOMFIELD, etc., cont.
William, ae. 30, with wife Sarah, ae. 25, and dau. Sarah, ae. 1, came in the Elizabeth of Ipswich April 30, 1634. Frm. Sept. 2, 1635. Propr., Cambridge. Sold house and lands before 1639.

BLOSSOM,
Thomas, Plymouth, who had been with the company in Holland, d. of an infectious fever in 1633. [B.] He wrote to Bradford from Leyden, Dec. 15, 1625, concerning Mr. Robinson's death. A son had d. since he left Plymouth; 2 children born since. [Mass. Hist. Coll. 3.] His widow Anna m. 17 Oct. 1633, Henry Rowley.

Thomas, (perhaps son of the above,) m. June 18, 1645, at Barnstable, Sarah Ewer. He was drowned at Nocett April 22, 1650. Admin. gr. 5 June, 1650, to his widow Sarah; she made over 5 li. to the ch. Sarah, whom she had by him.

BLOT, BLOTT,
Goodman, Reading, propr. 1647.

Johannah, maid servant to deacon Valentine Hill; adm. chh. 7 (7) 1644. "Now wife of one deacon Lovitt of Braintree." Dism. to Br. chh. 30 (1) 1645.

Robert, Charlestown, 1634; frm. March 4, 1634-5. With wife Susan adm. chh. Boston from Charlestown 28 (10) 1644. Sold land at Concord, gr. to Samuel Stretton, 29 (5) 1648. Dau. Mary m. Thomas Woodford. Wife Susanna d. in B. Jan. 20, 1659-60.
Will, dated 27 (3) 1662, codicil 27 March, 1665; prob. Feb. 2, 1665-6. Dau. Sarah, her husband Edward Ellis, and her ch. [?] whose names are Woodford; dau. Tosier and her ch. of whom the eldest is John Green; dau. Lovett of Braintree and her ch.; son-in-law Daniel Lovett; son-in-law Daniel Turin's ch. [Reg. XV.]

Thomas, Boston, 1636.

BLOWER, BLOWERS, BLORES,
John, Barnstable, atba. 1643.

John, cooper, Boston. Wife Tabitha, ch. Tabitha b. Feb. 12, 1654. Bought house and land Dec. 30, 1658.
Will dated 9 Sept. 1675, prob. 2 days later, beq. to wife Tabitha and ch. John, Tabitha, Mary and Thomas.

BLOWER, etc., cont.
Mrs., part of her money paid to Colonial treasurer 9 (7) 1639.

Thomas, ae. 50, came in the Truelove in Sept., 1635.

BLOYETT, see Blodget.

BOANES,
Elizabeth, maid servant to Richard Bellingham, adm. chh. of Boston 22 (6) 1635.

BOARDMAN, BORDMAN, BOORMAN, BOREMAN, BURMAN, (see also Boreman,)
Thomas, carpenter, from London. Wife Luce; ch. b. in London. Employed to repair fort at Plymouth, 1635, Sandwich, 1638. He m. 2, at Barnstable March 3, 1644-5, or March, 1645-6, Hannah Annable. Ch. Hannah b. May, 1646, Thomas b. Sept. 1648, Samuel b. July, 1651, Desire b. May, 1654, Mary b. March, 1656, Mehitabel b. Sept. 1658, Tristram b. Aug. 1661.
Will, (Thomas Burman of Barnstable,) May 9, prob. June 4, 1663. Wife Hannah; ch. Thomas, Trustrum, Samuel, Hannah, Desire, Mary, Mehitabel. Anthony Annibal and William Crocker adminrs. [Reg. VI, 95.]

William, Boston, apprentice of Richard Gridley to 17 (8) 1639; then of William Townsend, then of Thomas Witherley, mariner, from 30 (11) 1639. [L.] Rem. to Cambridge. A memb. of the chh. with his wife Frances; ch. Moses, Rebecca, Andrew, Aaron, Frances, Martha, Mary and William, all bapt. at Camb.; Elizabeth bapt. Aug. 26, 1660. [Mi.] He deposed 26 (6) 1672, ae. 57 years. [Mdx. Files.]
He d. 25 March, 1685, ae. 71. Inv. taken 28 May folg.; was filed by the widow Frances.

BOBBETT,
Edward, Taunton, atba. 1643. In court 8 June, 1649. He m. in Boston 7 (7) 1653, Sarah, dau. of Miles Tarne; ch. Edward b. July 15, 1655, Sarah b. March 20, 1657, (m. March 25, 1680, Samuel Pitts,) Hannah b. March 9, 1660, Damaris b. Sept. 15, 1663, Elkanah (dau.) b. Dec. 15, 1665, Dorcas b. Jan. 20, 1666 ,d. April 9, 1674, Esther b. April 15, 1669, Ruth b. Aug. 7, 1671, Deliverance b. Dec. 15, 1673.

BOBBETT, cont.
He was slain by the Indians. Admin. gr. to widow Sarah 6 March, 1676-7; eldest son double portion; other ch. equal shares.

BODFISH, BOTFISH,
Boniface, (residence not stated,) frm. May 6, 1635.

Robert, [Lynn,] juryman at Salem in 1636 and 1637. Of Sandwich in 1640; propr. and town officer; atba. 1643. Ch. Joseph b. April 3, 1651. (
Bridget, who m. Samuel Hinckley, and Mary, who m. Nov. 1659, John Crocker, Jr., may be connected with him.

BODINGTON,
John, merchant, Charlestown, contracted 15 (10) 1646, to deliver lot of fish at the new found land the next fishing season, and wrote his bro. at Mr. James Kirk's to buy the fish. [A.]

BODMAN, BADMAN, BOARDMAN,
John, shoemaker, Boston. Wife Sarah adm. chh. 23 (1) 1644. Ch. John b. (6) 1645, Manoah b. 6 (1) 1646, Sarah bapt. 13 (3) 1649, Samuel bapt. 23 (1) 1651, Joseph b. 17 Oct. 1653, Lydia b. 26 April, 1656.

William, Watertown. Wife Rebecca; ch. Rebecca b. 1643.

BOGGUST,
John, punished as accessory to a felony, 28 Sept. 1630.

BOLTER, BOULTER,
Nathaniel, [Hampton,] was before Gen. Court, 2 May, 1649. Rem. to Exeter.

BOLTON, BOULTON,
Nicholas, Dorchester, adm. chh. 8 (1) 1644. Frm. May 29, 1644. He was bellringer, and messenger for selectmen. Wife Elizabeth; ch. Thankful bapt. 4 (8) 1649, Elizabeth bapt. 18 (11) 1656, (m. Oct. 25, 1676, Experience Willis,) John, (ae. 16 in 1676).
He d. May 27, 1683. Nunc. will made 24 May, prob. 20 Sept. folg., beq. to wife, son John and dau. Experience Willis.

William, Newbury, propr. 1645. He m. 16 Jan. 1654-5, Jane Bartlett; she d. 6 Sept. 1659. He m. 2, 22 Nov. 1659, Mary Denison;

BOLTON, etc., cont.
ch. Mary d. Dec. 6, 1656, William b. 27 May, 1665, Ruth b. 1 Aug. 1667, Elizabeth b. 1672, d. 1674, Sarah b. 5 April, 1677, Hannah b. 18 July, 1679, Joseph b. 8 July, 1682.

He d. 27 March, 1697. Will dated 15 Feb. 1694-5, beq. to wife Mary, sons Joseph and Stephen, daus. Jane, Ruth, Elizabeth and Hannah. Son Stephen gave a bond 11 March, 1696-7, to care for his father and mother the rest of their lives.

BOND,
John, yeoman, Newbury, propr. 1642. Rem. to Rowley, and to Haverhill about 1667. He m. 5 Aug. 1649, Hester Blakeley; ch. John b. 10 June, 1650, Thomas b. and d. 1652, Joseph b. 14 April, 1653, Hester b. 25 Sept. 1655, (m. Aquila Chase,) Mary b. 16 Dec. 1657, Abigail b. 6 Nov. 1660, (m. Ezra Rolfe).

He d. Dec. 3, 1674. Will dated Oct. 31, 1674, prob. 13 April, 1675, beq. to wife Hester; daus. Mary and Abigail B. and Hester Chase; to son Joseph B. The widow m. May 5, 1675, John Williams.

William, Watertown, 1631. Town officer, deputy, and speaker of Gen. Court. He deposed 20 (10) 1681, ae. 55 yrs. He m. Feb. 7, 1649, Sarah, dau. of Nathaniel Biscoe. She d. Feb. 15, 1692-3; he m. in 1695, Elizabeth, widow of John Nevinson. Ch. William b. Dec. 1, 1650, John b. Dec. 1652, Thomas b. Dec. 23, 1654, Elizabeth b. Nov. 30, 1656, (m. Nathaniel Barsham,) Nathaniel b. Jan. 19, 1658, Nathaniel b. Jan. 9, 1659, Sarah b. July 27, 1661, (m. Palgrave Wellington,) Jonas b. July 13, 1664, Mary, (m. Richard Coolidge).

He d. Dec. 14, 1695. Agreement made 23 Jan. folg. between the sons William, Thomas, Nathaniel and Jonas B., Nathaniel and Elizabeth Barsham and Richard and Mary Coolidge, for division of the estate.

BONHAM, BONUM,
George, Plymouth, a suit of his arbitrated in 1640; atba. 1643. Ch. Sarah b. and d. in 1649, Sarah b. and d. 1650-1, Sarah b. Dec. 10, 1653.

BONNER,
Marie, servant to Mr. John Cotton, adm. chh. Boston 3 (6) 1634. Dism. to the

BONNER, cont.
chh. of Dover 18 (6) 1644, now wife to Mr. Daniel Mawd, teacher of the chh. of D.

BONNEY,
Thomas, shoemaker, of Sandwich, Eng., came in the Hercules in March, 1634. Settled at Charlestown; propr. 1635; sold house and lands in 1637. Perhaps the same man,

Thomas, Duxbury, prop. frm. 5 March, 1638-9. Propr. 31 Aug. 1640; town officer. In Court, 1645.

Will dated 2 Jan. 1688-9, prob. 1 May, 1693, beq. to wife Mary and son Thomas; est. to be divided between the children after the death of their mother.

BOOMER,
Matthew, Lynn, servant to Edmund Needham; called to court, 1647.

BORDEN, BOURDEN,
John, ae. 28, with wife Joan, ae. 23, and ch. Matthew, ae. 5, and Elizabeth, ae. 3, came in the Elizabeth and Ann in May, 1635. Settled at Watertown; took oath of fidelity in 1652.

BORDSALL, see Birchall.

BOREBANCKE, see Burbank,
Joseph, ae. 24, servant to George Hadbourne, came in the Abigail in June, 1635.

BOREMAN, see Boardman,
Samuel, Ipswich, a letter to him from his mother Julian, dated at [....] ydon, Eng. 5 Feb. 1641, addressed to him at Ips. proves his residence at that time. Mentions his 5 sisters; father dead 2 years; bro. Christopher dare not take upon him so dangerous a voyage as that to New England, as Samuel had desired.

He rem. to Wethersfield, Conn. where the letter has been preserved. [Genealogy.]

Thomas, Ipswich, frm. March 4, 1634-5. App. gager by Gen. Court 27 Sept. 1642. Sold land 27 (10) 1647. He built a bridge, which was protected by Gen. Court 6 May, 1657. He made a contract of marriage for his son Daniel with Hannah, dau. of Richard Hutchinson, testified to 27 (9) 1663. With wife Margaret sold land Dec. 9, 1667.

BOREMAN, etc., cont.
He testified to his signature, affixed to a document concerning the building of a mill at Ipswich in 1635, 28 Feb. 1671, being a very aged man.
The date of his death does not appear; but his widow Margaret made will in 1679, prob. March 30, 1680; beq. to kinsmen, Martha Low and Joanna Fellows; sons Daniel and Thomas B.; to Dinah, her son's maid. Inv. mentions Thomas Low.

Thomas, Yarmouth, taxed in 1632; atba. 1643.

BOSWELL, see Buswell,
John, Boston, memb. chh. 1630-1; "dead soon."

BOSWORTH, BOSEWORTH,
Benjamin, planter, Hingham, deposed 4 (4) 1639, ae. about 24, and Edward, or Edmund, one of the founders of Hull, may be presumed to be ch. of Edward, Sen., as well as Jonathan, tailor, propr. at Cambridge, 1633, who deposed 4 (4) 1639, ae. 26, and Nathaniel, of Hull, who joined with Benjamin 1 (7) 1640, in making a draft on Joseph B. of Coventry, Eng., shoemaker. [L.]

Edward, embarked in 1634 with wife and children; he d. on the way and the Gen. Court voted to maintain the widow and her family. Voted 7 July, 1635, that Mr. Henry Sewall should be paid for their transportation by Jonathan and Benjamin B. and William Buckland. The widow d. at Hingham May 18, 1648.

Haniel, Ipswich, came in 1638 from Boston, Lincolnshire, in the service of John Whittingham. Juryman, 1648. He deposed in 1681, ae. 66 years. Petitioned in 1683 for the appointment of Abiel Mercier as admin. of the est. of Theo. Shatswell, q. v.

His wife Abigail was one of the sisters of Thomas Scott who petitioned concerning his est. in 1684. [Es. Files.]

His will, not dated, prob. Sept. 25, 1683, beq. to wife and daus. Abigail and Elizabeth.

John, frm. May 14, 1634.

Zachariah, or Zaccheus, Boston, memb. chh. 1630-1; frm. May 25, 1636. Wife Anne; ch. Restored bapt. 26 (6) 1638, Elizabeth b. 24 (5) 1640, (m. John Morse,) [see Suff. De. III, 528, and IV, 144a.] Samuel bapt. 12 (1)

BOSWORTH, etc., cont.
1640, ae. about 6 days, Sarah b. and d. in 1645.

He. d. 28 (5) 1655; and the widow m. 17 (8) 1656, Thomas Cooper, of Rehoboth. His will, prob. 5 Oct. 1655, beq. to wife, to son Samuel and dau. Elizabeth.

BOULE,
Bridget, ae. 32, came as a servant with John Baker, in 1637.

BOUND,
William, Salem, memb. chh. 1636. He and his wife Anne were before the court for opposing infant baptism in 1642; were excommunicated from the chh. Child James baptized 25 (10) 1636, Andrew bapt. 12 (6) 1638, Peter bapt. 7 (4) 1640.

BOURNE, BORNE, BONE, BOWEN,
Garratt, Jarrett, Jared, or Jerauld, Boston, frm. May 6, 1635. He rem. to Rhode Island, for which the chh. excom. him 13 (2) 1654. Sold land at Cambridge in 1664, and at Boston in 1665. Wife Mary d. 30 (3) 1644. Ch. Jerauld or Gerard b. and d. 1643, [Rox. Rec.] Jarrett bapt. 7 (1) 1652.

Henry, Scituate, memb. chh. Jan. 25, 1634-5; frm. 7 Feb. 1636-7. He m. Sarah, ——, who was dism. from the chh. at Hingham and joined at S. Nov. 11, 1638. He rem. to Barnstable. Deputy, juror. Ch.: an infant bur. May 28, 1642, Ezra, (parent not given,) b. in Sandwich May 12, 1648.

His widow Sarah's will, prob. in 1684, beq. to John Hamline and John Phinney, Jr.

John, Salem, 1636, propr., memb. chh. 5 (3) 1644; before the Gen. Court, 1649. Ch. John bapt. 18 (3) 1645, Deborah bapt. 27 (4) 1647, Dorcas bapt. 26 (6) 1649. Propr. at Gloucester in 1650. Made contract with Nehemiah B. in 1639. [L.] Had business with Willoughby 8 (10) 1645. [A.] He was of Bermondsey, master of the Indevore of Cambridge.

John, Marshfield, propr. 1643. He m. July 18, 1645, Ales Besbege; ch. Elizabeth b. 31 May, 1646, Thomas b. Oct. 22, 1647, Alice b. March 4, 1649, Anne b. Nov. 1651, Martha b. 4 April, 1653, Mary b. June 5, 1660, Sarah b. Oct. 19, 1663.

He was bur. 8 Dec. 1684. Inv. taken May 12, 1686, after the death of the widow Alice;

BOURNE, etc., cont.
the eldest dau. Elizabeth had died, leaving 5 children; Thomas was only son and heir. John Mann was app. guardian to Joseph and Elizabeth Bent, who were to be maintained out of the estate.

Nehemiah, of White Chapel, Eng., white baker, had permission to travel to America April 10, 1638; came in the Confidence. Settled at Dorchester. Rem. to Dorchester, where he and his wife Hannah were adm. chh. and their son Nehemiah was bapt. 14 (4) 1640, ae. 4 days; ch. Hannah b. 10 (9) 1641 at Bo. They were rec'd to Bo. chh. in 1642. He was a debtor of Mrs. Elizabeth Poole of Westminster, Eng., 24 (9) 1646, called shipwright. Was about to build a ship of 250 tons, carrying 20 pieces of ordinance, May 8, 1646. [A.]

He went to Eng. in 1646 and became major of Col. Rainsborow's regiment in Cromwell's army. Ret. after good service. [W.] For notes on Eng. connections, see Reg. LI, 109-114.

Mr. Thomas, Plymouth, land gr. to his son Richard for him Jan. 2, 1636; frm. 7 Feb. 1636-7. He rem. to Marshfield. Propr. 1643. Wife Elizabeth was bur. July 18, 1660, ae. 70.

He was bur. May 11, 1664, ae. 83. Will dated May 2, prob. June 9, 1664, made son John right heir and exec., and beq. to him, to daus. [Martha] Bradford, [Anne] Smith, [Margaret] Winslow and [Lydia] Tilden; to son [Nathaniel] Tilden; to John, Thomas, Joseph and Robert Waterman; and to Mr. Arnold.

William. laborer, Duxbury, in Court 5 Nov., 1638. Rem. to Scituate. Ch. Lydia b. April, 1645.

BOWEN, BOWIN, BOWINE,
Griffin, or Griffith, gent., Boston, adm. chh. with wife Margaret 6 (12) 1638. Was from Langenith, Glamorganshire; had a bond from Henry Bowen May 15, 1640. [Suff. De. I.] Propr. 1644-1652. Ch. Esther bapt. 10 (12) 1638, Abigail bapt. 18 (2) 1641, Peniel b. 10 (3) 1644, Deriah bapt. 11 (2) 1647, ae. about 6 days. He rem. to London, whence he deeded his Boston lands April 17, 1669, to Isaac Addington, chirurgeon, who was contracting marriage with his dau. Elizabeth. Admin. gr. 3 Jan. 1676 to his

BOWEN, etc., cont.
son Henry. Division of his estate was made 6 Nov. 1683, to sons Francis, William and Henry; to Mr. John Weld and the widow Child. See Reg. XLVII, 453.

Obediah, Rehoboth, 1643-4. Ch. Obediah b. Sept. 18, 1651, Mary b. Jan. 18, 1652, Sara b. Nov. 6, 1654, Samuel b. July 16, 1659, Joseph b. June 26, 1662, Thomas b. Aug. 3, 1664, Hannah b. May 3, 1665, Lydia b. April 23, 1666, Marcy b. March 18, 1672, Isaac b. Sept. 30, 1674.

Will dated 11 Dec. 1708; grown ancient; prob. Oct. 14, 1710; beq. to sons Samuel and Joseph and dau. Hannah Brooks; gr. ch. Aaron, Daniel and Nathan, sons of dec. son Obediah; four pewter platters, given to him when he was baptized, he beq. to four gr. daus. Katharine, Sarah, Alice and Elizabeth B.; some land, recorded in Reh. he gave to James and Hezekiah B.; also beq. to Lydia Mason.

Richard, Rehoboth, town officer, prop. frm. 4 June, 1645, adm. frm. 5 June, 1651. He m. 4 (1) 1646, Esther Sutton. ,He was bur. Feb. 4, 1674. Will prob. 4 June, 1675, beq. to wife Elizabeth, ch. William, Obediah, Richard, Alice Wheaton, Sarah Fuller and Ruth Leverich. His widow was bur. in 1675.

Robert, cutler, Boston, contract after marrying his second wife, 3 (1) 1639. [L.]

Thomas, fisherman, Salem, Marblehead, deposed 26 (10) 1646, ae. 24 years; his wife Elizabeth confirmed the testimony which he gave. She deposed in March, 1654, ae. 26 years.

Admin. of his estate was gr. March 28, 1705, to John Roades of Marb. who had married his oldest daughter.

BOUTWELL, BOUTELL, BOUTLE, BOWTELL,
Edward, witnessed deeds in Boston in 1645.

James, Lynn, propr., frm. March 14, 1638-9. Mary, Lynn, before the court in 1640, may have been his first wife.

Will dated 22 (6) prob. 26 (9) 1651; wife Alice, ch. James, John and Sarah.

John, propr. at Cambridge in 1638. Had beq. from Edward Skinner in 1644.

BOUTWELL, etc., cont.
Bought land in 1648. Wife Margaret; ch. Mary b. Oct. 26, 1646, Margaret b. Jan. 4, 1649-50, John b. 1652.
He d. Aug. 30, 1676, ae. about 60. Inv. taken 23 Sept. folg.

Leonard, before Gen. Court 2 (4) 1640.

Thomas, memb. of the jury of the Quarter Court at Boston 2 (4) 1646, on the Hingham case. [Mass. Hist. Coll. 2-4.]

BOWDITCH, BOWDISH, BOWDISHE,
William, merchant, Salem, had lawsuit in 1640; propr. 1642. Sold house and land in Sal. to Philip Cromwell 26 Aug. 1680. Elizabeth, adm. chh. 10 (3) 1640, was probably his wife. Ch. Nathaniel bapt. 12 (12) 1642.
The inv. of his est. was taken 12 Nov. 1681; a Latin Bible, forty other books, etc.

BOWER, BOWERS,
Mr. George, planter, Scituate, frm. 7 March, 1636-7; town officer. Sold land in Sci. April 2, 1640. Rem. to Cambridge. Wife Barbarie d. March 25, 1644. He m. April 15, 1649, Elizabeth Worthington. Ch. Jerathmeel b. 1649. He was before the Court 31 May, 1652, for voting when not a freeman of this Colony. Deeded land to son Benannuel in 1656.
He d. 1656; in his will he beq. to wife; sons Benanuel, John and Jerathmeel, and daus. Patience and Silence. The widow m. Henry Bowtell.

Matthew, d. 30 (11) 1644, at Cambridge.

BOWLER,
Mary, in Gen. Court 7 March, 1636-7.

BOWLES, BOLDS,
John, Roxbury, ruling elder; frm. May 13, 1640. His wife Dorothy was buried 3 (9) 1649. He m. April 2, 1649 [1650] Elizabeth Heath; she d. July 6, 1655. Ch. Elizabeth bapt. Feb. 3, 1650, Isaac bapt. April 18, 1652, John bapt. June 27, 1653, Mary b. 20 (2) 1655.
Will dated Aug. 22, prob. Oct. 5, 1680. Wife Sarah to have what was promised at her marriage, less payment already made to Daniel Smith of Rehoboth and others; daus. Elizabeth White, Mary Gardner; son John; Mr. John Eliot. The widow d. 2 Sept. 1686.

BOWMAN,
John, Marshfield, propr. 1644.

Nathaniel, gent., appl. frm. Oct. 19, 1630. Propr. at Watertown, 1636. Rem. to Cambridge about 1650. Wife Anna; ch. Francis, Mary bur. Jan 1, 1637-8, Joanna bur. 20 (9) 1638, ae. 3 yrs., Dorcas bur. 6 (12) 1638, ae. 7 days, Nathaniel b. 6 (1) 1640, Joanna b. 20 (9) 1642, Dorcas, (m. Benjamin Blackleach). The wife Hannah, (Anna,) deposed in 1678, ae. 63.
He d. Jan. 26, 1681-2. Will dated 21 Oct. 1679, prob. April 4, 1682, beq. to sons Francis and Nathaniel, dau. Dorcas Marsh and gr. ch. Nathaniel and Benjamin Blackleach.

BOWSTREET, BOWSTRED,
William, Concord, frm. May 22, 1638.
He was bur. 31 (8) 1642. Will, (Suff. Prob.) dated 23 Oct. 1642, prob. 6 (1) 1643, beq. to the children of his sister Elizabeth Newman and to Richard Leton.

BOYDEN,
Thomas, ae. 21, came in the Francis of Ipswich April 30, 1634. As the servant of Mr. Gilson, he joined the chh. of Scituate May 17, 1635.

Thomas, planter, carter, Watertown, frm. May 26, 1647. Bought land in W. 16 (9) 1644. Wife Frances. Ch. Thomas b. 26 (7) 1639, Mary b. 15 (8) 1641, Rebecca b. Nov. 1, 1643, Nathaniel. He rem. to Boston; sold land in 1651 and 1653. Ch. b. in Bo.: John bapt. 21 (2) 1650, Jonathan b. 20 (12) 1651, Sarah b. 12 Oct. 1654. The wife Frances d. March 17, 1658. He m. Nov. 3, 1658, Hannah, widow of John Mosse, (Morse;) gave bond Oct. 18, 1661, for the bringing up of the ch., of John Morse, late of Medfield. He rem. to Medfield about 1662.
His wife Hannah made will Oct. 3, prob. Oct. 26, 1676; beq. to the 8 ch. she had by her husband, Joseph Morse, dec., viz. Samuel, Joseph, Jeremiah, Hannah Flood, Sarah Lawrence, Dorcas Clarke, Elizabeth Lawrence, Mary Plimpton.

BOYKIN, BOYKEN, BOYKETT,
Jarvis, or Gervaise, of Channington, Eng., carpenter, came from Sandwich, Eng., before June 9, 1637. Settled at Charlestown. Propr. Rem. to New Haven, Conn.

BOYLSTON, BOYLSTONE, BOILSTONE, BOYSTON,
Thomas, ae. 20, came in the Defense in July, 1635, cert., from parish of Fenchurch, London, Eng. Settled at Watertown, clothworker, planter. Owned considerable land. He gave a trust deed for the benefit of his wife and ch. 26 (5) 1652; mentioned kinsman Richard Boyson, citizen and cloth-worker, London. Wife Sarah; ch. Elizabeth b. 21 (7) 1640, (m. John Fisher of Medfield, who in his will beq. to her ch. her right in a legacie expected from their grandfather's uncle in Eng.;) Sarah b. 30 (7) 1642, Thomas b. Jan. 26, 1644-5.

He d. in 1653; his widow m. John Chinery; est. divided in 1668.

BOYNTON, BOINTON,
John, Sen., tailor, Rowley, propr. before 1643. Deposed to Wm. Bellingham's will in 1662, ae. 48 years. He m. in 1643 Ellen Pell of Boston, q. v.; ch. Joseph, John b. 17 (7) 1647, Caleb, Mercy b. 5 (10) 1651, (m. Josiah Clarke,) Hannah b. 26 (1) 1654, (m. Nathaniel Warner,) Sarah b. 19 (2) 1658, Samuel.
He was bur. 18 Feb. 1670. Will prob. 28 March, 1671. The widow m. 2, Maximilian Jewett.

William, tailor, Rowley, propr., frm. May 13, 1640. Schoolmaster. He deposed in 1662, ae. about 56 years. Wife Elizabeth; ch. John b. 19 (10) 1640, bur. March 26, 1665, Elizabeth b. 11 (10) 1642, (m. John Simmons,) Zachary b. 11 (8) 1644, bur. Aug. 4, 1660, Joshua b. 10 (6) 1646, Mary b. 23 (5) 1648, (m. John Eastman,) Caleb b. 7 (2) 1650, Sarah b. 1 (10) 1652, bur. 28 (6) 1654.
He d. 8 Dec. 1672.

BOYES, BOYSE, BOYCE,
Joseph, tanner, Salem, propr. 1638, adm. chh. 7 (2) 1640; frm. May 18, 1642. Sold house and land in 1657. Ch. Hester bapt. 21 (12) 1640, Eliza bapt. 6 (1) 1642, Joseph bapt. 31 (1) 1644, Benjamin bapt. 16 (3) 1647.
His will dated 4 (9) 1684, prob. Feb. 18, 1694-5, beq. to wife Ellennor, son Joseph, daus. Mary Southick, Hester [....] and Elizabeth Hanson; to Joseph's ch. Joseph and Benjamin.

Matthew, cloth-worker, Roxbury, frm. May 22, 1639. Rem. to Rowley. Deputy 1642. Ret. to Eng.; res. at Leeds. Deposed

BOYES, etc., cont.
16 Jan., 1661, ae. about 50 years. [Reg. XLI, 181.] Wife Elizabeth; ch. Samuel b. (7) 1640, Hannah b. 16 (4) 1642, Matthew b. 23 (1) 1644, Elizabeth b. 20 (3) 1646, Grace b. 2 (4) 1648, Elkanah b. 25 (1) 1650, Mercy b. 26 (2) 1650, (sic copia,) John b. 23 (5) 1651, Nathaniel b. 1 (7) 1653, Faith b. 28 (10) 1654.

Thomas, Dedham, in Court 5 (1) 1638-9. Wife Ann; ch. Ruth b. 2 (5) 1643.

BRABROOK, BRAIBROOKE, BRABROOKE, BRAYBROOK, BRAYBROOKE,
Ann, an old woman, d. at Roxbury May 20, 1648.

John, Watertown, 1640. Wife Elizabeth; ch. Elizabeth b. 4 (9) 1640, John b. 12 (2) 1642, Thomas b. 4 (3) 1643.
He d. in 1654. The widow and ch. Adam Draper, David Cummine, Thomas and Samuel Braybrook petitioned the Court with reward to the est., April 2, 1667.

Richard, yeoman, Ipswich, testified in 1659 that he had known a certain farm there 15 years. Deposed in 1679, ae. about 67. Gave marriage portion to dau. Mehitabel and her husband John Downing 20 Oct. 1669, his wife Jone consenting. [Es. Files.] Rem. to Wenham.
Will dated 17 July, prob. 23 Nov. 1681, beq. to wife, son and dau. Downing and their children; to the college and to his minister £6 apiece.

William, Sandwich, propr. 1640.

BRACEY, BRESSEY,
Thomas, Ipswich, propr. 1635.

BRACKETT, BROCKET,
Peter, Braintree, had land gr. for 12 heads 24 (12) 1639-40; frm. May 10, 1643. Deputy and magistrate. He deposed May 19, 1673, ae. 64 years. [Mdx. Files.] Wife Priscilla. He m. 2, Mary, widow of Nathaniel Williams. Ch. on rec.: John b. 30 (9) 1641, Joseph b. 13 (8) 1642, d. 24 (11) 1660, Hannah d. 15 (4) 1657, Mary d. 12 (11) 1660. From the will of his son John, prob. Jan. 30, 1667, we get these items: sister Upham, bro. Cooke, mother Williams' 5 ch., bro. Twelves, bro. Nathaniel Renolds, bro. Nathaniel Brackett, sister Sarah Brackett. [Reg. XV, 250.]

BRACKETT, etc., cont.
Richard, Braintree, memb. Boston chh. 1631-2; dism. to Br. chh. 5 (10) 1641; frm. May 25, 1636. Deacon, deputy, magistrate, captain. He deposed 2 July, 1668, ae. 56 years. [Suff. Prob.] Wife Alice d. 3 Nov. 1690, ae. 76. Ch. Hannah bapt. 4 (11) 1634, Peter and John bapt. 7 (3) 1637, Rachel bapt. 3 (9) 1639, Mary b. 1 (12) 1641, Josiah b. 8 (3) 1652.

He d. March 3, 1690, ae. 80; [gr. st.] Will prob. Dec. 19, 1690, beq. to wife Alice, sons John, Peter and James, sons-in-law Simon Crosby and Joseph Tompson, and their children; Elizabeth and Sarah, ch. of dec. son Josiah; son-in-law Joseph Crosby; daus. Hannah Blancher and Rachel Crosby; gr. ch. Abigail Tompson, and Hannah, dau. of John B.; son James exec. Houses and lands at Braintree and Billerica.

Thomas, Sen., Salem. Ch. Thomas bapt. 12 (10) 1645, Mary bapt. 4 (12) 1648, Joseph bapt. 15 (4) 1651. He admin. on est. of his son Thomas, 1 (5) 1668, for the benefit of himself and his now wife Alice.

BRADBURY,
Thomas, Salisbury, propr. 1639, frm. May 13, 1640. Clerk of writs, 1641, deputy, 1651; captain, judge, schoolmaster, recorder of Norfolk county. He m. Mary, dau. of John Perkins; ch. Wymond b. 1 (2) 1637, Judith b. 2 (8) 1638, (m. Caleb Moody,) Thomas b. 28 (11) 1640, Mary b. 17 (1) 1642, (m. John Stanyan,) Jane b. 11 (3) 1645, (m. Henry True,) Jacob b. 17 (4) 1647, William b. 15 (7) 1649, d. 4 Dec. 1678, Elizabeth b. 7 (9) 1651, (m. John Buss,) John b. 20 (2) 1654, d. 24 Nov. 1678, Ann b. 16 (2) 1656, d. in 1659, Jabez b. 27 (4) 1658, d. 28 April, 1677.

He d. March 16, 1694-5. His will dated 14 Feb. 1693-4, prob. March 26, 1695; aged and weak; beq. to gr. ch. Thomas and Jacob B., who shall pay a sum to their aunt True and give receipt to their bro. William about the admin. of their father's est. and pay their gr. mother an annuity; to daus. Mary Stanion and Jane True; to gr. ch. Elizabeth Buss; five pounds to the selectmen for the poor; wife Mary and dau. Judith Moody execs.

His wife was tried in 1692 for witchcraft; was convicted but not executed. She d. Dec. 20, 1700.

BRADE, BRAID, BROAD, see Breed.

BRADFORD,
Alexander, Dorchester, propr. 1641. Wife Sarah.

Will dated 16 (6) 1644, prob. 2 (8) 1645. Wife Sarah; bro. John B.'s children to inherit the mansion house, lands, etc. after her; bro. Walter Merry to help her in managing her affairs; to Robert Stowton. [Reg. III, 82.]

Robert, tailor, Boston, inhabitant, 1639; adm. chh. 4 (5) 1640. Wife Martha; ch. Moses b. 2 (1) 1644, Martha b. 9 (9) 1645, d. 13 Aug. 1661. Robert, who deposed in 1664, ae. 32, might have been a son.

Will dated 16 Nov. 1677, prob. 28 Dec. 1680; wife Margaret, (refers to marriage contract,) ch. Moses, Martha, (wife of Peter Maverick).

William, the distinguished governor of Plym. Colony and author of the remarkable history of its foundation, was the son of William and Alice (Hanson,) Bradford, of Austerfield, Eng., bapt. March 19, 1589-90. Resided at home till the Scrooby church, of which he was a member, removed to Holland, about 1607. He came to N. E. in the Mayflower, signed the Compact; and made his home at Plymouth.

No man did more than he in work as well as care, in the secular and religious life of the Colony. He wrote with his own hand a detailed history of the movement, from the time when the church was organized at Scrooby until the year 1650. Into this he introduced numerous letters and lists of names which bring the life of the Colony before the reader in a very vivid way. The book was kept in the hands of his descendants until the year 1728, when his grandson, Maj. John Bradford, lent it to Rev. Thomas Prince, of Boston, to be used in his preparation of a New England Chronology. At some later time it was carried from Boston to England, and placed in the library of the Fulham Palace. Thence it was brought, by the offices of of Hon. George F. Hoar and Hon. Thomas F. Bayard, lately Ambassador of the United States, and deposited in the office of the Secretary of the Commonwealth of Massachusetts, with appropriate ceremonies May 26, 1897. The State government has issued a very beautiful edition of the work, which is sold at the office of the Secretary at $1.00 a copy.

In Leyden, Holland, specified as a fustian-

BRADFORD, cont.
maker, he m. Nov. 8, 1613, Dorothy May. She came with him to Plymouth, but d. before landing, Dec. 7, 1620. He m. 14 Aug., 1623, Alice, dau. of Alexander Carpenter, b. at Wrentham, Eng., and widow of Constant Southworth; she survived him, and d. March 26, 1670-1, ae. about 80. Ch. John, left behind in 1620, came over later; William b. 17 June, 1624, Mercy b. before 1627, (m. Dec. 21, 1648, Benjamin Vermayes,) Joseph b. about 1630.

He made nunc. will May 9, 1657; had given John and William their portions of land and desired that Joseph's be equal to theirs. Gave to his wife Alice his stock in Kennebeck trade; desired that the promises he had made to his ch. and others should be made good. He commended to the supervisors of his est. some small books written by his own hand, to be improved as they should see meet. Mr. Thomas Prence, Capt. Thomas Willett and Lieut. Thomas Southworth, supervisors. Prob. June 3, 1657. [Reg. IV, 39, and V, 385.] The widow made will 29 Dec. 1669, prob. 7 June, 1670; beq. to sister Mary Carpenter; to son Constant Southworth and to gr. ch. Elizabeth Howland, dau. of son Thomas S. dec.; sons Joseph and William B.; maid servant, Mary Smith; a book out of her late husband's library to friend, Mr. Thomas Prence. [See John Cooper's will.]

BRADISH,
Robert, Cambridge, propr. 1635. He placed his dau. Hannah as an apprentice with Thomas Hawkins 12 (12) 1640. [L.] Wife Mary d. Sept., 1638. Second wife Vashti. Ch. Samuel b. 13 (12) 1639, d. 6 (5) 1642, Joseph b. (3) 1638, John b. 3 (10) 1645, Samuel b. and d. in 1648.

Will prob. Oct. 29, 1659. Widow Vashti; ch. James, John, Joseph, Mary (Gibbs,) and Hannah; son-in-law Ezekiel Morrell; bro. Isaac Morrell. [Reg. IX, 225.]

BRADLEY,
Daniel, ae. 20, came in the Elizabeth April 8, 1635. Res. at Ipswich in 1649. Was one of those who ran out the bounds between Ips. and Salem that year and in 1654.

He was slain by the heathen 13 Aug. 1689; widow Mary admin. Sept. 30, 1690.

John, Dorchester, propr. 1641, frm. May 18, 1642. Wife Katharine; ch. Salathiel b. 16 (1) 1641, d. 1 (3) 1642, Nathaniel, ae. 70 yrs., d. July 26, 1701.

John, Salem, 1636.
He d. (4) 1642. Nunc. will, (Suff. prob.) 29 (5) 1642. Deposition by Ursly Greenaway; he gave all to his wife except some of his clothes and tools to his bro.-in-law Wm. Allen. Inv. taken 21 (4) 1642; lot on Cape Ann side and at Jeffreys Creek. [Reg. II, 185, and VII, 32.]

Richard, shoemaker, Boston. He m. Anna (Hannah) widow of George Balden; she was adm. chh. 7 (3) 1648. Ch. John bapt. 1 (2) 1649, ae. about 6 days, Anna b. 16 (10) 1651, John bapt. 28 (10) 1651, Deliverance b. 3 April, 1655. Son John, merchant of ship Industry; his will prob. 6 Oct. 1676, by father Richard and wife Mary.

He d. before Nov. 10, 1679, when inv. of his est. was taken; filed Nov. 13 by the widow Hannah.

BRADSHAW, BREDSHA,
John, husbandman, Lynn, sued Thomas Willes for wages 29 (7) 1640. Rem. about that time. [L.]

BRADSTREET,
Humphrey, came in the Elizabeth in 1634, ae. 40, with wife Bridget, ae. 30, and ch. Anna, ae. 9, John, ae. 3, Martha, ae. 2, and Mary, ae. 1. Later ch. Sarah and Rebecca. Settled at Ipswich; propr. 1635. Frm. May 6, 1635; deputy. The son John res. at Marblehead in 1657; the dau. Hannah m. 1, Daniel Rolfe, and 2, Nicholas Holt; dau. Martha m. William Beale; another dau. m. Nicholas Wallis.

He d. before 1657, when the heirs receipted for their portions of his estate.

Simon, gent., son of a minister in Lincolnshire, [C. M.] b. at Hobling, Eng., in March, 1603; was one of the assts. of the Mass. Bay Co. in England in 1629. He came with governor Winthrop in 1630. With wife Anne joined the chh. at its organization. Rem. to Cambridge. Selectman in 1634; secretary of the Colony from 1630 till 1643. Asst., deputy governor and governor in successive years. Owned property at Ipswich in 1635. Resided at Andover. A man of discretion and fidelity.

BRADSTREET, cont.

He m. 1, Anne, dau. of Thomas Dudley, Esq., celebrated as the first poetess of N. E., who d. Sept. 16, 1672, ae. about 60 years. He m. 2, Ann, dau. of —— Downing. Ch. Samuel, Dorothy, (m. June 14, 1654, Mr. Seaborn Cotton,) Simon, Dudley, John b. 22 July, 1652, Hannah, (m. Andrew Wiggin,) Sarah, (m. Richard Hubbard,) Mercy, (m. Nathaniel Wade).

He d. at Salem March 27, 1697, ae. 94. His will, dated 23 Dec. 1689, and 27 Jan. 1692-3, prob. 2 April, 1697, beq. to wife Ann; to son Samuel, and his ch. Mercy, John, Simon and Anne; to the 3 ch. of dec. son Simon, Simon, John and Lucy; to son Dudley B. and each of his ch.; to son John, with entail to his ch.; to gr. ch. John Cotton, and to his 6 sisters, daus. of my dau. Dorothy; to son-in-law Andrew Wiggin, and his ch. by my dau. Hannah; to dau. Mercy and her husband, Mr. Nathaniel Wade, and to their ch.; to Mr. Samuel Willard. [Reg. I, 75, and VIII, 312.]

BRADWICKE,

Joyce, sentenced April 1, 1633, to pay 20 s. to Alexander Beck for promising him marriage without her friends' consent, and now refusing to perform the same. [Col. Rec.]

BRAGG,

Edmund, or Edward, Ipswich, servant to Mr. Symonds, 1642. Propr., town officer.

BRAKENBURY, BRACKENBURY,

Richard, Salem, frm. May 14, 1634; juryman 1637. Rem. to Beverly. He deposed 20 Jan. 1680, ae. 80 years, that he came to Salem with Endecott 6 Sept. 1628. [Es. Court Files; see Es. Inst. Coll. XIII.] Ellyn, [his wife,] memb. chh. before 1636. Hannah bapt. 1 (4) 1651.

His will dated 14 (1) prob. (4) 1684, beq. to gr. ch. Benjamin and Ellen Patch and Elizabeth Biles with her son Richard; Richard P.; son John P.; dau. Elizabeth; Katharine Kline, sister to gr. son John B.; Jonathan Biles.

William, planter, Charlestown, 1630; appl. frm. Oct. 19, 1630, adm. frm. March 4, 1632-3. Town officer. Wife Anne adm. chh. 5 (11) 1632. Wife Ales sold land with him in 1650. He sold house Nov. 1, 1639. He

BRAKENBURY, etc., cont.

res. at Malden. Ch. Anne b. about 1628, [W.] m. Wm. Foster, [Mdx. De. II, 125.] Mary bapt. June 29, 1634, (m. John Ridgeway,) Samuel b. Feb. 10, 1645-6.

He d. (6) 1668, ae. 66. Will dated 24 July, 1667, prob. 21 (7) 1668, beq. to wife Alice, son Samuel, daus. Anne Foster and Mary Ridgeway and their children; to cousin Richard Brakenbury, son-in-law Wm. Foster, Mr. Michael Wigglesworth and Mr. Benj. Bunker. Wife Alice d. Dec. 28, 1670, ae. 70.

BRAMPTON,

William, gent., bought Powderhorne Hill, Boston, of Harry Vane, Esq., (2) 1638. [L.]

BRANCH, see Baunsh,

Peter, carpenter, late of Holden in Kent, d. and his will was prob. in Suffolk co., dated June 16, 1638. Son John, eleven years old, was apprenticed to Thomas Wiburne, late of Tenterden, Kent, to whom the estate was committed for eleven years. Beq. to the widow of Stephen Ingleden or their children. If John die within 11 years the est. to go to the churches of Concord and Scituate. [Reg. II, 183.]

William, Springfield, propr. 1646, frm. April 13, 1648. He m. at Winsor, (rec. at Spr.) in 1643, Johan Farnam. She d. Oct. 12, 1675. His [second] wife Katharine d. Aug. 8, 1683.

He d. Sept. 16, 1683.

BRAND,

Mr. Benjamin, (residence not given,) appl. frm. Oct. 19, 1630.

George, baker, Roxbury, frm. May 22, 1650. He m. July 24, 1643, Martha Heath; he d. about Aug. 13, 1669; admin. gr. to his widow Martha; she d. Aug. 1, 1686,—old. [Reg. XLVIII, 325.]

BRANDISH,

John, (residence not given,) frm. March 4, 1634-5.

BRANDON, BRANDEN,

William, Weymouth, propr.

Will dated 31 (6) 1646, prob. 28 (8) 1647. Wife Mary; son Thomas, daus. Sarah, Mary, Hannah; bro. William's eldest son. [Reg.

BRANDON, etc., cont.
VII, 172.] Mary Branden, widow of Wm. B., late of Ashton Clinton, co. Bucks, constituted Richard Baldwin of Milford, N. E., her attorney to ask of Wm. B. and Thomas B., sons of Thomas Branden of Putnam, co. Herts, acct. of messuage and lands in Ashton Clinton, due to her and her son by virtue of her husband's will, 16 (9) 1647. [A.]

BRANE, BRAINES, BRAYNE,
Thomas, husbandman, ae. 40, came in the Abigail in July, 1635. Had beq. of 3 li. from Dennis Geere of Lynn, 10 Dec. 1635.

Agnes, widow, Salem, 1637, may be his relict.

BRANKER, BRANCKER,
Mr. John, Dorchester, propr., frm. Nov. 6. 1632. He sold his property Sept. 2, 1637. Rem. to Windsor, Conn.

BRASIER, BRAZIER,
Edward, husbandman, Charlestown, mentioned in will of Nathaniel Sparhawk of Watertown in 1647. Resident, 1653. He d. 3 May, 1689, ae. about 87.
Will dated 11 May, 1683, prob. Oct. 1, 1689, beq. to wife, son Thomas and dau. Abigail.

BRATCHER,
Austin, Charlestown, accidentally killed by Wm. Palmer. Inquest held Sept. 28, 1630.

BRATLEY,
John, Salem, propr. 1636.

BRAY,
Osomant, Weymouth.
Inv. of his est. presented 23 (12) 1648.

Thomas, Yarmouth, punished by the Court 7 Dec. 1641.

Thomas, ship-carpenter, Gloucester, propr. 1642. He deposed 30 (1) 1658, ae. about 54 years. He m. 3 (3) 1646, Marie Wilson; ch. Mary b. Jan. 16, 1647, Thomas b. March 31, 1649, John b. May 14, 1651, Thomas b. and d. in 1653, Nathaniel b. June 21, 1656, Thomas b. Jan. 19, 1658, Hannah b. March 21, 1662, Esther b. April 13, 1664.
He d. Nov. 30, 1691; Mary Bray, the aged, d. 27 (1) 1707. Will dated 20 Nov. 1672, prob. 29 March, 1692, beq. to wife Mary, ch. John,

BRAY, cont.
Nathaniel, Thomas, Mary Kinge, Sarah, Hannah and Hester B.; to dau. Mary's children.

BRECK,
Edward, Dorchester, propr. July 20, 1638; frm. May 22, 1639. A propr. and town officer at Lancaster in 1652.
He d. at Dorch. 2 (9) 1662. Will, Oct. 30, 1662; wife Isabel; ch. Robert, John, Mary, Elizabeth, and Susanna; dau. Blake's children. [Reg. IX, 338.] The widow m. 14 (10) 1663, Anthony Fisher, Sen., who d. April 18, 1671; she d. 22 (4) 1673.

BREDCAKE,
Mr. Thomas, had granted him from the Gen. Court 13 (9) 1644, 2 small guns from Winter Island by Salem, and a commission to capture any Turkish pirate.

BREED, BREAD, BRADE,
Allen, yeoman, Lynn, propr. 1638. An appraiser 9 (6) 1639. [L.] Ch. Miriam, Allen and John, whose mother d. before 1650. He deposed in 1671, ae. 70 years. He m. about 1650 Elizabeth, widow of William Knight. She was a witness to the will of Joseph How in 1650, and paid legacies of W. K. to his heirs in 1657. He deeded part of his est. to younger son John in 1655; refers to linen his mother left him, which is in possession of his sister Miriam. Deeds to son Allen B. and son-in-law William Meriam in 1666.

Thomas, cooper, engaged by the Mass. Bay Co. in England, March 23, 1628, to go to N. E.

BRELLES,
Robert, Scituate, atba. 1643.

BRENTON,
Mr. William, Esquire, merchant, Boston, adm. chh. (8) 1633, frm. May 14, 1634. Town officer, deputy, much in public business. Appointed to take charge of the House of Correction to be built at Boston Sept. 25, 1634. He rem. to Providence, R. I. before 10 (10) 1645. [A.] Wife Dorothie, adm. chh. 22 (1) 1635. His wife Martha joined him in a deed of land Feb. 16, 1666. Ch. Barnabas bapt. 24 (11) 1634, Mehetabel b. 28 Nov. 1652, Jaleham b. 15 Nov. 1655.
His will, dated 19 Feb. 1673, was prob. at

BRENTON, cont.
Newport, also recorded at Plymouth; beq. to sons Jahleel, William, Ebenezer, daus. Sarah, Mehitabel and Abigail; sons-in-law Peleg Sanford and John Poole; to cousin Philip Sandy; to sister Christian Sandy; to sister Katharine Cooke's children; to gr. ch. John Poole; to negro servants, who are to be freed in 5 years; to Mr. Roger Williams and other friends.

BRETT,
Isabel, Boston, memb. chh. 1630-1; "gone to Salem."

William, Duxbury, propr. 6 April, 1640, atba. 1643, frm. 2 June, 1646. Sold land Dec. 26, 1651. Rem. to Bridgewater; ruling elder.

Will dated 25 Nov., prob. 7 March, 1681, beq. to wife Margaret and ch. William, Elisha, Lydia and Hannah.

BREWER, BRUER,
Daniel, husbandman, Roxbury, embarked June 22, 1632, frm. May 14, 1634. Ch. Nathaniel b. May 1, 1635, Sarah b. March 8, 1638.

He d. March 28, 1646. Will prob. 20 (3) 1646. Wife Joanna; sons Daniel and Nathaniel, daus. Ann, Joanna and Sarah. Ann, dau. of widow Bruer, d. March 13, 1658. The widow Joanna d. 7 Feb. 1688, ae. 87 years.

John, Cambridge, propr. 1645. Wife Anne; ch. John b. 10 (8) 1642, Hannah b. Jan. 18, 1644-5.

Thomas, Ipswich, propr. 1639.

BREWSTER,
Mr. William, son of William Brewster, receiver of Scrooby, Nottinghamshire, Eng. and bailiff of the manor house. He deposed at Leyden June 25, 1609, ae. 42 years; his wife being then 40 and his son Jonathan 16. Educated sometime at Cambridge in Latin and Greek; private secretary to Davison, sec. of State; appointed post-master at Scrooby; the Pilgrim Church met at his house generally, and he entertained them. Was a leader in the removal to Holland; one of those imprisoned at Boston, Lincolnshire. Ruling elder at Leyden. His printing press was a great help. He bore his part with this poor persecuted church above 36 years. He often preached and otherwise greatly helped

BREWSTER, cont.
the church. He came in the Mayflower; signed the Compact. With him came his wife Mary and 2 sons, Love and Wrestling; the rest of his ch. were left behind and came over afterward. Wrestling d. a young man. The daus. that came over were d. in 1650, but left sundry children. With him came also Richard More, a boy apprenticed to him, who lived at Plymouth, and a bro. of Richard who d. the first winter. [B.] He res. at Duxbury. His wife Mary d. aged, before 1627. "He had many children." [B.] His dau. Fear m. Isaac Allerton. Patience m. Thomas Prence.

He d. April 10, 1644, ae. 80 years. Admin. gr. to his sons, Jonathan and Love June 5, 1644. The inv. showed 63 Latin books and between 300 and 400 English books. [Reg. IV, 174, and LIII, 109.]

BRIDGE, BRIDGES,
Edmund, or Edward, ae. 23, came in the James in July in 1635. Settled at Lynn; blacksmith; frm. Sept. 7, 1639; propr. Rem. to Rowley; suit in court at Ipswich in 1641; propr. The Gen. Court 26 May, 1647, ordered him to answer at Essex Court for neglect to further public service by delaying to shoe Mr. Symond's horse when he was about to come to Court. He deposed in 1658, ae. about 46 years. [Es. Files.] Rem. to Ipswich; later to Topsfield. Wife Alice; ch. Mehitabel b. 26 (1) 1641, Edward, Faith, (courted by Daniel Black in 1660; lawsuit).

He d. Jan. 13, 1684; his widow Mary d. Oct. 24, 1691.

Edward, Roxbury, frm. May 2, 1639. Wife Mary; ch. Mary b. Nov. 18, 1637, Thomas b. May 31, 1638.

He d. 20 or 23 (10) 1683, ae. about 82 years. Will dated 5 Dec. 1677, prob. 27 (10) 1683. Dau. Mary; Edward and other ch. of dec. son John; John Gay, son of dau. Mary.

Henry, Watertown, propr. 1636.

John, yeoman, Cambridge, propr. 1632, frm. March, 4, 1634-5. Deputy, town officer, deacon. He m. Elizabeth, widow successively of Roger Bancroft and Martin Saunders. Marriage contract 29 (9) 1658. [Mdx. De. II.] Ch. Matthew, Thomas, (who m. Dorcas ——, and left a dau. Dorcas). [Mi.] The widow m. Edward Taylor. [Endorsement on the Mar. Contr.]

BRIDGE, etc., cont.

Robert, Lynn, frm. June 2, 1641. Deputy, assistant. Special messenger of the Court to D'Aulnay in 1645. Capt. Bridges and wife were legatees of Capt. Robert Keayne in 1653. His wife Mary was a dau. of William Woodcock of London, gr. dau. of Mrs. Mary Washborne. [Es. Files 3, 5; Es. Inst. Coll. XVII, and W.]

William, Watertown, propr. 1636; Boston, 1643, Charlestown, 1643. Frm. May 26, 1647. He kept the ferry, his bro. Peter Tufts helping him. Wife Mary, dau. of John Oldham, d. about 1646. He m. 2, Persis Peirce, who survived him and m. John Harrison. She was adm. chh. 30 (9) 1643. Ch. Peter b. Jan. 1643-4, Rebecca b. and d. 1644, Samuel b. 19 (6) 1647, Mary, (m. John Knight).
He d. about 1648.

BRIDGHAM, BRIDHAM,

Henry, tanner, Dorchester, 1641, frm. May 10, 1643. He rem. to Boston; was adm. chh. a singleman 31 (1) 1644. Deacon. His wife Elizabeth gave letter of attorney 29 (9) 1645, to Francis Lyle of Boston to collect 56 li. due her from the est. of her father John Harding of Boreham in Essex, yeoman. Robert Harding a witness. H. B. gave letter of attorney 4 (9) 1646, for collection from his bro. Robert Bridgham of est. left by his father Henry B., late of Flotam in Suffolk. [A.] See Frary and Buttolph. Ch. John b. (7) 1645, Joseph 17 Jan. 1651, Benjamin b. 4 May, 1654, Hopestill b. July 29, 1658, Nathaniel b. 8 Dec. 1659, d. 1 June, 1660, Samuel bapt. 20 (11) 1660, Nathaniel b. April 2, 1662, James b. May 12, 1664. [Henry bapt. 16 (1) 1674, may have been a gr. ch.]

Will dated 8 (9) 1670, prob. 13 (2) 1672; inv. taken 31 (1) 1671. Wife and son Jonathan to carry on the tan yard and complete the instruction of sons Joseph, Benjamin, Samuel and James. Son John, already educated, to be joint exec. with his mother. Est. appraised at £3608.19. The widow Elizabeth made will, dated 2 Aug. prob. 5 Nov. 1672. Beq. to John, James, Jonathan and the 3 other sons; to sister Hannah Buttall.

BRIDGMAN, BRIDGEMAN, BRIGMAN,

James, Springfield, propr. 1643; town officer. Rem. to Northampton; sealer of weights and measures, 1661. Ch. John b.

BRIDGHAM, etc., cont.

7 (5) 1645, Thomas b. 14 (11) 1647, Martha b. 20 (9) 1649, Mary b. 5 (5) 1652. Wife Sarah d. 3 Aug. 1668.

His will, unsigned, beq. to ch. John; Sarah Tilestone and her son Cornelius; Martha, (wife of Samuel Dickinson,) and gr. ch. Mary B. Admin. gr. March 29, 1676, to son John.

John, Salem, propr. 1647. Wife Elizabeth memb. chh. 1 (7) 1650; ch. Mary bapt. 8 (7) 1650.

Will prob. (9) 1655; after settling Mr. Perkins' claim, the rest to daughter.

BRIGDEN, BRIGDON,

Thomas, husbandman, of Faversham, Eng., came with his wife in the Hercules in March, 1634. Settled at Charlestown. Propr. 1634. Frm. March 3, 1635-6. Cooper. With wife Mildred sold house in 1659. He and his wife Thomasine adm. chh. 5 (10) 1635. Ch. Thomas, Mary, (m. Henry Kemble,) Zachary bapt. 2 (6) 1639. Thomas deposed 22 (4) 1653, ae. 24. [Mdx. Files.]

He d. June 20, 1668. His widow d. March 12, 1669.

BRIGHAM, BRIGGAM, BRIGAM, BRIDGHAM,

Sebastian, Cambridge, propr. 1638. Rem. to Rowley; propr. 1643. Lic. to sell wine 13 Nov. 1644; deputy, 1646. Wife Mary; ch. Sarah b. 12 (5) 1640, Elizabeth b. 7 (4) 1643, Prudence b. 19 (1) 1646, Sebastian b. 2 (5) 1648.

Thomas, ae. 32, came in the Susan and Ellen in April, 1635; res. at Cambridge and Watertown. Propr.; frm. April 18, 1637. Wife Mercy; ch. John b. 9 (1) 1644, Hannah b. 9 (1) 1650. Town officer Camb. 1639.

He d. at Camb. Dec. 8, 1653. Will, dated 7 (10) 1653-4. Beq. to wife [Mercy], ch. Thomas, John, Mary, Hannah and Samuel. Prob. 3 (8) 1654. [Reg. XVII, 158.]

BRIGGS, BRIDGES, BRIGE,

Clement, felmonger, came to Plymouth in the Fortune in 1621. He was m. to Joane Allen by Mr. Thomas Stoughton of Dorchester, whom the Court fined for the act March 1, 1630-1. Res. at Weymouth from 1630 or thereabouts. He deposed 29 Aug., 1638, that he was dwelling about 22 years ago in South-

BRIGGS, etc., cont.

wark with Samuel Latham, felmonger; that Thomas Harlow was then dwelling with Robert Heeks at that place. Ch. Thomas b. 14 (4) 1633, Jonathan b. 14 (4) 1635, David b. 23 (6) 1640, Clement b. 1 (11) 1642.

Will prob. 24 (8) 1650; wife; sons Thomas, Jonathan, Clement, David, Remember. Prob. by widow Elizabeth July 28, 1659. [Reg. II, 144, VII, 233, and IX ,347.] The widow, in will dated 13 Nov. 1683, prob. Aug. 11, 1691, beq. to gr. ch. Clement and son Remember Briggs.

John, ae. 20, came in the Blessing in July, 1635. Watertown, propr. 1637. Sandwich, propr. 1640. Wife Katharine; ch. Samuel and Sarah.

Admin. on his est. June 1, 1641. [Reg. IV, 173.]

Matthias, yeoman, Hingham, m. May 9, 1648, Deborah, dau. of Matthew Cushing. She d. 25 Sept. 1700.

He d. 24 Feb. 1696-7. Will dated 11 March, 1686-7, beq. to wife Deborah, and to dau. Mary B. which I left in old England.

Walter, Scituate, atba. 1643.

BRIGHT,

Rev. Francis,, trained up under Mr. Davenport, came from Rayleigh, co. Essex, Eng. He was engaged by the Mass. Bay Co. 2 Feb. 1628-9, to come over to N. E. and preach to the Company's servants, to remain three years and be free to return at the end of that time. Transportation both ways, maintenance, and a salary of twenty pounds per annum to be provided. Similar arrangements were made with Messrs. Higginson and Skelton 8 April folg. They voted 6 April, 1629, to give him 5 li. toward his loss of wages in Eng., and his charge being in London. He came over in the Lyon's Whelp, arriving May 11, 1629. Preached to the settlers and workmen at Charlestown. [Char. town records.] Ret. to Eng. in 1630 in the Lyon in the summer of 1630. [Du.] He was the first person definitely engaged for clerical service in New England. He was a conformist; not agreeing with those that were for reformation, he returned for England. [Mor.]

Henry, Boston, memb. chh. 1630-1. Before the Gen. Court 7 Nov. 1634, and 6 (1) 1637-8. Rem. to Watertown; propr. 1642.

BRIGHT, cont.

Jan. 10, 1660, "aged about 80 years," he deeded his "mansion place" in Wat. to Thomas Hastings, the latter agreeing to care for him during the remainder of his life. [Mdx. De. II, 140.] Was assisted by the town in his age and sickness; d. Sept. 14, 1674, "aged 100 years and upward." [Town rec.] Inv. of his few effects was pres. 30 (11) 1674, by widd. Beers.

Henry, Jr., Watertown, frm. May 6, 1635. Town officer, deacon, surveyor of arms, com. of valuation, sergeant. He deposed about 2 (2) 1661, ae. about 60 years. [Mdx. Files.] His sister Mrs. Elizabeth Dell, widow, of Bow, co. Middlesex, Eng., left to his ch. a legacy, which was receipted for July 20, 1658. [Suff. De. III, 286.] He m. Anna, dau. of Henry and Anna Goldstone. Ch. Anna bur. 28 (8) 1639, ae. 4 yrs., Abigail b. Oct. 12, 1637, (m. Elisha Odlin,) Mary b. 23 (2) 1639, (m. Nathaniel Coolidge,) John b. 14 (3) 1641, Hannah b. 17 (1) 1643, Elizabeth, Nathaniel b. 5 (3) 1647, Beriah b. 22 (7) 1649.

He d. Aug. or Oct. 9, 1686. [Mdx. rec. and S.] Will dated 25 Jan. 1680, ae. 78 years, codicil 29 Oct. 1685, prob. Nov. 11, 1686. Sons John and Nathaniel, daus. Anna Ruggles, Elizabeth Hastings, Mary Coolidge, Abigail Awdley [Odlin,] and Beriah Fowle. Refers to father Goldstone. [See Bond's Hist. Wat. and Bright Genealogy.]

One of the above is called "my uncle" by Edward Parks, q. v.

Margaret, Mr. Holgraves' sister, had land assigned her in Salem in 1637, next to John Holgraves'. One of the first members of the church.

Samuel, Boston, servant to John Sweete, adm. chh. 1 (7) 1644. Frm. May, 1645.

Thomas, Watertown, "g.", mortgaged lands 30 (9) 1640. [L.] He sold house and 10 acres of ground 17 (10) 1640.

BRIGHTON, see Bright and Broughton,

Thomas, ae. 31, came in the Truelove in Sept., 1635.

BRIMSMEADE, BRINSMEADE,

John, Charlestown, inhab. 1636, adm. chh. 25 (1) 1638. He m. Mary Carter, who was adm. chh. 24 (8) 1639. Ch. Mary b. 24 (5) 1640, John b. 2 (1) 1643.

BRIMSMEADE, etc., cont.
William, Dorchester.
Will prob. 15 (3) 1648; ch. William, Alexander, Ebbett, Mary. [Reg. III, 266, and IX, 347.]

BRISCOE, BRISCO, BRISKOW, BISCOE, BISCO, see Bisco,
William, tailor, Boston, 1639, adm. chh. 30 (11) 1640; frm. June 22, 1641. Wife Cicely adm. chh. 4 (5) 1641. His son Daniel (or Nathaniel) adm. chh. 17 (2) was drowned (3) 1642. [W.] He had also sons Benjamin, Ezekiel, and Joseph. He and his wife were dism. to chh. of Milford 27 (6) 1648.

William Brisco, Sen., his inventory was taken 13 June, 1667, and admin. of his est. gr. to his son Benjamin.

Widow, sick at Winthrop's farm in 1636. [W.]

BRITTELL,
John, Salem, 1640. Rebecca, (Britt,) had child Ambross bapt. at Salem 30 (5) 1654.

BRITTERIDGE,
Richard, came in the Mayflower; signed the Compact; d. in Plymouth harbor Dec. 21, 1620.

BRITTON, BRITTAIN,
James, Weymouth, propr. He was punished for sympathy with Barnard and Lenthall, (12) 1638-9. A wrong done to him was acknowledged before the Gen. Court 2 (4) 1640. He rem. to Woburn, 1640. He was executed for alleged crime in 1643. [W.] Ch. James, d. at Wob. May 3, 1655, Jane, [dau.?] m. at Wob. Feb. 1, 1659, Isaac Cole.

BROAD, see Brade.

BROCK, BROOKE, BROOKS,
Henry, yeoman, clothier, Concord; frm. March 14, 1638-9. Rem. to Woburn; taxed in 1649; bought land in 1650. Ch. Joseph b. 12 (2) 1641. Wife Susanna d. 15 Sept. 1681; he m. 12 July, 1682, Annis Jaquith. He deposed 27 (10) 1658, ae. about 66 years. [Mdx. Files.]

Will dated 18 July, 1682, prob. 20 (2) 1683, beq. to wife Annes, as by marriage covenant; sons John, Timothy, and Isaac; son-in-law John Mousall and dau. Sarah; to dau. Les-

BROCK, etc., cont.
tor; to Isaac, Henry and Miriam, ch. of son Isaac; to pastors Thomas Cartor and Jabez Fox, and Lieut. Wm. Johnson.

Henry, Dedham, propr. 1638, adm. chh. 24 (10) 1641. Res. in Boston in 1639. [L.] Wife Elizabeth adm. chh. 29 (1) 1640; ch. John adm. chh. 3 (2) 1640. Mary Brock m. 5 (1) 1639, Henry Philips; Elizabeth Brock, adm. chh. 27 (8) 1643, m. 31 (8) 1644, Robert Gowing.

He d. in 1652. Will prob. Oct. 19, 1652; beq. to wife Elizabeth and ch. John, Elizabeth and Anne. [Reg. IV, 288.] Richard Barber calls him son-in-law.

Richard, carpenter, ae. 31, came in the Elizabeth and Ann April 27, 1635.

BROCKLEBANK,
Jane, widow, Rowley, propr. 1643, with sons Samuel and John. She was bur. 26 Dec. 1668.

John, Rowley, propr. 1650; town officer. He m. 26 Sept. 1657, Sarah Woodman; ch. John b. 26 (5) 1658, Elizabeth b. 20 Nov. 1660.

Will dated 30 Nov. 1665, prob. 25 Sept. 1666, beq. to wife Sarah and daus. Sarah and Elizabeth; to John Stevens and maid servant Mary Michill; father-in-law Archelaus Woodman and bro. Samuel B. overseers.

Samuel, Rowley, propr. 1649; town officer; captain. He deposed in 1665, ae. about 35 years. He m. 18 (3) 1652, Hannah ——; ch. Samuel b. 28 (9) 1653, Francis b. 26 (7) 1655 ,bur. July 22, 1660, Hannah b. 28 March, 1659, John bur. July 4, 1660, Sarah b. and d. 1666, Sarah b. July 7, 1668, Jane b. Jan. 31, 1670, Joseph b. Nov. 28, 1674.

Admin. of his est. was gr. to his widow Hannah; she pres. inv. 26 Sept. 1676; court ordered division to be made to ch. Samuel, Joseph, Hannah, Elizabeth, Mary and Sarah.

BROMFIELD, BRUMFEILD,
William, in Court 19 Sept. 1637. [See wills and notes on B. family in Reg. LII, 264, and LIII, 9.]

BROOK, BROOKE, BROOCK, BROOKS, BROOKES, see Brock,
Gilbert, ae. 14, came with William, in the Blessing in July, 1635; as servant to Mr.

BROOK, etc., cont.

Wm. Vassell, Scituate, before Plym. Court 5 March, 1638-9. Res. in Marshfield in 1645. Constable. He rem. to Scituate, then to Rehoboth. He gave power of attorney 20 March, 1694, to his son-in-law Robert Crossman of Taunton, who sold his land in Sci. in 1699. Ch. Elizabeth and Sarah bapt. at Sci. June 21, 1646, Mary bapt. July 15, 1649, Rachel bapt. July 7, 1650, Phebe bapt. Sept. 5, 1652, Bathsheba bapt. April 8, 1655, Rebecca bapt. April 12, 1657.
He d. 13 June, 1695. Will dated June 6, 1695, being aged; prob. July 7, folg.: beq. to wife Sarah; to Zachariah Carpenter that lives with me; gr. ch. Bathsheba Walker and Brook Thresher; to nine daughters, only Rachel's share to be given to my gr. son Benony Wigen. Son-in-law Robert Crossman and William Manle execs.

Richard, ae. 24, came in the Susan and Ellen in April, 1635. Propr. at Lynn in 1638; agreed to pay to Francis Godsome 9 (6) 1639. [L.] May be the same as

Richard, gunsmith, Boston, bondsman of Wm. Day, exec. of the will of Jane Woodcock, Aug. 10, 1666.

Robert, of Maidstone, Eng., mercer, with Anne his wife and 7 ch., came in the Hercules in March, 1634. Res. at Marblehead. Had a grant of land between his old house and new Nov. 16, 1657. Margaret, widow of Robert B., and mother of John B., m. 2, Captain George Corwin of Salem. Her first husband had a bro. John B. of London. [Es. Files, 4, 496.]

Thomas, ae. 18, came in the Susan and Ellen in April, 1635. Settled at Watertown. Frm. Dec. 7, 1636. Rem. to Concord; constable 4 (10) 1638; deputy; captain. Signed inv. of Thos. Atkinson's est. in 1646. Wife Grace d. May 12, 1664.
He d. May 21, 1667. Agreement between his heirs June 17, 1667; eldest son Joshua Brooks, Capt. Timothy Wheeler (husband of Mary B.,) Caleb and Gershom B.

Thomas, before Salem court in 1636; d. at sea before 1639. [L.]

William, ae. 20, came in the Blessing, in July, 1635. Settled at Salem, propr. 1639.

William, Marshfield, atba. 1643; town officer, juryman 1646. He was father-in-

BROOK, etc., cont.

law to Joseph, son of John Wiston of Sci. 6 March, 1665-6. Rem. to Scituate. Ch. Hannah bapt. Sept. 14, 1645, Nathaniel bapt. March 29, 1646, Mary bapt. Nov. 28, 1647, Sarah bapt. May 26, 1650, Miriam bapt. June 6, 1652, Deborah bapt. March 18, 1654, Thomas bapt. June 28, 1657, Johanna bapt. Oct. 16, 1659.
Will prob. 6 March, 1682-3, beq. to wife Susanna, sons Nathaniel and Thomas, daus. Hannah and Mary; wife's dau. Bathsheba, and gr. ch. Beriah.

BROOME,
Roger, ae. 17, came in the Truelove in Sept., 1635.

BROOMER,
George, tailor, Boston, bought house and land of James Stokes, and sold it 6 (7) 1642.

Joan, ae. 13, came in the Susan and Ellen in April, 1635.

Marie, ae. 10, came in the Elizabeth and Ann in April, 1635.

BROUGH, BROOFE,
Edmund, or Edward, Marshfield; had arbitration of a suit in Plym. Court, 1640. Atba. 1643. Was absent from town meeting 23 Aug. 1652.

BROUGHTON,
Mr. Thomas, merchant, Watertown. Rem. to Boston. He deposed in 1658, ae. about 44 years. [Es. Files.] He referred in 1646 to his bro. William res. in Bartholomew Lane, near the Royal Exchange, London. [Reg. XXXIX, 83.] He bought large tracts of land in Boston, Noddles Island, Quampegon and Kittery; erected mills, bakehouses, brewhouses, etc.; owned and operated shipping. Wife Mary, dau. of Nathaniel Brisco; ch. —— b. and d. in 1643, Elizabeth b. 15 (11) 1645, (m. Jacob Fowle.) Mary b. 5 (5) 1651, Thomas b. May 26, 1653, d. 1 (7) 1654, Nathaniel b. Dec. 5, 1654, Thomas b. Dec. 23, 1656, (became a gunmaker; d. in 1702; est. given to bro. Nathaniel and sisters Elizabeth Fowle and Abigail B.;) Hannah b. Dec. 28, 1658, Sarah b. June 9, 1660, Patience b. April 14, 1663, Abigail.
He d. Nov. 12, 1700, ae. about 87 years. [S.]

BROWN, BROWNE,

Abraham, Watertown, frm. March 6, 1631-2. Town officer, com. of Gen. Court. Wife Lydia; ch. Sarah, (m. George Parkhurst, Jr.,) Mary, (m. —— Lewis,) Lydia b. 21 (1) 1632, (m. Wm. Lakin,) Jonathan b. 15 (8) 1635, Hannah b. and d. in 1638, Abraham b. 6 (1) 1639.

He d. in 1650. The widow m. Nov. 27, 1659, Andrew Hodges of Ipswich. [Mdx. Files, 1670.]

Christian, widow, Salisbury, propr. 1640; d. 28 (10) 1641.

Rev. Edmund, came with Lechford, [see letter of L. to him, dated 10 (10) 1638, in Note-Book;] res. first at Plymouth. Rem. to Sudbury as minister; propr. 1639; frm. May 13, 1640.

He d. 22 (4) 1678. [S.] Will dated 24 May, prob. 9 July, 1678, beq. to wife Anne; to his kinsman Samuel Goffe of Cambridge, whom he adopts as son and heir; to Harvard College £ 100, and to the town of Sudbury £ 50 towards a school, after death of wife; to kinsmen John Browne of Bury St. Edmunds, co. Suff. Eng. and Thomas Reade of Sudbury; to man servant Richard Addams and maid servant Mary Plympton; to John Toll, James Whetcomb, Capt. John Greene and Thomas Walker.

Edmund, servant to Wm. Colborne, adm. chh. Boston 22 (4) 1634. He m. 14 (12) 1653, Elizabeth Oklye; ch. Mary b. 15 Dec. 1656.

He d. in Surinam about Michelmas, 1665. Admin. gr. to his wife 11 Oct., 1666. She d. and the 2 ch.'s grandmother, Mary, widow of Robert Boucier alias Garret, was made one of the trustees of his est. for the benefit of the ch., 2 Nov., 1666. [Reg. XV, 252, and XVI, 335.]

Edward, Boston, propr. 1635-1649; frm. May 6, 1635.

Edward, [Browne or Bourne,] Marshfield, propr. 1643.

Mr. Edward, or Edmund, Ipswich, propr. 1637.

Will, dated Feb. 9, 1659, prob. 27 (1) 1660. Sons Joseph and John; refers to a beq. given to dec. son Thomas by his aunt Watson in Eng.; bro. Bartholomew; wife Faith. The widow m. Daniel Warner; at her death she

BROWN, etc., cont.

beq. to these children, dau. Lydia and another dau.

Francis, servant to John Alby, d. in Braintree (1) 1640.

George, carpenter, came in the Mary and John March 24, 1633-4. Settled at Newbury. Propr. 1637; frm. May 13, 1640.

He d. 1 Aug. 1642. Will dated May 26, 1642, prob. March 28, 1643, beq. to wife, special bequest if she be with child; to bro. Richard B. of Newb.; to father and bro. Michael if they come over; nephews Margery and Joshua; to Joseph, son of bro. Richard, a share in mill at Salisbury.

George, Salisbury; rem. to Haverhill; propr., town officer. Deposed before selectmen Feb. 18, 1686-7, ae. about 60 years. Captain. He m. at Salis. June 25, 1645, (Court copy,) Ann Eaton; she d. Dec. 16, 1683. He m. March 17, 1683-4, widow Hannah Hazen, who d. Feb., 1715.

He d. Oct. 31, 1699, "ae. 76." Will prob. Nov. 6, 1699, beq. to wife; to her son Richard Hazen; her dau. Sarah, wife of Daniel Wiccomb, Jr.; to his bro. Henry B. of Salis. and his bro. William B. and some of their ch. and gr. ch.

Henry, shoemaker, Salisbury, propr. 1643. Wife Abigail; ch. Nathaniel b. 30 (4) 1642, Abigail b. 23 (12) 1643, (m. Samuel French,) Philip b. (10) 1646, Jonathan b. 25 (9) 1646, (sic copia,) Abraham b. 1 (11) 1649, Sarah b. 6 (10) 1654, (m. Andrew Greeley, Henry b. 8 (12) 1658. He and his wife Abigail deposed 11 (2) 1671, ae. about 56 years.

He d. Aug. 6, 1701; the widow d. Aug. 23, 1702.

Henry, mariner, of Line House, co. Middlesex, Eng., bought land in Boston in 1648. Mortg. it to Edward Budd, carver, Jan. 4, 1668.

Hugh, Salem, propr. 1636. He deposed 5 (8) 1657, ae. 39 years. [Mdx. Files.] He was sent with others in a boat to Ipswich about 1629 to help the friendly Indians against warlike tribes. [Depos. of W. Dixey.] Rem. to Boston. Wife Sarah; ch. Job b. 29 March, 1651, Hugh b. and d. 1652, Sarah b. and d. 1653, Sarah d. 3 (2) 1654.

BROWN, etc., cont.

Inv. of his est. presented 27 Jan. 1669-70. [Reg. XVIII, 325.]

James, Boston, memb. chh. 1630, frm. Sept. 3, 1634. Wife Grace; ch. James b. (7) 1645.
Will 9 (3) 1651. Beq. to wife Grace and son James; to the chh. of Boston of which he was a member; to the children of Thomas Stocker of Rumney Marsh.

James, Charlestown, propr. 1633, adm. chh. 10 (1) 1634, frm. May 25, 1636. Sold land in 1646. Wife Elizabeth adm. chh. 14 (4) 1634; ch. John bapt. 1 (1) 1639, Mary bapt. 3 (1) 1640. Elizabeth adm. chh. [bapt?] 31 (5) 1641.

James, a youth of about 17 yrs., from from Hampton, Eng., came in the James April 5, 1635.

James, glazier, Charlestown, frm. May 17, 1637. Hired Lovell's Island of the town in 1636. He rem. to Newbury; propr. 1637; town officer. Rem. to Salem. He deposed 28 (10) 1658, ae. about 53 years. [Mdx. Files.] He m. 1, Judith, dau. of Capt. John Cutting. He m. 2, Sarah, sister of his first wife. She was ae. 53 in 1658. Ch. John b. 4 (11) 1637-8, James b. in 1642, d. in 1643. James b. 19 (6) 1647, Nathaniel b. 21 (9) 1658, Samuel b. Jan. 14, 1656-7, Hannah bapt. Sept. 2, 1658, Abraham bapt. 14 (8) 1660, Mary b. May 25, 1663, Abigail b. Oct. 24, 1665, Martha b. **Dec. 22, 1667.**
He d. at Salem Nov. 3, 1676. Will prob. 29 (9) 1676; wife Sarah, bro. Nicholas Noyes; ch. John, James, Samuel, Abraham, Anna, Mary, Abigail, Martha, Sarah Beasly; to eldest son John est. left by Henry Bright of Watertown for money lent him many years ago; est. at Newbury left to wife by her father Cutting.

Jarrard, servant to Wm. Colborne, adm. chh. Boston 22 (4) 1634, with Edmund B.

John, Salem, one of the Assts. of the Mass. Bay Co. in Eng. and one of the Council of Governor John Endecott at the beginning of his term, April 17, 1629. He came in the Talbot; gave bond for return freight 28 Sept., 1629, being sent back with his bro. Samuel for speeches and practice tending to mutiny and faction. See Samuel, below. [Reg. XXXV, 250; Suff. De. 1.]

BROWN, etc., cont.

John, ae. 40, came in the Elizabeth April 17, 1635.

John, embarked June 22, 1632. Not identified.

John, tailor, ae. 27,, with servants Thomas Hart, ae. 24, and Mary Denny, ae. 24, cert. from Baddow, Essex, came in the Desire in June, 1635. Not identified.

Mr. John, gent. In his younger years, travelling in the low countries, he became acquainted with and took a good liking to the church at Leyden. [Mor.] Came therefore to Plymouth; taxed in 1632; frm.; Asst.; one of the comrs. of the United Colonies. Rem. to Rehoboth before 1646. [See Samuel Eddy.] Town officer, deputy, magistrate. Ret. to Eng. before 1659. [Letter of Thos. Mahew to J. Winthrop, Jr.] and became the steward of Sir Harry Vane. Came back to R. about 1661. John B. m. at Plymouth, 26 March, 1634, Phebe Harding. [Ply. Col. Rec.]
He d. in the spring of 1662. [Mor.] Will, dated April 7, 1662. Dau. Mary, wife of Thomas Willett, gr. ch. Martha, wife of John Saffin, gr. ch. John Brown, son of John; gr. ch. Joseph, Nathaniel, Lydia and Hannah B.; son James and wife Dorothy execs. [Reg. VI, 94, and XXXVI, 368. The widow d. at Swansey Jan. 27, 1673, in her 90th year. Her will dated 17 Dec. 1668, prob. 29 March, 1674, beq. to dau. Mary Willett and her ch.; to Sarah, dau. of dau. Sarah Eliot, dec.; to son James and daus.-in-law Lydia and Dorothy B. and their children.

John, mariner, Salem, propr. and memb. chh. 1637; frm. May 2, 1638. Chosen ruling elder 1660. Wrecked on return from Virginia; lost vessel and goods, but arrived at Sal. in 1661. Had new ship built by William Stephens. Ales (Alice) presumed to be his wife, memb. chh. in 1637. Ch. Jonathan, (d. 1667; est. admin. by his father;) John bapt. 16 (7) 1638, Jacob and Samuel bapt. 13 (1) 1641, John bapt. 1 (3) 1642, James bapt. 17 (5) 1642, Joanna bapt. 9 (2) 1643, Eliza bapt. 23 (10) 1643, Eliza bapt. 14 (2) 1644, Nathaniel bapt. 28 (5) 1644.
His will dated 2 Jan. 1683, prob. 24 Nov. 1684, beq. to gr. ch. John and Abiel B.; to 4 ch. of his dec. son James B.; to son-in-law Samuel Gardner, Jr. and his wife.

BROWN, etc., cont.

John, weaver, Duxbury, 1644, proposed for frm., but absent when action should have been taken 7 June, 1648. Brother of Peter. Bought land in Sandwich 31 Jan. 1649.

John, Watertown. Wife Dorothy; ch. Hannah b. 9 (7) 1634, Mary b. 24 (1) 1636. He was. bur. 20 (4) 1636, ae. 36.

Lydia, ae. 16, from the Parish of Little Minories, came in the Abigail in June, 1635.

Malachi, see Browning.

Margery, Newbury, d. March 26, 1650-1.

Nathaniel, Springfield. Ch. Nathaniel b. and d. 1649.

Nicholas, mariner, Lynn, propr. 1638, com. of Gen. Court 13 May, 1640. Rem. to Reading; propr. 1644; town officer. He and his wife and children were adm. from chh. of L. Ch. Edward b. Aug. 15, 1640, Joseph b. Dec. 10, 1647, Sarah b. June 6, 1650. He d. April 5, 1673. Will dated 9 (1), prob. 17 (4) 1673, beq. to ch. John, Josiah, Edward, Joseph, Cornelius and Elizabeth, and wife Elizabeth.

Peter, came in the Mayflower; signed the Compact; frm. 1633. Settled at Plymouth. Martha and Mary had divisions of cattle with him in 1627. See story of his getting lost. [Mou.]

He d. before Oct. 10, 1633. Est. settled by Court Nov. 11, 1633. Admin. gr. to widow Mary. Children by divers wives. Dau. Mary had 15 li. put into the hands of her guardian John Done for 9 years; dau. Priscilla had 15 li. in the hands of her guardian, Wm. Gilson, for 12 years; the rest to the widow for the bringing up of the 2 ch. she had by Mr. Brown. Oct. 10, 1644, Mary, ae. 17 years, chose her uncle, John B. of Duxbury, guardian. Priscilla also chose him Oct. 28, 1645. She m. Wm. Clark. [Reg. XXXVII, 276.]

Peter, Sudbury, propr. 1639.

Mr. Richard, Watertown, 1630, frm. May 18, 1631. Town officer, deputy, comr., ruling elder. Rem. from eldership for maintaining that the Romish chh. was a true chh., and for holding other heretical opinions. He made complaint when the red cross was cut out of the ensign at Salem Nov. 5, 1634. He

BROWN, etc., cont.

rem. to Charlestown in 1657. He was ae. 81 or 82 in 1657.

Will prob. March 20, 1661. Beq. to wife Elizabeth; servant Jonathan Simpson; to Phinehas Pratt; sons Richard and George B. in Eng. The widow m. Richard Jackson.

Richard, came in the Mary and John in 1633. Settled at Ipswich; sold the house he had built and rem. to Newbury before 1638. Propr. and town officer. Wife Edith d. April 12, 1647, and he m. 16 Feb., 1648, Elizabeth, widow of Giles Badger. Ch. Joseph, Joshua b. 10 April, 1642, Caleb b. 7 May, 1645, Elizabeth b. 29 March, 1649, Richard b. 18 Feb. 1650-1, Edmund b. 17 July, 1654, Sarah b. 7 Sept. 1657, Mary b. 10 April, 1660.

He d. 26 April, 1661. Will prob. June 24, 1661. Wife; son Joseph dec.; ch. Joshua, Richard, Edmund, Elizabeth, Sarah, and Mary (under aged and unmarried;) bro. George dec. Agreement made between John Badger and the Browne children 4 March, 1677-8.

Robert, ae. 24, came in the Truelove in Sept., 1635; frm. May 2, 1649. Settled at Cambridge; memb. chh. He m. May 8, 1649, Barbara Eden.

He d. Nov. 23, 1690, ae. 70 years. Barbara d. June 1, 1693, ae. 80 years. [Gr. St.]

Mr. Samuel, app. by the Mass. Bay Co. one of the Council of Governor John Endecott April 17, 1629. Was sent back with his bro. John within a few months, on charge of mutiny. One of them was a lawyer, the other a merchant. They gathered a company at sundry times and read the book of common prayer, and accused the governor and minister of being separatists, etc. [Mor.]

Susan, ae. 20, came in the Elizabeth and Ann in May, 1635.

Thomas, weaver, from Malford, Eng., came in the James in April, 1635, as servant to Thomas Antram. Settled at Newbury. Wife Mary d. 2 June, 1655. Ch. Mary b. 1635—"first white child born in Newbury," [Coffin,] (m. 13 May, 1656, Peter Godfrey,) Francis, Isaac. His wife Mary was a dau. of Thomas Newhall, of Lynn. See his will. Probably the Thomas B. who was a commoner at Ipswich, 1641.

He d. 8 Jan. 1686. "A kind of will," de-

BROWN, etc., cont.
fective in some points, was not recd. to probate Feb. 22, 1686, but admin. of the est. was gr. to his son Francis.

Thomas, Sudbury, propr. 1640. The Gen. Court 7 (8) 1640, granted him 200 acres of land for the 25 li. adventure of Mrs. Anne Harvyes. He seems to have rem. to Concord, where by wife Bridget he had ch. Boaz b. 14 (12) 1641, Mary b. 26 (1) 1646, Eliezer b. 5 (3) 1649. He is clearly the man who was adm. chh. Cambridge May 18, 1666; had m. before 1658 Martha, widow of Thomas Oldham; ch. Mehitabel bapt. June 2, 1661, Mary bapt. March 8, 1663, Ebenezer bapt. July 23, 1665, Ichabod bapt. Sept. 9, 1666. [Mi.]
Will dated Nov. 23, 1690, prob. in Jan. folg., beq. to wife Martha, daus. Mehitabel and Martha, and sons Ebenezer and Ichabod. The inv. shows house and land in Camb. and 300 acres at Worcester.

William, Boston, with wife Thomasine, servants to Governor Winthrop, adm. chh. 9 (11) 1633.

William, soap-boiler, Boston, 1634; Salem 1637. Perhaps a brief residence, from which he returned to Bo. Ch. Sarah bapt. 11 (3) 1634.
Will prob. Dec. 19, 1662. Wife Hannah exec; 12 pence apiece to his 6 children. A cow at Billerikey.

Mr. William, shop-keeper, Salem, 1636; frm. May 2, 1649. He deposed regarding the fishing business of Lord Brookes, Sayes and Sir Richard Saltonstall, 23 (6) 1645. [A.]
William, Esq. Salem, made will 12 March, 1686-7, prob. at Boston Feb. 1687, beq. to sons William and Benjamin, dau. Winthrop and her 3 children; to cousin Francis B., wine cooper in London; to pastor, Mr. Higginson; to the church; to the poor; to the school for the bringing up of poor scholars; to gr. ch. Sarah Deane; to cousin Thomas Smith; to Joseph Endecott and Wm. Redfurd. He d. 20 Jan. 1687, ae. 79. [Gr. st.]

William, fisherman, ae. 26, with [wife] Mary, ae. 26, came in the Love in July, 1635. Settled at Cape Ann 1644. [L.] Adm. chh. Salem 27 (10) 1641. Gloucester, town officer, 1647. He m. July 15, 1646, Mary "Robeson," perhaps widow of Abraham Robinson of

BROWN, etc., cont.
Gloc. Ch. Mary b. July 28, 1649, Mary bapt. 28 (11) 1656, James bapt. 2 (11) 1658.
He d. May 3, 1662. Will prob. 25 (4) 1662; wife Mary; son-in-law Abraham Robinson under 21 years and dau. Mary Browne under 18 years.

William, arrived June 22, 1639, apprentice to Mr. Vincent Potter, who released him to Thomas Joy, carpenter, Sept. 24, 1639. [L.]

William, Plymouth, 1644. Rem. to Eastham. He m. July 16, 1649, Mary Murcock. Ch. Mary b. May 14, 1650, George b. Jan. 16, 1651, William b. April 1, 1654, Samuel b. March, 1655-6.
Will 27 June, 1685, prob. 31 March, 1694, beq. to wife Mary, sons George, John, James and Samuel, and dau. Mercy.

William, gentleman, Sudbury, propr. 1639; frm. June 2, 1641. He petitioned the Gen. Court in 1649 for 200 acres of land due for 25 li. put into joint stock by his aunt Mrs. Ann Harvey, who authorized his application. Land laid out to him in Sudbury. Sold land in 1653. He m. 15 (9) 1641, "Mary Bisby of Duxbury;" ch. Mary b. 18 (3) 1643, Thomas b. 22 (3) 1645, Edmund b. 27 (9) 1643 [8?], Susanna b. 4 (12) 1646.
Will dated 20 May, prob. 25 Oct. 1676, beq. to his wife Mary his whole interest in the lands given to her by her father Beesbech at Hetcorne and Frittingden in co. Kent, Eng.; to sons Thomas, William, Edmund and Hopestill; to dau. Mary, wife of Benjamin Rice, and her son Ebenezer; to daus. Elizabeth and Sarah B.; to gr. ch. Mary, Thankful, Patience and Sarah B.

William, planter, Salisbury, bro. of George and Henry, propr. 1639. Memb. chh. 1677. He m. about 1645 Elizabeth Murford. She became insane in connection with the witchcraft delusion, 1661-1692. [Es. Files.] Ch. Mary b. 17 (4) 1647, (m. Thomas Hoyt,) William b. 24 (12) 1648, Ephraim b. 24 (4) 1650, Martha b. 5 (5) 1654, Elizabeth b. 6 (6) 1656, (m. Samuel Clough,) Sarah b. 12 (2) 1658, (m. Benjamin Brown).
He d. Aug. 24, 1706.

BROWNELL,
Thomas, planter, Braintree, sold land in 1640. [L.] Had accts. with Robert Keaine 22 (12) 1646. [A.]

BROWNING, BROWNINGE,
Malachy, gent., (called also Brown,) Watertown, propr. 1642. Signed as one of the appraisers of John Simson's estate (2) 1645. A letter of attorney was made 23 (10) 1644 to him to receive an annuity of 8 li. a year, to be paid by the com. of Chelmsford. He made Capt. Robert Harding of Boston his agent, 13 (8) 1647, to arrange with Mr. Thomas Browning of Mauldon in Essex, clerk, for reversion in Ratchford Hundred, Essex. [A.]
He d. at Mr. Robert Scott's house in Boston 27 (9) 1653.

Thomas, Salem, 1636, frm. April 17, 1637. Town officer. He deposed in 1660, ae. about 73 years. Rem. to Topsfield before 1661, and was dism. 9 Nov. 1663, to join in the forming of a chh. there. Ch. Mary bapt. 7 (11) 1637, Deborah bapt. 31 (11) 1646.
He d. Feb. 1670. Will, dated Feb. 16, 1670, prob. 28 (4) 1671. Gr. son Thomas Towne, daus. Towne, Simons, Williams and Meacham; wife exec. Joseph Williams and Isaac Meacham agreed on division of the est. 17 (2) 1675.

BRUEN, BREWEN,
Obediah, of Shrewsbury, Eng., draper, who had been a res. of Piscataqua. sold June 21, 1642, his share in that Patent which he had purchased of Richard Percyvall, draper, of Shrewsbury, May 4, 1640. [Mass. Arch.] Rem. to Plymouth; prop. frm. 1 March, 1640-1, but did not remain. Settled at Gloucester. Frm. May 19, 1642. Town officer, deputy, surveyor of the arms. Com. to end small causes. [See autograph in Es. Files I, 17.] Rem. to New London, Conn.

BRYANT, BRYAN, BRIAN,
John, Sen., Scituate.
He d. at Cohannack, (Taunton,) April 28, 1638. Will prob. June 17, 1638. All to son John except a gift to Richard Paul. Inv. taken by Mrs. Elizabeth Poole, Mrs. Jane Poole, Wm. Scradding and Richard Paul. Mr. John Gilbert to take care of the portion of the son John. [Reg. IV, 36.]

Stephen, Plymouth, 1638, Duxbury, atba. 1643. In Court in 1651. Frm. June 6, 1654. John Shaw, Jr., calls him bro-in-law. His dau. Abigail m. Lieut. John Bryant Nov. 23, 1665. [Reg. XXXV, 37.]

BRYANT, etc., cont.
Thomas, servant to Samuel Eedy, before Plym. Court in 1632. Servant to Mr. Allerton, before Boston Court 14 (4) 1642.

BUCK, BUKE,
Christian, ae. 26, came in the Blessing in July, 1635.

Isaac, blacksmith, Scituate, atba. 1643. Referred to in Plym. Col. Rec. in 1650 and 1655.

James, with his servant John Morfield, came from Hingham, Eng. in 1638 and settled at Hingham. Propr., frm. May 22, 1639. He m. at Dorchester June 4, 1639, name of wife not known. Ch. — bur. 13 June, 1640, James b. and d. 1642, Lydia bapt. Dec. 13, 1643, James d. 24 April, 1646, Abiel bapt. April 26, 1646, Lydia d. 19 April, 1667. Ch. Lydia, left without father or mother, was a charge of Hingham some years. Ann Bate had care of her. [Arch. 105.] [See Roger Williams.]

William, plow-wright, ae. 50, and Roger, ae. 18, came in the Increase April 15, 1635. Settled at Cambridge; res. in 1650.
He d. Jan. 24, 1657-8, ae. about 73. Inv. filed April 3, 1658, by his son Roger, admnr.

BUCKETT,
Marie, came in the Anne in 1623 to Plymouth; had lot adjoining that of Joseph Rogers.

BUCKLAND,
Thomas, frm. May 6, 1635. Rem. to Windsor, Conn.

William, carpenter, Hingham, (see Plaistow,) propr. 1635. [L.] Rem. to Rehoboth. Ch. Benjamin b. July 2, 1640. He sold land in Hing. May 25, 1661.

BUCKLEY, see Bulkley,
William, shoemaker, Ipswich, 1648, endorsed bond of John Johnson in 1654.

BUCKMASTER, BUCKMINSTER,
James, Sudbury, propr. 1640.

Thomas, laborer, Boston, had grant from Gen. Court 3 March, 1639-40; adm. chh. 4 (8) 1645, frm. May 6, 1646. Wife Joan adm. from chh. of Scituate 4 (8) 1645. Had

BUCKMASTER, etc., cont.
land at Sudbury in 1639. Son Lawrence d. 1645 or 1646; beq. to sister Elizabeth B.; Abigail Sherman; bro. Zachary B.; my father; Thomas Spaule and his dau. Mary.

He d. Sept. 28, 1656. Will mentions wife Joanna, ch. Zachary, Thomas, Joseph, Jabez; daus. Elizabeth Spowell (and her two ch.), Mary Stevens, Dorcas Corben, and Sarah B. [Reg. VI, 353, and XIX, 37.] The widow m. Sept. 1, 1661, Edward Garfield, q. v.

BUCKNAM,
William, carpenter, Charlestown, mentioned in inv. of Nathaniel Sparhawk in 1647. Rem. to Malden. He deposed 25 (7) 1665, ae. about 63 years. [Mdx. Files.] He m. Sarah, dau. of Prudence Wilkinson; she petitioned 16 (8) 1662. [Mdx. Files.] Petition concerning son John in 1641. [L.] Other ch. Mercie b. 14 (12) 1647, Sarah b. July, 1650, William b. Aug., 1652, Mehetabel b. Aug., 1654, Edward b. (7) 1657, Samuel d. 13 (7) 1658, Samuel b. Feb., 1659, (was apprenticed to John Atkinson, feltmaker, 3 July, 1678). [Es. Files.]

He d. March 28, 1679.

BUFFAM, BUFFUM,
Robert, Salem, 1638. Wife Thamesin; ch. Lydia b. 19 (12) 1646. [Es. Files.] Admin. gr. to widow Tamson 2 (10) 1669; deposition of Gertrude Pope. Petition of Robert Wilson, John Hill, Wm. Beanes and Jeremiah Neale, children and heirs of the deceased, Nov. 25, 1678, and deposition of his dau. Mary Neale, ae. about 30 yrs. Sons Caleb and Joshua referred to. The widow's will, dated 10 May, prob. at Boston 13 June, 1688, beq. to daus. Sarah Beans, Lydia Locker, Mary Neele; to the ch. of dau. Margaret Smith; to gr. ch. Deborah Forster and her bro. Robert Willson; Exercise Pope, Damaris Buffum, Sarah Darlin, Caleb and Tammasin B., Lydia Lennard and her sister Elizabeth Beckett, Tammazen and Robert Beans, Elizabeth Kellam, Jeremiah Neele; and to sons Joshua and Caleb.

BUGBEE, BUGBY, BUGBYE,
Edward, ae. 40, wife Rebecca, ae. 32, and dau. Sarah, ae. 4, came in the Francis of Ipswich April 30, 1634. Settled at Roxbury. Ch. Joseph b. June 6, 1640, an in-

BUGBEE, etc., cont.
fant b. and d. 1642. He was adm. chh., an old man, 20 (6) 1665.

He d. 27 (11) 1668, ae. above 80. Will prob. 30 Jan., 1668. Son Joseph dau. Sarah Chamberlain and her ch. Mary and Rebecca C. Son-in-law Richard Chamberlaine exec. [Reg. XIX, 163.]

Richard, Roxbury, frm. May 18, 1631. Wife Judith.

He d. before 1642. His widow m. Robert Parker, q. v.

BUITT, BEWYT,
George, Sandwich, propr. 1640, atba. 1643, constable, 1645.

BULFINCH,
John, Salem, propr., adm. chh. 21 (9) 1640, frm. May 18, 1642. Ann, [wife,] adm. chh. 4 (2) 1641.

BULGAR,
Richard, bricklayer, planter, Boston; paid for work at the fort by Mr. Pynchon in 1632; adm. chh. 13 (2) 1634. Ch. John bapt. at Bo. 20 (2) 1634.

He was dism. to chh. at the Falls of Paschcataqua 6 (11) 1638. Res. at Dover in 1640. [L.]

BULL,
Henry, ae. 19, cert. from St. Savior's, Southwark, Eng., named in list of the Elizabeth in April, 1635.

Henry, ae. 25, came in the James in July, 1635.

Thomas, ae. 25, came in the Hopewell in Sept., 1635. Rem. to Hartford, Conn.

William, Cambridge. He deposed 7 (8) 1656, ae. about 38 years, that in 1638 he was in the service of Capt. Cooke at his mill close by Major Gibbons' land. [Mdx. Files.] Wife Blyth; dau. Rebecca b. 22 (6) 1644.

Will dated 21 May, prob. 12 Oct. 1687, beq. to wife; to sons John, Samuel and Elisha; daus. Rebecca and Mary.

BULKLEY, BUCKLEY,
Rev. Peter, ae. 50, came in the Susan and Ellen in May, 1635, with John, ae. 15, Benjamin, ae. 11, and Daniel, ae. 9; Grace,

BULKLEY, etc., cont.

ae. 33, was enrolled in the list of the Elizabeth and Ann. Settled at Cambridge; householder 8 Feb. 1635. He was of an honorable family, a son of Edward B., D.D., and was b. at Woodhil (or Odel) in Bedfordshire, Jan. 31, 1682; grad. St. John's Coll. Cambridge; was silenced for non-conformity. His first wife was dau. of Mr. Thomas Allen of Goldington; by her he had 9 sons and two daus.; 8 years after her death he m. a dau. of Sir Richard Chitwood, by whom he had 3 sons and one dau. He brought large wealth and did great good. Gave many books to the library of Harvard College. Wrote The Gospel Covenant. [C. M.] [See Reg. 42, 45 and 52, and Genealogy.] He hal leave Sept. 1, 1635, with about 12 more families, to begin a town at Musketaquid, (Concord,) where he was pastor. Sons Edward and Thomas also came here and had families. Ch. b. at C.: Dorothie b. 2 (6) 1640, Peter b. 12 (6) 1643.

He d. 9 March, 1658-9. Will dated 14 April, 1658, prob. 20 (4) 1659; in his 76th year; beq. to wife; to sons Edward, Eliezer and Peter; to dau. Dorothy one hundred pounds in England which came by the death of one of wife's sisters; to son John in Eng. and son Joseph, res. not specified; to the widow of dec. son Thomas; to my lord Oliver St. John, Chief Justice of the Common pleas; to several individuals. [Reg. X, 167.]

BULLARD, BULWARD,

George, Watertown. He deposed 28 (10) 1658, ae. about 50 years. [Mdx. Files.] His wife, Mergrett, d. 8 (12) 1639. He m. 2, Beatrice Hall, (q. v.) Ch. Mary b. Feb. 12, 1639-40, Jacob b. 6 (2) 1642, Jonathan b. July 12, 1647. Beatrice d. at Dedham 29 (3) 1652. He m. April 30, 1655, widow Mary Maplehead.

He d. Jan. 14, 1688-9.

John, Dedham, propr., 1638; adm. chh. with wife Magdelen 2 (5) 1639. Ch. Abigail b. 8 (8) 1641, Joseph b. 26 (2) 1643, Hannah b. 1 (12) 1645, Michael b. 21 (1) 1648.

Robert, Watertown, before 1639.

"Robert Bullard, the husband of Anne Bullard, bur. 29 (4) 1639, 40 years old." The widow m. 2, Henry Thorp; she had grant of land in 1644. Ch. Benjamin, (m. in Dedham 5 (2) 1659, Martha, dau. of Thomas

BULLARD, etc., cont.

Pidge,) and two or more daughters. [See Thorp.]

William, Dedham, propr., 1638; with wife adm. chh. 13 (10) 1639. Rem. to Charlestown; propr.

He d. at Dedh. 24 Dec. 1686, ae. about 85 years. He made will July 5, 1679, codicil 22 May ,1684, prob. at Boston 17 March, 1686-7. Beq. to wife Mary; daus. Mary and Elizabeth; house and land at Dedham to son Nathaniel; grand child William, son of Isaac, dec.

N. B. Some William B. was memb. chh. of Cambridge in 1658, with wife Mary, formerly wife of Francis Grisold. [Mi.]

BULLEN, BULLEIN, [BOLEYN,]

Samuel, Dedham, 1639, propr. 23 (4) 1640; frm. June 2, 1641. Rem. to Medfield; deacon. He m. 10 (6) 1641, Mary, dau. of Samuel Morse; she was adm. chh. 7 (4) 1646. Ch. Mary b. 20 (5) 1642, Samuel b. 19 (10) 1644, Elizabeth b. 3 (12) 1646, (m. Benjamin Wheelock).

He d. Jan. 16, 1691-2; division of his est. was made June 24, 1697, to sons Samuel and Joseph and the other heirs, viz. Mary Clarke, John Bullen, Elisha Bullen, the children of Elizabeth Wheelock, the children of Ephraim Bullen, children of Melatiah Fisher; and Bethia Colburn.

BULLFLOWER, see Bellflower.

BULLOCK,

Edward, husbandman, ae. 32, came in the Elizabeth April 17, 1635.

Will, dated at Dorchester 25 (5) 1649. About to go to Eng. Beq. to wife and daughter-in-law Hannah Johnson. Prob. 29 Jan., 1656. List of debts. [Reg. VI, 355.]

Erasmus, Boston, 1632.

Henry, husbandman, ae. 40, with wife Susan, ae. 42 and ch. Henry, ae. 8, Mary, ae. 6, and Thomas, ae. 2, cert. from the parish of St. Lawrence, Essex, Eng., came in the Abigail in June, 1635. Settled at Charlestown, propr., 1638. Rem. to Salem about 1644. His wife Susan d. about 2 Nov. 1644. [Es Files.]

He d. 27 (10) 1663. Will dated Dec. 21, 1663, prob. 29 (4) 1664; wife Elizabeth, son Thomas, gr. ch. John and Elizabeth, ch. of his dec. son, Henry.

BUMPAS, BUMPASS, BOMPASSE,
Edward, came in the Fortune in 1621 to Plymouth. Settled at Marshfield, taxed in 1632, atba. 1643. Duxbury, propr., 1645. Took oath of fidelity in 1657. Ch. Sarah b. March 9, 1631, Elizabeth b. March 29, 1633, John b. June 2, 1636, Edward b. April 15, 1638, Joseph b. Feb. 15, 1639-40, Isaac b. last of March, 1642, Jacob b. March 25, 1644, Hannah b. April 3, 1646.

BUMSTEAD,
Edward, frm. May 13, 1640.
Thomas, brazier, pewterer, Roxbury. Rem. to Boston about 1644. Wife Susanna; ch. Anna b. June 20, 1639, Mary b. April 24, 1642, Joseph bapt. in Bo. 24 (9) 1644, ae. about 7 days, [W.] Mercy bapt. 20 (11) 1649, ae. about 5 days, Joseph b. Oct. 24, 1653. His dau. Hannah m. April 18, 1659, Thomas Shearer; his son Thomas d. May 3, 1661. With wife Susanna was adm. chh. 30 (10) 1660. Lydia, wife of Mr. John Miller of Yarmouth d. at his house Aug. 7, 1658.
Will dated 25 May, prob. 4 Aug. 1677; son Jeremy, daus. Hannah, wife of Thomas Sherwood; Mary, wife of Ambrose Dawse, and Mary, wife of Samuel Bosworth; wife Susanna.

BUNDY,
John, Plymouth, apprenticed to Griffin Mountague, carpenter, for 8 years from March 14, 1635, transferred to elder Wm. Brewster 6 March, 1636-7. In Court 21 Aug. 1637. Served 17 days against the Narragansetts from 15 Aug., 1645. Rem. to Boston; thence to Taunton. Wife Martha; ch. Martha b. in Boston Nov. 2, 1649, Mary b. 5 Oct., 1653, James b. 29 Sept. 1664, Patience d. March 27, 1655, Sarah b. 4 March, 1668, Samuel b. 4 Oct. 1670, John b. 6 Oct. 1677, Joseph b. 1 Jan. 1679, Edward b. 13 Aug. 1681. Wife Martha d. May 1, 1674; he m. 9 Jan. 1676, Jane Gurney of Mendon.
He made will in April, 1681;—Senior, ae. 64 years; beq. to wife and son James; other children by this wife.

BUNKER, BUNCKER, BUNCAR,
George, Charlestown, frm. March 4, 1634-5. Town officer. Gave marriage portion to his son John on his marriage with Hannah, dau. of Edward Mellows, dec. 4 (3) 1661. His wife Goodith (Judith) was adm. chh. 17 (2) 1636; she d. 10 (8) 1648. He

BUNKER, etc., cont.
m. 2, Margaret How. Her will prob. Dec. 18, 1660, beq. to heirs of her first husband in Watertown.
He d. at Malden in 1664. Will prob. 4 (8) 1664; sons Benjamin, Jonathan and John; and three daus. These were Mary, Martha and Elizabeth. [Wyman.]

BUNN, BUNNE,
Edward, Hull, one of the first planters, May 20, 1642. Propr. 1657. He, widower, m. in Boston 20 (6) 1657, Elizabeth Mason. Will dated 14 April, prob. 20 (8) 1673, beq. to cousin James Mason, now living with him; cousin Samuel Lee; wife Elizabeth; cousin Sarah Mason.

BUNTING,
Ann, [Boston?] her will presented for prob. 28 (11) 1640, in Gen. Court.

Thomas, apprenticed himself 5 Nov., 1644, to Phinehas Pratt for 8 yrs.

BURBANK, see Borebancke,
John, Rowley, propr., town officer, frm. May 13, 1640. First wife Ann; second wife Jemima; ch. John, ("little John," credited with work on fencing in 1648,) Timothy b. 18 (3) 1641, bur. July 14, 1660, Lydia b. 7 (2) 1644, Caleb b. 19 (3) 1646, Mary b. 16 (3) 1655, bur. July 12, 1660.
He made will 5 April, 1681, prob. 10 April, 1683; aged and decrepid; beq. to wife Gemina; sons Caleb and John; gr. son Timothy, son of John; and dau. Lydia. The widow Jemima d. 24 March, 1692-3.

BURCHAM, BURCHER, BURCHUM, see Birchall,
Edward, came in the Anne in 1623 to Plymouth; lot assigned for 2 persons. Land formerly his referred to in 1648. Rem. to Lynn; propr. 1638. Rem. to Salem; frm. 31 (1) 1640. [Es. Court.]

George, of Lincoln, mercer, directed payment to be made to Edward B. of Lynn, N. E. 23 (2) 1641. [L.]

BURDEN, BURDON,
George, shoemaker, tanner, Boston, adm. chh. 8 (11) 1636, frm. May 17, 1637. Wife Anne adm. chh. 6 (9) 1636. She sent power of attorney from Bristol, Eng.; to her

BURDEN, etc., cont.
husband April 8, 1652. Ch. Thomas b. and
d. 1637, Elisha b. 4 (12) 1638, Ezekiel b. 28
(1) 1641, Joseph and Benjamin b. and d. 1643,
Hannah bapt. 4 (3) 1645, Elizabeth bapt. 28
(9) 1647, ae. about 5 weeks, 4 days, Elisha
bapt. 8 (5) 1650.
Will dated 15 (8) 1652, prob. April 30, 1657;
wife and 2 ch. who may stay in England;
father Soulsby; his bro. Timothy. Estate
in Old and New Eng.

BURDENDON, see Bedortha.

BURDETT, BIRDETT, BIRDITT,
Mr. George, Salem, 1634. Frm. Sept.
2, 1635. Rem. to Dover, 1638. [W.]

BURDLEY,
Giles, Ipswich, resident, 1648-1656.
He d. before 1668, when his exec. Theophilus Wilson confirmed the sale of some
land.

BURG, BURGESS, BURGES, BURGIS, BURGE, BURDGE, BIRGE, BIRDGE,
James, ae. 14, came in the Hopewell in
April, 1635; settled at Boston. He m. 19 (8)
1652, Lydia Meed. She was adm. chh. 14
(5) 1661. Sara, adm. chh. 9 (4) 1661.
Inv. of his est. pres. by wife Lydia 31 (11)
1670.

John, Sen., Sandwich, 1638; made will
14 Aug. 1700, prob. July 3, 1701; beq. to sons
John, Thomas, Joseph, Samuel and Jacob;
daus. Martha and 4 others. Son Thomas
to have certain things till the death of his
aunt Martha Severance; wife Mary.

Richard, Sandwich, atba. 1643.

Robert, Lynn, a witness in 1648. Deposed in 1657, ae. about 36 years. Goodwife, deposed in 1663, ae. about 45 years.

Thomas, (Burg,) Sen., Duxbury, propr.
1637, juryman 1642. Rem. to Sandwich, atba.
1643; town officer, 1645; served against the
Narragansetts in 1645. Dau. Elizabeth m.
Feb. 12, 1651, Ezra Perry; son Thomas,
Sandwich, m. Nov. 8, 1648, Elizabeth Bassett. They were divorced 10 June, 1661, at
her desire.
Thomas, Sen. Sandwich, made will 4
Oct. 1684, prob. 2 March, 1684-5; beq. to
wife [Martha,] son Thomas B. of Rhode

BURG, etc., cont.
Island, sons Jacob, John and Joseph; son
Ezra Perry; gr. ch. Thomas, son of John.

BURGH,
Master Burgh, a minister out of office
at Dorchester, mentioned by Lechford in
Plain Dealing in 1642. May refer to Rev.
Jonathan Burr.

BURKBEE, BURPEE,
Thomas, Boston, watchman, before the
Court 3 Sept., 1639. Rem. to Rowley; propr.
1649. He deposed in 1671, ae. about 58 years.
He m. Martha, dau. of John Cheney of Newbury, widow of Anthony Sadler; she was
bur. Jan. 24, 1658, and he m. Sarah, dau.
of John Kelly. Ch. Hannah b. (1) 1655, John
b. 1656, d. 1657, Sarah b. 1658, d. 1660. Sarah
b. 15 (12) 1660, Thomas b. 25 (10) 1663.
He d. 1 June, 1701.

BURLEY,
Phebe, maid servant to Mr. John Cotton, adm. chh. Boston 31 (1) 1639.

BURMAN, see Boardman.

BURNELL, BUNNELL,
William, Pulling Point, Boston, juryman, 1630. Hired one third of the weir at
Menotomy in 1641. Wife Mary adm. chh.
11 (4) 1643; ch. Elizabeth bapt. 18 (4) 1643,
John b. (8) 1644. The wife Mary d. 16 (9)
1645; he m. 2, Sarah ——.
His will dated 16 (2) 1660, prob. May 17,
1661, beq. to wife Sarah, ch. John, Samuel
and Sarah. [Reg. IX, 230, and X, 270.]

BURNAP, BURNOP, BURNOPP, BURNETT,
Robert, Roxbury, propr. about 1640.
Rem. to Reading: propr. 1652. Mortg. farm
in 1655. Wife Ann d. at Read. April 27, 1681.
He m. 2, Mary ——. Ch. an infant bur. at
Rox. 1642. Thomas, a father in 1664, Sarah b. 6
(9) 1653. Robert B., Sen., with wife Mary,
R. B., Jr. with wife Sarah, and Thomas B.,
all of Reading, and Isaac Bullard of Dedham, with wife Ann, deeded to Elias Parkman in 1668 all their interest in half of a
farm in Salem, formerly in possession of
Isaac Burnap, dec. He deposed in his suit

BURNAP, etc., cont.
in court in 1653, ae. about 58 years. [Arch. 38 B.]
He d. Sept. 27, 1689. Will dated 15 Nov. 1688, prob. Oct. 1, 1689, beq. to sons Thomas and Robert; daus. Ann Goenes, [Jones,] and Sarah Browne; cousin Thomas B.; gr. ch. Joseph and Thomas, Sarah and Isaac Southericke.

BURNES,
Margaret, Boston, servant to Mr. John Cotton, adm. chh. 27 (5) 1634.

BURNHAM, BURNAM, see **Boardman,**
John, carpenter, Ipswich, propr.; served in the Pequot war and recd. pay from the town in 1639 and 1643. Recd. bequest from kinsman Robert Andrews. Sold house and lot 1 (4) 1648. Wife Mary deposed in 1670, ae. about 45 years; dau. Mary, at same time, ae. about 19.
His will signed 31 Dec. 1703, prob. Jan. 24 folg. beq. to sons John and Thomas; to wife Elizabeth; ch. Joseph, Jacob, Jonathan, David, Abigail and Mary. Owned ¾ of the brigendeen Swan.

Robert, yeoman, Boston, bought houselot in 1648. Bought land at Oyster River May 12, 1657. [Suff. De.] Wife Frances; ch. Robert b. 25 (7) 1647, Elizabeth b. 27 (8) 1651.

Thomas, carpenter, Ipswich, propr. 1647. Had land next to that of his brother in 1648. He deposed March 29, 1659, ae. about 40 years; called Simon Tuttle brother, and spoke of uncle John T. in England. His wife Mary, ae. 35, deposed concerning her mother, Mrs. T. at the same time. They testified 23 Jan. 1684, regarding the promises made by Thomas Clarke to his son John C. at the time the latter was about to marry their daughter.
His will dated 10 Jan. 1693-4, being aged and infirm; prob. 29 Sept. 1694; had formerly given to sons Thomas, John and James; gives to his six daus. Mary, Johannah, Abigail, Ruth, Sarah and Hester what his wife had desired; residue to wife Mary.

BURR, BURRE,
Benjamin, Cambridge, 1636.

Jehu, Springfield, one of the founders in 1635-6. [Reg. XIII, 297.] Was paid £18 for the carpenter work on the plantation

BURR, etc., cont.
house; signed the compact May 16, 1636. Measured land. Deputy.

Mr. John, frm. May 18, 1631.

Rev. Jonathan b. at Redgrave, Suff. about 1604; ministered at Horninger and Beckingshal; was silenced. Came to N. E. with wife and 3 children. [C. M.] Having been a minister in Eng., and of very good report there for piety and learning was invited to be asst. pastor at Dorchester 21 (10) 1639. Was charged with teaching familism, etc., and much discussion took place; he renounced his erroneous expressions in 1640. [W.]
He d. Aug. 9, 1641. [Blake's Annals.] His widow Frances m. Mr. Richard Dummer, and was dism. to Rowley chh. 25 (7) 1664. Ch. Mary bapt. 23 (10) 1639.

Rebecca, memb. chh. Dorchester 4 (12) 1639.

Simon, farmer, Hingham. Wife Rose d. 24 (4) 1647; he m. 2, Nov. 28, 1648, Hester ——; she d. 3 Feb., 1692-3. Ch. Esther d. 20 (10) 1645, Hannah b. 7 (6) 1646, Henry d. 14 (12) 1646, Simon and Hannah bapt. Feb. 25, 1654-5, John b. Jan. 6, 1659, Jonathan b. June 13, 1665, d. in Canada Exped. 1690.
He d. 7 Feb., 1691-2. Admin. gr. to son Simon.

BURRAGE, BORRAGE,
John, Charlestown, 1637. Clerk of market, ferryman. He was ae. 45 in 1662. [Mdx. Files.] Wife Mary adm. chh. with him 10 (2) 1642. He m. 2, Joanna Stower, (ae. 47 in 1671;) who d. Dec. 25, 1689. Ch. Mary bapt. 8 (3) 1641, (m. John Marshall,) Hannah b. 14 (10) 1643, (m. John French,) John, ae. 22 in 1668, Elizabeth, (m. Thomas Deane,) Nathaniel b. 1655, d. 1656, William b. June 10, 1657, Sarah b. 24 (11) 1658-9, (m. Wm. Johnson, Bethia bapt. 26 (8) 1661, Thomas b. May 26, 1663, Ruth b. Feb. 28, 1664-5, (m. Ignatius White,) Joanna d. 16 (4) 1668.
He d. 19 (8) 1685. Inv. filed by widow Joanna 15 Dec. folg. Her inv. was taken 13 (1) 1689-90. An agreement for division of the est. was made 2 May, 1694, by Mary Marshall, Hannah French, Elizabeth Poor, William, Bethiah and Thomas B., Sarah Johnson, Ruth White, and Susanna, dau. of John B. dec.

BURRELL, BURRILL, BURWELL,
George, Sen., Lynn, in Es. Court, 1637; propr. 1638.
Will, dated Oct. 18, 1653, prob. 21 (4) 1653; sons Francis, John and George; Francis, child. Ann Burt, in her will calls Francis Burrill her brother. Anne Burrell, widow, d. in Boston 3 Aug., 1659.
[Note. In Boston, Eng., Jan. 12, 1626, George Burrell, of Boston, ae. 26, and Mary Cooper of Appley, ae. 20, were lic. to marry.]

John, (Burules,) ae. 26, came in the Blessing in July, 1635.

John, shoemaker, Roxbury, 1634. Wife Sarah; dau. Sarah b. in July, 1634.
Will dated Aug. 3, 1654. Est. to be divided between his wife Sarah and dau. Sarah. Richard Davis, who had m. the dau. Sarah, was app. admin. jointly with the widow 19 Feb., 1656. [Reg. VI, 353.]

BURROUGHS, BURROWS, BURROW, BOROWE,
Edward, Marshfield, propr. 1650.

Jeremiah, Scituate, served against the Narragansetts in 1645. He m. May, 1651, —— Hewes; ch. Jeremiah b. March 11, 1651-2, John b. Nov. 1653, Elizabeth b. March 5, 1654-5, Mary b. Dec. 2, 1656. He rem. to Marshfield.
He was drowned. Inquest. Admin. gr. Dec. 3, 1660, to his widow for herself and children.

John, of Yarmouth, Eng., cooper, ae. 28, and Anne his wife, ae. 40, passed exam. to go to Salem, N. E. May 10, 1637. Propr. 14 (6) 1637; town officer.

John, servant to Mr. John Haule, was before the Gen. Court 6 (7) 1638, for seducing others to his opinions; and J. H. gave bonds for him. In Court 1 Sept., 1640.

Robert, Marblehead, propr. 1649.

William, ae. 19, came in the Susan and Ellen in April, 1635.

BURSALL, BURSELL, see Birchall,
James, Yarmouth, atba. 1643, town officer, 1645.
Admin. gr. 1 Nov., 1676, to widow Emmett, Enet or Euett, and Silas Saers. The 3 daus. to be joint heirs.

John, Yarmouth, atba. 1643.

BURSLEY, BURSLYNN, BURSLYN,
Mr. John, Dorchester, propr., frm. May 18, 1631. Deputy. See acct. of his servant Thomas Lane in 1634.

John, Sandwich, m. Mr. Hull's dau. about Nov. 28, 1639. [Sci. and Barns. Chh. Rec.] Rem. to Barnstable; his wife adm. chh. July 22, 1643. Constable, 1645. Ch. —— d. Jan 25, 1640, Mary bapt. July 29, 1643, John b. and d. 1644, Johannah bapt. March 1, 1645-6, Elizabeth bapt. March 24, 1649, John bapt. April 11, 1652.
The inv. of his est. rend. Aug. 21, 1660, by John Smith and John Chipman.

BURT, BURTES,
Edward, salter, shop-keeper, Charlestown. The Court ordered that he should keep Robert Way Aug. 5, 1634. He rec'd a legacie Oct. 24, 1653, from his uncle Thomas Burt, property at Darkin, co. Surrey, Eng. Carried on trade with the Barbadoes; dealt in sugar, etc. [Mdx. De. I, 136.]

Henry, Springfield, town officer, 1642; frm. April 13, 1648. Clerk of the writs. One of the four men who conducted Sabbath services in 1651, in absence of a minister. Wife Ulalia d. Aug. 19, 1690. Ch. Hannah b. April 28, 1641, (m. Dec. 24, 1657, John Bag,) a dau. b. 1643, Patience b. Aug. 18, 1645, (m. Oct. 7, 1667, John Bliss,) Mercy b. Sept. 27, 1647; sons named in admin. papers Jonathan and Nathaniel. [Reg. XXXII, 302.]
He d. April 31, 1662; had given part of his est. to son Nathaniel; wished his wife to have the rest.

Hugh, yeoman, ae. 35, with Ann, ae. 32, Hugh, ae. 15, Edward, ae. 8, and Wm. Bassett, ae. 9, came in the Abigail in July, 1635. Settled at Lynn. Propr. 1638. He deposed in 1661, ae. about 70 yrs.; had lived in Lynn about 25 yrs. He gave letter of attorney 19 (7) 1646, to receive of Susan, widow of Thomas Burt of Darkin, co. Surrey ,cordwinder, 20 li. as per his will, with annuities for 2 yrs., with legacies to Hugh, Jr., and Thomas B. [A.] The son Hugh d. in 1650, appointing his father overseer.
He d. Nov. 2, 1661; will dated 7 Oct., prob. 26 (9) 1661, gives to his son Edward all interest he has in housing or land in London or elsewhere in Eng., falling to him from his bro. John dec. Son William Bassett; gr.

BURT, etc., cont.
ch. Mary and Sarah, daus. of his dec. son Hugh. His wife was exec. She d. about 1673. Will dated 8 Jan. 1664, prob. 26 (4) 1673; beq. to Bassett ch., to Ellen, wife of Wm. and Hannah Bartrom, to Lydia Burrill and to bro. Francis Burrill.

James, Taunton. Town officer, 1645; juror. Guardian to Richard, son of his bro. Richard, late of Taunton, 26 Oct., 1647. Wife Anna d. Aug. 17, 1665.
His will prob. 2 March, 1680; aged and weak; beq. to eldest son James, son Thomas, daus. Hannah and Rachel and H.'s ch. Jacob Hathney (or Hackney).

John, ae. 29, came in the Defense in July, 1635. Settled at Springfield; taxed in 1638.

Richard, Taunton, his death referred to in Plym. Col. Rec. 1647; child Richard survived.

Roger, Cambridge. Wife Susan; ch. Samuel b. 6 (12) 1642.

BURTON,
Boniface, Lynn, frm. May 6, 1635. Juryman, 1636; propr. 1638. Rem. to Reading about 1644. In Essex Court 1643.
Old father Boniface Burton, aged 113 years, d. 13 (4) 1669. [S.] Will, dated 21 Feb. 1666-7, prob. (Suff.) 24 June, 1669. Wife Frances; niece, wife to Samuel Bennett, her husband and ch. [Reg. XX, 242.] The widow, of Boston, made will 11 Feb. 1669, prob. 17 April, 1679. Beq. to Mary and Hannah, daus. of Maj. Gen. John Leverett; to Sarah, wife of Hudson Leverett; to several other women; residue to be divided between Hannah and Rebecca Leverett, Rebecca Davenport and Sarah Addington.

Edward, Charlestown, before the Court Oct. 3, 1632, propr. 1633; rem. to Hingham.

John, Salem, 1636. Bought land in 1649. He deposed in 1666, ae. about 58 years.
Will, (John, Sen.) dated 14 Oct. prob. 16 Nov. 1684, beq. to sons John, Samuel and Isaac; dau. Hannah, wife of Wm. Osborne and her ch. Samuel O. and others.

Richard, before Plymouth Court 7 June, 1648.

BURTON, etc., cont.
Thomas, grocer, of London, res. in Boston in 1645 and signed petition for the removal of restriction upon freemanship, in 1645. [W.] His house at Strawberry Bank was sold by Wm. Brenton 4 (11) 1650.

Thomas, Hingham, m. Margaret, dau. of John Ottis; ch. Hannah b. May 30, 1641, Phebe b. May 12, 1644, Sarah b. Dec., 1645, Ruth b. Aug. 24, 1646, d. Aug. 17, 1647, Sarah b. May 13, 1049.
His widow d. 21 Oct. 1670.

BURWOODE,
Ales, before the Gen. Court 4 (10) 1638.

Thomas, defendant in a suit in Salem court in 1640. Went to England that year. [Es. Court Rec.]

BUSBY, BUSBEY,
Nicholas, weaver, ae. 50, with wife Bridget, ae. 53, and ch. Nicholas, John, Abraham and Sarah, of Norwich, Eng., passed exam. April 8, 1637, to go to Boston in N. E. and there inhabit. Settled at Watertown, propr., 1637, selectman. One of those who surveyed the line between Mass. and Plym. plantations in 1659. [Arch. Col. 23.]
Will, dated July 25, 1657, son Abraham, sons-in-law William and John Grout, all in N. E. and son John in Eng. Dec. son Nicholas; daus. Anne Nickerson and Katharine Savory and Sarah Grout. Books of Physic and Divinity; and weaver's tools. The widow Bridget deeded property to these ch., May 14, 1659. Inv. of her est. was presented July 3, 1660. [Reg. VIII, 278, and X, 173.]

William, presented to Gen. Court, for drunkenness, June 5, 1638, was found to have the falling sickness.

BUSCOTT, BUSKETT, BUSGUTT,
James, ae. 28, came in the Christian March 16, 1634.
Peter, smith, had lawsuit in Essex court in 1638.

BUSH,
Randolph, or Reynold, Cambridge, propr. 1641. Mortg. land in 1644 and redeemed it in 1657.

BUSHELL,
Ruth, ae. 23, came in the Abigail in July, 1635.

BUSHNELL, BUSHNALL,
Francis, carpenter, ae. 26, came in the Planter in April, 1635, with Marie, ae. 26, and ch. Martha, ae. 1 yr. Settled at Boston. Adm. inhabitant, Salem, 1636.
He d. at the Winthrop farm at Ten Hills 28 (1) 1636. The widow Martha, adm. chh. 3 (12) 1638. Her ch. Mary bapt. 17 (12) 1638, (m. 3 (8) 1657, George Robinson).

John, barber, glazier, came in the Hopewell in April, 1635, ae. 21. Settled at Salem. Was paid for glazing windows of meeting house in 1637. Rem. to Boston. Wife Jane; ch. Dorothy b. 19 (12) 1651, Sarah b. 24 March, 1655, Elizabeth b. Aug., 1657, d. 17 (2) 1662, John b. 19 Jan., 1659, Jane b. Dec. 18, 1662, William b. June 28, 1666.
He d. about 5 Aug. 1667; admin. gr. to widow Jane 14 (9) folg. Second admin. gr. 14 Dec. 1685, to son John, now of full age, for himself, his surviving sister and the child of his dec. sister. The widow had rem. out of this jurisdiction.

BUSHRODE,
Thomas, merchant; witness to deed of Robert Nash Sept. 24, 1642. Accts. with Val. Hill 18 (12) 1645. Was of Kikatan in Virginia in 1646. [A.]

BUSHOP, see Bishop,
Richard, Plymouth, hired with Love Brewster 3 Dec., 1638. Atba. 1643.

BUSSAKER,
Peter, before Gen. Court Sept. 6, 1636.

BUSSE, BUZIE,
Simon, Salem, a witness in court in 1645.

Ensign William, Concord, frm. March 14, 1638-9. Wife Ann d. Aug. 3, 1674. He m. 2, 24 Dec., 1674, Dorcas Jones; ch. Richard b. 6 (5) 1640, Ann b. 18 (12) 1641, (Hanna Busse m. Wm. Wheeler 30 Oct., 1659,) Nathaniel b. 15 (1) 1646, Joseph b. 4 (3) 1649.

BUSWELL, BOSWELL, BUZZELL,
Isaac, weaver, Salisbury, propr. 1639. Frm. Oct. 9, 1640. The Gen. Court allowed his removal to Hampton in 1639, but he returned. Frm. Oct. 9, 1640. Wife Margerite d. 29 (7) 1642. He m. 2, Susanna ——, who d. March 21, 1676-7. Ch. William, Samuel, Phebe, (m. John Gill,) Mary b. 29 (6) 1645, (m. Philip Brown,) Isaac b. 29 (5) 1650.
He d. 8 July, 1683. Will dated April 9, 1680, prob. Sept. 25, folg., beq. to son William and his wife, dau. Sarah, son-in-law John Gill, husband of dau. Phebe, Philip Browne, (husband of dau. Mary,) and son Samuel B.; to the three ch. left by son Isaac, and to gr. ch. Isaac, son of William.

BUTCHER, see Garrett.

BUTLER,
Giles, husbandman from Marlborough, Eng., came in the James, April 5, 1635.

John, Newbury, frm. May 2, 1649. He witnessed the will of Thos. Millard, 1653.

Mr., Haverhill, propr., 1647.

Nicholas, of Eastwell, Eng., yeoman, with wife Joice, 3 ch. and 5 servants, came from Sandwich, Eng., before June 9, 1637; settled at Dorchester; propr. before Sept. 10, 1637. Frm. March 4, 1638-9. Gent.; town officer; sold land in Roxbury in 1652, having removed to Martha's Vineyard; gave power of attorney to son John in 1651, for sale of lands, etc. Son Henry was schoolmaster at Dorch. in 1652 and proposed for minister at Uncatie in 1656.

Richard, Cambridge, propr. 1633; frm. May 14, 1634. Rem. to Hartford, Conn.

Stephen, Boston, 1648.

Thomas, laborer, Duxbury, in Court 7 June, 1637. Rem. to Sandwich, propr., 1640. Atba. 1643. Ch. (Patience b. Aug. 14, 1648,) Dorothy b. Jan. 23, 1650.

William, bro. to Richard, Cambridge, propr. 1635, frm. May 6, 1635. Rem. to Hartford and d. in 1648-9. Inv. brought in to Suff. Prob. by Increase Nowell, admin. about 1652.

BUTMAN, see Pickton,
John, Boston, 1649.

BUTTERICK, BUTRICK, BUTTRICK,

William, ae. 18, came in the Susan and Ellen in April, 1635. [Perhaps he entered in one ship and then changed to the other.]

William, an ostler, came in the Planter in April, 1635, ae. 21. Settled at Concord, frm. May 26, 1647. Sergeant. Rem. to Chelmsford; was one of the com. to invite the pastor and church of Wenham to remove to Chem. in 1654. [Wen. Chh. Rec.] He deposed 28 (1) 1659, ae. about 43 years, as to a house bought by Matthew Allen. [Mdx. Files.] John Hastings calls him son-in-law. Wife Mary; ch. Mary b. and d. 1648. Wife Sarah d. July 17, 1664. He m. 21 Feb., 1667, Jane Goodnow. Ch. John b. 21 Sept. 1653, Samuel b. 12 Jan., 1654, Edward b. and d. in 1656, Joseph b. 29 Dec., 1657, Sarah b. 27 July, 1662, Mary b. June 17, 1664, d. April 28, 1665.

Will dated 1 March, 1687, ae. about 71 years; prob. June 28, 1698; beq. to eldest son John a house he built in Stow; to son Samuel lands at Concord; to dau. Sarah Barritt; to the ch. of all three. Signed William Butterick.

BUTTALL, BUTTLE, BUTTLES, BUTTOLPH,

Leonard, bricklayer, brick-maker, Boston. His wife Judith adm. chh. 23 (3) 1641. Sold land at Muddy River 25 (5) 1643. Oct. 22, 1652, he deeded land to secure the payment of an annuity to the Free School of Boston. He deposed in the probate of Maj. William Holmes of Scituate, ae. 41 years, June 1, 1654.

Thomas, leather-dresser, glover, Boston, adm. chh. 22 (7) 1639; frm. June 2, 1641. Came in the Abigail in May, 1635, ae. 32, with wife Anne, (Annis,) ae. 24. Settled at Boston. Anne adm. chh. 28 (7) 1639. Ch. Thomas b. 12 (6) 1637, John b. 28 (12) 1639, Abigail b. 18 (12) 1642, (m. Aug. 15, 1660, David Saywell,) Samuel bapt. 19 (5) 1646, Samuel bapt. 15 (6) 1647, Samuel bapt. 12 (9) 1648, Mehetabel b. 26 (8) 1651. He signed bond with John and Elizabeth (Harding) Fraryc concerning Harding est. discharged 1 Oct., 1665.

Will, dated 25 (3) 1667. Prob. 18 June, 1667. Wife Anna, sons Thomas and John, daus. Abigail and Mehetabel, kinsman John Parker, bro. Henry Bridgham. [Reg. XVI, 159.] The widow Anna, or Hannah, made will 17

BUTTALL, etc., cont.

Sept., prob. 10 Nov. 1680; beq. to son John Bingley and his ch.; to the ch. of son Thomas, viz. Thomas, Marah, Abigail and Nicolas; to dau. Mehetabel Frost and her ch. Mehetabel and Elizabeth.

BUTTERFIELD,

Benjamin, Charlestown, 1638. Frm. May 10, 1643. Rem. to Woburn, propr. 1640; later to Chelmsford. Ch. Nathaniel b. at Woburn 14 (12) 1642, Samuel b. May 17, 1647, Joseph b. Aug. 15, 1649. He m. 2, at Chelm. June 3, 1663, Hannah Whittemore.

He d. March 2, 1688. Will dated 8 (3) 1677, prob. at Boston 7 June, 1688; beq. to sons Nathaniel, Samuel and Joseph; to Jonathan and Mary, ch. of his dec. son Jonathan; to Deborah, wife of Nathaniel.

Samuel, Springfield, propr., mentioned in the Compact in 1636.

BUTTERWORTH,

Samuel, propr. at Weymouth before 1651; frm. May 13, 1640. Taxed at Rehoboth, 1643. Propr., 1645.

Will, dated Oct. 13, 1684. Prob. March 3, 1685. To cousins: Abraham B. of Rhode Island and his dau. Ann B.; John B. of Swansey, and his 2 sons Samuel and Benjamin B.; Mary Mason, widow, of S., and her sons Noah and Samuel M. and William Hayward of Swansey. Mary m. Thomas Clifton, q. v. [Reg. XLI, 191.]

BUTTON,

John, miller, mylner, Boston, with wife Grace adm. chh. 22 (10) 1633; frm. May 14, 1634. He deposed 6 (4) 1667, ae. about 73 years. [Mdx. Files.] His wife d. 9 (1) 1638. His second wife Joan adm. chh. 25 (8) 1640. With wife Johanna sold land in B. Dec. 1, 1657. With wife Mary sold land 20 March, 1670-1. Bapt. in Boston 22 (3) 1670, Joseph and Mary of sister Simmons, now wife of John B.

Will dated 5 Nov. prob. 22 Nov. 1681, beq. to the church of Boston for the purchase of cups; to wife Mary.

Matthew, or Matthias, Boston. Wife Lettice, adm. chh. 26 (11) 1633, dau. Mary bapt. 23 (12) 1633, (m. at Haverhill Dec. 6, 1652, Edward Yeomans,) son Daniel bapt. 22 (12) 1634. He m. at Ipswich about 1639 Joane, widow of John Thornton. [Ips. Rec.]

BUTTON, cont.

Rem. to Haverhill about 1652. Wife Teagle or Tegell; ch. Hannah b. May 11, 1652, Daniel b. 10 April, 1654, d. about 25 (7) 1677, Samuel b. Sept. 1, 1655, Abigail b. 16 June, 1656, Thomas b. Dec. 6, 1657, Mathias b. 17 March, 1657-8, Elizabeth b. Jan. 10, 1659, Peter b. 17 July, 1660, Mehetabel b. Oct. 11, 1661, Patience b. 1 June, d. 30 Oct. 1662, Edward b. Feb. 6, 1663, Sarah, (m. 6 Jan. 1673, James Kingsbury). The wife Teagle d. Feb. 4, 1662; he m. June 9, 1663, Elizabeth Duston, who survived him and d. July 16, 1690. He conveyed land for the benefit of his wife to his bro.-in-law George Wheeler 11 (2) 1665.

He d. Aug. 13, 1672. The inv. of his est. was filed at Salisbury court 14 April, 1674, by Capt. Nath. Saltonstall, admin.

Robert, Salem, memb. chh. 1641; rem. to Boston; frm. May 18, 1642. Ch. Samuel bapt. at S. 27 (1) 1642, Abigail bapt. 17 (11) 1643, Hannah from the chh. of Salem bapt. at Boston 21 (10) 1645, ae. about 5 days, Sarah, do, ae. about 6 days, bapt. 16 (11) 1647, Samuel, do., ae. about 4 days, bapt. 24 (12) 1649, Hannah d. 20 (1) 1650.

Will prob. 28 (11) 1650; wife Abigail; son Samuel, daus. Abigail, Hannah and Sarah. The inv. was presented by his widow, now wife of Edward Hutchinson 21 (11) 1650. [Reg. VII, 334.]

BUTTRY,

Martha, Cambridge, propr. South Side Charles River 1636. [Court. Rec.]

Nicholas, ae. 33, with [wife] Martha, ae. 28, and [dau.] Grace, ae. 1, came in the James in July, 1635.

BUXTON,

Anthony, Salem, propr. 1636; cousin of William Vincent. Wife Elizabeth deposed in 1661, ae. 38 years; ch. Anthony b. 6 (7) 1653, Samuel b. 14 (6) 1655, James b. 8 (6) 1659, d. 15 (2) 1662, Thomas b. 24 (12) 1661, d. 20 (8) 1662, Joseph b. 17 (5) 1663, Hannah b. 27 Jan. 1665.

He d. in 1684. Will dated March 8, prob. 29 July, 1684, beq. to wife Elizabeth; dau. Elizabeth, wife of Isaac Cook; sons John and Joseph B.; daus. Lydia, Mary and Sarah and their ch.; dau. Hannah unmarried.

Ruth, the widow of Thomas Small had bro. John Buxton.

BUXTON, cont.

Thomas, Salem, 1638. Inv. 5 (4) 1654.

BYAM,

George, husbandman, Salem, propr., adm. chh. 27 (7) 1640; rem. to Wenham. With wife Susanna sold land 1657. Rem. to Chelmsford; frm. May 18, 1642. Ch. Abraham bapt. at Sal. 14 (2) 1644. He adopted Mary, dau. of Mary Harsey, Dec. 16 (7) 1646.

Will dated 10 March, prob. 15 (4) 1680, beq. to wife Susannah, son Abram and kinswoman Deborah Jaques.

Nathaniel, ae. 14, came in the Blessing in July, 1635. Nathaniel, Marshfield, witness to deed in 1644.

BYFORD, (Pyford,)

Peter, before Gen. Court in 1635.

BYLEY, BILEY,

Henry, tanner, Sarum, ae. 26, with [sister] Mary, ae. 22, Thomas Reeves, servant, and [bro.] John Byley, ae. 20, came in the Bevis in May, 1638. [Mary m. Samuel Dudley; John d. during 1638.] One of those the Court named as founders of Merrimack, (Salisbury,) 1638. He m. in Salisbury, Eng. Rebecca Swayne, who came to N. E. after him; ch. William bapt. 20 Aug. 1633, Rebecca bapt. 8 Dec. 1636, (m. 15 Dec. 1654, John Hale,) Henry bapt. 26 Aug. 1638.

He d. before 1641. The widow m. 2, 3 April, 1641, John Hall; m. 3, 22 July, 1650, William Worcester; m. 4, in 1663, Dep. Gov. Samuel Symonds. She d. 21 July, 1695. [See Batt and Byley Genealogy in Reg. LI and LII.]

BYRAM,

Nicholas, Weymouth, son-in-law of Abraham Shaw, and one of admins. of his est., appointed by the Gen. Court 29 (8) 1640. Witness to a deed of Kennebec property in 1649. Rem. to Bridgewater. Petitioned Plymouth Court about taxation in 1668. Town officer.

Will dated 13 June, 1687, beq. to wife Susanna and bro. John Shaw of Wey.; ch. not specified. The widow, aged, made will 7 Sept. 1698, prob. 18 Dec. 1699; beq. to son Nicholas, his wife Mary and ch. Nicholas and Mehetabel; to daus. Abigail Whitman, Deliverance Porter, Experience Willis and Susanna Edson; to gr. ch. Ebenezer Whitman, Mary Liech and Mary Willis; gave freedom to negro Tom and her maid.

CABELL, CABLE,
John, Dorchester, 1630. [See Col. Rec.] One of the founders of Springfield; signed the Compact May 16, 1636. [Reg. XIII, 297.] Was paid £11 for sawing the boards and making the locks and nails for the plantation house. Land-measurer. Ch. John b. 12 (11) 1640.

CADD,
Bartholomew, Boston.
Inv. presented by widow Mary June 16 1665. [Reg. XIII, 156.]

CADE, CADY,
James, shipwright, from Northam, Devon, Eng. Res. in Boston, with wife Margaret mortg. house and land in Northam, Eng., formerly of his father, Christopher Cade, and his mother Mary Hopper; his wife had a life interest in property at Biddeford, Eng., Dec. 4, 1638. [L.] [Reg. L, 505.] Prop. frm. of Plym. Colony, 1 Dec., 1640. His wife Margaret adm. chh. Boston 19 (1) 1643. Ch. Mary b. 4 (8) 1640.

Nicholas, planter, Watertown, bought land and house in partnership with John Knapp 8 (10) 1645, and sold his share to him 6 (1) 1650. Wife Judith, dau. of William Knapp; ch. John b. Jan. 15, 1650, Judy b. Sept. 2, 1653, James b. Aug. 28, 1655, Nicholas b. and d. in 1657, Daniel b. Nov. 27, 1659. He rem. to Groton.

CAINE, CANE, KENE,
Christopher, Cambridge, propr., 1633. Bought land 23 (12) 1642. Wife Margery memb. chh. Ch. Jonathan b. 27 (1) 1640, Nathan b. 5 (6) 1642, Deborah b. 17 (11) 1644, Ruth b. 6 (10) 1647, (m. Marmaduke Johnson; made will 3 April, 1676, prob. April 13, 1677, beq. to bros. Jonathan and Nathaniel, and sisters Easter and Deborah Cane and others;) Esther. [Mi.]
He d. Dec., 1653. Wife Margaret d. April 3, 1687.

CAKEBREAD,
Thomas, Watertown, frm. May 14, 1634; rem. to Dedham, propr., 14 (7) 1637. Sold in 1638, and rem. to Sudbury, propr. 1640. App. ensign and ordered to lead the company 27 Sept., 1642. He d. 4 (11) 1642. His widow Sarah had gr. of land in 1645. She m. 2, 7 Nov. 1649, Philemon Whale.

CALCOTT, see COLCORD, and COLLICOTT.

CALEM, see Kilham.

CALKIN, CAULKIN, CAUKIN, COUCKLYNE, CAWKIN,
Hugh, Plymouth, prop. for frm. 2 March, 1640-1, but did not remain. Settled at Gloucester. Selectman. Frm. Mass. Col. Dec. 27, 1642. Com. to end small causes. Wife Ann; ch. Deborah b. March 18, 1644, Rebecca d. 14 (1) 1651.

CALL, CALLE, CAUL,
John, Sen., Charlestown, 1637, adm. chh. 24 (8) 1639. Town officer, 1646. Rem. to Malden. His wife Joanna d. at Malden 30 (11) 1660.
He d. in 1677. John, of Charlestown, baker, [a son?] d. in 1697.

Thomas, Faversham, Eng., husbandman, with wife Bennett and 3 ch. came from Sandwich, Eng., before June 9, 1637. Settled at Charlestown; frm. May 13, 1640. Tile-maker, baker. He deposed [about 1663] ae. about 65 years. [Mdx. Files.] Lived near the ferry on Mystic side, (Malden). Wife adm. chh. 16 (12) 1639. He m. 2, Joanna Shepardson who d. Jan. 30, 1661. Ch. Thomas, John, Mary, Elizabeth bapt. 21 (12) 1640-1, (m. 1, Samuel Tingley, 2, Daniel Shepardson,) Mercy b. Nov. 7, 1643, (m. 1, Samuel Lee, 2, John Allen).
He d. May, 1676, ae. 79. Will dated 23 (9) 1670, date of probate not recorded; beq. to sons Thomas and John; daus. Mary, Elizabeth and Mercy; Thomas sole exec.

CALLOWE, CALLOWAY,
Oliver, mariner, Watertown, propr., 1642. He sent money by James Carle from Newfoundland 15 (9) 1647, to Sarah, wife of Henry Messinger. [A.] He m. in Boston Feb. 25, 1655, Judith Clocke, widow. She, as his widow, made will 7 April, 1681, prob. Aug. 14, 1684. Beq. to John Kneland, Sen., Ebenezer English, Jacob Gully; to Marah Hauckins and her five daus. named.

CANDALL,
Edward, Salem. The inv. of his est. was taken 15 Nov. 1646, by Wm. Ager and Peter Palfrey.

CAMPION, CHAMPION,
Thomas, of Ashford, Eng., came in the Hercules in March, 1634.

Clement, [what relation to Thomas?] res. at Strawberry Bank, (Portsmouth) he sold dwell-house and lands in Charlestown to Nicholas Davison April 13, 1647.

CANNON,
John, Plymouth, came in the Fortune in 1621.

CANTERBURY, CANTLEBURY, CANTILBURY,
William, Salem, propr. 1638; had a fishing lot. [Es. Files.] Daus. Rebecca, who deposed in 1658, ae. about 20 years, (m. Benjamin Woodrow,) and Ruth, (m. 1, Thomas Small, 2, William Sibley, of whose est. she was exec. 1691).

He d. 1 (4) 1663. Will prob. 3 (5) 1663. Wife Beatrice, son John, daus. Ruth and Rebecca, and the latter's children, Joseph and Mary. Division made 29 July, 1684, after the death of the widow.

Cornelius, cooper, Hingham, sold land in Hingham 3 (3) 1649; town officer, 1672. Wife Anna; ch. John bapt. July 7, 1652, Anna bapt. May 8, 1653, (m. July, 1679, Peter Barnes,) Mary bapt. Oct. 8, 1654, Cornelius bapt. Jan. 11, 1656, Elizabeth, Martha b. Oct. 7, 1665, Hannah b. June 29, 1669, (m. Stephen Stodder,) Hester b. Nov. 19, 1671, (m. Jan. 15, 1695, John Tower). Wife Anna d. 20 Dec., 1710.

His daus. Ann Barns, Mary, Elizabeth, Sarah, Hannah and Hester C. petitioned Jan. 29, 1683, for the division of his estate, as he was unable to make a will in his last sickness, and agreed that their mother should have one seventh of the estate and 20 s. a year from each of them. Stephen Stoddard, wheelwright, admin., rendered account after the widow's death.

CAPEN, CAPIN, GAPES,
Bernard, b. in Eng. in the year 1552, m. on Monday in Whitsun week, 1596, Joan, dau. of Oliver Purchase, ("Purchis"). Ch. b. in Eng.: Ruth b. 7 Aug., 1600, Susanna b. 11 April, 1602, d. 30 Nov., 1666, [believed by Stiles and others to have m. 1, Wm. Rockwell, and 2, Matthew Grant. Some discrepancy in dates.] John b. 26 Jan., 1612; (He came to this country with his parents, m.

CAPEN, etc., cont.
1, Redegon, dau. of Nicholas Clap of Venn Ottery, Oct. 20, 1637, m. 2, 20 Sept., 1647, Mary, dau. of Samuel Bass of Braintree). The family came from Dorchester, Eng., about Feb. 26, 1632. [See quotation from the diary of Wm. Whitway in Dorch. Pope Family, p. 13.] [See old family record in Reg. II, 80.] Settled at Dorchester; propr., 5 Aug., 1633, frm. May 25, 1636.

He d. 8 Nov., 1638, ae. 76. Will dated Oct. 9, 1638, prob. 19 Nov. 1652. Beq. to wife and son John. Makes his "brother dyer" one of the overseers of the estate. George Dyer deposed. The widow Joanna d. 26 March, 1653, ae. 75 yrs. [See Upsall.]

CARDER, KARDER,
Richard, Boston, frm. May 25, 1636-7. Was disarmed and banished with Hutchinson adherents. One of the subscribers to the constitution of Providence Plantation who bought lands of the Indians in March, 1637-8. Brought from R. I. to Boston in 1643 with Gorton et als; tried for alleged heresy and confined at Roxbury. [W.]

CAREW,
John, Plymouth, land gr. 2 Oct., 1637. Allowed to be for himself and to take Edmund Weston as a partner 7 Oct., 1639. He m. in June, 1644, Elizabeth ——.

CARLETON,
Mr. Edward, Rowley, propr., frm. May 18, 1642. Deputy, 1643-4. Wife Ellen; ch. Edward b. 28 (8) 1639, Mary b. 2 (4) 1642, John, (who gave deed of land in 1661 which his father had previously sold). He left some est. in N. E. when he went out of the country, part of which his son John obtained; Christopher and Hannah Babbage and Jeremiah and Nehemiah Jewett rec'd power of admin. on behalf of the ch. of Hannah, Mr. C.'s widow 29 (9) 1678. [Essex Court.]

CARMAN,
John, came to Plymouth in the Fortune in 1623; conveyed land with Wm. Tench before 1630.

John, Roxbury, "came to New England in the year 1631." [E.] Wife Florence.

John, Saugus, propr. at Sandwich 3 April, 1637. Com. on division of lands 1640.

CARLEY, see Kerley.

CARPENTER,
Gilbert, petitioned the Gen. Court 13 Nov. 1644, concerning the Dartmouth ship.

Mrs. Margaret, widow, Dedham, rec'd to chh. 29 (10) 1650.

Thomas, carpenter, Amesbury, Eng., came in the James April 5, 1635.

Thomazin, ae. 35, came in the Susan and Ellen in April, 1635.

William, carpenter, came in the Bevis in May, 1638. Settled at Weymouth. With him came his son William, William's wife Abigail, and 4 of their ch. under 10 yrs. of age. Settled at Rehoboth. Bought lands of Indians 30 (11) 1641. He was adm. frm. May 13, 1640. Constable, 1640; deputy, 1641. [Reg. IX, 52.] Ch. Hannah b. 3 (2) 1640, Abiah and Abraham b. 9 (2) 1643.

Will dated 10 (10) 1658, prob. 21 April, 1659, beq. to sons John, William, Joseph, Abiah and Samuel; daus. Hannah and Abigail; son John Titus. Wife exec. Large estate; many books. Widow Abigail's est. admin. 7 Sept. 1687, by son William.

CARR,
George, shipwright, Ipswich, propr. 1635; rem. to Salisbury; ferryman in 1641 at the island where he dwelleth, by permission of the court at Ipswich. Released his apprentice Thomas Coccrey about May, 1641. [L.] He and his sons carried on a large business in shipping, mills, etc. He m. Elizabeth ——; James Oliver of Boston was his bro.-in-law. Ch. Elizabeth, ae. about 6 years, bapt. at Boston 8 (7) 1650, (m. May 1, 1662, Mr. John Woodmansey,) George b. April 15, 1644, Richard and William b. March 15, 1646, James b. April 28, 1650, Mary b. Feb. 24, 1651, (m. James Bailey,) Sarah b. Dec. 17, 1654, (m. Thomas Baker,) John b. Nov. 14, 1656.

He d. April 4, 1682. Adjustment of his est. was made Sept. folg. Numerous papers on file, with accounts of the business. William C., James Bayley, Thomas Baker and Thomas Putnam petitioned. The widow d. May 6, 1691. Will prob. June 30 folg. Mentions sons George, William, John, Richard and James; daus. Mary Bayley, Sarah Baker and Anna Putnam; gr. ch. James Woodmansye.

CARR, cont.
Richard, ae. 29, came in the Abigail in July, 1635. Settled at Salisbury. Elizabeth, widow of George, calls him brother of her husband in 1682.

Robert, tailor, ae. 21, with Caleb, ae. 11, came in the Elizabeth and Ann in May, 1635.

CARRINGTON, see Cordington,
Edward, turner, Charlestown, 1633. Frm. May 25, 1636. Rem. to Malden. Deposed 24 Sept. 1653, ae. about 40. [Mdx. Files.] Ch. Elizabeth b. 11 (1) 1639, (m. Stephen Paine,) Mary, (m. Phinehas Sprague,) Sarah b. 9 (7) 1643. His wife Elizabeth, ae. 40 in 1658, d. 9 (7) 1684. [Second] wife Mary d. 9 (7) 1684. [Mdx. Rec.]

He d. 15 (7) 1684; beq. all to dau. Elizabeth Paine, her husband and her ch. Edward, and to gr. dau. Mary Sprague.

Thomas, embarked June 22, 1632.

CARSLEY, CASELEY,
John, Barnstable, in court with his wife Alis, 1 March, 1641.

William, planter, Hingham, propr. 17 July, 1637; rem. to Barnstable; frm. Nov. 2, 1637; constable, 1639. In court 7 Dec. 1641. He m. at Sandwich about Nov. 28, 1643, "Mrs. Matthews syster of Yarmouth." Atba. 1643. Ch. b. and d. May 7, 1641, 2 ch. b. and d. in 1649.

His widow Sarah admin. on his estate Jan. 26, 1693-4.

CARTER,
Joseph, son of —— and Elizabeth Carter, step-son of Francis Kirby, skinner, of London, came 11 April, 1639, with letter of introduction to Gov. John Winthrop. Bought land at Newbury in 1640. Ret. to Eng. [Reg. XXXV, 373.]

Joshua, Dorchester, frm. May 14, 1634, sold house and lands Sept. 15, 1637, and rem. to Windsor, Conn. [Reg. IX, 301.] Rem. to Deerfield. Admin. gr. to widow Mary March 27, 1677.

Martha, ae. 27, came in the Hopewell April, 1635.

Richard, carpenter, Boston, contracted to cut wood in Nov., 1639. [L.] Wife Anne

CARTER, cont.
had deed from her kinsman, John Gosmer, June 5, 1658. Ch. Mary b. 3 (5) 1641, brought suit in Gen. Court 22 May, 1651, against Mr. Charles Sanders for carrying his wife to Eng. without his consent. Sold house and land July 23, 1654.

Robert, servant of William Mullens, came in the Mayflower to Plymouth; d. soon after arrival.

Thomas, blacksmith, Charlestown, adm. chh. 8 (11) 1636, frm. March 9, 1636-7. Constable, 1640. [Wife] Hannah adm. chh. 2 (7) 1639; [second] wife Mary adm. chh. 4 (9) 1643; ch. Anna, b. 10 (1) bapt. 22 (1) 1640, (m. William Green,) Elizabeth b. 22 (2) 1642, bur. 12 (5) 1644. Son John deposed 4 (2) 1660, ae. about 40 years; refers to bro. Wm. Green; Joseph, currier, propr. 1646, Samuel and Thomas petition 18 (8) 1659, about the est. of their bro. W. G. [Mdx. Files.]

He made will 5 (3), inv. taken 25 (4) 1652; beq. to wife Mary; eldest son Thomas; other sons Samuel, Joseph and John; daus. Mary Brinsmead and Hannah Greene; gr. ch. [Caleb] and Joseph C., John G. and John B. Inv. mentions the shop, tools, iron and steel, etc. Samuel, shoemaker, referred in 1672, to land he had deeded to his honored father, T. C. of Char. before his death, some years past. The son Thomas, attorney for his bro. Matthew Williams, sold land at Marblehead 9 (10) 1662.

Thomas, servant of George Giddings, came in the Planter in 1635. Settled at Salisbury; planter; propr. 1639. Wife Mary; ch. Mary b. Oct. 6, 1641, (m. Joseph Lancaster,) Martha b. Feb. 1645, Martha b. March, 1647, Elizabeth b. April, 1649, John b. May 18, 1650, Abigail b. Feb. 1652, (m. Stephen Flanders,) Samuel b. Oct. 25, 1656, Sarah, (m. John Davis).

His will dated Oct. 30, prob. Nov. 14, 1676, beq. to wife and to ch. John, Samuel, Mary, Martha, Elizabeth, Abigail and Sarah. [See Reg. XXXVI, 319.]

Rev. Thomas, b. about 1608, as he deposed 17 (10) 1662, came first to Dedham, where he was propr. 25 (2) 1637. Rem. to Watertown; frm. May 21, 1638. Became the first minister of the church of Woburn, ordained Nov. 22, 1642. [W.] Sold land in Cambridge 18 (6) 1643. Was a much honored pastor, doing much to shape the character of the growing town. Wife Mary; ch. Samuel b. 8 (6) 1640, Judith b. 15 (1) 1642, Theophilus b. 12 (4) 1645, d. 19 (12) 1649, Mary b. 13 (3) 1648, [Mdx. Files.] Thomas, Timothy. He deeded lands to his children before his death; referred to this in nunc. will, prob. Sept. 4, 1684. Beq. library to his eldest son Samuel; rest to be divided between his three sons and his dau. Mary after the death of his wife.

He d. Sept. 5, 1684, "ae. 74." The sons Samuel, Thomas, and Timothy and their mother signed an agreement to abide by the will. The children of my brother Thomas Carter, who is now in New England, are mentioned in the will of James Carter of Hinderclay, Suffolk, Eng. 8 Sept. 1655. [Reg. XXXVI, 319.]

CARTHWICK, CARTRICK,
Michael, carpenter, Ipswich, propr. 1635; recd. pay for work at the bridge and for carriage for the gun in 1642. Constable in 1646.

Will dated 16 (11) 1646, prob. 1647, beq. all to the care of his wife till son John is 21 years of age and dau. Mildred is 22 years old or married, when they shall receive their portions.

CARTWRIGHT,
Bethia, Salem, made will May 2, prob. May, 1640; beq. to sister Elizabeth Capon in Walderswick, Sussex, Eng., Mary, wife of George Newton of Salem, John Jackson, Jr. of Exeter, Margaret, wife of John J. of Sal., Elizabeth Pellem and Elizabeth Nickson.

CARVER,
Mr. John, a worthy pioneer, a capable, self-sacrificing man; a native of England; he emigrated to Leyden, Holland. One of the deacons of the Pilgrim Church, sent to Eng. in 1617 to negotiate for an American home for the Colony; came in the Mayflower; signed the Compact in Cape Cod Bay Nov. 11, 1620; after the signing he was chosen the first governor of Plymouth Colony; served with ability, but d. of sun-stroke in April, 1621. His wife Katharine who came with him d. in June, 1621. No ch. mentioned in Plymouth documents. His man Roger White and a little boy, Jasper More, appren-

CARVER, cont.
ticed to him, d. in the winter of 1620-1. His other man-servant, John Howland, and a boy, Wm. Latham, who came with him, lived here; [see their names.]

Richard, husbandman, ae. 60, of Skratby, Eng., with wife Grace, ae. 40, ch. Elizabeth and Susanna, twins ae. 18, and servants Isaac Hart, ae. 22, Thomas Flege, ae. 21, Marable, (Mabel) Underwood, ae. 20, passed exam. to go to N. E. April 11, 1637. Settled at Watertown; yeoman.

Will dated 18 Dec., 1638, prob. 9 (7) 1641. Beq. to wife Grace and daus. Elizabeth and Susanna. [Reg. II, 262.]

Robert, planter, Marshfield, propr. 3 Sept., 1638, atba. 1643; frm. 7 June, 1648. Juryman, town officer.

He was bur. in April, 1680, "being 86 years old."

CARY,
James, draper, merchant, Charlestown, adm. chh. 3 (3) 1647. Clerk of writs 1650. He gave bond for the delivery of sugar Dec. 21, 1652. His wife Eleanor was adm. chh. 30 (9) 1642. She d. Nov. 9, 1697, ae. 80.

He d. Nov. 2, 1681, ae. 81. Will prob. April 4, 1682; wife and 5 ch.; Mehetabel, (m. Wm. Welstead,) (John b. 29 (5) 1642, James b. and d. in 1644,) Nathaniel b. 7 (1) 1645, Jonathan b. 15 (11) 1646, Elizabeth b. 23 (7) 1648, and Joanna. [Wyman.]

Nicholas, Salem, 1636. In court, 1637.

CASE,
Edward, Taunton, frm. Dec. 4, 1638; deputy, 1640.

CASSELL, CASWELL, CASEWELL,
Thomas, Taunton, atba. 1643. Ch. Stephen b. Feb. 15, 1648, Thomas b. Feb. 22, 1650, Peter b. Oct., 1652, Mary b. Aug., 1654, John b. July, 1656, Sarah b. Nov., 1658, William b. Sept. 15, 1660, Samuel b. Jan. 26, 1662, Elizabeth b. Jan. 10, 1664, Abigail b. Oct. 27, 1666, Esther b. June 4, 1669.

Will dated 28 Sept. 1691, codicil 16 March, 1696-7, inv. taken 30 March, prob. 14 Sept. 1697, beq. to ch. Stephen, Thomas, Peter, John, William, Samuel, Mary, Sarah, Hannah, Elizabeth, Abigail and Hester. Daniel Ramsdell was husband of Hannah.

CASTELL, CASTEELE,
Mr. John, a creditor of Wm. Swift of Watertown, 1642.

Robert, Ipswich, served in Pequot war; town voted him land in 1639, if demanded within a year.

CATLIN, see Kirtland.

CHACKSELL, CHACKSWELL, CHECKSELL,
John, Lynn, witness in court in 1647 and 1650.

CHADBOURNE,
William, Boston, 1644. Wife Mary; ch. Mary b. (10) 1644.

CHADWELL,
Richard, shipwright, Saugus, 1636. [Col. Rec.] Witness, Salem court, 1637. Law suit in 1641. [L.] See Sampson, John. Rem. to Sandwich. Propr. 3 April, 1637. He m. July 22, 1649, Katharine Presberry of S.

He d. Nov. 27, 1661. Will dated 22 (9), prob. 27 (10) 1681, beq. to son-in-law Lodewick Hawkse and his cosen Thomas, son of Moses Chadwell.

Thomas, bro. of Richard, shipwright, Salem, 1636; of Lynn; propr. 1638. Rem. to Sandwich before 1645. Res. at Charlestown in 1670; ret. to Lynn. [See George Davis.] Abigail, wife of Thomas, of Charlestown, made will 8 June, prob. 19 June, 1683; beq. to her husband; to sister Ann Pearson of Piscatag; to gr. son Joseph Goose and his sister Susanna Crosse; to sister Wheeler's daus.; refers to Joseph Goose's agreement, dated July 28, 1682.

He d. 27 Feb. 1683. Will dated 25 Feb., inv. taken June 18, 1684, beq. to son Moses; to M.'s wife Sarah and son Thomas; to dau. Ruth Needham.

CHADWICK,
Charles, Watertown, frm. May 18, 1631. Town officer, deputy.

He d. April 10, 1682, ae. 86. Will dated June 30, 1681, beq. to wife Elizabeth, (who d. Feb. 22, 1684,) kinsmen Thomas and John Chadwick; to the eldest son of Thomas, and to Charles, eldest son of John. Jere. Norcross mentions "bro. Charles Chadwick."

CHADWICK, cont.

John, Sen., Malden. Ch. Elizabeth b. April 1, 1648, John d. March 17, 1650, Sarah b. June 1, 1650, James b. April 15, 1653. His will dated 1 (10) 1680, prob. April 5, 1681, devised to sons John, James and Samuel and dau. Hannah; 3 daus. that are already married.

CHAFFIN, CHAFFEY, CHAFFE,

Matthew, ship-carpenter, Boston. Adm. chh. 7 (6) 1636. His wife Sarah adm. chh. 21 (12) 1640. They were dism. to (place not stated,) 10 (6) 1655. [Rem. to Newbury?]

Thomas, one of those the Gen. Court recognized as first planters of Hull, May 20, 1642. Propr. 1657. Rem. to Swansey. He made his will 25 July, 1680, being of great age; beq. to sons Nathaniel and Joseph. Inv. taken 15 May, 1683.

CHAIRYE,

John, his wife before Gen. Court 4 June, 1639.

CHALLIS, CHALICE,

Philip, planter, Ipswich ,propr. 1636. Lieut. Rem. to Salisbury. Propr. 1639. Was appointed by the Gen. Court to look after saltpetre breeding 27 Sept. 1642. He deposed in 1669, ae. about 52 years. Was referred to by his wife and others as Philip Watson Challis in some cases. He m. Mary, dau. of William Sargent; ch. Elizabeth, (m. 1, John Hoyt, 2, John Blaisdell,) John b. July 9, 1653, John b. June 26, 1655, William d. Dec. 19, 1657, Philip Watson b. Dec. 19, 1658, William b. May 28, 1663, Lydia b. May 31, 1665, (m. John Chase,) Mary b. Aug. 27, 1668, (m. Joseph Dow,) Hannah b. Sept. 20, 1675. He d. at Amesbury about 1681. Inv. presented April 22, 1691. The widow d. Sept. 27, 1716.

CHAMBERLAIN, CHAMBERLAYNE, CHAMBERLIN,

Abigail, bapt. at Dorchester 31 (1) 1644, her father being a memb. of the chh. of Concord but at present sojourning in D.

Edmund, Woburn. Rem. to Chelmsford before 1656, when he sold land at Billerica. Ch. Sarah b. Dec. 18, 1649, a dau. b. March 11, 1651-2.

Edward, Roxbury, m. Jan. 4, 1646, Mary Turner.

CHAMBERLAIN, etc., cont.

Elizabeth, adm. chh. Charlestown 29 (3) 1642.

Henry, shoemaker, from Hingham, Eng., came in 1638 with his wife, his mother and 2 ch. to Hingham. Propr., 1638, frm. March 13, 1638-9. Propr. at Hull in 1657. Mrs. C. joined the chh. at Barnstable Oct. 6, 1644. Mrs. C. widow, sister of Mr. Israel Stoughton, rec'd from Gen. Court a portion of Mr. Andrew's gift 14 May, 1645. Widow Christian C. d. 19 April, 1659, ae. 81 years.

Henry, blacksmith, Hingham, sold, Feb. 4, 1660, land gr. him by the town. Either he or his son Henry was town officer in Hull in 1670; son William town officer in 1669.

He d. in 1674. Will dated Nov. 8, 1673, prob. 29 July, 1674. Beq. to wife Jane, sons Henry and William, daus. Susan Carter, Ursley Cole, and Faith Patterson; gr. ch. John C. See Shelley, Sarah.

Richard, Braintree; ch. Richard b. and d. 1642. May be the same as

Richard, Sudbury, who made will Feb. 12 ,1672, prob. 18 (4) 1673; beq. to wife what she brought at marriage, etc.; eldest son Benjamin; daus. Rebecca, Mehitabel, Elizabeth Daniel, Mary Graives; son Joseph and gr. son John Graives.

Thomas, Woburn, taxed 1645; frm. May 29, 1644. Rem. to Chelmsford. Ch. Samuel b. Oct. 7, 1647, Mary b. Jan. 30, 1649. Hs m. at Chelmsford, Aug. 10, 1666, Sarah Proctor. He m. April 16, 1674, Mary, widow of John Poulter and of Sergt. John Parker. She d. Feb. 8, 1692-3, ae. 88. Her son John Poulter d. May 20, 1676; inv. mentions debts owing his mother Chamberlin and Mr. Samuel Whiting.

William, Woburn, taxed in 1648. Rem. to Billerica in 1654. Ch. Timothy b. Aug. 13, 1649, Isaac b. Oct. 1, 1650, John, [parent not stated,] d. March 3, 1652, Sarah b. May 20, 1655, (m. John Shed,) Jacob b. Jan. 18, 1657, Thomas b. Feb. 20, 1659, Edmond b. July 15, 1660, [1661?] Rebecca b. Feb. 25, 1662, (m. Thomas Stearns,) Abraham b. Jan. 6, 1664, Ann b. March 3, 1665-6, Clement b. May 30, 1669, Daniel b. Sept. 27, 1671. [See Shelley, Sarah.]

He d. May 31, 1706, ae. about 86.

CHALPIN, see Chapin.

CHAMBERS,
Amy, Boston, memb. chh., 1631.

Elizabeth, Boston, maid servant to Wm. Baulstone, adm. chh. 3 (6) 1634.

Robert, ae. 13, came in the Hopewell, 1635. Settled at Marshfield; atba. 1643. Servant of Mr. Edward Winslow; propr. 1644. Rem. and died; partnership acct. in Court 7 Aug., 1655.

Thomas, planter, Scituate, 1638, frm. 3 Dec., 1639; atba. 1643. Juror, town officer, deputy. Widow Richarden C. of Scl. made will 18 Nov. 1672, prob. June, 1673. Beq. to Abigail, wife of her son Thomas Curtice, and to Elizabeth his dau.; confirmed to her son John Curtice the bequest made by her husband, of the house and land after her death.

CHAMPNEY, CHAMPNIS,
John, Cambridge, propr., 1635. Wife Joanna; ch. Mary, (m. —— Richardson, living at Woburn in 1658;) Sarah, John, (d. Feb. 20, 1664;) all bapt in Camb. The widow m. 2, Golden Moore. [Mi.]

He d. about 1 (2) 1650, when permission was gr. for the sale of his house and land for the benefit of his widow, the wife of Golden Moore, and his children.

Mr. Richard, Cambridge, propr. 1635, frm. May 25, 1636. Ruling elder. Wife Jane. [Mi.] Ch. Esther, "living at Woburn in 1658; bapt. in England, aged about 6 years when her father joined here." [Mi.] Mary b. (8) 1633, Samuel b. (7) 1635, Sarah b. (3) 1638, Mary b. (9) 1639, John b. 28 (3) 1641, Lydia, Daniel b. 9 (1) 1644.

He d. Nov. 26, 1669. Will dated 30 June, prob. 21 Dec. 1669, beq. to wife Jane what she brought at marriage, etc.; to daus. Esther Converse, Mary French and Lydia C.; to sons Samuel and Daniel; to Josiah Converse; to Harvard College 40 acres of land; to Daniel Gookin, Jr., and Nathaniel Mitchell.

CHANDLER, CHAUNDLER,
Edmund, Plymouth, creditor of Godbert Godbertson, frm. 1633; res. at Duxbury 1636-7; constable; appraiser of est. of Wm. Thomas.

CHANDLER, etc., cont.
Will dated May 3, prob. 4 June, 1662, being old. Beq. to children Samuel, Benjamin, Joseph, Sarah, Ann, Mary and Ruth.

John, shoemaker, Boston, frm. May 13, 1640. He apprenticed his son John to William Webb, baker, of Roxbury, 28 (11) 1640-1. [L.] This son was bur. in R. Dec. 13, 1660. One of the com. app. by the Gen. Court 1 Oct. 1645, to lay out lots at Concord. Petitioner for the Nashaway plantation in 1645. Adm. inhabitant of Boston in 1647. Ch. Hannah b. at Concord 28 (12) 1640-1.

Nathaniel, Duxbury, atba. 1643. Served against the Narragansetts in 1645.

Roger, Duxbury, taxed in 1632; frm. 1633. Sold land in 1644. His dau. was in the service of Kenelm Winslow before May 5, 1646.

Samuel, Duxbury, taxed in 1632; in Court Oct. 2, 1637; atba. 1643. He m. at Dorchester, 21 (10) 1644, widow Sarah Davis. Inv. of his est. taken at Dux. 17 (9) 1683.

William, householder, Roxbury, propr., frm. May 13, 1640.

He was bur. 26 (11) 1641. His widow Annis m. 2, July 2, 1643, John Dane, and 3, John Parmenter. The Gen. Court gave Dane the house and land 17 Oct., 1642, for his payments on behalf of the wife and children. Ch. Thomas, William, Hannah, (m. George Abbot,) and Sarah, (m. William Cleaves,) were mentioned in the will of their mother. [See Parmenter.] Thomas deposed at Ipswich, March 29, 1692, ae. 64 years; William at same time, ae. 56 years.

CHAPFILL,
John, collier, Lynn, gave letter of attorney 4 (8) 1647, to his wife True C. of Bromley in Kent, to ask of John Waters, tailor ,of Chittington, Kent, an annuity of 3 li. passed due by deed of gift of said True to the ch. of her former husband, etc. [A.]

CHAPIN, CHAPUN, CHAPINNE, CHALPIN,
David, Springfield, frm. April 5, 1649. Adm. inhab. of Boston in 1658. He m. 29 (6) 1654, Lydia Crump. Ch. Lydia b. 19 (4) 1655, Caleb b. 2 (2) 1657, Sarah b. at Bo. 3 March, bapt. 6 (1) 1659, Hannah b. Oct. 23,

CHAPIN, etc., cont.
1661, Ebenezer bapt. April 3, 1664, Jonathan b. Feb. 12, 1665, Union b. Dec. 26, 1669, Ruth bapt. 8 (10) 1672, (m. Jan. 26, 1698, Wm. Twing).

Samuel, Springfield, frm. June 2, 1641; town officer, 1643; deacon, 1649; employed to conduct service part of the time, 1656-7, when there was no minister in town. Commissioner, 1651 and 1660. Ch. Japhet, Josiah, Catharine, ——, (m. —— Gilbert,) Hannah b. 2 (10) 1644, (m. Sept. 27, 1666, John Hitchcock,) Henry d. April 29, 1668, Henry, Sarah, (m. 14 (2) 1647, Rowland Thomas). He d. 11 Nov. 1675. Will dated 4 (1) 1674, prob. 24 March, 1676, beq. to wife, son Henry and gr. son Thomas Gilbert. Son Japhet C. with his wife Abilene, deposed. The widow Cicely d. Feb. 8, 1682; beq. to sons Henry C. of Spr. and Josiah C. of Braintree; daus. Catharine, wife of Samuel Marshfield, Sarah Thomas and Hannah Hitchcock; to Henry Gilbert, apprentice to John Hitchcock. Son Japhet C. exec.

CHAPLAIN, CHAPLAINE, CHAPLIN,
Rev. Clement, ae. 48, came in the Elizabeth and Ann in April, 1635. Settled at Cambridge; propr. and selectman Nov. 23, 1635; frm. March 3, 1635-6. Deputy 1636. Rem. to Wethersfield, Conn., and sold house and lands in C. 30 (7) 1645. Ret. to Thetford, co. Norfolk, Eng., and there d. in 1656. Will beq. to bro. Thomas C. of Bury St. Edmunds; mentioned kinsman Wm. Clarke of Roxbury, N. E. [Reg. XXXI, 413, and XXXVIII, 71.]

Mr. Hugh, Rowley, propr., frm. May 18, 1642. Wife Elizabeth; ch. John b. 26 (6) 1643, Joseph b. 11 (12) 1646, Thomas b. 2 (7) 1648, Jonathan b. 10 (10) 1651.

He was bur. 21 (1) 1653. Will dated 15 (1) 1654, prob. March 31, 1657; wife Elizabeth; eldest son John; three children mentioned in inventory. The widow Elizabeth m. 9 Dec. 1656, Nicholas Jackson.

CHAPMAN,
Edward, miller, Ipswich, propr. 1643. He m. Dorothy, dau. of Mark Symonds. Gave house and land to son John 1 Sept.

CHAPMAN, cont.
1677; had son Nathaniel who m. a dau. of Andrew Peters; testified 30 April, 1678. Will dated 9, prob. 30 April, 1678, beq. to wife Dorothy, as per mar. contract; to sons Symon, Nathaniel and Samuel; dau. Mary, wife of John Barry.

Florence, widow, adm. chh. Boston from chh. of Braintree 4 (8) 1645.

Henry, servant of Mr. Kean at Salem in 1641. [Es. Court Files.] Before Gen. Court for not obeying a press 2 (4) 1640.

Jacob, Boston, brought suit in Es. court in 1636. Propr. 1642.

John, Ipswich. Sold lumber Nov. 5, 1633. [Col. Rec.] Frm. May 14, 1634.
Inv. of his est. taken 1 March, 1677-8; admin. gr. to widow Deborah.

Ralph, ae. 20, cert. from St. Savior's, Southwark, Eng., came in the Elizabeth in April, 1635. Settled at Duxbury; bought land 8 Oct., 1639. Partner in ferry at Marshfield 11 Jan., 1641. Propr. 1644. He m. Nov. 23, 1642, Lydia Wills; ch. Mary b. 31 Oct. 1643, Sarah b. May 15, 1645, Isaac b. Aug. 4, 1647, dau. b. Oct. 5, 1649, son b. 1651. Sarah, John and Ralph bapt. Sept. 27, 1657. Will, dated Nov. 28, 1671, prob. June 4, 1672, beq. to dau. Sarah and her husband Wm. Norcut, or Norkett; to younger son Ralph; to ch. Isaac, John and Mary. Testimony that his hands were so swelled that he could not sign the will. [Reg. VII, 236.]

Robert, Marshfield, atba. 1643.

William, Hingham.
Old Chapman d. Nov. 1639. Will dated 16 Oct. 1639, prob. April 24, 1671. Beq. to dau. Elizabeth, wife of Thomas Huett, and her son Ephraim; to his son John Chapman, then in England.

CHAPPELL,
George, ae. 20, came in the Christian March 16, 1634.

Marie, Boston, servant to Mr. John Cotton, adm. chh. 31 (1) 1639.

Mary, widow, adm. chh. 4 (8) 1645.

Nathaniel, Boston, servant to Atherton Haulgh, adm. chh. 2 (8) 1634, frm. May 22, 1639.

CHARLES,
John, Charlestown, propr. 1636. Rem. to New Haven.

William, Salem, Marblehead, taxed in 1637. Wife Sarah adm. chh. 6 (4) 1647. He sealed the meeting house in 1656-7.
Will dated 31 Dec. 1672, prob. 27 (4) 1673; wife Sarah; cousins Robert C. and Mary, present wife of James Dennis. The widow's nunc. will prob. 29 (4) 1677, beq. to sister Tryphena Geer, and her ch. Tryphena, John and Sarah Fairfield; to Robert Charles' 2 daus. a legacy when he comes over for it; to goodmen Goldsmith and Haggett; to Mary, wife of James Dennis and her ch. James, Mary, Amos and Agnes.

CHARLETT, CHELLET,
Nicholas, Boston, servant to John Mylam, adm. chh. 10 (2) 1642. Frm. May, 1645. Wife Catharine adm. chh. 4 (8) 1645; ch. Elizabeth b. and d. 1645, Mary bapt. 3 (8) 1647, ae. about 5 days.
He d. and the widow m. Richard Haughton. She had permission from Gen. Court 14 Oct. 1651, to sell the house which N. C. had owned, and admin. on the est. for the benefit of her 2 children. [Arch. 15 B.]

CHARILBY,
Anthony, Boston, memb. chh. 1630-1.

CHASE, CHASSE, see Shaw,
Aquila, mariner, Hampton, 1640; rem. to Newbury; propr. 1646. He deposed in 1666, ae. about 48 years. Wife Anne; ch. Sarah, (m. C. Annis,) Anne b. 6 July, 1647, (m. Thomas Barber,) Priscilla b. 14 March, 1648, (m. Abel Merrill,) Mary b. 3 Feb. 1650, (m. John Stevens,) Aquila b. 27 Sept. 1652, Thomas b. 25 July, 1654, John b. 2 Nov. 1655, Elizabeth b. 13 Sept. 1657 ,Ruth b. 18 March, 1660, d. 30 May, 1676, Daniel b. 9 Dec. 1661, Moses b. 24 Dec. 1663.
He d. Dec. 27, 1670. The widow m. June 14, 1672, Daniel Mussiloway; she d. April 21, 1687.

William, planter, Roxbury, came with the first company, 1630, and went with a co. who made a new plantation at Yarmouth. [E.] Appl. frm. Oct. 19, 1630. Town officer. Served against the Narragansetts in 1645. Mary, dau. of goodman Chase the elder bur. at Barnstable Oct. 28, 1652.
Will, dated May 4, 1659, being aged; prob.

CHASE, etc., cont.
13 May. Beq. to wife Mary and 2 sons, Benjamin and William. [Reg. V, 388.]

CHAUKLEY, CHALKLEY,
Robert, weaver, from Spitalfields, London, Charlestown, 1645; town officer. Rem. to Woburn; taxed 1645; frm. May 26, 1647. He was ae. 55 in 1663; he d. Sept. 2, 1672. Will dated Charlestown, Aug. 27, 1672, prob. March 14, 1672-3; beq. to wife Elizabeth; to Henry Streeter and wife, to Nathaniel Smith of Haverhill, to John Whittemore, to the child Benoni, living in his family, to widow Mary Nash; residue to kinsman Robert C. in Eng. if he come for it within 3 yrs., or to his children; otherwise to "any brothers children of his that shall come for it. If no one come for it, this residue after the wife's death to go to the deacons of the poore of the Towne." The widow Elizabeth b. d. 13 (8) 1678.

CHAUNCEY, CHANSY,
Rev. Charles, "A great scholar and a godly man, procured from Eng. in 1639 by them of Plymouth." [W.] He was b. in Hartfordshire in 1589; studied at Westminster school; B. A. of Trinity college; became professor of Greek, preacher at Marston, afterward at Ware. Reproved for Puritanic teaching, he wrote a submission and afterward renounced it. Came to N. E., arriving a few days before Jan. 1, 1638. [C. M.] He acted as teacher of the chh. of Plymouth 3 yrs.; rem. to Scituate. Contended for immersion of infants in baptism. Brought into great controversy in both churches. [W.] Changed his views about 1654, and was elected president of Harvard College, where he rendered distinguished service. He and his wife adm. chh. of Cambridge (1) 1656. Wife Catharine, a dau. of Robert Eyre, Esq. [C. M.], d. Jan. 24, 1667. [Gr. St.] Ch. Barnabas, Sarah, both adm. chh. Camb. Dec. 10, 1658; Hannah, Nathaniel, Elnathan, Israel, these four bapt. at Sci. Other ch. Isaac and Ichabod. John Holmes, a student and servant to Mr. C., in full communion with the chh. of Camb., dismissed to the chh. of Duxbury. [Mi.]
He d. Feb. 19, 1671-2, ae. 82. [Gr. St.] [See wills of membs. of his family in Reg. XXXIX, 166.]

CHARWELL,
Thomas, a witness at Salem in 1641.

CHAUNER,
Margery, Boston, memb. chh. 1630-1.

CHEATER, CHATER, CHETER,
John, Newbury. Wife Alice; ch. Hannah b. 7 Aug. 1644, Lydia b. 12 Jan. 1647. [Es. Files.]

CHECKETT,
Josias, Scituate, took oath of allegiance 1 Feb., 1638. Constable, 1641-2.

CHECKLEY, CHEEKLEY, CHICKLEY,
John, merchant, suit in Es. court in 1640; res. at Boston, adm. chh. 4 (8) 1645, frm. May 10, 1648. An order drawn in his favor Sept. 8, 1640. [L.] He m. in Boston 5 (1) 1652, Ann, dau. of Mr. Simon Eires. Res. at Charlestown in 1664, at Bo. in 1670.

CHEESEBOROUGH,
William, blacksmith, Boston, with wife Anne adm. chh. 1630, juryman Nov. 9, 1630, frm. May 18, 1631. Dism. to Braintree 16 (12) 1639. Rem. to chh. of Rehoboth 1643, letters of dism. gr. 9 (2) 1648. Frm. Plym. Col. 2 May, 1648. Town officer 1634, deputy 1642. Ch. John bapt. 11 (9) 1632, Jabez bapt. 3 (3) 1635, Elisha bapt. 4 (4) 1637, Joseph b. 18 (5) 1640.

CHEESEHOLM, CHESHOLM, CHESSHAM, [CHISAM, CHISHOLM,]
Thomas, tailor, from Newcastle on Tyne, Eng., settled at Cambridge; frm. March 3, 1635-6. Inn-keeper 8 Sept., 1636. Deacon, steward of Harv. Coll.; town officer 1646. He deposed 2 (3) 1660, ae. about 56 years. [Mdx. Files.] Wife Isabel.
He d. Aug. 18, 1671. Will dated 17 Aug. prob. 4 (8) 1671, beq. to Elizabeth Sparhawk; to the children of Mrs. Witchfield, late of Windsor; to William Manning, Edmund Angier, Benoni Eaton and Mr. Urian Oakes' ch.

CHEEVER, CHEEVERS,
Bartholomew, shoemaker, Boston, frm. May 26, 1647; propr. Adm. chh. 31 (3) 1646. Will, dated Oct. 21, prob. Dec. 28, 1693,

CHEEVER, etc., cont.
beq. to wife Lydia, bro. Daniel, and his seven children, named; cousins Ezekiel C., schoolmaster, and Richard C. with his, son Bartholomew; to cousins Elizabeth Harwood, William and Samuel Barrett, Will. Twing, Benjamin Marsh; to Stephen Palmer that married bro. Daniel's dau. Elizabeth; to the ch. of cousin John Ballentine; to the poor of the old church. He left widow Lydia, sister of Wm. Barrett, but no ch. The widow's will was prob. March 14, 1701. [Reg. XXXVI, 305.]

Daniel, husbandman, Cambridge. He deposed 7 (2) 1664, ae. about 43 years. [Mdx. Files.] Wife Esther, (Hester) memb. chh. [Mi.] Ch. Mary b. 14 (12) 1645, Lydia b. 26 (9) 1647, James b. (rec. at Sudbury,) 7 Dec., 1649, John bapt. July 31, 1659, Esther b. and d. 1660, Israel bapt. Jan. 26, 1661, Hannah and Elizabeth b. and d. 1664, Elizabeth bapt. Aug. 6, 1665.
He d. March, 1703-4. Will, dated April 30, 1698, prob. June 21, 1704, refers to bro. Bartholomew C. of Boston, dec.; beq. to son Israel, James, daus. Lydia Luxford, Elizabeth Palmer and Hannah, wife of William Barrett, son-in-law Joseph Champney.

Ezekiel, the famous and worthy schoolmaster, b. in London Jan. 25, 1614-5. He res. at Boston in 1637; New Haven, 1638; Ipswich, 1650; Charlestown, Nov., 1661; Boston again Jan. 6, 1670. He petitioned Es. Court in 1675 respecting the est of Capt. Thomas Lowthrop, brother of his wife. He m. 1, in 1638, Mary ——; she d. at New Haven Jan. 20, 1649. He m. 2, Nov. 18, 1652, Ellen, sister of Capt. Thomas Lothrop of Beverly. She d. Sept. 10, 1706. Ch. Samuel, b. Sept. 22, 1639, Mary bapt. 29 (9) 1640, (m. Capt. Wm. Lewis,) Ezekiel bapt. 12 (4) 1642, Elizabeth bapt. 6 (2) 1645, (m. Samuel Goldthwaite, Sarah bapt. 21 (7) 1646, Hannah bapt. 25 (4) 1648, Abigail b. Oct. 20, 1653, Ezekiel b. July 1, 1655, Nathaniel b. June 23, 1657, Thomas b. Aug. 23, 1658, William b. and d. 1664, Susanna, (m. June 5, 1693, Joseph Russell).
He d. at Boston Aug. 21, 1708. [Reg. XXXIII, 164, and XXXVIII, 427, and XLI, 65.] His will dated 16 Feb. 1705-6. prob. 24 Aug. 1708, beq. to wife Ellen; to children Samuel, Mary, Elizabeth, Ezekiel, Thomas and Susanna; to grandson Ezekiel Russell.

CHENERY, CHINERY, GENERY, GINERY,
Lambert, Watertown; rem. to Dedham, 1636; frm. May, 1645. He deposed June 17, 1673, ae. 80 years. [Mdx. Files.] Wife — adm. chh. D. Dec. 4, 1640. He m. 2, 14 (3) 1658, Thomasine Hews; she d. Jan. 2, 1669. Ch. Isaac, John, Mary b. 24 (10) 1659.
He d. 30 (11) 1673-4. Will dated 17 (12) 1673, prob. 4 (12) 1674, beq. to sons John and Isaac, dau. Mary, son-in-law Richard Ellice, dau.-in-law Ruth Ellice, widow; to the church of Dedham.

CHENEY, CHEYNE, CHEYNEY, CHEANY, CHENY, CHANY, CHEINEY,
John, came into the land in the year 1635. He brought 4 children Mary, Martha, John, Daniel. Sarah, his 5th ch. was b. in the last mo. of the year, 1635, called February. He res. at Roxbury; he rem. from our church to Newbury the end of the next summer, 1636. Wife Martha. [E.] A prominent citizen of Newbury; town officer. Frm. May 17, 1637. He wrote his will 5 (4) 1666; (on file at Salem).

He d. July 28, 1666; his wife d. about 1684. Ch. Mary, (m. Sept. 3, 1645, Wm. Lawes,) Martha, (m. 1, Anthony Sadler, 2, Thomas Burkby,) John, Daniel, Sarah, (m. Dec. 23, 1652, Joseph Plumer,) Peter b. at Newbury, 1638, Lydia b. at N. 1640, (m. Nov. 12, 1657, John Kendricks,) Hannah b. Nov. 16, 1642, (m. Nov. 16, 1659, Richard Smith, Jr.,) Nathaniel b. at N. Jan. 12, 1644, Elizabeth b. at N. Jan. 12, 1647, (m. Stephen Cross).

William, planter, Roxbury, bought house and 40 acres of ground for 102 li. of Nicho. and Rich. Parker 18 (5) 1639, and a house and 61½ acres of Walter Blackbourne for 215 li. 30 (7) 1639, and contracted to keep 6 cows for him on shares. [L.] He was adm. chh. 5 (1) 1664-5, frm. May 23, 1666. Town officer; one of the feoffees of the Free School. Wife Margaret; ch. Ellen, (m. March 20, 1642-3, Humphrey Johnson,) Margaret (m., as his 2d wife and the mother of all his ch., Deacon Thomas Hastings,) Thomas, William, John b. Sept. 29, 1639, d. in 1671, Mehitabel b. June 1, 1643, (m. Thomas Wight, Jr.,) Joseph b. June 6, 1647.

He d. 2 (5) 1667 ,ae. 63 years. The widow m. 2, —— Burge, who d. before March,

CHENEY, cont.
1679-80. She rem. to Boston; made will Sept. 23, 1686, d. 2 or 3 (5) 1686. Genealogy.

CHERRALL,
William, baker, ae. 26, with Ursula, ae. 40, came in the Love in July, 1635.

CHESSON,
Roger, Ipswich, 1641.

CHESTER,
Leonard, Cambridge, propr. 1634; wife had grant of land which she sold in 1635. He rem. to Wethersfield, Conn. Wife Mary; ch. John b. Aug. 3, 1635; Dorcas b. Nov. 1, 1637, (m. at Salem, Nov. 12, 1656, Rev. Samuel Whiting, Jr.,) Stephen b. March 3, 1639, Mary b. Jan. 15, 1641, Prudence b. Feb. 16, 1643, (m. Thomas Russell,) Eunice b. June 15, 1645, (m. Richard Sprague,) Mercy b. Feb. 14, 1647; (see her will, prob. 21 (10) 1669, at Char.).

He d. Dec. 11, 1648. His widow m. Richard Russell, q. v.

CHICHESTER,
James, Taunton, atba. 1643. Rem. to Salem; adm. chh. 27 (2) 1651. Wife Mary, a witness in Es. court in 1645, adm. chh. Salem 14 (2) 1650; ch. John, James, Mary and Martha bapt. 21 (2) 1650, Sarah bapt. 4 (3) 1651, William bapt. 15 (3) 1653, Eliza bapt. 26 (1) 1654, Susanna bapt. 10 (3) 1657.

CHICKEN,
Joseph, ae. 16, servant to Robert Lovell, husbandman, came from Weymouth, Eng. before March 20, 1635.

CHICKERING, CHICKERIN, CHECKERY,
Francis, yeoman, Dedham, propr. 1638, frm. May 13, 1640. Memb. Court valuation com., ensign, selectman, deputy. Wife Amy or Ann adm. chh. 29 (10) 1640, d. 5 (10) 1649. He m. 11 (4) 1650, Sarah Sibble. Ch. Ann, (m. 3 (9) 1659, Stephen Paine,) Elizabeth b. 26 (7) 1638, d. 23 (5) 1642, Bethshua b. 23 (10) 1640, Easter b. 4 (9) 1643, John b. 19 (2) 1646, Mary b. 10 (2) 1648.

He d. 2 (8) 1658. Inv. presented by widow Sarah and Capt. Eleazer Lusher, Oct. 17, 1658. The Court allowed her 350 li., includ-

CHICKERING, etc., cont.
ing 150 li. contracted for at her marriage. [Reg. IX, 346.]

Henry, yeoman, Salem, propr. 1639; rem. to Dedham, adm. chh. with wife 29 (11) 1640; frm. June 2, 1641. Deputy, deacon. Was in the ship to go to Eng., and excused from service as deputy 27 (8) 1647.
He was bur. 22 (5) 1671, ae. 82 years. Will dated 23 (3) 1670, prob. 31 (6) 1671. Beq. to wife Ann; kinsman Nathaniel C., living with him; pastor John Allin; to the school and church of Dedham; to several individuals; to son, Mr. John Chickerin of Charlestown. See Mr. John Allin. Mary, Dedham, made over to John C., her cousin, son of Henry C. of D. in N. E., all her interest in a parcel of land belonging to the Manor of Benecar Hall in co. Suffolk, 20 (9) 1646. [A.]

CHIDLEY,
Mr. ——, before Boston Court 7 (7) 1641. [W.]

CHILD, CHILDE,
Ephraim, Watertown, frm. May 18, 1631. Town officer, deacon, deputy.
He d. 13 (12) 1662-3, ae. 70. Will dated Nov. 10, 1662, prob. April 2, 1663, beq. to Ephraim, son of Benjamin C.; to his cousin Wm. Bond, whom he app. co-exec. with his wife Elizabeth; to Richard and John C.; to Mary Rowles, wife of John Parker; to servant Davie; to Samuel Bush; beq. to her cousin William Bond, and made him exec. of her est.; beq. also to his wife and to Wm. junior, John, Thomas, Elizabeth and Sarah B.; to Ric. Child's wife and eldest and second son; to Ric. Beeres and wife and others.

Richard, Barnstable. Rem. to Yarmouth. He m. Oct. 15, 1648, Mary Linnell, or Linnett.

Robert, doctor, planter at Nashaway (Lancaster,) in 1644. One of those who petitioned for citizenship without church-membership in 1646; had a bro., Major of a regiment in Kent; a person of quality, and therefore not punished as severely as others for expressions and demeanor deemed disrespectful, but prosecuted repeatedly and confined sometime in his house (in Boston). [W.] A stockholder in the Iron Works Co.

CHILLINGWORTH, SHILLINGSWORTH,
Thomas, shoemaker, Sandwich, 1638, propr. 1640; rem. to Marshfield; frm. 5 June, 1644; town officer.
Admin. gr. to widow Joane March 1, 1652-3. [Reg. V, 259.] The widow m. Thomas Doged, and they secured to her 4 daus. their shares of the father's est. 7 March, 1653.

CHILSON,
Walsingham, Marblehead, a witness in 1647; owner of a swamp lot in 1649. With wife Mary he sold land in M. to Francis Johnson 13 July, 1655.

CHILTON,
James, came in the Mayflower; signed the Compact. Res. at Plymouth. Brought with him his wife Mary, who d. within a few months after arrival. He brought dau. Mary, who m. John Winslow. Another dau. came over afterward, that was married. [B.] He d. Dec. 6, 1620.

CHING, CHIN, CHYN,
George, Salem, Marblehead, taxed in 1638. Was appointed to receive money of John Lyon in 1638. [Court Files.] Witness in 1647.
Admin. of his est. gr. 6 (1) 1653, to widow, Elizabeth. [Es. Files X, 11.]

CHIPFIELD,
Edmund, ae. 20, came in the Hopewell in Sept. 1635.

CHIPMAN,
John, only son of Mr. Thomas Chipman of Brinspittal, Dorsetshire, Eng., b. about 1614, came to Plymouth 1630-1, in service of his cousin Richard Darby, whose father was custodian of certain money due him from the est. of his father. See his declaration and the deposition of Ann Hoskins in [Reg. IV, 23, and XXXV, 127.] He settled at Barnstable. He was adm. chh. Jan. 30, 1652; ruling elder, town officer, deputy. He m. Hope, dau. of John Howland, who was adm. chh. Aug. 7, 1650; she d. 8 Jan. 1683, ae. 54. [Gr. St.] Ch. Elizabeth b. June 24, 1647, Elizabeth bapt. Aug. 8, 1650, a ch. bur. Sept. 9, 1650, Hope bapt. Sept. 5, 1652, Lydia b. Dec. 25, 1654, John b. and d. 1656-7, Hannah b. Jan. 14, 1658, John, Samuel b. April 15, 1672.

CHITTENDEN, CHETTENDEN,
Thomas, ae. 51, with wife Rebecca, ae. 40, and ch. Isaac, ae. 10, and Henry, ae. 6, cert. by minister of Wapping, Eng, came in the Increase April, 1635. He settled at Scituate; linen-weaver. Took oath of allegiance 1 Feb. 1638. Will, dated Oct. 7, 1668, prob. June 4, 1669. Beq. all to sons Isaac and Henry. [Reg. VII, 178.]

CHITTWOOD,
Mary, ae. 24, cert. from St. Albons Herts, Eng., came in the Planter April 2, 1635.

CHOATE, CHOTE,
John, Ipswich, 1648; in court in 1650. Was living at Corporal Andrews' farm in 1658. Sergeant. He deposed in 1660, ae. about 30 years, in 1664, ae. about 40, and in 1683, ae. about 58. [Essex Files.] Wife Anne; ch. John b. June 15, 1661, Margaret, (m. Abraham Fitts,) Samuel, Mary b. Aug. 16, 1666, Thomas, Sarah, (m. John Burnham,) Joseph, Benjamin. He d. Dec. 4, 1695. Will dated 7 Dec. 1691; agreement made in place of the will 14 May, 1697. The widow d. Feb. 16, 1727, ae. upwards of 90. [Genealogy.]

CHOPPIN,
Philip, Marblehead, witness in court in 1639.

CHUBB,
Thomas, carpenter, Boston, freed from the service of Samuel Maverick, and engaged to Wm. Gaylord of Dorchester 3 May, 1631. [Col. Rec.] Rem. about 1636 to Salem. In court, 1639. Rem. to Beverly. His son William was apprenticed 25 April, 1672, to Zachery Herrick, carpenter. Sons Thomas, ae. 28, and John, ae. 24 or 5, deposed concerning William and their aged father and mother. [Es. Files.] He deposed in 1684, ae. about 75 years.

CHUBBUCK, CHUBBOCK, CHUBBEC,
Thomas, farmer, came with his wife in 1634 from Hingham, Eng. Settled at Charlestown. Wife Alice adm. chh. April 3, 1635. He rem. to Hingham; propr. Sept., 1635. Ch. Nathaniel bapt. 4 (3) 1635, Sarah bapt. Feb. 1637, (m. Sept. 25, 1657, Jeremiah Fitch,) John b. and d. 1639, Mary b. Oct. 13,

CHUBBUCK, etc., cont.
1642, (m. Feb. 18, 1663, Thomas Lincoln, Jr.,) Deborah b. July 6, 1645, d. March, 1650, John b. Dec. 30, 1648. Wife Alice d. 20 Feb. 1674-5.
He d. 9 Dec. 1676. Will prob. 27 Dec., 1676., beq. to children Nathaniel, John, Sarah, (wife of Jeremy Fitch,) Rebecca, (wife of William Hersey,) Mary, (wife of Thomas Lincoln).

CHURCH,
Garret, Watertown, contributed to the fort at Boston April 1, 1634; frm. May 2, 1649. He deposed 17 (10) 1662, ae. about 51 years. [Mdx. Files.] Wife Sarah; ch. John b. 10 (1) 1637-8, Samuel b. 12 (4) 1640, Sarah b. 10 (1) 1642, Mary b. 15 (3) 1644, Jonathan b. 13 (10) 1646, David b. 1 (7) 1657.

George, ae. 16, servant of Stephen Kent, came in the Confidence April 24, 1638. Before Boston Court 7 Sept., 1643, and sent to Ipswich.

Richard, carpenter, Boston, appl. frm. Oct. 19, 1630. Rem. to Weymouth, then to Plymouth before 1632. [B. in Reg. II, 243.] Volunteer for the Pequot War before 1637. Frm. 1633. Rem. to Charlestown. Bought one half of corn mill at Hingham Jan. 24, 1653, and rem. thither. Town officer. He deposed 15 (11) 1656, ae. about 47 years. [Mdx. Files.] He m. Elizabeth, dau. of Richard and Elizabeth Warren; she d. 4 March, 1670. Ch. Elizabeth, (m. Caleb Hobart,) Joseph, Benjamin, Caleb, Nathaniel, Hannah, Abigail b. June 22, 1647, (m. Dec. 19, 1666, Samuel Thaxter,) Charles, Richard, Sarah, (m. James Burross,) Mary d. 30 April, 1662, Deborah bapt. March 22, 1656, (m. John Irish, Jr.).
He d. at Dedham, (home of his son Caleb,) 26 Dec., 1668. His will, dated 25 Dec. 1668, gave lands in Hing., share in Iron Works at Taunton, etc., to wife Elizabeth; to son Joseph a double portion, on acct. of the lameness of his hand. [Reg. XIX, 163.]

CHURCHHILL, CHURCHALL, CHURCHWELL,
John, Plymouth, atba. 1643. Frm. 5 June, 1651. He m. 17 Dec., 1644, Hannah, dau. of Wm. Pontus; ch. Hannah b. Nov. 12, 1649, (m. John Rogers,) Eleazer b. April 20, 1652, Mary b. Aug. 1, 1654.
He d. Jan. 1, 1662. Nunc. will prob. May

CHURCHHILL, etc., cont.
3, 1662; sons Joseph, Eleazer, John, William to have estate, part now and the rest at his wife's death. Testimony of his kinswoman Abigail Clark, ae. 20 yrs. [Reg. VI, 94.] The widow, Hannah Churchill, Sen., m. 25 June, 1669, Giles Rickett. Her est. was distributed 17 March, 1691.

CHURCHMAN,
Hugh, Lynn. Presented in Essex Court in 1643, for living 7 or 8 yrs. without his wife.
Will, dated 4 (4) 1640, prob. 9 (5) 1644; to Wm. Winter, his son Josias Hale, and dau. Emma Hale; to Edward Burt.

John, embarked June 22, 1632.

CHUSMOR,
Richard, [Ipswich,] propr. 1637.

CHUTE, CHEWTE, SHUTE,
Lionell, b. at Dedham, Eng., 1580, son of Lionell C., clerk; came early to Ipswich; master of the Grammar School; frm. March 13, 1638-9. Bought house and land in 1639. Town officer. He m. Rose ——; ch. James bapt. in Dedham, Eng. Feb. 2, 1613-4, Mary bapt. do. Nov. 23, 1619.
Will dated 4 (7) 1644, prob. 7 (9) 1645, beq. to wife Rose and son James; to friend Joseph Mosse; to the poor of the chh. of Ips. Refers to dec. son Nathaniel.

CLAP, CLAPP,
Edward, son of William, of Salcombe Regis, Eng., came about 1633 to Dorchester where his bro. Roger had already settled. Propr., town officer, frm. Dec. 7, 1636; deacon. See Alderman. He m. 1, Prudence, dau. of Nicholas C. of Venn Ottery; he m. 2, Susanna, [perhaps dau. of Wm. Cockerell, q. v.] Ch. Elizabeth b. about 1634, [Gr. St.] (m. elder James Blake,) Prudence b. 29 (10) 1637, (m. at Dorch. in Feb. 1659-60, Simon Peck, [Hob.]) Ezra b. 22 (3) 1640, Nehemiah bapt. 10 (8) 1646, Susanna bapt. 10 (10) 1648, William bapt. 6 (5) 1651, Joseph bapt. 13 (6) 1654, Esther or Hester bapt. 3 (6) 1656, Abigail bapt. 1 (3), d. 8 (11) 1659, Joshua bapt. 12 (3) 1661, d. 22 (3) 1662, Jonathan b. and d. 1664.
He d. Jan. 8, 1664. Will prob. Feb. 17, 1664-5. Beq. to wife, sons Ezra and Nehemiah, daus. Susanna and Esther; portions of daus. to be equal with what they that are married have already received, that is £30 apiece. Inv. showed house and lands in Dorch. and Milton, 1-3 part of a house at Salem, etc. The widow Susanna d. June 16, 1668.

John, Dorchester, frm. 26 May, 1647. He d. July 24, 1655. Will prob. Aug. 30, 1635; bros. Nicholas, Thomas, Ambrose and bro. Richard in Eng.; bro.-in-law Edward C.; cousin John Capen, cousin Roger C.; widow Jone; bequests to church and school. The land sold in 1835, realized a large sum. The widow m. 26 (4) 1656, John Ellis of Medfield; was dism. to that chh. 3 (2) 1664.

Nicholas, son of Nicholas of Venn Ottery, Devon, Eng., came to Dorchester about 1633. Town officer, deacon. He m. 1, Sarah, dau. of William C. of Salcombe Regis; he m. 2, Abigail, widow of Robert Sharp. She witnessed probate papers as "Abigail Clapp" 15 Jan. 1656; also in 1665. He m. 3, Anna, widow of John Anniball, of Ipswich before April 15, 1667. [Ips. De.] Ch. Sarah b. 31 (10) 1637, Nathaniel b. 15 (7) 1640, Ebenezer bapt. 17 (1) 1644, Hannah bapt. 20 (7) 1646, (m. Ebenezer Strong.) Noah b. 15 (5) 1667, "of his 2d wife," says town record; but the mother was Anna, the third wife; Sarah b. Nov. 22, bapt. 11 (10) 1670, (m. Joseph Mather.)
He d. Nov. 4, 1679, ae. about 67. Admin. of his est. was gr. 18 Dec. 1679, to his sons Nathaniel and Ebenezer; but, after their death, the trust was given to their brother Noah, 26 Nov. 1716.

Capt. Roger, bro. of Edward, above, b. at Salcombe Regis, Eng. April 6, 1609, joined in the Church-Colony organized at Plymouth, Eng., in March, 1629; came in the Mary and John, arriving at Nantasket May 30, 1630. Settled at Dorchester. Propr., town officer, frm. May 14, 1634. He was capt. of the militia, deputy, authorized to join persons in marriage, and app. Aug. 10, 1665, capt. of the Castle, where he continued 21 years. Rem. to Boston in 1686. He m. Nov. 6, 1633, Johanna, dau. of Mr. Thomas Ford, a fellow passenger in the Mary and John. She was b. in Dorchester, Eng., June 8, 1617, and d. in June, 1695. Ch. Samuel b. 11 (8) 1634, William b. and d. in 1636, Elizabeth b. 22 (4) 1638, (m. Joseph Holmes,) Experience b. and d. in 1640, Waitstill b. 22 (8) 1641, d.

CLAP, etc., cont.

(6) 1643, Preserved b. 23 (9) 1643, Experience bapt. Dec. 21, 1645, Hopestill b. Nov. 6, 1647, Wait b. March 17, 1649, (m. Jonathan Simpson,) Thanks bapt. 25 (6) 1650, Desire b. Oct. 17, 1652, Thomas b. April, 1655, d. in 1670, Unite b. 13 Oct., 1656, d. March 20, 1664, Supply b. 30 (8) 1660, d. March 5, 1685-6.

He d. Feb. 2, 1690-1; was bur. in the old burying place, now called King's Chapel Burying-ground. He left an autobiography, which has been printed, and constitutes one of the most valuable memorials of the founders of New England. His will dated Nov. 19, 1690, beq. to his wife and surviving sons Samuel, Preserved, Hopestill and Desire, daus. Elizabeth and Wait, and cousins Ester Bissell and Constant Dewey.

Thomas, bro. of Nicholas, above, came early. Settled at Weymouth; frm. March 13, 1638-9. He rem. to Scituate; frm. Plym. Col. 5 June 1644. Town officer; deacon, deputy. Wife Abigail. Ch. Thomas b. March 15, 1639, Increase, Samuel, Eleazer, Elizabeth, (m. Thomas King,) Prudence, John b. 18 Oct. 1658, Abigail b. Jan. 29, 1659-60.

He d. April 20, 1684, ae. 87 yrs. Will dated 19 April, 1684, in the 87th year of my age, beq. to wife Abigail; ch. Thomas (of Dedham,) Samuel, Increase, Elizabeth (King,) Prudence, Abigail and Mary (Tilden;) gr. ch. Elizabeth. [See Clap Memorial, Dorchester Pope Family, and other works. The ancestry of Nicholas and Thomas Clap was discovered by Mr. J. Henry Lea.]

CLARE,

John, before Gen. Court 30 (2) 1640; Christopher Grant gave bonds for him.

CLARK, CLARKE, CLERK, CLERCKE, see Clooke,

Arthur, Hampton, frm. March 13, 1640. Rem. to Salem; adm. chh. 17 (8) 1641. Rem. to Boston; rec'd to chh. from chh. of H. 2 (10) 1643, with wife Sarah. Propr., 1645. Ch. Sarah bapt. 17 (1) 1644.

He d. ——. Admin gr. to widow Sarah on behalf of herself and her son Oct. 31, 1665. [Reg. XVI, 233.]

Barbary, a married woman, husband not named, tried in Es. court in 1639.

Bray, Dorchester, 1634.

CLARK, etc., cont.

Christopher, Boston, 1647. He went to England and returned, "ae. 38," passenger in the Speedwell May 30, 1656. He deposed 3 (2) 1660, ae. 42 years. [Mdx. Files.] Went to Barbadoes in 1650. [Arch. 15 B.] His wife Rebekah adm. chh. 25 (10) 1647; ch. Susanna, ae. about 8 days, bapt. 23 (2) 1648, Dorothie, ae. about 14 days, bapt. 20 (11) 1649, John b. 3 (12) 1651, Peter b. 14 June, 1653, Rebecca b. 4 May, 1657, Christopher bapt. 19 (12) 1659, Daniel b. Feb. 10, 1661, d. 16 March, 1662, Elizabeth b. Aug. 4, 1663.

Daniel, Ipswich, propr. 1634; before Gen. Court 4 (7) 1639; [L.] case referred to Ipswich Court. Rem. to Topsfield. Wife Damaris; ch. Mary b. 1 Nov. 1643, Elizabeth b. 10 Nov. 1647, Dority b. 10 Jan. 1649, Sarah b. 31 Jan. 1651, Samuel b. 5 Dec. 1663, Daniel d. 17 Jan. 1660.

Will dated Jan. 10, 1688, prob. 25 (2) 1690, beq. to sons John, Daniel and Humphrey; gr. ch. John Howlett; to son Horne's ch.; to all my daus.; to son Samuel C. in England.

Dennis, husbandman, of Dertford, co. Kent, Eng. hearing that his wife Anna was dead, betook himself to the company of Olave Peddington and had two children by her. Learning that Anna was still living, he made a written dismissal of Anna and declaration of adherence to Olave March 12, 1642, in presence of John Winthrop et als. [Suff. Prob. I, 31.[

Edward or Edmund, Sandwich, propr. 1640, atba. 1643.

Frances, Boston, maid servant to Mr. John Wilson, adm. chh. 1 (1) 1640. Now wife of one Mr. John Rayner, teacher of the chh. of Plymouth, dism. to Plym. chh. 18 (7) 1642.

George, Plymouth, 1637, atba. 1643. Propr. He m. 22 Jan. 1638-9, Allis Martin. He d. in 1644 and the widow m. Richard Bishop. She took the life of her dau. Martha Clarke, 4 yrs.old, July 22, 1648; was sentenced to death Oct. 4, 1648. The Court, 6 May, 1648, authorized John Churchil to dispose of the house and land that was John Clarke's for the benefit of his dau. Abigail Clark.

Hugh, Watertown; he rem. to Roxbury. Wife Elizabeth; ch. John b. 13 (8) 1641, Uri-

CLARK, etc., cont.

ah b. 5 (4) 1644, Elizabeth b. 31 (11) 1647. He deposed in 1681, ae. about 68. His wife d. 11 Dec. 1692. He d. July 20, 1693.

James, Boston, propr. at Braintree, 24 (12) 1639, of lot for 2 heads. Resided at Muddy River. Wife Jone, 1635. [Gen. Court Rec.] He m. in Roxbury Elizabeth Wright; ch. Elizabeth and Mary bapt. Jan. 8, 1645, Martha bapt. April 25, 1648, Hannah bapt. Dec. 23, 1649, James bapt. April 11, 1652, Samuel b. 9 (2) 1654. "My son James, now in N. E.," had beq. from John Clarke alias Kingman of Wells, Eng., yeoman, in will dated 24 Aug. 1646. [Reg. LI, 115.]

His will dated Sept. 11, 1667, was prob. 7 Jan. 1674. Beq. to wife and children, James, Samuel, John and Aaron. Cousin Peter Aspinwall, James Pemerton and son-in-law Walter Morse overseers.

Jeremy, agent of Wm. Coddington, 23 (4) 1642, to transact business in Mass. [Suff. De. I, 28.]

John, late citizen and chirurgeon of London in 1640, exec. of the est. of Anne Ward, late of Stratford, Es. [L.] Signed inv. of Wm. Hanbury in 1649. Settled at Newbury, frm. May 22, 1638. Propr.; town officer; exempt from taxes on account of pursuing his calling in town. Sold Newbury property 1 (10) 1651. Rem. to Boston. Deputy. The Gen. Court gave him a patent on his invention for sawing wood and warming rooms with little cost. The stoves he invented marked an era in N. E. history. He deposed as to being consulted professionally 6 May, 1662, ae. about 63. [Arch. 15 B.] Ch. John bapt. 8 (12) 1651; Jemina, (m. 6 (9) 1656, Mr. Robert Drue).

He d. in 1664. Will prob. Nov. 23, 1664; wife Martha, son John, dau. Jemimah Drew and her ch. John and Elizabeth. His widow d. 19 Sept. 1680, ae. 85. [S.] [See traditions and history in Reg. XXXIII, 19 and 226.]

John, ae. 22, came in the Elizabeth of Ipswich April 30, 1634.

John, Boston, memb. chh. 1631-2, frm. Nov. 6, 1632. Mr. John had lot at Braintree 19 (12) 1637, for 10 heads.

John, Cambridge, propr. 1633, frm. May 6, 1635. Agreed to build a weir, 1635-6.

CLARK, etc., cont.

John, Springfield, had leave to burn tar in 1646. Town officer. He m. 2, (1) 1646-7, Elizabeth Stebbins; ch. John b. 6 (1) 1647, Sarah b. 27 (10) 1649, Elizabeth b. 26 (10) 1651, Lydia bur. 1 (11) 1654.

Will dated Sept. 15, prob. Sept. 30, 1684, beq. to wife; son John; daus. Sarah Barnard and Mary Morgan. Son-in-law David Morgan deposed.

Jonas, or Jonah, mariner, Cambridge, propr., ruling elder. Appointed 13 Oct. 1654, with Samuel Andrew, to take observations at the northerly bounds of Mass. Plantation. Wife Sarah was bur. 20 (12) 1649, and he m. 30 (5) 1650, Elizabeth —. Ch. Thomas b. 2 (10) 1642, d. 20 (3) 1649, Sarah b. 15 (7) 1644, Jonas b 4 (7) 1646, Mary d. 15 (9) 1649, Elizabeth Thomas, Timothy, Samuel bapt. Nov. 6, 1659, Abigail bapt. May 4, 1662. [Mi.] The wife Elizabeth d. 25 March, 1673, ae. 41 years. [Gr. St.]

He d. Jan. 11, 1699, ae. 80. Will dated 19 Dec. 1699, prob. April 22, 1700, beq. to wife Elizabeth, sons Jonas, Timothy, Thomas, Joseph and Samuel; to daus. Susanna and Abigail; to dau. Bonner's 3 ch.; to dau. [dikaloon] and dau. Green; to Dorcas and Jonas Green; to son Timothy's son Samuel. Land in Camb., Groton and Dunstable.

Joseph, Dorchester, 1634; frm. March 4, 1634-5.

Goodman Clarke, the carpenter, had land at Dorch. Neck, adj. Thos. Makepeace, in 1649.

Joseph, Dedham, propr. 28 (7) 1640. Rem. to Medfield. Frm. May 18, 1653. Wife Alice; ch. Joseph b. 27 (5) 1642, Benjamin b. 9 (12) 1643, Daniel b. 29 (7) 1647, Mary b. 12 (1) 1649, Sarah b. 20 (12) 1650.

Martha, widow, 85 years old, d. [at Cambridge?] Sept. 19, 1680. [S.]

Mary, came in the Hopewell in Sept. 1635.

Mr. C., Mariner, Boston, ordered to clear the highway by his cellar 27 (6) 1649. [Town Rec.]

Nicholas, Cambridge, propr. 1634.

Richard, came in the Mayflower; signed the Compact; res. at Plymouth; but d. soon after arriving. [B.]

CLARK, etc., cont.

Richard, Plymouth, servant to Mr. Richard Derby, transferred to Mr. Atwood 1 Oct. 1638.

Richard, Rowley, propr. 1643; town officer. He m. (6) 1643, Alice ——; ch. Judah b. 5 (4) 1644, bur. July 28, 1660, Hester b. 10 (8) 1645, Mary b. 22 (10) 1648, John b. 26 (1) 1650, Martha b. 10 (1) [1652.] Will dated 7 Feb. 1673, prob. 31 March, 1674, beq. to son John and dau. Ester Hobkinson. Inv. taken 22 Feb. 1673.

Rowland, Dedham, propr. 11 (6) 1637. He d. 2 (12) 1638. Mary C., widow, adm. chh. 1 (2) 1642, d. 22 (3) 1642. Priscilla, who m. Nathaniel Colborn, Mary or Martha, who m. Benjamin Smith, and Elizabeth, who m. George Barber, were also in Ded. about 1639.

Thomas, came in 1623 to Plymouth; frm. 1633. Volunteered for the Pequot war in 1637. Town officer. Contracted marriage 20 Jan. 1664, with widow Alice Nicolls of Boston; her est. reserved for herself and her son John Nicolls, etc. She made will, after marriage, May 5, 1671, prob. 17 (4) 1671. Beq. to husband; to son John N.; to sisters Hannah Hollet, Elizabeth Welch ,and Susanna Hide; to bro. William Hollet. He d. March 24, 1697, ae. 98 years. [Gr. St.]

Thomas, late of Plymouth, witnesses a receipt of money paid to Richard Dole of Newbury in 1669. [Es. Files.]

Thomas, merchant, shop-keeper, Dorchester; frm. 1638-9. Propr.; rem. to Boston about 1643; town officer, deputy, captain. Signed inv. of John Hill in 1646. Wife Elizabeth, ch. Mehitabel b. 18 (2) 1640, bapt. 19 (2) 1640; her father being absent in England, Mr. Stoughton announced her name; Elizabeth b. 22 (3) 1642, (m. 28 May, 1661, Mr. John Freake,) Submit bapt. at Bo. 20 (6) 1646, ae. about 1 day; Submit, ae. about 14 days, bapt. 4 (1) 1649, Benjamin b. 4 May, 1656.

Thomas, locksmith, blacksmith, Boston, had land at Braintree 27 (11) 1639, for 8 heads. Wife ——; ch. Cornelius b. (10) 1639, Jacob b. (3) 1642, Deborah bapt. 9 (4) 1644, ae. about 6 days, Rachel b. 6 (5) 1646, Thomas bapt. 22 (6) 1647, ae. about 4 days, Thom-

CLARK, etc., cont.

as bapt. 17 (10) 1648, ae. about 5 days, Thomas bapt. 20 (8) 1650.

Thomas, residence not stated, deposed regarding the case of Robert Knight in 1655, ae. about 48 years.

Thomas, Sen. tanner, Ipswich, propr. 1634; frm. June 2, 1641. One of those who surveyed land up the Merrimac, to whom the Gen. Court voted payment 6 June, 1639.

Thomas, Ipswich, carpenter, gave land in Ips. Dec. 18, 1671, to his son Thomas, of same town, tailor.

Thomas, yeoman, Reading, propr. 1647; town officer; adm. chh. in 1662. He deposed in 1658, ae. about 40 years. [Es. Files 4, 12.] Wife Else d. June 28, 1658; son Thomas d. Nov. 1, 1673.

He d. Sept. 12, 1693; inv. filed.

Thurston, ae. 44, with Faith, ae. 15, came in the Francis of Ipswich April 30, 1630. Settled at Plymouth. Called also Tristram, Trustrum. Propr. 1636. Dau. Faith m. Edward Dotey. Son Thurston atba. 1643.

He d. about Dec. 10, 1661, of cold and exposure. Inquest. Admin. gr. to widow Faith 4 March, 1661. Her est. was divided June 1, 1663, between her dau. Faith Dotey and her sons Henry and Thurston Clarke.

William, Roxbury, frm. May 18, 1631, juryman, 3 May, 1631. Mr. William C., of Roxbury, N. E., mentioned in the will of Clement Chaplaine in 1656; q. v.

Mr. William, one of the first to plant at Agawam, (Ipswich,) April 1, 1633. [Col. Rec.] Had land assigned him Eastward of Labour in vane, southward of the town, Nov. 1634. Rem. to Salem, 1637; vintner. Part of his land fell within the limits of Lynn; for which he had another grant 13 (12) 1642. Dwelling between Linn and Ipswich, he had liberty from the Gen. Court to entertain passengers & cattle, 2 June, 1641. Ch. Bethiah bapt. at Salem 26 (6) 1638, Susanna bapt. 12 (1) 1642-3, Deborah bapt. 6 (6) 1645.

Admin. gr. to widow Katharine (5) 1647. Eldest son; another son and a m. dau. by a former wife; 4 younger (minor) children. The Gen. Court lic. the widow to keep the inn and sell wine, if she provide a fit man that is godly for the business.

CLARK, etc., cont.

William, came in the Mary and John March 24, 1633.

William, Dorchester, memb. chh. about 1636, with wife Sarah. Propr.; witnessed inv. of John Pratt in 1647. He was dism. 28 (2) 1661, to join in forming chh. at Northampton; wife Sarah and son Nathaniel dism. later. Ch. Sarah b. 21 (4) 1638, Jonathan b. 1 (8) 1639, Nathaniel z. 27 (11) 1641, Experience (dau.) b. 30 (1) 1643, Increase bapt. 1 (1) 1646, Samuel bapt. 23 (8) 1653, William b. 3 (5) 1656, Sarah bapt. 20 (1) 1658-9. Sarah, wife of W. C., d. at North. 6 Sept. 1675; Sarah, wife of Lieut. W. C., d. May 18, 1688. Lieut. W. C. d. at North. July 10, 1690; will dated 10 July, prob. 30 Sept. 1690; beq. to sons John, Samuel and William and daus. Rebecca and Sarah; to Mary and Sarah, daus. of son Nathaniel.

William, weaver, ae. 27, with wife Margaret, ae. 21, came in the Plain Joan in 1635; settled at Watertown; frm. May 22, 1639. He rem. to Woburn. Propr. 1651. He deposed 6 (2) 1664, ae. about 69 years. [Mdx. Files.] Ch. Mary b. 10 (10) 1640, (m. Nov. or Dec. 27, 1655, Wm. Locke,) Elizabeth b. 26 (9) 1642, (m. Dec. 28, 1659, George Brush,) Hannah b. 13 (12) 1645, (m. Joseph Buckminster,) Lydia, (m. —— Frissell).

He d. March 15, 1682. Will dated 10 (10) 1681, prob. April 4, 1682; weaver; stricken in years;beq. to wife; to gr. ch. John Locke, "who hath bin a liver with me many years;" to my three daughters; to the two daus. of my dau. Lidia; dau. frissell, dau. Brush, son George Brush, son William Locke. Margery d. Oct. 11, 1694.

William, Yarmouth, took oath of allegiance and was sworn constable 7 Oct., 1639; frm. 6 June, 1654.

He d. Dec. 7, 1688. Nunc. will prob. 28 (12) 1668-9; all to Joseph Benjamin, his son, who pres. inv. of the est. [Reg. VI, 178.]

William, Duxbury. He served against the Narragansetts 15 Aug., 1645. Had deed of land in D. March 6, 1649, from his kinsman Wm. Collier.

Will dated Jan. 3, prob. June 8, 1687; wife Martha; William Bonney, whom he had brought up. The latter renounced his claim Aug. 7, 1688 rather than remain with the widow. [Gen. Adv. I, 17.]

CLARY,

John, Watertown. He deposed July 10, 1672, ae. 60 years. [Mdx. Files.] He m. 5 (12) 1643, Sarah Cassell; ch. Sarah b. 4 (8) 1647, (m. Dec. 13, 1667, John Perry,) Gershom b. 7 (7) 1650.

CLAY,

Jonas, Wenham, 1643.

Thomas, Scituate, plaintiff in a suit before Gen. Court 29 (8) 1640; atba. 1643.

CLAYDON, CLADON, CLAYTON,

Richard, carpenter, wheelwright, ae. 34, of Sutton, Bedfordshire, made agreement 12 March, 1628-9, to go to Mass. for the Company, to work at his trade, taking with him his wife and one dau., his bro. Barnaby, ae. 23 yrs., and his sister 14 yrs. old. Came to Salem. [Suff De. I, XVI.]

CLEARE,

George, carpenter, Plymouth, had leave to build house April 3, 1637. Sold 1 Sept. 1638. He m. 20 Sept., 1638, Abigail ——.

George, Dedham, m. 26 (11) 1648, Martha Ward.

CLEEMOND,

John, Boston, servant to Jacob Eliot, adm. chh. 18 (5) 1640.

CLEMENT, CLEMENTS, CLEMANCE, CLEMONS,

Augustine, painter, of Redding, Eng., came in the James April 5, 1635. Settled at Dorchester. Propr., planter, frm. May 25, 1636. He employed John Tinker to sell for him property at Wockington, Berks, Oct. 18, 1638. [L.] Wife Elizabeth.

Will dated 31 Jan. 1671, prob. 31 (8) 1674. Beq. to son Samuel his house and lands in Boston, to wife Elizabeth house and lands in Dorch. with the moveable est.; to dau. Elizabeth Sumner and her children Hannah, William, Sarah, Experience, Ebenezer, Deliverance and Clement.

Mr. Robert, Haverhill. Deputy and com., 1647. Allowed by Salisbury Court to sell wine at H. in 1653. See Dummer.

He d. 29 Sept. 1658. Will dated Sept. 6, prob. 12 (8) 1658, beq. to wife; sons Job, John, Abraham and Daniel; sons [in law] Moses Pingrin, Abraham Morrill and John

CLEMENT, etc., cont.

Osgood; to my children's children that are in New England; to Mr. Ward, our minister. Another son Robert is mentioned under Fawne.

William, Cambridge, propr. on South side of Charles River in 1636. [Col. Rec.] He petitioned the Gen. Court for a divorce from his wife May, 1656. The wife Susan desired same. [Mdx. Files.]

The inv. of his est. taken 15 (12) 1669-70, was filed 21 (4) 1670, by Samuel Hide and John Jackson.

CLEVELAND,

Moses, Woburn, propr. 1649. He m. 26 (7) 1648, Ann Winn; ch. Moses b. Sept. 1, 1651, Hannah b. Aug. 4, 1653, Aaron b. Jan. 10, 1654, Samuel b. June 9, 1657, Miriam b. July 10, 1657, Joanna b. Sept. 19, 1661, d. March 12, 1667, Edward b. May 20, 1664, Josiah b. Feb. 26, 1666, Isaac b. May 11, 1669, Joanna b. April 5, 1670, Enoch b. Aug. 1, 1671. [Genealogy.]

CLEVIN,

Joan, ae. 16, came in the Hopewell in Sept., 1635.

CLIFFORD,

George, glover, servant to Mr. Thomas Buttall, Boston, adm. chh. 18 (1) 1643. Engaged by the town as a drummer for training-days and watches 27 (9) 1643. Wife ——; ch. John, bapt. 10 (3) 1646.

John, Salisbury, propr. 1640, rem. to Hampton.

Marie, ae. 25, came in the Susan and Ellen in April, 1635.

CLIFTON, CLIPTON,

Thomas, Weymouth, frm. June 2, 1641. Mr. James Parker was authorized by Gen. Court 28 (11) 1640, to m. Thomas Clifton and Mary Butterworth. Rem. to Rehoboth 1643. Juror, 1647; prop.; frm. 7 June, 1648.

CLOOKE, see CLARKE,

Jonah, frm. May 26, 1647.

CLOUGH, CLOW, CLUFF, CLUFFE, CLOUFE,

John, ae. 22, came in the Elizabeth April 11, 1635.

John, Boston, having served his master 4 yrs., had a lot gr. him by the Gen. Court, 13 March, 1638-9.

John, and Jone, at Charlestown, adm. chh. 21 (1) 1652. Elizabeth and Mary adm. chh. 9 (6) 1656.

John, tailor, Watertown, frm. May 18, 1642. Bought land in 1650. With wife Susan sold land in 1655.

John, house carpenter, Salisbury, propr. 1639. Frm. May 18, 1642. He deposed in 1691, ae. 77 years. Wife Jane d. Jan. 16, 1679; he m. Jan. 15, 1686, Martha Cilley or Sibley. Ch. Elizabeth b. Dec. 16, 1642, (m. —— Horne,) Mary b. July 30, 1644, Sarah b. June 28, 1646, (m. Daniel Merrill,) John b. March 9, 1648, Thomas b. May 29, 1651, Martha b. March 22, 1654, (m. Cornelius Page,) Samuel b. Feb. 20, 1656-7.

He d. July 26, 1691. Will prob. Nov. 3 folg. Beq. to now wife Martha; sons John, Samuel and Thomas; son-in-law Daniel Merrill; daus. Elizabeth Horne and Sarah Merrill; the children of dau. Martha, wife of Cornelius Page, late of Andover, and other gr. ch.

Richard, tailor, Plymouth, taxed in 1633, frm. 1634, propr. Volunteer for Pequot War 1637. Before Gen. Court 1 Sept., 1640.

William, Watertown, propr. 1645.
William, [Sen. or Jun.?] bricklayer, Charlestown, sold land in 1656; adm. chh. 25 (6) 1661. Ch. Benjamin bapt. 30 (1) 1662.
Will dated 24 Oct. prob. 17 Jan. 1684, beq. to wife Mary, sons William, John and Samuel, and dau. Mary.

CLOYCE, CLOYS, CLOISE,

John, mariner, Watertown, propr. 1638; took oath of fidelity 1652. He rem. to Charlestown before 1656, when he sold land at Wat. Wife Abigail; ch. John b. Aug. 26, 1638, Peter b. 27 (3) 1639, Nathaniel b. 6 (1) 1642. Second wife Jane; ch. Martha b. Oct. 13, 1659.

COACHMAN, see Cushman.

COATS,
Thomas, Lynn, 1646. Bought land in 1649. His wife was presented in Essex court in 1646 for interrupting Mr. Cobbett's preaching on Infant Baptism.

COBB,
Henry, Plymouth, taxed in 1632, frm. 1633. He rem. to Scituate; with wife Patience joined in the org. of the chh. Jan. 20, 1634-5. Rem. to Barnstable, propr. 2 Jan. 1638-9. Deacon, ruling elder. His wife d. May 4, 1648; and he m. 2, Sarah, dau. of Samuel Hinckley, Dec. 12, 1649. Ch. b. at Plymouth, recorded at Barnstable: John b. 7 June, 1632, James b. 14 Jan. 1634; b. at Scituate: Mary b. 24 March, 1637, bapt. 26 March, 1637, Hannah bapt. Oct. 5, 1639, Patience bapt. at Barnstable March 13, 1641, Gershom bapt. Jan. 12, 1644, Eleazer bapt. April 2, 1648, Mehetabel bapt. Sept. 7, 1651, bur. March 8, 1652, Samuel b. Oct. 12, 1654, Sarah b. and d. 1658, Jonathan b. Apr. 10, 1660, Sarah b. 10 March, 1662-3, Henry b. 3 Sept. 1667, Ephraim b. 11 Sept. 1671.

He made will 4 April, 1678, prob. 3 June, 1679; beq. to wife Sarah; sons James, John, Gershom, Eliezer, Samuel, Jonathan and Henry; to daus. Mary, Hannah and Patience.

COBBET, COBBITT,
James, ae. 23, came in the Elizabeth and Ann in April, 1635.

Rev. Thomas, b. at Newbury, 1608; studied at Oxford; came in 1637 to Lynn; [C. M.] associate minister with Rev. Samuel Whiting; frm. May 2, 1638; letter to Gov. Winthrop 13 (1) 1643. Wrote several books, of which his Practical Discourse on Prayer, pub. in 1657, is best known. Rem. to Ipswich not long after 1655.

He d. in 1685. His will, neither dated nor witnessed, was proved Nov. 22, 1685. In his cramped chirography it carries a copious creed and essay on life, showing his fine habits of mind and heart. Was drawing nigh to 75th [or 73d] year; 3 children and 2 grand ch. had died; he beq. to wife Elizabeth; refers to her ch. and gr. ch.; to son Belcher whose wife d. about a year and a half ago; and his ch. Samuel, whose wife d. about a year and a half ago; Elizabeth and [Bethia or] Bettris B.; to sons Samuel, Thomas and John C. [Es. Files 45, 30.] Had a quantity of malt, a farm of 500 acres near Haverhill; house and land at Lynn, etc.

COBHAM, alias Cobbitt,
Josiah, webster, clothier, Salisbury, propr. 1639. Must be considered the Josiah, ae. 21, who came in the Elizabeth and Ann in April, 1635. Settled at Cambridge; householder 8 Feb. 1635. Hingham; propr. 1637; frm. Oct. 7, 1640. He m. Mary, dau. of Richard Haffield, q. v. Sold land in 1642; rem. to Ipswich. Bought house and land at Boston March 7, 1658-9. Returned to Ips. He deposed in 1691, ae. about 70 years. Wife Mary; ch. Mary b. 25 (6) 1640, Josiah b. 12 (2) 1642, Martha b. 3 (5) 1643, Moses b. 3 (9) 1645, Sarah b. 25 (6) 1646, Joshua b. 15 (1) 1648, Marah b. 21 (3) 1652, Ruth b. at Boston Aug. 6, 1657.

COCKERELL,
William, fisherman, Hingham, propr. 1637; litigation in 1639. [L.] Presumably the same as William, admin. of whose est. was had at Essex Court, 11 (10) 1661. [Wife] Elizabeth; admin. of her est. 28 (4) 1664; Edward Clap, Francis Collins and Andrew Wood were appointed admins.; the est. was to be divided between them after all just debts were paid, [which may indicate that their wives were her daughters.]

COCCREY,
Thomas, Salisbury, released from apprenticeship to George Carr, shipwright, April 12, 1641. [L.]

COCK, COCKE, COX,
Oliver, Salisbury, app. Michael Powell his attorney to obtain houses and lands in Framlingham in Suffolk, and to require acct. of his grandfather Robert Merkant of Waybread, 5 (10) 1646. [A.]

Philip, apprentice to Capt. Wm. Couzens to learn the misterie of mariners, was transferred at Dorchester 24 (4) 1649, to John Gill, of Boston, mariner. [Suff. De.]

COCKERHAM, COCKRAM, COCKRAINE,
William, mariner, of Southold, co. Suffolk, Eng., ae. 28, with wife Christen, ae. 26, 2 children and 2 servants, passed exam. to go to New Eng. May 15, 1637. Came to Hingham; propr. Ret. to Eng. Oct. 3, 1642, and sent power of attorney to his son William March 25, 1657 to sell est. at H. [Hob.] [Suff De.] Had land next to his father-in-

COCKERHAM, etc., cont.
law Richard Eybrooke in 1637. [Hing. Rec.] Ch. Martha bapt. Aug. 19, 1638, Jonathan bapt. April 5, 1640, Mary bapt. Feb. 2, 1642.

CODDE,
Helen, maid servant of Mr. John Wilson, adm. chh. 6 (9) 1641.

CODDINGTON, COTTINGTON,
Mr. William, gent., of Boston, Eng., refused to contribute to the Royal Loan 9 March, 1626. [Reg. XXXVI, 138.] One of the assts. of the Mass. Bay Co. in Eng. March 18, 1629-30. Came to Boston, N. E., soon after. Memb. chh. 1630, frm. May 25, 1636. Asst. and town officer. Favored Mrs. Hutchinson, and was banished in 1638. Rem. to Newport, R. I.; sold Boston and Braintree property in 1639. John Beachampe calls him bro. in a letter to Wm. Paddy in 1649. [Freeman Genealogy, 23.] His first wife d. at Bo., N. E., in July, 1630. [Mass. Hist. Coll. 3.] Wife Mary adm. chh. 1632-3; ch. Mary bapt. 2 (1) 1634, Bedaiah bapt. 1 (3) 1636.

CODMAN, CODNAM,
Robert, mariner, Salem, had 5 acres of land and 5 for his mother 12 (5) 1637; town officer. Lawsuit, 1637. Rem. to Salisbury; propr. 1639. Salem voted 30 (7) 1647 to authorize the sale of the barque he goes in, the profits belonging in part to the town. Rem. about 1650 to Hartford, Conn. Ch. Benjamin bapt. at Salem Nov. 14, 1641, James b. April 15, 1644, at Salisbury. See Quodnam.

CODNER,
Christopher, Marblehead. He m. Mary, dau. of John Bennett, q. v.
Admin. (9) 1660; ch. Mary, [Jane!] ae. 5, and Christopher, ae. 3. Dau. Joane m. Joseph Bubier. The widow contracted marriage with Elias White of Marblehead in 1661. [Es. De. II, 31.] She afterward m. Richard Downing.

CODDINGTON, CORDINGTON, CARRINGTON,
Stockdale, Roxbury. He and his wife rec'd beq. from Elizabeth Hobbert in 1643.

CORDINGTON, etc., cont.
His wife Hannah, an ancient woman, was bur. July 20, 1644. He bought land at Hampton in 1648, and rem. thither.
He d. in 1650; admin. gr. to his eldest son John; who, residing in Boston, sold the Hampton land 15 (2) 1650.

COE, COOE,
Jane, ae. 30, came in the Susan and Ellen in April, 1635.
Robert, ae. 38, with wife Anne, ae. 43, John, ae. 8, Robert, ae. 7, and Benjamin, ae. 5, came in the Francis of Ipswich April 30, 1634. Frm. Sept. 3, 1634.
Matthew, fisherman, Gloucester, in court (10) 1647, propr. 1651. He m. 15 June, 1647, Elizabeth, dau. of Thomas Wakeley; [he m. 2, about 1657, Mary ——.] Ch. John b. last of June, 1649, Sarah b. 14 (1) 1651, Mary b. 15 (3) 1653, Abigail b. "of Matthew and Mary, his wife," June 5, 1658, Matthew b. and d. 1660.

COFFYN, COFFIN,
Mary, maid servant to Mr. Fowle, Boston, adm. chh. 20 (6) 1644.
Mr. Tristram, planter, came about 1642 to Haverhill; a witness to the Indian deed 15 Nov. 1642; propr. 1642-1647; rem. to Newbury. Kept an ordinary. Rem. about 1654 to Salisbury. Joined with other Salis. men in 1659 in buying land at Nantucket island and rem. thither in 1660. First magistrate of the island, and a capable officer. Wife Dionis [Stevens.] Ch. Peter, Tristram, (deposed in 1676, ae. about 44 years,) Elizabeth, (m. Stephen Greenleaf,) James, John d. at Hav. Oct. 30, 1642, Deborah b. and d. 1642, Mary b. Feb. 20, 1645, (m. Nathaniel Starbuck,) John b. Oct. 13 or 30, 1647, Stephen b. at Newb. May 11, 1652.
He d. Oct. 2 or 3, 1681. Admin. gr. 29 Nov. folg. to sons James, John and Stephen. See Genealogy, which shows descent from the C. family of Brixham, Devonshire, Eng.

COGAN, COGGAN,
Henry, Taunton, atba. 1643, Barnstable, took oath of fidelity 5 June, 1644. Wife Abigail; ch. Thomas bapt. March 2, 1639, bur. Jan. 26, 1658, John bapt. Feb. 12, 1642, Mary b. and d. 1645, Henry bapt. Oct. 12, 1646.
He d. in Eng. about 16 June, 1649. Inv.

COGAN, etc., cont.
rendered by his widow Oct. 29, 1649. The widow m. 2, John Fennye. [Reg. IV, 284.]

John, merchant; his mother Elinor d. in Tiverton, Devon, Eng., before Aug. 7, 1639. He sent power of attorney to Exeter, Eng., 7 (6) 1639, for collection of aught due to him, his wife or children from the est. of Ignatius Jordan of Exeter, Eng. [L.] He came to Dorchester about 1633. Frm. Nov. 5, 1633. Rem. to Boston and set up the first shop in town March 4, 1633-4. [W.] Wife Abigail memb. chh. Dorch.; ch. Abigail bapt. Second [?] wife Anne was adm. chh. Boston 27 (5) 1634. Ch. Annah bapt. 6 (9) 1636, Lydia b. 15 (1) 1639, Mary bapt. 30 (3) 1641, John bapt. 8 (3) 1642, Joshua b. Dec. 15, 1652, bapt. as Calib Dec. 20, 1652; Sarah b. Dec. 25, 1657, d. 12 (1) 1658. His dau. Mary m. 1, John Woodie, 2, Thomas Robinson; Elizabeth m. Joseph Rocke. His wife *Mary* or Anne d. 14 (11) 1651. He m. 10 (1) 1651-2, Mrs. Martha, widow of Gov. John Winthrop.

He d. April 27, 1658. Will prob. Aug. 3, 1658. Beq. to wife Martha, daus. Rocke and Robinson, and son Caleb. The widow d. about 24 Oct., 1660. [Reg. IX, 36, X, 175, and XXXI, 106.]

Thomas, Barnstable, atba. 1643.
He d. March 4, 1653. Inv. pres. by widow Joane 23 March folg.

COGGESHALL, COGGSWELL, COXALL,
John, merchant, embarked June 22, 1632; settled first at Roxbury; rem. to Boston. Adm. chh. with wife Marie and servant Anne Shelley from chh. of Rox. 20 (2) 1634. Frm. March 3, 1635-6. Deputy. Sympathized with Mr. Wheelwright and Mrs. Hutchinson in 1637, and was exiled to Rhode Island. Ch. Hannanell, (dau.) bapt. 3 (3) 1635, Wayte bapt. 11 (7) 1636, Bedaiah bapt. 30 (5) 1636.

COGGSWELL,
Mr. John, came in the Angel Gabriel, and was wrecked at Pemaquid 15 Aug., 1635. Settled at Ipswich; propr. 1635. Deeded house and lands at Chebacco Falls 2 (11) 1651, to son-in-law Cornelius Waldo. Ch. John, William, Mary, wife of Godfrey Armitage of Boston, and ——, wife of Cornelius Waldo. Abraham Wellman of Lynn gave re-

COGGSWELL, etc., cont.
ceipt to bros. John and Samuel C. in 1672. [See letter of John, Jr., in Reg. XV, 177.]

The inv. of his est. taken 27 Dec. 1669, was filed 29 March folg.

Mary, Boston, maid servant to Mr. Richard Bellingham, adm. chh. 29 (6) 1647.

COINTER, (see Winter,)
Christopher, Scituate, adm. chh. Dec. 24, 1637.

COIT, COYT, see Goit,
John, Marblehead, sold houses and lands 9 Feb. 1647; juryman, 1651. His bro. Solomon C. mentioned. Wife Mary; ch. (John C., the younger,) Abigail b. 3 (2) 1657, Nathaniel b. 13 (2) 1659.
Inventory of his estate filed with those dated 1663. [Es. Files.] The widow m. 3 (8) 1667, John Fitch. John C. d. 15 April, 1675.

COKE, see Cooke,
John, ae. 27, servant to Henry Collins, starch-maker, came in the Abigail in 1635.

Marie, ae. 14, came in the Hopewell in April, 1635.

COKER,
Richard, fined by the Gen. Court 3 March, 1634-5, for enticing certain servants to run away to the Dutch plantation.

Robert, came in the Mary and John in 1633. At Newbury, 1637; yeoman. Before Ipswich court, 1641. Propr., town officer. Wife Catharine d. 2 May, 1678. Ch. Joseph b. 6 Oct. 1640, Sarah b. 24 Nov. 1643, (m. James Smith,) Hannah b. June 9, 1644, Benjamin b. 30 June, 1650.

Will dated 20 Sept. 1678, prob. 29 March, 1681, beq. to sons Joseph and Benjamin; daus. Hannah Lunt and Sarah Smith; son-in-law James Smith; kinsmen Joshua and Caleb Moody.

COLBORN, COLBORNE, COLBURN, COALBORNE, COLBRON,
Nathaniel, Dedham, propr., 1637. Adm. chh. 29 (11) 1640, frm. June 21, 1641. Town Officer. He m. 25 (5) 1639, Priscilla Clarke; she was adm. chh. 23 (8) 1640. Ch. Sarah b 15 (2) 1640, Rebecca b. 17 (12) 1642, Nathaniel b. 3 (1) 1644, Priscilla b. 1 (2) 1646, (m.

COLBORN, etc., cont.
12 Nov. 1668, Joseph Morse;) John b. 29 (5) 1648, Mary b. 21 (11) 1650, Hannah b. 20 (11) 1652, Samuel b. 25 (11) 1654, Deborah b. 28 (11) 1656, Benjamin b. 24 (7) 1659, Joseph b. 1 (10) 1662.

Nathaniel, Sen., d. May 14, 1691. Will prob. April 26, 1692 ,beq. to wife Priscilla, sons Nathaniel, John, Samuel, Joseph and Benjamin; daus. Sarah Partridge, Rebecca Pratt, Priscilla Morse, Hannah Alderidge; to Deborah and Joseph, ch. of son-in-law Joseph Wight and my dec. dau. Deborah, Priscilla d. Aug. 12, 1692.

Robert, Ipswich, resident, 1648. He deposed in 1668, ae. about 60 years; wife Alice the same.

He d. May 2, 1685.

William; William Coleburn of Brentwood paid £ 25 into the stock of the Mass. Bay Co.; receipt dated 8 May, 1629. He petitioned in 1658 for a proper grant of land therefor, and recd. 300 acres. [Arch. 100.] Boston, appl. frm. Oct. 19, 1630, adm. frm. May 18, 1631. Town officer many terms. Will prob. 29 (8) 1662. Wife Margery; dau. Sarah Pierce and her dau. Sarah Colpit; dau. Mary Turand and her 5 ch. which she had by George Barrell, viz. James, William, John, Mary and Hannah; dau. Elizabeth Paine. [Reg. XI, 174.]

COLBY, COULBY,
Anthony, Boston, 1633. Frm. May 14, 1634. Propr. at Cambridge 1633; sold before 1640. Rem. to Salisbury about 1640. He was dism. from Boston chh. to chh. of Salis. 5 (5) 1646. Ch. John bapt. 8 (7) 1633, Sarah, (m. Orlando Bagley,) Samuel, (deposed in 1692, ae. about 53 years,) Rebecca b. March 11, 1643, (m. John Williams,) Mary b. Sept. 19, 1647, (m. Wm. Sargent, Jr.,) Thomas.

He d. Feb. 11, 1660; inv. and division of est. in 1662-3. The widow m. William Whittred; d. July 8, 1689, or thereabout. Her est. was admin. by son Samuel. List of ch. and gr. ch. [Es. Files, 38, 89.]

COLCORD, COLCOTT,
Edward, planter, Salem ,1637. Rem. to Dover, N. H. Deposed 8 April, 1673. Gave gifts of Mr. Bachiler to Chr. Hussey and wife, ae. 56 years. He contracted Nov. 5,

COLCORD, etc., cont.
1639, to deliver clapboards at Pascatt Rivers Mouth. [L.] He deposed 17 (9) 1669, ae. about 54 years.

See Page, Robert.

COLDHAM, COULDUM,
Thomas, miller, Lynn, frm. May 14, 1634. Propr., juryman. He deposed in 1662, about Mr. Humphrey's mill at L., which he tended 2 or 3 years; never kept a better mill in England. Was then ae. about 60 years. Ch. Thomas, Clement, (ae. about 37 yrs. in 1662,) Martha, wife of Richard Whitney, ment. by son Thomas, [Elizabeth, wife of John] Symonds. He admin. on the est. of his son Thomas 24 (4) 1673.

He d. April 8, 1675, ae. about 86 years. Will, dated March 14, 1674-5, beq. to wife Joannah, son Clement C., gr. ch. Samuel Symonds, bro. and friend Mr. Henry Rhodes. The son Thomas also referred to cousin Sara Harte.

COLE, COLES, COAL, COOLE, COOLLE,
Clement, ae. 30, came in the Susan and Ellen in April, 1635. Served with Mr. Robert Keayne in the business of tailor in 1639.

Daniel, tailor, Yarmouth, atba. 1643. Frm. 5 June, 1644. Had accts. with Thomas Hawkins for Mr. Pollington of London 23 (8) 1646. [A.] He rem. to Eastham; sold land at Marshfield June 8, 1649. Wife Ruth; ch. Mary b. March 10, 1658, William b. Sept. 15, 1663. The wife Ruth d. Dec. 15, 1694, ae. 66.

He d. Dec. 20, 1694. Admin. gr. 15 Jan. folg. to son Israel, at the request of his bros. and sisters. Agreement made between the children, John, Timothy, Israel, James, William, Daniel and Thomas, Daniel Dean and his wife Hephzibah, John Young and his wife Ruth, Joshua Hopkins and his wife Mary, and Medad Atwood and his wife Hester.

Henry, Sandwich, atba. 1643.

Isaac, carpenter, of Sandwich, Eng., with wife Joan and 2 children, came in the Hercules in March, 1634. Settled at Charlestown; frm. March 14, 1638-9. He deposed 2 (4) 1665, ae. about 58 years. [Mdx. Files.] Ch. Abraham b. 3 (8) 1636, Jacob b. 16 (5) 1641, Elizabeth b. 26 (7) 1643. His widow

COLE, etc., cont.

deposed 8 (6) 1674, ae. about 74 years; sons-in-law Samuel Bloghead and John Nutter petitioned concerning his estate. [Mdx. Files.]

James, shoemaker, inn-keeper, Plymouth, taxed in 1633, frm. 1633. Propr., town officer. Kept the famous tavern; lived on the side of the hill which still bears his name. Wife Mary; ch. James b. before 1627, Hugh b. before 1627, (both atba. 1643). He sold to his son Hugh of Swansey, shipwright, land at Saconnet "granted to the old servants, whereof I am one."

Job, Plymouth, 1634, Marshfield, 1638, Yarmouth later. Prop. frm. 5 March, 1638-9. He m. May 15, 1634, Rebecca Collier.

John, Plymouth. His will was prob. in 1637 or 1638. He beq. to bros. Job, and Daniel C.; to sister Rebecca; to Eliza Collyer; to each of Master Collier's men, viz. Edward, Joseph, Arthur, Ralph and John. Money paid goodwife Paddock for the child. [Reg. IV, 35.]

John, settled at Boston. Before the Court Nov. 3, 1635. Wife Joan; ch. Sarah b. 15 (11) 1641, John b. 17 (9) 1643.

John, ae. 40, came in the Confidence April 11, 1638. Settled at Salisbury; weaver; propr. 1639. Dau. Elizabeth m. William Carr. He d. in 1682. Admin. gr. to Maj. Robert Pike, who, in deed of 1703, refers to him as his uncle.

Margaret, a maid servant, Dedham, adm. chh. (3) 1639, was dism. in 1648 to the chh. of Watertown, having m. a bro. of that chh. named Dow.

Rice, or Ryse, Charlestown, memb. Boston chh. 1630; frm. April 1, 1633, propr. Char. 1634. Wife Arrold; ch. Robert, (d. about 1660,) John, James, Mary, (m. Richard Lowden,) Elizabeth, (m. Thomas Pierce). He d. 15 (3) 1646. Will dated (3) 1646, prob. April 1, 1662. To wife, sons Robert, John and James, and 2 daus. Richard Lowden and Thomas Peirce of Woburn, who m. the daus. asked for a division of the estate, the eldest and youngest sons having d. without heirs, leaving only one son. The widow, Arrold, wrote from Charlestown Aug. 28, 1655, to her son and dau. Jenks and dau. Ruth Coles, giving love of "your bro. John Cole

COLE, etc., cont.

and bros. and sisters Peirce and Lowden. She wrote 16 (10) 1661 to dau. Ruth Mood, referring to Ruth's former husband. Henry Mudd of Stepney, Eng., mariner, and Ruth his wife, gave power of attorney to John Smith of Charlestown 16 (—) 1661. [Mdx. Files.] Her will dated 20 (10) prob. 26 (10) 1662, beq. to son John C., sons Lowden and Perce and their ch.; bro. Solomon Phipps.

Robert, Roxbury, came with the first company. [E.]

Robert, [Boston?] punished by the Court in 1633. [W.]

Robert, Salem, 1637. Propr., 1638. Ann adm. chh. Sal. 1 (7) 1650.

Robert, Patuxet, with others, came under Mass. Jurisdiction 28 (8) 1642. [Suff. De.]

Mr. Samuel, confectioner, comfit-maker, inn-holder, Boston. Memb. chh. with wife Anne 1630-1. March 4, 1633-4 he set up the first house for common entertainment in Boston. [W.] His wife d.; he m. 2, Margaret, dau. of Isaac Greene, of Mersey, co. Essex, before 30 (7) 1647. [A.] He conveyed land in B. March 18, 1665-6, to Samuel, son of Wm. Royall, of Casco Bay, who had m. ffebee Greene, dau. of said Margaret. He made deed of gift Oct. 26, 1653, to Edmund Jackson and his dau. Mary, and to their ch. Elisha and Elizabeth, Oct. 6, 1666. Refers to gr. son Isaac Grose. He m. third, Oct. 16, 1660, Anne, widow of Robert Keayne.

Will, dated Dec. 21, 1666, prob. Feb. 13, 1666-7. To dau. Elizabeth, wife of Edward Weeden; to dau. Mary's ch. by Edmund Jackson, Elisha and Elizabeth; to gr. ch. Sarah Scenter and her husband John S.; to son John C.'s ch., the eldest of whom is Samuel; to gr. ch. Samuel Royal; to his old servant Elizabeth Ward. [Reg. XV, 249.]

Thomas, came in the Mary and John March 26, 1633-4. Settled at Salem. Propr. 1649. The following seems to refer to him: Bapt. at Navestock, Essex, Eng., Dec. 15, 1639, John, gr. ch. of Thomas Coale, ae. 3 yrs. which came out of N. E. [Reg. XXXI, 324.] His widow Anne made will 1 Nov. 1679, prob. 2 (5) 1680; beq. to sons Abraham and John C.

William, yeoman, gent., planter, Weymouth, late of Sutton in the parish of Chew

COLE, etc., cont.
Magna, Eng., and his wife Elizabeth, dau. of Francis Doughty, of Bristol, merchant, sued for the recovery of her inheritance 18 (8) 1626, and July 29, 1639. [L.] Mrs. Elizabeth Cole was allowed a bill of review by Gen. Court 29 May, 1644. She, a widow, petitioned the court 1 (4) 1647. [Arch. 38 B.] Suit with her bro. Mr. Francis Doughty of New Eng. and sister Bridget D. of Eng.

COLEMAN,

Anne, of Watertown, spinster, ae. 16, with her guardian, Samuel Hosier, sent letter of attorney to collect legacy of her dec. father, Wm. Coleman, saymaker, late of Colchester, Eng. 8 (6) 1639. [L.]

Edward, [Boston.] He m. at Eastham Oct. 27, 1648, Margaret Lumbard. [Scituate chh. Rec.] Ch. b. at Boston, Elizabeth b. 28 (11) 1651, Mary b. 12 Sept. 1653, d. 6 (7) 1657, Martha b. 8 Aug., 1655, James b. 31, Jan., 1656.

Inv. taken 28 Sept. 1691; widow Margaret deposed.

John, shoemaker, Charlestown, propr. 1637; perhaps a son of the following:

Joseph, shoemaker, of Sandwich, Eng., with wife Sarah and 4 children, came from S. before June 9, 1637. Res. first at Charlestown; rem. in 1638 to Hingham, then to Scituate. Took oath of allegiance 1 Feb. 1638. Will dated 30 (4) prob. March 4, 1674, beq. to wife Sarah, ch. Joseph, Zachariah ,Thomas ,Sarah, Abiah, Hannah and Mary.

Thomas, husbandman, Newbury; in partnership with Sir R. Saltonstall et als., keeping cattle, in 1635. Frm. May 17, 1637. Town officer. Rem. to Hampton, and later to Nantucket. He deposed Aug. 14, 1662, ae. 60 years. Wife Susanna d. 17 Nov. 1650. He m. 11 July, 1651, Mary, widow of Edmund Johnson, with whom he sold land in Hampton in 1652. Ch. b. at Newbury: Benjamin b. 1 May, 1640, drowned Oct. 1, 1650, Joseph b. 2 Dec. 1642, Isaac b. 20 Feb. 1646. Susanna, [his child?] d. 2 Jan. 1643.

Thomas, gave a letter of attorney 3 (8) 1646, concerning a house at [Esstum?] co. Worcester, and a legacie from John Coleman of Cotherstock, co. Northampton, carpenter. [A.]

COLEMAN, etc., cont.
Thomas, Wethersfield, Conn. 1639; deputy. Rem. to Hadley, propr. Will dated 29 Sept. 1674, prob. 29 March, 1676, beq. to wife; sons John and Noah; dau. Deborah; dau., the wife of Philip Davis; dau. Tratt's children; to son-in-law Thomas Wells my part of a house at Eversham, Eng.; to his son John now dwelling with me. The widow Frances made will, prob. March 26, 1678; beq. to son John Wells, daus. Mary and Deborah Wells; dau. Gilbert and son Jonathan G., and to gr. ch.

COLLAMORE, COLAMORE, COLIMORE, COLIMER, CULIMER,

Isaac, house-carpenter, Boston, 1636. Propr. He was adm. chh. 5 (12) 1642; frm. May 10, 1643; wife Margaret adm. chh. 22 (2) 1643. He served Mr. Abraham Mellows March 4, 1634-5; was employed by the government in making gun-carriages. He m. 22 (11) 1651, Margery Page.

Peter, Scituate, sold land due him for service in 1639; propr. 1640, atba. 1643, town officer 1650.

Will made 16 Jan. 1683, prob. 4 June, 1684, beq. to wife that now is—Mary; to Peter, John, Phebe and William Blackmore; to cousins Mary. Martha and Elizabeth, daus. of Anthony Collamore; to man, Wm. Clift; cousin Anthony C. exec.

COLLEN,

Sarah, Dorchester, memb. chh. before 1639.

COLLICOTT, COLLICOT, CALLACOTT,

Richard, tailor, Dorchester, frm. March 4, 1632-3. Deputy, 1636. Sergeant in Pequot War. In Indian trade monopoly 1641. [L.] Traded at the Eastward. [W.] Wife Joanna d. 5 (6) 1640. Wife Thomasin had ch. Experience b. 29 (7) 1641, Dependance b. 5 (5) 1643. He rem. to Boston. Deposed 20 (10) 1670, ae. about 67 years. [Mdx. Files.]

He was bur. July 9, 1686. [S.] Will dated 23 April, prob. 26 Aug. 1686, beq. to wife Thomezen; to dau. Experience Miles, and her son Richard; to dau. Bethiah C.; grandsons Richard and Samuel C.; to dau. Elizabeth, wife of Richard Hall, of Dorchester, her 3 daus. and her four sons Samuel, Rich-

COLLICOTT, etc., cont.
ard, Jonathan and Joseph. Lands near Dunstable and on the western side of the Kennebec river, above Abbacadussett's point, in Boston, etc. Refers to sister Moleford's house in Bo.

COLLIER, COLLYER, COLLER,
John, Hull, propr. at the founding of the town 2 May, 1642.

John, Watertown, took oath of fidelity in 1652. Deposed in April, 1657, ae. 25; wife Hannah ae. 20. Rem. to Sudbury.

Thomas, Hingham, propr. 1635; Hull 1642; propr. 1657; frm. May 6, 1646.
He d. 6 (2) 1647, ae. 71. [Hob.] Will prob. 29 (8) 1647; wife Susan, ch. Moses, Thomas and Susan. [Reg. VII, 173, and X, 88.] The widow d. 10 Dec. 1667.

Mr. William, one of the Adventurers to New Plimoth in Eng. 15 Nov. 1626; his brew-house in London mentioned in 1631; was agent of Mr. James Shirly. [B.] One of the "old comers," Plymouth, taxed in 1632, frm. 1633. Visited Boston with Gov. Bradford in 1634 to consult with authorities about the Hocking affair. [W.] One of the referees in adjusting partnership business between the English and Plymouth proprietors in 1641. [B.]
Rebecca m. May 15, 1634, Job Cole; Sarah m. the same day, Love Brewster; Mary m. April 1, 1636, Gov. Thomas Prence; Elizabeth m. 2, Nov. 1637, Constant Southworth.

COLLINS, COLLENS,
Christopher, shoemaker, Boston, 1639. Rem. to Braintree. Gave letter of attorney 15 (10) 1645, for the collection of money from Justinian Pearce of Plymouth, co. Devon, due to his wife, Jane Groope. [A.]

Edward, merchant, gent., Cambridge, propr. 1636; frm. May 13, 1640. Town officer, deacon. He and his children were legatees in the will of Daniel Collins of London in 1643. [E. and W.] Was of Medford in 1656. [Mdx. De. II.] He deposed 29 (2) 1660, ae. about 57 years. [Mdx. Files.] Was brought up by godly parents; father died and he was placed in a gentleman's house. Afterward spent a year with old Mr. Rogers of Wethersfield. Was apprenticed in a worthy family. Later went to Dedham, Eng. His wife relates that her father was careful in catechising her; at 19 began to seek the Lord for herself. Came to N. E. with her husband and child. [Rel.] He was attorney for Mrs. Elizabeth Poole of Westminster, Eng., 24 (9) 1646. [A.] He had a tripartite agreement with Richard Glover and Rebecca his wife and Thomas Andrewes and Damaris his wife, of London; and they sent 300 li. worth of cattle for the Craddock farm at Medford; Thomas Bridges and Edward Jackson of Cambridge, and Thomas Pierce and Edward Converse of Charlestown were appraisers, 12 Oct. 1647. [A.] Wife Martha; ch. Daniel, "living at Koningberg in Prussia in 1658, about 9 years old when his parents joined here;" [Mi.] John, "minister of God's word at Edinburgh in Scotland," [Mi.] Samuel, "living in Scotland," 1658, [Mi.] Sybil, ("m. Mr. John Whyting, preacher at Salem," in 1658,) [Mi.] Martha b. (7) 1639, Nathaniel b. 7 (1) 1642, Abigail b. 20 (7) 1644, Edward.

He d. 9 April, 1689, ae. about 86; will dated 20 Aug. 1683, and April 6, 1689, prob. 17 (10) 1689; beq. to wife Martha; she to distribute at her discretion to children and gr. ch.

Henry, starch-maker, ae. 29, with wife Ann, ae. 30, ch. Henry, ae. 5, John, ae. 3, and Margery, ae. 2, and servants Joshua Griffith, ae. 25, Hugh Alley, ae. 27, Mary Roote, ae. 15, John Coke, ae. 27, and George Burdin, ae. 24, came in the Abigail in June, 1635, cert. from the parish of Stepney, Eng. He settled at Lynn. Frm. March 9, 1636-7. Town officer.

Will dated 10 Feb. 1686, ae. about 82 years, prob. 31 March, 1687, beq. to wife; to son-in-law Johnson, sons Henry, Joseph and Benjamin, daus. Margery, Hannah and Elizabeth; refers to son John, dec.

John, shoemaker, Boston, 1639; adm. chh. 4 (2) 1646. Wife Susan; ch. John, Thomas b. 15 (8) 1645, Susanna, ae. about 3 yrs., 12 days, bapt. 5 (2) 1645, (m. 25 March, 1662, Thomas Walker).

He d. 29 May, 1670; admin. gr. to Gideon Allen. Inv. mentions shoemaker's stock and tools and 3 apprentices, etc.

John, Salem, 1642. Rem. to Gloucester; town officer 1647. He deposed 30 (1) 1658, ae. about 54 years. Wife Joane; ch.

COLLINS, etc., cont.
James b. Sept. 16, 1643, Marie b. March 8, 1646, Anna b. Sept. 26, 1649.

He d. March 25, 1675. Will dated Aug. 25, 1674, prob. April 21, 1675, beq. to wife Joane, sons John and James, and daus. Anna and Mary; to gr. dau. Mary Slampe. His daus. Mary, (with her husband James Davis,) and Anna, petitioned for another admin. after the death of their bro. John. The widow ret. to Salem church.

Rev. William, son-in-law of Mrs. Ann Hutchinson; preached some time at Barbadoes and did some good. Rem. to Newport. Was before Boston Court on religious matters in 1641. Was killed by the Indians at N. in 1643. [Col. Rec. and W.]

COLLISHAWE, COWLISHAWE,
William, Boston, adm. chh. with wife Anne and her dau. Sarah Morrice, (8) 1633. Frm. March 4, 1633-4.

COLTON, COULTON,
George, Hartford. Rem. to Springfield; propr. 1645; one of the chief citizens and officers of the plantation. Deputy, com. for laying out new plantations. Quarter Master of the Hampshire county troop; did important service in King Philip's War. Wife Deborah d. Sept. 5, 1689; he m. March 1, 1692, Lydia Wright, widow, successively, of Lawrence Bliss, John Norton and John Lamb; she d. Dec. 17, 1699. Ch. Isaac b. Nov. 21, 1646, Ephraim b. April 9, 1648, Mary b. Sept. 22, 1649, (m. Oct. 30, 1678, Samuel Barnard,) Thomas b. May 1, 1651, Sarah b. Feb. 24, 1652, (m. Oct. 30, 1678, Samuel Graves,) Deborah b. Jan. 25, 1654, (m. Dec. 28, 1676, Nathaniel Bliss,) Hepzibah b. Jan. 7, 1656, John b. April 8, 1659, Benjamin b. May 26, 1661.

He d. Feb. 13, 1699. [Reg. XXXIII, 202.] Will dated 2 April, 1699, prob. Jan. 11, 1699-1700, beq. to his four sons Isaac, Ephraim, Thomas and John and to their male heirs; to their three sisters, my daughters; to Rebecca, Samuel and Joseph, the children of dau. Sarah, deceased; to John's dau. Abigail. Isaac and Ephraim execs.

COLVER, CULVER, COLLIER,
Edward, wheelwright, Dedham. propr. 28 (9) 1637. He m. 19 (7) 1638, Anne Ellice; ch. John b. 15 (2) 1640, Joshua b. 12 (11) 1642, Samuel b. 9 (11) 1643.

COMPTON, CUMPTON,
John, laborer, Roxbury, rec'd from that chh. to chh. of Boston, 25 (7) 1642, his wife Susan adm. chh. 25 (12) 1642. Frm. Sept. 3, 1634. John, "of Boston, clothier," gave letter of attorney for recovery of "his title to certain lands to him descending," etc., 20 (10) 1645. [A.]

"Susanna, widow of the long since departed John Compton," beq. her est. to her little gr. ch., Joseph Brisco; prob. Nov. 12, 1664. [Reg. XIII, 153.]

COMSTOCK,
John, indentured servant of Henry Russell of Weymouth in 1639.

CONANT,
Christopher, Plymouth, came in 1623. Juryman at Charlestown Nov. 9, 1630.

Roger, son of Richard and Agnes, b. at Budleigh, Eng., bapt. 9 April, 1592, came, it is said, to Plymouth about 1622; rem. to Nantasket. Was recommended by friends in Eng. to the Western Adventurers as a successor to Mr. Thomas Gardner, (q. v.,) at the Cape Ann colony, and took charge there in 1625. [Hub.] On the failure of the colony at the end of a year he, with others, rem. to Naumkeag, which was later called Salem. He appl. for frm. 19 Oct. 1630. Adm. frm. 18 May, 1631. Town officer, deputy. Wife Sarah memb. chh. before 1636. Ch. Roger, ("first born child in Salem," recd. a grant of 20 acres of land 21 (11) 1639,) Exercise bapt. 24 (10) 1637, Lot, Sarah, Mary and others.

Will dated 1 (1) 1677, ae. about 85 years; prob. 25 (9) 1679, beq. to son Exercise and his children; son Lot and his ten ch.; dau. Sarah and her ch.; dau. Mary Dodge and her 5 ch.; to Adoniram Veren; to Hannah V. and her 2 ch.; to cousin Mary, wife to Hiller V.; to the daus. of cousin Jane Mason, including a share for the ch. of Love Stevens; to gr. ch. Rebecca C. and to Mary Leech. Capt. Roger Clap to pay a debt to the dau. of a Mrs. Pitts, living at Culliton in Devon; son Exercise to account for cattle left in his hands by Mr. Dudeny in Eng. for the benefit of his nephew Richard C. See Genealogy; but note statements here, carefully made.

CONCKLING, CONKLING, CONCLINE,
Annanias, glassman, Salem; propr., memb. chh., had additional land near his house in 1639. [See Southwick and Holmes.] Ch. Lewis bapt. 30 (2) 1643, Jacob and Elizabeth bapt. 29 (1) 1649. Susan adm. chh. 7 (12) 1650.

Note.—Capt. John C., who d. at Southold, Long Island, 6 April, 1694, in 64th year, is said in S. rec. to have been b. in Nottinghamshire, Eng. [Es. Inst. Coll. XXXI.]

CONDLIFFE, CUNDLIFFE, CUNLITHE,
Henry, Dorchester, memb. chh. about 1636; frm. May 29, 1644. Elizabeth, memb. chh. before 1639. Ch. Susanna, of wife Susanna ,b. 15 and bapt. 29 (1) 1643-4. He and his wife were dism. to join in the forming of a chh. at Northampton, 28 (2) and 1 (7) 1661.

He d. at N. Sept. 14, 1673. [Reg. III, 176.] Will dated 29 (5) 1669, prob. March 31, 1674, beq. to wife Susan; to her 2 gr. sons John and Henry Webb; to dau. Susan; to Warham, son of Mr. Eliezer Mather, his pastor; to the town of Northampton for a free school. The widow d. Nov. 19, 1675. She beq. to son-in-law John Webb, his wife Susan and their children.

CONEY, CONNY,
James, Braintree, 1640. Ch. Joshua b. (2) 1640, d. (10) 1642, Patience and Experience b. (6) 1642, James d. (10) 1642.

CONNELL, CONDELL,
Thomas, Boston, 1638. With wife Mary sold house and land July 7, 1645.

CONNER,
William, came in the Fortune in 1621; settled at Plymouth.

CONVERSE, CONVERS,
Allen, Salem, propr. 1639; rem. to Woburn. Frm. May 29, 1644. Taxed in 1645. Wife Elizabeth; ch. Zechariah b. Oct. 11, 1642, Elizabeth b. March 7, 1645, d. Aug. 2 ,1661, Sarah b. July 11, 1647, Joseph b. May 31, 1649, Mary b. and d. 1651, Theophilus b. and d. 1652, Samuel b. Sept. 20, 1653, Mary b. Nov. 26, 1655, Hannah b. March 13, 1660, (m. Nathaniel Pierce). The wife Elizabeth deposed 7 (8) 1668, ae. about 50 years. [Mdx. Files.]

CONVERSE, etc., cont.
He d. April 19, 1679. Will dated 14 April, prob. 17 (4) 1679, beq. to wife Elizabeth; to the 2 children of dec. son Zechariah; to the ch. of dau. Hannah Pierce; to son Samuel and daus. Sarah and Mary. The widow d. Aug. 9, 1691. [See Genealogy in Reg. L, 346.]

Edward, Charlestown, memb. chh. with wife Sarah, 1630, and of the re-organized chh. of Char., 1632. Frm. 18 May. 1631. Set up a ferry between Boston and Char. June 14, 1631. Juryman, 1630. Rem. to Woburn; propr. 1640. Deacon, town officer. He deposed 24 (1) 1661-2, ae. about 73 years. [Mdx. De. 11, 197.] Wife Sarah d. Jan. 14, 1662, and he m. 2, Joanna, widow of Ralph Sprague, who d. Feb. 24, 1670; (beq. to dau. Mary Edmunds and her dau. Mary; to sons Phineas, John, Richard and Samuel S., and to P.'s dau. Mary.) Ch. Samuel bapt. 12 (1) 1637, Josiah, (deposed 4 (2) 1660, ae. 41 years,) James, (depos. same time, ae. 39,) Mary, (m. Simon Tompson).

He d. Aug. 10, 1663.

COOK, COOKE,
Aaron, Dorchester, 1634; frm. May 6, 1635. Rem. to Windsor, Conn.; rem. before 1663 to Northampton; rem. to Westfield; keeper of the ordinary there in 1673. Major. Mary, [his wife?] memb. chh. of Dorch. about 1636. He m. 2, Joanna Denslow, who d. April, 1676; m. 3, Elizabeth Nash, who d. Sept. 1687; he m. 4, Rebecca Smith, who d. 6 April, 1701. Ch. Nathaniel, Joanna b. 5 Aug. 1638, Aaron bapt. 21 Feb. 1640-1, Miriam bapt. 12 March, 1642, Moses bapt. 16 Nov. 1645, Samuel bapt. 2 Nov. 1650, Elizabeth bapt. 7 Aug. 1653, Noah bapt. 14 June, 1657.

He d. 5 Sept. 1690.

Francis, came in the Mayflower; signed the Compact. He brought with him his son John. His wife Hester, a Walloon, a memb. chh. came in the Anne in 1623 with other of his children. [B.] Settled at Plymouth. Frm. 1633. Ch. named at the Division of cattle in 1627: John, Jacob, James, Hester, and Mary.

He d. April 7, 1663. Will, dated 7 (10) 1659, prob. 5 June, 1663; wife Hester and son John execs. and heirs. [Reg. VI, 95.]

COOK, etc., cont.

Col. George, gent., Cambridge, frm. March 3, 1635-6. He and his bro. Joseph came in the Defense July 4, 1635, registered as the servants of Roger Harlakenden; but bought property on their arrival, and occupied prominent stations in town and colony. Made contract Dec. 1, 1643, with Dr. Samuel Reade of Starford, Eng.; mortg. house at Camb. to S. Symonds of Ipswich. [Ips. De.] He ret. to Eng. and took part on the Parliamentary side in the Revolution. He d. in Ireland, and admin. on his est. was made here 4 (8) 1652. In 1690 John Quick, of London, husband of his dau. Elizabeth, gave power of attorney for the collection of est. in N. E. Wife Alice; ch. b. in Cambridge, Elizabeth b. and d. 1640, Thomas b. and d. 1642, Mary b. 15 (6) 1646.

Henry, butcher, Salem, propr., 1638. Mortg. house and land in 1649. He m. in June, 1639, Judith Birdsale. Ch. Isaac b. 3 (2) 1640, Samuel b. 30 (7) 1641, Judith b. 15 (7) 1643, (m. John Pudney,) Rachel b. 25 (7) 1645, (m. Elisha Kebed,) John b. 6 (7) 1647, Mary b. 15 (7) 1650, (m. Robert Moulton,) Martha b. 15 (7) 1650, Henry b. 30 (10) 1652, Eliza b. and d. 1654, Hannah b. in Sept. 1658, (m. Daniel Cannady).

He d. 25 Dec. or 14 (11) 1661. Admin. 26 (4) 1662. Widow Judith d. about (9) 1689. Inv of her est. taken Nov. 23, 1689.

John, ae. 17, a servant, came in the Abigail in 1635. Settled at Salem; propr. 1636; frm. May 18, 1642; in court, 1639; servant of Mr. Clark. Adm. chh. 21 (1) 1640; his wife adm. chh. 8 (7) 1640; ch. Sarah bapt. 19 (7) 1640, Eliza bapt. 16 (3) 1641, Mary bapt. 22 (8) 1643.

Joseph, gent., older bro. of George, above, came with him. Settled at Cambridge. Frm. March 3, 1635-6. Deputy, town officer; had charge of the military after his bro. ret. to Eng. He was a son of Thomas Cooke, of Great Yealdham, co. Essex, Eng., and made his bro. Thomas C. of Wormingfold his attorney, Nov. 5, 1639. [L.] He ret. to Eng.; deeded Cambridge lands from Stannaway, Essex. Wife Elizabeth; ch. Joseph b. 27 (10) 1643, Elizabeth b. 16 (1) 1644-5, Mary b. 30 (11) 1646, Grace b. 9 (10) 1648, Grace b. 1 (3) 1650, "Ruth bapt. at Camb." [Mi.] [See Epps.]

COOK, etc., cont.

Josias, yeoman, Plymouth, taxed in 1633, frm. 3 Jan. 1636; atba. 1643. He rem. to Eastham; propr. He m. 16 Sept. 1635, Elizabeth, widow of Stephen Dean. Had gr. of land for the Dean children 3 Sept. 1638. A dau. d. July 24, 1656.

Will dated 22 Sept., ae. about 63 years; prob. 29 Oct. 1673; beq. to wife Elizabeth, son Josias, sons-in-law Joseph Harding and Wm. Twining, dau. Bethia H., gr. ch. Joseph and Maziah H., gr. ch. Anna Shore; to gr. son Stephen T. a lot that was his gr. father Dean's; dau. Merriam Deane; gr. ch. Josias and Richard C. Widow Elizabeth's inv. was taken May 3, 1687.

Moses, plaintiff in a suit in Ipswich court in 1642.

Philip, Cambridge, propr., 1646; frm. May 26, 1647. He m. Mary, dau. of Barnabas Lampson; ch. Mary, Samuel, Hannah, Sarah, Philip bapt. May 5, 1661, John bapt. Aug. 30, 1663. [Mi.]

Will, dated July 18, 1666, prob. April 2, 1667; wife Mary; eldest son Samuel; ch. to be placed in families of friends and relatives if his wife approve: John, ae. 3, to his sister Singletary of Haverhill; Philip, ae. 5, to Richard Eccles; Hannah, ae. 9, to John Cooper; all to be brought up in Christian nurture and some honest employment; to kinsman Philip Eastman.

Margaret, Boston, memb. chh. 1630-1.

Rachel; she petitioned the Gen. Court, after the death of her husband, 23 May, 1650.

Richard, tailor, Boston, adm. chh. 28 (6) 1634, frm. March 4, 1634-5. Lieut. He deposed in 1658, ae. about 48 years. [Es. Files.] Owned lands in partnership with Arthur Perry in 1638. [L.] His wife Elizabeth rec'd 3 li. from the town of Boston 29 (8) 1660, for her services in curing the Spanish captives. Ch. Elhanan b. and d. 1636, Elisha b. 16 (7) 1637, Elkanah b. 14 (2) 1641, Joseph b. 1 (3) 1642, d. July 2, 1663, Benjamin b. (6) 1644, bur. (3) 1645, Elizabeth bapt. 25 (4) 1648, ae. about 5 weeks and 6 days, Mary bapt. 23 (4) 1650.

Will prob. 25 (10) 1673; wife Elizabeth, son Elisha, kinsman John C. and kinswoman Eleanor C.; Millicent, wife of Andrew Neale;

COOK, etc., cont.
to the College at Cambridge; to the children of his bros. William and Walter C. in Eng.

Richard, yeoman, Charlestown, Malden, propr. Lawsuit in Salem Court in 1640. His wife Frances, widow of Isaac Wheeler, deposed 5 (8) 1652, ae. 44, that she came in the same ship with Thomas Blanchard [the Jonathan] in 1639. [Mdx. Files.]
He d. 14 (8) 1658. Will dated 5 (7) prob. Dec. 28, 1658. Wife Frances and her ch. Isaac, Thomas, Elizabeth and Sarah Wheeler, and his dau. Mary C. The widow m. 5 (7) 1659, Thomas Greene, Sen.

Robert, apothecary, Charlestown, 1638; frm. June 2, 1641. Had an acct. with Elizabeth, widow of Henry Poole of Westminster 24 (9) 1646. [A.] The Gen. Court gr. him 800 acres of land 7 (8) 1640, in regard of his father's 100 li. adventured in the common stock. The father, Mr. Edward Cooke, Asst. subscribed 50 li. as a loan to the Company at a meeting in London 17 June, 1629. Sent letter by his son to Gov. Winthrop in 1638. Wife Sarah; ch. Samuel b. 10 (6) 1644.

Roger, Marshfield, propr. 1643; served against the Narragansetts in 1645. The Court paid the expenses of his sickness and burial 7 March, 1647-8.

Mr. Samuel, gent., from Ireland, invited to Dedham 26 (3) and made propr. 6 (5) 1640. See Smyth, John.

Susanna, Boston, now wife of one John Jenkins of Sandwich, dism. to that chh. 26 (1) 1648.

Thomas, mariner, Watertown.
He d. in Boston (12) 1645. Inv. May 16, 1646. [Reg. VII, 34.]

Thomas, Salem. He and his family were at the house of Nathaniel Stow of Ipswich in 1649. [Ips. Files.]
Inv. filed by Wm. Bartholomew and Wm. Varney, Essex Prob., (7) 1650.

Walter, Weymouth, 1643; frm. May 18, 1653. Rem. to Mendon, propr. 1663.
Will prob. Jan. 18, 1694-5; wife Katharine, eldest son John, other ch. Nicholas, Hannah, Samuel and Experience.

COOLEY, COOLY, COWLEY,
Benjamin, Springfield, propr. 1645; town officer many terms. Wife Sarah; ch.

COOLEY, etc., cont.
[perhaps Abelenah, (m. 22 July, 1664, Japhet Chapin,)] Bethia b. Sept. 16, 1643, (m. Dec. 5, 1664, Henry Chapin,) Obediah b. Sept. 27, 1646, Eliakin b. Jan. 8, 1648, Daniel b. May 2, 1651, Sarah b. Feb. 27, 1653, (m. Jan. 5, 1679, Jonathan Morgan,) Benjamin b. Sept. 1, 1656, Mary b. June 22, 1659, (m. April 21, 1687, Thomas Terry,) Joseph b. March 6, 1661.
He d. Aug. 17; his wife d. Aug. 23, 1684. His will and inv. filed Sept. 30 folg. and agreement for division accepted. [Reg. XXXIV, 266.]

John, Ipswich, propr. 1638.
Inv. taken 14 (1) filed 28 (1) 1654.

William, before Gen. Court Nov 5, 1633.

COMBE, COOMBS,
Mr. John, gent., Plymouth, frm. 1633, also adm. frm. 5 June 1644. He m. Sarah, dau. of Godbert Godbertson, q. v.; conveyed lands 24 Jan. 1633-4, which were her marriage portion. William Spooner paid certain debts of his in 1642, and had charge of his children in 1648.

COOMBS, COMBE,
Henry, fisherman, Salem, propr. 1635. Mortg. land, 1648. Rem. to Marblehead; propr. 1649.
Admin. Essex Prob. gr. to widow for herself and children 2 (10) 1669. She deeded land in 1670 to dau. Susanna and her husband Francis Grant.

COOLIDGE,
John, Watertown, frm. May 25, 1636, town officer, deputy. Wife Mary; ch. Stephen b. 28 (8) 1639, Obediah b. 15 (2) 1642, Jonathan b. 10 (1) 1645.
He d. May 7, 1691, ae. 88. Will dated Nov. 19, 1681, prob. June 16, 1691, names wife Mary, ch. John, Stephen, Simon, Nathaniel, and Jonathan; gr. daus. Sarah and Mary Mixer. The widow d. Aug. 22, 1691, ae. 88.

COOPER, COOP, COOPE,
Anthony, with wife and 4 sons, 4 daus. and 4 servants, came from Hingham, Eng., and settled at Hingham. [C.] Propr. 1635. Ch. Sarah, (m. Oct. 1648, Wm. Woodcock,) Rebeckah bapt. May 20, 1640, d. at Boston

COOPER, etc., cont.
22 Dec. 1643, Nathaniel bapt. March 26, 1643. Inv. taken Feb. 26, 1635.

Benjamin, husbandman, ae. 50, of Bramton, Suff., Eng., with wife Elizabeth, ae. 48, and ch. Lawrence, Mary, Rebecca, Benjamin; Francis Fillmingham, his son-in-law, ae. 32, his sister, ae. 48, and servants John Kilin and Philemon Dickerson, passed exam. to go to Salem, N. E. May 10, 1637. Settled at Salem.
Admin. Suff. Prob. 27 (7) 1637; son Lawrence, dau. Rebecca; and [sister?] Ester Cooper. [Reg. VII, 29.] Claim filed by Filmingham, approved by Gov. Endecott. Rebecca, ae. 15, was in Gov. E.'s family. [Mass. Hist. Coll. 4-6.]

Elizabeth, ae. 24, came in the Planter in April, 1635, cert. from Sudbury, co. Suffolk, Eng. Charlestown, adm. chh. 9 (10) 1643.

Humility, cousin to Edward Tillie, and his wife, came in the Mayflower to Plymouth. Ret. to Eng. after 1627, and d. there. [B.]

John, ae. 41, with wife Wibroe, ae. 42, and ch. Mary, ae. 13, John, ae. 10, Thomas, ae. 7, and Martha, ae. 5, from Olney, Bucks, Eng., came in the Hopewell April, 1635. Settled at Lynn; frm. Dec. 8, 1636; juryman, 1637. Rem. to Southampton, Long Island, at the beginning of that plantation in 1639-40. His dau. Martha m. Ellis Cooke, carpenter, of S.

John, planter, Scituate, frm. 1634; m. Nov. 27, 1634, Priscilla Wright. Rem. to Barnstable; deputy, deacon.
Will dated 28 Dec. 1676, prob. 25 Feb. 1683, beq. to wife Priscilla; after her death to the church of Barnstable, the surviving children of his sister Alice Bradford, and Lydia Morton.

John, Weymouth, sojourning at house of Mr. Henry Waltham.
He d., and inv. of his est. was rendered June 9, 1653; will prob. Oct. 21, 1653. To Hazilpenah Willcockes now dwelling with Mr. W.; to friend Thomas Dyer, whom he makes exec. [Reg. V, 303.]

John, son by former marriage of Lydia, wife of Gregory Stone ,b. in 1618, came to Cambridge about 1636. Yeoman; propr., deacon, town officer. He m. Anna, dau. of

COOPER, etc., cont.
Nathaniel Sparhawk; ch. Anna b. 16 (9) 1642 or 1643, Mary b. 11 (7) 1645, Samuel, John, Nathaniel bapt. May 8, 1659, Lydia b. April 13, 1665, Hannah bapt. Dec. 29, 1667. [Mi.]
He d. Aug. 22, 1691, ae. 73. Admin. of his est. gr. to his son Samuel, who gave bond May 1, 1693.

Mrs. Cooper, memb. Dorchester chh. in 1639.

Peter, ae. 28, came in the Susan and Ellen in April, 1635. Settled at Rowley; propr. Wife Emm or Amy; ch. Mary b. 2 (4) 1641, Samuel b. 8 (12) 1646, Deborah b. 30 (6) 1650, Sarah b. 14 (6) 1652.
He was bur. Jan. 15, 1657. Will dated 3 Jan. 1667, prob. 31 March, 1668; beq. to wife Emm, ch. Samuel, Mary, Deborah and Sara, and to the ch. of dau. Mary How. The widow was bur. April 18, 1689.

Thomas, Watertown.
He was bur. 20 (4) 1637-8, ae. 80 yrs.

Thomas, his wife, 2 ch., 2 servants and 2 other persons came from Hingham, Eng., to Hingham, N. E. in 1638; frm. March 13, 1638-9. Signature, "Thomas Coop." [Hing. Rec.] He rem. to Rehoboth 1643; propr. frm. Plym. Col. 4 June, 1645; town officer. Was attorney for Mrs. Anne Palsgrave to March 17, 1656. Son Thomas.

Thomas, carpenter, Windsor, Conn., bought land at Springfield Jan. 27, 1642; town officer, 1644. Employed to build meeting house Feb. 28, 1644. Signature in Town rec. Ch. Timothy b. 26 (2) 1644, Thomas b. 3 (5) 1646, Elizabeth b. 23 (12) 1648, Mary b. 15 (5) 1651, John b. 12 (2) 1654, Rebecca b. 15 (3) 1657, John b. 19 (3) 1659.
Lieut. Thomas C. was killed by the Indians Oct. 5, 1675. His widow Sarah pres. inv. and admin. March 28, 1676; was allowed the estate till son John was 21 years old.

Thomas, son of Henry C. of Little Bowden, Northampton, Eng., appr. to Leonard Buttolph, bricklayer, of Boston, 29 (6) 1639. [L.] May be the same as Thomas, of Boston, plasterer, who bought house and land Feb. 24, 1658. [See Matthew Smith.]

Timothy, Lynn, propr. 1638. Court com. 13 May, 1640. Rem. to Reading; propr. 1647. He and his ch. now in N. E. are named in

COOPER, etc., cont.
the will of his bro. John C. of Western Hall, 21 Nov. 1654. [Reg. XXXI, 413.]

He was slain by the Indians at Groton 2 March, 1675-6. Inv. on file.

Thomas, ae. 18, came in the Christian March 16, 1634.

COPIE,
James, frm. May 13, 1640.

COPP,
William, ae. 26, with Richard, ae. 24, came in the Blessing in July, 1635.

William, shoemaker, Boston, adm. chh. 4 (5) 1640, propr., frm. June 2, 1641. Wife Judith adm. chh. 24 (11) 1640. Ch. Johanna adm. chh. 26 (3) 1644, Naomi bapt. 5 (5) 1640, Jonathan b. 23 (6) 1640, Rebecca b. 6 (3) 1641, Ruth b. 24 (9) 1643, Lydia bapt. 9 (5) 1646, ae. about 3 days.

Will dated 31 Oct. 1662, prob. 15 March, 1669-70; wife Goodeth, dau. Tewxsbery, sons David and Jonathan, daus. Ruth and Lidia; gr. ch. William, Thomas, John and Mary Harvey, John and Sarah Atwood, Samuel and Sarah Norden. [Reg. XLVIII, 459.]

COPSE,
John, Watertown; he d., and inv. of his goods and est. was taken 14 (3) 1644, testified by Robert Nichols.

COREY, CORY,
Giles, Salem, watchman, 1647. [Es. Court rec.] Brought suit 26 (12) 1650. He deposed 17 (4) 1672, ae. about 55 years. Wife Margaret; ch. Deliverance b. 5 (6) 1658. He m. 2, Mary, who "was bought out of a London ship in Virginia by the father of Caleb More; who testified to this and to her good character when she was accused in 1678." [Es. Files.]

She d. Aug. 27, 1684, ae. 63 years. [Gr. st.]

CORLET, CORLETT,
Elijah, master of arts, schoolmaster, Cambridge, frm. May, 1645. He m. Barbara, dau. of —— and Elizabeth Cutter; ch. Rebecca b. 14 (6) 1644, Hephzibah and Ammi-Ruhamah also baptized here. [Mi.]

He d. Feb. 25, 1686-7.

CORLIS, CORLISS, CORLEE, CORLES, CORLY,
George, farmer, Haverhill, propr. 1645; town officer. He m. 26 Oct. 1645, Joanna, dau. of Thomas Davis; ch. Mary b. Sept. 28, 1646, (m. William Neff; she was captured by the Indians with Mrs. Hannah Duston in 1697;) John b. March 4, 1647-8, Johannah b. April 28, 1650, (m. Joseph Huckins,) Martha b. Jan. 2, 1652, (m. Samuel Ladd,) Deborah b. June 6, 1655, (m. Thomas Eastman,) Ann b. Nov. 8, 1657, (m. John Robie,) Huldah b. Nov. 18, 1661, (m. Samuel Kingsbury,) Sarah b. Feb. 23, 1663, (m. Joseph Ayer).

He d. Oct. 19, 1686. Will dated Oct. 18, prob. 23 Nov. 1686, beq. to son John, daus. Mary Neff, Johana Huckins, Deborah Esman, Martha Lad, dau. Roby and Sarah Corly, and to his wife Johanah.

CORNELIUS,
Daniel, sawyer, fisherman; Wm. Pierce, mariner, had power of attorney to collect money from him, Nov. 14, 1639. [L.]

CORNELL, CORNHILL, CORNISH, CONNELL, CONDELL,
Thomas, inn-holder, Boston, 1638. Sold lands in B. and Braintree Feb. 13, 1639. With wife Mary sold land July 7, 1645. Rem. to Gloucester; propr. 1649.

CORNING, CORNEY, CORNISH, CORNHILL,
Samuel, Salem, 1638, frm. June 2, 1641. An acre of land granted him for sowing hemp in 1641. Rem. to Wenham. Wife adm. chh. 5 (2) 1640; she was probably the Elizabeth Corning who was a witness to the will of Jane Comins in 1644. Ch. Remember bapt. 3 (3) 1640, Samuel bapt. 14 (1) 1640-1, Eliza bapt. 4 (4) 1643.

CORNISH,
Richard, Weymouth. His wife Katharine before Gen. Court Aug. 5, 1634. He rem. to Acomenticus; was drowned there in 1644.

CORNWALL, CORNEWELL,
William, with wife Joanne, adm. chh Roxbury in 1633. Genealogy in Reg. XLIX 39.

CORRINGTON,

John, ae. 33, and Mary, ae. 33, came in the Susan and Ellen in April, 1635.

CORWIN, CURWIN,

George, merchant, captain, Salem, propr. 1638. Town officer many years. He deposed 8 (5) 1667, ae. about 56 years. Deposed 27 (4) 1682, ae. about 70 years; came to the town near 44 years before. He m. Elizabeth, dau. of Mr. John Herbert, sometime mayor of Northampton, Eng. and widow of John White, by whom she had daus. Mary, (m. Samuel Andrews,) and Elizabeth, (m. Samuel Gardner). She d. 15 (7) 1668. He m. 22 (7) 1669, Elizabeth, dau. of —— Winslow, and widow of Robert Brooks. Mrs. C., b. and bapt. in Plymouth, was recd. to chh. of Sal. in 1672. Ch. John, "eldest son," Jonathan bapt. 17 (11) 1640, Abigail bapt. 30 (9) 1643, Hannah bapt. 4 (11) 1645, Eliza bapt. 2 (5) 1648, Penelope b. 7 (6) 1670, (m. 19 Feb. 1684-5, Josiah Walcott,) Susannah, "youngest daughter."

Admin. of his est. (4) 1685. The property, which had grown from the 400 pounds brought him by the widow White, was appraised at nearly 6000 li. Distribution was made to the widow, son Jonathan, the ch. of dec. son John, dau. Susanna, Josiah Walcott for his wife, James Russell for his wife, and to the widow for the other children. Samuel Gardner filed claims for portion due his wife. [Es. Files 44, 86-97; Es. Inst. Coll. IV, 169.] John Shatswell of Ipswich, in his will in 1646, mentions his "brother Curwin."

CORWITHEN, CARWITHEN,

David, Salem, Marblehead, constable, 1644; juryman, 1658. Grace, [his wife?] adm. chh. 18 (4) 1643. He and his dau. Curtis, with others, removing to Southold, L. I., had letters of dismission from the church granted 20 (6) 1665.

COSTONE, COSTIN,

William, carpenter, Concord, 1642. Rem. to Lynn, and rem. about 1654 to Boston. Ch. Sarah b. in Conc. 24 (1) 1642, Phebe b. in Conc. 10 (2) [1642?], Abigail, dau. of Mrs. Costone, of the chh. of Lynn, bapt. in Bo. 28 (11) 1654.

CORVANNELL, CORRANNELL, CORNELLY,

William, laborer, Duxbury, before the Court in 1637 and 1638. Servant of William Palmer.

COTTA, COTTY,

Robert, tailor, Salem, propr. 1636. Frm. May 6, 1635. Had lands for shop etc. at Gloucester; sold house and land in 1664. Johane, [wife?] one of the first membs. chh. of Salem; ch. a son bapt. 28 (11) 1637, Bethsua bapt. 24 (1) 1639, Mary bapt. 19 (7) 1640, Peter bapt. 1 (3) 1642, Obediah bapt. 10 (7) 1643, John bapt. 11 (3) 1645.

COTTLE, COTTELL,

William, a servant, ae. 12, came in the Confidence April 11, 1638. Settled at Newbury. He m. Sarah ——, who recd. legacy in 1664 from John Rolfe for herself and two children, Sarah and Ann C. She survived him and m. 2, John Hale. Ch. Sarah b. May 5, 1662, (m. William Titcomb,) Ann b. July 12, 1663, Susanna or Joanna b. Aug. 7, 1665, William b. Nov. 23, 1668.

He d. April 30, 1668; inv. Sept. 29, 1668.

COTTON,

Rev. John, son of Roland C., Esq., b. in Derby, Eng., Dec. 4, 1585, grad. Emanuel Coll., Cambridge. He was vicar of the parish of Boston, Eng., from 1626 till 1633. Declining to conform to some of the ceremonies then prescribed, he was reproved and fined. He went to Southampton in 1629 to see Mr. William Coddington and other friends and parishioners sail for N. E., and charged them to take advice of them of Plymouth and do nothing to offend them. [B.] He wrote Herbert Pelham Oct. 3, 1630, sending 3 pieces of gold to buy a hogshead of meal, etc. to send Mr. Coddington in N. E. [Mass. Hist Coll. V, 1.] He came in the Griffin, arriving Sept. 4, 1633. Was installed teacher of the chh. of Boston Oct. 17, 1633. He wielded a powerful influence for good, leaning to the side of Scriptural liberty rather than to that of severe restriction. He m. first Elizabeth Horrocks. He m. second in Boston, Eng., Mrs. Sarah Story, widow, who came with him to N. E., (whose dau. Elizabeth Story adm. chh. 24 (1) 1639, m. Wentworth Day q. v.) She survived him and m.

COTTON, cont.
26 (6) 1656, Mr. Richard Mather of Dorchester. She d. May 27, 1676, ae. 75. Ch. Seaborn, b. 12 (6) 1633, Sarah b. 12 (7) 1635, Elizabeth b. 9 (10) 1637, John b. 15 (1) 1639, Maria b. 16 (12) 1641, Rowland bapt. 24 (10) 1644, about 6 days old.

He d. in office 23 (10) 1652. Will dated 30 (9) prob. 27 (11) 1652. Beq. to son Seaborne "that south part of his house which Sir Henry Vane built while he sojourned with me, and gave by deed to Seaborne;" books to be divided between sons Seaborne and John; to two daus. Elizabeth and Mary; to wife his house and garden in the market place of Boston in Lincolnshire and moneys in the hands of his bro. Coney, his sister Mary C. or their son John C., together with property in Boston, N. E.; to grandchild Betty Day; to cousin Henry Smith, living with him, cousin John Angier, kinswoman Martha Mellowes and maid Elizabeth Clark; a silver tunn to the church of Boston, to be used among other Communion plate; beq. to Harvard College, and the free school of Boston in case his family return to England.

William, butcher, Gloucester, propr. 1642; settled at Boston; adm. chh. 15 (3) 1647, frm. May 26, 1647. Sergt. He deposed in Essex Court in 1661, ae. 43. He and his wife Ann witnessed the will of Thomas Millard of Newbury in 1653. Wife Anne; ch. William b. 31 (3) 1646; Mary, ae. about 5 yrs. 5 months, and John, ae. about 3 yrs. 5 months, both bapt. with William 16 (3) 1647; Sarah b. 18 (1) 1648, d. Jan. 22, 1663, William bapt. 23 (12) 1650, d. 29 (6) 1652, Rebecca b. Dec. 30, 1652, William bapt. 4 (12) 1654, Thomas bapt. 18 (11) 1656, Hannah b. Sept. 4, 1660, Benjamin b. March 18, 1665. Mary m. March 7, 1659, John Matson.

COURSER, COSSER,
William, shoemaker, ae. 26, came in the Elizabeth and Ann in May, 1635; settled at Boston; frm. May 25, 1636. Inn-holder, victualer. Wife Joan adm. chh. 12 (3) 1639. William and Hercules Cosser were members of the Scottish Charitable Society of Boston, 1658-1665; perhaps this William and Archelaus. Bought land at Chelmsford 10 Nov. 1664. He deposed June 16, 1663, ae. about 56 years. [Mdx. Files.] Ch. Deliverance b. 4 (1) 1638, Joannah b. 9 (12) 1639, John b. 3 (3) 1642; [Archelaus, husbandman, Lan-

COURSER, etc., cont.
caster, who sold land in B. 16 July, 1664, was he a son?]
Will dated 16 April, prob. 29 Sept. 1673. Beq. to wife Johanna, dau.-in-law Margaret C. and son John C.

COUSINS,
George, husbandman, from Marlborough, Eng., came in the James April 5, 1635.

Isaac, locksmith, Rowley, witness in court in 1649; with wife Elizabeth sold land in Rowley, Feb. 1651. With wife Ann sold land in Haverhill 4 Jan. 1657. Rem. to Boston. Sold land at Ipswich Feb. 1656; ch. Sarah b. 31 Aug. 1656. Wife Elizabeth d. 14 (10) 1656. He m. in 1657 Ann Hunt, formerly wife of John Edwards. Rebecca, of Isaac, and R. C. b. April 2, 1660.

COVELL, COUELL,
Cesora, ae. 15, came in the Abigail in July ,1635. Ezra, doubtless the person registered thus, settled at Plymouth; atba. 1643.

COVEY, COUVE,
James, Boston, had grant of land at Braintree for 4 heads 24 (12) 1639-40. Wife Mary; ch. Mary b. 7 (3) 1647.

John, Boston, witness to a deed 3 Oct. 1648.

COVINGTON,
John, Ipswich, propr. 1635; sold before 1639.

COWDREY, COWDRE, COWDERY,
Mr. William, Lynn, propr., 1638. Rem. to Reading. Deputy, town officer, deacon Deposed 7 (8) 1652, ae. about 54 years, and 27 (7) 1672, ae. 69 years. [Mdx. Files.] Wife Elizabeth d. Oct. 9, 1659; wife Joannah d. May, 1666; recd. from chh. of Lynn 16 (4) 1666. Wife Alse [Alice] named in will. Ch. Matthias b. 30 May, 1641, Bethiah b. 17 (2) 1643.

He d. Nov. 10, 1687. Will dated 12 Feb 1684, prob. 17 (10) 1689, beq. to wife Alse son Polly; dau. Hannah Polly's 7 ch.; to gr. ch. Bethiah Carter, Rebecca and Mary Cowdery; to son Nathaniel C., and to gr. ch. Nathaniel C.; mentions marriage of gr. ch. Nathaniel to Elizabeth Parker.

COWDALL,
John, Boston, mortgaged house and lands 8 (12) 1644. Sold land at Nashaway, (Lancaster,) 5 (8) 1647. He m. Mary, widow of William Davis, q. v.

COWELL, COWHELL,
William, "of New England, carpenter," gave bond for £ 10 Nov. 16, 1637, for his and his wife's passage; sued June 26, 1657. [Mdx. Files.]

COWLEY,
John, Ipswich, 1641.

COX, see also Cock,
Moses, Ipswich and Hampton before 19 (7) 1640. [L.]

COY,
Matthew, came from Boston, Eng. with his bro. Richard as a servant to John Whittingham. As a barber, servant to Mr. Atherton Haulgh, Boston, was adm. chh. 1 (11) 1641. Rem. to Wenham. Deposed in 1654, ae. about 33 years. [Es. Files 3, 4.] He m. 29 (6) 1654, Elizabeth Roberts.

Richard, Salisbury, propr. 1650. Rem. to Boston. Ch. Caleb b. Aug. 15, 1666.

COYTMORE, COYTEMORE, COITMORE, QUOTMORE,
Mr. Thomas, mariner, son of Rowland C. of Wapping, Eng., settled at Charlestown, 1636. Frm. May 13, 1640. Deputy, town officer. His mother Katharine, dau. of Robert Myles, yeoman, of Sutton, Eng., m. 1, Thomas Grey, of Harwich, Eng., and had dau. Parnell, who m. Increase Nowell; she m. 2, Dec. 23, 1610, Rowland Coytmore. He d. and she came to Charlestown; was. adm. chh. 7 (7) 1638; d. Nov. 29, 1659. She beq. to the ch. of her daus. Tyng, Nowell, and Graves; to gr. dau. Sarah Williams; to deacon Robert Hale; to Margaret Hutchinson, to Rev. Mr. Symes, pastor chh. of Char. He m. at Wapping June 24, 1635, Martha, dau. of Capt. Wm. Rainsborough; ch. Katharine b. and d. in 1636, Thomas bapt. 26 (12) 1641, William b. and d. 1643-4.

Capt. Coytmore made his will 25 (6) 1642, bound forth to sea. He was drowned in the wreck of Capt. Hawkin's ship 27 (10) 1644; a right, godly man and an expert seaman. [W.] The widow m. 2, Gov. John Winthrop and 3, John Cogan. No ch. that grew up. [Reg. XXXIV, 253.]

CRABB, CRABE,
John, appl. frm. Oct. 9, 1630.

CRABTREE,
John, joiner, Boston, propr., 1637. Sold land Sept. 25, 1654. Wife Alice; ch. John b. 25 (3) 1639, Deliverance b. and d. 1643.

The widow Alice m. 11 (12) 1656, Joshua Hewes.

CRACKBONE, CRACKBORNE,
Gilbert, planter, Cambridge, propr. 1635; frm. Dec. 7, 1636. Bought house and land in 1646. His first wife related (about 1646) that when young her brother sent for her to come to London; that she came to N. E. with husband and child. Their house was burnt. [Rel.] He m. 2, June 17, 1656, Elizabeth Coolidge.

He d. Jan. 2, 1671-2, leaving est. to his wife and to Joseph and Sarah, the ch. of his son Benjamin. His widow m. Richard Robbins.

CRACKSTON,
John, came in the Mayflower, signed the Compact, settled at Plymouth. He d. in 1621. With him came his son John who d. about 1626. [B.]

CRADOCK, CRADDOCK,
Isabel, ae. 30, came in the Rebecca in April, 1635.

Matthew, citizen and skinner of London, governor of the Mass. Bay Co. in Eng., prior to Mr. John Winthrop's election. Had a large plantation at Medford, mentioned in colonial records 28 Sept., 1630. Was fined 7 Nov. 1632, for his men's absence from training divers times, which gives some evidence that he had recently been or was then in Massachusetts. Letters from London to Gov. Winthrop, 1636-9.

He made will at London 9 Nov. 1640, probated in Charlestown 12 Feb. 1642, giving the following bequests among others: to the poor in Broadstreet where I served my apprenticeship; to the poor of St. Swithers where I dwelled; to wife Rebecca, dau. Damaris, brother Samuel C. and his sons Samuel and Matthew; to bro. and sister Sawyer. The widow m. 2, Richard Glover of London; they, as execs. of his will, gave power of attorney Feb. 12, 1645, to Nicholas Davison to settle all the N. E. affairs of the Cradock estate. [A.] She m. 3, Benja-

CRADOCK, etc., cont.
min Whitchcott. The Gen. Court considered her claims 13 May, 1648. His dau. Damaris m. Thomas Andrews, citizen and leather seller of London, and she and her mother sold the Medford estate to Edward Collins in 1652. [Mdx. De. II, 302.]

CRAFT, CRAFTS, CHROFT,
Griffin, or Griffith, Roxbury, came in 1630; frm. May 18, 1631; deputy, lieut. Wife Alice d. 26 (1) 1673, ae. 73. Ch. Hannah, (m. Nathaniel Wilson,) John b. July 10, 1630, Mary b. Oct. 10, 1632, Abigail b. March 8, 1634, Samuel b. Dec. 12, 1637, Moses b. April 28, 1641.
Will dated 18 May, 1689, prob. Dec. 9, 1690, beq. to wife Dorcas, son Moses, son-in-law Nathaniel Wilson, (and his wife Hannah,) and Edward Adams (with wife Abigail;) son Samuel exec. and residuary legatee. The widow Dorcas d. 30 Dec. 1697.

CRAGG,
Mary, Roxbury, m. Dec. 4, 1639, Thomas Stone.

CRAINE,
Elizabeth, Dorchester, memb. chh. 1641.

CRAM, CRAMME,
John, Boston, propr., 1635. Perhaps the J. C. who bought land in Hampton in 1658, and had deed of land 5 May, 1659, from Richard Swain for love and brotherly affection. Sons Benjamin and Thomas, dau. Lydia. [Norf. De., 1665.]

CRAMPTON,
Henry, Plymouth, rec'd pay from Raplh Smith and Edmund Tilson 3 May, 1641.

CRAMWELL, CROMWELL, CRANNIWELL,
John, Boston appl. frm. Oct. 19, 1630, adm. frm. March 4, 1633-4.
He d. in 1639, and his bro. Richard, of Woodbridge, co. Suff., Eng., made his bro.-in-law Thomas Marret attorney for sale of property beq. to him, April 16, 1642.

CRAVER,
Morgan, servant of Henry Waltham at Weymouth in 1640. [L.]

CRAWFORD, CRAFORD,
Mr., came in 1634; he was drowned, with bro. and servant in Charles river, Aug. 12, 1634. The Court app. commrs. Oct. 6, 1634, to take inv. of his est.

CRIBB, see Crips,
Benjamin, punished for stealing pigs in Dorchester March 22, 1630-1.
John, ae. 30, came in the Christian March 16, 1634.

CRISP, CRIPS, CRISPE,
Benjamin, mason, Watertown, propr., 1636, frm. May 4, 1646. He deposed 7 (8) 1656, ae. about 45 years, that he was servant to Maj. Gibbons 25 years agone. [Mdx. Files.] Wife Bridget; ch. Elizabeth b. Jan. 8. 1636-7, Mary b. 20 (3) 1638, Jonathan b. 29 (11) 1639, Eleazer b. 14 (11) 1641, Mehitabel b. 21 (11) 1645, [Zachariah.] His wife d. and he m. 2. Jonna Longley, who d. at Charlestown April 8, 1698, ae. 79. In her will she mentioned daus. Mary Leman, Sarah Rand and Lydia Nutting; gr. daus. Anna Lawrence, Lydia and Elizabeth Longley, Sarah Nutting, Mary and Elizabeth Shaddock; gr. son Wm. Longley; 3 children in captivity.
George, husbandman, planter, Plymouth. Rem. to Eastham. He gave letter of attorney to his bro. Robert C. of Southwark, Eng., mariner, to take possession for him of a legacy from his uncle, George C., land situated at Word, near Sandwich, co. Kent, 19 (1) 1640-1. [L.] He made the same bro. of St. Talwins in Southwark attorney for collection of legacy beq. by George C. late of Blackwall, Middlesex, shipwright, 22 (7) 1647. [A.]
Will dated 8 June, 1682, prob. 31 Oct. folg., beq. to wife Hephzibah and two minor children; mentions bro. Israel Cobb, and Samuel Berry (whom he had formerly looked upon as his own.)
Mr.; the Court app. commrs. chiefly of Watertown, c~ the inv. and distrib. of his est. Jan. 29, 1631-2.

CRITCHLEY, CRUTCHLEY, CRITHELEY, CROYCHLEY,
Richard, blacksmith, Boston, 1639, propr., adm. chh. 24 (2) 1642, frm. May 18, 1642. He m. 1. Alice, widow of Wm. Dyneley; contract made Aug. 15, 1639, [Suff. De. 11, 105.] She d. 26 (1) 1645. He m. 2. Jane

CRITCHLEY, etc., cont.

—; she was adm. chh. 27 (9) 1647. Ch. Samuel b. 25 (10) 1640, Joseph b. 3 (3) 1643, bur. 16 (6) 1645, Jane b. 15 (1) 1647, Elizabeth b. Nov. 28, 1653, Mary b. Jan, 18, 1655, Mary bapt. 2 (1) 1656, John b. Feb. 10, 1657, d. Sept. 25, 1658, Richard bapt. 6 (3) 1667, Rebecca, (of Richard and Elizabeth), b. March 1, 1674. Admin. of his est. gr. 10 (7) 1675 to his widow Elizabeth.

CROCKER, CROOKER, CROAKHAM, CROCUM, CROCKUM,

Francis, Barnstable, atba. 1643; served against the Narragansetts in 1645. He rec'd from Plym. Court 2 March, 1646-7, lic. to m. Mary Gaunt, kinswoman to Mr. Coggin of Bar. Rem. to Marshfield. Dau. Sarah m. 20 Jan. 1676, Thomas Macumber.

Francis, Marshfield, d. about 1700. He wrote his will Sept. 1700; beq. to wife Mary, son Jonathan, dau. Sarah Macumber, gr. ch. Daniel, Mary, Sarah, Ruth, Abigail and Mercy C. and Ursilla M.

John, Scituate, took oath of allegiance 1 Feb., 1638; rem. to Barnstable; atba. 1643; frm. 4 June, 1650. Juror, keeper of ordinary. Will dated Feb. 10, 1658; prob. 4 June, 1669, beq. to wife Jone; after her death to his bro. William C.'s ch. John, Job. Samuel, Josias, Eliezer, and Joseph; kinsman Job C.

William, planter, Scituate, memb. chh. Dec. 25, 1636. Took oath of allegiance Feb. 1, 1638. Rem. to Barnstable, propr., town officer; deacon. He deposed to the will of Dolor Davis in 1672, ae. about 65 years. Wife Alice. Ch. John b. May 11, 1637, Elizabeth b. Dec. 22, 1639, d. May, 1658, bur. May, 1658, Samuel b. July 3, 1642, Job b. March 9, 1644, Josiah bapt. Sept. 19, 1647, Eleazer b. July 21, 1650, Joseph b. 1654.

Will dated 6 Sept. prob. 19 Oct. 1692, beq. to wife Patience, ch. John, Josian, Eliazer, Joseph, and certain of their children.

CROFT, CROFTE, CROFTS,

William, yeoman, Lynn, propr. 1638. He deposed in 1682, ae. abopt 70 years.

Will dated 5 March, 1688-9, prob. 26 (9) 1689. Wife; son Thomas Ivory, dau. Sarah Chadwell, cousins, eldest ch. of Peter, Nathaniel and William Frottingham, sometime of Charlestown; Jonathan, son of James Thomson of Cburn, Hannah, dau. of Wm. Frottingham; dau. Ruth Bailey; wife's daus.

CROFT, etc., cont.

Sarah Chadwell and Lois Burrill; son-in-law John Burrill exec. His wife Ann deposed in 1667, ae. about 60 years. She made will 25 June, 1675, with his consent; mentions former husband Ivory, son Thomas Ivory, father South, dau. Sarah Chadwell, son Theophilus Baylye and wife, John Burrill, Sarah Farrington alias Potter. Prob. 26 (9) 1689.

CROMES,

Samuel, [Boston,] will prob. at court in Boston 2 (4) 1646, beq. all to Samuel Bitfield.

CROMWELL, CRUMWELL, CROMLON, see Cramwell,

Giles, propr. 1637. His wife Alice d. 14 June, 1648; he m. Sept. 1648, Alice Wiseman; she d. June, 1669.

He d. 25 Feb. 1672.

Peter, Salem, 1643.

Philip, butcher, Salem, propr. 1647; town officer. He deposed 30 (9) 1664, ae. about 50 years. Frm. May 3, 1665. He m. [2.] Dorothy, widow of Allen Keniston; marriage covenant 10 (2) 1649. [Es. De. 1, 7.] She deposed in 1662, ae. about 57 years.

She d. Sept. 27, 1673, ae. 67 years He m. 3, Mary —, who d. 14 Nov. 1683, ae. 72 He d. 3 March, 1693, ae. 83. [Gr st.]

Samuel (residence not stated,) frm. Sept. 3, 1634.

Thomas, Newbury. He and his wife died in 1635.

Thomas, [son of above?] Newbury, propr. 1643. He was one of the patentees of Hampton in 1638. He deposed in 1660, ae. about 43 years.

Thomas, mariner, Boston, 1636. Master of Ship Separation 26 (4) 1646. [A.] Went in a man of war and captured several Spanish vessels with great riches; stirred Plymouth and Boston on his return. [W.] He d. in 1649. See particulars in Bradford. Will prob. 26 (8) 1649; wife Anne exec.; dau. Elizabeth under 21,; goodwife Sherman, goodwife Spaule; to the town of Boston my six bells; refers to the ship Anne. [Reg. III, 268.] The dau. Elizabeth m. 18 Aug., 1659, Richard Price. The widow m. 2. Robert Knight; after his death she m. John Joyliffe.

CROSBY, see Pilsbury,
Constance, widow, Rowley, propr. 1643 or earlier, petitioned Ipswich Court 4 (3) 1674, on behalf of her gr. dau. Sarah Longhorne. In connection with this child we learn that Thomas, below, was a son of Constante, as well as Mary who m. Nicholas Longhorne. Anthony, chirurgeon, a propr. in R. later with wife Prudence, may have been a son.
She was bur. 25 Jan. 1683-4.

Simon, husbandman, ae. 26, with wife Anne ae. 25, and ch. Thomas 8 weeks old, came in the Susan and Ellen in April, 1635. Settled at Cambridge. Propr. February 8, 1635; town officer, frm. March 3, 1635-6. Ch. b. in Cambridge; Simon b. (6) 1637, Joseph b. (12) 1639.
He d. Sept., 1639, ae. 31. Inv. of his est. taken 15 (9) 1645, by John Bridge and Richard Jackson. Widow Ann yielded to the 3 sons, Thomas, Simon and Joseph certain portions 22 (7) 1645. She m. 2, Rev. Wm. Tompson of Braintree, who gave his consent to the arrangement. [Arch. 15 B.]

Thomas. Sen., Cambridge, had mortgage for money lent 16 (2) 1640. Propr. Residing at Rowley sold Camb. lands in 1649 and 1657.
He was bur. at R. 6 May, 1661; his widow Jane was bur. 2 May, 1662.

CROSMAN,
Robert, Dedham, townsman, 1642; before Gen. Court 10 May 1642. Had liberty to erect a water-mill in 1652 but declined. He m. 25 (3) 1652, Sarah Kingsbury. Ch. John b. March 16, 1654, Mary b. July 16, 1655, Robert b. Aug. 3, 1657, Joseph b. April 25, 1659, Nathaniel b. Aug. 7, 1660, Eleazer b. March 16, 1663, d. Oct. 26, 1667, Elizabeth b. May 2, 1665, Samuel b. July 25, 1667, Mercy b. March 20, 1669, Thomas b. Oct. 6, 1671, Susanna b. Feb. 14 1672. He rem. to Taunton.
Admin. of his est. was gr. 26 Nov. 1692, to John C. and John Thrasher. The est. was divided 25 July, 1696, to his ch. John, Robert, Sarah (Woodward,) Mary (Gould,) Elizabeth (Hayward,) Samuel and Mercy (Thresher;) to the ch. of son Joseph, dec.

CROSS, CROSSE,
Henry, carpenter, ae. 20, came in the Increase April 15, 1635.

CROSS, etc., cont.
John, Watertown. Wife Mary; ch. Mary b. 10 (3) 1641.
He was bur. 15 (7) 1640. The widow m. Robert Sanderson. [Mdx. De. VIII, 147.]

John, ae. 50, with wife Anne, ae. 38, came in the Elizabeth of Ipswich April 30, 1634. Settled at Ipswich; propr. 1635; frm. Sept. 6, 1639. His servant Clement Manning's case was before the Court in 1638. He was one of the proprs. of Hampton in 1638, but remained at Ips. Deputy, survveyor of the arms. Pledged ten shillings a year to the support of the free school 6 (10) 1650. Dau. Hannah b. in April, 1636, m. Thomas Hammond. [Testimony of Wm. English, Mdx. Files, 1658.] Her will, dated 19 March, 1656-7, beq. to her mother Hannah C. one sixth part of the rents of a farm in Ips.; to her son Thomas Hammond; to John Sherman and his ch. and to John Lithermore.
He d. about Jan. 18, 1650-1, last date in his will, which was prob. 25 (1) 1651; beq. to wife Anne and dau. Hannah; conditional bequest to Ipswich Free School. [See Files.] The widow d. in Watertown, Nov. 13, 1669; inv. of her est, filed 21 (4) 1670; the reversion of an old house and orchard mentioned.

Margaret, widow, Boston, adm. chh. 6 (11) 1638. Rem. to Rowley. Mentioned in will of Robert Hunter in 1647 and in that of Wm. Bellingham in 1650.

Robert, Ipswich, propr. 1635. Served in the Pequot war. His case referred to Ips. Court by Gen. Court 1 (10) 1640. His dau. m. William Nelson; son Stephen deposed in 1663, ae. 16½ years; son Robert, at same time, ae. about 21 years. Dau. Martha m. William Dirkee in 1664. He deeded land 13 (11) 1674, to son Stephen and his wife Elizabeth, to be given them at his death.

CROW, CROWE, CROE, CROWELL,
Mr. John, Charlestown, 1635. His wife had come the year before and bought a house of Mr. Wm. Jennings on her arrival. [Char. Rec.] Copy of list of his possessions in Char. (4) 1638, in Mdx. Files, 11. Town officer. He rem. to Yarmouth; took oath of allegiance to Plym. Col. Rec. Dec. 18, 1638; frm. and magistrate 2 June, 1640. Sold a farm in Dorchester to Thomas Makepeace before 1641. [L.] Wife Elishua adm. chh. Char. 4 (11) 1634-5; ch. Moyses (Moses,) bapt.

CROW, etc., cont.

24 (4) 1637. [John, propr. at Billerica, 1654, and Ylverton or Elverton, propr. at Yarmouth, have been conjectured to be sons.]

William, Plymouth, atba. 1643. Land allowed him 1 June, 1663, in respect of his uncle Mr. John Atwood dec.. He d. Jan. 1683-4, ae. about 55 years. [Gr. st.] Will dated 2 (11) prob. 6 (1) 1683, beq. to his brethren in Coventry, Samuel, Robert and Thomas Crow and John and Mary Harbert; to Ebenezer Spooner and Ephraim Thomas; remainder to wife Hannah.

CRUGOTT,

James, juryman, Gen. Court, 28 Sept., 1630.

CRUM,

Samuel, wine cooper, Boston, d. about (3) 1646; James Waker was recommended by Mr. Edw. Winslow to Gov. Winthrop for the administration of the est. [Mass. Hist. Coll. 4-6.]

CRUSE,

Richard, Boston, 1640.

Inv. of his est. (personal) taken by Simon Rogers and Richard Gridley 29 (2) 1640. [Reg. XXX, 80.]

CUDWORTH,

James, salter, gent., Scituate, frm. 1634. Rem. to Barnstable but returned after a few years. Stood for fair dealing toward the Quakers, and was much opposed for this by other magistrates; was deputy, Asst., Maj. General, com. of United Colonies; agent for the Colony in England and deputy governor in 1681. Wrote letters of historical importance; one to Dr. Stoughton of Aldermanbury in 1634, describes the state of affairs here; calls Rev. Zechariah Symmes cousin; refers to his uncles, apparently in N. E.; one of whom, Uncle Thomas, is about to be married to a widow that has means and 5 children; sends messages to bros. and sisters. Wife — joined the chh. with him Jan. 18, 1634; ch. James bapt. May 3, 1635, Mary bapt. July 23, 1637, Jonathan b. and d. 1638, Israel bapt. April 18, 1641, Joannah bapt. March 25, 1643, a child b. and d. 1644.

Will made 15 Sept. 1681, prob. 7 July, 1682, beq. to sons James, Israel and Jonathan; dau. Mary's 4 children, Israel, Robert, James and Mary Whetcombe; dau. Hannah Jones.

CULLICK, CULLICKE,

Capt. John, Charlestown, 1639; rem. to Boston in 1644. Adm. chh. with wife and adult ch. John and Eliazbeth 27 (9) 1659. Resided some time at Hartford, but ret. to Boston.

He d. Jan. 23, 1662-3. Will prob. Jan. 27, 1662; wife Elizabeth, son John and dau. Mary, minors. [Reg. XI, 338.] The widow m. Richard Ely; at her request a deed of porperty in Eng. to Henry Cullicke of Milton, Eng., was recorded in Boston in 1665. George Fenwick of Worminghurst, co. Essex, Eng., Esq. in his will, dated 10 March, 1656, beq. all his property in N. E. to his sister Cullick and her children; also 50 li, to her, 10 li. to bro. C., and a sum to each of their children. [Reg. XXXVIII, 199.] The dau. Elizabeth, when about to marry Benjamin Batten of Boston, merchant, rec'd. from him 23 Oct. 1671, security for her 2-3 share in the rents of houses and lands in Essex co. Eng., the other third belonging to her mother Elizabeth Ely. [Suff. De. VII, 285.]

CUMMINS, CUMMINGS, CUMMING, COMMINS, COMINS,

William, Salem, 1636, propr.; brought suit in court in 1637. His widow Jane or Jone's will was prob. 10 (5) 1644, inv. rend. -14 (11) 1646; beq. to son John; gr. ch. Mary and Joannah Bourn; to the church and Mr. Norrice; to goodman Cornish and others.

CURREN, CURWIN,

Matthias, Matthew, Ipswich, propr. 1634.

CURRIER,

Isaac, Watertown, propr. 1636.

Isaac, husbandman, Ipswich, propr. 1636 and onward. Frm. May 18, 1642. Rem. to Topsfield before 1660. Deeded land to son Isaac 16 July, 1663. He deposed in 1665, ae. about 65 years. Ch. a son d. at Tops. 28 July, 1660, a son b. and d. 1662.

Will dated 8 (3) prob. 14 (4) 1677, beq. to sons Isaac and John, son-in-law John Jewett; gr. ch. Isaac, son of Isaac.

Richard, millwright, Salisbury, propr. 1641. Taxed, 1650; town officer, etc. He deposed 12 (2) 1664, ae. about 47 years; was servant to Mr. Francis Dove at the time land was laid out to him. Built a saw-mill in 1656. Wife Ann joined in a deed in 1653;. d. after

CURRIER, cont.
1667. He m. 2. Joanna Pindar, widow of Valentine Rowell and Wm. Sargent. She d. Oct. 1690. Ch. Samuel, Hannah, m. Samuel Foot,) Thomas. Hannah joined with Sarah, widow of Philip Rowell 20 (4) 1691, in petitioning for a settlement of the estates of Richard and Joannah Currier, dec.

CURTIS, CURTICE, CUTTRIS, CORTIS,
Deodatus, planter, Braintree, bought land in 1640. [L.] Wife Rebecca; ch. Solomon b. 8 June, 1643, Ruth b. 8 (11) 1647. Rebecca, [widow?] m. 8 (4) 1648; Joseph Arnoll.

George, servant to Mr. John Cotton, adm. chh. Boston 4 (6) 1639; frm. May 13, 1640.

Henry, gent., ae. 27, came in the Elizabeth and Ann in 1635. Settled at Watertown; propr. 1636. Rem. to Sudbury; propr. 1639. Wife Mary; ch. Ephraim b. 31 (1) 1642. He d., and inv. of his est. was taken 27 Sept. 1678. "The housing and barn were burnt in the Indian warre time before his death." Filed by Joseph C. The widow Mary d. 3 (10) 1682.
Joan Parker of St. Saviour's, Southwark, Eng. in her will dated 24 Aug. 1674, beq. a silver tankard and 6 silver spoons to her bro. Henry Curtis of Sundbury in N. E.; and to his wife and 3 sons, Ephraim, John and Joseph, with him, 20 s. apiece. [Reg. XXXII, 337.]

Richard, Scituate, atba. 1643; town officer 1650. [See Chambers.] Ch. Anna b. 12 May, 1649, Elizabeth b. 12 Jan. 1651, John b. 9 Dec. 1653, Mary b. 9 Jan. 1655, Martha b. 15 March, 1657, Thomas b. 18 March, 1659, Deborah b. 16 April, 1661, Sarah b. 20 July, 1663.
Will dated 26 Oct. 1692, prob. Dec. 19, 1693, beq. to son John, who is to care for him and his wife Lydia the rest of their lives; son Thomas; daus. Hannah, Elizabeth Brooks, Mary Badcock and Sarah.

Richard, Salem, a witness in court in 1645. Ch. Caleb b. 24 (7) 1646, bapt. with Sarah 21 (2) 1650, Samuel b. 1 (2) bapt. 18 (3) 1651, Richard b. 14 (12) bapt. 20 (12) 1652, Sarah b. 19 (1) bapt. 15 (2) 1655, Hannah b. 16 (7) bapt. 28 (11) 1656, John b. and d. 1659, John b. and d. 1660, Mary b. 11 (12) 1662.

CURTIS, etc., cont.
Richard, cordwinder, Dorchester, propr.; town officer. Rem. to Milton, but came back in 1667. Wife Elizabeth d. 28 (3) 1657; he m. 25 (7) 1657, Sarah, widow of John Strange. Ch. Elizabeth b. 17 (5) 1643, Isaac b. 17 (4) 1658, Joseph b. 4 (7) 1661.

William, from Nasing, Eng., came to Roxbury in 1632, bringing 4 children, Thomas, Mary, John and Philip; his eldest son William came the year before, but died in 1634. [E.] Wife Sarah, sister to Rev. John Eliot, was bapt. 13 Jan. 1599-1600. He was propr.; frm. March 4, 1632-3. He conveyed lands to his son Isaac Feb. 11, 1669, on condition that he care for the father and mother the rest of their lives. Ch. rec. in Rox. Isaac b. July 22, 1641, Thomas d. 26 (4) 1650.
He d. Dec. 8, 1672, ae. 80; the widow d. March 26 or 28, 1673, ae. 73.

Zaccheus, of Downton, Eng., came in the James April 5, 1635. Settled at Salem; bought house near Brooksby, Marblehead; had grant of land 1646. See Corwithen. At Topsfield, wife Mary; ch. Mary d. 31 Dec. 1674, Mary d. Oct. 21, 1683, Zaccheus d. 7 Nov. 1683.

CURWIN, see Corwin.

CUSHING, CUSHIN,
Matthew, from Hingham, Eng., came in 1638 to Hingham, N. E. with wife, 4 sons and 1 dau., and his wife's sister, Frances Recroft, widow. Town officer, deacon. Wife Nazareth, (said by the family historian to have been a dau. of Henry Pitcher;) ch. Daniel bapt. April 20, 1619, Jeremiah bapt. July 21, 1621, Matthew bapt. April 5, 1623, Deborah bapt. Feb. 17, 1624-5, (m. Mathias Briggs,) John.
He d. Sept. 30, 1660, ae. 71 yrs. His heirs, Daniel, Matthew, John and Jeremiah C. and Matthias Briggs made agreement for a division of the est. to themselves and their mother Nov. 15, 1660. [Reg. IV, 88, and X, 173.] The widow d. 6 Jan., 1681-2, ae. 96 yrs.

Theophilus, bro. of Matthew, came from Hingham, Eng., to Hingham, N. E. in 1638 [?].
He d. March 24, 1678-9, ae. nearly 100 yrs.

CURWITHEN, see Corwithen.

CUSHMAN,
Robert, wool-carder, of Canterbury, Eng., m. at Leyden, Holland, June 3, 1617, Mary, widow of Thomas Chingleton of Sandwich, Eng. He was associated with Wm. Brewster as agent of the Leyden chh. in negotiations for removal. He came in the Fortune to Plymouth in 1621. See letters and details in Bradford. Though not ordained he did service as a preacher sometimes; and is regarded as the author of the sermon entitled The Danger of Self-love and the Sweetness of True Friendship, preached at Plymouth 9 Dec. 1621. He ret. to Eng. on business of the colony, and d. there in 1626.

Son Thomas came with him; became an important man here in church and colony.

CUSHMAN, *alias* **COACHMAN**,
James, planter, Scituate.
In his will dated April 25, prob. May 24, 1648, he beq. to his cousins John Twisden of Georgiana in co. of Devon, province of Mayne, and Mr. John Fernside of Duxbury; to Wm. Witherell of Scituate.

CUTHBERTSON, see Godbertson.

CUTLER, CUTLORE,
James, Watertown, propr. 1636. Propr. at Lancaster in 1645. Res. at Cambridge Farms (Lexington) afterward. Wife Ann; ch. James b. 6 (9) 1635, Hannah b. 26 (5) 1638, Elizabeth b. in 1639, d. in 1644, Mary b. 21 (9) 1643. The wife Anna was bur. 30 (7) 1644. He m. 9 (1) 1645, Mary, widow of Thomas King; ch. Elizabeth b. 20 (5) 1646. He d. May 17, 1694, ae. about 88. Will, dated Nov. 24, 1684, at Cambridge Farms, ae. 78, was prob. Aug. 20, 1694. He mentions ch. and gr. ch. of his wife formerly wife of Thomas King, viz. James, Thomas, John, John Collar, Richard Park's wife, John Parmenter's wife, Sarah Waite, Mary Johnson, Hannah Winter, Joanna, wife of Philip Russell, Jemimah, Samuel, Phebe.

John, Hingham, propr. 1636.
He d. Feb. 1638. His widow Mary m. second Thomas Huitt; ch. Thomas, who rem. to Charlestown. He gave a receipt 19 July, 1676, to the selectmen of Hingham for payment made to him for the care of his mother, Mary Huitt.

Richard, frm. June 2, 1641.

Robert, Charlestown, adm. chh. 6 (9) 1637, frm. May 2, 1638; deacon; town officer. The Gen. Court assumed the bills for his sickness 25 Oct. 1636. Ch. Nathaniel bapt. 8 (9) 1640.
He d. March 7, 1664-5. Will dated 1 May, 1664, prob. 20 (4) 1665, beq. to wife Rebecca, sons John and Nathaniel, dau. Rebecca, wife of Abraham Arrington, dau. Hannah, wife of Matthew Griffin, shop, tools of his trade, unwrought iron, share in ship Dolphin, etc. Note.—Stephen Fosdick, in his will in 1663, mentions "a falling ax that goodman Cutler made me." His wife Rebecca d. 18 (1) 1677. Her will dated 25 July, 1676, prob. April 3, 1678, beq. to the same and to gr. children.

Will, residence not stated, frm. April 18, 1637.

CUTTER,
Elizabeth, Cambridge; she related that she did not remember her father; mother placed her with a godly family at Newcastle (Eng.); had the ministry of Mr. Rodwell. Afterward her husband was taken away; she desired to come to N. E. [Rel.] She seems to have followed her sons, William and Richard, to this country. Lived in Cambridge with dau. Barbara, wife of Elijah Corlett. She made will Feb. 16, 1662-3, ae. about 87 years.

Richard, cooper, Cambridge, 1641, son of ―― and Elizabeth. Parents brought him up in the fear of the Lord. Though he had no opposition of heart against them he came to N. E. [Rel.] Frm. June 2, 1641. Mentioned as a res. in 1646. Wife Elizabeth d. March 5, 1662, ae. about 42 years. [Gr. St.] Ch. Elizabeth, Samuel, William b. 22 (12) 1648-9, Ephraim, Gershom, Mark,—all b. and bapt. at Camb.; he m. 2, widow Embsden, (who was adm. chh. Oct. 21, 1661, having *her* ch. Isaac and Jacob E. bapt. Nov. 3, 1661;) ch. Nathaniel bapt. Jan. 10, 1663, Rebecca bapt. **Oct. 8, 1665, Hephzibah** bapt. Dec. 1, 1667, (dec.) [Mi.] He d. 16 June, 1693, ae. about 72. [Gr. St.]

William, wine cooper, Cambridge, propr., town officer, 1639. Rem. to Charles-

CUTTER, cont.
town. Town officer, 1646. Ret. to England, to Newcastle on Tine. Gave power of attorney 12 (11) 1653, to Edward Goff and others. Gave another in 1674 to his brother R. C. of Camb., his friend Elijah Corlett of Camb. master of arts, and his friend Hugh Atkinson of the co. of Westmoreland, Eng. for sale of property in Char. Genealogy.

CUTTING, CUTTIN,
Mr. John, Sen., gent., mariner, Watertown, propr. 1636. Res. at Newbury in 1638; propr., town officer. Rem. to Charlestown, where he bought house and land in 1648. Was master of ship Advent of Boston 19 (8) 1647. [A.] Made many voyages to and from Eng. Sold his lands in Newbury to John Hull June 20, 1651. Ch. Judith and Sarah, who m. successively James Brown, q. v.; Mary, who m. Nicholas Noyes.

He d. at Newbury Nov. 20, 1659. His widow m. John Miller, and with him sold to their son-in-law Nicholas Noyes land formerly belonging to Stephen Dummer; which tract Dummer sold to Capt. Cutting, another document tells us. [To. Rec.]

Richard, wheelwright, came in the Elizabeth April 30, 1634, ae. 11. Settled at Watertown; bought house and land 16 (11) 1646. Wife Sarah; ch. James b. Jan. 26, 1657-8, —— b. Sept. 2, 1661, Lydia b. Sept. 1, 1666.

He d. March 21, 1695-6, an aged man; will beq. to sons Zachariah and James, daus. Susan Nucum and Lydia Spring, gr. ch. John Cutting and Elizabeth Barnard.

William, ae. 26, came in the Elizabeth of Ipswich April 30, 1634. Was agent of Ferdinando Adams to convey land in 1651.

DABYN,
Robert, servant to Mr. Joseph Hull, came from Weymouth, Eng., March 20, 1635.

DAGGETT, see Doggett.

DAKIN, see Deacon.

DADY, DADE,
William, butcher, Charlestown, 1630, adm. Boston chh. 1631-2, frm. April 1, 1633. Was one of the attorneys of Mrs. Palsgrave before March 17, 1656. Wife Dorothy, adm.

DADY, etc., cont.
chh. 31 (6) 1633; she d. March 8, 1670-1. Ch. William, Benjamin bapt. 24 (1) 1635, Nathaniel bapt. 22 (11) 1636, Zachariah b. 16 (3) 1644, Abigail.

He d. April 10, 1682, ae. 77. [Gr. St.] Will dated 3 Feb. 1681, prob. June 20, 1682, beq. to wife Martha and to her ch. by former husband; to son William and dau. Abigail.

DALLIBER, DOLLIBER, DOLLIVER, [Dolbear,]
Samuel, son of Robert of Stoke Abbot, Dorsetshire, Eng., bapt. Feb. 5, 1608, came to Marblehead about 1642; propr., town officer. Son Joseph, ae. 40 in 1669, was also propr. early.

He m. 2, Aug. 1, 1654, Mary, dau. of Robert Elwell; ch. William b. Aug. 17, 1656, Samuel b. July 9, 1658, Mary b. 26 March, 1662, Richard b. April 18, 1665, Sarah b. Dec. 24, 1667, John b. 2 (7) 1671.

He d. 22 July, 1683. Inv. of his est. filed by widow Mary 25 Sept. folg. Division was made to the eldest son Joseph; sons Richard, William and John; daus. Mary, widow of James Gardner, and her son Richard Dalliber; Sarah D.; Mary, wife of Richard Babson, and to son Richard Deike; who receipted for their portions at various dates, 1684-1696.

Tristram, bro. of Samuel, bapt. at Stoke Abbot 28 May, 1598, came to Salem before 1641. In fishing business at Marblehead and Gloucester. He returned to St. Ab., whence he wrote April 20, 1648, to John Balch and Wm. Woodberry of Sal. concerning his account with Wm. Vinson, Osman Dooch and John Stoodly; referred also to John Whitt and goodman Merry, and to Robert Elwell and his wife. Asks for the date of the death of his wife from the record; gave power of attorney to his bro. Samuel D. of Marb. for collection of money from John Whitt of Wenomen, [Wenham.]

He came again to Mass. He m. 1, Mary ——, who d. here 3 July, 1644. He m. 2, at St. Ab. Aug. 31, 1657, Sarah Peavie.

He d. at Gloc. 3 July, 1664. [Reg. VI, 251, XXXI, 312, and XXXII, 95.]

DALTON, DAULTON, DOLTON,
Philemon, linen weaver, ae. 45, with wife Hannah, ae. 35, and ch. Samuel, ae. 5½, came in the Increase, April 15, 1635. A

DALTON, etc., cont.
pioneer at Dedham, 1636. Rem to Hampton; had authority to perform marriages 14 May, 1645. Rem. to Ipswich. He d. in June, 1662.

Rev. Timothy, entered St. John's coll., Cambridge, Eng. Sept. 17, 1610, was ordained 19 June, 1614; vicar of Woolverstone, co. Suff. March 8, 1615; suspended by the bishop in April, 1636. Came hither soon after and settled at Watertown. Rem. to Dedham; adm. propr. 18 (5) 1637; frm. Sept. 7, 1637. Was one of the party sent by Ded. under permission of Gen. Court in 1638 to observe the southerly part of the patent. He contracted to saw 400 planks for a bridge, 1637. Sold his rights at Ded. in 1639. Rem. to Hampton, where he was elected "teacher" of the chh. June 2, 1639. He served with ability; opinions differ with regard to the issues which rose between him and Mr. Bachiler, "pastor" of the same chh. He gave certain lands to his kinsman Emanuel Hilliard, seaman, Jasper Blake, seaman, and to Nathaniel Bachiler, 10 (8) 1657. Wife Ruth; ch. Samuel bapt. at Woolv. 12 March, 1617, bur. same day, Deborah bapt. 3 June, 1619, bur. 19 May, 1624, Timothie bapt. 10 Nov. 1622, Ruth bur. 28 Aug. 1624-5.

He d. in 1661, ae. about 84 years. [Hampt. rec.] Beq. his est. to wife; to brother Philemon and his son Samuel.

The widow Ruth made, 22 March, 1663-4, to Nathaniel Bachiler, a deed of certain lands, conditioned on his providing for her in specified particulars till her death, and then paying legacies to Deborah, wife of John Smith; Elizabeth, wife of Joseph Merrie; Phebe, wife of Joseph Arnall; Joseph and George Parkers (Parkhurst;) Mary, wife of Thomas Carter of Woburn; Timothy and Benjamin Hilliard; Elizabeth Hilliard, dau. of Elizabeth Merrie; Abigail Ambross, dau. of the wife of John Severans; Mary, wife of William Fifield; Walter Roper and Hannah Willix. In her will, dated 8 (10) 1655, prob. 12 May, 1666, she beq. to her cozens, Nathaniel Batcheller and his wife Deborah; John Smith, Jr.; Mary, wife to Mr. Thos. Carter of W.; Samuel Dalton (for his son Timothie,) and Deborah Smithe.

DAMON, DAMMAN, DAMMANT, DAMING, see Eaton,
George, Scituate, atba. 1643.

DAMON. etc., cont.
John, planter, Scituate, 1644. He m. June 16, 1644, Katharine, dau. of Henry Merritt of Sci.; ch. Deborah b. April 25, 1645, John b. Nov. 3, 1647, Zechariah b. and d. 1649, Mary b. July, 1651, Daniel b. Feb. 1652. He m. [2,] 15 Jan. 1659, Martha, dau. of Arthur Howland; ch. Experience b. 17 April, 1662, Silence b. 2 Jan. 1663, Ebenezer b. 11 Jan. 1665, Margaret b. 20 July, 1670.

Inv. of his est. was taken 23 Oct. 1676; widow Martha and son Daniel deposed. A later agreement gave a share to son Zachary.

John, Reading, frm. May, 1645, propr. 1653; town officer. [Wife] Abigail memb. chh. 1648. Ch. John d. Jan. 14, 1651, John b. March 18, 1652, Abigail b. Aug. 26, 1654, Samuel b. June 23, 1656, Joseph b. Sept. 28, 1661.

DANA, DANIE, DANY,
Richard, planter, Cambridge, propr. before 1650. Wife Anne; ch. Anne, Jacob, Joseph and Abigail, all bapt. in Camb. before 1658; Benjamin bapt. April 8, 1660, Elizabeth bapt. April 27, 1662, Daniel bapt. April 3, 1664. [Mi.]

He d. April 2, 1690. Inv. filed. No will probated.

DAND,
Mr. John, [Boston] one of the petitioners for civil rights to be granted to non-church-members, in 1645; for this he was brought before the Court; discharged 10 May, 1648. [W.] [Col. Rec.]

DANE, DEAN, see Deane,
John, tailor, of Berkhamstead, and Bishops Stortford, Eng., came to Roxbury. Frm. June 2, 1641. In Court 1 (4) 1641. His wife died. **He m. July 2, 1643,** Annis, widow of Wm. Chandler. He rem. to Ipswich; propr. 1635; but ret. to Roxbury after some yrs, leaving his son John at Ips. He d. 14 (7) 1658. His will names wife Annice, sons John and Francis, and dau. Elizabeth How. Son John, ("Sen.,") deposed at Ips. Jan. 10, 1677, ae. upwards of 60 years; Francis deposed in 1673, ae. above 57 years. [Mdx. Files.]

Thomas, carpenter, ae. 32, came in the Elizabeth and Ann in May, 1635; settled at Concord. Wife Elizabeth;

DANE, etc., cont.
ch. a dau. b. 24 (12) 1642, Hannah b. 13 (1) 1645, Elizabeth b. 25 (10) 1648, d. 20 (4) 1649. His wife Mildred d. Sept. 15, 1673.

He d. Feb. 5, 1675. Will prob. June 24, 1676, beq. to son Joseph, daus. Sarah Heald, Mary Pellett and Hannah Page.

DANFORD,
John, his action against Richard Derby in Plymouth court in 1639.

DANFORTH, DAMPFORTH, DANFORD, DAMFORD,
Mr. Nicholas, yeoman, came in 1634 from Framlingham, Eng. [C. M.] Settled at Cambridge; propr. and selectman Nov. 23, 1635; frm. March 3, 1635-6. Town officer, deputy. A citizen of excellent qualities and efficiency. Wife Elizabeth d. in Eng. in 1629. Ch. Martha, (m. Richard French, and sold land with him inherited from her father in 1654,) Elizabeth, (m. Andrew Belcher, Thomas, (asst., deputy-governor, judge,) Anna, (m. Matthew Bridge,) Lydia, (m. William Beamans,), Samuel, (b. about 1627, became a celebrated minister, colleague of Rev. John Eliot at Roxbury; he d. 19 (9) 1674;) Jonathan, (became very prominent in colonial affairs; laid out and surveyed many tracts of land; deposed in 1677, ae. about 50 years.) [Es. Files.]

He d. (2) 1638. [See Hist. Billerica, Reports to Meetings of Danforth Family, etc.]

DANIEL, DANNELL,
Mrs. Alice, Salem, 1636. Lawsuit in 1638. See Beggarly.

Elizabeth, ae. 2 yrs. came in the Increase April 15, 1635; the name follows the family of Samuel Morse.

Robert, husbandman, Watertown, propr.; rem. to Cambridge 1636; frm. March 14, 1638-9. Town officer. Deposed 26 (4) 1652, ae. 60 years and upwards. [Mdx. Files.] Wife Elizabeth d. Oct. 2. 1643; he m. May 2, 1654, Reana, widow of Wm. Andrew. Ch. Mary b. 2 (7) 1642, Thomas bur. 6 (9) 1644.

He d. July 6, 1655. Will, dated 3 July, prob. Oct. 2, 1655. Wife Reana to have the est. he rec'd with her and additional. 5 children; eldest dau. Elizabeth now wife of Thomas Fanning; sons Samuel and Joseph, daus. Sarah and Mary; cousin Anna Newco-

DANIEL, etc., cont.
men. [Reg. XXX, 459.] The widow m. Edmund Frost.

William, inn-keeper, Dorchester, propr. 1646. Rem. to Milton. He m. Katharine, dau. of John Grenaway; ch. John bapt. 6 (6) 1648, Mary bapt. 7 (5) 1650, Susanna bapt. 18 (8) 1646, (m. John Kingsley;) Mary bapt. 10 (3) 1653, Hannah bapt. 22 (2) 1655, (m. Benjamin Badcock,) Samuel bapt. 24 (2) 1659.

Will dated 2 July, prob. 28 Sept. 1678. Beq. to wife Katharine, sons John and Samuel, daus. Hannah Badcock, son-in-law John Kinsley, grandchildren Susanna Kinsley and Silence [Woods]. Shop and blacksmith's tools to son Samuel.

DANTS,
Robert, frm. May 10, 1643.

DANVARD, DUNVARD,
John, Weymouth, before Gen. Court 3 March, 1639-40.

DARBY, DERBY,
Edward, referred to in the will of Agnes, widow of Augustine D. of Bisley, co. Surrey, dated 21 May, prob. 18 June, 1650. [Reg. XXXIX, 66.] Res. at Weymouth; rem. to Boston. He m. in Boston Jan. 25, 1659, Susanna Hooke.

Will dated 4 Jan. prob. 13 Jan. 1623-4, beq. to wife Rebecca, sons Jonathan and Samuel, daus. Sarah Cob, Jane and Ruth Derby; Jane to have silver spoons which her mother left.

John, son of Christopher D. of Sturtle near Bridport, co. Dorset, Eng., came to Plymouth. Propr. 6 Aug., 1637. Appl. frm. 6 March, 1637-8. Rem. to Yarmouth. Town officer. Ch. a son b. 28 Feb. 1647, Matthew b. Feb. 8, 1649.

He d. before 5 March, 1655-6, when admin. was gr. to his widow. After the death of Nicholas Nicarson in 1682 the Court ordered that the land on Monk's Hill in Plymouth should be divided between widows Blush and widow Nicarson who had rec'd nothing of her father John Darby, deceased, before.

Mr. Richard, gent., bro. of the foregoing, came to Plymouth about 1630, propr., juryman. Brought with him his kinsman John Chipman, q. v. [Reg. IV, 23, and XXXV, 127.]

DARLING, see Dorlon.

DARLOE, DARNO,
Penelope, ae. 29, came in the Defense in July, 1635, as maid-servant to Robert Keaine. She was adm. chh. Boston 24 (2) 1636.

DARRELL,
John, passed exam. to go to Salem, N. E. May 11, 1637.

DARVILL, DEVEL,
Robert, Sudbury, propr. 1639. Wife Esther; ch. Mary b. 10 (3) 1642.
Will dated 16 (11) 1661, prob. April 1, 1662, beq. to dau. Elizabeth Noice land in Norchurch, co. Hartford, Eng., and in Sudbury, to her daus. Elizabeth, Mary and Dorothy; to dau. Mary D.

DASSETT, see Dossett.

DASTIN, DAWSTIN, see **DURSTAN,**
Josiah, Charlestown, 1639; wife Lydia, ae. 26 years. [L.] Bought house and land at Medford April 26, 1641. Rem. to Reading; propr. 1647. He deposed 21 (1) 1669, ae. 66 years. [Mdx. Files.] Ch. Hannah b. 15 (7) 1645, Mary b. 1648, d. 1649, Mary b. Nov. 8, 1650, Sarah b. Sept. 25, 1653, Josiah b. May 14, 1656.
He d. Jan. 16, 1671.

DAVENISH,
Thomas, Salem, propr., 1638; frm. June 2, 1641. Mary adm. chh. 21 (1) 1640-1; ch. Mary bapt. 18 (5) 1641, Bethiah bapt, 30 (9) 1643.

DAVENPORT, DAMFORD, DAMFORTH,
Rev. John, b. at Coventry, Eng., in 1597, grad. at Magdalen Coll., Cambridge, A. B. 1615, A. M. and B. D. 1625; curate of St. Stephens, London. Went to Holland in 1633. Came to Boston in the Hector June 27, 1637. Settled at New Haven, Conn.; minister 1638-1667. Ret. to Boston, and was installed pastor of the First church Dec. 9, 1667. A hard student and a great preacher. [C. M.]
He d. March 15, 1669-70. His son John admin. 1 (7) 1670.

Richard, Salem, propr., lieut.; frm. Sept. 3, 1634. Chosen by the Gen. Court May 14, 1634, ensign to Capt. Trask. Rem. to Boston about 1643. He deposed in Salem Court 30

DAVENPORT, etc., cont.
(9) 1664, ae. about 58 years. Captain, deputy. He was the third commander of the fort on Castle Island, Boston Harbor. He was killed by lightning at the Island in July, 1665. Admin. gr. 30 Oct., 1665 to Wm. Stoughton, Nathaniel Davenport and Stephen Minot, at request of widow and her sons. [Reg. XVI, 233.] Wife Elizabeth one of the first members of the chh. Ch. Experience bapt. 27 (6) 1637, John bapt. 19 (7) 1641, Samuel bapt. at B. 5 (5) 1646, Sarah bapt. 30 (7) 1649, William b. May 11, 1656. Robert Hathorne of Bray, Eng., in a letter to his bro. Wm. H. in 1653, sends love to his bro. and sister Davenport.

Thomas, Dorchester, adm. chh. 20 (9) 1640, frm. May 18, 1642. Wife Mary adm. chh. 8 (1) 1644. Ch. Sarah b. 28 (10) 1643, Thomas bapt. 2 (1) 1645, Mary bapt. 21 (11) 1648, Anna bapt. 29 (10) 1650, Charles bapt. 7 (9) 1652, Abigail bapt. 8 (5) 1655, Mehitabel b. 14 (12) 1656, Jonathan b. 6 (1) 1658-9, Ebenezer b. 26 (2) 1661, John b. 20 (8) 1664.

He d. Nov. 9, 1685. His will, dated July 24, 1683, being aged, gave homestead to son John after the death of his wife. The widow d. Oct. 4, 1691. Genealogy. [Reg. XXXIII, 25.]

DAVIS, DAVIES,
Barnabas, from Tewksbury, Eng., ae. 36, came in the Blessing in July, 1635. Settled at Charlestown. Was in the employ of the brothers John and Wm. Woodcock; made several journeys to Conn., etc. Law suit in 1640-1 for payment of his salary. Refers to his father, James D. and his bro. Reade in Eng. [L.] He deposed 4 (2) 1659, ae. about 60 years. [Mdx. Files.] Elizabeth, [his wife?] adm. chh. Char. 8 (11) 1635.

He d. Nov. 27, 1685, ae. about 86 years.

Christopher, bondsman for John Davies before Gen. Court 13 Dec., 1636.

Dolor, carpenter, Cambridge, propr. 1635. He rem. to Duxbury. Propr. frm. [Plym. Col.] 5 March, 1638-9, adm. frm. 2 June, 1646. He and his wife were dism. from the chh. of Duxbury and joined that at Barnstable Aug. 27, 1648, whither he removed. Rem. to Concord.

He made will 13 Sept. 1672, prob. 2 July, 1673. Sons Symon and Samuel already had portions; wife Joanna; eldest son John; son-in-law Lewis and Mary his wife; dau. Ruth

DAVIS, etc., cont.
Hall; to the poor of the town where he may die. Refers to his sons Symon and Samuel as residing at Concord, and his having gone thither at the charges of Roger Chandeler.

George, blacksmith, Boston, adm. chh. 20 (6) 1644; frm. May 1645. Wife Barbara adm. chh. 22 (6) 1647. Ch. Samuel b. 17 Oct., 1651, John b. 3 June, 1652.
Will prob. April 25, 1655; to wife Barbara, sons Samuel and John. [Reg. V, 306, and IX, 35.] The widow m. 14 (11) 1655, John Brimblecombe, who gave bonds for the payment of the children's portions July 26, 1656. She afterward m. — Chadwell; her est. was admin. on 4 April, 1665, by Daniel Turrell and John Baker.

George, Salem, 1641. [Court Files.] Rem. to Reading; propr. 1644. Frm. May 26, 1647. Ch. Hannah b. May 31, 1648, Sarah b. Oct. 1, 1651, Elizabeth b. Jan. 16, 1654, Mary b. Jan. 6, 1657, John b. July 20, 1660, d. Nov. 4, 1660, Susanna b. May 11, 1662.
Will, dated Dec. 7, 1664, prob. Sept. 30, 1667. About to sail for Cape Fear, (where he d.); wife and son Benjamin, execs.; to son Joseph what he has in the ship and the weavers' loom; 5 daus. under age; bro. Wm. Clark of Lynn, one of the overseers. [Suff. Prob.; Reg. XVI.]
He d. July 14, 1667.

Isaac, Salem, 1636. Made a pair of stocks. He was ordered to be sent home to his wife in Eng., 15 June, 1637, and money raised for his passage.

James, Plymouth, propr. 6 Feb. 1636.

James, Braintree. Wife Mary; ch. Mary b. 7 (3) 1647.

James, Sen., Haverhill, propr. and purchaser of land in 1646. Town officer. He deposed 14 (2) 1663, ae. about 60 years. Excused by Hampton Court from training on account of his age in 1650. His sons James, Jr., and John were also proprs.; other ch. Judith, (m. Samuel Gile,) Ephraim, Samuel, Sarah, (m. John Page).
His wife Sissilla d. May 28, 1673; he d. ae. about 96 years, Jan. 29, 1678. Will March 17, 1675, codicil July 22, 1678, prob. 1680. Sons John, Ephraim, Samuel and James; dau. Sarah Page; gr. ch. James, son of John, Stephen and Ephraim, sons of Ephraim; James, son of Samuel Gilde.

DAVIS, etc., cont.
James, seaman, Boston, adm. chh. 7 (7) 1634, frm. March 4, 1634-5. Wife Joanna adm. chh. 6 (9) 1641; ch. Jacob b. 11 (5) 1639, Josebeth b. 20 (6) 1642, John d. 13 (9) 1653.
He d. Oct 17, 1661; admin. gr. to his wife Johanna 25 (11) 1661. John Wing, who m. one of the daus. of the said Wm. (sic,) resigned his claim.

Jenkin, joiner, Lynn, servant to Mr. Humfrey, frm. March 9, 1636-7. Juryman 1637, propr. 1638. Was punished for crime in 1642. The membs. of the chh. of Lynn petitioned the Gen. Court on his behalf Nov. 13, 1644. [Col. Rec., W. and Arch. 10, 26.] Mortg. house and land in 1661.

John, (Davy,) joiner, ae. 29, came in the Increase in April, 1635. Settled at Boston; frm. May 25, 1636; disarmed with others who favored Mrs. Hutchinson in 1637; propr. gave a bond 28 (5) 1640. Contracted to build a house for William Rix 31 Aug. 1640. Mr. John Davy, clarke, of Kenninghall, co. Norfolk, Eng., referred to in another document by Rix may be a connection. [L.]

John, Watertown; one of the petitioners for Lancaster, but not a settler there. [Arch. Eccl. I.] Wife Mary; ch. Mary b. 20 (1) 1642.
The widow Mary d. and Ephraim Child and Richard Davis were app. adminrs. June 19, 1656.

John, Ipswich, shoemaker, herdsman, before the Gen. Court 4 (10) 1638. Propr.; had additional land in 1651. Sold land at Jabaque, (Chebacco,) Ips. in 1648. John, Salisbury, ae. about 52 years, deposed 14 (2) 1664.
A John D. d. at Topsfield 24 Dec. 1672.
Will dated May 16, 1672, prob. 25 March, 1673; gave lists of debts and credits; beq. to his master and his family and others.

John, planter, Newbury, an early settler. Wife Elnor; ch. Mary b. 6 Oct. 1642, John b. 15 Jan. 1644, Zachary b. 22 Feb. 1646, Jeremiah b. 21 June, 1648, Mary b. 12 Aug., 1650, Cornelius b. 15 April, 1653, Ephraim b. 29 Sept. 1655.
He d. 12 Nov. 1675. Nunc. will and inv. filed Sept. 26, 1676. Son John to have 4 pounds; rest to remain in wife's hands for life, she paying 12 d. to each son and dau.; rest to them at her death.

DAVIS, etc., cont.

John* [Barnstable.] Brought goods from Weymouth to Sandwich in his boat for Michael Turner in 1637; did not deliver them at once because T. placed no signal to show the mouth of the harbor. [Court case.] He m. at Nocett March 15, 1648-9, Hannah Linnett or Linnell; ch. John b. at Barnstable Jan. 1649, Samuel b. Dec. 1651, Hannah and Mary b. Jan. 3, 1653, Joseph and Benjamin b. June 1656, Simon b. July 1658, Dolor b. Oct. 1660.

Will of J. D. Sen. of Barnstable dated 10 May, 1701, prob. April 9, 1703, beq. to sons John, Samuel, Benjamin, Dollor, Timothy and Jabez; daus. Mary Hinckley, Ruth Linel; dau. Hannah Jones' five ch:; gr. dau. Mary Goodspeed.

Margaret, ae. 32, with John, ae. 9, Marie, ae. 4, and Elizabeth, ae. 1, came in the Elizabeth April 17, 1635. Margery, a widow, at bro. Burdens, Boston, adm. chh. 15 (1) 1645. " Now wife of Charles Grist of Braintree," dism. to Br. 7 (3) 1648.

Nathaniel, came in the Hercules April 16, 1634.

Nicholas, ae. 40, Sarah, ae. 48, Joseph, ae. 13, with Wm. Lock, ae. 6, cert. from Stepney parish, came in the Planter March 22, 1634. Res. at Charlestown; rem. to Woburn, 1640. Wife Sarah d. 24 (3) 1643. He m. July 12, 1643, Elizabeth Isaac.

Nicholas, died; admin. of his est. in Plym. Col. given by Mass. Gen. Court to John Wales of Boston; inv. filed at Plym. 13 (5) 1673.

Philip, ae. 12, servant to John Ilsbey, came in the Confidence April 11, 1638. Philip, servant to John Cooke from 20 April, 1638, for 11 yrs. 2 months, from the first day of his arrival in N. E., was transferred Jan. 5, 1640-1, to Henry Samson.

Robert, ae. 30, with Margaret, came in the Confidence April 24, 1638, as servants to Peter Noyes. He settled at Sudbury. Wife Bridget; ch. Sarah b. 10 (2) 1646.

He d. 19 July, 1655; his will dated 17 July, prob. 2 (8) 1655, beq. to wife Bridget; dau. Sarah, under 21; bro. John D.; sister Margaret Bennett; apprentice Joseph Newton; to bro. Henry Loker; 10 s to Mr. Hunt. [Reg.

*This may be the son of Dolor.

DAVIS, etc., cont.

XIX, 43.] The widow m. Dec. 26, 1655, Thomas King.

Robert, Barnstable, 1645. Ch. Deborah b. Jan. 1645, Mary b. May 1648, Andrew b. May 1650, John b. March 1, 1652, Robert b. Aug. 1654, Josias b. Sept. 1656, Hannah b. Sept. 1658, Sarah b. Oct. 1660.

Will dated 14 April, 1688, prob. June 29, 1693, beq. to wife Ann; sons Joseph, Josiah, Robert and Andrew; daus. Deborah Geere, Sarah and Mary Davis and Hannah Dexter.

Samuel, Rumney Marsh, Boston. He was rec'd to chh. Boston 31 (3) 1646, from chh. of Watertown. Wife Anna adm. chh. 17 (2) 1646; ch. Susanna b. May 4, 1646, *Mary* bapt. 31 (3) 1646, ae. about 26 days, Susanna bapt. 28 (3) 1648, ae. about 3 days, Priscilla b. Aug. 3, 1650, Samuel b. at Braintree 22 (1) 1653, Sarah d. at Br. 29 (6) 1658, William d. 21 (7) 1657, Mary b. May 21, 1660, Sarah b. Sept. 11, 1661, Mary b. March 21, 1663, Elizabeth b. Oct. 6, 1664, Esther b. Jan. 19, 1665, Rebecca b. July 9, 1667, Nathaniel b. Nov. 26, 1669.

Will dated 2 May, prob. 4 July, 1672. Wife Anna; ch. Hannah Griggs, Abigail and Mary Townsend, Priscilla (lately married,) and Gershom.

Susan, ae. 16, came in the Blessing in July, 1635.

Thomas, sawyer, from Marlborough, Eng., came in the James April 5, 1635. Settled at Newbury. Frm. June 2, 1641. He deposed in 1662, ae. about 60 years. Rem. to Haverhill; mason, propr. 1646; town officer. He m. in England Christian —; [Hav. rec.] she d. April 7, 1668. His dau. Joanna m. George Corliss. His son Joseph d. Sept. 15, 1671.

Thomas himself d. July 27, 1683. Admin. gr. Oct 30 to Wm. Neffe; another admin. gr. in 1728 to his gr. gr. son John Corliss of Hav.

Tobias, Roxbury, 1646. Wife Sarah was bur. Feb. 15, 1648. He m. Dec. 13, 1649, Bridget Kinman. Ch. Sarah b. Feb. 10, 1646, John b. April 17, 1651, Tobias b. June 10, 1653, Isaac b. 7 (10) 1655.

He d. April 25, 1690. Will dated 9 June, 1684, prob. 14 July, 1690, beq. to wife; dau. Sarah Stephens and her ch. Sarah, John,

DAVIS, etc., cont.
Joseph, Mary, Hannah and Timothy; to son John and dau. Abigail.

William, smith, Boston, 1635. Wife Mary; ch. Abigail b. 31 (8) 1635, d. 24 (12) 1639, Thomas b. 15 (1) 1636, d. (5) 1638, Aaron b. 20 (5) 1638, d. 32 (8) 1639, John d. 20 (1) 1640, Trine (son,) b. 10 (6) 1640, Mary b. 3 (8) 1644.
He died in 1644; the widow m. 2. John Cowdall, who sold house and land which had been Davies' 8 (12) 1644. His son William petitioned the Gen. Court for the portions due to him and his bros. and sisters; referred to a deed of Cowdall and his mother. [Arch. 15 B.]

William, gunsmith, Boston, sold land in Bo. 27 (4) 1646. [Book of Poss.] Captain. He contracted at Springfield 31 (8) and m. at Bo. 6 (10) 1644, Margaret, dau. of Mr. John Pynchon. [Spr. and Bo. rec.] She d. 3 (5) 1653; he m. 2. Huldah, dau. of Rev. Zech. Symmes; after her death he m. Sarah —. Ch. Thomas b. 3 (7) 1645, Anna bapt. 5 (7) 1647, ae. about 8 days, Benjamin bapt, 19 (6) 1649, ae. about 2 days, Ephraim bapt. 18 (3) 1651, d .2 (6) 1652, William b. June 25, 1653, Sarah bapt. 3 (7) 1654, Joanna b. Aug. 16, 1655, *Elizabeth* bapt. 26 (6) 1655, Mary b. Dec. 3, 1656, Rebecca b. Aug. 3, 1658, Huldah b. Dec. 21, 1659, Ruth bapt. 17 (12) 1660, Ruth b. Feb. 12, 1662, Deborah b. April 13, 1665, Margaret b. Nov. 13, 1667.
He made will 17 May, prob. 26 May, 1676; beq. to wife Sarah; ch. Thomas, Benjamin, William, John, Elizabeth, Maria, Rebecca, Huldah, Ruth, Margarita and Hannah. The ch. he had by former wife Huldah to have what comes from the est. of her parents, Mr. Zechariah and Mrs. Sarah Symmes; his mother Elizabeth Davis is to be paid £ 4 per annum; beq. to bros. and sisters Brock, Savage, Willis, Prout, Usher and William Symmes; to mother ffarmer and sister Wyman, etc.

William, apothecary, Boston, adm. chh. 28 (5) 1644, frm. May, 1645. Bought land in 1648. [Book of Poss.] Appears to the writer to be William, merchant, late of Boston, now of Barbadoes, who, with wife Mary, sold land in Bo. 12 April, 1658. [Suff. De. III.]

N. B. William, Sen., and William, Jun., who are designated as propr.s in the Bk. of Pos. may be the two latter; descriptions of lands are not clear. A William D. was of Roxbury and Muddy River at a later period. He d. 18 (10) 1678, ae. 66 years.

DAVISON,
Nicholas, merchant, agent for Mr. Matthew Craddock, res. in Charlestown in 1639. Res. at Medford in 1642. [Mdx. De. I.] He ret. to Eng. and came again, ae. 45, in the Speedwell, May 30, 1656. He m. Joanna Miller; she was adm. chh. 14 (1) 1652.
Will dated 26 March, 1655, prob. 11 (5) 1664, beq. to wife Joan ,son Daniel and dau. Sarah; to bro. John D., whereabouts unknown; to sister Mary Hodges alias Anderson, wife to John A., and their children; to ch. of bro. Jeremy D. dec., who married and lived at Lin in old Eng.; to nephews Em and Joan Rash. One fourth part of the estate to the town of Charlestown, if wife and children die before inheriting it. She m. 2, Richard Kent, [Jr.] and, ae. about 65 years, sold land Mr. D. had owned, June 21, 1678.
The widow m. Richard Kent, Jr.

DAVY,
John, Boston. See Davis, John, above.

DAWE, DAWES,
John, before Gen. Court Sept. 6, 1631.

John, Boston. Will dated 13 Jan. 1682, prob. 18 (9) 1684. Wife Mary and children.

William, ae. 15, came in the Planter April 6, 1635; res. at Braintree. Frm. May 6, 1646. Rem. to Boston. Wife Susanna; ch. Ambrose b. in Br. 24 (5) 1642, Joanna bapt. 2 (4) 1650, Susan bapt. 17 (8) 1652, William b. 8 March, 1655, Johanna bapt. 2 (2) 1657, d. 14 Jan. 1659, Jonathan b. Nov. 3, 1661.
William, a mason, a good man, full of days, d. March 24, 1703-4. [S.]

DAWSE,
Priscilla, maid servant to Mr. Thomas Oliver, Boston, adm. chh. 14 (2) 1639. She was dism. 22 (9) 1640, as the wife of John Rogers, to chh. of Watertown.

DAWSON,
Henry, laborer, Boston, 1640, adm. chh. 16 (3) 1641, frm. June 2, 1641. Prosecuted by Gen. Court. [W.]

DAY, DEA,
Anthony, Gloucester, propr. before 1645. He signed the mill agreement in 1664, and deposed about the matter in 1695, ae. about 80 years. [Es. Deeds 39, 138.] Wife Susan; ch. John b. 28 (2) 1657, Ezekiel b. March 12, 1659, Ezekiel b. 19, (3) 1662, Nathaniel b. 9 (7) 1665, Elizabeth b. 2 (2) 1667, Samuel b. 25 (12) 1669, Joseph b. 4 (2) 1672. The bond of his admin. Ezekiel D. was signed May 13, 1708.

Hannah, ae. 20, came in the Elizabeth and Ann in May, 1635.

John, Watertown, propr. 1642.

Ralph, mason, Dedham, townsman 1 (11) 1644, frm. May, 1645. Beat the drum for meetings. He m. 12 (8) 1647, Susan Fairbank; she d. 8 (5) 1659; and he m. 15 (9) 1659, Abigail Ruggles; ch. Elizabeth b. and d. in 1648, Mary b. 9 (9) 1649, Susan b. 1652, John b. 15 (2) 1654, Abigail b. 22 (2) 1661.
Inv. of his est. taken 10 (11) filed 1 (12) 1677, includes mason's tools. In his will, dated Sept. 12, prob. Feb. 1, 1677, he beq. to wife Abigail, ch. John, Ralph, Mary, (wife of John Payn,) and Abigail. Tools and drum to Ralph; citterne to Abigail; one of his swords to son-in-law John Ruggles.

Robert, propr. 1634; ae. 30, came in the Hopewell in April, 1635; settled at Cambridge; frm. May 6, 1635.
He d. in 1648.

Robert, ae. 30, came in the Elizabeth of Ipswich April 30, 1637, with wife Mary, ae. 28; frm. June 2, 1641. Settled at Ipswich; res. before 1641; brickmaker, town officer. Will dated 11 Aug., prob. 25 Sept. 1683, beq. to son John, referring to his marriage with Sarah Pengry; to son James, and daus. Hannah Lord and Sarah Fiske.

Stephen, printer, locksmith, Cambridge, propr. 1636.
He set up his press in March, 1638-9, at the charge of Mr. Glover who d. on the way hither. Printed 1st the freeman's oath, next an almanac, then the Bay Psalm Book. [W.] Deposed April 6, 1656, ae. 62 yrs. Was one of the petitioners for a plantation at Nashaway (Lancaster) in 1648; had much land and was active in the affairs of the plantation, but did not remove thither. [Mdx. Files, 1662.] Wife Rebecca, widow of —

DAY, etc., cont.
Boardman and mother of William B., came to N. E. with him; she d. Oct. 17, 1658. Ch. Stephen d. 1 (10) 1639, Matthew d. 10 (3) 1649.
He d. before Jan. 27, 1668, when the inv. of his est. was taken, which was filed by William Boardman.

Thomas, Lynn, a witness in 1647. Inv. of his est. taken 9 (4) 1670, and admin. gr. to his widow Mary.

Wentworth, gent., a singleman, Boston, adm. chh. 12 (7) 1640. Propr. 26 (2) 1641, had land at Lynn about 1651. He m. Elizabeth, dau. of — and Sarah Story; her father d. in Eng. and her mother became the second wife of Rev. John Cotton, with whom she came to N. E. Ch. Elizabeth bapt. 26 (7) 1641, ae. about 4 days, Wentworth bapt. 13 (6) 1643, ae. about 6 days.

DEACON, DEAKIN, DAKIN, DEYKING,
John, ae. 28, came in the Abigail in July, 1635, with wife Alice, ae. 30. Settled at Lynn; propr. 1638; blacksmith. Witness in Es. Court in 1646. He deposed in 1662, ae. about 60. [Es. Files.] Wife Alice d. 27 (5) 1657, and he m. 2, 25 (10) 1657, Elizabeth, widow of John Pickering. Rem. to Boston. Sold land in Lynn 5 April, 1670.

DEACON, alias FRANCIS,
John, Plymouth, found dead in Feb. 1635-6. Property delivered by John Howland 2 July, 1640, to Daniel Salmon of Saugus for Richard Francis als. Deacon of Barnestone, co. Leicester, Eng., bro. of the deceased. [Plym. Col. Rec. XIII.]

DEANE, see Dane,
John, Taunton, frm. Plym. Col. Dec. 4, 1638.
Will prob. June 7, 1660; about 60 yrs. old. Wife Alice; ch. John, Thomas, Israel, Isaac, Nathaniel, and Elizabeth; bro. Walter D. [Reg. V, 388.]

Stephen, came in the Fortune in 1621 to Plymouth. Had liberty to set up a mill to beat corn in 1632; afterward a grindingmill. Frm. 1633. Bought house and land in 1633. He m. about 1627 Elizabeth, dau. of widow Mary Ring.
He d. Sept. 1634. Admin. Oct. 2, 1634; ch.

DEANE, cont.
Elizabeth, Miriam and Susanna. The widow m. Josias Cooke, and res. at Eastham. [Reg. III, 378.]
Rachel, ae. 31, came in the Planter, April, 1635.

Walter, bro. of John, tanner, Taunton, frm. Plym. Col. Dec. 4, 1638. Town officer. Walter D. with wife Eleanor joined in a deed Aug. 20, 1693. [Reg. III, 375.]

DEARE,
Philip, Salem, before the Gen. Court 6 March, 1637-8.

DEARING, DEERING,
Samuel, Braintree. He m. in 1647 Bethia, dau. of Gregory Baxter; ch. Bethia b. 6 (6) 1649, Mary b. 16 (11) 1652, Hannah b. 14 (12) 1654, Sarah b. and d. 1657, Elizabeth b. 12 (7) 1670. The wife Bethia d. 11 (3) 1649; he m. 5 (9) 1651, Mary Ray; she d. 5 (1) 1657. He m. 9 (10) 1657, Mary Nucome.
He d. 23 (8) 1671; admin. gr. 13 (1) 1671-2, to widow Mary. She m. 27 (2) 1675, George Speere.

DEEKES, see Dix.

DEIGHTON,
Thomas, merchant, Boston, witness to a document 27 (9) 1645. Had acct. with Mrs. Elizabeth Poole of Westminster, Eng. 24 (9) 1640. [A.]

DELANOY, DELANO, De La NOYE,
Philip, b. of French parents, [Wins.,] came to Plymouth from Leyden in the Fortune in 1621. Had lands assigned March, 1623; frm. 1633. Rem. to Duxbury; planter. He deposed 21 (4) 1641, ae. about 36 yrs. [L.] He volunteered for the Pequot War in 1637. He m. Dec. 19, 1634, Hester Dewsbery. He m. 2, Mary, dau. of William Pontus and widow of James Glasse; conveyed lands in 1664.
Nunc. will testified to 22 Aug. 1681, prob. 7 July, 1682. Sons Philip, Thomas, John and Samuel, (only son to the relict;) daus. Jane and Rebecca.

DELL, DILL,
Capt. George, mariner, Salem, propr. 1638. Boston 1645. Wife Abigail; ch. John b. (8) 1645, Samuel b. 31 (6) 1647, Joseph b. Feb. 1649, Benjamin b. 27 (2) 1652.
Will prob. Aug. 26, 1655. Beq. to sons; to bro. Ralph Dell; to bro. Mr. Richard Barachew of Hackney, near London. Essex Prob. [Reg. V, 443, and VIII, 77.] The widow m. 8 (9) 1655, John Hanniford.

DENING, DENIN, DENYN, [DENNE,]
William, Boston, servant to Wm. Brenton, adm. chh. 23 (1) 1634. Propr. 14 (10) 1635.
Will prob. Jan. 31, 1653; wife Ann; son Obediah in Eng.; kinswoman Mary Powell. [Reg. V, 302.]

DENLY, DONLY,
Jude, servant to Thomas Jones, came in the Confidence April 11, 1638.

DENNIS, DENNY, DINNY,
Edward, Boston, servant to Wm. Hutchinson, adm. chh. 29 (3) 1636; frm. April 17, 1637. Wife Sarah adm. 22 (7) 1639.

Edmund, Boston. Wife Sarah; ch. Sarah bapt. 9 (6) 1640, Mary b. 27 (4) 1642, Martha b. 1 (3) 1644, John b. 18 (12) 1645, Joseph b. 13 (4) 1648, Benjamin bapt. 22 (7) 1650.

Mary, ae. 24, servant to John Brown, came from Baddow, Essex, in June, 1639, in the Desire.

Robert, carpenter, planter, Yarmouth, brought suit in Court 2 March, 1640-1. Prop., frm. 4 June, 1650. Town officer. Juror. Ch. a son d. 1649, Mary b. Sept. 19, 1649.

William, shoemaker, Scituate; frm. Mass. March 9, 1637; bought land 24 March, 1638. Settled the affairs of his son William who had gone to Eng. in 1642.
Will, dated Feb. 16, 1649, prob. 5 March, 1656, beq. to son-in-law Wm. Parker and Judith his wife, my daughter; to Remember, Dependance and Experience Leichfield. [Reg. V, 335.] j

DENNISON, DENISON,
Mr. William, Roxbury, frm. July 3, 1632. He was b. at Bishop's Stortford, co. Hertford, Eng.; m. Nov. 7, 1603, Margaret [Chandler?] Monck. Ch. John, Daniel bapt. Oct. 18, 1612, Edward bapt. Nov. 3, 1616, George bapt. Dec. 20, 1620. He brought 3 children to N. E., all sons, Daniel, Edward and George. Daniel m. at Newtowne and was joyned to the church there. He afterwards moved to the chh. at Ipswich. [E.] These sons became very prominent citizens of the colony. He was chosen by the Court constable of Roxbury Nov. 5, 1633. Authorized to press men for the building of a bridge 27 (8) 1647. Deputy. He signed the inv. of Joseph Weld in 1646.

He was bur. Jan. 25, 1653. His wife Margaret was bur. Feb., 1645. His son, Maj. Gen. Daniel, left a sketch of the family history which is given in Reg. XLVI, and a pedigree is printed in same vol.

DENNY,
Mary, came as a servant, ae. 24, with John Brown, tailor, in 1635.

DENSLOW,
Nicholas, Dorchester, frm. March 4, 1632-3. Rem. to Windsor, Conn. Died 8 March, 1666, ae. 90 years. Old wido. D. d. 14 Aug. 1669.

DENT,
Francis, Salem, frm. May 14, 1634; propr. 1638.

Admin. of his goods granted by Gen. Court 5 (1) 1638-9, to Edmund Audeley.

DEORDALL,
Hugh, millwright, Hingham; gave a bond June 24, 1641. [L.]

DERBY, see Darby.

DERIFALL, DORYFALL, DERREFORD, DERISOULD,
Anne, ae. 24, came in the Elizabeth of Ipswich April 30, 1634. Maid servant to Wm. Coddington, adm. chh. Boston 2 (9) 1634.

Barnabas, Boston, adm. chh. 1632-3, frm. May 25, 1636; dism. to chh. of Braintree 24 (3) 1640. Propr. 1648. Propr. at

DERIFALL, etc., cont.
Lynn before 1655. [Suff. De. II, 267.] His wife Elizabeth d. at Br. 16 Sept. 1679; he d. Feb. 2, 1680.

Will dated 28 Jan. prob. 24 Feb. 1680, beq. to kinsman Samuel Spencer all his est. in consideration of his taking care of him the rest of his life; with small legacies to Samuel's bros. Obediah and Thomas S.

DESALLENOVA, see Salinovas.

DESBOROUGH, DISBOROUGH, DESBRO, DEESBURY,
Isaac, husbandman, ae. 18, of Ell-Tisley, co. Cambridge, came in the Hopewell in April, 1635. Settled at [Lynn.] Suit in Es. Court in 1638. Before Gen. Court 5 (1) 1638-9. [See Eng. Gl. by H. F. Waters in Reg. XLI, 353.]

Peter, Roxbury. He made Jonathan Pope of Rox. his attorney to receive wages due him from Griffith Bowen 28 (10) 1647.

Thomas, residence not given. Admin. gr. by the Court Sept. 3, 1633, to Mr. John Moody.

DEVEL, DEVILE, DEVAL, DEVOL,
Walter, Plymouth, in Court 2 Oct. 1637; brought suit, 1640.

William, Braintree. Rem. to Rehoboth; propr. 1643. Ch. John b. and d. 1643.

DEVEREAUX, DEVERIXE, DEVORUX,
John, fisherman, Salem, Marblehead. Deposed Dec. 24, 1694, ae. about 80, that he came from old England to Sal. about 1630 and had lived there and at Marb. ever since. [Es. Court Rec.] Servant of Joseph Dalliber in 1642. Had suit with Valentine Hill of Boston regarding his service in fishing at Monhegan about 1649. [Es. Files.] Wife Ann deposed in 1667, ae. about 46 years.

DEWER,
Thomas, tailor, Boston. He bought house, onsett and garden in B. May 15, 1648. One of the founders of the Scottish Charitable Society; member 1657-1665.

Admin. was gr. 15 Dec. 1694, to his son Sampson D., cooper.

DEVOTION,
Edward, planter, a singleman, adm. chh. Boston, 22 (1) 1645; frm. May 1645. Res. at Muddy River. Wife Mary; ch. Mary bapt. 25 (12) 1648, ae. about 4 days, Elizabeth bapt. 20 (2) 1651, (m. Joseph Weld,) Martha b. March 13, 1653, (m. John Ruggles,) Hannah b. Dec. 13, 1654, (m. John Ruggles,) Deborah bapt. 17 (3) 1657, John bapt. 26 (4) 1659, Sarah b. June 19, 1662, (m. Joseph Griffin).
He was bur. 23 (7) 1685, ae. 64. Will prob. 27 Oct. 1685. Beq. his est. to wife Mary, sons John, Edward and Thomas.

Margaret, ae. 9, came in the Abigail in July, 1635.

DEWEY, DUEE,
Thomas, Dorchester, frm. May 14, 1634. Rem. to Windsor, Conn. His son Thomas m. 1 (4) 1648, Constance Hawes. See Clap, Roger.

DEWING, DUIN,
Andrew, Dedham, adm. chh. 19 (2) 1646, frm. May 6, 1646. Wife Lydia d. 13 (8) 1651. He m. 10 (9) 1652, An Donstall. Ch. John b. 16 (12) 1649, John b. and d. 1651, Andrew b. 26 (11) 1655, Jonathan b. April 3, 1663, Deborah b. 1 (8) 1668.
He d. 16 (7) 1677. Will dated 8 (7) prob. 30 (8) 1677; wife Ann; eldest son Andrew, youngest son Jonathan; eldest dau. Lydia; other daus. Anne and Deborah.

DEWHURST,
Roger, Salem, called to court 3 (4) 1645.

DEXTER,
Francis, ae. 13, came in the Planter April 6, 1635.

Richard, planter, Boston, 1641. He rem. to Charlestown. He deposed 27 (6) 1666, ae. about 68 years. [Mdx. Files.] Wife Bridget; ch. Sarah b. 1 (9) 1644, (m. about 1666, Edmund Pinson,) Elizabeth.

Thomas, farmer, Lynn, in Court for battery on Capt. Endicott 3 May, 1631. He bought Nahant of an Indian about 1632, but the town claimed prior ownership. [Es. Files 29, 144.] Mortgaged his farm of 800 acres and his fishing weir at Lynn in 1640 and 1642. Gave property at Sandwich to son Thomas in Oct. 24, 1638, with the pro-

DEXTER, cont.
vision that Thomas should pay money to his daus. Mary and Frances. [L.] Mary m. John Frend, q. v. Rem. to Sandwich. Arbitrated a difference with alderman Hooke of Bristol, Eng. 30 (4) 1648. [A.] Rem. to Boston.
He d., and admin. was granted 9 Feb. 1676, to Capt. James Oliver and the son, Thomas D., Jr. Land at Lynn, debts at Barnstable, etc.

DIBBLE, DEEBLE, DYBELL,
Abraham, Dorchester. Rem. to Boston. Rem. to Southfield, (Suffield,) Conn. [See Allen, Henry.] Wife Lydia; ch. John b. 7 (5) bapt. at Bo. 16 (5) 1648, John bapt. 25 (6) 1650.

John, Springfield, propr. 1641. Ch. Zachary b. 4 (2) 1644, Elizabeth b. 11 (11) 1645, Sarah b. 26 (1) 1647.
He d. in 1646. The widow m. 2 (9) 1647, William Grave of Standford. [Spr. rec.]

Robert, Dorchester, propr., frm. May 6, 1635. Bailiff, 1638-1640. His son Thomas, to whom a house lot was gr. 17 Dec. 1635, on condition of his building within a year, is apparently the Thomas, husbandman, ae. 22, who, with Frances, "soror;" ae. 24, came from Weymouth, Eng., before March 20, 1635. Settled at Dorchester, propr., frm. May 17, 1637. Rem. to Windsor, Conn.

DICKERMAN,
Thomas, tailor, Dorchester, frm. March 14, 1638-9. Wife Ellen; ch. Abraham, Isaac b. (9) 1637, John bapt. 29 (7) 1644, Sarah b. at Malden, Oct. 1653, Thomas b. do. Aug. 1655.
He d. 3 (11) 1657. Inv. of his est, filed and admin. gr. to the widow 25 (11) 1657. Property at Dorch. and Boston. His widow m. John Bullard of Medfield before 1663.

DICKERSON, DICKARSON, DICKINSON, DIXISON, see DICKSON,
Philemon, tanner, servant to Benjamin Cooper of Branton, Eng., passed exam. to come to Salem, N. E. May 10, 1637. Propr. 1638. Had land granted for tan pits, etc., in 1639 Frm. June 2, 1641. Adm. chh. 7 (12) 1640, Mary adm. chh. 30 (2) 1648. Ch. Mary bapt. 20 (1) 1641-2, Thomas bapt. 10 (1) 1643-

DICKERSON, etc., cont.
4, Eliz. bapt. 28 (4) 1646, Peter bapt. 9 (5) 1648. Legatee of Edward Skinner in 1641.

Thomas, before Gen. Court 1639 and 1640. Rowley, propr. Wife Jennet; Ch. James b. 6 (7) 1640, Mary b. 27 (7) 1642, Sarah b. Oct. 18, 1644, Mercy b. (8) 1646, Martha b. 9 (12) 1648, Thomas b. 26 (8) 1655, bur. 30 March, 1659. He was bur. 29 (1) 1662.

Will dated 8 March, 1661, prob. 17 April, 1662, beq. to wife Jennet, son James daus. Sarah and three other daughters.

DICKSON, DIXON, DIXSON, see DICKINSON,

Rachel, came May 10, 1637, with her grandmother, Margaret Neave of Great Yarmouth, Eng., widow.

Rebecca, maid servant to Richard Bellingham, adm. chh. Boston 2 (3) 1634.

John, planter, Salisbury, propr. 1639. He m. 1 Mary —, who d. April 16, 1647; 2, Ann living in 1664; 3. April 14, 1681, Alice —, who survived him and m. William Allen. Ch. Mary b. March 12, 1639-40, John b. Oct. 20, 1642.

He d. Dec. 30, 1683.

Will prob. 1684. Mentions wife and her gr. ch. Samuel Adams; son John D. and dau. Mary Roe; to dau.-in-law Mary Pressie the great chest that was her mother's.

William, Cambridge, res. in 1633, [Col. Rec.] propr. 1641; frm. May 18, 1642. Wife Jane; ch. Mary b. 10 (6) 1644, Lydia, Abigail b. 10 (1) 1647, Mary bur. 21 (5) 1648, Hannah, John. The wife d. Dec. 4, 1689, ae. about 73. [Gr. st.]

He d. Aug. 5, 1692, ae. 78. [Gr. st.]

DIDCUTT,
John, mariner, Sandwich, took oath of allegiance 12 Feb. 1638-9.

DIFFY,
Richard, servant to Mr. Saltonstall, punished for misdemeanor Nov. 9, 1630.

DIKE, see Dix,

DILL, see Dell.

DILLINGHAM,
Edward, Lynn; witness at Salem Court in 1637; joined in the founding of Sandwich; propr. 3 April, 1637. Wife Ursula d. Feb. 9, 1656.

Will, May 1, 1666, prob. 5 June, 1667; was in the form of a deed of gift to his two sons Henry and John; property in his hands whose owners, specified, res. in Biteswell and other places in Lancashire, Eng. [Reg. VII, 225.]

John, Boston, memb. chh. 1630-1, juryman 1631, Ipswich, propr. 1634.

He d. before 6 Sept., 1636, when the Court app. adminrs. Wife Sarah d. soon. Her will dated 14 July, 1636, prob. at Es. Court, 2. (10) 1636, [original, with sundry papers, in Arch. 15 B.]; beq. to her only child Sarah D.; to her mother Thomasine Caly, bros. Abraham and Jacob C., sisters Bull and Bast, wives of John Bull and John Base, Rebecca and Emme C., all in England; to her pastor, Mr. Ward; to Richard Saltonstall and Samuel Appleton and their wives, committing her child and estate to their care. [Es. Ant. 1.]

DIMMOCK,
Rev. Thomas, Barnstable, frm., and deputy, 1639. Lieut. and drill-master, 1643. Ord. teaching elder of the chh. Aug. 7, 1650. Wife —; ch. Timothy bapt. Jan. 12, 1639, bur. June 17, 1640, twin infants bur. March 18, 1640-1, Mehetabel bapt. April 18, 1642, Shubael bapt. Sept. 15, 1644.

Nunc. will prob. 4 June, 1658. Left all to his wife, for the children were hers as well as his.

DIMOND, DIAMOND,
John, Salem or Lynn, in court in 1648; he and his man witnesses at court in 1649.

DINELY, DYNELEY,
William, barber, Boston, adm. chh. 10 (11) 1635, frm. April 17, 1637. Wife Alice; ch. John, Thomas b. 9 (11) 1635, d. 15 (11) 1654, Abigail b. (10) 1637, Fathergone b. 25 (10) 1638.

He died, and the widow m. second about Aug. 15, 1639, Richard Critchley.

DINGAM, DENGHAM, DENGAINE,
Mr. Henry, Watertown, propr. 1636, also propr. at Dedham. Rem. to Roxbury. Referred to as Doctor Dengham in Mdx. De. X, 52. He m. in April, 1641, Elizabeth Alcock.
He d. 10 (8) 1645.

DINGLEY,
John, smith, Sandwich, of military age 4 Dec., 1638, frm. 5 June 1644, town officer. Rem. to Marshfield. Deputy.
Admin. of his est. gr. March 18, 1689-90; distribution made to son Jacob, daus. Sarah, wife of Wm. Ford and Hannah, wife of Josiah Keane, and to gr. son Joseph D.

DINSDALE, DINSDELL,
William, cooper, Boston, adm. chh. 23 (1) 1657, frm. May 6, 1657, town officer. Wife Martha; ch. John b. (3) 1644, Martha b. 10 (11) 1648, Mary b. 24 (7) 1651, Sarah b. 7 Jan. 1657, John, Adam, William, Martha and Mary bapt. 5 (2) 1657, and Sarah bapt. 10 (11) folg.; Thomas b. and d. 1660, Joseph b. Nov. 21, 1661, *Jonathàn* bapt. 24 (9) 1661.
He d. 26 (3) 1675; and admin. was gr. to his eldest sons John and Adam in behalf of their mother; they joined with others in testifying that their father wished his est. to stand for his wife's maintenance, and be divided after her death. The wife Martha d. Aug. 7, 1696.

DITCHFIELD, DUTCHFIELD,
Mr. Thomas, Boston, before Gen. Court in 1641, res. 1644. Wife Anne; ch. Jone b. and d. 1644, Posthumus b. (6) 1645.
He was bur. 24 (2) 1645.

DIX, DIKE, DICKES, DEIKE, DEEKS, DIXE, DYKES,
Anthony, master of a vessel, Salem, had grant of land in 1636 for a home and for fishing trade. Was in business along the coast in 1632, etc., with Francis Johnson, q. v. Captured by the pirate Bull, he refused to act as pilot for him. [W.] He was cast away upon the head of Cape Cod in 1639. [C.] The widow's land is mentioned in a deed 25 (5) 1639. She m. 2. Nathaniel Pickman.

Edward, Charlestown, memb. chh. 1630; rem. to Watertown; frm. March 4, 1634-5. Town officer. Wife Jane; ch. Abigail b. 2 (3) 1637, Mary b. 2 (3) 1639, John b. 4 (7) 1640, Rebecca b. 18 (12) 1641.

DIX, etc., cont.
He d. July 9, 1660. Will mentions wife, and a bond given her for certain estate of hers; son John; dau. Abigail, wife to Thomas Parks; alludes to two other daus. The widow Susanna brought suit for dowry against Sergt. John Wincoll and John Dix April 2, 1661. She petitioned 18 (10) 1660, ae. between 60 and 70 years; youngest child about 16 years old. [Mdx. Files.]

Ralph, fisherman, Ipswich, was paid by the town in 1643 for service against the Indians. Propr. 1658. Had a bond for payment of money from Wm. White 2 Oct. 1647. Perhaps Ester, who was rec'd to the church of Reading, with her children, from the chh. of Ips. 30 (8) 1665, may be of this family.

Samuel, joiner, ae. 43, of Norwich, Eng., with wife Joane, ae. 38, ch. Priscilla and Abigail, and servants Wm. Storey, ae. 23, and Daniel Lindsey, ae. 18, passed exam. April 8, 1637 to go to Boston in N. E. to reside. But no record of them here. Widow, Ipswich, propr. 1639, may be the widow of Anthony, of Salem.

DIXEY, DIXIE, DIXER,
Thomas, Salem, 1637; rem. to Marblehead. Kept the ferry at Darby Fort side in 1644. Ensign. His wife adm. chh. 17 (7) 1643. Ch. Thomas bapt. 18 (4) 1643, Mary bapt. 12 (11) 1644, John bapt. 13 (10) 1646, Abigail bapt. 1 (8) 1648, Thomas bapt. 29 (11) 1653, Margaret bapt. 16 (1) 1655-6, John bapt. 26 (2) 1657, Samuel bapt. 20 (1) 1662-3.
Will dated 28 Feb. 1680, prob. at Boston 31 Aug. 1686, beq. to son-in-law Gabriel Holman; sons Thomas, John, and Samuel; wife Mary and daus. Mary Holman, Abigail Smith, Remember White and Hannah Bowin

William, Salem, propr. frm. May 14, 1634. Before the court for taking too high wages 27 (7) 1636. Sergeant. Authorized to keep a "horse boat ferry" 11 (10) 1639. Rem. to Beverly. [Wife] Anne memb. chh. before 1636. Ch. Abigail bapt. 25 (10) 1636, Anna bapt. 17 (4) 1638, John bapt. 19 (10) 1639, Eliza bapt. 3 (8) 1641, Sarah bapt. 2 (5) 1643. He deposed to the inv. of the est. of his son Samuel Dixer at Boston, Jan. 30, 1661. His dau. Elizabeth Stone was adm. to full com. in Salem chh. 20 (6) 1665, and had 4 ch. He deposed 16 Feb. 1680, ae. about 73 years;

DIXEY, etc., cont.
came to Salem in June, 1629. [Es. Files.] [Es. Inst. Coll. XIII.]

His will dated 21 Feb. 1684, prob. 24 June, 1690, beq. to 5 daus., Mary Woodberry, Hannah Judkin, Abigail Stone and Elizabeth Morgan; gr. ch. Elizabeth and Sarah D.; sons-in-law Samuel Morgan, Edmund Gale, Jonathan Stone and John Stone; other gr. ch.

DOBER, see Dover,

DOBSON,

Capt., set forth from Boston in a ship of 80 tons, double manned to trade at the eastward 19 (1) 1646; captured by D'Aulnay. [W.]

Charles. He mortg. his interest in the barque Charles 6 (9) 1649.

DODD, DOD,
George, mariner, Boston, 1647. Sold land in Cambridge in 1650. Wife Mary adm. chh. 15 (3) 1647; ch. Patience bapt. 16 (3) 1647, ae. about 1 yr., 35 days, Isaac b. 3 (7) 1651, Mary b. and d. 1653, Elizabeth b. 5 April, 1657, Mehetabel b. May 25, 1660.

He d. in Eng.; the Court gave the widow an allowance out of the est. for herself and the 4 children, July 23, 1663. [Reg. XII, 155.]

James, ae. 16, came in the Abigail in July, 1635.

John, residence not given. He was to receive payment from Chr. Lawson for Robert Saltonstall, May 15, 1648.

DODGE, DODS,
Richard, Salem. Adm. chh. 5 (3) 1644. Ch. Richard and Sarah bapt. 3 (5) 1644, Elizabeth adm. chh. 20 (2) 1645. Elizabeth adm. chh. 28 (12) 1657. He rem. to Wenham; propr. in 1644, Beverly.

Will, dated 14 (9) 1670, inv. June 27, 1671; wife Edith, ch. John, Richard, Samuel, Edward, Joseph, Mary Herrick, and Sarah; bro. Wm. D., Sen.; bro. Michael D. in Eng. to pay rent for land he occupies. The widow Edith, in will dated Feb. 14, 1677, gave her est. to daus. Mary (wife of Zachary) Herrick, Sarah, (wife of Peter) Woodbury, and their children; and to sons Edward and others.

William, husbandman, a passenger in the Lyon's Whelp in 1629 to Salem; recom-

DODGE, etc., cont.
mended by the Mass. Bay Co. to Gov. Endecott to have charge of a team of horses. He bought 200 acres of land in Salem bounds 28 (7) 1644. Ch. John bapt. 25 (10) 1636, William bapt. 19 (7) 1640, Hannah bapt. 24 (5) 1642.

DOGGETT, DOGGED, DOGED, DAGGETT,
John, Watertown, appl. frm. Oct. 19, 1630, adm. frm. May 18, 1631. Propr. Rem. to Rehoboth and then to Martha's Vineyard. Propr., frm. and deputy. He m. at Reh. 23 (9) 1651, Ann Sutton. He made will May 13, 1673; beq. to wife; to sons John, Joseph and Thomas; daus. Elizabeth and Hephzibah. Lands chiefly at "Martins Vineyard." Friend Isaac Robinson and son-in-law John Eedy overseers of his est. on the islands.

Thomas, ae. 30, servant to Thomas Olliver of Norwich, Eng., passed exam. to go to N. E. May 13, 1637. Settled at Concord. Rem. to Weymouth. Planter, town officer. Rem. to Marshfield; selectman. His wife d. at Conc. 23 (6) 1642. He m. 2. [Elizabeth] the widow of William Fry of Weymouth, and held the lands of her daus. till their majority. He m. 3. Joane, widow of Thomas Chillingworth, q. v. She was bur. Sept. 4, 1684. Ch. Rebecca b. at Mars. July 29, 1655.

He d. Aug. 18, 1692. Beq. to sons John and Samuel; to dau. Sarah Sherman's ch. Prudence, Sarah and Susanna; to daus. Hannah Blancher and Rebecca Wilder and their children. See Genealogy.

DOLE,
Richard, merchant, Newbury. He gave a release of a mortg. of Thomas Davis 22 Sept. 1673. [Norf. rec.] He deposed in 1676, ae. about 52 years. He m. 3 May, 1647, Hannah, dau. of widow Rolfe; she d. 16 Nov. 1678.. He m. 4. March, 1679, Hannah, widow of Capt. Samuel Brocklebank; she d. Sept. 6, 1690. He m. — Patience Walker. Ch. John b. 10 Aug. 1648, Richard b. 6 Sept. 1650, Anna b. and d. 1653, Benjamin b. 14 June 1654, Joseph b. 5 Aug. 1657, William b. 11 April, 1660, Henry b. 9 March, 1663, d. Sept. 13, 1690, Hannah b. 23 Oct. 1665, Apphia b. 7 Dec. 1668, Abner b. 8 March, 1672.

Admin. 30 July, 1705. Genealogy, [Reg. XXXVIII, 74.]

DOLIBER, see Dalliber.

DOLING, see Merry.

DOLTON, see Doten.

DONE, DOANE,
Mr. John, yeoman Plymouth, frm. and Asst. 1632-3, deacon 1633. Rem. to Eastham; townsman 1655.

John, ae. 16, who came in the Truelove in Sept. 1635; Lydia, m. 11 Sept. 1645, Samuel Hicks, probably his children.

He made will 18 May, 1678, ae. 88 years; prob. May 31, 1687; beq. to wife, sons John, Daniel and Ephraim, dau. Abigail; "all my sons and and daughters"; gr. dau. Margaret Hide [or Hix]. The inv. says he d. 21 Feb. 1685, ae. about 100 years. Abigail deposed 29 May, 1686.

DONN, see Dunn.

DORCHESTER,
Anthony, Windsor, Conn. 1644, rem. to Springfield; propr. about 1649. Town officer. Wife Sarah bur. 9 (9) 1649. Ch. John b. at W. 5 Nov. 1644, Sarah b. 12 (8) 1653, Hester b. 25 (8) 1656, d. 17 Nov. 1662 His [second] wife Martha d. 17 Dec. 1662. His son-in-law Samuel Kichwell was bur. 9 (4) 1651.

He d. Aug. 28, 1683. Inv. pres. Sept. 25, 1683, by son John. Agreement made between sons John and James, gr. ch. Benjamin, dau. Mary, wife of John Harmon, dau. Sarah, wife of Joseph Stebbins, and dau.-in-law Martha, wife of Abel Wright, who claimed something for what her mother, the relict of Samuel Kitcherell, once of Hartford, brought to the late Anthony D.

DORLON, DORLUM, DARLIN, DARLINE, [DARLING,]
George, yeoman, farmer, Salem, Lynn and Marblehead, 1647. Witness in John Hathorne case, with wife Kate, in 1657. He deposed in 1670, ae. about 50 years; in 1681, ae. about 66. Wife Katharine, dau. of Richard Gridley, living at the Eastward, mentioned in his will in 1674. She was a witness to the will of Robert Hawes in 1641.

He d. at Salem; inv. taken 13 Sept. 1693, will dated 12 April, prob. Oct. 9, 1693; beq. to wife Katharine, sons Jeames, John, Daniel, Thomas, Benjamin and Henry; daus. Hannah, Sarah and Margaret.

DORETY,
One D., an honest man, was drowned in Boston Bay, Nov. 21, 1634. [W.]

DORMAN,
Thomas, Ipswich, propr. 1634; rem. to Topsfield. Frm. March 4, 1634-5. Wife Ellen d. 27 Feb. 1667-8. Ch. John d. 16 (11) 1661-2, Daniel d. Aug. 10, 1673.

He d. 25 April, 1670. Will dated 24 April, prob. 3 May, 1670, beq. to sons Thomas and Ephraim, and cousin Daniel Bradley.

DORSET, DOSSETT, DASSETT, DUSSETT,
John, yeoman, locksmith, Boston, propr. 1639; rem. to Braintree. Frm. May 13, 1640. Signed petition about meadows in 1646. [Arch. 45.] He and son John, as execs. of the will of Mary Minot of Boston, sold land to his dau. Comfort D. 20 March, 1676. Ch. Jospeh bur. at Br. (10) 1642.

He d. about April, 1677; beq. all to son John and dau. Comfort.

DORYFALL, see Derifall.

DOTEY, DOTEN, DOLTEN, DOWTY,
Edward, planter, of London, servant to Stephen Hopkins, came in the Mayflower; signed the Compact; res. at Plymouth. Frm. 1633. He m. [second] Jan. 6, 1634, Faith, dau. of Thurston Clarke. "By second wife he hath seven children living in 1650." [B.] Ch. Edward, John, Thomas, Samuel, Desire, Elizabeth, Mary, Isaac b. Feb. 8, 1647, Joseph b. 30 April, 1651.

He d. Aug. 23, 1655. Will dated May 20, prob. Nov. 21, 1655; to wife and son Edward. The widow Faith m. March 14, 1666, John Philips of Plymouth. See Genealogy.

DOTTERIS,
John, son of Edward Andrew's wife, came from Eng. as an apprentice of Mr. Taylor; was passed over to the care of Mr Letherbee, who employed him in a bark to Boston. Allowed to remain with his mother 19 (8) 1637. [W.]

DOUGHTY, DOUGHTEY,
Mr. Francis, planter, from Bristol, Eng., at Dorchester 29 (5) 1639. [L.] Wrote Gov. Winthrop in Aug. 1640 from Taunton. Seems to be the minister who opposed the gathering of the church before 1642; he

DOUGHTY, etc., cont.

was obliged to leave the country with wife and children, and went to Aquithneck [L., P. D.] [Mass. Hist. Coll. ⅝.] Before Plym. Court 2 March, 1640-1. Was out of the country when his suit against his sister Mrs. Elizabeth Cole was acted on by Gen. Court 11 Nov. 1647.

James, Scituate; highway surveyor 1662; juryman, 1676. He m. 16 April, 1649, Lydia, dau .of Humphrey Turner. Ch. Mary b. 23 June, 1650, James b. 21 Feb. 1651, Elizabeth b. 5 Nov. 1654, Lydia b. 14 Feb. 1658, Sarah b. 2 April, 1662, Samuel b. 29 Sept. 1664, Robert b. 14 Feb. 1667, Susanna b. 15 Feb. 1670.

DOUNARD,

Marie, ae. 24, servant to James Hosmer, came in the Elizabeth April 9, 1635.

DOUGLASS, DUGLICE,

Henry, Boston, townsman, 30 (1) 1646. Propr. 1650, frm. May 6, 1657. Ch. Anne, (m. 1 Sept., 1660, Eliphalet Het.)

He d. about 17 May, 1667. Will dated 9 Feb. 1662, was prob. 31 July, 1667. 100 li. to the widow Judith; the rest to be divided between the 3 children, a double portion to the eldest son. Wife and son John admin. Land at Cape Fear to gr. ch. Samuel Het. [Reg. XVI, 227.] The widow Judith made will 30 Jan. 1679-80, prob. April 29, 1680; beq. to gr. ch. Samuel, John, Thomas, Hannah and Mary Hitt.

William, cooper, Boston, adm. inhab. 31 (6) 1640. Adm. chh. with wife Anne 7 (1) 1646. Also propr. at Ipswich, 1641. Bought land at Ips. in 1652. Ch. rec. at Boston: Elizabeth b. 26 (6) 1641, Sarah b. 8 (2) 1643, William b. 1 (2) 1645.

See Joan Drake.

DOVE,

Matthew, placed as a servant with John Blackleach of Salem for 4 yrs., June 1, 1640 [L.] Ch. (of sister Dove,) Hannah and Elizabeth bapt. 10 (7) 1654, Dorcas (of Matthew D.) bapt. 5 (8) 1656, Bethiah bapt. 30 (3) 1658, Daniel bapt. 3 (9) 1661, Deborah bapt. 20 (3) 1666, Matthew bapt. 10 (3) 1668.

DOVER, DOBER,

John, Springfield, propr. 1643-1664.

DOW, DOWE, DOUE, DOVE,

Mr. Francis, gent., Salisbury, propr. 1640, commoner, 1650. Ret. to Eng.; was of Salisbury, Eng. in 1664, when Robert Pike was his attorney. His son Peter sold the father's rights at Salis., N. E. in 1674.

Henry, husbandman, of Ormsby, Eng., ae. 29, with wife Joane, ae. 30, 4 ch. and servant Anne Maning, ae. 17, passed exam. to go to N. E. April 11, 1637. Settled at Watertown; frm. May 2, 1638. Rem. to Hampton; deputy, 1655. Gave land 3 (8) 1649 to Thomas Nudd, son of his former wife. Wife Jone, bur. 20 (4) 1640. He m. about 1642 Margaret Cole, q. v. Ch. Henry, (deposed in 1669, ae. about 35,) Thomas d. at Wat., bur. July 10, 1641, Joseph b. 20 (1) 1638, Daniel b. 22 (7) 1641, Mary b. 14 (7) 1643, Thomas b. at Hampton April 28, 1653, Jeremiah b. Sept. 6, 1657, and Hannah.

He d. April 25, 1659. Will dated 16 (2) prob. 4 (8)1659, beq. to wife Margaret, sons Henry, Joseph, Daniel, Thomas, Jeremie; daus. Mary and Hannah.

Thomas, Newbury, frm. June 22, 1642. He bought land and house in 1648. Rem. to Haverhill. Wife Phebe; ch. rec. at N.: Stephen b. 29 March, 1642, Mary b. 26 April, 1644, Martha b. 1 June, 1648.

He d. 31 May, 1654. Will dated 29 May, 1654, prob. 8 (2) 1656, beq. to wife Phebe; sons John, Thomas, Stephen, Mary and Martha, all under 21 years.

DOWNES, DOWNS,

William, servant, before Gen. Court in 1635. Settled at Boston; merchant; had large estate. He m. Hannah, dau. of Mr. Samuel Appleton. They sold to her bro. Samuel and sister Judith in 1676, her share in the est. of her gr. fa. Wm. Paine. [Ips. De. IV, 62.] Admin. of his est. granted 6 April, 1693, to Penn Townsend and others.

DOWNAN, DOWNHAM,

John, Braintree, before Gen. Court 2 (4) 1640. Wife Dorothy; ch. John b. and d. 1644, Joseph b. 30 (2) 1645, Mary bapt. in Boston 2 (11) 1647, ae. 10 days, Mercie b. 1 (7) 1652, Dorothy d. 18 (1) 1657-8, Benjamin b. 14 (8) 1659.

DOWNING,
Mr. Emanuel, gent., son of George Downing, gent., bapt. at Ipswich, Eng., 12 Aug., 1585, a lawyer till 1638, in London; came to Salem; frm. March 14, 1638-9. Deputy and influential citizen. Had large farm at Groton. His house was burned 6 (2) 1645. [W.] Had grant of land near Dover, N. H. Ret. to Eng. and came again, [then perhaps ret. permanently.] He m. at Groton, Eng., 10 April, 1622, Lucy, dau. of Adam Winthrop, Esq., and sister of Gov. John Winthrop, bapt. 27 Jan. 1601. His son George, about 20 yrs. of age, grad. Harv. Coll. 1642, went in a ship to instruct the seamen. Preached at various places on the way to Eng., and was there called to be a preacher in Fairfax's army. [W.] His dau. Ann m. Lieut. Joseph Gardner. Mary, kinswoman to Gov. John Winthrop adm. chh. Boston (9) 1633 . Lucy D., the younger, adm. chh. Salem 4 (2) 1647. Ch. recorded here: John bapt. 1 (1) 1640, Dorcas bapt. 7 (12) 1640, Theophilus bapt. 8 (7) 1644.

Mr. James, Salem, before Ess. court in 1639.

Theophilus, Salem, called to court, 1647. Wife Ellen. Ch. Benjamin bapt. 17 (11) 1646.

DOWSE, DOUSE,
Francis, tanner, one of George Burden's family, Boston, adm. chh. 20 (4) 1640; frm. June 2, 1641. Inhab. 30 (10) 1639. Constable. Wife Katharine adm. chh. 10 (4) 1643. He was dism. to Char. chh. 25 (3) 1651. Ch. Elizabeth b. 20 (6) 1642, (m. 16 Oct., 1659, Samuel Miles,) Mary bapt. 21 (2) 1644, ae. about 6 days, Hannah b. 7 (11) 1645, Sarah bapt. 7 (9) 1647, ae. about 6 days, Lydia bapt. 26 (3) 1650, d. 6 (8) 1651, Deborah b. 1 (11) 1651, Naomi b. 26 Oct., 1653, d. 14 (7) 1654, Lydia b. 10 (1) 1655, Sarah b. 2 (4) 1657 ,Mary b. 30 (11) 1658, Naomi bapt. 6 (12) 1658-9.

Will dated 13 Dec., prob. 23 Dec. 1680; son-in-law John Hill and dau. Mary, his wife; sons-in-law Matthew Ingram, Matthew Collins and Preserved Collicott; daus. Lydia Ingram, Naomi Collins, Deborah Collicott, Sarah Dunell and Hannah Homer.

Lawrence, carpenter, planter, Boston, adm. chh. 22 (1) 1645, frm. May 26, 1647. Rem. to Charlestown; propr. 1647; adm. chh.

DOWSE, etc., cont.
21 (1) 1652. Wife Margery; ch. John b. (8) 1644, bur. (6) 1645, Samuel ae. about 2 yrs. 3 weeks, and John, ae. about 22 weeks, bapt. 23 (1) 1646, Elizabeth b. 15 (1) 1647.

Will dated 25 Dec. 1691, prob. 21 Nov. 1692, beq. to wife Margery, sons Samuel, Joseph, Benjamin, Nathaniel, Jonathan and Eleazer; married daus. Elizabeth and Mary.

DRAKE,
Joan, widow, Boston, adm. chh. 3 (6) 1634.

Will prob. 5 (10) 1637; beq. to John Nott, to her sister Duglas, to her nephew; rest of goods in N. E. to Samuel Bellingham. All goods in Eng. to her 2 sisters there. Made her mr. (i. e. master,) executor.

John, [Dorchester,] appl. for frm. Oct. 19, 1630. Rem. to Windsor, Conn. He was bur. 18 Aug. 1659. [Wife] Elizabeth adm. chh. Dorch. 19 (4) 1640.

"Old widow Drake d. at Windsor, Oct. 7, 1681, at 100th year of age, having lived a widow 22 years." [Reg. XXXVI, 83.]

DRAP,
Cleare, ae. 30, came in the Francis of Ipswich April 30, 1634.

DRAPER,
Nicholas, Salem, 1636.

Roger, Concord, frm. March 14, 1638-9. He deposed 21 (1) 1658-9, ae. about 68 years. Son Adam. [Mdx. Files.] He m. 2, Mary, widow of Nathaniel Hadlock. Ch. Lydia b. 11 (9) 1641.

DRAYTON,
Henry, Marshfield, atba. 1643.

He was found dead 4 Dec. 1651, and the town app. Kenelm Winslow to admin. on their behalf. Inv. taken Dec. 12, 1651. [Reg. IV, 319.]

DRESSER,
John, Rowley, propr. 1642. He deposed in 1668, ae. about 61 years. Wife Mary; ch. Mary b. 23 (2) 1642, bur. Nov. 27, 1659, Samuel b. 10 (12) 1643, Jonathan b. 8 (11) 1646, bur. 10 (10) 1659, Elizabeth b. March 10, 1650, John, Jr. was a father in 1663.

He was bur. April 19, 1672. Will dated 5 March, prob.

DREW, DREWE, DREWES, DRUCE,
Vincon, (Vincent,) Hingham, propr. 1636. Ch. John bapt. April, 1641. Rem. to Boston. Bought, with Thomas Hammond, in 1655, a farm at Muddy River; deed 30 Aug. 1658.

His will dated Nov. 29, 1677, prob. Jan. 30 folg., beq. to son Vincent; to son John and his wife Mary and their children; to Rozman Druce.

DRINKER,
Nicholas, Charlestown, constable, 1646.

Philip, potter, ae. 39, with wife Elizabeth, ae. 32, and ch. Edward, ae. 13, and John, ae. 8, came in the Abigail in July, 1635. Settled at Charlestown; frm. May 17, 1637. Wife Elizabeth adm. chh. 6 (2) 1638. Town officer, 1646.

He d. 23 (4) 1647, beq. his est. to his wife Elizabeth and sons Edward and John, and apprentice, John Gouldsmith. Refers to his bro. James. [Reg. VII, 169.]

DRIVER, DRYVER,
Robert, tailor, Salem, frm. May 6, 1635. Juryman, 1637. Propr. at Lynn in 1638. He deposed on the Dexter case in 1657, ae. about 65 years. Wife Phebe; ch. Robert, Phebe b. about 1634, Ruth, (m. Robert Potter).

He d. April 3, 1680.

Robert, ae. 8, came in the Abigail in July, 1635, apparently with the family of Thomas Nore. Seems to be the R. D. a Scotchman, executed for murder in 1675. [S.]

DRURY, DREWRIE,
George, ae. 19, came in the Abigail in July, 1635.

Hugh, carpenter, Sudbury, propr. 1641; rem. to Boston, adm. chh. 16 (2) 1654, frm. May 3, 1654. Town officer. Wife Lydia adm. chh. 12 (1) 1648; ch. John b. at Sud. 2 (3) 1646, bapt. at Bo. 19 (1) 1649. They sold land in B. Nov. 16, 1660. Mrs. Mary, (whether Hugh's dau. or some other,) made nunc. will in 1680, beq. all to her cousin Samuel Shrimpton.

Will dated 1 Nov. 1687, prob. 30 July, 1689, beq. to Mary, widow of his son John, the est. of which he had been executor, for herself and her children; to sister Lydia Hawkins;

DRURY, etc., cont.
to sons Thomas; refers to dec. wife Lydia and to dau. Mary. Appoints his friend Henry Allen and brother Henry Rice executors, with his bro. Edward Rice alternate in case of the death of either.

DUCKET,
Mr., before Gen. Court in Boston in 1641. [W.]

DUDBRIDGE,
William, Gloucester, propr. 1649.

DUDLEY,
Mr. Thomas, gent., Esquire, son of Capt. Roger D., b. at Northampton, Eng.; a clerk to his mother's kinsman Judge Nichols; a capt. in the Low Countries; steward to the Earl of Lincoln; resident some time at Boston, Eng. One of the projectors of and later an undertaker in the Mass. Bay Co., 1 (10) 1629, Asst. March 18, and Deputy Governor March 23, 1629-30, at the last Court held in England. Came in the Arbella to Salem, then to Charlestown, in company with Gov. Winthrop. Was gov., dep. gov., or Asst. every year of his life thereafter. One of the 4 first signers of the covenant of the first chh. organized at Charlestown in July, 1630, which rem. to Boston, a few months later. Serg. Maj. Gen., 1644. Res. successively, at Charlestown, Cambridge and Roxbury. Built a house in Ipswich in 1635, but sold it to Mr. Hubbard. A man of large ability and noble character. Was in full accord with Gov. Winthrop in maintaining the domination of the estab. chh. (of New England) over civil and ecclesiastical affairs, after the English fashion. He m. in Eng. Dorothy —, "a gentlewoman whose extraction and estate were considerable." [C. M.] She was bur. Dec. 27, 1643; he m. April 4, 1644, Katharine (Deighton,) widow of Samuel Hagborne, who after his death m. Mr. John Allen, pastor at Dedham. Ch. Samuel, Anne, (m. Simon Bradstreet,) Patience, (m. 18 Oct. 1632, Daniel Denison,) Sarah, (m. 1, Benjamin Keayne, m. 2, Nicholas Pacy,) Mercy, (m. Mr. John Woodbridge,) Deborah b. 27 Feb. 1644-5, Joseph b. Sept. 23, 1647, Paul bapt. Sept. 8, 1650.

He was bur. July 31, 1653, ae. 76. Will dated 26 April, 1652, with additions 13 April, May 28 and July 8, 1653, prob. Aug. 15, 1653;

DUDLEY, cont.
desired to be buried near the grave of his first wife; beq. to all his children by both wives and to grand children Thomas and John D. whom he had brought up; son Joseph to have a double portion of the Roxbury lands, Paul and Deborah single portions of same; to the ch. of daus. Bradstreet, Denison and Woodbridge; to dau. Sarah Pacy; to his wife the remaining time of servant John Ranken; to the poor. Genealogy.

DUHURST,
Henry, ae. 35, came in the Defense in July, 1635.

DUKE,
John, ae. 20, came in the Elizabeth April 11, 1635.

DUMMER, alias PYLDRYM,
Mr. Richard, gent., arrived in the Whale 26 May, 1632, [W.] and settled at Roxbury. Frm. May 25, 1632. Built a water-mill in 1633. Rem. to Ipswich; res. afterward at Newbury. Went back to Eng. and ret. in the Bevis in May, 1638, ae. 40, with Alice, ae. 35, Thomas, ae. 19, Joane, ae. 19, Jane, ae. 10, Dorothy, ae. 6, Richard, ae. 4, and Thomas, ae. 2, and Stephen, husbandman, ae. 9; these were his brothers and members of their families. The ages were not correctly stated. Town officer, deputy. He m. first, Mary —; he m. second, Frances, wid. of Mr. Jonathan Burr; she d. 19 Nov. 1682. Ch. b. at Newbury: Shubael b. Feb. 17, 1635-6, Jeremiah b. 14 Sept. 1645, Hannah b. 7 Nov. 1647, Richard b. 13 Jan. 1650, William b. 18 Jan. 1659. His son Nathaniel was drowned; inquest 23 (7) 1658. [Es. Files.] He d. 14 Dec. 1679.

His will, dated 23 April, 1679, prob. April 1, 1680; wife Frances; dau.-in-law Elizabeth Paine; son Richard. The widow's est. was divided June 30, 1685, between her sons Shubael, Jeremiah and Richard D.

Stephen, bro. of Mr. Richard, youngest son of Thomas Pyldrym *alias* Dummer, was adm. to Middlestreet and Hole farms in Bishopstoke, Hants, on the surrender of his father, 24 Sept. 1625. These he surrendered 22 Feb. 1637-8, to his sons Stephen and Thomas. He came in the Bevis in May,

DUMMER, cont.
1638, with wife Alice; ch. Mehitabel b. at Newbury 1 Jan. 1639-40, Jane, Dorothy, Richard, and Thomas. The dau. Jane m. 25 March, 1646, Henry Sewall, Jr. He ret. to Eng. before 1648. [See letter to Henry Short in Ips. De. III, 256.]

He d. at Bishopstoke 6 Sept., 1670.

Thomas, gent., of Chicknell, in North Stoneham, co. Hants, seems to be the person who came in the Bevis in May, 1638, with dau. Joane, ae. 19, (who afterward m. Mr. Thomas Nelson of Rowley as his second wife). Res. at Newbury. Frm. May 13, 1640. Propr. also at Salisbury. Ret. to Eng. Will prob. 9 Nov. 1650 at London. Wife; eldest dau. Joane Nelson and her ch. Samuel and Mary N.; dau. Margaret Clements and her ch. now in N. E.; other ch. Thomas, Susan, Hester, Jane, and Mary, all under 21. Margaret m. Dec. 25, 1644, Job Clements of Haverhill. [See Reg. XXXIV, 390, and XXXV, 254, 269, and 321.]

DUNCAN, DUNCUN, DUNKAN, DUNKIN, DUNCUM, see Dunkin,
Mr. Nathaniel, merchant, Dorchester, one of the original church-colony who came in 1630; [Bl.] frm. May 6, 1635; one of the 7 signers of the second chh. covenant in 1636; selectman, auditor, deputy. He rem. to Boston; with wife was rec'd to chh. 7 (1) 1646. "Learned in Latin and French; a very good accountant." [J.] Wife Elizabeth; ch. Peter and Nathaniel. "My son Nathaniel D. and his children" are legatees in will of Ignatius Jurdaine, of Exeter, Eng. March 1, 1635, the sons Peter and Nathaniel, in that of Elizabeth J. of the same, in 1633. [Reg. XLIX, 493.]

The inv. of his est. was filed 26 Jan. 1668, by James Trowbridge, admin.

DUNFORD,
John, Plymouth, banished by the Court 4 June, 1639.

DUNHAM,
John, weaver, Plymouth, frm. 1633, deacon, deputy, town officer.

He d. March 2, 1668-9, ae. about 80. Will dated Jan. 25, 1668, beq. to sons John, Benajah and Daniel; son-in-law Stephen Wood; to the rest of my children that are not designated in this my last will twelve pence

DUNHAM, cont.
apiece if they demand it; to wife Abigail. [Reg. VII, 178.]

Samuel, who was in Plymouth, atba. 1643, prop. frm. 1 June 1647, and Joseph, ae. about 41, deposed 3 March, 1677, ae. about 51 years, that their father gave certain lands to their bro.-in-law-Benajah Pratt.

Thomas, Plymouth, atba. 1643, prop. frm. June 1, 1647.

DUNN, DONN,
Thomas, ae. 25, came in the Defense in July, 1635. Settled at —; frm. May 26, 1647.

DUNTON,
Robert, Reading, propr. 1644; town officer.

Edward and Elizabeth, Salem, membs. chh. 1639. "Removed."

Samuel, Reading, propr. 1644. Wife Ann. Ch. Samuel b. Oct. 15, 1647, Hannah b. Feb. 24, 1649, Nathaniel b. Jan. 16, 1655, Elizabeth b. March 25, 1658, Sarah b. March 28, 1660, Mary b. March 5, 1661-2, Ruth b April 4, 1664.

He d. Nov. 7, 1683. His will, prob. (12) 1684, beq. to sons Samuel, John and Nathaniel; daus. Hannah, Elizabeth, Sarah, Mary and Ruth; gr. son Samuel; refers to land which Thomas had to use. John was to maintain father and mother the rest of their lives.

Est. settled by son John. The account mentions payments to Hannah, Sarah, Nathaniel and Samuel D.; refers to death of his father, and to that of his mother in July, 1689.

DUNKIN,
Samuel, see Col. Rec. 1 (10) 1640.

DUNSTER,
Rev. Henry, Cambridge, propr., frm. June 2, 1641. He was president of Harvard College, 1640-1654. He leased Mr. Humphrey's mill at Lynn to Francis Ingalls in 1647. [Es. Files VIII, 75-8.] "An able proficient in Hebrew, Greek and Latin languages, an Orthodox Preacher of the truths of Christ." [J.] Became an Anabaptist. Rem. to Scituate. Was one of the revisers of the Bay Psalm Book. [C. M.] His wife

DUNSTER, cont.
Elizabeth d. 23 (6) 1643. He m. 2, Elizabeth, widow of Mr. Jose Glover. Ch. David b. 16 (3) 1645, Dorothy b. 29 (11) 1647.

He d. about 1659. Will dated 18 Feb. 1658, prob. June 21, 1659, beq. to wife; to sons David and Jonathan; to dau. Elizabeth, who is to be brought up by "my sister Mrs. Hills of Mauldon," or "my sister Williard of Concord," in case of her mother's death; to Mr. Chauncey, Mr. Mitchell, elder Frost; to cousin Bowers with her ch.; to cousin Faith Dunster; to sister Hills and to all her ch. born in this country; to sister Willard and all her ch.; to maid, Mary Russell.

DURAND, DURANT,
Mr. William, Boston, adm. chh. 7 (7) 1644. A witness to the will of Lawrence Sethick at Shelter Island in 1660.

DURDAL,
Hugh, came in the Bevis in May, 1638.

DUSTON, DURSTAN, DUSTIN, see DASTIN,
Thomas, Charlestown, propr. adjoining Ralph Hall in 1648.

DUTCH, DOUCH, DOUTCH, DOOCH,
Osmond, Osment, or Osman, mariner, Gloucester, sold property at Bridport, Eng., 18 (5) 1639, and arranged for the coming of his wife Grace and son Robert at an early day. [L.] Had lawsuit in Salem court in 1641. He deposed in 1663, ae. about 60 years. His wife Grace, in 1664, ae. about 50. Ch. Robert, (who deposed in 1658, ae. about 35,) Samuel, Hezekiah b. March 29, 1646, Alice, (m. — Meacham, of Ipswich,) Esther, (m. Samuel Elwell,) Mary, (m. Joseph Elwell,) Grace, (m. Christopher Hodgskins).

He d. in Nov. 1684. Admin. gr. to the widow and son Robert. The widow Grace d. Oct. 10, 1694. Will prob. March 28, 1704.

DUTTON,
John; he was before the Gen. Court 29 (8) 1640.

Thomas, Woburn; he deposed in 1658, ae. 39 years. Ch. Thomas, ae. 19, and Mary, ae. 17, in 1667. [Mdx. Files.] Ch. Mary b. 14 (9) 165[0], Susanna b. 27 (12) 1653.

DWIGHT,

John, yeoman, Watertown, propr. 1635; rem. to Dedham; pioneer; frm. March 13, 1638-9. Town officer. Bought one half of a water-mill 8 (6) 1642. Wife Hannah adm. chh. 9 (11) 1639. She d. 5 (7) 1656; he m. 20 (11) 1657, Elizabeth, widow successively of Thomas Thaxter and Wm. Ripley. She d. July 17, 1660.

He d. 24 (11) 1660. Will prob. March 5, 1660-1; wife Elizabeth; son Timothy, daus. Hannah Whiting, Mary Philips, and Sarah Reynolds. Sons-in-law Nathaniel Whiting, Henry Philips and Nathaniel Reynolds. [Reg. X, 264, and XXXI, 178.]

Timothy, Sen., Dedham, propr. 28 (6) 1638, having part of the lot of his bro. John. Adm. chh. 30 (6) 1640. Corporal, town officer. He rem. to Medfield. He m. 11 (9) 1651, Sarah Penman, who d. in 1652; he m. 3 (3) 1653, Sarah Powell. Ch. Sarah b. 6 (2) 1657, d. 9 (12) 1659, John b. 31 (3) 1661, Sarah b. 25 June 1664, Josiah b. 14 (8) 1665, and Nathaniel b. 20 (9) 1666. Samuel b. 2 Dec. 1668, Josiah b. 8 Feb. 1670, Seth b. 29 (5) 1673, Anna b. 12 (6) 1675, Henry b. 19 (10) 1676. The wife Sarah d. 27 June 1664. He m. 9 (11) 1664, Anna Flint. She d. 15 (8) 1675.

His will dated March 3, prob. March 15, 1676-7; ae. about 67 years; beq. to wife Dorcas, and sons Timothy and John.

DYER, DIER,

George, planter, Dorchester, juryman, 1630; frm. May 18, 1631. One of the attorneys for Thomas Purchase May 31, 1641. [L.]

Will dated 31 Dec. 1671, prob. 2 Aug. 1672; beq. to daus. Elizabeth, wife of Wm. Triscott, Mary, wife of Wm. Pond; to son-in-law James White of Dorch. his looms for weaving.

John, ae. 28, came in the Christian March 16, 1634.

Admin. of the est. of John Dyer of Boston, ironmonger, was gr. 11 June, 1695, to his widow Elizabeth and son John; division made to them and to ch. Benjamin, Joseph, Elizabeth, Mary and Sarah 9 March, 1698.

Thomas, cloth-worker, Weymouth, frm. May 29, 1644. Lic. inn-keeper; deputy; deacon; town officer. He m. 2, Elizabeth, widow successively of Abraham Harding and

DYER, etc., cont.

John Frary, Jr. Ch. Mary b. 3 (5) 1641, John b. 10 (5) 1643.

Will dated 3 Nov. prob. 13 Nov. 1676, beq. to wife £50 and the estate of her former husband (at Medfield;) to sons Joseph, John, and other children; to his gr. children; to pastor, Mr. Samuel Torrey, and to the church of Weymouth. The widow Elizabeth, in will dated 20 Nov. prob. 31 Jan. 1678, beq. to her sons Abraham and John Harding, dau. Elizabeth Adams, dau. Prudence, son Joseph Dyer, and grand children.

William, mylner, (miller) Boston, adm. chh. with wife Marie 13 (10) 1635; frm. March 3, 1635-6. He and his wife sympathized with Mrs. Hutchinson in 1638. [W.] Ch. Samuel b. 20 (10) 1635.

He d. in Dorchester 18 (4) 1672, in 93d year.

EAGLESFIELD,

Mary, Charlestown, adm. chh. 7 (8) 1639. She m. Samuel, son of Henry Adams, of Braintree. They gave letter of attorney 22 (8) 1646, to John Doe, salter at the Tonne in Wood st. London, for the collection of legacy from her father Emanuel E., late of London, haberdasher; later she sent for legacies from her gr. mother Elizabeth, her sister Hannah and her bro. Samuel E. [A.]

EALE, EALES, EELS, ILES, see Ely,

John, planter, Dorchester, frm. May 14, 1634. Sold house and land 28 (8) 1640. Bond given to John Iles concerning parties at Barnstable, Eng., in 1639, and to John Eels in 1641, show the identity of the man. [L.] He rem. to Windsor, Conn. about 1636; his son Samuel was bapt. at Dorch. 3 (3) 1640, "by communion of chhs. his father being a memb. of the chh. at Windsor."

John, bee-hive maker, Newbury. The Gen. Court sought to arrange for a suitable location for him 14 May, 1645.

He d. Nov. 25, 1653, ae. 78.

Richard, carpenter, Charlestown, 1638. [L.]

He d. 29 (8) 1639, leaving an unsigned will; inv. rendered Nov. 29, 1639. Beq. to bro. John and to John Keene in Eng.; to his aunt for her pains and love; to cousins Thomas and Daniel Harris, and to Anne, John and Abigail Maverick; to William, An-

EALE, etc., cont.
thony and John Harris; to goodwife Greenland; the rest to his 3 bros. and sister.

Samuel, Ipswich, servant of Mr. Natha. Rogers; went to Virginia in 1639. [Mass. Hist. Coll. 4-6.]

EAMES, AMES, see also Ames,
Anthony, Charlestown, propr. 1634; rem. to Hingham; propr.; frm. March 9, 1636-7. Assisted in laying out the line between Mass. Bay and Plymouth, patents. Petition, 2 (4) 1641. [L.] Town officer, deputy, captain; serious contention in Hing. and before the Court when he was chosen. [W.] Wife Margery, adm. Chsn. chh. 13 (7) 1635. Son Mark bought house and land with him in Marshfield 10 Dec. 1651. Dau. Margery m. Oct. 20, 1653, John Jacob. [Was John, who d. 29 Nov. 1641, his child?] He was called "Ames" in Marshfield records 1652; signatures as witnesses to will of John Rogers, copied by clerk of probate as Eames. Michael Peirse refers to father Eames, and calls Mark his brother. See Samuel Ward.

Thomas, brickmaker, Dedham, propr., 1640. Rem. to Medford. Deposed in 1651, ae. about 34 years. Wife Margaret adm. chh. 28 (11) 1641. [Reg. XXXII, 408.]

EARLY,
Robert, a passenger in the Hercules in April, 1634.

EARING, EARWINGE,
Mrs. Katharine, widow, Dorchester, memb. chh. before 1639; gave letter of attorney for collection of money due her in Eng. 27 (7) 1639. [L.] Rec'd to chh. of Boston 27 (9) 1642.

EAST, EASTIE, ESTIE, ESTEY, ASTYE,
Francis, carpenter, Boston, adm. chh. 11 (10) 1636; frm. April 17, 1637. [See Dedham chh. rec. 1638.] Wife Mary; ch. Samuel b. 11 (1) 1639, Mary b. 25 (1) 1642, Elizabeth b. 1 (9) 1644, David b. 26 (11) 1646, Sarah bapt. 11 (9) 1649, ae. about 2 days, Daniel b. 21 Sept. 1652, Rebecca b. 22 July, 1656, Hannah b. Sept. 4, 1658, d. 15 June, 1659.

EAST, etc., cont.
"Father East" d. March 17, was bur. March 19, 1686-7, said to be 94 years old. [S.]

Jeffrey, Salem, propr. 1636; brought suit in court in 1639 to recover pay for his service and for a boat. In court 12 (5) 1642. Sold 30 acres of land at Mackerel Cove for 30s. 6 Oct. 1651; went "out of this jurisdiction" so that his acknowledgment of the deed could not be recorded a month later, as William Dixie testified. Isaac, cooper, bought land in Salem, 1653, and in Topsfield, 1673; had son Jeffrey. Joseph, Salem, propr. 1639, rem. to Topsfield, weaver, constable. Both these may have been sons of Jeffrey.

Roger, Yarmouth, mentioned in inv. of Nath. Sparhawk of Wat. in 1647.

EASTON, EASON,
Joseph, Cambridge, propr. 1634; frm. March 4, 1634-5. Sold in 1639.

Mr. Nicholas, tanner, came in the Mary and John March 26, 1633-4. Settled at Ipswich; frm. Sept. 3, 1634. Deputy. Had liberty, Nov. 1634, to build a mill and weir. Testimony concerning his business in Ips. De. 1, 38. Rem. to Charlestown. Shared in the Hutchinson movement, and was banished to Newport in 1638. He m. second, widow Christian Beecher.

He d. Aug. 15, 1675, ae. 82.

Thomas, Newbury, d. Nov. 24, 1650.

EASTMAN, EASMEN, see East,
Roger, ae. 25, servant to John Sanders of Lanford, Wilts., Eng., came in the Confidence April 11, 1638. House carpenter. Settled at Salisbury; propr. 1639. Wife Sarah; ch. John b. March 9, 1640, Nathaniel b. May 18, 1643, Philip b. Dec. 30, 1644, Thomas b. Nov. 11, 1646, Timothy b. Nov. 29, 1648, Joseph b. Jan. 8, 1650, Benjamin b. Feb. 12, 1652, Sarah b. Sept. 25, 1655, (m. 1, Joseph French, 2. Solomon Shepherd,) Samuel b. Nov. 20, 1657, Ruth b. March 21, 1660. He deposed 11 (2) 1671, ae. about 60 years. Sarah deposed same day, ae. about 50.

He d. Dec. 16, 1694; will dated June 26, 1691, prob. March 27, 1695. Widow Sarah d. March 11, 1697-8.

EASTWICK, ESTICK, see **Estow,**

Edward, mariner, bought land in 1649. Widow, Salem, adm. chh. 21 (4) 1640. Goodwife — adm. chh. 29 (10) 1640. Inv. of his est. taken 22 June, 1666; admin. gr. to widow Hester. Ch. Elizabeth ae. 14, Sarah ae. 12, Hannah ae. 10, Esther ae. 7 and Edward ae. 4. Widow Esther made will 22 July, 1698, prob. June 31, 1708; beq. to gr. ch. Elizabeth Carle, Benjamin, Edward and Estwick Bush, and remainder to dau. Elizabeth Bush.

EATON, [see **Heaton,**]

Francis, carpenter, came in the Mayflower; signed the Compact; res. at Plymouth. Frm. 1633. Wife Sarah came with him, with ch. Samuel, and infant; Rachel b. before 1627; Benjamin apprenticed 11 Feb. 1635, for 14 yrs., including 2 yrs. school, to Bridget Fuller, widow; Samuel appr. for 7 yrs. Aug. 13, 1636, to John Cooke, Jr. The wife Sarah d. and he m. 2, Christian —.

He d. and admin, was gr. to Thomas Prence and John Done Nov. 25, 1633. [Reg. IV, 34, and Col. Rec.]

Jonas, Reading, 1647; propr., town officer; wife memb. chh. with him in 1648. Ch. Mary b. 8 (12) 1643, John b. 10 (7) 1645, Jonas b. and d. 24 (7) 1648, [Mdx. De. I.] Joshua b. 4 (10) 1653.

He d. Feb. 24, 1673; will prob. 7 (2) 1674; beq. to wife Grace, sons John, James, Joseph, Joshua and Jonathan, and dau. Mary.

John, Watertown, propr., frm. May 25, 1636. Rem. to Dedham; propr. 1637; town officer. Wife Abigail, ae. 35, with Mary, ae. 4, and Thomas, ae. 1, and Jane Dammant, ae. 9, came in the Elizabeth and Ann in April, 1635. Other ch. Abigail b. 6 (11) 1639, (m. 10 (9) 1659, Robert Mason,) Jacob b. 8 (4) 1642, d. 20 (1) 1646. The son Thomas d. 10 (7) 1649; the dau. Mary m. John Mason. Mrs. Eaton had ch. Jane and John Dammant by former marriage, who were rec'd to chh. of Dedh. 1640 and 1645.

He d. 10 (9) 1658. Will prob. 16 (10) 1658, beq. to wife Abigail; ch. John, Mary and Abigail; to John Dammant of Redding; to John Plimpton of Medfield; to kinsman Edward Hodson.

John, Sen., cooper, Salisbury, propr. 1639-1646. Rem. to Haverhill; propr. 1648;

EATON, cont.

town officer. With wife Martha sold land 20 (2) 1655. Ch. John, (deposed in 1660, ae. about 40 years,) Ann, (m. George Brown,) Elizabeth, (m. James Davis,) Thomas, Ruth, (m. Samuel Ingalls,) Hester. His wife Ann d. Feb. 5, 1660; he m. Nov. 20, 1661, Phebe, widow of Thomas Dow.

He d. Oct. 29, 1668; will prob. April 13, 1669, beq. to present wife; to sons John and Thomas; to daus. Brown, Davis and Ingalls; to gr. ch. Thomas, (son of John) and Thomas, (son of Thomas,) E., Hester and John Davis and John Ingalls. Widow Phebe d. Nov. 3, 1672. Inv. of her est, filed 25 Dec. 1672.

Nathaniel, bro. of Mr. Theophilus, b. about 1609, came to Cambridge about 1637; propr., frm. June 9, 1638. Became first master of the school which grew into Harvard College. A grant of land was made to him by the town of Camb. 2 (2) 1638, with this memorandum: "The two acres & two-thirds above mentioned to the Professor is to the Common use forever for a publicke scoole or Colledge. And to the use of mr. Nath Eaton as long as he shall be Imployed in that worke." Was tried by the Court 4 (7) 1639, on the charge of cruelty to his usher Mr. Nathaniel Briscoe, and to many of his pupils. He fled to New Hampshire; was sent back, afterward escaped to Virginia, leaving great debts, ill repute. As he had been initiated among the Jesuits, he took it upon him to be a minister there. His wife and ch. were drowned on a voyage thither. He afterward mar. a dau. of Mr. Thomas Graves of Va., formerly of Dorchester, and deserted her. [W.] He officiated at Northampton, Va., in 1642-3. and d. about 1646. [Reg. XL, 294.]

Benoni, son of Mr. Nathan Eaton, whose mother died a member of the chh. of Camb., was in the family of Thomas Cheeseholme and under his care in 1658. [Mi.] Inv. of his est. taken April 3, 1691, was filed by his widow Rachel.

Mr. Theophilus, son of Mr. Richard Eaton, clerk, (whose will may be seen in Reg. XXXVIII, 29,) a merchant of London of fair estate and great esteem for religion, and wisdom in outward affairs, [W.] arrived at Boston in June, 1637. Rem. very soon to Conn., where he was governor and a person of very great importance. See many sketches.

EATON, cont.

William, husbandman, of Staple, Eng., with wife Martha, 3 children and 1 servant, came from Sandwich, Eng., before June 9, 1637. Settled at Watertown; propr. 1642. He deposed in 1658, ae. about 54 years, and [his son] John, ae. about 22 years. Rem. to Reading; propr. 1644; town officer. He and his wife and 5 children were legatees in the will of the wife's sister, Margaret, widow of Edmund Lane of London, 3 Sept., 1662. [Reg. XXXVII, 378.] Ch. Daniel b. 20 (11) 1638, Mary b. 8 (2) 1643. He deposed in 1667, ae. about 60 years. [Es. files.]

He, d. at Read. May 13, 1673. His will dated 26 (7) 1672, prob. June 11, 1673, beq. to wife Martha, sons John and Daniel, dau. Mary, sons-in-law Thomas Browne and Francis Moore. [See Oldham.] The widow in her will, 24 Nov. 1675, prob. 21 (4) 1681, beq. to the same.

EBORNE, EABORNE, ABORNE,

Samuel, Salem, propr., memb. chh. 1636. He deposed 12 (9) 1666, ae. about 52. Wife Katharine adm. chh. 23 (5) 1648; ch. Samuel, Moses, and Mary bapt. 6 (6) 1648, Rebecca bapt. 23 (1) 1650-1, Sarah bapt. 15 (4) 1656, William bapt. 9 (6) 1668. He m. Katharine, dau. of James Smith of Marblehead, who mentions in his will in 1661, herself and her ch. Mary, Rebecca, Moses, Hannah, James and Sarah. He deposed in 1661, ae. 50 years.

Thomas, Salem, frm. May 14, 1634. Res. in 1642. [Essex Court files.]

ECCLES, ECKLES, ECKELS, EAGLES,

Richard, weaver, Cambridge. "Our bro. Jackson's man; brought up many years in Popery." [Rel.] He deposed in 1654, ae. about 40 years. Bought house and land in 1646. Frm. May 18, 1642. Wife Mary d. Aug. 23, 1675, and he m. 2, June 4, 1677, Susanna Carter. Ch. of Richard and Mary b. and bapt. in Camb.: Mary, Hannah and Martha. [Mi.]

He d. before March 10, 1696-7, when his est. was sold by his dau.

EDEN,

Barbara, Cambridge, m. in 1649, Robert Brown.

EDDENDEN,

Edmund, Scituate, propr., 1637; took oath of allegiance 1 Feb. 1638; frm. 1 June, 1641.

EDDY, EDDIE, EDY, EEDY,

John, son of Rev. William Eddy of Crainbrook, Eng.; came to Plymouth in the Handmaid, arriving Oct. 29, 1630. Rem. to Watertown; [see Bradford's letter, Reg. II, 244.] "A godly man, now and then a little distempered." [W.] Frm. Sept. 3, 1634. Town officer. He desired to be excused from training 15 (10) 1673, ae. 77 years. [Mdx. Files.] Wife Amy; ch. Pilgrim b. 25 (6) 1634, John b. 16 (12) 1636, Benjamin bur. in 1639, Samuel b. 30 (7) 1640, Abigail b. 11 (8) 1643. He m. 2. Joanna —, who d. Aug. 25, 1683, ae. 80.

He d. Oct. 12, 1684, ae. 90. Will dated 11 Jan. 1677, prob. Dec. 16, 1684; beq. to sons Samuel and John, sons-in-law John Miriam and Thomas Orton; and daus. Mary Orton, Sarah Miriam, Pilgrim Steadman, and Ruth Gardner; wife to have according to their contract.

Robert, ae. 25, came in the Hopewell in Sept., 1635.

Samuel, Plymouth, taxed 1632; frm. 1633; atba. 1643. Land grant 1636. Placed his son John, (7 yrs. old Dec. 25, 1644,) appr. with Francis Goulder, April 3, 1645, and "having many children and many wants," placed son Zechery (7 yrs. old) with Mr. John Browne of Rehoboth, 2 March, 1646-7. Wife Elizabeth; ch. rec.: Hannah b. June 23, 1647.

—, of Boxted, came to Plymouth in Nov. 1639. [W.] This may be Samuel, returning from a visit to England.

EEDES,

William, carpenter or wheelwright, came in the Lyon's Whelp to Salem, 1629. [Suff. De. I, XVI.]

EDGE, see Hedge.

EDMUNDS,

John, Boston, memb. chh. 1630, frm. May 18, 1631.

Walter, (Gualter,) Concord, 1639, frm. May 22, 1638; constable, 1640. Rem. to Charlestown. Adm. chh. 21 (1) 1652, with wife Dorothy; she d. Sept. 11, 1671. He de-

EDMUNDS, cont.
posed about 1662 that he served apprenticeship in England at selling strong waters, and desired relief from the prohibitory Act. [Mdx. Files.] Ch. Joshua, Mary, Daniel, John b. 2 (5) 1640.
He d. July 13, 1667. Will dated 30 (3), prob. Sept. 27, 1667, beq. to wife Dorothy, sons Joshua, Daniel and John, dau. Potter of Concord.

William, Lynn, propr.; frm. May 6, 1635. His wife in Court June 5, 1638. He deposed in 1659, ae. about 42 years. He m. in Boston 1 (7) 1662, Ann Martin, widow; his dau. Mary m., same date and place, Joseph Hutchins.
Inv. of his est. taken 8 Sept. 1693; admin. gr. to son John; division made Oct. 8, 1694, to ch. John, Joseph and Samuel E., and Mary Hitchins.

EDSELL, HEDSALL,
Thomas, ae. 47, came in the Elizabeth and Jane in April, 1635. Boston, He m. 16 (7) 1651, Elizabeth Ferman. Fined for voting though not a freeman 18 May, 1652. Bondsman for William Salter, as inhab., 1658.

EDSON,
Samuel, Salem, propr. 1639. May be Samuel of Bridgewater, who made will 15 Jan. 1688-9, prob. Sept. 20, 1692; having formerly deeded lands to children, now beq. to sons Samuel, Joseph and Josiah; to wife Susanna; to daus. Susanna, Sarah, Mary and Bethiah.

EDWARDS,
Alexander, Springfield, propr. 1643; town officer. He m. 28 (2) 1642, Sarah Searle, widow. Ch. Samuel b. 7 (1) 1642-3, Hanna b. 18 (12) 1644, Joseph b. 8 (1) 1647, Mary b. 20 (11) 1649, Benjamin b. 24 (4) 1652, Sarah b. 21 (9) 1654.
Will dated 30 Aug., inv. taken 24 Oct. 1690. Beq. to sons Samuel, Benjamin and Nathaniel, daus. Mary Field and Elizabeth Clark; to Sarah North, and John and Samuel Davis; wife to be well cared for.

Edmond, servant to Henry Feake of Sandwich, transferred to John Barnes 25 Sept., 1639.

EDWARDS, cont.
Edward, Plymouth, bought house and lands 31 Dec. 1642, to be paid for in money, stockings, shoes, or other merchantable commodities.

Henry, bondsman, Gen. Court, 29 (8) 1640.

John, apprenticed 24 Jan. 1638-9, to Edmond Chandler of Duxbury, for 5 years.

John, blacksmith, Charlestown, contract to learn gunsmithery 17 (7) 1640. [L.] Witness to indenture of Stephen Day of Cambridge, 16 (2) 1640.
His house and goods given by Gen. Court, 27 Sept., 1642, to (his partner) Harman Garrett and his heirs.

Matthew, Reading; before Gen. Court 3 (7) 1639; propr.
He d. 22 (10) 1683. He made will 18 Dec. 1683, prob. April 1, 1684; beq. to wife Mary; dau. Mary Polly and her ch.; daus. Tabitha, Sarah, Abigail and Elizabeth; son Matthew E.; farm on the other side of Ipswich river; to Nicholas Lun; hay and grass at certain places; debt to Capt. Walker for land; cousin Thomas Bancroft joint exec. with the wife. The son Matthew made will 30 July, 1689, and beq. to bro. John Polly, the sisters mentioned above, and other persons.

Nathaniel, merchant, Boston, adm. inhab. 1647. Legatee and admin. of est. of Nathaniel Smyth, 1651. [Gen Court.]
He d. 2 (11) 1653. Admin. gr. to Joseph Hills. Inv. taken 3 Feb. 1653-4, recorded with accounts of J. H. and Thos. Broughton.

Rice or Reece, joiner, Salem, propr. 1642. In court as of Wenham in 1647. His wife Joan adm. chh. Boston 9 (3) 1647. He deposed in 1680, ae. about 65 years.

Robert, ae. 22, came in the Hopewell in Sept., 1635. Settled at Concord; frm. May 18, 1642. Wife Christian; dau. Sarah b. and d. in 1640; dau. Christian b. 15 (1) 1645.
Nunc. will made before Goo. Heaward and Wm. Wood, prob. 2 (1) 1647, beq. all to his wife. Inv. taken 8 (10) 1646.

Thomas, shoemaker, Salem, propr 1637; frm. Feb. 28, 1642-3. Constable 25 (1) 1644. [Es. Court.] His wife Elizabeth sold land in 1649. Ch. Abr. "son of Edwards of Watertown," bapt. at Salem 19 (6) 1638, Jon, "son

EDWARDS, cont.
of sister Edwards," bapt. 2 (4) 1639, Joseph, do. bapt. 22 (3) 1642, Joshua bapt. 18 (4) 1643.

William, Lynn. Dealt in bees, 1641. [Es. Court rec.] Before the court in 1648.

EGGLESTONE, EGLESTON,
Bigot, Dorchester, frm. May 18, 1631. Rem. to Windsor, Conn.

EIRE, EYRE, EIRES, EYRES, AYER, etc.,
Mr. Simon, ae. 48, physician, came in the Increase, April 15, 1635, with wife Dorothy, ae. 38, and ch. Marie, ae. 15, Thomas, ae. 13, Simon, ae. 11, Rebecca, ae. 9, Christian, ae. 7, Anna, ae. 5, Benjamin, ae. 3, and Sarah, ae. 3 months. Settled at Watertown; propr. 1636; frm. April 17, 1637. Deputy. He rem. to Boston; rec'd chh. 17 (2) 1647. His wife Dorothy d. 11 (6) 1650; he m. 2. Martha —. Ch. Jonathan b. 20 (1) 1637, Dorothy b. 4 (4) 1640, Maria b. 26 (1) 1652; Ann m. John Checkley; John b. Feb. 19, 1653, John Whittingham, his son-in-law, d. 7 (9) 1653, Judith Whittingham, dau.-in-law, d. 27 (1) 1656.

He d. Nov. 10, 1658. Will prob. March 4, 1658-9. Beq. to wife Martha, to 2 youngest children, John and Maria, to eldest son Thomas and his dau. Dorothy; the rest of his children having had their portions. In the will of Wm. Paine other children are named, Benjamin, Rebecca, Christian. The widow Martha d. July 13, 1687.

ELDERKIN,
John, Lynn, propr., 1638. Rem. to Dedham; propr. 22 (12) 1641. Lot sold before 6 (12) 1642. He sold a new built mill at Lynn 16 (7) 1643. Mortg. half of a mill at Reading June 27, 1646. Wife —; ch. Abigail b. 13, bapt. 19 (7) 1641; John d. 1641.

ELDRED, ELDRECH,
Robert, servant to Mr. Nicholas Sympkins, transferred for 3 yrs. 25 May, 1639, to Mr. Thomas Prence. Plymouth, atha. 1643. Rem. to Yarmouth. He m. Oct. 1649, Elizabeth Nickarson; ch. Nicholas b. Aug. 18, 1650.

Inv. of his est. 18 Jan. 1682; some land given to the wife by her father Wm. Nickarson, Sen.; eldest son to have a double portion.

Samuel, Medford, resident before 1651. [Mdx. Files.] Deposed in 1652, ae. about 32 years. Cambridge, before Gen. Court Nov.

ELDRED, etc., cont.
22, 1659; deposed Ess. Court 1661, res. at Rumney Marsh. Wife Elizabeth; ch. Elizabeth b. 26 (8) 1642, Samuel b. 26 (8) 1644, Mary b. 15 (4) 1646, Thomas b. 8 (7) 1648.

William, Yarmouth. Wife Ann; suit to protect in 1645. Ch. Ann b. Dec. 1648, Sarah b. Oct. 10, 1650.

William Lumpkin of Y. in his will dated 23 July, 1668, beq. to gr. ch. Elisha and Bethia Eldred. Are they ch. of William and Ann? [Genealogy in Reg. LI, 46.]

ELFORD,
John, mariner, Salem; called to Court 1 March, 1630-1. Drew bill of exchange in 1639. [L.]

ELIOT, ELYOT, ELLIOTT,
Francis, son of Bennett and Lettice E., of Widford and Nasing, Eng., came as a planter to Braintree; frm. June 2, 1641. Became schoolmaster to the Indians under his bro. about 1650. [Reg. XXXVI, 292.] With wife Mary sold land in Br. May 4, 1662. Ch. Mary b. 27 (11) 1640, John b. 17 (2) 1650, Hannah b. 11 (8) 1651, (m. 6 (3) 1670, Stephen Willis,) Abigail b. 12 (11) 1658.

Inv. taken 29 Oct., pres. 13 Nov. 1677, by widow Mary. He beq. to his wife Mary; to daus. Rachel Poulter and Hannah Willis, and to Stephen Willis. Dec. dau. Mary Hubbart.

Jacob, son of Bennet and Lettice E., bapt. 21 Sept 1606, came early to Boston; deacon, ruling elder; frm. March 6, 1631-2. Wife Margery; ch. Jacob b. 16 (10) 1632, John b. 28 (10) 1634, Hannah b. 29 (11) 1636, [see W. vol. 2, p. 202.] (m. Theophilus Frary 4 (4) 1653,) Abigail b. 7 (2) 1639, Susanna b. 22 (5) 1641, Mehetabel b. (2) 1645, (m. Seth Perry,) Sarah bapt. 5 (10) 1647, Asaph b. 25 (8) 1651, and bapt. 2 (9) 1651, after his father's death.

Will prob. Nov. 20, 1651; the widow's will prob. 9 May, 1661. He beq. to wife, son Jacob and dau. Hannah; other ch. to have portions at majority or marriage. [Reg. IV, 53, X, 362, and XXX, 206.]

Rev. John, son of Bennett and Lettice (Aggar) Eliot, was bapt. at Widford, Eng., 5 Aug. 1604. [See wills of the father and others in Reg. XLVII, 397 *et seq.*]

"The Apostle to the Indians" came to N. E. Nov. 2, 1631; acting pastor of the Boston chh.

ELIOT, etc., cont.
in absence of Mr. Wilson; ord. over chh. of Roxbury in Oct. 1632; frm. May 6, 1631-2. In addition to a faithful performance of his parochial duties he found time for a thorough study of the language of the Indians of Massachusetts, so as to translate the Bible and other books into it; and achieved a great work in the conversion and education of many individuals. See many notices.

He m. in Rox. in 1632, Anne Mumford; she d. 22 March, 1686. Ch. Hannah b. Sept. 17, 1633, John b. Aug. 3, 1636, Joseph bapt. Dec. 20, 1638, Samuel bapt. Jan. 27, 1641, Aaron bapt. Feb. 19, 1643, d. 18 (9) 1655, Benjamin bapt. Feb. 29, 1646.

He d. May 20, 1690, in his 86th year.

Philip, son of Bennet and Lettice E., bapt. 25 April, 1602, came early to Roxbury; deacon. His wife, ae. 30, and ch.: Marie, ae. 13, Elizabeth, ae. 8, Sarah, ae. 6, Lydia, ae. 4, and Philip, ae. 2, came in the Hopewell in April, 1635.

He d. 22 or 24 (8) 1657. Will prob. Feb. 11, 1657. Wife Elizabeth, son Aldis and dau. Sarah Aldis; gr. ch. Henry Withington; dau. Lydia. [Reg. VIII, 281.] The est. of the widow was divided to her sons-in-law John Aldis, John Smith, of Dedham, and Rich. Withington of Dorchester, Feb. 2, 1660.

William, came in the Hercules April 16, 1634. "One Eliot of Ipswich" got lost in Nov. 1634. [W.] In Salem Court in 1660.

ELKIN, ELKINS, ELKYN,
Henry, tailor, Boston, adm. chh. 9 (9) 1634, frm. May 6, 1635. With wife Mary dism. to chh. of Exeter 3 (1) 1639.

Will dated 27 April, 1667, prob. 13 (2) 1669, "very aged;" beq. to sons Gershom and Eliezer.

Thomas, before the Court Aug. 5, 1634.

ELLENWOOD, ELWOOD,
Ralph, planter, ae. 28, came in the Truelove in Sept. 1635. Settled at Salem; rem. to Beverly; suit in Court, settled by arbitration, 1638. He deposed in 1669, ae. about 60. Adm. chh. 21 (1) 1647; goodwife adm. chh. 13 (6) 1648. He m. 14 (1) 1655, Ellen Lyn. Ch. Josiah bapt. 26 (3) 1644, Stephen bapt. 16 (1) 1656, Ralph bapt. 26 (2) 1657, Ralph b. 18 March, 1658, John b. 2 (5) 1659, Joseph b. 12 (3) 1662,

ELLENWOOD, etc., cont.
Mary b. 3 (2), bapt. 5 (4) 1664, Elizabeth b. 27 June, 1666, Sarah bapt. 7 (6) 1666, Benjamin b. 1 (2) 1668, David b. 6 July, 1670.

His will dated Jan. 7, 1673, prob. 3 (5) 1674, beq. to wife Helen and ch. Ralph, John, Joseph, Benjamin, David, Mary and Elizabeth. The widow Eleanor deposed.

ELLEN, ELLIN, ALLEN,
Nicholas, Dorchester, in Court 4 (4) 1639; propr. Feb. 2, 1646. [George Allen of Boston, son of Daniel and gr. son of Nicholas A. of Dorch. beq. in 1718 a small farm which had belonged to said gr. fa. N. A. This shows the double spelling of the name.] He deposed in 1656, ae. about 40 years. [Arch. 38 B.] He m. first Martha —; she d. Sept. 17, 1660; he m. 2, July 3, 1663, Mary, widow of Robert Pond, Jr. They sold the Pond est. Oct. 5, 1665. Ch. Ann b. 3 (11) 1657.

Will dated Nov. 16, 1667, prob. May 29, 1668. Wife Mary, eldest son Daniel, his other children; Martha and Mary Pond, his wife's daus. [Reg. XIX, 36.] Daniel admin. on the estate of his bro. Benjamin 11 Jan. 1677.

ELLERD,
Gartrud, Salem, member chh. before 1636.

ELLERY,
Henry, before Gen. Court 20 (3) 1640.

ELLET,
John, Watertown; wife Margaret; ch. Elizabeth b. 2 (12) 1633, John b. 12 (4) 1635-6, Anne b. 12 (5) 1638, Samuel and Martha b. and d. in 1640, Sarah b. 22 (10) 1643. Sold land, buildings and privileges 8 (3) 1646.

[Samuel?], Salem, witness at court in 1648.

ELLISON, ELLISIN,
Richard, Braintree; wife Thomasin; ch. Mary b. 15 (6) 1646, Hannah b. 24 (5) 1648, John b. 26 (6) 1650, Sarah b. 10 (4) 1652, Thomasin b. 1 (1) 1655, Experience (dau.) b. 6 (2) 1657, Richard b. 7 (2) 1642.

ELLIS, ELIS, ELCE, ELSE, ALICE,
Arthur, juryman, Gen. Court, Sept. 28, 1630.

Elizabeth, ae. 16, came in the Abigail in July, 1635.

Goodwife, Lynn, before the Court in 1647 for living 8 years from her husband.

John, Dedham, pioneer 1636, adm. chh. 17 (5) 1640, frm. June 2, 1641. He m. 10 (9) 1641, Susan Lumber; ch. John b. 26 (2) 1646. Rem. to Medfield. He m. 2, 26 (4) 1656, Joane, widow of John Clap of Dorchester. Will dated Sept. 24, 1690, prob. June 24, 1697; beq. to wife Jone; to eldest son John; to daus. Susanna Evins and Hannah Rocket articles that belonged to their mother, his first wife; to sons Joseph and Eleazer.

John, Sandwich, atba. 1643. Lieut. He m. Elizabeth, [dau. of Edmund Freeman;] in Court June 4, 1645. Ch. (parent not given) Bennett b. 27 Feb. 1648, Mordical (of John) b. March 24, 1650, Joel b. March 20, 1654, Matthias b. June 2, 1657. Inv. of his est. taken 23 May, 1677, pres. by his widow Elizabeth.

Mary, had deed of house in Boston 2 (1) 1645, from Maj. Gen. Gibbons. She afterward m. — Scarlet.

Lieut. Richard, wheelwright, Dedham, adm. chh. 5 (11) 1643. He m. 19 (7) 1650, Elizabeth French; ch. Elizabeth b. 23 (5) 1651, Sarah b. 23 (11) 1652, Mary b. 3 (12) 1654, John b. 31 (11) 1656, Anna b. 15 (1) 1659, Rebecca b. 30 (2) 1661, Eliezer b. Jan. 10, 1663, Joseph b. Oct. 1666, Abigail b. July 5, 1669.
He d. Oct. 21, 1694. Admin. gr. to his widow Elizabeth and son John 27 Dec. 1694.

Roger, weaver, Yarmouth, suit in court, 1641; atba. 1643; lic. by Gen. Court 12 (9) 1644, to m. Jane Lisham. Ch. John b. Dec. 1, 1648, bapt. at Barnstable April 15, 1649. He rem. to Boston; adm. inhab. in 1653. Bought house in Charlestown 25 (10) 1657. Nunc. will beq. all to his wife; this, with the inv. of his est., was filed 24 (1) 1668-9, by widow "Ales Elce."

William, see Allis.

ELITHORP, ELLITHORPE, ELLITHROP,
Thomas, Rowley, propr. 1643. His first wife d. and he m. 2, Abigail, widow of

ELITHORP, etc., cont.
Thomas Sumner. Ch. Nathaniel, (deposed in 1686, ae. about 55 years,) (m. Dec. 16, 1657, Mary, dau. of Nicholas Batt,) John b. 18 (3) 1643, Mary, (m. 12 (8) 1655, Henry Ryley,) Abigail, (m. Joseph Pickworth).
He d. about April, 1654. The Gen. Court adm. his will 3 May, 1654, but it does not appear. The widow m. 3, Thomas Jones; she joined with son Nathl. and daus. Mary Ryley and Abigail Pickworth 6 April, 1668, in appointing son John attorney for business at Rowley. [Es. Files XVIII and XXXI.]

ELLSLEY, see Ilsley.

ELMER,
Edward, embarked June 22, 1632. Settled at Cambridge, propr. 1635. Sold land before 1638.

ELMS, ELMES,
Ralph, (Radolphus) planter, Scituate, came in the Planter in April, 1635; atba. 1643. Gave bond to John Floyd Oct. 2, 1656, for money lent and paid for passage. He m. 25 Dec. 1644, Kateren Whitcombe. Ch. Sarah b. Sept. 29, 1645. See will of Sarah Elmes, widow of Southwark, co. Surrey, dated 25 Aug. 1653, prob. 20 April, 1654; son Radulphus Elmes now in parts beyond the seas; sons Jonathan and Henry Elmes. [Reg. XL, 306.] Ch. Sarah b. Sept. 29, 1645, Mary b. June 9, 1648, Joanna b. Mar. 28, 1651, Hannah b. Dec. 25, 1653, John b. July 6, 1655, Joseph b. March 16, 1658, Waitstill b. Feb. 9, 1660, Jonathan b. 27 Sept. 1663, Rodulphus b. 27 May, 1668.

ELSLY, ELUSLEY, see Ilsey.

ELSTON,
John, Salem, suffered shipwreck in Boston Bay 26 July, 1631, with two of Mr. Craddock's fishermen. [W.]

ELWELL, ELWAY,
Robert, Dorchester, propr. Sept. 1, 1634; frm. at Boston May 13, 1640; at Es. Court 30 (4) 1640. His wife had legacy from a bro. residing at Stoke Abbot, Dorsetshire, Eng., about 1648. [See Tristram Dalliber.] He sold before June 8, 1640, and rem. to Salem; adm. chh. 19 (12) 1642, and soon after to Gloucester. Town officer, comr. to end small causes. He m. 1, Joan —, who

ELWELL, etc., cont.
d. March 31, 1675. He m. 2, May 29, 1676, Alice, widow of Robert Leach, who had d. about (5) 1674. She d. April 10, 1691; she beq. her est. to her 5 daus., of whom Alice Bennett was one, and her 2 sons Samuel and Robert Leach.

Ch. Samuel, (deposed in 1694, ae. 60 years,) 2 children bapt. at Sal. 28 (6) 1639, John bapt. 23 (11) 1639-40, Isaac bapt. 27 (12) 1641, Josiah, Joseph, (who deposed March 28, 1664, ae. 16 years next May,) Sara b. and d. in 1651, Sarah b. May 12, 1652, d. Aug. 26, 1655, Thomas b. Nov. 12, 1654. bapt. 22 (2) 1655, Jacob b. June 10, 1657, d. May 21, 1658, Richard bapt. April 11, 1658, Mary, (m. Samuel Dalliber).

He d. in May or June, 1683. Will, dated 15 May, prob. 26 June, 1683. [See The Elwell Family.]

ELWOOD, see ELLENWOOD,

ELY, ELLY,
Edward, servant of John Scobell, carpenter, of Boston, in 1640. [L.]

One Ely, a seaman, came in the Mayflower, hired to stay in the country a year; when the time was out he ret. [B.]

Nathaniel, Cambridge, propr. 1634; frm. May 6, 1635. Rem. to Conn. where he held several important offices.

EMERSON,
John, came in the Abigail in July, 1635, at the age of 20 years. Settled at Scituate; yeoman, planter. Before the Gen. Court Jan. 3, 1636. Sold land in 1636 and 1639. Won a case in court 3 March, 1639-40.

He m. at Duxbury, July 19, 1638, Barbara, dau. of Mr. John Lothrop.

EMBERSON, EMERSON,
Thomas, baker, yeoman, Ipswich, propr. 1638; selectman, 1646. Conveyed his farm to his son John, for a yearly rental etc. during the lives of himself and his wife Elizabeth; many specifications. [Ips. De. I, 63.]

His will dated 31 May, 1653, prob. Jan. 4, 1660, beq. to sons Joseph, John and Nathaniel, daus. Elizabeth Fuller, and Susanna E.; to son James, if he shall come over into this country; to wife Elizabeth, whom he makes exec.

Genealogy.

EMERY,
Anthony, carpenter, of Romsey, came in the James in April, 1635. Settled at Newbury, 1637. Selectman, 1648. Rem to Dover and Kittery.

George, doctor, Salem, 1636. One of the appraisers of John Thorne's est. in 1646. The town agreed with him in 1647 about curing goody Lamberte. He deposed in 1662, ae. about 53 years. Wife Mary adm. chh. 1 (9) 1648. She d. about (9) 1673.

He d. 20 Feb. 1686-7.

John, carpenter, from Romsey, Eng., came in the James in 1635. Settled at Newbury. Frm. June 2, 1641. Town officer; kept the ordinary. His wife d. and he m. 2, Mary, widow of John Webster. Ch. Eleanor, (m. John Bayley,) Anne, (m. James Ordway,) John, Ebenezer, dau. b. 16 Sept. 1648, (m. John Hoag,) Jonathan b. 13 May, 1652, Hannah, (m. Michael Emerson).

He d. 3 Nov. 1683. Will dated May 12, prob. Nov. 27, 1683, in his 83d year; beq. to wife Mary, dau. Ebenezer Hoag, son Jonathan, gr. ch. Mary Emerson, to his six children; sons John E. and Abraham Merrill overseers. The widow Mary d. April 28, 1694. Will dated Aug. 1, 1693, prob. June 1, 1696, beq. to son Jonathan E.; to Israel's four daughters; to John Webster's son Israel; to daus. [Simons;] Abigail Merrill, Johannah — and Hannah Emerson; to son Stephen W.

EMMONS, EMANS,
Thomas, cordwainer, Boston, adm. inhabitant in 1647. With wife Martha adm. chh. 18 (11) 1651; frm. May 26, 1652.

He d. May 11, 1664. Will: Wife Martha; ch. Obediah, Samuel, Hannah Crab, Elizabeth Hincksman, Benjamin; kinswoman Martha Winsor; gr. ch. Thomas, son of Obediah, and Samuel Crab. The widow made will March 30, 1666, prob. Feb. 18, 1666-7; beq. to ch. Obediah, Samuel, Joseph, Benjamin, Alice; gr. ch. Thomas, Martha, Samuel, Mary, Elizabeth, and Samuel Crab; to kinswomen Martha and Hannah Winsor; son John Hincksman. [Reg. XII, 346.]

Edward, servant of John Scobell, carpenter, of Boston, in 1640. [L.]

Edward "Eymons," Haverhill, deposed in 1663, ae. 40 years.

ENDECOTT, ENDICOTT,
Mr. John; he arrived at Salem Sept. 6, 1628. He was chosen "Governor of the Plantation in the Mattachusetts Bay for the yeare following from the time he shall take his oath," by the Governor and Company in London, 30 April, 1629. He held the office until the arrival of Mr. John Winthrop, who had been chosen governor of the Company and also of the Plantation, in June, 1630. He took the oath of Asst. 7 Sept. 1630; was again elected governor March 26, 1649. Was captain of militia, magistrate and one of the most important statesmen of the Colony. He rem. to Boston in 1655. He calls Roger Ludlow "my brother" in a letter to Gov. Winthrop in 1644. [Mass. Hist. Coll. 4-6.] He m. first Anna Gouer, who came over in 1628 and d. in 1629. She was a "cousin" of Gov. Matthew Craddock; see his letter in Mass. Hist. Coll. 2-8. He m. second, Aug. 18, 1630, [W.] Elizabeth Gibson of Cambridge, Eng., member of the chh. before 1636. Ch. John and Zerubabel.

His will, dated 2 (3) 1659, presented but disallowed by the Court, mentions his farm at Salem which he had bought 4 (8) 1648, of Henry Chickering of Dedham; 2 farms on Ipswich River, bought respectively of Capts. Trask and Hawthorne.

ENFLING,
Nathaniel, servant of John Cogan, Boston, ae. about 18 yrs., deposed Aug. 8, 1639. [L.]

ENGLAND,
John, Plymouth, found drowned about June 5, 1638.

ENGLISH, ENGLIS, INGLISH, INGLIS, INGS, INGE, ENGES,
Maudit, (also called Madett, Maud, Maudie, Madot,) fuller, from Marlborough, Eng., came in the James April 5, 1635. Settled at Boston; propr. 1638. Adm. chh. "laborer," 5 (7) 1640. He deposed March 20, 1678-9, ae. about 70 years. [Supr. Court Rec.] Wife Joan adm. chh. 2 (10) 1643; ch. Hannah b. 2 (1) 1638-9, (m. 2 (5) 1657, Samuel Clement,) Mary bapt. 17 (9) 1644, ae. about 4 days, Samuel bapt. 7 (1) 1647, ae. about 9 days, (m. at Hingham Feb. 21, 1672-3, Mary, dau. of Nathaniel and Martha Beale).

His will dated 1 (10) 1684, prob. 18 July,

ENGLISH, etc., cont.
1685, beq. to son Samuel, dau.-in-law Mary, and gr. ch. Madet, Samuel and Nathaniel.

Thomas, mariner, came in the Mayflower to Plymouth, hired to go master of a shalop here; d. before the ship ret. [B.]

Sergt. William, cordwainer, Ipswich, propr. 1637; selectman; frm. Sept. 21, 1642. Rem. to Boston. Adm. townsman in 1652. Deputy. With wife Sara adm. chh. 15 (1) 1662-3.

Will dated 4 May, prob. 15 June, 1682, beq. to wife Mary, and to Sarah, dau. of Joshua and Sarah Windsor. Signed, William Inglish.

Bernard, husbandman, Pulling Point, Boston, bought land of James Bill in 1645, and rec'd deed July 6, 1666. He deposed 21 (4) 1664, ["Ingle,"] ae. about 57 years. [Mdx. Files.]

ENSIGN, ENSIGNE, INSIGN,
James, Cambridge, propr. 1634; frm. March 4, 1634-5.

Thomas, planter, Scituate, 1638, prop. frm., 5 March, 1638-9; atba. 1643; deacon in 1653. He m. 17 Jan. 1638, Eliza, dau. of widow Martha Wilder; ch. Hannah bapt. July 6, 1640.

Will, dated July 16, 1663, prob. 9 June, 1664. Wife Elizabeth; ch. John, Hannah and Sarah; wife's sister's dau. Sarah Underwood, not yet 15 yrs. old; to dau. Hannah's Son, Thomas Shepherd. [Reg. VI, 185.]

EPPS, EPES,
Mr. Daniel, gent., Ipswich, witness of a deed in 1641; propr.; town officer. Attorney for his cousin Joseph Cooke of Cambridge in a suit in 1658. [Es. Court files IV, 114.] He resided in London in 1621, when his wife recd. a beq. from her mother's father Thomas Cooke, yeoman, of Pebmershe, Essex. [Reg. XLVII, 128.] He m. Martha, dau. of Mr. Edmund Read, of Wickford, co. Essex, Eng.; she survived him and m. Deputy governor Samuel Symonds. Ch. Daniel, deposed in 1675, ae. about 50 years; Elizabeth, ae. 13, came in the Abigail in July, 1635; named in the will of her grandfather Reade in 1623; a dau. m. Peter Duncan of Gloucester. [Es. De. 1662.]

ERRINGTON, ERINGTON, ARRINGTON, [Harrington,]

Abraham, blacksmith, son of widow Ann, below, Cambridge, 1646. He deposed April 17, 1673, ae. about 53 years. [Mdx. Files.] He m. Rebecca, dau. of Robert Cutler of Charlestown; ch. Rebecca, Hannah, Sarah, Mary bapt. Jan. 13, 1660, Abraham bapt. Nov. 8, 1663. [Mi.]
He d. May 9, 1677, ae. 55 years. [Gr. St.] Admin. gr. to widow Rebecca.

Ann, widow, formerly of Newcastle-upon-Tyne; res. in Charlestown. [See Sill.] She was b. near Newcastle; the Lord gave her a good husband, but he died. [Rel.] She d. Dec. 25, 1653, ae. 77. [Gr. St.] Ch. Abraham, Rebecca, (m. John Watson). [Mi.]

Thomas, Salem; rem. to Lynn; mortg. house at Salem 10 (5) 1643. Res. at Charlestown, sold farm in C. 27 (9) 1649.

ESTIE, see East.

ESPY,
Robert, had an acct. with Gen. Court 5 (1) 1639. [Arch. 100.]

ESTOW,
William, Newbury, propr. about 1638, as John Emery deposed at Salisbury April 9, 1679. He was one of the first planters at Hampton 6 (7) 1638. Deputy. See Eastwick.

EUE, see Ewell, and Ewer,
Henry, ordered to leave Plymouth Colony bounds with his family 4 Dec. 1638. Propr. at Sandwich 16 April, 1640.

EVANS, EVINS, EUINS,
Mr. David, merchant, Boston. Ch. Nathaniel bapt. 26 (3) 1650, David d. 2 (9) 1653, Elizabeth b. 10 Aug. 1655, David b. 2 Feb. 1658, Martha d. 8 (7) 1658, Jonathan b. April 3, 1663.
He d. 27 July, 1663. Will, dated June 30, 1663; wife Mary; ch. David, Jonathan, Mary, Elizabeth; bro. John Clark. [Reg. XI, 344.]

Elizabeth, of Bridgend, Glamorganshire, articled as a servant with John Wheelwright, minister, 5 (5) 1639. [L.]

EVANS, etc., cont.
Henry, husbandman, Boston, adm. chh. 18 (4) 1643, frm. May, 1645. Wife Amy rec'd from chh. of Roxbury 23 (1) 1644.
He was drowned about March 1, 1666-7. Inv. of his est. filed in Mdx. court.

Richard, Dorchester, 1640; frm. May 10, 1643. Wife Mary.
Admin. gr. 11 (12) 1661, to eldest son Richard, for himself and bros. and sisters.

Thomas, [Plymouth.] He d. Jan. 27, 1634. Inv. filed at Plymouth. [Reg. IV, 35.] The court ordered that his debts be paid and the remainder be kept for his widow according to his will.

William, Dorchester, 1640. [L.] Wife Agnes a witness in 1640.

William, Gloucester, town officer, 1647.

William, Taunton, atba. 1643.
Inv. of his est. taken 15 Sept. 1671, pres. by Anna Evance 17 June, 1672.

EVELITH, EVELYTH,
Sylvester, baker, Boston, 1643. Rem. to Gloucester; his wife Susan, who had joined the chh. 19 (1) 1643, being dism. to join the chh. of Gloc. 12 (3) 1644. Town officer. The wife, ae. 50 years, testified before her husband and Wm. Vinson 30 (1) 1657, on the W. Brown case. She d. 7 (7) 1659. He m. 6 (7) 1662, Bridget Parkman. Ch. Joseph bapt. in Boston, 23 (1) 1643, ae. about 1 year and 9 months.
He d. Jan 4, 1689. Admin. of his est. was gr. to son Joseph, who filed at Boston 7 March, 1688-9, an inv. of the est., taken 9 Jan. previous.

EVERED, EVERARD, EVERETT, EVERITT,
Richard, (Everitt,) Springfield, a witness of the deed from the Indians in 1636; was the "chapman" of part of Henry Gregory's land, Jan. 24, 1638; propr. of other lands in 1646. Town officer. He m. 29 (4) 1643, Mary Winch.

Richard, farrier, Cambridge; propr.; pioneer at Dedham, 1636. He mortg. land in Camb. March 16, 1638-9. [L.] Frm. May 6, 1646. Wife Mary adm. chh. with him 6 (1) 1646; ch. Mary b. 28 (7) 1638, (m. (9) 1662, James Macharoy,) Samuel b. 31 (1) 1639, Sarah b. and d. 1641, James b. 14 (1) 1643,

EVERED, cont.

Sarah b. 12 (4) 1644, Abigail b. 1647, Israel b. 14 (5) 1651, Ruth b. 14 (11) 1653, Jedidiah b. 11 (5) 1656.

He d. 3 (5) 1682. Will dated 12 (3) 1680, prob. 25 July, 1682, beq. to wife Mary; sons Jedidiah, John and Samuel; daus. Abigail Puffer and Ruth; James, Daniel and Mary, ch. of dec. dau. Mary and James Mackerwithy; gr. ch. Sarah Fisher.

EVERED, *alias* WEBB,

John, husbandman, from Marlborough, Eng., came in the James April 5, 1635; merchant, Boston, m. Mary, widow of Thomas Fairweather in 1639. [L.] Memb. chh. 1639. Bought land in D. March 8, 1657. Called Ensign John Webb in an agreement 25 March, 1658. Owned a farm near Chelmsford and bought a neighboring island 9 (9) 1659. He deposed 20 (4) 1659, ae. about 46 years. [Mdx. Files.] He bought of the Indians 15 (6) 1666, the tract called Drawcutt or Augamtoocooke, upon Mynomack or Merrimack. [Norf. De. II.]

He was drowned while whaling 17 (8) 1668. [D.] Admin. gr. Dec. 15, 1668, to widow Mary, on petition of Thomas Hinksman. [Mdx. Files.] His autograph will dated at Drawcutt upon Merrimack, formerly of Boston, 10 Feb. 1665, prob. at Cambridge 13 (9) 1668, beq. to wife Mary; to the church of Boston; to the pastor of the chh. of Chelmsford; to bro. William Dinsdale of Bo.; to servants Henry Nelson, Hugh Stone, Samuel Mercer alias Watts, John Bennet, Peter Raghteliagh and Elizabeth Kilbourne; to cousins John, Robert, Thomas, Peter and Nathaniel Eayres, of Haverhill, and the wife of John [U]sleby and any other of that family; to the eldest son of John Bishop, late of Newbury, now of Nantucket.

Stephen, husbandman, came with John, above, in 1635. Was a servant of Lt. Wm. Phillips; died 18 Sept. 1659.

EVERILL,

James, leather-dresser, shoemaker, Boston, adm. chh. with wife Elizabeth 20 (5) 1634; frm. Sept. 3, 1634. Town officer. He and Richard Woody hired Bird island of the town 2 (2) 1658, for 60 years at 12 d. or a bushell of salt per annum. Allowance made to him and his dau. Manninge of 140 li. in rate pay in 1680 in consideration of their houses being blown up to stop the great

EVERILL, cont.

fire. Ch. Ezekiel bapt. 15 (3) 1636, Coneniah bapt. 4 (9) 1638, Elizabeth bapt. 3 (8) 1641, ae. 3 days. Abiel, who m. 6 (5) 1655, Elizabeth, dau. of Lieut. Wm. Philips of Boston and d. in 1660,—was he another child?

His will dated 11 Dec. prob. 2 Feb. 1682, beq. to wife Mary the est. she brought at marriage and more; to daus. Hannah Manning and Elizabeth Grant; to gr. ch. James Manning and Elizabeth Adkins; to the old church.

EVERT, EVART, EVARTS,

John, Concord, frm. March, 1637-8. Ch. John b. 29 (12) 1639, Judah b. 27 (8) 1642.

EWELL,

Henry, shoemaker, of Sandwich, Eng., came in the Hercules in March, 1634. Settled at Scituate; adm. chh. April 3, 1636. Volunteered for Pequot War in 1637. Rem. to Barnstable. Took oath of allegiance Feb. 1, 1638-9. Prop. frm. June 1, 1644; frm. 3 June, 1657. He m. at Green's Harbor Nov. 22, 1638, Sarah, dau. of Anthony Anniball; ch. John bapt. March 9, 1639, Ebenezer bapt. Feb. 12, 1642, Sarah bapt. Sept. 14, 1645, Hannah b. June 22, 1649, Gershom b. Nov. 14, 1650, Abiah b. Sept. 27, 1653 ,Ichabod b. June, 1659, Deborah b. June 4, 1663, Bethiah d. May 8, 1669.

He made will 16 Aug. 1681, being aged; prob. 13 March, 1688-9; beq. to wife Sarah; refers to a legacy given to dau. Hannah by Goody Woodfield; mentions that his house was burned by the Indians; beq. to sons Gershom and Ichabod, daus. Sarah [Northey,] Hannah, Eunice and Deborah.

EWER,

Thomas, tailor, ae. 40, with wife Sarah, ae. 28, and ch. Elizabeth, ae. 4, and Thomas, ae. 1½, came in the James in June, 1635. Settled at Charlestown; he and his wife adm. chh. 8 (11) 1635. Town officer, 1636.

He d. in 1638. Anthony Dyaper of London and Andrew Blake of Strowde, Kent, Eng., were empowered to collect money due him Oct. 31, 1638. [L.] Admin. gr. to the widow Sarah 4 (10) 1638. She m. 2, Thomas, son of Mr. John Lothrop of Barnstable. There the ch. Elizabeth d. April 9, 1641.

EWSTEAD, [see Husted,]
Richard, wheelwright, sent over to Salem by Mass. Bay Co. in 1639.

EYBROOKE, see Ibrook.

EXELL,
Richard, Springfield, propr. 1646-1672. He m. 4 (9) 1651, Hannah Reeves; ch. Mary b. 1 (1) 1652, John b. last of (1) 1655, Lydia b. 4 (9) 1657, Abigail b. 20 (3) 1660.

FABER,
Joseph, cooper, ae. 26, came in the Elizabeth and Ann in Apr. 1635. Settled at Boston, propr. He ret. to London and sold land and house in Bo. 7 (6) 1639. [L.]

FABINS, FABENS,
Elizabeth, ae. 16, came in the Elizabeth and Ann in May, 1635.

"Jon" [John or Jonathan] was one of the creditors of the est. of Thomas Dill of Marblehead in 1668.

FACE, see Veazie.

FAIRBANK, FAIRBANCK, FAIRBANKS, FAIRBANCKE,
Jonathan, Dedham, propr. 23 (1) 1636-7, adm. chh. 14 (6) 1646. Town officer. Wife Grace; ch. John, George, Jonas, Jonathan; Mary adm. chh. 11 (10) 1640 ,(m. 1, Michael Metcalf, 2, Christopher Smith,) Susan, (m. 12 (8) 1647, Ralph Day).

He d. 5 Dec. 1668; his will prob. Jan. 26, folg., mentions all the above-named and some of their children. The widow d. 28 (10) 1673. [Reg. XIX, 32.] See will of George Fairbanke of Sowerby in Halifax, Eng., dated May 28, 1650. [Reg. VII, 303.] Genealogy.

Richard, Boston, adm. chh. (8) 1633, frm. May 14, 1634. He had leave to sell his shop to Saunders, a book-binder, 7 (6) 1637. He was appointed by Gen. Court 5 (9) 1639, to have charge of all letters to and from Eng., voluntarily brought to his house. He made exchange of land 1 (2) 1652. Wife Elizabeth adm. chh. with him; ch. Constance bapt. 10 (11) 1635, (m. 30 (1) 1653, Samuel Mattocke,) Zaccheus bapt. 8 (10) 1639, d. 10 (9) 1653.

FAIRFIELD, FAYERFIELD,
Daniel, a half Dutchman, b. about 1601; Salem. Rem. to Boston. A convicted criminal in 1641. [W.] Wife Sarah; ch. Mary bur. (5) 1639, Elizabeth b. 30 (8) 1640, (m. 22 (8) 1657, Joseph Sowther,) Mary b. 7 (5) 1643, (m. 20 Aug. 1660, John Parker,) John b. Oct. 28, 1660, Daniel b. Sept. 18, 1662, Sarah b. Feb. 19, 1664, Abigail b. Feb. 22, 1673, Elizabeth b. March 1, 1674, Abigail b. Nov. 6, 1677, Daniel (of Daniel and Ruth) b. Dec. 1, 1680.

John, Charlestown, propr. 1638. Rec'd money from the town in 1656.

John, Salem, propr. 1638; frm. May 13, 1640. He rem. to Wenham. Wife Elizabeth adm. chh. 13 (4) 1641; ch. Walter b. about 1636, John bapt. 27 (4) 1641, Benjamin bapt. 27 (4) 1646.

He d. 22 (10) 1646. Will dated 11 (10) 1646, prob. at Ipswich 3 (5) 1647, (copy in Mdx. Files.) To wife Elizabeth; to sons Walter, ae. 8 years, and Benjamin, ae. 2 years; cousin Matthew Edward's land within my farm had from Salem; Henry Bartholomew and Robert Hawes of Salem, supervisors of will. The widow m. 2, Peter Palfrey, who gave bonds to pay the portions of the three children, Walter, John and Benjamin. [Es. Files VI, 119 and X, 49.] Walter sued Peter Palfrey 22 (7) 1660, for witholding the estate. [Mdx. Files.]

FALDOE,
Bartholomew, ae. 16, came in the Planter in April, 1635.

FALLAND,
Thomas, Yarmouth, frm. 7 Sept. 1641, atba. 1643; juryman, deputy.

FALLOWELL, FALLOWAY,
Gabriel, Boston, propr.; sold 2 (5) 1639, and rem. to Plymouth. Frm. 1 Sept. 1640; atba. 1643.

He d. Dec. 28, 1667, ae. 80. Will, dated Oct. 14, prob. Feb. 1667; wife Katharine, bro. Robert Finney, gr. ch. Jonathan F.; Sarah, dau. of John Wood. [Reg. VII, 177.] The widow Katharine d. 7 June, 1673. Her will was prob. 7 July, 1676. She beq. to her son John Fallowell's wife and children; to gr. ch. Jonathan and Hannah, wife of Jo-

FALLOWELL, etc., cont.
seph Bartlett; to her sister Anne Kinge and her ch. Samuel, Joseph and Isaac Kinge and Hannah May. Bro. Robert Finney.

William, [perhaps a son of Gabriel,] Plymouth, bought house and land July 5, 1636. He m. 16 May, 1640, Martha Beal. Martha [his widow?] m. June 29, 1649, Samuel Dunham.

FANE, [also called Vaine and Vane,]
Henry, turner, Boston, before the Court 13 (1) 1638, and in 1644. With wife Elizabeth sold house and land in B. Jan. 6, 1659. He deposed 30 (4) 1657, ae. about 72 years, regarding Dexter's ownership of Nahant. [Es. Files XXIX, 143.]

FARLEY,
George, [clothier,] Woburn, taxed in 1645. One of the incorporators of Billerica in 1654. He m. April 9, 1641, Christian Births; ch. James b. and d. 1643, Caleb b. April 1, 1645, Mary b. Feb. 27, 1646, Samuel b. March, 1654, Mehitabel b. April, 1656. He d. Dec. 27, 1693.

FARNHAM, FARNUM, FARMAN, VARNHAM,
John, joiner, Dorchester, 1638; frm. May 13, 1640. Rem. to Boston; bought shop and land about 1647. Town officer. Wife Elizabeth; son John d. 26 (6) 1652. He m. 7 (2) 1654, Susanna, dau. of Thomas Arnold of Watertown; ch. John b. May, 1655, dau. Elizabeth m. 6 (6) 1657, Joshua Carwithy; Joanna b. 3 (1) 1644, (m. 7 (11) 1657, James English;) Jonathan b. 13 Nov. 1659, Hannah b. 9 (9) 1642, David b. Oct. 30, 1662, Elizabeth b. Nov. 11, 1667, Thomas b. Sept. 17, 1670.

Ralph, barber, ae. 32, with Alice, ae. 28, Mary, ae. 7, Thomas, ae. 4, and Ralph, ae. 2, came in the James in July, 1638. Settled at Ipswich, propr. 1639; rem. to Andover. He (or the son Ralph) m. Oct. 26, 1657 or 1658, Elizabeth, dau. of Nicholas and Elizabeth Holt. Thomas, who deposed in 1657, ae. about 24 years, m. at Andover 8 July, 1660, Elizabeth Gibbons. Ralph, Jr. deposed in 1667, ae. about 30 years. [Es. Files.]

FARNWORTH, FARNSWORTH,
Joseph, cooper, Dorchester, frm. March 13, 1638-9; propr. Wife Elizabeth d.; he m. 2, Mary —. Ch. Hannah bapt. 30 (10) 1638, Mary bapt. 1638-9, Rebecca bapt. 5 (11) 1639, Ruth bapt. 10 (4) 1642, (m. Mr. Puffer,) Samuel bapt. 27 (8) 1644, Samuel bapt. 30 (3) 1647.

Will prob. Feb. 1, 1659; wife Mary and her sons by former husband, Joseph and Thomas Long; sons Joseph and Samuel; daus. Elizabeth, wife of John Mansfield, Ester; Mary, wife of Abraham Ripley; gr. son Joseph Peck, son of Simon Peck, who m. with my dau. Hannah, now dec.; dau. Rebecca. Genealogy.

FARR, FAROUGH, FARROWE, [see Fawer,]
George, Salem, frm. May 6, 1635. Had gr. of land at Lynn in 1638. He deposed on the Dexter case in 1657, ae. about 63 years. He m. 16 (11) 1643, Ann Whitmore; she deposed in 1658, ae. about 40 years. Ch. Mary b. Jan. 6, 1644, Martha b. Feb. 25, [1646,] Phebe b. May, [1650.] [Essex Court lists.] He d. 24 Oct. 1662. [Es. Files 41, 114.] The widow Elizabeth deposed 2 June, 1684; had lived 54 years in Lynn on a tract given to her husband George Farr by the townsmen of Lynn.

George, Ipswich, 1643, herd-keeper 1647; famous killer of foxes.

FARRAR, FARROW,
John, carpenter, with wife and ch. came from Hingham, Eng. and settled at Hingham in 1635; propr. 1636. Wife Frances d. Jan. 28, 1688. Ch. Mary, (m. 1, Samuel Stowell, 2, Joshua Beal,) John bapt. June 6, 1639, Remember bapt. Aug. 1642, (m. Henry Ward,) Hannah bapt. April 9, 1648, (m. Nathaniel Foulsham,) Nathan bapt. Sept. 17, 1654.

He d. 7 July, 1687; will prob. Aug. 17, 1687. Mentions all the ch. except Hannah; also gr. ch. John Garret, Frances and Nathaniel Ward. [Reg. VI, 315.]

Thomas, husbandman, Boston, son of Thomas F., of or near Burnley in Lanc.; husb. gave letter of attorney 2 (11) 1645, to his bro. Henry F., mariner, to sell or lease, etc. [A.]

FARRINGTON,
Edmund, [or Edward,] ae. 47, with wife Elizabeth, ae. 49, and ch. Sarah, ae. 14, Matthew, ae. 12, John, ae. 11, Eliza, ae. 8, from Olney, Bucks, Eng., came in the Hopewell April 1, 1635. Settled at Lynn; miller; propr. 1638; mentioned in inv. of Abraham Belknap in 1643. He deposed in 1661, ae. about 74 years. Son John rem. to Southampton, L. I. He deeded land to son Matthew in 1666.

He d. 20 (11) 1670. His will dated 12 Aug. 1667, prob. 28 March, 1671, beq. to wife Elizabeth his land and corn mill for her life; to sons Matthew and Edward, son Robert Terry, dau. Elizabeth Fuller.

John, gave bonds for Isaac Deesbro before Gen. Court 3 (10) 1639. Settled at Dedham, townsman 1 (11) 1646. Wife Mary; ch. Mary b. 5 (2) 1650.

Admin. gr. July 28, 1676, to his widow Mary and son John. Distribution was made 3 July, 1704, after her decease, to other children, viz. Nathaniel, Daniel and Benjamin Farrington, Sarah Witherley, Abigail Hoadley; and to Mary Kenney, dau. of Mary Farrington, another child, and John Abbot, in right of his mother, sometime Hannah Farrington, another child.

FARWELL, FAREWELL, FERWELL,
Henry, Concord, 1640. Rem. to Chelmsford. Ch. John, (ae. 50 in 1685,) Joseph b. 26 (12) 1640, Mary, Elizabeth, Olive, (m. at Chelmsford Oct. 30, 1668, Benjamin Spaulding).

Will dated 12 July, inv. taken 5 Aug. 1670, beq. to wife Ollife, son John, Joseph, daus. Mary Bates, Ollife Spalding and Elizabeth Wilkins.

Mr. Thomas, Taunton, atba. 1643. Made a contract with his servant James Bishop June 11, 1639. [Plym. Col. Rec.]

FAULKNER, FAWKNER,
Edmund, or Edward, Andover; licensed to sell wine, 1648. He m. at Salem Feb. 4, 1647, Dorothy Robinson. Ch. John b. 16 May, 1654, Hanna b. May, 1658. The wife Dorothy d. 27 Dec. 1668.

Francis Fawconer of Kingscleare, Hants, gent., beq. to my bro. Edmond Fawconer that is living in N. E. 200 li., in his will dated 1 Sept. 1662, prob. 21 May, 1663.

FAULKNER, etc., cont.
[Reg. XXXIX, 70.] Elizabeth, dau. of Francis and Abigail F. d. at Andover 17 Aug. 1678.

FAUNCE, PHANCE,
John, Plymouth, came in 1623: frm. 1633, propr. Ch. Elizabeth b. March 23, 1647, d. March 3, 1649, Mercy b. April 10, 1651, Joseph b. May 14, 1653.

He d. Nov. 29, 1654. [Plym. Col. Rec.] Inv. taken Dec. 15, 1653. [Reg. V, 259.] His heir apparent, Thomas Faunce, was recognized by Plym. Court 29 Oct., 1668.

Manasseh, yeoman, came in 1623 to Plymouth; propr.

FAWER, FAUER, FAUR, FARR,
Barnabas, came with Rev. Richard Mather in the James from Bristol, Eng., May 23, 1635. Settled at Dorchester. Wife Dinah d. 27 (7) 1642, leaving son Eleazer b. 18 (7) 1642. By second wife Grace Negoose, who was dism. from chh. Boston to Dorch. 10 (1) 1644, he had Abigail, bapt. 30 (5) 1644. He rem. to Boston; was rec'd to chh. 7 (1) 1646.

He d. 13 (10) 1654. Will prob. in Feb. folg. Wife Grace; son Eleazer to be kept at school with Mr. Cheever at Ipswich one year; etc. [Reg. V, 305, and IX, 135, Col. Rec.] His widow m. John Johnson, q. v.

FAUNE, FAWNE, FAWN,
Mr. John, gent., Ipswich, propr. 1634, frm. Sept. 2, 1635. Sold land 10 Oct. 1650. Rem. to Haverhill. Ch. Elizabeth, (m. Dec. 8, 1652, Robert Clement). Luke F., stationer, London, in 1665-6 beq. to Mrs. Elizabeth Clement, living near Boston, N. E., eldest dau. of my bro. Mr. John Fawne, and to her son Fawne Clement. [Reg. 1894.] "Robert Clements, of Haverhill in Norfolk, N. E., successor to Mr. Fawne, the father to the wife of said Robert," had deed of land in Ipswich May 18, 1674.

FAY,
Thomas, brought suit in Es. court in 1638.

FAYERWEATHER,
Thomas, Boston, propr. Inv. of his est. taken by Wm. Colborn and John Odlin 8 (11) 1638, included house and lands and personal effects. See Goodhue.

FEAKE, FEAKES, FREAKE,
Henry, Saugus, Lynn, frm. May 14, 1634. Juryman, 1636. He rem. to Sandwich; had land grant 3 April, 1637. Appl. frm. 4 June, 1639. Elizabeth, m. March 24, 1650, John Dillingham.

Robert, gent., son of James Feke of London, goldsmith, came to Watertown; frm. May 18, 1631. Town officer, deputy, lieut. He arranged for the sale of patrimony for himself and sister Judith Palmer, and bro. Tobias F., ae. 17, in 1639. [L.] He m. Elizabeth (Fones,) widow of Henry Winthrop.

He d. Feb. 1, 1660 or 1662. Admin. gr. Feb. 18, 1662-3.

FEAN,
Hannah, servant to Nathaniel Sparhawk, Cambridge, d. 11 (1) 1649.

FEARING, FERING,
John, servant to Matthew Hawk, came in 1638 from Cambridge Eng. and settled at Hingham; propr. 1635, frm. May 26, 1652. Selectman, deacon. Wife Margaret; ch. John, Israel bapt. Sept. 1644, Mary bapt. April 18, 1647, (m. James Hersey,) Sarah bapt. July 29, 1649, (m. Benjamin Lincoln.) He d. 14 May, 1665. Will prob. June 16, 1665, beq. all to wife and ch. [Reg. XIII, 331.]

FEASIE, see Veazie.

FEBAR, see Faber.

FELCH, FELT,
George, mason, Charlestown, 1633, resided at Mystic Side, 1640. He deposed 20 (11) 1654, ae. about 40 years. He removed about 1640 to Casco Bay, settling at Great Cove; was one of the founders of North Yarmouth, District of Maine. He made an agreement with his son George on the day of the latter's marriage, (9) 1662, to pay him £ 40. See also deed of Jane, widow of Arthur Mackworth, gent., of Falmouth, conveying to George Felt, husband of her dau. Phil-

FELCH, etc., cont.
lippe, land bounded by that of her dau. Purchas and that of her son James Andrews. [Norf. co. rec. IV, 75.] He removed to Malden, where he petitioned Gov. Andros in vain for assistance in 1688. The town aided him and his wife, 1681-1692. Wife Elizabeth, dau. of widow Prudence Wilkinson; adm. chh. Char. 19 (11) 1639. Ch. Elizabeth, (m. (9) 1655, William Leraby,) George, Mary, these three bapt. 26 (11) 1639; Mary, (m. (2) 1660, James Nichols,) Moyses, bapt. 20 (10) 1640.

He d. in 1693; the widow d. in 1694. Genealogy.

Henry, Gloucester, propr.; rem. to Reading; propr. 1644; sold Gloc. land before 1649. Town officer. Son Henry also a propr. in 1647.

He made will 4 July, 1670, prob. 27 (7) folg. Beq. to wife; sons Henry Felch and Samuel [....]ton; to each of his gr. ch. His dau. Mary and her husband John Wiborne deeded land 2 (6) 1671, to her mother Elizabeth F., widow.

FELLOW, FELLOWS,
Samuel, planter, weaver, Salisbury, propr. 1639; frm. May, 1645. Wife Ann d. Dec. 5, 1684. Ch. Samuel b. Jan. 13, 1646, Hannah b. Sept. 15, 1648, (m. Nathaniel Brown). He deposed Nov. 11, 1679, ae. about 60 years.

He d. March 6, 1697-8. Admin. of his est. June 30, 1698.

William, shoemaker, ae. 24, certified from St. Albons, Herts., came in the Planter April 2, 1635. Settled at Ipswich; propr.; herdsman, 1639; husbandman. He deposed in 1659, ae. about 50.

Will dated Nov. 29, 1676, prob. March 27, 1677, beq. to wife; sons Isaac, Ephraim, Samuel and Joseph; daus. Mary, Elizabeth, Abigail and Sarah.

FELMINGHAM, FILMINGAN,
Francis, came in 1637 to Salem; propr. 1637. Adm. chh. 16 (4) 1650. He m. Frances, dau. of Benjamin Cooper, who brought them over at his own charge. [Endecott; Mass. Hist. Coll. 4-6.] Ch. Mary, Frances, Rebecca and John bapt. 7 (6) 1650.

FELTON,
Benjamin, turner, Salem, propr. 1636, frm. 22 May, 1639. Constable; his shop mentioned in a deed in 1647. He deposed in 1668, ae. about 64 years; his wife Mary depos. in 1661, ae. about 35 years. Bought a house and land of Mr. Peter's attorney in 1659. Ch. John bapt. 26 (10) 1639, Remember bapt. 28 (3) 1643, Benjamin bapt. 18 (11) 1645. [Col. Rec. 29 (5) 1641.]

He d. in 1688. [See wills of supposed relations in Yarmouth, Eng. in Reg. LII.]

Nathaniel, Salem, son of widow Ellen, (who was adm. chh. before 1636,) had land assigned with her in 1636. He deposed 12 (9) 1666, ae. about 50 years. Adm. chh. 13 (6) 1648. Wife Mary; ch. John bapt. 30 (7) 1648, Ruth bapt. 29 (8) 1648, Mary bapt. 6 (2) 1651, Elizabeth b. 18 March, 1652, bapt. 1 (3) 1653, Nathaniel b. 15 (6) bapt. 28 (8) 1655, Mary b. 15 (11) 1657, bapt. 30 (3) 1658, Hannah bapt. 20 (4) 1663, Susanna bapt. 29 (1) 1665.

He d. July 30, 1705; will prob. May, 1706, beq. to ch. John, Nathaniel, Elizabeth, Ruth and Hannah.

FEN, FENN,
Benjamin, Dorchester, propr. 1637.

Richard, (Fen or Fennye,) ae. 27, came in the Planter April 7, 1635.

Robert, Salem. His wife Deborah adm. chh. 13 (4) 1641. Ch., a dau., bapt. 4 (5) 1641. Rem. to Boston about 1644. He placed his son Robert Twogood with Thomas Marshfield in 1640. He m. 1, Deborah —; he m. 2, 26 (4) 1654, Mary, widow of Capt. Thomas Hawkins. Ch. Robert bapt. in Bo. 16 (4) 1644, Deborah b. 15 (11) 1645, Elizabeth bapt. 26 (10) 1647.

He ret. to London and d. before June, 1657, when his widow bought land in Boston, which she sold to George Munjoy. She m. 3, 27 Feb. 1661, Henry Shrimpton.

FENNYE, see FINNEY.

FENNER, see Fenn and Venner,
Rebecca, ae. 25, came in the Truelove in Sept. 1635.

FENWICK, FENNICK,
Eliza, ae. 35, came in the Defense in July, 1635.

George, Esq., of Gray's Inn, London, came with wife to Boston in 1636. Went to Conn. in company with Rev. Hugh Peter (4) 1636. Mrs. Mary F. went from Bo. to Salem with Mrs. P. 13 (9) 1646. He ret. to Eng.; was made a colonel and gov. of Tinmouth Castle in 1648. [W.] His will dated 10 March, 1646, prob. 27 April, 1657, mentions dau. Elizabeth exec.; wife Katharine; father-in-law Mr. Clavering, and his wife Mrs. Dorothy C.; bro. Claudius; sisters Ledgard and Cullick; bro. Cullick; nephew Thomas Ledgard, niece Clifton; niece Rootflower's boy; daus. Elizabeth and Dorothy; their uncle Edward Apsley, Esq. All his est. in N. E. to sister Cullick and her ch., beside liberal money legacies. [Reg. XXXVIII, 199.]

FERGOOSE, see Vergoose.

FERMAES, FERMASE, FERMACE, FERMAYES, FORMAIS, VERMAES,
Abigail, Salem, adm. chh. 19 (7) 1640.

Benjamin, Salem, adm. chh. 6 (1) 1641-2. Boston, frm. May 18, 1642. Rem. to Plymouth. Bought house and garden in Plymouth 11 July, 1649. He m. Dec. 21, 1648, Mercy, dau. of Gov. Wm. Bradford.

Mark, Salem, 1638; frm. May 13, 1640. Alice, widow, Salem, propr. and memb. chh. Rem. to Boston; she d. 9 (12) 1655. Will prob. Feb. 8, 1656; beq. to sister Joan Towne, to daus. Sarah Langdon, Ester Estick, Susan Goose, and Abigail Hutchinson; gr. ch. Susan Goose; son-in-law Mr. Edward Hutchinson. Est. in Salem and Boston. Jonathan Negus [Negoose,[a witness.

FERNSIDE, FERNISIDE, FARNESEED, FURNESEY,
Mr. John, Boston and Duxbury. Suit vs. Bonney in Plym. Court, 1645. He deposed to the will of John Paybody in 1667. Wife Elizabeth; ch. Jacob b. 28 (5) 1642, Mary b. 8 (7) 1646, Hannah b. 8 (3) 1650, Lydia b. 3 April, 1653, *Abigail* bapt. 10 (2) 1653, Elizabeth b. and d. 1658, Ruth b. Aug. 20, 1661, Sarah bapt. 24 (2) 1664.

Will prob. at Boston 24 Feb. 1693-4, beq. to wife Elizabeth and son Jacob and each of the daus. now living.

FERRIS,
Jeffrey, frm. May 6, 1635.

FESSENDEN, FISSENDEN, FISHINGTON, PHESINGTON,
John, glover, Cambridge, propr. before 1636. Came to N. E. with his father's consent. [Rel.] Town officer. Frm. June 2, 1641. He and his wife Jane membs. of the chh. in 1658. [Mi.]

He d. Dec. 21, 1666. Nunc. will prob. April 2, 1667; beq. to his wife and his kinsman Nicholas F. Aid to be given to Hope Atherton if he came again to the college. His widow d. Jan. 13, 1682, ae. 80.

The widow, in her will dated Dec. 20, 1682, prob. 31 (1) 1684, beq. her whole estate to her cousin Nicholas Fessenden, he to pay legacies to cousin Hannah Sewall and her children, to sister More and other individuals. Judge Samuel Sewall in his diary calls Nicholas cousin, and mentions visiting "Aunt F. with her ch. John, Mary, Elizabeth and Jane at Canterbury, Eng. in 1688-9.

FIELD, FEILD,
Alexander, cordwinder, Salem, propr., 1642. His wife adm. chh. 1 (9) 1648. He sold house and land in 1652.

Darby, an Irishman, resident of Marblehead, 1637. Climbed the White Hill in 1642. [W.] Rem. to Dover.

Mrs. Mary, widow, Boston, adm. chh. 25 (10) 1647.

Robert, tailor, Boston, adm. chh. 14 (2) 1644, frm. May 29, 1644. Came from Yealing, Eng. in the James in April, 1635. Allowed to keep a cook's shop in 1652. Wife Mary adm. chh. 26 (9) 1648; ch. John bapt. 26 (3) 1644, Robert b. 30 (9) 1647, William bapt. 17 (1) 1650, Thomas b. 1 (10) 1651, Thomas b. 28 Nov. 1652, Robert b. 11 Sept. 1653, John b. June, 1656, Elizabeth b. June 17, 1658, Sarah b. Oct. 20, 1660, d. 30 Sept. 1661, Daniel b. Sept. 6, 1662, Sarah b. March 25, 1665.

Admin. gr. to widow Mary 30 (5) 1675.

FIFIELD,
William, came in the Hercules April 11, 1634. Settled at Hampton. Deposed 9 March, 1669, ae. about 55 years.

FILBERT, see Philbert.

FILBRICK, see Philbrick,
Robert, Ipswich, recd. land in 1639 for service in the Pequot War.

FILER,
Walter, Dorchester, propr., frm. May 14, 1634. Rem. to Windsor, Conn.

FINCH,
Abraham, frm. Sept. 3, 1634.

Arthur, witnessed a deed of Sir R. Saltonstall March 2, 1629. [Arch. 100, 1.]

Daniel, Watertown, frm. May 18, 1631. On a committee of Gen. Court in 1631. Rem. to Wethersfield, Conn.

John, Watertown; his wigwam and goods burned in Sept., 1630. Propr. 1636. Rem. to Conn.

Samuel, Roxbury, frm. May 14, 1634. His wife Katharine in Court 4 (7) 1638, for speaking against magistrates, etc. He m. Dec. 13, 1654, Judith Potter.

He d. 27 (11) 1673; old sister Finch d. 10 (8) 1683.

His will dated 10 Nov. prob. 26 Feb. 1673, beq. to the Free School of Roxbury; to the College; to wife's cousin Mary Fressell or to her children; to wife Judith; to Hannan, wife of John Mayo.

FINNEY, FENNEY, FENNYE, PHINNEY,
John, Plymouth, propr. 2 Dec. 1639; frm. 20 Aug. 1644. He rem. to Barnstable; joined the chh. Aug. 29. His wife Christian d. Sept. 9, 1649; he m. at Bar. July 9, or June 10, 1650, Abigail, widow of Henry Cogan; she was bur. May 7, 1653. He recd. a letter, dated at Burdport [Bridport] 10 April, 1654, from his father-in-law Tho. Bishop, asking him to send to him Abigail Coggan, his grand child, to Weymouth to his dau. Mrs. Sarah Lydds in Milcomb; wishes him to care for the other gr. ch. Thomas and Henry Coggan. [Ply. Rec. of Deeds, Vol. 2, folio 135.] He m. 26 June, 1654, Elizabeth Bayley of Bar.; ch. John, 14 years old, (b. 24 Dec. 1638, at Plymouth,) was bapt. at Bar. July 31, 1653, Jonathan b. 14 Aug. 1655, Robert b. 13 Aug. 1656, Hannah b. 2 Sept. 1657, Elizabeth b. 15 March, 1658-9, Josiah b. 11 Jan. 1660, Jeremiah b. 15 Aug. 1662, Joshua b. Dec. 1665. Mother

FINNEY, etc., cont.
Finney d. at Plymouth April 22, 1650, ae. upwards of 80. [Mother of John and Robert?]

Robert, bro. of John, planter, Plymouth, propr. Dec. 2, 1639; town officer; deacon. He m. 1 Sept. 1641, Phebe Ripley. He d. Jan. 7, 1687-8, ae. 80 years. [Chh. Rec.] Will dated 20 May, 1686, prob. at Plymouth 14 March, 1687; on file at Boston. Beq. to wife Phebe; to kinsmen Robert and Josiah F. of Ply.; to John F., Jr. of Barnstable, son of bro. John; to Charity May; to Hannah, wife of Ephraim Morton, Jr.

FIRMIN, FERMAN, FIRMAN,
Mr. Giles, apothecary, from Sudbury, Eng., came to Boston; adm. chh. 1632-3. Frm. March 4, 1633-4. Chosen deacon Oct. 10, 1633; town officer 1 (7) 1634.
He d. before 6 (8) 1634, when his successor in office was chosen. [For English connections see E. and W. and Reg. XXXVIII, 72.] Wife Martha Dogget. [D. Genealogy.]

Giles, [son of the above?] settled at Ipswich. Ret. to Eng. and became a preacher and writer. [C. M.]

John, came in 1630; settled at Watertown. His wigwam was burnt Nov. 10, 1630. Frm. May 18, 1631. He seems to have ret. to Eng. and to be the person, ae. 46, who came in the Elizabeth of Ipswich April 30, 1634. Propr., deacon, selectman.

Josiah, Boston, servant to John Winthrop, adm. chh. 6 (4) 1640.

Thomas, merchant, Ipswich, propr. 1635; bought and sold land in 1647. Inv. of his est. 10 (2) 1648, and admin. gr. to the widow Sarah.

FISH,
Gabriel, fisherman, Exeter, gave letter of attorney Aug. 3, 1639, for collection of money at Thorsthrop and Alford, co. Lincoln, Eng. [L.] Wife Elizabeth; ch. Deborah bapt. at Boston 11 (10) 1642, ae. about 8 days, Abel b. 15 (10) 1644, Elizabeth bapt. 4 (8) 1646, ae. about 5 days.

John, Sandwich, propr. 1640; atba. 1643. He and Jonathan F. drew a bill on their father, which was protested 17 May, 1643. [A.] Wife Cecilia; ch. Nathaniel, (par-

FISH, cont.
entage not stated,) b. at S. Nov. 27, 1648, Caleb b. and d. 1649.
He d., and admin. was gr. to the widow Lydia 3 May, 1664; the inv. was taken 18 Nov. 1663.

Jonathan, bro. of John, above, Sandwich, propr. 1640, atba. 1643. With wife Mary, called to testify in court 20 Aug. 1644. Ch. Nathaniel b. Dec. 18, 1650.

Nathaniel, Sandwich, propr. 1640. Ch. John b. April 13, 1651, Samuel b. Aug. 10, 1668; d. and beq. £ 8 to his aged father 2 Feb. 1691-2. Inv. of the est. of Nathaniel, Sen. taken 14 March, 1693-4. Widow Lydia and her bro. John Miller of Yarmouth admin.; engagement before marriage to pay her as much as he had with her, about £ 66.

FISHER,
Anthony, Sen., Dedham, propr. 18 (5) 1637. Deputy. He m. in Dorchester 14 (9) 1663, Isabel, widow of Edward Breck.
He d. April 18, 1671, in his 80th year. Admin. and division 26 (5) 1671. Sons Daniel, Nathaniel and Cornelius F. and Daniel Morse; dau. Joane, (widow of Anthony F., who had d. a year before). At some previous time, not given with the document, Daniel, Anthony, Nathaniel and Cornelius F. gave bond to their mother, to pay her ten pounds per year at 2 li. 10 s. the quarter of the yeare, in payment to her just content, dureing her naturall life. [Ded. Rec.] The widow d. June 21, 1673. Will dated 20 Sept. 1671, prob. 3 (5) 1673, beq. to Abigail, dau. of her dau. Turner; sons-in-law Turner and Samuel Paul; to every one of her gr. ch.; to son John Breck, son Samuel Rigby; rest to her 5 daus.; son-in-law Thomas Holman to pay dau. Susanna 3 pounds toward wedding outfit.

Joshua, Dedham, was allowed, 1 (11) 1637, to enter on the priveleges offered by the town to a smith, on behalf of his father, who is expected next summer; but must vacate if he come not in time to suit the town. The privileges were granted 28 (6) 1638, to Edward Kempe. Joshua, a servant, was adm. chh. (6) 1639. He (or his father) made a plot of ground in Braintree for the Iron Works Co. and the town 16 (9) 1647. Lieut. He m. 15 (1) 1643, Mary Aldis; she d. 3 (7) 1653. He m. 2, 16 (12) 1653-4, Lydia Oliver.

FISHER, cont.

Ch. Mary b. 23 (1) 1644, Joshua b. 30 (8) 1645, Abigail b. 29 (12) 1648, Joshua b. 9 (11) 1650, John b. 18 (12) 1651.

Admin. and division by agreement Nov. 23, 1672, sons-in-law Thomas Clap, John Holton and Daniel Fisher joining with the sons Joshua, John and Vigilant. The widow Lydia made will 29 (1) 1680, prob. 24 May, 1683. Son Vigilance, daus. Mary Clap, — Burroughs, Abigail Houghton and Rebecca Fisher; cousins Mary Clap and Jone Fisher; bro. Deacon Aldis, Mr. Adams of Ded., Mr. and Mrs. Man of Milton.

Joshua, Sen., smith, Dedham, adm. townsman, 1648; special grant of land 21 (7) 1650. He rem. to Medfield. Wife Anne; ch. Lieut. Joshua and John. He and his wife deed land and furnishings at M. to their son John, when about to marry Elizabeth, dau. of the late Thomas Boyleston, of Watertown, April 5, 1658. John's will gives important family items. [Reg. XIX, 34.]

Will dated 2 May, prob. 19 (9) 1674. Beq. to wife; dau. Mary, wife of Thomas Battle, and each of her children; gr. ch. Joshua Fisher; gr. ch. Mary, wife to Thos. Clap; gr. ch. Abigail, wife of John Houghton; gr. ch. John, son of Joshua Fisher; gr. ch. Hannah Burrowes; gr. ch. John, son of John Fisher; his sister Elizabeth and bro. Jonathan; to gr. ch. Vigilance, son of Joshua Fisher. Cousin Daniel F. of Dedham and gr. ch. Joshua F. execs.

The widow Anne, in will dated 8 April, 1675, prob. 1 Feb. 1676-7, beq. to dau. Battle, grand children John and Joshua, sons of her late son Lieut. Joshua F., and to John and Elizabeth, ch. of her late son John F.

John, Dedham, propr. 13 (5) 1637; d. 15 (5) 1637. His widow Elizabeth, adm. chh. 21 (6) 1640, d. 31 (11) 1651. Her small est. was admin. 10 (12) 1651, by Henry Chickering and Anthony Fisher. [Reg. VII, 58.]

Thomas, carpenter, Cambridge, propr. of house and land, 1634; frm. March 4, 1634-5. Rem. to Dedham; adm. propr. 18 (5) 1637.

He d. 10 (6) 1638. The town gave to his widow 40 shillings toward the bargain he had made in building the meeting-house, 25 (1) 1639. She paid to the attorney of Elisha

FISHER, cont.

Bridges, 4 (7) 1639, a legacy left by her husband for his dau. Sarah, wife of John Blackston. [L.] She had leave from Gen. Court 13 May, 1640, to admin. her husband's est., and to sell half of her lot for the bringing up of her children.

FISKE,

David, wheelwright, Cambridge, Watertown; frm. March 16, 1637-8. Town officer, juror. He deposed April 1, 1672, ae. about 49 years. [Mdx. Files.] Wife Lydia d. and he m. 2, Seaborne — after 1648; ch. Lydia b. 29 (2) 1647, Sarah bur. 8 (3) 1647, David b. 1 (7) 1648, d. 20 (7) 1649, David b. 15 (2) 1650, Elizabeth, Sarah, Hannah bapt. Nov. 27, 1659. [Mi.]

He d. about 1662. Will dated Sept. 10, 1660, prob. Jan. 22, 1662, beq. to dau. Fitch and son David.

James, Salem, adm. chh. 2 (5) 1641; frm. May 18, 1642. Rem. to Newbury; thence to Wenham. Recd. to chh. of W. from that of N. in 1644. Rem. to Haverhill; propr. 1646. Rem. to Groton. He m. Hannah Pike; [Hav. Rec.] ch. James b. Aug. 8, 1649, John b. Dec. 10, 1651, Ann b. and d. 1654, Thomas b. June 23, 1655, Ann b. Feb. 11, 1656, Samuel b. Nov. 1, 1658.

He d. at Groton 4 July, 1689; will dated 14 June, 1689, prob. at Cambridge; beq. to sons James, John, Samuel and Thomas, and dau. Hannah.

Rev. John, planter, minister, physician, b. at St. James, co. Suffolk, Eng., eldest of four children, all of whom afterward came to N. E. with him in 1637. Grad. at Cambridge. Preached three years at Salem; frm. Nov. 2, 1637. Brought letter of recommendation to Gov. Winthrop 19 April, 1637. [Mass. H. Coll. 4-6.] He made an agreement, ratified by Gen. Court 4 Sept. 1638, with his bro. William F., concerning est. and land. He ret. 200 li. of the est. to W. and became sole propr. of the land. William agreed to leave 100 li. to John in case he should die unmarried under 24 years of age. Rem. to Wenham; gave land for the meetinghouse 2 (1) 1642. Town officer; minister. About 1656 he rem. to Chelmsford, where he was pastor until his death. His wife d. Feb. 14, 1671, and he m. again. [C. M.]

FISKE, cont.
He d. Jan. 14, 1676. Will dated 8 June, prob. 22 Feb. 1676, beq. to wife Elizabeth, son John and his wife Lydia, daus. Sarah, wife of John Farwell, and Anna; younger son Moses; to William, eldest son of my bro. William, late of Wen.; to his widow and their other children. His ch. recd. legacies from the est. of their uncle John Clarke, physician, of Newport, R. I.

Nathan, Sen., Watertown, frm. May 10, 1642. He bought land 10 (7) 1643. Wife Susan; ch. Nathan b. 17 (8) 1642, John b. 25 (6) 1647, David b. 29 (2) 1650, Nathaniel b. 12 (5) 1653.
He d. June 21, 1676. His sister, Martha Underwood, deposed. Will dated 19 June, prob. 10 July, 1676, beq. to sons Nathan, John, David and Nathaniel, and dau. Sarah Gale. Beside the above-named children, he mentioned dau. Sarah.

Phinehas, Salem, frm. May 18, 1642. He rem. to Wenham. Mentioned in town rec. 21 (1) 1642; town officer. Son John adm. chh. 21 (11) 1648.
He d. 7 (2) 1673. Will prob. 26 (4) 1673; sons John and Thomas; nephew Samuel F.; Mara F.

William, bro. of John, above, Salem, frm. May 18, 1642. Lic. by Gen Court to sell wine, 13 Nov. 1644. Deputy. Rem. to Wenham. Constable 26 (12) 1643. [Es. Court.] Wife Bridget; ch. William bapt. 4 (4) 1643, Joseph bapt. 21 (3) 1648.
He d. about 1654. Inv. taken 16 (7) 1654.

FITCH, FITTS,
James, tailor, ae. 30, with wife Abigail, ae. 24, and John, ae. 14, came in the Defence in July, 1635. Settled at Boston. Adm. chh. with wife 27 (10) 1635. Ch. Elizabeth bapt. 15 (3) 1636, (m. John Parker, mariner, and sold land, April 27, 1659, which had belonged to James and Richard Fitch, and which was beq. to her by Richard).

Richard, Boston, propr. 1635.
He d. before 1659.

Zechariah, or Zachary, Salem, frm. Sept. 7, 1638. Propr. at Lynn in 1638, and at Reading from 1644. He and his wife rec'd to R. chh. from that of L. before 1648. He deposed 2 (2) 1661, ae. about 70 years; son Joseph at same time, ae. about 23. [Mdx.

FITCH, etc., cont.
Files.] Ch. Jeremy, propr., at Reading in 1647, Samuel b. at Lynn, (rec. at R.) March 6, 1644, Zechariah d. June 20, 1647.
He d. June 9, 1662. Will dated 10 (1) prob. June 17, 1662, beq. to wife Mary, sons Joseph, Samuel, Benjamin, Jeremiah and Thomas; dau. Sarah and her husband John Wesson.

FITCHENE,
Peter, came in the Champion in 1639. Was drowned at Boston. Inquest 3 (8) 1639. Inv. of goods rendered.

FITCHER,
Lieut., one of the colony at Mt. Wollaston about 1623. Left in charge by Rasdell, was ejected by Morton. Ret. to Eng. [B.]

FITTS, FFITT, FIT,
Richard, planter, bro. of Robert, Newbury, propr. 1637. He. m. 8 Oct. 1654, Sara Ordway; she d. 24 April, 1668.
He d. 2 Dec. 1672. In his will, prob. March 25, 1673, he beq. to bro.-in-law James Ordway; his sister Travisse's dau.; kinsman Abraham F. and his ch., Abraham and daus. all under age. Abraham, in a deed, calls Richard his uncle.

Robert, planter, propr. at Salisbury in 1639; rem. to Ipswich about 1652. He m. Grace, sister of Mr. Robert Lord. Son Abraham. They gave testimony 22 (10) 1664, as to the promise made by Simon Thompson desiring their son Abraham who married his daughter to come to Ipswich and reside. His cousin Isaiah Wood, son-in-law of Simon Tompson, also testified.
He d. May 9, 1665. Will dated Jan. 5, 1663, prob. June 26, 1665; beq. to wife Grace the goods and est. left to her by her mother, to dispose of among her kindred; son Abraham F. to have land at Salisbury which he purchased of his bro. Wm. Barnes, and other est.; wife to have remainder for life. Grace app. her bro. Robert Tounsend of Ipsw. her attorney in a suit vs. Samuel Gove, June 17, 1667. [Reg. XIII, 112, and XXXI, 323.] The widow Grace d. April 25, 1684.

Goodman Fitts, tailor, Charlestown, had liberty to set up a salt pan in 1637. [Town Rec.]

FFITZPEN, see Phippen.

FITZ RANDOLPH, FITZRANDOLPH, FITSRANDLE, FITZRANDALL, FITSRANDALL,

Mr. Edward, came from Nottinghamshire, Eng.; settled at Scituate; propr. 1636, adm. chh. May 14, 1637, frm. 4 Sept. 1638. He rem. to Barnstable in 1639; juryman, 1641. Sold house and lands 1 June, 1649. He m. May 10, 1637, Elizabeth Blossom, who was adm. chh. Aug. 27, 1643. Ch. Nathaniel b. and d. 1640, Nathaniel b. about 1642, (m. Mary, dau. of Joseph Holley,) Mary b. Oct. 6, 1644, Hannah bapt. April 23, 1648, Hannah b. April, 1649, Mary bapt. June 2, 1650, Mary b. May, 1651, John bapt. Jan. 2, 1652, John b. Oct. 7, 1653, Joseph b. March 1, 1656, Thomas b. Aug. 16, 1659, Hope b. April 2, 1661.

He removed to New Jersey about 1669. A descendant, Mr. H. C. F. Randolph, of New York city, has secured evidence regarding the English connections of the pioneer. N. B. The obnoxious Sir Edward Randolph, who came to N. E. in 1676 and returned with Gov. Andros, is a totally different person.

FLACK,

Cotton, yeoman, Boston, adm. chh., laborer, 5 (11) 1633; frm. May 13, 1640. Propr. Wife Jane; ch. Deborah bur. 1642, Deborah b. 5 (8) 1644.

Will prob. Aug. 5, 1658. Wife Jane; son Samuel. [Reg. VII, 353.]

FLACKMAN, FLATMAN,

Thomas, Braintree, frm. May 13, 1640. Wife —; ch. Elizabeth b. 7 (3) 1640, Thomas b. 3 (5) 1643.

FLAGG, FLEGG, FLEGE,

Thomas, ae. 21, came in April, 1637, as servant of Richard Carver. Settled at Watertown; yeoman, lieut., propr., town officer. He petitioned 4 (2) 1659, concerning the loss of his left eye by a gun. [Mdx. Files.] Wife Mary deposed in 1657, ae. about 38 years; ch. Gershom b. April 16, 1641, John b. June 14, 1643, Bartholomew b. Feb. 23, 1644, Thomas b. April 28, 1645, Michael b. March 23, 1650-1, Eleazer b. May 14, 1653, Elizabeth b. 22 (1) 1654-5, Mary b. Jan. 14, 1657, Rebecca b. 5 (7) 1660, Benjamin b. June 25, 1662, Allen b. May 16, 1665.

He d. Feb. 6, 1697-8. Will dated 5 March,

FLAGG, etc., cont.

1697, prob. Feb. 16, 1697-8, beq. to wife Mary, sons Michael, Thomas, Eleazer, Allen and Benjamin, daus. Mary and Elizabeth Bigelow and Rebecca Cooke; to gr. ch. John F., and the heirs of dec. son Gershom. The widow's will, prob. April 21, 1703, names ch. Mary and Elizabeth Bigelow, Rebecca Cook, and Benjamin F.

FLANDERS,

Stephen, planter, Salisbury, propr. 1646-1677. He m. Jane —, who d. Nov. 19, 1683. Ch. Mary d. May 4, 1650, Stephen b. March 8, 1646-7, Mary b. May 7, 1650, Philip b. July 14, 1652, Sarah b. Nov. 5, 1654, Naomi b. Dec. 15, 1656, John b. Feb. 11, 1658-9.

He d. June 27, 1684; will prob. Sept. 30, 1684. He beq. to eldest son Stephen; to daus. Mary and Naomi F. and Sarah Newhall; to gr. ch. Thomas F.; rest to be divided between sons Philip and John.

FLAUNE, FLAWNE,

Thomas, Yarmouth, atba. 1643; propr. 1648.

FLAVEL,

Thomas, with a son, came in the Fortune to Plymouth in 1621. Goodwife F. came in the Anne in 1623. All had lands assigned.

FLEMMING, FLEMING,

Abraham, husbandman, ae. 40, came in the Increase, April 15, 1635.

John, maulster, Watertown, 1647. Town officer. He bought land in 1651. Wife Anne; ch. Thomas, Mary, Elizabeth, Sarah b. at Wat. 1 (7) 1639, (m. John Barnard, Jr.,) John b. at Wat. 25 (1) 1642. Several of these ch. residing in Eng. sold their shares in the Wat. property at various dates. [Mdx. De.]

He d. June 4, 1657; the inv. of his est. was filed the 24th by the widow, who d. Nov. 11, folg. His will prob. 30 (10) 1658. Beq. to 3 children, viz. Thomas F., Elizabeth Neall and Mary Ruttriffe. [Mdx. Files.] Her will dated 4 (9) 1657, beq. to her dau. Sarah Barnard and her son John Fleming.

FLETCHER,

Edward, "cutler," Boston, adm. inhab. 24 (12) 1639; adm. chh. 18 (5) 1640, frm. Oct. 12, 1640. Propr. Sold house and shop Sept. 9, 1654. Wife Mary adm. chh. 8 (8) 1642. He returned to England; became a minister; came back again and d. here.

Edward F., now of Badgeden, co. of Gloucester, "clerke;" will, dated Feb. 20, 1659, prob. in Boston 12 Feb., 1666; admin. gr. to his widow Mary. Beq. to her a tenement in Gloc. within the precincts of the college, near the Little Cloisters, which is to be rented to Mr. James Forbes and his associates at 40 shillings per annum as long as they wish it for a place of worship; after her death this is to go to his sister Elizabeth Hooper; cousin Margaret Ellis. Goods and est. also in Boston, N. E. Mrs. Mary D. deposed. Inv. mentions nails, elephant's teeth and other goods in the shop. [Reg. XVI, 231.]

Moses, (Moyses,) came in the Mayflower, signed the Compact; res. at Plymouth; d. soon after arriving. [B.]

Robert, Concord, app. by Gen. Court constable, 2 Nov. 1637. Rem. to Chelmsford; joined with William F. and others in 1654 in inviting Mr. John Fiske and the Wenham church to remove to C.

He made will 4 Feb. 1672, ae. about four score years; commits his wife to the care of his son Francis and his wife; beq. to sons Francis, William and Samuel. Inv. taken 12 May, 1677.

Rose, widow, Boston, adm. chh. 10 (4) 1643.

William, Concord. Wife Rachel d. and he m. 2, 7 (9) 1645, Lydia Bats; ch. Joshua b. 10 (2) [1645], —, daughter, b. 30 (1) 1647. [Mdx. tr.]

FLINT,

Rev. Henry, came to N. E. in 1635; adm. chh. Boston 15 (9) 1635; frm. May 25, 1636; was dism. to ye gathering of a chh. at Mt. Wollaston, (Braintree,) 11 (6) 1639, and was ord. teacher in company with Mr. Wm. Tompson, pastor. He m. Margery, dau. of Charles Hoar, Jr., of Gloucester, Eng. Ch. Dorothy b. 11 (5) 1642, Annah b. 7 (11) 1643, (Hanna m. 15 (9) 1662, John Dassitt,) Josiah b. 24 (6) 1645, Margaret b. 20 (4) 1647,

FLINT, cont.

d. 29 (6) 1648, Joanna b. 18 (12) 1648, (m. 30 (10) 1669, Noah Newman,) David b. 11 (11) 1651, d. 29 (1) 1652, Seth b. 2 (2) 1653, Ruth b. 31 (11) 1654, Cotton and John b. 16 (7) d. 20 (9) 1656.

He d. April 27, 1668. Will, dated 24 (11) 1652, prob. 2 July, 1668. Wife Margery; sons Josiah and Seth; daughters. The widow d. March 10, 1686-7. [S.] [Reg. IX, 151, XVIII, 327, and LIII, 92.]

John, [Marblehead,] a witness at Es. court in 1639.

Mr. Thomas, bro. of Henry, Boston, 1637; frm. March, 1637-8; rem. to Concord. Deputy. Wife Abigail; ch. Ephraim b. 14 (11) 1641.

He d. Oct. 8, 1653, ae. 50. Will, dated 21 (10) 1651, left children to care of wife with counsel of Mr. Bulkley, teacher of chh. Conc.; his bro. Mr. Henry F., teacher of chh. Braintree; Capt. Simon Willard, and his uncle William Wood of Conc. [Reg. XVI, 72.] The widow d. Dec. 18, 1689, ae. 82.

William, Salem, with wife Alice and child, 3 (9) 1645; propr., overseer of fences and highways; juryman. He deposed in 1661, ae. about 58 years.

Will prob. Essex Court 27 (4) 1673; wife Alice; dau. Alice m. Henry Bullock, Jr. [Es. De. I, 39;] sons Thomas and Edward F.; son Joshua Ward, son Joshua; to John Hathorne; the court also gave a portion to son John Pickering. Widow Alice deposed in 1677, ae. about 70 years.

FLOOD,

Joseph, baker, ae. 45, with wife Jane, ae. 35, and ch. Elizabeth, ae. 9, Obediah, ae. 4, and Joseph, ae. 6 mos., came in the Abigail in July, 1635. Settled at Dorchester. Rem. to Lynn; propr. 1638. [Flood or Floyd] Juryman, 1639. In court for opposition to infant baptism in 1646.

Mr., Lynn, propr. in 1638.

Richard, Boston, propr. Wife Lydia; ch. Lydia b. in 1643.

He d.; the widow m. June 9, 1654, Joseph Gridley. Admin. was gr. to him on the est. of Flood 8 (7) 1662, for his wife and her 4 ch. [Reg. XII, 50.]

FLOYD,

John, citizen and haberdasher of London; his wife Anne gave power of attorney 28 (6) 1640, for the care and maintenance of their son Thomas, apprenticed to Arthur Howland of Duxbury, planter. [L.] He came to N. E. and res. at Scituate. Gave letters of attorney 4 (9) 1646, for collections in Eng. Released his servant Jane Duglas 26 Oct. 1647. [A.] Rem. to Boston; sold house and land Nov. 28, 1655.

FOBES, VOBES,

John, tailor, Duxbury, in Court 5 Aug. 1636; propr.; atba. 1643. Rem. to Bridgewater. Nunc. will July 31, 1662. Wife; two eldest sons John and Edward; dau. Mary. His bro. Experience Michell to help the wife and children. The son John died and his portion went to his bros. Edward and William; so George Allin of Sandwich wrote Exp. Michell. [Plym. Prob.]

FOGG,

James, Gloucester, a witness in 1648.

Ralph, Plymouth, gent., taxed 1632, frm. 1633. Was. ae. about 40 yrs. in 1640; testified that he saw specialties delivered to John Stratton at Dedham, Essex, Eng. Dec., 1631. [L.] Rem. to Salem. Secretary of Court 27 (10) 1636. Frm. Mass. Sept. 3, 1634; propr.; town officer. A town clerk was chosen to take his place in 1647. He applied to Gen. Court 1 (3) 1652, for permission to open "An office of Addresses," or medium of communication between employers and servants, sellers and buyers, etc. Letter in Arch. 105. Susanna, his wife, was a member of the chh. before 1636. Ch. Ezekiel bapt. 1 (2) 1638, David bapt. 15 (1) 1640. Susan, Salem, gave release to Richard Gibb, of London, refiner, 13 (8) 1647. [A.] Son John, with consent of his mother, sold land in 1648.

Ralph, of London, skinner, bought land and warehouses in Boston near his own property, in 1656. John of Barnstable, Eng., merchant, sold land at Salem, N. E., in possession of his father Ralph F., in 1665. [Es. De.]

FOKAR,

John, husbandman, ae. 21, came in the Increase April 15, 1635.

FOLGER,

John, proposed for a propr. at Dedham, 1638.

Peter, Martin's Vineyard, witness of a document Oct. 14, 1647.

FOLSAM, FOULSHAM, FOULCHER,

John, with wife and 2 servants, came from Old Hingham in 1638 and settled at Hingham. Propr., town officer; had liberty to erect saw-mill. Sold prop. in 1659, and rem. to Exeter. He m. in Eng. Mary, dau. of Edward Gilman, (who also came to Hing.). Ch. John; Samuel bapt. Oct. 11, 1641, Nathaniel bapt. June 2, 1644, Israel bapt. Sept. 1644, Peter bapt. April 8, 1649, Mary bapt. April 13, 1651, (m. George Marsh,) Ephraim bapt. Feb. 25, 1654-5.

He d. 27 Dec. 1681.

FOOKES, FOWKES,

Henry, Dorchester, propr. 1635; frm. May 6, 1635. Rem. to Windsor, Conn.

FOORTH, see Ford.

FOOTE, FOOT,

Joshua, citizen and iron-monger, of London, from 1645 onward did a large amount of business in N. E.; was a member of the Iron Works Co.; res. in Boston in 1653. Later at Roxbury, and Providence.

Will, Suff. Prob. Oct. 31, 1655. Wife and Children. Inv. of est. at Bo. Nov. 15, 1655. [Reg. V, 444, and IX, 137.]

Nathaniel, [Salem?] frm. Sept. 3, 1634. Rem. to Wethersfield, Conn. [Reg. IX, 272.]

Pasco, Salem, 1636. Adm. chh. 14 (9) 1652, and 8 ch. were baptized, viz. John, Malachi, Samuel, Elizabeth, Mary, Isaac, Pasca and Abigail.

He d. 28 (9) 1670; will dated 21 Sept. 1670; aged and weak; prob. 30 (4) 1671; sons Isaac, William and Pasco, daus. Elizabeth, Birtch, Mary and Abigail F.

FORD, FOARD, FOORD, FOORTH,

Barbara, ae. 16, came in the Susan and Ellen in April, 1635.

John, ae. 30, servant to Henry Kingman, came from Weymouth, Eng. before March 20, 1635.

Peter, see Sims.

FORD, etc., cont.

Roger, (Foorth,) Cambridge, d. 24 (2) 1644.

Thomas, from Dorchester, Eng., came in the Mary and John in 1630 to Dorchester. Frm. May 18, 1631. He rem. about 1635 to Windsor, Conn.; extensive land-holder; deputy. Rem. about 1672 to Northampton. Wife — d. 18 April, 1643; he m. 2, Mrs. Ann Scott, who joined him in deed 23 Aug. 1672. Ch. Johannah b. June 8, 1617, (m. Capt. Roger Clap,) Abigail, (m. John Strong,) Mary, (m. Aaron Cooke,) Hepzibah, (m. 1, Richard Lyman, Jr., 2, John Marsh). He d. 9 Nov. 1676. The inv. of his est. was pres. Jan. 10, 1676, by his son-in-law John Strong, to whom admin. was granted jointly with Preserved Clapp and goodwife Marsh.

Widow, came in the Fortune to Plymouth, and had 4 lots in 1623. Her ch. John and Martha had shares in cattle in 1627. Martha m. Wm. Nelson.

William, miller, Duxbury, atba. 1643; bought land 13 June, 1645; frm. 3 June, 1652. He deposed (to R. Chapman's will,) Oct. 30, 1671, ae. 67 yrs. Rem. to Marshfield.

He was bur. Sept. 18, 1676. Will dated 12 Sept. 1676, ae. about 72 years; beq. to wife Anna, sons William and Michael, daus. Margaret and Millicent, gr. ch. John Foard, William and John Carver.

FORDHAM,

Robert, gent., a witness to the will of Robert Hunt of Sudbury in 1640. Rem. to Southampton, [L. I. or Eng.?] and sold Sudbury lands in 1643; acknowledged in 1654. [Mdx. De. II, 65.]

Lechford calls him "a minister out of office" in 1642. [L., P. D.]

FORTEN,

John, ae. 14, came in the Hopewell in Sept. 1635.

FOSDIKE, FOSDICK, FOSDITCH, FORESDITCH,

Stephen, carpenter, Charlestown, inhab. 1635; frm. Sept. 7, 1638. Deposed 22 (4) 1653, ae. 70 years. [Mdx. Files.] Thomas, [his ch.?] d. 21 (4) 1650. [Mdx. Rec.] Mary, adm. chh. 4 (10) 1652.

He d. May 21, 1664. He left a widow,

FOSDICKE, etc., cont.

lame and infirm, ae. about 75 years, who was m. to him a maid about 1624, and took care of his six children by former wife. [Deposition of his "brother" John Witherall, Mdx. Files.] Will dated 23 Feb. 1663, prob. 21 (4) 1664, beq. to wife; to daus. Hannah, wife of James Barrett and Martha, wife of Richard Holding, and to their children; to dau. Marah, wife of Thomas Webb; to son John F. and to the two sons of my son Thomas F. deceased.

FOSTER, FORSTER,

Andrew, Gloucester, constable 1646. [Es. Files.] Rem. to Andover. Wife Ann; ch. Mary b. 9 July, 1652.

He d. 7 May, 1685, "ae. 106 years." His will dated 18 April, 1685, prob. 30 June folg.; "very aged;" beq. to wife Ann, sons Andrew and Abraham, and daus. Sarah and Mary; dau. Hannah had already recd. her portion.

Christopher, husbandman, ae. 32, with wife Frances, ae. 25, and ch. Rebecca, ae. 5, Nathaniel, ae. 2, and John, ae. 1, came in the Abigail in July, 1635. Settled at Lynn; propr. 1638. Lawsuit, 1637. Sold house and land 10 (1) 1645. He gave letters of attorney 9 (1) 1645-6, to Daniel King of Lynn, woolen draper, to collect legacy due his wife Frances from her mother Alice Stevens, late of Ewill in Surrey. [A.]

Edward, Scituate, 1632, frm. Jan. 3, 1636; atba. 1643. One of the founders of chh., Jan. 16, 1634. He rem. to Barnstable in 1638-9. He m. April 8, 1635, Lettice Handford. Ch. Timothy bapt. March 7, 1635, bur. Dec. 5, 1637, Timothy bapt. April 22, 1638.

Will, dated Nov. 24, 1643, prob. 20 Aug., 1644; wife Lettice, son Timothy, father Richard Sillis, bro. Isaac Robinson. [Reg. IV, 281.]

Hopestill, ae. 14, [19?] embarked on the Elizabeth 17 April, 1635, with his mother, the widow Patience, ae. 40. She was a dau. of widow Rachel Biggs. Settled at Dorchester. Both were adm. chh. before 1639. He was propr.; captain. He made an agreement May 10, 1646, with the sons of John Stowe about inheritance from their uncles Smallhope and John Bigg; lands in Cranbrook, Kent, Eng., and vicinity. [Suff.

FOSTER, etc., cont.
De. and A.] He m. Mary, dau. of James Bate; ch. Thankful bapt. 27 (10) 1640, (m. John Baker,) Hopestill bapt. 10 (1) 1644, Patience bapt. 16 (6) 1646, (m. Thomas Brown,) John bapt. 10 (10) 1648, James b. April 13, 1651, Elisha bapt. 24 (6) 1653, Mary bapt. 10 (12) 1655, (m. 1, Ephraim Sale, 2, Samuel Ward,) Comfort b. 28 (7) 1658, Standfast b. 13 (9) 1660, Richard b. and d. 1663.

He d. Oct. 15, 1676. Will dated 19 July, prob. Nov. 2, 1676, beq. to wife Mary; to son Hopestill and gr. ch. Hopestill; to sons John, James, Elisha, Comfort and Standfast; daus. Thankful Baker, Patience Brown, Mary (unmarried); to pastor Flint; to the free school; to the military company. His widow d. Jan. 5, 1703, ae. 83 yrs. [Reg. LII, 194.]

John, Salem, 1649. Deposed in 1670, ae. about 52 years. Conveyed land to son John in 1674. Wife Martha, dau. of Ralph Tompkins, deposed in 1670, ae. about 34 years. Ch. Mary bapt. 24 (1) 1649-50, Samuel bapt. 7 (1) 1652, John bapt. 3 (4) 1655, Benjamin, Jonathan and David bapt. 21 (5) 1667.

Reginald, or Reynold, Sen., husbandman, Ipswich, bought of John Tuttell, 26 Sept. 1638, a house and lands. [Ipsw. Rec.] Had charge of the town herd of cattle on South side of the river in 1643; work may be done by his son Abraham. Town officer. With wife Sarah sold land 2 Aug. 1676. His will dated 30 April, 1680, prob. 9 June, 1681, inv. taken 30 May, 1681, beq. to wife Sarah what she brought at marriage, and other things; to sons Abraham, Renold, Isaac, William and Jacob; to daus. Sarah, wife of William Story, and Mary, wife of Francis Paybody; to gr. ch. Hannah Story. The son Abraham d. 15 Jan. 1710-11, ae. about 90.

Richard, Plymouth, 1640. Served against the Narragansetts from 15 Aug., 1645. He m. 10 Sept. 1651, Mary Bartlett; ch. Mary b. March 8, 1652.

Samuel, sergeant, Wareham, frm. May 22, 1650. Rem. to Chelmsford.

Thomas, cannonier, passenger in the Hercules in April, 1634. Settled at Boston. Gunner at the Castle in 1639. Adm. chh. 26 (1) 1642, frm. May 18, 1642.

FOSTER, etc., cont.
Thomas, son of Mr. Thomas Foster, minister; gave letter of attorney in Boston to his bro. Richard F. of Ipswich, Eng., shipmaster, July 29, 1639. Gave letter of attorney concerning the inheritance of his wife Abigail, dau. of Matthew Wines, of Ipswich, co. Suffolk, Eng., 19 (1) 1640-1. [L.]

Thomas, Weymouth, frm. May 26, 1647. Ch. Thomas b. 18 (6) 1640, John b. 7 (8) 1642. [Mr. Thomas, mentioned in town records of Roxbury 18 (1) 1655, adm. chh. 18 (4) 1665, rem. to Dorchester, is likely to be this son.]

William, planter, came in the Hercules in April, 1634. Settled at Ipswich; propr. 1634. Took an apprentice 21 (4) 1639. [L.] He and his son William were taken prisoners at Sally and delivered after 18 months in 1673. [Rox. chh. rec.]

William, captain, Charlestown, adm. chh. 15 (6) 1652, Anne adm. 23 (7) 1652. Ch. Anna bapt. 5 (7) 1658, Richard bapt. 16 (6) 1663. Elizabeth Hailes, of Stepney, Eng., in her will, 28 Sept., 1664, beq. to her cousin Wm. Foster, of N. E. [Reg. XXXVIII, 422.]

FOULFOOT,
Thomas, ae. 22, came in the Christian March 16, 1634.

FOWNELL, see Furnell.

FOUNTAIN,
Edward, ae. 28, came in the Abigail in July, 1635.

FOWLE, FOULE,
Ann, ae. 25, came in the Susan and Ellen in April, 1635.

George, tanner, Concord, frm. March 14, 1638-9. Surveyor of the arms for C. 22 May, 1639. Rem. to Charlestown. Wife Mary; ch. Mary b. 24 (9) 1640, Peter b. 2 (10) 1641, James b. 12 (1) 1642, Mary b. 9 (12) 1644. A son Jacob, tailor, Boston, in will dated 14 Dec. prob. 17 Dec. 1678, beq. to bros. John, Peter, Isaac, James and Abraham Fowle, to cousins Samuel and Mary Rugels, to Richard Hincksman, Henry

FOWLE, etc., cont.
Philips and Thomas Skinner; his father Geo. Fowle, executor.
George's will dated 11 March, 1681-2, prob. Oct. 3, 1682, beq. to sons John, Peter, Abraham, Isaac, James, and to the ch. of son Zechariah.

Thomas, gent., armiger, merchant, 1639. [L.] Settled at Boston; adm. chh. 25 (1) 1643. Wife Margaret adm. chh. 31 (11) 1640. Ch. Elizabeth b. 14 (1) 1639, John b. 1 (5) 1641, Margaret b. 13 (2) 1643, Marie bapt. 16 (2) 1643, ae. about 4 days, James bapt. 8 (10) 1644, ae. about 5 days, Martha bapt. 25 (8) 1646, ae. about 7 days.

He was one of the petitioners for citizenship of non-church members in 1645. [W.] Shipping accts. 5 (7) 1645. Calls Vincent Potter bro.-in-law. [A.]

FOWLER,
Philip, came in the Mary and John March 24, 1633. Settled at Ipswich; propr. 1634; cloth-worker. Frm. Sept. 3, 1634. [See Sweetser.] He deposed 28 Feb. 1671, ae. above 80 years. He m. 1, Mary —, who d. Aug. 30, 1659; he m. 2, Mary, widow of George Norton; contract 27 Feb. 1659. Ch. Margaret, (m. Christopher Osgood,) Mary, (m. Wm. Chandler,) Samuel, Hester, (m. 1, Jathnell Bird, 2, Ezra Rolfe, 3, Robert Collins,) Joseph, Thomas. He adopted his son Joseph's son Philip, and deeded house and land to him 23 Dec. 1668.

He d. June 24, 1679; admin. gr. to gr. son Philip F., Sept. 1679.

Richard, Salem, in Court in 1641.

FOX, FOXE,
Daniel, Hingham, propr. 1636. Witness of a deed in Boston in 1648.

John, ae. 35, with Richard, ae. 15, came in the Abigail in July, 1635.

Thomas, Concord, servant to Mr. Cradock, was punished by Gen. Court 8 March, 1630-1, for suggesting that the Court had taken bribes in the Bratcher case. Propr.; frm. March, 1637-8. Rem. to Cambridge. Town officer. His wife Rebecca d. 11 (3) 1647; he m. May 24, 1650, Ellen, widow of Percival Greene; she d. May 27, 1682, ae. 82. [Gr. st.] He m. April 24, 1683, Elizabeth, widow of Charles Chadwick; she d.

FOX, etc., cont.
Feb. 22, 1684-5. He m. Dec. 16, 1685, Rebecca, widow of Nicholas Wyeth. Ch. Jabez, bapt. at Concord; in minority when his father joined the chh. of Camb. [Mi.], [Thomas, m. 13 (10) 1647, Hannah Brooks.] He d. April 25, 1693, ae. 85.

FOXWELL, FOXALL, FOXALLS,
Richard, tailor, [Boston,] frm. 18 May, 1631. Rem. to Plymouth; rem. to Scituate, being dism. to join in forming the chh. Jan. 16, 1634-5. Had probably been a memb. of the chh. in London, of which Mr. John Lothrop was pastor. [See Scituate chh. Rec. in Reg. IX.] He rem. to Barnstable in 1638-9. He m. first in Eng. and had child John, atba. 1643, who came here and d. Sept. 21, 1646. He m. second, Anne Shelley, who had been a maid servant to Mr. John Coggeshall of Rox. and Bo. and a memb. of the chh. in both places. [Rox. and Bo. chh. Rec.] She was rec'd to Sci. chh. June 14, 1635. Ch. Mary bapt. Aug. 30, 1635, (m. Jan. 8, 1654, Hugh Cole, of Plym.,) Martha bapt. April 22, 1638, Ruth bapt. April 4, 1641.

Will, dated April 7, prob. June 3, 1668; sons-in-law Samuel Bacon, Hugh Cole, and William Nelson, husband of his dau. Ruth; beq. to the chh., for the poor. A payment to be made to Mr. Adams, woolen draper, who did dwell at the lower end of Gratious st. in London. [Reg. VII, 179.]

FRANCIS,
Richard, brickmaker, Cambridge, propr., frm. May 13, 1640. Wife Alice; ch. Stephen b. 7 (12) 1644, Sarah b. 4 (10) 1646, John b. 4 (11) 1649.

He d. March 24, 1686-7, ae about 81 years. [Gr. st.] Admin. of his est. gr. to widow Alice April 5, 1687.

FRANCIS, *alias* DEACON, see Deacon.

FRANKLIN, FRANCKLIN, FRANCKLIJN,
Martha, Boston, m. 24 (8) 1650, William Phillips, Jr.

William, blacksmith, came in the Mary and John March 26, 1633-4. Settled at Ipswich. Rem. to Newbury, thence to Boston. Adm. chh. 30 (11) 1640. Town officer. Deposed 1 (12) 1652, ae. about 45 years, relative to Wm. Ting's gift of land to his cousin

FRANKLIN, etc., cont.
John Franckiln. [Book of Pos. 43.] He petitioned Parliament 6 July, 1655, for a position, in view of his losses within the territories of Portugal, etc. It was favorably reported. He m. before April 2, 1641, Alice, dau. of Robert Andrews, q. v.; he m. 2, Phebe —. Ch. Elizabeth b. in Bo. 3 (8) 1638, (m. 6 (8) 1656, George May,) Ebenezer d. 24 (8) 1644, Eliezer b. and d. 1645.
He d. in London. His est. was admin. in Boston July 28, 1658. The widow m. Augustin Lyndon; with whom she deeded one half of the houses and lands of the Franklin est. to George and Elizabeth May 2 June, 1660. [Reg. XXXVIII, 384.]

William, farmer, Newbury, 1638; rem. to Muddy River, Boston. He was executed in 1644 for the murder of his servant boy Nathaniel Sewall. Wife Joanna; ch. John b. 14 (5) 1642, Benjamin b. 12 (8) 1643, (cooper, Boston, had mortg. of land 16 Aug. 1677, from John Wampos alias White). [Mdx. De. VI, 84.] [Rox. Rec. and W.]

FRAILE,
George, wheelwright, Lynn, propr. 1638. Wife Elizabeth; ch. Elizabeth b. 30 March, 1641, Hanna b. Nov. 1642, d. 16 Nov. 1662, Eunice b. (10) 1644, Samuel b. 7 (1) 1645, Deborah b. Aug. 1648, Ruth b. April, 1652.
He d. 9 (10) 1663. Admin. 29 (4) 1664; wife Elizabeth, one son and four daus.

FRARY, FREARY, FRAY, FRAIRE, FRAYRYE,
John, cordwinder, Dedham, propr., frm. March 13, 1638-9. Rem. to Medfield about 1652. Wife Prudence; ch. John, Theophilus, Isaac b. 29 (10) 1638, Eliezer b. 14 (12) 1639, d. 1652, Samuel b. 27 (8) 1641, d. 1652.
Will dated 11 (4) 1675; in old age; beq. to wife Prudence, sons Theophilus, Eleazer, son Sampson, gr. ch. Hannah Walker, dau. of son Theophilus F.; apprentice Abigail Buckmaster. His widow m. Thos. Dyer.

FRATCHFORD,
Thomas, [Boston.] Inv. of his est. pres. by Robert Hull and James Johnson, 3 (3) 1648. [Reg. VII, 175.]

FREAKE, see Feake.

FREEBORN,
William, ae. 40, with wife Mary, ae. 33, ch. Mary, ae. 7, Sarah, ae. 2, and John Aldburgh, ae. 14, came in the Francis of Ipswich April 30, 1634. Settled at Boston; frm. Sept. 3, 1634. Was banished for upholding Mrs. Hutchinson in 1637, and was one of the founders of Rhode Island and Providence plantation.

FREEMAN,
Anthony, ae. 22, came in the Hopewell in Sept., 1635.

Edmund, husbandman, ae. 45, Thomas, ae. 24, Edmund or Edward, husbandman, ae. 34, Elizabeth, ae. 35, Alice, ae. 17, Edward, ae. 15, Elizabeth, ae. 12, and John, ae. 8, came in the Abigail in July, 1635. Making allowance for errors in age and the probable repetition of names, this record applies to Mr. Edmund F. and his family. He settled first at Saugus; rem. to Sandwich. [Plym. Col. Rec. I, 57.] Sold lands at Scituate 10 March, 1642, on behalf of his brother-in-law Mr. John Beauchamp, one of the adventurers of the Plymouth Colony. Frm. 7 Feb. 1636-7. Assistant. His dau. Alice m. William Paddy; Elizabeth m. John Ellis, and Mary m. Edward Perry. His wife Elizabeth d. Feb. 14, 1675.
Will dated 21 June, prob. 2 Nov. 1682; made his three sons, Edmond and John Freeman and Edward Perrey execs. Beq. to them; to gr. sons Matthias Ellis and Thomas Paddy; to dau. Elizabeth Ellis. Genealogy.

John, husbandman, ae. 35, with Sycilie, ae. 4, Marie, ae. 50, John, ae. 9, came in the Abigail in July, 1635. He settled at Sudbury; propr. 1639. Wife Elizabeth; ch. Joseph b. 29 (1) 1645, James b. and d. 1647.
Elizabeth Freeman, [his widow?] m. 13 Nov., 1649, Josiah Haine.

Mr. Samuel, gent., from Mawlyn, co. Kent, Eng.; had deed of English property July 22, 1640. [L.] His son Henry, gave letter of attorney 12 (10) 1646, for collection of legacy from his grandmother, Priscilla F. of Blackfriars in London, dec. [A.] His house in Watertown was burned Feb. 11, 1630. [W.] Wife Apphia; ch. Samuel b. May 11, 1638.

FREESTONE, FREISTON,
Anne and Frances, kinswomen of Wm. Hutchinson, adm. chh. Boston 9 (9) and 28 (10) 1634.

Elizabeth, late of Alford, co. Lincoln, now of Boston, N. E., spinster, dau. of Richard F. late of Horncastle, co. Lincoln, woolen draper, dec., gave letter of attorney Oct. 26, 1640, for collection of legacies left by her grandparents Robert and Mary F. [L.]

FRENCH,
Dorcas, maid servant to Mr. John Winthrop, adm. chh. Boston 10 (6) 1634; m. Christopher Peake of Roxbury.

Edward, tailor, Ipswich, propr. 1637. Rem. to Salisbury; propr. 1640; town officer. Wife Ann; ch. Joseph, John, Samuel, Hannah.
He d. Dec. 28, 1674. Will dated April 10, 1673, prob. April 13, 1675, of great age. beq. to Edward and Symond, sons of his son Joseph; to John, eldest son of his son John; to Samuel, eldest son of his son Samuel; to the new born son of his son John; to dau. Philbrick, and her sons John White and William P.; to son Joseph's dau. Anne; son John's daus. Abigail and Hannah; to his wife Anne, whom he appoints exec. The widow d. March 9, 1682-3; inv. April 10, 1683.

John, Boston, had land gr. at Braintree for 5 heads 24 (12) 1639-40. Adm. chh. of Dorchester 27 (11) 1642; frm. May 29, 1644. Wife Grace; ch. John b. 28 (12) 1640, John bapt. 12 (12) 1642, Thomas bapt. 2 (5) 1643. Other ch. recorded at Br.: Dependance, (son,) b. 7 (1) 1648, Temperance, (dau.) b. 30 (1) 1651, William b. 31 (1) 1653, Elizabeth b. 29 (7) 1655, Samuel b. 22 (12) 1659. Wife Grace d. 29 Feb. 1680, ae. 59 yrs. [Gr. St.] He m. 2, 8 July, 1683, Eleanor, widow of Wm. Veasey.
He d. 6 Aug. 1692, ae. 80 yrs. Division of the est. was made to his eldest son John, to Dependance, Thomas, Samuel, William, (son of William F., dec.;) to Temperance, wife of John Bowditch, to Elizabeth Wheelock of Mendon; and the ch. of Mary Lamb, dec. [Reg. XII, 353.]

John, Cambridge, propr. 1637. He and his wife *Sarah* membs. chh. and their ch. all bapt. at Camb. Dau. Sarah dism. to chh. of Billerica May 16, 1664. [Mi.] Wife Joanna [Mdx. Rec.] bur. 20 (11) 1645; ch. Sarah b. (8) 1637, Joseph b. 4 (2) 1640, Nathaniel b. 7 (4) 1643.
He was bur. 16 (12) 1645.

Stephen, Dorchester, propr., frm. May 14, 1634. Deputy. Rem. to Weymouth. App. one of the aids to Magistrates for Court matters 6 (7) 1638. Town officer, 1645.
Will dated 17 March, prob. 29 July, 1679; beq. to chh. of Wey.; to sister Mary Randall; to gr. sons Stephen, and Samuel, and gr. daus. Mary, Hannah and Elizabeth; to son Stephen. Land lately sold to bro. Searle.

Thomas, Boston, memb. chh. 1631, frm. Nov. 6, 1632. He was dism. to Ipswich 27 (11) 1638. Wife Alice; ch. Mary bapt. 23 (7) 1632, Mary bapt. 2 (1) 1634.
Admin. gr. by Gen. Court 5 (9) 1639, to his widow. She was dism. from the Boston chh. 16 (4) 1644, being now the wife of Thomas Howlett.

William, tailor, Cambridge, propr. 1635-6. Confirmed as lieut. 26 May, 1647. Deputy. Rem. to Billerica. His wife Elizabeth, ae. 30, with Francis, ae. 10, Elizabeth, ae. 6, Marie, ae. 2½, and John, ae. 5 mos. came in the Defence, July, 1635. John was bapt. by Mr. Hooker in Camb. [Mi.] Other ch. Sarah b. (1) 1638, Jacob b. 16 (11) 1639, Hannah b. 1641, d. 1642, Hannah, (m. John Bracket,) Samuel b. 1645, d. 1646, [Samuel,] Mary b. April 3, 1670, Sarah b. Oct. 29, 1671, Abigail b. April 14, 1673, d. 1674, Hannah b. Jan. 25, 1676. The wife Elizabeth d. March 31, 1668, and he m. Mary, widow of John Stearns, May 6, 1669.
He d. Nov. 20, 1681, ae. 77. His widow m. June 29, 1687, Isaac Mixer. His est. was divided 6 (10) 1687, between the widow and the three daus. Mary, (now Sharp;) Sarah and Hannah French. The instrument was acknowledged Aug. 26, 1722, by Sarah Crosbey, Mary, wife of Nathl. Dunckley, and Hannah, wife of John Child.

FRIEND, FREND,
Mr. John, Salem, 1638, propr. He m. in Oct. 1639, Mary, dau. of Thomas Dexter. Account in Lechford's Note Book. Propr. at Sandwich, 1640. Sold land in Sal. in 1652 to Edward Prescott of London.
Will dated 1 (11) 1655, prob. 27 (1) 1656;

FRIEND, etc., cont.
sons Samuel and James, daus. Elizabeth Pecker, Bethia and Hester.

John, carpenter, Boston, 1639. Bought land 1 (6) 1641, deeds made to his wife Mary. She was adm. chh., a widow, 8 (8) 1642.

FRISH,
John, one of the men with John Howland of Plymouth in the Kennebec affair in April, 1634.

FROST,
Edmund, Cambridge, frm. March 3, 1635-6; propr. 1636. Ruling elder. Wife Thomasine, "Thomas-Anne;" [Mi.] ch. John, "baptized in England," [Mi.] Thomas b. (1) 1637, Samuel b. (12) 1638, Joseph b. 13 (11) 1639, James b. 9 (2) 1643, Mary b. 24 (5) 1645, Ephraim, Thomas, Sarah. The wife Thomasine d., and he m. before 1669, Reana Daniel, widow successively of — James, Wm. Andrew and Robert Daniel. [Mdx. De. III, 364.]

He d. July 12, 1672. Will dated 16 April, "stricken in years;" prob. Oct. 1, folg. He beq. to wife Reana; to sons Ephraim, Thomas, John and Joseph; to his two daus. Sarah and Mary; to Jacob French and his wife, and the ch. of Golden More; to Harvard College and to Mr. Alcock's son there. The inv. of the est. of the widow was taken 3 (11) 1675.

FROTHINGHAM, FRODINGHAM,
William, Charlestown, propr. 1630; appl. frm. Oct. 19, 1630, adm. frm. March 6, 1631-2. Wife Anne also a memb. Boston chh. 1630; both joined in the organization of the Chasn. chh. in 1632. Ch. Bethia b. 7 (12) 1630, John b. 10 (6) 1633, Elizabeth b. 15 (1) 1635, Peter bapt. 15 (2) 1636, Mary bapt. 18 (2) 1638, Nathaniel bapt. 16 (2) 1640, Stephen bapt. 11 (9) 1641, Hannah b. 29 (11) 1642, Joseph b. and d. in 1645.

He d. 18 (8) 1651. Inv. of lands, farming effects and household goods. [See Croft.] The widow d. July 28, 1674, ae. 67.

FRY, FRYE, FRIE, FREY, FFREY,
George, husbandman, weaver, Weymouth, 1640; frm. May 7, 1651. He deposed 5 March, 1673-4, ae. about 58 yrs., that he

FRY, etc., cont.
was from Combe St. Nicholas, Eng., and came thence to Wey. in 1640; that he knew Wm. Torrey and his son Samuel there and ever since. [Suff. De. VIII, 392.] Will dated 6 July, prob. 30 Nov. 1676. Beq. to dau.-in-law Mary Smith, wife to James S., Sen.; daus. Ruth Torrey; Naomy Yeale and Mathiah Reed.

John, wheelwright, of Basing, Eng. with wife and 3 ch., came in the Bevis in May, 1638. Settled at Newbury, propr. 1638. Rem. to Salisbury, where he was propr. in 1639; thence to Andover. Wife Anne; ch. John, James b. 5 Feb. 1652, Sara d. 5 March, 1661-2, Elizabeth. The wife Anne d. 22 Oct. 1680.

He d. 9 Nov. 1693, ae. 92 years, 7 months. His will dated 16 March, 1685-6, prob. Dec. 5, 1693, beq. to eldest son John; son's Benjamin, Samuel and James; dau. Elizabeth Stiles. Signed John Frie.

Richard, Dorchester, propr. 1634.

William, Weymouth, one of the "passengers" to whom land was assigned in 1636,—12 acres for 2 persons. [See Hull, Joseph.] Wife [Elizabeth,] probably dau. of Jonas Humphrey of Dorchester; ch. Elizabeth b. 20 (10) 1639, (m. Nathan Fiske, Jr.,) Mary b. 9 (11) 1641, (m. Thomas Pierce of Dorchester).

He d. Oct. 6, 1642, [or was buried Oct. 26, 1642,] leaving nunc. will. Beq. to his wife, daus. Elizabeth and Mary; to Thomas Harris, Thomas Rawlens, and John Meggs, his 3 sisters' youngest children. The widow m. Thomas Dogget. [Reg. XXXIX, 230.]

FRYER, FRIER,
James, Cambridge. Wife Katharine d. July 28, 1640.

Elizabeth, Gloucester, propr. 1645; the Gen. Court, 13 Nov. 1644, annulled her marriage with John Richardson, who was proved to be a bigamist. She was living in 1668, deaf and in ill health. [Essex Arch.]

Frances, [a man?] Salem, one of the appraisers of the est. of Wm. Gouge in 1646.

Thomas, Salem, propr. 1639. Mr. Fryer was one of the "eight men" of Gloucester in 1642.

FULLER,

Ann, widow, ae. 79; will prob. at Salem 25 (4) 1662. Son Richard Leach; Bethia Farrow, John and Sarah Leach.

Edward, came in the Mayflower; signed the Compact. Res. at Plymouth. He and his wife who came with him d. in 1621. Their son Samuel, who also came, survived and res. in Plymouth.

Edward, Charlestown, before Gen. Court 3 (7) 1639.

Giles, prop. for propr. at Dedham, 1638. Rem. to Hampton. Near kinsman of Doctor Matthew, of Barnstable in 1673. [See Pettingall.]

Giles, weaver, Hampton, son of Roger, of Topcraft, co. Norf. Eng., yeoman. His only sister Susanna, wife of Tho. Thurton of Croydon, co. Surrey, tobacconist, applied for inheritance of his estate in London 5 April, 1677. [Norf. Co. Rec. Lib. III, folio 63.]

John, joiner, Boston, bought land at Lynn 9 (6) 1639, to be paid for by Edward Fuller of Olney, Bucks. [L.] See will of Edward, John's father, prob. 20 Sept. 1656. [Reg. L, 533.] He testified at Salem 25 (2) 1651, ae. 30 years, concerning his bro. Dexter's sale of Lady Moody's farm.

John, came in the Abigail in May, 1635, with William F. Settled at Ipswich, 1637; rem. to Salisbury, but ret. about 1648 to Ips. Wife Elizabeth; ch. John, James, William, Thomas, Nathaniel, Joseph, Susanna, Elizabeth, Sarah.

He d. June 4, 1666; will prob. Sept. 25, 1666. His will not dated, prob. 25 Sept. 1666, beq. to wife; to ch. James, William, John, Susanna, Elizabeth, Thomas, Nathaniel, Joseph and Sarah; another ch. expected. Their gr. father had lately given them portions. James, exec.; and he is to have a double portion of any est. that may be recovered in England.

John, farmer, maltster, Cambridge, propr. 1644. He deposed 16 (3) 1656, ae. about 40 years. [Mdx. Files.]

He d. Feb. 1697-8, ae. 87. Will dated 30 Jan. 1695-6, prob. Feb. 28, 1697-8, beq. to wife Elizabeth; ch. John, Jonathan, Joshua, Jeremiah, Bethia Bond; Jonathan Hide, son of dau. Elizabeth H., dec.; also to gr. ch. Mary Brown, Elizabeth and Hannah Hides.

FULLER, cont.

Matthew, planter, Plymouth; captain. Rem. to Scituate; rec'd to chh. Nov. 7, 1636, by letter from Plym. chh. Propr., sergeant, prop. frm. 7 Sept. 1642. Rem. to Barnstable. Physician. He, or his son Matthew, m. April 8, 1635, Jane, dau. of Mr. John Lothrop.

Will dated 25 July, prob. 30 Oct. 1678, gave to wife Frances; to gr. ch. Shubael, son of Ralph Jones; son John; Thomas, Jabez, Timothy, Matthias and Samuel, sons of his dec. son Samuel; daus. Mary, wife of Ralph Jones; Elizabeth, wife of Moses Rowley; and Anne, wife of son Samuel; to Bethiah, wife of his son John; to gr. ch. Sarah Rowley, Jedidiah Jones, and all the rest. To Robert Marshall, the Scotchman.

Robert, Salem, 1639; question whether he was to remove in 1643. [Town Rec.]

Robert, Dorchester, 1640. Rem. to Dedham. He and his wife rec'd to chh. from Dorch. chh. 19 (11) 1648. Wife Ann; ch. Jonathan b. 15 (6) 1643, Benoni b. 16 (4) 1646, d. 5 (7) 1647, Sarah b. 21 (7) 1647, John b. 26 (9) 1649, Mary b. 1 (1) 1653. His wife d. 4 (5) 1646. He m. 2, Sarah —; she d. 2 (4) 1686.

He d. Dec. 14, 1688. Will prob. 28 April, 1690, beq. to gr. ch. John and Prudence Ranger; to son Jonathan F. and dau. Mary Richards.

Samuel, physician, also say-maker, m. 1, in Eng. Elsie Glascock; m. 2, at Leyden, Holland, April 30, 1613, Agnes, dau. of Alexander Carpenter of Wrentham, Eng.; m. 3, in L. May 27, 1617, Bridget Lee. Came in the Mayflower, signed the Compact. Settled at Plymouth. Deacon, frm. 1633; an important citizen of Plymouth; aided the settlers at the Bay on their arrival in 1630. See his letters about these settlers at Boston and Dorchester to Bradford. [Mass. Hist. Coll. 3.] His wife and child came afterward; another ch. born here. [B.]

He d. in 1633, of an infectious fever, after he had much helped others. [B.] Will prob. July 30, 1638, mentions son Samuel, dau. Mercy, bro. Wm. Wright and his wife Priscilla; sister Alice Bradford. Refers to children, Sarah Converse and Elizabeth Cowles, committed to his care, the latter, at Charlestown, to be returned to her parents. His cosen Samuel is to remove from the estate.

FULLER, cont.

Servants Thomas Symons and Robert Cowles. To the church, to Wm. Brewster, Mrs. Heeks and others. [Reg. IV, 33.] [The widow] Bridget Fuller b. 30 Sept. 1641, Henry Sirkman.

Samuel, nephew of Doctor Samuel, was with his uncle at Plymouth before 1638; rem. to Barnstable. [Is he not son of Edward above?] Ch. Thomas b. 18 May, 1650, Sarah b. 14 Dec. 1654, a child b. and d. 1658.

Thomas, [smith,] Woburn, propr. 1640. He m. 1, June 13, 1643, Elizabeth Tidd; he m. 2, Aug. 25, 1684, Sarah Wyman. He m. 3, Hannah —, whose daus., wives of James Proctor, Aaron Cleveland and John Wilson, agreed to care for her in 1697. [Wob. Rec.] Ch. Thomas b. 22 or 30 (2) 1644, Elizabeth b. Sept. 12, 1645, Ruth b. May 17, 1648, Deborah b. May 12, 1650, John b. March 1, 1652-3, Jacob b. May 14, 1655, Joseph b. Aug. 8, 1658, Benjamin b. April 15, 1660, Samuel b. May 9, 1662.

He made will 9 June, prob. July 4, 1698; beq. to daus. Dean, Ruth Wilkins, Deborah Shaw, sons Thomas, Jacob and Benjamin F.; gr. ch. David Richardson, Ruth Wheeler and Bethia Fuller. Genealogy.

Thomas, Dedham, propr. Nov. 25, 1642. Ralph Fuller of Wortwell, Norfolk, linen weaver, in will dated 23 Oct. 1645, beq. to John, son of his son Thomas F., now in New England. [Reg. LII, 241.] He m. 22 (9) 1643, Hannah Flower; ch. John b. and d. 1644, John b. about 1645, Elizabeth b. 1 (2) 1648, Hannah b. 9 (9) 1650, Thomas b. 26 (12) 1652, Mary b. 25 (1) 1655, Samuel b. 25 (2) 1657, Sarah b. 3 (7) 1659, Thomas b. 23 June, 1662, Hannah Fuller d. April 11, 1672. Will dated 24 Sept. prob. 13 Nov. 1690; "aged;" beq. to wife Hannah, sons John and Thomas, daus. Elizabeth Meadcalfe, Mary Fisher and Sarah Day.

William, ae. 25, wih John, ae. 15, came in the Abigail in May, 1635. Settled at Ipswich; propr. 1635; sold house and land in 1639. App. gunsmith by Gen. Court 17 May, 1637. Frm. June 2, 1641. He kept the mill in 1639. [Col Rec.] Rem. to Concord. Perhaps he is the W. F., locksmith, who bought land at Hampton 9 (12) 1647. Wife Elizabeth d. 24 (5) 1642. Ch. Hannah b. 8 (6) 1641.

FURNELL, FUNNELL, FOUNELL, FOWNELL,

John, miller or millwright, Cambridge, 1638, propr.; frm. May, 1645. Bought share in a tide mill in 1650. He sold land in 1654, which he had received from the estate of Col. George Cooke for the education of his daughter. Rem. to Charlestown. "Friends dying, he was left under the care of his father-in-law;" apprenticed at 12 years of age. Went to Hartfordtown, (Eng.) to live with a carpenter; married. [Rel.] Wife Mary; ch. Sarah b. (6) 1638. He deposed at Salem in 1664, ae. about 57 years.

He d. March 19, 1673, ae. 65. Will dated 30 (7) 1663, prob. 1 (2) 1673, beq. all to his wife Mary for her life, and then to be at her disposing. Widow Mary d. Jan. 25, 1696, ae. 84.

Strong, soap-boiler, ship-carpenter, Boston; adm. chh. 18 (1) 1643; frm. May 10, 1643. Wife Eleanor; ch. Elizabeth b. 7 (3) 1643, Mary bapt. 10 (6) 1645, ae. about 8 days, Joanna b. 26 (12) 1646, John bapt. 20 (6) 1648, ae. about 5 days, Samuel bapt. 14 (2) 1650, Mary bapt. 1 (4) 1651, Susanna b. and d. 1652, John b. 28 June, 1653.

The widow Eleanor m. in 1659, Michael Lambert.

FUSSELL,

John, bought house and home lot in Weymouth 28 (7) 1640. Rem. to Medfield about 1651.

He d. Feb. 21, 1676.

GAGE, GADGE,

John, Boston, memb. chh. 1630-1, frm. March 4, 1633-4. One of the first to plant at Agawam (Ipswich,) April 1, 1633. [Col. Rec.] Dsm. from Boston chh. to that of Ips. 10 (7) 1643. Town officer; member of com. on allotments. With wife [Amee] sold land in Ips. 21 (12) 1653. He deposed in 1659, ae. about 50 years, and in 1662, ae. about 58. Rem. to Bradford; town officer. He m. 1, Anna or Amee, —, who d. in June, 1658; he m. 2, in Nov. 1658, Sarah —. Ch. Jonathan, Josiah, Benjamin, Samuel, Daniel, Nathaniel, Thomas. Having promised his son Benjamin, on his marriage to Prudence, dau. of Thomas Leaver, of Rowley, a certain gift of land, he deeded it to Benj.'s son John 12 Dec. 1672.

He d. March 24, 1672-3. Will prob. next

GAGE, etc., cont.
day. Beq. to wife Sarah, five sons and one gr. son. The widow d. July 7, 1681; her est. was given by the Court to her 3 daus., the wives of Wm. Smith, John French and Samuel Buswell.

Thomas, Yarmouth, debtor of Robert Button in 1650; took oath of fidelity, 1657. He m. Joane, dau. of Wm. Knight of Salem, and gave a release in 1655 to his mother-in-law Elizabeth K., now wife of Allen Breed, for his wife's patrimony. [Es. Files.] His son, ae. a year and a half, was drowned in a well in 1650; inquest. Other ch. John, William and Henry, who d. in the war of 1675-6; Thomas, Benjamin and Moses. [Genealogy in Reg. LIII, 201.] Rem. to Harwich.
In his will, dated 30 June, prob. 19 July, 1695, he beq. to sons Benjamin and Moses.

GAGER,
William, surgeon, came in the pay of the Mass. Bay government in July, 1630. Settled at Charlestown. Memb. chh. and a deacon.
He d. Sept. 20, 1630. His son John rec'd from the est. of Gov. Winthrop in 1649 a debt formerly due the father.

GAILDTHAIT, see Goldthwaight.

GALE, GAILE, GALL,
Edmund, Cambridge.
He d. 29 (5) 1642.

John, servant to John Button, Boston, adm. chh 3 (6) 1634. "Died soon."

Richard, yeoman, Watertown, propr. 1642. Wife Mary; ch. Sarah b. 8 (7) 1641.
He d. 22 March, 1679. Will prob. April 1, 1679. To wife; to sons Abraham and John, and daus. Mary Flagg and Sarah Garfield, and to Abraham's eldest children, Abraham and Richard.

GAINES, GAYNES,
Henry, Lynn, propr. 1638. Frm. March 14, 1638.

Jane, Lynn; inv. taken 14 (11) 1644.

GALLOP, GALOP,
Mr. Humphrey, Dorchester, one of the first company, 1630, propr., res. in 1633. Wife Anne; ch. Joseph b. in 1633.

John, mariner, fisherman, a trader along the coast; res. at Boston. Paid in 1632 by Mr. Pynchon for carrying a letter. Adm. chh. 5 (11) 1633. Aided the troops engaged in the Pequot War in 1637. [B.] [W.] Propr. at Gloucester before 1650. Wife Christobell, adm. chh. 24 (4) 1634.
He d. (11) 1649. His will, dated 20 Dec., was prob. 9 (12) 1649-50. He gave 40 s. towards building the new meeting-house; to wife; son John and his wife Hannah; sons Samuel and Nathaniel; dau. Joane Joy and her sons John and Joseph J. The widow d. 27 (7) 1655. Her will was prob. Oct. 31, 1655. [Reg. V, 444, and VII, 209 and 228.]

GALLEY, GALLY, GALLEE,
John, Salem, [Manchester,] 1636; lawsuit, 1637.
Will dated 22 May, 1683, ae. about 78 years; prob. 3 March, 1683-4. Sons-in-law Wm. Hoare, Gilacrus Ross and John Giles; dau. Elizabeth Giles; gr. ch. Sarah Ross, Mary Johnson and Elizabeth Trask.

GALLOWAY,
George, Lynn, was in possession of lands belonging to Thomas Hampton of Sandwich in 1637, as stated in Hampton's will.

GAMBLIN, GAMLIN, GAMLING,
Robert, planter, embarked March 7, 1631-2; came to Roxbury. He brought with him his dau. Mary, who was a maid servant in Pynchon's family, "a very gracious maiden;" she d. with the small pox in 1633. His son Robert came also, bringing wife Elizabeth, widow of Thomas Mayo of Town Marroling, co. Kent, and her son John Mayo. [See Lechford; Rox. chh. Rec.; Reg. XII, 274.]
Robert Gamblin was bur. at Concord 7 (7) 1642.

William, a witness to Winthrop and Dudley's Indian deed 28 (8) 1642; land at Concord.

GAME,
William, servant to Angell Hollard of Weymouth in 1641, then to John Crabtree. [L.]

GAMER,
Thomas, before Gen. Court 2 May, 1649.

GANNETT, GANNATT, GARNETT,
Judith, ae. 26, came in the Francis of Ipswich April 30, 1634. Judith, maid servant to John Coggeshall, adm. chh. Boston 7 (7) 1634; now wife of Robert Shelley, dism. to Barnstable 14 (5) 1644.

Thomas, Duxbury, atba. 1643, propr. 1642. Rem. to Bridgewater. Will, dated June 19, 1655. Prob. by widow Sarah 7 Aug., 1655. Beq. to wife and bro. Matthew G. [Reg. V, 261.]

GARD,
Roger, merchant, of the island of Fayall, now res. in N. E., was to receive goods on behalf of Abraham Shurt, as by the bond of Manning and Trerese, 13 May 1643. [A.]

GARDENER, GARDINER, GARDNER,
Sir Christopher, knighted at Jerusalem, came to Mass. in 1631. Made much trouble for the authorities. [B. and W.] See numerous sketches.

Lyon, ae. 36, with wife Mary, ae. 34, and Elizabeth Coles, their maid servant came in the Batcheler, arriving Nov. 28, 1635. Was an expert engineer, sent by the Lords Say and Seal to begin a fort at the mouth of the Connecticut River. But Mr. Winthrop had sent a bark with carpenters and other workmen 4 days before, to take possession of the spot. [W.] He volunteered to help in the laying out and building of the fortification upon Fort Hill in Boston 23 (11) 1635-6. [Town Rec.] He rem. to Conn., where he became a very valuable citizen.

Nathaniel, merchant, Boston. He bought of Capt. Thomas Lake 2 (9) 1649, several shares in the Swampscott and Dover patents.

Richard, came in the Mayflower to Plymouth; became a seaman. Ret. to England. [B.]

GARDNER, GARDINER, GARDENER, GEARNER,
Edmund, or Edward, ae. 25, came in the James in July, 1635. Settled at Cambridge; propr. Rem. to Ipswich; propr. 1635; frm. Oct. 7, 1640. Was rewarded by order of the Gen. Court in 1645 for making saltpetre. Mrs. Margaret, [his wife?] memb. chh. at Salem in 1639; testified 28 March, 1648, about goods transferred at Ipswich. [Ips. De. 1, 38.]

John, Plymouth, servant to Kenelm Winslow, was transferred to George Kenrick in 1635. Propr. 2 Nov. 1640. Settled at Hingham. Propr. 1656. Wife Mary; ch. John bapt. at H. July 17, 1652, Francis bapt. March 31, 1653, Mary bapt. Nov. 19, 1654, (m. Nathan Farrow,) Samuel bapt. March 23, 1655-6, Deborah bapt. July 5, 1657, James bapt. Feb. 4, 1659-60, Stephen bapt. Aug. 14, 1662, Thomas bapt. June 5, 1664, Benjamin bapt. April 7, 1666, Christian bapt. June 3, 1668, (m. Joseph Dunbar.)
He d. 24 Nov. 1668. Inv. filed 28 April, 1669.

Richard, yeoman, *not* the son of Thomas of Salem,] Woburn, propr. 1648. He deposed in 1658, ae. about 39 years. Bought lands of Thos Broughton in 1658. Rem. to Charlestown. Bought land in 1676. He m. Oct. 18, 1651, Anna Blanchard. Ch. John b. Aug. 14, 1652, Anna b. Jan. 17, 1654, Benjamin b. Dec. 26, 1656, Henry b. Feb. 12, 1657, Esther b. Oct. 15, 1659, Ruth b. April, 1661. He gave security 5 (2) 1653, to pay £108 to the 2 children his wife had by her former husband.
He d. May 29, 1698, ae. 79 years. Will dated March 15, 1696-7, prob. June 6, 1698, beq. to only son Henry; to his son John; to the ch. of daus. Hannah Coddington, Ruth Gypson, (Ruth and Anna); daus. Hester, Abigail, Rebecca and Mehitabel; gr. sons Benjamin Johnson, son to dau. Hester, John Whitmore, son to dau. Rebecca, John Connett, son of dau. Mehitabel, Richard and Simon Thompson, sons of dau. Abigail; Maj. William Johnson and pastor, Mr. Jabez Fox.

Thomas, householder, Roxbury, was buried in Nov. 1638. His widow, "aged sister" G., d. 7 (8) 1658. Children, Thomas, (m. July 4, 1641, Lucy Smith,) Peter, (came, ae. 18, in the Elizabeth, April 17, 1635; m. May 9, 1646, Rebecca Crooke; they made Michael

GARDNER, etc., cont.
Powell their attorney, 12 (10) 1646, to receive a legacy from her father Roger Crooke, of Hammersmith, tailor, dec.) [A.] Both Thomas and Peter had families.

Thomas, husbandman, came from Weymouth, Dorsetshire, in the spring of 1623-4 as superintendent of the planting of the colony sent out by The Western Adventurers of Dorchester, Eng. He spent the following summer and winter at Cape Ann, having 13 men under him. He was succeeded at the close of the year by Roger Conant, who also held office only one year, when the undertaking was abandoned. He settled at Salem, to which Conant and others had removed in 1626; appears in the earliest records extant, as proprietor. Juryman 27 (7) 1636; frm. May 17, 1637; town officer; deputy to Gen. Court. He deeded land 6 Dec. 1671, acknowledged 13 (1) 1672-3. First wife's name unknown, (unless she be the Margaret, mentioned above with Edmund.) He m. after 15 (3) 1642, Damaris, widow of — Shattuck, who was prominent among the Quakers of the town. She d. 28 (9) 1674. Ch. Thomas, George, (a father in 1644,) Richard, Samuel, (b. about 1627, per depos.) Joseph, John, Sarah, (m. — Balch,) Seeth b. 25 (10) 1636, (m. — Grafton,) Miriam, (m. John Hill); Joseph Pope calls George, Richard and Joseph "brothers."

He d. 29 (10) 1674. Will, dated Dec. 7, 1668, prob. March 29, 1675, beq. to wife, whom he calls the "mother in law" (stepmother,) of his son Thomas; to sons Thomas, Thomas of Salem, Woburn, propr. 1648. He George, Richard, Samuel, Joseph and John; to daus. Sarah Balch, Seeth Grafton and Miriam Hill, with the two daus. of the latter, namely Miriam and Susanna. [See The Planter's Plea, by Rev. John White, in Young's Chronicles and Hubbard.] Genealogy in preparation by Frank Augustine Gardner, M. D.

GARFIELD, GEARFIELD,
Edward, Watertown, propr. frm. May 6, 1635. Wife Rebecca; ch. Joseph b. 11 (7) 1637, Rebecca b. 10 (1) 1640, Abigail b. June 29, 1646. Older children, Samuel and Edward were proprs. in Wat. His wife d. April 16, 1661, ae. about 55 years; he m. Joanna, widow of Thomas Buckmaster, and conveyed, with her, 25 (4) 1663, land to her son Joseph B.

GARFIELD, etc., cont.
He d. June 14, 1672, [ae. about 97 years.] Will dated 30 Dec. 1668, prob. 11 (5) 1672, beq. to sons Samuel, Joseph and Benjamin; daus. Rebecca Mixter and Abigail G.; gr. ch. Sarah Parkhurst, and Sarah and Ephraim G., and to his wife. The widow made will 8 (1), prob. Suff. Aug. 17, 1676. Beq. to her three daus. Marie, Dorcas and Sarah, her dau.-in-law Elizabeth Spowell, her grandchild Johanna Lawrence and her son Jabez Buckmaster. [See hypothetical pedigree in Reg. XXXVII, 253.]

GARFOARD, GARSFORD,
Garvas or Jarvis, gent., Salem, 1634; propr. 1635; memb. chh. 1636; frm. at Salem 13 (1) 1639. He sold a buff coat for Mr. Gardiner in 1636 to Gov. Winthrop, q. v. His dau., Mrs. Ann Turland, is referred to in Sal. Rec. He sold house and land 26 (7) 1653.

GARLAND,
Peter, mariner, Charlestown, propr. 1637; Boston, 1638. [L.] Wife Joan; ch. Mary b. in 1654.

GARLIK, GARLIKE,
Joseph, called to Es. Court in 1639; servant of Moses Maverick at Marblehead, 1640.

GARRETT, GARRATT,
Herman, gunsmith, Charlestown, made agreement 17 (7) 1640, with John Edwards, blacksmith, to take him as partner. [L.] Rem. to Concord; propr. Jan. 20, 1643. One of the founders of Lancaster; named in an order of the Gen. Court regarding L. in 1653. Res. in Boston about 1659. [Suff. De. III, 388.] The same name used by the sachem of the Narragansetts in 1661. [Ib. 483.]

Hugh, Charlestown, inhabitant 1629-30.

James, mariner, Charlestown, with wife Deborah adm. chh. 7 (7) 1638; frm. June 6, 1639. Ch. Mary b. 4 (3) 1638, Priscilla b. 28 (4) 1640, James b. 6 (6) 1643, James b. 4 (6) 1646.

He was lost at sea Nov., 1657. The widow sold the est. March 30, 1663.

Richard, shoemaker, Boston, memb. chh. 1630, appl. frm. Oct. 19, 1630. Ch. Hannah d. (12) 1632.

He d. 28 Dec., 1630. [Deposition of James Hawkins; Suff. De. III, 344.]

GARRETT, etc., cont.

Mr. Richard, Scituate, before the Court 5 March, 1638-9; atba. 1643. Umpire in a land suit in 1650. Ch. Joseph b. 10 March, 1648-9, John b. 25 Nov. 1651, Mary b. 5 Nov. 1655.

Mr. Richard, Boston, d. 29 March, 1662; inv. filed 29 July folg. Admin. gr. to widow Lydia.

GARRETT, *alias* BUTCHER,

Robert, Boston, 1643. Wife Mary; ch. John b. 2 (4) 1643.

His will, dated Nov. 27, 1660, was prob. 15 Aug. 1668. On a voyage to Barbadoes; beq. to wife Mary for herself and his four ch. John, Robert, Mary and Sarah. His widow was one of the trustees of the est. of Edmund Browne 2 Nov., 1666, being grandmother to his 2 ch. [Reg. XVI, 335.]

GARY, GEARY, GERRY,

Arthur, Roxbury, frm. March 14, 1638-9. Ch. Samuel b. Sept. 22, 1638.

He d. Dec. 17, 1666, ae. 67 years. Will dated Nov. 18, 1664, prob. Jan. 30, 1666. Wife Frances; sons William, Nathaniel and Samuel. [Reg. XV, 248.]

GASCOYNE, GASKOYEE, GASKELL,

Edward, ship carpenter, Salem, propr. 1636. Bought house and land in 1659. Wife Sarah, Salem, memb. chh. 1639. Ch. "of Edward," Samuel and Preserved bapt. 7 (6) 1639, Daniel bapt. 10 (8) 1640, Sarah bapt. 14 (3) 1643, Hannah bapt. 1 (1) 1645-6, Edward bapt. 30 (2) 1648.

GATCHELL, GETCHELL, GATSHELL,

John, planter, Salem, Marblehead, propr. 1637; town requested him to cut off his long hair. He deposed in 1669, ae. about 53 years. Constable in 1657. [His wife.] Wyboro or Thribrough deposed in 1670, ae. about 50 years. She d. 11 Oct. 1684.

Richard, Marblehead, taxed in 1637.

Samuel, planter, Salem, 1637. Rem. to Hampton; sold land and house there 3 (17) 1648. Rem. to Salisbury; commoner, propr. 1650. Wife Dorcas d. Jan. 12, 1684. Ch. Susanna, (m. Joseph Norton,) Priscilla b. Feb. 26. 1648, (m. Solomon Rainsford,) Samuel.

He made will April 2, 1684, prob. Oct. 6, 1697.

GATES,

Stephen, with wife and 2 ch. from Hingham, Eng., came in 1638 to Hingham. Frm. May 14, 1656. Rem. to Cambridge about 1652; spent a few yrs. at Lancaster; Wife Ann; ch. Elizabeth, (m. in Hing. John Lassell,) Mary, (m. John Maynard,) Stephen, Simon, Thomas, Isaac, Rebceca bapt. at Hing. May 3, 1646, d. Jan. 1650.

His will, dated 9 (4) prob. 24 (9) 1662, beq. to wife; sons Simon, Stephen and Thomas, daus. Elizabeth, and Mary Mayner. Elizabeth Bradstare to abide with his wife. The widow m. 2, Richard Woodward; she d.— "Hannah G., widow"—Feb. 5, 1682; made will 18 April, 1682, prob. 9 (2) 1683; beq. to dau. Elizabeth Lazell; gr. ch. Mary, dau. of John Maynard, sons Stephen, Simon and Thomas G. "My last husband's name was Woodward, but I generally went by the name of Gates."

GATLEY,

Adam, Salem. Sold house frame, cellar and ¼ acre of land 11 (2) 1644.

GATLIFFE, GATLIVE, GETLIVE,

Thomas, miller, Dorchester, Braintree, 1653.

He d. before June 24, 1663. Admin. of his est. gr. 28 Oct. 1663, to his widow Prudence and only son Jonathan. Division agreed upon by them before the Court 30 (8) 1669. Daus. Prudence and Mary; the wife Prudence is called Jonathan's "mother-in-law."

GAULT, GALT, GOLT, GOLD, GOULT,

William, cordwainer, singleman, ae. 29, of Yarmouth, Eng., passed exam. May 11, 1637, to go to N. E. Settled at Salem; propr. 1638; adm. chh. 1639. Before the court in 1642 for speaking against the rule and the church. Ch. Deborah and Sarah bapt. 10 (7) 1648.

He d. 1 (2) 1659. Inv. April 22, 1660; children mentioned, Rebecca ae. 19, Deborah, ae. 15, Sarah, ae. 13. The dau. Rebecca m. 11 (9) 1663, John Bly, [Bligh.] The widow m. 2, Richard Bishop.

GAUNT,

Peter, Sandwich, 1638, propr. atba. 1643.

Lydia, [his widow?] made will 28 (10) 1691, prob. April 26, 1692; beq. to sons Israel, Hannaniah and Zachariah; dau. Lydia; gr. ch.

GAUNT, cont.
Mercy Hixe, Mary Thirston, James and John Easton and Deborah; to the meeting called quackers, for the service of the truth.

GAY,
John, Watertown, before 1635; rem. to Dedham in 1636. Frm. May 6, 1635. Town officer. Wife Joanna adm. chh. 25 (5) 1639. John Balducke, her son by former husband, was bapt. 8 (6) 1639. Ch. (of John and Joanna Gay,) Samuel b. 10 (1) 1639, Hezekiah b. 3 (5) 1640, Nathaniel b. 11 (11) 1642, Joanna b. 23 (1) 1644, (m. John Ware,) Eliezer b. 25 (4) 1647, Abiel (m. Daniel Hawes,) and Judith b. 23 (2) 1649, (m. John Ware,) John b. 0 (3) 1651, Jonathan b. 1 (6) 1653, Hannah b. 16 (8) 1656. Elizabeth, who m. Richard Martin at Salem, in 1660, is said to have been a dau.

He d. March 4, 1688; will prob. Dec. 17, 1689. [Genealogy in Reg. XXXIII, 45.]

Thomas, before Salem Court for defaming a man in 1636.

GAYLORD, GAYLARD, GALLARD, GALLERD,
Wiliam, planter, Dorchester, believed to have been one of the original chh. colony who came in the Mary and John in 1629-30, and one of the first deacons. Signed earliest land grants with the minister and Wm. Rockwell. Juryman Nov. 9, 1630. Town officer, deputy.

Re rem. about 1636 to Windsor, Conn. As agent of Mr. and Mrs. Warham, he leased lands in 1639. [L.] Deputy many terms. His wife d. 20 June, 1657.

He d. 20 July, 1673, ae. 88.

GEARE, GEARES, GEERE,
Dennis, ae. 30, with wife Elizabeth, ae. 22, and ch. Elizabeth, ae. 3, Sarah, ae. 2, came in the Abigail in June, 1635. Settled at Saugus. His will, dated Dec. 10, 1635, prob. Aug. 6, 1637, rec. in Boston and London, beq. to wife and daus.; to cousin Ann Pankhurst; to Elizabeth Tuesley; Roger Carver of Bridhemson and John Russell of Lewes in Sussex, to be overseers of his est. in Eng. Beq. out of the est. in N. E. to Thomas Topper, Thomas Braines, Thomas Launder, Benjamin Nye, and Thomas Grenvill; made provision for the ret. of his family to Eng. The residue to be bestowed on the plantations within the province of Mass. Bay. John Winthrop,

GEARE, etc., cont.
Sen., and others execs for N. E. The colony rec'd 300 li. [Reg. XXXVII, 239.]

William, Salem, 1638; frm. June 2, 1641. Rem. to Wenham before 1644. Wife Tryphena also memb. of chh. Ch. Samuel bapt. 14 (1) 1640-1, Mary bapt. 14 (3) 1643, John bapt. 23 (4) 1644, Ephraim bapt. 17 (2) 1647.

Widow Triphena, admin. of his est., sold land 15 May, 1676.

GEARNER, see Gardner,

GEDNEY, GIDNEY,
John, worsted weaver, of Norwich, Eng., with wife Sarah, ae. 25, and ch. Lediah, Hannah and John, and servants Wm. Walker and — Burges, ae. 26 years, passed exam. May 11, 1637, to go to Salem, N. E. Propr. 1637, frm. March, 1637-8. Inn-keeper, vintner. With now wife Katharine, he deeded lands to his son John, mariner, and his son-in-law Nicholas Potter, Sen., blacksmith in 1661. Mary, Salem, memb. chh. 1637. Ch. Bartholomew bapt. 14 (4) 1640, Eleazer bapt. 15 (3) 1642, Sarah bapt. 23 (4) 1644.

He d. Aug. 5, 1688. Will prob. Dec. 12, 1088, rec. at Boston. To dau.-in-law Rebecca Putnam; to Bethiah [Rebecca] dau. of Joseph Hutchinson; to the ch. of dau. Mary Potter; to son Bartholomew and his wife and ch.; ch. of son Eleazer G.; to dau. Susanna and ch. she had by son John G. dec. [Genealogy in Es. Inst. Coll. XVI.]

GELL, see Giles.

GENERY, see Chenery.

GENNISON, see Jennison.

GEOFFREY, GEOFFREYS, see Jeffreys.

GEORGE, GORGE,
John, Watertown, an early settler. Wife —, who d. about 1638; ch. Robert and Susan. He m. 2, Anne or Hannah, widow of Henry Goldstone. She deposed in 1654, ae. about 64 years. [Arch. 38 B.]

He d. before June 29, 1647, when the widow admin. on his est. She d. April 26, 1670, ae. 79. The inv. mentions debts he owed to his son Robert and dau. Susan. [Reg. VIII, 57.]

GEORGE, etc., cont.

John, apprenticed to Mr. John Winthrop for 8 yrs. before Gen. Court 2 (1) 1640-1, may have been a son of the above, and the person who beq. to his daus. Elizabeth Glasier, Martha Row, Ruth, Hannah and Mary, and son John G.

Nicholas, Dorchester, 1641; frm. May 23, 1666. Wife Elizabeth adm. chh. 1641; ch. Elizabeth bapt. 9 (1) 1641, (m. Samuel Rigby,) John bapt. 30 (3) 1643, Mary bapt. 21 (10) 1645, (m. James Bird,) Joshua b. about 1648, Nicholas. The son Nicholas d. in Guinea about 1666, acc. to testimony of Giles Young July 18, 1672, when admin. of his est. was gr. to his widow Abigail, with Nicholas, Sen., and John Greenland sureties.

His will was prob. 27 (2) 1675. Beq. to wife Elizabeth and to grandson Nicholas, now living with him; children all disposed of in marriage.

Peter, oatmeal maker, Braintree, with Mary his wife, dau. of John Rowneing of Hunden, co. Suff., dec. gave letter of attorney 19 (9) 1647, for coll. of dues from the ests. of her father and Symon Ray, her former husband. [A.] Ch. Susan b. (12) 1642, John d. 2 (9) 1653. He bought land in Br. in partnership with Henry Neale 14 (5) 1648. Rem. to Block Island. Sold land in Br. 5 July, 1670.

GETCHELL, see Gatchell.

GERRISH,

William, merchant, gent., [Ipsw. De. I, 81, Es. De. 1, 5.] Newbury. Capt., comr. of Court, town officer. He rem. to Boston. He m. 17 April, 1645, Joanna, dau. of Mrs. Elizabeth Goodall and widow of John Oliver. [See Lowell.] She d. 14 June, 1677. Ch. John b. "12 Feb. 1645," [Sal. rec.], 15 May, 1646, [Newb. rec.] Abigail b. 10 May, 1647, William b. 6 June, 1648, Joseph b. 23 March, 1649, Benjamin b. 13 Jan. 1651, Elizabeth b. 2 Sept. 1654, Moses b. 9 May, 1656, Mary b. April 1, 1658, (m. John, son of Richard Dole; marriage portion 3 May, 1676;) Anna b. 18 Oct. 1660, Judith b. 10 Sept. 1662.

He d. at Salem 9 Aug. 1687, "b. Aug. 19, 1620;" [Sal. to rec.] Will dated 16 July, 1687, prob. 5 Dec. folg., beq. to his former wife's dau. Mrs. Mary Appleton; to sons John, Joseph and Benjamin; to William, Bethiah and

GERRISH, cont.

Parson, ch. of his dec. son William; son Moses Greenleafe and dau. Elizabeth, his wife; dau. Mary Dole. His widow Ann, dau. and exec. of Richard Parker, of Boston, gent., made will 2 Feb. prob. at Bo. 21 March, 1687-8; beq. to dau. Ann Jones and her bro. Ephraim Manning; to gr. dau. Ann Sandys. Her death was Feb. 7, 1687-8. [S.]

GIBBONS, GIBBINS, GIBBON,

Edward, merchant, Boston, memb. chh. 1630-1, frm. May 18, 1631. Deputy, Major General. An important citizen. Res. at Charlestown sometime. Wife Margaret memb. chh. 1631. Ch. Jerusha b. 5 (8) 1631, Jotham b. 6 (8) 1633, Edward bapt. 3 (1) 1635, Edward bapt. 26 (1) 1637, Metsathiel bapt. 7 (8) 1638, John b. 30 (1) 1641.

He d. 9 (10) 1654. Inv. 15 (10) 1654. The widow ret. to Eng., and d. at Plymouth, co. Devon. Admin. gr. 28 Feb. 1656 to her dau. Jerusha, wife of Capt. Thomas Rea. Inv. filed in Boston 16 (10) 1658. [Reg. VIII, 275, IX, 346, and XXXVIII, 426.]

GIBBS, GIBB, GIBBE,

Giles, Dorchester, propr. 1633, frm. March 4, 1634-5. Rem. to Windsor, Conn. Ch. Gregory, Jacob, Samuel, Benjamin and Sarah.

He was bur. 21 May, 1641. Widow Katharine d. 24 Oct. 1660.

Henry, servant of Edmund Hubbard, Sen., came from Hingham, Eng., in 1633; res. at Charlestown a short time and rem. to Hingham. Mary adm. chh. Charlestown 23 (7) 1652.

He d. July 6, 1676. Will dated 15 June, prob. 31 Oct. 1676, beq. to the ch. of Samuel Stowell, Sen.

Thomas, Sandwich, atba. 1643, propr.. Ch. John b. Sept 12, 1634, Thomas b. March 23, 1636, Samuel b. 22 June, 1649, Sarah b. April 11, 1652, Job and Bethiah b. April 15, 1655, Mary b. Aug. 12, 1657, Samuel b. June 23, [1659].

Division of his est. was made April 14, 1693, between sons John, Thomas and Samuel; providing for their mother's maintenance.

GIBSON, GIFSON,
Christopher, chandler, Dorchester, probably of the first company, appl. frm. Oct. 19, 1630. Rem. to Boston in 1648; partner of David Selleck in the soap business. [Suff. De. II, 111.] Wife Marie.
Will undated, prob. 12 (1) 1674, beq. to cousin Hopestill Foster, Jr., and sister F.; cousin Thomas Dampford; Samuel and Clement Maxfield; cousin Williams; David Jones of Dorch.; Mr. Mather and Mr. Mayo; bro. Edward Sealle; Garratt Ingraham's wife Rebecca Seale; Gibson Farr that lives with his gr. fa. Pelton; James Priest; goodman Barker that rings the bell; William Ingraham; Alice and Ephraim Serle; Ebenezer Williams, beside what I have done for him since he came from Jamaica; the Second church of Boston, at the North End; Samuel Bedwell; cousins John, Elizabeth and Mercy Foster; cousin Joseph Alsop, Jr.; bro. James Brett and his son Samuel; bro. William Lane; sister Snelling; sister Mansfield; sister Preston and sister Ingraham; Mr. Houlsworth, a bro. of our church; John Withinton's wife; to the poor.

John, Cambridge, 1634; frm. May 17, 1637. Wife Rebecca; ch. John, (d. Oct. 15, 1679, ae. 48 years. [Gr. st.]) Rebecca, (m. Charles Stearns, ["now joined to the chh. of Watertown," Mi. in 1658.]) Mary b. (1) 1637, (m. John Ruggles,) Martha b. (2) 1639 (m. Jacob Newell,) Samuel b. 28 (8) 1644. Wife Rebecca was bur. at Roxbury Dec. 1, 1661, and he m. July 24, 1662, Joanna, widow of Henry Prentice.
He d. in 1694, ae. 93. [Genealogy, Reg. XXXVII, 388.]

GIDDINGS, GITTINGS,
George, husbandman, ae. 25, with Jane, ae. 20, and servants Thomas Carter, Michael Willmson, and Elizabeth Morrison, cert. from St. Albans, Herts, Eng., came in the Planter April 2, 1635. Settled at Ipswich; propr.; frm. Sept. 7, 1638. Memb. Court valuation com. 13 May, 1640; deputy, town officer. Gave land to son Samuel 30 March, 1675. He deposed March 29, 1659, ae. about 40 years; called Simon Tuttle bro.; his son Thomas was then 23 and John ae. 20.
Admin. gr. to his widow Jane 27 (4) 1676. [Es. Inst. Coll. III, 184, Reg. XXXVI, 319.] Agreement made by his sons Thomas, John, James and Samuel 26 Sept. 1676.

GIGGLES, see Jiggles.

GILBERT,
Humphrey, husbandman, Ipswich; paid in 1643 for service against the Indians. Bought land toward Wenham in 1650. Taxed at Wenham in 1655. He deposed in 1654, ae. about 38 years. [Mdx. Files.]
Will, dated 14 (12) 1657, prob. March 30, 1658; beq. to wife Elizabeth, son John, and dau. Elizabeth; to Abigail and 3 other daus. who were under age; to Peter Harvie, Richard Palmer, Richard Comer, Moses Ebberne. The 4 minor daus. petitioned that their husbands be app. adminrs. Jan. 1657-8. Evidence was given 27 (4) 1666, that the dau. Hannah had rec'd her portion.

John, Dorchester, a grave, honest gentleman; his son was arrested for drunkenness in 1636. [W.] He rem. to Taunton; frm. Plym. Col. 4 Dec. 1638. Propr., town officer.
Will, dated May 31, 1654, prob. June 3, 1657; to wife Winnifred, ch. Gyles, Joseph, Thomas, John, Mary Norcrosse, and her dau. Mary; to wife's gr. ch. Elizabeth Peslee. [Reg. V, 338.]

Nicholas, Watertown, ill-used by his master, Christopher Grant, who was before Gen. Court 28 (11) 1640.

GILD, GILE, see GUILD.

GILL,
Arthur, ship-carpenter, Dorchester, 1639. Frm. June 2, 1641. Rem. to Boston. Rec'd to chh. 27 (9) 1642. Wife Agnes; ch. John b. 16 (9) 1639, Thomas b. (8) 1644, Nathaniel bapt. 11 (2) 1647, d. 2 (7) 1652; dau. Frances m. 17 (8) 1656, Henry Boyen.
Admin. gr. to John Sweete for the children. The acct. rendered 19 March, 1656, mentions eldest son John, son Thomas gone to Eng., dau. Frances Gill and others. [Reg. IX, 228, and XXXI, 102.]

Isabel, memb. chh. Dorchester, 1639.

John, mariner, Dorchester, memb. chh. 20 (9) 1640, with goodwife Gill, name not given. He m. Elizabeth, dau. of William Ware; ch. Rebecca bapt. 7 (5) 1650. He m. Ann —. His dau. the wife of Joseph Belcher was dism. to Braintree chh. 6 (7) 1674. John adm. chh. 21 (7) 1662.

GILL, cont.

Widow Gill at liberty 13 Sept., 1680, to get trees from the common lands for the reparation of her mill. [Suff. De. VI, 158.] Wm. Ware beq. to his gr. ch. Obediah and Elizabeth Gill in 1658. The widow Ann's will dated 16 July, 1683, prob. 31 July, beq. to gr. ch. Ann, wife of Rowland Storey, and Joseph, Rebecca, Patience, Mary and Gill, ch. of dec. son-in-law, Joseph Belcher of Milton; to my bro. Roger Billing, Sen.

John, husbandman, Salisbury, propr., bought land 1646; commoner, 1650. He and his wife membs. chh. Wife Phebe joined him in a deed of land 26 Dec. 1659. Ch. Elizabeth b. Jan. 8, 1645, (m. Morris Tucker,) John b. Oct. 15, 1647, Phebe b. Jan. 6, 1649, (m. Isaac Morrill,) Samuel b. Jan. 5, 1651, Sarah b. June 27, 1654, Moses b. Dec. 26, 1656, Benjamin b. 1662, Isaac b. April 24, 1665.

He d. Dec. 1, 1690; will prob. March 31, 1691.

Thomas, Hingham, propr. 1635, town officer. Wife Hannah, dau. of John Otis, d. 25 Jan. 1675-6. Ch. Mary bapt. Jan. 1643-4, (m. John Beale, Jr.,) Sarah, twin of the above, (m. John Langlee,) Hannah bapt. Nov. 10, 1645, (m. Samuel Clap,) Elizabeth bapt. June, 1647, (m. Samuel Stodder,) Thomas b. March 8, 1648-9, John bapt. April 8, 1651, d. May 23, 1659, Deborah bapt. May 8, 1653, (m. Josiah Lane,) Samuel bapt. Dec. 16, 1655, Nathaniel b. and d. 1657, John b. and d. 1660, Rachel bapt. Oct. 3, 1661, (m. Samuel Stowell.)

He d. 24 Feb. 1704-5, ae. about 89 yrs.

GILLAM,

Benjamin, shipwright, Boston, adm. chh. 26 (8) 1634, frm. May 6, 1635. He bought ½ of ship Charitie April 8. 1652. Either he or his son of the same name was master of the ship Charles in Boston, 1665. [Suff. De. V, 69.] He deposed in 1653, ae. about 45 years. [Es. Files.] His wife Ann (Hannah) with son Benjamin, 1 yr. old, came in the Abigail in July, 1635. Was adm. chh. Boston 3 (11) 1635. Ch. Benjamin b. 1634, Zachary b. 30 (7) 1636, Hannah b. and d. 1638, Hannah b. (11) 1639, Elizabeth b. (11) 1641, Joseph bapt. 13 (8) 1644, ae. about 9 days, Elisha bapt. 21 (3) 1648, ae. about 8 days.

Admin. of his est. gr. 19 June, 1671, to

GILLAM, cont.

sons Benjamin and Joseph. The widow's will, dated 23 Feb. 1673, prob. 31 July, 1674, beq. to sons B. and J. and dau. Hannah, wife of Richard Sharp; gives to H. the care and education of the two motherless children of her dau. Gwinn.

Robert, mariner, Boston, 1637.

GILES, GILLES, GYLES, GELL,

Edward, apprentice boy of John Young, in court in 1640.

Edward, or Edmund, Salem, propr., memb. chh. 1636. Wife Bridget adm. chh. 26 (9) 1648. Ch. Mehitabel bapt. 2 (2) 1636, Remember bapt. 20 (11) 1638, Eleazer bapt. 27 (9) 1640, John b. 15 (2) 1645, [father's certificate in Es. files,] bapt. 11 (3) 1645.

The widow Bridget's will, dated 14 (11) 1668, prob. 30 (9) 1680, beq. to sons Samuel and Thomas Very; to sons Eleazer and John Giles; to Mary, wife of Thomas Cutler of Reading. [Es. Files XXXIV, 84.]

William, frm. May 14, 1634.

GILLETT, GELLETT, JELLET,

Jonathan, Dorchester, propr., frm. May 6, 1635. Rem. to Windsor, Conn.

Matthew, came in the Mary and John March 26, 1633-4. Was servant of George Williams of Salem, till his 7 years expired 30 June, 1641. In court (4) 1646. [Es. Court rec.]

Nathaniel, [Dorchester,] frm. May 14, 1634. Rem. to Windsor, Conn.

GILMAN, GILLMAN,

Edward, yeoman, wih his wife, 3 sons, 2 daus., and 3 servants came to Hingham in 1638. Propr., frm. March 13, 1638-9. He sold his est. in Hingham Oct. 1, 1652, having rem. to Ipswich, where he was a selectman in 1649. Settled later at Exeter, as did several of his children. Wife Mary; ch. Mary, (m. John Foulsham,) Edward, Moses, Lydia, (m. Jan. 19, 1644-5, Daniel Cushing,) Sarah, (m. John Leavitt,) John.

He d. before 10 (2) 1655, when admin. of his est. was gr. to his widow Mary, the sons and sons-in-law consenting. [Genealogy claims connection with the family of Caston, Eng.] See Smith, Richard.

GILLAWAY, GILLOW, GILLO,
John, Lynn. Owner of cattle in 1638. [W.] Constable, 28 (4) 1643, [Es. Court;] in court in 1648. His wife Rose, as his attorney, sold land in 1661.
Will dated 20 Feb. 1672, prob. 27 (4) 1673; wife; ch. John, Mary and Sarah and others; perhaps another. Widow Sarah deposed to the inventory.

GILPIN,
Anthony, brought several suits in Plymouth in 1641.

GILSON,
Ann, ae. 34, came in the Susan and Ellen in 1635.

Mr. William, Scituate; frm. and asst. 1632-3. Memb. chh. at its org. in 1634. Owned a wind-mill. Was one of those who undertook to cut a passage from Greene's Harbor to the bay in 1633. Propr. at Barnstable in 1639, but did not remove.
He d. Feb. 1, 1639. Will, dated Jan. 26, prob. 3 March, 1639-40. Wife Frances; no children; beq. to John and Hannah Dammon, the ch. of his sister, and to Daniel Romeball. [Reg. IV, 36, and Plym. Col. Rec.]

GIMSON, see Jimpson.

GILVEN,
Thomas, Ipswich, propr. 1639; land sold by widow Katharine at a later time.
N. B. Part of the grant seems identical with one made to Thomas Silver. Perhaps error of a colonial copyist of record.

GINGEN, GINGINE, GINGILL,
John, tailor, Taunton, atba. 1643, rem. to Dorchester about 1644; propr.; frm. May 6, 1646. Rem. to Lynn, then to Salem. Was a partner of Bray Wilkins.
Will, dated April 10, 1685, ae. about 70 yrs., prob. March 24, 1686, gave land to John Wilkins; beq. to his 3 sisters Elizabeth Baile, Mary and Abigail Wilkins; to Bray Wilkins' 4 children; to Samuel's children; to Thomas, Henry and Benjamin Wilkins' children; to the ch. of leadday knickels (Lydia Nichols,) and Margaret knit (Knight;) to the chh. of Dorch.; to Mr. Loson, minister of Salem village. [Reg. XL, 256.]

GINKINS, see Jenkins.

GINNER, see Jenner.

GINTHAM,
James, Dedham, adm. chh. 19 (2) 1646.

GIRLING, GURLING,
Richard, mariner, Cambridge, propr. 1635.
His land was sold in 1637 for the benefit of his creditors; only 4 shillings rem. to the widow 4 (4) 1639. [Gen. Court Rec.]

GLADWELL,
Amos, ae. 16, came in the Increase, April 15, 1635.

GLASSE, GLASS,
Henry, apprentice to Giles Rickard of Plymouth, who brought suit at Salem against Henry Phelps for his appearance 23 (4) 1645.

James, servant to Henry Barnes of Barnstable, was transferred, 13 Feb. 1639, to Manasseh Kempton. Settled at Scituate; atba. 1643. Rem. to Duxbury. He m. 31 Oct. 1645, Mary, dau. of Wm. Pontus; ch. Hannah b. June 2, 1647, Wybra b. Aug. 9, 1649, Hannah b. 24 Dec. 1651.
He was drowned Sept. 3, 1652. Admin. gr. to his widow Mary; she m. 2, Philip Delanoy.

Amey, see Richard Willis.

Roger, servant to John Crocker of Scituate, 1639-40, transferred to John Whetcombe.

GLEASON,
Richard, Sudbury, propr. 1640.

GLOVER, GLOWER,
Charles, embarked for N. E. June 22, 1632. Settled at Salem. Propr., ship-carpenter, 1638; adm. chh. 10 (3) 1640. Constable for Gloucester 31 (10) 1644. [Es. Court.] Elizabeth adm. chh. 23 (3) 1641; ch. Eliza bapt. 13 (3) 1640, Mary bapt. 24 (2) 1642, Samuel b. June 20, 1644, wife Elizabeth d. 6 (1) 1647. He m. 12 (11) 1649, Esther Saunders, widow.

Henry, ae. 24, came in the Elizabeth of Ipswich, April 30, 1634. Settled at Dedham. Adm. townsman 2 (11) 1642. Rem. about 1652 to Medfield.

GLOVER, etc., cont.
Admin. gr. to his widow Abigail Sept. 13, 1655.

Mr. John, gent., son of Thomas G. of Rainhill, Lancaster, Eng., came to Dorchester. He and his wife Anne joined the chh. soon after the re-organization in 1636. He carried on extensive operations in farming and tanning. Town officer, deputy. He rem. to Boston about 1652. Conveyed English est. to son Thomas. [Suff. De. I, 333.] Was called tanner in bond of Fowle and Hill, 14 (8) 1647. [A.]
Will prob. Feb. 9, 1653. Sons Thomas, Nathaniel, Habbakuk, John and Pelatiah.

Rev. Jose or Josse, of London, who had been much interested in the settlement of Massachusetts, died on the way hither in 1638. Brought a printing press. See Day.
He made will at London, 16 May, 1638, about to sail beyond the seas; prob. 22 Dec. 1638. Est. to wife for life; then to ch. Roger, John, Elizabeth, Sarah, Priscilla; to servant John Steadman; to sister Collins. Land in parishes of Durand and Stone, co. Kent. [Mdx. Files.] [Reg. XXXVIII, 72.] The widow Elizabeth sold land at Cambridge 17 (7) 1639, and recd. money from the execs. [L.] She m. 2, Mr. Henry Dunster, pres. of Harv. Coll. [Reg. XXX, 27, 136.] Suit brought 28 (1) 1655, by John Appleton and Priscilla, his wife, dau. of Mr. G. [Mdx. Files.] [See Humphrey, John.] Dau. Elizabeth m. Adam Winthrop. [Mdx. Court Rec. I, 103.]

Mr. Ralph, appl. frm. Oct. 19, 1630. Admin. of his est. gr. by Gen. Court, July 2, 1633, to Mr. Mahewe.

Stephen, Gloucester, propr. 1649. He m. [?]7 (8) 1663, Ruth Stevens, who, with her infant, d. in Aug. 1664.
He d. 10 Sept. 1686.

GOAD, see Gott,
Abigail, Salem, adm. chh. 8 (7) 1640.

Thomas, ae. 15, came in the Abigail in July, 1635.

GOADBY,
John, ae. 16, came in the Hopewell in April, 1635.

GOBE, see Gove.

GOBLE, GOBEL,
Thomas, Charlestown, propr.; town officer; with wife Alice adm. chh. 30 (6) 1634; frm. Sept. 3, 1634. Owned land at Cambridge in 1651. Rem. to Concord. Ch. John deposed 20 (4) 1654, ae. about 25 years, and Thomas, ae. about 20, [Mdx. Files.] Mary bapt. 27 (12) 1635, Sarah bapt. 27 (3) 1638.
Will dated 30 (9) prob. 29 (10) 1657, beq. to wife Ales, and to his 3 sons and 3 daus.; eldest son now in England; son Thomas' 2 sons, Thomas and Stephen.

GODBERTSON, CUTHBERTSON,
Godbert, or Cuthbert, a Dutchman, who came over to Plymouth in 1623 from Leyden, Holland, in full communion with the English Pilgrims. [Wins.] Had lands assigned in 1623. Frm. 1633. Wife Sarah or Zarah, a sister of Isaac Allerton, and son Samuel came with him. The latter was appr. April 1, 1634, to Richard Higgins, tailor, for 7 years.
He d. in 1633, and she d. soon after. Inv. rend. Oct. 23, 1633. Admin. of both ests. gr. to Wm. Bradford 25 Nov. 1633. [Reg. IV, 34.] Lands were confirmed by the Court 3 Aug., 1640, to John Combe, gent., and Phinehas Pratt, which Godbertson formerly gave to them at marriage with his daus.

GODDEN,
William, servant of Comfort Starr, ot Duxbury, in court 3 Aug. 1640.

GODFREY,
Francis, carpenter, Duxbury, land grant, 1638, laid out 28 Oct., 1640, atba. 1643. Referred to in inv. of John Hill of Boston in 1646. Rem. to Marshfield. Rem. to Bridgewater.
Will made Oct. 29, 1666; calls himself "an aged inhabitant of the town;" prob. July 30, 1669; wife Elizabeth, dau. Elizabeth Carye, son-in-law John Carye, grandchildren John and Elizabeth; servants John Pitcher and Richard Ginnings, a minor. Goods at Providence and Bridgewater.

John, came in the Mary and John March 24, 1638. Res. at Newbury, servant to John Spencer, as he deposed March 28, 1647. [Ips. De. I, 38.] Rem. to Andover; husbandman; lawsuit in Es. Court (7) 1648. Accused of witchcraft March 1, 1659. Deposed in 1661, ae. about 50 years.

GODFREY, cont.

Joseph, gave bond to James Astwood Aug. 24, 1647, for money to be paid in England. [A.]

William, husbandman, Watertown, frm. May 13, 1640. As guardian to John, his sonne, and Sarah, his late wife, he made Mr. Antoine Lawrence of London, linen draper, at the Boar's Head in Gracious street, his attorney 22 (4) 1648, to ask of the execs. of the will of Mrs. Key of Wooborne in Bedfordshire a legacy of 10 li. beq. to John. [A.] Rem. to Hampton; bought land there 3 (7) 1648; sold Wat. land in 1653. Deacon. [Second] wife Margaret; ch. John, Isaac b. 15 (2) 1639, Sarah b. 15 (3) 1642.

He d. March 25, 1671. Will dated 2 (8) 1667, prob. 11 (2) 1671; beq. to wife Margerie, sons John and Isaac, son-in-law Webster, and daus. Sarah and Deborah. His widow m., Sept. 14, 1671, John Merrian, [Marion.]

GODSON,
Francis, Lynn, propr. 1638.

GOFFE, GOUGH,
Edward or Edmund, Cambridge, also propr. at Watertown; frm. May 25, 1636. Deputy, town officer, 1636. With wife Margaret sold land to Thomas Woolson, planter, of Camb. 23 (10) 1653. He m. 1, Joyce —; she d. Nov. 1639. He m. 2, Margaret; ch. Samuel bapt. in England; about 7 years old when his father joined chh. of Camb. [Mi.]; he deposed in 1655, ae. about 27 years. [Mdx. Files.] Lydia, Deborah b. 15 (10) 1639, Hannah b. 23 (1) 1643, Nathaniel b. 23 (6) 1645, Abia b. 1 (2) 1646, Mary bur. 23 (2) 1646.

He d. Dec. 26, 1658. Will dated 2 April, 1657, mentions wife Margaret; son Samuel and his mother-in-law, widow Barnard; daus. Lydia, Deborah, Anna and Abia; wife's mother Isabella Wilkinson; gr. ch. Anna Goffe and John, Lydia and Jonathan Sprague. The widow m. Dec., 1662, John Witchfield, of Windsor, Conn. She d. in Camb. in 1669; her will mentions sister Jane, wife of Edward Winship.

Eliza, ae. 26, came in the James in July, 1635.

John, Newbury, propr. 1638.

He d. Dec. 9, 1641. Will dated Dec. 4, 1641, entered on Ipswich record. Beq. to

GOFFE, etc., cont.

wife Amy and 2 ch. Susan and Hanna, under 18 years of age. Inv. taken Dec. 16, 1641.

Samuel, petitioned the Gen. Court 22 (3) 1639 ,that land might be assigned to himself and his father, Thomas Gough of London, merchant. [L.]

GOLDON,
—, his house in Boston was adjacent to Thomas Joy's in 1649.

GOLDSMITH,
John, apprentice of Philip Drinker in 1647.

Richard, Salem, in Court 5 (5) 1643. Had grant of land at Wenham 23 (4) 1644. Wife Mary adm. chh. 31 (3) 1648; ch. Mary bapt. 15 (8) 1648, Sarah bapt. 14 (5) 1650.

Thomas, Salem, propr. 1643; took George Harris, apprentice. Witness in court, 1645.

GOLDSTONE, GOULDSTON, GOULDSON,
Henry, ae. 43, with wife Anna, ae. 45, and daus. Anna, ae. 18, and Mary, ae. 15, came in the Elizabeth of Ipswich, April 30, 1634. Settled at Watertown; propr. 1636. Was excused by the Court from training Nov. 7, 1634, on account of his age. The dau. Anna m. Dea. Henry Bright; Mary m. Lieut. Joshua Hewes of Roxbury.

He was bur. 25 (5) 1638. The widow m. 2, John George; and after his death presented the inv. of the est. left by Mr. Goldstone, 29 (4) 1647.

GOLDTHWAIGHT, GOULDTHWAIGHT, GOLDTHWAIT, GAILDTHWAIGHT,
Thomas, cooper, Salem, carried a suit against Mr. Pelham June 14, 1631. Frm. May 14, 1634. Propr. 1636; town officer. Clerk of the market, 1656-7. First wife [Elizabeth;] second wife Rachel, dau. of Lawrence Leach, widow of John Sibley. Ch. Samuel bapt. 20 (6) 1637, Mehitabel bapt. 27 (2) 1640, Eliza bapt. 20 (9) 1642.

His will dated 5 March, prob. 3 April, 1683, beq. to wife Rachel, son Samuel and son-in-law John King; to Joseph Sibley.

GOLDWYER, GOLDWIRE,
George, Haverhill, 1648, Salisbury, planter, bought house in 1648; propr. 1649; juryman, town officer. He m. Martha, dau. of the wife of Joseph Moyse; she survived him and m. 2, Maj. Robert Pike; in deeds he refers to her father-in-law Joseph Moys, sister Martha Greeley, and cousin Ephraim Winsley, Jr.
He d. April 12, 1684.

GOLT, see Gault.

GOOCH, GOUCH, GOOGE, GOUGE, GUTCH,
Robert, Salem, propr. 1637; had land by his father Holgrave. Frm. Dec. 27, 1642. Mentioned with wife Lydia in 1648; witness to a deed in 1647. Ch. John bapt. 3 (8) 1641, Patience bapt. 28 (3) 1643, Lydia bapt. 6 (2) 1645, Magdalen bapt. 17 (11) 1646, Eliza bapt. 19 (9) 1648, Deborah bapt. 16 (2) 1652, Sarah bapt. 4 (4) 1654.
He may be the Mr. G. of Newbury, who was before Gen. Court 4 (4) 1639.

William, Lynn, propr. 1638.
Inv. of his est. taken 28 (8) 1645; admin. gr. to widow Ann for herself and 3 small ch. 30 (4) 1646.

Note.—John Gooch, who took oath of fidelity at Wells, July 4, 1653, beq. to his son James, 7 May, 1667, a house in Slymbridge, Eng. [Reg. XXXIX, 184.]

GOOD, GOODE,
Thomas, ae. 24, came in the Bevis in May, 1635.

Richard, memb. jury at Boston in 1646 on the Hingham case. [Mass. Hist. Coll. 2-4.]

GOODALE, GOODELL, GOODHALL,
Elizabeth, of Newbury, late of Yarmouth, Eng., d. 8 April, 1647; admin. of her est. gr. March 27, 1648, and re-affirmed by Gen. Court 31 May, 1652, to her sons-in-law Abraham Toppan and John Lowle. Her dau. Susanna m. Abraham Toppan, Elizabeth m. John Lowle, and Joanna m. 1, John Oliver, and 2, Wm. Gerrish. [See Lowell.]

Richard, planter, turner, Newbury, 1638. Salisbury, propr. 1639. Wife Dorothy d. Jan. 27, 1664. Ch. Ann, (m. William Allen;) Richard; Elizabeth m. John Smith. [Es. De. I, 39.]

GOODALE, etc., cont.
He d. in 1666; will dated June 7 and Sept. 8, prob. Oct. 9, 1666. Beq. to son Richard, of Boston, and dau. Ann, wife of Will. Allin, of Salis.; to gr. dau. Hubbard, and to Cornelius Conner, formerly his servant. "Brethren" Edward French, Philip Challis and Richard Wells overseers.

Robert, ae. 30, with wife Katharine, ae. 28, and ch. Abraham, ae. 2, and Isaac, ae. 6 mos., came in the Elizabeth of Ipswich. Settled at Salem; farmer, planter. propr. 1636. In court in 1645. A child "of sister Goodell" bapt. 31 (3) 1640, Jacob "of Robert" bapt. 2 (11) 1641, Hannah bapt. 6 (6) 1645. He deeded land in 1668 to his dau. Hannah Killum. [Es. Files.] With wife Margaret sold land adjoining.
Will dated 12 Oct. 1682, prob. 27 June, 1683; "aged;" beq. to wife, dau. Elizabeth Bennett, gr. ch. John Smith. Widow Margaret deposed.

GOODENOW, GOODNOW, GOODINOW,
Edmund, husbandman, ae. 27, from Dunhead, Wilts., Eng., with his wife Anne and sons John and Thomas under 4 yrs. of age, with servant Richard Sanger, ae. 18, came in the Confidence April 11, 1638. Settled at Sudbury, propr. 1639, frm. May 13, 1640. Town officer, deputy. Lieut. 1 (2) 1651. [Mdx. Files.] Ch. Hannah b. 28 (9) 1639, Sarah b. 17 (1) 1642, Joseph b. 19 (5) 1645.
Capt. Edmund d. April 5, 1688.

John, husbandman, ae. 42, with wife Jane and daus. Lydia and Jane came from Semley, Wilts., in the Confidence April 11, 1638. Settled at Sudbury; propr. 1639.
He d. 28 March 1654. Will dated 2 (1) prob. 5 (3) 1654. Wife Jane; dau. Jane Wight, son-in-law Andrew Dunning; Abigail, dau. of his bro. Thomas G.; son-in-law Henry Wight of Dedham. [Reg. XIX, 43.] The widow made will July 7, 1662, prob. Oct. 2, 1666; beq. to gr. ch. John, son of Henry Wait, and Jane his wife, living at Dedham, and to their other ch. Joseph, Daniel Benjamin and a child, name not known.

Thomas, ae. 30, with wife Jane, son Thomas, ae. 1 yr. and sister Ursula, came from Shasbury, Eng., in the Confidence April 11, 1638. He settled at Sudbury, propr. 1639; selectman, 1639, etc. Rem. to Marlborough. Ch. Mary b. 25 (6) 1640, Abigail b. 11

GOODENOW, etc., cont.
(1) 1642, Susanna b. 20 (11) 1643, Sarah d. 7 April 1654, Samuel b. 26 (12) 1645, Susanna b. 21 (10) 1647, Elizabeth d. 28 (10) 1653. The sister Ursula d. at S. 23 (2) 1653.

He d. in 1666. Will dated Sept. 29, prob. 24 (8) 1666, beq. to daus. Susanna and Jane, loveing yoak fellow Joane, son Samuel and all his gr. children; bros. John Rudduck, Edmund G. and old bro. Ward overseers.

GOODNER,
Edmund, Ipswich, one of the men app. by Gen. Court 27 Sept. 1642, to look after the breeding of saltpetre.

GOODHUE, GOODHEWE,
Nicholas, clothworker, ae. 60, with wife Jane, ae. 48, came in the James in July in 1635. As no further record of him appears it may be supposed that he d. soon and that Jane was the "widow" G. who was reproved for not coming to the meeting in 1647.

William, weaver, yeoman, merchant, Ipswich, propr. 1635, frm. Dec. 7, 1636. Deacon. Bought the commonage of John Newman 1 (2) 1649. Bought land of Nathl. Browne April 1, 1673. He deposed 6 Jan. 1679, ae. 67 years, in favor of the formation of second (Chebacco) church. [Arch. Eccl. 1.] Wife Mary made will acc. to marriage contract 8 June, 1682, bequeathing her est. to Benjamin and Mary, 2 of the ch. of her son John Fayerweather of Boston. Made deed of gift to son William with consent of his now wife Bethia, May 1, 1686.

GOODMAN,
John, came in the Mayflower, signed the Compact, res. at Plymouth, d. soon after arrival, probaly from exposure when lost in Jan. 1620-1. [Mou.]

Richard, Cambridge, propr. 1633; frm. May 14, 1634; brought suit in Plymouth Court 4 March, 1638-9. Rem. to Hartford. Either he or a son of the same name m. at H. 8 Dec. 1659, Mary Terry and rem. to Hadley. Admin. of his est. gr. at Northampton court Sept. 26, 1676, to widow Mary and to her cousin Ensign Cooke. Her account specifies land at Hadley given to her husband by her father Stephen Terry; sons John, Richard, Thomas; daus. Mary and Elizabeth.

Thomas, a creditor of Thomas Watson of Duxbury in 1639. [L.]

GOODRICH, GOODRIDGE, GUTRICE, GUTRIG, GUTTERIDGE,
John, tailor, Watertown, propr. 1636; rem. to Boston. Adm. chh. 29 (11) 1641; frm. May 18, 1642. Wife Prudence adm. chh. 10 (4) 1643; ch. Joseph b. 1 (8) 1642.

William, Watertown, propr. 1636. Wife Margaret; ch. Jeremy b. 6 (1) 1637, Joseph b. 29 (7) 1639, apprenticed 8 May, 1645, by widow Margaret to Samuel Thatcher. [Mdx. De. I, 188.], Benjamin b. 11 (2) 1642.

He d. and inv. of his est. was taken April 3, 1647. [Reg. VIII, 57.] The widow m. John Hull of Newbury; she d. Feb. 3, 1682. Will dated Aug. 4, prob. 10 April, 1683, beq. to sons Jeremiah, Joseph and Benjamin; gr. son Benjamin G.; to dau. Mary Woodman; gr. ch. Mary Emry and Elizabeth Woodman.

GOODSPEED,
Roger, Barnstable, 1641; atba. 1643; adm. chh. July 28, 1644. Juror.

He m. Dec. 1641, Alice Layton; she was adm. chh. Dec. 31, 1643. Ch. Nathaniel b. Oct. 6, 1642, (d. before 3 May, 1670, when his est. was settled,) John b. June 15, 1645, Mary b. July, 1647, Benjamin b. May 6, 1650, (d. and beq. his est. in 1677,) Ruth b. April 10, 1652, Ebenezer b. Dec., 1655, Elizabeth b. May, 1658.

The widow Alice made will 10 Jan. 1688, prob. 4 Sept. 1689; beq. to ch. John, Ebenezer, Ruth (Davis,) and Elizabeth; dau.-in-law Lydia and gr. ch. Benjan. in.

GOODWIN, GOODIN, GOODING, GOODWYN,
Anne, ae. 18, servant of Abraham Toppan, came from Yarmouth, Eng., May 10, 1637, to Newbury.

Edward, lighterman, laborer, Boston, 1640; adm. chh. 26 (1) 1642; frm. May 18, 1642. Land transfers in 1644, 1668, etc. Wife Elizabeth; ch. Elizabeth b. Nov. 5, 1676, (m. May 11, 1693, Samuel Gardner,) Edward b. April 9, 1678.

Edward, of Boston, boatman, made will 5 Dec. 1693, being aged; prob. 3 Jan. 1694-5; beq. to wife Elizabeth and dau. Elizabeth, wife of Samuel Gardner. Bro. John Cleasby and Samuel Jackson overseers.

Susanna, Salem, memb. chh. 1637.

Mr. William, embarked June 22, 1632; came to Cambridge. Propr. 1633; frm. Nov.

GOODWIN, etc., cont.
6, 1632. Elder of the church. His dau. mentioned by Winthrop, vol. I, 142. He rem. to Conn.

GOOKIN, GOOKINS, GOOGAN,
Maj. Daniel, a Kentish soldier, migrated to Virginia with his father, Mr. Daniel G.; was attracted to New England by the influence of Rev. William Tompson and the others who visited Va. in 1643. He came to Boston the next year; was adm. chh. May 26, and made frm. May 29. Resided first at Roxbury; rem. to Cambridge in 1648. Was deputy, speaker of the Gen. Court, Asst., and com. on many important matters. A great patron of the work of Rev. John Eliot for the Indians, and a warm friend of theirs, though a sturdy soldier in the inevitable wars. Wrote several works of value. Wife Mary adm. Bo. chh. 7 (7) 1644; she deposed to the will of Mr. John Willett in 1663. ae. about 45 years. She d., and he m. 2, Hannah —, who d. Oct. 29, 1688, ae. 48 years. [Gr st.] Ch. Mary and Elizabeth, "bapt. elesewhere, not full 6 years old when their parents joined this church," [Mi.] Elizabeth bapt. at Rox. March 14, 1644, Hannah b. and d. 1647, Daniel bur. 3 (7) 1649, Daniel b. 12 (5) 1650. Other ch. named in will.
He d. March 19, 1686-7. His striking will, filed at Boston, beq. to wife Hannah the est. which was hers before marriage; to ch. Daniel, Samuel, Nathaniel; to Elizabeth Batter; to John Eliot, her son by her first marriage, and to her other ch.; to wife's son Thomas and daus. Hannah Gookin and Mary Savage. The dau. Mary m. Edmund Batter; [did she d. and he m. afterward her sister Elizabeth?]

GOORDLEY,
John, Boston, servant to Richard Tuttle, d. (10) 1638.

GOOSE, [see also Negoose,]
William, Boston, trustee for John Wallington of London, turner, to receive money 1 (8) 1645. Goody Goose adm. chh. Boston 24 (2) 1659. Ch. John bapt. at Salem 14 (2) 1644. In Salem Court 29 (4) 1664, the inv. of the est. of Mary, widow of Wm. G. was pres.: he had d. many yrs. before, intestate; the widow was distracted, and the town had borne the expense.

GORDON,
Edmond, ae. 18, came in the Susan and Ellen in April, 1635.

GORE, GOARE, GOARD,
Mr. John, Roxbury, frm. April 18, 1637. He sent letter of attorney 23 (10) 1644, to Joseph Browne of Southampton, malster, to prove the will of his father and to execute it for him. [A.] He bought land at Salisbury, the deed of which was made to his widow Rodah 20 Aug., 1658. Wife Rose, (Rhoda,) deposed May 19, 1655, ae. 45; [Suff. De. II.] Ch. John "b. in England, May 23, 1634," Obediah b. June 27, 1636, d. May 12, 1646, Abigail [Hanna] b. Aug. 5, 1641, d. April 13, 1642, Abigail bapt. May 7, 1643, Hannah bapt. 18 (3) 1645, Obediah bapt. 25 (1) 1648. The son John seems to be the master of the Mayflower, who deposed at Boston 25 (9) 1665, ae. 31 years.

He d. 4 June, 1657. Will prob. July 30, 1657; wife Rosa; 5 ch.: John, Samuel, Abigail and Hannah Gore, and Mary Mylame [?] The widow m. 2, John Remington; conveyed lands March 22, 1662; she m. 3, Edward Porter. [Reg. VIII, 382, XXXI, 104 and 177.]

Richard, ae. 17, came in the Elizabeth and Ann in April, 1635. Settled at Roxbury; frm. May 29, 1644. He m. Nov. 30, 1639, Phebe Hewes. Ch. Hannah b. June 1641, John and Hannah bapt. 1 (5) 1643, Mary b. June 23, 1644, Phebe b. March 12, 1645-6, Joseph b. Sept. 21, 1647, Sarah bapt. March 25, 1649, Joseph b. April 8, 1651, Lydia b. Feb. 20, 1652, Benjamin b. and d. 1654.

He d. 29 Sept. 1683.

GORHAM, GOARUM, GORUM, GOROME, GROOM, GROOME,
John, Plymouth, Duxbury. Frm. 4 June 1650. Had land gr. in Plym. 18 Dec. 1638; was partner with John Rogers at Duxbury in 1638-9. [L.] Built a bridge over South river with Joseph Beadle in 1650-1. He deposed 4 (1) 1674-5, ae. about 53 yrs. Was captain of a company for defence against the Indians 4 Oct. 1675. He m. Desire, dau. of John Howland. Ch. Desire b. at Plym. April 2, 1644, (m. at Bar. 7 Oct. 1661, John Hawes,) Temperance b. at Marshfield May 5, 1646, Elizabeth b. 2 April, 1648, James b. 28 April 1650, John b. 20 Feb. 1651, Joseph b. at Yarmouth 16 Feb. 1653, Jabez b. 3 Aug. 1656, Mercy b. 20 Jan. 1658, Lydia b. 11 Nov. 1661.

GORHAM, etc., cont.

He d. at Swansey 5 Feb. 1675. Admin. gr. to widow and sons James and John, March 1675-6; rights of younger ch. to be guarded. Division made to the widow Desire and ch. James, John, Jabez, Mercye, Lydia, Hannah and Shubael; £50 laid aside for the education of S. Admin. bond signed 9 March, 1675. [Plym. Scrap Book.] The widow d., and inv. of her est. was taken 3 Aug. 1683. [Genealogy.]

Ralph, Plymouth, had land gr. 2 Oct. 1637. In Court 4 June, 1639. He rem. to Swansey.

GORNELL, see Gurnell and Cornell.

GORNET, see Gurney.

GORTON,

John, Roxbury, 1636; frm. May 19, 1639. Wife Mary adm. chh. about 1640; ch. Mary d. Aug. 1636, Mary b. June 21, 1641, Sarah bapt. 21 (11) 1643, Hannah bapt. 5 (1) 1646, a dau. d. (9) 1646, Mary bapt. 7 (3) 1648, Alice bapt. March 8, 1651-2, Elizabeth b. and d. 1654, John bapt. 24 (12) 1655, drowned 15 (4) 1668, Abraham bapt. 8 (3) 1659.

Will dated 17 June, prob. Oct. 19, 1676, beq. to wife Alice, son Abraham, daus. Sarah, Mary and "cales" [Alice.]

Samuel, of London, clothier, came to Boston before 1636; res. in Plymouth in 1637; volunteered for the Pequot War. Put himself in conflict with the authorities of both colonies and caused and suffered much trouble. Was banished to R. I. in 1638. Went to Eng. in 1646, and obtained satisfactory documents from Parliament which protected him from further interference. [B., W., and Col. Recs.] Wife —; ch. Samuel, John, Benjamin, Maher, Sarah, Anna, Elizabeth, Susanna.

Thomas, Plymouth Colony, volunteer for the Pequot War in 1637.

GOSSE, GOFFE,

John, Watertown, propr.; frm. May 18, 1631. Wife Sarah; ch. Joseph bur. 10 (3) 1631, Elizabeth bur. 25 (10) 1641, Phebe, not recorded, sole surviving child.

He was bur. Feb. 15, 1643-4. Inv. 14 (3) 1644. The widow m. 2, Robert Nichols, who joned with her in a deed 14 (10) 1644. They rem. to Southampton, L. I.

GOSNALL,

Henry, Boston, memb. chh. 1630, with wife Mary.

GOTT,

Mr. Charles, Salem, deacon; deputy, 1634-5; propr. 1636. He wrote to Gov. Bradford July 30, 1629, an account of the ordination of Messrs. Skelton and Higginson. [B.]

Rem. to Wenham about 1651. Com. to end small causes in 1654. He and his wife and son Charles were dism. from Salem chh. to that of Wen. Dec. 10, 1663. Sarah, [dau. of Charles?] was adopted by Capt. Thomas Lathrop after the death of her mother, his wife's "cousin." Ch. Deborah bapt. 12 (12) 1636, Charles bapt. 2 (4) 1639, Daniel bapt. 28 (4) 1646.

He d. 15 (11) 1667. The widow deposed in 1667, ae. about 66 years.

GOULBE,

Thomas, glover, petitioned the Gen. Court in 1645.

GOULD, GOOLD, GOLD,

Edward, ae. 22, came in the Elizabeth April 9, 1635. Settled at Hingham; pail-maker. Had land grant at Boston in 1657. Wife Margaret; ch. Hannah b. March 12, 1643, (m. Samuel Hobart,) Sarah b. in 1648, Sarah bapt. Nov. 29, 1658, (m. Nov. 29, 1675, Arthur Cain.) The wife d. 6 Feb. 1682.

He d. 16 Feb. 1684-5.

Francis, Boston, a watchman, before the Court 3 (7) 1639.

Francis, Duxbury, atba. 1643.

Francis, Braintree; wife Rose; ch. Martha b. 18 (12) 1649, Mary b. 23 (10) 1651, Martha b. 15 (8) 1654, John b. 2 (6) 1657, Samuel b. 12 (6) 1658.

Goodman, Reading, propr. 1650.

Jarvis, shoemaker, ae. 30, came in the Elizabeth in April, 1635. Settled at Hingham; propr. 1636. Rem. to Boston. Wife Mary memb. chh. of Hing.; ch. John bapt. at Bo. 30 (6) 1646, ae. about 33 days, Joseph bapt. 25 (1) 1649-50.

He d. 27 (3) 1656; admin. gr. 4 July folg.

Jeremiah, Weymouth, propr. before 1644; rem. to Rhode Island. Attorney for Wm. Coddington in 1640, and for Henry Sandis in 1646. [Suff. De. and A.]

GOULD, etc., cont.

John, husbandman, ae. 25, with wife Grace, ae. 25, cert. from Towcester, co. Northampton, Eng., came in the Defense in July, 1635. He may be the

John, carpenter, Charlestown, frm. May 2, 1638. Wife Mary adm. chh 8 (11) 1636; she d. at Ten Hills Farm, Char. 14 (3) 1647. [W.] With wife Joane he sold land at Malden in 1658. He deposed in 1658, ae. about 47 years. Ch. John b. 1646, d. 1647, John b. 14 (3) 1647.

He d. March 21, 1690-1. Will dated 3 Jan. 1688, prob. 19 June, 1691, beq. to sons John and Daniel Gould and John Birbin; to gr. son Thomas G.

Nathan, in New England, legatee of his mother, Judith, of Watford, Eng., widow, by her will prob. 3 Sept. 1650; had rec'd. beq. from his bro. Zaccheus G. [Reg. XLIX, 267.] He was propr. at Salisbury, 1652. Wife Elizabeth; ch. Mary b. June 24, 1661, Elizabeth b. April 4, 1664, Samuel b. Feb. 3, 1667-8, Joseph b. Aug. 28, 1670, Hannah b. May 13, 1675.

He made will Dec. 12, 1692, prob. Sept. 27, 1693; wife Elizabeth.

Thomas, Charlestown, adm. chh. with wife Hannah 7 (4) 1640. He deposed 6 (2) 1652, ae. about 45 years. [Mdx. Files.] Seth Sweetser calls him brother. Ch. Hannah bapt. 11 (2) 1641, Jacob b. (rec. at Cambridge,) Sept. 16, 1643. He was opposed to the baptism of infants, and came under the discipline of the church in consequence; was expelled, and became the leader in the formation of the Anti-pedo-baptist (since called Baptist) church of Boston about 1665.

His will prob. 30 April, 1674, beq. to wife Mary, son Samuel, daus. Mary Skinner, Mehetable —, Mary Bunker, Abigail Shapley and Hannah Gold; son Nathaniel Hayward and his 2 children; gr. ch. Mary Skinner, Thomas G., the 2 ch. of Mary Bunker and the 2 ch. of Abigail Shapley.

Zaccheus, husbandman, Lynn, headed a petition that husbandmen be excused from training in seedtime and harvest; dated 7 (8) 1640. [L.] Rem. to Ipswich; sold land at Weymouth which had belonged to Jeremy Gould 26 (9) 1644. Rem. to Topsfield. He deposed in 1661, ae. about 72 years. His wife Phebe d. 20 (9) 1663. Ch. [Phebe, (m. Thomas

GOULD, etc., cont.

Perkins,) Mary, (m. John Reddington,) Martha, (m. John Newmarch.) [So stated by the Genealogy of the Family.]

GOULDER, GOOLE,

Francis, Plymouth, propr. 1638, atba. 1643; frm. 4 June, 1650. Wife Katharine d. 16 March, 1650.

He d. May 17, 1664.

GOULWORTH,

John, punished for felony 28 Sept. 1630.

GOVE, GOBE, GOFFE,

John, Charlestown; frm. May 22, 1638. Adm. chh. Char 3 (3) 1647. Bought house and land 29 Sept. 1647.

Will 22 (11) 1647. Wife, sons John and Edward; dau. Mary to be adopted, with his wife's full consent by Ralph Mousall and his wife, to whom he gives a silver porringer and 5 li. Legacies to be paid out of the brass in the house or that which is to come out of Eng. by Mr. James Allen. Edward deposed in 1667, ae. about 28 years. [Norf. files.] [Reg. VII, 170.] The widow m. 2, John Mansfield, who joined her in paying the sons their portions 5 Dec. 1655. [Char. Rec.]

Obediah, before Gen. Court 1 Oct., 1645, and Essex in 1646.

GOYT, GOYTE, GOIT, see Coit,

John, Dorchester propr. 1632; land gr. to others in 1634, if he come not over the next summer. John, perhaps the same, Salem, Marblehead, 1640. [Es. Court rec.] Mary adm. chh. 18 (4) 1643. Ch. Joseph and Mary bapt. 30 (5) 1643, Mary bapt. 17 (1) 1643-4.

Admin. Ess. Court, (1) 1663.

GOWING, GOWEN,

Robert, Dedham, a man servant, adm. chh. (5) 1639; propr. Dec. 23, 1640. Rem. to Wenham before 1651. He m. 31 (8) 1644, Elizabeth Brock; ch. John b. 13 (9) 1645, Elizabeth bapt. (2) 1647, Hannah bapt 21 (12) 1648-9.

Robert, Wenham, petitioned the Gen. Court 23 May, 1650.

GRAFTON,

Joseph, mariner, Salem, 1636. Master of the bark Endeavor in 1641. [L.] Made a successful voyage to Pemaquid and Boston in 1639. [W.] Goodwife Grafton desired of the town a lot for her mother at the end of her husband's lot in 1637. [See Scarlet.] Ch. Joseph bapt 24 (11) 1636, John bapt. 28 (2) 1639, Nathaniel bapt. 24 (2) 1642.

Two imperfect wills were set aside, and distribution made by consent of heirs as follows: to Bethia Goodhue, John Grafton, John Gardner (for his ch. by wife Priscilla,) the two sons of Joseph, Jr., dec.; the three daus. of Nathaniel; to Mary Meade, William and Edmund Herfield, Robert Kitchin and his three sisters, Mary Fox, Elizabeth Colyer and Samuel Gardner, Jr.

Joshua, Salem, 1649.

GRAME, GRAMES, GREAMES, GRIMES,

Samuel, pewterer, Boston 1638; accounts with him in 1640. [L.] Bondsman for John Hogg in Gen. Court 28 (11) 1640, adm. chh. 26 (1) 1642; frm. May 18, 1642. Lot gr. him at Braintree in 1639. Wife Frances; ch. Mary b. 27 (2) 1639, bapt. 27 (1) 1642, ae. about 3 yrs.

Thomas, Charlestown. Wife Katharine; ch. Susan b. 8 (5) 1643.

GRANGER, GRAUNGER, GRANGE,

Bryan, Salem, propr. 1637.

Launcelot, Ipswich, res. 1648; rem. to Newbury. Leased farm of Stephen Kent. [Es. files 3, 98.] He m. 4 Jan. 1653-4, Joanna, dau. of Robert Adams; ch. John b. 15 Jan. 1655, George b. 28 Nov. 1658, Elizabeth b. 13 March, 1662, Dorothy b. 15 Feb. 1663, a dau. b. May 15, 1666, Samuel b. Aug. 2, 1668, Abraham b. 17 April, 1673.

Thomas, Scituate. His son Thomas was executed in 1642. [W. and Plym. Col. Rec.]

He d., and admin, was gr. 3 Jan. 1642-3, to Timothy Hatherly and Edmund Eddenden on behalf of his wife and children and to pay debts. Widow Grace d. in 1648; will dated Nov. 24, 1648; son John, under age; dau. Elizabeth. Witnessed by Timo. Hatherly. [Reg. IV, 283.]

GRANT, GRAUNT,

Christopher, glazier, Watertown, propr. 1634. Deposed 6 (2) 1658, ae. 48 years. [Mdx. Files.] Wife Mary; ch. Abigail b. 6 (12) 1634, Joshua b. 11 (4) 1637, Caleb b. 8 (7) 1639, Benjamin b. 6 (7) 1641, Sarah b. 1 (12) 1642-3, Joseph b. 28 (7) 1646, Mary, Mercy, Christopher b. 1649.

He d. Sept. 6, 1685; admin. to sons Christopher, Caleb and Joseph; the daus. Sarah Seaverns and Mary Smith deposed, after the death of their mother, Jan. 19, 1691-2.

Matthew, b. in England, Oct. 27, 1601, came to Dorchester, probably one of the original church-colony that came in the Mary and John in 1629-30; frm. May 18, 1631. He rem. to Windsor, Conn., in 1635-6; was clerk of the chh. there. Ancestor of President Ulysses S. Grant. He m. 1, Priscilla—, Nov. 16, 1625; she d. April 27, 1644, ae. 43 yrs. 2 mos.; he m. 2, May 29, 1645, Susanna, dau. of Bernard Capen, and widow of William Rockwell, who was b. April 5, 1602; she d. Nov. 14, 1664. Ch. Priscilla b. Sept. 14, 1626, Samuel b. Nov. 12, 1631, Tahan b. Feb. 3, 1633, John b. April 30, 1642. [From his own rec.. See Stiles' Windsor.]

He d. 16 Dec. 1681.

Seth or Zeth, embarked June 22, 1632. Settled at Cambridge; propr. 1634.

Thomas, came from England in same ship with Samuel, son of Wm. Stickney, i. e. before 1638, as S S. deposed at Salem Prob. Court 20 July, 1698. Jane, widow, Rowley, propr. 1643. Ch. John, Hannah, (m. — Brown,) Frances, (m. — Keyes,) Ann, (m. 11 (4) 1658, Robert Emerson).

GRAUSE,

William, Yarmouth, atba. 1643.

GRAVES, GRAVE,

John, cow-leech, householder, [See Es. Inst. Coll. XXXI.] Roxbury, a goodly bro. of the chh., arrived (3) 1633; he brought 5 ch.: John, Samuel, Jonathan, Sarah and Mary; his wife quickly d. and he m. Dec., 1635, Judith [Alward.] [E.] He arranged Nov. 23, 1638, for collection of rents upon his dau. Sarah's legacy from Thomas Finch of Hertford, Eng., from his sister Lydia Ford of Nasing, Eng., [L.] See will of Anne G., widow, of St. Botolph without Algate, dated 10 Feb.

GRAVES, etc., cont.
1675. [Reg. L., 423.] Ch. Hannah b. in Rox. Sept. 8, 1636.

He d. 4 (9) 1644. Will, dated Nov. 1, 1644. Beq. to ch. John, Samuel, Jonathan, Hanna and Mary; the latter to have the bed her grandmother now lieth upon; if wife live 5 yrs. after the death of my mother, she shall pay 6 li. to my dau. Hannah. "Old mother Graves, of fourscore yeares," was bur. Feb. 24, 1644-5. The son John d. in 1645, and beq. 26 (9) 1645, to bros. Samuel and Jonathan; sisters Sara, Hanna and Mary, and his mother.

Richard, husbandman, ae. 33, came in the Abigail in July, 1635. Settled at Salem, propr. 1637; fisherman. His wife adm. chh. 23 (6) 1640; 3 children bapt. 14 (1) 1640-1, Joseph bapt. 16 (8) 1642, Benjamin and Elizabeth bapt. 6 (6) 1645, Mary bapt. 26 (2) 1648, Richard bapt. 6 (8) 1650, Hannah bapt 15 (6) 1652, Deliverance bapt. 16 (5) 1654, Joan, ae. 30, and Mary, ae. 26, who came in the Hopewell in Sept., 1635, may have been his wife and dau.; the ages of passengers being very carelessly recorded.

Samuel, Plymouth, sold house July 4, 1636.

Samuel, hatter, Ipswich, propr. 1635, (goodman,) bought house and land 1 Dec. 1654, rented land, 1660.

Mr. Thomas, gent., of Gravesend, co. Kent, an expert in mines, minerals, fortifications and surveys, made a written agreement with the Mass. Bay Co. in Eng., March 5, 1628, for transportation of himself, his wife, 5 children, a boy and a maid servant; was app. a memb. of Gov. Endecott's Council, and came with him to Salem. Rem. to Charlestown; laid out the town before the coming of Winthrop. Frm. May 18, 1631. One of the com. to lay out the town of Woburn in 1640, and one of the first town officers there.

Mr. Thomas, sea-captain, b. June 6, 1605 at Ratcliffe, near London, res. at Charlestown in 1638. Adm. chh. with wife 7 (8) 1639. Made report concerning stormy weather in the Downs 12 (4) 1644. Had charge of ship Tryall 3 (10) 1645. [A.] Rearadmiral.

He m. Katharine Gray; she d. 21 (12) 1681, ae. above 76. Ch. Rebecca adm. chh. 9 (5)

GRAVES, etc., cont.
1648, John, Thomas adm. chh. 17 (7) 1665, Susanna adm. chh. 17 (2) 1664, Nathaniel bapt. 5 (9) 1639, Joseph b. 13 (2) 1645.

He d. 31 (5) 1653. His will dated 13 June, 1652, was prob. 1 (10) 1653; he had left it in the care of his bro. Abram G.; was presented to the Court by the widow. Beq. to wife Katharine; ch. Rebecca, John, Thomas, Nathaniel, Susanna and Joseph. His inv. shows 1-5th part of a house at Ham, near London, in England; a share in the ship called Trades-Increase, etc.

"Mr. Thomas Graves, a member of Dorchester, and a very understanding man, would needs leave the church, and go to Virginia against all counsel, etc. He and his wife and divers of his children died, and his whole family was ruined about a year after. Only one daughter escaped, who, being left a maid with a good estate, married after to that apostate, Nathaniel Eaton, who, having spent all she had, fled away, and left her miserable, 1646." [W.]

William, ae. 12, came with John Upham, husbandman, from Weymouth, Eng., before March 20, 1635. Perhaps the person who res. at Dover in 1659.

GRAY, GREY,
Edward, yeoman, Plymouth, 1646, propr. 1650. Became very wealthy and was an active and useful citizen. He m. 1 Jan. 16, 1650-1, Mary Winslow; m. 2, Dec. 12, 1667, Dorothy, dau. of Thomas Lettice. Ch. Desire b. 6 Nov. 1651, (m. 10 Jan. 1671, Nathaniel Southworth,) Mary b. 18, Sept. 1653, Elizabeth b. 11 Feb. 165[5], Sarah b. 12 Aug. 1659, John b. 1 Oct. 1661, Edward b. 31 Jan. 1666, Susanna b. 15 Oct., 1668, (m. John Cole.) Other ch. mentioned in probate rec.: Hannah, Thomas, Rebecca, Lydia and Samuel.

27 Oct. 1680, "Edward Gray, yeoman," sold his one-thirtieth share in Taunton lands; his widow Dorothy and son John receipted for the purchase-money 12 Oct. 1682. [Plym. Scrap Book.] He d. 30 June, 1681. [Gr. St.] One third of his corn was given to his children by first wife, the rest to the widow and the children he had by her. Her account was allowed 5 March, 1684-5. [Plym. Col. Rec. vol. VI, 149.] The widow m. 2, Nath-

GRAY, etc., cont.

aniel Clarke, and sought divorce from him June 2, 1686. [Col. Rec. VI.]

Henry, tailor, citizen and merchant of London, came to Boston; propr. 1637. Arranged for marriage in 1639. [L.]

Katharine, before Gen. Court Aug. 5, 1634.

John, planter, of Boston, N. E. with his wife Elizabeth sold a house and lot in Lynn 1 (6) 1639. [L.] "My bro. John Grey of New England" had beq. in will of William G., of London, citizen and merchant tailor, dated 1 Sept. 1657. [Reg. XLII, 72.] Mr. John, Yarmouth, before Gen. Court March 1, 1641, and 3 March, 1645-6. Lands granted about 1642; atba. 1643. Ch. Benjamin b. Dec. 1648, William b. Oct. 5, 1650.

Inv. of his est. taken 10 Feb. 1674; widow Hannah.

Robert, Salem, had liberty to come and dwell in Ipswich in 1646; but he did not remove. Wife Elizabeth, adm. chh. 16 (4) 1650. Ch. Eliza. bapt. 9 (1) 1650-1, Joseph, bapt. 9 (3) 1652, Bethiah bapt. 11 (4) 1654, Thomas bapt. 11 (3) 1656, Robert bapt. 23 (3) 1658, Hannah bapt. 26 (4) 1659.

Thomas, Plymouth, servant of Mr. John Atwood, transferred 16 May, 1639, to Job Cole, who had paid his passage.
He d. Nov. 29, 1652. [Plym. Col. Rec.]

Thomas, fisherman, Salem, Marblehead. Before Gen. Court Sept. 28, 1630, and 1638; before Es. Court in 1642.

Widow, Salem, 1637.

GRAYGOOSE,

Nathaniel, Boston, "a singleman," adm. chh. 2 (6) 1640.

GREELEY,

Andrew, blacksmith, Salisbury, propr. 1643; constable. Rem. to Haverhill; one of the owners of a mill in 1665. He deposed 9 (2) 1672, ae. about 52 years. Wife Mary; ch. Phillip b. Sept. 21, 1644, Andrew b. Dec. 10, 1646, Mary b. July 16, 1649,(m. Ephraim Winsley,) Joseph b. Feb. 5, 1651, Benjamin b. Dec. 9, 1654, Westwood b. March 29, 1659.

He d. June 30, 1697; admin. gr. to son Philip May 20, 1703. Widow Mary d. Dec. 24, 1703. [See Goldwyer.]

GREEN, GREENE,

Bartholomew, Cambridge, propr. 1634; frm. May 14, 1634. Wife Elizabeth; ch. [Samuel,] Nathaniel, [Sarah.]

He d. before 1642. His widow Elizabeth d. Oct. 28. 1677, ae. 88, "after a widowhood of about 40 years." Will dated 8 (4) 1672, prob. Nov. 20, 1677, beq. to son Nathaniel her whole est. for his long care of her.

Rev. Henry, scholar, minister, Ipswich, frm. May 13, 1642; was paid in 1643 for service against the Indians. Was invited to be minister at Martin's Vineyard in 1643, but went not. Was ordained pastor at Reading 5 (9) 1645. [W.] Mrs. G. memb. chh. Read. He d. in May, 1648.

Henry, propr. Watertown, 1642. He deposed in 1652, ae. about 30 years. [Arch. 38 B.] Perhaps he is the Henry, millwright, who res. at Hampton in 1652, and sold land there.

James, Charlestown, adm. chh. 7 (12) 1646, frm. May 26, 1647. Rem. to Malden.
He d. March 29, 1687. Will dated 2 Sept. 1682, prob. 5 May, 1687, beq. to wife Elizabeth and sons John and James.

John, with wife Perseverance, ch. John, Jacob, Abigail, Joseph, and maid, Sarah Johns, embarked for New England April 12, 1632. Settled at Charlestown. Adm. chh. with wife 29 (1) 1633; frm. May 18, 1642. Ruling elder, town clerk. Signed inv. of Abram Hawkins in 1647. Mary bapt. (2) 1634. Jacob deposed in 1657, ae. 36.
He d. April 22, 1658, ae. 65; will dated 21 (2) prob. 15 (4) 1658, beq. to wife Joane; ch. John, Jacob and Mary. Refers to wife's est. before marriage with him.

John, ae. 27, with Dorcas, ae. 15, came in the Francis of Ipswich April 30, 1635.

John, surgeon, came in the James April 5, 1635.

John, Sandwich, atba. 1643.

He was bur. April 4, 1660; will dated 28 Feb. 1659, prob. June 7, 1660, beq. to his sister and her children; James Skiffe, Sen., exec. and residuary legatee.

John, Roxbury, d. at Daniel Brewer's house; the Court appointed D. B. adminr. 4 (10) 1638, debts paid to several persons; he had worked at Castle Island.

GREEN, etc., cont.

Joseph, Plymouth, arbitration of certain business 2 Nov. 1640; atba. 1643.

Percival, husbandman, ae. 32, with wife Ellen, ae. 32, came in the Susan and Ellen in April, 1635. Settled at Cambridge; frm. March 3, 1635-6. Mrs. G. told in the chh. that she was born of godly parents; father suffered imprisonment, and was taken away while she was young. [Rel.] Ch. John b. (4) 1636, Elizabeth b. (2) 1639.
He d. 25 (10) 1639. The widow m. 2, Thomas Fox who arranged for the est. of Mr. G. to pass to her and her children, 24 (3) 1650.

Ralph, Boston, child John b. 22 (10) 1642. Ralph, Malden, ch. —, b. Jan. 1653.

Rebecca, Malden, widow; the inv. of the est. filed 4 (1) 1674-5 by Thomas Newell on behalf of his wife and the other children.

Samuel, Cambridge, propr. 1634, frm. March 3, 1635-6. Doorkeeper of the Gen. Court in 1644. Wife Jane; ch. Elizabeth b. 16 (2) 1640, Sarah b. 7 (8) 1642, Lydia b. 23 (1) 1644-5, Lydia b. 13 (2) 1646, Samuel b. 6 (1) 1647, Joseph b. 7 (9) 1649.

Solomon, apprenticed to John Crabtree, joiner, for 7 years, and to remain 1 year as a journeyman, 12 (6) 1639. Agreement made by Elizabeth Leger, widow of John Greene of Hadley in Suffolk, Eng., clothier. His sister Mary G. was placed at the same time with William Hudson, fisherman. [L.] See Leager, Jacob.

Thomas, ae. 15, cert. from St. Albons, Herts., Eng., came in the Planter, April 2, 1635. Same name and age given in the Hopewell later in the same month. Probably the same person, and he the son of the folg.

Thomas, Sen., Malden, lived at Lady Moody's farm at Lynn about 1646; depos. 16 (6) 1662, ae. about 62 years. [Mdx. Files.] His wife Elizabeth d. (6) 1658, and he m. 5 (7) 1659, Frances, widow of Richard Cooke. Ch. rec: at Mal.: Dorcas b. May 1, 1653, John b. Jan. 26, 1658.
He d. Dec. 19, 1667. Will dated 12 Nov., prob. 15 Jan. 1667, beq. to eldest son Thomas; to sons John, William, Henry and Samuel; daus. Elizabeth, Mary, Hannah, Martha and Dorcas, and to his wife.

William, Charlestown, adm. chh. 8 (5) 1643, frm. May 29, 1644. Rem. to Woburn,

GREEN, etc., cont.

propr. 1640. He m. Johannah, dau. of Mr. Thomas Carter, sister of Mrs. John Tuttle of Ipswich; she deposed in 1659, ae. 59 years. [Es. Files.] Ch. Mary b. 20 (11) 1644, Hannah b. Feb. 7, 1646, John b. Oct. 11, 1649.
He d. 7 (1) 1653-4. Will dated 6 (11) prob. 4 (2) 1654, beq. to wife Hannah; to eldest son John a double portion and what his gr. father had beq. to him; other sons and daus. to share alike; wife exec. Bro. John C. and Capt. Edward Johnson overseers. [Reg. XVI, 74.]

GREENFIELD, GRENFEILD,

Samuel, weaver, ae. 27, of Norwich, Eng., with wife Barbara, ae. 35, and servant, John Teed, ae. 19, passed exam. May 12, 1637, to go to N. E. Recd. inhabitant and propr. at Salem 14 (6) 1637. Rem. to Ipswich. His wife d. and he m. Susan, widow of Humphrey Wyth or Wise, with whom he sold land 4 March, 1638. Was one of those licensed by the Court 6 (7) 1638, to begin the plantation at Hampton. Rem. to Exeter.

GREENLEAF, GRENLEFE,

Edmund, dyer, gent., Newbury, frm. March 13, 1638-9. Kept a house of entertainment in 1639. Com. of the Gen. Court to end small businesses in 1642. Captain. Rem. to Boston; his dyehouse located by the spring 30 (5) 1655. His wife Sarah d. Jan. 18, 1662-3. He m. 2, Sarah, widow of William Hills, q. v. Ch. Enoch, Judith, (m. 1, Henry Somerby, m. 2, Tristram Coffin, Jr.,) Stephen, Elizabeth, (m. 1, Giles Badger, m. 2, Richard Browne,) Daniel d. Dec. 5, 1654, Sarah, (m. William Hilton,) [John.]
His will dated 22 Dec. 1668, prob. 12 (2) 1671, beq. to son Stephen; daus. Elizabeth Browne, widow, and Judith Coffin; to gr. ch. Elizabeth Hilton and Enoch G.; to Enoch's eldest son James. Cousin Thomas Moon, mariner, overseer; sons Stephen G. and Tristram Coffin execs. Refers to William, Ignatius and James Hill, his wife's sons, and to £50 apiece beq. to them by their aunt.

GREENLAND,

John, carpenter, Charlestown, propr. on Mystic Side in 1638. Deposition. [L.] Gen. Court gr. him leave to plant on a five acre lot, 7 Oct. 1640. Town officer. He

GREENLAND, cont.
deposed 29 (10) 1657, ae. about 50 years, and 17 (4) 1662, ae. about 60. [Mdx. Files.] Wife Lydia; ch. John b. 16 (8) 1641.
Will dated 1 May, 1685, prob. 27 March, 1691, beq. to wife Lydia, sons John and Daniel, dau. Abigail Ireland and Daniel's dau. Elizabeth.

GREENOUGH, GREENOW,
Mary, Sandwich, memb. chh. before 1644, m. Capt. Bezaleel Peyton and rem. to Boston.

William, mariner, brother of the above, deposed 23 July, 1678, ae. about 51 years, relative to her property. Came to Boston, (perhaps from Sandwich,) about 1650; m. July 4, 1652, Elizabeth, dau. of Micholas Upsall. Had deed of land from him April 7, 1660, and sold it in 1674. Captain. Ch. William b. April 12, 1656, d. (6) 1657, William b. 1658, d. 1659, Israel b. and d. 1660. He m. 2, Oct. 10, 1660, Ruth, dau. of Thomas Swift; ch. Samuel b. and d. 1661, Mary b. Nov. 28, 1662, Dorothy b. March 16, 1663, Elizabeth b. Nov. 30, 1664, Anna b. May 20, 1665, Luke b. Feb. 10, 1667, William b. Feb. 20, 1670, John b. Feb. 17, 1672, Samuel b. Aug. 31, 1676, Consider b. March 7, 1677. He d. Aug. 6, 1693.

GREENSLADE, see Averitt.

GREENSMITH,
Mr. Stephen, Boston, censured by Gen. Court 9 March, 1636-7, for criticising the ministers; appealed to the king 3 (6) 1637. [W.] Contracted for purchase of clapboards Nov. 5, 1639.

GREGORY,
John, Duxbury, propr. 1638. May be the same as John, Weymouth, whose est. was admin. 30 Nov. 1692, by John Taylor. [See will of William G. of Nottingham, gent., in Reg. XLVII.]

Henry, Springfield, res. 1640, propr. Made request through his son Judah, March 14, 1642, for leave to sell land. The town bought it.

GRENVILL,
Thomas, rec'd beq. from Dennis Geere of Lynn in 1635.

GRENAWAY, GREENAWAY, GRENEAWAY, GREENWAY,
John, millwright, Dorchester, probably came in the Mary and John in 1629-30; appl. frm. Oct. 19, 1630; frm. May 18, 1631. Town officer. Wife Mary; ch. Ann. (m. Robert Pierce,) Elizabeth, (m. — Allen,) Ursula, ae. 32, came in the Elizabeth in April, 1635, (m. Hugh Batten,) Susanna, (m. Nathaniel Wales,) Katharine, (m. William Daniels,) Mary, (m. Thomas Millett). He deeded his lands to his daus. Ursula, Ann, and Katharine in 1651 and 1652, providing for contingent payments to be made to his daus. Elizabeth Allen (and her children,) and Susanna Wales (and her children if she have any).

He d. soon after making these deeds; his wife d. Jan. 23, 1658. [Reg. IX, 348, and XXXII, 55.]

Richard, Salem, Marblehead, propr. 9 (8) 1637.

GRESHOLD, see Griswold.

GRIDLEY,
Richard, brick-maker, bricklayer, Boston, 1631. Propr.; frm. April 1, 1634. Town officer. Sympathized with the Hutchinson party, and was disarmed as many others were. He deposed July 2, 1660, ae. about 59 years.

Wife Grace adm. chh. 29 (10) 1633. Ch. Joseph, deposed 29 (7) 1663, ae. about 35 years. [Mdx. Files.] [Katharine, (m. George Dorlon,)] Mary b. 14 (2) 1632, Sarah b. 14 (2) 1634, Hannah b. 10 (2) 1636, (m. 16 (7) 1657, Edward Davis,) Returne b. 14 (1) 1637-8, (m. 9 (2) 1656, John Davis,) Believe b. 1 (3) 1640, Tremble b. 14 (1) 1642-3.

His will, dated 19 (8) was prob. (9) 1674. Wife Grace; dau. Dorlum that lives at the Eastward; the ch. [Hannah,] of his dec. son Tremble; gr. ch. Mary and Believe G. Had given lands to some of his ch. before. The widow d. soon. In her inv. taken 3 June, 1675, a house is mentioned that Roger Billing is to have.

Thomas, Windsor, Conn. 1639; served in Pequot war and recd. bounty lands. Rem. to Northampton.

GRIFFIN, GRIFFYN, GRIFFON,
Hugh, Sudbury, propr. 1639; town marshall and clerk of the writs; frm. May, 1645.

GRIFFIN, etc., cont.

Wife Elizabeth; ch. Abigail b. 3 (9) 1640, Sarah b. 20 (9) 1642, Shemuel b. 9 (11) 1644, Jonathan b. 22 June, 1647.

He d. 21 June, 1656. Will dated 6 (1) prob. 16 Dec. 1656, beq. to wife Elizabeth, sons Shemuel and Jonathan, and daus. Abigail and Sarah.

Humphrey, butcher, Ipswich, came to the place in 1639. His application for a lot was refused at first "because the town was full," but he bought a house and lot of Daniel Denison 19 Jan. 1641; afterward had grants of land as other proprs. Town officer. He m. Elizabeth, dau. of Robert Andrews, who beq. to her sons John and two others not named, whom we know to have been Nathaniel and Samuel. They had daus. Lydia and Elizabeth, the latter m. Edward Deare. He deposed 18 Dec. 1658. ae. about 53 years; his son John depos. in 1659, ae. about 24.

The inv. of his est. was presented in court 25 March, 1662. The widow m. 2, Hugh Sherratt, q. v.

Richard, Concord, frm. March, 1637-8. Deputy and comr. of Court 1639. He deposed 21 (1) 1658-9, ae. about 67 years, about a house, bought by Matthew Allen. He m. 10 Dec. 1660, Mary Haward or Harrod, widow.

He d. 5 April, 1661. Will dated 19 (1) 1661, ae. about 70 years, prob. June 25, 1661; beq. to wife Mary; to kinsman Matthew G. of Charlestown; to Christopher Wooly. Admin. gr. to widow for herself and children. Second admin. and bond by his son Joseph G. of Boston, tailor, 26 March, 1680.

Thomas, Boston, part owner of wharf property in 1639. [L.]

He d. at Roxbury; inv. July 18, 1661. Letter of Thomas Parke of southertowne to his bro. Wm. Parke at Rox., asking his help in settling the est. of G. for the benefit of creditors. [Reg. X, 359, and XXXI, 176.]

GRIFFITH,

Henry, Cambridge, d. 12 (9) 1639.

Joshua, ae. 25, servant to Henry Collins, starch-maker, came in the Abigail in June, 1635, cert. from the parish of Stepney, Eng.

GRICE, GRISE, GRIST,

Charles, Braintree, before 1648, frm. May 7, 1651. He m. Margery Davis, widow, of Boston, who was dism. to chh. of Br. 7 (3) 1648.

He d. 9 (9) 1663. Will prob. 12 Nov. 1663; wife Margery, son-in-law Wm. Owen, son David G., and bros. John and William G. in Eng. [Reg. XII, 273.] The widow d. 13 (7) 1669.

GRIGGS,

George, of Landen, co. Bucks, Eng., ae. 42, with wife Alice, ae. 32, and ch. Thomas, ae. 15, William, ae. 14, Elizabeth, ae. 10, Mary, ae. 6, and James, ae. 2, came in the Hopewell April 1, 1635. Settled at Boston. Propr. 1635. Ch. b. in Bo.: Elizabeth b. 14 (3) 1636, d. (3) 1640, Sarah b. 15 (3) 1637, William bur. (10) 1638.

He d. June 23, 1660. Will dated 4 (5) 1655, prob. 3 Aug. 1660. Wife; son James, daus. Anne Jones, Mary Brooks, Sarah King. The widow Alice d. July 19, 1662. Admin. of her will granted to her son-in-law Robert Lattimore in right of his wife Anne and to Roger Burgis in right of his wife Sarah; the son James having been absent many years, and supposed to be dead, the Court divided the est. to the daus. Sept. 6, 1665. [Reg. IX, 343, anr XII, 48.]

Humphrey, Braintree, made Isaac Martin of Hingham his attorney 2 (10) 1646, to collect of Wm. Griggs of Cavendish in Suff. 5 li., a legacy from Thomas G. of Sudbury, Suff., tallow-chandler. [A.] He m. 1 (9) 1655, widow Grizzell Jewell.

Inv. of his est. taken 18 (6) 1657, and admin. gr. to his widow Grizzell. She m. Henry Kibbe, of Dorchester.

John, Watertown, propr. 1636. He m. at Roxbury Nov. 11, 1652, Mary, dau. of William Pattin. Ch. John bapt. Aug. 10, 1653.

He d. 23 Jan. 1691-2.

Thomas, householder, Roxbury. Wife Mary bur. Nov. 29, 1639; he m. Aug. 26, 1640, Mary Green. His dau., ae. about 12 yrs., d. in 1645.

He d. May 23, 1646. [E.] Inv. taken 25 (3) 1646. The widow m. Jasper Rawlings.

William, Boston, Rumney Marsh. Wife Rachel; ch. William b. April 2, 1640, Sarah b. Oct. 6, 1642, Rachel b. Oct. 13, 1644,

GRIGGS, cont.
Isaac b. Oct. 5, 1646, Elizabeth b. Oct. 3, 1648, Jacob b. Nov. 30, 1658, (all bapt. in Boston July 31, 1659;) Hannah b. March 12, 1660, Rebecca b. April 3, 1662, *Mary* bapt. 18 (3) 1662.

GRIMES, see Grame and Gryme.

GRIMSTEAD, GRIMSTONE, see Glinsted,
Margaret, widow, Boston, d. 20 (11) 1649; inv. filed 7 (12) 1649, by Thomas Clarke and Edmund Eddenden.

GRINDER,
Alice, servant, appr. to Isaac Allerton for 5 yrs. Nov. 24, 1633; left here by Mr. John Graunt, master of the —. [Plym. Col. Rec.]

GRINE,
Anthony, Charlestown, resident in 1634.

GRISWALD, GRISSELL, GRISSOLL, GRESHOLD, GRISWOLD,
Francis, Cambridge, drummer, had land grant in 1636. Propr. also at Charlestown; frm. May, 1645. Bought house and lands in Cambridge March 16, 1651. Wife Mary; ch. Mary b. 28 (8) 1639, Hannah b. 1642 and d. 1643, Hannah b. March 4, 1644-5.
He d. Oct. 2, 1652. Nunc. will prob. Mdx. court 1 (2) 1653, on testimony of his wife. Beq. all to his two daughters. [Mdx. Files.] His widow m. 2, Wm. Bullard, [Mi.] and at her decease the daus. Elizabeth, (wife of Jonah Palmer of Rehoboth,) and Hannah, received their portions. [Mdx. De. I, 168.]

GROCE,
Simon, Salem, 1650.

GROOM, see Gorham,
Mr. Samuel, mariner, Salisbury, propr. 1650. Ret. to Eng. and from London, 20 Aug. 1658, gave power of attorney to Phillip Worlidg of Boram, Essex, yeoman, to sell his lands in Salis.; this was done by Thos. Bradbury as attorney for Daniel Pierce of Newbury, whom W. made *his* attorney for the purpose.

GROSSE, GROSS, GROWSE, GROSE,
Edmund, a sea-faring man, Boston, propr. 1639, adm. chh. 22 (1) 1645, with wife Katharine. Ch. Isaac b. 1 (8) 1642, Susanna b. (6) 1644, both bapt. 23 (1) 1645; Hannah bapt. 15 (6) 1647, ae. about 3 days, Lydia bapt. 10 (1) 1650, ae. about 4 days, Mary b. 9 Sept. 1652, John b. 21 April, 1655.
Will prob. 3 May, 1655, beq. to wife, son Isaac, dau. Susanna and 3 other children.

Isaac, brewer, husbandman, Boston, adm. chh. 17 (2) 1636. He was dism. to Exeter chh. with the Wheelwright party 6 (11) 1638. Ret. to Boston.
Will prob. 5 (4) 1649; wife; ch. Edmund, Clement and Matthew G.; gr. ch. Isaac, Hannah and Susanna G.; Mr. John Cotton, Mr. Philemon Pormort, *et als.* [Reg. VII, 228.] The son Matthew deposed May 19, 1655, ae. about 25 yrs. The widow Ann m. 15 (6) 1658, Samuel Sheere, of Dedham.

Joseph, of Plymouth, servant of John Winslow, transferred 28 July, 1640, to John Howland.

William, Yarmouth; question raised in Plym. Court in 1645 as to his maintenance.

GROUT,
John, yeoman, Watertown, propr. 1642. Rem. to Sudbury and later to Cambridge. Frm. May 3, 1665. Deposed 6 (2) 1652, ae. about 37 years. [Mdx. Files.]
Petition, signed by neighbors, at Sudbury, Oct. 7, 1662, that he be allowed to "practice the mistery of chirurgery." [Mdx. Files.] Wife Mary d. about 1641, and he m. 2, Sarah, dau. of Nicholas Busbey, who rec'd a tract of land in Wat. May 26, 1660, from her father's est.; they then res. at Sudbury. Ch. b. in Wat.: John b. 8 (6) 1641, Sarah b. 11 (10) 1643, Joseph b. at S. 21 July, 1649, Abigail b. 14 Oct. 1655, Mary b. at Sud. Aug. 1, 1661.
He d. July 25, 1697. Will prob. Aug. 16, 1697. Sons John, Jonathan and Joseph; son-in-law John Livermore; dau. Susanna; dau. Abigail Curtis, wife of Joseph; dau. Mary Knap, wife of Thomas, dau. Elizabeth's 5 children by Samuel Allen. Son-in-law, John Woodward, husband of Susanna, mentioned in the inv. The widow Sarah d. 25 April, 1699.

GROVE, GROVES,
Edward, entertained to serve at the Fort (Boston) from 24 July, 1636, at 10 li. per annum. [W.]

Edward, sailmaker, Boston; is he the same as the foregoing? Will dated 22 Sept. prob. Dec. 16, 1686, beq. to dau. Mary, wife of William Hirst of Salem, gr. son Groves Hirst, wife Elizabeth, residue to grandchildren.

GROVER,
Edmund, Salem, propr. 1636. He deposed in 1660, ae. about 60 years. Testified in 1678 that he worked on Mr. Endecott's farm about 45 years before. [Wife] Margaret adm. chh. 3 (3) 1646; ch. Naomi, Mary and Lydia bapt. 17 (3) 1646, Deborah bapt. 26 (1) 1648.

Inv. of his est. taken 2 Aug. 1682; admin. gr. to son Nehemiah.

John, Charlestown, 1640; Rumney Marsh, 1656. Rem. to Malden. Wife Elizabeth; ch. John b. 18 (12) 1640, Elizabeth b. 1 (7) 1642, Lydia b. 28 (2) 1644.

John d. at Malden Feb. 19, 1673-4. [See Atwood.] Elizabeth d. March, 1673-4. Note also the folg.: John, ae. about 80 years, made will before Aaron Way, James Bill and Wm. Ireland of Boston 1 Sept. prob. 16 Dec. 1686. Beq. to dau. Elizabeth gencks [Jenks;] gr. son Paul; grand children; grand dau. Lydia Moral, now wife of Joseph Bill.

Ould goodwife Grover adm. chh. Charlestown 30 (9) 1643.

Samuel, ae. 16, came in the Truelove in Sept. 1635.

Thomas, Charlestown, rem. to Malden. Wife Elizabeth; ch. Lazarus b. 5 (2) 1642, Elizabeth b. at Malden Dec. 27, 1652, Grace d. 3 (3) 1658.

He d. 28 (8) 1661. The inv. of his est. was filed Dec. 17, 1661, by his widow Elizabeth and son Lazarus. Admin. on the est. of John, ae. 17 years, and his sister Elizabeth, was gr. 16 (4) 1674, to their bro. Lazarus.

GRUNDY,
Thomas, sailor, Boston, servant to Mr. James Smith, shipmaster, adm. chh. 12 (8) 1644.

GRUBB,
Thomas, leather-dresser, Boston, with wife Anne adm. chh. 1632-3; frm. March 4, 1633-4. He drew on his father-in-law, Jeffrey Salter, of Kingslynne, co. Norfolk, tanner, Sept. 1, 1640. [L.] He conveyed land at Muddy River 31 (3) 1652, to Margery, widow of Jacob Eliot, for the use of her children. Wife Anne; ch. Abiah b. and d. 1637, John b. (6) bapt. 2 (7) 1638, Samuel b. 5 (10) 1641, John b. and d. 1644, Elizabeth bapt. 30 (4) 1644, ae. about 6 days, Heman b. 21 (12) 1645, d. 29 (7) 1647.

GRYME,
Elizabeth, an ancient maid, Boston, adm. chh. 15 (7) 1639.

GUILD, GUIL, GUILE, GUYLES, GILE, GILD,
John, Dedham, adm. chh. 17 (5) 1640, propr.; frm. May 10, 1643. He m. 24 (4) 1645, Elizabeth Crooke; she d. 31 Aug. 1669; ch. John b. 22 (6) 1646, Samuel b. 7 (9) 1647, John b. 29 (9) 1649, Eliezer b. 30 (9) 1653, Ebenezer b. 21 (10) 1657, d. 21 (2) 1661, Elizabeth b. 18 (11) 1660, Benjamin b. 25 May, 1664.

Will dated 3 Oct. prob. 3 Nov. 1682, beq. to his three children Samuel, John and Elizabeth.

Samuel, Haverhill, propr.; town officer; frm. May 18, 1642. He m. Sept. 1, 1647, Judith Davis; she d. May, 1667. Ch. Samuel b. Aug. 30, 1648, Judith b. April 5, 1650, John b. Dec. 8, 1652, Hannah b. Oct. 12, 1654, Sarah b. 1 March, 1657-8, James b. Aug. 27, 1660, Ephraim b. March 21, 1661-2.

He d. Feb. 21, 1683. Will dated 16 Feb. 1683, prob. March 21 folg., beq. to ch. John, Samuel, Ephraim, Sarah, and gr. ch. Judith Page; had given portion to Thomas Clough upon marriage with daughter.

GULLIVER, GULLIFORD,
Anthony, yeoman, Dorchester, bought land 15 (11) 1644. Bought ½ interest in the Hutchinson farm in 1656. Res. in Milton; frm. May 23, 1666.

He d. Nov. 28, 1706, ae. 87. [Gr. st.] [Reg. VII, 89.] Will dated 20 Jan. 1703, prob. 23 Dec. 1706, beq. to wife Elinor, as by agreement; to sons Samuel, Jonathan, Nathaniel; daus. Hannah Tucker, Lydia Leonard, Eliza G. and Mary Atherton.

GULTHROP,
Ralph, Boston, adm. inhab. 28 (1) 1642.

GUN, GUNN, GONN,
Jasper, ae. 29, with Ann, ae. 25, came in the Defense in July, 1635. Settled at Roxbury. Propr.; frm. May 25, 1636.

Thomas, Dorchester, 1634, frm. May 6, 1635. Rem. to Windsor, Conn.

GUNISON, GUNNISON, GULLISON,
Hugh, vintner, Boston, servant to Richard Bellingham, adm. chh. 22 (1) 1635. Frm. May 25, 1636. He rec'd 20 li. of Mr. John Bewford of Middlesex, gent., 7 (11) 1644. [A.] Sold his house called the King's Arms, and brew houses, etc., April 7, 1651. His wife Elizabeth d. 25 (11) 1645; he m. 2, Sarah, widow of Henry Lynne, who was adm. chh. 15 (3) 1647. Ch. Sarah b. 14 (12) 1637, Elizabeth b. 25 (2) 1640, Deborah b. (8) 1642, Hester bapt. 20 (12) 1647, Joseph b. 31 (1) 1649, Elihu b. 12 (12) 1649.

He d. before 1660. [Suff. De. III, 481.] His widow m. — Mitchell; petitioned Gen. Court for adjustment of matters connected with H. G.'s est. 30 May, 1663; in letter to Capt. Davenport 26 (3) 1660, she says he "may ask need money of my father Tilly." See Tilly, Wm.

GUNLITHE, see Condliffe.

GURNELL, GORNELL, GORNHILL, GORNETT, GURNIT,
John, Dorchester, memb. chh. about 1637, frm. May 10, 1643, town officer. He had John, (son of Sampson) Mason, dwelling then with him, bapt. 23 (7) 1660, ae. 4 yrs.

He d. July 30, 1675, ae. 64. His will dated 19 (11) 1674-5, prob. 19 Aug., 1675, beq. to wife; to bros. Richard and George G., sister Clements, cousin Jonas Prisse in Eng. if they come here; to Robert Prisse if he remain in N. E.; to several individuals; to the school; £40 to be kept as a stock to be loaned to a poor, honest and godly tradesman, to help set him up; he to return it, and the fund to be loaned again. His widow Jane m. 2, John Burge; she d. April 4, 1678, ae. 78. Will beq. 3 li. to the chh. to buy Communion cups; rest of her est. to John Mason, or, in event of his death, to the poor of the town. [Reg. XL, 258.]

GUNTER,
Lester, ae. 13, came in the Truelove in Sept. 1635.

GUPPY, GUPPEE,
Reuben, Salem, suit at Ipswich, 1641. He deposed in 1665, ae. about 60 years. Wife Ellen; ch. John b. 12 (8) 1646, Reuben b. 6 (11) 1650. His two eldest children were placed, by order of the town 18 (8) 1647, the girl with Philip Verin, the boy with Robert Lemmon.

GURGEFIELD, see Bennett.

GURNEY, GORNET,
John, Sen., tailor, Braintree. [N. B. He is called John Cheny, Sen., in the printed records of Braintree, by a typographical error.] Was an apprentice of John Newgate, 29 (7) 1636, ae. 21 years; had 3 years longer to serve. [W.] Signed a petition about the meadows in 1646. [Arch. 45.] Sold land in Br. 12 Feb. 1661. His wife d. 20 (7) 1661, and he m. 12 (9) 1661, Grizzell, widow of Henry Kibbee.

He d. in 1662-3; inv. March 16, 1663. [Reg. XII, 53.]

GUTCH, see Gouch.

GUTSALL,
Walter, husbandman, ae. 34, came in the Abigail in July, 1635.

GUTTERIDGE, see GOODRICH.

GUY, GUYE,
John, Lynn, contracted for a boat in May, 1640. [L.]

Nicholas, carpenter, ae. 50, came in the Confidence April 11, 1638, with wife Jane ae. 30, dau. Mary and servants Joseph Taintor and —, from Upton Gray, Southampton, Eng. Settled at Watertown. Frm. May 22, 1638. Deacon.

He d. July 6, 1649. Inv. taken Oct., 17 folg. The Court gr. admin, to the widow Jane Oct. 14, 1651. Ch. Mary m. Henry Curtis and res. at Sudbury. Another dau. m. Joseph Taintor. The widow beq. her est. Aug. 16, 1666, to these daus. and their husbands and children, making her gr. son Ephraim Curtice exec.

GYLES,
William, residence not specified, frm. May 14, 1634.

GWIN,
John, before Boston Court 10 May, 1643.

Mary, Charlestown, adm. chh. 7 (12) 1646.

Thomas, Boston, witness to deed of John Lee in 1647. He m. Elizabeth, dau. of Benjamin Gillam; ch. Thomas b. Nov. 3, 1661, Elizabeth b. Oct. 16, 1668. She d. before 16 Jan. 1669; [inv. in Suff. De. V, 30.]

GUILLAM, GWILLING,
James, Dedham; by one record he was bur. (9) 1646; by another he d. 29 (9) 1647.

GYVER,
Bridget, Boston, memb. chh. 1631-2.

HABBELL,
Elizabeth, servant of Mr. Wm. Brewster, Plymouth, 21 Aug. 1637. [Col. Rec.]

HACKFORD,
William, fisherman, Salem, propr. 1636.

HACKET, HACKETT,
A servant in Salem, about 18 years of age, executed for crime in 1641. [W.]

Jabez, Lynn, gave bond to Susanna, dau. of Adam Hawkes, for money now in the hands of Boniface Burton, 5 (9) 1644. Testified in Court in 1647. Was to have a legacy paid him by the admin. of Thos. Leverett in case of the death of John Hackett.

Jabez, Taunton, 1654. [Is he the Lynn man?] Ch. John b. 26 Dec. 1654, Jabez b. 12 Sept. 1656, Mary b. 9 Jan. 1659, Sarah b. 13 July, 1661, Samuel b. 29 July, 1664, Ha[....] b. 25 Jan. 1666.

HACKWELL,
John, ae. 18, came in the Increase April 15, 1635.

HADAWAY, see Hathaway.

HADBOURNE,
George glover, ae. 43, with wife Anne, ae. 46, ch. Rebecca, ae. 10, and Anna, ae. 4, and servants Joseph Borebancke, ae. 24, and Joane Jordan, ae. 16, came in the Abigail in June, 1635, cert. from the parish of Stepney, Eng. See George Hauborne, of Hampton, N. H.

HADDEN, HADDON, HADEN,
Ferman, Duxbury, atba. 1643; action in his behalf in Plym. Court in 1650. Rem. to Charlestown. He m. at Boston 5 (3) 1657, Elizabeth —. Ch. Samuel b. Dec. 15, 1657, Samuel b. 27 (12) 1658.

Jarrett, Jared, Garret or Gerhard, tailor, planter, Boston, memb. chh. 1630-1, frm. May 14, 1634. Propr. Cambridge 1633. Rem. to Salisbury; dismissed to the chh. of Salis. from that of Boston with wife Margaret 11 (8) 1640. Propr., town officer. He deposed 14 (2) 1668, ae. about 60 years. Wife d. March 20, 1672-3. Ch. Mary, (m. Henry Blesdall,) Sarah b. Jan. 15, 1639, (m. 1, Edmund Eliot, m. 2, Samuel Younglove.)

His will, dated 20 Jan. 1686-7, prob. March 20, 1689-90, beq. to son-in-law Henry Blaisdell; gr. sons John Eliot, Ebenezer, Henry and Ralph Blaisdell and Mary Rawlins; to Elizabeth, wife of John Huntington; to daus. Mary and Sarah.

Katharine, Cambridge, propr. 1639.

HADLEY,
George, planter, yeoman, Ipswich, propr. before 1639. Rem. about 1655 to Rowley. He conveyed property 9 June, 1670, to wife Deborah, and made contract with her relative to what she brought with her at marriage. Ret. to Ipswich. Ch. [John, Samuel, Martha, Abigail,] Elizabeth d. at Topsfield 2 March, 1660-1, and Abigail d. 12 Sept. 1662.

HADLOCK,
Nathaniel, Charlestown, adm. chh. 10 (7) 1644, frm. May 6, 1646. Had care of the sweeping of chimneys in the town in 1648. Was one of the incorporators of Lancaster, 1653. Wife Mary adm. chh. of Char. 30 (9) 1643; ch. Mary b. 31 (3) 1641, Nathaniel b. 5 (4) 1643.

He d. before 1667, when the widow, who had m. Roger Draper, sold land in Char.

HAFFIELD, HAFFELL, HALFIELD, HAYFIELD,
Richard, currier, ae. 54, with wife Martha, ae. 42, ch. Marie, ae. 17, Sarah ae. 14, Martha, ae. 8, Rachel, ae. 6, and Ruth, ae. 3, cert. from Sudbury co. Suff. Eng., came in the Planter, April 10, 1635. Settled at Ipswich; propr. 1635.
He d. about 1639; beq. his est. in equal portions to the daughters above named. Rachel and Ruth chose their bro. Richard Coy guardian 8 April, 1652. [Reg. III, 156.] See petition of Josiah Cobbet and wife Mary, and John Ilsley and wife Sarah, April 29, 1668. [Mass. Arch. XV, 115,] and deposition of Simon Tompson, [Ips. De. II, 61.]
His widow was made a commoner in 1641. She d. at Wenham 22 (12) 1667. Richard Coy and his wife Martha sold her share in the estate 15 June, 1668.

HAFORD,
Nathan, servant to John Tuttell, ae. 16, cert. from St. Albons, Herts., Eng., came in the Planter April 2, 1635.

HAGBORNE,
Samuel, Roxbury, propr. He m. Katharine, dau. of John Deighton of Gloucester, Eng., bapt. Jan. 16, 1614, named in her fathers will in 1640. [Reg. XLV, 303.] Ch. Elizabeth "b. in England" May 7, 1635, Samuel b. Jan. 20, 1637, John b. March 26, 1640, Hannah b. Jan. 5, 1642.
He was bur. Dec. 27, 1642. Will dated 19 Jan. prob. 8 (1) 1642-3. Beq. to eldest dau. Elizabeth articles her grandfather left her; to bro. Abraham H.; to bro. Lugg; to maid Alice and man Nathaniel, wife, son Samuel, son John, younger dau.; to the free school of Rox. The widow m. 2, Gov. Thomas Dudley and 3, Rev. James Allen, q. v.

HAGER, AGER,
William, Watertown. He m. March 20, 1645, Mary Bemis. Ch. Mary b. Dec. 25, 1645, Ruhama and Samuel b. Nov. 20, 1647, Hannah b. Nov. 21, 1641, Sarah b. Sept. 1 1651, [Susanna,] William b. Feb. 12, 1658, Rebecca b. Oct. 28, 1661, [Abigail, Mehetabel.]
He d. Jan. 10, 1683-4. His widow Mary, an aged woman d. Dec. 1695.

HAILSTONE, see Halston,
William, [tailor,] Taunton, frm. 5 June 1644. Juryman.

HAGGIT,
Henry, Salem, 1642, frm. May 11, 1670. Rem. to Wenham.
Will dated 12 (12) 1676; ae. about 83 years; beq. to ch. Henry, Moses, Mary, Deliverance and Hannah. Prob. 26 March, 1678.

HAINES, HAYNES, HAINE, HAYNE,
Edmund, Springfield, propr. 1646. Ch. Ruth b. 27 (2) 1647. He was bur. about that time, and his widow m. 29 (4) 1648, George Lancton of Wethersfield, Conn.

John, Esquire. When young was under Mr. Dod's ministry; later in Essex, under Mr. Rogers. [Rel.] Was a gentleman of great estate. [W.] Came in the Griffin Sept. 4, 1633; settled at Cambridge; adm. frm. May 14, 1634. Selectman 3 Feb. 1634. Was chosen Asst. of the colony in 1634, and governor 3 (6) 1635. Rem. soon after to Conn., where he was gov. several terms, and rendered large service to that colony. [Reg. XVI, 167; many notices.]

Mark, Boston, 1647. Wife Mary; ch. Elizabeth bapt. 10 (8) 1647, ae. about 5 days, Mehetabel bapt. 7 (9) 1652, John bapt. 10 (7) 1654.

Richard, husbandman, Salem, was bondsman for Daniel Hutchins before Gen. Court 20 (3) 1640. With William Haines, sold their two-thirds part of a farm in Salem 29 (4) 1648.

Ralph, Salem, petitioned Gen. Court in 1645.

Robert, a witness to a deed in Boston in 1648.

Sarah, Salem, adm. chh. 4 (1) 1649.

Walter, linen weaver, ae. 55, from Sutton Mandifield, co. Wilts., came in the Confidence in 1638 with wife Eliza; sons under 16 years of age, Thomas, John and Josias; daus. Suffrance and Mary; and servants John Blandford, John Riddet and Richard Biddlecome. Settled at Sudbury. Selectman, 1639. Com. to end small causes, 1645. Deputy, 1641. A Thomas H. d. at Sud. 28 July, 1640.
He d., 14 Feb. 1664. Will dated 25 May 1659, codicil March 4, 1663-4, prob. April 4, 1665, beq. to wife Elizabeth; sons Thomas, John and Josiah; son-in-law Thomas Noyes; to son-in-law Roger Gourd and my dau., his

HAINES, etc., cont.
wife, a tenement in Shaston, Dorsetshire, Eng. See will of Alice H., perhaps mother of Walter, in Reg. XXXIX, 263.

William, husbandman, Salem, 1644, adm. chh. 14 (9) 1647. He gave a letter of attorney 25 (9) 1647, to Thomas Haynes, merchant, London, for collection at Danes Halle, Bedfordshire. [A.] He mortg. land in 1647; discharged the mortg. in 1660. See Richard, above.

HAIT, HAITE, HAYTE, HETT, HITT,
Simeon, Scituate, adm. chh. with wife April 19, 1638. His brother, the smith, had a house there in 1636. [Lo. in Reg. IX.] See Tilden.

Thomas, cooper, planter, Hingham, 1633; propr. 1635; frm. Sept. 14, 1642. Residing at Cambridge, sold property before 1638. At Rehoboth, 1643; frm. Plym. Col. 4 June, 1645. Of Boston, 1639 to 1649. He deposed Oct. 1, 1661, ae. about 50 years. [Mdx. Files.] He m. Ann —; she d. Nov. 30, 1688, ae. about 75 years. [Mdx. Files.] Ch. rec. in Boston; Eliphalet bapt. 26 (9) 1639, Mehetabel bapt. 23 (2) 1648, Mary bapt. 15 (5) 1649; ch. rec. at Malden, Israel b. March, 1652-3.

HALE, HAILE, HAYLE, HALES, see Hall,
John, [Lynn,] lawsuit in Es. Court, 1638.

Robert, carpenter, Charlestown, inhab. and memb. chh. 1630, frm. May 14, 1634. Deacon, town officer, ensign. Res. at Malden. Wife Jone; ch. John b. 3 (4) 1636, adm. chh. 22 (6) 1658, became minister at Beverly. [See Reg. XIII, 315;] Mary b. 17 (3) 1639, Zecharias b. 3 (2) 1641, d. 1643, Samuel b. 9 (2) 1644, Joanna, Zechary.

He d. 16 (5) 1659. Will dated 26 (4) 1647, prob. Oct. 4, 1659, beq. to wife; to minor children John, Samuel, Mary and Joanna. [Mdx. Files.] In the inv. the widow mentions that her dau. Mary Wilson rec'd. part of her portion at marriage. The widow m. 2, Richard Jacob. Her sons John Hale and Edward Wilson rec'd a deed from her in 1669.

Sarah, ae. 11, came in the Truelove in Sept., 1635.

HALE, etc., cont.
Thomas, Roxbury, frm. May 14, 1634. He m. about (12) 1639, Jane Lord. He rem. to Hartford, Conn.

Thomas, glover, leather dresser, Salem, frm. Sept. 7, 1634. Sergeant. Sold land in 1658-9. He deposed in 1660, ae. 50 years.

Thomas, son of Thomas H. of Watton at Stone, Herts, bapt. 15 June, 1606, came in the Hector from London, 10 May, 1637, bearing a letter from his mother's bro., Francis Kirby to Gov. John Winthrop. Settled at Newbury. Sold land in N. in 1640; [rec. at Ipswich.] Bought land at Haverhill in 1646; town officer. With wife Thomasine sold land at Salem in 1667. [Thomas Halle deposed 27 (9) 1671, ae. about 67 years.] Wife Thomasine; ch. Thomas bapt. at Watton Nov. 18, 1633, John bapt. do. April 19, 1635. [Reg. XXXV, 367.]

He d. 21 Dec. 1682; the widow d. 30 Jan. 1682-3.

William, planter, [Charlestown,] gave security for Francis Willoughby July 22, 1640. [L.] Wife Sarah before the Court 7 Sept., 1641.

William, Marshfield, one of the arbitrators of the case of John Cogan et als. June 2, 1635; atba. 1643, propr. 1644. Served against the Narragansetts in 1645.

HALFORD,
Thomas, ae. 20, came in the Christian March 16, 1634.

HALL, HALLE, HOLL, HAULE, see also Hale and Hawley,
Bettrice, Boston, maid servant of Jacob Eliot, adm. chh. 20 (4) 1640; now wife of one George Bullward of Watertown, dism. to that chh. 17 (9) 1644.

Edmund, gent., Boston, bondsman July 25, 1640. [L.]

Edward, Plymouth, propr. 1637; servant to Francis Doughty of Taunton in 1640-1; sold house and land in 1642. Rem. to Duxbury; atba. 1643; served against the Narragansetts 1645. Rem. before 1652. [Plym. Col. Rec.] Wife Hester; ch. John b. at Braintree 23 (11) 1650, Hester b. 23 (8) 1654,

Will dated at Rehoboth Nov. 23, 1670; inv.

HALL, etc., cont.
March 6, 1670-1; wife Esther, son John; [Reg. VII, 236.]

Edward, late of Henborough, Eng., carpenter, son of Francis Hall, yeoman, now of Duxbury, N. E., a certificate of his health made July 15, 1640. [L.]

Edward, carpenter, Lynn, servant to Mr. Friend, in Court in 1637, had bequest from Robert Keayne in 1653. Ch. ["Hale" in Salem rec.] Joseph b. 3 (5) 1646, Ephraim b. 8 (7) 1648, Sarah b. (6) 1651, Elizabeth b. 30 (2) 1654, Rebecca b. 30 (2) 1657. Edward gave letter of attorney 12 (10) 1646 to receive legacies from est. of his father Edward H. of Amsbury in Gloucestershire; Eleanor H. of Hill and John Moore of Stapleton in the same county to give acquittance. [A.]

He d. middle of June, 1669. Will undated, prob. 28 Sept. 1669; beq. to wife Sarah, sons Joseph and Ephraim, and daus. Sarah, Elizabeth, Rebecca and Martha.

Edward, Cambridge, frm. May 2, 1638. Was in the congregation of Mr. Glover, of Mr. Tenner and afterward of Mr. Shepard at Heddon, Northumberland, Eng. [Rel.] Wife Margaret, memb. chh., d. Dec. 7, 1666, and he m. June 18, 1667, Mary Rayner.

He d. Oct. 20, 1680, ae. 73. Will dated 30 Jan. 1678, prob. April 5, 1681, beq. to wife Mary, who may dispose of the est. to his relations and kindred as she shall judge best.

George, lands assigned at Duxbury before 1639, not occupied. Taunton atba., 1643, town officer 1645.

Will dated 26 Oct. prob. 1 March, 1669. Wife Mary, sons John, Samuel and Joseph; daus. Charity and Sarah; 40 s. to chh. of Taunton to buy cups with; to William Evens. [Reg. VII, 180.]

John, Charlestown, memb. chh. 1630, frm. May 14, 1634. Wife Joanna adm. chh. 6 (2) 1638; ch. John bapt. 13 (3) 1638, Samuel (son of widow Jone) bapt. 24 (12) 1639-40.

He d. about (10) 1639.

John, Charlestown, frm. May 6, 1635. Rem. to Nashaway. [Mdx. Files, 1651.] Wife Elizabeth; ch. Shebar bapt. 9 (11) 1639, John b. 21 (7) 1645, Elizabeth b. 4 (7) 1647, Elizabeth b. 2 (9) 1648.

John, Saugus, Salem, 1637; frm. May 13, 1640.

HALL, etc., cont.
John, Salisbury, propr. 1641; selectman. He m. April 3, 1641, Rebecca, widow of Henry Biley, q. v. After his death in 1647 she m. Mr. Wm. Worcester and later Dep. gov. Samuel Symonds. She sold house left by Mr Hall 10 May, 1648. [Col. Rec.] Ch. John b. March 18, 1641-2. He rem. to Eng., and wrote to his mother, Mrs. Symonds, letters which are on file. [Reg. 1893.]

John, Barnstable, atba. 1643. Rem. to Yarmouth. Ch. Joseph bapt. July 3, 1642, Benjamin b. and d. 1644, Gershom bapt. March 5, 1647, William bapt. June 8, 1651, Benjamin bapt. May 29, 1653.

Will dated 15 July, 1694, prob Aug. 25, 1696, beq. to sons Samuel, Joseph, William, Benjamin, Elisha, John, Nathaniel, and Gershom.

Mr. Nathaniel, Dorchester, propr. (1) 1634.

Ralph, pipe stave maker, Charlestown. Sold land with wife Mary, 1648. She may be the widow Mary, memb. chh. of Cambridge before 1658; her ch. were all adult at the time of her joining; two of them, John and Susanna, since joined to the chh. of Concord. [Mi.]

Richard, Dorchester, memb. chh. 1644. Lieut. Ch. Martha b. 12 (6) 1648, (m. Sept. 18, 1674, Ebenezer Williams,) Samuel b. 1 (1) 1651, Elizabeth b. 20 (10) 1653, Jonathan b. 8 (2) 1659, Experience b. 30 (11) 1661.

He d. June 23, 1691; his widow d. Oct. 8, 1693.

Samuel, of Canterbury, Eng., yeoman, with wife Joan and 3 servants, came from Sandwich, Eng., before June 9, 1637.

Samuel, gent., Ipswich, before Gen. Court Oct. 13, 1634; propr. 1636. Rem. to Salisbury; propr. 1639; deputy 1655. Treasurer of Norf. co. Sold land in 1657. [Arch. 15 B.]. He ret. to England.

H d. at Langford, Essex, in 1680, leaving a widow Sarah but no child. Will dated Nov. 13, 1679, prob. Jan. 25, 1680; beq. to those who had lost by the great fire in Boston and by Indian wars in the colony. He also beq. to the poor of Newbury, Hampton and Amesbury. Mr. John Hall of Islington, near London, exec. The latter sent an order to his mother, Mrs. Rebecca Symonds of Ips., who

HALL, etc., cont.
gave a sum to widow Susanna Ayres, a great sufferer by the Indian wars; for which her son Thomas A. gave receipt Oct. 19, 1682. [Ips. De. IV, 473.]

Thomas, Cambridge, propr. 1645. Wife Isabel; ch. Hannah b. 4 (1) 1648. Elizabeth, (second) wife of Thomas H., memb. chh. Camb., and her ch. Mary, Hannah and Lydia all bapt. in this chh. before 1658. [Mi.]

Admin. of his est. was gr. to Israel Mead and Ephraim Cutter; inv. taken Oct. 5, 1691.

HALLETT, HALLITT, HELLOT, HOLLETT,
Andrew, ae. 28, servant to Richard Wade, cooper, of Simstuly, (sic.,) came from Weymouth, Eng., before March 20, 1635. Settled at Dorchester; propr. 1638. Rem. to Yarmouth; propr. 6 May, 1639. He gave a cow to the poor of the town in 1643. Schoolmaster in 1646. [A.] Ch. Dorcas bapt. at Barnstable June 1, 1646, Jonathan b. 20 Nov. 1647, John b. 11 Dec. 1650, Hannah, (m. 1 July, 1656, John Hadaway of Bar.)

His will dated 14 March, 1682, prob. 31 May, 1684, beq. to wife Ann, ch. Jonathan, John, Ruhannah (Bourne,) Abigail (Aldin,) and Mehetabel; to gr. ch. Timothy, Hannah, Hezekiah, Eliezer and John Bourne, and to the ch. of Abigail Aldin. The widow made will 3 June, 1684, prob. 20 June 1694; beq. to daus. Mehitabel Dexter, Ruhannah Bourne and Abigail Aldin; and to gr. ch. John Bourne.

Samuel, Yarmouth, atba. 1643. He was drowned at Nocett April 22, 1650. Admin. of his est. was gr. 5 June folg. to Thomas Howes and Samuel Mayo.

John, planter, Scituate, atba. 1643.

HALLOWAY, see Holloway.

HALSALL, HALSEY, HALSYE,
George, blacksmith, Dorchester. Rem. to Boston about 1642. Frm. May, 1645. Wife Elizabeth rec'd with him to chh. of B. 23 (1) 1644; ch. Mehetabel bapt. in Bo. 1 (11) 1642, ae. about 13 days, d. Oct., 1643, Joseph b. 3 (10) 1644, Hannah bapt. 10 (11) 1646, ae. about 4 days, Elizabeth bapt. 11 (1) 1649, ae. about 10 days, Sarah b. and d. 1650-1, Benjamin b. 18 Sept. 1652. Wife Joane joined him in a deed Nov. 24, 1654. They were divorced

HALSALL, etc., cont.
and she (called Joan Swan) m. again. [Arch. Dom. 9.] See Swan, Henry.

John, ae. 24, came in the Elizabeth and Ann in May, 1635.

Thomas, Lynn, propr. 1638. Rem. to Southampton, L. I.?

William, planter, Boston, inhab. 1646, dism. from Boston chh. to that of Lynn, being to dwell there for a season, 5 (10) 1647, with wife Sarah. Ret. to Boston; res. at Pulling Point. Wife Sarah; ch. Asa b. Jan. 1, 1654, Joseph b. May 29, 1657. See Hasey, Wm.

HALSTEAD,
Nathan, Concord, frm. June 2, 1641. Wife Isabel d. 15 (1) 1641.

Inv. of his est. taken 5 (12) 1643; it shows books, £ 16, 17, 6; "Pothecarie ware" £ 3.

Susanna, Charlestown, adm. chh. 8 (11) 1635. She d. at Watertown July 5, 1669; beq. her estate and debts due her to her sister Grace, wife of Michael Berstow, and other persons; will dated Jan. 11, 1667, prob. 9 (8) 1669.

William, Concord, see Bayley.

He d. 27 (5) 1645. Will prob. 13 (4) 1646; to bro. Henry and sister Edna; 15 li. to poor of the town, to be laid out in a cow. [Reg. VIII, 177.]

HAMLET, HAMLETT, HAMBLETT,
William, carpenter, Watertown, propr. 1642, bought land in Charlestown, and in Cambridge, 1645; frm. May 7, 1651. Rem. to Billerica in 1656, and to Woburn in 1679. Wife Sarah, (widow of Hubbard, who had ch. James, Sarah and Thomas H.;) ch. Jacob and Rebecca b. and bapt. in Camb. [Mi.]

HAMLIN, HAMBLIN, HAMLEN, HAMLING,
James, Sen., Barnstable, propr. frm. 1 March 1641-2, atba. 1643, town officer. Ch. Bartholomew bapt. April 24, 1642, John bapt. June 30, 1644, an infant bur. Dec. 2, 1646, Sarah bapt. Nov. 7, 1647, Eleazer bapt. March 17, 1649, Israel bapt. June 25, 1652, Israel b. 25 June, 1655.

Will dated 23 Jan. 1683, prob. Oct. 22, 1690, beq. to wife Anne, and ch. Bartholomew, Hannah, John, Sarah, Eleazer and Israel.

HAMMERSTON,
Edward, Cambridge, was bur. 24 (—) 1646.

HAMMOND, HAMMON, HAMMERS,
Benjamin, Salem, servant of Joseph Hardy, in Court in 1640; man of same name at Yarmouth, atba. 1643. Mary, Yarmouth, [wife of Benjamin?] before Plym. Court, 1648.

Frances, maid servant to Thomas Leverett, Boston, adm. chh. (9) 1633.

Martha, maid servant to Mr. Edward Hutchinson, Boston, adm. chh. 15 (6) 1641.

Philip, widow, Boston, memb. chh., 1631-2. May be the "widow," propr. at Lynn, 1638. She m. Robert Harding, q. v.

Thomas, planter, Hingham, propr., frm. March 9, 1636-7. Sold house and lands March 28, 1651, the deed being endorsed by his wife Elizabeth 14 (3) 1656. Bought land at Muddy River, Boston, in partnership with Vincent Drewse. Rem. to Cambridge.
He d. 30 Sept. 1675. Will, undated and unfinished, on file; aged; beq. to wife Elizabeth, whom he appoints exec.; to daus. Elizabeth Woodward and Sarah Stedman; to Sarah and Elizabeth, daus. of the latter; to sons Thomas and Nathaniel.

William, from Lavenham, Eng., came before 1635 to Watertown; frm. May, 25, 1636. Propr.; town officer. Became surety for a debt in England of his son William, who d. in 1636. [Letter of Robert Ryece to Gov. Winthrop.] He gave letter of attorney 22 (9) 1647, to his son Thomas, to obtain possession of lands at Lavenham, which were the possession of his mother, Rose Steward. [A.] Elizabeth, ae. 47, Elizabeth, ae. 15, Sarah, ae. 10, and John, ae. 7, came in the Francis of Ipswich, April 30, 1634. Elizabeth, called by Rev. John Lothrop "my sister," was recd. by him to the chh. of Scituate April 14, 1636, having a dismission from the chh. of Wat.; which seems to be the dau. Elizabeth, m. about that time to Samuel House.
He d. Oct. 8, 1662. Will dated July 1, 1662, ae. about 90 years, beq. to wife; son John; the 4 children of dec. dau. Elizabeth House; dau. Sarah Smith and her son Adam; dau. Barnes; gr. son Thomas, son of dec. son Thomas. [See Cross, John.] The widow d. Sept. 14, 1674, ae. about 90.

HAMBRO, see Hanbury.

HAMPTON,
James, bought dwelling house and land at Salem in 1650.

Thomas, Sandwich.
Will, dated March, 1637, prob. 5 March, 1638-9, inv. 4 Sept. 1638. Beq. to wife; to Mr. Leverich and his wife; to Wm. Harlow and others. [Reg. IV, 36.] Land and goods at Saugus alias Lynn in hands of George Galloway, etc.

HANBURY, HAMBURY, HAMBRO, HENBURY,
Daniel, ae. 29, came in the Planter April 6, 1635.

Luke, residence not stated, before Gen. Court 1637.

Peter, Sandwich, atba. 1643. In Court 5 June, 1644.

Mr. William, merchant, Plymouth, prop. frm. 7 March, 1642-3. He rem. to Boston about 1648. He m. at Plymouth 28 Sept. 1641, Hannah, dau. of Nathaniel Souther; ch. William bapt. at Bo. 11 (12) 1648, ae. about 6 days.
Nunc. will 12 (12) 1649; beq. all to wife, trusting his children to her care. The inventory refers to a question about a farm at Joanes River betwixt him and his bro. John; money to come at the death of old Mrs. H. in Eng. [Reg. VII, 231.] The widow allowed two thirds of the estate to the 4 children; refers to her sister Stroude in London. Hannah m. in Bo. 24 (8) 1656, Francis Johnson.

HANDMER, HANDMORE, HANMER,
John, planter, Scituate, 1638, propr. Rem. to Duxbury, 1640.
Elizabeth m. 19 Sept. 1657, Daniel Hicks of Sci.
His will dated 4 Dec. 1676, prob. 1 March, 1676-7, beq. to wife Hannah, eldest son John, sons Joseph and Isaac.

HANCOCK,
Elizabeth, Charlestown, adm. chh. 23 (7) 1640.

Nathaniel, Cambridge, propr. 1634. Wife Joanna; ch. Mary b. (9) 1634, Sarah b.

HANCOCK, cont.
(1) 1636, Nathaniel b. 18 (10) 1639, John b. in 1641, d. 1643, Elizabeth b. 1 (1) 1644, Lydia b. 5 (2) 1646.
He d. about 1648.

HANCHET, HANDSET, HANSETT,
John, Boston, servant to Mr. John Wilson, adm. chh. 13 (5) 1634, yeoman, planter; frm. May 17, 1637. Rem. to Braintree in 1640 and to Roxbury in 1644. [Boston chh. Rec.] He m. April 2, 1644, Elizabeth Perry. Wife Elizabeth adm. chh. 18 (6) 1639; ch. John b. 15 (5) 1641, Thomas b. Oct. 1645, Hannah b. in 1647, d. in 1648, Hannah b. and d. 1649, Peter bapt. 6 (5) 1651, John d. 2 (2) 1654, Elizabeth d. 9 (4) 1668.
He d. Feb. 21, 1683.

John, Ipswich, propr. and resident 1638.

HANDS, HANNES,
Mark, smith, nailer, Boston, 1645. Wife Mary adm. chh. 17 (2) 1647; ch. Mary b. 1645, d. 1646, Mehitabel b. Oct 21, 1652, John b. Sept. 10, 1654.
He made will July 15, 1661, bound on a voyage to Barbadoes; prob. June 17, 1664. Beq. to dau. Mehitabel articles left for her by her dec. mother; to son John; to kinsman Joseph Dill and his mother Abigail Hanniford; to Samuel and Benjamin Dill; 5 li. toward the building of a school house at the North end of the town. [Reg. XIII, 9.]

HANGERT,
Henry, servant, ae. 23, came in the Confidence April 11, 1638.

HANNADOWNE, see Amadown.

HANNIFORD, HANFORD, HONNIFORD, HANNIFALL, HANDFORTH,
Egglin, ae. 46, with daus. Margaret, ae. 16, and Elizabeth, ae. 14, came in the Planter in April, 1635. She was adm. chh. Scituate Nov. 21, 1635, with the memorandum "Mr. Hatherly's sister." She m. Dec. 15, 1637, Mr. Richard Sealis; rec'd gift of land in Sci. from Mr. Hatherly 3 March, 1640.

John, mariner, Boston. Wife Hannah adm. chh. 11 (2) 1647, d. 16 (6) 1653; he m. 8 (9) 1655, Abigail, widow of George Dill, sister of Mark Hands; ch. Samuel b. 1 (3) 1645, Samuel bapt. 18 (2) 1647, ae. about 36

HANNIFORD, etc., cont.
weeks, John bapt. 7 (11) 1648, ae. about 12 days, Hannah bapt. 5 (11) 1650, Sarah b. Aug. 8, 1656, Abigail b. March 8, 1660.
Will prob. April 15, 1661; beq. to wife, children, father-in-law John Button, sister Mary French, sister Rose Morrish. [Reg. XIII, 149.]

Nathaniel, (Handforth,) of London, haberdasher, bought house and land in Lynn 6 Sept. 1638; constable 10 (5) 1645. [Es. Court.] He deposed in 1665, ae. 50 years and upward.

Thomas, Scituate, atba. 1643.

HANNUM, HANNAM, HAMMON,
William, Dorchester, propr. 1635. Sold 10 Sept. 1637, and rem. to Windsor, Conn.; thence to Northampton. Ch. at W.: Abigail b. 22 Nov. 1640, Joanna b. 24 July, 1642, Elizabeth b. 24 April, 1645, Mary b. 5 April, 1640.
He d. June 1, 1677. Widow Honor d. at Westfield in 1680. [Reg. XL, 253.] [See Upsall.]

HARBIE, see Harvey.

HARBOUR, HARBAR,
John, Boston, land granted him at Braintree 24 (12) 1639, for 3 heads. His son John joined him in a deed of land in 1657; his wife Hannah conveying her right of dower.
He d. 1 (4) 1675; the widow d. 6 (3) 1677.

HARDIER,
Richard, Braintree, frm. May 10, 1648. Dau. Lydia m. April 1, 1651, Martin Saunders, Jr.
He d. 27 (10) 1657. Will prob. Oct. 6, 1664; beq. to wife Elizabeth; refers to John Hardier and his wife. The widow d. 4 (7) 1664; beq. to her only child and her gr. child, Elizabeth Saunders; beq. to John and Joseph Kent, and to Joseph Kent's 3 daus. [Reg. XIII, 12, and XXXI, 105.]

HARDING,
Abraham, glover, planter, Boston, Braintree, Medfield; frm. May, 1645. He gave letter of attorney 28 (6) 1640, for the collection of legacy left by his father John Harding of Boram, co. Essex, Eng., husbandman, dec., from Agnes Greene of Tarl-

HARDING, cont.
ing, Essex, the widow and exec. of his father. [L.] [See Bridgham.]
Will prob. April 24, 1655; wife Elizabeth, son John and other ch. [Reg. IX, 35.] The widow m. 2, John Frary, Jr., and 3, Thomas Dyer. Thomas Buttolph signed prob. bond, and petitioned Court with herself, her husband and her son John Harding, (then 21 yrs. of age,) Oct. 1, 1665, for distribution of the est. John became guardian of his sister Elizabeth and the other 2 children. [Reg. XVI, 160.]

Elizabeth, ae. 12, came in the Abigail in May, 1635; as maid servant of Capt. Edward Gibbons, Boston, she was adm. chh. 17 (12) 1643.

George, Salem, called to court in 1647.

John, Salem, [compare with John Hardy,] frm. May 13, 1640. Bought land at Gloucester in 1652. Town officer 1654. He m. 22 (2) 1652, widow Tibbit.

John, Weymouth, selectman, 1643.
Admin. on his est. was gr. 2 Nov. 1682, to his son-in-law John Whitmarsh, housewright.

Widow Martha, Plymouth, taxed 1632. She d., leaving 1 son in the custody of Mr. Done. Inv. Oct. 8, 1633. [Reg. IV, 34.] John, of Duxbury, atba. in 1643, may be this son. Phebe, who m. John Brown in 1634, and Winyfride, who m. Thomas Whiton in 1639, are not accounted for.

Robert, merchant, captain, Boston, frm. May 18, 1631. Was in partnership with Robert Scott sometime. Res. at Newport in 1640. [L.] [See Bridgham.] Was paid for services by Gen. Court in 1645. Ret. to Eng.; sold the house he had built in Boston Oct. 1, 1651. He m. Philip Hammond, widow, who was disciplined by the chh. of Bo. for her defense of Mrs. Hutchinson 1 (7) 1639.

HARDMAN, HEARDMAN,
John, Lynn, witness at court in 1647.

HARDY, see Harding and Hart,
John, fisherman, Salem, frm. Sept. 3, 1634. A vessel of his was wrecked in 1641; the "wrack" referred to in Gen. Court records. He desired land about Bass River for his son Joseph in 1643. Goodwife, adm. chh.

HARDY, cont.
14 (2) 1650. His dau. Elizabeth Haskell was recd. to full communion in the chh. 22 (11) 1661.
His will, signed 30 (1) prob. 30 (4) 1652, beq. to wife Elizabeth; dau. Elizabeth Haskell, with her husband Roger H. and their 4 ch., John, William, Mark and Elizabeth; son Joseph and his dau. Elizabeth; gave the time of his apprentice, Thomas Varney, to R. Haskell; the boy's parents may buy the rest of the term. The widow made will 7 (6) 1654, prob. 11 (9) folg.; beq. to the same persons.

Thomas, one of the first to plant at Ipswich, April 1, 1633. [Col. Rec.] Propr. Presumably the same as Thomas, Haverhill, who gave land 1 July, 1670, to dau. Mary, wife of Samuel Currier.
He made will at Merrimack Village, near Haverhill, (Bradford,) 4 March, 1671-2, with postscript Dec. 12, 1677, when he was ae. about 72 years; prob. March 7, 1677-8; beq. to wife; sons Thomas, John, Joseph, Jacob and William; son-in-law William Hutchins; dau. Mary and her children.

HARKER, HEARKER,
Anthony, yeoman, Boston, servant to Thomas Leverett, adm. chh. (9) 1633, frm. May 25, 1636. Propr. He deposed in 1657, ae. about 48 years, concerning the receipt of iron at Edw. Hutchinson's warehouse. Wife Mary adm. chh. 21 (1) 1641; ch. John bapt. 14 (2) 1639, Mary bapt. 17 (8) 1641, ae. about 5 days, John bapt. 30 (2) 1643, ae. about 10 days, Sarah b. 30 (7) 1646, Mercy bapt. 12 (6) 1649, ae. about 10 days, Elizabeth bapt. 7 (1) 1652.

John, Scituate, volunteer for the Pequot war, 1637. Before the Court 2 June, 1640. Land confirmed to him 7 Nov. 1643. Partner in land with Peter Collymer in 1642.

William, Lynn, propr. 1638. In court for withdrawing from baptizing of infants, 1646. He deposed 17 (5) 1659, ae. about 65 years. His son William rem. to Southampton, L. I.; deposed before N. Y. officials, 16 May, 1641, that he was b. in Cincenshier, [Lincolnshire?] and was ae. about 24 years.

HARKET, HARKOT, see HACKETT,
Richard, Salem, before Gen. Court 17 Oct. 1643.

HARLAKENDEN, IRLAKINGTON,
Richard, Esq., Cambridge, propr. 1638.

Roger, Esquire, gent., b. in Erlescolne, co. Essex, Eng., came in the Defense July 3, 1635, with wife Elizabeth, ae. 18, sister Mabel H., ae. 21, and servants, Anne Wood, ae. 23, Samuel Shepherd, ae. 22, Joseph Cocke, ae. 27, George Cocke, ae. 25, (see Cooke,) William French, ae. 30, and his wife Eliza, ae. 32, Robert —, and Sarah Simes, ae. 30. Settled at Cambridge. Propr.; town officer. Ch. Elizabeth b. (10) 1636, Margaret b. (7) 1638.

He d. Nov. 17, 1638, ae. 27. Will engrossed Dec. 3, 1639, [L.] beq. to wife Elizabeth, dau. Elizabeth, bro. Richard H., bro. John Haynes, sister Neville, cousin Sarah; to his pastor, Mr. Shepherd; to the poor of the chh.; to the library, etc. [Reg. II, 181.] His widow m. 2, Herbert Pelham, Esq.

HARLOW,
William, cooper, Sandwich, prop. frm. 5 March, 1638-9; frm. 6 June, 1654, propr.. Rem. to Plymouth. Sergeant. He m. Dec. 20, 1649, Rebecca Bartlett; ch. William b. and d. 1650, Samuel b. 27 Jan. 1652, Rebecca b. 12 June, 1655, William b. 2 June, 1657. He m. 2, July 15, 1658, Mary Faunce; ch. Mary b. 19 (..) 1659, Repentance b. 22 Nov. 1660, John b. 19 Oct., 1662, Nathaniel b. 30 Sept. 1664. His wife Mary d. Oct. 4, 1664; he m. Jan. 20, 1665, Mary Shelley; ch. Hannah b. 28 Oct. 1666, Bathshua b. 21 April, 1667, Joanna b. 24 March, 1669, Mehitabel b. 4 Oct., 1672, Judith b. 2 Aug. 1676.

His est. settled Sept. 18, 1691; division made to four sons, Samuel, William, Nathaniel and Benjamin, and to his seven daughters not named. The widow made oath to the inv. at home, on account of her weakness.

HARMAN, HARMON, HERMON,
Francis, ae. 43, John, ae. 12, and Sarah, ae. 10, came in the Love in July, 1635.

John, Springfield, propr.; taxed in 1644; town officer. Ch. Sarah b. 24 (11) 1644, Joseph b. 4 (11) 1646, Elizabeth b. 1649, d. 7 (4) 1652, Mary b. 12 (9) 1651, Nathaniel b. 13 (1) 1654, Ebenezer b. 12 (6) 1657, d. 7 (1) 1660, Sarah b. Oct. 14, 1649, Mary b. Oct.

HARMAN, etc., cont.
23, 1671, d. 13 Nov. 1673, Sarah b. Feb. 1, 1675.

Nunc. will made 4 March, 1660, beq. all to his wife.

John, son of Edmund Harmon, of London, tailor, acknowledged himself apprentice of Francis Cooke of New Plymouth for 7 years from Oct. 1, 1636. Atba. 1643. Served 17 days against the Narragansetts from 15 Aug., 1645.
John d. 16 (1) 1661.

Widow, had grant of land at Lynn in 1638.

HARNETT,
Edward, tailor, Salem, 1638; adm. chh. 1 (8) 1643; took Jeremiah, son of William and Alice Chichester, as an apprentice 31 (6) 1658. Wife Scicillea or Cicely, memb. chh. 1639; joined him in deed in 1657. Edward, Jr., adm. chh. 3 (3) 1645. Ch. Jonathan bapt. 17 (9) 1650, Eunice bapt. 3 (7) 1654.

HARADEN, HARRADEN, HARRENDEN, HARANDINE,
Edward, Ipswich, about 1650. Rem. to Gloucester; testified in 1656 to the standing of certain line trees before the year 1652. He deposed in 1677, ae. above 50 years. Wife Sarah; ch. Elizabeth, (m. 27 (7) 1676, Thomas Prince, Jr.,) Edward b. about 1650, as he deposed in 1727; Andrew b. 13 (11) 1658, d. March 4, 1683, Ann b. 2 March, 1660, John b. Aug. 7, 1663, Thomas b. 8 (7) 1665, d. April 26, 1683, Joseph b. 18 (6) 1668, Sarah b. 30 July, 1670, d. 3 (7) 1672, Benjamin b. 11 (7) 1671.

Admin. on his est. was gr. to the widow and son Edward; they sold land in 1694.

HARPER,
William, lawsuits in Salem Court in 1641.

HARRIMAN,
Leonard, Rowley, propr. about 1648. Wife Margaret.

He d. 6 May, 1691. Will prob. 29 Sept. 1691, beq. to sons Matthew and Jonathan; daus. Hannah Boynton and Mary H.

HARRINGTON, ARRINGTON, HER-RINGTON, ERRINGTON,
Edward, Charlestown, adm. chh. 3 (3) 1647.

Joseph, servant to Capt. Keane. Lynn, lawsuit in 1641.

Richard, lime-burner, Charlestown, inhab. 1643; frm. May 26, 1647. Wife Elizabeth adm. chh. 9 (10) 1643; ch. Mary, (m. Seabred Taylor,) Elizabeth b. 15 (1) 1643, (m. Wm. Vine).
He d. in 1659; admin. gr. to the selectmen.

Robert, Watertown, propr. 1642; took oath of fidelity in 1652; frm. May 27. 1663. Town officer; mill-owner. He m. Oct. 1, [1647,] Susan George; ch. Susan b. Aug. 18, 1649, John b. Aug. 24, 1651, Robert b. 31 (6) 1653, George b. Nov. 24, 1655, Daniel b. Nov. 1, 1657, Joseph b. Dec. 28, 1659. The wife d. July 6, 1694.
He d. May 11, 1707, ae. 91. Will names sons John, Daniel, Benjamin, Samuel, Thomas, Edward; daus. Susanna Beers, Mary Bemis, Sarah Winship; Joanna Ward, late wife of his son Joseph, and her son Joseph.

HARRIS, HARRICE,
Anthony, Ipswich, res. 1648. Referred to in the will of Richard Eels in 1639.

Arthur, (called also Harrison,) Duxbury, atba. 1643. Propr. 1 June, 1640. He res. at Boston.
Will dated 17 March, 1673, prob. 7 July, 1674, beq. to eldest son Isaac, son Samuel and dau. Mary; rest to wife who was to care for the other children. The son Samuel d. in 1678, and beq. to his wife Hannah, his bro. Isaac, sisters Martha Snell and — Winchcorne, and their children.

George, Salem, propr. 1636. His house by the Cove, the common landing place of the North river. [Es. Court rec.]

George, a child about 8 years of age, apprenticed (11) 1643, for 12 years to Thomas Goldsmith to learn his trade. [To. rec.]

Jane, ae. 28, came in the Christian March 16, 1634; settled at Scituate; adm. chh. June 21, 1635.

John, mariner, Rowley, propr. 1643; frm. May 26, 1647. Bought land of Daniel H. of R., carpenter, (artificer, wheelwright,)

HARRIS, etc., cont.
5 Aug. 1652. Wife Bridget bur. Aug. 4, 1672; ch. John b. 8 (8) 1649. He consented 28 June, 1680, to the prob. of the will of his "last wife." [Ips. De. IV, 345.] His ch. Elizabeth, Nathaniel, John and Mary recd. bequests from Mr. Nathaniel Rogers, who calls him cousin. Made deeds of gift to sons Nathaniel and Timothy in 1680 and 1682.
He d., aged, Feb. 15, 1694. Will dated 8 Jan. 1691-2, prob. 27 March, 1695, beq. to wife Alice, referring to their marriage contract; to son Nathaniel and his son John; sons John and Timothy; dau. Mary Allen.

Joseph, Salem, 1643.

Joshua, apprenticed for 5 years to Thomas Weston, Nov. 5, 1633. In Gen. Court.

Parnel, of Bow, London, came in the Hercules in March, 1634.

Richard, gent., Cambridge, sold house 6 (1) 1642, which had belonged to John Moores.
He d. Aug. 29, 1644.

Robert, Roxbury; the Gen. Court freed him from his master 10 (10) 1641. Propr.; frm. May 22, 1650. He bought land at Muddy River 9 Feb., 1659. He m. Jan. 24, 1642, Elizabeth Boffee or Boughey, who had bros. Bold, Timothy and Thomas, and sisters Katharine Thorpe, Hannah Wilding, Mary Roe, and Priscilla Bruce. [Reg. V, 307, and XXXIX, 331.] Ch. Elizabeth b. Nov. 9, 1644, John bapt. 8 (6) 1647, Timothy bapt. 14 (5) 1650, Daniel b. May 14, 1652, Priscilla bapt. 19 (8) 1653.

Thomas, Roxbury, servant to John Johnson, d. 2 (7) 1640. See Frye, William.

Thomas, fisherman, seaman, Ipswich, served against the Indians and was paid by the town in 1643; propr. at Rowley 1643; sold land in R. in 1643, giving deed with wife Martha 22 (12) 1654. He m. Nov. 15, 1647, Martha Lake; ch. Thomas b. Aug. 8, 1648, Martha b. 8 Jan. 1650, John b. 7 Jan. 1652, Elizabeth b. Feb. 8, 1654, Margaret b. 6 Aug. 1657, Mary b. last Jan. 1659, William b. 12 Dec. 1664. He deposed in 1658, ae. 40 years.
Will dated 16 July, prob. Sept. 14, 1687; beq. to Wife Martha, sons John, William

HARRIS, etc., cont.
and Ebenezer. Refers to oldest son who d. beyond the sea.

Walter, embarked March 6, 1631, came to Plymouth upon an engagement with Mr. John Atwood of London, under command of Mr. John Done of Plym. for 5 years; was transferred to Henry Howland April 8, 1633.

Walter, of Dorchester, frm. June 2, 1641, signed the inv. of John Pope in 1649.

William, Charlestown, Rowley, propr. 1643. Wife Eedy, or Edee, adm. chh. Charlestown 30 (9) 1642; ch. b. at Rowley 1 (5) 1645. Amy adm. chh. Charlestown 9 (6) 1656.

HARRISON,
Arthur, (called also Harris, q. v.)

Rev. Edward, Boston, adm. inhab. in 1645. Wife Eleanor; ch. Joseph b. 20 (3) 1646; John bapt. 21 (3) 1648, his father being pastor of the church at Virginia; Elizabeth bapt. 28 (8) 1649, ae. about 7 days.

John, gent., an attachment granted for him by Gen. Court 4 (10) 1638.

John, rope-maker, cordish maker, Salisbury, propr. 1639, frm. June 2, 1641. Sold lands in Salis. to Ralph Blasdale 25 (1) 1643. Rem. to Boston. Rec'd to chh. from S. with wife Grace 17 (12) 1643. One of the attorneys of John Hodges, citizen and cooper of London in 1647. [Norf. rec.] Ch. John b. 2 (2) 1652, Elizabeth b. 2 Aug. 1653, Eliashib bapt. 18 (1) 1655, Anna b. 21 (10) 1656, Bethiah b. Sept. 7, 1658, Ebenezer b. May 31, 1660, Abraham b. Sept. 3, 1661, Rebecca b. Feb. 2, 1662, d. July 25, 1663, Isaac b. June 18, 1664. He m. 2, Persis, widow of Wm. Bridges, who was adm. chh. as his wife, 9 (2) 1654; she d. March 7, 1682-3. He d. Dec. 11, 1684.

Richard, Charlestown, witness to a deed in 1647.

HARROD,
Winnifred, adm. chh. Charlestown 12 (12) 1636.

HARSON,
Christopher, Wenham, 1643. [Essex Court files.]

HART, HEART, compare with Hardy,
Edmund, or Edward, Dorchester, propr. 1632; frm. May 14, 1635. Weymouth, propr. 1636. Ch. Martha b. 12 (8) 1640.

Isaac, yeoman, Watertown, before Gen. Court 30 (5) 1640; propr. 1642. Sold land in 1656. Rem. to Lynn, afterward to Reading. Propr. 1647. Wife Elizabeth memb. chh. R. 1648; petitioned Mdx. Court with him in 1656. Ch. Elizabeth b. Dec. 11, 1651, Samuel b. Feb. 9, 1656, (m. 29 Jan. 1673, Mary Witterige; he d. 25 June, 1683. He, ae. about 40, and she, ae. about 35, deposed in 1658. [Es. files.]

His will dated Feb. 6, 1697, prob. Feb. 19, 1699, beq. to wife Elizabeth, sons Thomas, John, Samuel and Adam, and daus. Elizabeth Wenborn and Dabra (Deborah) Proctor.

John, embarked March 7, 1631.

John, shoemaker, ae. 40, with Mary, ae. 31, came in the James in July, 1635. Settled at Salem, Marblehead; propr. 1636; Mary memb. chh. 1637; he was adm. chh. 1638. Witness at Court 1645.

Admin. gr. to widow Florence 26 (4) 1656. Inv. 14 (1) 1655-6. Edward Flint, Jeremiah Neale, Joseph Morgan and John Trask gave power of attorney 1 March, 1672-3, to their bro.-in-law Jonathan Hart, to act for them as husbands of the daughters of the late John and Florence Hart of Marblehead. [See also Es. files XVIII, 58.]

Nicholas, Taunton, atba. 1643. [See Rossiter.]

Stephen, Cambridge, propr. 1633; frm. May 14, 1634. Propr. Sold in 1635. Rem. to Conn.

Thomas, ae. 24, servant to John Browne, tailor, cert. from Baddow, Essex, came in the Desire in June, 1635. Settled at Ipswich; propr. 1639; town officer.

HARTOPP, HARTUB,
William, Plymouth, Duxbury, atba. 1643.

HARTSHORN,
Thomas, Reading, propr., frm. May 10, 1648. Deposed 3 (2) 1654, ae. about 40 years. [Mdx. Files.] Wife Susanna d. March 18, 1659-60. He m. Hannah —, who was recd. from the chh. of Ipswich 6 (2) 1663; she d.

HARTSHORN, cont.
July 20, 1673. Ch. Thomas b. Oct. 30, 1646, Thomas b. 30 (7) 1648, [Mdx. De. I.] John b. May 6, 1650, Joseph b. July 2, 1652, Jonathan b. Aug. 20, 1656, Susanna b. March 2, 1659, Timothy b. Feb. 3, 1661, Mary b. Aug. 19, 1672.

He d. about 18 May, 1683, when inv. of his est. was taken. Will dated 26 Oct. 1681, prob. 19 June, 1683, beq. to sons Benjamin and Thomas, dau. Susannah and wife Sarah.

HARTWELL,
William, Concord, frm. May 18. 1642. Wife Jasan, Jassin, or Jezan, deposed 11 (3) 1675, ae. 67 years, concerning the will of her dau. Sarah Parker, widow. Ch. John b. 23 (12) 1640, Samuel b. 26 (1) 1645, Martha b. 25 (2) 1649, Sarah, (m. — Parker; made nunc. will, as above; beq. to her children and to her sister, wife of Jonathan Hill, of Billerica; inv. mentions her youngest son John P.).

HARVARD,
REV. JOHN, FOUNDER OF HARVARD COLLEGE, was bapt. at Southwark, co. Surrey, Eng., Nov. 29, 1607, son of Robert Harvard, (name sometimes spelt Harvie, Harvye, Haverede, Harwar and Haward,) citizen and butcher; and of his wife Katharine Rogers, a native of Stratford on Avon. The father was bur. Aug. 24, 1625; his widow m. 19 Jan. 1625-6, John Elletson, citizen and cooper, who d. in June, 1626; she m. 28 May, 1627, Richard Yearwood, citizen and grocer, who d. in Sept. or Oct., 1632. The wills of these persons, of the father of Mrs. Harvard, and of Thomas, bro. of John, discovered and collated by Mr. Henry F. Waters, are presented in the Register for July, 1885.

Mr. Harvard was matriculated at Emanuel Coll., Cambridge, 7 July, 1631, A. B. in 1632 and A. M. in 1635. He married Anne, dau. of Mr. John Sadler, vicar of Patcham, co. Sussex, b. Aug. 24, 1614.

He sold some of his lands 16 Feb. 1636-7, and sailed for N. E. soon after. He settled at Charlestown, where he was adm. a townsman 6 (6) 1637, a special vote giving him "promise of such accommodations as best we can." He and his wife were adm. chh. 6 (9) 1637. As the pastor, Mr. Thomas James, had recently gone away, Mr. Harvard officiated in his place, in conjunction

HARVARD, cont.
with the teacher, Mr. Symmes, though his ill-health forbade his being installed. Johnson speaks highly of his preaching. The town chose him a memb. of a com. to consider something tending towards a body of laws 26 April, 1638.

The Gen. Court had voted to establish a college at Newetowne, (Cambridge;) and he, being one of the teaching elders of a neighboring church, must have felt the needs and realized the importance of the infant institution. He d. of consumption Sept. 14, 1638; and left to the college at Cambridge one half of his estate, a sum amounting to 700 li. [S.] In consideration of this gift the Gen. Court ordered 13 March, 1638-9, that " the college formerly agreed upon to bee built at Cambridg shalbee called Harvard Colledge."

He left no issue. The widow married early in 1639 Mr. Thomas Allen, who was installed shortly after as colleague pastor at Charlestown. The Court granted to him 500 acres of land 6 June, 1639, "in regard of Mr. Harvard's gift." They returned to England about 1650.

HARVEY, HARVIE, HARVY, HARBIE,
Joseph, husbandman, of Gamscolne, Essex, Eng., died on the voyage to this country. Bequeathed his estate to be lent to poor christians in these plantations for two years; then to be returned to his bro. John Harvie of Wethersfield, Eng. and his sister goodwife Burke in Eng. Dated June 26, 1638; inv. in Boston Court 4 June, 1639, 48 li., 2 s., 9½ d.

Richard, ae. 22, with Ann, ae. 22, cert. from St. Albans, Eng., came in the Planter April 2, 1635. Settled at Salem; tailor, propr. 1638. Adm. chh. 5 Oct. 1661. Ch. Anna, Eliz. and John bapt. 8 (10) 1661, dau. Jehodan bapt. 13 (5) 1662, Abigail bapt. 6 (9) 1664. Bro. and sister Harvey were dism. with others to Southold, L. I., 20 (6) 1665.

Richard, Concord. Twin daughters b. and d. (9) 1639; wife Margaret d. 2 (10) 1639.

Thomas, yeoman, Taunton, atba. 1643; deposed 8 Nov. 1638, ae. about 21 years.

William, tanner, Taunton, 1639. Rem. to Boston. He m. 2 April, 1639, Joane Huck-

HARVEY, etc., cont.

er of Cohannett; she was adm. with him to the chh. of Boston in 1643. His [second] wife, Martha, was adm. chh. 16 (2) 1654. Ch. Abigail b. 25 (2) 1640, Thomas b. 13 (10) 1641, Experience, dau., b. 4 (1) 1644, Joseph b. 8 (10) 1645, William b. 27 Aug. 1651, Thomas b. 16 Aug. 1652, John b. 5 Feb. 1654, Mary bapt. 2 (6) 1657.

He d. Aug. 15, 1658. Admin. gr. to widow Martha for herself and 4 young ch. April 28, 1659. [Reg. IX, 346.] The widow m. 10 Nov. 1659, Henry Tewxbery.

HARWOOD, HARWOODE, HARDWOOD, HARROD,

Emm, Salem, deposed Jan. 28, 1701-2, ae. about 71 years, that she lived with Thomas Flint from 1649 to 1653.

George, house-carpenter, Boston, 1636. Wife Jane adm. chh. 25 (12) 1642; dism. to chh. at Pequot 26 (8) 1651. Ch. John b. 4 (5) 1639, Deliverance d. (12) 1640, Joanna b. 10 (10) 1642, bapt. with John 5 (1) 1643.

Henry, Boston, 1630, herdsman; appl. frm. Oct. 19, 1630, adm. frm. March 4, 1632-3. Wife Elizabeth adm. chh. 1632. Ch. John bapt. 3 (4) 1632. [W.] Rem. to Charlestown; herdsman, 1632. [Wife] Winnifred adm. chh. 12 (12) 1636.

Inv. presented in Gen. Court 5 (10) 1637.

Henry, shoemaker, Salem, 1638, frm. Feb. 28, 1642-3. Constable. Goodwife adm. chh. 31 (11) 1640.

Nunc. will prob. 29 (4) 1664; est. to go to wife for her life, then to his kinswoman Jane, wife of Richard Flinders, last to his wife's dau. Elizabeth, wife of Matthew Nixon; £4 "to the church, to help the poor in bearing the charge of the Lord's supper." Prob. acct. (9) 1671. The widow Elizabeth sold certain lands 1 Nov. 1669. [Es. files.]

Mr. John, tailor, merchant, Boston, adm. chh. 25 (10) 1647, frm. May 22, 1649. Referee in Burt and Rayner acct. in 1655. [Suff. De. II, 170.] Deposed in Gifford case in 1653, ae. about 27 years. [Es. files.] Ch. Elizabeth bapt. 17 (1) 1650, Hezekiah b. April 27, 1653, d. 25 (4) 1654.

HASELTINE, HAZELTINE, HAZELTON, HASELDON,

Francis, Boston, memb. chh. 1630-1. "D. soon."

John, Rowley, propr. 1643. He m. Joan Anter, q. v.; ch. Mary b. 9 (10) 1648, Nathaniel b. 20 (7) 1656. Rem. to Haverhill. He deposed in 1663, ae. about 40 years. With wife Joanna he sold land in Bradford to David H. of Bradford, 4 Jan. 1674.

He d. Dec. 23, 1690, ae. about 70 years. Will dated 17 Aug. 1689, prob. 31 March, 1691, beq. to wife; sons Samuel, John and Nathaniel, and dau. Mary. The widow d., aged, July 17, 1698.

Robert, Rowley, propr., memb. grand jury 1641. Rem. to Bradford. He m. 23 (10) 1639, Anna —; ch. Anna b. 1 (2) 1641, Mercy b. (8) 1642, Samuel b. 20 (12) 1645, Mary b. 14 (2) 1646, Abraham b. 23 (3) 1648, Deliverance b. 25 (1) 1651, Elizabeth b. Jan. 15, 1652, both d. 14 (5) 1654, Robert b. 7 (9) 1657, Gershom b. Jan. 31, 1661.

He d. 27 Aug. 1674. Will dated 25 Oct. 1673, prob. 29 Sept. 1674, beq. to wife Anna, sons David, Abraham, Robert and Gershom, daus. Deliverance and Marey [or Mercy]; to minister Symmes and to the town.

HASEY, HESYE, HACY, see Halsall,

William, yeoman, Pulling Point, Boston. Rem. to Rumney Marsh. Wife Sarah adm. chh. 9 (1) 1650; ch. Elizabeth, Sarah and Hester bapt. 23 (1) 1651, William b. 15 Sept. 1652, Susanna b. May 30, 1660, Martha bapt. 24 (2) 1664.

Admin. of his est. gr. to widow Judith 4 July, 1695. She had letter of dismission from Ipswich to Bo. chh. 12 (9) 1675. [Mass. Hist Coll. 4-8.]

Hester or Esther, b. 20 March, 1650-1, m. 11 Jan., 1672, Henry Green of Malden. [See her own account of her family in Reg. LIV, 211.]

HASKELL, HASCALL, HOSKELL,

Roger, planter, Salem, 1636. He deposed in 1664, ae. about 50 years. His wife Elizabeth was a dau. of John Hardy, who beq. to her and her 4 ch. John, William, Mark and Elizabeth in 1652.

He d. in 1667; will dated 27 May, prob. 26 (4) 1667; wife Elizabeth; ch. Mark, Wil-

HASKELL, etc., cont.
liam, John, Roger, Josiah, Samuel, Elizabeth, Hannah and Sarah; bros. William and Mark H.; sister Jone; son-in-law Wm. Dodge; father in law John Stone. The widow m. 2, Edward Berry of Salem, weaver. [Es. files XIX, 47, Es. De. III, 45.] The bro. Mark may be he who was in court in 1652 for wearing broad lace, and in 1661 called to account for the ketch Francis and Hanna.

William, husbandman, Gloucester, propr. 1645. He deposed in 1672, ae. about 55 years. He m. Nov. 6, 1643, Mary, dau. of Walter Tybbott; ch. William b. Aug. 26, 1644, Joseph b. June 2, 1646, Benjamin, (ae. 92 in 1741,) Ruth, (m. Nehemiah Grover,) Mary, (m. Wm. Dodge,) Mark b. April 8, 1658, Sarah b. June 28, 1660, (m. Jacob Griggs).

The wife Mary d. Aug. 16, and he d. Aug. 20, 1693. Will prob. Sept. 4, 1693, mentions all these ch. and Mark and William, ch. of his son William, dec. [Hist. Gloucester.] [See Genealogy in Es. In. Coll. XXXI.]

HASLEWOOD, HAZELWOOD,
John, before Gen. Court 6 (10) 1638.

HASSARD, HASARD, HAZARD,
Thomas, ship carpenter, Boston, adm. chh. 22 (3) 1636, frm. May 25, 1636. Ch. Hannah bapt. 10 (7) 1637.

HASSELL, HASEWELL, HAZELL,
John, Ipswich, propr. 1635, frm. March 9, 1636-7.

John, Sickunke, (Rehoboth,) lawsuit, 1641, summoned to Plymouth 2 Aug. 1642, to own jurisdiction; lands at R. confirmed to him 6 June, 1649. Prosecuted for attending house meetings Oct. 2, 1650.

He made will 17 (7) 1651, prob. 2 March, 1651-2; beq. to any of his kindred who may demand it 12 pence; to Wm. Howell; to John Clarke of Rhode Island; to Nathaniel Biscoe of Watertown. All the rest to the procuring of liberty for the churches and people of God.

Richard, Cambridge, frm. May 26, 1647. He deposed 17 (10) 1662, ae. about 40 years. [Mdx. Files.] Wife Joanna or Jane; ch. Elizabeth b. 20 (7) 1643, Joseph b. 20 (7) 1645, Hester b. 6 (10) 1646-7, Annah, (of Richard and Anna,) b. Oct. 6, 1669.

HASSEN, see Hazen.

HASTINGS,
John, tanner, Braintree, frm. May 10, 1643. Rem. to Cambridge; propr. 1648; rec'd to chh. Feb. 1656. [Mi.] Ch. Elizabeth b. at Br. 2 (5) 1643. His wife d. and he m. 2, Anne, widow of John Meane. Ch. Walter, Samuel, (bapt. in England,) John, Seaborne and Elizabeth. [Mi.]

He d. Dec. 2, 1657. Will, dated July 26, 1657, mentions wife Anne, sons Walter, Samuel and John, dau. Elizabeth, dau.-in-law Mary Meane, son-in-law Wm. Buttricke. The widow Ann d. 25 (1) 1666, ae. about 60. The inv. of her est. was filed by son Walter April 3, 1666. Walter and Samuel, who had married her two daughters, agreed on division of the est. with John Hastings and Elizabeth Billings.

Thomas, ae. 29, with wife Susan, ae. 34, came in the Elizabeth of Ipswich April 30, 1634. Settled at Watertown; frm. May 6, 1635. Yeoman, selectman, deacon, town clerk, deputy. Non-resident propr. at Dedham, 1636. Signed inv. of Wm. Goodrich in 1647. His wife d. Feb. 2, 1650; he m. 2, Margaret, dau. of Wm. Cheney, of Roxbury. Ch. Thomas b. July 1, 1652, John b. March 1, 1653-4, William b. Aug. 8, 1655, Joseph b. Sept. 12, 1657, Benjamin b. Aug. 9, 1659, Nathaniel b. Sept. 25, 1661, Hephzibah b. Jan. 31, 1663-4, (m. Deacon Wm. Bond,) Samuel b. March 12, 1665-6.

Will dated 12 March, 1682, prob. 7 (7) 1685, beq. to wife Margaret life use of all in her possession; to sons Thomas, John, Joseph, Benjamin, Nathaniel and Samuel; to dau. Hephzibah Bond and to two daus. of son Thomas.

HATCH,
John, yeoman, Scituate, endorsed a bond Jan. 3, 1636.

Jonathan, Plymouth, before Plym. and Gen. Courts in 1640. Sent to Lieut. Davenport at Salem in 1642. Afterward placed in care of Stephen Hopkins. He served against the Narragansetts in 1645. Hired land of Indians in 1651. Res. at Barnstable. He m. 11 April, 1647, Sarah Rowley; ch. Mary b. 14 July, 1648, Thomas b. 1 Jan. 1649, Jonathan b. 17 May, 1652, Joseph b. 7 March, 1654, Benjamin b. 7 Sept. 1655, Nathaniel

HATCH, cont.

b. 5 June, 1657, Samuel b. 7 Oct. 1659, Moses b. 4 March, 1662, Sarah b. 21 March, 1664.

In his will, dated 15 Sept. 1705, he beq. to all these sons but Nathaniel and to daus. Mary Weeks, Sarah Wing and Mary Rowley, wife of Nathan R. Lydia, sister of Jonathan, before Court 1641-2.

Thomas, Dorchester, propr., frm. May 14, 1634. Sold house and lands, except his commons in the Neck, Oct. 31, 1639.

Thomas, Yarmouth, propr., frm. 7 Jan. 1638-9.

Thomas, Barnstable, atba. 1643. Rem. to Scituate.

He d. before June 14, 1646, when ch. Hanna was bapt. Inv. presented by widow Grace May 27, 1661. Working tools, timber, an instrument called a violin, etc. [Reg. V, 338.]

The widow of Thomas Hatch of Scituate had lived there 4 or 5 years in 1659, though married to John Spring of Watertown. [Plym. Col. Rec.] Daniel Pryor had ch. Daniel bapt. at Second chh. Sci. July 6, 1656, "grand child to our sister Spring."

William, merchant, of Sandwich, Eng., with wife Jane, 5 children and 6 servants, came in the Hercules in March, 1634. Settled at Sandwich. Ret. to Eng. and came again, a joint undertaker in the Castle in 1638. [L.] Planter; frm. Jan. 5, 1635-6. Lieut., 1643; elder.

He d. at Scituate Nov. 6, 1651. Will dated Nov. 5, 1651; wife Jane; daus. Jane Lovell, and Ann Torrey; gr. ch. John Lovell, James, William, Joseph and Damaris Torrey; sons Walter and William, execs. [Reg. IV, 320.] The widow m. 31 March, 1653, Thomas King.

HATCHET,

William, before Boston Court 7 Oct., 1641. Executed.

HATHAWAY, HATHWAY, HADAWAY,

Arthur, Marshfield, atba. 1643. Plymouth, 1646. He m. 20 Nov. 1652, Sarah Cooke of Plym.; ch. John b. 17 Sept., 1653, Arthur b. 28 Feb., 1655.

Arthur, Dartmouth, made will 9 Feb. 1709-10, prob. Feb. 6, 1710-11; beq. to sons John, Thomas and Jonathan, daus. Mary Ham-

HATHAWAY, etc., cont.

mond, Lydia Sisson and Hannah Cadman; to wife Sarah.

John, ae. 18, came in the Blessing in July, 1635. Before Gen. Court 6 June, 1637. Res. at Taunton, 1649. Before Plym. Court for lending a gun to an Indian. Res. at Barnstable 1656. Ch. John b. 16 Aug. 1658, Hannah b. May 1662, Edward b. 10 Feb. 1663. He rem. to Yarmouth.

Will dated 3 Aug. 1689, prob. Feb. 15, 1696-7; beq. to wife Elizabeth, sons Thomas, John, Gideon and Edward; daus. by a former wife; wife to bestow on her two daus.

Nicholas, Braintree, had land grant for 4 heads 24 (12) 1639-40.

Susan, ae. 34, came in the Abigail in July, 1635.

HATHERLY,

Timothy, felt maker, merchant, gentleman, from the parish of St. Olaves, Southwark, London, [see Irish, John,] came in the Anne in 1623, [Mor.] but returned the folg. winter; came again in the Friendship, about the middle of the summer of 1630, [B.] to Plymouth. Was one of the leading partners in Plymouth Colony. Returned to England, and came again in the William and Francis June 5, 1632. Settled at Scituate. Frm. Jan. 5, 1634-5. He and his wife joined the church Jan. 11, 1634, and his sister, Egglin Handford, joined Nov. 21, 1635. He was an active and influential citizen, an officer in town, Asst. and treasurer of the Colony, and com. of the United Colonies. He did not consent to the persecution of Quakers, and was left off the bench in consequence. He m. 2, Lydia, widow of Nathl. Tilden. Deeded land, etc., in 1666 to Joseph Tilden, conditioned on life-care of himself and wife.

He d. Oct. 24, 1666. Will dated Dec. 20, 1664, prob. Oct. 30, 1666, beq. to wife Lydia; Edward Jenkins, his wife and ch.: Nicholas Wade, wife and ch.; Susanna, wife of William Brooks and her ch.; Timothy and Elizabeth Foster; Mr. Thomas Hanford; Fear Robinson, now wife of Samuel Baker, and the other three ch. of Isaac Robinson, John, Isaac and Mercy; wife's ch. Lydia Garratt, and her four ch.; the wife of Wm. Bassett; the widow Preble; George Sutton, his wife and ch.; to Lydia and Thomas Lapham;

HATHERLY, cont.
Stephen Tilden; servant Thomas Savory; Mr. Nicholas Baker; Lydia, dau. of Wm. Hatch; friend Joseph Tilden, exec. [W., B., Cudworth, etc.]

HATHORNE, HAWTHORN, HAUTHORNE,
John, Salem, memb. chh. 1637. Rem. to Malden; Gen. Court licensed him to keep the ordinary. Rem. to Lynn. He deposed in 1665, ae. about 42 years. A brother of Major William. Wife Sarah; ch. Sarah bapt. 2 (4) 1644, John bapt. 14 (8) 1646, Priscilla bapt. 22 (5) 1649.
Will dated 19 Oct. 1676, prob. 27 (4) 1677, beq. to wife Sarah; ch. Ebenezer, Priscilla Shore, (and her dau. of same name,) Marah, Phebe, and Nathaniel.

Mr. William, Dorchester, propr. and frm. May 14, 1634; town officer. Rem. to Salem in 1636, he and his wife being adm. to the chh. in 1637. Major, town officer, deputy, Asst., com. of United Colonies. One of the most sagacious and efficient of the colonial leaders. He deposed in court at Salem 2 (10) 1658, ae. about 51 years. Had letters from his bro. Robert H. of Bray, Eng., April 1, 1653, with message to bro. John H. [Reg. XII, 295.] His wife Anna was called "sister" by Mrs. Lydia Banks; but in what way meant does not appear.
A list of his children, in his own hand, has come down, being entered in a volume which he owned. [Es. Inst. Col. III, 66.] Ch. Sarah b. 11(1) 1634-5, Eleazer b. 1 (6) 1637, Nathaniel b. 11 (6) 1639, John b. 4 (6) 1641, (John bapt. 3 (5) 1644,) Anna b. 12 (10) 1643, William b. 1 (2) 1645, (William bapt. 8 (2) 1646,) Elizabeth b. 22 (5) 1649, (Mary bapt. 1 (3) 1653.) Those in parenthesis are taken from Salem records. His dau. Mrs. Helwis was recd. to full com. in the chh. in 1661.
He d. in 1681. Will dated 17 Feb. 1679-80, inv. taken 10 June, 1681. Wife Ann exec.; beq. to her, to William, Samuel and Abigail, ch. of dec. son Eleazer; son John; Sarah, widow of dec. son William; gr. ch. Jervice Helwyde, land at Groton if he come over from "Urop" to enjoy it; dau. Sarah Coaker's two eldest sons by her husband Coaker; to the rest of his gr.ch. Sons John H. and Israel Porter execs.

HAULGH, see Hough.

HAULTON, see Holton,
William, ae. 23, came in the Francis of Ipswich April 30, 1634.

HAVEN, HAVENS,
Richard, Lynn, 1645. Wife Susanna, dau. of Thomas Newhall, who names her and her ch. in his will. He deposed in Prob. court in 1691, ae. 74 years. Record in Book II, "copied out of the old book." Ch. Hannah b. 22 (12) 1645, Mary b. 12 (1) 1647, Joseph b. 22 (12) 1649, Richard b. 25 (3) 1651, Susanna b. 24 (2) 1653, Sarah b. 4 (4) 1655, John b. 10 (10) 1656, Martha b. 1658, d. 1659, Samuel b. and d. 1660, Jonathan b. 1660, d. 1662, Nathaniel b. 30 July, 1664, Moses b. 20 May, 1667. The wife Susanna d. 7 Feb. 1682.
He made will 21 May, 1701; aged; beq. to sons John, Nathaniel and Moses; gr. ch. Joseph, son of son Richard, dec.; dau. Hannah Goodell; son-in-law John Tarbox; dau. Sarah Whitney; gr. ch. [Westol] Cogswell, Hannah Parker, Hannah Goodell and the ch. of son Moses.

HAWLEY, HAWLY, HAULE, see Hale and Hall,
John, Charlestown, with wife Bethiah, dism. from Boston chh. 14 (8) 1632, and joined that of Char.

Jonathan, Charlestown, propr. 1635.

Richard, residence not stated, frm. May 29, 1644.

Samuel, Charlestown, died before 16 (—) 1637, when the inv. of his est. was presented, taken by Raphe Sprage and Raphe Mousell. It included house and land at Mystic side; land in England which was part of his wife's "ioynter."

Thomas, Roxbury. Wife Emm, bur. Nov. 29, 1651; he m. Feb. 2, 1651-2, Dorothy (Harbittle,) widow of Thomas Lamb; ch. Thomas bapt. Oct. 8 or 16, 1651, Joseph bapt. 30 (11) 1652, bur. Nov. 3, 1653, Joseph b. 4 (7) 1654, Elizabeth bapt. 29 (4) 1656, Dorothy bapt. 20 (4) 1658.
He was slain at Sudbury April 21, 1676 Widow Dorothy d. Jan. 28, 1697-8.

HAWES, HAWS, HAUS,

Edmund, of London, Eng., came in the James April 5, 1635. Plymouth, propr. 2 Oct. 1637. Rem. to Duxbury; frm. 5 June, 1644. Town officer. Sold lands at Marshfield in 1649 and rem. to Yarmouth.

Will signed 5 May, 1692, being aged; prob. July 20, 1693; beq. to son John and his wife Desire; to gr. ch. Joseph, Desire, Jabez, Edmund, Ebenezer, Isaac and Benjamin Hawes, Elizabeth Doged and Mary Baron; gr. ch. Experience; to gr. gr. children; to John Hathaway.

Edward, Dedham, 1648. He was employed to plaster the meeting-house in 1648. He m. 15 (2) 1648, Eliony Lumber; ch. Lydia b. 26 (11) 1648, Mary b. 4 (9) 1650, Daniel b. 10 (12) 1651, Hannah b. 1 (12) 1654, John b. 17 (10) 1656, Nathaniel b. 14 (6) 1660, Abigail b. 2 (8) 1662, Joseph b. 9 Aug. 1664, Deborah b. 1 Sept. 1666.

He d. June 28, 1686. Will prob. 17 Dec. 1689, beq. to wife Eliony, ch. Daniel, John, Nathaniel, Joseph, Lydia Gay, Hannah Mason, Abigail Vales and Deborah Pond.

Richard, ae. 29, with Ann, ae. 26, and ch. Anna, ae. 2½ and Obediah, ae. 6 mos., came in the Truelove in Sept., 1635. Settled at Dorchester, propr.; frm. May 2, 1638. Other ch. rec. in Dorch., Constance, (m. 1 (4) 1663, Thomas Dewey,) son Eleazer.

Admin. gr. on his est. 27 (11) 1656. [Reg. XI, 342.]

Robert, a soap-boiler, ae. 19, came in the Elizabeth and Ann in April, 1635. Settled at Roxbury. Rem. to Salem. His mill referred to in 1648. [Es. files.] Rem. to Wenham; propr. 1654. His wife Frances made nunc. will June 12, prob. Essex Court, Sept. 10, 1645; beq. to sons Robert and Mathew Edwards, to the young ch. Thomas she had by Robert Hawes; to Alice, dau. of Robert Hawes; to her sister Ellen [Hiler] in Eng.; to Katharine Dorlon and Sarah Bartett, the two maids that kept her in her sickness; four pounds to a child in old England. He d. 29 (10) 1666, ae. about 84. Will prob. Jan. 18, 1666-7; sons Thomas and John Hawes; dau. Mary; wife; son Humphrey Barrett, exec.; bro. John Pierpont and friend Edward Dennison, overseers.

HAWK, HAWKS, HAWKES,

Adam, Charlestown, 1634; rem. to Lynn; propr. 1638. He deposed in 1658, ae. about 50 years; his son-in-law Thomas Hutchinson dep. in same case. [Es. Files, IV, 12.] Wife Anne adm. chh. 21 (9) 1634; she d. 4 (10) 1669. He m. June, 1670, Sarah Hooper. Ch. Sarah b. June 2, 1671.

He d. 13 (1) 1671. Division of his est. was made 27 March, 1672, between the widow Sarah, son John, dau. Sarah (under 18 years); to Wm. Coggswell for his wife; to Frances, Samuel, Thomas and Edward Hutchinson; to Elizabeth Hart, and to Moses, son of John H.

Isaac, Lynn, called to court 29 (10) 1646.

John, [Dorchester?] frm. Sept. 3, 1634. Rem. to Windsor, Conn., thence about 1660 to Hadley. Ch. John b. 13 Aug. 1643, Nathaniel bapt. 16 Feb. 1644, Elizabeth bapt. 10 Jan. 1646, (m. Joseph Gillett,) Ann bapt. 1 Oct. 1648, Isaac bapt. Aug. 1650, Mary b. May 23, 1652, Joanna b. Feb. 8, 1653, Eleazer b. 20 Dec. 1655, Sarah b. 29 Sept. 1657, Gershom b. 12 April, 1659.

He was bur. June 30, 1662. His widow Elizabeth m. — Hinsdale, after whose death she returned to the Hawks homestead; her sons Eliezer and Gershom Hawks had portions assigned Sept. 27, 1681.

Matthew, with wife and servant John Fearing, came from Cambridge, Eng., and settled at Hingham, 1638. Frm. May 18, 1642. Town officer, schoolmaster. Ch. Elizabeth bapt. July 14, 1639, (m. Stephen Lincoln,) Sarah bapt. Aug. 1, 1641, (m. John Cushing,) Bethiah bapt. Jan. 21, 1643, (m. Benjamin Stetson,) Mary bapt. Aug. 2, 1646, (m. Benjamin Loring,) Deborah bapt. March 22, 1651, (m. John Briggs,) Hannah bapt. July 22, 1655, (m. Peter Cushing). His wife Margaret d. 18 March, 1683.

He d. 11 Dec. 1684, ae. 74 years.

Samuel, before Gen. Court 28 (11) 1640.

HAWKINS,

Abraham, Charlestown, ae. about 28 years, deposed to the list of goods of his master, Thomas Rucke, July 19, 1639. [L.] Adm. chh. 30 (9) 1643; propr.; frm. May, 1645. Town officer. Elizabeth adm. chh. 13 (2) 1643.

He d. 6 (11) 1647. Inv. of his est. presented

HAWKINS, cont.
by widow Elizabeth 18 (1) 1648-9; working tools, house, land, etc.

George, ship-wright, Boston, attorney of George Richardson, of Wapping, mariner, May 1, 1641.

James, bricklayer, Boston, before the Court 4 Aug. 1635, for taking too high wages. Had land grant at Braintree 19 (12) 1637, for 4 heads. Sold dwelling-house in Bo. 5 (9) 1638. He deposed 1 (12) 1659, ae. about 56 years, that he saw and read in 1636 an indenture of Thomas Munt with his master, Richard Garritt. He deeded land 31 Jan. 1667, to his son-in-law Bartholomew Threadneedle. Wife Mary; ch. Susan b. 13 (12) 1645, Peleg b. 9 (1) 1648, James b. July 3, 1652, James b. March 18, 1653, Sarah b. March 18, 1656, Elihu b. Sept. 22, 1658, James, Elizabeth and Sarah bapt. 29 (2) 1667.
Will dated 25 June, 1669, prob. 30 April, 1670. Wife Mary; son James; 5 daus., Mary, Ruth, Damaris, Elizabeth and Sarah; to 10 gr. ch. a Bible apiece. [Reg. XLVIII, 460.]

Job, ae. 15, came in the Planter April 10, 1635, cert. from Sudbury, Eng. Res. at Boston. Wife Frances; ch. Martha b. 26 (1) 1646, Job b. April 20, 1658.

Mary, probably of one of these families, m. in Boston 21 (9) 1654, John Aylett.

Richard. No evidence of his residence here. His wife Jane was forbidden by Gen. Court, 12 March, 1637-8, to meddle in surgery, phisick or religion except with the elders, for satisfaction. Her sons James, Job and Thomas petitioned the Court in 1650 that she might be allowed to live in this jurisdiction; but were denied. She was, however, allowed to come to Boston on her way to England, 23 May, 1655.

Thomas, carpenter, captain, shipwright, of White Chapel, had permission to travel to America May 8, 1632. He res. first at Dorchester, then at Charlestown, (propr. 1636,) and afterward at Boston. Engaged extensively in shipbuilding and commerce. Built ship Seafort, of 400 tons, at Boston, and sailed in her 23 (9) 1644 for Spain; there she was wrecked, and 19 persons drowned. He was wrecked at the same place in another ship 2 (12) 1645. His wife Mary was with

HAWKINS, cont.
him in the Dorchester chh.; ch. Sarah bapt. 24 (1) 1638-9, (m. 4 (11) 1653, Robert Breck, merchant, of Galway, Ireland,) Abigail bapt. 1642, (m. May 13, 1660, Samuel Moore). His son Thomas sold land about 1666.
He d. on the ret. voyage of his ship from Eng. in 1648. Inv. filed 26 July, 1654. Est. divided between his wife, son Thomas and 4 daus. [W.] The widow m. 2, Robert Fenne before 29 (8) 1657.

John, Boston, memb. chh. 1631-2; d. soon after.

Richard, ae. 15, came in the Susan and Ellen in April, 1635.

Robert, husbandman, ae. 25, with wife Mary, ae. 25, came in the Elizabeth and Ann in April, 1635. Settled at Charlestown. Frm. May 25, 1636. He was adm. chh. 17 (2) 1636. His wife Mary adm. chh. 8 (11) 1635. Ch. Eleazer bapt. 25 (10) 1636, Zachary bapt. 25 (8) 1639, Joseph bapt. 3 (2) 1641.
Robert H. d. 11 (7) 1704. [S.]

Thomas, baker, Boston, propr. 1636. Purchaser 28 (4) 1645. Wife Hannah adm. chh. 15 (6) 1641; she d. 27 (3) 1644. He m. 2, Rebecca —; ch. Abraham b. in 1637, bapt. ae. 4 years, 22 (6) 1641, Thomas b. 1 (11) 1636-7, Hannah and Job b. 20 (11) 1640, Hope b. 2 (2) 1643, Hannah b. 1644, (m. June 7, 1661, Edward Howard,) Mehetabel b. Jan. 27, 1656, Richard b. Feb. 20, 1659, Ephraim b. April 5, 1664, Ephraim b. Oct. 15, 1665, Melatiah b. Nov. 12, 1666.

Timothy, weaver, Watertown, had grant of trees from Cambridge to pay for timber he used about John French's house, 13 (1) 1647-8; bought land in 1651.
Inv. of his est. taken 27 Sept. 1651.

HAWKSWORTH,
Nathaniel, Lynn, appraiser of est. of Jane Gaines in 1644.

Thomas, ae. 23, came in the Christian March 16, 1634. Settled at Salisbury; planter; propr. 1640. Ch. Mary b. April 22, 1641 (m. Onesiphorus Page,) Susanna d. Nov. 17 1655.
He d. Nov. 8, 1642; inv. Oct. 8, 1651. Widow Mary was propr. 1650. She m. 2, Belshazzer Willix.

HAY,
Samuel, lawsuit in Essex Court in 1641.

HAYDEN, HAYDON, HEYDEN, HOIDEN, HOYDEN,
James, Charlestown, adm. chh. 13 (7) 1635; frm. March 9, 1636-7. Ferryman. Wife Elizabeth; ch. James b. 13 (12) 1637, John b. 26 (10) 1639, Ruhamah b. 18 (9) 1641, Elizabeth, Joshua, Mercy, Thomas.
The inv. of his est. taken Dec. 12, 1667, was filed by his wife Elizabeth; that of John, [his son?] was taken 3 Dec. 1675.

John, Dorchester, propr. 1632, frm. May 14, 1634. Before Gen. Court and acquitted 6 June, 1639. Rem. to Braintree. Gen. Court assisted him in the care of a distracted child 1647-1653. Wife Susanna; ch. Jonathan b. 19 (3) 1640, Hannah b. 7 (2) 1642, Ebenezer b. 7 (12) 1645, Nehemiah b. 14 (12) 1647. Samuel and John, Jr., of Braintree, may have been older sons.
Will dated 31 Oct. 1678, prob. 26 July, 1682, beq. to wife Susanna, sons Ebenezer, Joseph, Nehemiah and John, dau. Hannah and the ch. of dec. son Samuel. Joseph to be maintained.

HAYFIELD, see **HAFFIELD.**

HAYLE, see **HALE.**

HAYWARD, HAWARD, HEYWARD, HAYWOOD, HEYWOOD, HOWARD,
George, "Heward," Concord, frm. March 1637-8. One of the appraisers of the estate of Wm. Halsted 10 (10) 1645. Wife Mary; ch. John b. 20 (10) 1640, Joseph b. 26 (1) 1643, Sarah b. 19 (1) 1645, Hannah b. 22 (2) 1647, Simon b. 22 (11) 1648, George b. 2 July, 1654.
He was drowned March 29, 1671, while helping Wm. Frizzell over the river in a canoe. His estate was divided between his widow Mary and his children John, Joseph Simeon, George, Elizabeth Wheeler, Sarah Prescott and Hannah Farrar. Joshua Wheeler, John Prescott and Jacob Farrar signed, Sept. 23, 1671. [Mdx. Files.]

Henry, ae. 7, came with John Barnard in 1634-5.

James, tailor, came in the Planter in 1635, ae. 22 years. Cert. from Stepney parish. Settled at Charlestown in 1636. Rem. to Woburn; propr. 1642. Ch. Rebecca b. 4 (10) 1641, d. 4 (10) 1642. Brought suit in Ipswich Court in 1642.
He d. 20 (9) 1642. [The widow] Judith, Woburn, m. Jan. 18, 1643, William Simonds.

John, ae. 22, cert. from Stepney parish, Eng., came in the Planter March 22, 1634. John, Concord, m. 17 Aug., 1656, Rebecca Atkinson; ch. Rebecca b. and d. 1657, John b. 5 April, 1661, Persis b. 24 April, 1664, Benoni b. and d. 1665. The wife Rebecca d. Aug. 5, 1665. He m. Nov. 30, 1665, Sarah Simond; ch. Sarah b. Aug. 30, 1666.

John, Watertown, frm. May 14, 1634-5, ae. 43. Propr. 1636. Constable 1638. Rem. to Dedham; rec'd to chh. 19 (11) 1644 from chh. of Wat. Will dated at Charlestown, July 31, 1672, ae. 79 years; prob. 19 (12) 1672; beq. to Thomas and Samuel Aldredge, Sarah and Esther Judson, Henry During; to Geo. Westbrook; to Andrew During's 5 ch.; to Mr. Samuell Phillips of Rowley, his 5 ch.; to the Colledge at Cambridge a house at Wat.; rest of est. at Ded., Wat., and elsewhere to wife and Samuel Phillips, whom he made execrs.
The widow d. at Dedham 23 (2) 1684. She beq. to eldest son Thomas Aldridge and his dau. Mary; son Samuel Aldridge; dau. Sarah Woodcock, (wife of John); gr. dau. Sarah (Westbrook) Woodcock; dau. Esther Kingsbury, (wife of Eleazer).

John, Plymouth. Volunteer for Pequot War 7 June, 1637. Duxbury, atba. 1643. Rem. to Bridgewater; ensign, 1664. Ch. Sarah b. at Plymouth 20 Aug. 1647. Elizabeth, [a dau.?] m. John Ames.

Nicholas, fisherman, Salem, propr. 1642. [Called also Howard.]
Will dated Jan. 6, 1682, "aged;" prob. 10 April, 1683; beq. to sons Nathaniel and the ch. of dec. son Nehemiah; to Nathl's sons Nathaniel and Nicholas; dau.-in-law Hannah Judkins; to gr. ch. Samuel, Elizabeth, Abigail and Sarah, J. and Hannah H.; to Annah Sargent and Rose H.

Richard, (Awards) from Bedfordshire, Eng., sent over with his family to Salem in 1629, by Mass. Bay Co. [Suff. De. I. xvi.] Boston, had grant of house-plot 19 (12) 1637-8.

Robert, Scituate, atba. 1643.

HAYWARD, etc., cont.

Samuel, ae. 22, came in the April 11, 1635; settled at Boston; carpenter. Wife Isabel; ch. James b. 16 (10) 1645.

Samuel, Sen., Charlestown, frm. May 2, 1649. Rem. to Malden. Wife Sarah adm. chh. 9 (5) 1648. Ch. Samuel b. 4 (3) 1646, Hannah, Martha b. 15 (11) 1652-3, Mary b. Aug. 1654, Sarah b. Feb. 1655-6, Elizabeth b. Sept. 25, 1658, Richard bapt. 22 (5) 1660, Deborah bapt. 6 (5) 1662, Nathaniel, Abigail, Jonathan. Will dated 5 (1) 1680-1, prob. 20 (4) 1681, beq. to sons Samuel, Nathaniel and Jonathan; dau. Hannah's ch.; remaining daus. Martha, Mary, Sarah, Elizabeth, Deborah and Abigail.

Widow Elizabeth d. May 12, 1686. Her will dated 11 (3) 1686, prob. 5 May, 1687, beq. to dau. Abigail her share in the est. of her first husband Oaks; to the wife of Samuel Haward.

Thomas, tailor, of Aylesford, Eng., with wife Susannah and 5 children, came in the Hercules in March 1634. Settled at Cambridge; propr. 1635-6. Rem. to Duxbury, propr. and purchaser 5 Nov. 1638. In Court 1644. Frm. 1 June, 1647. Rem. to Bridgewater.

Will dated June 29, 1678; yeoman, Sen.; beq. to sons Elisha and Joseph and gr. ch. Joseph.

William, Charlestown, propr. 1637; rem. to Braintree, deputy, 1641. Bought land in 1648. Signed his name "William Haywood," as witness to deed of James Everill in 1654. Ch. Huldah, (m. 14 (11) 1652, Ferdinando Thayer,) Jonathan, (m. 6 (3) 1663, Sarah Thayer).

He was drowned 10 (3) 1659. Admin. gr. 14 June 1659, to widow Margery for herself and children. [Reg. IX, 346.] The widow d. 18 (5) 1676. Admin. of her est. gr. 1 Aug. 1676, to her son Jonathan.

HAZELL, see HASSELL.

HAZARD, see HASSARD.

HAZEN, HASSEN,

Edward, Rowley, propr. about 1646. Town officer. Wife Elizabeth was bur. Sept. 18, 1649. He m. 2, in March, 1649-50, Hannah, dau. of Thomas Grant; ch. Eliz-

HAZEN, etc., cont.

abeth b. March 8, 1650-1, (m. Nathaniel Harris,) Hannah b. Sept. 1653, (m. William Gibson,) John b. Sept. 22, 1655, Thomas b. Feb. 29, 1657-8, Edward b. Sept. 10, 1660, Isabell b. July 21, 1662, (m. John Wood,) Priscilla b. Nov. 25, 1664, (m. Jeremiah Pearson,) Edney b. June 20, 1667, (m. Timothy Perkins,) Richard b. Aug. 6, 1669, Hephzibah b. Dec. 22, 1671, Sarah b. Aug. 22, 1673, (m. Daniel Wicom, Jr.).

He was bur. July 12, 1683; his widow m. 2, George Browne of Haverhill; she d. in Feb., 1715. [Genealogy in Reg. XXXIII, 229.]

HEALD, HELD,

John, Concord, frm. June 2, 1641. He rem. to Roxbury, then to Cambridge. Wife Dorothy; ch. Dorcas b. 22 (3) 1645, d. 1 (3) 1650, Gershom b. 23 (1) 1647, Dorothy b. 16 (8) 1649, Israel b. 30 July, 1660.

He d. 24 May, 1662. Autograph will dated 19 April, prob. 16 June, 1662, beq. to wife Dorothy, ch. John, Timothy and Hannah, and five younger.

HEALY, HEAY, HEILY, HEALIE, HELY, HALY, HEALE, HELYE, see also HALE,

Edward, merchant, res. not given. Gave bond to Wm. Pester of Salem Sept. 2, 1638; action against him Nov. 5, 1639. [L.]

Richard, ae. 22, came in the Christian March 16, 1634.

Robert, Watertown, propr., 1643.

William, Roxbury, frm. May, 1645. Endorsed a bond of J. Scarborough 15 (11) 1645. Signed as witness to will of John Graves in 1645. Rem. to Lynn and then to Cambridge before 1658. His wife and infant ch. d. 8 (9) 1649. Second wife Grace, dau. of Miles Ives. Ch. Hannah bapt. 7 (5) 1644, Samuel b. and d. in 1646, Elizabeth b. 9 (9) bapt. 14 (9) 1647, Sarah bapt. 2 (12) 1650, William bapt. 11 (5) 1652, Grace b. and bapt. at Camb.; Nathaniel bapt. Feb. 6, 1658, Martha bapt. Sept. 9, 1660.

He d. Nov. 28, 1683, ae. 70. Inv. taken 28 March folg., and admin. gr. to Daniel Cheever.

HEARD, HERD, HARD, HORD, HOORD, HURD,

John, tailor, having served with Mr. Wm. Hutchinson for divers years was adm. inhab. of Boston in 1639. Adm. chh. with wife Mary 7 (5) 1639. She deposed in 1662, ae. about 40 years. [Arch. 15 B.] He was to receive 40 s. from Mr. John Beauford 23 (10) 1644. Had accts. with Thomas Footman of Gorgeana 5 (2) 1648. [A.] Ch. John bapt. 18 (6) 1639, Hannah bapt. 20 (7) 1640, John bapt. 17 (5) 1642, ae. about 4 days, Joseph b. 10 (7) 1644, Mary bapt. 8 (9) 1646, ae. about 7 days, Benjamin bapt. 27 (6) 1648, ae. about 7 days, Mary bapt. 20 (8) 1650, Benjamin bapt. Nov. 28, 1652, Samuel b. March 14, 1655, Jacob (of Ann and John) bapt. 18 (1) 1655, Mehetabel (of John and Mary) b. Dec. 21, 1657, Mehetabel (of Ann) bapt. 27 (10) 1657.

John Hurd, Sen., d. Sept. 23, 1690. Will prob. Oct. 2, 1690, beq. to wife Mary; sons John and Jacob; gr. dau. Elizabeth, dau. of Benjamin, dec.; dau. Hannah Cowell; Jacob's son Jacob.

Luke, linen-weaver, Newbury, propr. 1638. Salem, frm. Sept. 6, 1639. Rem. to Salisbury; propr. 1640. Rem. to Ipswich; d. in 1647. Ch. John b. Feb. 4, d. Feb. 25, 1643; John b. March 6, 1644-5, Edmund.

Nunc. will prob. 28 (7) 1647; wife Sarah, sons John and Edmund.

At the request of the ch.'s grandfather John Wyatt, Joseph Bigsby, intending marriage to the widow, and about removing from this jurisdiction, gave bonds with her 15 (10) 1647, for maintenance of the ch.; their gr. father Wyatt to advise. Sarah was to receive land at Asington, co. Suff., Eng., after her mother's death, if not entailed.

William, Plymouth, came in the Ann in 1623.

HEARNDALE,

Benjamin, Lynn, accused of wife-beating in 1647.

HEATE, see HAIT.

HEATH,

Bartholomew, Newbury. Rem. to Haverhill; propr. 1646; town officer. He deposed in 1657, ae. about 41 years. Deeded land 12 March, 1668-9, to his sons John, Joseph and

HEATH, cont.

Josias H. He m. Hannah Moyce; ch. b. at Newb.: John b. 15 Aug. 1643, at Hav. Joshua b. and d. 1647, Hannah b. May 7, 1648, d. Nov. 9, 1668, Josiah b. Sept. 4, 1651, Elizabeth b. and d. 1654, Benjamin b. 1656, d. 1657, Elizabeth b. 1658, d. 1659. Wife Hannah d. July 19, 1677.

He d. Jan. 15, 1681. Inv. March 28, 1682.

Isaac, harms maker, (armourer?) ae. 50, Elizabeth, ae. 40, Martha, ae. 30, and Elizabeth, ae. 5, came in the Hopewell in Sept., 1635. Settled at Roxbury; frm. May 25, 1636. Ruling elder, town officer, deputy. His dau. Elizabeth m. John Bowles, and d. 7 (5) 1655.

He was bur. 23 (11) 1660. Will prob. 2 days later. To wife; son; cousin Martha Brand; kinsman Edward Morrice; Mary Mory. The widow Elizabeth d. 14 (11) 1664. Her will mentions sister Burnett and her son Isaac B.; Jacob Newell's wife; Isaac Johnson's dau. that he had by Hannah Heath; cousin Gary, the old man; goodmen Frysell that m. goodman Buskett's dau.; cousin Capt. Johnson, and sister Waterman. [Reg. X, 65, and XIII, 150.]

William, embarked June 22, 1632, came to Roxbury; frm. March 4, 1632-3. Court com. and deputy in 1634; householder.

He d. 29 (3) 1652. His will mentions wife, sons Isaac and Peleg, daus. Mary Spere, and Hannah Tenne, and bro. Elder Heath. [Reg. IV, 287.] The widow was bur. 15 (10) 1660.

HEATON, called also EATON,

Nathaniel, mercer, Boston, propr. Adm. chh. with wife Elizabeth 2 (9) 1634. Had accts. in 1639 with Lechford. Frm. May 25, 1636. Ch. Eleazer b. 22 (7), bapt. 2 (8) 1636, Nathaniel b. 31 (6) bapt. 1 (7) 1639, Elizabeth b. 13 (8) bapt. 8 (8) 1639.

The widow m. 2, Joseph Pell, and 3, John Minor. Jabesh "Eaton" and Mary who m. John Gilbert 5 (3) 1653, seemed to be older ch. The widow conveys her right of dower in certain land May 13, 1660. Nathaniel and Elizabeth petitioned Feb. 1, 1664, for a division of the est., which was allowed. [Reg. XIII, 338.] Inv. mentions something which had been given to Cornelius Fisher's wife Leah.

HEBBERT, HIBBIRD, HEBARD, HEBART, HEBERT, HIBBARD,
Robert, Salem, bricklayer, adm. chh. with wife Joanna May 3, 1646. Bought land in 1659. Rem. to Beverly. Ch. Marie b. Nov. 27, 1641, (m. Nicholas Snelling,) John b. Jan. 24, 1642-3, Sarah b. and d. 1644, Joseph and Robert bapt. May 7, 1648, Johanna b. Feb| 23, 1651, (m. John Swanton,) Elizabeth b. May 6, 1653, Abigail b. May 6, 1655, (m. Thomas Blackford of Beverly,) Samuel b. June 20, 1658.
He d. May 7, 1684; will prob. 24 June, 1684, beq. to wife and children. The widow d. 1696. [Genealogy in Reg. LI, 316.]

HECKNELL,
John, Braintree. Ch. John b. 3 (10) 1638.

HEDGE, EDGE, HEDGES,
William, gent., capt., brought a suit in Es. Court in 1637. Settled at Sandwich; sold the time of his servant Robert Wicksen Nov. 8, 1638. Propr. 1640. Frm. 5 June, 1651. Town officer. He rem. to Yarmouth. Ch. Elizabeth b. 21 May 1647, (m. Jan. 4, 1665, Jonathan Barnes of Plym.,) Mary b. 1648. Will dated June 30, prob. 11 Aug. 1670. Wife Blanch; ch. Abraham, Elisha, William, John, Elemuel, Sarah Matthews, Elizabeth Barnes, Mary Sturges and Marcye; sister Brookes to have a livelyhood among his children so long as she continues a widow. [Reg. VII, 235.]

William, Taunton, frm. Mass. Col. May 14, 1639.
He d. April 2, 1654. Wife Mary, (dau. of Henry Andrews,) sons John and Henry. [Reg. V, 261.] The widow m. 2, Peter Pitts, and deeded her part of the estate to her sons, her husband endorsing the bond, 15 March, 1654.

HEDSALL, see Edsall.

HEFFORD, HEIFER,
Henry, transferred by permission of Gen. Court from the service of Mr. Jonathan Wade of Ipswich to that of John Johnson, 1 (10) 1640.

Samuel, Ipswich, res. 1648.

HEILAND, HEYLAND, HILAND, HYLAND,
Thomas, planter, Scituate, propr. 1637; took oath of allegiance 1 Feb. 1638; atba. 1643. Juryman; town officer. His son Thomas was his partner in a suit at law in 1653. Dau. Sarah m. 6 Jan. 1651, Thomas Turner.
His will dated 14 Feb. 1682, inv. taken 3 May, 1683, beq. to son Thomas; gr. sons Thomas and John; daus. Elizabeth James, Sarah Turner, Mary Bryant and Deborah Ticknor; Isabel Witherell, sometime wife to son Samuel, now wife to Samuel W.; gr. ch. Benjamin and Elizabeth Bryant, Philip, son of Francis James of Hingham, and Joseph Studson. Lands at Waldern in Old England, against Waldern Down towards Herffields, and a house at Tenterden in Kent, to son Thomas.

HEMAN,
Francis, residence not stated, frm. May 6, 1646.

HEMENWAY, HEMMENWAY, HENINGWAY, HINNINGWAY,
Ralph, a man-servant, Roxbury, frm. Sept. 3, 1634. Memb. chh. 1633. [E.] Propr. He m. July 5, 1634, Elizabeth Hewes; she d. Feb. 4, 1684, ae. 82. Ch. Marah b. and d. 1635, Samuel b. June, 1636, Ruth b. Sept. 21, 1638, John b. April 27, 1641, Joshua b. April 9, 1643, Mary b. April 7, 1644, Elizabeth b. May 31, 1645, Mary b. April 7, 1647.
He d. June 1, 1678. Will dated 4 May, 1677, prob. 11 July, 1678, beq. to wife Elizabeth; sons John, Samuel, Joseway; dau. Elizabeth Holbrook.

HENDRICK, HENDRICKS,
Daniel, planter, Haverhill, propr. 1645; sold land in Hampton 8 (8) 1649; town officer. He deeded land 25 March, 1662, for his seven eldest ch. (specified,) in trust to his bros.-in-law John and Robert Pike. He m. Dorothie, dau. of John Pike, Sen. She d. June 5, 1659. He m. 2, Mary Stockbridge. Ch. Daniel, Hannah b. June 4, 1645, John b. May 23, 1648, Jotham b. March 21, 1649-50, Jabez b. Dec. 3, 1651, Israel b. Nov. 11, 1653, Dorothie b. May 31, 1659, Sarah b. Aug. 8, 1661, Abraham b. Aug. 2, 1663, d. Dec. 1, 1690, Deborah b. Nov. 25, 1666.

HEMPENSTALL,
Robert, shipwright, Boston, son of Thomas, of Southold, Eng., mariner, sold est. in Eng. to his father-in-law Henry Harwood 1 (1) 1640-1. [L.]

HENDRICKSON,
Peter, Boston; wife Margaret; ch. Mary b. 21 (1) 1639, John b. 22 (12) 1642.

HEPBURN, HEIPBOURNE, HEYPBOURNE,
George, glover, Charlestown, frm. May 25, 1636. Bell-ringer, 1657. Wife Hannah adm. chh. 6 (2) 1638; ch. Rebecca, Hannah, Sarah.
He d. Feb. 9, 1665-6. Will dated 27 (6) 1665, no date of prob., beq. to son Wright, he to pay to each of the ch. viz. Richard, John, and Abigail W.; son Ludkin to secure to his wife what I gave her on her marriage to her first husband; to Sara and Rebecca Sally. Aaron Ludkin was his partner in his trade.

HERBERT, HARBERT, HURBERT, HIRBERT,
John, shoemaker, ae. 23, cert. from Northampton, Eng., came in the Abigail in June, 1635. Settled at Salem; propr. 1637, frm. June 2, 1641. The Gen. Court gr. him land Oct. 7, 1640, on account of the £50 adventure of John Harris. Was one of the appraisers of the est. of John Thorne in 1646. Mary, [his wife?] adm. chh. 1639. Ch. Mary bapt. 29 (1) 1640, John bapt. 15 (8) 1643.
He rem. to Southold, L. I.; sold Salem land in 1656. [Es. De.]

HERMAN,
Nathaniel, Braintree, frm. May 10, 1643. Ch. Nathaniel b. 8 (12) 1640, Mary b. 15 (12) 1642.

HERMITAGE, see Armitage.

HERN, HERNE, HURNE,
George, residence not stated, before Gen. Court 2 (4) 1640.
Is this the man "Hern" associated with the Hutchinsons at Newport, who taught that women have no souls, etc., in 1638, according to Winthrop?
Matthew, Hingham, propr. 1635; ret. to Eng. before 1640. [L.]

HERRICK, HERRICKE,
Henry, yeoman, Salem, propr. 1635, frm. May 18, 1631. Rem. to Wenham, and later to Beverly. Wife Edith memb. chh. before 1636. Ch. Zechariah bapt. 25 (10) 1636, a son bapt. 11 (12) 1637, Henry bapt. 16 (11) 1639, Joseph bapt. 6 (6) 1645, Eliza bapt. 4 (5) 1647, John bapt. 26 (3) 1650, Lydia and Joseph, of — H., bapt. 26 (7) 1666.
Inv. of his est. taken 15 March, 1670-1, presented by son Henry; land, books, etc. The widow Edith deposed 28 (9) 1672, ae. about 60 years, that her father Hugh Laskin sold land before he went away about 25 years ago.

William, of Boston in 1640. [L.]

HERRING, HEARING, HEERING,
James, Cambridge, propr. Rem. to Dedham; propr. 19 (5) 1639.

Thomas, Dedham, adm. townsman 1643, frm. May 3, 1654. He m. 15 (2) 1650, Mary, dau. of Robert Pierce of Dorchester; he and his wife rec'd from Dorch. chh. 19 (8) 1651. Ch. Mary b. and d. 1651, Thomas b. 13 (5) 1654, James b. 5 (9) 1656, Sarah b. 14 (11) 1658, Deborah b. 16 Oct. 1666, Martha b. 11 July, 1668, Thomas b. 28 April, 1670.
He d. 27 (6) 1684. Will dated 18 (2) 1673, prob. 7 Nov. 1684, beq. to wife Mary, and to children at her discretion.

HERSEY, HEARSEY, HARSYE,
William, husbandman, Hingham, propr. 1636, frm. March, 1637-8. Court com. of valuation, 1640; town officer. Dau. Elizabeth m. Moses Gilman; Judith m. Humphrey Wilson.
He d. March 24, 1658. Will mentions wife Elizabeth; ch. William, John, James, Frances, Elizabeth, Judith; gr. ch. John Croade and William Hersie. Cousin John Farrington, Thomas Marsh and son-in-law Richard Croade, overseers. [Reg. VIII, 354.] The widow's will, dated 26 Aug. 1670, prob. 25 (8) 1671, beq. to ch. William, John, James, Frances Croade, Judith Wilson and Elizabeth Gilman.

HEWARD, see Haward,
John, in Court 7 April, 1635.

HERSOME, HERSONNE, HERSOINE, HARSAY, see Winsley,
Christopher, Salem, 1643. Rem. to Wenham. Ch. Mary bapt. (3) 1646.
Mary, widow, d. 2 (7) 1646; admin. 29 (10) 1646.

HETHERSAY, HETHERSEE, HEATHERSYE, HITHERSEA,
Robert, Concord, propr., rem. to Charlestown; mortg. house in Conc. 20 (11) 1640. Called into Essex Court 1643; had lived many years from his wife. Brought suits in Norf. court in 1648.

HEWES, HUGHS, HUES, see Huse,
Abel, frm. May 18, 1642.

John, Scituate, taxed in 1632; appl. frm. 6 March, 1637-8; atba. 1643. Wife Jone. [Plym. Col. Rec. 1634.]
Will dated 6 Feb. 1671, prob. 22 Feb. 1674, beq. to wife Joanna, son James H. and son-in-law Jeremiah Hatch.

John, Watertown, propr. 1642.

Joshua, iron-monger, merchant, Roxbury, came about (7) of the year 1633; his wife (Mary), dau. of [Henry] Gouldstone, came the next summer to Watertown, where she joined the chh.; they were m. Oct. [8] 1634. [E.] Propr., town officer, deputy. He rem. to Wickford in the Narragansett country, whence he gave deeds relating to the est. of Joshua Foote 14 Nov. 1665. He res. in Boston 1645-1657. His wife Mary d. in Bo. 23 (6) 1655; and he m. 11 (12) 1656, Alice, dau. of John Crabtree. Ch. Joshua b. and d. 1639, Mary b. Dec. 29, 1641, Joshua b. May 25, 1644, Hannah b. 28 Oct. 1657.

HEWETT, HUETT, HUITT,
Humphrey, Duxbury, took oath of fidelity 3 Jan. 1636.

James, Plymouth, juryman, 1636.

Nicholas, Boston. Ch. Zebulon b. (11) 1644.

Robert, punished by the Court March 6, 1632-3.

Thomas, tailor, Hingham, propr., frm. 26 May, 1647. He deposed June 15, 1663, ae. about 54 years, upon marriage of his dau. Elizabeth with Thomas Hubert. [Mdx. Files.] Wife Elizabeth, dau. of Wm. Chap-

HEWETT, etc., cont.
man, (who. beq. to her in 1639,) d. 22 May, 1649. He m. 2, Mary, widow of John Cutler. Ch. Ephraim bapt. July, 1639, Jary bapt. May 2, 1640, John bapt. July 18, 1641, James bapt. March 12, 1642-3, Elizabeth b. and d. 1643, Thomas bapt. May 12, 1644, Elizabeth bapt. March 3, 1644-5, Timothy bapt. Feb. 21, 1646-7.
He d. 24 May, 1670, ae. about 61 years. Inv. taken 12 Aug. 1670, and admin. gr. to son Ephraim. The est. recd. from Wm. Chapman is mentioned. The widow was living with her son Thomas at Charlestown in 1674. [Town Rec.]

HEWLETT,
Lewis, Charlestown, propr. 1636; before Gen. Court 3 (10) 1639. Rem. to Salisbury; propr. 1640.
Matthew, came in the Hercules in April, 1634.
Mr., Salem; resided at Saugus; desired land at Marblehead in 1636.

HEWSTEAD, HUSTEAD, HUSTED, HUSTE,
Robert, husbandman, ae. 40, came from Weymouth, Eng., before March 20, 1635. Settled at Braintree; propr. 1639.

HIBBARD, see Hebbert.

HIBBENS, HIBBINS,
Mr. William, gent., Boston, came in the Mary and John March 26, 1633-4; frm. May 13, 1640. Asst., deputy, town officer, agent for the Colony in England, etc. Was adm. to the chh. with wife Anne 28 (7) 1639. The church gave him general letters of introduction and recommendation to churches in Eng. 25 (5) 1641. He rendered most important service to the Colony in Parliament, in connection with Messrs. Peter and Weld in 1641 and 1642. Made public expression of his gratitude to God for remarkable preservation and prosperity, on his return. [W.]
He d. July 23, 1654.
His widow was adjudged a witch, and executed in 1656. Her will, prob. July 2, 1656, beq. to her sons John, Joseph and Jonathan Moore; to cousin Mark Cooe. [Reg. VI, 283.]

HICKE, HICKS, see HIX.

HICHBORN,
David, Boston, a servant, before the Court 1 (4) 1641. Wife Catharine; ch. Catharine b. 2 June, 1654, Solomon and David b. and d. in 1661.

HIDE, see HYDE.

HIGDON,
Peter, servant to Anthony Thatcher, of Sarum, tailor, came in the James, April 5, 1635.

HIGGINS, HUGGINS,
Alexander, Duxbury, took oath of fidelity 3 Jan. 1636.

Alexander, Salem, 1637.

Richard, Eastham, propr. 1650 or earlier. He m. Oct. 1651, Mary Yates; ch. Mary b. Sept. 1652, Eliakim b. Oct. 20, 1654, Jedaiah b. March, 1656, Ezra b. June, 1658, Thomas b. Jan. 1661, Lydia b. July, 1664.

John, Dedham, pioneer, 1636; sold land in 1639.

John, Hampton, mortg. house and land to secure delivery of pipe staves 22 (1) 1643-4. [Ipswich rec.]

Will dated May 31, prob. Oct. 11. 1670; ae. about 61 years; beq. to wife Bridget and son John. The widow m. 2, John Clifford, q. v.

Richard, tailor, Plymouth, taxed in 1632; frm. 1634; atba. 1643. Took Samuel Godbertson apprentice in 1634. He m. Dec. 11, 1634, Lydia Chandler; he m. 2, Mary, widow of John Yates; ch. Jonathan b. July, 1637, Benjamin b. July, 1640, Mary b. 27 Sept. 1652, Eliakim b. 20 Oct. 1654, William b. 15 Dec. 1655, Jedidiah b. 5 March, 1656.

Thomas, Plymouth, apprenticed for 8 years, Jan. 1, 1633-4, to John Jenney. Rem. to Barnstable. He m. at Nocett, Nov. 3, 1648, [Rose,] widow [of Hugh] Tillye.

HIGGINSON,
Rev. Francis, one of the first ministers of the chh. of Salem, b. in 1587, grad. at Emanuel Coll., Cambridge, Eng., A.B. 1609, A.M. 1613; preached at Claybrook in Leicester. Was sought by the Mass. Bay Company 23 March, 1628-9, for service in New England. Came in the Talbot, June 29,

HIGGINSON, cont.
1629, to Salem, where he did important, though brief work, as teacher of the church. "A good man, full of faith and full of work." [C. M.]

He d. in Aug. 1630. His widow rem. to Charlestown, then to New Haven, Conn. She d. in 1640. Ch. John, Francis, Timothy, Theophilus, Samuel, Anne, Mary, Charles, Neophytus. [Reg. VI, 105.] [Es. Inst. Coll. V, 33.] [See Lord, William.]

HILDRETH, HILDRICK, HILDRICKE,
Richard, Cambridge, frm. May 10, 1643; town officer, 1645. Rem. to Woburn. One of the founders of Chelmsford; had a special grant of 150 acres of land in 1663 on account of having lost his right hand. His son James, ae. 20, deposed concerning his father's corn, 30 (7) 1651. [Mdx. Files.]

He d. in 1688, ae. 83. [Reg. XI, 7.]

HILL, HILLS, ILLS, HULL,
Abraham, carpenter, Charlestown, adm. chh. 3 (4) 1639; frm. May 13, 1640. Town officer. Sold house 1646. Rem. to Malden. Deposed 2 (8) 1660, ae. about 45 years; referred to father Robert Longe of Charlestown. [Mdx. Files.] Wife Sarah; ch. Ruth b. 2 (4) 1640, Isaac b. 29 (8) 1641, Abraham b. 1 (8) 1643, Sarah b. 19 (6) 1647, d. Oct. 1649, Sarah b. in Malden Oct. 1649, Mary b. 9 May, 1652, Jacob b. (1) 1656-7.

He d. Feb. 13, 1669-70. Inv. filed 5 (2) 1670, by widow Sarah.

Bartholomew, mentioned in Col. Rec. 3 Nov. 1630.

Elizabeth, widow, Boston, adm. chh. 5 (3) 1639.

Hercules, Scituate, [see William Hatch,] served 13 days against the Narragansetts in 1645.

John, Dorchester, propr. 1633. Wife Frances adm. chh. before 1639; ch. Samuel bapt. in 1638, Samuel b. in 1640, Jonathan bapt. 12 (5) 1640, Hannah b. in 1641, Mercy b. 8 (11) 1642, [Ebenezer] bapt. 15 (12) 1645, Martha bapt. 20 (6) 1648, Mehitabel bapt. 18 (12) 1650, Mary m. 12 (2) 1656, Thomas Brecke, Ruth m. 19 (5) 1654, Roger Willis, Rebecca adm. chh. 11 (7) 1664.

HILL, etc., cont.

He d. 31 (3) 1664. Will prob. 30 (4) 1664, beq. to wife Frances, sons John and Samuel and dau. Mary; at his wife's death the est. to be divided to the "nine youngest children," or so many as may survive. A son-in-law of the widow came from Boggerstow to sojourn at her house 12 (4) 1675. She m. 2, Jonas Austin, and rem. to Taunton, being dism. from the chh. 28 (4) 1674. She d. at Dorch. Nov. 18, 1676.

John, blacksmith, Boston, adm. chh. with wife Margaret (5) 1641; frm. May 18, 1642. One of the founders of Lancaster accepted by Gen. Court in 1645.

He d. July 21, 1646. [Col. Rec.] Inventory filed 11 Nov. 1646. [Reg. VII, 35.]

John, carpenter, Boston, bond, 14 (6) 1639. [L.] Frm. May 6, 1646.

John, merchant, Boston, adm. chh. 15 (3) 1647.

John; he rem. to Newbury; the Gen. Court confirmed his sale of land at Watertown 15 May, 1654.

John, wheelwright, Salem, propr. 1649, 1658, etc. He m. 1, Miriam, dau. of Thomas Gardner, Sen.; m. 2, Lydia Buffum 26 (6) 1664. Ch. Miriam b. 24 (1) 1658, Susanna b. 31 (5) 1660, Lydia b. March 30, 1666, Elizabeth b. Dec. 15, 1667, John b. 22 (11) 1670, Robert b. 11 (9) 1676.

His will dated 29 Sept. prob. 30 Nov. 1680, beq. to ch. Miriam, Susan, Lydia, Elizabeth, John and Robert.

John, Plymouth, rem. before 1631; see letter of Bradford in Reg. II, 244.

Joseph, (Hills,) Sen., woolen draper, from Malden, co. Essex, Eng., deposed 30 July, 1639, that he came in the Susan and Ellen in 1638, as an undertaker, (i. e. stockholder). [L.] Settled at Charlestown; adm. inhabitant in 1636; res. in the part which became Malden. Adm. chh. with wife Rose, (sister of Mr. Henry Dunster,) 2 (12) 1639; frm. May, 1645. Deputy. He deposed 16 (10) 1662, ae. about 60. Joseph, Jr., deposed same day, ae. about 32. [Mdx. Files.] His note-book, containing business memoranda from 1627 down, is in the possession of the N. E. Hist Gen. Society. His wife Rose d. March 24, 1650. He m. June 24, 1651,

HILL, etc., cont.

Hannah, widow of Edward Mellows; he petitioned the Court, with her uncle, Mr. Peter Bulkeley, and recd. authority to sell est. for the benefit of her children, 27 May, 1652. After her death he m. (11) 1655, Helen Atkinson, who d. Jan. 6, 1663, and he m. Anne, widow of Henry Lunt, of Newbury, 8 March, 1665. She deposed in 1671, ae. about 50 years. Ch. Gershom b. 27 (5) 1639, Mehetabel b. 1 (11) 1640, d. July, 1653, John d. June 28, 1652, Samuel b. July, 1652, Nathaniel b. and d. in 1653-4, Deborah b. (1) 1656-7, d. Oct. 1, 1662, Abigail b. 6 (8) 1658, d. Oct. 9, 1662, Abigail b. in Boston Jan. 5, 1663.

He d. at Newbury 5 Feb. 1686-7, or 1687-8. Will prob. March 14, 1687-8, beq. to wife Anne; ch. Samuel, Wayte, Gershom, Elizabeth, Hannah; ch. of his dec. son Joseph; gr. ch. Hannah and Elizabeth Blanchard, Hannah Winton and Samuel Green; to Rebecca Newhall; son-in-law Abiel Long and son Samuel execrs.

Ralph, yeoman, Plymouth, 1638; sold land 16 Sept. 1643. Rem. to Woburn, propr. 1643, frm. 26 May, 1647. Town officer. One of the incorporators of Billerica in 1654. Gave land for a burying place. He m. at Plymouth, 21 Dec. 1638, Margaret, widow of Roger Toothaker; ch. Jonathan b. at Wob. April 20, 1646.

He d. 29 April, 1663. Will dated 18 Nov. 1662, prob. 12 (9) 1663, beq. to wife Margaret; ch. Ralph, Martha, Rebecca, Nathaniel and Jonathan; gr. ch. Mary Littlefield and Elizabeth Hill; son-in-law Roger Toothaker. The widow Margaret d. 22 (9) 1683, ae. 88.

Richard, cooper, Charlestown, propr. 1638.

Robert, servant to Mr. Craddock, ae. 20, came in the Defence in July, 1635.

Tobias, and wife, [Lynn,] lawsuit in Es. Court, 1640.

Thomas, Roxbury, a servant in Mr. John Eliot's family, came in 1633; d. about (12) 1634; faithful, prudent, good. [E.]

Mr. Thomas, Plymouth, frm. 7 March, 1636-7. Propr. 1638. Sold house and garden, 1640.

Valentine, merchant, Boston, adm. chh.

HILL, etc., cont.

12 (4) 1636, frm. May 13, 1640. Propr., town officer, deacon. Was chief owner of a large wharf property. Bought lands at Oyster River, (Dover,) before 1649; rem. thither. Wife Frances d. 17 (12) 1644 or 5; he m. 2, Mary —, who was adm. chh. 15 (3) 1647. Ch. Hannah b. 17 (1) 1638, (m. Jan. 24, 1659, Antipas Boyce,) John b. and d. in 1640. Elizabeth b. 12 (10) 1641, d. 9 (2) 1643, Joseph and Benjamin b. and d. in 1644, Joseph bapt. 26 (5) 1646, ae. about 8 days, John bapt. 2₂ (6) 1647, ae. about 3 days, Samuel bapt. 10 (10) 1648, ae. about 2 days, Mary bapt. 30 (10) 1649, ae. about 1 day, Elizabeth bapt. 25 (3) 1651.

He d. before Aug. 3, 1663, when the widow made her friend Mr. Joseph Hill of Malden her attorney for certain business.

Mr. William, merchant, Dorchester, one of the first company; [Bl.] frm. Nov. 5, 1633. He sold his property July 20, 1638.

William, embarked March 7, 1631; came to Roxbury in 1632, a man-servant. Frm. May 14, 1634. He m. Phillis, dau. of Richard Lyman, and rem. to Hartford, Conn. [E.] Wife Sarah; ch. William, Ignatius and James were legatees of his sister, Mary Goodwyn, widow, of Lyme Regis, Dorset, Eng. in will, 31 March, 1665. [Reg. XXXIX, 79.] His widow m. 2, Edmund Greenleaf of Boston, q. v.

William, wheelwright, ae. 70, came in the James in July, 1635.

Zebulon, cooper, Gloucester, propr. 1649; having formerly lived in Bristol, Eng., he deposed at Salem 27 (7) 1652, concerning Thomas Wathing. His wife Elizabeth was dismissed from the chh. of Salem to that of Saybrook, Conn. in 1662. Ch. John b. 2 (4) 1659, Philip b. 24 (10) 1662, Zebulon b. 5 (4) [....], Elizabeth b. 1 (12) 1664, Abigail b. 24 (7) 1670, Sara b. 22 June, 1675.

Will dated 29 March, 1699, prob. 11 March, 1699. Refers to the will of dec. son Zebulon; beq. to son Philip, daus. Elizabeth Marston, Abigail Allen, Sarah Morgan; to gr. ch. Benjamin and Elizabeth Ashby.

HILLIARD, HILLER, HILLYARD, HILLIER,

Anthony, Hingham, propr. 1639.

Hugh, residence unknown, frm. Sept. 3, 1634.

HILLIARD, etc., cont.

William, ae. 23, carpenter, came in the Elizabeth and Ann in May, 1635. Settled at Duxbury; before the Court 12 March, 1638-9. Juryman 1638; atba. 1643. Owned a mill with George Pollerd in 1640. Propr.

William, Boston. Rem. to Hingham. Wife Hester; ch. Hester or Esther b. 25 (1) 1642, (m. at Hingham Jan. 9, 1657, Joseph Bate,) Mary bapt. 7 (4) 1644, (m. at H. Aug. 14, 1664, John Farrow, Jr.,) William bapt. with the others at Hing. March 25, 1655.

HILMAN,

Ellner, ae. 33, came in the Abigail in July, 1635.

HILTON,

William, came in the Fortune to Plymouth, Nov. 1621; his wife and children came in the Anne in 1623. Lands assigned them in 1623. [Plym. Col. Rec.] Rem. to Newbury; in acct. with the est. of Joseph Avery in 1635. [Col. Rec.] Frm. May 19, 1642. Deputy, 1642-3. Rem. to New Hampshire. Ch. Sarah b. June, 1641, Charles b. July, 1643, Ann b. 12 Feb. 1648, Elizabeth b. 6 Nov. 1650, William b. 28 June, 1653.

HINCKLEY, HINKLY,

Samuel, from Tenterden, co. Kent, came in the Hercules in March, 1634. Settled at Scituate. Frm. 7 Feb. 1636-7. Rem. to Barnstable in 1638-9. Juror, town officer. His wife Sarah came with him; was adm. chh. Aug. 30, 1635; they brought four children: Thomas, (who became governor of Plymouth Colony,) Susanna, (m. Rev. John Smith,) Sarah, (m. Henry Cobb,) and Mary; other ch. b. here were Elizabeth bapt. Sept. 6, 1635, (m. 15 July, 1657, Elisha Parker,) Samuel bapt. 24 July, 1642, John bapt. 26 May, 1644. His wife d. Aug. 18, 1656; he m. Dec., 1657, Bridget Bodfish.

He d. Oct. 31, 1662; will dated 8 Oct. 1662, prob. 4 March, 1662-3, beq. to wife Bridget, sons Samuel, John and Thomas, daus. Susannah, Sarah, Mary and Elizabeth, and to his grandchildren. [Reg. VI, 95.]

HINDERSAM,

Margaret, before Gen. Court 3 (10) 1639; her husband gave bonds.

HINDS, HINDES, HYNDS, HAYNES, HAINES, HINDE,

Elizabeth, a maid servant, came in 1633 to Roxbury; memb. chh.; m. Alexander Beck, and was recd. to chh. of Boston 27 (9) 1642.

James, Salem, memb. chh. 25 (2) 1637, frm. March, 1637-8. Sold land in Marblehead in 1649. Rem. to Southold, L. I. Wife Mary; ch. John bapt. 28 (6) 1639, James bapt. 2 (6) 1641, Benjamin bapt. 26 (6) 1643, Mary bapt. 19 (2) 1646, James bapt. 27 (12) 1647, Jonathan and Sarah bapt. 11 (4) 1648, Thomas bapt. 4 (3) 1651.
Will, dated 1 March, 1652, inv. dated 18 (9) 1655, beq. to wife Mary; to eldest son John his tools and a double portion; other children not specified. [Reg. XXXVII, 161.]

Margery, maid servant to John Underhill, adm. chh. Boston 29 (10) 1633.

HINSDALE, HINSDELL, HENSDELL,

Robert, Dedham, propr. 1637, memb. chh. 1638. Town officer. Rem. to Medfield. Mortg. land in 1656. He and his wife Ann conveyed lands in M. to Jeremiah Tauke, citizen and cloth-worker of London, Aug. 20, 1663, as security for the payment of certain sums. Wife Ann adm. chh. 2 (4) 1639; ch. Barnabas b. 13 (9) 1639, Gamaliel b. 5 (1) 1642, Mary b. 14 (12) 1643, Experience, son, b. 27 (11) 1645, John b. 27 (11) 1647, Ephraim b. 26 (7) 1650.
He rem. to Hadley and later to Deerfield, where he and his sons Barnabas, John and Samuel were slain by Indians. Inv. of his est. taken Oct. 22, 1676; Ephraim was surety for the widow Elizabeth.

HINSTOON,

Teague, Charlestown, resident in 1634.

HITCHCOCK,

Richard, residence not given, was before Gen. Court Aug. 5, 1634.

Matthew, ae. 25, came in the Susan and Ellen in April, 1635. Settled at Watertown; propr. 1636. Had a grant of land in payment for his care of the dry herd Sept. 16, 1639. Rem. to New Haven, Conn.

HITCHIN, see HUTCHINS and HUTCHINSON,

Edward, a singleman, adm. chh. Boston 3 (6) 1634; frm. March 4, 1634-5.

HIX, HICKS, HICKE, HEEKS, HEECKS,

Richard, Boston; gave bond with Isaac Walker for the security of the ship Beginning; cleared by Henry Parks 27 Oct. 1651. Wife Mary; ch. Timothy b. 2 May, 1649, Mary b. Dec. 1654, Richard b. 20 Jan. 1656, d. July 27, 1658, Elizabeth b. July 25, 1659, Thomas b. Feb. 23, 1661, Elizabeth and Thomas bapt. 16 Oct. 1664, Rebecca b. March 26, 1665, Timothy bapt. 25 (4) 1665.

Robert, felmonger, from Southwark, co. Surrey, Eng., came in the Fortune in 1621 to Plymouth. Drew lots for himself, his wife and two children in 1623. (See Clement Briggs.) Frm. 1633. At the division of Cattle in 1627 he had wife Margaret, ch. Samuel, Ephraim, Lydia and Phebe.
He d. March 24, 1647. Will dated May 28, 1645, prob. May 15, 1648, beq. to wife Margaret, sons Samuel and Ephraim, gr. son John Bangs; to John Watson and other persons. The widow made will July 8, 1665, giving her est. to son Samuel, dau.-in-law Lydia, gr. ch. John Bangs; to the son of her son Ephraim, now dec.; to the son of George Watson, husband of her dec. dau. Phebe. [Reg. 11, 244, IV, 282, and VI, 187.]

Thomas, Marblehead, a proprietor in 1649. [Rem. to] Scituate.
Will dated Jan. 10, 1652, prob. Oct. 3, 1653. Wife Margaret, sons Zachariah, Daniel and Samuel. The widow being unable to come to Plymouth to prove the will, on account of her age and weakness, the Court ordered that her deposition be taken at home. [Reg. V, 260, and Plym. Col Rec.]

HOAR, HORE, HOARE,

Joanna, widow of Mr. Charles Hoar, brewer, of the city of Gloucester, Eng., came to N. E. about 1642. Her dau. Margery m. Mr. Henry Flint, who was the assoc. minister of the chh. of Braintree, and there she made her home. She brought with her sons John, Daniel and Leonard, and dau. Joanna, b. about 1625, (m. at Br. 26 (5) 1648, Edmund Quinsey, Jr.) A son Thomas was mentioned in her husband's will, who seems

HOAR, etc., cont.

to have rem. in Eng. She d. 21 (10) 1661. [See Genealogy in Reg. LIII.]

Daniel, son of the above, came to Boston; in partnership with Richard Cooke, recd. mortg. of land in Bo. 26 (10) 1650. His bro. John conducted a suit for him against Cooke, 1665; he then res. in Hull, Eng. He calls Richard Cooke cousin, in letter dated April 20, 1663. [Mdx. Files.] [Suff. De. IV, 317, and Col. Rec.]

Hezekiah, Taunton, atba. 1643; town officer. Ch. Mercy b. Jan. 1654, Nathaniel b. March, 1656, Sarah b. 1 April, 1658, Elizabeth b. 26 May, 1660, Edward b. 25 Sept. 1663, Lydia b. 24 March, 1665, Hezekiah b. 10 Nov. 1668, Mary b. 22 Sept. 1669.

John, son of Charles and Joanna, b. about 1623, settled at Scituate; atba. 1643; juryman, 1646; prop. frm. 5 June, 1651. Lawyer, farmer, propr. Sold land in 1659, and rem. to Concord. Remonstrated to the Court about 1665, that he could not obtain justice for his bro.'s interests which he was representing; and was disbarred temporarily from pleading any case except his own. He rendered ever memorable service in protection of the praying Indians, and in obtaining the deliverance of captives held by hostile Indians in 1675, in consideration of which he recd. a grant of land in 1682. Ch. Elizabeth, (m. Dec. 23, 1675, Jonathan Prescott,) Mary, (m. Oct. 21, 1668, Benjamin Graves,) Daniel b. 1650.

He d. April 2, 1704. His wife Alice d. June 5, 1696.

Rev. Leonard, son of Charles and Joanna, b. at Gloucester, Eng. about 1632, came to N. E. about 1642. Was grad. at Harvard College in 1650; became its third president, constituted 10 (10) 1672. [S.] He m. Bridget, dau. of Lord John and Alicia Lisle. Ch. Bridget b. March 13, 1673, (m. Mr. Thomas Cotton; res. at Shoreditch, London, in 1695, her mother then dwelling with her).

He d. in Boston 28 Nov., and was bur. at Braintree 6 Dec. 1675, ae. 45 years. Will dated 25 Oct. 1675; beq. to dau. Bridget and wife; to bros. Daniel and John Hoar, sisters Flint and Quinsey; cousins Josiah Flint and Noah Newman. To be interred at Braintree. The widow m. Hezekiah Usher. She d. May 25, 1723. [Reg. IX, 154, and 377.]

HOAR, etc., cont.

Richard, Yarmouth, frm. 7 Sept. 1641; atba. 1643; propr.; elder; com. for Court business; schoolmaster.

HOBART, see HUBBARD.

HOBBY,

John, apparently of Dorchester, arrested for selling beaver skins he found, 20 (3) 1637. [W.] Murdered by John Williams about (7) 1637.

HOBLE,

John, ae. 13, (sic) husbandman, came from Weymouth, Eng. before March 20, 1635. The son of widow Hoble was presented in Plym. Court 2 March, 1640-1. John d. at Springfield 24 (2) 1644.

HOBBS,

Maurice, Newbury, before Ipswich court in 1642; witness in 1663.

Thomas, Salem, a witness in court in 1648. He deposed in 1679, ae. 54 years, concerning matters at Wenham in 1651.

HOBSON,

William, Rowley, recd. bequest from Wm. Bellingham in 1650; propr.; selectman 1652. He m. 12 (9) 1652, Ann, dau. of Humphrey Raynor.

He was bur. 17 July, 1659. His wife, as adm. of his estate, confirmed in 1661 a deed of land he had formerly sold; and sold a lot which had been her father's. She sold other land in 1682.

In the admin. of the est. of John Hobson in 1684 reference is made to his father and mother and bro. and sister Hobson.

HODSHEN, HOCHENS, HODCHENS, HODCHEN, HODSON, HUTCHEN, see HUTCHINS,

George, Cambridge, propr. 1636, frm. March, 1637-8. Town officer. Returned to Newcastle on Tyne, Eng. before 1652; gave power of attorney for sale of Camb. property, etc. [Mdx. De. II.] Wife Jane; ch. Joseph b. 28 (10) 1639, Luke b. 6 (2) 1644, Anna b. 30 (7) 1645, Abiah b. 3 (2) 1648.

HODGES, see Hodsden, Hedges and Miller.

Andrew, husbandman, Ipswich, propr. 1639; frm. June 2, 1641.

Will dated Oct. 11, 1665, prob. 27 (1) 1666. Wife and her gr. child; cousin Giles Birdley, and others; to the poor of the town; to the college at Cambridge.

John, mariner, Charlestown, inhabitant, 1633. He gave letter of attorney 23 (6) 1645, for business at Bermuda. [A.]

Wife Mary survived him and m. John Anderson, q. v.

John, cooper, Salisbury, propr. 1639. Was of London, Eng. in 1647, when his land was sold by John Harrison, agent.

Nicholas, (Miller *alias* Hodges,) Plymouth, served against the Narragansetts from 15 Aug. 1645. [See Hosdone.]

Admin. of his est. was gr. to Wm. Hoskins, Sen. 6 Feb. 1665. Will dated Oct. 24, 1665, beq. to Peter Reife, John and Wm., Jr. Hoskins, to Mary Cobb, Daniel Ramsden and Hannah Reife. [Reg. VI, 187.]

William, Taunton, atba. 1643. [See will of Anthony Silpin of Barnstable, Plym. Prob. lib. II, p. 6.]

Richard, witness to a deed in Boston, 17 (8) 1645.

HODGKINS, HODGKINSON, HODGSKINS, HOSKINS.

Mr. William, planter, Plymouth, frm. 1634, juryman 1636. Propr. He m. Nov. 2, 1636, Sarah Cushman. He m. 21 Dec. 1638, Ann Hynes. Rem. to Ipswich about 1641. He deposed Sept. 29, 1691, ae. about 69 years; had occupied beach privileges fifty years. Placed his dau. Sarah with Thomas and Winnifride Whitney 2 Jan. 1643, to remain till 20 years of age. Wife Ann deposed 2 March, 1641; had lived before marriage at the house of Mr. Derby, father of John and Richard D. Ch. — b. 30 Nov. 1647, Samuel b. 8 Aug. 1654.

HOGG,

John, residence not given, before the Court in 1637.

Richard, tailor, Boston, propr. 1639. Adm. chh. with wife Joan 18 (6) 1639; frm. May 13, 1640. Ch. Joseph b. (10) 1636, bapt. 25 (6) 1639, Mary bapt. 22 (5) 1641, ae. about 6 days, John b. 4 (1) 1643, Mary b. 3 (11) 1646.

HOMAN, HOEMAN,

Nathaniel, took oath of freemanship May 10, 1643.

William, husbandman, ae. 40, with wife Winnifred, ae. 35, and children Hannah, ae. 8, Jeremy, ae. 6, Mary, ae. 4, Sarah, ae. 2, and Abraham, ae. 3 months, and Alice Ashby, servant, cert. from the parish of All Saints, Northampton, Eng., came in the Desire in June, 1635.

HOLBECK,

Grace, one of John Sampford's family, adm. chh. Boston 16 (6) 1635.

William, servant to William White, came in the Mayflower to Plymouth; died soon after landing. [B.]

HOLBIDGE,

Arthur, before Gen. Court Aug. 7, 1635, for taking too high wages.

HOLBROOK,

John, Sen., yeoman, Weymouth, frm. May 13, 1640. Bought ½ of a house, land and mill in W. 10 (10) 1656. Bought the other half of the heirs of Thomas Gatlive in 1668-9. With wife Elizabeth sold property in 1669. John, Jr., being one of the witnesses. A com. was chosen by the town, 22 Jan. 1674, to confer with him about the mill. Deputy, 1651. His [first] wife Sarah d. 14 (11) 1643.

Richard, Dorchester, propr., signed agreement 2 (12) 1646. [Town Rec.] Frm. May 10, 1648. Ch. Abigail bapt. 21 (3) 1648, Mary bapt. 17 (1) 1650, John, (m. 24 (9) 1663, Elizabeth Hemenway).

Thomas, ae. 34, of Broadway, Eng., with wife Jane, ae. 34, ch. John, ae. 11, Thomas, ae. 10, Anne, ae. 5, and Elizabeth, ae. 1, came from Weymouth, Eng. before March 20, 1635. Settled at Weymouth. Memb. of com. to lay out way from Br. to Dorchester, 1640. Frm. May, 1645. Town officer, 1648. Of Dorchester, planter, bought land beyond Neponset 31 (6) 1649.

Inv. of his est. taken 10 March, pres. 26 April, 1677, by son, Capt. John H. Will dated 31 (12) 1668, prob. April 24, 1677, beq. to wife Jane, sons John, William and Thomas, daus. Anne Rennolds, Elizabeth Hatch and Jane Drake, gr. ch. John, Peter and William H.

HOLCOMB, HOLCOMBE,
Thomas, Dorchester, propr., frm. May 14, 1634. He sold his property Aug. 12, 1635, and rem. to Windsor, Conn.

William, residence not stated, frm. May 26, 1647.

HOLDEN, HOULDEN, HOULDING, HOLDER,
Justinian, ae. 23, came in the Francis of Ipswich April 30, 1635. Settled at Watertown. Frm. May 6, 1657. Rem. to Cambridge; carpenter. He deposed in 1679, ae. about 66 years. Ch. Ebenezer (of Justinian and Mary) b. at Woburn May 11, 1690.

He d. in 1691. Will dated 12 Aug. prob. Oct. 6, 1691, beq. to wife Mary; ch. Samuel, John, Isaac, Joseph and three daus. The exec. Isaac Amsden and the dau. Mary were appointed guardians in 1698 for the daus. Grace and Elizabeth.

Randall, residence in Mass. not stated. He was brought from Rhode Island to Boston to be tried by the Gen. Court with Gorten *et als.* in 1643; imprisoned at Salem. Obtained protection from Parliament in 1646. [W.]

Richard, ae. 28, came in the Francis of Ipswich April 30, 1634. Settled at Watertown. Rem. to Woburn; propr. 1658. Rem to Groton. Deposed Dec. 1658, ae. about 50 years. Wife Martha; ch. Stephen b. 19 (5) 1642, Martha b. 15 (11) 1645, John b. March 17, 1649-50. His wife d. Dec. 6, 1681. He d. at Groton March 1, 1696, aged, infirm and a widower.

HOLDER, HOULDER,
Nathaniel, Dorchester, memb. chh. about 1636.

HOLDRED, HOLDROYD, HOLDRIDGE,
William, ae. 25, tanner, came in the Elizabeth, April 18, 1635. Settled at Ipswich. The Gen. Court admitted him to have a lot, (place not stated,) 2 Nov. 1637. Sold 10 April, 1639; propr. at Salisbury. Rem. to Haverhill; propr. 1650. Wife Isabel; ch. b. at Salis.: Sarah b. 1640, d. 1641, Mary b. and d. 1641, Rebecca b. June 20, 1643, (m. Richard Margin, of Dover,) William b. March 15, 1647, Sarah b. Dec. 26, 1650, d. Jan. 4, 1651, Mehitabel b. April 14, 1654, d. June 13, 1657, Mary b. Dec. 24, 1656.

HOLGRAVE,
Mr. John, fisherman, mariner, Salem, frm. Nov. 5, 1633. Deputy; town officer. Before Gen. Court 4 (10) 1638. Inn-keeper 1639. Elizabeth his wife one of the first members of the chh. Ch. Joshua, a propr. in 1635; Lydia, memb. chh. 1639. Ch. Eliza bapt. 1 (9) 1640, (m. Robert Gooch).

HOLLAND, HOLLON,
Christopher, lighterman, taxed at Woburn in 1645; rem. to Boston, res. 1647; bought house in 1652. Wife Ann; ch. John b. Feb. 6, 1647, Bridget b. March 14, 1649, Joanna b. 1650, and d. in 1652, Elizabeth b. Feb. 17, 1654.

Will dated 3 Feb. 1700-1, prob. 29 March, 1705, beq. to wife Ann and dau. Hannah Senter; had given portions to children; son-in-law John Tuder of New York mentioned.

John, ferryman, Dorchester, frm. Dec. 6, 1636. Made voyages to the Eastward; gave testimony in Court in 1635 concerning Wonnerton. Owner of the bark Endeavor. Town officer. Wife Judith; ch. Thomas, John, Nathaniel bapt. 30 (10) 1638, Deliverance bapt. 21 (1) 1641, Prudence bapt. 25 (3) 1645, Relief bapt. 16 (3) 1650.

Will dated 16 (10) 1651; bound for Virginia; beq. to wife half of his est. exc. the island of Munings Moone, which he gave to his eldest son John in addition to a double share in the rest of the est.; the other half to be divided among the children. Prob. 16 Sept. 1652. [L.] [Reg. IV, 287.]

Thomas, Yarmouth, "still a member of a separated church in Old England," had his child Thomas bapt. at Barnstable May 9, 1641.

He made will Oct. 1, 1686, prob. 31 May, 1687; beq. to ch. Thomas, Mary, (wife of John Whilding,) Elizabeth, (wife of Samuel Hall,) and Deborah.

HOLLARD, HOLLETT, HOLLAND,
Angell, shoemaker, ae. 21, with his wife Katharine, ae. 22, embarked from Weymouth, Eng. before March 20, 1635. Settled at Weymouth; frm. March 3, 1635-6; propr. 1643. Rem. to Boston. Wife Katharine; ch. Hannah b. 8 (8) 1635, (m. 23 (5) 1652, Wm. Ballentine,) Elizabeth b. (5) 1638, Thomas b. and d. in 1641, [George?] Hephzibah b. 10 (6) 1642, Thomas b. 8 (8), bapt. 10 (9) 1644, Sarah b. 5 (1) 1646, John bapt. 27 (3) 1649,

HOLLARD, etc., cont.
Mary bapt. 14 (7) 1641, Joanna b. and d. in 1653-4.
He d. in Boston last of June, 1670. Inv. pres. by widow Catharine 28 (5) 1671. The est. owed to Mr. Thos. Hollard in England. The widow m. 2, John Upham.

HOLLETT, see HALLETT.

HOLLEY, HOLLY,
Joseph, Dorchester, 1634. Rem. to Sandwich, atba. 1643.
His est. was divided in May, 1665, and these ch. receipted for their portions: Joseph Holley, Jr., Mary, wife of Nathaniel Fitsrandall, Sarah, wife of Joseph Allen, Experience Holley, and Hopestill, wife of Samuel Worden.

Samuel, Cambridge, propr. 1639. [Wife] Elizabeth, ae. 30, came in the 'Blessing in July, 1635.
Will, dated Oct. 22, 1643, mentions wife and son, without giving names. [Reg. II, 385, and XXX, 81.] The son John sold his share 4 Oct. 1645. [Camb. Propr. rec.] His widow Elizabeth m. John Kendall.

HOLLIDGE,
Richard, laborer, Boston, adm. chh. 3 (1) 1639; frm. May 22, 1639. Wife Anne adm. chh. 10 (1) 1639. Her will made 7 Dec. 1681, prob. 24 Aug. 1682, beq. to Madame Bradstreet; Mr. John Cotton of Plymouth and his wife; goodwife Rust; the wife of Roger Burgis; rest to cousins Abraham and Mary Browne.

HOLLINSWORTH, HALLINGWORTH, HOLLINWOOD,
Richard, ae. 40, with Susan, ae. 30, Christian Hunter, ae. 20, Elizabeth Hunter, ae. 18, Thomas Hunter, ae. 14, Wm. Hollingsworth, ae. 7, Richard, ae. 4, Elizabeth, ae. 3, and Susan, ae. 2, came in the Blessing in July, 1635. Res. at Salem. Shipwright, [L.] built the ship Sara in 1641. His son Richard testified in 1673 that his father arrived about 40 years ago with a family of 12 and a good est., and was first builder of vessels. [Mass. Arch. LIX, 127.] Susan, adm. chh. 20 (5) 1651.
He d. in 1654. Inv. taken 26 (3), filed 25 (4) 1654. He gave land to his sons William

HOLLINSWORTH, etc., cont.
and Richard and dau. Susanna. [Deposition of his son-in-law Richard Moore.] His dau. Katharine m. John Gedney, Jr. [Es. De. I, 31.]

HOLLOWAY, HOLWAY, HALLIWAY, HALOWAY,
John, ae. 21, came in the Elizabeth and Ann in April, 1635. Of Boston, tailor, in 1656. [Suff. De. II, 333.]

Joseph, millwright, Sandwich, ae. about 35 yrs. in 1640. [L.] Mortgaged house and lands in 1639, released 2 (1) 1640. Wife Rose called to testify in Court 20 Aug. 1644.
Inv. rendered Dec. 4, 1647. [Reg. IV, 282.] The widow m. 19 May, 1648, Wm. Newland.

Thomas, Plymouth, soldier in the Pequot war in 1637. In court at Plym. and Boston in 1638.

Timothy, Taunton, atba. 1643.

William, tailor, mercer, Taunton, atba. 1643. Rem. to Boston, sold house and lands at Taun. 6 (12) 1650; bought house and land in Bo. 28 (4) 1650. He deposed Sept. 6, 1658, ae. 72 years. He admin. on the estates of his sons Joseph, John and Symeon H., long since deceased, in 1662. [Arch. 15 B.] Wife Mary; ch. Timothy, Elisha, Malachi, Nehemiah and Esther, bapt. at Dorchester 7 (2) 1650, Mary b. in Bo. April 2, 1653. He was dism. from Dorch. chh. to that of Boston 6 (11) 1660.
Will dated 9 May, 1664, prob. April 6, 1665, beq. to wife Elizabeth and ch. mentioned above, excepting Mary, his est. in old and New England. [Reg. XIII, 156.] Her will dated 23 Aug. 1679, prob. 15 July, 1680, beq. to son-in-law Timothy H. of Taunton land wh. had belonged to her husband William H.; to son-in-law Samuel H. and his wife Jane; to Mary, wife of son Elisha H.; to son Mallachy H. of Taunton.

William, servant to William Bassett, Marshfield, 1637, [Plym. Col. Rec.] atba. 1643, frm. 5 June, 1644.
Admin. gr. March 1, 1652-3, to widow Grace; she m. 2, 6 July, 1654, John Phillips, who secured to her 2 daus. their shares of their father's est. She was killed by lightning; was buried June 24, 1666. The dau. Grace m. in Nov. 1666, Josiah Read.

HOLLISTER,
John, Weymouth, deputy and frm. May 10, 1643. Town officer, 1648.

HOLMAN, HOLMAR, HOLDMAN,
Edward, Plymouth, came in the Anne in 1623; probably returned to Eng. and was the Edward who embarked June 22, 1632, for N. E. Sold house, land and shallop Jan. 10, 1633-4, and received land at Scituate in part payment. Volunteer for the Pequot war in 1637. He m. before 1645 Amey Glasse, widow of Richard Willis, q. v.

John, gent., Dorchester, propr., town officer, ensign. Was authorized to receive a payment for the Gen. Court Oct. 3, 1632. Associated with Simon Willard and Richard Collicot in monopoly of Indian trade in 1641. [L.] Gave power of attorney 17 (9) 1647, to Thomas Bishop of Bredport, co. Dorset, for collection of rents of Barwick farm in parish of Swyer, co. Dorset, by virtue of the will of his father Morgan Holman. [A.] Wife Anna adm. chh. 4 (9) 1639, d. 1 (10) 1639. He m. 2, —. Ch. John b. 23 (12) 1637, Thomas b. 6 (6) 1641, Abigail bapt. 20 (10) 1642, Anna bapt. 29 (7) 1644, Samuel bapt. 6 (10) 1646, Patience bapt. 28 (11) 1648, Mary.
He d. about 1652. Will, dated 10 (4) 1652, proved April 7, 1653, gave est. to wife and ch. named above; wife exec., brethren Richard Collicot and Wm. Robinson overseers.

William, Cambridge, propr. before 1639.
He d. Jan. 18, 1652-3, ae. 59. The widow Winnifred d. Oct. 16, 1671, ae. 74. Inv. of her est. filed 20 Dec. 1671. Ch. [Hannah], Jeremiah Mary, [Sarah], Abraham, [Isaac], [Seeth]. The dau. Mary d. in 1673; admin. gr. to her brothers Jeremiah and Abram H. 18 Dec. 1673.

HOLIMAN, HOLYMAN, HOLLE,
Ezekiel, entertained to serve at Castle Island for a year at 10 li. per annum. [Col. Rec.] Settled at Dedham, 1636; sold in 1637. Rem. to Salem. Censured by the Court March, 1637, for non-attendance at meetings of the church, and for influencing others. Rem. to Newport; re-baptized Mrs. Scott. [W.]

HOLMES, HOMES, HULME, HOME,
Christopher, residence not stated, before Gen. Court 17 Oct. 1643.

Deborah, Salem, asked for grant of land 6 (1) 1636; not granted because it was not thought becoming for a maid to have solitary habitation. Memb. chh. 1637.

George, householder, Roxbury, frm. May 22, 1639. His wife Deborah was bur. Feb. 5, 1641. He m. —. Ch. Nathaniel b. Feb. 1, 1639, Deborah b. and d. in 1641, a ch. bur. Oct. 30, 1642, Sarah bapt. 7 (11) 1643, Deborah bapt. 9 (9) 1645, d. 29 (7) 1646.
He was bur. Dec. 18, 1645. Will prob. 30 (11) 1651; wife; eldest son Joseph, other ch. The widow d. 6 (11) 1662. [Reg. VII, 30.]

Margery, Boston, adm. chh. 1630.

John, gent., Plymouth, taxed in 1632, frm. 1634; messenger of the Court in 1638. Mrs. Sarah, d. Aug. 18, 1650.
He d. Oct. 13, 1667.

John, see Chauncey.

Obediah, glassman, Salem, propr. 1638 and 1639. Constable 1642. [See Conckling and Southwick.] Katharine memb. chh. 1639. Ch. Martha bapt. 3 (3) 1640, Samuel bapt. 20 (1) 1641-2, Obediah bapt. 9 (4) 1644.

Obediah, Rehoboth, prop. frm. 7 June, 1648. Suit vs. Mr. Samuel Newman, 1650.

Richard, millwright, Rowley, town officer. He deposed at Ipswich March 29, 1692, ae. about 88 years; worked for Mr. Thomas Nelson in building dam, grist-mill and saw-mill, and in making the stones for said grist-mill, in Rowley about 50 years ago. Wife Alice.
Will dated 15 July, 1695, prob. 13 Jan. folg.; aged; beq. to dau. Elizabeth, her husband John Pearl and their ch. Alice, Edmund, Timothy, Mary and John. Mentions her former husband John Knight, of Kettle Cove.

Robert, husbandman, Cambridge, propr. before 1636. Relates that after 20 years of age he removed from his father's house to Northumberland; Bought cattle. Came to N. E. His wife lost her mother when young; her mother-in-law had many children. She lived with the vicar of the place; heard much said against Puritans. [Rel.] Wife Jane; ch. Dorcas b. (6) 1638, d.

HOLMES, etc. cont.
1642, John b. (4) 1639, [Joseph,] Elizabeth b. 2 (1) 1644, Mehetabel b. and d. 1645, Sarah b. 13 (9) 1646, Ephraim b. 1647, d. 1648, [Samuel.] Wife Jane d. Oct. 28, 1653.
He d. in 1663. Will dated 20 (3), inv. taken 13 (4) 1663; beq. to sons John and Joseph and dau. Elizabeth.

William, major, Plymouth, frm. 1633; leader of the Plymouth colony forces in the Pequot War 1637. He ret. to Eng. and served the king and Parliament; came again in 1649. Had relatives in Eng. and Antigua.
He d. at Boston Nov. 12, 1649. Will names Margaret and Mary, daus. of dec. bro. Thomas H., res. in the island of Antego, and his widow Margaret Webb, and her daus. Rachel and Bathsheba, now living in London; the widow and two last named to have the farm if they come to N. E. Kinsman, Job Hawkins, of Boston. [Reg. V, 386, and VII, 230.]

William, Scituate, 1636; Marshfield. Prosecuted Dinah Silvester for calling his wife a witch; D. S. retracted May 9, 1661.
He was bur. 9 (9) 1678, ae. 86; widow Elizabeth bur. Feb. 17, 1689, in 86th year of her age. He beq. his est. to his wife and ch. Israel, Isaac, Josiah, Abraham, Elizabeth, Mary, Sarah and Rebecca.

HOLT, HOLTE, HOULT,
Nicholas, tanner, from Romsey, Eng., came in the James April 5, 1635. Settled at Newbury; husbandman, propr., town officer. Rem. to Andover; sold Newb. property 14 Nov. 1652. He deposed 11 (2) 1671, ae. about 63 years. Wife Elizabeth d. and he m. 12 or 20 June, 1658, Hannah, dau. of Humphrey Bradstreet, and widow of Daniel Rolfe (Rofe); she d. 20 June, 1665, and he m. 21 May, 1666, Martha, widow of Roger Preston. Ch. Elizabeth b. March 30, 1636, Mary b. Oct. 6, 1638, (m. 5 July, 1657, Thomas Johnson,) Sarah b. June 2, 1640, Samuel b. 6 Oct. 1641, Henry, (a father in 1670,) James, (a father in 1679,) Nicholas, (a father in 1680,) Priscilla b. and d. 1653, Rebecca b. 14 Nov. 1662, John b. 11 Jan. 1663.
He d. 30 Jan. 1685.

HOLTON, HOULTON,
Robert, slater, Boston, adm. chh. 9 (1) 1634, frm. May 14, 1634. Wife Anne adm. chh. 10 (11) 1635; ch. James bapt. 5 (8) 1634, Jabez bapt. 2 (2) 1637.

Joseph, servant to Richard Ingersoll before 1644, Salem; deposed in 1669, ae. about 48 years. Wife Sara; ch. on record: Joseph bapt. 15 (3) 1653, Benjamin b. 14 (12) 1657, Henry bapt. 24 (3) 1663, James bapt. 20 (3) 1666.
Will dated 24 May, 1703, prob. 27 June, 1705, beq. to sons Henry, John, Joseph, James; daus. Elizabeth Buxton and Sarah Needham; gr. ch. Benjamin H.

HOLYOKE, HOLIOAK, HOLLIOCK, HOLLIOCKE,
Rev. Edward, Lynn, frm. March 14, 1638-9. Had power from Gen. Court 13 March, 1638-9, to manage the lands of Lord Brooke. Was one of the adventurers in the Piscataqua plantation; sold his share to Robert Saltonstall Oct. 25, 1644. He was deputy for Springfield in 1650, though not resident there; but because his son Elizur was one of its chief citizens.
He d. at Rumney Marsh May 4, 1660. Will dated 25 Dec. 1658, prob. June 25, 1660. Only son Elizur; sons-in-law George Keyser, — Prenam, — Andrews, — Tuttle; dau. Hannah Keasur, dau. Martin; kinswoman Mary Mansfield; kinsman Thomas Morris of Newham; cousin Davis.

HOMSTED, see OLMSTEAD.

HOMWOOD,
William, Cambridge. Wife Winnifred; ch. Elizabeth b. 19 (3) 1644.

HONYWELL, HUNNIWELL,
William, Plymouth, made agreement with Thomas Prence for 7 years from 24 June, 1633; was freed 28 Feb., 1639, and took land of Mr. P. to plant on shares. Land granted to him 1 June, 1641.

HOOD,
John, weaver and planter, from Halstead, Essex, Eng., res. at Cambridge, N. E. 20 (8) 1638, leased property in H. [L.] Res. at Lynn; took as an apprentice Abraham, son of widow Tilton of L., 5 Dec. 1653. Ret. to Eng., and sent word to his wife Elizabeth to deliver him to his mother (widow Tilton;) the latter had meantime m. Roger Shaw of

HOOD, cont.
Hampton and had died; and Elizabeth delivered the boy to his bro. Peter T. of Conn. This act she revoked 10 Nov. 1655, on learning that Hampton Court had assigned the lad to Shaw. [Norf. De. I, 103.] Leased property in H., in possession of his mother Anne and her (second) husband, Thomas Beard. See will of his father, John H. in Reg. L., 423. [L.] He rem. to Lynn. Sold 14 (6) 1654, to William Crofts of L., yeoman, 3 tenements in Halstead, etc., 40 shillings to be paid to each of John's sisters, according to the will of their father. [Ess. De.]

HOOK, HOOKE,
Charles, Lynn, a witness in court in 1647.

John, servant to Isaac Allerton, came in the Mayflower to Plymouth; d. soon after arrival. [B.]

Mr. William, merchant, Salisbury, frm. Oct. 12, 1640. Had interests at Agamenticus in 1640. [L.] Came to N. E. about 1634. [W.] Sold land to Samuel Bennett March 15, 1649, referring to his father Humphrey and his uncle William Hooke. Humphrey was of Bristol, Eng. in 1646. [A.] Ch. Jacob b. at Salisbury Sept. 15, 1640; William.

He d. before 4 (8) 1653, when admin. of his est. was gr. to his widow Elinor; she petitioned Gen. Court 23 May, 1655, for right to sell lands at the Eastward belonging to her first husband Capt. Norton; granted. She also received power to manage the est. of her late husband Wm. Hooke for herself and youngest son, but not to sell.

Rev. William, minister, ordained at Taunton "by master Bishop a schoolmaster and one Parker a husbandman." [L., P.D.] A sermon of his July 23, 1640 entitled "New England's Teares for Old England's Feares." [J., Introd.] Rem. to New Haven.

HOOKER,
Rev. Thomas, b. at Marfield, Leicestershire about 1586; fellow of Emanuel Col., Cambridge; assistant to Mr. Mitchell, the incumbent of Chelmsford, Essex, about 1626; kept school at Little Baddow, having Mr. John Eliot (afterward of our Roxbury,) for a tutor. Spent some time in Holland. [C. M.] Came in the Griffin, with Cotton and Stone Sept. 4, 1633; was ordained pastor at Newe-

HOOKER, cont.
towne (Cambridge) Oct. 11, 1633; frm. May 14, 1634. He rem. with part of the church to Hartford, Conn. about May 31, 1636. [W.]
He d. at H. July 7, 1647, ae. 61. His will named wife Susanna, ch. John, Samuel, Sarah and Joanna and Mary dec. A sister m. Mr. George Alcock.

HOOPER, HOUPER,
William, ae. 18, came in the James in July, 1635. Settled at Reading, 1644; frm. May 10, 1648. Wife Elizabeth also memb. chh. of R.; ch. Mary b. Nov. 1647, James b. and d. 1649, Sarah b. Dec. 7, 1650, Ruth b. April 15, 1652, d. 15 (2) 1653, William b. Nov. 3, 1658, Hannah b. March 31, 1662, Elizabeth b. Aug. 20, 1665, Thomas b. April 2, 1668, John b. July 5, 1670.

He d. Dec. 5, 1678. Will dated 5 Aug. 1678, prob. 17 (4) 1679, beq. to wife and 6 children that are unmarried. Son William adult. Bro. Capt. Marshall and cousin Ensign Bancraft overseers.

HOOPER, alias POTTLE, alias WARR,
Abraham, Plymouth, in Court Oct. 2, 1637.

HOPCOTT,
Sarah, Salem, adm. chh. 8 (7) 1640, m. Thomas Macy.

HOPKINS,
John, Cambridge, propr. 1634, frm. March 4, 1634-5. He rem. to Hartford in 1636; d. in 1654. Ch. Stephen and Bethiah. The widow Jane m. 2, Nathaniel Ward of Hadley.

"Mr., a merchant of London, of fair estate and of great esteem for religion and wisdom in outward affairs," came to Boston in June, 1637. [W.]

Richard, Watertown, for selling gun and ammunition to Indians, was sentenced to be whipped and branded on the cheek, Sept. 4, 1632.

Mr. Stephen, gent., of London, came in the Mayflower; signed the Compact; settled at Plymouth. Frm. and asst. 1632-3. Volunteer for the Pequot War, 1637. He brought with him his wife Elizabeth, son Giles, and dau. Constanta, (ch. of a former wife,) and Damaris and Oceanus (b. at sea,)

HOPKINS, cont.
by this wife. [B.] Ch. Caleb and Deborah also drew shares in the cattle in 1627.
He d. in 1644. Will, dated June 6, prob. Aug. 20, 1644. Sons Giles and Caleb; daus. Constance, (wife of Nicholas Snow,) Deborah, Damaris, Ruth and Elizabeth; to Stephen, son of Giles. Est. divided May 19, 1647. The widow Elizabeth's est. was admin. Oct. 6, 1659. Agreement made between Andrew Ring, Jacob Cooke and Gyles Hopkins regarding the estate. [Reg. IV, 281, and V, 387.]

HOPKINSON,
Michael, Boston, servant to Jacob Eliot, adm. chh. 6 (11) 1638, frm. May 13, 1640. He was dism. "to the gathering of a church at Rowley," 24 (9) 1639. Wife Ann deposed March 30, 1675-6, ae. 60 years. Ch. Jonathan b. and d. 1641, Jonathan b. 9 (2) 1643, Jeremy b. 26 (1) 1645, John b. 7 (11) 1646, Caleb b. 19 (12) 1648.
He was bur. Feb. 28, 1648. Inv. filed 29 (7) 1657. The widow m. afterward John Trumble, and later Richard Swan. She made her will 4 July, 1678, prob. 24 Sept. 1678. Beq. to sons Caleb, John and Jonathan Hopkinson, and others. [Reg. XXXI, 115.]

HOPPEN, HOPPIN, HOPPIE,
Stephen, weaver, planter, Dorchester, 1646. [See John Pope.] Res. on Thompson's Island in 1659, and had mortg. of land in Boston. Bought house and lands at Roxbury May 13, 1653. He deposed 30 Oct. 1666, ae. about 40 years; helped to run the line from the top of the Blue Hills southward about 1642, and had run other lines. [Arch. 30.] Ch. Thomas b. 21 (1) 1655, Opportunity b. Nov. 15, 1657.
He d. Nov. 1, 1677. Will prob. 9 May, 1678; beq. to wife Hannah; to sons John, Thomas, Joseph and Benjamin; dau. Opportunity; son Seaver and dau. Hannah; son-in-law Richard Butt.

HORNE, ORNE, see LAHORNE,
George, servant to Wm. Denne, Boston, in Court 4 (7) 1638.

John, carpenter, Salem, propr. on a court com. in 1638; deacon. Wife Ann memb. chh. before 1636; wife Frances adm. chh. 30 (1) 1656. She joined in a deed in 1659. He deposed in 1662, ae. about 60 years. Ch.

HORNE, etc., cont.
Recompense bapt. 25 (10) 1636, Simon bapt. 28 (8) 1649, Benjamin bapt. 25 (12) 1654, Ann bapt. 22 (1) 1657, Jonathan bapt. 1 (6) 1658.
His will dated 8 Oct. 1679, being aged; codicil 27 Feb. 1683-4, prob. Nov. 25, 1684; beq. to sons John, Symond, Joseph and Benjamin; daus. Elizabeth Gardner, Jehoadan Harvey, Mary Smith and Ann Felton.

HORSEFORD, HORSFORD, HOSFORD,
William, Dorchester, propr. 1633, frm. April 1, 1634. Rem. to Windsor, Conn.

HORTON,
Barnabas, baker, Ipswich, sold land 12 (1) 1641.

Thomas, Springfield, a witness of the Indian deed in 1636; propr., taxed in 1638.
He d. in 1640. His widow Mary was examined Oct. 9, 1640, for selling her husband's piece to the Indians. She made marriage contract with Robert Ashley Aug. 7, 1641, reserving the rights of her son, Jarmy [Jeremiah,] 3 years old, and her other son, an infant. [Reg. XXXIII, 310.]

Walter, Plymouth, juryman 5 June, 1638.

HOSIER,
Samuel, planter, Watertown, frm. May 18, 1631; propr., town officer. He was guardian of Anne, dau. of Wm. Coleman of Colchester, Eng., 8 (6) 1639. [L.] He m. [2,] Oct. 13, 1657, Ursula, widow of Stephen Streeter of Charlestown.
He d. July 29, 1665. In his will dated July 28, he beq. to Charles Stearns; to bro.'s son in Eng.; to his sister and Mrs. Prout; to the church and pastor; to son Holland's ch., Joseph and Sarah; to wife Ursula's children; residue to wife, and after her death to Stephen Payne and his children; to my brother's son in England, and to my sister if she be living. The widow m. William Robinson of Dorchester, and sold her Wat. property June 27, 1671.

HOSKINS, HOSKINE, see also HODGKINS,
John, Dorchester, juryman Nov. 9, 1630; frm. May 18, 1631, propr. Rem. to Windsor, Conn. John, adm. frm. May 14, 1634, and Thomas, frm. May 6, 1635, may be sons. [See Hist. Windsor.]

HORWOOD,
James, ae. 30, came in the Christian March 16, 1634.

HOSDONE, see HODSEN.

HOSMER, HOSMORE, OSMER,
James, clothier, ae. 28, came in the Elizabeth April 9, 1635, with wife Ann, ae. 27, ch. Marie, ae. 2 years, and Ann, ae. 3 mos., and servants Marie Dounard, ae. 24, and Marie Martin, ae. 19. Settled at Cambridge; sold land before 1638; rem. to Concord. Frm. May 17, 1637. Wife Mary bur. 11 (3) 1641; second wife Alice; ch. Mary b. 1639, d. 1642, Stephen b. 27 (9) 1642, Hannah, b. 16 (6) 1644, Mary b. 14 (2) 16—. James, Jr., was slain in the engagement with the Indians at Sudbury 21 (2) 1676. His wife "Elinne," d. 3 March, 1664-5.

James H., Sen., d. Feb. 7, 1685.

Thomas, Cambridge, propr. 1633-1642; frm. May 6, 1635. Town officer. Rem. to Hartford.

HOUCHIN, HOWCHIN, HUTCHINS,
Jeremiah, tanner, Dorchester, propr. before 1639. Adm. chh. with wife 4 (12) 1639; frm. May 13, 1640. He rem. to Boston. Town officer. Deputy. He deposed Jan. 29, 1664-5, ae. about 49 years. [Arch. 15 B.] Wife Esther (Hester;) ch. Mary b. 18 (1) 1640, bapt. at Dorch. 14 (1) 1641, (m. 22 (4) 1657, Nathaniel Greene,) Jeremy b. and d. 1643, Mehetabel bapt. 30 (4) 1644, ae. about 7 days, William bapt. 1 (5) 1649, ae. about 3 days, Hannah bapt. 19 (3) 1650, Jeremiah b. and d. 1651, Jeremiah b. 26 Nov. 1652, Sarah b. 10 March, 1653, Elizabeth, (m. 9 (9) 1653, John Endecott, Jr.,) Sarah bapt. 12 (1) 1654, John b. 27 Oct. 1655, d. 2 (5) 1657, Nathaniel b. July 24, 1658, Richard b. Dec. 16, 1660.

Will dated 7 April, 1670, prob. 3 March, 1670-1; beq. to wife Esther life use of houses, lands, tanyards, etc., entrusting to her care his two youngest children Nathaniel and Rachel; to ch. Elizabeth, wife to Mr. James Allen, Esther, wife to Samuel Wheelwright, Mary, wife to Nathaniel Greene, Nathaniel and Rachel H.; to Mr. John Westgate of Harliston, co. Norfolk, Eng., who had charge of his business in Eng. The widow Esther

HOUCHIN, etc., cont.
deeded land 24 June, 1670. She d. July 2, 1693.

Daniel, deposed before Gen. Court in 1640 about 2 children in his charge on the ship.

HOUGH, HAUGH, HAULGH, HOFFE,
Atherton, gent., a prominent citizen of Boston, Lincolnshire, Eng., one of those who refused the Royal Loan in 1626, a parishioner of Mr. John Cotton, having borne with him the burdens of non-conformity, accompanied him to N. E. in 1633. Res. first at Cambridge, but was a citizen of Boston. Adm. chh. with wife Elizabeth (9) 1633. Deputy, town officer. Was a man of great strength of character. Had grant of land, 130 acres, in Grave's Neck, between Oyster Bank bay and Gibbons' creek, where he had house, etc., in 1635. Had also a farm at Braintree. His wife Elizabeth d. 14 (8) 1643; his second wife Susanna was adm. chh. 4 (2) 1646. The inv. of her est. was filed 29 (3) 1651. His son Samuel, b. about 1621, adm. Boston chh. 12 (8) 1644, was a pupil of Mr. Nathaniel Eaton at Cambridge in 1639. [L.]

He d. Sept. 11, 1650.

William, house carpenter, Gloucester, town officer 1650. He m. Oct. 28, 1645, Sarah, dau. of Hugh Calkin; ch. Hanna b. July 31, 1646, Abiah (a son) b. Sept. 15, 1648, Saray b. 23 (1) 1651.

HOUHTON, HAUGHTON,
Henry, Salem, appointed to supply the place of Mr. Sharpe as ruling elder in case of absence or sickness, in 1629. [Suff. De. XVIII.] He d. the first winter. [C. M.]

John, ae. 4 years, came in the Abigail in June, 1635, cert. from Eaton Bray, co. Bedford, Eng. He seems to be the John, of Dedham, who m. Beatrix —, and had ch. Robert b. 28 (1) 1659, Mary b. 22 March, 1661-2; rem. to Lancaster, and there had Beatrix b. 3 (10) 1665, (m. Sept. 20, 1683, John Pope,) Benjamin b. 25 (3) 1668, Sarah b. 30 (5) 1672.

Will dated 8 April, 1684, prob. June 17 folg., beq. to wife Beatrix and ch. John, Robert, Jonas, Benjamin, Mary and Sarah. April 4, 1721, after the death of the widow, division was agreed upon by John, Robert, Jonas, John Harris and Beatrix Pope.

HOUHTON, etc., cont.

William, butcher, ae. 22, came in the Increase April 15, 1635. Settled at Boston. Ch. Sarah bapt. 6 (2) 1651.

HOUSE,

Samuel, ship-carpenter, Scituate, memb. chh. Jan. 16, 1634, frm. 1634. He rem. to Cambridge; sold land at Sci. 13 Nov. 1643. Rem. to Barnstable; 18 (9) 1645, he gave letter of attorney to Hez. Usher to collect 20 li. left him by Thomas —. [A.] He ret. to Sci. Wife Elizabeth; ch. Elizabeth bapt. Oct. 23, 1636, Sarah bapt. Aug. 1, 1641, John b. at Camb. 6 (10) 1642, d. 22 (2) 1664, John bapt. at Bar. May 18, 1645.

He d. in 1661. Inv. of his est. taken at request of his ch. Samuel and Elizabeth, Sept. 12, 1661. [Reg. VI, 95.] Elizabeth m. 1 Jan. 1661-2, John Sutten.

HOVEY,

Daniel, planter, Ipswich, propr. 1636. He m. Abigail, dau. of Robert Andrews about 1642. Ch. Daniel, John, Thomas, James, Joseph, Nathaniel, Abigail, Priscilla. Letter to Essex Prob. Court, vol. 2, page 244, dated Sept. 27, 1683, names wife and 6 sons and 1 dau., her children. All the sons except James then living. [Reg. XXXVI, 195.]

Daniel, Sen. d. May 29, 1695. Will dated 18 March, 1691-2, aged "seventy thre gointo seventy fower," beq. to sons Daniel, John, Thomas, Joseph and Nathaniel; gr. ch. Daniel, son of dec. son James; daus. Priscilla, wife of John Aires, and Abigail, wife of Thomas Hodgkins. The son-in-law John Ayres deposed in 1693, ae. about 44 years.

HOW, HOWE, HOWES, HOWS,

Abraham, Roxbury, about 1636, frm. May 17, 1637, propr. Ch. Elizabeth, memb. chh. 1644, Sarah, Isaac b. June 24, 1639, Deborah b. Sept. 2, 1641, Israel b. July 7, 1644, Abram bapt. Sept. 25, 1653, Hester, (m. 1 Henry Mason, 2, John Sears,) Isaac bapt. 30 (1) 1656. His wife d. 7 (10) 1645, and he m. —.

His will dated 26 May, prob. 2 Nov. 1676, beq. to ch. Abraham, Israel, Isaac, Hester Mason and Deborah; to the ch. of dau. Elizabeth; to dau. Sarah's ch. Joseph, Isaac and Sarah.

HOW, etc., cont.

Daniel, Saugus, (Lynn,) lieut., ordered by Gov. Vane to command and train his company 16 (4) 1636. [W.] Frm. May 14, 1634, propr., deputy, town officer. Comr. of Es. Court in 1637.

[Ephraim and Joseph, sons of somebody in Lynn, probably of Daniel, proprs. in 1638.]

Edmund, Plymouth Court, requested land 1 April, 1639.

Edward, Watertown, 1633. [Court Rec.] Frm. May 14, 1634. Ruling elder, town officer, deputy.

He d. 24 (4) 1644. Will prob. next day. Beq. to Nathaniel Treadway; Anne, wife of John Stonne of Sudbury; and Mary and Elizabeth Knowles; residue to wife. Widow Margaret m. 2, George Bunker; in her will, prob. Dec. 19, 1660, she gave to her sister Mary Rogers, and her [ch.] John and Elizabeth, of Boxstead, Eng.; to John Stone, of Sudbury, and to Nathaniel Treadway of Wat. Daus. Suffrana, wife of N. Treadway, and Anna, wife of J. Stone. [Reg. III, 77, and VII, 60.]

Edward, husbandman, ae. 60, with Elizabeth, ae. 50, Jeremy, ae. 21, Sarah, ae. 12, Ephraim, ae. 9, Isaac, ae. 7, and William, ae. 6, came in the Truelove in Sept., 1635. Settled at Lynn; frm. Dec. 8, 1636, propr. 1638; deputy.

He d. suddenly at Boston (2) 1639. Admin. gr. to his widow Elizabeth 22 May, 1639. The widow had a claim upon Mrs. Philips on behalf of children; seems to refer to Samuel and Elizabeth Philips, gr. ch. of Richard Sergeant. [Col. Rec. 1644 and 1645.]

James, Roxbury, frm. May 17, 1637, propr. Wife also, name not recorded, memb. chh. about 1635. Rem. to Salem; resident in 1648. Rem. to Ipswich. James, Sen., Ipswich, memb. jury in 1641. He deposed in 1665, ae. about 61 years.

John, Sudbury, frm. May 13, 1640. Town officer 1657. He petitioned 30 (7) 1662, to be excused from training because he was aged, thick of hearing, and maintained 3 soldiers in his family. [Mdx. Files.] Wife Mary; ch. John b. 24 (8) 1640, Samuel b. 20 (8) 1642, Mary b. 1646, d. 1647, Mary b. 15 (11) 1653, Isaac b. 8 (6) 1648.

He d. 28 (3) 1680. Will dated 24 May, prob. 15 June, 1680, beq. to wife; ch. Samuel,

HOW, etc., cont.
Isaac, Josiah, Thomas, Eleazer, Sarah Ward, Mary Witherby; gr. ch. John, son of John.

Mr. Thomas, (Howes,) planter, Yarmouth, took oath of allegiance 18 Dec. 1638, prop. frm. 3 Sept. 1639; propr.; com. of division 1639.
Will, dated Sept. 26, prob. Oct. 1, 1665. Wife Mary; sons Joseph, Thomas, Jeremy; gr. ch. Samuel to be taught the trade of a cooper by [his father] Thomas. [Reg. VI, 187.]

HOWARD, HAWORD, HAWARD, HAWOORTH,
Nathaniel, Dorchester, adm. chh. 28 (12) 1641; frm. May 10, 1643. Rem. to Salem. Ch. Eliza bapt. 26 (6) 1666.

Robert, Dorchester, propr., 1639; frm. Feb. 1652. Town officer. He rem. to Boston about 1668. Wife Mary; ch. Bethiah bapt. 16 (12) 1639, Nathaniel bapt. 6 (12) 1641, Jonathan bapt. 25 (4) 1643, Hannah bapt. (12) 1643, (m. Samuel Minot,) John bapt. 4 (11) 1645, Abiel bapt. 8 (6) 1647, and Sarah bapt. 20 (5) 1651.
His will dated 28 May, prob. 29 Jan. 1683, beq. to wife Mary, son Jonathan and other children. The widow Mary made will 2 July, prob. 19 July, 1683; beq. to son-in-law Wm. Clarke of Bo.; daus. Bethiah Messenger, Hannah Minot, Mary Jones and Temperance Smith; Samuel Bass; gr. ch. John, Amee and Mary; the ch. of my son Jeremiah H.; rest to son Jonathan H..

Samuel, tailor, Braintree, had lands 19 (12) 1637, for 3 heads. See Hayward, Samuel.

William, Salem, and Wenham; rem. to Topsfield. Signed—William Howard—as witness to the inventory of Samuel Smith in 1642. Frm. 13 (3) 1640. He deposed in 1661, ae. about 52 years. Rose adm. chh. Salem 10 (3) 1640, Nathaniel, son of sister H., bapt. 13 (9) 1642.

William, Ipswich, sold land 11 (8) 1649. Signed bill against Wm. Payne in 1649. [Es. Files.]

William, Hampton, propr. 1650; lieut., deputy, 1644.

HOWARD, etc., cont.
William, Boston, attorney for R. Bellingham and deputy marshall general in an action in Es. court in 1666; deposed, ae. 57 years.

HOWELL,
Mr. Edward, gent., late of Marsh Gibbon, Bucks, 1638; settled at Lynn; propr. 1638; frm. March 14, 1638-9; juryman, 1639. He gave letter of attorney in 1640 for the collection of annuity and the sale of lands and tenements in Watton Underwood, Bucks.
He rem. about 1641 to Southampton, L. I.

Thomas, brick-layer, Marshfield, in co. with Robert Barker and others bought land, ferry and boat 11 Jan. 1641.
He d. at Boston. Will declared on his death-bed June 8, 1647, forwarded by Mr. Aspinwall to Plymouth Prob. court. Est. to be equally divided between his wife and 2 sons; kinsman Job Lane, exec.; Edmond Weston to have charge till Lane ret. from Eng. Inv. filed May 31, 1648; admin. gr. 7 June ,1648. [Reg. IV, 282.] [See Daniel Cole.] Job Lane, having returned, refused in writing 19 Oct. 1647, to accept the exec.-ship of the will of his uncle.

HOWEN, HOWING, HOWYN,
Robert, cutler, Boston, adm. chh. 13 (4) 1641, frm. May 18, 1642. Wife Elizabeth adm. chh. 17 (2) 1642; ch. John b. (4) 1643, Israel bapt. 14 (6) 1642, ae. about 7 days.
The widow d. 27 (7) 1653; inv. taken 6 (8) 1653, by Richard Truesdell. [Reg. VII, 338.]

HOWLAND,
Arthur, planter, yeoman, Duxbury, propr. 1640; see some of his accounts in 1640. [L.] Prop. for frm. 1 March, 1641-2. Brought suit 5 Nov. 1644, for goods brought from Eng. for him by the wife of Robert Mendam. Rem. to Marshfield.
He d. Oct. 30, 1675. Will prob. 7 March folg., beq. to wife Margaret; son Arthur; gr. ch. Assadiah Smith and his 3 bros.; daus. Mary Williamson, Martha Daman and Elizabeth Low; gr. ch. Mary Walker and Timothy Williamson. The widow Margaret was bur. Oct. 23, 1683. Her will prob. 5 March, 1683-4, beq. to gr. son John Walker; to Ebenezer, Thomas and Arthur, ch. of her son Arthur, whom she made exec.

HOWLAND, cont.

Henry, yeoman, Duxbury, taxed in 1632, frm. 1633, atba. 1643; town officer. His will dated 28 (9), prob. 8 March, 1670, beq. to wife Mary; ch. Zoeth, Joseph, John, Samuel, Sarah, Elizabeth, Mary and Abigail. The widow made will 3 May, 1674, prob. 26 same month; beq. to sons named above and to daus. Abigail Young, Mary Cudworth, Sarah Dennis and Elizabeth Allin.

John, came in the Mayflower, as servant (or steward) of Mr. John Carver. Signed the Compact; took an active part in the early explorations. Settled at Plymouth. Town officer; a partner in the Trading Company of the Colony; Asst. or deputy almost continually. Prominent in the church, so that he "assisted in the imposition of hands" upon Rev. John Cotton, Jr. when he was ordained pastor 30 (6) 1669. He m. Elizabeth, dau. of John Tillie. [B.] Ch. John b. Feb. 24, 1626, [S.] Desire, (also named at the division of cattle in 1627; she m. John Gorum,) Hope, (b. about 1630, [Gr. st.]; m. John Chipman,) Deborah ,(m. 4 Jan. 1648, John Smith, Jr. of Plym.,) Elizabeth, (m. 13 Sept. 1649, Ephraim Hicks,) Ruth, (m. 17 Nov. 1664, Thomas Cushman). Others named in will.

He d. Feb. 23, 1672-3; "a profitable instrument of good; the last man that was left of those that came over in the ship called the May Flower that arrived at Plymouth." [Plym. Col. Rec. VII, 34.] He made will 29 May, prob. 6 March, 1672. Grown aged; beq. to wife Elizabeth his house in Rockey Nook in the town of Plymouth, and made her residuary legatee; beq. to sons John, Jabez, Isaac, Joseph; to daus. Desire Gorum, Hope Chipman, Elizabeth Dickerson, Lydia Browne, Hannah Bosworth and Ruth Cushman; to gr. ch. Elizabeth, dau. of his son John. Signed and sealed, (but only copies of Plym. wills extant). The widow d. 21 (12) 1687, ae. 80. [Swansey rec.] Her will dated 17 Dec. 1686, aged 79 years; beq. to sons named by her husband, and daus. Lydia, Elizabeth and Hannah; to gr. ch. Elizabeth Bursley, Nathaniel Howland, James, Jabez and Dorothy Browne, and Desire Gorum. Son-in-law James Browne and son Jabez execs.

Genealogy and sketches.

HOWLETT,

Thomas, carpenter, [Ips. rec.], Boston,

HOWLETT, cont.

memb. chh. 1630-1; frm. March 4, 1633-4. One of the first planters at Agawam, (Ipswich,) April 1, 1633. [Col. Rec.] "Having lived sundry years at Ips.," he was dism. to that chh. 10 (7) 1643. [Bo. chh. rec.] Deputy, ensign, deacon. He deposed in 1658, ae. about 52 years. He m. about 1644 Alice, widow of Thomas French. He m. 2 or 3, Rebecca, widow of Thomas Smith. Will dated 4 Nov. 1677, prob. 24 Sept. 1678, beq. to wife Rebecca what she brought with her and other items; to son Samuel and daus. Sarah Comings and Mary Perly; to Alice Comings; to Mary, dau. of his son John, or to his wife; to son Thomas' wife and ch.; rest to son William. The widow d. 1 Nov. 1680, and her est. was given to her two sons James and John Smith.

HOYDEN, see HAYDEN.

HOWMAN,

John, appl. frm. Oct. 19, 1630. [See Holman.] Rem. to Topsfield; selectman, 1661.

HOWSEN, HOWSON,

Peter, ae. 31, and wife Ellen, ae. 39, cert. to come to N. E. March 11, 1634. Captain; his est. in Suff. Prob. Court 13 (10) 1652. Owner of ship Brocke, etc. [Reg. VIII, 59.]

HOYT, HOIT, HOYTE,

John, planter, Salisbury, propr. 1639; owned land also at Ipswich in 1641 and at Haverhill in 1650, but resided at Salis. in the section which became Amesbury. Wife Frances d. Feb. 23, 1642-3; he m. 2, Frances —; ch. Frances, (m. 1, John Colby, 2, John Barnard,) John; Thomas and Gregory b. Jan. 1, 1640-1, Elizabeth b. Feb. 23, 1642, Sarah b. Jan. 16, d. Feb. 26, 1644-5, Mary b. Feb. 20, 1645-6, (m. Christopher Bartlett,) Joseph b. and d. 1648, Joseph b. and d. 1649, Marah b. and d. 1653, Naomi b. Jan. 23, 1654, (m. John Lovejoy,) Dorothy b. April 13, 1656, Mehitable b. Oct. 25, 1664.

He d. Feb. 28, 1687-8; admin. of his est. gr. May 8, 1697.

Simon, Charlestown, propr. 1630; rem. to Dorchester; propr.; frm. May 18, 1631. Rem. to Windsor, Conn.

HUBBARD, HUBBERT, HOBART,
Ann, Dedham, m. 8 (5) 1638, Wm. Barstow.

Anthony, Dedham. He m. 14 (2) 1648, Sarah Bacon; ch. John b. 14 (2) 1649, Abraham b. and d. 1650. Sarah d. 1652.

Mr. Benjamin, "artist," Charlestown, adm. chh. with wife Alice 30 (6) 1633, frm. Sept. 3, 1634. Wrote Roger Williams in 1637 about finding a place there. Accompanied the surveying party who laid out the town of Woburn. [To. rec.] He (or one of the name) wrote from London 25 (12) 1644, to Gov. Winthrop; good voyage and favorable acceptance by many gentlemen through W.'s influence. Had not yet made trial before artists of his invention concerning longitude. [Mass. Hist. Coll. 3-1.]
Ch. Benjamin bapt. 30 (1) 1634, Elizabeth b. 4 (2) 1636, Thomas b. 31 (3) bapt. 24 (4) 1639, Hannah b. 16 (10) 1641.

Elizabeth, widow, Boston, d. 6 (11) 1643. Her will dated 29 (10) 1643, was prob. (Suff.) 4 (7) 1644. Ch. Hannah and Benjamin Hobert execs.; other ch. Richard, Sarah and Rachel. Money to be paid to Stoctdell and Hannah Carrington. Signed Elizabeth Hobbert.

Edmund, Sen., (wrote his name Hubbard and Hubberd,) from Hingham, Eng., came in 1633 with his wife, son Joshua, daus. Rebecca and Sarah, and servant Henry Gibbs. Settled at Charlestown. Was adm. chh. 19 (6) 1633, with son Edmund and his wife Elizabeth. Benjamin and Alice his wife, and Joshua and his sister Rebecca, were also adm. chh. within a few days. Frm. March 4, 1633-4. Constable March 3, 1634. He rem. to Hingham. Deputy. He m. 1, in Eng., Margaret [Dewey]; she d. and he m. 2, Oct. 10, 1634, Sarah, widow of Mr. John Lyford. Ch. Nazareth, (m. John Beal,) Edmund, Peter.
(The latter, Rev. Peter, grad. Magdalen Coll., Cambridge, 1625, minister at Hingham 44 years; kept a careful diary of baptisms, admissions to chh. and local items of great historical value;—wrote his name *Hobart*; but records: "March 8, 1646, father Hubbeard dyed; June 23, 1649, mother Hobart dyed.") Other ch. of Edmund: Thomas, Rebecca, Sarah, Joshua. [See Hist. Hingham, etc.]

HUBBARD, etc., cont.
James, Lynn, accused of opposing the baptism of infants; was called before Gen. Court and acquitted 1 (10) 1640. In Essex Court 29 (4) 1643. Rem. to Long Island and sold house and land at Charlestown, 27 (8) 1643.

James, Watertown. Wife Sarah; ch. Thomas b. 10 (6) 1633, James, Sarah, (m. — Champney). [Mi.]
He d. 26 (11) 1638, ae. 30 years; his will in Court at Boston 10 (10) 1641. His widow m. William Hamlet.

Joseph, Newbury, propr. 1637.

Robert, a witness to a deed of Hill and Leverett of Boston, 1649.

Samuel, Springfield, frm. March 4, 1634-5; town officer; kept the ordinary, 1640. Ch. Ruth b. 10 (2) 1640, Rachel b. 7 (1) 1642-3, Bethiah b. 29 (10) 1646.

William, appl. frm. Oct. 19, 1630; probably ret. to Eng., and was the

William, husbandman, ae. 40, who came with Judith, ae. 25, Mary, ae. 20, Martha, ae. 22, John, ae. 15, William, ae. 13, Nathaniel, ae. 6, and Richard, ae. 4, who came in the Defense in July, 1635. Settled at Ipswich. Propr.; bought house and land of Thomas Dudley in 1635; frm. May 2, 1638; member of the Particular Court of Ips. 1639; had grant of land from the Gen. Court on the North side of Quochecho river, which he sold Oct. 15, 1656, to Capt. Thomas Wiggin of Quomscooke. Gent.; wife Judith signed with him. He rem. to Boston. Sold land to son Richard 24 June, 1662.
He made will 8 June, prob. 19 Aug. 1670; beq. to son William lands at Tendring Hundred, Eng. and at Ipswich, N. E.; referred to lands already given to sons Richard and William; gave more to the latter.
Rev. William, the son here mentioned, was grad. at Harvard coll. 1642; pastor at Wenham, 1643, at Ipswich, 1656; wrote a History of New England, of standard value.

William, ae. 35, Thomas, ae. 10, and John, ae. 10, came in the Elizabeth and Ann in April, 1635. Mary, ae. 24, came in the Hopewell in Sept. 1635. Grant of land made to Mr. Hubbard for his family upon conditions referred to 12 (3) 1643, by the town of Wenham.

HUCKINS, HUCKINGS, HUGGINS,
Thomas, planter, Barnstable, atba. 1643, frm. 3 June, 1652; town officer. He m. in 1642, Mary Wells of Bar. She was bur. 28 July, 1648, and he m. at Nocett Nov. 3, 1648, Rose Hellier, *als.* widow Tillye. Ch. Lydia b. and d. 1644, Mary b. 29 March, 1646, Elizabeth bapt. Feb. 27, 1647, bur. 8 Dec. 1648, John bapt. Aug. 5, 1649, Thomas bapt. April 27, 1651, Hannah bapt. Oct. 16, 1653, Joseph b. 21 Feb. 1655.

He was cast away 9 Nov. 1679, in 62nd year; son Joseph lost with him. Inv. of his est. taken 10 Feb. 1679; agreement made 14 March folg. between the widow Rose, son Thomas, Hope, relict of eldest son John, and her five daughters, Samuel Stores and Mary his wife, James Gorham and Hannah his wife, and Jabez Serjeant, in full of legacy given him by his grandfather, the said Thomas H.

HUDD, see HOOD,
Marie, maid servant to Mr. John Winthrop, Sen., adm. chh. Boston 28 (6) 1634.

HUDSON,
James, laborer, Boston, propr. 1641. Wife Anne adm. chh. 3 (2) 1642; ch. Lydia b. 27 (2) 1643, Deborah bapt. 20 (8) 1644, James b. 25 (6) 1646, Lydia b. 15 (1) 1648. He m. 3 (12) 1652, Rebecca, dau. of Wm. Browne of Bo.; ch. John b. and d. 1653. The wife Rebecca d. 14 (9) 1653. He m. Mary —, who was adm. chh. 17 (1) 1661; ch. John b. and d. 1654, Mary b. July 27, 1656, Lazarus b. Oct. 22, 1658, Bethiah and Abigail b. Dec. 13, 1659, Samuel b. March 23, 1661, *Mary* bapt. 28 (2) 1661. Ebenezer b. March 4, 1662, Elizabeth bapt. 6 (9) 1664, Eleazer b. June 19, 1668.

John, household servant to Mr. Humphrey, Salem, 1642. Punished in 1649 by Gen. Court. Rem to Manchester; sold house. He deposed in 1670 ,ae. 57 years, Mary, ae. about 50, and Samuel, ae. about 21.

John, husbandman, Duxbury.
Will, dated Nov. 20, 1683, prob. Sept. 12, 1688; wife Anne; daus. Hannah Turner, Rhoda Palmer, Elizabeth Vicory, Abigail Stetson; son Japhet Turner. [Gen. Adv. I, 42.]

Mary, widow, Boston, adm. chh. 19 (11) 1639.

HUDSON, cont.
Nicholas, residence not stated, frm. March 9, 1636-7.

Ralph, woollen draper, ae. 42, with wife Marie, ae. 42, and ch. Hannah, ae. 14, John, ae. 12, Elizabeth, ae. 5, came in the Susan and Ellen in April, 1635. Settled at Cambridge; householder 8 Feb. 1635. Rem. to Boston; adm. chh. 17 (2) 1636, frm. May 25, 1636.
Will prob. 20 (9) 1651, names dau. Hannah who m. Capt. John Leverett; bro. John Hudson; wife's sister, the wife of Mr. Peacock. [Reg. IV, 54.]

Thomas, Lynn, propr. in 1638. Sold lands 22 (10) 1645.

William, baker, Boston, memb. chh. 1630, frm. May 18, 1631. Went to Eng. in 1645; became ensign of a foot company in Col. Rainsborow's regiment. Returned after good service. [W.] Went again to Chatham, co. Kent, Eng.; gave power of attorney concerning property in Boston to his sons William H., inn-holder, and Francis H., fisherman, both of B. April 29, 1656. Wife Susan adm. chh. 1630-1; ch. Nathaniel b. 30 (11) 1633, Richard d. 26 (8) 1641, Hannah, (m. Oct. 10, 1661, Benjamin Richards).

HUGGEN, see HIGGINS.

HUGHES, HUGHS, HEWGHES, see also HEWES,
Parnell, Lynn; fine for selling strong water without lic. remitted 15 Oct. 1650.

William, of "New Medows," sold animals and farm produce Aug. 13, 1643, to Richard Barker; witness, John Hughes. [Es. Court files.] Of Lynn, 1646; refused to pay toward maintenance of ministry. [Es. files.]

HUGHSON, HEWSON,
John, merchant, Boston, signed inv. of Wm. Hanbury in 1649.

HUIT, see also HEWETT,
Ephraim, residence not stated. His widow Isabel sold a 100 li. share in the patents of Piscataqua and Swamscot Sept. 22, 1647. [Suff. De. I, 90.] She seems to be referred to on the same page as Mrs. Isabel Willett, q. v.

HULBURT,
William; rem. to Windsor, Conn.; thence about 1654 to Hartford; thence rem. to Northampton.

HULL,
Mr. George, Dorchester, one of the first company 1630, [Blake.] Frm. March 4, 1632-3. Town officer, deputy. Rem. to Windsor, Conn.

John, Dorchester, propr., frm. Aug. 7, 1632. [Perhaps this name was a clerical error for Hill.]

Rev. Joseph, (called Hall in passenger list,) of Somerset, a minister, ae. 40, with wife Agnes, ae. 25, ch. Joane, ae. 15, Joseph, ae. 13, Tristram, ae. 11, Elizabeth, ae. 7, Temperance, ae. 9, Grissell, ae. 5, Dorothy, ae. 3; and servants Judith French, ae. 20, John Wood, ae. 20, and Robert Dabyn, ae. 28, came from Weymouth, Eng., March 20, 1635. He was allowed by the Gen. Court 5 (8) 1635, to sit down at Wessaguscus, after called Weymouth, and 21 families with him. Frm. Sept. 2, 1635. He rem. to Hingham. One of the com. to assist magistrates 6 (7) 1638; deputy. "Gave his farewell sermon May 5, 1639." [Hob.] Rem. to Barnstable. Frm. and deputy Plym. Col. 1639. Rem. to Yarmouth and became pastor of the chh. Ch. Benjamin bapt. at Hing. March 24, 1639, Naomi bapt. in 1639, Ruth bapt. May 9, 1641, Sarah d. in 1647.

Richard, carpenter, Boston, frm. April 1, 1634.

Robert, blacksmith, chandler, Boston, adm. chh. 29 (3) 1636, frm. March 9, 1636-7. He gave to his son John, when 21 years of age and about to marry, a house and lands in Boston and elsewhere, reserving life use for himself. Referred to in Suffolk deeds III, 300. This son became the celebrated mint-master. Son Edward was commander of Rhode Island forces against the Dutch in 1653. [Es. Files 2, 95-102.] Wife Elizabeth adm. chh. 23 (4) 1639.
Will dated 20 (3) 1657; son John, son Edmund Quinney and his son John; son Richard Storer; son Edward H. Admin. gr. Feb. 12, 1666, to John, only surviving son. [Reg. XV, 322.]

Samuel ae. 25, came in the Elizabeth and Ann in May 1635.

HULLING, HULING,
—, residence not stated, frm. May 22, 1638.

HUN, HUNNE,
George, tanner, Boston, adm. chh. 22 (3) 1636, frm. May 17, 1637. Wife Anne adm. chh. 3 (1) 1639.
He d. (4) 1640. He beq. to wife Anne; son Nathaniel to be servant 5 years to James Johnson, who was made his guardian; land in Boston and Braintree. Nathaniel signed the agreement. [Reg. VII, 31.] The widow m. 16 (10) 1651, Wm. Philpot.

HUNNIWELL, see Honywell.

HUMPHREY, HUMPHREYS, HUMFREY,
Mr. John, Esquire, a magistrate, had grant of land at Saugus 6 March 1632-3. Frm. May 25, 1636. Had sad experiences in regard to some of his ch. in 1641. [W.] He brought into this country an est. of 2,000 li.; was a very useful ruler. [W.] App. by Gen. Court 2 June 1641, sergeant major general.
He d. poor in 1653. Admin. gr. to his son Joseph 13 (10) 1661. The Court gave him a grant of 300 acres which he sold June 25, 1664. Litigation over the farm in 1662 in Es. Court; important documents. Ch. Theophilus bapt. 24 (11) 1636, Thomas bapt. 26 (6) 1638, Joseph bapt. 5 (2) 1640, Lydia bapt. 25 (2) 1641, Dorcas b. about 1632, Sarah b. about 1634.

"July," 1634. Mr. Humphrey and the lady Susan, his wife, one of the Earl of Lincoln's sisters, arrived at Boston, bringing military supplies, 16 heifers given by Mr. Richard Andrews to the plantaton, one for each of the ministers and the rest to the poor; etc., and mesages from people of quality who desired to come over." [W.]

Jonas, from Wendover, Eng., where he had been a constable, [Family Papers,] came to Dorchester about 1637. Memb. chh. 1639, frm. May 13, 1640. Propr.; son James propr. 1646. Wife Frances memb. chh. 1639. Ch. Sarah bur. (7) 1638. The wife d. and he m. 2, Jane (Clap), widow of George Weeks; she d. 2 (6) 1668.
He d. March 19, 1661-2; will dated March 12, prob. April 17, 1662. Copy in possession of descendants. Beq. to wife; to sons James

HUMPHREY, etc., cont.
and Jonas; to dau. Susanna, wife to Nicholas White; to gr. child Elizabeth Frie a chest that was her grandmother's. [See William Fry.]

HUNT,
Edmund, or Edward, Cambridge, propr. 1634; sold house and land in 1636-7. Rem. to Duxbury; land grant Oct. 2, 1637, atba. 1643. Town officer.
Inv. taken 20 March, 1656, filed 24 (8) 1657. [Reg. V, 386.]

Enoch, from Titenden in the parish of Lee, Eng., [Mass. Arch. 129, 16,] Weymouth; 1640; town officer, 1651. In Court 1 (2) 1641. Wife Dorothie, widow of — Barker; she survived him, and m. John King. In her will, dated 14 (4) 1652, prob. 21 (8) 1652, she beq. to dau. Sarah Hunt, referred to Ephraim H., and to ch. Joseph and Ruth Barker and Susanna Heath. Ch. Sarah b. 4 (5) 1640.
He d. before 1647, when Dorothy's lands are mentioned in deeds of abutting tracts. Admin. gr. to son Ephraim 18 (9) 1652; [Reg. V, 239.] The son Ephraim, blacksmith, Weymouth, gave letter of attorney 5 (10) 1646, for collection of property in Beaconsfield, Bucks, formerly of John Hunt of Winchmore Hill in Agmondsham parish. [A.]

Mary, Salem, adm. chh. 21 (1) 1640-1.

Peter, lieut., Rehoboth, 1643; prop. frm. 4 June, 1645., adm. frm. 5 June, 1651; town officer. He m. Dec. 14, 1646, Elizabeth Smith; ch. Sarah b. Jan. 21, 1646-7, Judah b. April 21, 1648, Peter b. June 14, 1650, Enoch b. Feb. 28, 1652, Elizabeth b. March 1, 1654, John b. Oct. 15, 1656, Mary b. June 15, 1658, Ephraim b. March 31, 1661, Tabitha b. Sept. 14, 1663, Daniel b. Feb. 14, 1665, Benjamin b. Sept. 29, 1668, Nath. b. Dec. 31, 1670, d. Aug. 28, 1671. Peter, Morah and Tabitha bur. 1676. He was bur. Oct. 21, 1692.
Will dated 19 June, 1689, prob. 26 Dec. 1692; beq. to sons Enoch, John, Ephraim, Benjamin; dau. Judith Williams and her sons Nathaniel and Thomas Cooper; gr. ch. Ann Paine and Sarah Pecke; sons-in-law Samuel Peck and James Willett. Certain land he had of father Bowen.

Robert, yeoman, Charlestown, inhabitant 1638; rem. to Sudbury. Propr. 1640. Will dated 2 Oct. 1640; wife Susanna exec.

HUNT, cont.
for herself and the [three] minor children; friends Sedgwick and Lyne of Char. overseers. The widow d., and inv. of her est. was filed 24 (9) 1642. [Reg. VII, 32, and XXX, 80.]

William, Concord, rem. to Marlborough; frm. June 2, 1641. Witness to will of Wm. Bowstred of Concord, 23 Oct. 1642.
He signed his will Oct. 23, 1667, date of probate not given; beq. to wife Mary, and sons Samuel, Nehemiah and Isaac, and dau. Elizabeth Barnes.

HUNTER,
Robert, Rowley, propr., frm. Oct. 7, 1640.
He was bur. 5 (6) 1647. Will dated 5 (6) prob. 28 (7) 1647, beq. to wife Mary; to Thomas Birkby his shop gear, etc.; to certain poor of the chh.; to Abel Langley, conditionally; otherwise to the church.

HUNTING,
John, Dedham, propr. 28 (6) 1638, frm. March 13, 1638-9. Wife Esther adm. chh. April 24, 1639; ch. Samuel b. 22 (5) 1640, Nathaniel bapt. 24 (10) 1643, Mary adm. chh. 30 (2) 1643.
Will dated 15 Dec. 1684, prob. 26 March, 1691; affirms bequests made by wife Hester in her will Jan. 4, 1675; refers to his bro. Francis Seaborne; beq. to son Samuel, living in Charlestown; to ch. John, Mary Buckner, (widow in Boston,) and to her dau. Mary White; to son-in-law Robert Ware, in right of his first wife Margaret; to dau. Hester Fisher; to son-in-law John Peck of Rehoboth, in right for his eldest dau. Hester, of his first wife Elizabeth.

HUNTINGTON,
Margaret, widow, Roxbury, came in 1633; brought children with her. [E.]

William, planter, Salibsury, 1643, propr. 1650. He and his wife Joannah exchanged land in Salis. with John Bayley of Newbury and Elnor his wife 1 (10) 1652. Ch. John b. Aug. 1643, James d. Feb. 5, 1646, Mary b. July 8, 1648, (m. Joshua Goldsmith.) He d. about 1689.

HUNTLEY,
John, Lynn, in court, 1650.

HURD, see Heard.

HURST,
James, planter, Plymouth, taxed in 1632, frm. 1633, propr. 1638. His dau. Mary m. Oct. 16, 1657, Jonathan Dunham. Will dated Dec. 10, prob. 2 March, 1657; wife Gartend, [Gertrude;] gr. ch. John, Gershom, James, Eleazer, Hannah and Patience Cobb, and Mary Dunham. [Reg. V, 386.] The widow Gartheren d. before March 30, 1670, when the inv. of her est. was taken.

Margerite, Charlestown, adm. chh. 30 (9) 1642.

William, Sandwich; had a suit in court in 1637. He m. 17 March 1639, Katharine Thickston. Admin. gr. to the widow 1 June, 1641. [Plym. Col. Rec.]

HUSE, see Hewes,
Abel, Newbury, propr., frm. May 18, 1642. He deposed in 1666, aged about 64 years. Wife Eleanor d. 1 March, 1663; he m. 25 May, 1663, Mary Sears. Ch. Ruth b. 25 Feb. 1663-4, Abel b. 19 Feb. 1664, Thomas b. 9 Aug. 1666, William b. Oct. 12, 1667, Sarah b. Dec. 8, 1668, John b. 20 June, 1670, Amy b. 8 Sept. 1673, d. May 12, 1675, Ebenezer, a dau., b. 10 Aug. 1675.

He d. 29 March, 1690. Will dated 7 March, prob. Sept. 30, 1690; to wife Mary that which was her former husband's, etc.; sons Abel, Thomas, William, John; daus. Ruth Browne, Sarah and Ebenezer H.

HUSSEY,
Christopher, Saugus, 1632, frm. May 14, 1634. Rem. to Newbury; propr. 1637. One of the first planters at Hampton, 6 Sept., 1638. He m. 1, Theodate, dau. of Rev. Stephen Bachiler, who gave to them his cattle, goods and debts on his return to Eng. [Deposition of Colcord in 1672.]

Robert, carpenter, Duxbury, atba. 1643. Sold houes, lands, etc., to Mr. Ralph Partrich 10 (7) 1654.
Inv. taken by Ensign John Haward Oct. 30, 1667. [Reg. VII, 177.]

HUTCHINS, HUCHENS, see Hochens,
John, Newbury, brought suit in Ipswich Court in 1642. Rem. to Haverhill. Gave house and land at Newb. to wife Frances, and cattle to dau. Elizabeth and son William, 23 Nov. 1654. Conveyed land to son Joseph 29 April, 1661. Ch. recorded: Joseph b. 15 Nov. 1640, John b. Oct. 10, 1641, Benjamin b. 15 May, 164[4], Love b. 16 July 1647.

He d. Feb. 6, 1685. Will prob. March 30, 1686, beq. to wife Frances; sons William, Joseph, Benjamin and Samuel; daus. Elizabeth Ayres and Love Sherburne. The widow d. April 5, 1694, and beq. her est. to several of these children.

HUTCHINSON,
Edward. son of Edward and Susanna, of Alford, co. Lincoln, Eng., came to Boston about 1633, adm. chh. (8) 1633, frm March 4, 1633-4. Town officer. He deposed 25 March, 1658, ae. about 56 years. Possessed considerable wealth and transacted a large amount of business. Acted sometimes for bro. Richard H., ironmonger, of London. Was involved in the troubles which grew out of the preaching of his bro. William's wife and his bro.-in-law, Mr. John Wheelwright in 1637 and 1638; and rem. to Newport. Ret. to Eng. Wife Sarah adm. chh. 18 (10) 1633; ch. John bapt. 31 (6) 1634, Ichabod bapt. 3 (7) 1637.

George, Charlestown, propr.; memb. chh. 1630, frm. April 1, 1634. Town officer. Wife Margaret; ch. Nathaniel bapt. 9 (8) 1633.

He d. Dec. 11, 1660. Will prob. 18 (10) 1660, beq. to wife; son Nathaniel; apprentice boy Eleazer White. Brother John Penticost and Thomas Lynde overseers.

John, carpenter, ae. 30, came in the Bevis in May, 1638.

Richard, yeoman, Salem, propr. 1636; adm. chh. 4 (2) 1647. Bought a farm in 1648 and sold half of it to Nathaniel Putnam in 1651. [Es. De. and Files.] He deposed 11 Feb. 1681-2, ae. about 80 years. Wife Alice memb. chh. before 1636. He m. 2, Oct. 1668, Susanna, widow of Samuel Archard; she d. Nov. 26, 1674. He m. 3, Sarah, widow of James Standish. Ch. Abigail bapt. 25 (10) 1636, Hannah bapt. 20 (11) 1638, John b. in

HUTCHINSON, cont.
May, [Es. Files,] bapt. 2 (5) 1643, (had a deed of part of his father's est. in 1666.)

Will dated 19 June, 1679, prob. 26 (7) 1682; wife to be made comfortable for one of her age by son Joseph; to have what she had when they married if she wish to remove; he beq. to son-in-law Anthony Ashby and dau. Abigail, his wife; son-in-law Daniel Boardman and dau. Hannah, his wife; sons-in-law Nathaniel Putnam, Thomas Hale and James Hadlock; gr. ch. Bethia Hutchinson and Sarah Hadlock; servant, Black Peter; son Joseph exec. [Genealogy in Es. Inst. Coll. IX.]

Samuel, bro. of Edward, above, settled at Lynn; propr. before 1638. He deposed in 1658, ae. about 40 years.

Will dated 17 April, prob. 16 July, 1667, gave beq. to the son Samuel and six daus. of his sister Wheelwright and other relatives, but did not mention wife or child.

Susanna, widow of Wiliam, of Alford, Eng., came to N. E. in company with her son-in-law Mr. John Wheelwright and his wife Marie, her dau., in 1636. Was adm. to Boston chh. 12 (4) 1636. She rem. with them to Exeter; was dism. from Bo. chh. 3 (1) 1639.

William, eldest son of William and Susanna, of Alford, Eng., came to Boston in 1634, bringing his wife, Anne, dau. of Francis and Bridget (Dryden) Marbury, b. at Alford 20 July, 1691; who was destined to take a very significant part in the affairs of the new country. She made numerous addresses or sermons on religious subjects in a very earnest spirit, but presented a number of doctrines quite out of harmony with those held by the churches of New England; gathered about her a large number of men, as well as women; placed the ministers and officials of the colony in a position or embarrassment and opposition to herself; and drew down on herself and her brother-in-law, Mr. John Wheelwright, a storm of persecution. She was banished to Rhode Island, but not there relieved from pursuit of the Mass. authorities. To this was added the affliction of Indian atrocities; and she was killed by the savages in Sept., 1643. Her husband was a business man of large ability; and no fault was found with him except for hs sympathy and aid to his wife,

HUTCHINSON, cont.
whom he nobly supported, however his views may have differed from those she maintained.

Children: Edward bapt. 28 May, 1613, Susanna bapt. Sept. 4, 1614, bur. Sept. 8, 1630, Richard bapt. 8 Dec. 1615, Faith bapt. 14 Aug. 1617, (m. Capt. Thomas Savage,) Bridget bapt. 15 Jan. 1618-9, Elizabeth bapt. 15 Feb. 1621-2, bur. Oct. 4, 1630, William bapt. 22 Jan. 1623, Samuel bapt. 17 Dec. 1624, Anne bapt. 5 May, 1626, Mary bapt. 22 Feb. 1627-8. William bapt. 28 Sept. 1631, Susanna bapt. 15 Nov. 1633, Zuriel b. in Boston 13 (1) 1636. Of these Richard, Francis, Bridget and Faith were adm. chh. Boston in 1634. Edward, Jr., a singleman, was adm. chh. 10 (6) 1634.

HUTLEY, HUTLIFFE, see Utley,
Richard, ae. 15, came in the Hopewell in Sept. 1635. Settled at Ipswich; propr., 1639. Was paid in 1643 for service against the Indians. Bought land 20 Nov. 1645.

HYDE, HIDE, HIDES, IDE,
George, ship carpenter, mariner, Boston, 1642. Wife Anne adm. chh. 14 (4) 1645; ch. Mary b. 3 (6) 1642, Timothy b. (6) 1644; both bapt. 15 (4) 1645.

He d. in 1645. The widow m. Daniel Weld of Braintree.

John, tailor, from Marlborough, Eng., came in the James, April, 1635.

Jonathan, Cambridge, joined with his bro. Samuel in the purchase of land in 1647. Rec'd to full communion in the chh. with wife Mary Jan. 8, 1661. He deposed 2 (1) 1673, ae. 47 years. Ch. Jonathan, Samuel, John and Elizabeth bapt. in Feb. 1661, William bapt. [....]

Nicholas, Rehoboth, see Ide.

Richard, carpenter, Salem, 1642. Sold house and land in 1659. He deposed in 1674, about 60 years old. Ch. Isaac bapt. 17 (5) 1642, Rebecca bapt. 31 (1) 1644, Ephraim bapt. 12 (2) 1646, Mary bapt. 2 (11) 1647, Hannah bapt. 7 (2) 1650, Richard bapt. 6 (4) 1652, dau. Christian bapt. 20 (6) 1654.

Samuel, planter, Cambridge, came in the Jonathan in 1639, as he deposed in 1652. Settled at Cambridge. Propr.; frm. May 2,

HYDE, etc., cont.

1649. Deacon. Wife Temperance; ch. Samuel, Joshua, b. 12 (1) 1642, Job, Sarah b. 19 (3) 1644, Elizabeth. [Reg. XXXII, 409.]

He d. Sept. 14, 1689, ae. about 80. Will dated 10 July, prob. Oct. 1, 1689, beq. to wife; son Samuel and son-in-law Samuel Woolson; gr. ch. Samuel, John and Sarah H. Bro. Jonathan H. one of the overseers.

HYRICKE, see Herrick.

HYNDS, see HINDS.

IBROOK, IBROOKE, EYBROOKE, [town rec.]

Richard, Hingham, propr. 1635, in connection with William Cockraine, Sen., his son-in-law. Before Gen. Court 5 (1) 1638-9. Ch. Rebecca, (m. Mr. Peter Hobart, widower, and d. 7 (7) 1693, ae. 72 years,) Ellen, (m. at Cambridge, March, 1638, Capt. Joshua Hobart,) Margaret, (m. at Charlestown, Feb. 13, 1638-9, John Tower of Hing.). [Hob.]

He d. Nov. 14, 1651.

Robert, who, at Southold, Eng., March 25, 1657, witnessed a deed of Wm. Cockraine, [Suff. De. I, 62,] may be supposed to be a relation of the above.

IDE, IYDE, [HYDE,]

Nicholas, Rehoboth, propr. 1645, frm. 7 June, 1648. He petitioned the Court in 1648 for a child's portion of the est. of Thomas Bliss, who called him son-in-law. Wife Mary bur. Sept. 9, 1690. Ch. Nathaniel b. Nov. 11, 1647, Mary b. Dec. 10, 1649, John b. Dec. 1652, Nicholas b. Nov. 1654, Martha b. Oct. 1656, Elizabeth b. April 6, 1658, Timothy b. Oct. 1660, Dorothy b. May 11, 1662, Patience b. May 25, 1664, Experience b. Oct. 1665.

He was bur. Oct. 18, 1690.

ILES, see EELS.

ILSLIE, ILSLY, ILSBY, ILSBEY, ELSLY, ELUSLEY,

John, shoemaker, came in the Confidence April 11, 1638, with wife Barbara, ae. 20, and a servant. Settled at Salisbury; barber; propr. 1639; frm. Sept. 6, 1639. He deposed in 1660, ae. about 50 years. His wife Barbara d., and he m. 2, Sarah, dau. of Richard Haffield, q. v. Wife Sarah, who signed

ILSLIE, etc., cont.

deed in 1652, d. Aug. 3, 1673. Ch. John b. March, 1642, Sarah b. Aug. 31, 1644, (m. Philip Greeley,) Ruth b. March 6, 1647, d. May 2, 1650, Jonathan b. Nov. 2, 1652.

He d. Dec. 10, 1683; inv. pres. March 25, 1684.

William, shoemaker, ae. 26, came in the Confidence April 11, 1638. Settled at Newbury; propr., juryman. One of the witnesses to the will of John Cheney 5 (4) 1666. Wife Barbara. Ch. Mary, (m. Samuel Moore,) Elisha, John b. 11 Sept. 1641, William b. 23 Feb. 1647, Joseph b. 3 Oct. 1649, Isaac b. 23 June, 1652, Sara b. 8 Aug. 1655, (m. Samuel Hale,) a son b. and d. 1658.

He d. July 22, 1681; will dated Feb. 26, 1679, prob. July 28, 1681, beq. to wife Barbary, sons John, Joseph, Isaac, Elisha and William; to Samuel Moores, husband of Mary, and Samuel Hale, husband of Sarah I.; to the wife and ch. of son John.

INGALLS, ENGALS,

Edmund, (Edward,) Lynn, propr., 1638. In court (4) 1646.

His death was caused by a defect in Lynn bridge, for which a jury was called by Gen. Court 18 Oct. 1648, at the request of his son Robert. Will dated Aug. 28, prob. 14 (9) 1648; wife Ann; ch. Robert, John, Samuel, Henry, Elizabeth, Mary, Faith, (wife to Andrew Allen,) Sarah, (wife to Wm. Bitnar;) bro. Francis Ingalls; son-in-law Francis Dane. Leaves Katharine Skippee with his wife. To John 3 acres of land he hath in England.

Francis, tanner, Lynn, propr. 1638. His account with John Humphrey about purchase of farm, 1648-1656, in Es. files VIII, 75. He deposed 26 (9) 1662, ae. about 60 years. Rem. to Boston.

Will dated 10 Aug. prob. 1 Nov. 1672, beq. to wife Mary and son Joseph Belknap; residue to Elizabeth Farnam of Andover, after wife's death.

INGHAM,

Thomas, Scituate. Ch. Sarah b. 21 Jan. 1647, Sarah bapt. March 2, 1656.

INGS, see ENGLISH.

INGERSOLL, INKERSALL,
Richard, from Bedfordshire, Eng., sent over to Salem with his family by the Mass. Bay Co. in 1629. [Suff. De. I, xvi.] Propr. Maintained a ferry over North river in 1636. Wife Anne memb. chh. before 1636. Ch. John b. middle of (7) 1644. [Es. files.]
Will prob. Jan. 2, 1644-5; wife Ann, sons George, John, and Nathaniel; sons-in-law Richard Pettingell, (husband of Joanna,) and William Haines; dau. Alice Walcott and youngest dau. Bathsheba. The widow m. 2, John Knight of Newbury. [Es. files XIV, 29.]

INGOLDSBY, INGLESBY,
John, sawyer, Boston, singleman, adm. chh. 6 (9) 1641; frm. May 18, 1642. Bought house and lot Jan. 26, 1651. Wife Ruth; ch. John b. and d. 1649, John bapt. 15 (7) 1650, John b. 10 July, 1653, John b. 2 (8), bapt. as William 7 (8), d. as John 15 (10) 1655; Ebenezer b. 13 Dec., 1656, Peter b. 8 March, 1658, Peter bapt. 13 (1) 1659.

INGRAHAM, INGRAM,
Edward, ae. 18, came in the Blessing in July, 1635. Settled at Salem; propr. 1638, swine-keeper 1640.

Richard, Rehoboth, propr. 1645.

INMAN,
Edward, Braintree. Ch. John b. 18 (7) 1648.

IRELAND,
Samuel, carpenter, ae. 32, with wife Marie, ae. 30, and ch. Martha, ae. 1½, came in the Increase April 15, 1635.

William, yeoman, Dorchester, 1648; frm. May 22, 1650. He was dism. to the new chh. in Boston 3 (12) 1660. Ch. Rebecca bapt. 10 (1) 1649, Rebecca bapt. 20 (8) 1650, Ann bapt. 13 (12) 1652, William bapt. 16 (10) 1655.

IRESON, IERSTON,
Edward, ae. 32, came in the Abigail in July, 1635, with Elizabeth, ae. 27. Settled at Lynn; propr. 1638. He deposed in 1663, ae. about 62 years.
He d. Dec. 1675. Will dated Oct. 26, 1674, prob. 27 (4) 1676; wife Alice, sons Samuel and Benjamin; daus. Elizabeth and Ruth.

INNES, see IRONS.

IRISH,
John, of the parish of Clisdon, co. Somerset, laborer, was indentured to Timothy Hatherly of the parish of St. Olaves in Southwark, co. Surrey, as a servant, to go to Plymouth in N. E. April 10, 1629. Witness, Robert Winsor, Jr. [Suff. co. files; Reg. XXXIX, 28.] Settled at Duxbury. Inherited land of Henry Wallis. Volunteer for the Pequot War, 1637. Land grant 5 March, 1643. Atba. 1643.

IRONS, IONS, IANS, IJONS, JIONS,
Edward, Salisbury, took oath of fidelity in 1645.

Matthew, servant to William Colborn, Boston, adm. chh. 20 (2) 1634. Propr. 1637. Kept an ordinary in 1653. Wife Anne; ch. Elizabeth b. 15 (2) 1631, John b. 16 (7) 1638, Elizabeth bapt. 18 (2) 1641, Thomas bapt. 5 (12) 1642, ae. 18 days, Thomas b. 18 (4) 1643, Rebecca b. 26 (12) 1644, Matthias bapt. 14 (1) 1647, ae. about 6 days, Edward bapt. 11 (12) 1648, ae. about 3 days, Samuel bapt. 24 (9) 1650, Ann bapt. 8 (12) 1651, Anne b. 6 June, d. 26 June, 1654, William d. 1 (9) 1654, Katharine b. 1 June, 1655, Matthew d. 13 (3) 1656.
He d. in 1661. Will prob. Jan. 30, 1661; sons John, Thomas, Samuel, daus. Elizabeth and Rebecca. [Reg. XII, 36.]

ISABEL, ISBELL,
Robert, carpenter, Salem, propr. 1636. Lawsuit, 1641. Ann, his wife, deposed in case of Margaret Pease in 1645. Rem. to Manchester. Sold house and land in 1651.

ISAAC, ISACKE,
Joseph, Cambridge, propr., frm. March 9, 1636-7; town officer, 1638. Deputy. Rebecca, ae. 36, [perhaps his wife,] came in the Elizabeth of Ipswich April 30, 1634.
He d. 11 (3) 1642.

ISLIN, ISLYN,
Thomas, Sudbury, frm. May 13, 1640. Town officer, 1643.

IVER,
Michael, in Es. Court in 1639; before Gen. Court 3 March, 1639-40.

IVES,

Miles, Watertown, propr. 1636. [Not unlikely he is the man enrolled as Mathias Ives, frm. May 25, 1638.] He sold house and land in Newton village in 1639. See will of John Ive of Naylonde, co. Suffolk, Eng., prob. 17 June, 1619; beq. to son Miles and his children. [Reg. XXXVIII, 416.] Wife Martha; ch. Sarah b. 11 (8) 1639, Mary b. 10 (5) 1641, Hannah b. 9 (3) 1643.

He d. Aug. 26, 1684, ae. 76. [Mdx. rec.] Will mentions son-in-law John Polly; son-in-law Luse Allen, and his ch. Abel and Sarah; gr. child Nathaniel Healy; Mary Allen and Martha Healy; sister Grace Ireland; son James Hubbard.

IVEY, IVIE, IVY,

James, Braintree.

He d. March 3, 1653-4; beq. to his children and to his bro.'s son John Ivey. [Reg. VIII, 128 w.]

John, Newbury; the only record is the birth of his son John b. Nov. 6, 1643.

IVORY, IVORYE,

William, Lynn, propr. 1638; lawsuit, 1639. Petitioned the Gen. Court in 1645 regarding his long absence on military service.

Inv. of his est. taken 26 (1) 1653, filed at Ipswich, showed carpenters' tools, etc.

JACKLING, JACKLINGE, JACKLYN, JAGLIN,

Edmund, glazier, Boston, adm. chh. 31 (6) 1634, frm. May 6, 1635. Paid a bill to Robert Tainton, merchant, of London, in 1659. [Suff. De. III, 336.] Wife Susan, dau. of Henry Pease; ch. Samuel b. 19 (2) 1640, Susanna b. and d. 1643, Susan b. and d. 1644, Hannah b. 12 (9) 1645, Susan b. 16 (11) 1648, Mehetabel b. 15 Feb. 1653, Marah b. 15 June, 1655, Ruth b. Aug. 4, 1658, Mehetabel and Mary bapt. 8 (2) 1660.

Will dated Dec. 23, 1672, prob. 29 Sept. 1681; about to take a voyage to sea; beq. to wife, to daus. Mehetabel and Mary; to son Samuel. The widow, in her will dated 14 March, 1686-7, beq. her est. to dau. Mary Parris.

JACKMAN,

James, Newbury. Ch. Mary b. 1644, Sarah b. 18 Jan. 1647, Hester b. 12 Sept. 1651, James b. 22 June, 1655, Joanna b. 14 June, 1657, Richard b. Feb. 6, 1659.

He d. 30 Dec. 1694.

JACKSON,

Edmund, shoemaker, Boston, adm. chh. 15 (9) 1635, frm. May 25, 1636. Wife Martha d. 12 (9) 1652; he m. 7 (11) 1652, Mary Gawdren, widow, dau. of Samuel Cole; she d. 18 Jan. [Feb.] 1658-9. He m. 27 Oct. 1659-60, Elizabeth Pilkenton. Ch. Hannah b. 1 (1) 1636-7, John b. 20 (8) 1638, Thomas b. 1 (1) 1640-1, Samuel b. 27 (4) 1643, Jeremiah b. (5) 1645, Mary bapt. 17 (2) 1647, Isaac b. 22 (9) 1651, Edmund b. 30 (8) 1654, Elizabeth b. 11 Feb. 1656, Elisha b. 12 Feb. 1658, Sarah b. Sept. 24, 1660, Martha b. Feb. 11, 1661-2, Susanna b. Dec. 2, 1663, Susanna b. Sept. 19, 1666, Edmund b. Oct. 5, 1668. Samuel Cole gave land to his gr. ch. Elisha and Elizabeth J. 6 Oct. 1666.

Will, dated 2 May, prob. 28 July, 1675. Beq. to wife Elizabeth and ch. Samuel, Jeremiah, Hannah, (wife of John Andrews,) Sarah, Martha, Susanna, Edmund and Mary. The widow Elizabeth m. Wm. Beal, Sen., of Marblehead, and d. 5 Nov. 1683.

Edward, gent., Cambridge, frm. May, 1645. Propr. Deputy. Witness to deed and appraiser of the est. of Samuel Holly in 1643. Bought land in 1656. Wife — d. and he m. 14 (1) 1648-9, Elizabeth, dau. of John Newgate and widow of John Oliver; they sold land in Boston June 2, 1666. Ch. Jonathan, Hannah, Rebecca, Sebiss, Frances d. 5 (8) 1649, Sarah b. in Camb. 5 (11) 1649, bapt. in Boston 21 (2) 1650, Edward, Lydia, Elizabeth, Hannah, Ruth.

He d. June 17, 1681, ae. 79; will dated 11 June, prob. 26 Aug. folg., beq. to wife; sons Edward, Jonathan and Sebiss; daus. Ruth J., Hannah Ward, Rebecca Prentice, Lydia Fuller, Sarah Hobart, and Hannah Wilson; gr. ch. and great gr. ch. to the number of 36; sons-in-law John and Thomas Oliver and dau.-in-law Elizabeth Wiswall; to the College; to the use of the ministry; to friend Capt. Thomas Prentice; sons-in-law Joseph Fuller, John Prentice, Nathaniel Wilson, John Ward, Nehemiah Hubart. His widow d. Sept. 30, 1709, ae. 92. Her will mentions

JACKSON, cont.,
dau. Elizabeth Bond in addition to persons named in her husband's will.

Henry, planter, ae. 29, came in the Elizabeth and Ann in April, 1635. Settled at Watertown; gave letter of attorney to Edward How of Wat. to receive debts in N. E. 26 (7) 1639. [L.]

John, fisherman, ae. 40, with Margaret, ae. 36, and John, ae. 2, came in the Blessing in July, 1635. Settled at Cambridge, propr., deacon. Ch. Caleb b. and d. 12 (10) 1645, Anna b. 8 (1) 1647, Abigail b. 4 (6) 1648.
The inv. of his est. taken 30 Jan. 1674, was filed April 6, 1675. Agreement made 20 Dec. 1676, between the widow Margaret, James Trowbridge, Noah Wiswall, Samuel Truesdall, Daniel Preston and Elijah Kendrick, who had married daughters of the deceased, his son Abram and daus. Deliverance and Sarah, for the partition of the estate.

John, wholesale man in Burchen Lane, ae. 30, came in the Defense in July, 1635. Settled at Salem. Memb. chh. with wife Margaret, 1639. Frm. June 2, 1641. Sold lumber to go to Conn. June 2, 1644.

Will dated 31 (1) prob. (4) 1655; wife Mary; son John J.; Margaret Nouel.

John, Ipswich, propr. 1635.
Inv. of his goods and est. 18 (7) 1648. Admin. gr. to widow Katharine; one son and 5 daus., all under 21 years; her *husband* to be possessed of the est., bring up the children, and pay them their portions when due.
Evidently she had married again before she settled the estate, but we do not find record of it.

John, his house burned in 1636. [W.]

John, carpenter, Boston, frm. May 10, 1643. Wife Abigail adm. chh. 12 (7) 1640. She d. and he m. 14 (9) 1657, Jane, dau. of Evan Thomas. Ch. of John and Abigail: Sarah b. 15 (6) 1639, Abigail b. 24 (6) 1641, John b. 26 (4) 1643, Hannah b. 2 (5) 1645, Peter bapt. 12 (7) 1647, d. 5 (9) 1653, Mary bapt. 4 (9) 1649, ae. about 6 days, Benjamin bapt. 23 (12) 1650, d. 11 (9) 1653, Mary bapt. 25 Oct., 1652, *Sarah* bapt. 31 Oct., 1652; ch. of John and Jane: John b. and d. 1658, John b. Feb. 24, 1662. He deposed to admin. of Thomas Millard in 1669-70, ae. about 60 years; Abigail deposed, ae. same.

JACKSON, cont.,
Will dated 10 Dec. prob. 29 Jan. 1672. Wife Abigail, son John, dau. Sara Eustace; youngest dau. Mary; working tools to grand child John Eustace.

Manus, Charlestown, propr. 1640. Wife Rebecca; ch. Rebecca b. 25 (10) 1643.

Richard, yeoman, Cambridge, propr. 1636. Town officer, deputy. Wife Isabell d. Feb. 12, 1661; he m. 2, Elizabeth, widow of Richard Browne of Charlestown; she d. Jan. 11, 1676-7.
He made will 22 June, 1672, ae. about 90 years; prob. Oct. 10, 1672. Beq. to wife Elizabeth what she had by former husband R. B.; to the church of Camb.; to Richard Eccles; kinswoman Sarah Childs; Samuel Platts; after his wife wife's decease certain items to kinsman John J. The widow Elizabeth, in will dated 14 (4) 1676, prob. 6 (1) 1677, beq. to the ch. of her husband's kinswoman Mary Eccles, dec.; to Sarah, wife of Joseph Childs, and to his kinsman John J.; to dau. Wakefield; to Sarah, wife of John J.; to Richard and Martha Eccles; to John and Jonathan Simpson. Refers to former husband Mr. Wm. Browne.

Samuel, yeoman, a bondsman in Court Jan. 3, 1636. Scituate; adm. chh. Feb. 25, 1637. Rem. to Barnstable; prop. frm. 1 June, 1641, atba. 1643. Ret. to Sci. in 1646. Town officer. Attorney for Thomas Bell 20 (6) 1647. [A.] His wife d. March 4 or 5 1638. He m. Nov. 20, 1639, Hester, dau. of Richard Sillis. Ch. Anna bapt. March 25, 1638, several years old; Bethiah bapt. March 14, 1640, Hester bapt. Feb. 5, 1642, Samuel bapt. (7) 1646, Jonathan b. 7 May, 1647.
Will dated 28 Aug. prob. Oct. 30, 1682, beq. to wife and son Jonathan.

Nicholas, Rowley, m. (5) 1646, Sarah Reilly; m. 2, 9 Dec. 1656, Elizabeth, widow of Hugh Chapman, who petitioned Gen. Court regarding H. C.'s est. 6 (2) 1657. [Arch. B, 2.]

Thomas, Plymouth, executed in 1638 for complicity in the robbery and murder of an Indian.

William, Rowley, propr. 1639. Wife Joane bur. Nov. 20, 1680; ch. Mary b. 8 (12) 1639, Deborah b. 24 (11) 1644.
Will dated 6 Dec. 1680, being aged and

JACKSON, cont.,
decrepid; prob. 4 (3) 1681. Wife had lately died. He beq. to only son John what he promised him on his marriage with bro. Poore's dau., and to his son John that he had by Elizabeth, his late wife; to eldest dau. Elizabeth How; to dau. Mary Foster; to son John Thrumble and dau. Deborah, his wife.

JACOB, JACOBS,
Nicholas, husbandman, came from old Hingham in 1633 with his wife and 2 children and their cousin Thomas Lincoln, weaver, and settled at Hingham. He owned a homestall at Watertown, but sold it before 1636. Kept an ordinary in H. in 1640. Comr., deputy, town officer. Wife Mary; ch. John b. about 1630, Elizabeth, (m. 1, Dec. 4, 1648, John, son of Thomas Thaxter, m. 2, March 23, 1690-1, Daniel Cushing; she d. 24 Nov. 1725, ae. 93 years;) Mary, (m. John Otis, Jr.,) Sarah, (m. Matthew Cushing, Jr.,) Hannah bapt. Feb. 23, 1639, (m. Thomas Loring,) Josiah b. and d. 1642, Deborah bapt. Nov. 6, 1643, (m. Nathaniel Thomas,) Joseph bapt. May 10, 1646.

He d. 5 (4) 1657. Will provided for the whole family. [Reg. VIII, 280.] The widow m. 2, March 10, 1659, John Beal; she d. 15 June, 1681.

Richard, yeoman, came in the Mary and John March 24, 1633; settled at Ipswich; frm. May 6, 1635. Town officer. He m. 1, Martha, dau. of Samuel Appleton. He m. 2, Johanna, widow of Robert Hale of Charlestown; contract 6 Oct. 1662. [Mdx. Files.] Son Richard's will dated 8 June, prob. 26 Sept. 1676, beq. to bros. Thomas, John, Joseph and Nathaniel; sisters Martha and Judith. Desires his "two uncle Appletons" to be overseers. Samuel Appleton was a witness, and John A. one of the appraisers.

JAMES,
Edmund, planter, Watertown, appl. frm. Oct. 19, 1630. Propr., town officer. [His widow] Reana entered into marriage contract with Wm. Andrew of Cambridge 11 (6) 1640. [Mdx. De. III, 7.]

Erasmus, Salem, Marblehead, 1637. Lawsuit, 1639. He deposed in 1654, ae. 49, and his wife Jane, ae. 53.

Admin. of his est. June 26, 1660. Ch. Erasmus J. and Hester, wife of Richard Road,

JAMES, cont.,
made agreement for division of the est. of their mother Jane J. 30 (4) 1669.

Gardey, or Gaudy, husbandman, Charlestown. Adm. chh. 15 (3) 1641, frm. May 18, 1642. Anna adm. chh. 28 (11) 1641. He deposed 17 (4) 1654, ae. about 50 years. [Mdx. Files.]. Rem. to Boston and was adm. inhab. in 1657. Ret. to Winfarthing, co. Norfolk, Eng., for a short time, but came again in 1661.

Will dated Dec. 26, prob. Jan. 31, 1683. Beq. his house and land in Winowfarthing to Benjamin Smith and John Curtis, after life use by his wife; beq. to several other persons and to the church of Boston.

Francis, with wife and 2 servants, Thomas Sucklin and Richard Baxter, came from Hingham, Eng., in 1638 and settled at Hingham; propr.; frm. May 10, 1643. His house was burned in May, 1647.

He d. 27 Dec. 1647. Francis, Hingham, est. admin. by widow Elizabeth 5 May, 1685; 9 shares in first and third divisions at Conyhasset, 1 planting lot at Planting Hill, 1 acre fresh meadow bought of Thomas Minor, 9 acres of commons, etc. She admin. July 12, 1688, on the est. of her son Philip.

Philip, with wife, 4 children and 2 servants, William Pitts and Edward Mitchell, came from Hingham, Eng., and settled in Hingham in 1638. He d. soon after he came. Widow [Jane] m. Feb. 14, 1640, George Russell. [Hob.]

Ralph, Plymouth, m. 17 April, 1650, Mary Fuller.

Rosamond, Marblehead, taxed in 1638.

Thomas, tailor, [Boston,] was blown up in the ship Mary Rose in Boston Harbor July 27, 1640. [L.]

Rev. Thomas, b. about 1563. [Hub.] came about 1631 to Charlestown. With wife Elizabeth adm. chh. Boston 1631-2; frm. Nov. 6, 1632. He was ordained minister of the church of Charlestown, Nov. 2, 1632. Ch. John b. at Char., bapt. 9 (11) 1632, Thomas became minister at Easthampton, L. I., in 1651. A council of churches met at Chsn. to consider differences between Mr. James and the church 11 (1) 1635-6, which supported certain crticisms which had been made regarding his melancholy and

JAMES, cont.,
jealous disposition; and, in accordance with its advice, he removed during the succeeding year.

He went to New Haven, Conn.; had land grant in 1639. Visited Virginia with Tompson and Knowles in 1642; ret. to New Haven, and went back to England about 1648; became minister of Needham Market, co. Suffolk; there he died.

Will dated 5 Feb. 1682, prob. 13 Feb. 1683, beq. all books, household effects and clothes which could be sent, to son Thomas James of Easthampton, Long Island in New England. In case Thomas be not living est. to be divided between grandchildren or great-grandchildren. Beq. to individuals; 10 li. for the binding out of 3 poor widows' sons. [Reg. LI, 422.]

Thomas, Salem, gave letter of attorney 27 (6) 1645 to Thomas Burges of Charlestown to recover a debt of Francis Spicer of Eckton, Northamptonshire, and to sell land in Earles Barton in same co. [A.] This may be the

Thomas, Lancaster, who made will 13 (1), prob. 12 (3) 1660; beq. to cousins Lydia, Mary, Hannah, Christopher and John Lewis; to wife's mother in England, if living, his housing and land in Eng.

William, Salem, appl. frm. Oct. 19, 1630. With wife Elizabeth before Salem Court 27 (7) 1636.

William, embarked for N. E. June 22, 1632.

William, mercer, of Boston, N. E., son of Albon James, late citizen and mercer of London, gave letter of attorney to his uncle George Strange, gent., to sell land left him by his uncle, William James, 9 (8) 1640. [L.]

JAQUES, JAQUITH, JAQUISH, JAQUE, JACKEWISH,
Abraham, Charlestown, adm. chh. 9 (10) 1643, frm. May 14, 1656. Anna adm. chh. 13 (2) 1643. Ch. Abraham b. 19 (10) 1644, Mary b. 3 (9) 1646. These children recd. a legacy from their mother's father, James Jordan of Dedham, in 1655.

Will dated 16 (9) 1675, prob. Decd. 19, 1676, beq. to wife Hannah or Anna, son Abram and daus. Lydia, Sarah and Deborah.

JAQUES, etc., cont.
Henry, carpenter, Newbury, 1648. He deposed in 1663, ae. about 44 years. He m. 8 Oct. 1648, Anne Knight; ch. Henry b. 30 July, 1648, Mary b. 1651, d. 23 Oct. 1653, [Richard,] Stephen b. 9 Sept. 1661, Sara b. 20 March, 1654, Daniel b. 20 Feb. 1667, Elizabeth b. 28 Oct. 1669, Ruth b. 14 April 1672, Abigail b. 11 March, 1674, [Hannah.]

He d. 22 Feb. 1686. His will was presented in court 8 March, 1686-7, and admin. gr. to his son Stephen.

JARMAN,
Priscilla, ae. 10, came in the Susan and Ellen in May, 1635.

JARRETT,
John, Salem, frm. May 13, 1640. Probably rem. to Rowley, where J. J. was propr. and juryman in 1641. Wife Susanna; ch. Elizabeth bur. July 13, 1660.

He was bur. 11 (12) 1647. Will dated 11 (11) 1647, prob. 27 (7) 1648, beq. to wife Susanna and dau. Elizabeth.

JARVIS,
Mr. John, juryman, Gen. Court, Sept. 28, 1630.

Inv. Suff. Prob. Sept. 26, 1656; had the acct. books of Mr. Robert Patteshall in his charge. The est owed Wm. Blanten for 24 weeks board. [Reg. XII, 50.]

JEFFREY, JEOFFREYS, GEOFFREYS,
Edward, ae. 24, came in the Truelove, in Sept. 1635.

Robert, ae. 30, wife Marie, ae. 27, with ch. Thomas, ae. 7, Elizabeth, ae. 6, and Mary, ae. 3 came in the Elizabeth and Ann in May, 1635. Settled at Charlestown. Wife Mary adm. chh. 17 (12) 1636. Sold house and land in 1637.

Thomas, Dorchester, frm. May 14, 1634.

Mr. William, gent., Weymouth, an old planter, [W.] frm. May 18, 1631. Was deputed with Mr. Wm. Blackstone to put Mr. J. Oldham in possession of his grant. [Suff. De. I. XIII.] Signed a bond for Jeremy Gould in 1641. [L.] Brought a letter from Morton to Gov. Winthrop Aug. 4, 1634. Ch. Mary b. 20 (1) 1642.

"— Jeffrey," did valiant service in the Pequot War in 1636-7. [W. in B.]

JEFFS, JEFFES, JEFTS, JEFTES, JESS,
Henry, Woburn, propr. 1640. One of the incorporators of Billerica, 1654. He m. Sept. 13, 1647, Anna Stowers. He m. 2, May 21, 1649, Hannah Births, who d. Sept. 15, 1662. He m. 3, Oct. 3, 1666, Mary, widow of Simon Bird; she d. April 1, 1679, and he m. 4, May 5, 1681, Mary Baker, widow, of Concord. Ch. John b. at Wob. May 11, 1651, Hannah d. May, 1653, Hannah b. Feb. 14, 1654, (m. April 30, 1674, Andrew Spaulding,) Joanna b. May 24, 1656, (m. John Dunkin,) Henry b. March 21, 1658-9.

He d. May 24, 1700, [ae. about 94.] Will dated March 4, 1691-2, prob. June 17, 1700, beq. to eldest son John and his son Henry; to son Henry; daus. Hannah Spalding and Joannah Button; gr. ch. Mary and John, ch. of John Dunkin, Henry, son of Andrew Spalding, Alice, John, Mary and Hannah Jefts; son-in-law William Baker of Concord.

JEGGLES, JIGGLES, GIGGLES,
William, ship-carpenter, fisherman, Salem, propr. 1636; adm. chh. 26 (9) 1648. Sold land in 1658. Wife Elizabeth; ch. inferred from various circumstances; Daniel, (propr. 1638,) Thomas, (m. by special permission of the Gen. Court, by Capt. Hathorne 27 Oct. 1647, to Abigail Sharpe; had ch. Abigail, Thomas, Samuel, Elizabeth, William, Daniel, Nathaniel and Mary bapt. Nov. 22, 1668, John bapt. May 13, 1669;) Mary, (memb. chh. 1636).

He d. before 28 (4) 1659, when his widow Elizabeth presented inv. of his estate; three of the ch. long ago married, the other abroad at sea; eldest son in England, master of a ship.

JELLIT, see Gillett.

JEMSON, JEMPSON, GIMSON, JAMESON,
James, laborer, Boston, 1647; propr.; inspector of the flats. Wife Sarah adm. chh. 27 (9) 1647; ch. Marie bapt. 28 (9) 1647, John bapt. 3 (7) 1648, James b. 22 (10) 1651, Sarah b. 2 Jan. 1654, Joseph bapt. 20 (4) 1658.

He d. Jan. 1661. Inv. 21 (11) 1661; admin. gr. to widow Sarah. [Reg. XI, 341.] The widow d. March 25, 1696.

JENKS, JENCKES, JINKS,
Joseph, blacksmith, of Hammersmith in Lynn, 1645, propr.; one of the petitioners for a plantation at Nashaway, but not a settler. The Gen. Court granted him a patent for 14 years from May, 1646, for engines for water mills; the selectmen of Boston were authorized in 1658 to make arrangements with him for construction of fire-engines. He had liberty from the Iron Works Co. in 1656 to set up a mill for making scythes or other iron-work by water. [Es. De. 1, 32.] He assigned a note to his son Joseph 12 April, 1655. His first wife did not come over with him. After her death he m. Elizabeth—. Ch. b. here, Sarah, Deborah, John and Daniel. The wife d. July, 1678. He deposed 17 Sept. 1681, ae. about 81 years, concerning Mr. Leader's coming over to the Iron Works 33 years before, and employing Samuel Bennett to buy land for him.

He d. in March, 1683.

JENKINS, JENKIN,
Edward, planter, Scituate, servant of Nathl. Tilden, 1641, atba. 1643, frm. 1 June, 1647. Sold land June 9, 1660. Joseph, son of John Whetstone of Sci. calls him uncle. Wife Lettice.

Will dated 2 March, 1699,—very aged,—prob. Aug. 9, 1699, beq. to wife, son Thomas, dau. Mary Cock; to gr. ch. Edward, Mary and Daniel Jenkins, Hannah Turner, Mary Brown and Ruth Cock. Widow Mary made will 26 Jan., 1704-5, bequeathing to son Isaac Ripley, the ch. of son Abraham R., dec., to daus. Mary Wade and Rebecca Smith. Debt due from son Thomas Jenkins.

Joel, Braintree, before Gen. Court in 1640, frm. May 6, 1646. Rem. to Malden. Ch. Lydia b. 13 (8) 1640, Theophilus b. 7 (2) 1642, Ezekiel bapt. in Boston 16 (7) 1649, Obediah bapt. 13 (8) 1650.

He d. in Mald. Will dated July 4, 1687, prob. 2 (9) 1689, beq. to sons Lemuel, Ezekiel and Obediah; daus. Lydia, wife of John Paul, Hannah, wife of — Parker, and Hannah, wife of Joseph Merriam; gr. ch. Lemuel and Ezekiel, sons of Lemuel. Lands in Mald. and Reading.

John, ae. 26, came in the Defense in July, 1635. Elizabeth, ae. 27, came in the Truelove in Sept., 1635.

JENKINS, etc., cont.,

John, Plymouth, propr., frm. 3 Jan. 1636. Volunteer for Pequot War, 1637, and a soldier in the Narragansett War in 1645. Town officer, juror. Rem. to Sandwich. Propr. He m. 2, Feb. 1652, Mary Ewer of Barnstable. Ch. Sarah b. at Bar. 15 Nov. 1653, Mehetabel b. 2 March, 1654-5, Samuel b. 12 Sept. 1657, John b. 13 Nov. 1659, Mary b. 1 Oct. 1662, Thomas b. 15 July, 1666, Joseph b. March, 1669.

Inv. pres. 28 Oct. 1684, by his son Zechariah.

"One Jenkins, late an inhabitant of Dorchester, and now removed to Cape Porpus, was killed by the Indians in 1632." [W.]

JENNER, GINNER, see Trerice and Lynde,

Rev. Thomas, Roxbury, frm. Dec. 8, 1636. Rem. to Weymouth. He and Thomas, Jr., were proprs. in 1636. Was called to be pastor of the church and he and his people were brought into harmony by a gathering of elders 9 (11) 1637. [W.] Frm. Sept. 6, 1639. Deputy; arbiter in a case before Gen. Court, 1640.

He rem. to the district of Maine before 1644. [Mass. Hist. Coll. 4-7.] Thomas of Charlestown sold house and lands at Weymouth which had been his father's 28 (10) 1649, and Mrs. Jenner consented to the deed. Esther adm. chh. Char. 9 (5) 1648.

JENNEY, JENNY, [JENNINGS,]

John, brewer's man, of Norwich, Eng., m. at Leyden, Holland, Sept. 5, 1614, Sarah Carey, of Monksoon, Eng. Came to Plymouth in the James in 1623. [Mor.] Drew lots for 5 persons. His wife Sarah and ch. Samuel, Abigail and Sarah had shares in cattle in 1627. He was frm. in 1633. Carried on a corn-mill in 1638, which the widow continued in 1644.

Will dated 28 Dec. 1643, inv. taken 25 May; will prob. June 30, 1644; gives to wife and children mentioned above, also dau. Susan. Dau. Abigail had rec'd something by the will of her grandmother; and he consents to her marriage with Henry Wood after one year. The widow's will, prob. Aug. 18, 1655, mentions daus. Sarah Pope and Abigail Wood, son Samuel and son Benjamin Bartlett, and friends. [Reg. IV, 174, and V, 262.] Sarah m. Thomas Pope; Susan m. Benjamin Bartlett.

JENNINGS, JENNISON, GENNINGS, GENNISON,

Nicholas, ae. 22, came in the Francis of Ipswich April 30, 1634.

Robert, Watertown, app. ensign to Capt. Patrick in the military company Aug. 16, 1631; propr.; frm. May, 1645. Deputy. As attorney for his bro. William J., formerly of Wat. but now of Colchester, Eng., he sold land in 1657. Wife Elizabeth d. Oct. 30, 1638, ae. 30. He m. Grace —. Ch. Elizabeth b. 12 (2) 1637, Michael b. 17 (10) 1640, Samuel b. 15 (10) 1642. Wife d. Nov. 26, 1686.

He d. July 4, 1690. Will dated 15 Sept. 1683, and 2 April, 1687, prob. Oct. 7, 1690, beq. to wife; to dau. Michall Warren; son-in-lad George Reed; son Samuel exec; gr. sons William and Robert J.

Mr. William, captain, Charlestown, built a house in 1630; sold, and rem. to Watertown, frm. May 18, 1631. Formerly a partner of Richard Spitty of Grey's Inn, gent. [L.] Was one of the first selectmen; deputy. "Ensign Jenyson went for a pilot in the Thunder to Bermuda Oct. 17, 1633," and reported improved conditions there on his return. [W.] Commanded a company against the Pequots in 1636. Was called to the Court in July 1644 for a slight difference of opinion on the question between the Parliament and the king; proved to be most loyal to the Colony and the Commonwealth. [W.] Was employed by the Earl of Warwick to see to his vessel at Boston June 27, 1646. [Suff. De. I, 77.]

He ret. to Colchester, Eng. See Robert, above.

JERNELL, see Jewell.

JEWELL, JERNELL,

Thomas, ae. 27, miller, came in the Planter in April, 1635. Settled at Braintree. Lands assigned him 24 (12) 1639-40, for 3 heads. Wife Grizzell; ch. Joseph b. 24 (2) 1642, Thomas and Hannah b. 27 (12) 1643, (Hannah m. 30 (6) 1664, John Parris, Nathaniel b. 15 (2) 1648, Grizzell b. 19 (1) 1651, Mercy b. 14 (2) 1653.

He d. in 1654. Will prob. July 21, 1654, beq. to wife and children. The widow Grizzell about to marry Humphrey Griggs, admin.. She afterward m. John Gurney, Sen., Henry Kibbe and John Burge. [Reg. V, 305.]

JESS, JESSE,
William, Springfield, 1644, town officer. Ch. Abigail b. 1 (1) 1644-5. He was drowned 1 (1) 1644-5.

JESSUP, JESOP,
Walter, weaver, ae. 21, came from Weymouth, Eng., before March 20, 1635.

JEWETT,
Joseph, yeoman, clothier, Rowley, frm. May 22, 1639. Propr.; deputy. Bought a farm of Samuel Bellingham 23 July, 1653. He arranged with John Hull of Newbury 6 March, 1656, for payment of an annuity to himself and wife. Wife Mary was bur. 12 (2) 1652. He m. May 13, 1653, Ann, widow of Capt. Bozoan Allen; she d. 4 Feb. 1661. [Hob.] Ch. Hannah b. 15 (4) 1641, Nehemiah b. 6 (2) 1643, Faith and Patience b. 5 (3) 1645, Jeremiah, Mary b. 4 (2) 1654, Joseph b. 1 (2) 1656.

He was bur. 26 Feb. 1660. Will dated 15 Feb., prob. 26 March, 1661, beq. to five ch. by former wife and two by last wife; eldest son Jeremiah to have double portion, and he, with sons Philip Nelson and John Carlton to be execs. [See Blodgette's Rowley Settlers.]

Maximilian, bro. of the above, Rowley, frm. May 13, 1640. Deacon. Deputy. Wife Ann was bur. Nov. 9, 1667. Ch. Ezekiel b. 5 (1) 1643, Anna b. 26 (12) 1644, Mary b. 18 (12) 1646, Elizabeth b. 22 (3) 1650, Faith b. Oct. 8, 1652, Sarah b. 17 (1) 1658, bur. June 19, 1660, Priscilla b. and d. 1664.

He d. 19, Oct. 1684. Will prob 25 (9) 1684. Wife and her son John Boynton; dau. Elizabeth; sons Ezekiel and Joseph; daus. Anna (and her son Jonathan Barker,) Mary Hazeltine, Sarah, Elizabeth Hazeltine and Faith Dowse.

JOCELYN, see Joslin.

JOES,
William, ae. 28, came in the Truelove in Sept. 1635.

JOHNSON, JONSON, JANSEN,
Davy, frm. May 18, 1631. Is believed by some to be the "Mr. Johnson," who came to Dorchester in the Mary and John in 1630, [Bl.] and settled at Dorchester. Propr. 1633-1636. Apparently he d. early in that year and his widow m. again; for the town

JOHNSON, etc., cont.,
granted land June 27, 1636, to "Mrs. Johnson that was."

Edmond, ae. 23, came in the James in July, 1635. Settled at Hampton. Wife Mary; ch. Peter, John, James and Dorcas. He d. about 1651, and the widow m. 2, Thomas Coleman, of Newbury, who gave security 7 (8) 1653, for the portions of the ch.

Edward, licensed by Gov. Winthrop to go forth on trading to Merrimack; of which Dep. gov. Dudley complained in Aug. 1632. [W.] Had accounts with the Court July 1, 1634.

Edward, joiner, of Canterbury, Eng., came from Sandwich, Eng., before June 9, 1637, with wife Susan, 7 children and 3 servants. Settled at Charlestown. Propr. 1638. Adm. chh. 25 (1) 1638. [Incorrectly copied "William."] Shipwright. Was one of the six persons appointed by the town of Char. to erect a church and town at Woburn, 14 (3) 1640. Became a leader in the town, selectman, clerk, captain, and deputy. Residing at Char., he sold ⅞ of a vessel now on the stocks before his dwelling house in 1654. His wife Susan deposed 21 (4) 1664, ae. about 66 years, concerning the match between Matthew J. and the dau. of Peter Palfrey. [Mdx. Files.] Ch. Edward, George, William, Martha, (m. March 18, 1649, John Amee,) Matthew, John, Susan, (m. James Prentice.) He deposed in 1659, ae. about 60 years.

It is generally believed that he was the author of "The Wonder Working Providence of Zions Saviour." [See Introduction to Poole's imprint of that work, Andover, 1867.]

He d. April 23, 1672. Will dated 15 (3) 1671, prob. May 11, 1672, beq. to wife Susan and all these children with some of their ch.; specifies est. at Heron Hill, Eng., etc. The widow, in will dated Dec. 14, 1689, beq. all to son John.

Francis, gent., Salem, frm. May 18, 1631. Traded at the Eastward in 1632-3. Partner about 1632 with Conant, Palfrey, Dike and Pickman. [Es. Files, III, 30 and 80.] Mortg. his farm in Salem 28 (9) 1649. Res. at Marblehead. Town officer, 1657. Lieut. He deposed in 1672, ae. about 66 years. Wife Johane memb. chh. in first list.

JOHNSON, etc., cont.,
Ch. Naomi bapt. 1 (2) 1638, Ruth bapt. 29 (1) 1640, Eliza bapt. 24 (2) 1642, Francis bapt. 16 (4) 1644, Samuel bapt. 20 (3) 1649, Joanna bapt. 5 (8) 1651, Sarah bapt. 19 (12) 1653. His dau. Mrs. Sherman was recd. to full com. in Sal. chh. Oct. 5, 1665, and had her child bapt. His sister Mrs. Dorothy Norrice referred to him in a deposition. He m. at Boston 24 (3) 1656, Hannah Hanbury.

Admin. of his est. was gr. at Bo. March 23, 1690-1, to Thaddeus Mackartey and Elizabeth, his wife.

Mr. Isaac, gent., of Sempringham, Eng., ae. 22, was lic. April 5, 1623, to marry Lady Arbella Fynes, ae. 22, dau. of Thomas, Earl of Lincoln. Became a large adventurer in the Mass. Bay Co. in 1629; was chosen one of the Assistants. Came to Boston in the ship Arbella in 1630. One of the members of the church at its foundation. His wife came with him; but d. at Salem in Aug., 1630. He d. Sept. 30 following, leaving some part of his substance to the colony. [W.] [Reg. LIII, 70.] See numerous sketches.

James, leather-dresser, glover, capt. of a foot company, Boston, adm. chh. 10 (2) 1636, frm. May 25, 1636. Town officer. He signed inv. of John Oliver in 1641. Wife Margaret d. 28 (1) 1643; he m. Abigail —. Ch. James; Joseph b. and d. 1644, Abigail b. 25 (9) 1645, Abigail b. 12 (12) 1646, Elizabeth bapt. 29 (2) 1649, d. 11 (9) 1653, Samuel bapt. 16 (1) 1651, John bapt. 13 (1) 1653, Elizabeth b. 12 April 1655, d. 23 (12) 1663, *James* bapt. 15 (2) 1655, Mary b. 27 March 1657, Hannah b. 23 Nov. 1659, d. 3 Aug. 1660, Hannah b. June 12, 1661.

Mary, widow, Boston, made will Feb. 11, prob. 24 (12) 1669-70. Son Samuel Johnson, daus. Rebecca, wife of William Allen, and Hannah, wife of John Liskcom. Inv. shows goods in shop, household effects, house and land, etc.

John, yeoman, Roxbury, chosen by the Gen. Court 19 Oct. 1630, constable of Rox. and surveyor of all the arms of the Colony, a very industrious and faithful man in his place, [W.]; frm. May 18, 1631; town officer, deputy. His house was burned, 2 (6) 1645, with 17 bbls. of the country's powder and many arms. [W.] Agent for Mrs. Katharine Sumpner of London in 1653. He signed

JOHNSON, etc., cont.,
the inv. of Joseph Weld in 1646. His wife Margaret d. 9 (4) 1655. He m. 2, Grace, widow of Barnabas Fawer. [Gen. Court Rec., May, 1656.] Ch. John, Isaac and Humphrey, who came to Rox. and were efficient citizens.

He d. 30 (7) 1659. Will prob. Oct. 15 folg.; est. to be divided between his 5 children, eldest son to have a double portion. His eldest dau., Mary, m. Roger Moorry, and res. at Providence; sold her share in her father's est. Oct. 12, 1659. [Reg. IX, 224.] The widow Grace made will 21 Dec., prob. 29 Dec. 1671. All to bros. Jonathan and Benjamin Negus.

John, ae. 23, came in the Elizabeth, April 15, 1635.

John, ae. 26, with Susan, ae. 24, Elizabeth, ae. 2, and Thomas. ae. 18 months, came in the James, in July, 1635.

John, sail-maker, mentioned in the inv. of Bozoun Allen in 1652.

John, Watertown, made an indenture with Daniel Pierce of Watertown, blacksmith, 25 (4) 1639. [L.] He m. 19 (8) 1659, Mary Kinge. Ch. Hannah, whom Parson Bailey calls "a good girl whom I love," when recording her baptism and adm. to chh., Feb. 27, 1686. Her father deeded to her land and houses at Cambridge Farms Nov. 6, 1697, he then res. at Camb.

John, shoemaker, Ipswich, propr. 1635. Bought house and land in 1654. Rem. to Rowley; captain. He deposed in 1671, ae. 67 years, regarding son Thomas and *his* wife Mary.

He d. 29 Jan. 1685-6. Inv. of his est. taken 19 March, 1685-6, presented by his widow Hannah; the est was given to her and her ch. Hannah, (wife of Thomas Palmer,) Elizabeth, (wife of James Baily,) and Samuel, ae. 14 years. The three signed agreement for division 23 May, 1703.

Peter, with Bryon Bincks, in Court July 3, 1632. Peter, the Dutchman, Boston, 1638.

Richard, Charlestown, propr. 1630; had an acct. with Mr. Saltonstall in Gen. Court March 22, 1630-1. Salem 1637; frm. May 17, 1637. Rem. to Lynn. Had grant of land

JOHNSON, etc., cont.,
in 1638. Constable 8 (5) 1645; [Es. Court.] He deposed in 1663, ae. about 51 years. Will dated 20 Aug., prob. 27 (9) 1666; wife; ch. Daniel, Samuel, Abigail Collins and Elizabeth Tolman. The widow Alice deeded land to her son Samuel and son-in-law John Collins 24 (10) 1666.

Mr. Robert, Jr., [sic?] Rowley; will dated 13 (7) 1649, prob. 26 (1) 1650; beq. to the poor of R. church; to be distributed at the discretion of cousin Thomas Barker and Humphrey Reyner. Inv. shows 3 black hats, 6 bands, hour-glass, books, etc.

Samuel, punished by the Court with Coaker 3 March 1634-5, for enticing others to run away to the Dutch plantation. Res. at Boston. Wife Mary; ch. Peter b. 2 July, 1653, d. 19 (1) 1654.
He d. 23 (11) 1656. Inv. presented by widow Mary. She was adm. chh. 14 (12) 1656.

Solomon, Sen., Sudbury, propr., 1639; Solomon, Jr., also propr. 1645. S. J., tailor, sold land in 1653. Rem. to Marlborough. Wife Eleanor; ch. Joseph and Nathaniel b. 3 (12) 1639, Johana b. 16 Feb. 1641, Mary b. 23 (11) 1643, Caleb b. 1 (12) 1645, Samuel b. 6 March 1654.
His will dated 28 March, 1686, prob. 6 Oct. 1687, beq. to wife Eleanor; son Nathaniel and his 3 sons, Joseph, Samuel and John; sons Solomon and John; son-in-law John Barnes.

Thomas, Sandwich, atba. 1643, served against the Narragansetts in 1645. Ch. Priscilla b. Nov. 20, 1657; deputy, Plym. Court, 1637-8.

Thomas, Hingham, propr. 1636, drowned 29 (3) 1656. [Boston Rec.] His widow Margaret d. at Hing. 7 Jan. 1659-60. Nunc. will prob. Jan. 25, 1659-60; beq. to Mary, dau. of John Tucker, Sen., Thomas Lincoln, weaver, and Richard Wood deposed. Reference to her late husband T. J. [Reg. X, 84.]

William, planter, Charlestown, adm. chh. with wife Elizabeth 13 (12) 1634; propr., frm. March 4, 1634. He deposed 29 (10) 1657, ae. 54 years. [Mdx. Files.] Ch. Ruhama bapt. 21 (12) 1634, Joseph bapt. 12 (12) 1636, Elizabeth bapt. 13 (1) 1639, Jonathan bapt. 14 (5) 1641. James b. ("of William and Jud-

JOHNSON, etc., cont.
ith,") 21 (6) 1643. William adm. chh. 25 (1) 1638.

Will dated 7 Dec. 1677; beq. to wife Elizabeth, ch. John, Joseph, Jonathan, Nathaniel, Zachariah, Isaac, Elizabeth; dec. dau. Ruhama's dau. Elizabeth Bacon. [Genealogy Reg. XXXIII, 81.] Inv. of est. of William and Elizabeth J. taken April 12, 1686. John J. of Haverhill and Zechariah J. of Char. being appointed admins. of the est. of their father William and mother Elizabeth, made division of the same between themselves and their bros. Joseph, Isaac, Jonathan and Nathaniel, 13 April, 1686.

JOLLIFFE, JOYLIFFE,

Mr. John, merchant, Boston, 1636, agent of Matthew Craddock. [Letters of C. to W.] Mortg. land in B. 27 (4) 1638. [L.] Town officer. Frm. May 7, 1673, memb. 3d chh. He deposed 2 (1) 1673, ae. 57 yrs. [Mdx. Files.] He m. 28 (11) 1656, Anne, widow, successively, of Capt. Thomas Crumwell and of Robert Knight. Ch Hannah b. May 9, 1660.

He d. Nov. 23, 1701, [Sewall.] Will dated 7 Feb. 1699, prob. 27 Dec. 1701; house to Martha, dau. of his late wife and wife of Jarvis Ballard; power of redemption to the heirs of Richard Price; beq. to Katharine Bowles, dau. of his bro. Dr. George Joyliffe, and other Eng. relatives; to Mr. Simon Willard of Bo. and to the poor. [See Reg. XLII, 71.]

JONES, JOANES, JOHNS, JOHNES, JONS,

Bithia, Boston, memb. chh. 1630-1; "gone to Salem."

Charles, ae. 21, came in the Abigail in June, 1635, cert. from Little Minories, Eng.

Mr. Edward, (Johnes,) Charlestown, inhabitant 1630, frm. May 18, 1631. Adm. chh. Charlestown 9 (1) 1633; Anna adm. 25 (1) 1638. Their dau. Mary bapt. 8 (11) 1636. Susanna adm. chh. 5 (5) 1641. Sold lands and house 24 (7) 1644.

Edward, carpenter, Boston, came from Tichmersh, co. Northampton, Eng., about May, 1639, intending to come an apprentice to Anthony Stanyon at Exeter; his father, Edward Jones, of Wellingborow, North., giv-

JONES, etc., cont.,
ing his outfit into the hands of William Leeke. Lawsuit June, 1641. [L.]

Griffin, or Griffith, Springfield, propr. 1646, frm. April 5, 1649. Ch. Mercy b. 5 (4) 1647, Hephzibah b. 26 (11) 1648, Samuel b. 19 (11) 1650, Ebenezer b. 14 (5) 1653, Thomas b. 9 (4) 1655, Griffith b. 4 (4) 1658, Griffith b. 28 (1) 1660, Experience b. 12 Aug. 1652, Pelatiah b. July 22, 1664. His wife d. May 6, 1665.
He d. Feb. 19, 1676. Admin. of his est. gr. 23 (7) 1677, to his sons Samuel and Ebenezer.

James, residence not stated, frm. May 29, 1644.

John, (Johnes,) ae. 18, came in the Hopewell in April, 1635.

John, ae. 20, came in the Susan and Ellen in April, 1635.

John, Plymouth, before Court 2 June, 1640.

John, Concord. Wife Dorcas; ch. Eliphalet b. 9 (11) 1640, Samuel b. (at Cambridge) 8 (8) 1648, Ephraim b. 6 Jan. 1650, Elizabeth b. Feb. 11, 1652, Joseph b. 8 June, 1654, John b. 6 July, 1656, Dorcas b. 29 May, 1659, Rebecca b. 28 March, 1662-3.
He d. June 22, 1673.

Lewis, Roxbury, memb. chh. about 1640. Rem. to Watertown about 1651. Wife Ann; ch. Phebe b. Jan. 21, 1645, d. 6 (5) 1650, Shubael b. 14 (8) 1651.
He d. April 11, 1684. Will mentions wife Anna, ch. Shubael, Josiah and Lydia Whitney; friend and bro. John Stone.

Matthew, Boston, propr., 1649.

Mary, in charge of Alexander Beck, provided for by the Gen. Court 1 (10) 1640.

Mr. —, tried in Es. Court in 1639.

Mr., a minister, came to N. E. at the same time as Mr. Wilson, Mr. Shepherd, Mr. Peter and others, arriving at Boston 6 (8) 1635. Mr. Buckly and Mr. Jones, two English ministers, attempted to organize a church at Concord 5 (5) 1635; organization completed 6 (1) 1637, and Mr. Jones ordained pastor. [W.] He went with part of the people to a new plantation. [J.] See Charles, above.

Ralph, Plymouth, atba 1643. Rem. to

JONES, etc., cont.,
Barnstable. Ch. Shobal b. Aug. 27, 1654, Jedidiah b. 4 Jan. 1656, John b. 14 Aug. 1659, Mercy b. 14 Nov. 1666, Ralph b. 1 Oct. 1669.
He made will 11 (3) 1691, being aged; prob. April 29, 1692. Beq. to my friends called Quackers; to wife land bought by my father Fuller, etc.; to sons Shubael, Ralph, Samuel, Matthew, Ephraim and John; to daus. Mercy, Mary and Hittable.

Richard, of Dinder, Eng., embarked from Weymouth before March 20, 1635. Settled at Dorchester; bought house and land in 1635. Richard, Salisbury, witness in Es. court in 1648, may be the same. Alice, ae. 26, who came in the James in July, 1635, was doubtless his wife.
He d. intestate, leaving ch. Timothy, Samuel, Elizabeth and Mary. The widow Alice conveyed the est. 2 (12) 1642, to Anthony Thatcher of Yarmouth, Richard Baker, Thomas Millett and George Weeks of Dorchester for her son Timothy. Reference in the inv. of her est. to her bro. Thatcher and her man John March. [Suff. De. I, 41.]

Morgan (John), Springfield, propr. 1643, taxed 1664. Widow Katherine, perhaps his mother, taxed in 1646. She was bur. 2 (9) 1657.

Robert, planter, Hingham, propr. 1636; a witness in 1639. [L.] His daus-in-law Elizabeth and Jane Curtis, gave him power of attorney 4 (10) 1646, to collect legacies from their grandmother, Jane Alexander, late of Reading, co. Oxford, Eng. [A.] Either he or his son Robert m. Anna, dau. of John Bibble. Wife Elizabeth; ch. Robert, Joseph, Sarah, (m. — Belknap,) Jane, (m. Thomas Collier,) Benjamin bapt. March, 1638, Ephraim bapt. July 29, 1649, John bapt. July 17, 1652, Elizabeth bapt. Aug. 1662, Benjamin bapt. Oct. 27, 1666.
He d. 17 Nov. 1691. In his will, dated 20 April, 1688, he beq. to each of the above said ch. except Robert and Ephraim, specifying Benjamin the elder and Benjamin the younger; beq. to the ch. of Robert, dec. The widow d. 25 Sept. 1712.

Sarah, ae. 34, with Sarah, ae. 15, John, ae. 11, Ruth, ae. 7, Theophilus, ae. 3, Rebecca, ae. 2, and Elizabeth, ae. 6 mos., came in the Defense in July, 1635.

Sister, Cambridge, memb. chh. about

JONES, etc., cont.,
1641. Came to this country with her parents. [Rel.]

Teague, Yarmouth, served against the Narragansetts in 1645; res. in 1649.

Thomas, husbandman, ae. 40, came in the Abigail in July, 1635, with Ellen, ae. 36, John, ae. 15, Isaac, ae. 8, Hester, ae. 6, Thomas, ae. 3, and Sarah, ae. 3 mos. Settled at Dorchester. One of the signers of the church covenant Aug. 23, 1636. Town officer. Wife Ellen d. Feb. 2, 1678. Ch. Thomas d. in 1635, Hannah b. 28 (1) 1636, Rebecca b. 9 (12) 1641.

He d. 13 (9) 1667, ae. 75. Will prob. Jan. 15, 1667-8. Wife Ellen, son Isaac, dau. Hannah, and her children, Henry, Richard, and Elizabeth Way; gr. ch. James and Thomas Greene. [Reg. XV, 325.]

Thomas, butcher, from Elsing, co. Norfolk, came in the Mary and Ann in 1637, ae. 25. Settled at Newbury; propr. 1637. Rem. to Exeter, and sold land in 1639. Rem. to Charlestown, and sold land in Newb. 6 July, 1650. Deposed in 1654, ae. 45.

He d. Oct. 24, 1666. Will dated Sept. 24, prob. (Mdx.) Dec. 18, 1666, beq. to wife Abigail and dau. Susanna Goose; son-in-law William G. mentioned in inv.

Thomas, Hingham, propr. 1637. With son Abraham, propr. at Hull in 1657. His son Abraham sold land May 3, 1658, which his father had given him. Ch. bapt. at Hing., parentage not specified: Thomas bapt. March 29, 1640, Mary bapt. May 28, 1643.

Thomas, of Manchester, dying in Hull; inv. of est. at M. and at H. taken in March, 1680-1, presented at Ipswich. Wife Elizabeth, sons Abraham, Thomas and Ephraim, (who call her their "mother-in-law,) John (incapable,) daus. Sarah Chamberlain and Hannah Goding.

Thomas, Gloucester, freed by the Court from the service of Wm. Richardson 2 (3) 1642. Propr. 1643. He deposed in 1665, ae. 67 years, regarding the first laying out of the marsh of the long cove in Squam. Wife Marie (Mary); ch. Thomas b. March 25, 1640, Ruth b. Feb. 22, 1644, Samuel b. Aug. 1647, Ephraim b. April, 1649, Benjamin b. July, 1651, Remember b. Aug. 1, 1653.

He d. 15 (7) 1671; will prob. at Ipswich 26 (7) 1671; inv. filed at Salem same date; wife

JONES, etc., cont.,
and dau. Winslow of Salisbury mentioned. The widow d. 4 (12) 1681.

William, Cambridge, propr. 1635. Probably he is the "Will Johns, painter, late of Sandwich, Eng., now of New England," whose wife Margaret came in the Hercules in March, 1634. She was accused of being a witch; tried and hung in 1648. Her husband desired soon after to ship for Barbadoes, but was imprisoned. [W.]

JOPE, see JUPE.

JORDAN, JORDAINE, JURDEN, see COGAN,

Francis, Ipswich, propr. 1635. Propr. in Plum. Island, etc. in 1665. Prosecuted for entertaining a sick stranger. [Arch. 38 B.] He m. 6 (9) 1635, Jane Wilson; ch. Sarah b. 8 (9) 1636, Hannah b. March 14, 1638, Mary b. and d. 1639, Mary b. May 16, 1641, Lydia b. Feb. 14, 1643, Deborah b. Dec. 4, 1647. [Ess. Court Rec.]

He d. April, 1672-3. Will dated April 23, 1672, prob. Sept. 24, 1678; beq. to wife Jane; to gr. ch. Mary Simson; ch. and gr. ch. to have what wife may leave.

James, Dedham, probably before 1650. He d. 29 (1) 1655. Will prob. Aug. 1, 1655; son Thomas J.; dau. Mary, who was bried; the 5 ch. of his dau. Anne, late wife of Abraham Jaquith of Charlestown. [Reg. V, 441.] Mary d. 12 (8) 1681.

Joane, ae. 16, servant to George Hadbourne, came in the Abigail in June, 1635.

John, tailor, Plymouth, in Court 1 Dec. 1640; atba. 1643. Sold land in 1653. Ch. Barak b. 24 Feb. 1650.

John, Medford, gave letter of attorney 19 (12) 1645, for collections in Eng. [A.]

Stephen, came in the Mary and John in March, 1633-4; settled at Ipswich, propr. 1636; additional grant in 1639. Herd-keeper, 1645; res. in 1649. Sold land in Ips. 20 (10) 1653. Rem. to Newbury. He m. Susanna, widow of Nathaniel Merrill.

He d. 8 Feb. 1669; widow Susanna d. 25 Jan. 1673; admin. gr. to her son Abel Merrill.

JOSLIN, JOCELYN, JOSELYN, JOSSELYN,

Thomas, husbandman, ae. 43, with wife Rebecca, ae. 43, ch. Rebecca, ae. 18, Dorothy, ae. 11, Nathaniel, ae. 8, Eliza, ae. 6, and Mary, ae. 1, and Elizabeth Ward, servant, ae. 38, came in the Increase April, 1635. Settled at Hingham; propr., town officer. Bought land of his son-in-law Thomas Nichols in 1638. [Town rec.] Rem. about 1654 to Lancaster. The widow Rebecca m. 2, William Kerly; deeded lands in 1664 to sons Nathaniel J. and Roger Sumner. Rebecca m. Thomas Nichols; Elizabeth m. in Boston June 12, 1652, Edward Yeomans.

His will dated 9 May, 1660, prob. 29 (1) 1661, beq. to wife Rebecca, sons Abram and Nathaniel, daus. Rebecca Nichols and Elizabeth Emmons, son-in-law Roger Sumner, gr. son Abram J. Signs his name Thomas Joslin.

JOY, JAY,

Thomas, carpenter, Boston, propr., 1636. He built the town house in 1640. Was arrested in 1646 for helping to get signers to the petition for enlarged franchise, and for questioning the Court's authority in arresting him. Released soon. [W.] Rem. to Hingham. Owned tide-mill and other property 1650. Bought lands of the Indians June 26, 1668. Wife Joane, dau. of John Gallop, deposed 2 (4) 1652, ae. about 34 years. [Arch. 38 B.] Ch. Samuel b. 26 (12) 1639, John b. 10 (8) 1641, Thomas b. 3 (1) 1642, d. 2 Dec. 1648, Joseph b. 1 (2) 1645, Ephraim b. 7 (12) 1646, Sarah bapt. 23 (5) 1648, ae. about 31 days, Benjamin bapt. 12 (3) 1650, Elizabeth bapt. 17 (8) 1652, Elizabeth bapt. 7 (11) 1654, (m. Nathaniel Beal,) Ruth b. Feb. 28, 1658, bapt. 1 (3) 1659, (m. 1, John Low, 2, John Curtis).

He d. in 1678. Will prob. 31 Oct., 1678. The widow d. 20 March, 1690-1.

JOYCE,

John, Sandwich, propr. 1638, atba. 1643. Rem. to Yarmouth, atba. 1643. Constable 2 June, 1646. Ch. Abigail bapt. at Barnstable June 1, 1646.

Will dated Nov. 20, prob. 5 March, 1666; wife Dorothy, only son Hosea; daus. Mary and Dorcas. [Reg. VI, 188.]

William, [Boston,] inv. pres. by Thomas Savage and Anthony Stoddard 25 (8) 1648; wife in Rattliffe, London. [Reg. VII, 175.]

JUDD,

Thomas, Cambridge, propr. 1635, frm. May 25, 1636. Sold before 1638. Rem. to Hartford, Conn.

JUDKIN, JUDKINS, JURKIN,

Job., sawyer, Boston, propr. 1637. He gave his eldest son Samuel land in B. Aug. 7, 1662. Wife Sarah adm. chh. 8 (6) 1641, d. 26 (9) 1657. Ch. Job b. and d. 1637, Samuel b. 27 (9) 1638, bapt. 15 (6) 1641, Job. b. and d. 1641, Joel b. 30 (7) 1643, Sarah b. 7 (10) 1645.

Thomas, Gloucester, propr. before 1645, a witness in 1647. He m. 25 Nov. 1685, widow Anna Heeward.

He d. 23 Feb. 1694-5; will prob. 26 March folg.; beq. to wife Anna and gr. sons Thomas Sergent and Thomas Alling; after her death to her children. She d. 27 Jan. 1706.

JUDSON,

Samuel, Dedham, townsman 1 (11) 1644. Rec'd April 20, 1651, John Judson, ae. 14 years, son of Michael J. of Horton in Bradford dale, co. of York, Eng., to be an apprentice. He m. 2 (2) 1644, Bridget Warne; she d. 28 (1) 1646. He m. 6 (8) 1646, Mary, widow of Henry Aldridge. Ch. Mary b. 20 (8) 1647, Sarah b. 24 (5) 1651, Easter b. 10 (4) 1654.

He d. 11 (5) 1657. Will prob. July 30, 1657; daus. Mary, Sarah and Ester Judson; wife Mary with her 2 sons, ch. of a former husband, Henry Aldridge. [Reg. VIII, 280.] The widow m. John Hayward.

William, before the Court and discharged 5 (1) 1638-9.

JUPE, JOPE,

Alice, wife of one —, Boston, adm. chh. 24 (11) 1640. Her husband may have been Benjamin, a nephew of Roberk Keayne, living at his house in 1656.

William, ae. 40, came in the Batcheler in 1635.

JUSALL,

Sara, a sufferer from ill-treatment in 1638. [Gen. Court Rec.]

KADE, see Cade.

KARDER, see Carder.

KEAYNE, KEAINE, KAINE, KANE, KEENE, KENE, see Caine,

John, ae. 60 years, with Martha, Eliza, Josias and Sarah *Keene*, came in the Confidence April 11, 1638. Settled at Hingham. He d. 14 (11) 1649.

Mr. Robert, citizen and merchant tailor of London, ae. 40, came in the Defense in July, 1635, with wife Ann, ae. 38, and son Benjamin, ae. 16. Settled at Boston, after a short residence at Lynn. Adm. chh. with wife 20 (1) 1636, frm. May 25, 1636. Deputy, town officer. Carried on large business and left great est.

He d. 23 (1) 1656. Will prob. May 2, 1656. Left bulk of property to widow and son; made large bequests to the town of Boston and Harvard College; also beq. to the ch. of his dec. sister Mrs. Grace Jupe, namely, Anthony, (in Eng.,) Benjamin, living in his house, and Mary, wife of John Mosse, (Morse,) of Boston; to his wife's sister, the wife of Mr. John Wilson, and to her bro. John Mansfield, and several other persons. His cousin Edward Lawson was one of the overseers. [Reg. VI, 89.] The widow m. 2, Samuel Cole of Boston.

William, (Keene,) Salem, Marblehead, taxed in 1638.

William, (called also Keeny,) Boston. Wife Agnes adm. chh. 31 (3) 1646; ch. Mary, ae. about 7½ years, and John, ae. about 3, years 10 mos., bapt. 31 (3) 1646. The wife was dism. to the chh. at Pequot 10 (5) 1653.

KEITH,
John, Plymouth, 1646.

KELLY, KALY, KEELE, KEYLE, KEYLEY,

Abel, Salem, adm. chh. 7 (12) 1640; frm. June 2, 1641.

David, yeoman, of Hog Island in the precincts of Boston, bought land in the town 13 May, 1656. Wife Elizabeth; ch. David b. 18 Dec., 1647, Samuel b. 9 Oct. 1657, d. Sept. 11, 1658, Samuel b. Nov. 30, 1661. He d. in 1662. Admin. gr. Oct. 23, 1662 to his widow Elizabeth for herself and 5 children. [Reg. XII, 5.] The widow m. Robert Smith, seaman, of Boston, and joined with her son David in a deed of land Aug. 20, 1666.

KELLY, etc., cont.,

Edward, ae. 14, came in the Hopewell in April 1635. Settled at Boston. Took John Berry as an apprentice 30 (1) 1646. [Town rec.] Wife Elizabeth; ch. Edward b. Nov. 4, 1664.

John, Newbury, propr. before 1640. Ch. Sarah b. 12 Feb. 1640, (m. Thomas Burkbee,) John b. 2 July, 1642, Mary, (m. April 12, 1666, John Belconger.) He d. 28 Dec. 1644.

John, Marblehead, in court in 1646.

KELSEY,
William, Cambridge, propr., 1633; frm. March 4, 1634-5. Sold meadow 19 (2) 1636. Rem. to Hartford.

KEMP, KEMPE,
Edward, blacksmith, Dedham, propr. 28 (6) 1638; frm. March 13, 1638-9. Rem. to Wenham; declined office of deacon in 1651. Rem. to Chelmsford in 1655. Esther, m. at Dedham, 15 (9) 1648, Samuel Foster.
Will dated 27 Jan. 1667, prob. April 6, 1669, beq. to Esther, her husband S. F. and son S. F.; to kinsman Samuel Kemp of Groton.

John, before Gen. Court 3 (7) 1639.

Robert, Dedham, adm. chh. April 24, 1639, his wife adm. chh. 11 (8) 1639.

Mr. William, came in the James April 5, 1635. Settled at Duxbury. Juryman. Prop. frm. 5 March, 1638-9; had land grant 7 Jan. 1638-9.

Inv. taken Sept. 23, 1641, and admin. gr. to his widow Elizabeth Nov. 2, folg. [Reg. IV, 173.]

KEMPSTER,
Daniel, carpenter, Cambridge, propr. 1642, frm. May 26, 1647.

He d. in 1666-7, ae. about 80. He made will 27 Sept. 1665, prob. April 2, 1667. Beq. to Rev. Mr. Mitchell; to cousin Thomas Moulton; to the children of kinsman Samuel Andrew; to the dau. of bro. John Kempster, dec. of Needum, Eng.; to Anna, dau. of Thomas Packe, of Dunstall, Eng.; to elder Frost.

KEMPTON,
Ephraim, tailor, Scituate, an early settler.

He d. May 5, or June 24 [To. rec.] 1645. Inv. filed and admin. gr. 28 Oct. 1645 to

KEMPTON, cont.,
Manasseh and Ephraim K. His son Ephraim had been in partnership with him from the time of their coming to N. E. Est. set off June 4, 1645. Manasseh K. of Scit. and Thomas Rawlins, Sen., of Boston arranged for the apportionment of the estate to Ephraim and the other three children 8 (4) 1658. [Ply. Deeds II.]

Manasseh, yeoman, Plymouth, one of the purchasers or old-comers, shared in the division of cattle in 1627, taxed in 1632, frm. 1633.

He d. Jan. 14, 1662-3. "He did much good in his place in the time God lent him." His wife Julian d. Feb. 19, 1664-5, ae. 81.

KENDALL, KENDALL *alias* **MILES,**
Francis, miller, Woburn, 1640, frm. May 26, 1647. Town officer. He deposed in Dec. 1658, ae. about 38 years, and 2 (2) 1662, ae. about 48 years. [Mdx. Files.] He m. Dec. 24, 1644, Mary Tidd; ch. John b. May or July 2, 1646, Thomas b. Jan. 10, 1648-9, Mary b. Jan. 20, 1650-1, [m. Israel Reed,] Elizabeth b. Jan. 15, 1652-3, (m. James Pierce,) Hannah b. Jan. 26, 1654-5, (m. Wm. Greene,) Rebecca b. March 21, 1656-7, (m. Joshua Eaton,) Samuel b. March 8, 1659-60, Jacob b. Jan. 25, 1660-1, Abigail b. April 6, 1666, (m. Wm. Reed.) His wife Mary d. 1705. He d. 1708.

Will, dated May 9, 1706, mentions ch. above-named and several gr. ch.; also the 8 ch. of his bro. Thomas K. that were living when Thomas d. [Reg. XXXVI, 17.]

John, Cambridge, 1644-6. He m. about 1644, Elizabeth, widow of Samuel Holly, and sold the H. estate with her in 1646.

Presca, Salem, memb. chh. before 1636; "dead" before 1659.

Robert, residence not stated frm. May 6, 1647.

Thomas, Reading, propr. 1644; bro. of Francis, frm. May 10, 1648. Wife Rebecca. Ch. Elizabeth b. 17 (8) 1642, (m. John Eaton,) Rebecca b. 10 (12) 1644, (m. James Bowtell,) Mary b. 24 (10) 1647, (m. Abraham Bryant,) Hannah b. 27 (11) 1649, (m. John Parker, [Mdx. De. I.] Sarah b. 22 (4) 1653, (m. Samuel Dunton,) Abigail b. 20 June, 1655, (m. John Nichols,) Susanna, (m. Nathaniel Goodwin,) Tabitha, (m. John Pearson.)

KENDALL, etc., cont.,
He d. 22 July, 1681. Agreement for division made 30 Sept. folg. between his widow Rebecca and sons-in-law John Eaton, Abraham Briant, John Parker, John Person, Nathaniel Goodwin, James Bowtell, Samuel Dunken and John Niccolls. The widow d. in 1703, ae. 85. [Hist. Reading.]

KENDRICK, KENRICK, KENERICK, KINRICK,
George, came in the ship with Rev. Richard Mather from Bristol, Eng., May 23, 1635. Settled at Scituate; yeoman, took John Gardiner as an apprentice 22 Feb. 1635-6. Frm. Jan. 5, 1635-6. Adm. chh. with wife April 9, 1637. Rem. to Barnstable, then to Boston. Volunteer for the Pequot War 1637. Town officer 1640. Ch. bapt. at Sci. Deborah Nov. 25, 1638, d. Feb. 21, 1638-9, Deborah b in Bo. 16 (6) 1646, Priscilla bapt. do. 21 (4) 1650. Wife Jane mentioned in Bo. Rec. He m. at Rehoboth April 23, 1647, Ruth Bowen.

John, laborer, yeoman, Boston, adm. chh. 11 (6) 1639, frm. May 13, 1640. Sold house and lands in B. Jan. 8, 1652. He rem. to Cambridge village (Newton). Wife Anne adm. chh. 18 (5) 1640, d. Nov. 15, 1656. Second wife Judith d. at Roxbury Aug. 23, 1687. Ch. Hannah b. 9 (12) 1639, John b. 3 (8) 1641, Elizabeth bapt. 21 (11) 1643, Elisha b. 18 (8) 1645, Maria bapt. 10 (7) 1648, Hannah b. 20 (1) 1651-2.

He d. Aug. 29, 1686. Will dated Jan. 21, 1683, ae. about 78 years, prob. 23 Sept. 1686, beq. to wife Judith; son John; son-in-law Jonathan Metcalf; John, and other ch. of son Eliah K.; to Mr. Nehemiah Hobart, his pastor. The widow "Judah" d. 23 Aug. 1687.

KENNEY, KENEY, KENNY, KENNINGE,
Henry, (Kenninge), placed as an apprentice with Wm. Parke of Roxbury 21 (4) 1639, by Vincent Potter. [L.] Rem. to Salem. [Wife] Ann, Salem, adm. chh. 24 (6) 1654. Ch. John bapt. 10 (7) 1654, Mary bapt. 3 (5) 1659, Sarah bapt. 29 (4) 1662, Elizabeth, of sister K., bapt. 1 (3) 1664, — bapt. 12 (3) 1666.

William, Marblehead, before Court in 1642.

Admin. of his est. 30 (9) 1670.

KENNEY, etc., cont.,
KENNISTON,

Mr. Allen, Salem, propr., 1638, frm. May 18, 1642. Wife Dorothy memb. chh. 1636.

Will dated 10 (9), prob. 28 (10) 1648. Wife Dorothy; beq. to various friends. The widow m. 2, Philip Cromwell.

KENT,

Edward, Newbury, propr. 1637.

Joanna, formerly widow of Nicholas Davison, m. Mr. Richard Kent, [Jr.] and d. his widow Oct. 30, 1699. [Es. Files 46, 20; Newbury rec.]

John, probably one of the bros. of Joshua, Dedham, 1645, adm. chh. 18 (5) 1652, frm. May 3, 1654. He m. 21 (3) 1662, Hannah Griswold; they rem. to Charlestown, and were recd to that chh. from Ded. chh. April 13, 1673. Ch. Hannah, John, Mary, Joshua bapt. 5 (6) 1673, Joseph bapt. 17 (8) 1675, Samuel, Ebenezer bapt. 22 (6) 1680, Lydia, Mary.

Joshua, Dedham, townsman 2 (3) 1643, adm. chh. (9) 1644, frm. May 6, 1646. Went to Eng in 1644; brought back with him two bros. in 1645. Went again in 1647 with his wife, but returned (8) 1648, to stay. [Chh. rec.] Wife Mary adm. chh. 2 (2) 1654; ch. Lydia b. 17 (12) 1646, Sarah b. 27 (1) 1650, Mary b. 15 (10) 1651.

His will prob. 14 (9) 1664; beq. all to wife. [Reg. XIII, 13.] Her will prob. 1 Feb. 1676-7, beq. to eldest dau. Mary [Tumbers] and other daus. Lydia, Sarah and Mary.

Richard, yeoman, came in the Mary and John March 26, 1634. Settled at Ipwich; built a weir on Chebacco river in 1634. Rem. to Newbury; frm. March 4, 1634-5. One of the first planters at Salisbury, but did not remove thither. Comr. 1650; town officer. Ch. Rebecca, (m. Samuel Scollard,) John b. 10 July, 1645.

He d. 14 June, 1654. Inv. filed at Ipswich 26 (7) 1654, and at Salem 14 Sept. 1667.

Stephen, came in the Confidence April 24, 1638, with wife Margery and servants, among whom was Rebecca Kent, ae. 16. Settled at Newbury. Frm. May 22, 1638. Rem. to Haverhill about 1651. Before Gen. Court 18 May, 1663. He deposed in 1667, ae. about 60 years. Rem. about 1670 to Wood-

KENT, cont.,

brdge, N. J.; [Ips. De. II, 389.] He m. Ann —, who d. Aug. 3, 1660; he m. May 29, 1663, Ellenor Scadlock. His son-in-law Robert Ford of Hav. sold land on his account 17 March, 1671. Ch. Elizabeth b. 1 March, 1641, d. Feb. 27, 1652, Hannah b. 20 March, 1643, Stephen b. 6 March, 1647, Rebecca b. 3 Aug. 1650, Elizabeth b. Dec. 4, 1653, David b. May 26, 1657.

Thomas, Sen., Gloucester, propr. 1643. He d. 1 May, 1658. His widow d. 16 Oct. 1671.

KERBY, KIRBY,

John, ae. 12, came in the Hopewell in Sept. 1635. Settled at Plymouth; atba. 1643.

Richard, Sandwich, one of the legatees of Thomas Hampton in 1637, atba. 1643. Wife Jane called to testify in Court 20 Aug., 1644. Ch. Abigail, Jane and Increase d. in 1649. The wife was bur. 23 March, 1649.

William, fisherman, planter, Boston, propr. 1639. Wife Elizabeth; ch. Elizabeth b. 20 (10) 1640, d. 12 (5) 1642. Wife Annis, Anne or Hannah joined him in a deed of land April 1, 1652.

KERLY, KERLEY, CARLEY,

Edward, ae. 22, husbandman, from Ashmore, Eng., came in the Confidence, April 1, 1638.

William, one of the first planters at Hull, 20 May, 1642. Rem. to Sudbury, bought land in 1643, and settled there. Frm. May 26, 1647. One of the founders of Lancaster, 1653. He m. at Sud. 6 (8) 1646, Hannah King; she d. 12 (1) 1658, and he m. 31 (3) 1659, Bridget, widow of Thomas Rowlandson; she d. 14 (4) 1662. He m. 6 (3) 1664, Rebecca, widow of Thomas Joslin. Ch. William, propr. at Sud., 1646, [Mary, (m. 6 Oct. 1647, Richard Smith,)] Henry.

He d. Jan. 11, 1683. Will dated 26 (5) 1669, inv. taken 19 July 1670, beq. to sons William and Henry K. and John Devall. Certain goods which came to him by his last wife appraised by Nathl. Joslin, etc.

KERSLEY, see Carsley.

KERTLAND, see Kirtland.

KETCHERING, CETCHERIN, KEDG-
ERER, see Kitcherin,
Joseph, Charlestown, inhab., 1636, propr. 1638. Adm. chh. 8 (11) 1636; [wife] Sarah adm. chh. 30 (9) 1643, Salem, fishing lot granted him at Winter Harbor, 1639.

KETTELL, KETTLE,
John, Watertown, land laid out for him and a house ordered to be built May 10, 1642.

John, Salem, a boy, apprentice to John Lovett of Mackerel Cove, before the Court in 1641. Res. at Gloucester; propr. 1649. Deposed 10 (3) 1653, ae. about 32 years. Wife Elizabeth; ch. John b. March 26, 1654, William b. April 1, 1656, d. 12 Jan. 1676, Elizabeth b. 15 (12) 1657, Mary b. 5 March, 1659, Samuel b. 2 (2) 1662, James b. 20 March, 1664.
He d. 12 Oct. 1685. Nunc. will prob. March 30, 1686, beq. to wife Elizabeth for life; then to their children. Admin. gr. to Samuel Corning, Sen., and wife.

Peter, ae. 10, came in the Abigail in May, 1635.

Richard, cooper, Charlestown. Adm. chh. with wife Hester 30 (5) 1633; frm. March 4, 1634-5. He m. Esther or Hester Ward, who as maid servant of Atherton Haulgh was adm. Boston chh. 26 (11) 1633, and was dism. to the chh. of Charlestown 17 (5) 1642 as wife of R. K. Ch. Hannah bapt. 29 (8) 1637, John bapt. 8 (10) 1639, Joseph bapt. 2 (12) 1640, Samuel b. 19 (9) 1642, Nathaniel b. 11 (8) 1644, Jonathan, a father in 1677.
He d. June 28, 1680. Will dated 13 May, prob. 5 (8) 1680, beq. to ch. John, Joseph, Samuel, Nathaniel and Jonathan K. and Hannah Call, and their ch.

KEY, KEYES,
Robert, Lynn and Watertown. Before Gen. Court 5 June, 1638. Rem. to Newbury about 1644. Wife Sarah; ch. Sarah b. 26 (3) 1633, Rebecca b. 17 (1) 1638, Phebe b. 17 (4) 1639, Mary b. in 1641, d. in 1642, Elias b. May 20, 1643, Mary b. at N. 16 June, 1645. [Solomon, Newbury, m. 2 Oct. 1653, Frances Grant; was he an older child?]
He d. at Newbury, July 16, 1647. His widow Sarah gave answer to a bill drawn on him, Aug. 10, 1647. [A.]

KETCHAM, CACHAM,
Edward, Ipswich, propr. 1638; frm. Dec. 8, 1636-7.
Hester, freed from service with John Woolridge by Gen. Court 3 March, 1639-40.

KEYSER, KESAR, KEISAR, KEZAR,
George, tanner, Lynn, frm. March 14, 1638-9. Constable 31 (10) 1644. [Es. Court.] Owner of a boat. [W.] Mate of Capt. James Smith's ship; traded for negroes at Guinea in 1644; had difficulty with Smith about the cargo, and was prosecuted at home for kidnapping. [W.] He gave letter of attorney 18 (10) 1645 for the collection of a legacy from the est. of his father, George Kesar of Leighton Bussard, Bedf., tanner. [A.] Wife Elizabeth joined him in a deed in 1653. She d. 24 (4) 1659. He deposed in 1664, ae. about 50 years. Ch. George b. (3) 1657, Edward b. and d. 1659. Rem. to Salem; recd. to chh. May 2, 1680, by dism. from that of Lynn.
He made will Feb. 16, 1686, being full of years; wife Rebecca; sons Eleazer, John and Benjamin; dau. Hannah; son-in-law Thomas Mold and his wife Mary; son Eleazer's ch. Mary and Sarah; son John's ch. John, George and Tmothy; gr. ch. Robert and Sarah Gilloway; Sarah, wife of Robert Cannon; Edward and Susanna Martin of Boston, his first wife's sister's ch.; wife's dau. Elizabeth Ashbey.

Thomas, shipmaster, Lynn, contracted for a pinnace in May, 1640. [L.] Lawsuit at Salem in 1641. Wife Mary adm. chh. Boston 14 (4) 1645; ch. Rebecca, ae. about 4 years, 7 mos. and Thomas, ae. about 2 years, 5 weeks, bapt. 15 (4) 1645; Timothy b. 15 (12) 1645.

KIBBE, KIBBEY, KEBY, KEBBEY, KIDBY, KIDBYE,
Edward, sawyer, Boston, propr. Wife Mary adm. chh. 29 (9) 1645. Ch. Mary, ae. about 5 yrs. 7 mos., 2 weeks, James, ae. about 3 yrs. 6 mos., Elisha, ae. about 10 mos., 10 days, all bapt. 30 (9) 1645; Deborah bapt. 7 (9) 1647, John bapt. 27 (5) 1649, bur. Feb. 8, 1652, Reuben b. and d. 1652, Elizabeth, rec. in Roxbury, b. 27 (11) 1654.

Henry, tailor, Dorchester, propr. 1639. Frm. May 18, 1642. Wife Rachel d. 16 (5) 1657. He m. 8 (8) 1657, Grissel, widow suc-

KIBBE, etc., cont.,
cessively of Thomas Jewell, Humphrey Griggs and John Gurney, Sen.; ch. Sherebiah b. 2 (10) 1659.
He d. 10 (6) 1661. Admin. gr. 15 Aug. 1661 to his widow, who presented Oct. 30, folg. an inv. of est. which she brought her husband at marriage. [Reg. X, 360.] She m. John Gurney, Sen.

John, Duxbury, propr., 1640, sold land 10 Dec., 1650.

Lewis, fisherman, Boston, propr., 1639. Lewis, mariner, of London, with whom Wm. Hudson, Jr., had accts. in 1647, [A.] may be the same person.

KIDDER,
James, Cambridge, 1649. Rem. to Billerica about 1659. Ensign. Wife Anne memb. chh. with him, dism. to chh. of Billerica. Ch. Hannah b. 1 (1) 1649,, Dorothy James, John, Thomas, all bapt. at Camb.; Nathaniel bapt. Feb. 27, 165[8]. Ephraim bapt. May 26, 1661. [Mi.]
He d. April 6, 1676; inv. filed June 1, 1677.

KILBORNE,
George, Rowley, propr., frm. May 13, 1640. James Barker calls him brother. Wife Elizabeth; ch. Mary b. May 3, 1649, Joseph b. 5 (2) 1652, Jacob b. 10 (6) 1654, Samuel b. 11 (9) 1656, Isaac b. 26 Jan. 1659, Elizabeth b. 2 (1) 1653.
He d. 14 Oct. 1685. Inv. ret. by widow Elizabeth Nov. 20, 1685.

Thomas, ae. 24, with wife Elizabeth, ae. 20, came in the Elizabeth of Ipswich April 30, 1634.

Thomas, husbandman, ae. 55, with wife Frances, ae. 50, ch. Margaret, ae. 23, Lydia, ae. 22, Marie, ae. 16, Francis, ae. 12, and John, ae. 10, came in the Increase April 15, 1635.

KILCUP, KILLCUP,
William, sieve maker, Lynn, gave bond for Daniel Hutchins to the Gen. Court 20 (3) 1640. Bought land at Lynn with minerals and privilege of mining in 1650. Rem. to Charlestown. With wife Grace sold char. houses and lands in 1653. Rem. to Boston. His wife d. Jan. 2, 1678-9, ae. 80.
He d. June 9, 1689, ae. 87.

KILHAM, KILLAM, KELHAM, KALEM, KILLIN, KULEM,
Augustine, Austin, measurer, Salem, 1637. Goat keeper, 1640. Rem. to Dedham; adm. chh. with wife Alice 28 (6) 1640. Frm. June 2, 1641. Rem. to Wenham before 1653. Ch. Lot b. 11 (7) 1640, Sarah bapt. 9 (11) 1641.
He d. 5 (4) 1667; the wife "Als" d. 18 (5) 1667. His will dated 2 (4), prob. 24 Sept. 1667, beq. to wife, sons Lot and John.

John, came May 10, 1638, as servant of Benjamin Cooper of Branton, Eng., to res. at Salem. Rem. to Dedham; propr. 1648.

KILLINGHALL,
Margaret, ae. 20, came in the Truelove in Sept. 1635.

KILMASTER,
John, before Gen. Court 7 Sept., 1641.

KIMBALL, KEMBLE, KEMBALL, KEMBOLD, KIMBOLD,
Henry, ae. 42, with wife Susan, ae. 35, and ch. Richard Cutting, ae. 11, Elizabeth K. ae. 4, and Susan K. ae. 1½ came in the Elizabeth of Ipswich April 30, 1634. Settled at Watertown; propr. 1636, frm. May 2, 1638. His dau. Elizabeth m. Thomas Straight and Susanna m. John Randall. [John also said to be a child.]
Admin. on his est. 22 (5) 1648. [Reg. VII, 174.] Genealogy.

Richard, ae. 39, with wife Ursula and ch. Henry, ae. 15, Elizabeth, ae. 13, Richard, ae. 11, Mary, ae. 9, Martha, ae. 5, John, ae. 3, and Thomas, ae. 1, came in the Elizabeth of Ipswich April 30, 1634. Settled at Watertown; propr.; frm. May 6, 1635. Rem. to Ipswich. Propr. 1637; wheelwright. One of the execs. of the est. of his bro. Thomas Scott. He m. 2, Oct. 23, 1661, Margaret, widow of Henry Dow, who d. 1 1(1) 1675-6. Younger ch. Sarah, Benjamin and Caleb. He had a deed of land and cattle 12 Jan. 1650, from his son-in-law Joseph Fowler. Ursula was a dau. of Henry and Martha Skott [Scott] of Rattlesden, Suffolk, Eng.; her mother and bro. Thomas came in the same ship. [Reg. LII, 248.]
Will dated 5 March, 1674, prob. 28 Sept. 1675. Beq. to wife the fulfilment of marriage contract, etc.; to sons Henry, Richard, John, Thomas, (and his ch.,) Benjamin, (and

KIMBALL, etc., cont.,
his ch.,) Caleb (and his 7 ch.;) to son-in-law John Severans; to daus. Elizabeth, Mary and Sarah (and her ch.;) to wife's ch. Thomas, Jeremiah and Mary; to the two eldest daus. of Giles Cowes by his first wife; and to cousin Haniell Bosworth. The widow's est. was appraised March 1, 1675-6; admin. gr. to Daniel and Thomas Dow. [Es. Inst. XVIII.] Genealogy.

KIMBERLY,
Thomas, Dorchester, 1635. Alice [wife of Thomas?] memb. chh. about 1639.

KINDE, KYNDE,
Arthur, Boston. Wife Jane; ch. Sarah b. (9) 1646, James d. 19 (5) 1654, James b. 29 Oct. 1654, Mary d. 27 (8) 1655, Nathaniel b. Aug. 1, 1658, Thomas b. 26 Sept. 1659, Mary b. and d. 1662, William b. Feb. 26, 1664.

The widow Jane made will 18 March, prob. 20 April 1710; beq. to the North church in Boston her silver tankard marked I. K.; to the wives of Increase and Cotton Mather and Stephen French, Jr.; to Sarah Knight; to gr. dau. Mary Harison; to gr. gr. daus. Sarah and Katharine Guille; to gr. gr. dau. Mary Crapo, dau of gr. dau. Jane; to her bro.'s dau., cousin Hannah Hardman; to gr. daus. Rachel Toker and Sarah Guille; to Thos. Barnard, Sen.; to the ch. of her son John Kind and dau. Sarah Rouse, both deceased; William and James Kind, ch. of John and William and Michael Rouse and Sarah Guille being the ch. of Sarah.

KING, KINGE,
Daniel, woolen draper, gentleman, Lynn, see accts. 1639. [L.] See Christopher Foster. He mortg. property at Lynn to secure bills of exchange drawn on his wife 23 (11) 1661. A bill signed by Daniel King of Uxbridge, Middlesex, drap. 6 April, 1639, copied in Note Book 7 (8) 1647. [A.] His son Daniel, of Beconsfield, co. Bucks, Eng., bound for N. E., rec'd money as an adventure from his cousin Wm. Guy, May 16, 1653. [Ess. Court files IX, 45 and 46.] Daniel deposed Nov. 6, 1655, ae. about 30 [Mdx. Files.] He sold land with consent of Elizabeth his now wife, 1 Aug. 1661.

He d. May 27, 1672. Will dated 7 (12) 1671, prob. 26 (4) 1672; "of Swampscott;" beq. to wife Elizabeth, son Daniel and daus.

KING, etc., cont.,
Hannah Blaner, Elizabeth Redden, Sarah Nedom; son Blaner, son Nedom.

George, came in the Hercules April 16, 1634. Frm. April 18, 1637.

Henry, of Brencsley, came in the James April 5, 1635.

Joanna, Boston, servant to Gov. Winthrop, adm. chh. 16 (4) 1639.

John, Sen., Weymouth, seaman, before Gen. Court 4 (10) 1638, master of a fishing boat in 1640. [L.] Propr. He deposed 24 (4) 1657 in the Tidd case, ae. about 57 years. [Mdx. Files.] His wife d., and he m. Dorothy, widow successively, of — Barker and Enoch Hunt. [See her will under Hunt.] Ch. Mary b. 15 (4) 1639, Abigail b. 14 (1) 1641.

Mr. Joseph, before Boston Court 29 (2) 1641.
Admin. gr. 30 (4) 1676 on the est. of Joseph K. who was slain in the war.

Percy, (Persis,) ae. 24, maid servant to Mr. Robert Crowley, came in the Elizabeth and Ann April 15, 1635.

Robert, ae. 22, a servant, came in the Confidence April 11, 1638.

Samuel, Plymouth, bought land in 1639; atba. 1643. Allowed to build and plant on land he had bought 27 Feb. 1639-40; and to live in the house with his father-in-law, Giles Rickett. Ch. Samuel b. 29 Aug. 1649, Isaac b. 24 Oct. 1651.

Sara, the Gen. Court ordered her goods ret. to her 9 (7) 1639.

Thomas, ae. 15, came in the Elizabeth with John Barnard, April 30, 1634.

Thomas, ae. 21, [31?] came in the Blessing in July, 1635, with Susan, ae. 30. Settled at Scituate, adm. chh. Feb. 25, 1637. Atba. 1643. Wife Suza adm. chh. before 1639. Ch. Rhoda b. 11 Oct. 1639, George b. 24 Dec. 1642, Thomas b. 21 June, 1645, Daniel b. 4 Feb. 1647, Sarah b. 24 May 1650, John b. and d. 1652, Ann d. about July 26, 1652. The wife Sarah d. June 6, 1652. He m. 31 March 1653, Jane widow of Wm. Hatch. She d. Oct. 8, 1653. He d. 24 Sept. 1691. He made will 30

KING, etc., cont.,
June, 1691, prob. March 16, 1691-2; beq. to wife Anne, dau. Sarah Besbey, grandsons John and Thomas Rogers. Set his negro servant Roben free and gave him his bed and five pounds in money. Residue to son Thomas.

Thomas, ae. 19, came in the Francis in 1634. Settled at Watertown; propr. 1640. One of the founders of Nashaway. Wife Mary; ch. Thomas b. 16 (1) 1640-1, bur. 28 (10) 1644, Mary b. 2 (12) 1641-2, (m. Oct. 19, 1659, John Johnson.)
He was bur. 3 (10) 1644. Inv. rendered 24 (10) 1644 and 23 (2) 1645. The widow m. in 1645 James Cutler.

Thomas, before Boston Court with his wife 14 June, 1642; referred to Salem Court.

Thomas, Sudbury, 1642. Wife Anne; ch. Thomas b. and d. 1642; the mother d. 24 (10) 1642. He m. 2, Dec. 26, 1655, Bridget, widow of Robert Davis. She d. a widow, March 1, 1685.
Note. Peter King the elder of Shaston, Dorset, gent., named his bro. Thomas K., now dwelling in N. E., in his will of May 30, 1658. [Reg. XLIX, 509.]

William, ae. 40, with wife Dorothy, ae. 34, ch. Mary, ae. 12, Katharine, ae. 10, William, ae. 8, and Hannah, ae. 6, embarked from Weymouth, Eng., before March 20, 1635. Settled at Salem, propr., frm. May 25, 1636; juryman 1637. Had land at the head of Bass river, 1638. Ch. William, (m. about 1652 Katharine, dau. of Michael Shafflin, q. v.), Mehitabel bapt. 25 (10) 1636, John bapt. 11 (9) 1638, Deliverance bapt. 31 (8) 1641.
He d. before 1652.

William, ae. 28, came in the Abigail in July, 1635.

KINGMAN,
Henry, ae. 40, with wife Joane, ae. 39, ch. Edward, ae. 16, Joane, ae. 11, Anne, ae. 9, Thomas, ae. 7, John, ae. 2, and servant John Ford, ae. 30, embarked from Weymouth, Eng., before March 20, 1635. Settled at Weymouth, frm. March 3, 1635-6. Lic. as ferryman 3 March, 1635-6. Deputy, 1638. Town officer. His wife Joan d. April 11, 1659.
He d. 5 (4) 1667. Will, dated 24 May, prob. 31 July, 1667. Aged 74 years or thereabout;

KINGMAN, cont.,
sons Edward, Thomas and John K.; daus. Holbrook, Davis and Barnard. [Reg. XVI, 226.]

KINGSBURY,
Henry, came from Eng. in the Talbot; had a ch. or two sick with the measles March 28, 1630. [W.] Joined chh. Boston with wife Margaret, and the clerk marked the names "dead since." Henry, of Ipswich, propr. before 1638, res. in 1656; called kinsman by John K. of Dedham, was probably a son; he deposed in 1669, ae. about 54 yrs. He rem. to Rowley, thence to Haverhill. [Reg. XIII, 157.] Bought house and land in Hav. 31 March, 1648.
He d. 1 Oct. 1687. Inv. ret. 10 Oct. by Joseph.

John, Watertown, frm. March 3, 1635-6; propr. Rem. to Dedham, 1636. Propr., town officer, deputy.
He d. after long weakness, 12 (7) 1660. [1669?] Will prob. 2 (10) 1659. To bro. Joseph, wife Margaret, kinsman Thomas Cooper of Seaconque, and Henry K. of Ipswich. The widow made will, prob. 20 (8) 1662; kinsmen Thomas Fuller and Hannah, his wife. [Reg. X, 176, and XI, 40.]

Joseph, Sen., yeoman, Dedham, frm. June 2, 1641. Wife Millicent adm. chh. April 24, 1639; ch. Mary b. 1 (7) 1637, Elizabeth b. 14 (7) 1638, Joseph b. 17 (12) 1640, John b. 15 (6) 1643, Eliezer b. 17 (3) 1645, Nathaniel b. 26 (1) 1650, Sarah, (m. Robert Crossman.)
He d. in 1676. Will dated 22 (3) 1675, prob. 1 June, 1676, beq. to sons Joseph, John Eliezer and Nathaniel; wife Millicent; dau. Sarah Crosemen; son-in-law Thomas Cooper of Rehoboth; to gr. ch. Elizabeth Brewer; sons-in-law Robert Croseman and Nathaniel Brewer. Refers to dec. bro. John K.

William, Dedham, app. by Gen. Court 6 (7) 1638, to report about unlicensed newcomers. Sarah, [his wife?] adm. chh. 18 (10) 1643, d. 24 (11) 1645.

KINGSLEY, KINGSLY, KINGESLEY, KINSLEY,
John, husbandman, Dorchester, frm. March 4, 1632-3. One of the 7 signers of the church covenant Aug. 23, 1636. Sold meadow land in Dorch. April 14, 1655. [Rem.

KINGSLEY, etc., cont.,
to Rehoboth?] Wife Elizabeth; ch. Eldad b. in 1638, Renewed b. 19 (1) 1641.

John, of Rehoboth, made will 2 (9) 1677, prob. 5 March, 1678-9. Beq. to wife Mary and son Eldad.

Mary, Reading, bought one half of the Sawmill in R. of John Elderkin, 5 (6) 1646.

Stephen, husbandman, Braintree, 1637, Propr. Frm. May 13, 1640. Rem. to Dorchester and bought ½ of the Hutchinson farm Feb. 23, 1656. Ret. to Braintree and sold land in Milton May 11, 1670. Elder of the chh., deputy. Ch. Mary b. 30 (6) 1640. Will dated at Milton 27 (3) prob. 3 (5) 1673; beq. to son John; sons-in-law Henry Crane, Anthony Gollifer and Robert Mason; to the three children of his son Samuel, to the son at the age of 21 and the daus. at the age of 18.

KINGSMAN, KINSMAN,
Robert, came in the Mary and John May 24, 1633. Settled at Ipswich. Propr. before 1635. Bought house and land in 1642.

KINHAM,
Alice, ae. 22, came from Weymouth, Eng., before March 20, 1635.

KIRK,
Judith, ae. 18, came in the Susan and Ellen in April, 1635.

KIRMAN, KERMAN,
John, Cambridge, frm. March 4, 1632-3. App. to receive money from Mr. Crispe's estate Oct. 18, 1631. Deputy 1634-5. John, Sandwich, debtor of Thos. Hampton, 1637; propr. 3 June, 1640.

Mr., master of Hawkin's ship Seafort, drowned in the wreck off the coast of Spain in 1644. [W.]

KIRTLAND, KERTLAND, KYRTLAND, KIRKLAND, CARTELYN, CATLIN,
Nathaniel, ae. 19, came with his bro. Philip in the Hopewell April 1, 1635. Settled at Lynn. Rem. to Southampton, L. I. Deposed at New York May 16, 1641, ae. 22 years. Returned to Lynn. Wife Parnell; ch. John b. (6) 1659, Hannah b. 15 (2) 1662, Elizabeth b. 20 (1) 1664.

His will made 17 Aug. 1685, ae. about 72;

KIRTLAND, etc., cont.,
prob. 31 March, 1687; beq. to wife; sons Nathaniel, John and Philip; daus. Hannah and Mary; gr. ch. of Lee and Collins names.

Philip, Sen. propr. Lynn, 1638. No further particulars.

Philip, Jr. ae. 21, came in the Hopewell in 1635, from Shortington, Buckingham, Eng.; settled at Lynn. Went with the colony to Southampton, L. I.; deposed at New York May 16, 1641, ae. 26 years. Ret. to Lynn. Shoemaker. Bought land in 1652. Wife Alice; ch. Mary b. 8 (4) 1640, Sarah b. 27 (7) 1646, Susanna b. 8 (1) 1651, Hannah b. 12 (4) 1654, Ebenezer b. 11 (4) 165[6]. Admin. of his oral will gr. 17 (5) 1659, to his bro. John. Beq. to wife Alice and ch. Mary, Sarah, Susanna, Hannah and Ebenezer. The widow m. Evan Thomas of Boston. [Suff. De. III, 447 and 484.] The bro. John, (time of arrival here not known), deposed June 26, 1661, ae. about 52 years.

KITCHELL,
Robert, Braintree, one of the appraisers of the est. of Mose Paine, 30 (8) 1643.

KITCHEN,
John, ae. 21, came as servant to Zachary Bickwell from Weymouth, Eng. before March 20, 1635. Settled at Salem, shoemaker. Before Gen. Court with certain books 3 (7) 1639; propr., 1640, frm. Feb. 28, 1642, constable 1648. Suit against him in 1650. He deposed in 1661, ae. about 42. His wife adm. chh. 26 (12) 1642; ch. Eliza and Hannah bapt. 12 (1) 1642-3, Joseph bapt. 20 (2) 1645, John bapt. 28 (4) 1646, Mary bapt. 23 (2) 1648, John bapt. 21 (1) 1652, Robert bapt. 15 (2) 1655.

Will dated 20 Dec. 1675, prob. 30 (4) 1676, beq. to wife and son Robert; other children to inherit after wife.

KITCHERIN, see **KETCHERING.**

KINRICK, see **KENDRICK.**

KITSON,
Ales, Duxbury, m. Wm. Renolds.

KNAPP, KNAP,

Nicholas, Watertown, propr.; fined for selling a medicine for the scurvy which the Court had judged worthless, 1 March, 1630-1. He sold lands and privileges 6 (3) 1646. Wife Elinor; ch. Jonathan bur. 27 (10) 1631, ae. 7 weeks, Timothy b. 14 (10) 1632, Joshua b. 5 (11) 1634, Caleb b. 20 (11) 1636, Sarah b. 5 (11) 1638, Ruth b. 6 (11) 1640, Hannah b. 6 (1) 1643.

William, carpenter, Watertown, referred to in Col. Rec. 3 Nov. 1630, with his son. Propr. 1636. Deed of gift to son John in 1655.

He d. Aug. 30, 1659, ae. about 80 yrs. Will mentions wife Priscilla, widow of Thomas Akers, ch. William, John, James, Mary Smith, Judith Cady, Anne, (wife of Thomas Philbrick,) and Elizabeth Buttery, widow, of Buers St. Mary, co. Suffolk, Eng. [See Mdx. Files and De.] The latter sent power of Attorney 27 Dec. 1660, for collection of her dues. Herbert and Waldegrave Pelham witnesses. [Mdx. Prob. files.]

KNEVITT,

Ruth, Boston, maid servant to Henry Webb, adm. chh. 2 (3) 1641.

KNIGHT,

Athagered, [Watertown]. Inv. made by Lieut. Hugh Mason and goodman John Coolidge, filed in Suff. Prob. 25 (5) 1643. [Reg. III, 81.]

Alexander, Ipswich, propr. 1635. Child Nathaniel, left alone in the house, was burned to death; inquest April 27, 1648.

Ezekiel, Salem, 1637. Rem. to Braintree. Wife Elizabeth bur. 28 (2) 1642. Ch. Ezekiel b. 1 (12) 1640, d. 29 (7) 1641.

George, (with) his wife and child came from Barrow, Eng., 1638, and settled at Hingham.

Goodman —, Reading, propr. 1644.

John, Dorchester, 1634; frm. May 25, 1636. Mrs. Knight, memb. chh. about 1636. He d. Nov. 1632. Admin. gr. to Roger Ludlow March 4, 1632-3.

John, tailor, of Romsey, Eng., came in the James April 5, 1635.

KNIGHT, cont.,

John, carpenter, came in the Bevis in May, 1638.

John, carpenter, Cambridge, householder 1635. Watertown, propr. 1636. Gave bond for a payment in 1641. [L.] Sold land at Wat. 4 (6) 1640. Bought land in Sudbury, 1640. With wife Mary sold Wat. lands in 1652. Propr. at Sudbury; and rem. to Charlestown. Rem. to Woburn; propr. 1650. Wife Mary d. May 16, 1676.

He d. 29 (3) 1674. Will dated 14 (12) 1672, prob. June 10, 1674; confirmed deed of gift to gr. ch. Elizabeth, dau. of son John K., Jr.; beq. to her sister Abigail and to son-in-law Robert Peirse of Woburn and my dau. his wife.

John, Newbury. A witness in the case of Joseph Avery before Gen. Court, 1635. Propr. 1638; town officer. Wife Elizabeth d. 20 March, 1644.

Inv. of his est. taken 15 March, 1677-8, was presented by his widow Bathsheba.

Macklin, Matling, Boston, contracted in Nov. 1639, to cut wood. [L.] Adm. inhab. in 1645. Wife Dorothy adm. chh. 18 (4) 1643.

Master Knight, Ipswich, a minister out of employment in 1642. [L., P. D.]

Philip, cooper, Charlestown, inhab. in 1637; a house-lot and other land was voted to him for keeping the ferry in 1651. Wife Margery adm. chh. 7 (3) 1650.

Admin. Ess. Court 23 (9) 1665, gr. to widow Margery. Ch. [Jonathan], ae. 26, Philip, ae. 23, Rebecca, ae. 17, Eliza, ae. 13, and Mary, ae. 11. Son Jonathan a witness in court with him 26 (2) 1662. [Mdx. Files.]

Richard, tailor, of Romsey, Eng. came in the James April 5, 1635.

Richard, tailor, Newbury, 1635, frm. May 25, 1636; propr., town officer. Bought land 5 March, 1648. Rem. to Salisbury. He deposed April 3, 1680, ae. about 78 years. Ch. rec. at N.: Rebecca b. March 3, 1642, Sara b. 23 March, 1647-8.

Richard, Weymouth, gave bonds 15 (6) 1637, for the appearance of Robert Corbin, master of the Speedwell, at the next Court. [W.]

KNIGHT, cont.,

Richard, slater, Boston, 1641, adm. chh. 26 (1) 1642, frm. May 18, 1642. Wife Dinah adm. chh. 15 (3) 1642. Ch. Samuel b. 18 (12) 1642, bur. 25 (7) 1643, Joseph b. 15 (3) 1645, Jonathan bapt. 11 (1) 1649, ae. about 8 days, John bapt. 1 (10) 1650, Joanna b. 24 Jan. 1652.

Robert, carpenter, came in the Bevis in May, 1638. Res. at Marblehead, propr. 1649. He deposed 19 (2) 1673, ae. 58 years, regarding a neighbor's possession of land many years.

Robert, merchant, Boston, formerly of Bristol, Eng., was app. attorney for Abraham Shurt of Pemaquid 22 (9) 1647, to collect money. [A.] He m. about 1651, Anna, widow, of Thomas Cromwell. Ch. Edward b. Feb. 5, 1652, Martha b. Sept. 1, 1653.

He d. 27 (4) 1655. Will prob. Aug. 1, 1655; beq. to wife Anna and ch. Edward and Martha. [Reg. V, 442.] The widow m. 3, John Joyliffe.

Walter, Duxbury, appl. for land 3 Sept. 1638. A resident in 1640.

Walter, was living in Salem before the arrival of Gov. Endecott in 1628. [Deposition of Rich. Brackenbury.] Lawsuits in Es. and Gen. Court 1640 and 1641.

William, slater, Charlestown, adm. inhab. 1637.

William, Ipswich, propr. 1638.

William, Salem, 1636; Lynn, juryman, propr., 1638, frm. May 2, 1638. Constable in 1641. [Es. Court rec.] According to the testimony of widow Martha Williams he was a mason and a deacon of a dissenting congregation in England; that he came to N. E. with one Hathorne and others for liberty of conscience, leaving estates in Eng.; that his son John ret. to Eng. in the time of the civil wars. John Porter testified to the same. [Es. Court files; Es. Inst. Coll. II, 102.]

Will dated 2 Dec. 1653, prob. 28 (4) 1655. Wife Elizabeth, sons John and Francis, dau. Anne and her ch., dau. Hannah, and John and Nathaniel Ballard. After legacies are paid to these the residue goes to the 4 ch. he had by last wife Elizabeth; eldest son Jacob to have double portion. "Our brother Nicholas Potter" one of the overseers. The widow m. 2, Allen Breed; the dau. Joane m.

KNIGHT, cont.,

Thomas Gage of Yarmouth. Receipts in 1657. John Farrington and John and Nathaniel Ballard, as sons-in-law, and Mary K., as dau. also receipted for their portions. [Es. Deeds II, 52.]

KNOCKER, KNOKAR,

George, Charlestown, mentioned in inv. of his bro. Thomas in 1641. He deposed 3 (2) 1666, ae. about 55 years. [Mdx. Files.]

Thomas, Charlestown, d. 1641. Inv. 19 (9) 1641. His bro. George Knocker and other persons are mentioned. [Reg. III, 80.]

KNOLLEYS, KNOWLES,

Rev. Hansard, came to N. E. in 1638. Took the side of Mrs. Hutchinson in the theological controversy then raging, and was allowed or compelled to rem. to Piscataqua. Wrote to England letters of criticism upon the Mass. authorities. Was called to answer for them at Boston, and apologized publicly 20 (12) 1639. Was accused of criminal deeds. [W.] Ret. to Eng.

KNOTT, KNOT,

George, Sandwich. He made will in May, prob. 8 June, 1649; beq. to wife Martha, son Samuel and dau. Martha; to Thomas Dunham, in case he and the dau. marry.

KNOWER, KNORE, KNOWE,

George, Charlestown, Mystic side, [L.] 1631-1640. Res. at Malden.

He d. Feb. 13, 1674. Will dated 3 (11) 1674, ae. 67 years. Beq. to wife Elizabeth, son Jonathan, dau. Mary Merrable, gr. ch. Hannah and Elizabeth Bucknam.

Thomas, clothier, Charlestown, inhabitant and propr. in 1630. Set in the bilboes 8 April, 1632, for some offence, and for threatening that if punished here he would have the case tried again in Eng. [Col. Rec.] An account book, used in London in 1593 and 1594, by Thomas Knower and Abraham Cartwright of London, clothier, was used as a record book by the first town clerk of Charlestown; it gives many names of clothiers and others who had dealings with them.

Thomas, husbandman, ae. 33, with Noel, ae. 29, and Sarah, ae. 7, came in the Abigail in July, 1635.

KNOWER, etc., cont.,

Thomas, found dead in his boat on Mystic Side in 1641. [W.]

KNOWLES, KNOLLS,

Alexander, frm. Dec. 6, 1636.

Henry, ae. 25, came in the Susan and Ellen in April, 1635.

Rev. John, came to Boston about 1638; adm. chh. as "a studyent," 25 (6) 1639. Was dism. to the chh. of Watertown 1 (1), and ordained colleague pastor to Mr. Phillips 10 (9) 1640. A godly man and a prime scholar. [W.] He was selected to accompany Mr. William Tompson to Virginia in 1642, in the effort to plant churches of the New England type there. Returned to his work at Wat. for a time, then ret. to Eng. He sold land in Lynn to the Iron Works Co. 24 Oct. 1651. [Es. Files XXI, 85.] Residing at Bristol, Eng. 30 March, 1655, sold land in Lynn. [Es. De. II, 97.] [See Bills.] Wife Elizabeth; ch. Mary b. 9 (2) 1641, Elizabeth b. 15 (3) 1643, Hannah, (m. Benjamin Eyres; petitioned for divorce 18 March, 1684-5. [Arch. Dom. 9.]

Richard, Plymouth, before the court and acquitted Jan. 2, 1637-8. Propr. 1638-9. He m. 15 Aug. 1639, Ruth Bower. Ch. Samuel b. 17 Sept. 1651, Mehitabel b. at Eastham 20 May, 1652, Mehitabel b. and d. 20 May, 1653, Barbara b. 28 Sept. 1653. He had land at the head of George Bowers' meadow in 1640.

Will, "the Lady Moodie's man," Lynn, resident April 28, 1639. [Mdx. Files.]

KNOWLTON, NOLTON, see KENNING,

John, shoemaker, Ipswich, propr. 1639; frm. June 2, 1641.

Will dated 29 (9) 1653, prob. 28 (1) 1654, beq. to wife Margery; ch. John, Abraham and Elizabeth; bros. Thomas and William K. The widow made will 20 Feb. 1653, prob. 28 (1) 1654, making bro. Thomas K. exec. of her own and her husband's wills; bro. Wilson one of the overseers; Theophilus W. deposed.

Thomas, shoemaker, Ipswich, propr. 1641; bought land in 1641; deacon. Wife Susanna.

He d. April 3, 1692.

KNOWLTON, etc., cont.

William, bricklayer, Ipswich, propr. 1641; sold land in 1643.

The account of the est. of W. K. was presented in Essex Prob. by his bro. Thomas in 1678. He had kept two boys from the age of five to eight and a girl from one year old till she married.

William, Hingham, propr. died before June 11, 1649, when his widow Anne m. John Tucker.

Admin. of his est. was gr. 23 Oct. 1667, to his widow Anne and only dau. Susannah; inv. presented 26 May, 1668.

KULEM, see Kilham.

KYRTLAND, see Kirtland.

KNOWNE,

William, Salem, 1642.

LACOCK,

Lawrence, ship-carpenter, Boston. Wife Alice adm. chh. 22 (1) 1644.

LADD,

Daniel, husbandman, came in the Mary and John March 24, 1633. Settled at Ipswich; propr. Feb. 5, 1637. Rem. to Salisbury; husbandman; propr. 1639. Rem. to Haverhill before 1648. Wife Ann; ch. Elizabeth b. Nov. 1, 1640, (m. Nathaniel Smith,) Daniel b. July 6, 1642, Lydia b. 8 (8) 1645, (m. Josiah Gage,) Mary b. Feb. 14, 1646, (m. Caleb Richardson,) Samuel b. Nov. 1, 1649, Nathaniel b. March 10, 1651, Ezekiel b. Sept. 16, 1654, Sarah b. Nov. 4, 1657, (m. Onesiporus Marsh). The widow Ann d. Feb. 10, 1693-4. [Reg. XXXVIII, 345.]

He d. July 27, 1693. Will dated Jan. 30, 1692, prob. Jan. 9, 1694-5, beq. to wife; referred to deeds of land he had given to his ch.; beq. to son-in-law Josiah Gage. Admin. gr. to son Daniel.

LAHORNE, LAHERNE, LEIGHORNE, LEYHORNE, [see HORNE,]

James, Duxbury, hired to serve Francis Sprague for 1 year from Feb. 1, 1638-9.

Rowland, planter, Duxbury, propr., 1636. Debtor of John Atwood of Plymouth in 1642. Rem. to Charlestown; cow-keeper in 1645; bought land in 1648. He m. Jan. 14, 1635, "Flower," [Flora] —; she joined him in a deed of land in 1654.

LADDON, see **LUDDON.**

LAKE, LEAKE,

Anne, ae. 19, came in the Desire, cert. from Baddow, Essex, Eng., in June, 1635.

John, tailor, Boston, adm. chh. 2 (10) 1643, frm. May 29, 1644. Bought land June 26, 1648. He deposed to the admin. of Thos. Millard in 1669-70, ae. about 51 years. Wife Mary; ch. Caleb b. 27 (3) 1645, Persis bapt. 31 (8) 1647, ae. about 13 days, Mary bapt. 3 (4) 1649, ae. about 4 days.

He made will 3 Aug., prob. 9 Aug. 1677; beq. to wife Lucy; bro-in-law Matthew Coy and his wife; cousin Lake; cousins John and Mary, ch. of bro. Luke L.; Mary Saxton. Widow and said John L. execs. James Taylor was appointed guardian to the nephew John Lake, 6 Oct. 1677.

Capt. Thomas, son of Richard, of Erby, Eng., b. in 1615, m. Mary, dau. of Stephen Goodyear, deputy gov. of New Haven Colony; came early to Boston. Was engaged in trade and had extensive land interests in Maine. He deposed in Boston July 30, 1663, ae. about 48 years, about Penobscot lands, for which he had paid rent to Col. Temple. Wife Mary; ch. Stephen b. 13 (12) 1649, Mary b. and d. 1653, Mary b. and d. 1659, Edward b. and d. 1662, Ann b. Oct. 12, 1663, (m. Mr. Increase Mather,) John b. Feb. 22, 1665, d. June 27, 1690, Nathaniel b. July 18, 1668, Rebecca b. July 6, 1670, Sarah b. Sept. 14, 1671.

He was slain by the Indians at Kennebec Aug. 16, 1676. Will dated 27 Feb. 1663, prob. 20 Feb. 1676, beq. to sister Lydia Goodyeare, to Sam. Sheepheard, pastor at Rowley, to cousin George Rokesby, Mr. John Shearman, pastor at Wat., Mr. Henry ffrencham; to wife Mary; to ch. Steven, Thomas and Anne. The widow d. in 1705; beq. her est. to cousins John and Richard Watts and Mary Treworthy.

Thomas, husbandman, Dorchester, adm. chh. 20 (9) 1640, frm. June 2, 1641, propr., town officer. Wife Alice d. Oct. 20, 1678, ae. 70. His kinsman and servant, Thomas Lake, called before the church 19 (12) 1659.

He d. Oct. 27, 1678, ae. 80. Will prob. 14 Nov. 1678, beq. to the church a piece of plate for the Lord's table; to his bro. Henry Lake and his children; to one of them, his cousin Thomas L.; to the overseers of the will.

LAKIN, see **Larkin.**

LAMB, LAMBE,

Edward, Watertown, propr., sold house and land in 1647-8. Wife Margaret; ch. Hannah b. 27 (10) 1633, Mary b. and d. 1635, Samuel b. 3 (2) 1637, Mary b. 30 (2) 1639, John and Increase b. and d. 1640, Elizabeth bapt. in Boston 27 (6) 1648, ae. about 11 days.

He d. about 1650. The widow m. 2, Samuel Allen, and with him as adminr. sold house to Thomas Boyden, 19 Oct. 1650, by order of Gen. Court.

Roger, residence not stated, frm. May 18, 1631.

Thomas, Roxbury, came in 1630; brought ch. Thomas and John. [E.] Frm. May 18, 1631. Rec'd the right July 2, 1633, to take slate on Slate Island for 3 years at yearly rent of 2s., 6d. Wife Elizabeth was bur. Nov. 28, 1639; he m. July 16, 1640, Dorothy Harbittle. Ch. Thomas and John mentioned above, Samuel b. (8) 1630, (bapt. at Dorchester,) Abel b. (6) 1633, dau., Decline b. (2) 1637, Benjamin b. Nov. 27, 1635, Caleb b. 9 (2) 1641, Joshua b. Nov. 27, 1642, Mary bapt. 29 (7) 1644, Abiel b. Aug. 15, 1646.

He d. April 3, 1646. The widow m. Thomas Hawley and sold lands 4 (4) 1669. [Suff. De. VI, 42. Col. rec. 1633.]

LAMBERT,

Francis, Rowley, propr., frm. May 13, 1640. Wife Jane. Ch. Jonathan b. 20 (11) 1639, Gershom b. 16 (1) 1643, Thomas b. and d. 1644-5, John, (m. 14 May, 1662, Abigail Hutchinson,) Ann, (m. Dec. 16, 1659, Thomas Nelson, Jr.). Gershom in his will in 1664 mentions "Aunt Rogers and cousin Elizabeth Pratt." See Barker, Thomas.

He d. Sept. 21, 1647. Will dated the day before, was prob. 28 (1) 1648. He beq. to wife Jane, ch. John, Jonathan, Gershom, and Ann. Jonathan to be brought up as a scholar; bro. Thomas Barker and wife Jane execs. The widow was bur. June 7, 1659.

Michael, Salem, lawsuit in 1637, propr. 1648. Wife Elizabeth in 1647. [Es. Files.] He m. [at Boston] in 1659 Elinor Furnell, widow.

Admin. of his est. gr. 29 (9) 1676, to widow Ellinor; minor ch. Michael, Abigail, Moses, Rebecca.

Richard, joiner, Salem, propr. 1636.

LAMBERT, cont.,
Before Gen. Court Oct. 6, 1634; before Essex Court in 1637 and 1648.

William, ae. 26, came in the Susan and Ellen in April, 1635.

LAMBSON, LAMSON, LAMPSON,
Barnabas, Cambridge, propr. and town officer, 1635.

Will undated, prob. Suffolk co. about 1640. He disposed of his ch. thus: Mary to bro. Sparhawk, Sarah to bro. Isaac, Barnabey to bro. Parish, [Martha] to bro. Stone, Joseph to bro. Bridge. [Reg. II, 104.]

William, Ipswich, propr., frm. May 17, 1637. He had liberty from Gen. Court 7 Sept., 1641, to fell trees on the other side of Chebacco, not within limits of any town. Inv. of his est. was taken 14 Feb. 1658. Admin. March 29, 1659; widow Sarah and 8 children; bros. John Ayres and Wm. Fellows. The widow being about to marry Thomas Hartshorne of Reading, he gave security 11 (10) 1659, for the payment of the children's portions. Eldest son 16 yrs. old, next 9, third 2, and youngest 24 weeks; daus. aged 14, 7, 5 and 4, respectively. Account against John and the other children by Anthony Potter, March 29, 1682. [Es. files XXXVII, 18.] John deposed in 1682, ae. 39 years.

LAND, see LANE.

LANE, LAINE, LANNE, LAND,
Job, carpenter, Dorchester, son of James L. of Great Misenden, Bucks, made Mr. Lenthall, minister of Little Haunden, Bucks, his attorney 20 (9) 1647, with reference to the lands at Rickmansworth in same co., now or late in possession of Henry or John L., which rightly descend to Job. [A.] Frm. May 14, 1656. Rem. to Malden, remaining a memb. of the Dorch. chh. Deposed 20 (11) 1654, ae. 30 years. [Mdx. Files.] Wife Sarah d. about May 19, 1659. He m. (7) 1660, Anna, dau. of Mr. John Reyner of Plymouth and Dover. Ch. Sarah bapt. 28 (3) 1648, Mary bapt. 7 (6) 1653, Rebecca b. at Malden (3) 1658, bapt. at Dorch. 4 (5) 1658, John bapt. 17 (9) 1661, "above ¼ of a year old, their dwelling soe remote," Anna b. and d. 1662, Jemina b. Aug. 19, 1666. [See Lane papers in Reg. XI.] Sarah m. Oct. 1655, James Lewis of Barnstable.

LANE, etc., cont.,
William, Dorchester, propr., 1637. Wife Agnes memb. chh. about 1637. Ch. George, ae. 22, came as a servant to Angel Hollard in 1634-5, with "kinswoman," [sister] Sarah, ae. 18; she m. Nathaniel Baker, Jr.; Annis or Avith, (m. Thomas Lincoln the cooper;) Mary, (m. Joseph Long,) Elizabeth, (m. Thomas Rider;) Andrew.

Will prob. July 6, 1654; house to son-in-law Thomas Rider and my dau. Elizabeth, his wife; dau. Mary Long; sons George and Andrew Lane, and Thomas Linckhorne and Nathaniel Baker, all of Hingham; faithful servant, Freedome Kingley; loving bro. Joseph Farnworth and John Wiswell, exec. [Reg. V, 304.]

William, Boston, 1649; chimney-sweeper, 1655. Frm. May 6, 1657. He m. 21 (6) 1656, Mary, dau. of Thomas Brewer of Roxbury; she was adm. chh. 4 (5) 1661. Ch. Samuel b. 23 (11) 1651, John b. 5 Feb. 1653, Mary b. 15 May, 1656, Sarah b. 15 June, 1657, William b. 1 Oct., 1659, Elizabeth b. Feb. 3, 1661, Thomas b. March 8, 1663, Ebenezer b. March 27, 1666.

LANG, LANGE,
Richard, clapboard-ryver, Weymouth, came about 1634; made complaint against town officers for failure to allot him a due proportion of land. Case heard by Mr. Stoughton Nov. 23, 1640. [Col. Rec. and L.]

LANGDON, LANCKTON, LANGTON,
John, sail maker, Boston, witnessed a bond of John Purse in 1645. [A.] Mortg. land March 22, 1661. Wife Sarah; ch. Abigail b. Aug. 5, 1660.

Admin. of his est. Essex Court gr. 30 (9) 1677, to Stephen Haskett, to whose children, it was proved, he beq. his estate.

George, Wethersfield, Conn., rem. to Springfield; town officer 1650. He m. 29 (4) 1648, the widow Haynes of Spr. Ch. Hester b. 22 (6) 1649. Rem. to Northampton.

Will dated Nov. 28, 1676, beq. to wife; to son Thomas Hanchet; daus. Corber, Pritchet and Easter Hannam; son John and gr. son Samuel L.

Roger, Ipswich, propr. 1635; frm. March 4, 1634-5. Rem. to Haverhill. Town officer, 1665. Inv. of his est., taken 24 Jan. 1671, was filed by Edmond Bridges.

LANGEMORE,
John, servant to Christopher Martin, came in the Mayflower to Plymouth; d. soon after arriving. [B.]

LANGER,
Richard, Hingham, propr. 1636. Will, dated Feb. 20, 1659, prob. 2 May, 1661. Inv. taken Feb. 18, 1660. All his lands in Hingham, N. E. which he bought of his son-in-law Thomas Lincoln, and land at Great Rocke and Conyhasset to his dau. Margaret's oldest son, Joshua Lincoln; beq. to daus. Margaret, Dinah and Elizabeth. Witness, Nicholas Baker. [Reg. X, 269, and XXXI, 178.]

LANGFORD, LANCKFORD,
John, residence not stated, frm. May, 1645.
Richard, Plymouth, taxed in 1632. He d. 14 Sept.; inv. taken by Joshua Pratt and Edw. ffoster, pres. 28 Oct. 1633.

LANGHORNE, see LONGHORNE.

LANGLEY, LONGLEY,
Abel, Rowley, propr. about 1647; town officer; wife Sarah bur. 16 May, 1666. He m. 21 (10) 1666, Mary Dickinson; 3d wife Sarah was bur. June 20, 1683. Ch. Sarah b. Nov. 7, 1675, Abel b. 31 (1) 1677, John b. 31 May, 1681.
He d. before 7 Oct. 1693, when Joseph Quilter, exec. of his est., conveyed land on behalf of his cousin, Abel L., Jr.

Richard, Lynn, propr., 1638.

William, Lynn, son of John Longley, clerk, of Frisby, co. Lincoln, made letter of attorney Aug. 8, 1639, to Thomas Meeke of Waynflete St. Mary, co. aforesaid, gent., to sell and rent lands, goods, and legacies descended to him from his said father. [L.] Frm. March 4, 1638-9. Town officer. Deposed in 1661, ae. 47. Rem. to Groton.
He d. Nov. 29, 1680. Will made 3 Nov. 1680, recorded 10 (2) 1681; beq. to wife Joanna, sons John and William, daus. Mary Lemmond, Hannah Tarbell, Lydia Nutten and Sarah Rand and their children specified.

LANNIN,
James, glover, ae. 26, cert. from Stepney parish, came in the Planter March 22, 1634.

LANOE, see DELANO.

LAPHAM,
Thomas, Scituate, adm. chh. April 24, 1636, prop. frm. 5 March, 1638-9. He sold house and ½ acre of land in Tenterden, Eng., near to Sir Edward Hales' place called Bures Ile, to Thomas Hiland; confirmed by the widow 22 June, 1650. He m. March 13, 1636, Mary, dau. of Nathaniel Tilden; ch. Elizabeth bapt. May 6, 1638, Rebecca bapt. March 15, 1645, Joseph bapt. Sept. 24, 1648.
Will dated Jan. 15, 1644, prob. Oct. 1, 1652; inv. taken Jan. 23, 1648; wife Mary, ch. Elizabeth, Mary, Thomas and Lydia. [Reg. IV, 319.]

LARGE,
William, and his wife came to Hingham in 1635; propr. 1636.

LARKIN, LARGIN, LAUKIN, LAWGIN, LASKIN,
Edward, turner, wheelmaker, Charlestown, adm. chh. 23 (7) 1639, frm. May 13, 1640. Wife Joanna adm. chh. 11 (8) 1638. Ch. John b. and bapt. 10 (1) 1640, Sarah bapt. 4 (7) 1641, Elizabeth b. 5 (7) 1641, (sic,) Hannah b. 16 (1) 1643, "of John and Joane," Thomas b. 18 (8) 1644, Joanna, Sarah b. 12 (1) 1647. The son John, in his will, calls John Nowell his brother.

Henry, Boston. Wife Anna; ch. Susanna b. 16 (11) 1645. He m. 2, Alice, widow of Jeremiah Moore; ch. Joseph b. in 1653, d. in 1654. [Suff. De. VI, 7.]

Hugh, (Laskin,) Salem, propr. 1635, memb. chh. 1636. Servant boy named Eliot in court in 1641. His dau. Edith m. Henry Herrick, q. v.
Inv. of his est. March 21, 1658-9.

William, Reading, propr. 1647; town officer. Rem. to Groton. He receipted June 10, 1646, for a legacy from his father William L., late of Reading, Eng., paid to him by his father-in-law, (step-father,) William Martin. Similar legacy was paid Aug. 5, 1673, to his bro. John L., of Groton. [Wife] Lydia memb. chh. 1648; ch. Mary b. 7 (9), d. 3 (11) 1649, [Mdx. De. I.] William b. May 6, 1655, John b. Jan. 3, 1657, Jonathan b. June 28, 1661, Mary b. Feb. 16, 1662.

LARY,
Sarah, Charlestown, adm. chh. 2 (7) 1639.

LASSELL, LAZELL,
Henry, Scituate, memb. chh. 1637.

John, Hingham; town officer. He m. Nov. 29, 1647, Elizabeth, dau. of Stephen Gates; she d. 3 Aug. 1704. Ch. John bapt. Sept. 8, 1650, d. 14 May, 1665, Thomas b. Sept. 15, 1652, Joshua b. Nov. 17, 1654, Stephen b. Oct. 6, 1656 ,Elizabeth b. Feb. 28, 1657-8, d. 7 April, 1676, Isaac b. July 10, 1660, Hannah b. Aug. 31, 1662, (m. — Turner,) Mary b. Sept. 2, 1664, (m. Simon Burr, Jr.,) Sarah b. Nov. 29, 1666, (m. Peter Ripley,) John b. April 25, 1669, Israel b. Sept. 24, 1671.

He d. Oct. 21, 1700. Will dated 2 Sept. 1695, prob. 16 Jan. 1700-1; sons Thomas, Stephen, John and Israel, and the ch. of Joshua and Isaac, dec.; daus. Hannah Turner, Mary Burr and Sarah Ripley.

LATCOME,
William, came in the Hercules in April, 1634.

LATHAM, LATHOM, LATHUM, LATHRUM,
Cary, or Carath, Cambridge, propr. Sold house in 1645-6 and rem. to New London, Conn. Wife Elizabeth, dau. of John Masters; ch. Thomas b. (9) 1639, Joseph b. 2 (10) 16[..].

Mary, executed as a criminal in 1643. [W.]

Robert, Marshfield, propr. 1650, punished for causing the death of his servant, John Walker in Jan. 1654-5. Wife Susanna; ch. Mercy b. 2 June, 1650.

William, a servant boy in the family of Gov. John Carver, came in the Mayflower; was taxed in Plymouth in 1632; planter. Rem. to Duxbury . Deposed in 1641, ae. about 32. [L.] He went to Eng. and afterward to the Bahama Islands. [B.]

LATON, LAUGHTON, see LEIGHTON.

LATHROP, see LOTHROP.

LAUNDER, LAUNDERS,
Thomas, ae. 22, came in the Abigail in July, 1635. Had beq. of 3 li. from Dennis Geere of Lynn 10 Dec., 1635. Settled at Sandwich; propr., 1640, atba. 1648. He m. July 2, 1651, Jane Kerbie. Ch. John b. Jan. 2, 1653, Martha b. March 7, 1654, Mary b. Jan. 23, 1656.

He d. Nov. 11, 1675. Inv. of his est. taken 15 Nov. 1675.

William, Marshfield, servant to Mr. John Combe, transferred 5 April, 1642, to Mr. Wm. Thomas, and Nov. 9, 1643, to Thomas Bourne.

Inv. filed Jan. 1, 1648, and will dated 19 Dec. prob. 8 March, 1648. Beq. to the children of Robert Waterman; to Roger Glase, and to Jonathan Brewster and his wife.

LAVER, LAUER, LEVVER, see Leaver,
Margery, Dorchester memb. chh. about 1639.

Will, dated 4 (6) 1664, prob. 10 (9) 1664, beq. to Mr. William Tompson, Mr. Richard Mather, Daniel Preston and his wife and children, Jane Gurnet, Mr. John and Thomas Wiswall. [Reg. XIII, 13.]

LAWRENCE, LARRENCE, LAWRENSON, LAWRUN, see Lary,
Henry, Charlestown, propr. before 1638. Christian, [his widow?] with her son John sold house and land July 22, 1646. This John deposed 4 (4) 1639, ae. 24 years. The widow d. March 3, 1647-8.

James, a servant, before Boston Court, 29 (5) 1641.

John, carpenter, Watertown, propr., 1636, frm. April 17, 1637. He deposed 20 (1) 1657, ae. about 35 years. [Mdx. Deeds] He sold mansion and land at Wat. in 1662 and rem. to Groton. Wife Elizabeth d. Aug. 29, 1663, and he m. Susanna, dau. of Wm. Bachiler of Charlestown. Ch. John b. 14 (1) 1635, Nathaniel b. 15 (8) 1639, Joseph b. and d. 1642, Joseph b. 30 (3) 1643, Jonathan bur. 6 (2) 1643, Mary b. 16 (5) 1645, Peleg b. 10 (11) 1647, Enos b. 5 (1) 1648, Zechariah b. 9 (1) 1658.

He d. July 11, 1667; the widow d. July 8, 1668. In his will he appoints his wife and sons Nathaniel and Joseph execs.; names also ch. Enoch, Samuel, Isaac, Jonathan, Zechariah, Elizabeth and Mary; the widow

LAWRENCE, etc., cont.,
in her will adds daus. Abigail and Susanna, her own children; beq. to her sisters Rachel Atwood and Abigail Asting.

Nicholas, of Charlestown, sold land adjoining that of John L. 24 (12) 1648. Rem. to Dorchester. Ch. Samuel bapt. 10 (8) 1652, Thomas bapt. 28 (3) 1654, Mary b. 1656, Patience bapt. 20 (4) 1658, Nathaniel bapt. 12 (6) 1660, Nicholas bapt. 29 (4) 1662, Rebecca bapt. 11 (7) 1664, Ebenezer b. about 1666, Benjamin bapt. 31 (10) 1671.

Inv. of his est. includes carpenter's tools; filed 21 May, 1685, by widow Mary. He beq. to wife Mary; to eldest son; to the other four children, Mary Rebecca, Nicholas and Benjamin.

Robert, Marshfield, propr. 1644.

Thomas, Hingham, propr. 1637. Wife Elizabeth; ch. Elizabeth, (m. 31 (10) 1658, William Smead,) Mary, (m. 28 (8) 1658, Thomas Modesley,) Sarah bapt. March 4, 1643-4.

He d. 5 (9) 1655. Nunc. will made in presence of his wife's brother elder Edward Bates of Weymouth and John Smith of Hing., beq. to wife Elizabeth; cert. 16 (3) 1675. The widow rem. to Dorchester, where the daus. married; deposed to a transfer of land in 1675, referring to her children. She d. Feb. 18, 1679.

William, Duxbury, atba. 1643; a son-in-law of Francis Sprague, who sold him land at Dux. April 1, 1644.

LAW, LAWS, LAWES,
Francis, weaver, born in Norwich, Eng., and there living, passed exam. in April, 1637, to go to N. E. with wife, child Mary and servants Samuel Lincorne, ae. 18, and Anne Smith, ae. 19. Settled at Salem. Propr. His wife adm. chh. 19 (7) 1640. Dau. Mary deposed in 1663, ae. about 48 years.

His will dated 6 Nov. 1665, prob. 28 (4) 1666, beq. to dau. Mary, her husband John Neale and their ch. Jeremiah, John, Jonathan and Lydia.

William, ae. 12, with Marie, ae. 9, and John, ae. 17, apparently registered as the ch. of John Tuttell, came in the Planter in April, 1635. Settled at Rowley; propr., town officer. He m. Sept. 3, 1645, Mary, dau.

LAW, etc., cont.,
of John Cheney and widow of Anthony Saddler; she died, and he m. 2, May 2, 1666, Faith, widow of John Smith. Ch. Rebecca b. 9 (7) 1646, John b. March 20, 1648, both bur. 9 (7) 1652; Mary b. 23 (3) 1650, bur. 29 (3) 1653, Rebecca b. 1 (4) 1655, Mary b. 15 (8) 1657, John b. 1 March, 1659, bur. 23 (5) 1661, Priscilla b. 18 (9) 1662, Aquila b. July 26, 1667, d. April 15, 1669.

He was bur. March 30, 1668. Widow Faith testified about sale of land by him 29 Sept. 1668.

LAWSON,
Christopher, cooper, Boston, 1643. Propr. Many transactions in merchandise and real estate. Propr. at Piscataqua. His wife Elizabeth gave power of attorney 20 (8)1646, to Barnabas Fawer for collection of legacies from Henry and Thomas James of Filton, co. Gloc. Eng. [A.] He deposed in 1671, ae. about 55 years. [Es. Files.] Propr. at Haverhill, 1649. His wife deserted him and returned to Eng.; he petitioned for divorce 11 Oct. 1670. Ch. Thomas b. 4 (3) 1643, Mary b. 27 (8) 1645. Admin. of his est. was gr. 20 Nov. 1682, to Edward Thyng.

Henry, his creditors called to prove their claims at Gen. Court June 14, 1631.

LEDAGE,
Henry, tailor of Sarum, came in the James April 15, 1635.

LEECH, LEACH,
Ambrose, carpenter, Sudbury, propr., contracted in 1641 to build a bridge over the river. Was one of the sureties for Charles Dobson at Boston 6 (9) 1649. Res. at Narragansett Nov. 9, 1663, when he sold land at Boston. [Mdx. Files, 1650.]

Mr. John, bro. of Lawrence, Salem, recd. for an inhabitant in 1636. Presented at court in 1647, for not living with his wife. Frm. May 29, 1644.

His nunc. will was prob. 20 (10) 1658. He was occupied at the Iron Works. Beq. all to John, son of Richard Leech.

Lawrence, sent over to Salem by the Mass. Bay Co. in 1629. [Suff. De. I.] Juryman Nov. 29, 1630. Frm. May 18, 1631. Propr.; town officer repeatedly. Lands gr. to

LEECH, etc., cont.,
his sons Robert and John, 1636-7. A way laid out in 1657 from the meeting-house on Cape Ann side to his mill. Wife Elizabeth memb. chh. in earliest list.

His nunc. will prob. 25 (4) 1662. He was 85 years old. Beq. all to his wife. Owed £30 for the mill. Admin. gr. to widow Elizabeth.

Margaret, ae. 22, came in the Susan and Ellen in April, 1635.

Richard, Salem, 1638; frm. May 3, 1665. He deposed in 1678, ae. about 60 years. Wife Sarah adm. chh. 1 (9) 1648 or 13 (6) 1648. Ch. John bapt. 3 (7) 1648, John and Sarah bapt. 19 (9) 1648, Rachel bapt. 6 (2) 1651, Eliza bapt. 27 (9) 1653, Mary bapt. 3 (7) 1654, Richard bapt. 15 (4) 1656.

His will dated 17 June, prob. Nov. 25, 1687, beq. to wife Sarah; son John; daus. Elizabeth, wife of Benjamin Collins, Mary, wife of Benjamin Ireson, Hannah and Rachel; Joseph, Sarah and John Herrick, ch. of dau. Sarah; young Pascho Foote, now living with him. [Original, written on parchment, in Es. Files, 47, 87.] See Fuller, Ann.

Robert, collar maker, Charlestown, 1637. Propr. He deposed in 1663, ae. about 57 years. Sarah adm. chh. 9 (7) 1639. Mary d. Feb. 11, 1658. Ch. Elizabeth m. John Fosket.

He d. May 22, 1688, ae. about 80. Will prob. at Boston 14 June, 1688, beq. to the 7 children of John Foskit and dau. Mary; chiefly to Thomas F. and his wife Miriam.

LEADER,
Richard, gent., merchant, Lynn, agent for the Iron Works Co., in Sept., 1645. He had formerly been employed about mines in Ireland. Covenanted with the Adventurers in Iron Works in 1644 to take charge of their affairs 7 years at £100 per annum, with house, ground for horses and cows and passage for himself, wife, 2 children and 3 servants. [Mass. Hist. Coll. 4-6.] [Suff. De. 1, 62.] Propr., Boston, Aug. 24, 1653. [W.] Sold the slitting mill in Lynn to Capt. Wm. Hathorne in 1650. Sold lands in Boston in 1655.

Thomas, Dedham, propr. 21 (7) 1638; his wife adm. chh. 30 (2) 1641. Rem. to Boston; adm. townsman 31 (2) 1647. Had charge of the yoking and ringing of swine

LEADER, cont.,
for the town. Wife Rebecca d. 16 (10) 1653. He m. 2, Susanna, widow of George Hauborne. He m. 3, Ales —, who survived him. Susan, wife of Thomas Leader of Boston made will 24 May, 1657, prob. at Hampton 6 (8) 1657; beq. to her husband; to Edward Rishworth, Thomas Wheelwright, Merabah Smith, Hannah Clifford, Samuel Dalton, Robert Smith, Henry Elkins, Henry Robie and Mary Wedgewood. Inv. shows house and land in H., etc. Edward Rishworth receipted 31 (9) 1659, for his share of that est. which was given him by Susanna Habborne of Hampton.

He d. 28 Oct. 1663. Will dated 17 Oct. 1663, prob. Nov. 3, 1663. To wife Ales the house he used to let; to son Samuel dwelling house, land tools, etc.; to Thomas, Abigail and Rebecca ch. of his late son John. [Reg. XII, 156.]

LEAGER, LEGER, LEDGER, LEAGUER, LEGAR, LEGARE,
Jacob, husbandman, Boston, 1638; adm. chh. 14 (1) 1641, frm. June 2, 1641. He m. 1, Elizabeth, widow of John Greene of Hadley, Eng., who brought over her son Solomon and dau. Mary. [L.] She was adm. chh. Boston 12 (3) 1639. He m. 2, Ann, dau. of Wm. Blake of Dorchester. Ch. Bethia bapt. in Dorch. 10 (6)1651, (m. Fearnot Shaw,) Hannah b. Nov. 14, 1655, (m. John Walker.)

He d. Feb. 24, 1662-3; will dated Nov. 10, 1662, prob. March 19, 1662-3. Beq. to wife and daus.; to my sister Marie's ch. in Eng.; to Jacob and Joseph Walker and Elishua Thurston; 12 d. apiece to second wife's children. [Reg. XI, 340; "Increase Blake," p. 23.] The widow d. July 12, 1681, ae. 63 years.

LEARNED, LERNED, LARNED, LARNET,
William, Charlestown, propr. 1630; adm. chh. with wife Goodith 6 (10) 1632; frm. May 14, 1634; memb. of the com. to propose to the Court a body of laws in 1638. One of the founders of the town and chh. of Woburn, 1640. Town officer. Wife Goodith (Judith,) d., and he m. 2, Sarah or Jane —. Ch. Isaac and Sarah.

He d. March 1, 1645. Widow "Sarah" or "Jane" L., d. at Malden 24 (11) 1660. Admin. gr. to Ralph Shepherd April 2, 1661.

LEATHERLAND,
William, carpenter, Boston, one of Mr. Roe's servants, adm. chh. 24 (9) 1633. He may be the frm. adm. March 4, 1634-5, enrolled as "Netherland." He gave half of his house to his sister, the wife of Nathaniel Patridge, and to her husband, about 1647. Perhaps he is the William Lullaby who was in the service of Mr. Hill of Boston (12) 1649. [Es. Files I, 142..] Wife Margaret joined him in a deed to Peter Tyll, sawyer, Feb. 5, 1662. He deposed 25 Jan. 1670, ae. 62 years.

LEATHERMORE, see Livermore.

LEAVES,
Ellen, ae. 17, came in the Hopewell in Sept., 1635.

LEAVITT, LEVITE, LEVET,
John, tailor, Dorchester, 1634, propr., frm. March 3, 1635-6. Rem. to Hingham; propr. 1636; deacon, town officer, deputy.

Wife — d. 4 July, 1646. Perhaps Mary "Lovitt," memb. Dorch. chh. before 1639, was this person. He m. Dec. 16, 1646, Sarah, dau. of Edward Gilman. Ch. John, Hannah bapt. April 7, 1639,(m. John Lobdell,) Samuel bapt. April, 1641, Elizabeth bapt. April 8, 1644, (m. Samuel Judkins,) Jeremiah bapt. March 1, 1645-6, Israel bapt. April 23, 1648, Moses bapt. Aug. 12,1650, Josiah b. May, 1653, Nehemiah b. Jan. 22, 1655-6, Sarah b. Feb. 25, 1658, (m. Nehemiah Clap,) Mary b. June 21, 1661, (m. Benjamin Bates,) Hannah b. March 20, 1663-4, (m. Joseph Loring,) Abigail b. Dec. 4, 1667, (m. Isaac Lassell.) See letter concerning the will of John Lobdell in 1673.

He d. Nov. 1691, ae. 83. Will prob. 27 Jan. folg. To wife Sarah; gr. ch. Samuel Judkin; 9 children, viz.: Samuel, Israel, Moses, Josiah, Nehemiah, Sarah, (wife of Samuel How,) Mary, (wife of Benjamin Bate,) Hannah, (wife of Joseph Loring,) Abiell, (wife of Isaac Lazell.) Refers to money lent his dau. Sarah when she was a widow by the name of Clap; gr. ch. John, son of Israel; Bathsheba, wife of Joseph Turner, formerly wife of his son John Leavitt.

LECHFORD,
Thomas, gent., Clements' Inn, London, practiser at law, arrived at Boston 27 (4) 1638. Kept careful record of papers drawn by or executed before him until his ret. to Eng., Aug. 3, 1641. This Note Book, published by the American Antiquarian Society in 1885, is a mine of wealth to students of the colonial period. At his suggestion public record of deeds and wills was begun in Boston. He was not in accord with the prevalent ideas of church and state here, and after returning to Eng. he published in 1642 "Plain Dealing: or Newes from New England," a book full of criticism of the colonial governments. His wife Elizabeth was here with him; after his death she m. Samuel Wilbore. She was adm. chh. Nov 29, 1645.

Inv. of Lechford's est. was filed in B. 3 (3) 1648, and admin. gr. to S. W. After Mr. Wilbores death she m. Henry Bishop, and d about 1655. [Reg. XXX, 201.] [Mass. Hist. Coll. 3-3.]

LEE, LEA, LEIGH,
John, fined 1 April, 1634, for calling Mr. Ludlow names, Ipswich, propr. 1640. He deposed in 1658, ae. about three score years. [Es. Files.]
Will dated 12 June, prob. 26 Sept. 1671, beq. to wife; to sons John and Joseph, to Sarah Hungerfoot a portion to be paid her at marriage, beside what I have already given her, provided she continue to live with my wife till that time. His son John sold land 28 Nov. 26, [1674,] which his late father had purchased.

Robert, Plymouth, frm. Jan. 3, 1636. He and his wife Mary called bro. and sister by Mr. John Atwood; their ch. Anne and Mary also remembered in his will, in 1643. Juryman in 1646. Town officer. The widow Mary d. in Oct. 1681, having spent the last 8 years in the family of her son Ensign John Howland of Barnstable. Inv. pres. 8 March, 1681-2.

Thomas, Ipswich, propr. 1641. Sold house and lot 2 May, 1659, wife Alice consenting.
He d. 23 March, 1661-2. Will dated 19 March, 1661, prob. 17 April, 1662, beq. to wife Alice; gr. son Richard Lee; dau. Susanna, now in Eng. or her children, if any of

LEE, etc., cont.,
them shall be here to demand it within 7 years.

William, ae. 16, came in the Planter in April, 1635.

LEAVER, LEVER, see Laver,
Thomas, linen weaver, Rowley, propr. Bought land 21 (12) 1650. He deposed in 1682, ae. 67 years. He m. 1 Sept., 1643, Mary Bradley; ch. Prudence b. 11 (6) 1644, Thomas b. 2 (5) 1647, Mary b. 5 (7) 1649, Jonathan b. 28 (6) 1657, bur. Aug. 8, 1660.
He was bur. Dec. 27, 1683. His inv. mentions only son Thomas, who had been in partnership with him; daus. Prudence, wife of Samuel Stickney, and Mary, wife of Samuel Dressar. The widow Mary testified 15 April, 1674, to her husband's promise to Thomas on the day of his marriage.

LEEDS,
Richard, mariner, ae. 32, of Great Yarmouth, Eng., with wife Joane, ae. 23, and 1 child, passed exam. to go to N. E. April 12, 1637. Settled at Dorchester, propr. 1638, frm. May, 1645. Ch. Joseph and Benjamin, twins, bapt. 4 (2) 1639, Hannah bapt. 6 (12) 1639-40, m. (Samuel Clap 18 (11) 1658.) Wife Joan d. Feb. 9, 1682.
He d. March 18, 1693-4, ae. about 98 years. Will dated 2 March, prob. 30 March, 1692-3, near an hundred years old; beq. to ch. Joseph and Benjamin Leeds and Hannah Clap; to the heirs of his dau.-in-law Mrs. Miriam Leeds his land at Northampton; to gr. ch. Joseph L.; to pastor, Mr. Danforth.

LEGG, LEDG,
John, in service of Mr. Humphrey at Lynn 3 May, 1631. [Col. Rec.] Frm. May 6, 1635. Before the Court in 1638. Rem. to Marblehead; propr. 1649. He deposed in 1657, ae. about 45 years, as to the fencing of Nahant by Mr. H. and others. The wife Elizabeth deposed in 1665, ae. about 57 years; son John, ae. about 21.
Will prob. 2 (5) 1674; wife Elizabeth and ch. Samuel, John and Daniel.

LENNER, LEONARDSON,
Solomon, Duxbury, propr. 7 May, 1638, atba. 1643. He rem. to Bridgewater.
His est. was settled upon sons Samuel and John and other ch. 27 Oct., 1675.

LEIGHORNE, see Lahorne.

LEIGHTON, LIGHTON, LATON, LAYTON, LAUGHTON, LETTIN, LETTYNE,
Alice (Laton), Barnstable, m. in 1641 Roger Goodspeed.

John, Ipswich, was paid for Indian service in 1643. Allowed to build a weir in 1648. Constable. John, [the same?] m. at Boston Sept 1, 1659, widow Johannah Mullings.

Richard, Concord, propr. before Jan. 20, 1643, Rowley, propr. about 1643; was paid in 1654 for underpinning the meetinghouse. He m. 14 Nov. 1650, Mary —; ch. Josiah b. at Conc. 20 (12) 1640, a son b. 12 (7) 1643; b. at Rowl., John b. 12 (2) 1651, Mary b. 16 (10) 1654, Ezekiel b. 12 (8) 1657, Richard bur. June 2, 1660, Richard b. Dec. 9, 1664.
He was bur. 2 June, 1684. Will prob. 26 Sept.; beq. to wife, sons John and Ezekiel, and daus. Mary and Sarah.

Thomas, ae. 23, came in the Elizabeth April 15, 1635; settled at Lynn; propr. 1638; selectman 1643. Frm. March 14 1638-9. Licensed to sell wine 14 May, 1645. Deputy 1646.
He made will 27 July, 1697, prob. Aug. 30 folg.; beq. to eldest son Thomas Laughton; to son Samuel, dau. Rebecca Ingalls and gr. dau. Margaret L.; to the three ch. of son Thomas and to each of son Samuel's ch.

LEMON, LEAMON, LEOMON,
Robert, Salem, propr. 1636, frm. Dec. 27, 1642. His wife Mary was memb. chh. 1639. Ch. Grace and Mary bapt. 1 (2) 1639, Martha bapt. 22 (1) 1639-40, John bapt. 27 (1) 1642, Eliza bapt. 17 (10) 1643, John bapt. 12 (8) 1645, Hannah bapt. 7 (6) 1650.
Will dated Aug. 2, 1665, prob. 25 (4) 1667; beq. to wife Mary; to ch. Sarah and Hannah; "to he that did marry with my dafter Mathe;" to Thomas, Robert and Mary Sallows; to Benjamin L. his sea-chest and sea instruments. Martha's husband was Bartholomew Gale. [Es. Files XXX, 7.] The widow Mary, with Charles Knight, husband of her dau. Sarah, Samuel Beadle, husband of the dau. Hannah, agreed upon a final division 16 (9) 1674.

LENTHALL,
Rev. Robert, Weymouth. Of good report in Eng.; held some of Mrs. Hutchinson's opinions as of justification before faith; opposed mutual stipulation (covenant) of chh. membs.; maintained that baptism was the only door of entrance to the churches, etc. The magistrates called him to account and he retracted. The church was gathered there with approbation of the magistrates and elders 30 (11) 1638. He rem. to Newport; adm. frm. of R. I. Aug. 6, 1640. Taught school; had land grants. Ret. to Eng. in 1642. [W.]

LEPINGWELL, LAPPINWALL, LEPPINGWELL,
Michael, carpenter, Cambridge. Rem. to Woburn. Taxed in 1645. Wife Isabel; ch, Naomi b. Nov. 8, 1638, Hannah b. and d. 1643, Sarah b. 22 (2) 1644, Hannah b. Jan. 6, 1645, (m. April 15, 1668, Gershom Flagg,) Thomas b. Jan. 13, 1648, Ruth b. Jan. 2, 1649, Michael b. and d. 1651.

He d. March 22, 1686-7. Will dated April 2, 1686, prob. April 14, 1687, beq. to son Thomas; to Gershom, son to dau. Flagg; to other daughters. Son-in-law Gershom Flagg exec.

LEONARD,
John, Springfield, propr. 1638; town officer. He m. 12 (9) 1640, Sarah Heald. Ch. John b. 25 (6) 1641, d. 22 (4) 1648, Joseph b. and d. 1643, Joseph b.. 20 (3) 1644, Sarah b. 13 (10) 1645, Mary b. 14 (7) 1647, Martha b. 15 (2) 1649, Lydia b. 2 (8) 1650, John b. 10 (7) 1652, Benjamin b. 5 (7) 1654, Abel b. 22 (5) 1656, Josias b. 28 (1) 1658, Hannah b. 19 (12) 1659, Rebecca b. 26 (3) 1661, John d. 13 March, 1662-3, Deborah b. 1 Oct. 1663, Rachel b. Nov. 8, 1665.

Admin. of his est. gr. March 28, 1676 to his widow Sarah. The agreement between the heirs names sons Joseph, Benjamin, Abel and Josiah L., John Keep and Samuel Bliss.

LESTER,
Andrew, Gloucester, constable 7 (11) 1646. [Es. Court.]

LETTIN, see Leighton.

LETTICE, LETTIS,
Thomas, carpenter, Plymouth, 1636, propr. 2 Dec, 1639, atba. 1643, frm. June 6, 1653. Juryman, town officer. Took as an apprentice Thomas, son of Thomas Savory, ae. 5 years, 2 Aug. 1653. Wife Anne; ch. Elizabeth, (m. 18 Oct., 1655, Wm. Shirtley,) Dorothy, (m. Dec. 12, 1665, Edward Gray,) Thomas d. 3 Nov. 1650.

He made will in 1678, *declared* Oct. 25, 1681, prob. Oct. 1682. Beq. to wife Anne; daus. Anne, wife of Samuel Tenney, Elizabeth Cook, widow, and Dorothy, wife of Edward Gray.

LEVENS, LEAVENS,
John, embarked for N. E. March 7, 1631, came to Roxbury. Arrived in 1632 and adm. chh. [E.] Wife Elizabeth was bur. Oct. 10, 1638; he m. July 5, 1639, Rachel Wright. Ch. John b. April 27, 1640, James b. April 16, 1642, Peter and Andrew (Caleb) b. Sept. 11, 1644, Peter d. (11) 1644, Rachel b. Aug. 1646.

He d. Nov. 16, 1647, ae. 65. Admin. 30 (6) 1648. [Reg. VII, 175.]

LEVERETT, LEVERITT,
Mr. Thomas, from Boston, Eng., one of those who refused the Royal Loan 9 March, 1626. [Reg. XXXVI, 138.] A memb. of Mr. Cotton's congregation. Came to Boston, N. E. in 1633. Adm. chh. with wife Anne (8) 1633 and chosen ruling elder; frm. March 4, 1633-4. Propr., town officer, an important citizen. Ch. Anne adm. chh. 20 (12) 1641, (m. Isaac Addington,) Jane, adm. chh. 26 (3) 1639, John adm. chh. 14 (b) 1639,(went to Eng. in 1644; was captain of a foot company in Col. Rainsborow's regiment; ret. after good service;) [W.] another ch. John b. here 7 (7) 1633.

He d. 3 (2) 1650. Nunc. will made 1 (2) inv. taken 6 July, 1650. All to his wife Ann. The widow Anne d. 15 Oct. 1656. Will prob. 29 Jan. 1656-7 beq. to her son Capt. John; dau. Anne Addington; cousin Elizabeth Fich; gr. ch. Isaac Addington; to Hudson Leverett; to Sarah Shelly, Francis Langome and Margaret, the maid. [Reg. IV, 121 and 125, and VII, 234.]

LEVERICH, LEVERIDGE,
Rev. William, "a godly minister," came in the James to Salem Oct. 10, 1633. [W.] Went with Capt. Thomas Wiggin, who ret.

LEVERICH, etc., cont.
from Eng. in the same ship to Piscataqua. Was adm. chh. Boston 9 (6) 1635; frm. 7 Feb. 1636-7. After a brief ministry at Piscataqua he rem. to Sandwich where he ministered well. He rem. about 1658 to Oyster Bay, L. I.

LEWIS, LEWES,
Edmund, ae. 33, wife Mary, ae. 32, and ch. John, ae. 3 years, and Thomas, ae. 9 months, came in the Elizabeth of Ipswich, April 30, 1634. Res. at Watertown. Propr.; frm. May 25, 1636. In company with Henry Dow he bought land at Newbury 16 (8) 1644. He rem. to Lynn. Ch. rec. at Wat.; James b. 15 (11) 1635, Nathaniel b. 25 (6) 1639, a child bur. 6 (9) 1642, ae. 10 days.
He d. in 1650. Will signed 13 (1), prob. 25 (12) Wife Mary; sons John the eldest, Thomas and 4 others; land at Wat. The widow d. Sept. 7, 1658.

George, clothier, Plymouth. Rem. to Scituate; adm. chh. Sept. 20, 1635. His house and that of goodman Lewis, Jr., mentioned by Parson Lothrop as being in Sci. in 1636. Rem. to Barnstable. Frm. 3 June, 1657. Wife Mary; ch. John bapt. March 11, 1637, Ephraim bapt. July 25, 1641, Sarah bapt. Feb. 11, 1643.
Will prob. March 3, 1663; wife Mary; ch. Ephraim, George, Thomas, James, Edward, John, Sarah. His dau. Mary m. Nov. 14, 1643, John Bryant, Jr. [Reg. VI, 185.]
Note. The identification of the ch. is difficult, owing to the similarity of names in the several families.

John, of Tenterden, Eng., with wife Sarah, came in the Hercules in March, 1634. Settled at Scituate. Frm. Plym. Col. 7 Feb. 1636-7. Butcher, rem. to Boston, 1652; ch. Sarah bapt. at Bo. o (11) 1650. Wife Sarah d. 12 (5) 1657; he m. 22 Nov. 1659, Alice, widow of Nathaniel Bishop, who joined him in a deed of land 24 Aug. 1659. Ch. Samuel b. Jan. 18, 1661, Joseph b. Feb. 4, 1662, Benoni b. 25 (11) 1664.

John, carpenter, late of Tanton, N. E., transferred Wm. Roberts an apprentice, to John Crabtree, 16 (4) 1640. [L.]

John, planter, Charlestown, inhabitant, 1634, adm. chh. 10 (7) 1644. He rem. to Malden. Wife Margerite adm. chh. 7 (7) 1638; she d. March 10, 1649. He m. April

LEWIS, etc., cont.
10, 1650, Mary Brown. Ch. John b. 12, bapt. 14 (7) 1638, Joseph and Mary bapt. 29 (1) 1640, Samuel b. 24, bapt. 27 (4) 1641, Elizabeth b. 10 (7) 1642, Sarah b. Dec. 24, 1647, Abraham b. Dec. 10, 1650, Jonathan b. and d. 1651, Mary b. Jan. 1652-3, Hannah, Isaac, Trial b. (11) 1657.
He d. (7) 1657. The widow m. before 1667 — Cutler. [Mdx. De. III, 203.]

Mary, Springfield, had lived 7 years from her husband, and claimed the right by English laws to marry again. She m. in 1645 "a brickmaker" of Spr. [Mass. Hist. Coll. 4-6.]

Robert, sawyer, ae. 28, with Elizabeth, ae. 22, came in the Blessing in July, 1635. Settled at Salem. Rem. to Newbury; propr. in the new town, 1643.
He d. May 4, 1643. Will referred to in Ess. Court 6 (5) 1644, when inv. was filed.

Thomas, Dorchester, memb. chh., land granted him conditioned on his keeping cattle for the plantation, Sept. 10, 1637.

William, embarked for N. E. June 22, 1632; came to Roxbury. Frm. 18 May, 1642. Ch. John b. in Eng. [Rox. Rec.] Nov. 1, 1635, Christopher, b. do. in 1636, Lydia b. at Rox. Dec. 25, 1640, Josias b. July 28, 1641, Isaac b. 15 (2) 1644.

William, Cambridge, propr. 1635; frm. Nov. 6, 1632. Rem. to Hartford, then to Farmington, Conn., whence he or his son of same name rem. to Hadley, and was deputy in 1662. Ret. to Farmington, Conn., and d. Aug. 2, 1683.

LEWSON,
John, residence not stated, frm. March 13, 1638-9.

LEYHORNE, see Lahorne.

LIGHTFOOT, LIGHTFOOTE,
Francis, Lynn, frm. Dec. 8, 1636. Propr., juryman, 1638. Selectman, 1643.
He d. Dec. 10, 1646. Will prob. 29 (1) 1646. To wife Anne; to bro. John L. of London and sister Isabel L. of Freston, near old Boston in Lincolnshire; to bro. Pell and Hannah Pell; to Dorothy and Elizabeth Whiting; to Samuel Cobbett. Bro. Handfurth one of the overseers.

LIGHTON, see LEIGHTON.

LILFORD, LILLFORTH, see LINFORD.

LILY, LILLYE,
Luke, propr. at Marshfield, atba. 1643; served against the Narragansetts in 1645.

LINCOLN, LINCORNE, LINKHORN, LINKUM,
Daniel, seaman, sergeant, Hingham, 1644; propr., town officer. Deposed 27 Sept. 1695, ae. 75 years. [Hist. Hing.] Wife Susanna d. 20 Feb. 1703-4. Ch. Susanna b. 14 May, 1654, (m. Robert Waterman,) Daniel b. 1657, d. 1658, Hannah b. Sept. 10, 1659, (m. John Lewis,) Daniel b. 1661, Sarah b. Sept. 7, 1664, (m. Nathaniel Nichols,) Ephraim b. May 26, 1667, a son b. and d. 1669, Rachel b. June 27, 1671, (m. Israel Lassell).

Will dated 16 Sept. 1692, prob. 18 May, 1699, beq. to wife Susanna; sons Daniel and Ephraim; daus. Susanna, Hannah, Sarah and Rachel.

Samuel, mariner, came from Hingham, Eng. as a servant to Francis Laws in 1635, and settled at Salem. [Cushing.] Rem. to Hingham in 1637. Propr. 1649. Wife Martha; ch. Samuel b. Aug. 25, 1650, Daniel b. Jan. 2, 1652, Mordecai b. and d. 1655, Mordecai b. June 14, 1657, *(the great-great-great-great-grandfather of President Abraham Lincoln,)* Thomas b. 1659, d. 1661, Mary b. March 27, 1662, (m. Joseph Bate,) Thomas b. Aug. 20, 1664, Martha b. Feb. 11, 1666, Sarah b. and d. 1669, Sarah b. June 17, 1671, Rebecca b. March 11, 1673-4, (m. 1, John Clark of Plymouth, 2, Israel Nichols, widower).

He d. 26 May, 1690, ae. 71 years; the widow d. 10 April, 1693.

Stephen, from Windham, Eng. came in 1638, with wife and son Stephen, and settled at Hingham. Propr. 1638. Wife Margaret was bur. 13 June, 1642. Ch. Stephen, (m. Feb. 1660, Elizabeth, dau. of Matthew Hawk,) Sarah bapt. 22 May, 1642, d. 4 Nov. 1649.

He d. 11 Oct. 1658. Will, made 11 days before, beq. to mother Joan L., son Stephen, and to Susanna, dau. of his bro. Thomas L., husbandman.

LINCOLN, etc., cont.
Robert, laborer, Boston, (Winnisimet,) 1647. Wife Anne rec'd to chh. 9 (3) 1647. Admin. gr. to the widow July 29, 1663. [Reg. XII, 154.]

Thomas, Charlestown, propr. 1634; probably one of the following:

Thomas, miller, Hingham, propr. 1635. Rem. to Taunton. Name of first wife unknown; he m. Dec. 10, 1665, Elizabeth, widow [of Francis] Street. He gave land in Hing. to his son Thomas, who sold it 11 Oct. 1662, specifying these facts. Ch. Thomas bapt. Feb. 1637, John and Samuel bapt. Feb. 1639, Mary bapt. Oct. 6, 1642, Sarah bapt. Dec., 1645.

He made will 23 Aug. 1683, ae. about 80 years; prob. 5 March 1683-4. Beq. to wife Elizabeth, ch. Thomas, John, Samuel, Mary; dau. Sarah's son Thomas; son-in-law Joseph Willis; William Hack; Mary Street.

Thomas, cooper, malster, Hingham, propr. 1636. Wife Annis or Avith, dau. of Wm. Lane, d. Feb. 13 or 14, 1682-3. Ch. Thomas bapt. May 6, 1638, Joseph bapt. Nov. 20, 1640, Benjamin bapt. May 7, 1643, Deborah bapt. Aug. 3, 1645, (m. Samuel Thaxter,) Sarah bapt. Oct. 5, 1650, d. 7 July, 1658. He d. 28 Sept. 1691. Will prob. 27 Oct. 1692, beq. to ch. Thomas, Joseph, Benjamin, and Deborah, wife of Samuel Thaxter.

Thomas, weaver, cousin of Nicholas Jacob, and his wife, came with them from Hingham, Eng. and settled at our Hingham in 1633. Propr. 1635. Frm. March, 1637-8. Wife Susanna d. March, 1641; second wife Mary d. 21 Dec. 1683, an aged woman. No children known. He d. 2 Sept. 1675.

Will prob. 26 Oct. 1675; beq. all to wife Mary; after her death to his bro. Samuel and 7 specified ch. of his. Widow Mary d. 21 Dec. 1683.

Thomas, husbandman, bro. of Stephen, came from Windham, Eng. in 1638 and settled at Hingham. Frm. May 18, 1642; propr., town officer. Wife Margaret, dau. of Richard Langer; ch. Caleb b. Oct. 8, 1643, d. before 1659, Joshua b. May 3, 1645, Susanna b. Aug. 16, 1646, (m. Joseph Barstow,) Mary b. Feb. 10, 1648, (m. Thomas Marsh,) Thomas b. Sept. 29, 1650, Daniel b. May 14, 1654, d. 14 Feb. 1669-70, Elizabeth b. Dec. 2, 1656,

LINCOLN, etc., cont.
(m. Daniel Lincoln,) Ephraim b. and d. 1659, Ruth b. Nov. 19, 1662, (m. Samuel Gill).

He d. 16 Aug. 1692. Will dated 24 May, 1681, prob. 3 Nov. 1692, beq. to wife Margaret, daus. Susanna Barstow; Mary, wife of Francis Barber; Sarah, wife of Thomas Mash; Elizabeth, wife of Daniel Lincoln, and Ruth L.; sons Joshua, Caleb and Thomas. The widow d. 5 March, 1693-4.

LINFORD, LINCEFORD, LINSFORD, LINFURTH, LILFORD, LILFORTH,
Thomas, Yarmouth, suit in Es. Court by his attorney Tho. Brook, 1638. Suit brought concerning his goods in Plymouth Court 7 Dec. 1641. His wife Anne punished for crime.

Thomas, Rowley, propr. 1643. Bought land in Haverhill in 1648, and had grants of land beside. He deposed in 1662, ae. about 47. He m. Eliz. Emerson; ch. Elizabeth b. April 12, 1648, Mary b. Feb. 7, 1649, Martha b. March 12, 1654, d. June 7, 1660.
He d. Nov. 15, 1672; inv. taken 3 days later. His widow Elizabeth d. Feb. 20, 1692-3.

LINDALE, LINDELL, LENDALL,
James, tailor, Duxbury, propr. 1640. Sold land to Edmund Chandler shortly before his death.
Will prob. March 4, 1652; wife Mary, son Timothy, dau. Abigail. Admin. gr. after the death of the widow, Feb. 8, 1652-3, on behalf of the children. [Col. Rec., Reg. IV, 320, and VII, 15.]

LINDSEY, LINSEY, LYNSIE, LYNSEY,
Christopher, Lynn. He deposed in 1657 that he worked for Thomas Dexter in fencing Nahant when D. bought it of "Blacke Will or Duke William." He served in Pequot War in 1637; was wounded and disabled from service 20 weeks. For this the Gen. Court, 23 May, 1655, allowed him 3 li. Lawsuit in 1641. Built house on the common in 1647. [Es. Files.]
He d. April 11, 1669; will prob. 29 (4) 1669. Widow; ch. Eliezer, John and Nahomie.

Daniel, ae. 18, servant to Samuel Dix, passed exam. to go to Boston, N. E. April 8, 1637.

LINGE,
Benjamin, Charlestown, inhab. 1636.

LINKES, LINCKS,
Philip, Scituate, slain by the bow of a tree March 10, 1637. Admin. gr. 4 Dec. 1638, to Mr. Timothy Hatherly.

LINN, LINNE, LYNNE,
Henry, Boston, propr., punished for felony 28 Sept. 1630; whipped and banished in Sept. 1631, for writing letters to Eng. full of slander against government and churches. [W.] He ret. to Boston before 1636. Wife Sarah; ch. Sarah b. 20 (6) 1636, Elizabeth b. 27 (1) 1638, Ephraim b. 16 (11) 1639, Rebecca b. 15 (12) 1645; all bapt. 23 (3) 1647.
He d. about 1646; the widow m. 2, Hugh Gunnison.

LINNELL, LINNETT, LENNET, LARNETT,
Robert, called "my brother," by Mr. John Lothrop, adm. chh. Scituate with his wife Sept. 16, 1638, "having a letter of dismission from the church in London." Took oath of allegiance 1 Feb. 1638. Propr. at Barnstable 22 Jan. 1638-9. Ch. Hannah, (m. 15 March, 1648, John Davis of Bar.,) Abigail, (m. May, 1650, Joshua Lombard,) David, (m. March 9, 1652, Hannah Shelley).
He made will 23 Jan. 1662, prob. 12 March, 1662-3; beq. to wife; to son David; to Abigail and Bethya; to John Davis. The widow Penninnah petitioned the Court 29 Oct. 1669, to recover the house her husband had left her from the hands of David L.

LINTON, LYNTON,
Richard, Watertown, juryman, Gen. Court, Sept. 28, 1630. He rem. to Lancaster; sold house and lot (7) 1645, testified 6 (10) 1646, by his son-in-law Lawrence Waters. Deed of gift to dau. Ann, wife of L. W. 13 March, 1659; one to George Bennett and Lydia his wife my gr. ch. and to their son John, 7 (11) 1662.
He d. 30 (1) 1665. Inv. of his est. filed June 20, 1665.

LIPPINCOTT,
Richard, barber, Dorchester, frm. May 13, 1640. Rem. to Boston. Rec'd to chh. with wife Abigail 28 (10) 1644. Ch. Remembrance bapt. 19 (7) 1641, John b. 6 (9) 1644, Abigail b. and d. 1646.

LISHE,
Sarah, residence not stated, admin. of her est. gr. to Lieut. Duncan in Gen. Court 3 (10) 1639.

LISLE, LYSLE, LYLE, LYALL, LYOLL, LOYALL,
Francis, barber-surgeon, Boston, adm. inhab. 7 (6) 1638, adm. chh. 29 (7) 1639. Had lot at Braintree for 5 heads 25 (9) 1639. Bought house and shop in Bo. 10 (6) 1641. He went to Eng. with Stoughton and others in 1645; was made surgeon of the Earl of Manchester's Life Guards; did not ret. [W.] Wife Alice adm. chh. 29 (11) 1641; ch. Joseph b. 10 (8) 1638, Joseph bapt. 6 (8) 1639, Benjamin b. 1 (11) 1639, Mary bapt. 14 (12) 1640, Joseph b. 14 (1) 1642. The widow d. 30 (3) 1666, and admin. of her est. was gr. to Freegrace Bendall Nov. 1, 1666, on behalf of his wife Mary, the dau., and Joseph the son. of Francis and Alice Lisle. [Reg. XVI, 335.]

LISCOM, LISKUM,
Thomas, witness in Boston 25 (9) 1645. [A.]

LISTEN, LISSON,
Nicholas, Salem, 1637, propr. at Marblehead; named in the acct. of George Pollard in 1646. Sold land before 1649.

LISTER, LYSTER,
Andrew, Gloucester, frm. May 10, 1643; propr. 1649. A witness for Mr. Blinman in 1647. [Wenham rec.] Wife Barbara; ch. Daniel b. April 15, 1642, Andrew b. Dec. 26, 1644, Mary b. Dec. 26, 1647, Anne b. March 21, 1651.

LITCHFIELD, LEICHFIELD, LECHFIELD,
Lawrence, Scituate. Dau. Dependance b. 15 Feb. 1646. Wife Judith, dau. of Wm. Dennis, married after his death William Peaks; she testified 20 March, 1657-8, that her husband, on his death-bed, consented that John Allen of Scituate might adopt his son Josias.

LITTLE,
George, tailor, Newbury, propr. 1638. One of the early members of the Baptist church of N. Wife Alice d. 1 Dec. 1680. He m. 19 July, 1681, Eleanor Barnard. Ch. Sarah b. and d. 1652, Joseph b. 22 Sept. 1653, John b. 28 July, 1655, d. 20 July, 1672; Moses b. 11 March, 1657, Sarah b. 24 Nov. 1661.

He d. about 1694; widow Eleanor d. at Amesbury 27 Nov. 1694.

Thomas, Sen., Plymouth, taxed in 1632; bought a shallop in 1633. Atba. 1643. Rem. to Marshfield. He m. April 19, 1633, Ann Warren. She deposed to the will of Ralph Chapman, 6 June, 1672, ae. 60 years. Her son Ephraim, (b. 17 May, 1650,) deposed same day, ae. 22.

Thomas, Sen. made will 17 May, 1671, prob. with inv. 1 July, 1672. Beq. to wife; to sons Isaac, Ephraim, Thomas and Samuel; gr. ch. John Jones; servant Sarah Pomrey.

LITTLEFIELD,
Annis, ae. 38, with 6 children, and servants John Knight and Hugh Durdal, came in the Bevis in May, 1638.

Francis, Woburn, propr. 1646. Ch. Mary b. Dec. 14, 1646; wife Jane d. Dec. 20, 1646. Rem. to Wells, Maine.

John, Dedham, inhab. 31 (6) 1650. He m. 9 (3) 1650, Mary Mere; ch. Rebecca b. 26 (1) 1651, Expedience b. and d. 1659, John b. 5 Oct. 1664, Ebenezer b. 13 Oct. 1669.

LITTLEHALE, LITTLEHALL,
Richard, came in the Mary and John March 24, 1633. Settled at Newbury; propr. 1638. Rem. to Haverhill. He m. 15 Nov. 1647, Mary Lancton; ch. dau. b. and d. 1648, Mary b. Sept. 11, 1649, d. June 8, 1650, John b. Nov. 27, 1650, Richard b. and d. 1652, Ebenezer b. and d. 1654, Richard b. Aug. 24, 1655, Joseph b. 1656, d. 1657, Joseph b. and d. 1658, a son b. and d. 1659, Isaac b. July 9, 1660, Mary b. Jan. 31, 1661, Sarah b. and d. 1663. He mortg. house and 4 acres of land in Haverhill 27 (8) 1648. [Suff. De. I.]

He d. Feb. 18, 1663. The inv. of his est. is on file.

LIVERMORE, LEATHERMORE,
John, ae. 28, came in the Francis of Ipswich April 30, 1634. Settled at Watertown; potter; town officer, propr. 1636. Rem. to New Haven, Conn. before 1639 and ret. about 1653. Wife Grace; ch. recorded at New Haven: Samuel bapt. Aug. 15, 1641, Daniel bapt. Oct. 6, 1643, a dau. bapt. June 4, 1645, Mary bapt. Sept. 12, 1647; ch. rec. at Wat.: Edmund b. and d. in 1659.
He d. April 14, 1684. His will, dated 4 Jan. 1682, ae. 77 or 78 years; prob. 16 (4) 1684; beq. to wife Grace; to eldest son John; son-in-law John Coolidge's ch. by my dau. dec.; to only surviving dau. Martha; to sons Samuel and Nathaniel, and to the latter's daus. Hannah and Grace. The widow Grace made will 19 Dec. 1690; beq. to gr. son James Townsin, the ch. of dau. Hannah Coolidge, and dau. Martha, wife of Abraham Parker of Chelmsford; to sons John, Samuel and Nathaniel.

LLOYD,
Walter, ae. 27, came in the Hopewell in Sept. 1635.

LOBDELL, LOBDEN,
Nicholas, (Lobden,) Hingham, propr. June, 1635. Witness to the will of Thomas Mussell 27 July, 1640. [Reg. III, 179.] His wife d. in March, 1641. [Hob.] [Children] Isaac, (m. Martha, dau. of Samuel Ward; rem. to Hull); John, (m. 1, Hannah, dau. of John Leavitt, 2, —, dau. of Nathaniel Bosworth; rem. to Hull). See will of John, witnessed by Isaac, 26 Oct. 1673.

LOCK, LOCKE,
William, came in the Planter May 22, 1634, ae. 6 years, in care of kinsman Nicholas Davis. Res. at Woburn. Bought land of goodman Persons of Boston about 1651. [Mdx. De. IV, 229.] Deacon. Deposed 29 (10) 1658, ae. about 30 years. [Mdx. Files.] He m. at Woburn Nov. or Dec. 27, 1665, Mary, dau. of Wm. and Margery Clarke; she d. July 18, 1715. Ch. William b. Dec. 27, 1657, d. Jan. 9, 1658, William b. Jan. 18, 1658, John b. Aug. 1, 1661, Joseph b. March 8, 1663-4, Mary b. Oct. 16, 1666, Samuel b. Oct. 14, 1669, Ebenezer b. Jan. 8, 1673, James b. Nov. 14, 1677, Elizabeth b. Jan. 4, 1680, William b. June 28, 1684.
He d. June 16, 1720. See Trerice.

LITSTER,
Edward, servant to Stephen Hopkins, came in the Mayflower to Plymouth; completed his time, went to Virginia and d. there. [B.]

LOCKWOOD,
Edmund or Edward, Cambridge, juryman Nov. 9, 1630, frm. May 18, 1631, constable May, 1632. Wife Elizabeth; ch. John b. (9) 1632.
He d. before March 3, 1634-5, when the Court asked his widow Ruth to bring in writings left in his hands. Admin. gr. to Robert Lockwood on the children and estate.

Robert, sergt. Salem, frm. March 9, 1636-7. Appl. in 1637 for a lot next to his father Norman.

Robert, Watertown, propr. 1636. Sold marsh in Cambridge before 1638. Sold lands 30 (2) 1646, and rem. to Norwalk, Conn. Wife Susan; ch. Jonathan b. 1 (7) 1634, Deborah b. 12 (8) 1636, Joseph b. 6 (6) 1638, Daniel b. 2 (1) 1640, Ephraim b 1 (10) 1641, Gershom b. 6 (7) 1643.

LODGE,
Grace, Boston, maid servant to Mr. John Wilson, adm. chh. 28 (7) 1633.

LOMBARD, see LUMBARD.

LONG, LONGE,
John, husbandman, Weymouth, ae. 24, deposed June 24, 1641. [L.] Before Gen. Court 1 (4) 1641.

John, Plymouth, hired with Mr. Atwood Oct. 24, 1638.

Nathaniel, merchant, Boston, bought of John Turner 15 (12) 1647, one fourth part of the ship Charles, and of John Milom one eighth of the John. [A.] Owned house and land, 1645.

Philip, Ipswich, bought land 27 (10) 1647; Boston, propr. He deposed in 1658 concerning the death of David Selleck in Virginia; ae. about 40 years. Wife Anne adm. chh. 2 (1) 1650. Ch. Joseph b. and d. 1652.
He made will Oct. 27, 1658, bound to sea. Wife Anne deposed Nov. 13, 1659, as exec.

LONG, etc., cont.

Robert, came in 1623 to Plymouth; lands assigned to him in the section with Patience and Fear Brewster.

Robert, innholder, ae. 45, with wife Elizabeth, ae. 30, ch. Michell, ae. 20, Sarah, ae. 18, Robert, ae. 16, Eliza, ae. 12, Anne, ae. 10, Mary, ae. 9, Rebecca and John, ae. 8, Zachary, ae. 4, and Joshua, ae. 9 mos., with servant Luce Mercer, cert. from Dunstable, Eng., came in the Defense July 7, 1635. Settled at Charlestown. Adm. chh. with wife Elizabeth 17 (2) 1636. Joanna adm. chh. 4 (10) 1652. Hannah b. 2, bapt. 12 (1) 1637, Ruth b. and bapt. 3 (4) 1639, Deborah b. 10, bapt. 23 (6) 1642, Samuel b. 23 (2) 1647. He deposed 21 (1) 1655, ae. about 65 years. Abraham Hill calls him father. [Mdx. Files.]

He d. Jan. 9, 1663. Will dated July 10, 1658, prob. 6 Feb. 1663, beq. to wife; ch. Joshua, John, Michael, Zechariah, dau. Kempthorne, Ruth, Deborah, Hannah, Rebecca Rooe, Sarah Hill, Elizabeth Parker and Anna Converse; gr. son Samuel L. to have his portion when of age. Refers to bro. Johnson. The widow Elizabeth had a grandson Henry Cookery, an apprentice in 1673. She d. May 29, 1687, ae. 84.

Robert, Newbury, deacon. He deposed 7 (4) 1653, ae. about 32 years. He m. at N. in 1647, Alice Short; ch. a dau. [Mary,] b. Feb. 24, 1647, Abiel b. 19 Feb. 1648, Susanna b. 14 Nov. 1656, a dau. b. and d. 1661, a son [John,] b. April 16, 1664, a son b. March 18, 1665-6.

He d. 27 Dec. 1690. Widow Alice d. 17 Jan. 1690-1. Division of his est. agreed on Sept. 28, 1691, by his ch. Abiel, Mary, Rebecca, Susanna, Martha, Shubael and John, and signed by Abiel Long and Daniel Mushelaway, Nicholas Rawlings, Susanna Blandford and Martha, Shubael and John Long.

Nicholas, ae. 19, came in the Blessing in July, 1635.

LONGHORNE, LANGHORNE,

Richard, Rowley. He deposed to Bellingham matters in 1662, ae. 45. He m. 16 (11) 1647, Mary Crosby; ch. Elizabeth b. Sept., 1649, Constance b. Sept., 1652, Thomas bur. 8 (12) 1653, Samuel b. 1654, bur. 1660, Thomas b. 1657, bur. 1660, Sarah b. 16 (12) 1660, Bethiah b. 9 (4) 1662, Richard b. 20 May, 1665, Thomas b. 1667, d. 1668.

LONGHORNE, etc., cont.

He d. at Haverhill 13 (12) 1668; will dated Feb. 10, 1668, prob. 30 March, 1669, beq. to dau. Elizabeth a double portion; the other three daus. to have single shares; beq. to servant Samuel, son of Obadiah Wood. Testimony was given that he desired his bro. Thomas L. to be one of the execs., but he declined on account of the distance of his abode; also that he sent for his bro., John Pickard, to visit him, and asked him to confer with the children's grandmother and their two aunts, to whose care he left them. The dau., Sarah, petitioned Ipswich Court 4 (3) 1674; referred to her grandmother Constante Crosby, and to her uncle Thomas L. of Cambridge.

Thomas, butcher, and town drummer, Cambridge. He deposed 2 (1) 1671-2, ae. about 50 years. [Mdx. Files.] He m. about 1646, Sarah, dau. of Bartholomew Green; ch. Thomas b. and d. 1647, Sarah b. 26 (12) 1648, Elizabeth, Mary, Samuel bapt. Dec. 9, 1660, Mercy bapt. May 11, 1662, [Mi.] Patience.

He d. May 6, 1685. Will dated April 24, 1685, ae. about 69 years, beq. to wife [Sarah] and three daus. Sarah, Elizabeth and Mary. Prob. 16 (4) 1685.

LONGLEY, see Langley.

LOOFE, see Luffe.

LOOK, LOOKE, LOOKER, LOKER, LOCKER, LUCAR, LUKER,

Elizabeth, widow, Sudbury, d. 18 (3) 1648.

Henry, Sudbury, propr. 1639, frm. May 10, 1643. He m. 24 (1) 1647, Hannah Brewer.

He d. Oct. 14, 1688.

John, Sudbury, took oath of fidelity in 1645; frm. May 6, 1646. Wife Mary; ch. Mary b. 28 (7) 1653.

He d. 18 (4) 1653. The widow bought house and lot in 1654.

Robert, [Sudbury.] He witnessed Webcowites' deed to Jotham Gibbons 13 (11) 1639. Was bondsman for John Griffin 20 (3) 1640. [L.]

LORD,

Richard, Cambridge, propr., frm. March 4, 1634-5.

Robert, Senior, Ipswich, frm. March 3, 1635-6. Town officer. Recorder, deputy. He was a cousin to John L. of Sudbury, Suffolk, Eng., to whom he and his mother Katharine sold a tenement in S. shortly before the date of his will, 1 March, 1640. The mother came to Ipswich; propr. 1637; was made a commoner in 1641. [Reg. XXXI, 160, and L. 111.] He wrote a letter to Wm. Bartholomew, calling him brother; mentioned his own wife and son Thomas Lord; letter presented in Mdx. Court Feb. 2, 1673. He deposed July 30, 1660, ae. 57 years. [Es. Files.]
He wrote his will 28 June, 1683; it was probated 25 Sept. folg.; he beq. to his wife Mary, mentioning that they had lived together in marriage almost 53 years; to eldest son Robert; to sons Thomas and Samuel, living at Charlestown; to son Nathaniel; to dau. Sarah Wilson; to Mary, William, Joseph and Samuel, the ch. of dau. Chandler, dec.; to dau. Abigail Foster and her ch. and to dau. Hannah Grow and her ch. provided that they pay a certain sum to their sister Susanna Osgood and her ch.; to gr. son Samuel Lord, now living with me; to gr. son Robert Lord "tersha," (*tertius*.)

Robert, Boston, 1650. Wife Rebecca, dau. of Christopher Stanley; her mother gave her part of a house she was already living in, adjoining her sister Thurston's Aug. 18, 1652. Ch. Robert b. (2) 1651.

Thomas, smith, ae. 50, with wife Dorothy, ae. 46, and ch. Thomas, ae. 16, Ann, ae. 14, William, ae. 12, John, ae. 10, Robert, ae. 9, and Dorothy, ae. 4, came in the Elizabeth and Ann in April, 1635.

William, cutler, Salem, propr. 1635. Bought of John Woolcut 23 (9) 1635, the house built for Mr. Francis Higginson, later occupied by Mr. Roger Williams. [Es. Inst. Coll. VIII, 252.] Frm. Sept. 6, 1639. Town officer. His wife Abigail memb. chh. 1636.
Will dated March 2, 1668, prob. 24 (4) 1673; "ancient;" beq. to wife Abigail; kinsman William Lord, with his ch. William and Abigail; Mrs. Felton, widow; Joseph Grafton, Sen. and Richard Prince. The widow made will 26 April, prob. 15 June, 1682; beq. to all the ch. of her husband's kinsman W. L. by

LORD, etc., cont.

name; and to her second husband, Resolved White.

William, Salem, frm. Es. Court 1 (5) 1640. He deposed in 1680, ae. about 60 years; his wife Jane, ae. about 56.
Will dated 10 Nov., prob. 24 Nov. 1685; beq. to wife Jane; sons Joseph, William and Jeremiah; daus. Dinah, Abigail, Margaret, Elizabeth Godsoe and Jane.

LORING,

Thomas, Hingham, propr., frm. March 3, 1635-6. Deputy, deacon. His house was burned 15 March, 1645-6. Rem. to Hull. Propr. 1657. Son John was also propr. at the time. Wife Jane; ch. Thomas, John b. 22 Dec. 1630, [Hing. rec.] Isaac bapt. Jan. 20, 1639-40, d. Feb. folg., Isaac bapt. Jan. 9, 1641-2, d. 2 March, 1644-5, Josiah bapt. Jan. 9, 1641, Benjamin bapt. Nov. 24, 1644.
He d. 4 April, 1661. Inv. taken 27 June, 1662. The widow d. 25 Aug. 1672. Will dated 10 July, prob. 23 Oct. folg., beq. to eldest son Thomas L. and Hannah, his wife; to sons John and Benjamin; to son Josiah's wife.

LOOMAN, LUMAN, LUME,

Mrs. Anne, Roxbury. The Court ordered inv. of her goods made March 3, 1634-5. This may mean the goods of her husband, of which she was to be admin. If so she probably rem. to Weymouth, and it was her nunc. will which was prob. 21 (8) 1659; gr. ch. Hannah Jackson, heir and exec.; gr. ch. John Monticue (Montague) that dwells at the Eastward. Inv. taken by Maximilian Jewett and Samuel Brocklebanke, ret. in Essex Court April 17, 1662.

LOOMIS, LOMAS, LUMMAS, LUMMUS,

Edward, ae. 24, embarked on the Susan and Ellen in April, 1635; Edward, ae. 27, embarked on the Elizabeth April 17, 1635. Both entries probably refer to the same person, who settled at Ipswich; weaver; commoner in 1641. Wife Mary deposed in 1672, ae. about 66 years.
He d. 29 Aug. 1682. Will prob. 26 Sept. beq. to sons Jonathan, Samuel and Nathaniel, son John Sherrin and my dau. his wife; son Samuel's children.

LOTHROP, LOWTHROP, LATHROP, LOTHROP, etc., cont.
LOTHROPP,

Rev. John, was minister at Egerton in Kent. Rem. to London in 1624, and was pastor of a Congregational church. The archbishop caused the arrest of himself and 43 members of the church April 29, 1632, and most of them were imprisoned for 2 years for the simple offense of practising the teachings of the New Testament. His first wife died while he was in prison. [Mor.] He and some others were released on condition of leaving the country, and came to N. E.; he arrived with his family 18 Sept. 1634, and soon after organized a church at Scituate. "So many of us as had been in covenant before" united Jan. 8, 1634-5, and others were added shortly. He was adm. frm. Plym. Col. 7 Feb. 1636-7. Two years later he, with the principal part of the church, rem. to found the church and town of Barnstable. His record of the two congregations was copied in 1769 by Rev. Ezra Stiles; the original having since been lost, this copy has been printed by the Hist. Gen. Society, in Reg. IX and X. Mr. Lothrop was a man of deep piety, great zeal and large ability. He m. a second wife, whose name is not on our records, who came here with him, joined the chh. June 14, 1635, and survived him. Children: Jane, (m. April 8, 1635, Samuel Fuller, Jr.,) Barbara, (m. July 19, 1638, John Emerson,) Thomas, (m. Dec. 11, 1639, "brother Larnett's daughter, widow Ewer in the Bey,"—Sarah, widow of Thomas Ewer of Charlestown,) Samuel, (m. Nov. 28, 1644, Elizabeth Scudder,) Joseph, (m. Dec. 11, 1650, Mary Ansell,) John, (named in the father's will, believed by descendants to be the John bapt. at Barn. Feb. 9, 1644-5,) Benjamin, (named in the will,) Barnabas bapt. June 6, 1636, Abigail bapt. Nov. 2, 1639, Bathshua bapt. Feb. 27, 1641, and two others who d. in infancy.

His will dated Aug. 10, prob. Dec. 8, 1653, beq. to wife; to eldest son Thomas; to son John who is in England; son Benjamin, daus. Jane and Barbara; to each of the rest of his children, both his and his wife's.

Mark, Salem, propr. 1642; a kinsman of Thomas L.

Capt. Thomas, Salem, Beverly, propr., frm. May 14, 1634; town officer, deputy. Suit in court, 1659. Served in Acadia in 1654-5. He m. Bethia, dau. of Daniel Rea; left no child, but adopted a dau. of a cousin of his wife, Sarah Gott.

He d. in the war in 1675; nunc. will prob. 22 (10) 1675; beq. a farm to his sister, the wife of Ezekiel Cheever; another to his dau. Sarah Gott Lothrop; land to the town for the use of the ministry; to his bro. Joshua Rea and his 4 youngest ch.; to Noah Fisk; to his wife. [Es. Inst. Coll. II, 177; Reg. XXXVIII, 332.] The widow m. 2, Joseph Grafton, and 3, Wm. Goodhue.

LOTTES,
John, Springfield, propr. 1645.

LOVE,
Hezekiah, Taunton, juryman, Plym. Court, 1650.
John, Boston, in Court 7 July, 1635.

LOVEJOY,
John, Andover, propr. 1650. He deposed in 1669, ae. about 47 years. He m. at Ipswich, Jan. 1, 1651, Mary Osgood; ch. Mary b. 11 April, 1652, Sara b. 11 April, 1654, William b. 21 April, 1657, Ann b. 21 Dec. 1659, Christopher b. 1 March, 1661, Joseph b. 8 Feb. 1662, Benjamin b. 4 Dec. 1664, Nathaniel b. 29 May, 1667, Abigail b. 20 Aug. 1669, Debora b. 4 Nov. 1671, Ebenezer b. 22 Jan. 1673. The wife Mary d. 15 July, 1675. He d. 7 Nov. 1690.

His will dated 1 Sept., codicil 23 Oct. 1690, prob. March 31, 1691, beq. to wife Hannah, with whom he had lived in a married condition about 13 years, abundant provision, referring to marriage contract; portion already given to William, eldest son now living; to other sons Christopher, Nathaniel, Joseph and Ebenezer; to daus. Sarah Johnson, Ann Blancher, and Abigail and Deborah L. Refers to son Benjamin, for whom certain lands had been intended, and to gr. son John L. Desires his bro. Thomas Osgood and sons William and Joseph L. to have charge of son Ebenezer and gr. dau. Frances.

LOVELL, LOWELL, see LOVETT,
Robert, husbandman, ae. 40, with wife Elizabeth, ae. 35, children Zaccheus, ae. 15, Anne, ae. 16, John, ae. 8, Ellen and James, ae. 1 year, and servant Joseph Chickin, ae. 16, embarked from Weymouth, Eng., before

LOVELL, etc., cont.
March 20, 1635. Settled at Weymouth; recd. arms from Pynchon in 1636; propr. 1643.

Will dated 3 (2) 1652, prob. 25 June, 1672; beq. to wife; sons John and James; son-in-law Andrew Ford and his eldest and youngest sons; to son John's son.

Thomas, Sen., came from Dublin, Ireland, where he had lived in the house with William and Rebecca Bacon in 1639. Settled at Salem about 1641. Rem. to Ipswich, propr. 1647. Deposed 25 Dec. 1694, ae. about 74 years. [Reg. XXXIX, 28.]

William, captain, Dorchester, one of the original company who came in 1629-30. [Bl.] His wife Wybro before Gen. Court 7 (1) 1636-7. Suit at Salem Court 28 (1) 1637.

LOVERING, LOVERUN,
John, Watertown, yeoman, frm. May 25, 1636. Town officer.

Nunc. will, dated Oct. 4, 1638, prob. 9 (9) 1644, beq. 100 li. to his bro. that had children; 20 li. to the church after his wife's death; rest to his wife Ann. She m. June 19, 1639, Mr. Edmund Browne; they gave power of attorney 25 (5) 1639, for the collection of what was due him in Eng. [Reg. III, 79 and Suff. De. I, 59.]

LOVET, LOVETT, LOVITT, LOVELL,
Daniel, Salem, res. 1638. Rem. to Braintree. He and his mother had grant of land in 1639, 12 acres for 3 heads. Leased 60 acres of land from the town of Boston 30 (7) 1650. Son-in-law of Robert Blott. Rem. to Mendon. Wife Joanna deposed June 18, 1670, ae. about 50 years; ch. James b. 5 (8) 1648, Mary b. 1 (7) 1651, Martha b. 4 (7) 1654, Hannah b. 30 (1) 1656.

He made will 26 Dec. 1691, prob. April 28, 1692; beq. to wife Joannah, son James, and daus. Mary Tyler, Martha Fairbank and Hannah Ryder.

John, Salem, 1638. Res. at Mackerel Cove in 1641; see Kettle, John. Mary [his wife?] adm. chh. Salem 1 (7) 1650. Ch. Symond, Joseph and Mary bapt. 8 (7) 1650, Bethiah bapt. 13 (4) 1652, Abigail bapt. 18 (1) 1654-5.

Mary, memb. Dorchester chh. before 1639. [See Leavitt.]

LOW, LOWE, LOE,
John, wheelwright, Boston, 1640. [L.] [Suff. De. VI, 230.] Bought land 1645. Wife Elizabeth adm. chh. 15 (3) 1642. A son d. 1 (10) 1653. His son Anthony gave letter of attorney 22 (9) 1647, to John Prick, tallow-chandler, Alderman Bury, to receive legacy from Mary Smith, late of Aldermanbury or Cheapside. [A.]

He d. 1 (10) 1653. Admin. gr. to son Anthony, he to provide for his mother during her life. [Reg. VIII, 128 v.]

John, Hingham, propr. 1648. Sold home lot and other lands 7 March, 1654-5. He m. Feb. 28, 1648, Elizabeth, dau. of John Stoddard; she d. 14 Sept. 1658. Ch. Elizabeth b. July 16, 1650, Tabitha b. Jan. 7, 1652, d. 9 (6) 1654, John b. April 3, 1655, Tabitha b. June 5, 1658.

He d. 25 Jan. 1696.

Susannah, ae. 86, d. at Watertown 19 (6) 1684.

Thomas, Ipswich, propr. 1641, bought land in 1647. His son Thomas m. Martha, dau. of Thomas Boreman, q. v. He deposed in 1660, ae. about 55, and Sarah, ae. about 23.

His will dated 20 April, prob. 6 Nov., inv. taken 5 Nov. 1677; beq. to wife Susannah; sons John and Thomas; daus. Margaret and Sarah; gr. ch. Thomas Low, Margaret Davison, Sarah Safford and Sarah Low.

LOWDEN,
Richard, husbandman, Charlestown, adm. chh. 15 (11) 1641, frm. May 18, 1642. Propr. at Woburn 1640, but res. at Char. Bought house and land 27 (8) 1643. Town officer, 1654. [Mdx. Files.] He deposed in 1662, ae. about 44 years. Wife Mary, dau. of Rice Cole; ch. John b. 10 (3), bapt. 15 (3) 1641, Jeremy b. and d. in 1643, Mary b. 24 (12) 1644.

LOWELL, LOWLE,
John, Newbury, propr. 1638. Frm. June 2, 1641. Deputy, comr., clerk of the writs. He m. Elizabeth, dau. of the widow Elizabeth Goodale, formerly of Great Yarmouth, Eng. Ch. rec. at N.: Joseph b. 28 Nov. 1639, Benjamin b. 12 Sept. 1642, Thomas b. 4 June, 1644, Elizabeth b. 16 Feb. 1646.

LORD, cont.

He d. 10 July, 1647. Will dated 9 (4), prob. 27 (8) 1647, inv. taken 30 (4) 1647. Beq. to wife Elizabeth one half of his est. and 20 li. out of what came from her mother; to his first wife's children, John, Mary, Peter, James and Joseph; to his second wife's children, Benjamin and Elizabeth; daus. Elizabeth and Mary to have of their own mother's clothes. Sister Johan Gerrish and bro. William G.; other persons. [Reg. VII, 35.] The Court decided that Elizabeth should have clothes which had belonged to her gr. mo. Elizabeth Goodale, in possession of her mother now living; Mary, ae. about 17 years, was permitted 15 Oct. 1650, to receive her portion and go to her friends in Eng. Account rendered in Es. prob. (9) 1684. Elizabeth m. 1 Jan. 1667, Philip Nelson.

The widow Elizabeth's will, made 17 (1) 1650, was proved 28 (8) 1651. She beq. to her sister Tappine; to her sons-in-law John, James and Joseph Lowle; to son Benjamin and dau. Elizabeth. Bro. Thomas Millard to keep Benjamin till he go forth to be an apprentice. Bros. T. M., Richard L., Abraham T. and Wm. Gerrish overseers to see Elizabeth brought up to her needle and suitably instructed.

Percival, merchant, Newbury, propr. 1638. Wife Rebecca d. Dec. 28, 1645. He d. 8 Jan 1664.

Richard, bro. of John, Newbury, propr. 1637. He admin. on the est. of his bro. John; was relieved by the Court 18 May, 1653, being very sickly. He deposed in 1674, ae. 72 years. Wife Margaret. Ch. [Percival b. 1639,] Rebecca b. 27 Jan. 1641, Samuel b. 1644, Thomas b. 28 Sept. 1649.

He d. 5 Aug. 1682. Will dated June 25, 1681, prob. Sept. 26, 1682. Beq. to wife Margaret, sons Percival, Thomas, Samuel.

LUDDAM, LUDDEN,

James, servant to William Almy and David Johnson; the Court ordered payment to be made to him March 1, 1635-6. Settled at Weymouth; corporal, town officer. Ch. Mary b. 17 (10) 1636, Sarah b. 15 (9) 1639, Sarah b. 5 (4) 1642.

Will prob. Feb. 16, 1692-3; "in old age;" beq. to sons Benjamin, Joseph and James; wife to have life use of est.

LUCAS, LUKAS,

Marie, maid servant to Mrs. Anne Newgate, adm. chh. Boston 29 (10) 1633.

LUDDINGTON, LOUDDINGTON,

Christian, ae. 18, came in the Hopewell in April, 1635.

William, weaver, Charlestown, his house beyond the half-mile limit from the village which had been set by the Gen. Court; law repealed 13 May, 1640. Res. at Malden. He deposed in 1657, ae. 50 years. [Mdx. Files.] Ch. Thomas, ae. 20 and John, ae. 17, deposed same day. Wife Ellen; ch. Mary b. 6 (12) 1642, Matthew b. at Malden 16 (10) 1657, d. 12 (11) 1657.

He rem. to New Haven, and d. there. Petition for admin. made in Mdx. co. 1 (8) 1661, by John Wayte. James Barrat, admin. filed inv. 1 (2) 1662.

LUDKIN, LUCKIN, LUTKINE,

George, with wife and son, came in 1635 and settled at Hingham. [Cu.] Propr. Frm. March 3, 1635-6. Rem. to Braintree. He was bur. 22 (12) 1647. Admin. gr. 31 (6) 1648 to Aaron Ludkin. [Reg. VII, 175.] Aaron, tanner, Charlestown, 1648; town officer 1649; m. Hannah, dau. of Geo. Hepburn, was probably this son and administrator.

Job, Boston. Wife Sarah; ch. Sarah b. 7 (10) 1645.

William, b. at Norwich, Eng., locksmith, ae. 33, with wife Elizabeth, ae. 34, with one child and one servant, Thomas Homes, passed exam. April 8, 1637, to go to Boston in N. E., to reside; mortg. two houses at Marblehead in possession of Wm. Chichester 18 (5) 1643. Purchased in 1647 a house and shop of John Button, who confirmed the title to the widow and children 28 May, 1656. Ch. Esther bur. (8) 1645.

He was drowned 27 (1) 1652. Admin. gr. to widow Elizabeth. Two children, a son and a daughter. [Reg. VIII, 58.] She d. Aug. 20, 1676; made will 18 Aug., prob. Dec. 6, 1676, bequeathing all to her dau. Lydia Alleyn, and her children; admin. gr. to her son-in-law Edward Alleyn, shop-keeper.

LUDWELL,

John, ae. 50, came in the Confidence, April 11, 1638.

LUDLOW, LUDLOWE,
Col. George, Esquire, Dorchester, appl. frm. Oct. 19, 1630. Ret. to Eng. soon; then went to York, Virginia. Will, dated 8 Sept. and 23 Oct. 1655; prob. at London 1 Aug. 1656. Wife Elizabeth; nephew Thomas L.; bro. Gabriel, dec.; nephew Jonathan, son of his bro. Roger L., now living at Dublin, Ireland; residue to the ch. of Roger, who admin. [Reg. XL, 300.]

Mr. Roger, gent., merchant, chosen an Asst. of the Mass. Bay Co. in Eng. 10 Feb. 1629-30, came over in 1630. Settled at Dorchester. Appld. for frm. Oct. 19, 1630. Town officer, deputy governor. Rem. to Windsor, Conn. in 1636. One of the comrs. of the United Colonies, 1651-3. Rem. to Virginia. Children named in the will of his bro. George: Jonathan, Joseph, Roger, Anne, Mary, and Sarah.

LUFFE, LUFF, LOOF,
John, came in the Mary and John May 24, 1633. Settled at Salem. Propr. 1636; weaver. Lawsuit in 1641. Sold land in 1648. [Wife] Bridget adm. chh. 16 (3) 1647.

LUGG, LUGGE,
John, Boston, had a grant of land at Braintree 27 (11) 1639 for 9 heads. Wife Jane adm. chh. 10 (12) 1638; ch. Elizabeth b. 7 (1) 1638, Mary bapt. 25 (7) 1642, (m. 11 Feb. 1658, Nathaniel Barnard,) John bapt. 4 (6) 1644.

LUMPKIN, LUMKIN,
Richard, Ipswich, propr. 1638, frm. March 2, 1638. Deputy 1638-9; deacon. Inv. of his est. taken 23 (9) 1642. His widow Sarah, mentioned in Ipsw. rec. Dec. 25, 1643, m. 2, Dea. Simon Stone, of Wat., and sold lands in Topsfield in 1660. She was related to the Anglers. [Mdx. Files, 1663.]

William, weaver. One of the frm. and proprs. of Yarmouth, 7 Jan. 1638-9. [Plym. Col. Rec.] Constable, 1639-40.
Will, dated July 23, 1668, prob. 29 Oct. 1671. Wife Thomasin; dau. Thomasin, wife of John Sunderling; gr. ch. William Gray and Elisha and Bethia Eldred. [Reg. VII, 236.]

LUSE,
Harke, Scituate atba. 1643.

LUMBERT, LUMBARD, LUMBAR,
John, Springfield, propr. 1646; town officer. He m. at New Haven, [rec. at Spr.] 1 (7) 1647, Johan Prichard. Ch. John b. 20 (5) 1648, David b. 16 (8) 1650, Nathaniel b. 6 (7) 1653.

He d. in May, 1672; inv. pres. Sept. 24 folg.

Thomas, Dorchester, propr., frm. May 18, 1631. Rem. about 1639 to Barnstable. Inn-keeper, 1639. Ch. Bernard, (deposed in 1668, ae. 60 years; adm. chh. Sci. 23 (4) 1639;) Joshua, (adm. chh. Bar. March 14, 1646;) Joseph, (deposed in 1667, ae. 29 years;) Jobaniah, (bapt. at Dorch. 23 (4) 1639;) Jedidiah, (bapt. at Bar. Dec. 5, 1641;) Benjamin, (bapt. at Bar. Aug. 5, 1643.)

Will dated March 25, 1662, prob. 7 March, 1664. Wife Joyce; ch. Bernard, Joshua, Joseph, Jedidiah, Benjamin, Caleb, Jemima, and Margaret Coleman; sons-in-law Joseph Benjamine and Edward Coleman; gr. ch. Abigail Benjamin. [Reg. VI, 186.]

LUND, LUNDE,
Thomas, merchant, late of Hingham in N. E., made letter of attorney Oct. 24, 1640, to Thomas Grubb of Boston, to receive moneys due to him. App. attorney for London parties March 28, 1646. [Suff. De. II, 74.] Called also "leather-dresser, of London." [L.] A Thomas Lund was an early settler of Dunstable, a generation later.

LUNT,
Enoch, blacksmith, Weymouth, recd. a letter of attorney to collect money at Comberton, co. Cambridge, Eng., 25 (5) 1641. [L.]

Henry, came in the Mary and John, March 26, 1633; settled at Newbury in 1635; frm. May 2, 1638; propr. Ch. Sarah b. Nov. 8, 1639, Daniel b. 17 May, 1641, John b. 30 Nov. 1643, Priscilla b. 16 Feb. 1645, Mary b. 13 July, 1648, Elizabeth b. 29 Dec., 1650, Henry b. 20 Feb. 1652. He d. July 10, 1662. Will prob. Sept. 30, 1662; wife Anne; sons Daniel, John and Henry; daus. Sarah, Priscilla, Mary and Elizabeth. The widow m. 2, Joseph Hills. [Reg. IX, 33.]

LUSH,
Henry, ae. 17, servant of Richard Wade, came from Weymouth, Eng. before March 20, 1635.

LUSHER,
Eleazer, Dedham, adm. propr. 18 (5) 1637, memb. chh. 1638, frm. March 13, 1638-

LUSHER, cont.

9. Town officer, major, deputy, Asst. Wife adm. chh. 1639. She d. and he m. in Charleston Aug. 8, 1662, Mary, dau. of George Bunker and widow of John Gwinn. Samuel, [his son?] d. 30 (10) 1638.

He d. 3 (9) 1672; [S.] his relict Mary d. 26 (12) 1672-3. No child referred to in their wills; Lydia, dau. of John and Martha (Bunker) Starr, was practically an adopted dau. and recd. beq. from both. [See introduction to Dedham Town Records.]

LUSON,

John, Dedham, propr. 18 (5) 1637, memb. chh. 1638; his wife soon after. Town officer; com. to end small businesses.

Will, dated 15 (12) 1660, prob. May 25, 1661, inv. taken 18 (3) 1661. "Age and infirmities increasing daily;" beq. house, lands, etc., to kinsman Thomas Battely of D. for Thomas, Robert, Susan, Mary and John, ch. of Robert L. in Old Eng., after death of Martha, the testator's wife; kinswoman Anne, wife of William Bearstowe of Scituate. [Reg. X, 267, and XXXI, 178.] The widow d. 5 (5) 1679.

LUST,

John, Salem; he and his wife living separately in 1648. [Es. files.]

LUTHER,

— The Gen. Court decreed 22 May, 1646, that the widow Luther should have the balance of her husband's wages according to sea custom, after allowing to the merchants what they had paid for the redemption of her son.

LUXFORD,

James, herdman, servant to Gov. Winthrop, [L.] Charlestown; propr. 1637; propr. at Cambridge before 1638. Res. at Duxbury, 1641. Wife Elizabeth; ch. Elizabeth b. (7) 1637, Reuben b. (12) 1640. Divorced, fined and punished in 1639 and 1640, for bigamy and other offenses.

LYDGET, see Alford.

LYFORD,

Ann, ae. 13, came in the Susan and Ellen in May, 1635.

Rev. John, went from Eng. to Ireland about 1620; came to Plymouth in 1624. Proved wicked and treasonable. Rem. to

LYFORD, cont.

Nantasket, then to Cape Ann with Conant, [Hub.] thence to Virginia; d. before Oct. 10, 1634, when his worthy widow Sarah m. Edmund Hubbard, Sen. of Hingham. His ch. Ruth and Mordecai receipted in 1641-2 for legacies left them in the will of their father. Ruth m. April 19, 1643, James Bate. [B.] [Suff. De. I, 27.] His son Obediah, clerk, d. in Ireland, and Mr. Hubbard was chosen guardian 6 Aug., 1639, of Mordecai, then 14 yrs. old, who was to receive property which Obediah had left. Their mother Sarah, "widow of John Lyford, clerk," dec., and wife of Edmund Hubbard, planter, ae. about 53 years," testified. [L.]

LYMAN,

Richard, came to Roxbury (9) 1631; brought children Phillis, Richard, Sarah and John. Rem. to Conn. [E.] Frm. July 11, 1633. Wife Sarah, dau. Phillis m. William Hills.

He d. in 1640. Genealogy.

LYNDE, LINDE, LINE, LYNE,

Mary, ae. 6, came in the Abigail in July, 1635.

Thomas, malster, Charlestown, adm. chh. with wife Margerite 4 (12) 1634. Frm. March 4, 1634-5. Propr.; deputy. He gave letter of attorney 30 (10) 1647, to John Allen of Char. to ask of the Chamberlain of the city of London, Eng. the spending money due Henry Jordan, whose guardian he was, on account of £ XL paid into the Chamber 8 Oct. 1633, by Margaret Jordan (now his wife) for the use of Henry, son and orphan of Henry Jordan, late citizen and cutler of London. A receipt to her, as widow of H. J., dated 15 May, 1632, and one to Thomas Lynde of Dunstable, co. Bedford, yeoman, her husband, 8 Oct., 1633, are annexed. [A.] He and his wife Rebecca made deed of gift to her dau. Rebecca, wife of Thomas Jenner in 1670. His wife d. Aug. 23, 1662; he m. Dec. 6, 1665, Rebecca Trerice; she d. an aged woman, Dec. 8, 1688. Ch. Thomas adm. chh. 4 (9) 1643, Henry d. 9 (2) 1646, Mary, Joseph b. 3, bapt. 5 (4) 1636, Sarah b. 16 (2) bapt. 14 (2) 1639, Hannah b. 2, bapt. 8 (3) 1642, Samuel b. 14 (8) 1644, Elizabeth b. at Malden April 20, 1650, Joseph b. Dec. 13, 1652.

He d. dec. 30, 1671. Will dated 21 Dec. prob. 2 (12) 1671, beq. to wife Rebecca, sons

LYNDE, etc., cont.

Joseph, Samuel and Thomas, son-in-law Robert Pierpoint in right of his wife, dau. Hannah Trerise, dau. Mary Wicks of Succenessett; to the teaching elder of the church; to widow Syms.

LYON, LION,

John, Marblehead, taxed in 1637; gave note in 1638 for payment of money to George Ching of Salem. Propr. 1649.

Peter, weaver, Dorchester, 1639, propr., frm. May 2, 1649. Susanna, [his wife?] memb. chh. before 1639. His wife "Ann" d. Nov. 26, 1689. Ch. Mary b. 4 (9) 1650, Elhanan b. 23 (7) 1652, Nathaniel b. 28 (10) 1654, Susanna bapt. 28 (1) 1658, Ebenezer b. 20 (12) 1660, Peter bapt. 6 (7) 1663, Israel b. 21 (8) 1666, Mehetable b. 23 (8) 1669, Eliab b. July 12, 1673, Freefrace b. Aug. 18, 1677. Admin. of his est. was gr. 8 Jan. 1694-5, to his son-in-law Daniel Morey, carter, of Boston.

Mr. Richard, sent over to Cambridge from England about 1641 by Mr. Henry Mildmay as a tutor to his son, assisted in revising the Bay Psalm Book. [C. M.]

William, husbandman, Roxbury, memb. chh. with wife (Sarah) about 1647. He m. June 17, 1646, Sarah Ruggles; she d. 9 Feb. 1688-9. He m. 2, Martha —. Ch. John bapt. April 10, 1647, Thomas bapt. Aug. 8, 1648, Samuel bapt. June 16, 1650, William bapt. 18 (5) 1652, Joseph bapt. Nov. 30 or 3 (10) 1654, Sarah bapt. 8 (1) 1657, Jonathan bapt. 9 (7) 1666, d. 30 (3) 1668.

He was bur. 21 May, 1692. Will prob. 20 Oct. 1692, beq. to sons John, Thomas, Samuel, William and Joseph; to wife Martha. The widow d. 4 Aug. 1694.

LYTHERLAND, see LEATHERLAND.

LYVARS,

Judith, Boston, maid servant to Robert Harding, adm. chh. 3 (1) 1635.

MACY, MACIE, MASIE, MASSY,

George, Taunton, atba. 1643; in court 20 Aug. 1654. Town officer; captain. Will dated 20 June, prob. 5 Sept. 1693, beq. to wife Susanna; daus. Elizabeth Hodges, Sarah Black, Mary Williams, Rebecca Williams and Deborah Macy.

MACY, etc., cont.

Thomas, clothier, merchant, Newbury, propr., frm. Sept. 6, 1639. Rem. to Salisbury. Was servant and agent to Mr. Francis Dow about 1640. [Depos. of Richard Currier.] Propr. 1640; town officer; deputy. Rem. about 1659 to Chilmark; his was the first family on Nantucket Island. A friend to the Quakers. He sold certain lands 18 Dec. 1657, to Peter Gee of Newton Ferris, co. of Devon, fisherman. He m. Sarah Hopcott, q. v. who d. in 1706, ae. 94. Ch. Sarah b. July 9, 1644, d. 1645 or 1646, Sarah b. Aug. 1, 1646, (m. William Worth,) Mary b. Dec. 4, 1648, (m. Wm. Bunker,) Bethia, (m. Joseph Gardner,) Thomas b. Sept. 2, 1653, John b. July 14, 1655, Francis b. 1657, d. 1658.

He d. 19 June, 1682. Admin. of his est. 1 Aug. folg. See Genealogy.

MACUMBER, MAYCUMBER,

John, carpenter, Taunton, atba. 1643, in Court 20 Aug. 1644.

William, cooper, Dorchester, in company with Henry Madeley of the same town, carpenter, had liberty to dwell at Plymouth 2 April, 1638. Rem. to Duxbury, atba. 1643. Rem. to Marshfield.

Inv. taken May 27, rendered 7 June, 1670; Priscilla, Thomas and Matthew Macumber deposed. [Reg. VII, 180.] The son Matthew of Taunton, ae. about 25 years, made will 9 Dec. 1675, bequeathing to mother and bros. John, Thomas and William.

MADDOX, see MATTOCKS,

John, sawyer, cert. from Stepney parish, Eng., came in the Planter March 22, 1634. Settled at Salem.

He d. April 22, 1643. Will prob. 6 (5) 1644, referred to in Court files.

MADER,

Robert, Boston, servant to Wm. Franklin, adm. chh. 16 (2) 1643.

MAGGOTT, MAGIT,

Joseph, Watertown, frm. May 6, 1635; mentioned in inv. of Nathl. Sparowhauke in 1647.

MAGSON, or MAYSON,

Richard, Boston, servant to James Everill, adm. chh. 2 (8) 1634.

MAHEW, MAHU, MAYHEW, see **MAYO,**

Thomas, gent., merchant, Watertown, chairman of com. of Gen. Court on boundary in 1631. Deputy; frm. May 14, 1634. Of Medford in 1635. [Plym. Col. Rec. XII.] Recd. a grant of land at Nantucket and Martha's Vineyard in 1641, and rem. thither later. He m. Jane, widow of Thomas Paine, of London, whose son Thomas, ae. 15, chose Mr. and Mrs. M. his guardians Oct. 14, 1647. He was to receive the reversion of lands at Whittlebury, Northamptonshire, 23 (8) 1646. [A.] [L.]

Rev. Thomas, his son, adult in 1641, was the noble preacher to the Indians at the Vineyard. Other ch. rec. at Wat.: Hannah b. 15 (4) 1635, Bethia b. 6 (10) 1636, Mary b. 14 (11) 1639.

MAHOON, MAYHOONE, MATHEWE,

Dermont, Dorman, a servant, his affairs with his master adjusted by the Gen. Court 14 June, 1642. Res. at Boston. Propr. of house and garden. Wife Dinah d 8 (11) 1656. Ch. Daniel b. 4 (10) 1646, Honour b. 29 (8) 1648, Margaret (of Dorman and Margaret,) b. June 3, 1661. Son Teg, 9 yrs. old, appr. 9 May, 1640, to George Strange, transferred to Mr. Browne of Salem. [L.]

Admin. of his est. gr. to his widow 17 May, 1661. Widow Margaret m. July 20, 1661, Bryan Morfrey, an Irishman.

MAKEPEACE,

Thomas, gent., Dorchester, propr. 1635. Of independant opinions. He was informed by the Court 13 (1) 1639, that "Because of his novile disposition they were weary of him unless he should reform." He witnessed a deed in London June 12, and in Boston 21 (7) 1654. He deposed 2 (2) 1662, ae. near 70 years. [Mdx. Files.] His first wife died. He m. 2, Elizabeth, widow of Oliver Mellowes, who was dism. from Boston chh. to Dorch. 25 (5) 1641. Ch. Wait-a-while bapt. 22 (3) 1641, (m. 15 Sept. 1661, Josiah Cooper,) Joseph bapt. 20 (7) 1646, Ester, (m. 24 (2) 1655, John Browne,) Mary, (m. 5 (7) 1656, Lawrence Willis of Bridgewater).

Will, dated June 30, 1666, prob. Aug. 1, 1667; beq. a house and lands in Eng. to eldest son Thomas, who had long possessed his portion; to son William; to son-in-law Lawrence Willis and his dau. Mary W.; to

MAKEPEACE, cont.

eldest dau. Hannah, wife of Stephen Hoppin, of Thompson's Island, and their ch. Deliverance, John, Stephen, Hannah, Sarah, Thomas, Opportunity, Joseph and Benjamin; to dau. Hester, wife of John Browne of Marlborough, and their ch. Elizabeth, Joseph, Sarah, Mary and John; to dau. Waytawhile, wife of Josiah Cooper of Boston, and their ch. Elizabeth and Thomas; to kinswoman Mary, wife of John Pearce of Rhode Island; to his wife's 3 daus. viz. Mary, wife of James Dennis of Boston, Martha, wife of Joseph Walters of Milford, and Mary, wife of Emanuel Sprinckfield in Old Eng.; to son-in-law Abel Langley. Wife Elizabeth and son-in-law Cooper, execs. [Reg. XV, 323.]

MAN, MANN,

Richard, planter, Scituate, had deed of land in 1648. Ch. Nathaniel b. 25 Sept. 1646, Thomas b. 15 Aug. 1650, Richard b. 5 Feb. 1652, Josiah b. 10 Dec. 1654.

He was drowned 16 Feb., 1655. Inv. taken April 14, 1656. [Reg. V, 262.] Admin. gr. to the widow, who agreed to give 3 li. to each of her 3 youngest ch. 6 May, 1656. [Was Rebecca M. who m. John Cowen in March, 1656-7, his widow?]

William, Cambridge, propr. 1634. He m. in 1643, Mary Jarrad. [Reg. XIII, 325.] He m. in Cambridge, June 11, 1657, Alice Tiel. His child Samuel was b. in July, 1647, and became first minister of Wrentham.

In his will, dated Dec. 10, 1661, prob. 1 (2) 1662, he beq. to his wife goods she brought from former marriage; and to his only son Samuel some clothes that were his former wife's, etc.

MANIFOLD,

John, ae. 17, came in the Blessing in July, 1635.

MANNERING,

Joseph, embarked for N. E. March 7, 1631. Mentioned in Court Rec. Nov. 5, 1633, but residence not stated.

MANNING,

Clement ,servant to John Cross of Ipswich in 1638. [Court Rec.]

George, shoemaker, Sudbury; propr. 1640. Rem. to Boston, m. 15 (5) 1653, Mary Haroden. He m. in Boston, 13 (1) 1655, Hannah Blanchard, widow. Ch. Elizabeth b. March 19, 1657, Mary b. Dec. 15, 1659, Elizabeth d. Feb. 4, 1660, Elizabeth b. Oct. 13, 1661, James b. March 6, 1663, Mary b. Nov. 3, 1666, Sarah b. March 19, 1668, John b. Oct. 11, 1671; Hannah Manninge of sister Dinsdale was bapt. 23 (12) 1672, and Adam Dinsdale, of the same; Joseph b. Nov. 6, 1674.

John, Ipswich, propr. 1634. Susan, Ipswich, propr. 1638.

John, merchant, Boston, 1643. Had acct. with Nicholas Treroise 26 (3) 1645. Bond of theirs made at the Island of Fyall 22 (9) 1647. [A.] His son John was b. 25 (3) 1643; dau. Mary was b. 4 (3) 1644, and his wife Abigail d. 25 (3) 1644. By second wife Anne, who was adm. chh. 15 (3) 1647, he had son Ebenezer b. about 3 (1) 1646-7, and bapt. 16 (3) 1647, John bapt. 24 (7) 1648, ae. about 4 days, Anne b. March 13, 1651, Ephraim b. Aug. 10, 1655.

Thomas, husbandman, Ipswich, propr. 1638. Sold house and land 15 March, 1647. Deposed in 1671, ae. about 76 years. Inv. of his est. taken 30 Sept. 1675, presented by Daniel M.

William, Cambridge, propr. 1638, frm. May 13, 1640. Apprenticed at 15 years of age. Came to N. E. with wife. Spent some weeks at Roxbury; came to Cambridge. Lost wife and child. [Rel.] [Second] wife Susanna d. Oct. 16, 1650. [Third] wife Dorothy. Ch. William, Jr., (propr. 1646, d. 14 March, 1690, ae. 76 years, m. 21 (4) 1642, (m. David Walsbie,) Samuel b. 21 (5) 1644, Sarah b. 28 (11) 1645, Abigail b. in 1647, d. in 1648; John b. 31 (1) 1649, and Mary also bapt. at Camb. [Mi.] He rem. to Boston. Made will 17 Feb. 1665, prob. April 28, 1666; two thirds of the est. he had before his last marriage, he beq. to his son William Manning; rest to his gr. son Samuel Walsbie. [Reg. XV.] The widow Dorothie d. at Camb. July 26, 1692, ae. 80 years. [Gr. St.]

MANSFIELD, MANSFELT,

Andrew, Lynn, town clerk, attested to records of land grants made in 1638, in Essex Court files, vol. VI, fol. 77. Deposed 30 (4) 1669, that he was about 49 years old. Wife Bethia joined him in deed to Charles Gott in 1663. Second wife Mary, widow of John Neale, q. v. Deposed in 1663, ae. about 48 years.

Arthur, Lynn. Deposed March 26, 1661, that he was about 38 years old; that he had been an inhab. there 22 or 23 years.

Daniel, Boston, "being so frozen," was treated by Mr. Thomas Oliver whom the Court paid 13 May, 1640.

Elizabeth, Lynn, ae. about 87 yrs., d. Sept. 1, 1673; will dated 20 (2) 1667, prob. 26 (9) 1673; sons Joseph and Andrew; gr. ch. Elizabeth, Deborah, John and Joseph Mansfield. [See Farnsworth.]

John, ae. 34, came in the Susan and Ellen in April, 1635. Served with his bro.-in-law, Robert Keayne, tailor; had lands assigned him in Boston in 1637. Rem. to Charlestown. He was a son of Sir John Mansfield. Frm. May 10, 1643. [Reg. VI, 156.] He applied to Gen. Court in 1654, to be employed in the mint with Hull and Sanders. [Arch. 105.] He deposed June 21, 1659; had served at the goldsmith's trade 24 years. His father was a rich man, a justice of the peace, a knight. [Mdx. Files.]

He m. Mary, widow of John Gove, and joined with her 5 Dec. 1655, in paying to her sons John and Edward Gove their portions. [Char. Rec.] [Col. Rec. 1650.]

His son John and dau. Elizabeth, twins, ae. 8 years, were placed Dec. 30, 1656, with his sister Mrs. Keaine and Mr. Samuel Whiting, Jr., to be brought up. [Mdx. Court Rec.]

They made a joint will 21 Aug. 1665, securing to her one third of £600 a year in lands left him in York, Eng., and debts due to him there; the rest to his lawful heirs, after life use by themselves; estate in Char., Boston, Braintree. Refers to his mother, sister Coale and bro.-in-law Robert Keayne. (Not perfect, wanting executors and witnesses not sworn.)

One Mansfield, a poor, godly man of Exeter, aided to come to N. E. by a rich merchant of Eng. named Marshall; came in the Regard to Boston 13 Nov. 1634; grew rich. Lost godliness and wealth. [W.]

MANSFIELD, etc., cont.
Robert, yeoman, Lynn; constable 1647. [Es. Court rec.]
He made a deed of gift in 1666 to sons Andrew, Joseph; refers to Joseph's wife Elizabeth, dau. of Edmund Needham.

MANTELL,
Robert, of Dorchester, intending to go to Eng., borrowed money, for which he gave bond. Oct. 15, 1640. [L.]

MANTON,
Edward, Seaconck, lands confirmed to him 2 May, 1643.

MAPES,
John, ae. 21, came in the Francis of Ipswich April 30, 1634.

MARBLE, MARRABLE, MIRABLE,
John, Boston. Wife Judith; ch. John b. 10 (9) 1646.

William, planter, Charlestown, 1642; frm. May 3, 1654. Wife Elizabeth; dau. Mary b. 10 (2) 1642. They deposed in Blanchard case in 1652, ae. "about 40 yrs. apiece." [Reg. XXXII, 408.] He deposed alone at same Court, ae. about 36 years.

He went to England about 1656, and Richard Stowers petitioned for liberty to keep an ordinary in his place at Malden. [Mdx. Files.]

MARCH, see MARSH and MEECH,
Hugh, ae. 20, came with Stephen Kent in the Confidence April 24, 1638. Settled at Newbury; propr., town officer, carpenter. Sold land with wife Judith 14 (1) 1651. Wife Judith d. 14 Dec. 1675; he m. 29 May, 1676, Dorcas Blackleach, who d. 22 Nov. 1683; he m. 3, Dec. 1685, Sara Healy, who d. 25 Oct. 1699. Ch. [George b. 1646,] Judith b. 3 Jan. 1652, Hugh b. 3 Nov. 1656, John b. 10 June, 1658, James b. 11 Jan. 1663.

He d. 12 March, 1693.

John, Charlestown, adm. chh. 15 (3) 1642; frm. May 18, 1642. Town officer. [Wife?] Rebeckah adm. chh. 29 (3) 1642. His son Edward d. 4 (8) 1636; son John d. 2 (3) 1641.

Will prob. 17 (11) 1665, beq. to wife Ann the est. she brought at marriage; dau. Frances Bucke and her ch.; son Theophilus M. and his son John; wife's gr. ch. Sarah Bickner.

MARGESON,
Edmund, came in the Mayflower to Plymouth; d. soon after arrival. [B.]

MARION, MARRION,
John, shoemaker, Watertown. Wife Sarah; dau. Mary bur. 24 (11) 1641, ae. 2 mos., son John b. and bur. in 1643. Rem. to Boston; frm. May 26, 1652. Bought house and lot Feb. 18, 1648; another in 1661; other lands in 1674; deed witnessed by sons Samuel and John, Jr. Ch. rec. at Boston: Joseph b. Oct. 14, 1666, Benjamin b. Aug. 25, 1670. He d. 27 Jan. 1705, ae. 86 years. Will prob. 12 Feb. beq. to wife Sarah, sons John, (cordwainer,) Samuel, (tailor,) Isaac, Joseph and Benjamin; daus. Sarah, (wife of John Balston,) and Thomazin Penniman; gr. son John, son of Samuel.

MARPORT,
Mabel, Boston, adm. chh. 1632 3.

MARRET, MARRIOT,
Thomas, cordwinder, shoemaker, Cambridge, propr. 1635. Attorney of his bro.-in-law, Richard Cranniwell of Woodbridge, Suffolk co., Eng., April 16, 1642. Deacon, selectman. Wife Susanna; ch. John bapt. in England, about 5 years old when his father joined chh. of Camb., [Mi.] Thomas bapt. in England, Abigail, Susanna, Hannah, adm. chh. Dec. 15, 1658.

He d. June 30, 1664. Will dated 15 Oct. 1663, in 75th year; he beq. to aged wife Susanna, and to children John, Thomas, Abigail and Hannah, and to their children; to the ch. of son George Baisto, dec.

MARRINER,
Mr., his company had accts. adjusted in Court July 1, 1634.

Thomas, Cambridge, propr. 1638.

Thomas, propr., Boston, freed from service to Robert Smyth 31 (8) 1639. Frm. March 3, 1635.

Thomas, of Newfoundland, paid money to John Phillips of Boston in 1652. [Es. De. I, 27.]

MARRIOT, MARRYOTT, MERRIOT,
Nicholas, fisherman, Salem, 1635, propr. at Marblehead, 1637.

MARRLEY, see MORLEY.

MARSE,
Thomas, a witness to a deed of Sir R. Saltonstall March 2, 1629. [Arch. 100, 1.]

MARSH,
Lieut. Alexander, yeoman, Braintree, frm. May 3, 1654. Owned a house and land at Boston.

He d. March 7, 1698, ae. about 70 years. [Gr. st.] Will dated 19 March, 1696-7, prob. 31 March, 1698, beq. to wife Bathsheba; daus. Rachel and Phebe; dau. Anna and her husband Samuel French; sons-in-law Dependance French, and Samuel Bass; son John Marsh under age; dau. Mary French; gr. dau. Mary French.

George, Hingham, propr. 1635, frm. March 3, 1635-6. Town officer.

He d. July 2, 1647; will dated same day; wife Elizabeth; sons Thomas and Onesiphorus, daus. Elizabeth Turner and Mary Padge. (See Page, Abraham.) The widow m. 2, Nov., 1648, Richard Bowen. [Reg. VII, 36.]

John, cordwinder, Salem, came in the Mary and John May 24, 1633; propr. He and his wife Susanna joined with Nathl. Felton and Mary his wife in a deed in 1661. She was adm. chh. 30 (2) 1648. Ch. Zachariah bapt. 30 (2) 1637, John bapt. 19 (3) 1639, Ruth bapt. 5 (3) 1641, Elizabeth b. 8 (5) 1646, [Es. Files,] bapt. 13 (7) 1646, Ezekiel bapt. 29 (8) 1648, Bethiah bapt. 1 (7) 1650, Samuel bapt. 2 (8) 1652, Susanna bapt. 7 (3) 1654, Mary bapt. 14 (7) 1656, Jacob b. 6 (6) 1658, Jacob bapt. 10 (2) 1659, a dau. bapt. 12 (4) 1664. His son John d. in 1669, leaving a widow Sarah.

He d. about 1674. Will, dated 28 March, 1672, prob. 26 (9) 1674; wife Susanna, ch. Zechary, Samuel, Jacob, Ezekiel, Benjamin, Bethiah. Note.—"My son John Marsh, now in New England," was a legatee in the will of Grace, widow of John Marsh, of Branktry, Essex, clothier, dated 29 Jan. 1657, prob. 22 May, 1667. The father's will was prob. 29 May, 1627. [Reg. XLIX, 370.]

John, Charlestown, inhab. 1638. See March.

MARVILL,
Thomas, before Gen. Court 11 Nov. 1647.

MARSHALL, MARTIAL, MARSHAL,
Christopher, Boston, singleman, adm. chh. 28 (6) 1634, frm. May 6, 1635. Ch. Anna bapt. 13 (3) 1638. He was dism. to Paschataqua, 6 (11) 1638.

Edmund, weaver, Salem, 1636; frm. May 17, 1637. Rem. to Ipswich. Sold land in Gloucester 31 March, 1663. He deposed in 1668, ae. 70, and his wife Millicent, ae. 67. Millicent memb. chh. Salem, 1637. Ch. Naomy bapt. 24 (11) 1636, Ann bapt. 15 (2) 1638, Ruth bapt. 3 (3) 1640, Sarah bapt. 29 (3) 1642, Edmund bapt. 16 (4) 1644, Benjamin b. 7 (9) bapt. 27 (9) 1646.

Francis, ae. 30, came in the Christian March 16, 1634. Perhaps this is the "Frauncis, seamester," of Boston, who had mortg. of house and land from Elizabeth Wood June 7, 1659.

John, husbandman, Boston, having served with our bro. Mr. Edward Hutchinson, was adm. inhab. 24 (12) 1639-40. Propr. Wife Sarah; ch. John b. 10 (10) 1645, bapt. 12 (6) 1655, with Joseph, Samuel, Sarah and Hannah; Thomas bapt. 11 (3) 1656, Christopher bapt. 21 (6) 1659, Benjamin b. Feb. 15, 1660-1, Christopher b. Aug. 18, 1664.

Thomas, planter, Dorchester, frm. March 4, 1634-5. (Name sometimes spelt Marshfield.) Rem. to Windsor, Conn. Gave bond to John Iles July 29, 1639. One of the undertakers of ships Charles and Hopewell in 1640. [L.] Extract from a letter of his in Suff. De. I, 12.]

Thomas, Boston, adm. chh. 3 (6) 1634, a widower; frm. March 4, 1634-5. Deacon, town officer, deputy. Chosen to keep the ferry to Charlestown and Winnisimmet 23 (11) 1635. With wife Alice conveyed his homestead to son Samuel M. of Windsor, Conn. July 4, 1663. Signed inv. of John Hill in 1646. He m. 2, Alice —; ch. Eliakim b. 1 (1) 1637, Thomas bapt. 7 (11) 1643, ae. about 5 days. The wife Alice d. May 20, 1664. Four days later he deeded effects to her daus. Sarah, wife of James Pemberton, and Francis, wife of Joseph How; refers to his sons Eliakim and Thomas M.

He d. before Dec. 8, 1664. Admin. gr. Jan. 31, 1664-5, to James Pemberton. [Reg. XVI, 163.]

MARSHALL, etc., cont.

Thomas, shoemaker, ae. 22, came in the James in 1635. Settled at Boston, adm. chh. 17 (12) 1643. Frm. May 29, 1644. Had grant of land 15 ft. square 26 (6) 1644. Dism. to chh. of New Haven 26 (2) 1646; letter of dismission given 2 (2) 1648.

Thomas, tailor, Lynn, propr. 1638; and rem. before 1643. [Mass. Arch.]

Thomas, carpenter, Lynn. Rem. to Reading; captain, carpenter. He deposed 2 (2) 1661, ae. about 45 years. [Mdx. Files.] Wife Joan memb. chh. 1648. Ch. b. at Reading: Hannah b. 7 (4) 1640, Samuel b. and d. 1643, Abigail b. 16 (2) 1644-5, Thomas b. 20 (12) 1647, Elizabeth b. 12 (10) 1649, Sarah or Susanna b. 18 (10) 1650, Susanna b. April 2, 1652, Sarah b. Feb. 14, 1654, John b. 14 Jan. 1659.

[See Notes on Persons of the name Marshall connected with America, in Reg. XXXIII, 217.]

He d. 23 Dec. 1689. Wife Rebecca d. Aug. 1693. [Lynn Rec.]

William, ae. 40, came in the Abigail in June, 1635.

MARSHFIELD,

Samuel, Springfield, propr. 1648. Was marshall of the county many years; deputy, town officer. He m. 18 (12) 1651, Hester Wright. He m. 2, Dec. 28, 1664, Katharine Chapin, widow successively of Nathaniel Bliss and Thomas Gilbert. Ch. Mercy b. 1 (3) 1653, Thomas b. 6 (6) 1654, Sarah b. 2 (12) 1656, Samuel b. 25 (1) 1659, Hannah b. 20 (5) 1661, Abilene b. April 2, 1664, Josias b. Sept. 29, 1665, Hester b. Sept. 6, 1667, Margaret b. Dec. 23, 1670. The wife Hester d. 3 April, 1664.

Inv. of his est. was taken in May, 1692, Josias, son and heir, admin.

MARSTON, MASTON, MARSON,

Elizabeth, in court June 11, 1633.

John, ae. 20, servant of Mary Moulton, passed exam. to go to N. E. April 11, 1637. Settled at Salem. Propr., frm. June 2, 1641. He deposed in 1666, ae. about 50 years, being master of John Ruck's ketch called the Returne; brought certain goods from the Barbadoes. Wife Alice; ch. John b. 29 (6) bapt. 12 (7) 1641, Ephraim b. 30 (8) bapt. 10

MARSTON, etc., cont.

(10) 1643, Manasses bapt. 7 (7) 1645, Sarah bapt. 19 (1) 1647, Benjamin bapt. 9 (1) 1651, Hannah bapt. 17 (2) 1653, Thomas bapt. 11 (12) 1654, Eliza bapt. 30 (6) 1657, Abigail b. 19 (12) 1658, bapt. 10 (2) 1659, Mary b. 23 March, 1661. He d. Dec. 19, 1681, ae. 66. [Gr. st.]

He made will Dec. 18, 1681, prob. 30 (4) 1682; beq. to wife; sons John, Manasseh, Ephraim and Benjamin, and daus. Sarah and Abigail.

Thomas, Salem, propr. 1636; frm. June 2, 1641. May be the Thomas, of Hampton, who deposed 9 March, 1665, ae. about 52 years.

William, Salem, propr. 1636; frm. May 23, 1666. He deposed 2 (5) 1674, ae. about 52 years; had been a servant of Capt. Corwin at some time. His wife (Sarah), adm. chh. 20 (1) 1659; ch. Sarah b. 12 (12) 1654, d. July, 1655, Hannah b. 1 (7) 1655, Elizabeth bapt. 10 (2) 1659, Mary b. 2 (2) 1661, dau. Deliverance b. 15 (3) bapt. 20 (4) 1663, William b. 19 (7) bapt. 20 (7) 1668.

William, Sen. Hampton, made will 25 June, prob. 8 Oct. 1672; beq. to sons Thomas, William and John; daus. Prudence Cox and Trifana M.; wife Sabina exec.

MARTIN, MARTYN, MARTEN,

Mr. Ambrose, Dorchester, 1637. Fined 10 li. and sent to Mr. Mather for instruction, for opposing covenant and ministry, 13 (1) 1638-9. [Col. Rec.] Rem. to Concord. Ch. Joseph b. 8 (9) 1640, Sarah b. 27 (8) 1642.

Abraham, weaver, Hingham, propr. 1635; rem. in 1643, to Rehoboth. Prop. frm. Plymouth Col. 4 June, 1645.

Will dated Sept. 9, 1669, prob. 6 Oct. 1670, beq. to the children of bro. Richard and of John Ormsby; to Mr. Hubbert, pastor at Hing. et als.; left money for a bell to call people to worship, for the burying-place and for a bier. [Reg. VII, 235.]

Mr. Christopher, from Billerica, Eng., [B.] was treasurer of the Plymouth Company; came in the Mayflower; signed the Compact; settled at Plymouth. Brought with him his wife and 2 servants, Salamon Prower, and John Langemore.

He d. Jan. 8, 1620-1; and all his dyed in the first infection. [B.]

MARTIN, etc., cont.

Edward, ae. 19, came in the Abigail in July, 1635.

George, came as a servant to Samuel Winsley about 1639; bought Job Cole's rights at Salisbury about 1643. [Depos. of Robert Pike, 1695.] Propr. 1642-1664. Took oath of fidelity in 1646. His petition to Gen. Court in 1648 was referred to Hampton Court. Blacksmith. He m. 1, Hannah; m. 2, Aug. 11, 1646, Susanna, dau. of Richard North. Ch. Hannah b. Feb. 1, 1643, (m. Ezekiel Wathen or Worthen,) Richard b. June 29, 1647, Geo. b. Oct. 21, 1648, John b. Jan. 26, 1650, Esther b. April 7, 1653, (m. John Jameson,) Jane b. Nov. 2, 1656, (m. Samuel Hadley,) Abigail b. Sept. 10, 1659, (m. James Hadlock,) William b. Dec. 11, 1662, Samuel b. Sept. 29, 1667.

Will dated Jan. 19, 1683, prob. Nov. 23, 1686. The widow Susanna was executed July 19, 1692, at Salem, for alleged witchcraft.

Isaac, a witness in a Hingham lawsuit in 1639. [L.] Rehoboth, propr. 1643.

John, ship-carpenter, Charlestown, 1635; deputy; adm. chh. with wife Rebecca 2 (7) 1639; frm. May 13, 1640. Adm. inhab. Boston 1658. Res. at Charlestown in 1650, and with wife Sarah sold land at Malden. Ch. Sarah bapt. at Char. 9 (7) 1639, Mary bapt. 14 (1) 1640-1, Mehetabel bapt. 1 (8) 1643.

John, yeoman, Chelmsford, sold land June 30, 1664.

John, Marblehead, admin. of his est. gr. at Boston 9 July, 1688, to Wm. and Benj. Browne of Salem.

Marie, ae. 19, servant to James Hosmer, came in the Elizabeth April 9, 1635. Maid servant of John Coggeshall, adm. chh. 6 (10) 1635.

Richard,* ae. 12, came in the Elizabeth and Ann in April in 1635. Witnessed deed at Boston in 1651. Richard, mariner, of Bo. bought house Nov. 3, 1655, near land of R. M. ship-carpenter. Richard, of Boston, ship-carpenter, with wife Mary sold land 9 Feb. 1658. He m. at Salem in 1660, Elizabeth, dau. of John Gay of Dedham. They sold land in Boston 24 Aug. 1666.

Will dated 19 July, prob. 6 (9) 1671, beq.

MARTIN, etc., cont.

to wife Elizabeth for herself and their children.

*Richard, Rehoboth, aged, made will, prob. May 7, 1695; beq. to sons Richard and Francis and Richard's eldest son John, who are in old England; to son John now with me; to John Ormsby, dau. Grace's eldest son; to daus. Grace Ormsby and Annis Chaffee.

Robert, of Badcombe, husbandman, ae. 44, with wife Joane, ae. 44, embarked from Weymouth, Eng., before March 20, 1635. Settled at Weymouth, frm. May 13, 1640. App. by Gen. Court 6 Sept. 1636, to view the land beyond Monotoquid River. Prop. frm. Plymouth Col. 1645. Selectman, 1643. One of those who surveyed the line between Mass. and Plym. colonies; report accepted by Gen. Court 31 May, 1659. Rem. to Rehoboth. [Arch. Col. 23.]

Will, dated 6 (3) 1660; wife Joan and children; bro. Richard Martin and his children in Eng.; bro. Abraham M.; cousin Roger Clap of Dorchester. The widow Joanna's will, prob. April 6, 1668; sister Smith; cousin Clap and the ch. he had by my kinswoman [Jane] Clap; kinsmna John Ormsbey; cousins Grace, Thomas and Jacob Ormsbey, bro. Upham's children at Mauldin, et als. [Reg. VI, 93, and VII, 178.]

Solomon, ae. 16, came in the James in July, 1635. Settled at Gloucester; propr. 1649. Rem. to Andover, frm. May 26, 1652. His wife Alice consented 8 (3) 1652 to the sale of his house and land at Gloster. [Ips. De. I, 95.]

Thomas, planter, Charlestown, inhab. 1638, adm. chh. 12 (3) 1639. Gave bond to Solomon Saffery in 1639. [L.] Rem. to Cambridge. He m. at Woburn 1 (4) 1650, Alce Ellett. [See will of Henry Martin of Wapping, Mdx. Eng. mariner, 1655.] [Reg. LI, 116.]

William, Reading, propr. 1644; town officer. He and "sister Martin," memb. chh. 1648.

MARVIN, MARVYN,

Matthew, husbandman, ae. 35, with wife Elizabeth, ae. 31, (children) Elizabeth, ae. 13, Matthew, ae. 8, Marie, ae. 6, Sarah, ae.

MARVIN, etc., cont.
3, and Hannah, ae. ½ yr., came in the Increase April 15, 1635.

Thomas, Newbury, propr. He d. 28 Nov. 1651.

MASIE, see MACY.

MASCALL, MASKALL,
Robert, Boston, "One of Mr. Wm. Peirce's family," adm. chh. 20 (4) 1640; dism. 5 (5) 1646, "to the church of Christ at Dover in England."

John, Salem. He m. March, 1649, Ellen Long; she was adm. chh. 16 (4) 1650; ch. John b. 25 (10) bapt. 23 (12) 1650, Stephen b. 15 (12) 1652, bapt. 13 (1) 1653, Mehitabel b. 15 (3) bapt. 3 (4) 1655, Thomas bapt. 10 (3) 1657, James b. 16 (1) 1661, James bapt. 26 (3) 1662, Nicholas b. 14 (2) 1661, Nicholas bapt. 5 (4) 1664.

MASON,
Elias, [see widow, below,] Salem, 1649. Ch. Martha bapt. 18 (3) 1651, Elias bapt. 29 (3) 1653, Jane adm. chh. 2 (3) 1647, and her ch. Sarah and Mary bapt. 3 weeks later, Hannah bapt. 14 (11) 1648.

Will dated 1 May, 1684, prob. at Boston June 13, 1688, beq. to daus. Sarah, wife of John Robinson, Mary, wife of George Cox, and Hannah; Elizabeth Baxter and Love Stephens and their children.

Henry, Scituate, atba. 1643; probably the same as Henry, brewer, Boston, frm. May 22, 1650. Adm. inhab. in 1657. With wife Easter sold his dwelling house and land in Dorchester 3 April, 1668.

Will dated 6 (8) prob. 17 (9) 1676, beq. to cousin Mercy, dau. of Joseph Eliot; to wife Hester. The widow m. 2, John Sears of Woburn; her will dated 2 March, 1679, and July 12, 1680, prob. 2 Sept. 1680, beq. to Joseph and Mercy Ellit for the bringing up of their child Joseph, and to his sister Deborah Skelton's ch.; to the ch. of bros. Isaac and Abraham How; to Sarah, Abraham and Hester Parker; to Mary Grandee's ch.; to her husband John Seirs; to her bro. Israel How. A lot of land at Dorchester, the gift of her father How. [Es. Files XXXIII, 123-4.]

Hugh, yeoman, tanner, captain, came April 30, 1634, ae. 28, with wife Hester, ae.

MASON, cont.
22, in the Francis of Ipswich. Settled at Watertown, frm. and deputy, March 4, 1634-5. Town officer. Com. to end small causes. Ch. recorded at Wat.: Hannah b. 23 (7) 1636, Mary b. 18 (10) 1640, Ruth bur. 17 (10) 1640, Joseph b. 10 (6) 1646, Daniel b. 19 (12) 1648, Sarah b. Sept. 25, 1651. The widow d. May 1, (21) 1692, ae. 82.

He d. Oct. 10, 1678, ae. 73. Will dated 13 (12) 1677, prob. 22 (11) 1678, beq. to wife and ch. John, Hannah and Sarah; son Daniel had recd. a liberal education; son Joseph exec.

John, Dorchester, frm. March 4, 1634-5. Agreement with certain settlers on his lands March 4, 1634. [Arch. 3, 347.] He rem. to Hingham. Capt., chief commander in the Pequot War. Rem. to Windsor, Conn.; sold house and lot at Hingham 5 (5) 1647. He m. at Hing. July, 1639, Anne, dau. of Mr. Robert Peck, q. v. Ch. Priscilla, Samuel, John, Rachel, Anne, Daniel, Elizabeth. [Hist. Hing.]

Ralph, joiner, ae. 35, with wife Anne, ae. 35, and ch. Richard, ae. 5, Samuel, ae. 3, and Susan, ae. 1, came in the Abigail in July, 1635. Settled at Boston. He mortg. his house June 5, 1638. Deeded land to his eldest son Richard and Sarah his wife, dau. of Henry Messenger, April 20, 1661. Son Zuriell b. 14 (2) 1637, John b. 15 (8) 1640, Jacob b. 12 (2) 1644, Hannah b. 23 (10) 1647, Susanna m. Dec. 14, 1659, William Norton.

Will dated 11 Jan. 1672, prob. 23 Jan. 1678, beq. to aged wife Anne, children Richard, Samuel, Susanna, John and Jacob. Land at York at the eastward and in Boston.

Robert, Roxbury; his wife was bur. in April, 1637. He sold his lands in R. Nov. 24, 1640. Rem. to Dedham, propr. 29 (9) 1639. Mortg. dwelling house and lands Feb. 2, 1646. John M. of Dedham, Robert and Thomas of Medfield, gave bond 14 Nov. 1667, to admin. on the estate of their father Robert M. of Dedham. John, son of widow Margery M. of Medfield, was slain in battle at the Eastward, and inv. of his est. pres. Nov. 29, 1679.

Widow, Emma, of Eastwell, Eng., came in the Hercules March, 1634. Settled at Salem.

She d. about 26 (3) 1646; inv. taken 26 (3)

MASON, cont.
was filed 30 (10) 1646; est. to be divided between her ch., the eldest son to have a double portion. See Elias.

MASSEY, MASSIE, see MACY,
Jeffrey, Sen., Salem, frm. May 14, 1634. Deputy 1638-9. Memb. Court valuation com. 13 May, 1640. Town officer. Constable 15 (2) 1645. [Es. Court.] He deposed 30 (9) 1664, ae. 73 years; had lived in Salem about 34 years. Wife Ellen adm. chh. 26 (9) 1648. He d. 9 (9) 1676. Will, dated 6 (9) 1676, prob. 29 (4) 1677; wife Ellen, son John and other children. John deposed 28 (4) 1672, ae. 41 years. He rendered his account 1 July, 1680.

MASTERS, MAISTERS,
Mr. John, Watertown, frm. May 18, 1631. Rem. to Cambridge, propr., 1633. Protested against the admission of unworthy members into the church in 1631. [W.] Member of a com. to advise respecting the raising of a public stock in 1632. He undertook to make a passage from Charles River to the New Town, 12 feet broad and 7 feet deep, in 1631; and the Court promised him satisfaction. [Prince.]
He d. Dec. 21, 1639. His wife d. Dec. 10, 1639. His will, dated 19 (10) 1639, beq. all his est. to his wife for her life; after her death to his daus. Sarah Dobyson and Lidya Tabor, and to his gr. ch. John Lockwood and to Nathaniel Master ten pounds apiece; to Abraham M. ten shillings. The rest to dau. Elizabeth Latham. [Reg. II, 180.]

Nathaniel, legatee of Mr. John in 1639; res. at Salem; tailor. Sold land in 1667. Wife Ruth signed.

MASTERSON,
Richard, wool-carder, of Sandwich, Eng., m. at Leyden, Holland, Nov. 26, 1619, Mary Goodall of Leicester, Eng. See a joint letter of his with others from Leyden in 1625. [Hist. Coll. 3.] He came to Plymouth; d. of fever in 1633. [B.] His widow Mary m. Mr. Ralph Smith; she deeded to her son Nathaniel and her dau. Sara, wife of John Wood, a house in Leyden, Holland, which had belonged to her dec. husband R. M.; deed recorded in 1649.

MATHER,
Rev. Richard, b. at Lowton in the parish of Winwick, Eng., in the year 1596, son of Thomas and Margarite Mather. Schoolmaster at Toxteth Park in 1611. Converted in 1614; studied at Brazen Nose Coll., Oxford; was ordained by the bishop of Chester, and became vicar of Toxteth in 1618. [Journal and Life.]
Having been suspended in 1633 and 1634 for non-conformity, being thoroughly convinced of the errors of the Established church, he decided to rem. to New England for liberty and opportunity of doing good unhindered. He sailed from Bristol May 23, 1635, in the ship James; arrived in Boston Aug. 17, 1635. Was adm. chh. with wife Katharine 20 (7) 1635. Became teacher of the chh. at Dorchester, where he remained till his death. Had the respect of all for pure, sagacious and consecrated character and was very successful in his ministry. He wrote a journal of his voyage. With Rev. Wm. Tompson he composed an Answer to Mr. Charles Herle; he was the chief author of The Elders' Discourse about Church Government in 1639, and the Cambridge Platform in 1647.
He m. Katharine, dau. of Edmund Hoult, of Bury, Lancaster, Sept. 29, 1624. She d. in 1654-5. Ch. Samuel, Timothy, Nathaniel and Joseph b. in Eng.; Eleazer and Increase b. in Dorch., the former in 1638, the latter bapt. 23 (4) 1639. He m. 2, 26 (6) 1656, Sarah, widow of Mr. John Cotton, who survived him and d. May 27, 1676, ae. about 75 yrs. [Record of her son Seaborn; Reg. XXXIII, 34.]
His will, dated 16 (8) 1661, ae. almost 65 yrs., gave to his wife Sarah 100 li. being double what she brought him; to her dau. Mary Cotton and gr. child Elizabeth Day; to the ch. of his sister Ellin Worseley; to son Timothy Mather, his wife Elizabeth, his son Samuel and his other ch.; to sons Samuel, Nathaniel, Eliazer and Increase Mather; to son Timothy Mather and his son Samuel. [Reg. XX, 250, and July, 1900.]

MATTHEW, MATTHEWS, MATTHIS,
Dorman, (see Mahoone.)

Edmund, before Gen. Court 1 Sept., 1640.

James, Yarmouth, atba. 1643. Constable 1639-40. Charlestown, inhab. 1634; of Yarmouth prior to 1639. [See Carseley.]

MATTHEW, etc. cont.
Ch. Samuel b. 1 May, 1647, Sarah b. 21 July, 1649, Esther b. 8 Jan. 1650-1.

John, Roxbury, propr. 1640, frm. May 18, 1642. Sold his house in R. 19 (10) 1645. Endorsed deed of land in Charlestown, 1648. Ch. Gershom b. July 25, 1641, Elizabeth b. Oct. 14, 1643.
He d. intestate 20 Nov. 1658. Attest Edwd. Burt. [Mdx. Files.]

John, of Boston, tailor, sold house and ground Oct. 10, 1649.
Will prob. 11 April, 1670. Wife Elizabeth to have the dwelling house; son John; dau. Wigeer living in Dartmouth, Eng. [Reg. XLVIII, 459.]

John, cooper, Springfield, propr. 1645; beat the drum to call people to meetings; town officer. He m. 24 (12) 1642, Pentecost Bond; she was killed by the Indians Oct. 5, 1675. Ch. Abigail bur. 25 (5) 1646, Sarah bur. 7 (11) 1649.
He d. Aug. 25, 1684. Admin. gr. to Nathaniel Burt.

John, Rehoboth, propr. 1643.

Rev. Marmaduke, Boston, "A godly minister, one Mr. Matthews," arrived in a ship of Barnstable which brought about 80 passengers, near all Western people. [W.] His wife Katharine adm. chh. 6 (12) 1638, dism. to Yarmouth 27 (6) 1643. Settled at Yarmouth, took oath of allegiance to Plym. Col. 7 Feb. 1638-9. Ch. Manasseh bapt. at Bar. Jan. 24, 1640. Inhabitants of Hull petitioned Gen. Court in 1649 that he might be their minister. He went to them, but was recalled by the Court for erroneous and unsafe expressions. Was ord. at Malden in 1651 and fined therefor by the Court; remitted 23 Oct. 1652. Letters in Mass. Hist. Coll. 3-1. Mary, of Mr. Marmaduke Matthews of the chh. of Yar. bapt. at Boston, 29 (6) 1647.

Mary, Boston, servant to Thomas Leveritt, adm. chh. 4 (5) 1640.

Thomas, Boston. His widow Margery admin. on his est. 7 (7) 1641. [Court Rec.] She was a sister of Au. Clement, from Wockingham, co. Berks, 1638. [L.] Was adm. chh. Boston 10 (8) 1641. She d. 3 (9) 1655.

MATSON, METSON,
Thomas, gunsmith, settled at Braintree,

MATSON, cont.
Boston, rec'd to chh. "by Communion of churches from a chh. in London," 1630-1. His wife Amy or Anne was sister of Abigail, first wife of Theodore Atkinson. [Suff. De. VI, 333.] Ch. who rec'd deed of gift from Theodore Atkinson April 13, 1670: Thomas, John, Joshua, Abigail. They were dism. to chh. of Mt. Wollaston 16 (12) 1639. With Anne his wife receipted to their sister-in-law Mrs. Chambers, widow of Thomas Chambers, citizen and clothworker of London, dwelling at the sign of the golden key in Sherborne lane, 28 (5) 1640. [L.] Ch. Thomas bapt. 27 (8) 1633, John bapt. 10 (5) 1636. Inv. of his est. was filed by his widow Amy April 26, 1677.

His will dated 9 June, 1676, prob. April 26, 1677; "aged;" beq. to wife Amy; sons Thomas, Joshua and John M.; dau. Abigail, her husband Lyonel Wheatley and their ch. The widow made will 28 Feb., prob. 1 May, 1677-8; beq. to her son John's ch. Amy, Thomas and Hannah, and to his wife Mary; to Abigail and Mary, daus. of dec. dau. Abigail Wheatley.

MATTOCKS, MATTOCKE, MATTOX, see Maddox,
David, Roxbury, frm. May 22, 1650.
He d. about (3) 1654. The magistrates gave the est. to his widow Sarah, a son and a decrepit dau. May 25, 1654. [Reg. VIII, 276.] The widow m. 2, Thomas Rawlin, Sen. His dau. Elizabeth b. and d. 1655.

James, cooper, Boston, had liberty to live with his bro. John Spoore or elsewhere 18 (4) 1638; adm. chh. 24 (12) 1638, frm. March 13, 1638-9. Dism. to chh. at Mt. Wollaston for ye winter season 24 (9) 1639. Bought a house lot of Anthony Stoddard 28 (10) 1644, and sold it to John Synderland Dec. 30, 1644. Bought house and land April 25, 1653, and gave it to his son Samuel who was about to marry Constance, dau. of Richard Fairbanks. Dau. Mary m. 9 July, 1661, Samuel Browne.

Will, dated Jan. 21, 1666, prob. Aug. 1, 1667. Wife Mary, son Samuel Mattock, daus. Alice, wife of John Lewes, and Mary, wife of Samuel Browne. [Reg. XV, 325.] The widow Mary, aged, made will 8 Jan. 1680, prob. 11 April, 1682; beq. to son Samuel, and his ch. James and Samuel; dau. Alice How; gr. ch. Samuel and Joseph Lew-

MATTOCKS, etc., cont.
is; dau. Mary Bishop; gr. ch. James, Mary and Samuel Browne and Hannah Byshop.

John, Salem, worked with Robert Lewis on the ship Sara for Richard Hollingsworth, ship-builder, who gave them an order for the money 19 Aug. 1641.
He d. April 22, 1643; inv. 6 (5) 1644.

Stephen, sent over by Mr. Peter and Mr. Weld in 1643, a servant, assigned to Elder How of Watertown, lived with Nathaniel Treadway of Wat. 5 (2) 1653. [Mdx. Files.]

MAUDE,
Rev. Daniel, came in the ship James from Bristol, Eng., in company with Richard Mather in May, 1639. Adm. chh. 20 (7) 1635; frm. May 25, 1636. Was chosen schoolmaster at Boston Aug. 12, 1636. Was dism. to the chh. of Dover 17 (1) 1644, where he was settled as minister; vote to build him a house passed 1 (6) 1648. He m. Mary (Marie) Bonner; q. v.

MAUDESLEY, MOSELEY, MODSLEY,
Henry, carpenter, ae. 24, came in the Hopewell in July, 1637. Settled at Dorchester. Had leave to dwell in Plymouth colony 2 April, 1638. Frm. May 6, 1646. Rem. to Braintree. Ch. Mary b. 29 (7) 1638, Samuel b. 14 (4) 1641. Res. in Boston in 1639 and in 1652.

John, Dorchester, frm. March 14, 1638-9. His first wife was Elizabeth; son Joseph b. in 1638.
He d. 27 (8) 1661. His widow Cicery admin. Oct. 29, 1661. She made will Nov. 28, 1661; sons Thomas and John; dau. Elizabeth. She d. 3 (10) 1661. [Reg. XI, 170.]

MAULDER,
Ffebe, ae. 7, came in the Defense in July, 1635.

MAURICE, see Morris.

MAURY, see Morey.

MAVERICK,
Elias, Charlestown, 1630, adm. chh. 9 (12) 1632-3, frm. June 11, 1633. He is men-

MAVERICK, cont.
tioned in both Salem and Boston in 1636. He m. Anna Harris, who was adm. chh. 7 (8) 1639; she d. Sept. 7, 1697, ae. 84, at Reading. Ch. James, (d. and his father admin. on his est. 31 Oct. 1671;) John b. 13, bapt. 27 (12) 1635, Abigail b. 10, bapt. 14 (6) 1637, Elizabeth b. 2 (4) 1639, Sarah b. 20 (12) 1640, Elias b. 17 (1) 1643, Peter, Mary, Ruth, Paul b. 10 June, 1657, Rebecca.

Will prob. Nov. 6, 1684. Beq. to wife Anna; sons Elias, Peter and Paul; daus. Abigail Clark, Sarah Walton, Mary Waye, Ruth Smith and Rebecca Thomas; to gr. ch. Jotham, son of his son John, James, son of Peter, Ruth Johnson, and others; refers to Jemima, dau. of Lieut. John Smith, wife of his son Paul. Gives to his servant Jonas Holmes the rest of his time. Makes his father-in-law, Dea. William Stitson, Aaron Way, Sen. and Wm. Ireland, Sen. overseers.

Rev. John, a native of co. Devon, was matriculated at Exeter Coll., Oxford, 24 Oct. 1595, ae. 18, and took degree of A.B. 8 July, 1599, and A.M. 7 July, 1603; was ordained deacon at Exeter, Eng. July 26, 1597, and preached in Devonshire. He was chosen one of the ministers of the church-colony which organized at Plymouth, Eng. in March, 1629, and came to our Dorchester, arriving May 30, 1630. Was a propr. and signed the earliest orders for distribution of lands in the town, with his colleague Warham and Gaylord and Rockwell, believed to have been deacons. He remained in Dorchester when half of the church went with the other minister to colonize Windsor, Conn., in 1635-6; but d. 3 Feb. 1635-6. [Hub.] "Was near 60 years of age; a man of very humble spirit and faithful in furthering the work of the Lord here, both in the churches and civil state." [W.] We have no record of his family. [Reg. XLIII, 326.]

Moses, Dorchester, propr. 1633. Rem. to Salem, propr. at Marblehead in 1637; constable in 1643, [Es. Court rec.] a business man of much enterprise. He deposed in 1662, ae. about 50 years. He m. 1, Remember, dau. of Isaac Allerton, who conveyed to him in May, 1635, property at Marb. He and his wife and children were recd. to the chh. in 1637. She was living in 1650; [B.] but d. after 1652. He m. 2, 22 (8) 1656, Eu-

MAVERICK, cont.
nice, widow of Thomas Roberts; she deposed in 1671, ae. about 43 years. Ch. recorded: a dau. bapt. 7 (6) 1639, Mary bapt. 14 (12) 1640, d. at Boston 20 Feb. 1655, Abigail bapt. 12 (11) 1644, Eliza bapt. 8 (9) 1646, Samuel bapt. 19 (10) 1647, Eliza bapt. 30 (7) 1649, (m. 1, John Turner, 2, Charles Redford,) Remember bapt. 17 (7) 1652, Mary bapt. 6 (7) 1657, Aaron bapt. 20 (1) 1662, Rebecca, (m. John, son of Adam Hawks).

He d. 28 June, 1686, ae. 86 years, Will dated March 30, 1686, admin. gr. 15 July, 1686, to widow Eunice; beq. to wife; to Moses Hawke, only surviving child of his late dau. Rebecca; to Samuel and Mary Ward, Abigail Hinds and Mary Dallabare, ch. of his dec. dau. Abigail; to daus. Eliz: Skinner, Remember Woodman, Mary Ferguson and Sarah Norman. In 1691 Edward Woodman of Boston, husband of Remember, petitioned for full settlement of the est. [Es. Files 46, 28.]

Mr. Samuel, (said by Jocelyn to be a son of Mr. John, above,) came in 1625 to Noddles Island, now East Boston, where he was found by the Dorchester and Boston colonists in 1630. Frm. Oct. 2, 1632. Carried on fishing, trading and farming. He was paid in 1632 by Mr. Pynchon for a month's wages of Elias M. [Mass. Hist. Coll. 2-8.] Did noble work in caring for the Indians when they were suffering from small pox in 1633. He deposed Dec. 7, 1665, ae. 63 years. With wife Amias sold messuage at Winnisimmet and interest in the ferry Feb. 27, 1634. They, with their son and heir apparent, Nathaniel, sold Noddles Island, bake house, mill, etc. in 1649. John Thompson calls him father, in 1646. [A.] His dau. Mary m. 1, 8 (12) 1655, John Palsgrave; m. 2, 20 Sept. 1660, Francis Hooke; lived at Kittery.

He rem. to New York. Was one of the comrs. of king Charles II in 1664. Took strong ground against the Mass. Bay Company; [see his letters in N. Y. Hist. Soc. Coll. See deed of his house to dau. Mary; N. Y. De. 1, 133.] A son Samuel d. in 1663, whose widow m. Wm. Bradbury of Salisbury.

MAYCOCK, MEACOCK,
Peter, Plymouth, sold the 25 acres of land due to him for service 25 Aug. 1638; made bargain with Jonathan Brewster to keep the ferry at North river. Before the court, 1640.

MAWER, see MOORE,
William, a stranger in Boston, 1636.

MAY, MAYES, MAIES,
John, Roxbury, frm. June 2, 1641. Sister M. d. 18 (4) 1651. [Second wife] Sarah, an aged woman, recd. from chh. of Dorchester 29 (2) 1660. Sarah, wife of J. M., d. May 4, 1670.

John M., Sen. d. April 28, 1670, ae. about 80. His nunc. will, made Sabbath morning, April 24, prob. April 29, 1670, beq. to son John all the tools and ½ a tract of land; son Samuel to have the other half; household goods to be divided between the sons after the death of his wife. [Reg. XLVIII, 460.]

MAYER,
Thomas, servant to Henry Smith, came to Hingham in 1638.

MAYNARD, MYNARD, see MINOR,
John, carpenter, Duxbury, witness to will of John Cole in 1637; contracted to build a prison at Plymouth 4 March, 1638-9; had land grant at Dux. in 1640; town officer, 1645. Rem. to Boston; sold Dux. land 20 Aug. 1647. He m. 16 May, 1640, Mary, dau. of Comfort Starr; ch. Hannah and Lydia, ae. about 4 days, bapt. 26 (9) 1648. Inv. of his est. filed 7 (9) 1658. List of debts, 25 (9) 1659. [Reg. IX, 347, and XXXI, 175.]

John, Cambridge, propr. 1634; frm. May 29, 1644. May be the folg.:

John, maulster, Sudbury, propr. 1639 selectman, 1646; frm. May 2, 1649. He m 16 (4) 1646, Mary, widow [or dau.!] of Thomas Axtell; ch. Elizabeth b. 26 May, 1649 Hannah b. 30 (7) 1653.

Will dated 4 Sept. 1672, prob. April 1, 1673 beq. to wife Mary; sons John and Zechary daus. Elizabeth, wife of Joseph Graves, Lydia, wife of Joseph Moores, and Mary, unmarried.

MAYO,
Rev. John, Barnstable, frm. 3 March 1639-40.
Rev. John, ordained minister of the North church, Boston, Nov. 9, 1655; dismissed Apr 15, 1672.
Mr. John, late of Yarmouth, a com. wa appointed to settle his est. upon his wi

MAYO, cont.

and children 7 June, 1676. Inv. presented by his widow Thamasin, not including goods she brought at marriage; division agreed upon between the widow; the son John; Samuel, Hannah and Bathsheba, ch. of the son Nathaniel, dec.; Joseph Howes signed on behalf of Hannah Bacon; Thomas Huckens subscribed. The dau. Hannah had m. 4 Dec. 1640, Nathaniel Bacon. Nathaniel d. in 1661. John m. at Eastham 1 Jan. 1650, Hannah Reycraft, or Lecraft.

John, Roxbury, son-in-law of Robert Gamlin, arrived 20 (3) 1632. [E.] Propr. Wife Sarah; ch. Hannah b. April 24, 1657, John b. Feb. 15, 1658, Hannah b. Feb. 16, 1660. Joseph bapt. 13 (11) 1666, Mehetabel bapt. 28 (12) 1668, Thomas bapt. 20 (9) 1670, Benjamin bapt. 1672, Thomas bapt. 16 (9) 1673.

He was bur. April 28, 1688. Will prob. June 11, 1691, beq. to wife Hannah; sons John, Thomas and Joseph; daus. Hannah Morrice and Mehetabel Mayo. The widow d. Oct. 5, 1699.

Rev. Samuel, Barnstable, ordained a teaching elder (minister) April 15, 1640. Atba. 1643. His wife joined the chh. Jan. 20, 1649. Ch. Mary and Samuel bapt. Feb. 3, 1649, Hannah bapt. Oct. 20, 1650, Elizabeth bapt. May 22, 1653.

MEACHAM, MACHAM, MECHUM,

Jeremiah, clothier, Salem, sold dwelling house and land in 1650. He m. Alice, dau. of Osman Douch of Gloucester. [Ess. De.]

Will dated 12 April, 1694, prob. Nov. 18, 1695; "very ancient;" wife Margaret deceased; now wife Alice; dau. Rhoda dec.; beq. to her son Samuel West; fulling-mill to son Jeremiah; to all my children and their children. Agreement for division made June 26, 1696, between Jeremiah and Isaac M., Sarah, (wife of Joseph Boyce,) Rebecca, (wife of John Mecarter,) Bethiah, (wife of George Hacker,) and Hannah Gill, widow.

MEAD, MEED, MEADE, MAID,

Gabriel, Dorchester, frm. May 2, 1638. Wife Joanna memb. chh. about 1638. Ch. Lydia, named in her father's will, Israel bapt. 2 (7) 1639, Experience bapt. 23 (11) 1641, (m. 4 (10) 1663, Jabez Eaton,) Sarah bapt. 4 (11) 1643, (m. 31 (9) 1664, Samuel Ed-

MEAD, etc., cont.

dy,) Patience bapt. 29 (1) 1646, (m. 28 (2) 1669, Matthias Evans,) David bapt. 7 (5) 1650.

He d. 12 (3) 1666, ae. about 77. Will prob. 17 July, 1667. Wife Joanna; ch. Lydia, Experience, Sarah and Patience, all under age. [Reg. XV, 163.]

William, propr. Roxbury.

He—, an aged man, was bur. 3 (9) 1683; old sister M. was bur. 9 (9) 1683. His will dated 29 Oct. prob. 29 Nov., beq. to wife Rebecca, and after her decease to the Free School of Roxbury; to son-in-law Joseph Stanton; to bro. Richard M. The widow beq. to the school; to bro. and sister M., and to a number of friends.

William, husbandman, Gloucester, lawsuit in 1639, constable 22 (9) 1648. [Es. Court rec.] [See Southmeade.]

MEADCALFE, see Metcalf.

John, called to Gen. Court 5 (1) 1638-9, being not yet returned from Piscataqua.

MEADOWS,

Philip, Roxbury, propr. He m. in April, 1641, Elizabeth Ingulden; ch. Hannah b. Feb. 1, 1642-3.

MEAKINS, MEKINS, MEKIN,

Thomas, Boston; he and his wife Katharine, servants to Edmund Quinsey, adm. chh. 2 (12) 1633, dism. to Braintree 6 (4) 1641. He was adm. frm. March 9, 1636-7. Son Thomas, adm. chh. 30 (1) 1634, recd. beq. from Mr. Thomas Bell, of London, a bro. of Katharine, in 1670. Another child was also a legatee. [See Bell.] Katharine d. Feb. 3, 1650. Ch. rec. at Br.: Sarah b. 24 (2) 1641, Thomas b. 8 (4) 1643, Helen drowned 3 (10) 1638. [It is difficult to distinguish records relating to Thomas, Sen., and Thomas, Jr.]

MEANE, MEENE, MEAN,

John, Cambridge, propr. Wife Anne; ch. John b. 3 (12) 1638, d. 16 (6) 1639, Sarah b. 12 (....) 1639-40, (m. Walter Hastings,) Mary b. 3 (2) 1644, (m. Samuel Hastings,) John b. and d. 1646.

He d. 19 (1) 1645-6. The widow m. John Hastings, q. v.

MEARS, MEARES, MERE, MERES, MEERE, MEERES,

Robert, husbandman, ae. 45, with Elizabeth, ae. 30, Samuel, ae. 3, and John, ae. 3 months, came in the Abigail in July, 1635. Settled at Boston. Propr. Jan. 1635-6. Elizabeth adm. chh. 24 (5) 1636. Ch. b. in Bo.: Stephen bapt. 10 (7) 1637, Stephen b. 25 (10) 1638-9, d. Dec. 10, 1661, Samuel b. 7 (4) 1641, James b. 9 (1) 1644.

Will dated Feb. 20, 1666, being aged; wife Elizabeth to have life use of est.; beq. to sons Samuel and James and to the first-born ch. of each; to James, son of dec. son John; wife exec., bro. James Johnson and Mr. Thomas Wilder, overseers. Prob. Nov. 13, 1667. [Reg. XVII, 346.]

MEECH,

John, Charlestown, inhabitant, 1630. See March.

MEGGS,

John, Weymouth. He m. a sister of William Fry, who beq. to her son John in 1643. Ch. John b. 29 (12) 1641-2.

MELLOWS, MELLOWES, MELLHOUSE,

Mr. Abraham, invested 50 li. in the stock of the Mass. Bay Co. about the year 1630. Came to N. E. Settled at Charlestown; adm. to ch. with wife Martha and son Edward 19 (6) 1633; frm. May 14, 1634. Town officer.

He d. in 1638. Will mentioned in Gen. Court 4 June, 1639. Serg. Edward, "heir and assignee," petitioned the Court 9 (4) 1641, for 300 acres more of land. [L.]

Oliver, Boston, adm. chh. with wife Elizabeth 20 (5) 1634. Propr. He was one of the partisans of Mrs. Hutchinson whom the Court disarmed in 1637. Ch. Samuel bapt. 7 (10) 1634, Martha bapt. 6 (1) 1636, Mary bapt. 26 (6) 1638, (m. 13 (7) 1655, Emanuel Springfield).

He d. at Braintree. Admin. gr. to his widow Elizabeth 5 (10) 1638. [Reg. XXX, 78.] The widow m. 2, Thomas Makepeace; who petitioned the Court 22 May, 1651, for power to sell land at Br. for the 6 ch.'s benefit, and gave security, with the eldest son John, for the payment of the younger ch.'s portions. John deposed in prob. of Thomas Blackley 30 Jan. 1673, ae. about 53 years, and his wife Martha, ae. about 43 years.

MELLEN, MELLIN, MELLERS,

Richard, Charlestown. Rem. to Weymouth; frm. Sept. 7, 1639. Ch. James b. at Char. 3 (4) 1642, Sarah b. at Wey. 4 (2) 1643.

MENDALL, MENDILOUE, MENDLOUE, MENDLOVE, MENDAM,

Mark, laborer, Plymouth, in Court 12 July, 1637. Bought land in 1639.

Robert, Duxbury, volunteer for the Pequot war in 1637. Had land grant 2 Oct. 1637. Sold house and land in 1639. His wife Mary was punished 3 Sept. 1639. She brought goods out of Eng. which were for Arthur Howland, and kept or sold them, for which her husband paid by sale of lands 5 Nov. 1644.

William, Plymouth, servant of Wm. Palmer, transferred in 1633 to Richard Church to learn the trade of carpenter.

MERCER,

Luce, ae. 19, came in the Defence in July, 1635.

Thomas, called to Salem Court in 1639.
Thomas, Boston. Wife Edith. Their son Samuel apprenticed to George Carr of Salisbury 20 Oct. 1676.

MERCHANT, MERCHAND, MARCHANT,

John, Braintree. Had grant of land for 2 heads 24 (12) 1639. Wife Sarah d. 3 (10) 1638.

John, Watertown, propr. 1642.

John, Yarmouth, constable, 7 June, 1648. Ensign of the town company, approved by the Court 8 June, 1664. Lieut. 11 Aug. 1670, called Senior. Ch. Mary b. 20 May, 1648, Abijah b. 10 Jan. 1650.

William, Watertown. Wife Mary; ch. Mary b. 24 (1) 1641. He and his wife were legatees in the will of Edward Skinner of Cambridge in 1641.

William, Ipswich, fence-viewer in 1656. His widow Mary made will 25 June, 1679; admin. gr. to Henry Osborn 30 March, 1680; beq. to the ch. of her dau. Mary Osborn; refers to the inv. of her dec. husband W. M.

MERIAM, MERRIAM, MERION, MIRIAM,

George, Concord, frm. June 2, 1641. Wife Susanna; ch. Elizabeth b. 8 (9) 1641, Sarah b. 17 (5) 1649, Samuel b. 21 (5) 16—, Hannah b. 14 (5) 16—, Abigail b. 15 (5) 16—, Mary d. 10 (6) 1646.
He d. Dec. 29, 1675. Inv. filed by Samuel M. exec. 4 (2) 1676.

John, Boston, frm. May 26, 1647. Wife Sarah adm. chh. with him 15 (12) 1651; ch. John bapt. 22 (12) 1651, Isaac b. Jan. 20, 1652.

Joseph, planter, came as an "undertaker" in the Castle, arriving at Charlestown in July, 1638. Settled at Concord. [L.] Suit in Plym. court for money in 1639. Wife Sarah; ch. John b. 9 (5) 1641.
He d. 1 (11) 1640-1. Will prob. Suff. 26 (8) 1642. Wife to have the whole est. for the bringing up of all the ch. until they are 21 years of age; she may sell the house and provide a lesser one. Est. to be appraised when oldest ch. is 21, and wife to have one third; the same if she marries. Brethren Mr. Thomas Flint, Simon Willard and Robert M. overseers. [Reg. II, 184, and L, 506.[

Robert, planter, Concord, bro. of Joseph, ae. 26 in 1639, frm. March 13, 1638-9. Owned land at Charlestown in 1638. Deputy 1655.
Will dated 10 Dec. 1681, prob. April 4, 1682, beq. to wife; cousin Isaac Day in old England, son of sister Joan D., dec., provided he come to possess it; otherwise to cousin Robert, son of Joseph M. of Concord, dec.; cousin Jonathan Hubbard; Joseph French and Sarah Wheeler who formerly lived with me. Rest to the ch. of two dec. bros. George and Joseph M., specifying 8 persons.

William Mirriam, of Hadloe, Kent, clothier, in will dated 8 Sept., prob. 27 Nov. 1635, beq. to sons Joseph, George and Robert; which seems to apply to these Concord pioneers. [Reg. L, 506.]

MERICK, MERRICK, MIRICK, MIRACK,

Henry, Scituate, took oath of allegiance 1 Feb. 1638.

James, Charlestown, propr. 1648.

John, cooper, Charlestown, 1642. He deposed in 1660, ae. 46 years. [Mdx. Files.]

MERICK, etc., cont.

He apprenticed son Benjamin to Henry Kembie, blacksmith, Dec. 6, 1657. Wife Judith; ch. Hopestill b. 20 (2) 1642. Wife Hopestill adm. chh. 10 (7) 1644; ch. Benjamin b. 22 (4) 1644. He m. at Cambridge 3 (2) 1655, Elizabeth, dau. of Thomas Weyborne of Boston. Ch. Abigail bapt. 17 (12) 1660.
He d. 15 Feb.; inv. of his est. taken 22 Feb. 1675.

John, Hingham, propr. 1637.
He d. 2 July, 1647. Will prob. 9 (7) 1647. Wife Elizabeth; sister Elizabeth Hilliard and her children; niece Elizabeth M.; servants John Skathe and Ann S.; John and Ann Fisher in Eng. [Reg. VII, 173.] The widow rem. to Roxbury, and sold lands at Hing. 13 (10) 1649.

Thomas, Springfield, frm. Oct. 11, 1665. Taxed 1638. Sergeant; much in town office. He sold his dwelling house and other buildings, with lands, in Spr. 2 (2) 1651. He deposed 9 Feb. 1690, ae. about 70 years. He m. 14 (2) 1639, Sarah Stebbins. Ch. Thomas b. 12 (2) 1641, Sarah b. 9 (3) 1643, Mary b. 28 (7) 1645, bur. 28 (5) 1646, Mary b. 27 (6) 1647, Hannah b. 10 (12) 1649. He m. 21 (8) 1653, Elizabeth Tilley. Ch. Elizabeth b. 26 (6) 1654, Miriam b. 1 (3) 1656, John b. 9 (9) 1658, Elizabeth bur. 11 (11) 1659, Elizabeth b. 4 (5) 1661, Thomas b. 2 Jan. 1663, Tilly b. Oct. 20, 1667, James b. March 2, 1669-70, Abigail b. 7 (7) 1673. Wife Elizabeth d. Aug. 21, 1684.

William, Duxbury, in court 5 Oct. 1636. Town officer 1646.

William, Eastham; suit in court in 1641; townsman 1655; ensign. Ch. William b. 15 Sept. 1643, Stephen b. 12 May, 1646, Rebecca b. 28 July, 1648, Mary b. 4 Nov. 1650, Ruth b. 15 May, 1652, Sarah b. 1 Aug. 1654, John b. 15 Jan. 1656, Isaac b. 6 Jan. 1660, Rebecca b. 28 Nov. 1668.
Will dated 3 Dec., prob. 6 March, 1688; about 86 years old; beq. to wife Rebeccah, sons William and Stephen; the rest of my children.

MERRIFIELD, MERRYFIELD,

Henry, husbandman, Dorchester, 1649. Ch. Mary, John, Elizabeth, (m. Thomas Pope,) Ruth, all bapt. 16 (2) 1649; Mary bapt. 18 (2) 1652, Thomas bapt. 30 (5) 1654,

MERRIFIELD, etc., cont.
Abigail bapt. 3 (6) 1656, Benjamin bapt. 27 (12) 1658, Martha bapt. 28 (2) 1661, Henry bapt. 31 (5) 1664.

He d. April 14, 1687. The widow Margaret d. July 6, 1688.

MERRILL, MERRELL, MERIAL,
John, Ipswich, had grant of land before 1636. Rem. to Newbury, propr. 1638; town officer; frm. May 13, 1640. Conveyed lands to bro. Nathaniel M. and son-in-law Stephen Swett; [no date; town rec.] Wife Elizabeth; dau. Hannah, (m. May 24, 1647, Stephen Swett.)

He d. 12 Sept. 1673. Beq. to gr. ch. John Swett and his bros. and sisters. Widow Elizabeth sold land Nov. 20, 1673; she d. July 14, 1682; beq. to son-in-law and gr. ch.

Nathaniel, Newbury, propr. 1638. Wife Susanna; ch. rec. at N., Daniel b. Aug. 20, 1642, Abel b. Feb. 20, 1643.

He d. March 16, 1654-5. Will prob. March 27, 1655. To wife Susanna, dau. Susanna; son Nathaniel to have est.., subject to wife's life-interest; he to pay to his sister as directed, and to his bros. John, Abraham, Daniel and Abel at 22 years of age. Bro. John M. and Anthony Somerby overseers. The dau. Susanna m. Oct. 15, 1663, John Burbank. The widow Susanna m. 2, Stephen Jordan. [See deed of land by her son Nathaniel 16 Aug. 1661.]

MERRITT, MERRETT, MERRICK,
Henry, planter, Scituate, took oath of allegiance 1 Feb. 1638; atba. 1643. Town officer 1642. Goody M. joined the chh. April 16, 1637. His dau. Katharine m. June, 1644, John Dammon.

He d. 30 Nov. 1653. Admin. gr. Jan. 24, 1653-4, to his bro. John M. [Reg. V, 260.]

John, Scituate, atba. 1643.

He d. about the latter part of Feb. 1676. Inv. taken 15 March folg.; mentions his wife Elizabeth; ch. Deborah ae. 21 years last March, John ae. 16, last Feb., Henry ae. 14 last Jan., Jonathan ae. 12 last July, Mary ae. 9 last Dec. and Elizabeth ae. 6 last July.

MERRY, MERRIE,
Nicholas, before Gen. Court 3 (7) 1639.

Joseph, Haverhill, propr. sold Dec. 22, 1644, and in 1648. Rem. to Hampton.

MERRY, etc., cont.
Contract of marriage with Elizabeth Hillier, widow, 13 (10) 1659.

Walter, or Waters, shipwright, Boston, adm. chh. 9 (12) 1633, frm. March 4, 1633-4. Wife Rebecca adm. chh. 29 (10) 1633; ch. Jeremy b. and d. 1633, Rebecca b. and d. 1635, Jeremy b. and d. 1637. The wife Rebecca d. 4 (5) 1653, and he m. 19 (6) 1653 Mary Doling; ch. Silvanus b. and d. 1655, Walter b. 3 June, 1657.

He was drowned 28 (6) 1657. Admin. gr. Oct. 27, 1657. Wife Mary and son Walter med. [Reg. IX, 230.] The widow m. 13 (9) 1657, Robert Thornton.

MESSENGER, MESSINGER,
Henry, joiner, Boston, had a great lot at Muddy River, for 2 heads, 11 (9) 1639. Frm. May 3, 1665. Wife Sarah, [see Callowe,] adm. chh. 1 (9) 1640; ch. John b. 25 (3) 1641, Sarah b. 12 (1) 1643, (m. Nov. 20, 1660, Richard Mason,) Simeon b. (1) 1645, Maryah bapt. 15 (6) 1647, Anne bapt. 20 (11) 1649, Rebecca b. 26 (4) 1653, Henry bapt. 3 (7) 1654, Lydia and Priscilla b. Nov. 22, 1656, Priscilla d. 21 (4) 1657, Priscilla b. 1659, Thomas b. March 22, 1662, Ebenezer b. Oct. 25, 1665, Martha, (m. Sept. 5, 1689, Jeremiah Fitch.) Old Mrs. Messenger, (Sarah M.,) d. June 6, 1697; (twice recorded.)

His will dated 25 March, prob. 9 April, 1673, beq. to wife Sarah for herself and the children; to son John.

METCALF, MEDCALF, see Meadcalfe,
Joseph, seaman, Ipswich, propr. 1634; called to Gen. Court 5 (1) 1638-9. Deputy 1635, 1643-4. With wife Elizabeth sold land in Ips. to Edward Neland a certain Irishman, 5 June, 1665.

Will dated June 3, 1665, ae. about 60; prob. 26 Sept., 1665; beq. to wife Elizabeth, son Thomas and gr. ch. Joseph, Mary and Elizabeth.

Michael, dornix weaver, of Norwich, Eng., ae. 45, with wife Sarah, ae. 39, children Michael, Thomas, Mary, Sarah, Elizabeth, Martha, Joane and Rebecca, and servant, Thomas Comberbach, ae. 16, passed exam. April 18, 1637, to go to N. E. Settled at Dedham; propr. 18 (5) 1637, adm. chh. 24 (6) 1639, frm. May 13, 1640. See letter of his, describing the religious persecutions he

312

METCALF, etc., cont.
had borne in Eng., [Reg. XVI, 279.] Town officer, school-master. Wife adm. chh. 11 (8) 1639. She d. Nov. 30, 1644, ae. 51 years, 5 months, 13 days; was b. at Wagnham, near Norwich, June 17, 1593, married Oct. 13, 1616. [Ded. chh. rec.] He m. 2, Mary, widow of Thomas Pidge.

He d. Dec. 27, 1664. Will dated 15 (9) 1664; refers to the covenant made with his wife Mary before their marriage, namely 13 Aug. 1645; sons John and Thomas M.; Michael, son of his dec. son Michael; daus. Mary, (wife of Henry Wilson,) Elizabeth, (wife of Thomas Bancroft,) Martha, (wife of Nathaniel Stow,) Joane, (wife of — Walker,) Rebecca, (wife of John Mackintosh,) Sarah, (wife of Robert Onion;) his wife's dau. Martha, (wife of Benjamin Bullard;) his dau. Stowes eldest son which she had by her first husband Wm. Brignall, to have four pounds when he shall attayne to lawful age; gr. ch. John Mackintosh and Robert Onion. [Reg. VI, 172.] Prob. Feb. 1, 1664-5.

Theophilus, Salem, 1636.

METHER,
Henry, Boston, made indenture with Thomas Cornish 24 (3) 1639. [L.]

MICHELL, MITCHELL, MICHEL,
Edward, came from Hingham, Eng., to Hingham, N. E., as a servant of Philip James, in 1638. Before the Court in 1641-2.

Experience, planter, came to Plymouth in 1623; frm. 1633. He rem. to Duxbury; juryman, town officer, propr. in 1623 with George Morton. Rem. to Bridgewater.

Will dated 5 Dec., 1689, [1688], inv. taken 14 May, 1689, prob. Sept. 4, 1689; beq. to wife Mary, sons Edward and John, daus. Mary Shaw, Sarah and Hannah Haward, and gr. ch. Experience, Thomas and Mary M.

George, house-carpenter, Boston. Sold house and land Oct. 21, 1654. Wife Mary; ch. Elizabeth b. Aug. 26, 1645, Mercy b. Aug. 25, 1648, John b. June 3, 1650, Sarah b. Dec. 8, 1652.

Rev. Jonathan, b. 1624, at Halifax, Yorkshire, [Mor.] came as a child of 11 in the ship James, from Bristol, Eng., in 1635, in company with Mr. Richard Mather, with his parents Matthew and Susan Michel, who

MICHELL, etc., cont.
settled in Connecticut. He grad. at Harvard in 1649 and was installed pastor at Cambridge 21 Jan. 1650. He was adm. frm. May 2, 1645. He was a very acceptable preacher and pastor. He left a valuable record of the families of the church, containing memoranda about times of arrivals, ages, etc. He m. Nov., 1650, Margaret, widow of his predecessor, Mr. Thomas Shepard. Ch. Margaret, Nathaniel b. 1656, d. 15 (5) 1673, John d. Oct. 29, 1659, Samuel b. Oct. 14, 1660, Margaret, Jonathan.

He d. 9 (5) 1668. [Rox. rec.] Admin. gr. to widow Margaret. Her est. was admin. by son Jonathan April 7, 1691.

Matthew, came in the James from Bristol, Eng., in 1635, in company with Mr. Richard Mather. Settled at Charlestown. Rem. to Springfield, and was one of the founders of the plantation in 1636. [Reg. XIII, 29.]

Susan M., also mentioned by Mather as being on board the James.

Thomas, Charlestown, adm. chh. with Anne 11 (4) 1636. Deputy, 1648. Thomas m. at Malden, (9) 1655, Mary Molton.

Thomas, Boston, [is it the foregoing?] Admin. gr. Feb. 28, 1677, to his widow Anna.

William, Newbury. He m. 7 Nov. 1648, Mary Sawyer; ch. Mary b. 31 Aug. 1649, John b. 21 May, 1651, William b. 1 March, 1653, Elizabeth b. 15 March, 1654-5. He d. 16 July, 1654.

MICHELSON, MICHISON, MITCHELSON,
Edward, gent., Cambridge, propr. 1636; marshall of the Gen. Court, 1637, also in 1660; ordered to apprehend Whalley and Goffe. [Suff. De. V, 1.] He m. Ruth Bushell; ch. Ruth b. 9 (9) 1638, Thomas b. (7) 1639, Bethia b. 6 (10) 1642, Edward b. 11 (9) 1644, Elizabeth b. 29 (6) 1646, Deborah, (m. — Wells, adm. chh. Jan. 1, 1664.) [Mi.] The wife d. June 15, 1664, ae. about 52.

He d. March 7, 1680-1, ae. 77. [Gr. st.]

MICKLTHWAITE,
Mr. Nathaniel, Boston, factor for Mr. Richard Hutchinson in 1639. [L.]

MIGHILL, MIHILL,
Thomas, Roxbury, Rowley, frm. May 13, 1640. Deputy 1648; deacon; town officer. He and his wife members chh. Rox. about 1637. Ch. Thomas b. 29 (8) 1639, Ezekiel b. 6 (8) 1642, Timothy b. 21 (4) 1644, Nathaniel b. 1646, Stephen b. 27 (12) 1651, Anna b. 8 (7) 1654. Wife Ellen was bur. 12 (5) 1640. He m. 2, Ann Parratt.
He was bur. 14 (5) 1654. Will dated 11 June, 1654, prob. 27 (1) 1655; beq. to wife Ann, sons Samuel, John, Thomas, Ezekiel and Stephen, and dau. Mary; to sister Ann Tenny; to Faith Parratt, Sen.; to the church.

MILDMAY,
William, son of Sir Henry, came over to study at Harvard College about 1641, where he remained till 1651, with a tutor, Mr. Richard Lyon, q. v. [C. M.]

MILES, MYLES, see Mills,
Edward, Boston, adm. townsman, 1644.

John, Boston, frm. March 14, 1638-9. Residing at Concord, he had ch. Mary b. 11 (12) 1639.

Joseph, came in the Mary and John March 26, 1634. Joseph at Salem in 1657.

Samuel, Boston, frm. May 1645. He m. at Boston, Oct. 16, 1659, Elizabeth, dau. of Francis Dowse.

MILLARD, MILLWARD, MILLER,
John, Salem.

George, Lynn, freed from his master, Captain Bridges by the Gen. Court 27 Sept. 1642.

Thomas, husbandman, planter, Boston, propr. 1639. Sold land May 2, 1668. Admin. of his est. gr. 4 Feb. 1669-70, to John Miller of Rehoboth. Testimony that he had no kindred in this country except this cousin J. M., and that he wished him to be his heir.

Thomas, mariner, fisherman, Cape Ann, Gloucester, deposed Aug. 25, 1640, ae. about 40 years. Selectman 1642. Partner with Osman Douch in fishing, with headquarters at Noddles Island, in 1639. [L.] Selectman in 1641. He rem. to Newbury; bought house and land in N., 1650, and sold Gloc. land 9 June, 1652. Wife Isabel in

MILLARD, etc., cont.
1640. Ch. Ann b. Nov. 1, 1642, Elizabeth b. 1644, (m. Daniel Pierce, Jr.)
He d. at Boston, Sept. 2, 1653. Will made 30 Aug., prob. 25 (9) 1653. Wife Anne; ch. under 18 years of age, Rebecca and Elizabeth. Rebecca m. May 27, 1656, Thomas Thorpe. See Pierce, Daniel.

MILLER,
Alexander, servant to Mr. Stoughton Dorchester, 1632, propr. 1634. Frm. May 2, 1638. Rem. to Boston.

Rev. John, Dorchester, propr. 1635. Rem. to Roxbury. Elder in the chh., afterward preached at Rowley. [E.] Frm. May 22, 1639. Became minister at Yarmouth. Still later pastor at Groton. Propr. at Sandwich in 1640. Was app. one of the ministers to visit Virginia in 1642, but declined. Gen. Court gave order for his accommodation at Y. 14 May, 1648. Prop. for frm. Plym. Col., 4 June, 1650.

He d. at Gr. June 14, 1663. Wife Lydia, with him in the chh. of Rox., d. at Boston Aug. 7, 1647 at the house of Thomas Bumstead. Ch. Mehitophal b. at Rox. July 12, 1638, Lydia b. at Rowley 2 (12) 1640, Susanna b. at Y. 2 May, 1647, rec. at Rox. Aug. 24, 1647, Elizabeth b. at Y. 13 Oct. 1649. Admin. gr. July 3, 1663, to his son John; books appraised by Anthony Thatcher and Edmund Hawes; other est. by John Larance and James Fiske, Sen.

John, Sen., Rehoboth, propr. 1643, town officer 1648. Ch. Hannah b. Dec. 23, 1653, Sarah b. Oct. 15, 1655, Samuel b. Oct. 5, 1658, Joseph b. Aug. 1660, Benjamin b. Sept. 22, 1662. He was cousin and heir of Thomas Millard, of Boston, in 1669.

Joseph, ae. 15, came in the Hopewell in Sept. 1635. [See Millard.]

Richard, Charlestown, 1637. Rem. to Cambridge. Wife Eleanor adm. chh. Char. 4 (9) 1643; ch. Joseph, James, Hannah. Was Joanna, who m. Nicholas Davison, this Hannah? Elizabeth, widow of Henry Herbert, James Miller and Joseph M., husband of Mary, only dau. of Walter Pope, made an agreement about lands 7 Nov. 1677.

Robert, before Gen. Court 7 Oct. 1646. Robert, Concord, inv. taken 26 (12) 1646, showed house, lands and farming tools.

MILLER, cont.

William, Ipswich, paid for service against the Indians in 1646; a resident in 1648.

Thomas, tailor, ae. 30, with wife Mary, ae. 29, and son Thomas, ae. 2, cert. from the parish of St. Saviours, Southwark, Eng., came in the Elizabeth, in April, 1635. Settled at Dorchester. [L.] Propr., town officer. Frm. May 17, 1637. Removed to Gloucester. Bought house and land there in 1655. Wife Mary, dau. of John Grenaway, q. v.; ch. Thomas, came with them from Eng., John b. 8 (5) 1635, Jonathan b. and d. 1638, Mary b. 26 (6) 1639, Mehitabel b. 14 (1) 1641, bapt. 20 (1) 1642.

Inv. of his est. taken 23 (7) 1676, was presented by the widow Mary at Ipswich 3 days later. Agreement for division made 27 Sept. 1682, after her death, between Thomas and Nathaniel M., Sarah, widow of John M., Thomas Riggs [husband of —] and Isaac Elwell, [husband of —].

MILLS, MILLES,

John, Boston, appl. frm. Oct. 19, 1630, frm. March 6, 1631-2. Rem. to Braintree in 1641; he and his wife Susan and their son John had letters of dismission 14 (6) 1656. Town officer. Had accts. with Edward Witheridge in 1648. [A.] Ch. Joy and Recompense, daus. bapt. 25 (10) 1631, John bapt. 3 (4) 1632, (d. at Br. 27 Feb. 1684-5, ae. 62;) Jonathan bapt. 30 (6) 1635, James bapt. 3 (4) 1638.

He d. 5 July, 1678. Mrs. Susanna d. 10 (10) 1675, ae. 80 years. His will dated 12 Jan. 1677, prob. 10 Sept. 1678, beq. to only son John and daus. Mary Hawkins and Susanna Dawes; desires that one of John's sons may be fitted for the work of the ministry, "which was the employment of my predecessors unto the third if not the fourth generations."

Samuel, Weymouth. He deposed 11 (1) 1640, ae. 21, servant to Henry Waltham. [L.] Rem. to Dedham; townsman 1 (11) 1644, memb. chh. before 1646. Wife Frances; ch. Samuel b. and d. 1646, Samuel d. 15 (10) 1649, Benjamin b. 20 (1) 1651, Elizabeth b. 10 (9) 1652, Stephen d. 3 (10) 1653, Sarah b. 5 (9) 1654, Rebecca b. 10 (2) 1657.

The wife Mary d. Oct 30, and he d. Jan. 1694-5.

MILLER *alias* **Hodges, see Hodges.**

MILLETT,

Richard, appl. frm. Oct. 19, 1630, frm. June 11, 1633.

MILNER,

Michael, ae. 23, came in the James in July, 1635.

MINGO,

—, Boston, a neger, his child Hope b 19 (3) 1641.

MINGY, MINGEY,

Jeffrey, Dedham, propr. 11 (6) 1637, sold (8) 1639; frm. May 13, 1640. Rem. to Hampton. Beq. his est. in 1658 to his wife and Eliakin Wardwell.

MINOR, MINARD, MINORD, MINORT, MYNARD, see Maynard,

James Boston. Wife Mary; ch. Amander b. (7) 1645. Mary Mynate, ae. about 45, deposed to the will of Mary Truesdell, Nov. 26, 1674.

John, carpenter, Boston, bought land 1 April, 1648. His widow Elizabeth and James Johnson, adminrs., sold his house and land Dec. 19, 1659. May 13, 1660, she sold her right of dower in land previously belonging to her former husband, Nathaniel "Eaton;" [see Heaton.] Sold land to her son-in-law John Barnes of Boston, cooper, March 1, 1669-70. Her will, dated 11 March, 1671, prob. 27 (10) 1683, beq. to ch. Jabez, Nathaniel and Eleazer Eaton; to cousin Mary Bartholomew; to the 5 ch. of her dau. Fisher; to dau. Elizabeth Barnes. Admin. gr. to her sons Cornelius Fisher and Nathaniel Heaton of Wrentham.

Thomas, [signature "Minor,"] Charlestown, memb. chh. 1632; propr. 1634; rem. to Hingham, propr. 1636. He m. April 23, 1634, Grace, dau. of Walter Palmer; ch. Clement bapt. March 18, 1638, Thomas bapt. May 10, 1640, Ephraim bapt. May 1, 1642, Joseph bapt. Aug. 25, 1644. Rem. to Hingham. Signed petition for liberty to plant at Whitehead Neck in 1645; also for Nashaway same year. Rem. to New London, Conn.

MINOT, MYNOT,
George, son of Thomas, of Saffron-Walden, Eng., b. Aug. 4, 1594, came to Dorchester before 1634; frm. April 1, 1634, one of the ten men same year, and afterward; ruling elder 30 years. Deputy. Wife Martha; ch. John b. 1626, James b. 31 (10) 1628, Stephen b. (3) 1631, Samuel b. (10) 1635, Hannah b. (2) 1637, (m. Mr. William Stoughton.) His wife d. 23 (10) 1657.

He d. 24 (10) 1671. Will dated Sept. 10, 1669, prob. 2 Feb. 1671. Beq. to sons James, Stephen, Samuel, and to Stephen and Samuel, sons of his deceased son John.

MINTER,
Desire, came in the Mayflower to Plymouth in the family of Mr. John Carver. Ret. to her friends in Eng. after his death, and d. there. [B.]

MIRIAM, see Meriam.

MITCHELL, see Michell.

MIXER, MIXTER,
Isaac, ae. 31, with wife Sarah ae. 33, and son Isaac, ae. 4 embarked for N. E. at Ipswich, Eng., April 10, 1634. Settled at Watertown; propr. 1636. Frm. May 2, 1638. Town officer, clerk of train-band.

He d. in 1655. Will prob. June 19, 1655; beq. to wife Sarah; to son Isaac; to dau. Sarah, wife of John Sterns; owned a share in the schooner Diligent. [Reg. XIX, 42.] The widow deposed 23 (4) 1657, ae. about 58. [Mdx. Files.]

MOLL,
Adam, tailor, ae. 19, came in the Bevis in May, 1638.

MONDAY, MONDE, MONDEY,
Henry, Salisbury, gent.; frm. May 13, 1640; propr.; appointed by the Gen. Court, 6 (9) 1639, on the com. on division of lands at S. Juryman. Wife — d. July 22, 1654. Gave his house, lands and commonage in S. to his nephew Philip Wollidge Aug. 3 and 27, 1655.

MONJOY, see Munjoy.

MONISH,
Lieut., second commander of the fort on Castle Island in Boston Harbor. [C.]

MONTAGUE, MOUNTAGUE,
Griffin, carpenter, Muddy River, Boston, 1635. [Col. Rec.] Sold the time of his apprentice, John Bundy, to William Brewster of Plymouth 6 March, 1636-7.

Rem. to Cape Porpoise, Maine. Took oath of fidelity July 5, 1653. Mrs. Anne Looman, of Weymouth, beq. to her gr. son, John Monticue, that dwells at the Eastward.

Richard, Boston, 1646. Rem. to Salem; witness in 1647. Wife Abigail adm. chh. Bo. 4 (2) 1646; adm. chh. Salem 31 (8) 1647; ch. Sarah b. and d. 1646, Martha bapt. 20 (4) 1647. His wife was dism. 25 (3) 1651, to the chh. of Wethersfield, Conn., whither he rem. Thence about 1659 he rem. to Hadley. Clerk of writs 1680.

He d. Dec. 14, 1681. Will dated 8 July, 1681, prob. 28 March, 1682, beq. to wife Abigail, sons Peter and John, daus. Mary and Abigail Warriner; dau. Martha White and the two ch. she had by Isaac Harrison. Genealogy.

MOODY,
Mr. John, Roxbury, frm. Nov. 5, 1633. Deputy 1634-5. Wife Sarah.

The Lady Deborah, "a wise and anciently religious woman," [W.] came to Lynn before 1638, when she is recorded as a propr. Rem. to Salem. Adm. chh. 5 (2) 1640. Was presented in court in 1641 for opposing Infant Baptism. Her house was unroofed in a tempest 4 (9) 1646. [W.] Had a grant of 400 acres of land from Gen. Court in 1640. Rem. to Long Island. [See E's Files 2, 20.] Her house attacked by Indians in 1643. One of the patentees of Gravesend, L. I., living there in 1654. Her son Henry was also a grantee, and sold land which he had recd. from his mother Deborah Modye deceased, May 11, 1659.

William, came in the Mary and John May 22, 1633-4; settled at Ipswich; land grant 1634. Rem. to Newbury; frm. May 6, 1635. Town officer at N. Saddler. Gave land and goods to son Samuel 8 Sept. 1673. His wife Sarah d. Jan. 13, 1672. Ch. Samuel, Joshua, Caleb. [See will of Samuel.]

He d. Oct. 25, 1673.

MOON, MOONE,
Robert, tailor, Boston, had accounts with Wm. Gibbones, and gave power of attorney to Joseph Howe 7 (3) 1645. [A.]

MOORE, MOOR, MORE, see Morrey and Mawer,

Edmund, Newbury, propr., petitioned Gen. Court 18 Oct. 1648, for full title to lands bought of John Lowle, dec. Wife Ann d. 17 June, 1676. Ch. Martha b. 12 Dec. 1643, Jonathan b. 23 April, 1646, Mary b. 30 Nov. 1656, Hannah b. April 2, 1661, d. 25 March, 1665. He deeded land to son Edmund with consent of son Jonathan, 20 Dec. 1677.

Ellen, a little girl, in charge of Mr. Edward Winslow, came in the Mayflower to Plymouth; she d. soon after arrival. [B.]

Enoch, Cambridge, propr. 1637.

Francis, Sen., Cambridge, propr., frm. May 22, 1638. He m. 1, Katharine, who was bur. 3 (2) 1643; he m. 2, Elizabeth. Ch. Francis, Samuel, (9 years of age when his father joined the chh. of Camb., having been bapt. in Eng.; was in Barbadoes in 1658;) Anne, (now Kidder,) Rebecca; ("Elizabeth, wife of F. M. hath 3 children at the time of her joining Camb. chh., the youngest, Rebecca, being 15 at the time of her joining the chh. which was (1) 1657." [Mi.]

He d. 20 Aug. 1671, ae. 85 years. Inv. of his est. taken 24 (8) 1671, was burnt with the records of the court, and a copy which had been made was afterwards filed. The widow Elizabeth d. 5 Nov. 1683, ae. 84 years. [Gr. st.]

George, Scituate, propr. 1636; rem. to Duxbury. Servant to Edward Dotey, 1638. Ferryman over Jones River. See Morrey.

Golden or Goulden, Cambridge, propr., frm. June 2, 1641. Rem. to Billerica about 1658. Was of Medford in 1664. [Mdx. De. II.] Wife Joane, widow of John Champney, d. Feb. 18, 1675; ch. Hannah b. 15 (1 or 9) 1643, Lydia, Ruth. [Mi.]

He d. Sept. 3, 1698, ae. about 89.

Hannah, perhaps the same as Anne, memb. chh. Salem, 1636, sold land on Darby Fort side in 1660.

Hugh, embarked for N. E. April 12, 1632.

Isaac, ae. 13, came in the Increase April 15 1635.

Jasper, a child in charge of Mr. John Carver came in the Mayflower; d. in 1621. [B.]

MOORE, etc., cont.

Jeremiah, came from Windham, Eng., to Hingham in 1638. Rem. to Boston. Was adm. to chh., a singleman, 4 (4) 1643; frm. May, 1645. Ch. Samuel bapt. 29 (6) 1647, Jeremiah b. 17 (10) 1648, Mary bapt. 16 (12) 1650, (m. John Cotta.)

He d. in 1650. Inv. taken 13 (11) 1650. [Reg. VII, 34.]

John, Dorchester, propr. before 1634; frm. May 18, 1631; town officer to 1638.

John, Cambridge, propr. before 1636; frm. July 3, 1632. Agreed to keep cattle in 1636. Memb. valuation com. for Camb. 13 May, 1640. Deacon.

John, Salem, suit against him in court in 1636. Frm. Dec. 8, 1636. Ch. Jerusha bapt. 25 (10) 1636, Benjamin bapt. 18 (5) 1641, Ephraim b. or bapt. 10 (10) 1643.

John, ae. 24, a servant, came in the Planter in March, 1634, certified from Stepney parish.

John, the governor's servant, mentioned in Boston records in 1639.

John, Sen., yeoman, Sudbury, propr. 1640; John, Jr., also propr. Bought land in 1642; town officer. He m. Elizabeth, dau. of Philemon Whale, q. v.

John, Sudbury, made will 25 Aug. 1668, prob. 7 April, 1674. Beq. to eldest son John, of Lancaster; sons William, Jacob, Joseph and Benjamin; daus. Elizabeth, wife of Henry Rice; Mary, wife of Daniel Stone, and Lydia, wife of James Cutler, who rec'd a portion upon her marriage with her former husband, Samuel Wright. Refers to his "age."

John, Braintree, wife Bridget d. in 1643.

Old John Moore of 100 years died 27 (8) 1679. [Roxbury Records.]

John Mendon, d. 25 (8) 1679; nunc. will prob. 19 Feb. 1679. Beq. to wife Elizabeth and sons and daughters.

Richard, came as a boy, apprenticed to William Brewster, in the Mayflower to Plymouth. He deposed 27 Sept. 1684 ae. about 70 years, that he came from the house of Mr. Thomas Weston in London; that he knew of the arrival of Mr. Weston's colony in Mass. Bay about two and a half years later, the—

MOORE, etc., cont.

coming of Weston a short time afterwards, and the desertion of the colonists soon after by reason of Indians and sickness; etc. [Reg. L., 203.] A brother and a sister Ellen came with him. He settled at Duxbury; yeoman; propr. Rem. to Salem. Mariner; adm. chh. 27 (12) 1641; was a retainer and servant of Richard Hollingsworth, whose dau. he m. as a second wife. Deeded land in 1675 to his sons Caleb and Richard and daus. Susanna and Christian. Deposed April 1, 1690, ae. about 78 years. [Es. Files, 48, 75.] He m. at Dux. Oct. 20, 1636, Christian Hunt; she was adm. chh. Sal. 16 (4) 1650; she d. Oct. 5, 1686. He m. 2, Susanna, dau. of Richard Hollingsworth. Ch. Samuel and Thomas bapt. 6 (1) 1642, Caleb bapt. 31 (1) 1644, Joshua bapt. 3 (3) 1646, Richard bapt. 2 (11) 1647, Susanna bapt. 12 (3) 1650, Christian bapt. 5 (7) 1652, Mary b. 15 (11) 1661.

Samuel, Salem, propr. 1636; frm. May 18, 1631. Ch. Samuel bapt. 25 (10) 1636, Remember bapt. 9 (10) 1638.

Thomas, Dorchester, propr., town officer, 1634; frm. May 18 1631. Thomas and Elizabeth Moore are recorded among the children bapt. at Dorch. about 1636, by communion of churches, one or both of their parents being membs. of the chh. at Windsor or Hingham. He rem. to Windsor.

Thomas, Salem, propr. 1636; wife Martha joined chh. with him in 1639. They were dismissed to some other church not specified. He rem. to Southold, L. I., and sold land at Sal. in 1656. Ch. Thomas and Martha bapt. 21 (8) 1639, Benjamin bapt. 2 (6) 1640, Nathaniel bapt. 3 (5) 1642, Hannah bapt. 29 (10) 1644, Elizabeth bapt. 31 (11) 1646, Jonathan bapt. 3 (4) 1649, Mary bapt. 15 (4) 1651.

William, Salem, 1638.

William, Ipswich, deeded land on east side of the river of Exeter to his dau. Mary, wife of Robert Powell, 22 Jan. 1660.

MOORECOCK, MORECOCK,

Bennett, ae. 16, Nicholas, ae. 14, and Marie, ae. 10, came in the Elizabeth and Ann in May, 1635. See Thomas Whiton and John Smith, Plymouth. Mary m. 16 July, 1649, William Browne of Plym.

MOOTEHAM,

Thomas, [Boston,] chosen ensign in place of sergt. Morris, Nov. 5, 1633. [Col. Rec.]

MORDEN,

Jane, ae. 30, came in the Christian March 16, 1634.

MORECROFT,

Mr. John, before Boston Court 2 (1) 1640-1. [Col. Rec. and L.]

MOREY, MAURY, MORIE, MAURIE, MORREY, MORY,

George, Duxbury, propr. 31 Aug. 1640.

John, ae. 19, came in the Blessing in July, 1635.

Roger, Salem, propr. 1636; "neatherd;" memb. chh.; [wife] Elizabeth adm. chh. 17 (8) 1641. Ch. Jonathan bapt. 2 (2) 1637, Apphia bapt. 17 (4) 1638, Mary bapt. 16 (11) 1639, Benjamin bapt. 20 (3) 1641 or 1649.

MORFIELD,

John, servant of James Buck, came in 1638 from Hingham, Eng. to Hingham, N. E.

MORGAN,

Bennett, came to Plymouth in the Fortune in 1621. Had lands assigned in 1623.

James, husbandman, Roxbury. frm. May 10, 1643. Mortg. land in 1644; sold land in 1651. He m. Aug. 6, 1640, Margery Hill. Ch. Hannah b. July 18, 1642, James bapt. 3 (1) 1643-4, John bapt. Sept. 30, 1645, Joseph bapt. 29 (9) 1647, Abraham bapt. 3 (7) 1648, d. 2 (6) 1649, a dau. bapt. 17 (9) 1650.

Miles, Springfield, propr. 1645. Town officer. Ch. Mary b. 14 (12) 1644, Jonathan b. 16 (9) 1646, David b. 23 (7) 1648, Pelatiah b. 7 (5) 1650, Isaac b. 12 (3) 1652, Lydia b. 8 (2) 1654, Hannah b. 11 (12) 1656, Mercy b. 18 (5) 1658, Nathaniel b. June 14, 1658. The inv. of his est. was taken July 12, 1699; presented by Jonathan, David and Isaac; division made to them and their bro. Nathaniel; Samuel Terrey assented to this in right of their sister, his first wife; his dau. Hannah to have a good cow upon the day of her marriage.

Robert, Salem, 1636. Adm. chh. 16 (4) 1650. He deposed in 1671, ae. 70 years. Ch.

MORGAN, cont.
Samuel, Luke, Joseph and Benjamin bapt. 23 (4) 1650, Robert bapt. 15 (10) 1650, Bethiah bapt. 29 (3) 1653, Aaron bapt. 24 (3) 1663.

Will dated 14 (6) 1672, prob. 24 (4) 1673, beq. to wife Margaret and her father Norman; ch. Samuel, Benjamin, Robert, Joseph, Moses and Bethia.

MORLEY, MORLY,
Doctor John, Braintree, frm. May, 1645. He m. 20 (2) 1647, Constant Starr. Dr. Comfort S. calls him bro.-in-law. He was a legatee in the will of his uncle Thomas Burnall, citizen and cloth-worker of London, 19 Aug. 1661. [Reg. XXXVIII, 419.]

He made will 18 Jan. 1660, prob. April 2, 1661; beq. property in N. E. and at Chesthunt, co. Hartford, Eng. to wife Constant, and after her death to his sister Ann Farmer; refers to the will of his dec. mother Katharine M. The widow made will April 6, 1667, prob. June 14, 1669; beq. to bro. Joy Starr, sisters Ann Farmer, Suretrust Rouse; to Mrs. Dorothy Shepard of Rowley; to cousins John Starr, Sen., Simon Eyres, Elizabeth Farmise, Elizabeth Edmunds; kinswoman Lydia Minard.

Ralph, Charlestown, d. (7) 1630. Widow at house of John Greene; inhabitant in 1630; was cared for by the town in 1635.

Robert, servant to Mr. Andrew Mathews late barber surgeon, was appointed by the Mass. Bay Co. March 5, 1628, to serve the plantation as barber and surgeon for 3 years.
Did he come here?

Sarah, appr. for 9 years to Mr. Nathaniel Turner of Saugus, 8 April, 1632.

MORRELL, MORRILL,
Abraham, blacksmith, Cambridge, propr. 1636. Rem. to Salisbury. Propr. 1640. Had land at Haverhill in 1649. Wife Sarah; ch. Isaac b. July 10, 1646, Jacob b. Aug. 24, 1648, Sarah b. Oct. 14, 1650, (m. 1, Philip Rowell, m. 2, Onesiphorus Page, m. 3, Daniel Merrill,) Abraham b. Nov. 14, 1652, Moses b. Dec. 28, 1655, Aaron b. Aug. 9, 1658, Richard b. and d. 1659, Lydia b. March 28, 1660-1, (m. Ephraim Severance,) Hephzibah b. Jan. 1662-3, (m. Capt. John Dibbs).

He fell sick and d. at Roxbury; was bur. 20 (4) 1662. Will not dated, prob. at Hamp-

MORRELL, etc., cont.
ton 14 Oct. 1662, beq. to wife and minor ch. Isaac, Abraham, Jacob, Sarah, Moses and Lydia. The widow conveyed 1 (9) 1665, to Thomas Bradbury and her bro. Job Clement certain property in trust for her dau. Hephzibah who was b. after the father's death.

Edward, laborer, Yarmouth, deposition 7 Oct. 1639; in Court and indicted in 1641.

George, before Gen. Court 6 (7) 1638. Plymouth Court provided for him 31 Aug. 1638.

Isaac, blacksmith, embarked for N. E. June 22, 1632. Came to Roxbury; frm. March 4, 1632-3. Propr. Wife Sarah; ch. Isaac b. and d. 1632, Isaac b. and d. 1633, Hannah b. Sept. 12, 1636, (m. Daniel Brewer,) Elizabeth b. and d. 1638, Isaac bur. Jan. 31, 1639, Abraham b. June 6, 1640, d. 13 (9) 1661. The wife Sarah d. 9 (11) 1672, ae. 72.

He d. Dec. 18, 1661. Will prob. Jan. 23, 1661-2. Sons-in-law John Smith, Tobias Davis and Daniel Brewer; dau. Katharine Smith; cousin Isaac M.; gr. ch. [Reg. XI, 36.]

Mr., a minister, brought over to Massachusetts by Robert Gorges, who had been appointed by the Council governor for New England, in 1623. He had power and authority of superintendencies over other churches, but made no use of it; only spoke of it as he was about to return a year after the governor. He resided at Wessaguscus. [B.]

MORRICKE,
John, Hingham.
Will dated 24 June, prob. 9 Sept. 1647. Beq. to his sister Elizabeth Hiller, and her ch. John and Anne Scathe; to wife Elizabeth; to Wm. Heley; if his "neese" Elizabeth Morricke, John and Anne Fisher shall come over, etc. His widow Elizabeth sold land at Hing. 13 (10) 1649. She d. 25 (6) 1650. Will dated 14 March, 1649, prob. 5 (7) 1650. At Hingham, but now dwelling in Roxbury; Robert Hull of Boston and Leonard Fellowes of Great Bowden in old England execs.; to William F. of Ipswich, Richard F. of Conn., Samuel F. of Salisbury, William Healy of Roxbury and his two eldest children, Mr.

MORRICKE, cont.
Eliot and Mr. Danforth of Rox., Mr. Hubbert of Hing., Ann Hillard of Hing., John and Ann Scath; my sister Grace Allam in Lincolnshire. [Reg. VII, 232.]

MORRIS, MAURICE, MORES, MORRICE, MORUS,
Ademia, Rehoboth, propr. 1646.

Edward, carpenter, from Keniton Magna, Dorset, came in the confidence April 11, 1638. Settled at Roxbury; mentioned in town records 23 (12) 1652. Probably the person who, at Boston, m. 20 (9) 1655, Grace Bett.
Admin. of his est. gr. Jan. 27, 1690-1, to his eldest son Isaac M.

Rice, Charlestown, inhabitant 1634. Wife Hester —; ch. Hannah, Hester b. 6 (1) 1641.
He d. 25 (2) 1647.

Richard, Boston, memb. chh. with his wife in 1630; juror Nov. 9, 1630; frm. May 18, 1631. Res. some time at Roxbury; deputy 1634-5. Was dism. to the chh. of Paschquataqua (Exeter,) 6 (11) 1638. Was of Dover in 1639, shipping clapboards. Ensign, lieut. Wrote an address concerning Capt. Underhill in Latin in 1640. [L.] Wife Lenora dism. to chh. of P. 3 (1) 1639.

Robert, Rehoboth, Seacunck; suit in Plym. court in 1641; lands confirmed to him 2 May, 1643.

Sarah, dau. of Mrs. Anne Cowlishawe, adm. chh. Boston (8) 1633.

Thomas, Seacunk, rem. to New Haven and sold house and lands at S. 26 Nov. 1640. [Plym. Col. De.]

William, of Royston, co. Hartford, butcher, apprenticed to Wm. Collier, gent. for 5 yrs. from April 4, Charles 13, was transferred 6 Aug. 1637, to Love Brewster of Duxbury, yeoman.

William, bricklayer, Boston; [compare with the preceding.] He deposed 4 (2) 1659, ae. 45 years. [Mdx. Files.] With wife Dorcas mortg. land in Bo. Jan. 13, 1664.

MORRISON,
Elizabeth, ae. 12, came with the family of George Giddings in the Planter April 2, 1635, cert. from the parish of St. Albons, Herts., Eng.

MORSE, MORSS, MOSS, MOSSE,
Anthony, shoemaker, of Marlborough, Eng., came in the James April 5, 1635. Settled at Newbury. Frm. May 25, 1636. Propr.. He deposed 9 May, 1665, ae. about 58 years. Wife [Mary?] Ch. recorded: Benjamin b. 4 March, 1640, Sarah b. 1 May, 1641, Hannah b. 1642, Lydia b. and d. 1645, Lydia b. 7 Oct. 1647, d. May 19, 1648, Mary b. 9 April, 1649, d. 14 June, 1662, Hester b. 3 May, 1651, Joshua b. 24 July, 1653.
He d. Oct. 12, 1686. Will dated 29 April, 1680, prob. 23 Nov. 1686, beq. to sons Robert, Peter, Anthony, Joseph, Benjamin and Joshua and their children; to daus. Thurlo, Stikny, Newman and Smith, or their ch.; to dau. Rebecca Homs; to gr. ch. Rich. Thurlo. Signed Anthony Morse.

Joseph, ae. 24, came in the Elizabeth of Ipswich April 30, 1634. Settled at Watertown; propr. 1636. Wife Esther, dau. of John Peirce of Wat.; ch. Joseph b. 30 (2) 1637, John b. 28 (12) 1638, Jonathan bur. 12 (3) 1643, Jonathan b. 7 (9) 1643, Hester b. 7 (1) 1645.
He d. March 4, 1690-1. Admin. gr. to his son John.

Joseph, [Mosse,] planter, Ipswich, propr. 1637.
Will dated 24 (2) prob. 29 (7) 1646; beq. to wife Dorothy, sons Joseph and John, dau. Hannah.

Samuel, husbandman, ae. 50, with wife Elizabeth, ae. 48, and (son) Joseph, ae. 20, came in the Increase April 15, 1635. Settled at Dedham. Propr. 1636. Frm. Oct. 8, 1640. Town officer. Rem. to Medfield.
He d. April 5, 1654. Will prob. 30 (11) 1654. To wife Elizabeth; to sons John and Daniel, and to Ann, wife of son Joseph, dec.; to dau. Mary Bullen. Inv. taken 10 (5) 1654. [Reg. V, 299, and IX, 141.] The widow d. June 20, 1654.

Thomas, Dedham, proposed for memb. in chh. at its formation in 1638; adm. chh. 28 (4) 1640.

MORSE, etc., cont.

William, shoemaker, from Marlborough, Eng. came in the James April 5, 1635. Settled at Newbury. Frm. March 3, 1635-6. Propr. Wife Elizabeth; ch. Hannah b. 6 March, 1641, Timothy b. 10 June, 1648, d. 10 Dec. 1659, Abigail b. 14 Feb. 1651, [Jonathan, Obediah, Elizabeth.] Elizabeth M. d. March 18, 1655.

He d. 29 Nov. 1683. Will signed 8 Aug. 1683, prob. March 25, 1684, beq. to wife; dau. Abigail and her husband John Kendrick with their children; sons Jonathan and Obediah, daus. Elizabeth (and her 4 ch.) and Hannah (and her son John Stiles).

MORTON, MOURTON, MOURT,

George, of York, Eng., m. at Leyden, Holland, July 23, 1612, Julia Ann, dau. of Alexander Carpenter; came to Plymouth in the Anne in 1623; 8 lots were assigned to him and Experience Mitchell. No further record of him found. Ephraim and John are believed to be his sons.

His son Nathaniel, b. at Leyden, (m. at Plymouth Dec. 22, 1635, Lydia Cooper; see John Cooper;) became secretary of Plym. Col.; wrote a valuable history, (based largely on Bradford's work,) called New England's Memorial, or Moort's Relation.

Mary, adm. chh. of Boston in 1630-1.

Thomas, came in the Fortune in 1621; res. at Plymouth. Had share of cattle in 1627. Propr.; sold land in 1639. Thomas, Jr., came in 1623; parentage not stated.

Thomas, of Clifford's Inn, gent. in company with Capt. Wollaston, arrived in N. E. in 1622, with 30 servants. Settled at Mount Wollaston, afterward included in Braintree. His dissipations and riotous dealings with both whites and Indians were utterly disgusting to the settlers at Plymouth and Boston, and endangered the peace and welfare of the whole region. He was remonstrated with to no effect; then punished in 1630 for wordy attacks on the government and people of Mass. Bay, for injuries done to the Indians and for selling weapons to them, etc. Wrote a hostile book, "The New English Canaan." Was sent to Eng.; lay a long time in Exeter jail. Came to Boston in 1644; was tried; freed on acct. of his age and poverty, and allowed to go out of the jurisdiction. Rem. to Agamenticus, and d. about 1646. [W. and B.] See Fitcher and Wollaston.

MORY, see Morey.

MOSELEY, see Maudesley.

MOSES,

John, shipwright, Duxbury, sued for pay for a pinnace he had built, 21 (4) 1641. [L.]

MOTT, MOTE,

Adam, tailor, ae. 39, with wife Sarah, ae. 31, and children John, ae. 14, Adam, ae. 12, Jonathan, ae. 9, Elizabeth, ae. 6, and Mary, ae. 4, came in the Defence in July, 1635. Settled at Roxbury; frm. May 25, 1636. Rem. to Hingham; called to Gen. Court 6 (7) 1638.

Nathaniel, Scituate, atba. 1643; served against the Narragansetts in 1645. He m. at Braintree 25 (10) 1656, Hannah, widow of Peter Shooter; ch. Nathaniel b. 28 (10) 1657, d. 13 (1) 1660, John b. 19 (6) 1659, Mary b. 15 (10) 1664, a dau. b. 5 (12) 1666, Elizabeth b. 17 (3) 1671, Experience d. 24 (10) 1672, Edward b. 11 (3) 1673, Ebenezer b. 7 (10) 1675.

He was killed by the Indians Feb. 23, 1675.

MOULTON, MOLTON,

James, Salem, propr., frm. March, 1637-8. Res. at Wenham in 1644. Constable 29 (10) 1646. [Es. Court.] Wife Mary also memb. chh. Ch. James bapt. 7 (11) 1637, Samuel bapt. 25 (10) 1642, Elizabeth bapt. 9 (5) 1647.

His will dated 26 Feb. 1678, prob. March 30, 1680, beq. to wife; sons James and Samuel and dau. Mary Friend; to the college; to the church, and to the minister, Mr. Joseph Gerrish.

John, of Ormsby, Eng., husbandman, ae. 38, with wife Anne, ae. 38, children Henry, Mercy, Anne, Jane and Bridget, and servants Adam Goodens, ae. 20, and Alice Eden, ae. 18, passed exam. April 11, 1637, to go to N. E. Settled at Newbury; frm. May 22, 1638. One of the founders of Hampton named in Col Rec. 6 (7) 1638.

Will dated 23 Jan. 1649, prob. 1 (8) 1650; wife Ann, sons Henry and John; daus. Ann, Jane and Bridget; son Samborne; Mary Samborne.

Mary, widow, ae. 30, with servants John Maston, ae. 20, and Merrean Moulton, ae. 23, and Ruth Moulton, singlewoman, ae.

MOULTON, etc., cont.
20, passed exam. at the same time as John, above. Settled at Salem; memb. chh. 1637.

Robert, Mr., carpenter, shipwright, sent over in 1628-9 by the Mass. Bay Co., came to Salem; frm. May 18, 1631. Deputy. Was of Charlestown in 1634. Ret to Sal. Propr., town officer. Ch. Abigail bapt. 22 (3) 1642, Robert bapt. 23 (4) 1644.
Will prob. 26 (4) 1655. Son Robert M.; dau. Dorothy Edwards; gr. son Robert M.; Joshua and goodwife Buffum. The son Robert's will was prob. 28 (9) 1665.

Thomas, fisherman, Charlestown, master of Ralph Glover's boat 3 Nov. 1630. [Col. Rec.] He deposed 4 (4) 1639, ae. about 30 years. [L.] He rem. to Malden. Sold land in 1656. Wife Jane adm. chh. 2 (12) 1632; deposed 20 (11) 1654, ae. 45 years; [Mdx. Files.] ch. John bapt. 16 (1) 1633, Martha bapt. 24 (5) 1635, Hannah bapt. 20 (9) 1641, Elizabeth bapt. 24 (2) 1642.
He d. 24 (10) 1657. Will dated 5 (8) prob. 24 (10) 1657, beq. to son Winslow and Sarah his wife; to sons Michell and Adams, rest to wife and sons John and Jacob.

Thomas, Newbury, propr. 1638. Rem. to Hampton. Deposed in 1655, ae. about 50 years. [Arch. 38 B.]

MOUSALL, MOUSELL, MOWSALL,
John, husbandman, Charlestown. adm. chh. with wife — 23 (6) 1634; frm. Sept. 3, 1634. Deputy, 1634-5, deacon. Rem. to Woburn; propr. 1640. He deposed in 1663, ae. about 67 years. Ch. Eunice, (m. at Wob. Nov. 1, 1649, John Brooks).
He d. March 27, 1665. Will dated 19 (4) 1660, prob. April 4, 1665, beq. to wife Joanna; son John; son John Brooks ch.; Ephraim Bucke and Hannah Lippenwell. Bro. James Tomson one of the overseers.

Ralph, carpenter, Charlestown, memb. original chh.; was dism. with wife Alice and others Oct. 14, 1632, to form the local chh. of Char. Town officer, deacon, deputy. Ch. Thomas bapt. 25 (3) 1633.
He d. April 30, 1657. Will dated 13 April, prob. 23 (4) 1657, beq. to ch. John, Thomas, Elizabeth, Mary, Ruth Wood and Marie Gove; cousins Nathaniel Ball and Mary Waine; Thomas Osburne, Wm. Crouch, widow Streeter; dear friend and countrywoman Mrs. Green. Rest to wife Alice.

MOUSALL, etc., cont.
The widow d. 1674. Inv. of her est. taken 4 Feb. 1674.

Ruth, Salem, recd. to chh. by letter testimonial 31 (11) 1640.

MOUSAR,
John, Salem, propr. 1639.

MOUSGRAVE, MUSGRAVE,
Mary, Concord, d. 25 (10) 1649.

MOXAM, MOXOM, MOXON,
Rev. George, was adm. to the chh. of Dorchester at the same time with Revs. Samuel Newman and William Tompson, about 1636. Rem. to Springfield, where he was the first minister. Frm. Sept. 7, 1637. House built for him in 1638. He sold house and lands to the town Sept. 14, 1652. No further record of him there. Ch. Union b. 16 (12) 1641, Samuel b. 10 (3) 1645, a son b. 19 (3) 1647. His daus. Martha and Rebecca were among the persons who accused Mary Parsons of witchcraft in 1651.

MOYCE, MOICE, MOISE,
Joseph, joiner, Salisbury, propr. 1640-1658. He was a legatee in the will of Mr. Nicholas Stanton of Ipswich, Eng. in 1648. [E. and W.] He and his three sons had lands assigned them at Haverhill in 1649. Wife Hannah d. at Salis. in 1658. Martha, wife 1, of George Goldwyer, and 2, of Robert Pike, calls Joseph Moys father-in-law, and Mary, wife of Andrew Greeley, sister.

MUDD,
Peter, engaged as servant with Ralph Woory of Charlestown, 29 (5) 1647, for one year, to go with him in the ship. [A.]

MUDGE,
Jarvis, called to the Court 4 (10) 1638. The name appears at Hartford, 1640.

MULLINS, MULLINES, MOLINES,
Mr. William, came from Leyden, Holland in the Mayflower; signed the Compact; res. at Plymouth. Brought with him his wife, son Joseph and dau. Priscilla, and a servant Robart Carter.
He d. Feb. 21, 1620-1; his wife, son and servant d. during that winter. The dau. survived, and m. John Alden. [B.]

322

MUN,
Benjamin, Springfield, res. 1649, propr. 1651. He m. 12 (2) 1649, Abigail, widow of Francis Ball. Ch. Abigail b. 28 (4) 1650, John b. 8 (12) 1652, Benjamin b. 1 (1) 1655, James b. 10 (12) 1656, Nathaniel b. 25 (5) 1661. He d. Nov. 1675. Admin. gr. to widow Abigail. She m. Thomas Stebbins, Jr. [See Ball.]

MUNDAY, see Monday.

MUNDEN,
Abraham, Springfield, propr. 1644. He m. 16 (3) 1644, Anne Munson. Ch. Mary b. 8 (6) 1645.
He was drowned Oct. 29, 1645.

MUNJOY, MONJOY,
George, mariner, ship-carpenter, came from Falmouth, in Casco, province of Maine, to Boston; was adm. chh. 5 (3) 1647; frm. May 26, 1647. He sold, Aug. 18, 1667, property left him by his father John M. of Abbotsham, co. Devon, Eng. to William Tytherley, of Bythefoard, co. Dev., mariner, now res. in Boston; his sister Mary, wife of John Sanders of Braintree, N. E., joined in the deed; reference made to their sister Martha M. of Abbotsham. [Suff De.] He m. Mary, dau. of Dea. John Philips, q. v. Ch. rec. at Bo.: John b. 17 April, 1653, George b. 21 April, 1656, *John* bapt. 27 (2) 1656, Josiah b. April 4, 1658, Philip bapt. 1 (4) 1662, Mary bapt. 1 (5) 1665, Hephzibah bapt. 9 (9) 1673, (m. Oct. 1, 1691, Nathaniel Alden,) Pelatiah and Gershom bapt. 20 (4) 1675. [Were any of these ch. of George, Jr.?]

MUNKE,
Ann, Roxbury, m. April 17, 1644, John Stebbin.

MUNNINGS, MANNING,
Edmund, ae. 40, with wife Mary, ae. 30, and children Mary, ae. 9, and Mehetabel, ae. 3, came in the Abigail in July, 1635. Settled at Dorchester. Ch. rec. at Dorch.: Hopestill b. 5 (2) 1637, Returned b. 7 (7) 1640, Take-heed b. 20 (8) 1642.
He ret. to Eng. Will dated at Onge, Essex, Oct. 1, 1666, prob. July 18, 1667. [Reg. XXXVII, 378.]
George, ae. 37, with wife Elizabeth, ae. 41, and children Elizabeth, ae. 12, and Abigail, ae. 7, came in the Elizabeth of Ips-

MUNNINGS, etc., cont.
wich, April, 1634. Settled at Watertown; propr. 1636. He deposed 23 (4) 1657, ae. 58; his wife Johanna, ae. 45. [Mdx. Files.] The Gen. Court allowed him 5 li., Oct. 28, 1636, in regard of the loss of his eye in the voyage to Block Island. He rem. to Sudbury. Propr. 1639. Acted for the plantation in buying land of the Indians 25 (5) 1639. [L.] He rem. to Boston; cordwinder; sold land at Wat. in 1652. Ch. George b. at Bo. Nov. 24, 1655.
He d. Aug. 24, 1658. Will prob. Sept. 16, 1658; wife Johannah, formerly wife of Symon Boyers. [Reg. VIII, 354.] The widow m. Sept. 21, 1659, John Laughton.

MUNSON,
Susan, ae. 25, came in the Elizabeth of Ipswich April 30, 1634.

Thomazin, ae. 14, came in the Blessing in July, 1635.

MUNT, MOUNT, MUNTE,
Thomas, brick-layer, mason, Boston, served as an apprentice first with Richard Garrett, with whom he came from Eng. in 1630, afterward with Gov. John Winthrop; had land in Bo. in view of this service. [Suff. De III, and W.] Sold property at Braintree in 1653. Wife Dorothy d. 28 (12) 1639; he m. 2, Faith —; he m. 3, Elinor —. Ch. Faith b. 24 (2) 1645, (m. Nov. 21, 1660, Clement Short,) Mary, (m. Thomas Kingston,) Patience.
He d. July 27, 1664. Admin. gr. to widow Elinor, on behalf of herself and three daus. [Reg. XII, 346.] The widow m. Thomas Hill, and joined him in a deed of land 10 March, 1667-8. Distribution of est. made April 28, 1666. [Reg. XVI, 162.]

MUSSELWHIT, MUSSELWHITE, [MUSSILOWAY?]
John, of Langford, Eng. came in the James April 5, 1635. Settled at Newbury; memb. jury at Ipswich in 1642.
He d. Jan. 30, 1669-70. Will dated 30 Aug. 1669, prob. 29 March, 1670, beq. to John M. of Ba[nn]stock in Wilshire, gr. son of my bro. David; to Thomas M. and Eda his sister.

MUSSEY, MUZZALL,

Abraham, came in the Mary and John March 26 1633-4; John, came with him.

Robert, Ipswich, frm. Sept. 3, 1634. Com. on allotments. Wife Bridget; ch. Mary, Joseph, (eldest son,) Benjamin, Ellen; all mentioned in his will dated Jan. 5, 1642, and March 18, 1643-4; prob. May 16, 1644. Refers also to a former wife; to brother Dane the elder. Additional inventory presented 17 (2) 1648, by Bridget Rowlison, late wife of R. M.

MUST, MUSTE, MUSSE,

Edward, residence not known, frm. May 14, 1634.

Hester, Cambridge, propr. 1635. She m. William Reskew, and with him sold land March 24, 1635-6.

MYGATT,

Joseph, Cambridge, propr. 1634 and 1635.

MYLAM, MILAM, MILOM,

Humphrey, cooper, Boston, bought land of his bro. John 7 (12) 1650. Wife Mary; ch. Mary b. 23 (3) 1652, Constancy b. 15 Dec. 1653, Sarah, incorrectly rec. "of John and Mary," b. 6 April, 1656, Abigail d. 7 May, 1659, Abigail b. Oct. 10, 1660, Hannah b. June 27, 1663, Ruth b. 26 April, 1666.

He d. in April, 1667. Will dated Feb. 14, prob. 3 May, 1667, beq. to wife Mary, ch. Mary, Constance, Sarah, Abigail and Hannah; to apprentice Nath Claddis. [Reg. XV, 326, and XVI, 56.]

John, cooper, Boston, with wife Anne adm. chh. 3 (11) 1635; frm. May 25, 1636. Had liberty to wharf before his property 27 (9) 1643. Made agreement with Wm. Franklin to pay certain tolls for vessels coming up the stream for his use or for the mill. Wife Christian; ch. Benjamin bapt. 10 (11) 1635, Constance b. 25 (10) 1638, John b. 18 (7) 1640, Eleazer b. 30 (7) 1642, Samuel b. 15 (6) 1644, Ebenezer b. 6 (3) 1646, Elizabeth bapt. 30 (11) 1647, ae. about 9 days, Samson bapt. 2 (6) 1649, ae. about 2 days, Joseph b. 26 (12) 1651.

NANNEY, NANNY, NANNYES,

Robert, ae. 22, "sent away," [fitted out?] by Robert Cordell, goldsmith, Lombard st., London, came in the Increase April 14, 1635. Rem. to Dover; returned to Boston. He m. about 1652 Katharine, dau. of Mr. John Wheelwright; ch. John b. Feb. 16, 1653, d. 20 (7) 1654, John b. Aug. 12, 1655, John b. Aug. 12, 1656, bapt. Aug. 17, 1656, d. 11 (10) 1658, Joseph b. and d. 1658, Samuel b. Aug. 27, 1659, Mary b. June 22, 1661, Elizabeth b. Jan. 2, 1663-4. He conveyed to Mr. W. and his son Samuel W. 19 (2) 1663, certain pieces of property in trust for his wife and the children she had borne him.

He d. Aug. 27, 1663. Will mentions property at Hampton, Wells, Boston, etc. and at Barbadoes in company with his uncle Richard Hutchinson of London. [Reg. XII, 155, Suff. and York Deeds.] The widow m. 2, Edward Naylor, from whom her father desired her divorce Sept. 11, 1673. [Arch. Dom. 9.]

NASH, NASHE,

Gregory, Charlestown, memb. chh. 1630; he and his wife d. (12) 1630.

James, Sen. shoemaker, yeoman, Weymouth, frm. May, 1645. Town officer, 1648. Sold land and wharf at Boston Jan. 29, 1651. Deputy 1655. Wife Alice; ch. Jacob. Had water works at Marshfield in 1651.

Admin. of his est. was gr. 31 Dec. 1680, to sons John, of Boston, cooper, and Jacob, of Weymouth.

Robert, butcher, free victualer, Boston, 1640. Wife Sarah adm. chh. 25 (12) 1642. House at Bendall's dock in 1647. Bought half of a vessel of George Dod in 1650; mortg. house and land in 1652. Was trading with Thomas Follit of Pascataqua in 1652. [Es. Files II, 39.]

Samuel, yeoman, Duxbury, frm. 1633, volunteer for the Pequot war in 1637; served against the Narragansetts in 1645; app. lieut. 1645. He deposed 6 July, 1682, ae. about 80 years. [Plym. Col. rec.]

Will dated 2 June, 1681, beq. to dau. Martha Clark; to Samuel and Ichabod, ch. of his dec. gr. son Samuel Samson; gr. daus. Elizabeth Dillano and Mary Howland.

Samuel, shoemaker, Weymouth, late of Burrough Green, co. Cambridge, Eng. gave

NASH, etc., cont.
letter of attorney 25 (5) 1641, to Enoch Lunt of Wey., blacksmith, to rec. a debt in Eng.

William, Charlestown, adm. chh. with wife Mary 30 (6) 1634; propr. 1635. He d. about 1637. Widow Mary was recognized as a propr. in his place in 1638. She d. June 18; will prob. July 3, 1674; beq. to son Peter and dau. Marie, wife of Thomas Hale; to next kinswoman Hanna Eddenden.

NEAL, NEALE,
Henry, carpenter, Braintree, had land grant for 3 heads 24 (12) 1639-40. Town officer. He deposed in Mdx. court 30 (4) 1654, ae. about 35 years. Rem. to Providence, R. I., about 1657; bought house and land, which sold in 1661, after returning to Br. [Prov. rec.] Active in town business to old age. Wife Martha was bur. 23 (5) 1653. He m. 11 (12) 1655, Hanah, dau. of Quinton Pray. Ch. rec. at Br.: Martha b. 16 (11) 1642, Samuel b. 31 (5) 1647, Henry b. 19 (1) 1649, Hannah b. 2 (2) 1651, bur. 20 (9) 1657, Sarah b. and d. 1653, Joseph b. 6 (8) 1660, Mary b. 1 (11) 1664, Rachel b. 12 (1) 1665, d. 15 (10) 1675, Deborah b. 7 (1) 1667, Benjamin b. 7 (1) 1668-9, Ruth b. 25 (10) 1670, Lydia b. 8 (10) 1672, Elizabeth b. 28 (4) 1675, Joanna b. May 27, 1680, Rebecca, Rachel, (m. 24 (1) 1697-8, Ralph Pope). He d. Oct. 16, 1688, ae. 71 years. [Gr. St.] The statement is made on his gravestone that he was the father of 21 children. Will dated Aug. 11 and Sept. 12, 1688, prob. Feb. 27, 1690-1, beq. to wife Hannah; sons Samuel, Joseph, Benjamin and Henry; daus. Abigail Scott, Hannah, wife of Nehemiah Heiden, Sarah Merryfield, Mary Thyre, Ruth Thayre, Deborah, Lydia, Rebecca, Rachel, Elizabeth and Joanna; calls Samuel Allis the cousin of his son Henry.

James, witness of a deed of Mrs. Stoughton at Dorchester, in 1649.

John, Salem, before Boston court 3 (7) 1639; frm. May 18, 1642. He m. Mary, dau. of Francis Laws, q. v.; she was adm. chh. 21 (1) 1647; ch. John bapt. 22 (3) 1642, John bapt. 24 (1) 1643-4, Jeremiah bapt. 18 (11) 1645, Lydia bapt. 7 (2) 1650, Jonathan bapt. 15 (6) 1652, Mary bapt. 29 (2) 1655, John bapt. 24 (11) 1657, Joseph b. or bapt. 14 (1) 1659. He d. 12 May, 1672. Will dated 3 May, prob. 28 (4) 1672, beq. to wife Mary; sons

NEAL, etc., cont.
Jeremiah, John, Jonathan and Joseph; dau. Lydia Hart; gr. ch. John, Mary and Sarah N. and Lydia H. The widow m. 2, Andrew Mansfield. Her est. was divided to sons Jeremiah, Jonathan and Joseph 7 (7) 1681.

William, [Boston,] made nunc. will 5 (8) 1646; goodwife Mylom and John Harwood deposed.

NEAVE, NEAUE, NEVE,
Margaret, of Great Yarmouth, widow, ae. 58, and Rachel Dixson, her grand-dau. passed exam. May 10, 1637, to go to N. E. Settled at Salem; adm. chh. 21 (1) 1647; she d. 1 June, 1658.

Richard, entered a case in Court, but failed to prosecute 1 (10) 1640.

NEEDHAM, NEADHAM, NEEDAM,
Anne, Boston, memb. chh. 1631-2.
Elizabeth, gave a letter of attorney 25 (3) 1648, to John Scott to receive goods belonging to her husband in Virginia, being credibly informed of his death. [A.]

Nicholas, Braintree, propr. 1636.

William, cooper, Braintree, propr. 1639, frm. May 10, 1648.

William, cooper, Boston, aged, made will 10 June, prob. 26 Dec. 1690; beq. to Wm. and John N., ch. of his dec. kinsman John N., late of Boston; to bro. Andrew N., a tailor, living in London, and to his son Thomas; to the Third church of Boston; to Mr. Samuel Willard, teacher; to Edward Spaulding; to Joseph Thompson, Sen. of Billerica.

NEGOOSE, NEGUS, GOOSE,
Benjamin, salter, husbandman, Boston, propr. 1639; adm. chh. 10 (4) 1643, frm. May 10, 1648. Wife Elizabeth; ch. Elizabeth b. 14 (2) 1640, bapt. 11 (4) 1643, (m. 2 March, 1659, Richard Barnard,) Benjamin b. (7) 1641, bapt. 11 (4) 1643, Mary b. 7, bapt. 8 (8) 1643, Samuel b. 17 (10) 1645, Jabez bapt. 9 (2) 1648, ae. about 9 days, John bapt. 31 (6) 1651, Hannah b. 2 Oct. 1653.

Will made 17 Sept. 1684, "being aged;" prob. 19 Jan. 1693-4; beq. to dau. Elizabeth Barnard, to her youngest dau. Elizabeth, and her 3 other daus.; to son Jabez N. and 3 other children not named. Signed Benjamin Negus.

NEGOOSE, etc., cont.
Grace, Boston, adm. chh. with her bro. Jonathan 27 (5) 1634. She m. Barnabas Fawer, and was dism. to the chh. of Dorchester 10 (1) 1643. After his death she m. John Johnson, Sen., of Roxbury; in the division of Fawer's est. she retained a woodlot in Boston which came from Thomas Negus to her. [Gen. Court, 14 Oct. 1656.]

Jonathan, Boston, adm. to chh., a singleman, 27 (5) 1634, frm. Sept. 3, 1634. Town officer. He deposed in 1657, ae. about 50 years. [Copy in Es. Files, 1678.] Ch. Isaac bapt. 3 (1) 1650, ae. about 10 days, Maria bapt. 10 (5) 1653.

NELSON,
Mr. Thomas, gent., the wealthiest of the Yorkshire men who founded Rowley. Came first to Boston. Lent money on mortgage to Richard Evered of Cambridge. [L.] Was one of the chief town officers of Rowley from 1638. Deputy, com. of Court, etc. Built mills in 1640-2; [see Holmes, Richard.] He went to England on business, and died there. He m. first —, who came with him and d. soon. He m. 2, Joane, dau. of Mr. Thomas (and niece of Mr. Richard) Dummer. Contract in Es. Files 3, 67, dated 15 (12) 1641. Ch. Philip and Thomas came with him; Mercy b. 26 (12) 1643, Samuel.

He made will here, adding to it when about to start for home; dates, Dec. 4, 1645, and 6 (6) 1648; prob. 21 Feb. 1650. Beq. to eldest son Philip a double portion; to sons Thomas and Samuel and dau. Mercie. Refers to his aunt Katharine Witham, and to a legacy she had left to Philip; Richard Bellingham and Richard Dummer execs. and to have charge of the education of the three eldest children; to wife Joane his mill, millhouse and lands in Rowley for her life; the reversion to his children. The commissioners of the estate found in Mr. D.'s hands £ 1685-14-09. Division of the houses and lands was agreed upon Sept. 16, 1676, between the sons Philip and Thomas and John Stocke who had married their sister Mercy, his attorney, Benjamin Alford, acting for him. The prob. account shows that the admin. went to York and Hull to collect moneys due the est.; and proved the will and had it recorded in Eng.

William, Plymouth, before 1636; land grant 3 Aug. 1640, atba. 1643. Juryman,

NELSON, cont.
1648. He m. 29 Oct. 1640, Martha Ford; ch. Joane b. 28 Feb. 1650.

Will dated 31 Oct. 1679, prob. 5 March, 1679-80, beq. to wife Martha, sons John and William; dau. Martha Cobb. Inv. of the widow's est. was taken 7 March, 1683-4.

NETHERLAND,
William, residence not stated, frm. March 4, 1634-5. See Leatherland.

NEVILL,
William, singleman, Ipswich, in the service of Mr. Whipple. Will dated 15 (2) 1643, prob. (7) 1643; beq. to his master's ch. Mary, Ann and others; to his partner William Robinson; William Gooderson, goody Langton, to Mary and Sarah L. and Jane Woodam. Roger Langton exec.

NEWBERRY, NEWBURY,
Richard, Weymouth, propr. 1643, town officer 1652.

Mr. Thomas, Dorchester, frm. Sept. 3, 1634. Bought the house Mr. Pynchon built; had with it 80 acres of land, and 20 acres at Squantum. Deputy. Had charge of the work at Castle Island. Rem. to Windsor, Conn. Ch. Sarah, (m. Henry Wolcott,) Mary, (m. Daniel Clark,) Benjamin. [Suff. De. III, 525.]

He d. in 1635 or 1636. Will dated 12 (10) 1635, prob. Jan. 28, 1636-7. Beq. to wife Jane 200 li., with all which she brought with her at marriage; rest to be equally divided among his children, except that three of his younger daus. should have 50 s. apiece less than the others. Wife exec.; Mr. John Warham and William Gaylord overseers. The widow m. Mr. John Warham, and with him leased Neponset lands to Richard Wright 1 (3) 1639. [L.] Feb. 6, 1669, his sons Joseph and Benjamin N. and sons-in-law Henry Wolcott and Daniel Clark, with Mr. Warham and William Gaylord in behalf of the three youngest children, petitioned for lands in W. which properly belonged to his estate. [Arch. 15 B.]

NEWBEY,
William, came in the Mary and John, March 26, 1633-4.

NEWCOMB, NEWCOME, NUCOM,

Francis, husbandman, ae. 30, with wife Rachel, ae. 20, and children Rachel, ae. 2½, and Joan, ae. 9 months, came in the Planter, April 6, 1635. Settled in that part of Boston which became Braintree. Wife Rachel adm. chh. 28 (12) 1635. He was dism. to chh. of Br. 16 (12) 1639. Ch. Hannah bapt. 15 (8) 1637, Mary b. 31 (1) 1640, (m. 9 (10) 1657, Samuel Dearing,) Sarah b. 30 (4) 1643, Judith b. 16 (11) 1645, Peter b. 16 (3) 1648, Abigail b. 16 (5) 1651, Leah b. 30 (5) 1654, Elizabeth b. 26 (6) 1658.

He d. June 13, 1672, accounted 100 years old.

NEWCOMIN,

John, a young man, murdered by John Billington of Plymouth in 1630.

NEWELL,

Abraham, ae. 50, with wife Frances, ae. 40, and children Faith, ae. 14, Grace, ae. 13, Abraham, ae. 8, John, ae. 5, and Isaac, ae. 2, came in the Frances of Ipswich April 30, 1634. Settled at Roxbury. Frm. March 4, 1634-5. Son Jacob also mentioned by Eliot as coming with him. Faith, servant to Robert Scott, was adm. chh. Boston 14 (4) 1645. He deeded lands to son Abraham 4 Sept. 1665, in consideration of an annuity to be paid himself and wife. [Suff. De. IV, 96.]

He d. June 13, 1672, ae. 91 years. "Mother" Frances Newell, neere 100 yeare old, d. 13 or 16 (11) 1682. His will, dated 8 Feb. 1669, prob. 4 (5) 1672, beq. to sons Abraham, John, Isaac, Jacob, William Toy, wife Frances.

NEWGATE,

John, hatter, merchant, Boston, adm. chh. 3 (6) 1634, frm. March 4, 1634-5. Deputy, town officer. Wife Anne, [Johannah?]; ch. rec. at Bo.: Elizabeth, (adm. chh. 30 (1) 1634, m. 1, John Oliver, 2, Edward Jackson,) Sarah, (adm. chh. 20 (4) 1640,) Hannah b. and d. 1633, Hannah b. 1 (6) 1635, (m. 22 (12) 1652, Simon Lynde,) Joseph d. 14 (10) 1658.

He made a will Oct. 2, 1638, when expecting to go to Eng.: lands at Horningerth, co. Suff., Eng. to eldest son John; other ch. Sarah, Hannah, Nathaniel, Joseph, Elizabeth Oliver; servant Theodore Atkinson. [L.] This was not probated.

He d. about 1665. Will prob. Sept. 11, 1665. Wife Ann, son Nathaniel N., sons-in-

NEWGATE, cont.

law Peter Oliver, Simon Lynde, John Oliver, dec. and Edward Jackson; daus. Elizabeth Jackson, Sarah Oliver, Hannah Lynde; bro.-in-law Thomas Townsin of Lynn; wife's sister that married with my uncle's son, William Newgate, living in London; 5 li. per annum to Harvard Coll.; etc. [Reg. XIII, 333.]

Widow Ann's will dated 6 Aug. 1676, prob. 8 April, 1679, beq. to son Nathaniel's son Nathl.; gr. dau. Elizabeth Lind and her bros. and sisters; Jonathan and Sebise Jackson; Hannah Smith, once my maid; goodman Hale; to brethren that are of our private meeting; to sister Madson, the elder woman, sister Alcock that was.

A John Newgate, of Bury St. Edmunds, Eng., in his will prob. 5 Oct. 1649, beq. to his bro. John Newgate now living resident in parts beyond the seas called New England; also to bro. Joseph Newgate. [Reg. XXXIII, 57.]

NEWLAND,

Anthony, Salisbury, 1649, propr.

John, Sandwich, atba. 1643. Elizabeth, widow of John, bur. May 24, 1671.

Jeremy, Ipswich, was paid for Indian service in 1643.

Jeremiah, Taunton, ch. Anthony b. 1 Aug. 1657, Elizabeth b. 18 May, 1659, Susanna b. 15 July, 1664, Jeremiah b. 8 Feb. 1667, John b. 25 March, 1669, Mary b. 17 July, 1671, Benjamin b. 1 Oct. 1673, Mercy b. 25 March, 1676.

He d. 25 July, 1681. His children Jeremy, Benjamin and John Newland, William and John Witherly, William Cobb and Nicholas Smith, gave their discharge to Anthony Newland as admin. of the estate of their father Jeremiah and mother Katharine N., 10 Jan. 1701.

William, Weymouth, 1640. [L.] Rem. to Sandwich. Propr.; juryman, 1640; frm. 7 Sept. 1641. Allowed to train the townsmen June, 1645. Lieut. 1647. Deputy. He m. 19 May, 1648, Rose, widow of Joseph Holloway; ch. Mary b. 16 April, 1649, Elizabeth bur. Sept. 4, 1658.

He d. in April, 1694; beq. to wife Rose, dau. Mercy, wife of William Edwards and her dau. Elizabeth; to his bro. John N.; bro.-in-law William Allin.

NEWHALL, NEWILL,

Anthony, Lynn, propr. 1638. Will dated 14 Jan. 1656, prob. March 31, 1657. Grandchildren Richard and Elizabeth Hood; son John, dau. Mary and her husband.

Thomas, Lynn, propr. 1638. Wife Mary d. 25 Sept. 1665. His son Thomas deposed 10 (9) 1683, ae. about 50 years; refers to his father and uncle Anthony N.
He d. 25 May, 1674. Will dated April 1, 1668, prob. 1 (5) 1674. Sons Thomas and John; bro. Farrington; son Thomas Browne's children; son Richard Haven's ch. Joseph, Richard, Sarah, Nathaniel and Moses; daus. Susanna Haven and Mary Browne.

NEWMAN, NUMAN,

John, husbandman, came in the Mary and John March 26, 1634; settled at Ipswich; propr. 1634; was paid for work at the watchhouse in 1647. Sold house and land in 1646.
His will dated Nov., 1673, prob. 31 March, 1674, beq. to wife for life, and to his children what she might leave. Called Senior. Widow Alice deposed.

Elizabeth, ae. 24, came in the James in June, 1635. Robert and Thomas came with John in 1635.

Rev. Samuel, [b. at Banbury, Eng. about 1600,] came to Dorchester about 1636 or 1637, and joined the chh. in company with Revs. Moxam and Tompson. Remained there a year and a half; was then pastor at Weymouth five years. [C. M.] Rem. to Rehoboth; was ordained pastor in 1644. A man of admirable scholarship and a very acceptable preacher. He revised here a work on which he had been some time engaged, and which was published at London, a Concordance of The Bible in English, the best book of the kind up to that day. He also performed a large ministerial service.
He d. July 5, 1663. Will dated Nov. 18, 1661, prob. March 3, 1663-4, beq. to wife Sybil; sons Samuel, Antipas and Noah; dau. Hopestill and two others; to old servants, Mary Humphreys of Dorchester, Elizabeth Cubby, of Wey., Elizabeth Palmer, of Reh., and present servant Lydia Winchester. The dau. Hopestill m. Rev. George Shove.

Thomas, Ipswich, propr. 1638. Will dated Jan. 8, 1675, beq. to wife Sa-

NEWMAN, etc., cont.

rah; sons Thomas, John and Benjamin, the latter "gone to the wars." Inv. and will filed 28 March, 1676.

NEWTON,

Anthony, Dorchester, propr. 1637, herdsman, 1653. Had grant of land at Braintree for 3 heads in 1639, but did not reside there. Additional land in 1667. Rem. to Milton. One of the seven first members of the church there, 24 (2) 1678. His wife dism. to join the same 18 (7) 1681. Ch. Hannah and Mary bapt. 6 (1) 1641, Mary d. 31 (11) 1663, John bapt. 8 (11) 1642, Ephraim bapt. 19 (7) 1647, Abigail bapt. 18 (12) 1650, (m. 17 (10) 1695, James Puffer). Son John's est. was admin. by the father 23 May, 1678. "My son Anthony and dau. Joane, now in N. E.," mentioned in will of John Newton of Colliton, Devon, chirurgeon, 3 April, 1646. [Reg. XLIX, 384.]

Ellen, came to Plymouth in the Anne in 1623, and had one lot of land assigned her.

John, Dorchester, propr., frm. March 4, 1632-3. John, of Dedham, townsman 2 (11) 1642, frm. May 10, 1643. A kinsman and legatee of Edward Allen. John, a witness in Boston in 1645. [A.]

Richard, Sudbury, propr. 1639; frm. May, 1645. One of the founders of Marlborough. [Arch.] Wife Anne; ch. John b. 20 (8) 1641, — b. Oct. 20, 1643, Mary b. 22 (4) 1644, Moses b. 26 (1) 1646, Hannah b. 13 April, 1654, Daniel b. 21 Dec. 1655.

Richard, husbandman, Marlborough. His will dated 8 Sept. 1693, prob. 17 Nov. 1707, beq. to wife Hannah; ch. John, Mary, (wife of Jonathan Johnson,) Joseph, Moses, Daniel, Elizabeth Dingley, and Sarah Taylor.

NICHOLAS,

Austin, Plymouth, came in the Fortune in 1621.

Elizabeth, ae. 25, came in the Susan and Ellen in April, 1635.

One Nicholas, servant to Mr. Thatcher at Yarmouth, 1640. [L.]

Nicholas, the Swede, Scituate, propr. Scituate, 1636; called Nicholas Albeson the Swede in report of soldiers of Sci. in Phillip's war in 1676. [Hist. Sci.]

NEWMARCH,
John, Ipswich, propr. 1648; propr. also at Rowley, 1643. Sold to Richard Longhorne. Martha deposed at Ipswich 29 (1) 1654. [See Zaccheus Gould.]

NICHOLS, NICOLES, NICKOLDS,
Jane, "servant to our teacher," adm. chh. Boston, 7 (2) 1639.

John, Watertown, propr. 1636.

Randolph or Randall, biscuit baker, Charlestown, adm. chh. 3 (3) 1647. Signed inv. of Abr. Hawkins in 1647. Bought land in 1657. Wife Elizabeth; ch. Sarah b. 27 (11) 1642, Hannah b. 4 (2) 1647, John b. Jan. 1653. Will dated 4 Dec. 1688, prob. Nov. 9, 1691; housing and lands in Uxbridge, co. Midd., Eng., beq. him by his father William N., he beq. to son John and to Elizabeth and Hannah, ch. of son Nathaniel, dec.; the est. in Uxbridge given him by uncle Robert N., dec., he beq. to son Randall; Char. property to wife Elizabeth and his 9 gr. ch., the ch. of his daus. Hammond and Elizabeth Tuck with those of Nathaniel. Refers to son-in-law Thos. Tuck, dec.; David, son of the late David Anderson and of Katherine his wife, now wife of Capt. Richard Sprague.

Richard, Ipswich, propr.; before Gen. Court 1 (10) 1640. Rem. to Reading; sister N. adm. chh. R. from that of I. in 1666. He d. 22 Nov. 1674. Will dated 19 Nov. prob. 11 Dec. 1674, beq. to wife Ann, sons John, Thomas and James, and daus. Mary and Hannah.

Robert, Watertown, gave a letter of attorney 27 (1) 1644, to Rufus Barton to recover a debt of George Roome of Rhode Island. [A.] He rem. to Southold, L. I., sold land at Wat. in 1648. He m. about 1644 Sarah, widow of John Gosse. [Suff. De. I, 55.] Sarah, adm. chh. Charlestown 4 (9) 1643.

Walter, Cambridge, householder 8 Feb. 1635, frm. Dec. 7, 1636.

Thomas, planter, Cambridge, propr., sold before 1638. Rem. to Hingham; propr. 1637-8. Town officer. He drew exchange, 15 (8) 1639, on his bro. George N., the exec. of the est. of his father Walter N., clothier, late of Coggeshall, co. Essex, Eng., who d. 1 April, 1639. [L.] He m. Rebecca, dau. of Thomas Jocelyn; she d. 22 Sept. 1675, ae. 58 years. He m. Sept. 23, 1681, Dorcas —. She

NICHOLS, etc., cont.
d. 15 Oct. 1694. Ch. Thomas, Rebecca and Elizabeth bapt. Jan. 1643; Hannah b. Feb. 18, 1645, Ephraim b. May 14, 1648, Israel b. Sept. 1, 1650, Nathaniel and Mary b. July 3, 1653, Sarah b. July 15, 1655, Charity b. May 3, 1658, Patience b. Dec. 25, 1660. He d. 8 Nov. 1696.

William, Salem, propr. 1638. Rem. to Topsfield; propr. 1651. He deposed in 1652, ae. about 53 years; and again, in 1661, ae. about 63; again 14 May, 1694, ae. upwards of 100 years, that he had lived more than 42 years on a farm which he bought of Henry Bartholomew. [Reg. IX, 377.]
Wife Margaret in 1661. Will dated April 26, 1693, prob. Feb. 17, 1695, mentions wife Mary and children. Mary, (wife of Thomas Cane or Cave,) Hannah, (wife of Thomas Wilkins,) and John: these children petitioned the court about the estate.

NICHOLSON, NICKERSON,
John, Watertown, propr. 1637.

William, weaver, ae. 33, of Norwich, Eng., with wife Anne, ae. 28, and ch. Nicholas, Robert, Elizabeth and Anne, passed exam. in April, 1637, to go to N. E. Settled at Boston. Frm. May 22, 1638. He rem. to Yarmouth. Bought lands of the Indians at Manamoiet before 1 Dec. 1663. His sons-in-law Robert Eldred, Nathaniel Covell and Tristram Hedges were in Court with him 31 Oct. 1666, on acct. of a letter he had written, defaming Gov. Hinckley. His sons Nicholas, Robert, Samuel, John, and Joseph joined with them in a petition for land at Man., 5 June, 1667. His dau. Elizabeth m. at Y., last week of Oct. 1649, Robert Eldred. His wife Anne recd. a legacy from her father Nicholas Busbey in 1660.

NIDDES,
Anne, Boston, maid servant to William Brenton, adm. chh. 13 (2) 1634.

NILES, NYLES,
John, Braintree. Frm. May 26, 1647. Wife Jane; ch. Hannah b. 16 (12) 1636, John b. 1 (4) 1638, Joseph b. 15 (6) 1640, Nathaniel b. 16 (6) 1642, Samuel b. 3 (12) 1644, Increase b. 16 (10) 1646, Benjamin b. 1 (11) 1648. The wife d. 15 (3) 1654.
He d. 8 Feb. 1693-4, ae. about 91.

NILE, see Neal and Niles,
John, Dorchester, propr. 1634-1638.

NICHOSON, see Nicholson.

NIXON, NICKS,
Matthew, fisherman, Salem, propr. 1638. [See Es. Files, 1647.]

NODDLE,
William, Salem, frm. May 18, 1631. Is believed to have owned or lived on the island which has born his name since 1630, now East Boston.
The only record of him beside his freemanship is the folg.: One Noddle, an honest man of Salem, carrying wood in a canoe in the South River, was overturned and drowned in 1632. [W.]

NORCROSS,
Mr. Jeremiah, Cambridge, propr. before 1642, frm. Feb. 1652. Bought house and land at Watertown (3) 1649. Town officer. His acct. with his son John Smyth before Gen. Court 1 (10) 1640. [See Smith, John.]
He d. in 1657. Will pres. at Court Oct. 6, 1657; declared before he went to England; wife Adrean; son Nathaniel and his wife Sarah; son Richard and his wife Mary; Mary, wife of my wife's son John Smith; bro.'s dau. Anne, wife of Samuel Davis; bro. Charles Chadwick; Sarah, wife of Francis Macy; to gr. ch. in old England. The son Nathaniel, a university scholar, was called to be minister of Nashaway [Lancaster] in 1643. [W.]

NORDEN, NORTHEND.
Hugh, Boston. He m. Joanna, formerly Copp; ch. Hannah bapt. 30 (3) 1647, ae. about 5 days.

Samuel, shoemaker, Boston, propr.; frm. May 23, 1666. Town officer, frequent witness of deeds. Wife Joanna; ch. Sarah bapt. 12 (6) 1649, Samuel b. 8 (9) 1651, Nathaniel b. 27 Nov. 1653, Benjamin b. 15 June, 1656. The wife Joanna d. 29 (4) 1656, and he m. in 1656, Elizabeth, dau. of Philemon Pormort; ch. Elizabeth b. 2 Sept. 1657, Susanna b. 26 Nov. 1659, Joseph b. 28 Feb. 1663, Abigail bapt. 10 (10) 1665, Joshua b. July 3, 1666, Mary b. March 22, 1669, *Marah* bapt. 27 (1) 1670, Isaac b. March 8, 1672.

NOLTON, see Knowlton.

NORMAN,
Hugh, Yarmouth, atba. 1643. He m. 8 Oct. 1639, Sarah White. In Court 1650. He returned to England, to Orchyard, a parish near Taunton, and abandoned his family here. [Testimony of Thomas Allyn and Thomas Richards in 1654.] [Plym. De. II.]

John, Sen., Salem, probably son of Richard, below, summoned to Court 3 May, 1631. Propr. 1636. Rem. to Manchester. Contracted 23 March, 1657, to build a house for the use of the ministry. He certified to the Court the births of four children 29 (11) 1644. Wife Arabella adm. chh. 21 (3) 1637, or 25 (12) 1637. Ch. John b. in Aug. 1637, bapt. 4 (1) 1637-8, Lydia b. middle of Jan. 1639, bapt. 23 (11) 1639, Hanna b. 14 Jan. 1642, Ann bapt. 1 (3) 1642, Arabella b. 14 (2) 1644, Martha bapt. 17 (3) 1646, Richard bapt. 5 (8) 1651, Joseph bapt. 8 (7) 1653, Joseph bapt. 7 (7) 1656.
The inv. of his est. was filled 26 (7) 1672. Widow Arabella d. 23 Nov. 1679; her inv. was filed by John 29 (4) 1680.

Richard, presumed to be the "old goodman Norman," who, "with his son," was living at Salem Sept. 6, 1628, as Richard Brakenbury testified. Sergt. Lockwood declined a lot adjoining his "father Norman," 17 (2) 1637.
His "son" may be John, above, or Richard, who deposed in 1673, ae. about 50 years; but evidence is wanting. Lieut. Richard, Marblehead, inv. taken Nov. 20, 1683, had ch. there mentioned, Rebecca Richard, William, John, Elizabeth, Joseph, Benjamin and Jonathan; widow Margaret. Part of her portion in Edward Diman's hands.

NORRICE, NORRIS,
Mr. Edward, minister, Boston, adm. chh. 21 (5) 1639; frm. May 13, 1640. His wife Elinor adm. chh. 18 (6) 1639. He was granted leave to reside at Salem where he was teacher of the church, 15 (7) 1639; and letters of dismission for both were granted 26 (10) 1639. "A grave and judicious elder." [W.] The town of Salem chose "yong Mr. Norris to teach skoole" (11) 1639; and granted "Mr." N. 116 acres of land 21 (11) 1639. Dorothy N., Salem, adm. chh. 18 (1) 1655, deposed March 22, 1655-6, as to being at the house of

NORRICE, etc., cont.
her bro. Francis Johnson at Marblehead three or four years before. [Reg. XXXIX, 386.]

He d. 23 (10) 1659.

Will prob. 27 (4) 1660; son Edward N.

NORTH,
Alice, memb. chh. Dorchester, before 1639.

John, ae. 20, came in the Susan and Ellen in April, 1635. Settled at Ipswich; propr. 1637. Sold land 7 (1) 1642.

Mr., called captain, Plymouth, came over in 1643; called into Court for seditious, boastful speeches 5 March, 1643-4, and required to leave the jurisdiction within 2 months. [Plym. Col. Rec.]

Richard, husbandman, Salisbury propr. 1639, frm. June 2, 1641. Wife Ursula; ch. Mary, (m. Thomas Jones,) Sarah, Susanna, (m. George Martin.) [See suit of the latter couple vs. Nathaniel Winsley in Supr. Court, Boston.] [Testimony in Norf. Files, 80.]

He d. March 1, 1667; will dated Jan. 26, 1648, prob. April 14, 1668. Widow Ursula made will May 19, 1668, codicil 24 June, 1669, prob. April 11, 1671; beq. to gr. ch. Mary, wife of Nathl. Winsley, and her dau. Hephsibah; to Mary, wife of Thos. Jones, and to Susannah, wife of George Martyn.

NORTHEND, NORDEN,
Ezekiel, Rowley, propr. before 1648; corporal, town officer. He deposed in 1662, ae. 40 years, and in 1692, ae. about 64 years; worked in the building of mills by Thomas Nelson in 1640, etc. He m. Dec. 1, 1648, Edna, widow of Richard Bayley; ch. Edna b. July 1, 1649, (m. 1, Thomas Lambert, m. 2, Andrew Stickney,) Elizabeth b. Sept. 17, 1651, Elizabeth b. Oct. 19, 1656, (m. 1, Humphrey Hobson, m. 2, Thomas Gage,) John b. Jan. 18, 1658, Sarah b. Jan. 3, 1661, (m. Thomas Hale,) Ezekiel b. Nov. 8, 1666.

He d. Sept. 7, 1698. Will dated Feb. 8, 1697-8, prob. in 1678, beq. to wife Edna, son Ezekiel, daus. Edna Stickney, Elizabeth Gage, and Sarah Hale.

Jeremiah, Rowley, servant of Mr. William Bellingham, recd. beq. from Mr. B. in 1650.

NORTHCOATE, NORTHCUTT,
William, Yarmouth, atba. 1643; served against the Narragansetts in 1645.

NORTHEY,
John, Marblehead, a witness in court in 1646.

Will dated 8 Nov. 1688, prob. June 30, 1691, beq. to son John; daus. Sarah Martin and Dorothy Pickett; gr. ch. John, Peter, Samuel, Robert and Thomas N. and John P.

NORTON,
Francis, of London, came to Charlestown; resident in 1630; adm. townsman 1637; town officer, 1646. Adm. chh. 10 (2) 1642; frm. May 18, 1642. Lieut., deputy. Brought suit for money at Salem 25 (9) 1641. Wife Mary adm. chh. 10 (1) 1639. She recd. a bequest by the will of her father, Nicholas Houghton of London, 2 March, 1648, and by that of her bro. Robert H. of St. Olave's, Southworth, co. Surrey, brewer, 25 Dec. 1653. Ch. Abigail, (m. John Long,) Mary, (m. Joseph Noyes,) Deborah, (m. Zechary Hill,) Elizabeth, (m. 1, Timothy Symmes, m. 2, Ephraim Savage.) [Reg. XLII, 65.] Capt. Francis N. had charge of the armory at Boston in 1659. [Town rec.]

George, carpenter, probably the "Norton, carpenter," sent over to Salem by the Mass. Bay Co. in 1629; settled at Salem. Frm. May 14, 1634. Town officer. Rem. to Gloucester. One of those to whom the Gen. Court gave permission to erect a village at Jeffreys Creek, (Manchester,) 13 May, 1642. Deputy. He leased "Groton Farm" of Lucie, widow of Emanuel Downing in 1656. [Es. Files XI, 39.] Rem. to Wenham chh. 21 (7) 1645. Wife Mary adm. chh. 1637; ch. Freegrace b. about 1635, John bapt. 2 (8) 1637, Nathaniel bapt. 19 (3) 1639, George bapt. 28 (1) 1641, Mary b. about 1643, Mehitabel b. about 1645, Sarah bapt. 15 (12) 1646, Hannah b. about 1648, Abigail bapt. 14 (7) 1651, Elizabeth bapt. 7 (6) 1653.

Inv. of his est. 22 (7) 1659; list of children attached.

Henry, placed under bonds by the Gen. Court 4 March, 1634-5.

Rev. John, "b. at Startford in Hartfordshire, 6 May, 1606," [C. M.] a godly man and preacher in England, came with his family at the invitation of Mr. Edward Winslow, to the Massachusetts in the autumn of 1635;

NORTON, cont.
preached at Plymouth, where their pastor, Mr. Smith, gave over his place to him; but he left them to came to Mass. [W.] Removed to Ipswich where he was invited by sundry of his acquaintance; so he went to them and became their minister. [B.] Had grant of lands at Ips. 16 (2) 1638. Rem. to Boston as teacher of the First church. Was sent to England as an agent of the colony in 1662.

He d. 5 April, 1663. He made will 14 Jan. 1661, prob. 16 April, 1663; refers to a call to England he had recd.; beq. to his wife, and after her death to the children of his bro. William N. of Ipswich, N. E.; to William; to my mother, bro. Thomas, and sisters Martha Wood, Mary Young and Elizabeth N., all to be paid at bro. Thomas' house in London; to the poor of the First chh. of Boston; library to go to any son of bro. William who may enter the ministry. Mrs. Mary, his widow, sold land in Ips. Sept. 8, 1671. She d. Dec. 17, 1677. [L. H.] A man of eminent ability and learning. Author of several books. His Answer to Appollonius on Church Government, written in 1645, was the first Latin book written in this country, according to C. M.

Nicholas, Weymouth, bought, Feb. 20, 1639, of Richard Standerwick of Broadway, co. Somerset, clothier, all the cattle in the hands of Mr. Hull in N. E. [Plym. Col. rec.] Town officer, 1646. Ch. Isaac b. May 3, 1641, Jacob b. March or April, 1643.

Richard, cooper, Boston, resident, 1649-1654. Wife Dorothy; ch. Richard d. 10 (12) 1649.

Inv. of his est. taken 8 Aug. 1657, and filed by Hugh Williams, admin.

William, ae. 25, came in the Hopewell Aug. 29, 1635; settled at Ipswich. Bro. of Mr. John. Bought house and land 4 Sept., 1648. He deposed Dec. 18, 1658, ae. about 50 years.

His will dated 28 April, 1694 prob. May 15 folg., beq. to son John only 10 shillings because he had recd. his portion "in Larning and bringing up at the colleage;" dau. Elizabeth Wainrite; son Bonase to take care of his mother.

William, Hingham. Propr., frm. March 3, 1635-6.

He d. June, 1639. His widow Anne brought

NORTON, cont.
suit in 1641 against Samuel Ward, concerning a piece of land which he had bought of her late husband. [L.] She m. 2, John Tucker.

NORWICK,
John, residence not stated, frm. May 13, 1640.

NOTT,
John, legatee of widow Joane Drake in 1637. His portion ordered to be placed in the hands of William Cheeseborough 4 Sept. 1638.

NOURSE, NURSE,
Francis, a youth, in court in 1639; res. at Salem; propr. 1647. In court, 1658. He deposed 26 (9) 1666, ae. about 45 years.

NOWELL, NOELL,
Increase, a member of the Mass. Bay Co. in England, came in the fleet with Winthrop in 1630. Settled at Charlestown. Joined in the first church organization, with wife Parnell, in July, 1630, and in the re-organization at Char. in 1632. Was elected ruling elder 27 July, 1630; Asst., deputy, secretary of the Colony, town officer. Wife Parnell was dau. of Thomas Grey, mariner, of Harwich, Eng., by his first wife, Katharine, dau. of Robert Myles, of Sutton. [L.] She d. March 25, 1687, ae. 84. Ch. Increase b. 19 (9), bapt. 21 (9) 1630, d. 6 (1) 1632, Abigail b. 27 (2) bapt. 3 (4) 1632, d. 6 (1) 1634, Samuel bapt. 22 (9) 1634, Eliezer b. and d. 1636, Mehitabel bapt. 4 (12) 1637-8, Increase bapt. 23 (3) 1640, Mary b. 26 (3) 1643, Alexander; Mary, adm. chh. Charlestown, 7 (12) 1646, may be error of record for baptism.

He d. Nov. 1, 1655. Will dated 23 (4), prob. 25 (10) 1655, beq. to wife Parnell, mother Coitmore, sons Increase, Alexander and Samuel, daus. Mehetabel and Mary, and to personal friends. The widow d. March 25, 1687. [S.] [Reg. XXXIV, 253.]

NOYES, NOYCE, NOYS, NOIES, [sig.]
Rev. James, son of Rev. William, rector of Cholderton, co. Wilts., Eng., and of his wife Anne, sister of Mr. Robert Parker; in her will, prob. April 27, 1658, she beq. to sons James and Nicholas in New England. Rev. Thomas Parker of Newbury calls him and his bro. Nicholas "cousins." [Reg. XLIX,

NOYES, etc. cont.

261.] He was matriculated at Brasenose coll. Oxford, 22 Aug. 1627. He m. about 1633 Sarah, dau. of Mr. Joseph Browne of Southampton. He came in the Mary and John March 26, 1633-4; frm. Sept. 3, 1634. Res. a while at Ipswich. Came to Newbury about March, 1634-5, and was associated in the work of the ministry with his kinsman Rev. Thomas Parker. Ch. Joseph b. 15 Oct. 1637, James b. 11 March, 1639, Sarah b. 12 Aug. 1641, d. 21 Feb. 1653, Moses b. 6 Dec. 1643, John b. 3 June, 1645, Thomas b. 10 Aug. 1648, John b. June 4, 1649, Rebecca b. 1 April, 1651, William b. 22 Sept. 1653, Sarah b. 21 March, 1655-6.

He d. Oct. 21, 1656. Will signed 17 Oct. prob. (9) 1656. Wife and children; bro. Nicholas N.; cousin Thomas Parker. The widow Sarah d. 13 (7) 1691. Her will, dated 11 Nov. 1681, being aged, was prob. 29 (7) 1691. Sons Joseph, James and Moses; dau. Sarah, wife of her son John, and their ch. Sarah, John and Oliver; sons William and Thomas; daus. Rebecca and Sarah.

Nicholas, bro. of James, came with him in the Mary and John March 26, 1633-4. Settled at Newbury on the beginning of the plantation a year later. Frm. May 17, 1637. Propr., town officer, deacon. Ret. to Eng. and came again in 1639. See his deposition with that of Peter, below. He m. Mary, dau. of Capt. John Cutting; ch. Mary b. 15 Oct., 1641, (m. John French,) Hannah b. 30 Oct. 1643, (m. Peter Cheney,) John b. 20 Jan. 1645, Nicholas b. 22 Dec. 1647, Cutting b. 23 Sept. 1649, Sarah b. 13 Sept. 1651, d. Feb. 21, 1652, Sarah b. 22 Aug. 1653, (m. Matthew Pettingell,) Timothy b. 23 June, 1655, James b. 16 May, 1657, Abigail b. 11 April, 1659, (m. Simeon French,) Rachel b. 20 March, 1661, (m. James Jackman,) Thomas b. 20 June, 1663, Rebecca b. 18 May, 1665, d. 1 Dec. 1683. He d. 23 Nov. 1701, ae. 83. [Genealogy in Reg. L. 35.]

Peter, yeoman, from Penton, co. Hants, ae. 47, with son Thomas, ae. 15, and dau. Elizabeth, came in the Confidence, April 24, 1638. Settled at Watertown; "gent;" propr. 1642; frm. May 13, 1640. App. by Gen. Court Surveyor of arms, 13 May, 1640. Settled at Sudbury; lands assigned to him and Thomas in 1639. Selectman 1639, et seq. Ret. to Eng. and came again in the Jonathan in 1639; deposed in the Blanchard

NOYES, etc. cont.

case in Salem Court, in 1652. Nicholas, Dorothy and Peter, Jr., came with him. [Reg. XXXII, 407.] Deputy. He gave by deed to his second son Peter, June 24, 1654, a tract of land in Andover, Eng., adjoining land of Mr. Thomas Noys; the elder son Thomas, to whom a share in the land had been given before, now conveyed his title to Peter, Jr. [Suff. De. II, 32.]

Will dated 22 Sept., prob. Oct. 5, 1657, beq. to sons Thomas, Peter and Joseph, and daus. Elizabeth, wife of Josiah Haines, Dorothy, wife of John Hayne, and Abigail, wife of Thomas Plimpton; to kinsman Shadrach Habgood and pastor, Mr. Edmond Browne.

NUDD,

Thomas, son of Jone, [first] wife of Henry Dow, who gave him a tract of land at Hampton in 1649. Came to Watertown in 1637; rem. to Hamp.

NUNN,

Richard, ae. 19, came in the Increase April 15, 1635.

NURTON, see Norton.

NUTBROWNE,

Francis, ae. 16, came in the Defence in July, 1635.

NUTT, NUTTE, NUTE,

Miles, Watertown, propr. 1636; frm. May 17, 1637. Rem. to Woburn; propr. 1645. Wife Sybil, widow of John Bibell, adm. chh. Charlestown 29 (6) 1660; ch. Sarah, (m. Nov. 5, 1644, John Wyman, and afterward Thomas Fuller,) Anna, sometime of Lancaster.

He d. July 2, 1671, ae. about 73. He and his wife Sybil made a mutual agreement or will 4 Jan. 1658; her dau. Anne, wife of Robert Jones and her ch. to inherit certain property. He made will 1 Feb., prob. 15 (10) 1674; beq. to wife Sybil and dau. Sarah, wife of John Wyman, and to her ch. The widow m. 3, John Doolittle of Rumney Marsh; she d. Sept. 23, 1690, ae. 82.

NYLES, see Niles.

NYE, NOY,

Benjamin, Sandwich, had bequest of 30 shillings from Dennis Geere of Lynn 10 Dec. 1635. Propr. 1640. He m. 19 Oct. 1640, Katharine Tupper. Ch. Jonathan b. 20 Nov. 1649, (parents not stated,) Mary b. April 8, 1652. Goodwife Nye was a member of the chh. in 1694.

OAK, OAKS, OAKES, OKES,

Edward, merchant, Cambridge, propr., 1640; town officer. Frm. May 18, 1642. He deposed 3 (2) 1660, ae. about 56 years. [Mdx. Files.] He was attorney for Mrs. Elizabeth Poole of Westminster, Eng., 24 (9) 1646. Ch. Urian bapt. in England; about 10 years old when his father joined Camb. chh.; [Mi.] afterward president of Harvard College; Edward bapt. in England, Mary and Thomas bapt. in Camb. [Mi.] Thomas b. 18 (4) 1644.

He d. at Concord Oct. 13, 1689, ae. 85 years. Inv. of his est. taken Jan. 30, 1691-2. [See records of the family in Reg. XXXI, 324.]

Richard, Boston, propr. before 1636; lot was forfeited because not built upon.

Thomas, Cambridge, frm. May 18, 1642. Wife Elizabeth; ch. Elizabeth b. 3 (9) 1646, Thomas b. and d. 1648, Elizabeth b. 26 (3) 1649, Hannah bapt. at Camb. (no date given,) Thomas b. after his father's death, bapt. March 20, 1658-9.

He d. in 1658. The widow m. Samuel Hayward or Howard; her dau. Abigail H. bapt. at Camb. Sept. 23, 1666, rem. to Malden. [Mi.] Will dated Sept. 22, prob. 28 (10) 1658, beq. to wife Elizabeth and children not specified; bro. Edward O.

OAKLEY, see Oateley.

OATES, see Otis.

ODDINGSELL, ODDINGSELLE,

Thomas, gent., Salem, drew exchange on his father, John O. of Epperston, co. Nottingham, Esquire, Aug. 28, 1640. [L.] John Blackleach sued him at Salem; payment in part made in 1642. [Es. Files.]

ODELL, ODLE,

William, Concord. Ch. James b. 1639, bur. 1641, Rebecca b. 17 (5) 1642.

ODLIN, ODLYN, AUDLYN, AUDELYN, AUDLEY,

John, armourer, cutler, Boston, frm. May 14, 1634. "One of the very first inhabitant of Bo." [S.] One of the richer inhabitants who subscribed to the Free School in 1636. He deposed 10 June, 1684, concerning the town's purchase of the rights of Mr. William Blackstone. Wife Margaret; ch. John b. and d. 1635, Hannah b. and d. 1637, Elisha b. 1 (5) 1640, John b. 3 (12) 1641, Hannah bapt. 29 (8) 1643, ae. about 8 days, (m. Jeremiah Bumstead,) Peter b. 2 (6) 1646.

He d. Dec. 18, 1685. Will signed imperfectly "John Odlin," dated "fift day of month one thousand six hundred eight foure ore five," prob. 11 Jan. 1685, beq. to sons John, Peter and Elisha; to grandchild Hannah Bumsted; great Bible to Peter; Bible—Geneva translation, and Calvens Institutions; the rest of his books to be divided between the three.

OFFIT,

Thomas, with wife Isabel, members of the chh. of Roxbury about 1632. [E.]

OFFLEY,

Mr. David, gent., Boston, propr. 1638. Mortg. house and garden in security for bills of exchange payable by his mother to Mr. Robert Houghton 10 (6) 1641. Partner with Samuel Hosier in the business of taking and curing sturgeon at Yarmouth, 16 (6) 1639. Had accts. with Mr. Robert O., citizen and mercer of London, and with Stephen O. Joined in a letter of attorney with his wife Elizabeth, 26 (7) 1639, concerning est. at Glaston, Eng., to Edward or Henry Woolcott, or others. [L.] Was a propr. at Watertown in 1644.

OLBON, see Albon.

OLDHAM, OULDAM,

Mr. John, came to Plymouth in 1623. Was associated with Lyford in schemes to overthrow the government and substitute episcopal rule; wrote letters to persons in England who were hostile to the Colony; was detected and banished. The Western Adventurers of Dorchester, Eng., sent him to Cape Ann in 1625, but he accomplished nought. He went to Eng., and came again in 1630. Settled at Watertown. Frm. May 18, 1631. Deputy, 1634-5. Gen. Court

OLDHAM, etc., cont.
granted him a farm at Wat.; this he mortg. to Mr. Craddock. Was on important committees. Had grants from the Indians of islands in Narragansett Bay. Was slain by Indians while on a trading voyage at Block Island in July, 1636. [W. and B.]

John, ae. 12, came in the Elizabeth and Ann in May, 1635, res. at Duxbury, atba. 1643; and Thomas, ae. 10, who came at the same time, res. at Scituate; m. Nov. 20, 1656, [1657] Mary Witherell; had ch. Mary b. 20 Aug. 1658, Thomas b. 30 Oct. 1660; may both be children of John, above.

OLIVER, OLLIVER, OLYVER,
Christopher, residence not stated, before Gen. Court Nov. 7, 1634.

John, linen draper, of Bristol, Eng., came to Newbury about April 9, 1639. He deposed Sept. 17, 1640, ae. 27 years. Frm. 13 May, 1640. [Suff. De. I, 51.] He m. Joanna, dau. of Mrs. Joanna Goodale. Ch. Mary b. June 7, 1640, (m. 8 Dec. 1656, Samuel Appleton of Ipswich.)

He d. 1642, intestate. The Gen. Court 14 June, 1642, gave the est. to the widow, Joane, on condition that she pay 100 li. to the dau. at her marriage or at 18 years of age; the widow m. 17 April, 1645, William Gerrish. The Gen. Court allowed him, 2 May, 1649, to take charge of the portion of the dau. Mary, and to pay it to her when she is 14 years of age. Joseph Perry of Bristol, Eng., mercer, deposed 16 Jan. 1642, concerning the matter; a letter of attorney was sent to Francis Brewster to receive certain money of the widow of John Oliver or of Mr. Gerrish, her husband, 30 (9) 1646. [A.]

Mr. Thomas, embarked for N. E. March 7, 1631; settled at Boston; adm. chh. with wife Anne in 1632; frm. Nov. 6, 1632. Became ruling elder of the chh. Town officer, a man of great influence in the community. His wife Anne d. (3) 1635; he m. about 1637, Anne, widow [of Oliver Purchase, Sen.] His dau.-in-law, Sarah Purchase, was adm. chh. 31 (3) 1646. The wife was adm. chh. 27 (9) 1642. Ch. John, (adm. chh. in 1632,) Peter, (adm. chh. 23 (4) 1639,) Samuel, (adm. chh. 21 (3) 1643,) Abigail, (adm. chh. 30 (5) 1643,) James, (deposed in 1655, ae. about 35 years. [Es. Files.] adm. chh. 13 (4) 1640,) Nathaniel d. (9) 1633, Daniel d. (4) 1637.

OLIVER, etc., cont.
His will dated March 13, 1652, prob. Jan. 27, 1657. Wife; sons John, Peter, James, Samuel; dau. Abigail, wife of James Johnson; daus. Woodfall and Havens; Richard Woodfall at Muddy River; Hannah Tarne. To all gr. ch. in Old and New England 10 s. apiece. [Reg. VIII, 351.]

Thomas, calinder, ae. 36, of Norwich, Eng., with wife Mary, ae. 34, children Thomas and John, and servants, Thomas Doged, ae. 30, and Mary Sape, ae. 12, passed exam. May 13, 1637, to go to N. E. Settled at Salem. Propr. Sold land in 1659. His wife who had suffered somewhat in Eng. for refusing to bow at the name of Jesus, did not join the chh. of Salem, but publicly demanded to receive the Lord's Supper, etc., in 1639. Was incessant in her demands and reproaches, and was repeatedly punished. [W.] The husband was in court for his protests in 1646.

OLMSTEAD, OMSTED, HOLMSTEAD,
James, embarked for N. E. June 22, 1632. Propr. at Cambridge 1633; frm. Nov. 6, 1632; constable, 1634. Rem. to Hartford.

Nicholas, Cambridge, propr. of a house-lot and other land 1635; sold 20 Feb. 1636:

OLNEY, ONE,
Thomas, shoemaker, ae. 35, with [wife] Marie, ae. 30, and [sons] Thomas, ae. 3, and Etnetus (sic) cert. from the parish of St. Albons, Herts, came in the Planter April 2, 1635. Settled at Salem, propr. 1636. Frm. May 17, 1637. For his agreement in belief with the Hutchinson party in 1638, he was ordered to depart from the colony. Son Nabadiah bapt. 27 (6) 1637.

ONG, ONGE,
—, came with his wife in the Lyon in 1630. [W.] Probably his widow Frances O., of Wat., fermerly of Lavenham, Eng., is referred to as a witness to conversation which took place in her shop in L., by Robert Ryece, in letter to Gov. Winthrop in 1636. She was bur. at Watertown (9) 1638. John White, who owed her 25 li., gave security to John Sherman 20 July, 1643, for the payment of this etc. in the behalf of the children. Simon O., who may have been one of these ch., sold a house at Wat. 20 (12)

ONG, etc., cont.
1646. He deposed 8 (2) 1672, ae. about 50 years. [Mdx. Files.]
His est. was admin. by his bro. Jacob O., Nov. 8, 1678.

ONION, ONYON,
John, Braintree, propr. for 2 heads 24 (12) 1639.

Robert, ae. 26, came in the Blessing in July, 1635. Settled at Roxbury; his wife Mary and infant child were bur. 4 (2) 1643. [W.] He rem. to Dedham. Townsman 1 (11) 1644, adm. chh. 23 (1) 1645, frm. May 6, 1646. He m. 3 (10) 1643, Grace Ebrew; she d. 16 (12) 1647. He m. Sarah —. Ch. Sarah b. 23 (3) 1649, *Susan* bapt. 27 (3) 1649, Mary b. 12 (12) 1650, Hannah b. 29 (4) 1656, Benjamin b. 24 (10) 1659, Joseph b. 10 March, 1662-3, Grace b. 22 March, 1665-6, Sarah, (the wife,) d. Feb. 25, 1671; he d. Nov. 21, 1673.
Admin. of his est. was gr. 30 Jan. 1673, to Thomas Medcalfe.

ORCHARD, see ARCHER.

ORDWAY,
Abner, suit in Plymouth Court, 1650.

James, Newbury, propr. 1648. He deposed, 1669, ae. about 45 years. He m. 25 Nov. 1648, Anne, dau. of John Emery; she d. March 31, 1687. Ch. Ephraim b. 25 April, 1650, a child d. June 18, 1650, James b. 16 April, 1651, Edward b. 17 Sept. 1653, Sarah b. Jan. 14, 1655, Sarah b. 14 Sept. 1656, John b. 17 Nov. 1658, Isaac b. 4 Dec. 1660, d. 16 Jan. 1669, Jane b. 22 Nov. 1663, Hannaniah b. 2 Dec. 1665, a child d. June 6, 1668, [Anne b. 12 Feb. 1670, Mary b. 5 April, 1672.]

ORMSBY, ORMESBY, ARMSBEY, ORMSBEY,
Anne, widow, had lands assigned her in Boston in 1635, confirmed in 1638. She was adm. chh. 28 (6) 1639, and dism. with Jane Wilkes and Elizabeth Tuttle 8 (7) 1639, to [Ipswich] church.

Edmund, Boston, had a great lot at Muddy River for 3 heads, 16 (2) 1638.

Richard, planter, Haverhill; propr. 1650; town officer; also lived at Salisbury some time. He deposed in 1660, ae. 52 years.

ORMSBY, etc., cont.
Rem. to Hehoboth; sold lands to Robert Pike in 1663. Wife Sarah; ch. John, Thomas b. Nov. 11, 1645, Jacob b. March 6, 1647-8.
Inv. of his est. taken 30 (5) 1664. Debts by book left at Salisbury, etc. Widow Sarah deposed.

ORNE, see HORNE.

ORRIS ORRICE, ORRYS,
George, ae. 21, came in the Elizabeth and Ann in May, 1635. Res. at Boston; blacksmith. Wife Elizabeth adm. chh. 15 (1) 1645; ch. Mary bapt. 23 (1) ae. about 1 year, 7 months, John b. 1 (1) 1646, Bethiah bapt. 30 (5) 1648, ae. about 6 days, Experience bapt. 25 (3) 1651, Sarah b. 16 (Nov.) 1653, Jonathan bapt. 8 (12) 1656, Samuel b. 20 Dec. 1659, Nathaniel b. April 27, 1664.

ORTON,
Thomas, Charlestown. Wife Mary adm. chh. 12 (2) 1650; ch. Mary b. 27 (6) 1648, William bapt. 5 (12) 1659, Ebenezer bapt. 17 (11) 1663, Thomas bapt. 7 (3) 1665, Anne bapt. 5 (6) 1666, Abigail bapt. 19 (7) 1668.

OSBORN, OSBORNE, OSBURN, OSBURNE, OZBAN,
Christopher, Duxbury, called into Plymouth Court 4 Dec. 1638, but marked in the record "dead."

James, Springfield, propr. 1646. He m. in 1645 or 1646 Joyce Smith. Ch. Elizabeth b. 27 (3) 1647, Mary b. 16 (1) 1649, James b. 8 (3) 1654, Sarah b. 3 (12) 1657, Samuel b. 1 Feb. 1663.
His est. was divided by agreement Sept. 29, 1685, between his sons James and Samuel.

John, Braintree. Ch. John b. 2 (12) 1639, Matthew d. (3) 1641.

Mary, indicted for the murder of her dau.; was acquitted 19 (7) 1637.

Mary, fined by the Gen. Court for giving quicksilver to her husband 29 (5) 1641.

Matthew, Weymouth, appr. to John Reade 14 Sept. 1637, transferred to John Done of Plymouth 21 Aug. 1637.
He d. at W. (3) 1641.

OSBORN, etc., cont.

Richard, before Gen. Court 19 (7) 1637.

Thomas, Charlestown, adm. chh. 10 (7) 1644. Rem. to Malden, but returned after some years. He and his wife were recd. to the chh. of Char. from that of Malden 23 (12) 1661. Ch. Sarah b. 29 (1) 1647, Thomas b. June 26, 1649, Mary b. March 11, 1651-2, — b. April 30, 1654.

William, merchant, Hingham, propr. 1635; Salem, propr., town officer, frm. May 22, 1639. He went to Braintree to become clerk of the Iron Works; son —, b. at Br., bapt. at Dorchester May 26, 1644, being born at the house of his brother. [Dorch. Chh. Rec.] He rem. to Boston about 1652. Wife Frediseed adm. chh. 23 (3) 1641; ch. Recompense bapt. May 26, 1644, Hannah b. 24 (6) 1646, Bezaleel b. 8 (1) 1649, Joseph b. 6 (2) 1652, Jonathan b. Nov. 16, 1656.

Admin. gr. Aug. 26, 1662, to the widow for herself and 5 children; eldest son had taken one degree; land at Wenham and Dorchester. [Reg. XI, 345.]

OSGOOD,

Christopher, came in the Mary and John March 24, 1633-4. Settled at Ipswich; brickmaker; propr. 1634. Frm. May 6, 1635. Will dated April 19, prob. 10 (8) 1650, beq. to wife Margery; son Christopher; daus. Mary, Abigail, Elizabeth and Deborah; wife exec.; father Philip Fowler one of the overseers. The daus. Mary m. John Lovejoy, Abigail m. Shoreborne Wilson, Deborah m. John Ross or Russ. The widow m. 2, Thomas Rowell of Andover; she m. 3, Thomas Coleman of Newbury. Residing at Nantucket, she deeded 27 May, 1673, to her son Thomas O. of Newbury, the house and land where she dwelt in the time of her former husband, Thomas Rowell, which is now in possession of Christopher O.; he to pay certain sums to her son Jacob Rowell and her daus. Abigail Wilson and Deborah Russ. She made another deed to him of the nature of a will, 8 June, 1675. [See Reg. XIII, 200.]

John, yeoman, Newbury, 1638. One of the original settlers of Hampton, allowed by the Gen. Court 6 (7) 1638. Res. at Newbury in 1648. Rem. to Andover; deputy, 1651. Sergeant, 1658. [See petition of 17 settlers of And. in Es. Files IV, 127.] His wife Sarah came in the Confidence April 11, 1638,

OSGOOD, cont.

with 4 children, hailing from Horrell, Eng. William O., William Jones and Margery Parke, a servant, were fellow passengers. Ch. Sarah, (m. John Clement,) John, Mary, (m. Henry Ingalls, Elizabeth, (m. John Browne of Reading,) Stephen, Hannah, (m. Samuel Archer).

He d. in 1651. Will signed April 12, 1650, prob. Nov. 25, 1651; in his 54th year; born July 23, 1595; beq. to wife Sarah; ch. Stephen, Mary, Elizabeth, Hannah, Sarah Clements and her dau. Bakah; servant Caleb Johnson; to the chh. of Newbury 18 shillings to buy a cushion for the minister to lay his book upon; rest to son John and wife Sarah, whom he makes execs. [Reg. XIII, 117.] The widow d. April 8, 1667.

William, Salisbury, 1650. Testified 1 (3) 1654, ae. about 45 years, about Anthony Sadler's purchase of a house in the year 1650. [Arch. 38 B.]

Will dated 15 March, 1700, beq. to son William, his wife Abigail and his son John; to gr. dau. Elizabeth, wife of John Flanders; to gr. ch. William, Hannah and John, ch. of dec. son John; to gr. son Thomas Quimby, son of dec. dau. Elizabeth; to daus. Joanna, wife of Robert Jones, and Sarah, wife of John Colby; to his dau. Mary and her husband Thomas Currier.

OTIS, OTTIS, OATES, OATISE,

John, planter, Hingham, propr. 1635. Frm. March 3, 1635-6. Town officer. His buildings burned March 15, 1645-6. He rem. about 1655 to Weymouth. Wife Margaret d. 28 (4) 1653.

He d. May 31, 1657, ae. 76. [Hob.] Will prob. July 28, 1657. To wife; to son John, who was made exec.; to dau. Margaret Burton and her three children; to dau. Hannah Gile; to Mary and Thomas Gile, Jr.; to daus. Anne and Alice. [Reg. VIII, 279.] Elizabeth, Weymouth, widow, made will 12 Sept. 1672, prob. 17 July, 1676. Beq. to son John Streme, dau. Elizabeth and son-in-law Lt. John Holbrook.

John, Scituate, bur. May 8, 1641.

OVELL,

Nathaniel, cordwinder, of Dover, embarked for N. E. from Sandwich, Eng. before June 9, 1637.

OTLEY, OATLEY, OAKLEY, UTLEY,

Mr. Adam, Lynn, fined by the Court 7 (7) 1641, for aiding Thomas Owen to escape from prison. Represented his father-in-law, Mr. John Humphrey, in lawsuit in 1642. [Suff. De. I, 33; Col. Rec., W.]

Sarah, perhaps his wife, adm. chh. Charlestown 30 (6) 1634. [Es. Files VII, 128.]

OWEN,

Thomas, merchant, Boston, attorney of Mrs. Anne Stratton in 1640. [L.] Punished for misconduct 7 (7) 1641. Sheltered by Maverick. [W.]

William, Braintree, 1650; frm. May 7, 1651. He m. 29 (7) 1650, Elizabeth Davies; Charles Grice calls him son-in-law. Ch. Daniel bur. 14 (8) 1651, Deliverance, dau., b. 15 (12) 1654, Ebenezer b. 1 (3) 1657, d. of small pox on Canada expedition in Aug. 1690, Daniel b. 23 (9) 1659, a son b. 1 (6) 1667, Obediah b. 1 (12) 1670.

He d. 17 Jan. 1702. The widow d. 3 June, 1702.

PACKARD, PACKER,

Samuel, came from Windham, Eng. in 1638, with wife and child, and settled at Hingham. Propr. 1638. Rem. to Bridgewater. Ch. Elizabeth, Samuel, Hannah and Israel bapt. 19 July, 1646, Zaccheus, Jane and Abigail bapt. April 20, 1651; Deliverance bapt. July 11, 1652.

Will dated 29 Oct. 1684, prob. 3 March, 1684-5, beq. to wife Elizabeth, ch. Samuel, Zaccheus, John, Nathaniel, Mary, (wife of Richard Phillips,) Hannah, (wife of Thomas Randall,) Jael, (wife of John Smith,) Deborah, (wife of Samuel Washburn,) and Deliverance, (wife of Thomas Washburne;) gr. ch. Israel and Deliverance Auger, and others.

PACY,

Nicholas, Salem, propr. 1638. He m. 1, Katharine —, who had plighted her troth to Mark Vermais; both confessed their error before the Court 28 (10) 1640. She was adm. chh. 23 (3) 1641. Ch. Hannah bapt. 29 (3) 1642. He m. 2, Sarah, dau. of Gov. Thomas Dudley, who had been the wife of Benjamin Keayne, Jr., and had been divorced from him. She was admitted inhabitant of Bos-

PACY, cont.

ton in 1655. She d. Nov. 3, 1659. Will prob. 26 (9) 1659, gave all to her dau. Anna Keayne.

PADDOCK,

Robert, smith, Plymouth, creditor of Job Cole, 1638; atba. 1643, Duxbury, propr. 1638. Goodwife rec'd money from est. of Job Cole "for the child." Ch. Zachariah b. 20 March, 1636, Mary b. 10 March, 1638, Alice b. 7 March, 1640, a dau. b. 1641. John b. 1 April, 1643.

He was bur. July 25, 1650; on his death-bed he gave his son John to Capt. Thomas Willett; the widow Mary confirmed this in Nov. folg. She sold house and shop to Stephen Wood Dec. 3, 1650. The dau. Alice m. 24 March, 1650, Thomas Roberts. William Palmer, b. 27 June, 1634, was his son-in-law. [Plym. Col. Rec. vol. VIII.]

PADDY,

William, skinner, merchant, from London, came in the James April 5, 1635. Settled at Plymouth; frm. Jan. 3, 1636; deputy, 1639. Rem. to Boston. He was one of the lessees of the trade at Kennebeck up to 1650. Mr. John Beauchamp, one of the partners in Plymouth Company, calls him cousin in letter in Plym. Deeds, II; refers also to bro. Freeman, Paddy's father, and to bro. Coddington. He m. 24 Nov. 1639, Alice, dau. of Edmund Freeman; she d. 24 April, 1651, and he m. 2, 3 (10) 1651, Mary, sister of Wm. Greenough, and widow of Bezaleel Payton. Ch. Elizabeth b. 12 Nov. 1641, John b. 25 Nov. 1643, Samuel b. 1 Aug. 1645, Thomas b. 6 Sept. 1647, Joseph b. and d. 1649, William b. 16 Sept. 1652. Other ch. named in his will: Mercy, (m. Leonard Dowden,) Nathaniel, Hannah, Benjamin.

Will prob. Sept. 9, 1658. Beq. to wife and children; also to Sarah and Mary Payton, ch. of his wife by former husband. Other bequests. Leonard Dowden and Thomas Paddy gave bonds July 19, 1680, to admin. on the remaining est. of their father, Wm. Paddy, dec. [Reg. VII, 339, VIII, 335, and XXXI, 321.]

PAGE,

Abraham,, tailor, of Great Baddow, Essex, Eng., had a bond Aug. 25, 1636, from Wm. Vincent, for £ 20 when he should be 21 years old; otherwise to his bros. Isaac and

PAGE, cont.

Jacob P. [Suff. De. I, 66.] He settled at Boston; gave letter of attorney 23 (10) 1645, for collection of dues in Eng. [A.] Wife Mary; see Col. Rec. 1638.

Edward, cooper, Boston, was freed from his master 29 (2) 1641. Gave a bond for the payment of money April 8, 1663. He was bur. Aug. 16, 1693. Admin. of his est. gr. to his widow Abiah 22 Dec. 1693.

John, Hingham, signed a petition to Gen. Court 4 Nov. 1646. Rem. to Haverhill about 1652. Wife Mary [Marsh?] d. Feb. 15, 1696. Ch. John bapt. July 11, 1641, Onesiphorus bapt. Nov. 20, 1642, Benjamin bapt. July 14, 1644, Mary bapt. May 3, 1646, (m. 1, John Dow, 2, Samuel Shepherd,) Joseph bapt. March 5, 1647, Cornelius bapt. July 15, 1649, Sarah bapt. July 18, 1651, (m. James Sanders,) Elizabeth b. and d. 1653, Mercy b. April 1, 1655, (m. John Clough,) Ephraim b. and d. 1659.

He d. Nov. 23, 1687. Admin. gr. to gr. son Thomas, March 12, 1721-2; division Nov. 1723.

John, came in 1630, with wife and 2 children from Dedham, Eng.; had relief sent him in the hard times of 1630 by his minister, Mr. John Rogers. [W.] Settled at Watertown. Constable Sept., 1630. Propr. house burned April 21, 1631. Wife Phebe; ch. Samuel b. 20 (6) 1633, Daniel bur. 10 (6) 1634. Son John refers to his father's lands in a deed in 1662.

He d. Dec. 18, 1676, ae. about 90; inv. filed. His widow d. Sept. 25, 1677, ae. about 87.

Margaret, Salem, a town charge; money was voted 30 (7) 1647, to pay her passage to England.

Robert, husbandman, ae. 33, with wife Lucy, ae. 30, ad children Frances, Margaret and Susanna, and servants William Moulton, ae. 20, and Anne Wad, ae. 15, of Ormsby, Eng., passed exam. April 11, 1637, to go to N. E. Settled at Salem. Wife Lucy adm. chh., 1639. He was adm. frm. May 18, 1642. Rem. to Hampton; deputy, deacon. He secured the claims of his brother Edward Colcord and his wife Ann, in 1654 and 1679. Ch. Rebecca and Samuel bapt. at Sal. 1 (7) 1639.

He d. Sept. 22, 1679. Will dated 9 Sept., prob. 29 Sept. 1679, beq. to sons Francis and Thomas; daus. Mary Fogg, Margaret San-

PAGE, cont.

borne, and Hannah, wife of Henry Dow; gr. ch. Seth, James, and Hannah Fogg; Joseph, Benjamin, Robert, Hannah, Sarah and Ruth Moulton; Jonathan Samborne; Rebecca, Hannah, Samuel, Lucie and Meriah Marston; Joseph, Samuel, Symon and Jabez Dow; Robert, Samuel, John, Mary and Lucie Page; (some of these gr. ch. called by their marriage names in the will.

Thomas, tailor, ae. 29, with wife Elizabeth, ae. 28, and children Thomas, ae. 2, and Katharine, ae. 1, and servants Edward Spurks, ae. 22, and Kat: Taylor, ae. 24, cert. from All Saints, Stayning, (London,) came in the Increase in April, 1635.

We note that Thomas, gent., Saco, (Maine,) gave bond 22 (1) 1640-1. [L.]

William, Watertown, planter, bought land in 1650. Wife Anne; ch. John b. and d. 1642. They took John, son of George Parkhurst, Jr., to bring up in 1646. [Suff. De. I, 78.]

He d. 9 (10) 1664. He made will 16 Dec. 1664, prob. April 4, 1665; beq. to wife Hannah; at her death to each of his kindred now in N. E., to kinsman Thomas Leason; to Edward L. now living with me.

PAGRAM,

Mr. Richard, Charlestown, propr. 1635.

PAINE, PAYNE,

Edward, of Wapping, mariner, Charlestown, inhabitant, 1638. He sold, by his attorney, George Arnell, land at Char. 19 (1) 1640-1. His son Joseph, ae. 22 years, sold land and houses at Char. 2 (9) 1649.

Moses, gent., Cambridge, propr. before 1638; rem. to Braintree. Ensign; frm. June 2, 1641. He m., as his last wife, Judith, widow of Edmund Quinsey. Ch. Moses, Stephen, Elizabeth, (m. Nov. 17, 1643, Henry Adams).

He d. 21 (4) 1643. Will prob. 30 (8) 1643; beq. to wife Judith; to sons Moses and Stephen, and dau. Elizabeth. Goods and lands at Br., Camb., Concord and Pascataqua, and in Old England. [Reg. II, 263.]

Mr. Robert, Ipswich, propr. 1639, one of the com. for furthering trade in 1640. Frm. June 2, 1641. He deposed in 1667, ae.

PAINE, etc., cont.
about 65 years. Deputy 1647-8. [Suff. De. III, 357.]

Thomas, of Wrentom, co. Suff, Eng., weaver, ae. 50, passed exam. May 10, 1637, to go to Salem in N. E., with wife Elizabeth, ae. 53, and children Thomas, John, Mary, Elizabeth, Dorothy and Sarah. Settled at Salem; propr. 1637. Son Thomas bound to Nich: Poore; suit in Es. Court in 1637. Will dated 10 (2) 1638; inv. 10 (5) 1644; beq. to wife, son Thomas, dau. Mary, kinsman Henry Blomfield.

Thomas, Dedham, propr. 28 (9) 1640; with wife Rebecca adm. chh. 23 (2) 1641; frm. June 2, 1641. Ch. Rebecca b. 19 (7) 1642, Thomas b. 29 (1) 1644, John b. 27 (2) 1646, Elizabeth b. 6 (1) 1648. Will dated 26 July, prob. Sept. 23, 1686, beq. to wife Rebecca; sons Thomas and John; son-in-law Thomas Patten on behalf of his wife Rebecca, dec.; gr. ch. Rebecca Patten; dau. Elizabeth Hunting. Inv. shows weaving implements, etc.

Thomas, Yarmouth, inhabitant 1641; land confirmed 1648. Rem. to Eastham; townsman 1655, or earlier. Is perhaps the Thomas, mariner, whose widow Hannah admin. on his est. at Boston 29 July, 1667. [Reg. XVIII, 154.]

Thomas, son of Thomas Paine, of London, merchant, came to N. E. with his mother Jane, who had m. 2, Mr. Thomas Mahew; he chose them his guardians Oct. 14, 1647, being 15 years old and upwards. [Suff. De. I, 86.]

Walter, Charlestown, resident, 1635.

William, husbandman, ae. 37, with wife Anna, ae. 40, children Susan, ae. 11, Anna, ae. 5, John, ae. 3, and Daniel, ae. 8 weeks, came in the Increase April 15, 1635. William, ae. 15, came in the Abigail in July, 1635. Resided at Salem, Ipswich and Boston. Frm. May 13, 1640. Paid for work done on the ship Sara at Salem in 1641. Of Ipswich, merchant, propr. 1639. Town officer. His dau. Hannah m. April 2, 1651, Samuel Appleton, Jr. William Payne, late of Lanham, now of New Eng., mentioned in letter to Gov. Winthrop 17 Jan. 1636. [Mass. Hist. Coll. 4-6.] In a deposition in Es. Files, 1658, he calls Anthony Stoddard cousin.

PAINE, etc., cont.
Will made at Boston, 2 Oct. 1660. Long infirm; beq. to wife Hanna dwelling house at Boston, mill at Watertown and household effects; to Hanna, Samuel and Judith, ch. of his dec. dau. Hanna Appleton; to Benjamin, Mary, Rebekah, Christian, Ann and Dorothy, ch. of Symond Eyers, dec., and to Symond, son of Symond E., Jr., dec.; to sister Page, and to her ch. John, Samuel, Elizabeth, Mary, Phebe; to the ch. of his sister Hament, viz. John, Elizabeth and Hanna; to kinswoman Elizabeth House, dau. of Samuel and Elizabeth H.; to two daus. of his cosan John Tall, when of age; to son-in-law Samuel Appleton; to William Howard, Jerimy Belcher, Anthony Stodder, Christopher Clarke, Oliver Purchase, (whom he requests to be helpful to his son John concerning the accounts of the Iron worke;) to Mary Ingion; to the ministers, Norton and Wilson of Boston, Shirman of Wat., Browne of Sudbury, Cobbit of Ips., Fisk of Chensford, Phillips of Rowley, Mayhoo of the new chh., Boston. To the Colledge at Cambridge, 20 li. to be kept as a stock forever. Made his son-in-law Samuel Appleton, son John, and Mr. Anthony Stodder execs., and Mr. Christopher Clarke, Mr. Joseph Taintor and Mr. Oliver Purchase overseers and feofees in trust. Gave his execs. power to expend 100 li. out of the est. for some pyous use and necessary worke. In a postscript he gave 5 li. to Doctor Clarke and 5 li. to Capt. Thomas Clarke Company to buy them Cullers. Witnesses John Mayo, Christopher Clarke and Will: Howard. [Reg. X, 85.]

William, shoemaker, Salem, bought shop of John Baylyes in 1649.

PAINTER, PAYNTER,
Thomas, joiner, Boston, juryman 28 Sept. 1630; adm. chh. 5 (7) 1640; frm. Oct. 12, 1640. Had a grant of land from Gen. Court at Rowley 6 June, 1639. Gave letter of attorney 5 (11) 1647, for collection of money from Wm. Withington of Rhode Island. [A.] Wife Katharine; ch. William d. 30 (7) 1639, Thomas b. and d. 1639, Elizabeth d. 24 (2) 1640. The wife d. in 1641. He m. a second wife, and had an other child. One Painter of Hingham, who had lived at New Haven and Rowley and Charlestown, wa-

PAINTER, etc., cont.
whipped in 1644 for refusing to have his child baptized at the church where his wife was a member. [W.]

PAKES,
William, Scituate, atba. 1643. His dau. was drowned 15 Nov. 1653; inquest.

PALFLIN,
John, before Gen. Court 4 (4) 1639.

PALFREY,
Jane, widow, m. George Willowes or Willis of Cambridge; had ch. John and Elizabeth Palfrey. [Mi.]

Peter, yeoman, planter, Salem, juryman, Gen. Court, 1630; frm. May 18, 1631. One of the settlers before the arrival of Endecott. (Depos. of Brakenbury.) Had land at the head of Bass river. Rem. to Reading. Town officer at both places. [Wife] Edith memb. chh. before 1636. After her death he m., about 1646, Elizabeth, widow of John Fairfield. Ch. Jonathan and Jehodan bapt. 25 (10) 1636, Remember bapt. 16 (7) 1638, Mary bapt. 15 (10) 1639; other ch. were the wives of Samuel Pickman, Matthew Johnson and Benjamin Smith, mentioned in the father's will; Johnson sued the est. in 1663 for a portion promised him at marriage. [Mdx. Files.] Remember went to Roxbury to live, and m. Peter Aspinwall. See Fairfield.

He d. Sept. 15, 1663. Will dated Oct. 21, 1662, codicil added 19 May, 1663, prob. 15 (10) 1663; far stricken in years; beq. to son-in-law Matthew Johnson; to youngest dau. Mary P.; to sons-in-law Samuel Pickman, Peter Aspinwall and Benjamin Smith.

PALGRAVE, PALSGRAVE,
Mr. Richard, physician, Charlestown, propr. 1630; with wife Anne adm. chh. 1631, frm. May 18, 1631. Ch. John, (who quitclaimed land in 1657,) Mary, (m. Roger Willington,) Sarah, (m. Dr. John Alcock; d. 29 (9) 1665, ae. 44 years,) Rebecca b. 25 (5) 1631, John b. 6 (1) 1634, Lydia b. 15 (11) 1635, Bethiah b. and d. 1638, Elizabeth.

He d. about 1655. His widow, dwelling at Stepney, Eng., made a letter of attorney March 17, 1656. [Midx. De. II, 32.] She ret. to N. E. and d. at Roxbury 17 (11) 1669, ae. 75. Will prob. May 13, 1669. Beq. to eldest

PALGRAVE, etc., cont.
dau. Mary, wife of Roger Willington; to Anna and other children of her son and dau. Alcock; to John Heylet, eldest son of her dau. Lydia, he to be educated in physick; to Mary, wife of John Maddox; to grandchildren. A debt due to John Pattison in old England.

PALMER,
Abraham, Charlestown, with wife Grace adm. chh. in 1630. Frm. May 18, 1631. Town clerk, deputy. Sold lands, houseinge, timber and accommodations 30 (1) 1647. Engaged in trade at Barbadoes and other W. I. ports. [Suff. De. II, 163.]

He d. at Barbadoes; admin. gr. to his wife Grace 23 (7) 1653. [Reg. VII, 338.] The widow d. Dec., 1660. Inv. of her est. taken 20 Dec., 1660, filed 2 (2) 1661.

Edward, carpenter, [Boston.] He was fined by the Gen. Court in 1639-40, for asking too high a price for a piece of timber for the stocks. [L., and Col. Rec.]

George, wine-cooper, Boston, propr.; in court 30 (2) 1640. Was of Ipswich in 1650, and contracted to deliver pipe-staves. Mortg. his house and land Feb. 11, 1655. Wife Elizabeth.

Henry, Newbury, 1638-1642; frm. June 22, 1642. Before Boston court 2 (1) 1640-1. Rem. to Haverhill; propr. 1644; town officer. Com. to end small causes 26 May, 1647. Excused by Hampton court in 1650 from training, on account of infirmities. He m. Elizabeth; ch. rec. at Hav.: Bathshua d. Feb. 26, 1654. His wife d. Nov. 22, 1664.

He d. July 15, 1680. His will dated 10 July, prob. 28 Sept. 1680, beq. to gr. ch. John Dalton, Elizabeth Ayer, now wife to John Clements, Samuel and Timothy A.; to son and dau. Robert and Elizabeth A.; son and dau. Samuel and Mehitabel Dalton.

John, Boston, 1636; had lands at Braintree; frm. March 13, 1638-9. Audrey, widow, Boston, had the house of her son John as a part of what he had recd. from his father; Gen. Court, 22 May, 1650. This she sold March 11, 1652. [See Book of Poss., p. 36 and 37, and Suff. De. I, 313.]

John, ae. 24, came in the Elizabeth of Ipswich April 30, 1634. Perhaps the seaman who res. at Hingham; propr. 1635; who

PALMER, cont.
deposed in 1641 that he came to dwell at H. about 4 years before; propr. He was wrecked but not drowned in 1639. [W.] Rem. to Scituate. In court 1650. Yeoman. Ch. John, Elnathan, Samuel bapt. Feb. 1640, Josiah bapt. June 7, 1643, Elizabeth d. 6 July, 1647, Hannah bapt. May, 1647. Will dated 7 Feb. 1675, prob. 7 March, 1676; beq. to eldest son John and his ch. Sarah, Hannah, Elizabeth and Bezaleel; to second son Samuel, third son Josiah, and dau. Hannah.

John, Rowley, propr. 1643. He deposed in 1693, ae. about 70 years. He m. 17 (7) 1645, Ruth —; she was bur. Oct. 13, 1649. He m. 2, 14 (5) 1650, Margaret —. Ch. Hannah b. 1 (7) 1647, bur. 25 Oct. 1670, John b. 7 (8) 1649, bur. Aug. 6, 1683, Elizabeth b. 1 (8) 1652, John b. 15 (1) 1656, Francis b. 4 (10) 1657, Sarah b. 13 (11) 1661.

He d., aged, 17 June, 1695. Will dated 23 Aug. 1693, prob. July, 1695.

Richard, ae. 29, came in the James in July, 1635.

Thomas, Rowley, propr. 1643. He m. (6) 1643, Ann —; ch. Samuel b. 20 (6) 1644, Timothy b. 2 (2) 1647, Thomas b. (6) 1650. The wife Ann was bur. 22 Feb. 1686.
His will dated 2 Aug., prob. 28 Sept. 1669.

Walter, Charlestown, accused and acquitted of causing the death of Austen Bratcher, Sept. 28, 1630; frm. May 18, 1631. Constable, 1633-1636. Rem. to Seakonk. Frm. Plym. Col. 28 Oct. 1645. Deputy, town officer, juryman. Wife Rebecca and dau. Grace, (who m. Thomas Minor,) adm. chh. Char. 1 (4) 1633. Ch. Hannah bapt. 15 (4) 1634, Elihu bapt. 24 (11) 1635, Nehemiah bapt. 23 (9) 1637, Moses bapt. 6 (2) 1640, Benjamin b. 30 (3) 1642.
He d. at Sothertowne, in the county of Suffolke, about 1662. Will prob. 11 May, 1662; wife and son Elihu execs.; children John, Grace, Jonas, William, Gershom, Nehemiah, Moses, Benjamin, Hannah, Rebecca, Elizabeth. [Reg. XI, 39.]

William, nailer, came in the Fortune to Plymouth in 1621; taxed at Duxbury in 1632; frm. 1633. Wife Frances and son William had shares in the cattle in 1627.
Will prob. Dec. 4, 1637; wife, a young woman; son Henry, dau. Bridget, grand child Rebecca; Moyses Rowly; Stephen Tracy; the

PALMER, cont.
church of Plymouth. [Reg. IV, 35.] John Willis brought suit against the executors of this will, having m. Elizabeth, formerly wife of William the younger, son of the above.

William, yeoman, Newbury; one of those licensed by Gen. Court to begin a plantation at Hampton 6 (7) 1638; frm. March 13, 1638-9. He conveyed all his property in Hampton and Newbury, March 10, 1645, to John Sherman of Watertown, and Martha, his dau., Sherman's wife, in lieu of est. in Great Ormesby, Eng. which was her inheritance. J. and M. S. sold all their share in his est. to his youngest son Joseph P. in 1661.

William, divorced by Gen. Court 19 Oct. 1650, from his wife Elinor who had married another man in England.

William, Yarmouth, with wife Judith, dau. of James Feke of London, goldsmith, gave letter of attorney Dec. 5, 1639, to Tobias Dixon, citizen and mercer of L., to sell a house and shop in Lumbard street, late in occupation of one Brampton. [L.] He was allowed to train the inhabitants of Y. in 1639 and 1643; lieut., deputy.

PALMERLEY,
John, ae. 20, came in the Elizabeth and Ann in April, 1635.

PANCRUST,
Ann, ae. 16, came in the Abigail in June, 1635.

PANTRY, PANCRY, PEYNTREE,
William, Cambridge, 1633, propr. 1635, frm. March 4, 1634-5. Was excused by the Court from training, on account of his age, Nov. 7, 1634. [See Tuttle, Richard.]

PARDON,
William, laborer, Weymouth, frm. May, 1645. [See Collins and Poole.]

PARIS,
John, merchant, Charlestown, gave power of attorney March 3, 1645, to Maj. Edward Gibbons, specially to recover his wife's portion from Mr. Wm. Barnard of Char. Mortg. house at Barbadoes and certain shipping property to John Allen of Char. 4 (4) 1650.

PARISH, PARRIS,
Thomas, clothier, ae. 22, came in the Increase in April, 1635. Settled at Watertown; propr. 1636; rem. to Cambridge; frm. April 18, 1637. Town officer, 1639. Contracted to sell lands at Halstead, Eng. for John Hood, Oct. 22, 1638. Ret. to Eng. before 1654. Was described in a deed as "gent," of Nayland, Suffolk co. Wife Mary; ch. Mary b. 3 (2) 1638, Thomas b. 21 (5) 1641.

PARK, PARKE, PARKS, PARKES,
Edward, [Watertown?] a "cousin" of Gov. Winthrop, wrote him from London 8 March, 1647, asking his aid and advice for his "uncle" Henry Bright and son Henry Parks about land ordered to himself by the Court. [Mass. Hist. Coll. 4-7.]

Joseph, Hingham, propr., suit about fences in 1639. [L.]

Richard, Cambridge, householder 1635. [See Edward Winship.]

Robert, residence not stated, had leave of the Gen. Court 30 May, 1644, to marry Alice Tompson without further publishment.

William, Roxbury, came, a single man, in the 12th month, 1630. [E.] Deacon, town officer, deputy, commissioner; frm. May 18, 1631. He owned land also at Stonington. Signed inv. of John Levens in 1648. He m. Martha, dau. of John Holgrave, of Salem; she d. Aug. 25, 1708, in her 94th year. Ch. Theoder b. July 26, 1637, (m. Samuel Williams,) Hannah b. Aug. 28, 1639, d. 26 (4) 1665, Martha b. March 2, 1641, Sarah bapt. 19 (9) 1643, bur. 8 (9) 1644, John b. June 30, 1645, d. 16 (4) 1646, John bapt. 13 (3) 1649, Deborah bapt. 6 (2) 1651, William bapt. 8 (8) 1654, d. 14 (5) 1656, John d. 4 (3) 1663. See letter from his bro. Thomas P. of Southertowne in 1661.

He d. May 11, 1685. Will prob. 30 July, 1685, beq. to wife Martha; son Samuel Williams and his children, Samuel, John, Park, Ebenezer, Deborah, Martha and Abigail; son Isaac William's ch., especially William whom I have brought up; refers to land that belonged to bro. Thomas Parks; son John Smith and dau. Smith; bro. Samuel Parks and his sons Robert and William; Hannah Williams. [Reg. XXXI, 176.]

PARILL,
Edward, Watertown. Admin. of his est. June 2, 1644. [Reg. VIII, 56.]

PARKER, PARKE, PARKES, PARKERS,
Abraham, Woburn, taxed, 1645; rem. to Chelmsford. He m. Nov. 18, 1644, Rose Whitlock; ch. Hannah b. Oct. 29, 1645, John b. Oct. 30, 1647, Abraham b. March 8, 1649, d. Oct. 20, 1651, Mary, (m. at Chelm. Dec. 11, 1678, James, son of Capt. James Parker).
The inv. of the estates of Abraham and Rose was taken March 23, 1696, admin. gr. to son Moses.

Edmund, Roxbury, propr., rem. to Lancaster. He m. at Rox. May 31, 1647, Elizabeth, [dau. of Abraham] How; ch. Elizabeth bapt. 2 (2) 1648, Elizabeth bapt. 29 (2) 1649, Abraham bapt. 5 (7) 1652, Mercy and Esther b. at Lanc. 28 (8) 1654, Deborah b. 6 (11) 1655, *Mary*, Esther and Deborah bapt. at Rox. 22 (4) 1656.

George, carpenter, ae. 23, came in the Susan and Ellen in April, 1635. A George Parker took oath of fidelity at York, Nov. 22, 1652.

Rev. James, Weymouth, a godly man and a scholar, many years a deputy of the Court, was called to Pascataqua to be their minister in 1642. Had good success. [W.] Sold houses and lands at Wey. 26 (9) 1644, res. at Strawberry Bank. Frm. May 29, 1644.

James, Woburn, 1640, taxed 1645. Rem. to Billerica in 1654, to Chelmsford in 1658. He m. May 23, 1643, Elizabeth Long; ch. Elizabeth b. March 12, 1645, Ann b. Jan. 5, 1646, John b. Jan. 18, 1648, Sarah b. Aug. 29, 1650, d. Oct. 15, 1651, James.
He d. at Groton in 1701, ae. 83 years. [Hist. Billerica.]

John, carpenter, from Marlborough, Eng., came in the James April 5, 1635. Settled at Boston. Wife Jane adm. chh. 8 (11) 1636. Ch. Thomas b. 2 (8) 1635, bapt. 22 (11) 1636, Noah b. 3 (2) bapt. 8 (2) 1638. Jane, of Boston, widow, by deed of gift, 15 (5) 1646, gave to her eldest dau. Margaret and her heirs 21 feet square in the angle at the meeting of the streets out of her house-lot; the house and rest of lot to sons John, Thomas, and Noah; 6 li. apiece out of her chattels

PARKER, etc., cont.
to daus. Sarah and Alice at 18 years of age, or marriage; property to remain in the hands of her husband in case of her death before the sons became of age. She m. Richard Tare (Thayer); made a conveyance of land to Clement Corbin Oct. 7, 1656. The dau. Sarah m. 22 (4) 1653, Isaac Bull.

John, Hingham, propr. 1636.

John, Taunton, frm. 7 Sept. 1641; atba. 1643. He d. Feb. 26, 1657. Will: wife Sarah; children Samuel, Elizabeth, Mary, Abigail; bro. Mr. John Summers, minister; wife's sister's son Nathaniel Smith and her other ch.; sister Elizabeth Philips and James Ph. of Tau. and ch.; cousin James Walker's ch.; mentions house at Boston, share in Tau. iron works, lands of bro. Parker. [Reg. VII, 177.]

John, shoemaker, Boston; wife Sarah adm. chh. 20 (6) 1644. Is he not the son of John and Jane?

John, Woburn, propr. 1649; Billerica, 1654; sergt. Built first meeting house; town officer. He m. Mary, widow of John Poulter of Raleigh, Essex, Eng., whose dau. Elizabeth m. Jonathan Danforth. He m. 3, Thos. Chamberlin.

He d. June 14, 1667. [Hist. Billerica.]

Joseph, tanner, ae. 24, from Newbury, Eng., came in the Confidence April 11, 1638. Settled at Newbury. Propr. at Salisbury 1639, carpenter. Rem. to Andover. Memb. chh. 1645. He was a witness in Salem Court in 1642. Soldier in King Philip's War, 1675-6. Wife Mary; ch. John, Joseph b. May 1642, Thomas, Sarah, Stephen b. 1 March, 1651, Hester b. 12 May, 1654, John b. 30 June, 1656, Samuel b. 14 Oct. 1659, Ruth b. 2 June, 1661.

He d. Nov. 5, 1678. Will prob. 29 (9) 1678. Wife Mary; children Joseph, Thomas, Stephen, Samuel, Sarah, Mary, Ruth; bro. Nathan P.; est. in England, some at Rumsey. Widow Mary d. Oct. 2, 1695; admin. April 6, 1696.

Judith Parker, widow, of Charlestown, sold a house and land in Hampton 23 (3) 1645, to John Marian of Watertown; payment to be made at either of her dwellings in any of the 6 towns in the bay, namely Char., Bo., Camb., Wat., Rox., or Dorch.

PARKER, etc., cont.
Mr., Salem. Ch. Mary bapt. 13 (10) 1646.

Nathaniel, baker, of London, ae. 20, came in the Bevis in May, 1638.

Nathan, bro. of Joseph, Newbury. Rem. to Andover. He deposed in 1662, ae. about 40 years. One of the 10 first members of the chh. in 1645. He m. at N. 20 Nov. 1648, Susanna Short, who d. 26 Aug. 1651. He m. 2, Mary —. Ch. Nathan, John b. 20 Dec. 1653, James b. 14 Aug. 1655, Mary b. 14 April, 1657, Hanna b. 14 May, 1659, Mary b. 1660, Elizabeth b. 20 Jan. 1663, Robert b. 26 Feb. 1665, Sarah and Peter b. April 3, 1670.

He d. 25 June, 1685.

Nicholas, yeoman, Roxbury, came to N. E. about the 3d month, 1633 . [E.] Frm. March 4, 1633-4. With Richard P., he sold house and land at R. to William Cheney July 18, 1639. He mortg. land to Henry Symons of Boston; testified to 5 (6) 1643. Rem. to Bo. about 1642. Wife Anne joined chh. of Bo. with him by dism. from chh. of Rox. 25 (12) 1642. Ch. Joanna bapt. at Bo. 1 (4) 1635, Jonathan b. 1 (12), bapt. 2 (12) 1639, Abiel b. 15 (11) 1641, *Abiah* bapt. 27 (1) 1642, ae. about 9 weeks, Joanna, (m. 5 (5) 1655, Arthur Mason).

Ralph, Gloucester, propr. 1649.

Richard, merchant, Boston, 1639, or earlier: adm. chh. 23 (11) 1640; frm. June 2, 1641. [He may be the Richard Parke who was. propr. at Cambridge in 1636.] Bought house and land at Braintree 3 (1) 1640. [L.] With wife Ann he sold, May 8, 1653, land in the woods on the westerly side of Charles river, about 3 miles from Natick. Deeded land to his dau. Ann Manning, about to marry John Sands, Oct. 9, 1669. Wife Anne adm. chh. Bo. 24 (11) 1640. Ch. Joseph b. and d. 1638, Sarah b. 8 (5) 1641.

Will dated 3 Jan., prob. 21 Feb., 1672-3, beq. to gr. ch. Ephraim Manning, son of his dau. Ann M., Ann, wife of John Sands, and the 3 daus. of his dec. dau Payne; to the poor of the church of which he was a member; dau. Ann M. exec.

Robert, planter, servant to William Aspinwall, Boston, adm. chh. 9 (1) 1634, frm. March 4, 1634-5. Was disciplined by the chh. "for selling the inheritance of his wife's chil-

PARKER, etc., cont.

dren," but was restored to fellowship 24 (5) 1636. Rem. to Cambridge. Was dism. to that chh. 1 (12) 1656. [Rox. and Camb. chh. rec.] Propr., but not resident of Billerica in 1654. Deposed in 1670, ae. about 66. Wife Judith; ch. Benjamin b. (4) 1636, Nathaniel b. 28 (5) 1638, Sarah b. (2) 1640, John, "of Judith, widow of Richard Bugby, who God tooke," bapt. at Roxbury 27 (1) 1642, Rachel. He made will 21 March, 1682, ae. about 82 years; beq. to dau. Sarah Foster and her ch. Sons Benjamin and John, dec., had rec'd. full portions. Prob. 7 (2) 1685. The widow d. May 8, 1682, ae. 80.

Rev. Thomas, son of Rev. Thomas P. the eminent preacher and writer, "natus et baptizatus die Pentecoste, anno 1575, being June 8th, as I take it," [S.] came to Ipswich in the Mary and John March 26, 1634. Rem. with the first settlers to Newbury, of which he was the minister until his death. He maintained a policy which was more Presbyterian than that of the churches of New Eng. in general and was somewhat opposed by certain parishioners; yet all conceded him a pure, unselfish, capable minister. He never married. His mother, Mrs. Dorothy P. of Mildenhall, Wilts. in her will, dated 10 Oct. 1649, beq. £200 to him; mentions daus. Sarah, wife of Thomas Bayley, Elizabeth, wife of Timothy Avery; the 4 ch. of Sarah B.; John and Benjamin Woodbridge, Sarah Kerridge and Lucy Sparhawke. [Reg. XXXII, 337.]

He d. 24 April, 1677; will dated 12 Sept. 1663, prob. 23 May, 1677, at Boston, beq. to nephews John and Benj. Woodbridge and Nicholas and Sarah [widow of James] Noyes.

Thomas, ae. 30, came in the Susan and Ellen in April, 1635. Settled at Lynn; propr. 1638. Frm. May 17, 1637. Rem. to Reading, propr.; deacon. Ch. Mary b. Dec. 12, 1647, Martha b. March, 1649, Nathaniel b. May 16, 1651, Sarah b. Sept. 30, 1653, d. Oct. 20, 1656, Jonathan b. May 18, 1656, d. June 10, 1680, Thomas b. Aug. 9, 1668, Samuel b. March 26, 1670, Sarah b. Feb. 28, 1671, Deborah b. Aug. 15, 1674.

He d. Aug. 12, 1683. Will dated 3 Aug., prob. Dec. 18, beq. to wife Amy; sons John, Thomas, Nathaniel and Hananiah; daus. Mary and Martha; gr. ch. Samuel and Sarah

PARKER, etc., cont.

P.; to John "a great Bible that Boniface Burton gave me."

Walter, ae. 18, came in the Love in July, 1635.

William, Watertown, deputy, 1635, frm. June 2, 1641. Propr. at Sudbury, 1639. Wife Elizabeth; ch. Ephraim bur. 12 (6) 1640, ae. 6 months; Ruhama b. 19 (7) 1641, Palti, dau. of William P. of the chh. of Wat., bapt. in Boston 4 (12) 1648, ae. about 1 month.

William, husbandman, Scituate, 1637; took oath of allegiance 1 Feb. 1638; prop. frm. 1 Dec. 1640; had grant of land as an old resident, in 1674. He m. April, 1639. Mary Rawlins; she d. Aug. 1651; ch. Mary b. 1 Jan. 1639-40, William b. Dec. 1643. Martha bapt. June 13, 1647, Patience b. Feb. 1648. He m. 2, Nov. 3, 1651, Mary, dau. of Humphrey Turner. Ch. Lydia b. May 9, 1653, Miles b. June 25, 1655, bapt. April 6, 1656, Lydia bapt. April 13 folg., Joseph b. Oct. 4, 1658, Nathaniel b. March 8, 1662.

Will dated 1 July, 1684, prob. 3 Oct. folg., beq. to wife Mary; ch. Miles, Nathaniel, Lydia, Joseph, Mary, Judah, Patience (Randall;) gr. ch. Stephen Totman.

William, inn-keeper, Taunton, constable March 1, 1641. Frm. 2 March, 1640-1. Will dated March 15, 1659, being 60 years old; prob. 4 June, 1662. Wife Alice; James Philips; Elizabeth, wife of James Walker. Inv. taken 10 (12) 1661. [Reg. VI, 93.] James Phillips receipted for his uncle's bequest 3 (7) 1662, at the hand of his aunt Allis Paine.

PARKHURST, PARKUST, PARKIS,

George, yeoman, Watertown, propr. 1642; frm. May 10, 1643. He m. about 1644, Susanna, widow of Mr. John Simson. Rem. to Boston, where his wife confirmed deeds of land in 1651 and 1655. Ch. Daniel bapt. at Bo. 10 (4) 1649, Joshua bapt. 7 (1) 1652, Caleb bapt. 26 (12) 1653, George, Jr., of Wat., a father in 1646, [Suff. De. I, 78,] and Phebe, (who m. Thomas Arnall,) were older children.

PARKMAN, PARKEMAN,

Elias, mariner, Dorchester, propr. 1633, frm. May 6, 1635. Had servant Richard Serle in 1637. [W.] Rem. to Windsor, Conn. [See L.] Was afterward at Saybrook. Rem. to Boston about 1648. Bought land and

PARKER, etc., cont.
house Aug. 7, 1652. Wife Bridget; ch. Mary bapt. 24 (7) 1648, Deliverance b. 3 (6) 1651, Nathaniel b. June 24, 1655; Sarah, (m. Sept. 18, 1661, John Jarvis.

Admin. was gr. Aug. 20, 1662, at the request of the widow, Bridget, and her eldest son, to Thomas Rawlings, on behalf of the family and creditors of Elias Parkman, Sen., supposed to be deceased 28 of July, 1662. [Reg XII, 50.]

PARMENTER, PARMITER, PALMENTER, PALMITER, PARMINSTER,
Benjamin, Salem, propr. 1637. Took —, apprentice, to teach him his trade. Deposed in 1666, ae. 57 years; his wife Mary, in 1667, ae. about 57.

John, yeoman, Roxbury, resided for some time, then rem. to Sudbury, where he was a deacon. [E.] Propr. and selectman, 1639. Son John also propr. Com. to end small causes, 1640. He m. Aug. 9, 1660, Annis, widow of Wm. Chandler and of John Dane. She d. March 15, 1683; he d. 1 (3) 1671, ae. 83.

Will dated 25 March, prob. 25 (5) 1671, beq. to gr. son John P.; to wife Annie; to dau. Woods and son-in-law John Wood of "Malbery." Cousin Cheevers, shoemaker, in Boston, one of the execs.; cousin John Stibbins one of the overseers. The widow's will, dated Nov. 1, 1672, prob. Nov. 15, 1683, beq. to her son John Chandler the estate left her by her husband Dane; he to pay to John Dane, and to her sons Thomas and William Chandler, certain sums; to her daus. Hannah Abbot and Sarah Cleaves. Cousin Elizabeth Denison, Anna Stebbins and sister Wise to aid in division of estate. Sons Thomas and John Chandler, execs.; sons Wm. Chandler, George Abbot and William Cleaves. Timothy Stevens and Mary Wise overseers.

Robert, Braintree, deacon, frm. May 22, 1650. He m. 3 (2) 1648, Leah Wheatley; ch. John b. 1653, Elizabeth b. 22 (8) 1657, Hannah b. 17 (11) 1658.

He d. June 27, 1696, ae. 74 years. Will dated 23 Feb. 1693-4, prob. July 9, 1696, beq. to only son Joseph, wife Leah, and daus. Elizabeth Peniman and Hannah Tompson.

PARRIE, see Perry,
Edward ae. 24, came in the Truelove in Sept. 1635.

PARR,
Abel, residence not stated, frm. June 2 1641.

James, residence not stated, having his house burned, was aided by the Gen. Court 17 Oct. 1643.

PARRATT, PARRETT,
Francis, Rowley, propr. Deputy 7 (8) 1640; clerk of the writs 10 (10) 1641; deacon. Wife Elizabeth; ch. Elizabeth b. 1 (3) 1640, Faith b. 20 (1) 1642, Sarah b. 22 (12) 1643, Mercy b. 23 (1) 1646, Mary b. 15 (5) 1647, Martha b. 9 (8) 1649, Hannah b. 21 (12) 1651.

Made will Nov. 18, 1655, intending a journey to England; prob. 30 (7) 1656. Beq. to wife and six daus.

PARRISE,
Christopher, Boston, propr. 9 (2) 1649.

PARSONS,
Benjamin, Springfield propr., deacon, town officer 1651. He m. 1, 6 (8) 1653, Sarah, [dau. of Richard Vore, of Windsor, Conn.] who d. Jan. 1, 1676; he m. 2, Sarah, widow of John Leonard Feb. 21, 1677. Ch. Sarah b. Aug. 18, 1656, (m. James Dorchester,) Benjamin b. Sept. 15, 1658, Mary b. Dec. 10, 1660, d. Jan. 27, 1662, Abigail b. Jan. 6, 1662, (m. 1, John Mun, 2, John Richards,) Samuel b. Oct. 10, 1666, Ebenezer b. Nov. 17, 1668, Mary b. Dec. 17, 1670, (m. Thomas Richards,) Hezekiah b. Nov. 24, 1673, Joseph b. Dec. 1675.

He d. Aug. 29, 1689.

Hugh, sawyer, bricklayer, Springfield, propr. 1646, town officer. He m. 27 (8) 1645, Mary Lewis. Ch. Samuel b. Oct. 4, 1648, bur. 1 (8) 1649, Joshua b. Oct. 26, 1650, d. June 4, 1651. The wife was accused of wtchcraft and of the murder of her babe. Condemned to death 22 May, 1651. [Reg. I, 263.] He was also tried and convicted on the charge of witchcraft; but his sentence was set aside by the Gen. Court.

Joseph, Springfield, propr., town officer, 1645; cornet of the company. A witness of Pynchon's purchase from the Indians, July 15, 1636. Town officer. Rem. to Northampton; kept an ordinary in 1661; ret. to Spr. He m. Nov. 26, 1646, Mary, dau. of Thomas Bliss, of Hartford, she d. Jan. 29, 1712. Ch. Joseph, John, Benjamin bur. 22 (4) 1649, Samuel, Ebenezer, Jonathan b. June 6 1657, David b. April 30, 1659, Mary b. June 27,

PARSONS, cont.
1661, (m. 1, Joseph Ashley, 2, Joseph Williston,) Hannah, (m. Pelatiah Glover,) Abigail b. Sept. 3, 1666, (m. John Colton,) Hester, (m. Joseph Smith.)
He d. Oct. 9, 1683. [Reg. I, 266.]

Robert, Lynn, propr. 1638; frm. March 14, 1638-9. Robert, servant to Martin Saunders, Braintree, d. 26 (10) 1665.

William, carpenter, "sley maker," Boston, adm. chh. 20 (2) 1644, frm. May, 1645. He deposed at Salem in 1680, ae. about 60 years. With wife Ruth, he sold land at Bo. July 21, 1654. Ch. Ruth b. 3 (8) 1645, Naomi bapt. 6 (2) 1651.

He d. at Boston, Jan. 31, 1701-2, ae. 88 years. [See S.] Will dated 20 Dec. 1695, prob. Nov. 6, 1702, beq. to Ruth Swift, Naomi Young, Sarah Lorell and gr. ch. Susanna Young, whom he makes exec. Susanna Codner of Roxbury requested prob. of the will.

PARTRICH, PARTRIDGE, PATRIDGE,
Capt. John, his account with Capt. Clarke before Gen. Court 17 Oct. 1649. May have lived here. Perhaps the father of William, below.

Nathaniel, tailor, Boston, adm. chh. 21 (3) 1643, frm. May 29, 1644. His wife —, adm. chh. 23 (2) 1643, was a sister of William Leatherland, who gave them half of his house about the year 1647. [Deposition, Suff. De. III, 382.]

Rev. Ralph, came to N. E. in 1636. [W.] Settled at Duxbury. Frm. 6 March, 1637-8. See his letter in 1642. [B.] Was from Sutton, co. Kent; see deed of portion to his dau. Mary on her marriage with John Marshall, Nov. 29, 1631. [Suff. De. III, 417.] His dau. Elizabeth m. Mr. Thomas Thatcher, pastor at Weymouth and Boston. [A.] His son George had grant of land at Dux. He was a very efficient and useful man; practised medicine beside pastoral duties.
Will, dated Sept. 29, 1655, prob. May 4, 1658; spoke of dec. wife Patience; beq. to daus. Mary, wife of John Marshall, and her sons Robert and John, and Elizabeth Thatcher, and her ch. Thomas, Ralph, Peter and Patience; to his sister Elizabeth Tidge; to William Brett; to his servants Joseph Prior and Anna Reiner. [Reg. V, 387.]

PARTRICH, etc., cont.
William, Lynn, propr. 1638, frm. March 14, 1638, Salisbury, propr. 1640-1654. He m. Ann —. Ch. John, Rachel d. April 19, 1650, Hannah, Elizabeth b. Feb. 14, 1642, (m. Joseph Shaw,) Nehemiah b. May 5, 1645, Sarah b. Aug. 24, 1647, Rachel b. June 19, 1650, (m. Joseph Chase,) William. He recd. a legacy of 43 pounds for his children from the est. of John Partridg of Olney, Buckingham, Eng., declared at Hampton Court 5 (8) 1652. [Norf. co. rec.]

He d. July 5, 1654; admin. Oct. 3, folg. The widow Ann m. 2, Jan. 1, 1655, Anthony Stanyan, who conveyed land 11 June, 1659, to her son John, of Boston, seaman, for legacies left John and his sisters Hannah and Elizabeth by their gr. father John P.

PARRYER, see Perry and Purrier,
William, ae. 36, with wife Alice, ae. 37, and children Mary, ae. 7, Sarah, ae. 5, and Katharine, ae. 18 months, came in the Hopewell April 1, 1635, from Olney, Bucks, Eng.

PASMER,
Bartholomew, Boston; ch. Abigail b. (4) 1641.

PATCH,
Edmund, Salem, propr. 1638. Wife —, memb. chh.; ch. Abram bapt. 5 (6) 1649. Elizabeth, the first born English female of Salem and of the Massachuestts colony, died at Beverly Jan. 14, 1714-5, [Boston News Letter; Reg. IV, 289.] James, in will in 1658, names bros. John Patch and Nicholas Woodbury. Rem. to Wenham. He gave bond Feb. 20, 1673, to Richard and Samuel Dodge of Wen., that he would not sell any of his property; this was for the security of himself, his dau.-in-law and the children.
Inv. of his est. was taken 10 Nov. 1680; admin. gr. to his nephew Thomas Patch; mention made of his two gr. sons, Edmund and Abraham, sons of his son Abraham. [Es. Files, XXXIV, 88-9.]

Nicholas, Salem, propr., 1639; adm. chh. 14 (2) 1650. From the reference to [his son] Thomas in the admin. of Edmund, it may be inferred that they were brothers.
The inv. of his est. was presented in court 27 (9) 1673, and division made to his two sons John and Thomas by mutual agreement.

PATCHIN,
Joseph, Roxbury; goodwife adm. chh. in 1649. Ch. Joseph b. 14 (2) 1643, John b. 20 (10) 1644, bapt. 24 (1) 1650; a child d. (3) 1649.

PATIENCE,
Thomas, Salem, presented to the court for opposing infant baptism 1 (4) 1641; referred to Mr. Endecott. Hindered his child from baptism. Marked "gone" in Es. Court Files, 12 (5) 1642.

PATRICK,
Capt. Daniel, Watertown, engaged by the government to make shot 7 Sept. 1630; frm. May 18, 1631. Town officer; captain of a company of soldiers. Rem. to Cambridge, propr. 1633; later to Stamford, Conn. His wife was a Dutch woman. [W.]
He was murdered about March 1643-4. [New Haven Col. rec.]

PATTEN, PATTIN,
Nathaniel, gent., yeoman, planter, late of Crewkerne, Eng., bought house and land at Dorchester 28 (4) 1640; propr., town officer. Brought suit, and presented accts. against the undertakers of ships Charles and Hopewell in 1640. [L.] Bought wharf, land and buildings in Boston in 1654. His wife, Mrs. Patten, adm. chh. 29 (8) 1641.
He d. Jan. 13, 1671. Admin. gr. to his widow Mrs. Justin (sic) Patten Aug. 2, 1672. Her will dated 2 Jan. 1673, prob. 3 Feb. 1675, beq. to the church to be laid out in plate; to sister Pike and her dau. and the dau.'s children; cousin Benjamin Bate; to several friends.

Thomas, Salem, propr. 1642.

William, Cambridge, agreed to keep 100 cattle March 13, 1635; propr. 1636, frm. May, 1645. One of the incorporators of Billerica, 1654, but did not remove to it. Wife Mary; ch. Mary, bapt. in England; about 4 or 5 years old when her parents joined the chh. of Camb. [Mi.] William bur. 22 (1) 1645-6, Thomas b. (8) 1636, Nathaniel d. (11) 1639, Sarah b. 27 (11) 1641, Nathaniel b. 28 (5) 1643.
He d. Dec. 10, 1668. Est. divided April 6, 1669, to widow and ch. Thomas, Nathaniel, and Sarah Patten and Mary Griggs. [Mdx. Files.] His widow d. Sept. 20, 1673. Admin. gr. to Thomas and Nathaniel 8 (2) 1674.

PATTESON,
Edward, ae. 33, came in the Christian March 16, 1634. Res. at Rehoboth; propr. 1643; grant forfeited.

PAUL, PAULLE, PALLE, see Poole,
Daniel, mariner, from Ipswich, co. Suffolk, Eng., of Boston, N. E., gave letter of attorney for the sale of lands in I., and the delivery of money to his wife Elizabeth, Aug. 26, 1640. [L.]

Richard, entertained to serve at the fort in Boston from 29 July, 1636, at 10 li. per annum. [W.] Settled at Taunton, planter. Lic. to keep an inn, 1640. He m. 8 Nov. 1638, Margery Turner of T. Mrs. Margerie Paul was remembered in the will of Elizabeth Poole. She m. 2, Henry Withington, of Dorchester; Samuel, her only son, m. 9 (11) 1666, Mary Breck, of Dorch.; he d. Nov. 3, 1690.

PAULMIN,
Sebastian, brought to N. E. by his uncle, Nicholas Simpkin, was left in apprenticeship with Robert Keayne, and money with him, until his mother could be heard from; 28 (5) 1636. [W.]

PAYBODY, PEABODY,
Francis, husbandman ae. 21 years, cert. from the parish of St. Albons, co. Herts, Eng., came in the Planter April 2, 1635, settled at Ipswich; propr. 1636; rem. to Topsfield. Lieut.; frm. 18 May, 1642. He deposed 24 (4) 1662, ae. "about fifti yeares." He m. Mary, dau. of Reginald Foster; she d. April 9, 1705. Ch. [John, Joseph, William, Isaac, Jacob, Sarah, Hepsibah, Lydia, Mary,] Ruth b. 22 May, 1658, Damaris b. and d. 1660, Samuel b. 4 June, 1662, d. 13 Sept. 1677, Jacob b. 28 July, 1664, Hannah b. 8 May, 1668, Nathaniel b. 29 July, 1669. [Genealogy in Reg. II, 153.]
He d. Feb. 19, 1697-8.

John, planter, Duxbury, frm. 7 Feb. 1636-7, propr.
Will dated at Duxbrook, Plym. Col. July 16, 1649, prob. at Boston, April 27, 1667, recorded at Plymouth; beq. to wife Isabel; sons Thomas, Francis and William; to John, son of William Paybody; to dau. Annis Rouse, and to John, son of John Rouse. [Reg. XII, 312.]

PAULLY, POLLY,
Benjamin, before Gen. Court 29 (8) 1640; Salem, herdsman, 1647-1657.

PAYSON, PASON, PAISON,
Edward, a man servant, memb. chh. Roxbury, 1634. [E.] Propr., frm. May 13, 1640. He m. Aug. 20, 1640, Ann Parks; she was bur. Sept. 10, 1641. He m. 2, Mary Eliot, Jan. 1, 1642. Ch. Marah b. Sept. 2, 1641, John b. June 11, 1643, Jonathan b. Dec. 19, 1644, d. 7 (11) 1666, Ann b. April 22, 1647, Johanna bapt. 25 (1) 1648, d. 16 (6) 1650, Joanna bapt. Feb. 5, 1649, bur. Feb. 15, 1650, Anne bapt. 30 (9) 1651, Susanna bapt. 28 (6) 1653, d. 29 (7) 1654, Susanna bapt. 1 (5) 1655, Edward bapt. 28 (4) 1657, Ephraim bapt. 20 (12) 1658, Samuel bapt. 21 (7) 1662, Mary bapt. 19 (1) 1664-5.

Will dated 10 Nov. 1688, prob. Sept. 3, 1691. Beq. to wife Mary; sons John, Ephraim, Edward and Samuel P.; sons Benjamin Tucker and Preserved Capen; a Bible to each grandchild.

Giles, ae. 26, came in the Hopewell in April, 1635, from Nazing, Eng.; settled at Roxbury. Deacon; husbandman; frm. April 18, 1637. He m. in April, 1637, Elizabeth Dowell; she d. Jan. 8, 1677. Ch. Elizabeth b. and d. 1639, Samuel b. Nov. 7, 1641, Elizabeth b. 4 (12) 1644, Sarah bapt. July 16, 1648.

He d. 28 Jan. 1688, ae. 78 years. Admin. of his est. was gr. 29 April, 1697, to daughters Elizabeth Brown of Boston, widow, and Sarah Wiswall of Newton, widow.

PAYTON, PEYTON, PAITON,
Bezaleel, mariner, Boston, adm. chh. 7 (7) 1644. Narrowly escaped wreck at Conyhasset, on his way home from Barbadoes, in a vessel of 60 tons, in 1648. [W.] Wife, sometime called Mary Greenow, recd. to chh. from ch. of Sandwich 28 (5) 1644; ch. Sarah b. 9 (6), bapt 13 (6) 1644, Mary b. 7 (3) 1646, Abigail bapt. 23 (5) 1648.

Admin. of his est. 21 (9) 1651. [Reg. VIII, 58.] The widow m. 3 (10) 1651, William Paddy.

PEACH,
Arthur, Plymouth, a young man, served in the Pequot War; committed crime; on his flight from Plym. in 1638, he killed an

PEACH, cont.
Indian, and was executed. [Plym. Col. Rec. and B.]

John, Sen., fisherman, Salem, 1630; rem. to Marblehead; propr., town officer. He deposed 25 (1) 1672, ae. about 60 years; had lived in town 41 years. Several other depositions confirm this.

He d. 20 Aug. 1683. Will dated 2 Oct. 1682, prob. Sept. 30, 1683, beq. to John Squire, my sister's son in Barbadoes; to bro. Thomas' widow and sister Margery's ch. in England, under the direction of cousin John Minson of Simborough; to cousin William Peach's two sons, John and Thomas; cousin John Legg to pay; to cousin William Hine, his wife Abigail and their ch.; to cousin Peter Dallivar and his dau. Margaret; rents due in England.

John, Junior, brother of the above, Marblehead. He deposed 25 (1) 1672, ae. about 58 years; had lived in M. about 33 years. Both he and his bro. John were selectmen at the same time. Wife Alice a witness in 1644.

His will dated 10 Jan. 1687-8, prob. May 21, 1694, beq. to wife Alice; to gr. ch., the children left by dau. Waters; to daus. Mary Woods and Elizabeth Legg; to my only son William Peach, his wife Emme and two sons John and Thomas; house and lot to be held in feetail by J. and T. and their male heirs forever.

PEACOCK,
Marie, ae. 15, came in the Hopewell, April, 1635.

Richard, glazier, Roxbury, frm. May 22, 1639. He rem. to Boston about 1654. Wife Jane d. 9 (5) 1653; and he m. 17 (6) 1654, Margery Shove, widow. Ch. Samuel b. Feb. 18, 1639, Caleb b. March 1, 1641, d. Sept. 26, 1659.

Inv. taken last of April, 1669; admin. gr. to his son Samuel. The widow d. at the house of her son, Mr. George Shove, in Taunton; bur. 17 April, 1680.

William, ae. 12, came with Marie, above. Settled at Roxbury; yeoman; adm. chh. Feb. 21, 1660. He m. April 12, 1653, Mary Willis. Ch. William b. and d. 1655. Another "son" William m. 3 Aug. 1681, Sarah Edsall.

PEAKE,
Christopher, Roxbury, frm. March 4, 1634-5. He m. Jan. 3, 1636, Dorcas French; she d. Oct. 14 or 15, 1694. Ch. Jonathan b. Dec. 17, 1637, Dorcas b. March 1, 1639, Hannab b. Jan. 25, 1642, bur. 5 (8) 1660, Joseph b. Feb. 12, 1644, Ephraim bapt. 11 (2) 1652, [March 16, 1652,] Sarah bapt. 9 (1) 1656.

Will dated 2 (2), prob. 2 (6) 1666; wife and children as above-mentioned. The inv. mentions land where he had intended to set up tan-fats. [Reg. XV.]

Note. Thomas Peake of Birmingham, Eng., in his will in 1654, beq. to "the daus. of my brother Peake which dwell in Eng. and every of those which dwell beyond the sea." [Reg. XXI, 413.]

William, Scituate, m. May 6, or Oct. —, 1650, Judith Lechfeelde; ch. Israel b. 22 Feb. 1655, Eleazer b. 3 May, 1657.

Will dated 31 Oct. 1682, inv. taken 14 Feb. 1682-3, beq. to wife Judith; sons Israel, Eleazer and William; dau.-in-law Dependance Leichfield and her ch. Dependance and Remember Luce. The widow, in her will of Sept. 5, 1685, beq. to the same children.

PEARCE, PEARS, see Pierce.

PEARSON, PEIRSON, PIERSON, PERSON, PERSONS, PERSUNE,
Rev. Abraham, adm. chh. Boston 5 (7) 1640; as "a studyent," had "leave to join in ye gathering of a church at the Long Island" 11 (8) 1640. Was minister at Southampton, L. I., till 1644, when he rem. to Branford, Conn.; thence he rem. to Newark, N. J. "'A godly, learned man." [W.] "A Yorkshire man, pious and prudent. [C. M.]

Bartholomew, Watertown, bought land in 1644; frm. May 10, 1648. Rem. to Woburn. Wife Azlee, Uzlah, or Ursula; ch. Bartholomew b. and d. 1640, Bartholomew and Jonathan b. 26 (12) 1641, Martha b. 17 (7) 1643, Joseph b. 8 (9) 1650.

John, Reading, propr. 1644; frm. May 26, 1647. Town officer. He deposed 2 (2) 1661, ae. about 45 years. His wife Madeline depos. in 1669, ae. about 50 years. Ch. Mary b. 20 (4) 1643, Bethiah b. 15 (7) 1645, Sarah b. 20 (11) 1647, John b. June 22, 1650, James b. Nov. 2 1652.

Will dated 19 April, 1679, prob. 25 (4) 1679; wife Maudlin, son John, daus. Mary Burnap,

PEARSON, etc., cont.
Bethiah Carter and Sarah Townsend; servant John Lilly.

John, Rowley, propr., town officer, 1649; deacon. Wife Dorcas; ch. Mary b. 26 (3) 1643, John b. 27 (10) 1644, Samuel b. 29 (5) 1648, Mary b. 17 (12) 1651, Jeremy b. 25 (8) 1653, Joseph b. Aug. 21, 1656, Benjamin b. 6 (2) 1658, Phebe b. April 13, 1660, Sarah b. May 6, 1666.

Will referred to but not extant; the widow Dorcas declined to admin. May 19, 1694, the son John did the same 28 July folg.; sons Jeremiah and Stephen undertook the charge, and gave bond Aug. 6. Inv. taken Jan 11, 1693-4, shows nearly the time of his death.

Richard, salter, ae. 30, came from Weymouth, Eng., March 20, 1635, as servant to M. Bernard of Batcombe, Eng.

PEASE, PEAS,
Henry, at some time a servant to Gov. Winthrop, was adm. to the chh. of Boston with wife Susan in 1631 or 1632. Frm. Sept. 3, 1634. They were dism. to the chh. of Braintree "for this winter," 22 (9) 1640, but are afterward mentioned in Bo. records as res. there still. Dau. Susan adm. chh. 16 (6) 1635. The wife was bur. 25 (10) 1643. His [second] wife Bridget was adm. chh. 15 (3) 1647. His son John, in his will dated 23 Feb. 1682, mentions father Henry and bro. Henry.

He d. in 1648. Will dated 3 Aug., prob. 26 (11) 1648-9. Wife; sons John and Henry; dau. Susanna Jacklin and her two children. Land in Bo. and Br., the latter in possession of Richard Tare. The widow d. before 6 Feb. 1683, when the surviving son, Henry, admin. on her est. [Reg. XXX, 203.]

John, ae. 27, with child Robert, ae. 3, and Dorcas Greene, ae. 15, came in the Francis of Ipswich April 30, 1634. Settled at Salem; before Gen. Court Nov. 3, 1635, for treatment of his mother, Mrs. Weston, (who is mentioned below.) Sold house and land to Richard Ingersoll 18 (4) 1644. [Suff. De.]

John, Salem; wife Mary; ch. John b. 30 (3) 1654, Robert b. 14 (3) 1656, Mary b. 8 Oct. 1658, Abraham b. 5 (8) 1662.

Luce, wife of — Pease, before the Court at Boston 17 Oct. 1643, for alleged sympathy with Gorton's opinions.

PEASE, etc., cont.

Margaret, widow, Salem, memb. chh. 1639; will dated 1 (7) 1642, prob. 1 (11) 1645; beq. to grandchild John, son of her son Robert Pease, and to Faith Barber. [Court Files I, 35.] She seems to have married Francis Weston, and to have been called "Pease" again after his death.

Robert, ae. 27, came in the Francis of Ipswich April 30, 1634. Settled at Salem; adm. chh. 1 (18) 1643. Ch. John, Robert, (deposed in 1670, ae. about 41 years,) Nathaniel, Sarah and Mary bapt. 15 (8) 1643.

Admin. of his est. gr. 3 (11) 1644, to widow Maria; sons John and Robert mentioned.

PEASELEY, PEASLE, PEASLY,

Joseph, Newbury, propr.; frm. June 22, 1642. He bought land of Mr. Stratton which he afterward resigned to the town. [No date.] Rem. to Haverhill; propr. 1646; town officer. Rem. to Salisbury. Wife Mary; ch. Elizabeth, Jane, (m. John Davis,) Mary, Sarah b. Sept. 20, 1642, (m. Thomas Barnard,) Joseph b. Sept. 9, 1646.

He d. Dec. 3, 1660; will, prob. Nov. 11 folg., beq. to wife Mary; son Joseph; daus. Elizabeth, Jane and Mary; gr. ch. Sarah Sawer. Admin. of the est. of widow Mary was gr. to her son Joseph Sept. 27, 1694.

PEAT,

John, husbandman, from Duffill, Derby, Eng., ae. 38, came in the Hopewell in April, 1635.

PECK,

Mr. Joseph, from Hingham, Eng. came to Hingham, N. E. in 1638, with wife, 3 sons, a daughter, and 5 servants. Frm. and deputy March 13, 1638. Commissioner. Rem. to Seaconk in 1645. Prop. frm. Plym. Col. 4 June, 1641; lic. to marry persons 2 Oct. 1650. Ch. recorded here: Simon, Samuel bapt. Feb. 3, 1638-9, Nathaniel bapt. Oct. 31, 1641, Israel bapt. March 31, 1643, Samuel, Hannah and Israel bapt. July 19, 1646.

He d. Thursday, Dec. 22, 1663. Will prob. 3 March, 1663-4. Beq. to sons Joseph, John, Nicholas, Samuel and Nathaniel, and dau. Hubbert. The sons united in a statement Dec. 24, 1663, of an amplification of the written will which was made on their father's death-bed; which the Court accepted. See Farnworth.

PECK, cont.

Rev. Robert, preacher of the Gospel in the town of Hingham, Eng., came in 1638, with his wife, two children and two servants, and settled in Hingham; where he was ordained teacher of the church Nov. 28, 1638. [Hob. and W.] He sailed for England with wife and son Joseph 27 Oct. 1641, and returned to his former parish.

Will dated at Hingham, Eng. 24 July, 1651, prob. 10 April, 1658; sons Thomas, Samuel, Robert, dec., and Joseph; children of his dau. Anne, wife of Capt. John Mason of Seabrooke, Conn. river, N. E.; wife Martha. [Reg. XXXIX, 65.]

Thomas, shipwright, Boston, resident before 1650; bought land in 1656. His wife Elizabeth petitioned the Gen. Court in his absence 23 May, 1650. Ch. Elizabeth b. Jan. 19, 1652. He deposed 17 (4) 1673, ae. 54 years. [Mdx. Files.]

His will dated 3 March, 1698, and 20 Jan. 1699-1700, prob. 15 Feb. folg., beq. to wife Elizabeth; daus. Elizabeth Fisher, Rachel Potter and Faith Waldo; gr. ch. Elizabeth and James Gooch and William and Mary Peck, ch. of son John P., dec.; Benjamin and Samuel, ch. of son Benjamin P.; had taken two of son Nathaniel's ch. to bring up since he came home; gr. ch. Joseph, Elizabeth and Sarah P.; principal heir and exec. son Thomas P. of Bo. shopkeeper.

PEIRCE, see PIERCE.

PELHAM, PELLUM,

John, ae. 20, came in the Susan and Ellen in April, 1635. Settled at Rehoboth. Town officer 1648.

Mr. Herbert, Esquire, Cambridge, 1635, propr. 1638; frm. May, 1645. His sister Penelope, ae. 16, came May 15, 1635, to pass to her bro.'s plantation in N. E.; (she m. Gov. Richard Bellingham 9 (9) 1641.) He m. Elizabeth —; ch. rec. at Camb.: Mary b. 12 (9) 1643, Frances b. 9 (9) 1645. He was town officer, deputy, Asst.; chosen treasurer of Harvard College 27 (10) 1643. [W.] Land adjoining in and near Sudbury. [Sud. Rec.]

He ret. to Eng. Will, dated at Ferrers in Bewers Hamlet, co. Essex, 1 Jan. 1672, gave to sisters Elizabeth Pelham and Penelope, wife of R. Bellingham, Esq.; to his sons Waldegrave, Edward, Nathaniel and Henry

PELHAM, etc., cont.
P.; to his daus. Penelope, wife of Josias Winslow, Anne P., Katharine Clark, and —, the wife of Cuthlach Eliot, (Guthlach Tolliot,) and her dau. Elizabeth; to son Jeremiah Stonnard. Son Edward to have the property in N. E. Prob. 30 March, 1676. [Reg. XVIII, and XXXIII.]

Mr. William, may be the passenger left behind by the Arbella. [W.] [Watertown.] Appl. frm. Oct. 19, 1630. One of the bondsmen of Nicho. Knapp 1 March, 1630-1. Rem. to Sudbury; propr. and selectman, 1639. The Gen. Court established him as captain 12 Aug. 1645.

PELL,
Ellen, maid servant of Atherton Haulgh, adm. chh. Boston 4 (5) 1641; dism. 1 (8) 1643, to Rowley, where she went in a way of marriage; letters of dism. to same granted 21 (2) 1644, being now wife to one John Bointon, member of that chh.

Joseph, butcher, Boston, frm. March 14, 1638-9. He m. Elizabeth, widow of Nathaniel Eaton.
Admin. on his est. was gr. 23 (2) 1650. Agreement between the widow and children of the deceased. [Reg. VII, 234.]

— Pell, Lynn, propr. 1638; Reading, propr. 1644.

Thomas, tailor, ae. 22, came in the Hopewell in April, 1635.

Thomas, chirurgeon, Boston, app. attorney for Edmund Leach, gent., Oct. 29, 1651. May be the Lynn and Reading man.

William, chandler, Boston, adm. chh. 7 (7) 1634; frm. May 6, 1635. With wife Alice sold land April 17, 1655. Ch. Mary b. 30 (4) 1634, (m. 1 (9) 1655, Richard George,) Nathaniel b. and d. 1638, Hannah b. 14 (11) 1640, Deborah bapt. 2 (4) 1644, ae. about 6 days.
Will dated 22 (12) 1671, prob. 4 (3) 1672. Wife Alice; son-in-law Richard George and his wife Mary; sons John and Samuel, and grand sons John and William, sons of his son Samuel.

PELTON,
John, Dorchester, propr. Ch. John bapt. 2 (1) 1645, Samuel bapt. 25 (11) 1646, Mary bapt. 18 (12) 1654.
He d. Jan. 23, 1680; inv. of his est. filed June 9, 1681. In his will, prob. 10 March, 1680-1, he beq. to wife Susanna, and ch. John, Samuel, Robert and Mary. Old mother Pelton was bur. May 10, 1706.

PEMBERTON, PEMMERTON,
Mr. James, Charlestown, appl. frm. Oct. 19, 1630. Propr. 1633. One of those who had "planted" at Mystic side; petitioned Gen. Court 14 (12) 1640. [L.] [Wife] Alice adm. chh. 31 (6) 1633. James, with [second] wife Marget and son-in-law Edward Barlow, referred a controversy with the Dexters to Capt. Robert Keayne and others 9 (1) 1653. Margaret deposed Dec. 15, 1662, ae. about 50 years. [Mdx. Files.] Ch. James bapt. 14 (7) 1633, Mary bapt. 3 (2) 1636, Sarah bapt. 30 (10) 1638, John bapt. 24 (2) 1642.
He d. at Malden Feb. 5, 1661-2. Will dated 23 (1) 1659-60, prob. April 1, 1662, beq. to wife Margit, son John, daus. Marie, wife of Edward Barlow, and Sara.

James, laborer, Boston, adm. chh. 25 (10) 1647, frm. May 10, 1648; brewer. Appears to be the man who is mentioned in the will of Robert Keayne as his servant and afterward his partner. Wife Sarah, dau. of Alice, wife of Thomas Marshall; q. v. Ch. John bapt. 26 (10) 1647, Sarah bapt. 28 (11) 1648, ae. about 6 weeks, James bapt. 13 (2) 1651, Thomas bapt. 27 (1) 1653, d. 29 Sept. 1661, Joseph b. 2 July, 1655, Elizabeth b. 26 Dec. 1657, Benjamin b. April 26, 1660, Mary b. July 13, 1662, Benjamin b. March 11, 1665, Jonathan b. Aug. 28, 1668, Ellener b. Feb. 3, 1671. [A James P. had son John b. at Newbury 10 Feb. 1647, which corresponds to the baptism of John, above.]
Will dated 12 Feb. 1695, prob. Oct. 29, 1696, beq. to wife Sarah and children John, Joseph, Benjamin, Jonathan, Ebenezer and Mary Pemberton and Elizabeth Elatson; to gr. ch. James and George, sons of dec. son Thomas.

John, Boston, memb. chh. 1632, frm. April 1, 1634. Propr. 1635. Rem. to Newbury; propr. 1638; was admonished for some offence against the chh. of N. by Boston

PEMBERTON, etc., cont.

chh. 25 (9) 1639; but was reconciled and dism. "recomendatorily" to that chh. 4 (8) 1640. Before Ipswich court in 1641. Constable 1647. His wife Elizabeth d. at N. 22 Feb. 1645.

He ret. to Eng. and d. at Lawford, co. Essex. Will dated 9 Sept. 1653, prob. 25 March, 1654. Goods in N. E. in charge of Hercules Woodman; beq. to dau.-in-law Deborah Goffe, there born; in case of her death to his bro. James Pemberton and his sister Robinson. Other goods to bros. William, Richard and Thomas. [Reg. XXXIX, 61.]

PEMBROOKE, PENYBROOK,

Francis, Dedham, testified to Mr. Edw. Allen's will, 29 (8) 1642. Adm. chh. 30 (5) 1643.

PEMTREE, PEMTRE, PEINTRE, PENTRY,

William, Cambridge, propr. 1633.

PEN, PENN, PENNE, PENNY,

Christian, came to Plymouth in 1623. Had one lot assigned to her.

Ellene, m. at Plymouth, 20 July, 1639, Thomas Riddings.

Hannah, sister of James, "servant to James Everill," adm. chh. Boston 15 (1) 1635; m. William Townsend.

James, came in the first company; appointed beadle to attend the governor Aug. 23, 1630; messenger of the Court in 1634. Settled at Boston; propr., town officer, ruling elder of the church. Appl. frm. Oct. 19, 1630. Was sent as messenger of the chh. to carry contributions to "ye poore church of Christ yt was banished from Bermudas to Segoton or Segotea," 28 (1) 1650; his detailed report is in the records of the church. Deputy, 1647. Wife Katharine adm. chh. with him in 1630. She survived him; she beq. her est. to Mr. James Allen's ch. 25 Oct. 1679.

He made will 29 (7) prob. 23 (8) 1671. Beq. to kinsmen Mr. James Allin and Penn Townsend; for the maintenance of poor scholars at the College; to the first church of Boston; to his sister Hannah Townsend and her ch. Peter, James and Deborah; to the ch. of Hannah Hull, viz. Thomas, Mary and Han-

PEN, etc., cont.

nah; to sister Mary Min[er], and to Sarah Sheally; to wife, life use of estate.

William, a son of Anthony, of Birmingham, Eng., shoemaker, as per deposition in Mass. Arch. VIII, 92; came early to Charlestown. Rem. to Braintree. Gave a general acquittance and deed of 120 acres of land at Br. 23 (12) 1647. [A.]

William, sawyer, Braintree, bought land in Br. April 21, 1653.

PENDLETON,

Capt. Bryan or Brian, Watertown, frm. Sept. 3, 1634. Town officer, deputy, memb. artillery co., etc. Rem. to Sudbury; propr. and selectman, 1639. Appointed by the Court to train the company 13 May, 1640. With wife Eleanor sold land and housing at Wat. March 20, 1648. Res. at Sud. 2 years. Rem. to Portsmouth, N. H.; deputy, councillor, major. Rem. to Saco and Kennebunkport, Maine. Ret. to Portsmouth, where he d. He deposed 2 (5) 1669, ae. about 70 years, concerning boundary line of Portsmouth. [Norf. De. II.]

Will dated Aug. 9, 1677, schedule dated April 5, 1681. Wife Eleanor; son James and his children; gr. ch. Pendleton Fletcher. [Reg. III, 122.]

PENMAN,

Sarah, Dedham, m. in 1651 Timothy Dwight.

PENNAIRE, PENNAIRD, PENYER, PENOIRE,

Robert, ae. 21, came with Capt. Babb Sept. 8, 1635. Was before the Court at Boston 3 (7) 1639. May be the same as Robert Pen or Penny, at Salem, 1638. Thomas, ae. 10, came with Robert.

Robert, late of Stanford, appointed Jonathan Sellick his attorney, 18 Oct. 1671, for collection of a legacy left him by his bro. Mr. Wm. Penoyer, late of London. [Suff. De VI, 280.]

PENNIMAN, PENNYMAN,

James, Boston, adm. chh. with wife Lydia, 1631. Rem. to Braintree. Frm. March 6, 1631-2. Ch. James bapt. 26 (1) 1633, Lydia bapt. 22 (12) 1634, John bapt. 15 (11) 1636, Joseph b. at Br. 1 (6), bapt. at Bo. 29 (7) 1639, Sarah b. 16 (3) 1641, Hannah b. 26

PENNIMAN, etc., cont.
(3) 1648, Abigail b. 27 (10) 1651, (m. 18 (2) 1678, Samuel Neale,) Mary b. 29 (7) 1653, (m. April 4, 1678, Samuel Paine,) Samuel b. 1 (9) 1655. He d. 26 (10) 1664. Will prob. Jan. 31, 1664. Beq. his moveable est. and half his land and buildings to his wife Lydia, for the support of herself and the lesser children; the other half to son Joseph, he to help his mother; eldest son James hath already had his portion; to youngest son Samuel and three youngest daus. 20 li. apiece. [Reg. XIII, 151.] The widow m. 2, Thomas Wight, in whose will and her own are proofs that she was a dau. of Bennett Eliot of Widford and Nasing, Eng.

PENNINGTON,
Deborah, Salem, propr. 1636.

PENTICUS, PENTICOST, PENTECOST,
John, rope-maker, Charlestown, adm. chh. with wife Joanna 16 (7) 1639; frm. May 13, 1640. Constable, 1657. Ch. John, Joanna, (m. John Larkin; see his will). Wife Joanna d. Jan. 27, 1685, ae. about 70. He d. Oct. 19, 1697, ae. near 90.

PEPPER, PEEPER,
Francis, Springfield, propr. 1645.
Will dated Dec. 5, 1685, prob. March 30, 1686, beq. to cousins Joseph, Samuel, Marah, Benjamin and Jeremiah Northrop, who are specified in prob. papers as living at Seaside, Conn.

Phillis, a maid servant, memb. chh. Roxbury about 1637. [E.]

Richard, ae. 27, with wife Mary, ae. 30, child Mary, ae. 3½, and Stephen Brackett, ae. 11, came in the Francis of Ipswich April 30, 1634. Settled at Roxbury; frm. March 4, 1634-5.

Robert, Roxbury, frm. May 10, 1643. He m. March 14, 1642, Elizabeth Johnson; she d. Jan. 5, 1683. Ch. Elizabeth b. and d. in 1643-4, Elizabeth b. May 25, 1645, John b. April 8, 1647, Joseph bapt. 18 (1) 1648-9, Mary bapt. 27 (2) 1651, Benjamin bapt. May 15, 1653, bur. 16 (11) 1669, Robert bapt. 29 (2) 1655, Sarah b. April 28, 1657, Isaac bapt. 1 (3) 1659, Jacob bapt. 4 (6) 1661. The son John, in will, 3 March, 1669-70, calls Isaac Johnson his uncle. [Reg. XLVIII, 458.]

PEPPER, etc., cont.
He d. July 7, 1684. Will prob. 17 July, 1684, beq. to sons Isaac and Jacob, daus. Elizabeth Everet, Mary Everet of Dedham, Sarah Mason of Boston, and Bethiah, dau. of his son Joseph P. dec.

PERCIE, see PIERCE.

PERK,
Richard, miller, ae. 33, with [wife] Margery, ae. 40, and [ch.] Isabel, ae. 7, and Elizabeth, ae. 5, came in the Defence in July, 1635.

PERKINS, PERKEINGS, PERKUS, PARKINS,
Isaac, yeoman, Ipswich, propr. 1637. His widow Alice sold land and house 15 (4) 1639. [Ips. Rec.] Ch. Isaac, (rem. to Hampton,) Jacob, (sold land recd. from his father, 23 (2) 1674, after removing to Holmes Hole).

John, Boston, adm. chh. with wife Judith in 1631. Frm. May 18, 1631. One of the com. to settle bounds between Roxbury and Dorchester in 1632. Rem. to Ipswich; propr. 1634; deputy, 1636; town officer. Freed from training in 1651. Ch. John, Lydia bapt. at Bo. 3 (4) 1632, (m. Henry Bennett,) Thomas, (paid in 1643 by the town of Ipswich for service against the Indians,) Elizabeth, (m. William Sargent,) Mary, (m. Thomas Bradbury.)
Will dated 28 (1) prob. 26 (7) 1654. Wife Judith; eldest son John and his two sons John and Abraham; son Thomas and his son John; son Jacob; daus. Elizabeth Sargent, Mary Bradbury, Lydia Bennett and their ch.; gr. ch. Thomas Bradbury. Genealogy. [Reg. X, 211-216.]

Rev. William, son of William, of London, merchant tailor; [see copy of an ancient manuscript in Topsfield town records,] embarked March 7, 1631; came to Roxbury. Frm. Sept. 3, 1634. Deputy, 1644. Captain. Was one of the first to plant at Agawam or Ipswich, mentioned in Gen. Court rec. April 1, 1633. Propr. 1635. Res. at Weymouth from 1643 to 1648; selectman 1647, schoolmaster 1651. Had deed from Zaccheus Gould, of land at Wey. April 2, 1645. Rem. to Gloucester. Capt. Perkins lot mentioned in 1648. Land given to him by the town in 1650. He bought house and lands which had

PERKINS, etc., cont.
been occupied by his predecessor, Mr. Obediah Bruen. Was schoolmaster; pastor afterwards. He sold 5 Oct. 1655, and rem. to Topsfield, whose first minister he then became. In 1641 he had a grant of 400 acres of land from the Court, "for his fathers fifty pounds." See reference to him in the will of Samuel Purchas. [Reg. XXXVIII, 320.] He deposed 26 (7) 1671, ae. about 64 years. He m. at Roxbury, Aug. 30, 1636, Elizabeth Wooton; ch. William b. and d. 1639, William b. Feb. 26, 1641, Elizabeth b. June 18, 1643, (m. John Ramsdell,) Tobijah, Katharine b. Oct. 29, 1648, (m. John Baker,) Mary b. Feb. 17, 1650-1, "baptized by my ministry," says the father, (m. Oliver Purchis,) John b. April 2, 1655, Sarah b. March 2, 1656-7, (m. John Bradstreet,) Timothy b. 11 Aug. 1658, Rebecca b. May 4, 1662, (m. Thomas Fiske).

He d. May 21, 1682, ae. 75.

PERLY, PERLEY, PEARLEY,

Allen, husbandman, ae. 27, cert. from St. Albons, co. Herts, came in the Planter April 1, 1635. Settled at Ipswich; propr. 1635. Frm. May 18, 1642.

He d. 28 Dec. 1675. Will dated 23 June, 1670, and 16 Nov. 1671. prob. Feb. 3, 1675-6. Wife Susannah; sons John, Thomas, Samuel, Timothy; daus. Sarah and Martha; son Nathaniel, dec.

PERRIN, PERREN,

Mr., of Salem; reference to him in 1639. [L.]

John, Braintree. Rem. to Rehoboth. Ch. Mary b. 22 (12) 1640.

Will dated June 16, prob. 23 Nov. 1674, beq. to wife Anna, sons John and Abraham; daus. Anna and other children.

PERRY, PURY, PARY, see Parrie, Parryer, and Purrier,

Arthur, tailor, Boston, propr., adm. chh. 16 (4) 1639, frm. May 13, 1640. Partner of Richard Cooke. [L.] Wife Elizabeth adm. chh. 13 (12) 1643; ch. Elishua b. Dec. 20, 1637, d. April 10, 1639, Seth b. 7 (1) 1639, Sarah b. 30 (9) 1644, Elizabeth b. 28 (11) 1646, Deborah bapt. 1 (5) 1649, ae. about 4 days, Arthur bapt. 27 (5) 1651.

PERRY, etc., cont.
He d. 9 (8) 1652. The widow m. 2, 22 (10) 1653, John Gillett.

Francis, wheelwright, Salem, punished for ill speches to his master and behaviour to his master July 5, 1631. Propr. 1636. Lawsuit, 1639. Sold houses and land 5 Nov. 1645. Wife Jane, adm. chh. 13 (4) 1641; ch. Sarah and Benjamin bapt. 18 (5) 1641, David bapt. 2 (6) 1641, Samuel bapt. 10 (2) 1642, Elisha bapt. 11 (6) 1644.

George, Marshfield, propr. 1645.

Isaac, Boston, memb. chh. 1630; frm. March 6, 1631-2.

John, householder, Roxbury. Ch. Elizabeth b. Jan. 25, 1637, John b. Sept. 7, 1639, Samuel b. March 1, 1640. He was bur. Sept. 21, 1642. Will dated 4 June, 1642, was prob. 24 (5) 1643. Beq. house, land and goods to wife, to bring up his 3 children. Brethren Wm. Heath and Philip Eliot overseers.

John, Taunton, atba. 1643. Of Marshfield, propr. 1645. His son William, 7 years old Dec. 1, 1649, was placed as an apprentice with John Bradford of Dux. 21 May, 1650.

John, yeoman, Newbury, propr. 1648. Sold land April 1, 1651.

Richard, Charlestown, propr. 1636. Richard, Jr., recd. money through the Gen. Court 3 (7) 1639.

Thomas, Ipswich, propr. 1641. Propr. at Haverhill in 1652.

William, planter, Scituate, took oath of allegiance 1 Feb. 1638. Lawsuit about a well 7 Jan. 1644. He rem. to Marshfield. Wife Susanna was a legatee of Michael Barstow.

Admin. of his est. gr. 4 April, 1693, to his eldest son Thomas.

William, tailor, Watertown, (see Parryer,) propr. 1642, frm. May 6, 1646. He was ae. 66 in 1672. Wife Anne; ch. Elizabeth b. 12 (6) 1641.

He d. Sept. 9, 1683; will, made Jan. 8, 1681, at age of 75 years; beq. to wife; at her death to be divided between his ch. Obediah, Samuel, Sarah, Anna, Elizabeth, Abia.

PERSONS, see Pearson.

PESTER,
William, merchant, Salem, propr. 1636. A bond to him dated Sept. 2, 1638. [Suff. De. I, 17.] He mortg. house and land Oct. 20, 1641. He drew on his uncle William Pester, Esq., at Barnard Castle, my Lord Chamberlaynes house in Thames street, London, Aug. 28, 1640. [L.] Dorothy, whose husband went to Eng. 10 years since, had liberty from Gen. Court 31 May, 1652, to marry again.

PETER, [incorrectly called Peters,]
Rev. Hugh, b. in 1699 at Fowy, Cornwall, grad. Trinity Col., Cambridge, A.B. 1617, A.M. 1622; preached at St. Sepulchres, London. Subscribed toward the stock of the Mass. Bay Co. in 1628. Became a puritan. Was pastor of the English church at Rotterdam; came to Boston 6 (8) 1635. He was ordained pastor of the church at Salem, where he did an excellent work. He took a broad interest in all New England, and was an active promoter of many movements which helped on the civil, social and religious welfare of the people. He returned to England as one of the representatives of the Colonies at the opening of the Great Revolution, and became one of the foremost leaders of the Parliamentary party. After the Restoration he was brought to trial for treason, and, in particular, for being one of the chief movers for the execution of king Charles I. Of course he was condemned; was hung, drawn and quartered Oct. 16, 1660. His first wife, Elizabeth, widow of Edmund Reade, mother of the wife of Gov. Samuel Symonds, came to N. E. with him or very soon afterward; was recd. to the chh. of Salem. She died, and he m. 2, Mrs. Deliverance Sheffield, who was dismissed from the chh. of Bo. 2 (11) 1639, and rec'd at Salem as his wife. She became insane at some time not long after, and remained so to the close of her life, so far as is known. His child, Elizabeth, was bapt. at Salem 8 (1) 1640; she m. — Barker, and as his widow was living at Deptford, Eng. in 1703, when she gave a letter of attorney for collection of property at Salem which had belonged to her father. He was "father" to John Winthrop, Jr., as appears from a phrase in a letter from Roger Williams to the latter in 1660. Gov. Winthrop speaks of him as "my brother Peter." [Felt's memoirs of Mr. Peter in Reg. V; Winthrop, and Col Rec.]

PETTINGELL, PETTINGALL, PETTENGILL, PETTINGAILE, PATTENGELL,
Richard, Salem, propr., frm. June 2, 1641. Rem. to Wenham; recd. to chh. by letter 4 (6) 1649. Rem. to Newbury; bought land 8 April, 1651. He deposed at Hampton court 14 (8) 1673, ae. about 52 years, that he knew Giles Fuller, late of Hampton, and Mr. Matth. Fuller of Barnstable, doctor, both of them in old England and in N. E., and that they were near kinsmen. Wife Joanna, dau. of Richard Ingersoll, q. v.; ch. Samuel bapt. 9 (12) 1644, Mary b. at Newb. 6 July, 1652, Nathaniel b. 21 Sept. 1654, a child b. Nov. 15, d. 17, 1657, Henry d. Jan. 20, 1659.

PETTIS,
John, Ipswich, commoner, 1641.

PETTIT,
Anne, Boston, recd. chh. 1630-1 from chh. of Salem.

Thomas, Boston, having served with Oliver Mellowes this 3½ years, had a houseplot granted him 8 (11) 1637. The lot is referred to in a deed of Geo. Griggs' 8 (8) 1650.

PEYNTREE, see Pantry.

PEYTON, see Payton.

PHANCE, see Faunce.

PHESE, see Veazie.

PHELPS, see Phillips,
George, Dorchester, also called Phillips, propr. 1632, frm. May 6, 1635. Rem. to Windsor, Conn. and later to Westfield. Will dated April 24, 1683, prob. June 6, 1687, Beq. to wife; to son Joseph of Windsor; sons Isaac, Jacob, John and Nathaniel; to Isaac's son Isaac.

Henry, came in the Hercules April 10, 1634. Res. at Salem. Lawsuit, 1645. [Es. Files.] He was charged in 1660 with entertaining Quakers. His son John was placed in care of an uncle, Edmund Batter; and to have a portion which had been left him by his grandmother. [Es. Files.]

William, Dorchester, propr., juryman Nov. 9, 1630, constable in 1631, frm. May 18, 1631; deputy 1634. Rem. to Windsor, Conn.

PHESINGTON, see Fessenden.

PHILBERT, PHILPOT, PHILPOTT, FILBERT,

Thomas, Watertown, propr. 1644. He became distracted, and was placed in prison. Bryan Pendleton and Machael Bairstow were allowed by the Court 27 Oct. 1647, to take out of his house and sell sufficient to discharge their engagement of about 6 li. for him.

William, salt-maker, Boston, townsman, 1642, adm. chh. 29 (9) 1645. He m. 16 (10) 1651, Anne, widow of George Hunn. Mary Philberd, who was m. 20 (11) 1652, to Wm. Hinckesman, may have been of his family.

PHILBRICK, see Filbrick,

Thomas, Watertown, propr. 1636. He sold house and land Jan. 23, 1645, and rem. to Hampton. He deposed 11 (2) 1667, ae. about 42 years. Wife Elizabeth d. 19 (12) 1663. Ch. James, John, Thomas, (deposed in 1666, ae. 42,) Elizabeth, (m. Thomas Chase,) Mary, (m. Thomas Tuck,) Martha, (m. John Cass).

Will dated March, 1663-4, "very aged;" prob. 8 (8) 1667. Mentions ch. James, Thomas, Elizabeth, Hannah, Mary, Martha, and gr. ch. John. [Reg. VII, 358, and XXXVIII, 279.]

PHILIPS, PHILLIPS, PHILIP,

George, Dorchester; see Phelps.

Rev. George, b. at Raynham, co. Norfolk, Eng. grad. at Gaius Coll., Cambridge, A.B. 1613, A.M. 1617; preached at Boxford, Eng.; came to N. E. in the Arbella in 1630. Was the first minister of Watertown, and was "especially gifted and very peaceful in his place." [W.] Frm. May 18, 1631. His first wife, a dau. of Richard Sergeant, came with him, and d. at Salem soon after arrival. He m. 2, Elizabeth —. Ch. rec. at Wat.: Zorubabel b. 5 (2) 1632, Elizabeth, (m. Job Bishop,) Jonathan b. 16 (1) 1633, Theophilus b. 28 (3) 1636, Anniball bur. 17 (2) 1638, ae. 2 months, Ephraim b. and d. 1640, Obediah bur. 5 (2) 1641.

He d. July 1, 1644. Will prob. 6 (7) 1644. Beq. to wife a third part; the rest to the children; eldest son to have a double portion. The widow d. Jan. 27, 1681. Will: sons Samuel, Zerubabel, Jonathan and Theophilus; Job Bishop; James Barnard who m. dau. Abigail. [See Bond.]

PHILIPS, etc., cont.

Hannah, Watertown, m. Sept. 1, 1638, Joseph Morse, who settled at Dedham, [son of Joseph of Ipswich.]

Henry, butcher, Dedham, propr. 14 (7) 1637, adm. chh. April 24, 1639, frm. March 13, 1637-8. Town officer, ensign. Rem. to Boston about 1656; adm. chh. 11 (2) 1658. He m. 5 (1) 1639, Mary Brock, who was adm. chh. 5 (2) 1640, and d. 2 (5) 1640. He m. 1 (3) 1641, Ann Hunting; ch. Eliezer b. and d. 1641, Hannah b. 25 (3) 1643, Abigail b. 2 (8) 1645, John b. 2 (4) 1648, Sarah b. 30 (6) 1650. The wife Ann d., and he m. Mary, dau. of John Dwight; she was adm. chh. Bo. 23 (1) 1656-7; ch. Henry b. Oct. 1, 1656, Timothy b. Sept. 15, 1658, Mary b. Nov. 28, 1660, Samuel bapt. 2 (9) 1662, Elishu bapt. May 15, 1665, Jonathan b. Sept. 12, 1666, Mehetabel bapt. 21 (5) 1667, John b. Jan. 22, 1668-9, John b. July 9, 1670, Elizabeth b. Aug. 29, 1672.

He signed his will 4 Dec. 1685; "preserved to old age;" prob. 18 Feb. folg. Beq. to wife Mary; daus. Hannah Negus and Abigail East and son Eleazer P. have already had their portions; beq. to other ch. Timothy, Samuel, John, Mehitabel and Elizabeth; the est. left by sons Nathaniel and Henry to be divided to the survivors. A payment to be made to Francis East.

John, yeoman, Dorchester, appl. frm. Oct. 19, 1630; frm. Aug. 7, 1632. He rem. to Boston; sold Dorch. property 25 (12) 1651. Deacon. Deposed 25 April, 1660, to the declaration of Thomas Johnson, being 51 years old or thereabout. Wife Joanna d. in Bo. 24 Oct. 1675, ae. 80 years. [Copp's Hill gr. st.] Ch. John; Mary b. 1633, d. 1640, John b. (2) 1640, Israel b. 1642, d. 1643, Mary bapt. about 1638, ("m. Mr. Mountjoy of Boston;" note in Dorch. chh. Rec).

Will dated 15 March ,1680-1, prob. 27 Dec. 1683. Beq. to son-in-law George Munjay, his wife and children; to present wife Sarah; to Huldah, dau. of his grand son John Munjoy, dec.; to the military company of the North end of Boston in which he was an officer. Mary Lawrence, late Munjoy, deposed to the inventory of her late father, 27 Dec. 1683.

Mr. John, minister, from Wrentham, Eng.; came before 1638, when he was associated with Mr. Ezekiel Rogers and others in the company for Rowley, to whom the

PHILIPS, etc., cont.

Gen. Court granted land 13 March, 1638-9. The town of Salem offered "a village to him and his company." The chh. of Dedham desired him for its pastor in 1638; but, in view of "the service of the church of Cambridge and the foundation of the colledge," he declined the call. Yet he was adm. to Ded. chh. with his wife (3) 1640; they had leave of the chh. to return to England a year later, and sailed 26 (8) 1641. He is mentioned by Lechford as "a minister out of office" in 1641-2. [L., P. D.] [W., Col. Rec., Ded. Chh. Rec. and Salem Town Rec.]

John, Duxbury, a volunteer for the Pequot War in 1637; propr. 1640; atba. 1643. He bought, 19 Oct. 1639, a house in D. of Robert Mendall, for which annual payments were to be made at Boston. He m. at Marshfield July 6, 1654, Grace Holloway. He m. March 14, 1666, Faith, [widow of Edward] Doten. She d. Dec. 21, 1675; made will Dec. 12, 1675, giving her est. to h er daus. Mary, Elizabeth and Desire. Admin. was gr. to John Rouse, husband of Mary, Nov. 4, 1676. Ch. Joseph b. last of March, 1655.

He made will 20 Oct. 1691, ae. about 89 years; beq. to eldest son Samuel, and son Benjamin, and each of their sons. Prob. 16 May, 1692.

Martin, Dedham, propr. 11 (6) 1637; sold in 1642.

Nicholas, butcher, Dedham, pioneer, 1636; frm. May 13, 1640. Sold land about 1641. Memb. Court Valuation com. 1640. Rem. to Weymouth; town officer, 1648. Rem. to Boston about 1651. Ch. Experience, dau., b. 8 (3) 1641, Caleb b. 22 (11) 1643. He m. 4 (10) 1651, Hannah Salter; ch. Elizabeth b. Feb. 24, 1652, Hannah b. Nov. 25, 1654, Nicholas d. 1 (6) 1657, Nicholas b. May 12, 1660, d. Aug. 18, 1661, Abigail b. Feb. 20, 1661, Sarah bapt. 6 (3) 1666, Thomas b. Oct. 19, 1667.

He d. Thurs., 15 March, 1669-70; inv. 24 April folg. The widow m. John Ruggles. [Reg. XLVIII, 460.]

William, Taunton, atba. 1643.

Will dated April 16, 1654. Aged threescore and ten at least; wife Elizabeth, son James, son-in-law James Walker, dau. Elizabeth Walker, and their little dau. Hester and other children. [Reg. V, 260.]

William, vintner, inn-holder, Charlestown, adm. chh. with wife Mary 23 (7) 1639,

PHILIPS, etc., cont.

frm. May 13, 1640. Daniel Field, of Tring, Eng., in a letter to Seth Sweetser, May 10, 1642, sent love to Wm. Philips and his wife. He rem. to Boston. His wife Mary d. 1 (3) 1646; he m. 2, Bridget, widow of John Sanford. Mortg. his house, called Ship Tavern, March 10, 1657, for the payment of certain sums to her children. She d. and he m. 3, Susanna, widow of Christopher Stanley. She d. 16 (4) 1655, leaving a will, dated same day as his, 10 (7) 1650; prob. Aug. 2, 1655. To dau.-in-law Mary Feild, dau. Martha Thurston, dau. Rebecca Lord, sons William and Nathaniel P., daus. Elizabeth and Phebe P., dau. Sarah; to Elizabeth and William Aspinwall; to any of her bros.' or sisters' children that may come over; to Richard and George Bennitt who were her servants. Residue to her husband, Wm. Philips. [Reg. V, 447.] Capt. Richard Thurston and Martha, his wife, and Mr. Robert Lord and Rebecca, his wife, living in Eng., sold their rights in a certain house in Boston in connection with Lieut. Philips, Jan. 8, 1656. Ch. rec. in Boston: Elizabeth, (m. 6 (5) 1655, Abiel Everill, and 2, John Alden, [Reg. X, 269.] Phebe bapt. 16 (2) 1640, (m. July 26, 1659, Zechariah Gillam,) Nathaniel bapt. 19 (2) 1641, Mary b. 17 (12) 1643.

He d. Aug. 1657.

PHINNEY, see Finney.

PHIPPEN, PHIPPENY,

David, son of Robert Fitzpen or Phippen of Weymouth, Eng., came early to Hingham; propr., frm. March 3, 1635-6. Rem. to Boston before 1637. Wife Sarah; ch. John b. and d. 1637, John b. and d. 1640.

Will prob. 31 (8) 1650; to wife Sarah house, shop, store, and tools; a house-lot to each of the sons Benjamin, Gamaliel and George, and to son-in-law, Thomas Yeo. A cow to son George Vickars. Son Joseph joint exec. with the wife.

His three eldest sons were legatees in the will of his brother George, rector of St. Mary's chh., Truro, Eng., 20 July, 1650. [Reg. XLIX, 244.]

Judith, ae. 16, came in the Planter March 22, 1634, cert. from the parish of Stepney.

PHIPPS, FIPPS,

Solomon, Charlestown, adm. chh. 15 (11) 1641; frm. May 18, 1642. Town officer. "Mother Phipps" adm. chh. 15 (3) 1642. Wife Elizabeth; ch. Elizabeth b. 23 (2) 1643; Joseph bapt. 13 (8) 1661.

Will dated 24 May, 1670, prob. 14 (10) 1671; beq. to wife Elizabeth; ch. Solomon, Samuel, Joseph, Elizabeth Roy; to dau.-[in-law?] Mary P. Elizabeth P., an aged widow, d. Nov. 1, 1688.

William, Plymouth, closing a term of service to the partners, sold the portion of land due to him to John Winslow, 31 Aug. 1636.

PICKARD, PICKETT,

John, carpenter, Salem, propr., adm. chh. 1 (9) 1648. Rem. to Rowley; town officer and propr. 1648. He deposed in 1664, ae. about 42 years. First wife Jane; second wife Ann; ch. rec. at R.: Rebeca b. 3 (8) 1645, John b. 1 (1) 1653; ch. rec. at Salem: John, Thomas and Sarah bapt. 9 (9) 1648, Rebecca bapt. 30 (4) 1650, Daniel bapt. 25 (11) 1651, Jacob bapt. 3 (7) 1654; ch. b. at Rowley: Sarah b. 3 (11) 1656, Ann b. 15 (5) 1659, Samuel b. (3) 1663.

He d. Sept. 1683. Will prob. 27 (9) 1683. Wife Ann; sons John and Samuel P., Thomas Hammond and Solomon Phipps; daus. Rebecca, Sarah, Mary, Ann, Jane and Hannah.

PICKERING, PICKE,

John, Cambridge. Wife Mary; ch. Lydia b. Nov. 5, 1638, Abigail b. 22 (2) 1642.

John, carpenter, Salem, propr. 1636. Contracted 4 (12) 1638, to build the new meetng-house, and was employed 25 (1) 1644 to keep the bridge in repair for 16 years. Wife Elizabeth memb. chh. 1639. Ch. Eliza bapt. 3 (1) 1643-4, Elizabeth b. 17 (6), bapt. 31 (6) 1646, [certificate in Es. Files.]

Will dated 30 (5) 1655, prob. 1 (5) 1657. Wife Elizabeth; sons John and Jonathan, minors. The widow m. 25 (10) 1657, John Deacon. Genealogy.

PICKETT. alias PARKUS,

Christopher, planter, Boston. He m. in Roxbury in June, 1647, Elizabeth Stone.

PICKMAN, see Pitman.

PICKRAM, PICKROM,

John, Watertown. Wife Esther; dau. Jone bur. 13 (10) 1630, ae. 20 years; son John bur. 6 (5) 1639. The widow was propr. in 1636. She and her son George sold a piece of land Sept. 1, 1646, to Joshua Stubbs and his mother-in-law Abigail Benjamin.

John, ae. 30, d. at Wat. 10 (10) 1650.

PICKRYN,

John, punished by the Court Sept. 28, 1630, as accessory to a felony.

PICKWORTH,

John, Salem; he went to Plymouth and got a wife before 1631. [B. in letter to W. See Reg. II, 243.] Propr. at Jeffrey's Creek in 1637. Ch. Ruth, Hannah and John bapt. 14 (3) 1638, Joseph bapt. 12 (12) 1642, Rachel bapt. 3 (3) 1646, Benjamin bapt. 2 (5) 1648, Sarah bapt. 6 (8) 1650, Abigail bapt. 2 (8) 1652.

His will prob. 25 (9) 1663, names wife Ann; sons Samuel, Joseph, Benjamin; daus. Ruth Masterson, Hanna Callem and Abigail P. The widow Ann beq. her est. 10 May, 1682, to daus. Ruth Mastons and Rachel Sible; son Joseph P.'s dau. Ann; gr. ch. Ann, dau. of John Killem and dau. Rachel's youngest dau. Ann S. Prob. 3 April, 1683.

PICKTON, PICDEN, PIGDON,

Thomas, Salem, propr. 1638. A witness in court in 1647.

Will prob. 28 (9) 1677. Wife Ann exec. and heir. She d. 25 Dec. 1683. Her will dated 29 Dec. 1677, prob. (4) 1684, beq. to Wm. Cash, Sen.; to Jeremiah Butman and wife and their ch. Jeremiah, Matthew, John, Joseph and Benjamin B.

PID,

Richard, residence not given, frm. June 22, 1642.

PIDCOCK,

George, tailor, Duxbury. He m. 16 May, 1640, Sarah Rickard. Before Court 1641. Exempt from training 1643. Constable 1656.

PIDGE, PIGGE, PIG,
Thomas, householder, "a godly, Christian man," [E.] Roxbury. Frm. May 14, 1634. Propr. Wife Mary; ch. Martha b. 12 (1) 1642, bapt. 12 (1, 1643, (m. in Ded. 5 (12) 1659, Benjamin Bullard.) A dau. m. Wood of Braintree, and had ch. Mary and Sarah, twins, b. and bapt. at Rox. 25 (10) 1642. Son Thomas, ae. 18, testified for Nicholas Wood 20 (4) 1653. [Mdx. Files.]
He d. and was bur. Dec. 30, 1643. Will prob. 7 (12) 1644. Beq. to wife, sons Thomas and John, daus. Hannah, Sarah, Martha and Mary. [Reg. III, 78.] The widow m. 2, Michael Metcalf.

PIERCE, PEARCE, PEARS, PEARSE, PEIRCE, PIERS,
Abraham, Plymouth, one of the "purchasers or old-comers," had share in cattle in 1627; frm. 1633. Settled at Duxbury. His dau. Alice was taken to Barnstable for baptism by his wife's sister, goody Scudder, and bapt. July 21, 1650.
Admin. of his est. gr. 3 June, 1673, to his son Abraham, who was allowed to take the remainder of the est. after paying portions to his bro. Isaac P. and his sisters Rebecca Wills and Alice Baker.

Anthony, weaver, Watertown, frm. Sept. 3, 1634. Bought land, 1655. Seems to be the son of John of Wat.

Daniel, ae. 23, came in the Elizabeth of Ipswich, April 30, 1635. Settled at Newbury. Frm. May 2, 1638, blacksmith. Propr.; town officer. Wife [Sarah] d. July 17, 1654. He m. 2 ,Dec. 26, 1654, Anne, (widow of Thomas) Milward. Ch. Daniel, Joshua b. 15 May, 1642, Sarah, (m. Caleb Moody,) Martha b. 14 Feb. 1648, (m. Thomas Noyes.)
He d. 27 Nov. 1677. Will prob. March 26, 1678, beq. to wife Ann according to marriage contract; to her son-in-law Thomas Thorpe; rest to son Daniel Pierce and his male heirs.

John, cooper, Dorchester, propr., frm. May 18, 1631. Town officer. Rem. to Boston. Sold Dorch. property 28 (12) 1642. Adm. it hab. Bo. 28 (12) 1641. Wife Parnell d. (8) 1639; he m. 2, Mary —; she d., and he m. 3, 10 (6) 1654, Rebecca Wheeler, widow, of Boston. Ch. Joseph b. 30 (8) 1631, Abigail b. 17 (5) 1633, John b. 3 (1) 1634-5, Nehemiah b. 1637, d. 1639, Mary b. 6 (1) 1640, Nehemiah b. 17 (11) 1641.

PIERCE, etc., cont.
Will prob. Oct. 11, 1661; wife Rebecca; sons Samuel and Nehemiah, daus. Mary, Mercy and Exercise. Est. at Bo. and Dorch. [Reg. X, 359.]

John, weaver, ae. 49, of Norwich, Eng., with wife Elizabeth, ae. "36," and children John, Barbara, Judith and Elizabeth, and servant John Gedney, passed exam. to go to Boston, N. E., April 8, 1637. Settled at Watertown. The dau. Judith m. at Woburn Jan., 30 or Dec. 30, 1644, Francis Wyman.
He d. Aug. 19, 1661. Will dated 7 (1) 1657-8, prob. 1 Oct. 1661, beq. to wife Elizabeth, son Anthony and "the rest of" his children. The widow d. March 12, 1666, ae. about 79 years. Her will names children Anthony, Robert, John, Esther Morse and Mary Coldham; gr. daus. Mary and Esther Ball, ch. of her dau. Elizabeth; John, son of Anthony, and Judah, dau. of Robert. [The son] Robert deposed 29 (10) 1658, ae. 38 years; Robert deposed at Ipswich in 1663, ae. about 50 years.

John, wife Elnor, before Gen. Court, Boston, in 1639 and 1641. John, wife Elizabeth; ch. John and Elizabeth b. at Bo. 16 (4) 1643. Elizabeth the wife d. at Sudbury 12 June, 1655. [This may be the son of John of Wat.]

Mark, Cambridge, propr. 1642. Rem. to Conn. [Reg. XLIX, 500.]

Marmaduke, tailor, came before June 9, 1637, from Sandwich, Eng., with wife Mary and one servant. Settled at Salem; had serious trouble with his "boy;" testimony given before Gen. Court 3 (10) 1639. [Col. Rec. and L.]

Michael, Hingham, 1645. Rem. to Scituate. Took John Reade as an apprentice July 15, 1653. His wife d. 31 Dec. 1662; he m. Ann —. Ch. Persis bapt. Jan. 7, 1645, Benjamin, John, Ephraim, Elizabeth, Deborah, Anna and Abigail, all bapt. at Hing. May 9, 1665; Abiah, Ruth. [Hist. Hing. and Col. Rec.]
He was a captain in King Philip's War, and was slain in battle. His will dated 15 Jan. 1675, prob. 22 July, 1676, made his son Benjamin exec.; beq. to wife Annah, son John; to son Ephraim, and his ch. Eliakim and Ephraim; refers to a gift from father Eames, and calls Mark E. and Charles

PIERCE, etc., cont.

Stockbridge brothers; to ch. Abigail and Mary Holbrook, Elizabeth, Sarah, Annah, Abiah, Ruth and Persis Peirse; to gr. ch. Elizabeth and Abigail Holbrook.

Phebe, ae. 18, came in the Increase April 15, 1635.

Robert, Dorchester, made a commoner, Oct. 31, 1639, adm. chh. 9 (4) 1640. Frm. May 18, 1642. Res. on Pine Neck in 1644, and on his "great lot" the latter part of his life. He m. Ann, dau. of John Grenaway, who conveyed land to her in 1651. She d. Dec. 31, 1695, ae. about 104 years. [Gr. st.] Ch. Thomas, b. about 1635, [Gr. st.], Deborah b. (12) 1639, d. 15 (2) 1640, Mary, (m. Thomas Herring,) and Sarah who d. before 1658.

He or his son Thomas built the dwelling, still known as "The Old Pierce House."

He d. 5 (11) 1664. Will dated 13 (8) 1664, prob. 2 March, 1664-5; desired to leave est. so that it might be enjoyed by his survivors "with comfort and peace." To wife one-half of real est. for life, and half the personal to dispose at her death; son Thomas to have half the land now and the rest at his mother's death; he paying 20 li. to his sister Mary, wife of Thomas Herrin of Dedham and 10 li. to be divided between her 5 children. A worthy charge to his children. [Reg. XIII, 154.]

Thomas, Charlestown; wife Elizabeth adm. chh. 10 (11), and he adm. chh. 21 (12) 1634. Frm. May 6, 1635. He rem. to Woburn; propr. 1643; town officer. Signed a petition in 1663, ae. about 46 years old. [Mass. Arch. vol. 106.] Wife Elizabeth was ae. 71 in 1667. Ch. Abigail bapt. 17 (4) 1639, a son John b. at Wob. 7 (1) 1643, Thomas b. Jan. 21, 1644, Elizabeth b. Dec. 25, 1646, Joseph b. Sept. 22, 1648, d. Feb. 27, 1648-9, Joseph b. Aug. 14, 1649, Stephen b. July 16, 1651, Samuel b. 1654, d. 1655, Samuel b. April 7, 1656, William b. March 7, 1656-7, James b. May 7, 1659, Abigail b. Nov. 20, 1660.

He d. Oct. 7, 1666. Will dated Nov. 7, 1665, ae. about 82 years; beq. to wife Elizabeth; gr. ch. Mary Bridge and Elizabeth Jeffs, now dwelling with me; to all gr. ch.; to Harvard College. The widow deposed to the inv. March 22, 1666-7, ae. 71 years.

William, Barnstable, atba. 1643, of Yarmouth, atba. 1643.

PIERCE, etc., cont.

Mr. William, mariner, master of the Lyons' Whelp and other ships, made many voyages across the Atlantic, bringing passengers and supplies. Came to Boston to reside about 1632. Adm. chh. 1632; wife Bridget adm. chh. 2 (12) 1633. Town officer, colonial officer. One of the most influential citizens. He was shot 13 (5) 1641 by people of Providence Island, Bermuda, as he was taking a load of colonists from Massachusetts colony to the island. [W.] [See Pearce, Peirce and Pierce Genealogies.]

PIERPOINT, PEIRPOINT, PEIRPOYNTE, PEARPOINT,

James, Ipswich, herdsman, 1646.

John, malster, Ipswich, 1648, had deed of land in Roxbury from his father-in-law John Stow. He bought land in Ips. 15 Nov. 1649. Memb. chh Rox. Nov. 17, 1650; frm. May 26, 1652. Town officer. Ch. Thankful b. Nov. 26, 1649, John b. July 22, 1651, John b. Oct. 28, 1652, dau. Experience b. 4 (11) 1654, infant b. and d. 1657, James bapt. 8 (11) 1659, Ebenezer bapt. 22 (10) 1661, Jonathan d. 23 (8) 1663, Thankful bapt. 27 (10) 1663, Joseph bapt. 12 (6) 1666, Benjamin bapt. 2 (6) 1668. He deposed in Essex Court in 1670, ae. 51 years.

He d. at Rox. Dec. 7, 1682, ae. 64 years. Will, written by himself, 12 Oct. 1681, prob. 21 Dec. 1682, attested by his brother Robert P., his widow Thankful, his ch. John, James and Ebenezer, the guardians of his sons Joseph and Benjamin, John Hayward, husband of his dau. Experience, and Dea. Wm. Parke. Beq. lands, mills, malthouse, etc. Refers to cousin Baret.

Robert, Ipswich, maulster, resident, 1648. Rem. to Roxbury; wife Maria adm. ch h. 20 (6) 1665. Ch. Jonathan d. 23 (8) 1663, Jonathan bapt. 20 (6) 1665, Thomas bapt. 6 (11) 1667, Ezra d. 21 (9) 1669, James bapt. 25 (8) 1674, Sarah bapt. 29 (3) 1680.

Admin. of his est. was gr. 12 July, 1694, to Sarah and Jonathan P.

PILBEAME,

James, Boston, inhabitant, 1649. Rem. to Rehoboth. Admin. of his est. gr. 6 (3) 1653, to his son-in-law Leonard Rice. [Reg. V, 261.]

PIKE, PYKE,
James, Charlestown, adm. chh. 3 (3) 1647, frm. May 26, 1647. Rem. to Reading. Ch. John b. 1 (11) 1653.

John, Ipswich, propr. witness in Court at Cambridge Aug. 4, 1635. Rem. to Newbury in 1635, with sons John and Robert who became also proprietors at once and town officers. Attorney for Mr. Eson [Easton] at Salem Court 28 (1) 1637. [Es. Files.] In 1669 John, Jr., gave testimony concerning the organizing of town and chh.. He deposed 30 (1) 1648, respecting a payment made as constable of Ips.

He d. at Salisbury 26 May; will signed 24 May, prob. Oct. 3, 1654.

PILSBURY, PEELSBURY, PILSBERY,
William, yeoman, husbandman, Dorchester, resident, 1648. Bought house and land at Newbury of Edward Rawson, Dec. 10, 1651. Bought land at Salisbury 8 (1) 1658. He m. Dorothy Crosby. [Court Rec. 1 (4) 1641.] Ch. Deborah b. 16 (2) 1642, Job b. 16 (8) 1643, Caleb b. at N. 28 Jan. 1653, d. 4 July, 1680, William b. 27 July, 1656, Experience b. 1 April, 1658, Increase b. 10 Oct. 1660, Thankful b. 22 April, 1662, Joshua d. 20 June, 1674, [Moses, Abel.]

He d. 19 June, 1686. Will dated 2 April, prob. 10 Sept. 1686, beq. to wife Dorothy, ch. Moses, Abel, William, Increase, Job, Deborah Evens, Experience and Thankful P.

PIN, PINE, PINNE, PINNEY, PYNEY, PYNNY,
Mr. Humphrey, Dorchester, one of the original colony that came in the Mary and John in 1629-30. Propr.; frm. May 14, 1634. Rem. to Windsor, Conn.

He d. 20 Aug. 1683; his widow d. 18 Aug. 1684.

Thomas, Weymouth, gave letter of attorney July 31, 1640. [L.] Frm. May, 1645.

PINCHON, see Pynchon.

PINDAR, PYNDAR,
Henry, carpenter, Ipswich, commoner, 1641; one of the builders of the prison in 1652. Sold house and land and commonage 20 Jan. 1657. The widow Elizabeth gave land to Edward Deare and his wife Elizabeth, her granddaughter, Aug. 24, 1666.

Mary, ae. 53, Francis, ae. 20, Marie, ae.

PINDAR, etc., cont.
17, Joanna, ae. 14, Katharine, ae. 10, and John, ae. 8, came in the Susan and Ellen in April, 1635.

Richard, Gloucester, in court 1647.

PINGREE, PINGRY, PENGRY,
Aaron, Ipswich, 1640, propr. He m. Jennet, widow of Robert Starkweather.

He beq. to her son John S. and to the 3 sons and 3 daus. of his bro. Moses P. in his will dated May 4, 1684, prob. Nov. 17, 1696.

Moses, saltmaker, Ipswich, bought land in 1641. Town officer, deacon. He deposed in 1661, ae. about 50 years. Wife Lydia, dau. of Mr. Robert Clement; ch. Sarah, (m. John Day,) Lydia, (m. Thomas Burnam,) Moses, Aaron, John, Thomas, Mehitabel, Abigail b. Jan. 30, 1666.

He d. Jan. 2, 1695.

PINION, PYNION, PINGON,
Nicholas, Lynn, with wife Elizabeth, called to court several times in 1647-8. Testified 1 April, 1661, ae. about 53 years, against the loyalty of a neighbor. [Arch 106.]

PINSON, PYNSON, PINCIN,
Thomas, Scituate, took oath of allegiance 1 Feb. 1638, atba. 1643; memb. of a board of arbitration, 1648. He m. 10 Nov. 1639, Joane Stanley. Ch. Thomas b. May 15, 1640, Hannah b. Dec. 4, 1642, (m. Jan. 15, 1661, George Young.)

Will made 4 April, 1689, being aged; prob. 27 June, 1694; beq. to son Thomas, son-in-law John Witherell, gr. ch. Thomas, Hannah, Margery, Elizabeth and Patience Young, Thomas P. and Joshua W. Dau. Hannah Morey consented to the probate.

PITCHER, PICHER,
Andrew, Dorchester, propr., frm. June 2, 1641. Wife Margaret; ch. Samuel bapt. 18 (2) 1641, Experience bapt. 25 (7) 1642, Mary bapt. 30 (9) 1644, (m. Isaac Rush,) Ruth bapt. 25 (5) 1647, John bapt. 11 (6) 1650, Nathaniel bapt. 18 (2) 1652, Jonathan.

He d. 19 (12) 1660. Will prob. 9 (3) 1661. To wife and children. [Reg. X, 266, and XXXI, 177.]

Note. The will of William Pitcher was prob. Es. co. 30 (4) 1676. Bro. John Pitcher living at Kenton, Devonshire, Eng.; friend Andrew Tucker.

PITFORD, PETFORD,
Peter, Marblehead; was plaintiff or defendant in several suits in Es. Court, 1641. Weigher of fish in 1648. [Es. Files.]

PITMAN, PICKMAN,
Nathaniel, witnessed a bond given to Wm. Pester of Salem, Sept. 2, 1636. Propr. 1639. Partner with Conant and others in Eastern trade. Deposed in 1662, ae. about 47 years. He m. Tabitha, widow of Anthony Dikes, as she deposed in 1657.

Will dated Sept. 23, 1684, prob. Nov. 24, 1685. Wife deceased. Daus. Mary Hodges, Hannah, wife of John Sanders, and Tabitha ffeveryeare; Bethiah Cole; son Nathaniel's children. The dau. Tabitha m. 30 (6) 1664, Edmond Feveryear.

PITNEY, PITTNEY,
James, Ipswich, propr. 1639. May be the same as

James, feltmaker, Marshfield, atba. 1643; propr. Rem. to Boston. Adm. inhabitant in 1652.

Will dated March 14, prob. March 21, 1663, 80 years old. Son John Thomas, Sen., and dau. Sarah Thomas; son James Pitney and dau. Abigail. [Reg. VI, 185.]

Sarah, ae. 22, with children, Sarah, ae. 7, and Samuel, ae. 1½, and Margaret, ae. 22, came in the Planter in April, 1635.

PITHOUSE,
John, husbandman, of Marlborough, Eng., came in the James, April 5, 1635.

PITTS, PITT, PIT, PYTT,
Edith, servant of Samuel Jackson of Scituate, in 1636. [Plym. Col. Rec.]

Edmund, linen weaver, came with his wife and child and his bro. Leonard P. and Adam Foulsham, from old Hingham, and settled in Hingham. Propr. 1637. Frm. May 13, 1640. Town officer. Wife Ann d. Nov. 1686. Ch. Mary bur. 15 June, 1641, Sarah bapt. Dec. 29, 1639, Mary bapt. Sept. 8, 1642, Ann bapt. Dec. 22, 1644, Isaac bapt. April 12, 1646, Elizabeth b. April 23, 1648, Deborah b. Nov. 6, 1651, John b. Nov. 27, 1653, Jeremiah b. Jan. 25, 1656. Edmund gave letter of

PITTS, etc., cont.
attorney in 1646 for the collection of 20 li. due L. P. from John [ffitling] of Hingham in co. Norfolk. [A.]

He d. 13 May, 1685, ae. about 72, [Hob.] Will prob. 26 May, beq. to wife Ann; daus. Elizabeth, wife of Thomas Joanes, Sarah, wife of Abraham Hollman, Mary, wife of John Bull, Anne, wife of Benj. Eastman, Deborah Witton and her sons John and David; gr. ch. Benj. and Thomas Eastman, Thomas Joanes and Samuel Jay.

Elizabeth, memb. chh. Dorchester before 1639. She signed a receipt for money recd. from Daniel Salmon, 21 (9) 1639. [Es. Court Files.] Elizabeth was adm. chh. Charlestown 13 (2) 1639. Mrs. Elizabeth, Weymouth; admin. of her est. was gr. Aug. 1, 1655, to her dau. Elizabeth and her husband, William Holbrook.

Leonard, bro. of Edmund, servant to John Burrell, d. at Boston 13 Feb. 1645.

Peter, Taunton, atba. 1643. Note the following:

Peter, Bristol, made will 9 June, 1692, prob. 12 Jan. folg.; beq. to sons Samuel, Peter and Ebenezer, daus. Alice, Mary and Sarah; wife Mary.

William, came in the Fortune to Plymouth in 1623.

William, came in 1638 from Hingham, Eng., and settled at Hingham.

William, Marblehead, merchant, bought houses and land at M. in 1647. Propr. 1649. He m. 7 (10) 1655, Susan, widow of Philip Aealy. Rem. to Boston. Susanna made nunc. will prob. Sept. 29, 1668, ½ of her est. to dau. Mary Lattimore, the other half to her husband. Admin. on est. of Susanna Ely, since Pitts, was gr. 25 (1) 1670, to John Bundy of Taunton, who appeared to be nearest of kin.

PITTY, PETTEE,
William, Weymouth, propr. Ch. John b. 28 (11) 1638, Joseph b. 16 (5) 1639, Mary b. 13 (11) 1642.

His will dated 14 April, 1679, prob. 29 July folg., beq. to wife Mary; eldest son Joseph; sons Samuel and William; dau. Mary, wife to Henry Adams.

PLACE, PLAICE, PLAISE, PLASSE, PLASE,

Peter, laborer, yeoman, Boston, adm. chh. 4 (2) 1646, frm. May 6, 1646. Wife Alice adm. chh. 18 (1) 1643; ch. Hannah b. 20 (11) 1642, (m. Stephen Talby,) Elizabeth b. 29 (7) 1644, Joseph b. 19 (8) 1646, Peter bapt. 30 (11) 1647, ae. about 3 days, Peter bapt. 17 (4) 1649, ae. about 2 days, John bapt. 1 (7) 1650, Elizabeth b. Oct. 21, 1652, d. 8 (6) 1654, Sarah b. Sept. 3, 1657.

Admin. of his est. gr. 22 April, 1675, to his widow Alice, and was assumed by her son John, mariner, after her death, Oct. 1, 1681.

Thomas, Cambridge, propr., sold before 1639, Boston, frm. May 13, 1640.

William, gunsmith, from the parish of St. Botolph, Aldersgate, London, came to Salem about 1637. Had special arrangements made for his residence and shop because of his business. His wife was Phebe (Manning), widow of James Waters of the same parish, and mother of Richard Waters of Salem.

He d. April 15, 1646, at the house of Thomas Weeks of S.; admin. of his est. 5 (6) 1646.

PLAISTOW,

Josias, gent., came early to N. E. He took 4 baskets of corn belonging to Chickatabot in Sept. 1631. For this he was compelled to restore 8 baskets, to pay a fine of 5 li., and be degraded from the title of gentleman; and his men, William Buckland and Thomas Andrew to be whipped for being accessory. [W .and Col. Rec.]

PLANTAYNE, see Blanton.

PLAYER,

Giles, before Gen. Court in 1638 and 1640.

PLIMPTON, PLYMPTON, PLIMTON, PLUNTON,

Elizabeth, came in the Jonathan in 1639. See depositions in the case of Blanchard vs. Barnes, Mdx. Court, 1652. [Reg. XXXII, 407.] She m. John Rutter.

John, Dedham, adm. chh. 20 (11) 1642; propr., frm. May 10, 1643; town officer. Sergeant. He m. 13 (1) 1644, Jane Dammin; [see Eaton, John;] ch. Hannah b. 1 (1) 1645, John b. 21 (1) 1646, d. 26 (2) 1647, Marah b.

PLIMPTON, etc., cont.
9 (2) 1648, John b. 5 (6) 1649, Peter b. in 1651, bapt. 7 (1) 1652.

He rem. to Deerfield. Was slain by the Indians in 1676. Inv. of his est. filed at ᴗuffield, Sept. 24, 1678, by widow Jane.

Thomas, Sudbury, servant of Peter Noyes, bought land of him in 1643. Wife Abigail; ch. Abigail b. 30 (7) 1653, Jane b. 18 Aug. 1655, Peter b. Jan. 4, 1666.

He was killed by the Indians and his house and barn burned. Inv. of the remainder taken 11 Sept. 1676. Agreement for division made 29 March, 1697, by the children, Thomas, (the eldest son,) Jane, (wife of Joseph Dabe,) Elizabeth, (wife of John Lock,) Mary, (wife of Matthew Stone,) Hannah, (singelowman,) and Peter.

PLUMER, PLUMMER,

Anne, Plymouth, m. 6 Feb. 1635-6, Henry Samson.

Francis, linen weaver, Newbury, propr., frm. May 14, 1634; town officer. Bought land 5 March, 1648. Wife Ruth d. 17 or 18 Aug. 1647. He m. widow Ann Palmer 31 March, 1649, who d. 18 Oct. 1665. He m. 29 Nov. 1665, Beatrice, widow of Wm. Cantlebury of Salem. Agreement 25 Nov. 1670. Ch. Samuel, Joseph, Mary, (m. April 20, 1660, John Cheney, Jr.)

He d. 17 Jan. 1672. Inv. of his est. and what Beatrice brought filed together 25 March, 1673.

Mary, Plymouth, m. Sept. 12, 1633, John Barnes.

PLUMLEY, PLIMLEY,

Alexander, Boston, Braintree, had been in the employ of Mr. Colbron; had grant of land at Br. 26 (6) 1639, for 3 heads. Wife Hester; son Submit b. 8 (11) 1653.

Will dated 8 March, prob. 30 March, 1681-2, beq. to wife Easter, sons Joseph and Submit, daus. Easter, Hannah and Elizabeth; son Winter.

POCHER,

George, Braintree, d. 29 (7) 1639.

POD, PODD,

Samuel, ae. 25, came in the Susan and Ellen in April, 1635, Ipswich, propr. 1641. Widow Grace, Ipswich, d. May 31, 1695.

PODGER, PODYER, PODYERD, PODYEARD,

John, miller, Hingham, brought suit in Es. court (11) 1641; and [his widow] Jane made Roger Clap of Dorch. her attorney in the same suit 27 June, 1646. Witness Geo. Weeks. [Es. Files.] Ch. Mary bapt. April 27, 1644, Mehitabel b. and John b. and d. 1644, Mehetabel and John bapt. Dec. 1645. See Ward, Samuel.

POFFER,

George, Braintree, had grant of land 24 (12) 1639, for 5 heads. James, ae. about 68, d. 25 July, 1692. Widow, aged, d. 18 (12) 1676.

POGET,

Thomas, residence not stated, frm. May 26, 1647.

POLLARD,

George, miller, Duxbury, attorney for John Pollard of Boston, 19 (4) 1641. [L.] Yeoman, formerly of Stoke Clere, Eng., in partnership with William Hiller, he agreed with the inhabitants of Dux. 7 Nov. 1639, to erect and maintain a water milne for grinding and stamping English and Indian corn. He rem. from the town before 10 Nov. 1646. [Ply. Col. Rec.] A natural inference is that he is

George, Marblehead, his will, dated 13 (3) prob. 31 (10) 1646, beq. to goodman Tiler of Lynn, John Hart, the younger, and Christopher, son of Edmond Nicolson.

John, husbandman, merchant, Boston, late of Belcham, co. Essex, Eng., receipted for cheese 3 (10) 1640. [L.]

Katharine, a maid, Boston, adm. chh. 15 (10) 1639.

William, shepherd, carter, ordinary keeper, Boston, 1644. Wife Anne; ch. John b. 4 (4) 1644, Samuel b. 24 (11) 1645, Hannah b 10 (11) 1648, d. 2 (6) 1662, William b. 20 March, 1652, Elizabeth b. 13 Jan. 1653, Joseph b. 15 March, 1657, Sarah b. 20 Oct. 1659, Benjamin b. April 22, 1663, Ann b. Oct. 18, 1664, Jonathan b. April 12, 1666. William, Jr. d. Jan. 24, and the son Joseph d. Dec. 30, 1690.

Will dated 15 Oct. 1678, prob. June 3, 1686, beq. to eldest son John and the rest of my sons and daughters; to wife Anne.

POLLEY, POLLY,

George, Woburn, propr. 1649. He m. May 21, 1649, Elizabeth Winn; ch. John b. Dec. 16, 1650, Joseph b. Dec. 25, 1652, George b. Jan. 4, 1655, Elizabeth b. April 14, 1657, Samuel b. and d. 1660, Hannah b. and d. 1662, Hannah b. June 28, 1663.

He d. Dec. 22, 1683. Will dated June 5, 1683, prob. April 1, 1684, beq. to wife Elizabeth, sons John, George, Samuel and Edward, daus. Elizabeth, Hannah and Sarah. Widow Elizabeth d. May 2, 1695.

John, Roxbury, propr. His wife Susanna was adm. chh. in 1650, d. 30 (2) 1664; wife Mary adm. chh. 8 (5) 1666, d. 30 (6) 1666; wife Hannah d. June 8, 1684. Ch. John; Mary and Sarah bapt. June 2, 1650, Hannah bapt. 15 (12) 1651, Abigail b. 4 (4) 1654, Bethiah bapt. 20 (12) 1658, Susanna bapt. 22 (10) 1661, Rebecca bapt. 16 (6) 1668, Joanna bapt. 13 (1) 1669-70, Mehitabel bapt. 18 (12) 1671, Rhoda bapt. 25 (11) 1673, Sarah bapt. 25 (5) 1680. Hannah, m. Isaac Curtis; was adm. chh. 30 (2) 1671.

He d. April 2, 1689, ae. 71. Will dated 17 Dec. 1688, prob. March, 1690-1 ,beq. to son-in-law John Peelam and Mary his wife, of Rehoboth; to son John under 21 years of age; son-in-law John Lion; wife Jane to have according to contract; to his 7 daus. by first wife Susanna; dau. the wife of Benjamin Saben; to his 6 daus. by his third wife Hannah, viz. Rebecca, Johanna, Mehitabel, Rhoda, Patience and Sarah; the 4 motherless ch. of dau. Saben.

POMEROY, POMROY, PUMROY, PUMMERY,,

Eldad or Eltweed, Dorchester, frm. March 4, 1632-3. Appointed by Gen. Court constable of Dorch. June 3, 1634. Rem. to Windsor, Conn., then to Northampton. His wife d. 5 July, 1655, and he m. widow Lydia Parsons. He deeded land in W. to his son Caleb in 1664, upon C.'s marriage. His son Joseph was apprentice to goodman Gunn. Ch. Eldad d. at Nor. in 1660, Medad bapt. 19 Aug. 1638, Caleb b. 6 March, 1641, Mary bapt. April 21, 1644, Joshua bapt. Nov. 22, 1646.

POND,

John, came with Winthrop in 1630; was sent back to his father by him for more provisions; another son came also. Winthrop

POND, cont.

afterward sent love to William Pond, one of his neighbors in England, in a home letter.

Robert, the elder, Dorchester. Wife Mary; ch. Mary m. John Blackman. The inv. of his est. was taken 27 (10) 1637. A chest of carpenter's tools and pump tools are mentioned. [Reg. VII, 30.] Mary and William petitioned the Court for admin. of the est. and it was ordered 10 May, 1648. His widow m. in 1649 or 1650, Edward Shephard of Cambridge; who conveyed, 24 Feb. 1650-1, to John Blackman, son-in-law to the late Robert P., one half the house and lands which W. P. had owned. Robert, who had ch. Mary b. 14 (5) 1657, and Martha b. 13 (2) 1660, and whose widow Mary m. Nicholas Ellen, relationship not stated.

William, Dorchester, adm. chh. with "goody" Pond, 28 (12) 1641. Contracted to lay the ground-sills of the meeting-house 10 (7) 1655. Ch. Sarah bapt. 6 (12) 1641, Abigail bapt. 19 (1) 1646, Samuel bapt. 16 (1) 1655, Elizabeth and Martha b. 17 (12) 1657, Judith b. 16 (8) 1659, Thankful b. 15 (11) 1661, George b. 20 (11) 1665, Mindwell b. 24 (6) 1667.

PONNT,

Thomas, ae. 21, came in the Elizabeth and Ann in 1635.

PONTON, PONTING,

Richard, apprenticed to John Reade of Braintree for 8 years, before Boston Court 2 (1) 1640-1. Boston, husbandman, adm. chh. 28 (10) 1644.

PONTUS,

William, probably the William Pantes (as copied), fustian maker, from near Dover, England, who m. at Leyden, Holland, Dec. 4, 1610, Wybra Hausen, a maid; William Brewster being a witness. Came to Plymouth early. Had lands at Thorp, near Windberry Hill, referred to in a Court order as gr. to him "long since." Propr.; frm. 1633. Juryman, 1636.

He d. Feb. 9, 1652-3. Will dated Sept. 9, 1650, prob. Feb. 20, 1652. Beq. to daus. Mary, (wife of James Glasse; had a child Wybra;) and Hannah, (wife of John Churchill). [Reg. V, 259.]

POOLE, POOL, POLE, see Paul,

Edward, sawyer, ae. 26, came as servant to George Allen from Weymouth, Eng. before March 20, 1635. Settled at Weymouth. Sought to obtain Mary Lane, servant of Richard Silvester for a wife (1) 1641. [L.] He gave letter of attorney to William Pardon to collect legacies due his wife Sarah from Edmund Pinney and Elizabeth Standerwick, of Broadway, Somersetshire, 5 (10) 1645. [A.]

Will prob. Oct. 26, 1644; beq. to wife, sons Samuel, Isaac, Joseph, Benjamin, John, Jacob, and dau. Sarah. [Reg. XIII, 12.]

Mrs. Elizabeth, an ancient maid, chief founder of the Plantation of Taunton, came in 1637. She lost much cattle and endured many hardships. [W.] Plymouth Court ordered lands laid out for her 3 March, 1639-40.

She d. May 21, 1654. Will dated 17 (3) 1654, ae. about 65 years; beq. to her bro. Capt. William P. of Tau.; to her cousin John, her bro.'s eldest son; and to his bros. Timothy and Nathaniel; to cousin Mary P.; to her kind old friend, sister Margery Powle, widow. [See Richard Paul.] [Reg. V, 262.]

Henry, girdler, London, came early to N. E.; resided at Boston. The only mention of him on B. records is this: he died 14 (7) 1643. His will dated 20 Aug. 1643, was prob. in London. He beq. to wife Elizabeth; to sons Henry, Robert and Edmund; to father Rowland Poole and sister Martha Castle; to bro. Randall P. and his children; to Anna Paullmoore; to Wm. Bartholomew; to the Colledge of Cambredg in New England ten pounds; to Robert Castle, Thomas Bendish, and Mr. Peter, whom he appointed overseers of his est. in England; made Nehemiah Bourne, William Davis, Robert Cooke and Thomas Dayton overseers for N. E.; wife Elizabeth exec. Richard Shearman, Thomas Bartholomew, Jo Wakelin and George Story witnesses. J. H. S. Fogg, M.D. furnished copy of the foregoing to the Reg. for July, 1892. Descendants of Mr. Poole, residing in Eng., have corresponded recently with officers of the Hist. Gen. Society.

John, yeoman, miller, Cambridge, mentioned about 1633; res. at Lynn, propr. before 1638; witness in case in Ess. court 27 (4) 1637; before Gen. Court 4 (10) 1638. Rem. to Reading. Made contract with the town

POOLE, etc., cont.

in 1644 to build a dam, turn the course of a stream, erect and maintain a water-mill for the use of the inhabitants. Proprietor: town officer. Lawsuit about mill in 1652. [Mdx. Files.] His servant John England in court 1637. With wife Margaret sold house and land in 1653. [Es. De. II, 105.] [Judith, first wife?] memb. chh. of Reading, 1648.

He d. 1 (12) 1667. Will dated 14 (12) 1666, beq. to son Jonathan; dau. Mary, wife of Matthew Edwards; son-in-law William Barrett; gr. ch. John and Lydia Barrett, Marey, Sarah and Elizabeth Edwards; to bro. and sister Armitage and their children; cousin Godfrey A.; Mr. and Mrs. Dane of Andover.

Samuel, Boston; his child Anne bapt. 7 (6) 1642, ae. about 8 days.

William, servant to Col. John Endecott, Salem, in Es. Court, 1638 and 1641.

William, gent. Taunton, frm. Dec. 4, 1638. He and his wife made Mr. John Dore of Axmouth, co. Devon, their attorney for the collection of a legacy from the est. of her bro. John Greene, of Milton, Somersetshire, dec. [A.] See wills of Devonshire Pooles, [Reg. XLVIII, 490.] The wife and son Theophilus were named in the will of her kinswoman Katharine Northcote, widow, of Hoxton, co. Mdx., Eng., dated 11 March, in 1685. He removed to Dorchester and was schoolmaster from 1659. He and his wife were recd. to the chh. from that of Tau. 31 (1) 1672. Ch. John, Timothy and Nathaniel, named in will of Elizabeth in 1654; William bapt. at Roxbury 20 (4) 1658, d. at Dorch. April 21, 1687, Mary, (m. 28 March. 1672, Daniel Henchman).

He d. Feb. 24 or 25, 1674, ae. 81 years. [See epitaph in Reg. II, 381.] The widow Jane made will at Dorchester 29 Aug. 1690, prob. June 25, 1691; beq. to son John and daus. Bethesda Filer and Mary Henchman; to gr. son John, or his sister Jane her share in the Iron Works at Taunton; to every one of her gr. children; to her minister, Mr. John Danforth.

POOR, POORE, POER, PORE,

Alice, ae. 20, came in the Bevis in May, 1638.

Daniel, came in the Bevis in 1638, ae. 14 years. Settled at Andover. He m. at

POOR, etc., cont.

Boston Oct. 20, 1650, Mary Farnum. Ch. Sara b. 28 Dec. 1652, Matthew, dau. b. 4 Nov. 1654, Daniel b. 5 Sept. 1656, John b. 5 Sept. 1658, d. 24 Dec. 1690, Hanna b. 6 May, 1660, Elizabeth b. 15 April, 1661, Deborah b. 18 April, 1664, Ruth b. 16 Feb. 1665, Priscilla b. 22 June, 1667, Lucy b. 28 Sept. 1670.

Will dated 7 June, 1689, prob. 24 June, 1690. Wife Mary; sons Daniel and John, daus. Ruth, Lucy, Martha, Mary, Sarah, Hannah, Deborah, Elizabeth and Priscilla; bro.-in-law John Farnum.

John, Lynn, propr. 1638, rem. to Newbury. Ch. John b. 21 June, 1642, Hannah b. 14 Oct. 1645, Elizabeth b. 8 Nov. 1647, Mary b. 15 July, 1648, Hannah b. 25 March, 1649, Henry b. 13 Dec. 1650, Mary b. and d. 1652, Joseph b. 4 Oct. 1653, Sarah b. 5 June, 1655, Lydia b. 5 Dec. 1656, Edward b. 5 April, 1658, Abigail b. 26 March, 1660, Abigail b. 5 Aug. 1661.

He d. 23 Nov. 1684. Inv. filed by widow Sarah.

Nicholas, Saugus, sued by his apprentice or workman Thomas Paine in Es. court in 1637.

Samuel, ae. 18, came in the Bevis in May, 1638; settled at Newbury. Bought land April 15, 1652. Ch. Rebecca b. 7 Feb. 1648, Mary b. 21 March, 1650, Samuel b. 14 Oct. 1653, Edward b. 27 May, 1656, Elizabeth b. 20 Jan. 1658, Joseph b. 10 June, 1661, Sarah b. 4 June, 1664, Edward b. 22 Feb. 1667, Mary b. 21 Feb. 1671.

He d. 31 Dec. 1683. Nunc. will dated 25 March, 1684, beq. to ch. Samuel, Edward, Elizabeth, Sara, Hannah, Mary, Benjamin, Joseph P. and Rebecca Smith; gr. ch. Mary Parson; to wife Rebecca.

POPE,

Anthony, embarked at London, in the Falcon, Dec. 25, 1635. Settled at Charlestown.

He d. Feb. 1, 1712-3.

Ephraim, Boston, propr., 1637. He m. widow Ann Bacon, who was adm. chh. 4 (8) 1657; her son John Bacon and Ephraim and Elizabeth P. were bapt. Oct. 18, folg.

His will, dated Jan. 24, 1676, gave est. to his ch. named above.

POPE, cont.
John, Sen., weaver, Dorchester, frm. Sept. 3, 1634, propr., selectman; one of the seven signers of the chh. covenant Aug. 23, 1636. Ch. rec. at Dorch.: John b. 30 (4) 1635, Nathan b. (5) 1641.

He d. 12 (2) 1646. Will prob. 5 (4) 1649. Beq. to wife Jane and dau. Patience, to bro. Thomas, to Joshua, his sister's husband, to William Smead, his apprentice boy, to Stephen Hoppin, a weaver, and to Hannah Jansen, (Johnson,) his servant. The widow Jane (dau. of Nicholas Clap, of Venn Ottery, co. Devon,) d. 12 (11) 1662. Beq. her est. to her dau. Patience, (wife of Edward Blake,) and her children Mary, Sarah and Jane.

John, husbandman, Dorchester, believed to be a son of John, Sen., though not named in the wills of the Senior or his wife; had land at Salem in 1636, and was proposed for propr. at Dedham in 1639; settled at Dorchester before 1643. His home was on Squantom. Had extensive lands. He m. Alice —, living in 1651; then Margaret —, who survived him and d. Oct. 20, 1702, ae. about 74 years. Ch. Thomas b. Nov. 27, 1643, Margaret, (m. — Peirce,) William, John b. March 5, 1658, Susanna, (m. John Cock,) Mary, (m. Thomas Cock,) Ebenezer, (served in the war of 1690,) Thankful, (m. Smith Woodward,) Ralph b. in 1673, Jane, (m. John Munning,) Joseph b. and d. 1679.

He d. 18 Oct. 1686. Admin. gr. to widow Margaret 11 Nov. 1686. Order for division April 4, 1700. Eldest son Thomas had receipted for his portion; other heirs: ch. of son John, dec.; sons William and Ralph; Margaret Peirce, only ch. of dec. dau. Margaret; daus. Susanna, wife of John Cox, Mary, widow of Thomas Cox, Thankful, wife of Smith Woodward, and Jane, wife of John Munnings.

John, carpenter, Boston, before the Court 30 (2) 1640, for ill-behaviour while an apprentice or servant; rem. to Bristol.

He d., unmarried, April 2, 1686. Inv. shows carpenter's tools, etc.; had worked on the meeting house.

Jonathan, Roxbury, a witness, 1647. [A.] He deposed 22 May, 1650, ae. about 24 years, to the nunc. will of John Woodey. [Arch. 15 B.]

Joseph, came in the Mary and John March 26, 1634-5; settled at Salem. Propr.;

POPE, cont.
husbandman; frm. May 17, 1637. Became a Quaker. Wife Gertrude adm. chh. 4 (1) 1649; ch. Damaris bapt. 22 (2) 1643, (m. Joshua Buffum,) Hannah bapt. 20 (5) 1645, Hannah bapt. 26 (1) 1648, (m. Caleb Buffum,) George bapt. 8 (5) 1649, Joseph bapt. 27 (8) 1650, Benjamin bapt. 17 (2) 1653, Enos, Samuel bapt. 18 (3) 1656.

All these are mentioned in his will, dated Sept. 11, 1666. He requested his bros. George, Richard and Joseph Gardner and his cousin, Samuel Shattok the elder to be overseers of the will. Lieut. George Gardner deposed 27 (4) 1667.

Thomas, cooper, Plymouth, taxed in 1632; house-lot granted in 1636; volunteer in the Pequot war in 1637; constable, 1645; propr. at Plymouth and Dartmouth. Gave receipt to George Bonum 30 Oct. 1652. Rem. to D. about 1674. He m. July 28, 1637, Ann, dau. of Gabriel Fallowell; he m. 2, May 29, 1646, Sarah, dau. of John Jenney. Ch. Hannah b. in 1639, (m. Joseph Bartlett,) Seth b. Jan. 13, 1648, Susanna b. in 1649, (m. Jacob Mitchell,) Thomas b. March 25, 1651, Sarah b. Feb. 14, 1652, (m. 1, Samuel Hinckley, 2, Thomas Huckins,) John b. March 15, 1653, d. July, 1675, Joanna b. about 1657, (m. John Hathaway,) Isaac.

Will dated July 9, 1683; aged. Beq. to son Seth and grandson Thomas; to gr. son Jacob Mitchell, dau. Deborah Pope and other daus.; son Isaac, not yet 2 years old. Prob. Nov. 2, 1683.

Thomasin, widow, of Bristol, Eng., gave power of attorney 4 March, 1645, to Robert Knight, to collect anything due her from Richard Russell of Charlestown. [A.] It is not certain whether she had lived here. See the following.

Walter, Charlestown, propr., bought house of John Wignall, 1630. Ch. Mary m. Joseph Miller, and sold land, inherited from her father, Nov. 7, 1677.

PORMORT, PORMONT, PURMORT,
Philemon, school-master, Boston, adm. to chh. with wife Susann, 28 (6) 1634. Frm. May 6, 1635. Intreated to become scholemaster 13 (2) 1635. Propr. Sympathizing with Mrs. Hutchinson and Mr. Wheelwright, he rem. to Exeter; was dism. from the chh. 6 (11) 1638. Ret. to Bo. and was in the em-

PORMORT, etc., cont.
ploy of Valentine Hill 9 (8) 1645. [A.] Subsequently rem. to Wells, Me. His wife Susan d. 29 (10) 1642. He m. Elizabeth —. Ch. Lazarus b. 28 (12) 1635-6, Anna b. 5 (2) 1638, Pedajah b. 3 (4) 1640, Borshuah bapt. 4 (5) 1647, Mary, (m. 24 (9) 1652, Nathaniel Adams, Jr.,) Elizabeth, (m. in 1656 Samuel Norden,) Martha b. 16, bapt. 19 June, 1653.

PORTER,
Abel, having served our bro. Grubb 4 years, had a grant of land in Boston, in 1637. He was adm. chh., a singleman, 23 (11) 1640. He m. in 1642-3 Anne, widow of William Simmons; who was adm chh. 23 (2) 1643.
Will dated 15 Sept. 1685, prob. 6 May, 1686, beq. to wife Ann; sons Abel and John; dau. Abigail; dau. Low.

Edward, chandler, husbandman, came in 1636; brought children, John, ae. about 3 years, and William, ae. about a year. [E.] Settled at Roxbury. Frm. May 17, 1637; deputy, 1638-9. Bought house and land in Boston Nov. 28, 1655. Sold Rox. property in 1659. Rem. to Boston. Signature in inv. of Daniel Brewer, 1647. Wife Anna; ch. Elizabeth bapt. Dec. 25, 1637, (m. — Nash,) Hannah b. Oct. 18, 1639, (m. Fathergone Dineley,) Mary b. and d. 1642, Joseph b. 5 (3) 1644, Deborah b. April 26, 1646. He m. Rhoda, widow of John Remington and of John Gore. She sold land in Rox. 7 Dec. 1677.
His est. was appraised 3 Aug. 1677; inv. filed by widow Rhoda. His will dated 28 July, 1677, beq. to his wife and four children; servant Thomas Watts.

Elizabeth, Roxbury, m. Jan. 20, 1636, Isaac Johnson.

John, farmer, Roxbury, frm. Nov. 5, 1633. Rem. to Hingham p;ropr. 1635; deputy; town officer. Rem. to Salem about 1644. Town officer many times. Sold house and and at Hing. 15 (1) 1648. Adm. chh. 29 (2) 1649. He deposed in 1669, ae. 73 years. He testified concerning Wm. Knight, Jan. 1672-3, ae. about 85 years. [So recorded.] Rem. to Wenham. Sergeant. Wife Margaret, widow of — Odding, memb. chh. of Rox. with him. [E.] She d. and he m. 2, Mary —, who was adm. chh. Salem 5 (3)

PORTER, cont.
1644. Ch. John, Samuel, Joseph bapt. Sept. 9, 1638, Benjamin bapt. Nov. 1639, Israel bapt. Feb. 12, 1642, Mary bapt. 12 (8) 1645, Jonathan bapt. 12 (1) 1648, Sarah bapt. 3 (4) 1649.
He d. 6 Sept. 1676. Will dated 28 April, 1673, prob. 26 (7) 1676, beq. to wife Mary; sons John, Benjamin, Israel and Joseph; dau. Mary, wife of Thomas Gardner, and her 3 children; dau. Sarah; John, son of son Samuel; to Mr. Higginson and to the poor of Salem.

Nathaniel, Salem, propr., frm. April 17, 1637. Bell-ringer, 1638. Signed as witness the will of John Sanders in 1643. Mary, [his wife?] adm. chh. before 1639.

Richard, husbandman, embarked at Weymouth, Eng. before March 20, 1635. Settled at Weymouth. Frm. May 18, 1653. Ch. Ruth b. 3 (8) 1639.
Will dated 25 Dec. 1685, prob. 26 Dec. 1689, beq. to Thomas, only son of dec. son Thomas; to son John; gr. ch. Ruth Richards and Samuel Bayly; dau. Mary Bicknell.

Robert, Concord, was complained of in 1650 by the selectmen of Sudbury for burning down their woods, making tar.

Roger, husbandman, ae. 55, from Long Sutton, Hants. Eng., with daus. Joane, Susan, Mary and Rose, came in the Confidence April 11, 1638. Settled at Watertown. Frm. May 2, 1639.
He d. 3 (2) 1654, ae. about 71 years. Inv. taken 14 (2) 1654. His widow Grace d. June 3, 1662, ae. about 70 years. Her will mentions daus. Elizabeth, wife of Daniel Smith, and Martha, wife of Capt. John Sherman, and their ch., and her bro. John Coolidge.

POSMORE, see Pasmer, also Hosmer,
James, Concord. Wife Alice; ch. Stephen b. 13 (9) 1642.

POST, POAST,
Stephen, Cambridge, propr. 1634. [Rem. to Hartford?]

Richard, Lynn, Woburn, taxed, 1645. He m. Feb. 27, 1649-50, Susanna Sutton. He m. Nov. 18, 1662, Mary Tyler.

POTTER,
Anthony, Ipswich, resident, 1648. Mentioned in will of Edmund Bridges, 1660.

John, Charlestown, inhabitant 1636. John, Sudbury, propr. 1640.

Luke, yeoman, Concord, frm. March 13, 1638-9. Deacon. Wife Mary d. 3 (2) 1644; he m. 2, 19 (8) 1644, Mary Edmands. Ch. Eunice b. 2 (1) 1640, Eunice b. 2 (2) 1641, Rebecca b. and d. 1643, Luke b. 30 (3) 1646, Dorothy b. 9 (2) 1650, Bethia b. 4 Nov. 1659, Luke d. 13 Aug. 1661.
Will dated 11 June, 1695, codicil dated 15 Sept. 1697, prob. Nov. 1, 1697, beq. to wife; to son Judah Potter; daus. Unis Fry, Elizabeth Jones, — Barrett and Dorothy Brooks.

Nicholas, bricklayer, Lynn, propr. 1638. Lic. to draw wine in 1646. Wife Alice d. 28 (12) 1657, or 26 (11) 1658. He m. 2, Mary, dau. of John Gedney. Ch. Mary b. and d. 1659, Hannah bapt. 25 (1) 1661, Sarah b. 4 Oct. 1662, Mary b. 10 (9) 1663, Samuel bapt. 10 (1) 1664-5, d. 10 (1) 1665, Hannah bapt. 8 (2) 1666, Lydia bapt. 10 (12) 1666, d. 17 (7) 1668, Bethiah bapt. 12 (5) 1668, Samuel bapt. April 25, 1669, Lydia bapt. July 17, 1670.
He d. 18 (8) 1677. Will dated 10 (8) prob. 29 (9) 1677, beq. to children by his late last wife, Samuel, Benjamin, Sarah, Mary, Hannah and Bethiah; to son Robert and dau. Elizabeth Newell; father John Gedney, and bros. Bartholomew and Eleazer G.

Robert, householder, Roxbury, frm. Sept. 3, 1634. Wife Isabel; ch. Deliverance bapt. at Boston 5 (1) 1637. He was banished for alleged sympathy with Mrs. Hutchinson in 1638. Was brought back from Rhode Island in 1643 with Gorton and others, and tried for alleged heresies; was confined at Rowley. [W.] Bur. at Rox. June 17, 1653.

Vincent, gent., ae. 21, came in the Elizabeth and Ann in May, 1635. Had apprentices, John Johnson, Stephen Barrett, Henry Kenninge and William Browne, whom he placed with new masters in 1639. [L.] [See Thomas Fowle.] He was entertained to serve at the fort in Boston for one year from 13 (8) 1636, at 10 li. wages. [W.]

William, ae. 25, came in the Increase, April 15, 1635.

POTTER, cont.
William, ae. 27, with wife Frances, ae. 26, and ch. Joseph, ae. 20 weeks, came in the Abigail in July, 1635.

William, Braintree, had grant of land 30 (10) 1639, for 11 heads.

William, Watertown, propr., 1638; sold land and house 8 (9) 1645.

William, Roxbury, propr., frm. May 13, 1640. He m. June 2, 1645, Judith, widow of John Graves.
He d. 17 (11) 1653. Will beq. to wife's dau. Hannah Grave; to his bros. John and George and sister Jane, and to sister Anne's dau. the wife of John Coking, in Eng.; to the minister of Braintree; to the College; to the school of Roxbury.

POTTLE, see Hooper.

POWELL,
Michael, merchant, Dedham, propr. 1639, adm. chh. with wife Abigail 16 (2) 1642. Town clerk, deputy. Rem. to Boston. Was one of the creditors of Thomas Yeow, 17 Dec. 1651. He and Thomas Lake gave bonds to Es. Court in 1649. [Files I, 113.] Declined to accept the position of elder of the second chh. to which he, though a layman, was called, after he had preached to them sometime, unless the Court approved, 6 Sept. 1653. They disapproved, "because it tended to discourage learning," since he had neither the learning or abilities requisite for the office. [Arch. Eccl. 1.] He deposed 18 Sept. 1662, ae. 56. [Es. Files.] Ch. Elizabeth b. 10 (4) 1641, (m. 23 Aug. 1659, Richard Hollingworth,) Dorothy b. 2 (5) 1643, Michael b. 12 (8) 1645, Margaret bapt. 14 (11) 1648, ae. about 8 days, Sarah, (m. at Dedham, 3 (3) 1653, Timothy Dwight,) Mary, (m. at Boston, 27 (3) 1657, Edward Wright). The two last are not rec. as his daus.
He d. Jan. 28, 1672-3. [W.] Admin. gr. March 20, 1672-3, to his widow Abigail. Her will dated 14 March, prob. 28 April, 1677, beq. to daus. Abigail Howlett, Elizabeth Hollingsworth, Dorothy Perry and Margaret Howard; to Samuel Howlett and others. Inv. filed 28 April, 1677, by sons Anthony Hayward and Seth Perry.

William, cooper, Charlestown, 1636. As tenant to Edward Payne, he sold land

POWELL, cont.

16 (5) 1642. Wife Elizabeth d. 3 (10) 1644. Ch. Mary b. 30 (2) 1637, Martha b. 29 (2) 1639, Joshua b. 15 (9) 1641, Elizabeth b. 22 (6) 1642.

William, Taunton, atba. 1643; defendant in a lawsuit in 1644.

POWER,

John, hosier, Charlestown. Wife Sarah; ch. Peter b. 4 (9) 1643. The wife sold house and land in his name 3 (10) 1645.

Nicholas, brought to Boston from Rhode Island in 1643 with Gorton and others, to be tried for heresy; dismissed with an admonition. [W.]

POWNING,

Henry, Dover, frm. May 29, 1653. Rem. to Boston; recd. to chh. from D. chh. 15 (8) 1648. Wife Elizabeth; ch. Elizabeth bapt. 3 (12) 1649, Mary bapt. 5 (8) 1651, Henry b. 28 April, 1654, Hannah b. 8 April, 1656, d. 6 (5) 1657, Hannah b. and d. 1658, Sarah b. 3 Aug. 1659, Daniel b. Aug. 27, 1661, Anna (Hannah) b. Feb. 29, bapt. 6 (1) 1664.

Inv. of his est. rendered July 27, 1665, by widow Elizabeth. Land at Kittery, etc. [Reg. XVI, 228.]

Robert, Dorchester, occupant of land adjoining John Glover's land on North side of river Neponset in 1649.

POYETT,

Lucy, spinster, ae. 23, passed exam. May 10, 1637, to go to N. E.

PRATT, PRAT,

Mr. Abraham, appointed surgeon for the plantation by the Mass. Bay Co. in Eng., 5 March, 1628. Settled at Roxbury. Juryman 1630; appl. frm. Oct. 19, 1630. Was propr. at Charlestown in 1638; chirurgeon. Rem. to Cambridge; a member of the church there in Mr. Hooker's time; an experienced surgeon; was drowned with his wife on the coast of Spain 27 Oct. 1644, ae. above 60 years. Left no children. [W.]

John, Cambridge, propr. 1634, frm. May 14, 1634. Was called to account by the Gen. Court Nov. 3, 1635, for statements in his letters to England, such as that "this country was nothing but rocks, sands and marshes." Apologized. Sold lands before 1638.

John, Dorchester, adm. chh. 27 (11) 1642; frm. May 10, 1643. His dau. Elizabeth bapt. 19 (12) 1642, m. Roger Billings. Will prob. 27 (11) 1647. Beq. to wife and children. [Reg. VII, 36.] The widow Mary m. William Turner, who joined her in a deed of land formerly Mr. Pratt's, April 1, 1671.

Joshua, came in the Anne in 1623, in company with his bro. Phinehas. Settled at Plymouth. Frm. 1633; constable and messenger Jan. 1, 1633-4; juror, com. Admin. of his est. gr. 5 Oct. 1656, to widow Bathsheba.

Bathsheba, m. 29 Aug. 1667, John Dogged.

Matthew, Weymouth, frm. May 13, 1640. See account of Matthew P. and his wife Sarah, deaf and dumb, membs. chh. of Wey. [C. M.] Ch. Joseph b. 10 (6) 1667.

Phinehas, joiner, came in the Anne in 1623 to Plymouth; frm. 1633. Sold land near the high cliff in 1633-4. He m. a dau. of Godbert Godbertson, q. v. Hannah, [his dau.?] m. 18 March, 1651, William Spooner. He d. at Charlestown April 19, 1680, ae. about 90 years. [Gr. St.] Will dated 8 Jan. 1677, prob. 15 (4) 1680, beq. to wife Mary and son Joseph. His son Samuel had d. in 1679, bequeathing to bros. Joseph Pratt and John Rogers, and to his own wife and children.

Richard, Charlestown, propr. 1649; rem. to Malden. Ch. Mary b. 30 (7) 1643, Thomas b. 5 (3) 1646, Mercy b. June 15, 1650.

Thomas, residence not stated, frm. May 26, 1647.

PRAY,

Quinton, fineryman, Lynn, in the employ of the Iron Works Co. before 1646. In court, 1647. Deposed 27 (8) 1653, in the case of John Gifford vs. the I. W. Co., ae. about 53 years. Rem. to Braintree, and continued in the same business. Wife Joan; ch. Richard, [See Es. Court Rec.], John, Hannah, (m. as his second wife, Henry Neale,) Dorothy, (ae. about 16 years in 1650, m. Richard Thayer, Jr.).

He d. 17 (4) 1667. Inv. of his est. taken 21 (5) 1667, and admin. gr. to widow Joan.

PREBLE,
Abraham, Scituate, witnessed a deed in 1639; took oath of fidelity about 1644. Rem. to York in the district of Maine. He m. at Sci. Judith, dau. of Nathaniel Tilden. Ch. Nathaniel bapt. at Second chh. of Sci. April 9, 1648.
[See wills of Prebles, residing at several points in Kent, Eng., in Reg. L, 118; see Genealogy.]

PRENCE, PRINCE,
Mr. Thomas, gent., came in the Fortune in 1621 to Plymouth. Was chosen governor in 1633; re-elected repeatedly. A partner in the Trading Co. [B.] "A wellwiller to all that feared God and a terrour to the wicked." [Plym. Col. Rec.] Rem. to Eastham before 1649. Wife [Patience] d. in 1634. [B.] He m. April 1, 1635, Mary Collier. Ch. Rebecca, (m. 22 April, 1646, Edmund Freeman, Jr.,) Mercy, (m. Feb. 13, 1649, John Freeman,) Hannah, (m. Feb. 13, 1649, Nathaniel Mayo,) Jane, (m. 9 Jan. 1660, Mark Snow,) Judith, (m. 28 Dec. 1665, Isaac Barker). Other ch. named in the will.

He d. March 29, 1673, in his 73d year. Will dated 13 March, prob. 5 June, 1673, beq. to wife Mary goods that were hers before marriage; to his seven daus. Hannah Marcye, Jane Marsh, Jane, wife of Mark Snow, Mary Tracye, Sary Howes, Elizabeth Howland and Sary Howes, Elizabeth Howland and Judith Barker; to gr. ch. Theophilus Mayo and Susanna Prence, dau. of his son Thomas, deceased; to son John Freeman. Bro. Thomas Clarke to be a help to the wife.

N. B. Thomas Prince of All Saints Barking, London, carriage maker, in his will, dated 31 July, prob. 14 Aug. 1630, beq. to "my son Thomas *Prence* now in New England" a silver bowl and a seal ring of gold, to be delivered to him at his next return; also beq. to dau. Rebecca, wife of Thomas Dipple, citizen and merchant tailor, of London, etc. [Em. and W.]

PRENTICE, PRENTISS,
Henry, Cambridge, planter, propr.; also at Sudbury, 1639. Frm. May 22, 1650. Wife Elizabeth d. May 13, 1643; he m. Joane —; ch. Mary b. 25 (9) 1644, (m. Nathaniel Hancock,) Solomon, Abiah b. 22 (3) 1648, Samuel b. 3 (6) 1650, Sarah, Henry; all born and bapt. in Cambridge. [Mi.]

He d. June 9, 1654. His widow m. John Gibson; they admin. on the est. 6 (8) 1663.

Robert, Roxbury, propr. 1639.

He d. 3 (12) 1665. Admin. was gr. April 26, 1666, to Capt. Thomas Prentice. [Reg. XVI, 334.]

Capt. Thomas, yeoman, Cambridge. Wife Grace; ch. Grace, bapt. in England, and about 4 years old when her parents joined here; Thomas and Elizabeth b. 22 (11) 1649, memb chh. with Mary, John. [Mi.]

He d. July 7, 1709, ae. 89. The wife Grace d. Oct. 9, 1692.

Valentine, Roxbury, came to this land in 1631; joined the chh. in 1632; brought but one son, John; buried another at sea; lived a godly life. [E.] Wife Alice; son John adm. chh. 24 (7) 1665. An Alice d. at Concord 8 (1) 1643.

He d. in 1633. The widow m. 2, John Watson.

PRESBURY, PRESBERRY,
John, Sandwich, atba. 1643. Ch. Mary b. 10 (3) 1641.

He was bur. May 19, 1648. Katharine, [his widow?] m. July 22, 1649, Richard Chadwell of Sandwich.

PRESCOTT,
John, blacksmith, Watertown, bought house and land at Lancaster, (Nashaway,) 5 (8) 1647. Took oath of fidelity 1652. Petitioned Gen. Court 19 June, 1650. He finished his mill and began to grind corn 23 (3) 1654. [Mdx. De. III, 406.] Wife Mary. Dau. Mary m., 1648, Thomas Sawyer.

Will dated 8 (8) 1673; in old age; prob. April 4, 1682; beq. to wife, sons John, Jonathan and Jonas; to James Sawyer his gr. ch. and servant; to daus. Mary, Sarah and Lydia; to gr. ch. Martha Ruge.

PRESGRAVE,
Peter, servant to Mr. Samuel Maverick, before Gen. Court 6 (7) 1638.

PRESLAND, PRESTLAND,
Nicholas, Plymouth, engaged with Edward Winslow to saw boards in 1634. Volunteer for the Pequot war in 1637.

PRESTON,

Daniel, husbandman, Dorchester, propr., deacon, town officer. Ch. — bapt. 15 (12) 1645, Daniel bapt. 7 (8) 1649, John bapt. 14 (7) 1651, Mary, (m. 28 May, 1662, Eliezer Fawer). His wife Mary d. 5 Oct. 1695. He was bur. Nov. 12, 1707, ae. 86 or 88 years. [Chh. rec.] Admin. of his est. was gr. 18 March, 1707-8, to his son Daniel.

Edward, Boston. He gave letters of attorney 20 (9) 1645, to Hugh Williams to collect dues in England. [A.] Wife Margaret; ch. William b. 30 (11) 1651, Mary b. 1 Jan. 1653.

John, and his wife, membs. chh. of Reading, 1648.

Roger, tanner, ae. 21, came in the Elizabeth April 8, 1635. Settled at Ipswich; propr. before 1639. Wife Martha sold house and land 11 March, 1657-8. He leased the Em. Downing farm of George Norton in 1659. [Es. Files XI.] His widow m. 2, Nicholas Holt. She deposed in 1666, ae. about 44. [Es. Files XI, 106.] Ch. Thomas and Samuel.

William, ae. 44, with wife Marie, ae. 34, and children Elizabeth, ae. 11, Sarah, ae. 8, Marie, ae. 6, and John, ae. 3, came in the Truelove in Sept. 1635. Settled at Dorchester. Propr. 18 Feb. 1635. Sold before 1639. Rem. to New Haven. [Reg. XXXIII, 421.]

PRICE,

David, Dorchester, propr. 1635, frm. Dec. 7, 1636.

John, Duxbury, hired with Stephen Tracy for 4 months, June, 1638. [Plym. Col. Rec.]

Rebecca, ae. 14, came in the Abigail in July, 1635.

Richard, tailor, b. at Shrewsbury, Eng.; a man of middle stature, black hair, thin face, etc.; charged with having left Jo: Pickering of Piscataqua, having 4 years yet to serve from 25 April, 1639; sued at law 5 (7) 1640. [L.] Merchant, Boston, frm. Oct. 19, 1644. Sold land Sept. 16, 1669, reserving remainder for wife Elizabeth and their children. Made will at the island of Nevis 16 April, 1674, prob. at Boston 31 July, 1674; beq. to wife Elizabeth; ch. Thomas, Jolliffe, Elizabeth and Richard.

Walter, shop-keeper, Salem. He admin. on the est. of his servant John Watkins in 1641; propr.; frm. Dec. 27, 1642; juryman, town officer. He deposed in 1658, ae. about 45 years. Was one of the purchasers of Noddle's Island in 1659. Owned largely in vessels and lands. Wife Elizabeth adm. chh. with him 6 (1) 1642, deposed in 1668, ae. about 51 years. Ch. Eliza bapt. 13 (1) 1641, Theodore bapt. 30 (9) 1643, John bapt. 18 (11) 1645, Hannah bapt. 30 (11) 1647, William bapt. 24 (1) 1649-50, Samuel bapt. 12 (1) 1653-4, Walter bapt. 16 (1) 1656. Will dated 21 May, prob. 1 (5) 1674, beq. to wife Elizabeth; sons William and John; daus. Elizabeth Rucke, Hannah Veren, Anne Bradstreet; gr. ch. Elizabeth and Anne Price, Elizabeth, John and Hannah Croad; bro. William Gerrish and Capt. Thomas Lothrop overseers.

Capt. Hugh, came to Plymouth; was prop. for frm. 1 March, 1640-1, but did not remain. Re s. a while at Cape Ann, (Gloucester.) Rem. to Roxbury about 1642. Frm. May 18, 1642; deputy 1643 and 1647. One of the chief in the town. [W.] Wife Elinor; ch. Abiel or Abigail bapt. 26 (10) 1641, Zebadiah b. and d. 1643, Phebe bapt. 20 (8) 1644, an infant b. and d. 1649, Mary —, a servant of his, was bur. Jan. 10, 1643. Ret. to Broughton, co. Denbigh, Wales; sold (by his attorneys) his property at Rox. June 8, 1656.

Richard, shoemaker, Yarmouth, prop. frm. March, 1642-3, adm. frm. 5 June, 1644. Propr. Bought house and land at Charlestown 12 (12) 1652, and rem. thither. Was recd. to chh. with wife Anne and dau. Templar, by dism. from the ch'h. of Y. 29 (5) 1660. Will dated 22 Jan. 1668, prob. 20 (2) 1669, beq. to wife Margerie; to gr. ch. Hannah, wife of Alexander Stewart, and her ch. James and John; gr. ch. James, and Samuel Templar; Richard Taylor and his ch. Richard and Ann; to dau. Hannah, wife of Richard Templar, and her children. Receipts for their portions were given by Alexander Stewart, son of Ane Templar; John Chamberlin, husband of Deborah T., in behalf of his wife and her bro. Samuel T. [Ply. and Es. Prob.]

PRICE, cont.

Roger, Springfield, propr. 1643; frm. April 13, 1648. Town officer. His wife Frances was bur. 9 (1) 1651. Alice, of Spr. was m. 18 (12) 1644, to William Bradley of New Haven. Nathaniel, also of Spr., m. 12 (4) 1651, Hannah Lanckton.

William, Ipswich, witness in 1640; propr. Bought house and land at Topsfield in 1660. Rem. to Brookfield or Quaboag. Had a mill. Sold Ips. land 10 Nov. 1673. Sergeant.

Was killed by the Indians, with his son Samuel, Aug. 3, 1675. Inv. filed at Ips. 27 (1) 1677, by son William. Est. divided to widow and 8 children, who were John, William, Joseph, (b. March 1, 1658,) Elizabeth, Sarah, b. Jan. 22, 1662,) Mary, Hannah and Esther.

PRIDE,

John, Salem, propr. 1636. Suit in Es. Court in 1636.

Admin. of his est. gr. and inv. filed (10) 1647.

PRIEST,

Degory, of London, adm. frm. of Leyden, Holland, Nov. 16, 1615; m. in Leyden, Nov. 4, 1611, Sarah, dau. of John Vincent of London, Mr. Allerton's sister. Came in the Mayflower; signed the Compact; settled at Plymouth, but died Jan. 1, 1620-1. His wife and children came to Plym. at a later time. Mary and Sarah recd. shares in the cattle in 1627. [B. and Col. Rec.]

James, Dorchester, propr. 1637, frm. May 10, 1643. Rem. to Weymouth; child James b. 8 (3) 1640.

His will dated 4 March, 1675, prob. 28 April, 1676, beq. to wife and son-in-law Sidrach Thayer. Inv. mentions a debt due from his son-in-law Henry Turbifield. The widow, in will dated at Boston 24 May, 1676, beq. to son Joseph Priest and his son James; to daus. Hannah Rust, Elizabeth Hollice, Deliverance Thare and Mary Turbifield; to son-in-law Richard Rust; to Sarah Bagley or Bayley, whom she had brought up from a child.

PRIME,

Mark, Rowley, propr. before 1650. Town officer. Res. 1672. Wife Ann; ch. Samuel b. 14 (6) 1649, Mary bur. 6 (11) 1653. He was bur. 21 Dec. 1683. Will signed but not dated, prob. April 15, 1684, beq. to son Samuel, his wife Sara and their children. Samuel died soon and the two estates were settled upon his widow Sarah and her ch, Samuel, Sarah, Marke and Ann.

PRINCE, see also Prence,

John, Cambridge, propr. 1634, frm. March 4, 1634-5. Rem. to Hingham; propr. 1635. Rem. to Hull; propr. 1642; town officer; ruling elder. He m. at Watertown, May, 1637, Alice Honor; she died, and he m. Anna, widow of William Barstow. Ch. all bapt. at Hingham: John bapt. May 16, 1638, Elizabeth bapt. Aug. 9, 1640, (m. Josiah Loring,) Joseph bapt. Feb. 26, 1642, Martha bapt. Aug. 1645, Job bapt. Aug. 2, 1647, Samuel bapt. Aug. 19, 1649, Benjamin bapt. April 25, 1652, Isaac bapt. July 9, 1654, Thomas bapt. Aug. 8, 1658.

He d. 16 Aug. 1676, in his 66th year. Will dated 9 May, prob. Oct. 18, 1676, beq. to wife Anne; ch. John, Joseph, Elizabeth, (wife to Josiah,) Martha, (wife to Christopher Wheaton,) Job, Samuel, Isaac and Thomas.

John, Hingham, propr., town officer. Wife Margaret, ch. Mary b. 8 (2) 1649, (m. Joseph Joy,) Sarah b. Feb. 22, 1652, d. 21 (3) 1653, Sarah, (m. Thomas Sayer,) Deborah b. Aug. 23, 1657, (m. Wm. King).

His will dated June 10, 1689, prob. Feb. 5, 1696-7, beq. to the above-named; to gr. ch. Wm. and Deborah King, Thomas Sayer and Joseph "Jay."

Richard, tailor, Salem, propr. 1638, recd. inhabitant 1639; frm. Dec. 27, 1642. Town officer many times; deacon. He deposed in 1672, ae. about 59 years. Wife Mary adm. chh. 1 (9) 1648. Ch. John bapt. 20 (12) 1641, Joseph bapt. 10 (7) 1643, (died, and beq. to bros. and sister and her children, Nov. 14, 1677;) Mary bapt. 26 (2) 1648, (m. Stephen Daniel,) Samuel bapt. 18 (3) 1651, Richard bapt. 18 (1) 1654-5, Jonathan bapt. 15 (1) 1656-7.

Will signed 21 (4) 1675, ae. about 61 years; prob. 22 (10) folg.; beq. to wife; sons Joseph, Samuel, Richard and Jonathan; dau. Mary Daniel; gr. ch. Stephen and Mary Daniel. [Es. Files XXIV, 56.]

Robert, Salem, propr. 1649. He m. 5 (2) 1662, Sarah Warren; ch. James b. and d.

PRINCE, cont.
1664, James b. 15 Aug. 1668, Elizabeth b. 19 (12) 1669.

Will prob. 30 (4) 1674, beq. to wife; to children James, Joseph, Elizabeth, and to Henry Brag.

Thomas, Wenham, propr. 1644. Rem. to Gloucester; propr.; sold certain lands before 1649. [Es. Files.] Deposed in 1659 concerning William Brown. Wife Margaret deposed in 1666, ae. about 40 years. Ch. Thomas b. 24 (10) 1650, (m. 27 (7) 1676, Elizabeth, dau. of Edward Harraden,) John b. 12 (9) 1653, Mary b. July 19, 1658, (m. 16 (7) 1675, Hugh Row,) Isaac b. Nov. 7, 1663.

He d. 17 Jan. 1690. Will dated 14 Jan. 1689, prob. 25 (1) 1690, beq. to wife Margaret; sons Thomas and Isaac; dau. Mary Rowe, and gr. ch. John Prince, Abraham Rowe and others; to cousin Abraham Patch.

PRIOR, PRYOR,
Thomas, Scituate, took oath of allegiance 1 Feb. 1638.

He was bur. June 22, 1639; will prob. Sept. 28, 1639. Son John exec.; probably the John who came in the Hopewell in Sept. 1635, ae. 16 years;) other sons Joseph and Daniel here, and Samuel and Thomas, and daus. Elizabeth and Mary in England; [Reg. IV, 36.] He was formerly of Watford, co. Herts, maulster; sons John and Daniel sold property there 28 (6) 1640. [L.] Joseph, not yet 20 years old, sued Daniel and his wife Mary 5 Nov. 1644, for his portion of the patrimony.

PROCTOR, PROCTER,
George, Dorchester, propr. 1634; frm. May 17, 1637. Wife Edith; ch. Sarah, Mary, Hannah, Abigail b. 24 (6) 1637, Thomas b. 16 (10) 163[9], Samuel b. 8 (9) 1640, (became a cooper; joined his mother in a deed of land in 1668.)

He d. 29 (11) 1661. Will dated 27 Jan., prob. 27 Feb., beq. to wife Edith; son Samuel; daus. Sarah, Mary, Hannah and Abigail. [Reg. IX, 173.]

John, husbandman, ae. 40, with Martha, ae. 28, John, ae. 3, and Marie, ae. 1 year, came in the Susan and Ellen in April, 1635. Settled at Ipswich; propr. 1635; bought additional land in 1647. Rem. to Salem. He deposed in 1667, ae. 75 years; mentioned bro. Giddens.

PROCTOR, etc., cont.
Will dated 18 Aug., prob. 28 (9) 1672; aged and infirm; beq. to wife Martha the house that was George Stevenson's; to four daus., Martha White, Abigail Varney, Sara Dodge and Hanna Weeden; to three sons, John, Joseph and Benjamin Proctor; to gr. ch. John and Martha Hadley. Benjamin deposed in 1668, ae. about 17 years. Testimony was given 17 Oct. 1672, that he gave his wife's clothing to his daus. and Martha Hadley; and gave a pair of oxen to son James White.

Robert, Salem, frm. May 10, 1643. Seems to be the Robert, of Concord, who m. 31 (10) 1645, Jane Hildreth; had ch. Sarah b. 12 (8) 1646, Gershom b. 13 (3) 1648, and Mary b. 8 (2) 1650. Rem. to Chelmsford.

His will, dated 10 March, 1695-6, prob. July 13, 1697, beq. to wife Jane; sons Gershom, Peter, James, John, Samuel, Israel and Thomas, (if he live and return from sea to N. E.;) daus. Dorothy Barrett and Elizabeth Proctor.

PROUT,
Timothy, ship-carpenter, mariner, Boston, adm. chh. 20 (2) 1644, frm. May 29, 1644. He deposed in 1661, ae. about 40; was at Barbadoes the last summer. Wife Margaret adm. chh. 2 (3) 1646; ch. Timothy b. 10 (1) 1645, Susanna b. 26 (2) 1647, John bapt. 11 (12) 1648, ae. about 8 days, Joseph bapt. 9 (2) 1650, William b. 23 May, 1653, Benjamin b. 6 July, 1655, Ebenezer b. 14 March, 1656, d. 5 April, 1659. The wife Margaret d. 29 Oct. 1685. Elizabeth, wife of T. P., d. Jan. 19, 1693-4, in her 57th year. [Copp's Hill Epitaphs.]

He d. Nov. 3, 1702, ae. above 80 years. [S.] Will dated 7 March, 1699, prob. 17 Dec. 1702, beq. to sons John, Joseph, Ebenezer and Timothy, (if alive and shall return,) cousin Mary Jackson; to grand and great grand children.

PROWER,
Salamon, servant of Christopher Martin, came in the Mayflower to Plymouth; died not long after arriving. [B.]

PRUDDEN,
Rev. Peter, came from Eng., July 26, 1637, with 15 or more associates. Dedham offered them lands 11 (6) 1637, but they declined them. He went with Mr. Davenport and Mr. Eaton (by water) to Quineplack 30 (1) 1638. [W. and Reg. XI, 238.]

PUFFER, see Poffer.

PURCHASE, PURCHAS, PURCHIS, PURCHES,
Oliver, of Dorchester, Eng., came in 1633 to our Dorchester. He died soon, as a grant of land was given to his widow in 1633. His son Oliver came with him; res. first at Dorch., then rem. to Taunton; later to Lynn, and finally to Concord; was frm. Dec. 7, 1636; deposed at Lynn in 1665, ae. about 48 years. His dau. Joan, b. about 1578, m. in Eng., Whit Monday, 1696, Bernard Capen, and came with him to Dorch. in 1633. The widow seems to be the person who m. ruling elder Thomas Oliver, of Boston, as his second wife, about 1642; and his dau.-in-law Sarah Purchase, adm. chh. Boston 31 (3) 1646, her child.

Mr. Thomas, gent., came at an early day to Maine. He sold to Gov. John Winthrop and the Mass. Bay Co. 22 (5) 1639 a tract of land at Pagiscot 4 miles square, with provision for their jurisdiction. He sued certain men for taking from his premises at P. some moose skins that belonged to Abacodusset, an Indian sagamore, May 31, 1641. [L.] He rem. to Lynn. Sold three-eighths of the Blessing to Valentine Hill 29 (8) 1644. [A.] His wife Mary d. at Boston 7 (11) 1655.

He d. May 11, 1678, ae. 101 years; will dated 2 May, 1677, prob. 25 (5) 1678. Widow Elizabeth and five children; had lost most of his est. at the Eastward. Widow and son Thomas execrs.. Friends Mr. Henry Jocelin, cousins Oliver Purchase of Hammersmith, and Edward Alline of Boston overseers.

William, a witness to deed of Wm. Potter of Watertown 8 (10) 1645.

PURRIER, see Perry,
William, Ipswich, propr. 1638; Salisbury, 1639.

PURTON,
Elizabeth, widow, adm. chh. Boston (9) 1633.
Will prob. 29 (2) 1650; son John, heir; feather bed to Mr. John Cotton in case son John should die; Bible to Robert Blott; rest to the church. [Reg. VII, 233.]

PUTNAM,
John, formerly of Abbotsason in Buckinghamshire, England, [town record,] came early to Salem. Planter, yeoman. Had grants of land in 1640 and onward; was adm. chh. 4 (2) 1647. His wife Priscilla was adm. chh. 21 (1) 1640-1. His sons John, Nathaniel and Thomas came also to Salem, and were enterprising citizens. John (who deposed March 30, 1685, ae. about 68 years,) m. 3 (7) 1652, Rebecca Prince; Nathaniel (who deposed 30 (1) 1685, ae. about 65 years, that he had lived 46 yrs. in Salem,) m. Elizabeth, dau. of Richard Hutchinson; Thomas m. 1, 17 (8) 1643, Ann, dau. of Mr. Edward and Prudence Holyoke, who d. 1 (7) 1665; he m. 2, 14 (9) 1666, Mary Wren, widow. [Salem town rec.] He deeded lands to his son John, referring to lands given to son Nathaniel, 3 (1) 1653, and to the bounds of his brothers. Other deeds in 1662.

He d. 30 (10) 1662.

PUTTELL,

PYCE,
Alice, maid servant to Judith Quinsey, adm. chh. Boston 4 (7) 1636.

PYFORD, see Byford.

PYNCHON, PINCHON, PINCHIN, PYNSON, see Pinson,
Mr. William, Esquire, came in the Arbella in 1630. Assistant. Settled first at Dorchester; sold house in 1634; res. at Roxbury till he had arranged for the beginning of the plantation at Agawam, (Springfield,) for which the Gen. Court made him chief commissioner 3 March, 1635-6. Bought lands of the Indians. See agreement of the first settlers in article on Mr. Pynchon in Reg. XIII, 289. Frm. Aug. 2, 1642. He was the leader in the new settlement. Wrote a book on Justification, printed in 1650, which recd. severe criticism from the most prominent ministers and statesmen of the Colony. He ret. to England in 1662, and died there. His wife d. soon after he landed, and he m. Mrs. Frances Sanford of Dorchester. His son John, b. in Eng., became a very influential man, whose stamp is left on the history of the Conn. Valley for the remainder of the century. Valuable papers of his in Mass. Hist. Coll. 2-8.

PYE,
George, a More, with Mr. Cradock; the Court decided 5 June, 1638, that advice must be had from Rye about his case.

PYKE, see Pike,
Tabitha, maid servant of Richard Bellingham, adm. chh. Boston 1 (9) 1640.

PYNE, see Pin.

QUICK,
Anne, sold house and garden in Charlton (Charlestown,) late the property of Will: Studson, 23 (10) 1640.

John, Lynn, propr. 1638.

William, seaman, Charlestown, 1638. Was in the Narragansett country in 1638. [Mass. Hist. 37, 323.] Sold house and land 26 (11) 1643.

QUILTER,
Mark, planter, Ipswich, propr. 1636. His wife Frances deposed concerning his sickness, etc. [Es. Files 4, 127.]

He made will Feb. 7, 1653, prob. 28 March, 1654; to wife, sons Mark and Joseph, daus. Mary, Rebecca and Sarah. Widow Thamar Q. deposed in 1661 regarding the sickness of her only son Joseph Q. She d. July 2, 1694.

QUINSEY, QUINSYE, QUINCY,
Mr. Edmund, Boston, adm. chh. with wife Judith (9) 1633; frm. and deputy March 4, 1634. Memb. of com. to assess rates 10 (9) 1634. The town voted that his lands and those of Wm. Coddington at Mt. Wollaston, (Braintree,) should be bounded out, 14 (10) 1625. Memb. of com. to lay out others' lands there 4 (11) 1635-6. Ch. Edmund, a prominent citizen of Braintree, d. 7 Jan. 1697-8, in his 68th year. [Hob.]

He d. before April 9, 1639, when Judith Q.'s lands are referred to in deed of adjacent tract. The widow m. Moses Paine, and was dism. to chh. of Br. from Bo. chh. 30 (1) 1645.

See wills of Anne Quinsie, of Lillford, and John Quincey, of Widgthorpe, co. Northampton, Eng., in Reg. XLVII, 525. Genealogy.

QUODNAM, see Codman,
Robert, brought suit in Es. Court in 1638. Perhaps it was his—"Quodnam's"—pinnace by which Mr. William Pynchon sent a letter from Springfield to Gov. Winthrop in 1645.

QUOTMORE, see Coytmore.

RABEY, RABBE,
Katharine, of Yarmouth, Eng., ae. 68, a waterman's widow, passed exam. April 12, 1637, to go to N. E. to remain with her son. She settled at Salem; was adm. chh. 2 (5) 1641.

RAINBOROW, RAYNBOROWE, RAINSBOROUGH,
William, merchant, Charlestown, 1639, mortg. house and 10 acres of land in Watertown which had been the home of Robert Feakes, 17 (10) 1640. [Suff. De. and L.]

He ret. to Eng. 1644; became colonel of a regiment in Cromwell's army, having Israel Stoughton as Lt. col., Nehemiah Bourne a major, John Leverett a captain, and Wm. Hudson an ensign.

RAINSFORD, RAYNESFORD,
Edward, merchant, Boston, memb. chh. 1630; res. at Dorchester before 1632, but ret. to Bo. Frm. April 17, 1637. He deposed to the will of Rich. Truesdell 29 (10) 1671, ae. about 60 years. Edward, passenger in the Abigail in July, 1635, is probably this man returning from a visit to Eng. Wife — d. (4) 1632. His second wife, Elizabeth, adm. chh. Bo. 15 (10) 1633; ch. Josiah or Joshua and Mary bapt. 17 (4) 1632, J. d. (7) 1632, John b. 30 (4) 1634, Jonathan b. (8) 1636, Ranis b. 4 (4) 1638, (m. Josias Belcher,) Nathan b. (6) 1641, David b. (7) 1644, Solomon bapt. 25 (8) 1646, Elizabeth bapt. 25 (12) 1648, Hannah bapt. 12 (11) 1650, Anna b. 1 (12) 1651, bapt. 8 (12) 1651 or 1652, Edward bapt. 15 (8) 1654.

His will dated 3 Aug., prob. 28 Aug. 1680, beq. to wife Elizabeth; to dau. Mary Parcyfull; to the ch. of son Jonathan R., dec., viz.: Jonathan, Dorothy and Mary; to sons John, Solomon, David, and Nathan R.; to daus. Reanus Belcher, Elizabeth Greenough and Anna Hough. Raynsford's island and other lands, vessels, etc., mentioned in inventory.

John, Lynn, juryman, 1638. He deposed 30 (4) 1657, ae. about 55 years, that about 25

RAINSFORD, etc., cont.
years before he was servant to Capt. Torner, who, with other men, fenced in Nahant, and kept cattle there in common.

RAMSDEN, RAMESDEN, RAMSDELL,
Joseph, Plymouth, planted a piece of land on shares in 1641; atba. 1643. He m. 2 March, 1645, Rachel Eaton; she deposed in 1648, ae. about 23 years. He m. 16 Oct. 1661, Mary Savory, of Plymouth. Ch. Daniel b. 14 Sept. 1649.

RAND, RANDE,
James, Plymouth, came in 1623.

Robert, husbandman, Charlestown, 1635, rem. to Lynn; he recd. a beq. from Robert Keayne, his former employer. Wife Alice adm. chh. 8 (11) 1635; ch. Margery, adm. chh. 9 (10) 1643, Thomas, Susanna, Alice, Nathaniel bapt. 3 (9) 1636, Elizabeth bapt. (11) 1639, Hannah, dau. of Robert, b. at Salem (4) 1657.

His widow, Alice, d., and her will, dated 22 (6) 1663, was prob. Aug. 17, 1691; beq. to sons Nathaniel and Thomas; gr. ch. John, Edmund, Samuel, Thomas, and the 4 daus. of her son Thomas.

RANDALL, RANDOLL,
—, of Mt. Wollaston, one of those banished in 1638 for supporting Mrs. Hutchinson's party.
C. A. S.,

Philip, Dorcheste:, 1633; frm. May 14, 1634. Rem. to Windsor. Was bur. 26 Sept. 1648. Ch. Philura, (m. George Phelps,) and Abraham.

Robert, formerly of Wendover, as he deposed, b. about 1606. [Mass. Arch. 125, 16,] settled at Weymouth; wife Mary bur. 3 (7) 1640. He m. 2, —; ch. Mary b. 20 (1) 1642.

He d. 3 May, 1691; inv. taken 16 May. John Randall exec.

His will dated 27 March, prob. 25 May, 1691, beq. to ch. John, Thomas, Mary, now wife to Abraham Staple of Mendon, Hannah, now wife to John Warfield of same.

William, Scituate, suit in court, 1641, atba. 1643, Marshfield, propr. 1645, frm. 6 June, 1654. His wife Elizabeth was legatee in the will of Michael Barstow. Ch. Sarah bapt. with two folg. Nov. 23, 1645, Joseph b. March, 1642, Hannah b. March, 1644, William

RANDALL, etc., cont.
b. Dec. 1647, John b. April, 1650, Elizabeth b. Oct. 1652, Job b. 8 Feb. 1654-5, Benjamin bapt. Nov. 8, 1659, Isaac bapt. Jan. 9, 1658.

He d. Widow Elizabeth d. at Wat. Dec. 24, 1672, ae. about 80.

William, Newbury. He deposed in 1661, ae. about 40 years. He m. 4 Oct. 1649, Elizabeth —. Ch. Elizabeth b. 13 May, 1650, William b. 2 March, 1653, John b. and d. 1655, Mary b. 26 March, 1656, Hannah b. 7 Jan. 1658.

RANDOLPH, see Fitz Randolph.

RASDELL,
Mr., a partner of Capt. Wollaston in the colony at the Mount about 1623. Went to Virginia. [B.]

RASHLEY,
Henry, Boston, had accts. with Capt. Hawkins, and was in his employ 22 (10) 1645. [A.] Bought house and land Nov. 28, 1648. His wife Susanna recd. from the Gen. Court title to his land 14 Oct. 1651, as he had departed long since and was never heard of. [Arch. 15 B.]

Rev. Thomas, Boston, adm. chh. 8 (1) 1640, as "a studyent." Ch. John bapt. 18 (3) 1645, ae. about 6 weeks. He was "chaplain" at Cape Anne in 1642. [L., P. D.] Rem. to Exeter where he was minister about 1643. [Mass. Hist. Coll. 4-7.]

RATCLIFFE, RATLIFFE,
Philip, Salem, was ordered to be punished for malicious and scandalous speeches against the government and the chh. of S. June 14, 1631. Capt. Roger Clap writes that he saw the sentence carried out by whipping and cutting off his ears. Such punishments were common in Europe at that period.

RAWLINGS, RAWLEN, RALLENES, ROLLINS,
James, Newbury, propr. 1637, 1638; frm. May 14, 1634.

Jasper, brickmaker, Roxbury, frm. Sept. 3, 1634. Rem. to Boston. His wife Jane came in the Increase in April, 1635. He m. 2, June 8, 1651, Mary, widow of Thomas Griggs.

RAWLINGS, etc., cont.
He d. in 1665. Will dated 17 (11) prob. 18 (4) 1665, gave all to wife Mary; he gives a house-lot to any of his children who may come over to settle here.

Richard, plasterer, Boston, adm. chh. 18 (1) 1643; frm. May 10, 1643. Wife Mary adm. chh. 8 (8) 1642.

Thomas, Sen., carpenter, planter, Roxbury, came with the first company, 1630; he brought 5 children, Thomas, Mary, Joane, Nathaniel and John. He rem. to Scituate; his wife Mary, after great suffering, d. there about 1639. [E.] Propr., frm. May 18, 1631. He rem. to Boston. Emm, wife of Thomas R. d. at Bo. 27 (10) 1655. He m. 2 (3) 1656, Sarah Maddox. His dau. Joane m. at Sci. Jan. 28, 1645-6, Ephraim Kempton. Mary m. April, 1639, William Parker. Thomas, fisherman, seaman, of Weymouth and Boston, who deposed April 12, 1641, ae. about 32 years, appears to be the son of the above. He d. 15 March, 1660; will prob. April 4, 1660. Wife Sarah; sons Thomas and Nathaniel. House and land in Bo. and farm at Sci. [Reg. IX, 226.]

RAWLINSON, see Rowlandson.

RAWSON,
Edward, gent., son of David R., citizen and merchant tailor of London, b. in Gillingham, Eng., April 16, 1615. [Genealogy.] He deposed May 4, 1687, ae. about 55 years. [Suff. De. VI, 174.] Came to Newbury about 1637; town clerk, deputy, clerk of the court. Rem. to Boston in 1650, being chosen secretary of the Colony. An efficient official and important citizen. He m. Rachel, dau. of Richard and Rachel Perne, of Gillingham, gent.; ch. b. at Newb.: [Edward, Rachel,] David b. 6 May, 1644, Perne b. Sept. 16, 1646; b. in Boston: William b. May 21, 1651, Hannah bapt. 10 (8) 1653, d. 27 (3) 1656; Rebecca b. Oct. 19, 1654, Rebecca b. May 21, 1656, (m. an imposter; went with him to Eng. and was lost on the ret. voyage;) Elizabeth b. Nov. 12, 1657, Grindall bapt. 30 (11) 1658, John bapt. 14 (5) 1661.
He d. Aug. 27, 1693. Admin. gr. 4 Jan. 1693-4, to son William. Warrant to distribute est. April 6, 1695; partial acct. Jan. 14, 1722. Genealogy. [Reg. III, 201, and XXXVIII, 308.]

RAVENSDALE,
John, residence not stated, frm. May 6, 1635.

RAY, RAYES, REA, REY, WRAY,
Daniel, bought house in Plymouth in 1630. Rem. to Salem before Feb. 6, 1631; so Bradford says in letter to Winthrop; [Reg. II, 240.] Frm. May 14, 1634; propr. 1636; town officer. [Dau.] Bethia memb. chh. 1637.
Agreement made between his heirs 26 (4) 1662, in accordance with a will he began but did not finish. Son Joshua and his son Daniel; daus. Rebecca and Sarah, under age; son Thomas Lothrop and his wife.

Simon, Braintree.
He d. 30 (7) 1641. Inv. taken Feb. 20, 1641.

RAYMOND, RAYMENT,
Richard, mariner, Salem, frm. May 14, 1634; propr. 1636; town officer. Bro. R. and his wife dism. to chh. of Seabrook in 1662. He deeded land in 1668 to his son-in-law Oliver Mannering. [Es. De. III, 44.] [Wife] Judith memb. chh. 1636. Ch. Barsheba bapt. 11 (5) 1636, Joshua bapt. 3 (1) 1639, Lemuel bapt. 3 (11) 1640, Hannah bapt. 12 (12) 1642, Samuel bapt. 13 (5) 1645, Richard bapt. 2 (11) 1647, Eliza bapt. 28 (2) 1650, Daniel bapt. 17 (2) 1653.

REYNOR, RAYNER, RAYNOR, REYNER,
Humphrey, Rowley, bro. of Mr. John, frm. May 18, 1642, deputy 1649; ruling elder. Ch. dau. Ann, (m. 12 (9) 1652, William Hobson;) Jachin, (m. Nov. 12, 1662, Elizabeth Denison).
He was bur. 14 Sept. 1660. Will dated 10 Sept. 1660, mentions daus. Whipple and Hobson; son Wigglesworth; gr. ch. Humphrey, John and William H., and Mary W.

Rev. John, b. at Gildersome, co. York, came in 1635 or 1636 to Plymouth. Was chosen teacher; lands granted him Feb. 6, 1636. Frm. 6 March, 1637-8. Wrote a letter on Moral Laws in 1642. [B.] Was called to be pastor at Dover, N. H. and rem. thither. He m. 1st a dau. of — Boyes; he m. 2, Frances Clarke, who had been a maid servant in the family of Rev. John Wilson, and was dism. to the chh. of Plym. 18 (7) 1642. Ch. Jachin, Anna, (m. Job Lane,) John, Eliz-

379

REYNOR, etc., cont.
abeth, Dorothy, Abigail, Judith, a dau. b. 26 Dec. 1647, Joseph b. 15 Aug. 1650, d. 3 Nov. 1652.

Mr. John Reynor, teacher of Dover church, d. 21 (2) 1669; Mr. J. R. pastor of do. d. 21 (10) 1676. [S.] [See Lane Family Papers in Reg. XI, and B.]

Thurston, ae. 40, with wife Elizabeth, ae. 36, and children Thurston, ae. 13, Joseph, ae. 11, Elizabeth, ae. 9, Edward, ae. 10, and Lydia, ae. 1, came in the Elizabeth of Ipswich April 30, 1635. Settled at Watertown. Propr. 1642. Rem. to Wethersfield, Conn.

READ, READE, REED, REEDE, REID, etc.,
Benjamin, Duxbury ,atba. 1643.

Esdras, (Ezra,) tailor, Boston, 1638, frm. June 2, 1641. Of Salem, propr. 1638; adm. chh. 10 (3) 1640; [wife] Alice adm. chh. 29 (10) 1640. Deputy 1648. Had grant of land at Wenham, 1643; juryman, deacon. Rem. to Chelmsford in 1655 Adm. inhabitant of Boston again in 1658.
Admin. on his est. was gr. 17 Dec. 1680, to his son Obediah of Boston.

John, Rehoboth, innkeeper, 1649, prop. frm. 4 June, 1650. Town officer.
Admin. of his est. was gr. to widow Rachel and Thomas R. 7 June, 1676.

Goodman, Scituate, atba. 1643. Ch. Israel bapt. at Dorchester 31 (5) 1642; "his father sent him by his mother from Scituate whereof himselfe was member." [Dorch. Chh. Rec.]

John, of Weymouth, planter, took a 10 years lease of Capt. Tyng's farm at Mt. Wollaston 14 (2) 1639. [L.] Frm. May 13, 1640. Propr. Rem. to Braintree. With wife Sarah gave letters of attorney 27 (9) 1645, to receive gift to her from her father, William Lessie, of Blyborough, co. Suff. Eng. [A.] Ch. John b. 29 (6) 1640, Thomas b. 20 (9) 1641.

Matthew, Salem, servant to Charles Gott, in court, 1638.

Philip, Weymouth, propr. 1641; frm. May 30, 1660. Ch. Philip b. 24 (8) 1641.
Will dated 15 Dec. 1674, prob. 5 May, 1676, beq. to son Philip, wife Mary and son-in-

READ, etc., cont.
law John Vining. Bro. Thomas Dyer and friend Richard Porter overseers.

Robert, Boston, frm. April 17, 1644. Land gr. in Bo. 1637, having been a res. in 1635. Sealer of leather. Rem. to Exeter, N. H. Wife Hannah d. 24 (4) 1655. Second wife Susanna survived him and m. John Presson or Preston of Bo. with whom she conveyed land 11 June, 1668. Ch. Hannah, (m. John Souter,) Mary, Rebecca b. and bapt. at Bo. 29 (7) 1646, Deborah bapt. 28 (11) 1648, ae. about 3 days, Sarah bapt. 1 (7) 1650, Samuel bapt. 3 (2) 1653, d. 31 (1) 1654, Samuel b. Feb. 28, 1654.

Thomas, ("red,") apprentice of Thomas King of Watertown, with 2 years time unexpired 24 (10) 1644. [King's Inventory.] Thomas and Mary had dau. Elizabeth d. in Boston March 28, 1658, and son Thomas d. 11 May, 1661. Widow Mary m. 14 Aug. 1660, Thomas Matson.

Thomas, Salem, propr., juror at Gen. Court Sept. 28, 1630; frm. April 1, 1634. Ensign, 1636. [Wife] Sarah adm. chh. 7 (12) 1640; second wife Mary. Ch., two bapt. 31 (3) 1640, Aaron bapt. 18 (1) 1648-9, Susanna bapt. 23 (7) 1649, John b. 1651, d. 1662, Mary bapt. 10 (2) 1653, Eliza bapt. 13 (3) 1655, Remember bapt. 26 (2) 1657, Sarah bapt. 15 (1) 1659-60, Jacob b. 1662, d. 1663, Jacob bapt. 7 (9) 1663, Sarah bapt. 19 (6) 1666.
Admin. of his est. 25 (4) 1667. Children by the first wife 4 sons and 1 dau.; by his second wife 7 ch.: 2 sons about 20 and 4; 5 daus. ae. 17, 14, 12, 10, and 1½ years.

William, ae. 48, with Mabel, ae. 30, and George, ae. 6, Ralph, ae. 5, and Justice, ae. 18 months, came in the Defence in July, 1635. Settled in Boston; frm. Sept. 2. 1635. He bought of Nicholas Davis, of Charlestown, his house and 60 acres of land at Wooborne 7 (5) 1648, and removed thither.
His will dated 9 April, was prob. in London 31 Oct. 1656; recorded at Charlestown. Admin. gr. to widow Mabel. He beq. to wife; to the four youngest ch.; to his three ch. that are married in N. E. viz. George, Ralph and Michael (sic;) Money due him frcm Wm. Brenton and others. [Reg. XVIII, 381.] The widow m. Henry Summers.

William, of Batcome, tailor, ae. 28,

READ, etc., cont.
with wife Susan, ae. 29, ch. Hannah, ae. 3, Susan, ae. 1, and his servant Richard Adams, ae. 29, and his wife and child, came from Weymouth, Eng. before March 20, 1635. Settled at Weymouth. Deputy, 1636. Town officer. Frm. March 14, 1638-9. Rem. to Boston in 1646; bought land, etc. Adm. chh. with wife Susanna 15 (3) 1647. She d. 12 (8) 1653, and he m. 20 (1) 1654, Ruth Crooke. Ch. William b. 15 (10) 1639, Esther b. 8 (3) 1641, John b. 25 (7) bapt. at Bo. 27 (7) 1646, William b. Feb. 3, 1654-5, Isaac b. April 18, 1656, Hannah d. 25 (9) 1656, Susanna m. Dec. 13, 1659, Samuel Smith, Isaac b. April 18, 1656, Ephraim b. Nov. 23, 1657, (bapt. as ch. of "Ephraim of Wey.,") Jonathan b. and d. 1659, Timothy b. Aug. 11, 1660, William b. May 7, 1662, Hezekiah b. July 6, 1663, Sarah b. June 26, 1665, Elizabeth b. Dec. 22, 1666, Elizabeth b. April 22, 1669, *John* (of Wm. and Hannah,) bapt. 25 (2) 1669.

Admin. of his est. gr. 28 Nov. 1667, to John Wiswall, Jr.

REAPS, see Ropes.

RECROFT, RICROFT,
Frances, widow, sister of Matthew Cushing's wife, came with him to Hingham in 1638. [See Ward, Samuel.]

RECKSWELL,
John, Lynn, witness at court in 1649.

REDAWAY, RUDWAY,
James, Rehoboth, propr. 1646. Town officer 1653; juror. Ch. John b. Dec. 10, 1644, Mary b. May 27, 1646, Martha b. March 15, 1648, James b. last of March, 1650, Liddia b. May 30, 1652, Rebecka b. middle of Feb. 1654. Son James was bur. Oct. 1676. Admin. gr. 6 March, 1676-7, to his bro. John, who was allowed a double portion; his 3 sisters to have the rest.

James, Sen. was bur. March 31, 1684. Will dated 26 July, 1677, being aged, prob. June 18, 1684, beq. to daus. Sarah, Martha and Rebecca, to David, son of Samuel Carpenter, Rebecca, dau. of Abiah C., and John, son of William C.; rest to son John R.

REDDING, READING, RIDDINGS,
Joseph, Boston, memb. chh. 1631-2; propr. at Cambridge before 1633; frm. May 14, 1634. Rem. to Ipswich; propr. 1639.
His will was brought into court 29 (1) 1681, and the widow Annice's est. was appraised 1 April, 1681.

Miles, cooper, Boston, frm. May 14, 1634. His lands referred to in a deed in 1658, as "of old in his possession."
He made will 23 Oct. prob. 6 (9) 1671. Beq. to the deacons of the First church of Boston for the poor and for the use of the church; books to goodman Dowse, Thos. Matson, Sen. and Robert Bradford.

Thomas, Plymouth (town or colony,) volunteer for the Pequot war in 1637. He m. 20 July, 1639, Ellene Penny. Placed his male child, about 5 years old, in care of Gowen White 4 June, 1645, to be brought up to the age of 21 years.

REDDINGTON,
Abraham, Topsfield, propr. 1645. His wife Margaret was dism. from chh. of Salem to that of Tops. 19 (1) 1664. He deposed in 1673, ae. 58 years. Ch. Elizabeth b. 18 Feb. 1645, Abraham b. 25 Nov. 1647, Thomas b. 25 July, 1649, Sarah b. 15 March, 1654, Isaac d. May 4, 1657, Isaac b. 27 June, 1657, Isaac bapt. 18 (5) 1658, Benjamin b. April 19, 1661.

Will dated 14 Oct. 1693, prob. Nov. 8, 1697, beq. to sons Abraham and Thomas, daus. Elizabeth Prescutt and Sarah Row and wife Margaret.

John, Salem, 1646; rem. to Topsfield. Town officer 1661. Wife [see Gould, Z.]; ch. Eliza bapt. 8 (9) 1646, John b. 20 June, 1649, Mary b. 4 May, 1651, Martha and Phebe b. 7 April, 1655, Daniel b. 17 March, 1657, Sarah b. 12 March, 1658-9, John d. March 8, 1659.

He d. 15 Nov. 1690. He made will 7 Nov. 1690, ae. about 70 years; prob. 25 of same month; beq. to son Daniel; to the ch. which dau. Mary R. had by her first husband John Herrick and her last husband Robert [Cue]; to daus. Martha, wife of John Gould, and Phebe, wife of Samuel Fisk; wife to have what was promised her by writing.

REDDOCKE, see Ruddock.

REDIAT, REDYATE, RIDDETT, RIDDET, RYDEAT,
John, ae. 26, came in the Confidence in 1633, from Sutton Mandifield, Wilts, as servant to Walter Hayne. Settled at Sudbury; propr. 1644; frm. May, 1645. Rem. to Marlborough. [Arch. Eccles. I.] He m. 26 (6) 1643, Anne Volt; ch. John b. 19 (2) 1644, Mehitabel b. 26 (10) 1645, Hannah b. 12 (2) 1648, Samuel b. 22 (8) d. 9 (9) 1653.

REDFEN, REDFYN, REDSEN, REDSYN,
William, Cambridge, propr. 1642; sold 8 (7) 1646.

REDNAP, REDNAPE, REDKNAPP,
Joseph, late of Hampton, co. Middlesex, and citizen and cooper of London, came early to Lynn. Frm. Sept. 3, 1634; propr. before 1638. Juryman, 1638. He sold land called Blackbush, near Hampton Court, Mdx. co. Eng., now in possession of his mother, Elizabeth Redknap, Oct. 26, 1640. [L.] [Suff. De. I, 99.] He deposed 30 (4) 1669, ae. between 70 and 80 years old.

He was bur. Friday, Jan. 22, 1684-5; "a man of 110 years old." [S.] Made will 20 May, 1681, prob. at Boston 28 Oct. 1686, beq. to sons Nathaniel and Benjamin.

REDMAN,
Richard, before Gen. Court 3 (7) 1639. Ransomed from the Indians, and discharged by the Court 4 Nov. 1646.

Robert, Dorchester, propr.; his land adj. to that of some of Mrs. Stoughton's in 1649. Rem. to Milton. He deposed in 1656, ae. about 45 years. [Arch. 38 B.]

He d. 13 (11) 1678. Will dated 30 Dec. prob. 31 Jan. 1678, beq. to wife Luce; youngest son Charles and dau. Mercy; son Everinden and dau. Ruth, his wife; eldest son John; son-in-law William [Delene.]

REEVE, REEVES,
John, came in the Christian, March 16, 1634. Salem, propr. 1642. Jane, [his wife?] adm. chh. 23 (6) 1640.

Margery, m. Francis Weston, at Plymouth, 1639.

Thomas, servant of Henry Byley came in the Bevis in May, 1638. Settled at Roxbury; set free from the service of John Gore by the Gen. Court, 1644. Frm. May, 1645.

REEVE, etc., cont.
He m. April 15, 1645, Hannah Rowe. He rem. to Springfield. Propr. 1646; drummer, town officer. Ch. Hannah b. 11 (12) 1648, John b. 1651, d. 1652.

He was bur. 5 (9) 1650.

William, ae. 22, came in the Elizabeth and Ann in April, 1635. Before Gen. Court 4 (10) 1638; before Es. Court 1640.

REMICK, REMICKE,
John, Boston, had grant allowed him at Muddy River 30 (10) 1639, for 4 heads.

REMINGTON, RIMINGTON,
John, carpenter, Newbury, 1637; frm. May 22, 1638. Rem. to Rowley and was appointed to train the company there 13 May, 1640. [Col. Rec.] Lieut.; propr. 1643. Rem. to Roxbury; re-constructed the meetinghouse in 1658. Propr. "Late inhabitant of Rowley, now of Roxbury," he sold land 1659-1662. Wife Elizabeth d. at Rowl. Oct. 24, 1658; he m. 2, Rhoda, widow of John Gore; she survived him and m. 3, Edward Porter. Son John, carpenter, propr. at Rowl. 1652, had large family; difficult to separate the two sets of children's births. Son Thomas also res. at Rowl., and Jonathan at Cambridge at the death of the father.

He d. at Rox. June 8, 1667. Admin. gr. to son Jonathan and John Steadman.

RENNELL, see Reynolds,
James, Plymouth, atba. 1643.

RESKEW, RUSKEW,
William, Cambridge, appointed to make a pound, 1636. He m. widow Hester Must before March 24, 1635-6, when he sold a piece of land by her consent. [Camb. Propr. Rec.]

REVELL,
Mr. John, one of the Adventurers of the Mass. Bay Co., came in the Jewell, in the fleet with Winthrop in 1630; returned with Capt. Peirce in the Lyon. [Du.]

REW, REWE,
Edward, Taunton, atba. 1643; town officer 1647.

He d. 26 July, 1678. Will dated July 18, prob. 30 Aug. 1678. Beq. all to wife Sarah.

REX, see RIX.

REYNER, see RAYNER.

REYCRAFT, see Mayo.

REYNOLDS, REINOLDS, REIGNOLDS, RANOLDS, see Rennell,
Henry, tailor, Salem, 1641. Adm. chh. 6 (1) 1653. His wife mentioned in 1648. [Es. Files.] With wife Sarah sold land in 1665.

John, Watertown, propr., town officer 1635, frm. May 6, 1635.

Richard, came in the Mary and John March 24, 1633-4.

Sarah, came in the Elizabeth of Ipswich April 30, 1634.

Robert, shoemaker, Boston, adm. chh. 10 (6) 1634, frm. Sept. 3, 1634. Sold land at Muddy River in 1645 and 1653. Wife Mary adm. chh. 4 (8) 1645.
Will prob. July 27, 1659; wife Mary; son Nathaniel; dau. Ruth Whitney and her eldest son; dau. Tabitha Abda and her son Matthew; dau. Sarah Mason and her son Nathaniel. [Reg. IX, 138.]

William, Plymouth, one of the party with John Howland at Kennebeck, in the Hocking affair in 1634. Recd. land on Duxbury side Feb. 6, 1637. Owned cattle in 1638. He m. 30 Aug. 1638, Alis Kitson. Sold land in 1640.

William, Salem, adm. chh. 10 (3) 1640.

RHODES, ROADS, RODES,
Henry, Lynn, witness in court in 1647.

Zachary, Rehoboth, propr. 1643, prop. frm. Plymouth Col. 4 June, 1645.

RICE, RISE, RYCE, RYSE,
Edmund, yeoman, Sudbury, propr. and selectman, 1639; frm. May 13, 1642, deputy 1643. Memb. of com. to convey lands at Whip Sufferage in 1657. He deposed 3 (2) 1656, ae. about 62 years. [Mdx. Files.] Rem. to Marlborough. Thomas, Samuel and Joseph R. were also petitioners for church privileges there. [Arch. Eccl. I.] Sold land to his sons Edward and Henry R. 20 Feb. 1654. Wife Tamazine d. 13 June, 1654. Ch. Benjamin b. 31 (3) 1640. He m. 1 March, 1655, Mercy Brigham.
He d. in May, 1663. Petition for division of his estate was signed 16 (4) 1663, by widow

RICE, etc., cont.
Mercy, 8 elder and 2 younger children. [Mdx. Files.]

John, Dedham. Wife Ann; ch. John b. 26 (8) 1650, Mary b. 6 (7) 1652, Sarah b. 2 (4) 1654, John b. 18 (6) 1656, Rachel b. 3 Sept. 1664.

Philip, tailor, Boston, 1640; adm. chh. 21 (9) 1641.
Admin. of his est. Feb. 3, 1664, to Dea. R. Truesdale and Richard Tailor. [Reg. XIII, 338.]

Richard, Cambridge, agreed to keep 100 cows for town 1 March, 1635; frm. June 2, 1641. Rem. to Concord. Deposed 21 (4) 1670, ae. 60 years. [Mdx. Files.] Ch. Elizabeth b. at C. 27 (8) 1641, John b. 23 (12) 1643. He d. June 9, 1709, ae. nearly 100 years.

Robert, Boston. Wife Elizabeth; ch. Joshua b. 14 (2) 1637, Nathaniel b. 1 (2) 1639, Patience b. and d. 1632.

Widow —, propr. at Sudbury, 1639. She appears to be the person who m. Miles Tarne of Boston about 1652. See his will.

RICHARD, RICHARDS, RICHES,
David, Roxbury, a witness to deed of Joseph Wise in 1650.
Old Davy R. was bur. 1 (7) 1680.

Edward, joiner, miller, Lynn, wtness in court in 1639. Lawsuit in 1646. He deposed in 1662, ae. about 40 years. He and his wife Ann wrote, 12 June, 1668, to their son William R., living in Philadelphia or elsewhere, asking him to come home and settle, as they were getting old; would give him half the place. They refer to other children, Daniel, Mary and Abigail. [Es. Prob.]

Edward, shoemaker, Dedham, propr. 1638, adm. chh. 17 (5) 1640, frm. June 2, 1641. Selectman. He m. 10 (7) 1638 Susan Hunting; she was adm. chh. 19 (11) 1644; ch. Mary b. 29 (7) 1639, John b. 1 (5) 1641, Dorcas b. 24 (7) 1643, d. 12 (8) 1648, Sarah b. 25 (3) 1651.
He d. 25 (6), and his wife Susanna d. 9 (7) 1684. His will, attested 25 Sept. 1684, beq. to his wife; to sons John and Nathaniel R.; to son Bullard and dau. Mary Bullard; to son Hearsey; to gr. dau. Mary Gay.

RICHARD, etc., cont.

George, called before Gen. Court 4 (10) 1638.

John, laborer, Plymouth, had grant of land at Mannammet Pond 5 Nov. 1638.

Nathaniel, embarked for N. E. June 22, 1632. Settled at Cambridge. Propr. 1633. Frm. Nov. 6, 1632.

Mr. Thomas, one of the original colony of Dorchester, [Bl.] frm. May 18, 1630. Propr. Rem. about 1639 to Weymouth. [L.] Owned a mill in com. with Henry Waltham; in his absence, his wife Welthia (Welthiann,) adjusted partnership matters before Gen. Court 28 (11) 1640. Selectman, 1643. Will prob. 28 (11) 1650. Wife Welthian; sons John, James, Samuel Joseph and Benjamin; daus. Mary, Ann, Alice and Hannah. [Reg. VII, 232.] The dau. Hannah d. at Boston 10 (9) 1651. The widow's will dated at Boston, 3 July, prob. 4 Nov. 1679, beq. to children John, James; to Thomas, Alice, Hannah, William, Mercy, John, Samuel, Melatiah, Mary and Sarah Bradford, children of William Bradford of Plymouth Colony and my daughter Alice, deceased; to Samuel, Thomas, Jr., Bathsheba and Mehetable Hinckley, Hannah Glover, Melatiah Crocker, Sarah Bacon and Mary Wiborne, ch. of Thomas Hinckley of Plym. Col. and my dau. Mary, dec.; to Ephraim and John, sons of Ephraim Hunt and my late dau. Anne; to children of these grandchildren; to the poor of Boston; to Harvard College; to Sarah Leverett, widow of our late honored governor; to each of the overseers of the will.

William, Plymouth, taxed in 1632.

William, Weymouth, sold house and lands in Wey. and in Braintree 12 (2) 1648. William, his business with John Turner referred to in Gen. Court 1 Sept. 1640. Wife Grace. Ch. James b. June 2, 1658, Benjamin b. May 19, 1660.

Admin. on est. of W. R. of Wey., gr. 24 April, 1683, to widow Mary for herself and children.

RICHARDSON, RICHESON, RICHISSON,

Amos, Boston, propr. 1645. Acct. of merchandise in Suff. De TI, 176. Admin. on est. of James Smith in 1653. Wife Mary adm. chh. 25 (10) 1647. Ch. Mary bapt. 26 (10) 1647, John, ae. about 29 days, bapt. 26

RICHARDSON, etc., cont.

(10) 1647, Amos bapt. 20 (11) 1649, ae. about 6 days, Stephen b. 14 (4) 1652, Catharine b. 6 Jan. 1654, Sarah b. 19 July, 1657, Samuel b. 18 Feb. 1659, Prudence b. Jan. 31, 1662.

Edward, Newbury. Ch. Edward b. 21 Dec. 1649, d. 25 March, 1655, Caleb b. 18 Aug. 1652, Ruth b. 23 Nov. 1655, Moses b. 4 April, 1658, Mary b. 2 Sept. 1660.

He d. 14 Nov. 1685.

Ezekiel, planter, Charlestown, memb. chh. with wife Susanna 1630, frm. May 18, 1631; deputy. One of the founders of the (re-organized) chh. at Charlestown, Nov. 14, 1632. Rem. to Woburn. Propr. 1640. Town officer. Ch. Phebe bapt. 3 (4) 1632, (m. Nov. 1, 1649, Henry Baldwin,) Theophilus bapt. 22 (10) 1633, Josiah bapt. 7 (9) 1635, John bapt. 21 (5) 1638, d. 7 (11) 1642, Jonathan bapt. 13 (12) 1639, James bapt. 11 (5) 1641, Ruth b. and d. 1643.

He d. Oct. 21, 1647. Will prob. 1 (4) 1648. Wife Susanna; sons Theophilus, Josias and James; dau. Phebe; bros. Samuel and Thomas R. [Reg. VII, 172.] The wdow m. Henry Brooks. Deed made to her from Samuel R. 27 (1) 1651. [Char. Rec.]

George, ae. 30, came in the Susan and Ellen in April, 1635. Settled at Watertown; propr. 1636; before Gen. Court 1 (10) 1640.

George, of Wapping, mariner, bought 13 (3) 1639, and sold, per his attorney, May 1, 1641, 200 acres of land at Salem, lately in possession of Peter Palfrey. The Gen. Court ordered a trial of the case of the Dartmouth ship which he had, and which had recently been lost, 12 (9) 1644.

Henry, carpenter, of Canterbury, Eng., came in the Hercules in March, 1634, with wife Mary, 5 children, and 1 servant.

John, Woburn. The Gen. Court heard the testimony of Nelson Hutchinson, 13 Nov. 1644, that he had seen, within 12 months, the wife of John R., living in England; the Court, therefore, adjudged his last marriage with Elizabeth Frier to be void. Ruth, of Elizabeth R., b. at Wob. 31 (6) 1643.

Samuel, yeoman, Charlestown, adm. chh. 8 (12) 1667, frm. May 2, 1638. Rem. to Woburn, 1640; town officer. With wife Joanna brought suit again John Marble June 7, 1658. [Mdx. Files.] Ch. John bapt. 12 (9)

RICHARDSON, etc., cont.
1u͡o9, Hannah b. and d. 1642, Joseph b. 27 (5) 1643, Samuel b. May 22, 1644, S†· Aug. 15, 1649, Thomas b. Dec. 31, 1651, d. Sept. 27, 1657.

He d. suddenly March 23, 1657-8, leaving 4 sons and 2 daus., of whom the eldest John, was 19; Joseph, Samuel, — about 13, Stephen about 8. Petition for settlement was filed after 3 years. [Mdx. Files.] Joanna, in will prob. 1677, beq. to these sons an͏ͅ to dau. Mary Mousall.

Thomas, Charlestown, frm. May 2, 1638. Rem. to Woburn, 1640; propr., town officer. Wife Mary adm. chh. 21 (12) 1635; ch. Mary bapt. 17 (9) 1638, (m. May 15, 1655, John Baldwin,) Sarah bapt. 22 (9) 1640, Isaac b. 24 (3) 1643, Thomas b. Oct. 4, 1645, Ruth b. April 14, 1647, Phebe b. Jan. 24, 1648, Nathaniel b. Jan. 2, 1650.

He d. Aug. 28, 1651.

William, Newbury; his servant, Thomas Jones, freed from service 20 May, 1642. Ch. Sarah b. May 15, 1655.

RICKARD, RICKETT, RICARD,
Giles, Sen., weaver, Plymouth, propr., frm. 7 Sept. 1641; juror, town officer. Brought suit at Salem 23 (4) 1645, concerning his apprentice boy, Henry Glass. Recd. letter of attorney for collection of a debt 13 (4) 1646. [A.] Samuel King was his son-in-law. His wife Judith d. Feb. 6, 1661-2; and he m. 20 May, 1662, Jone Tilson. He m. 25 Jan. 1669, Hannah Churchill, Sen.

Will dated 8 Jan. 1684, prob. 5 March, 1684-5, beq. to wife Hannah; to gr. son John, son of dec. son John; gr. sons Gyles, and John, sons of Gyles, whom he made exec. and residuary legatee. The inv. of the widow Hannah's est. taken March 17, 1691, names articles at houses of her ch. Joseph, Eleazer, John, William, and John Drew; things given to gr. ch. Hannah Dotey and to Martha Dotey.

Sarah, Plymouth, m. 16 May, 1640, George Pidcock.

Thomas, Scituate, town officer, 1639-40. Will dated 14 Nov., prob. 8 June, 1648. Beq. to Thomas Pinchin and others; to cozen Henry Borne. [Reg. IV, 283.]

RICKDALE, see Rigdale.

RICROFT, see Recroft.

RICKS, see Rix.

RIDER, RYDER,
Samuel, Yarmouth, one of the frm. and proprs. of Yarmouth, 7 Jan. 1638-9. Town officer; captain, reduced to ranks in 1654. He m. 23 Dec. 1656, Sarah Bartlett. Ch. Mary b. 6 Sept. 1647, Samuel b. 18 Nov. 1657.

Will dated 20 Nov., prob. 2 March, 1679. beq. to wife Anne, sons Benjamin, Samuel, Zachary and Joseph, daus. Jane, Elizabeth and Mary.

Thomas, came in the Hercules, April 16, 1634. Settled at Weymouth, rem. to Boston. Wife Elizabeth, dau. of Wm. Lane of Dorchester; ch. Elizabeth bapt. at Bo. 14 (8) 1649, Jacob bapt. 10 (6) 1651, Nathaniel bapt. 4 (10) 1653, Hannah b. 7 March, 1655.

He d.; the widow, being left with 5 small children, the Court allowed her, 23 May, 1655, to sell a house at Dorch. which had been left by her father to her and her children.

RIDDLESDEN,
Marie, ae. 27, came in the Susan and Ellen in April, 1635.

RIDGE,
Mary, before the Gen. Court March 6. 1632-3.

RIGBY,
John, Dorchester, propr. 1637, frm. 18 May, 1642. Wife Isabel also memb. chh.; ch. Elizabeth bapt. 1 (3) 1638, Samuel bapt. 20 (8) 1640, Mehetable bapt. 3 (2) 1643, Abigail bapt. 22 (4) 1645.

He d. in 1646. His widow Isabel signed an agreement of proprs. 2 (12) 1646-7. Inv. taken 16 (2), filed 9 (10) 1647.

RIGDALE, RICKDALE,
John, came in the Mayflower to Plymouth; signed the Compact. Both he and his wife Alice d. in the first sickness in the next spring. [B.] Alice, memb. chh. of Dorchester before 1639, may be a relation.

RIGGS,
Edward, Roxbury, propr., frm. May 14, 1634. He m. April 5, 1633, Elizabeth Roos; she d. Oct. 1635. He m. 2, Elizabeth —, who d. 2 (7) 1669. Ch. Lydia bur. Aug. 1633, Elizabeth bur. May, 1634, John bur. (8) 1634, Edward, Mary.

He d. 5 (1) 1671. Will dated 2 Sept. 1670, prob. 6 (1) 1671-2; son Edward and his wife and children; dau. Mary Twitchell and her ch. Rachel and Haup; to Hannah Twitchell; gr. ch. Elizabeth Allen.

RIGHT, see Wright.

RING, RINGE, RINDGE,
Andrew, Plymouth, son of widow Mary; propr. 2 Nov. 1640; atba. 1643; frm. 2 June, 1646; juror, 1650. He m. 23 April, 1646, Deborah, dau. of Stephen Hopkins.

Will made 14 Dec. 1691, stricken in years; prob. 22 March, 1692-3; beq. to sons William and Eleazer; daus. Mary, Deborah and Susanna; John, son of dau. Elizabeth Mayo, late of Eastham, and Mary, dau. of dau. Mary Morton.

Daniel, fisherman, Ipswich, propr. 1648. Wife Mary [Kinsman.] Ch. Daniel, Mary, Susanna, Roger b. June 19, 1657, Sarah b. Aug. 7, 1659, Isaac.

He d. Feb. 1661. Will prob. March 25, 1662. The widow m. before 1665, Uzzall Wardwell, and rem. to Bristol. The dau. Susanna had her uncle Robert Kinsman appointed guardian in 1669.

Widow Mary, Plymouth, made will Oct. 28, 1633. Beq. to son Andrew and dau. Elizabeth, wife of Stephen Dean. [Reg. IV, 34.]

Robert, came as a servant of John Sanders, in 1638; settled at Salisbury; cooper. Propr.; frm. Oct. 9, 1640. He ret. to Eng. in 1643. Came back about 1650. Lost some rights thereby in the town. [See suits in Norf., Suff. and Supr. court files.] Carried on fishing business at Ring's Island. Wife Elizabeth; ch. Hannah, (m. — Harrison,) Elizabeth, (m. Nathaniel Griffin,) Martha b. Dec. 2, 1654, (m. Henry Trussell,) Jarvis b. Feb. 1657, John b. Feb. 27, 1661, Joseph, Robert.

He d. Nov. 25, 1690. Will dated Jan. 23, 1687, prob. March 31, 1691, beq. to sons John, Joseph, Robert, and Jarvis; daus. Hannah Harrison, now in Eng., Elizabeth Griffen

RING, etc., cont.
and Martha Trueswell; to gr. ch. Elizabeth and Mariah Griffen, Sarah Trueswell and Jarvis Ring; to Will Cottle, son to Sarah, now wife of John Hale of Newbury, and to her dau. Joanna; to Rev. Thomas Wells and his son Titus.

RIPLEY,
William, weaver, from Lynn, Eng., came in 1638; settled at Hingham. Propr. 1638. He m. 2, Sept. 29, 1654, Elizabeth, widow of Thomas Thaxter.

He d. 20 (5) 1656. Will prob. Jan. 24, 1656-7, beq. to sons John and Abraham. [Reg. VI, 354.] The widow m. 3, John Dwight.

ROBBINS, ROBINS, see also Roberts and Robinson,
Nicholas, shoemaker, Cambridge, propr., sold about 1638. Rem. to Duxbury; bought land 4 Oct. 1638.

Will prob. 4 (1) 1650. Wife Ann; children John, Katheren, Mary and Hannah. [Reg. IV, 319.]

Richard, (on town records called Roberts,) Charlestown, with wife Rebecca adm. chh. 24 (3) 1640. Ch. John bapt. as of R. and R. "Robinson," 31 (3) 1640. Rem. to Cambridge. Ch. John bapt. at Char. [Mi.], Samuel b. 22 (3) 1643; other ch. Nathaniel and Rebecca. His wife d. and he m. March 26, 1673, Elizabeth, widow of Gilbert Crackbone. See deeds.

Thomas, Duxbury, atba. 1643.

Thomas, Salem, served a Court warrant in 1641. Propr. 1650. He deposed March 29, 1675, ae. about 55 years.

Will dated 18 April, 1680, prob. Suff. co. 18 Jan. 1688, and admin. gr. to Wm. and Rebecca Pinson. Beq. to cousin Wm. Pinson and his wife Rebecca; my sister's dau.; to wife Mary; to Wm. Trask, Jr.

ROBERTS, ROBERT, see Robins,
Hugh, Gloucester, witness in court, 1647.

John, Roxbury, frm. May 22, 1639.
He d. 27 (9) 1651. Admin. Feb. 2, 1653. Bro. Samuel R. at Salisbury. [Reg. VII, 337, and IX, 142.] List of debts filed 22 (6)

ROBERTS, etc., cont.

1655, mention 2 months' wages for service in the ship Goodfellow.

Joseph, embarked for N. E. June 22, 1632.

Nicholas, Cambridge, propr. 1635.

Samuel, see Robins, Samuel.

Old mother Roberts, a Welsh woman, d. at Rox. 1 (7) 1645, in the 103d year of her age.

Robert, Ipswich, was paid for service against the Indians in 1643. Sold house and land in 1658. Wife Susan consented. He deposed in 1659, ae. about 40; had known of the Denison farm above 24 years.

Inv. of his est. filed 29 Sept. 1663. Land at Chebacco.

Thomas, Plymouth, servant of Mr. Atwood, in Court in 1637 and 1640. Bought house and land 8 Jan. 1639; atba. 1643 at Marshfield. He m. 24 March, 1650, Mary Padduck of Plymouth.

Thomas, (see Rodbard,) hatter Roxbury, frm. May, 1645. Rem. to Boston in 1646. Wife Eunice adm. chh. Bo. 15 (3) 1647. Ch. Timothy b. 7 (6), bapt. 9 (6) 1646, Elizabeth bapt. 11 (4) 1648, Lydia bapt. 18 (3) 1651, Eunice b. 18 Aug. 1653.

He d., and the widow m. 22 (8) 1656, Moses Maverick. As admin. of her former husband's est. she sold certain lands March 6, 1666, for the benefit of the four abovementioned children.

William, was assigned by Robert Lewes of Boston, carpenter, 16 (4) 1640, to John Crabtree. Of Weymouth in 1646. [Mdx. Files.] William, wine-coop, *alias* mariner, of Wapping, co. Mdx., Eng., sold land in Char. 18 (8) 1646; [Char. rec.]; and of Charlestown, sold one-half of his house to John Thomson 23 (3) 1648. [A.] Admin. of his est. was gr. 8 May, 1680, to Richard Way, cooper of Boston.

ROBINSON, ROBERSON, ROBERTSON,
see also Robins and Roberts,

Abraham, fisherman, Cape Ann, Gloucester, part owner of a boat in 1641; propr. before 1649. [L.] Abraham R., "son-in-law" of William Brown of Gloc., under 21 years of age in 1662. Was he not a son of this man?

ROBINSON, etc., cont.

Abraham, Sen., d. 23 Feb. 1645.

Anna, widow, memb. chh. Salem, 1637.

Anthony, before the Gen. Court 6 (10) 1636.

Ellen, passed exam. April 11, 1637, to go to N. E.

Isaac, son of the beloved pastor of the Pilgrim church at Scrooby and Leyden, Holland, came to N. E. in 1631, according to a note of Judge Sewall's conversation with him. He was b. in Leyden in 1610; res. at Plymouth a short time, but rem. to Scituate. Frm. 1633. Rem. with the chh. to Barnstable in 1639; deputy, collector of excise, juror. He m. June 27, 1636, Margaret, dau. of Egglin Hanford, Mr. Hatherly's sister. She was bur. June 13, 1649, and he m. a second wife whose name does not appear. Ch. Susannah bapt. Jan. 21, 1637-8, John bapt. April 5, 1640, Isaac bapt. Aug. 7, 1642, Feare bapt. Jan. 26, 1644, (m. Isaac Baker,) Mercy bapt. July 4, 1647, Israel bapt. Oct. 5, 1651, Jacob bapt. May 15, 1653.

Isaac, ae. 15, came in the Hopewell in Sept. 1635. Settled at Lynn. Servant of Mr. Wood. In Court in 1637.

Jane, before Gen. Court 3 (10) 1639, regarding her house.

John, millwright, Ipswich, propr. 1635-1639. Will dated 27 Feb. 1657, prob. 30 March, 1658, beq. to Alice, wife of Thomas Howlett, and to Thomas Howlett, Jr.

John, blacksmith, Haverhill, bought house and land of Joseph Merry in 1644. Bought house and land in Exeter 20 (12) 1651. Residing in Hav. sold house and land there 5 Aug. 1651, wife Elizabeth joining.

John, late servant to our bro. Newgate, Boston, had grant of a house-plot 28 (8) 1639. Perhaps he is the person called John Robertsonne, to whom a lot was granted 27 (2) 1640. It is not unlikely that he is the John Robison, servant to Wm. Philips, who made will 2 June, 1653, prob. 9 June folg., and beq. to his mother and sister in case they be alive and claim it; otherwise to W. P. and Robt. ffeild.

John, Salem, propr., memb. chh. 1639. Lawsuit in 1641. Witness, 1647.

Will dated 22 Sept. Inv. taken by Elias

ROBINSON, etc., cont.

Stileman and Richard Prince 28 (9) 1653. Beq. to wife Eleanor for her life; then to the first one of his kindred that shall come to seek it; beq. to Elder Samuel Sharpe, and John Jackson of Boston.

Robert, ae. 41, came in the Christian, March 16, 1634.

Mr. Thomas, Roxbury, propr. about 1636; wife Silence memb. chh. Rem. to Boston. Sold all his remaining right and interest in lands at Rox. 11 Nov. 1662.

Thomas, mariner, Boston, sold the Speedwell to Thomas Witherley of Southwark, co. Surrey, 27 (5) 1640. [L.] Ch. Ephraim d. 22 Sept., and Samuel d. 16 Jan. 1661-2. He declined to admin. on est. of his son Samuel R., 28 Oct. 1662, and the trust devolved on his son John. [Reg. XII, 51.]

He made his will 17 March, 1665, prob. 27 April, 1666. Beq. to wife; to ch. Thomas, James, Joseph and Mary R.; son John supposed to be in Eng.; to bro. Joseph Rocke. [Reg. XV.] Peter Oliver and Joseph Rock, admins. petition Gen. Court for leave to sell a house and land in 1667. [Arch. 15 B.] Compare with following.

Thomas, gentleman, Scituate, bought house and land in 1642. Com. of town, 1643. Acct. with widow Alice Thompson Sept. 2, 1640. [L.] Juryman 1644; took oath of fidelity 3 March, 1644-5; prop. frm. 4 June, 1650. Bought houses and land in Boston Aug. 29, 1654. He m. in Bo. 10 (11) 1652, Mary, dau. of John Cogan, and widow of John Woodey. She d. 26 Oct. 1661. He m. Elizabeth, widow of Richard Sherman, q. v.

"Robinson, that lived at Little Waldenfield, Eng.," came with wife and 6 children in company with Mr. Nathaniel Rogers, in 1636. Letter of Brampton Gurdon to Gov. Winthrop. [Mass. Hist. Coll. 4 series, IV, 560.]

William, husbandman, yeoman, Dorchester, rented premises 30 (7) 1639. [L.] Frm. Dec. 27, 1642. With wife Margaret sold land Oct. 1664. He m. 2, Ursula, widow of Samuel Hosier, q. v. Ch. —, Samuel bapt. 14 (4) 1640, Increase bapt. 6 (1) 1642, Prudence bapt 17 (10) 1643, m. John Bridge of Roxbury,) Waiting bapt. 26 (2) 1646, (m. Joseph Penniman.)

His will not dated, was prob. 31 July, 1668,

ROBINSON, etc., cont.

by consent of widow Ursula and ch. Samuel, and Increase R., John Bridge and Joseph Peniman; beq. to the ch. above-named and to his wife's dau. Mary Streeter.

William, tailor, Salem, frm. May 18, 1642; propr. 1637; another grant to him and his son in 1649. Sold land in 1660. Wife Isabel memb. chh. 1637. Ch. Anna bapt 3 (10) 1637, Samuel bapt. 26 (10) 1639, Mary bapt. 12 (1) 1642-3, Timothy bapt. 28 (4) 1644, Mark b. and d. 1645, [certificate in Es. Files.] Hester bapt. 28 (3) 1654.

Will dated Feb. 9, 1676-7, prob. 29 (9) 1678. Son Joseph at Barbadoes; sons Samuel and John execs.; dau. Sarah Newbury; gr. ch. Timothy R.

ROCKE,

Joseph, shop-keeper, merchant, Boston, probably a resident in 1649, adm. chh. 18 (11) 1651, frm. May 26, 1652. He deposed 16 (9) 1670, ae. about 51 years. [Arch. 15 B.] He m. Elizabeth, dau. of John Cogan, who was adm. to chh. with him; ch. Elizabeth b. 5 (12) 1651, Sarah b. Jan. 17, 1652, d. 27 (4) 1654, Elizabeth bapt. 29 (11) 1653, Rebecca b. and d. 1655, John b. Nov. 2, 1656, Joseph b. Feb. 1, 1657, d. Sept. 10, 1660, Hannah, (m. 9 (8) 1657, James Breding,) Samuel b. May 17, 1662, Benjamin b. Sept. 3, 1663, Elisha b. Feb. 16, 1666.

The widow m. 2, Wiliam Clements. [Suff. De. IV, 225.]

Thomas, Weymouth, servant to Edward Smith, d. 15 (5) 1642.

ROCKETT,

John, Dorchester, propr. 1633; his land transferred to another in 1634.

Richard, Dorchester, propr. 1633-1638; Braintree, had grant of land for 5 heads, 24 (12) 1639-40. He and his wife Agnes sold house and land, formerly of Zachary Bicknell; Gen. Court gave decision upon it March 9, 1636-7. Ch. John b. 1 (10) 1641.

ROCKWELL,

William, Dorchester, probably one of the original church-colony; juryman Nov. 9, 1630; deacon; one of the leaders in granting lands to settlers. Rem. to Windsor, Conn., in 1636-7 with Mr. Warham and half of the church.

ROCKWELL, cont.

He d. 15 May, 1640. His widow Susanna thew Grant, q. v.. Ch. Joan b. April, 1625, (probably dau. of Bernard Capen of Dorchester, Eng., m. there 14 April, 1624,) m. 2, Mat-John b. 18 July, 1637, Samuel b. 28 March, 1631, Ruth b. Aug. 1633, (m. Christopher Huntington,) Joseph, Sarah b. 21 July, 1638, (m. Walter Gaylord.) [Genealogy.]

ROCKWOOD, see Rockett,
Richard, Braintree.
Inv. of his est. taken 7 (6), admin. gr. 15 (9) 1660; Elder Kingsley and Anne Rockett deposed. Payment made to his dafter; another made for a cow that was killed by John Rockwood. Admin. of the est. of the widow Anne Rockwood was gr. 29 April, 1664, to John Taylor that m. her dau. Phebe. Inv. taken at her decease, March 1, 1664. [Reg. X, 175, and XIII, 333.]

RODBARD,
Thomas, Boston, sold share in a house by his attorney 16 Dec. 1646. See Roberts, Thomas.

RODES, see Rhodes.

ROGERS,
Daniel, sawyer, Braintree sold land 14 (5) 1642.

David, Braintree, had gr. of land 24 (12) 1639, for 2 heads. Ch. Ruth b. 3 (11)1640. He d. 24 (7) 1642.

Rev. Ezekiel, b. in Wethersfield, Eng., in 1590, son of Richard Rogers; B. A. at Bennett's Coll., Cambridge, 1604, M. A. at Christ's Coll. 1608; settled at Rowley, Eng. Came with a colony to N. E. in 1637-8, and founded Rowley. Frm. May 23, 1639. Was installed pastor 10 (3) 1639. [W.] He m. 1, Joane Hartopp, dau.-in-law of Thomas Dampier of Stratford at Bow, gent., who beq. to her in his will 26 March, 1617; he m. 2, a dau. of Mr. John Wilson, who came with him to N. E. and was bur. 8 May 1649; he m. 3, Mary, widow of Thomas Barker, 16 July, 1651; who was bur. 12 Feb. 1678-9. All his children died young.

He d. Jan. 23, 1660-1. His will, dated 17 April, 1660, prob. 26 March, 1661, refers to his father Mr. Richard Rogers; and to his 17 years' pastorate at Rowley, Eng.; to his suspension and to his rest and comfort in

ROGERS, etc., cont.

his N. E. parish, in the church way he believed to be the purest in the whole world. Beq. to wife Mary; to nephew Mr. Samuel Stone of Conn.; to my consen, his son; dear bro. and fellow-servant, Mr. Philips; to his sometime servant Elizabeth Tenney, ells Parratt; to niece Mrs. Mary Matosius of Malden, Essex, Eng.; to niece, Mrs. Elizabeth C..ton, wife of the preacher of Rotterdam in Holland; to the wife of cousin Rogers of Billerica; books to Harvard coll.; to Ezekiel, son of the late Mr. Nathaniel Rogers of Ipswich; to the church and town of Rowley for support of two teaching elders, conditioned on their election of an elder to fill a vacancy within 4 years after it occurs, the bequest to go to Harvard coll. in default of this condition. [See Reg. V, 125, and XLI, 158-188.] The widow Mary made will 22 July, 1678, prob. 1 April, 1679; beq. to cousins Thomas and Ann Nelson of Rowley; to Thomas Lambert; to Mr. Cobbitt. Philip Nelson, exec.

James, ae. 20, came in the Increase April 15, 1635.

John, Dedham, pioneer, 1636. App. to go upon the discovery of Charles river, 21 (7) 1638. Frm. May 17, 1637. He gave power of attorney 17 (7) 1639 to Arthur Draper and Daniel Rogers to receive money from Thomas Rogers. [L.]

John, clothier, Watertown, son of Thomas Rogers of Moulsham in the parish of Chelmsford, co. Essex., sheomaker, dec., gave letter of attorney 16 (10) 1645. [A.]

John, Weymouth, propr. 1643; deacon, town officer. Ch. Lydia b. March 27, 1642. He d. Feb. 11, 1660-1. Will prob. April 13 folg., beq. to wife Judith; ch. Mary, wife of John Rane, Lydia, wife of Joseph White, Hannah, wife of Samuel Pratt, and Sarah R., under 18 years of age.

John, and wife Priscilla (Dawse), dism. from chh. of Boston to that of Watertown 22 (9) 1640. He m. Nov. 3, 1653, Abigail Martin. Rem. to Wenham; recd. to the chh. by letter from Wat. in 1654. Ch. (rec. at Wat.): John b 11 (7) 1641, Mary b. 26 (8) 1643, Abigail b. Jan. 21, 1655.

He d. Dec. 22, 1674, ae. about 80 years. [Reg. XLI, 168.]

John, weaver, planter, Duxbury, taxed in 1632, frm. March 1, 1641-2. Town officer,

ROGERS, etc., cont.

com., juror. Suit at law in 1639. [L.] He m. 16 April, 1639, Ann Churchman. Lived at Scituate about 1647. [Depos. of son John in 1699.] Rem. to Marshfield.

John R. of Marshfield, Sen., will dated Feb. 1, 1660, prob. 5 June, 1661; wife Frances exec.; sons John, Joseph, Timothy; daus. Ann (Hudson,) Mary, Abigail; gr. ch. George and John Russell. John Hudson lived on his land at Namasakeeset. [Reg. VI, 93.]

Joseph, came in the Mayflower to Plymouth; had lands assigned in 1623; frm. 1633. Rem. to Duxbury. Allowed to keep a ferry over Jones' river, near his house, 2 March, 1635-6. He and his bro. John R. had grant of land 6 April, 1640. Rem. to Eastham; appointed lieut. of the company at Nawsett in 1647. Ch. Sarah b. and d. 1633, Joseph b. 19 July, 1635, Thomas b. March 29, bapt. at Scituate May 6, 1638, Elizabeth b. 29 Sept. 1639, John b. 3 April, 1642, Mary b. 22 Sept. 1644, James b. 18 Oct. 1648, Hannah b. 8 Aug. 1652.

His will dated 2 Jan., prob. 5 March, 1677-8, beq. to sons Thomas, John and James, daus. Elizabeth Higgins and Hannah R.; to wife Beriah Higgens to have a share with the children because he had lived with him a great while, etc.

Rev. Mr., a minister, brought in 1628 by Mr. Allerton to Plymouth for the people to hear, proved to be crased in his braine, and was sent back. [B.] [Mass Hist. Coll. 3-1.]

Rev. Nathaniel, minister, b. about 1598 at Haverhill, Eng., son of Mr. John Rogers, the famous preacher of Dedham; grad. at Emanuel coll., Cambridge; preached at Assington, Eng. Came thence to N. E. June, 1636, arriving here 17 Nov. 1636. [See letter of Brampton Gurdon to John Winthrop in Reg. XLI, 183.] Settled at Ipswich, where he was minister till his death, 3 July, 1655. He m. Margaret, dau. of Robert and Mary [Sparhawk] Crane of Great Coggeshall, co. Essex; ch. Mary bapt. Feb. 1628, (m. Mr. William Hubbard, of Ipswich, N. E.), John b. 23 Jan. 1630, (became pres. of Harvard coll.;) Nathaniel b. 30 Sept. 1632, Samuel b. 16 Jan. 1634-5, Ezekiel, d. in N. E. 5 July, 1674, Timothy b. at Ips. 9 Nov. 1638.

He d. July 3, 1655. His nunc. will was prob. 25 (7) 1655. Beq. to wife Margaret; to sons John, Nathaniel, Samuel, Timothy and

ROGERS, etc., cont.

Ezekiel; to dau. — money had been paid already; to gr. ch. John, Nathaniel and Margaret Hubbard; to cousin John Rogers; to Elizabeth, Nathaniel, John and Mary, ch. of his cousin John Harris, of Rowley; to maid servants Mary Quilter and Sarah Fillebrown; to Harvard coll. 5 li. The widow deposed, March 30, 1665, ae. about 55 years; she d. 23 Jan. 1675.

Robert, Boston, ae. 23 years, deposed Nov. 23, 1640, to a claim put forward by his kinsman, John R. of Agamenticus, ae. about 27 years, concerning goods lost in the ship Rose. [L.] He resided at Newbury. Bought part of Plum Island, final deeds of which are in Es. Files XI, 61-3. Susanna, widow, Newbury, made will 3 July, 1665, prob. Sept. 24, 1677; beq. to sons Robert, Thomas and John, and dau. Elizabeth.

Simon, ae. 20, came in the Defence in July, 1635.

Simon, Concord, wife Mary; d. 1 (6) 1640.

Simon, tanner, cordwinder, Boston, adm. inhabitant 25 (5) 1642; bellmann 1653. With John Parker, sold land in Bo. June 16, 1649. Adm. chh. 10 (4) 1644. Wife Susan adm. chh. 10 (4) 1643; ch. Nathaniel b. 14 (11) 1642, bapt. 12 (1) 1643-4, Lydia b. 1 (10) 1645, John bapt. 23 (5) 1648, ae. about 5 days, Elizabeth bapt. 3 (6) 1651, Simon b. 28 April, 1654, Gamaliel b. 26 March, 1657, Joseph b. July 29, 1662 .

Will dated 1 April, 1678, prob. 30 Jan. 1679, beq. to wife Susannah; to eldest son Gamaliel, son Joseph and dau. Elizabeth Rust.

Thomas, came in the Mayflower to Plymouth, bringing his son Joseph; his other children came afterwards. He died in the first sickness, but his son Joseph was married and had 6 children; and the rest of his ch. were married and had many children (in 1650. [B.] Probably Joseph (foregoing) and John of Duxbury were his ch., but proof is incomplete. See Genealogy by Drummond.

ROLFE, ROALFE, ROAFE, ROFFE,

Barbary, ae. 20, came in the Hopewell in Sept. 1635.

Daniel, (called Rofe, Rose and Ro-se,) Ipswich, 1648, taxed in Rowley in 1650. He m. Hannah, (Anna) dau. of Humphrey Bradstreet.

ROLFE, etc., cont.

He d. and inv. of his est. was taken June 24, 1654. The widow m. 2, Nicholas Holt.

Henry, Newbury, propr. Wife Honour; ch. Anna, (m. 1, Thomas Blanchard, 2, Richard Gardner,) Hannah, (m. Richard Dole,) John, Benjamin.
He d. 1 March, 1642-3. Will, dated 15 (12) 1642, beq. to wife, eldest son John and other children under 21 years; brother John R., cousin John Sanders of Salisbury, and kinsman Thomas Whiteer. The widow Honour made nunc. will at the house of Thomas Blanchard in Charlestown; prob. at Ipswich 20 (12) 1650. Beq. to sons Benjamin and John, dau. Hannah Dole that lives at Newbury, and another dau.; to her 4 grand children; 3 pounds, ten shillings due her in England.

John, husbandman, ae. 50, with wife Ann, dau. Hester, and servant Thomas Whittle, (Whittier,) ae. 18, came from Melchior Parke, Eng., in the Confidence, April 11, 1638. Settled at Salisbury; propr. 1639-1652. He removed to Newbury.
Will dated Feb. 4, prob. March 29, 1664; beq. to dau. Hester, wife of John Sanders, and her ch.; to Sarah, wife of William Cottell, and her ch. Sarah and Ann C., in addition to his former gifts to her; to gr. ch. Isaac, and Joseph Ring; to Elizabeth Shropshire and Esther Ring; to Thomas Whittier's ch.; to children at Newbury; to son, and to his ch. Marie and Rebecca; to Benjamin R's. sons John and Benjamin; to Ann, wife of Richard Gardner; to the 6 ch. of Richard Dole, whom he appoints exec. Oct. 22, 1668, claim was made for these legacies by Richard Ring of Marlborough, Eng., and his ch. Joseph, Isaac and Esther R. and Elizabeth Shropshire; and they sent Joseph over to collect them. [Es. De.]

ROMAN,

John, Cambridge, d. 19 (10) 1638.

ROMEBALL, see Rumball.

ROODE,

Thomas, Salem, in court, 1641; Boston, attorney for Nicholas Roe of Glasten in Somersetshire, yeoman, son of John Roe, dec.

ROOK,

James, Watertown. Wife Honor; ch. Mary b. May 5, 1646.

ROOKMAN,

John, ae. 45, with Elizabeth, ae. 31, and John, ae. 9, came in the Abigail in July, 1635.

ROOS,

Elizabeth, Roxbury, m. in 1633, Edward Riggs.

ROOT, ROOTS, ROOTES,

Ralph, husbandman, ae. 50, with Mary, ae. 15, came in the Abigail in June, 1635. Settled at Boston. He sold land estated upon his dau. Sarah by Edward Whitfield; deed confirmed by Gen Court Feb. 28, 1649. His wife Mary was adm. chh. 3 (12) 1638; she d. 15 (9) 1655. He, being stricken in age, deeded his house and land March 14, 1659-60, to his dau. Sarah, wife of James Balston. His nunc. will was prob. March 29, 1666. Beq. to son and dau. Balston: to dau. Jeane Buttell, and to dau. at Linn. [Reg. XV.]

Joseph, of Great Chart, Eng., came in the Hercules in March, 1634. Settled at Salem. Lawsuit, 1640. [Josiah?] adm. chh. 13 (6) 1648. Ch. Josiah, Bethiah, John and Susanna bapt. 24 (7) 1648, Thomas bapt. — 1650, Jonathan bapt. 28 (8) 1665.

ROPER, ROAPER,

John, carpenter, ae. 26, from New Bucknam, Eng., with wife Alice, ae. 23, and children Alice and Elizabeth, passed exam. April 13, 1637, to go to N. E. Settled at Dedham. Frm. June 2, 1641. Propr. 11 (6) 1637. Wife Alice adm. chh. 13 (7) 1639. He rem. to Charlestown before 1649. Ch. b. here: Mary bapt. 22 (7) 1639, Rachel b. 18 (1) 1639, d. 16 (5) 1641, Hannah b. 5 (2) 1642, Ephraim and Benjamin b. 23 (12) 1644. Sarah, m. at Dedham April 18, 1669, James Maknab. [See William Allen.]

Walter, carpenter, Ipswich, rem. to Topsfield; frm. May 13, 1642. Agent for William Payne in 1653. He deposed in 1661, ae. about 48 years.
Will dated 15 July, prob. 28 Sept. 1680, beq. to wife Susan, son John and Nathaniel, daus. Mary, Elizabeth and Sarah, gr. ch. Elizabeth, Susan, Margaret, Rose and Sarah Sparkes and Elizabeth and Susan Dutch.

ROOTEN, ROOTON, ROOTENS,
Richard, Salem, propr. 1636. Lynn, propr. 1638. Katharine, [his wife?] adm. chh. 20 (5) 1651.

He d. 20 (7) 1663. Will dated June 12, prob. 25 (9) 1663. Wife; kinsman Edmund R.; to Jonathan Hartshorne, if he continue with my wife; to pastor Mr. Whiting; to Henry Rhodes and John Taylor.

ROPES, ROAPES, ROPPS,
George, servant to Mr. Garfoard, Salem, before Gen. Court in 1636. Lawsuit, 1637. His time expired in 1638; he went to Eng.; was to have 20 acres of land on his return. Carpenter. Wife Mary adm. chh. 15 (3) 1642; ch. Jonathan bapt. 5 (4) 1642, Mary bapt. 3 (9) 1644, John bapt. 4 (5) 1647, William bapt. 26 (8) 1651, Abigail bapt. 29 (8) 1654, Samuel bapt. 15 (1) 1656-7.

Admin. gr. to his widow Mary 3 (10) 1670. Ch. John and George Ropps, and John Norman.

ROSCOE, see Ruskew.

ROSE, see Row and Rolfe,
Ezra, Ipswich, propr. 1648.

George, Concord.
He d. 20 (2) 1649. [Mdx. Files.]

John, Watertown, propr. 1636; Cambridge, d. Dec. 12, 1640.

ROSSITER,
Bray, [Brian?] gent., physician. Dorchester, came in the Mary and John in 1629-30. Propr. Sold land to Wm. Hutchinson. [L.] Rem. to Windsor, Conn., where he witnessed a deed Sept. 12, 1647. [Suff. De. I, 98.] Rem. to Guilford, Conn. [Mass. Hist. Coll. 3-10.]

Mr. Edward, one of the Assistants, came to N. E. in 1630.
He d. before Nov. 29, 1630. [W.] His dau., widow Jane Hart, petitioned Gen. Court for aid in 1685, being 70 years old. [Reg. XXXIII, 242.]

Hugh, Dorchester, had grant of land adjoining "Mr. Rosciter's ground," Feb. 10, 1634.

Jane, Taunton, m. 23 March, 1639-40, Thomas Gilbert.

ROUSE, ROWSE, see Rowes,
Faithful, sadler, Charlestown, adm. chh. 1 (5) 1643; frm. May 29, 1644. Town officer, 1646. Wife Suretrust, a sister of Dr. Comfort Starr, adm. chh. 30 (9) 1642; Mercie adm. chh. 9 (10) 1643.

He made will 9 April, 1664, prob. 21 June; beq. to wife; dau. Mercy Sweat; sister Morley; Hannah Mainer now with me; to the church, the college and the Grammar school. The widow Suretrust d. Jan. 8, 1685, ae. about 86 years. Her will dated 20 (8) 1679, prob. April 6, 1686, beq. to son-in-law John Sweat and dau. Marie his wife; to kinswomen Elizabeth Fernside, Elizabeth, wife of Joshua Edmunds, Marie, wife of John Pell, and Elizabeth and Lydia, daus. of Samuel Hale; to James, son of kinsman James and Hanna Hayden; to Elizabeth F.'s 3 daus.; to John, son of Comfort Starr.

George, Plymouth, had grant of land 3 Sept. 1638.

George, Braintree, had grant of land for 5 heads 24 (12) 1639. Frm. May 13, 1640.

George, (Rose,) Concord, d. 20 (3) 1649.

John, Marshfield, servant to Thomas Prence, transferred in 1634 to John Barnes; atba. 1643; propr. 1640. Had lic. to marry 7 Jan. 1638-9. Town officer 1645. Ch. Mary b. Aug. 10, 1640, John b. Sept. 28, 1643, Simon b. 14 June, 1645, George b. May 17, 1648.

He d. Dec. 16, 1684. Will dated May 30, 1682, beq. to wife; ch. John, Simon, Mary, Anna and Elizabeth. Bro. William Paybodie one of the overseers. The court allowed the widow to take oath to the will and inv. at home on account of her age and weakness. His widow Annis made will Nov. 10, 1687; prob. Sept. 12, 1688. Daus. Mary Price, Anna Holmes and Elizabeth Bourne; sons John and Simon Rows; servant Samuel Cornish. [Gen. Adv. I, 41.]

ROW, ROWE, ROE, ROWES, see Rouse,
Edward, Gloucester, propr. 1650. Hugh and John, brothers, [his sons?] made agreement in 1662.

Elenor, widow, adm. chh. Boston 2 (10) 1643.

Henry, from Platford, Eng. came in the James, April 5, 1635.

ROW, etc., cont.

"Mr. Owen Roe, of London, having house and lott and certain cattele among us, had a grant of 200 acres of land at Mt. Wollaston for the present releife of his cattell, and for him to injoy whenas he shall become an inhabitant amongst us, and not otherwise," 20 (4) 1636. William Leatherland, one of his servants, was adm. chh. in 1633.

Robert, ae. 40, with wife Margery, ae. 40, and children John and Robert, ae. 15, Elizabeth, ae. 13, Mary, ae. 11, Samuel, ae. 9, Sarah, ae. 7, Daniel, ae. 3, and Dorcas, ae. 2, came in the Francis of Ipswich April 30, 1634.

ROWELL, ROWHEEL,

Thomas, carpenter, Salisbury, propr. 1639-1641. Rem. to Ipswich. Was employed to build a prison in 1652. Rem. to Andover. First wife d., and he m. [2,] Margaret, widow of Christopher Osgood; contracting, Feb. 24, 1650-1, to bring up her 2 sons and 2 daus. Ch. Valentine, (adult in 1646,) [and Jacob b. about 1660.]

He d. about 8 May, 1662. Will dated Feb. 24, 1650-1, prob. Sept. 30, 1662. Second inv. made after the widow's death, June, 1681.

ROWLAND,

William, Plymouth, taxed in 1632; suit in court in 1640.

ROWLANDSON, ROWLINGSON, ROLENSON, RAWLINSON,

Thomas, Ipswich, propr. 1637, frm. May 2, 1638, constable, 1645. Rem. to Lancaster. He m. between 1644 and 1648 Bridget, widow of Robert Mussey, who survived him and m. 2, May, 31, 1659, Wm. Kerley, Sen.; she d. June 14, 1662. Ch. Thomas, Elizabeth, (m. Richard Wells,) Martha, (m. John Eaton,) Joseph.

He d. Nov. 17, 1657. Inv. of his estate taken 27 (11) 1657; certain tools injured by being lost at Charlestown by the sea-shore a long season; oxen at Salisbury. Mr. Joseph R., the son, deposed.

ROWLEY,

Henry, planter, Plymouth, taxed in 1632; frm. 1634. Rem. to Scituate, where he and his wife joined the chh. Jan. 8, 1634. Rem. to Barnstable; propr. 22 Jan. 1638-9.

ROWLEY, cont.

Town officer. Son Moses, ["Moyses?"] He m. Oct. 17, 1633, Ann, widow of Thomas Blossom. See will of William Palmer. He m. 2, 22 April, 1652, Elizabeth Fuller; ch. Mary b. 20 March, 1653, Moses b. 10 Nov. 1654, child d. 15 Aug. 1656, Shobal and Mehitabel b. 11 Jan. 1660, Sarah b. 16 Sept. 1662, Aaron b. 1 May, 1666, John b. 22 Oct. 1667.

ROWTON, ROOLTON,

Richard, husbandman, ae. 36, with wife Ann, ae. 36, and child Edmund, ae. 6, came in the Susan and Ellen in April, 1635. The son Edmund d. at Lynn 4 March, 1674-5

He d. about 1683; a will dated 21 April, 1682, bequeathing to wife Mary, and adopted son Daniel Poole was not allowed; will dated Oct. 12, 1683, giving est. to Nathl. Felton, Sen. on condition of his caring for the wife Mary, was prob. 27 (9) 1683.

ROYAL, ROYALL, RYALL, RIALL,

William, cooper and cleaver of timber, engaged March 23, 1628, sent over by the Mass. Bay Co. to Salem. Res. at Casco Bay in 1636. Royall's river in what is now Yarmouth, Me. flowed by his house, and recd. his name. About 1675 he rem. to Dorchester, where he d. June 15, 1676. He m. Phebe, second wife of Samuel Cole of Boston, dau. of Margaret Greene, who survived him, and d. July 16, 1678. Ch. John, Samuel, Isaac, Joseph, Mary and Mehetabel. [Gen. by E. D. Harris in Reg. XXXIX, 348.]

ROYCE, ROISE,

Robert, Boston, memb. chh. 1632, frm. April 1, 1634. Ch. Joshua bapt. 16 (2) 1637, Nathaniel bapt. 24 (1) 1639.

ROYLE,

Gabriel, Plymouth, atba. 1643.

ROYLEY, see Riley.

RUCK, RUCKE,

Mr. Thomas, came from Malden, co. Essex, in April, 1638; made a list of goods brought with him, to which he deposed 19 July, 1639, ae. about 48 years. [L.] Settled at Charlestown. His wife adm. chh. with him 5 (2) 1640; frm. 13 (2) 1640. Rem. to Salem. Propr., town officer. Rem. to Boston. Was a draper, distiller, and inn-keeper.

RUCK, etc., cont.
Had a house called the Swan in 1651. Ch. Stephen bapt. at Salem. Son Thomas was lost at sea; will prob. June 26, 1653, beq. to bros. John and Samuel, of Sal., sister Joane Kalsoe, and to father Thomas.

His will dated 7 Dec. 1662, prob. 1 May, 1668, beq. to wife Elizabeth, ch. John, Samuel, Joane, wife of Henry Farnham and her son Thomas Swan. Admin. of the est. was gr. 3 (10) 1670, to the widow.

RUCKMAN,
George, a creditor of Thos. Hampton of Sandwich in 1637.

RUDDOCK, RUDDYK,
Jolliff, Boston, merchant, attorney for John Crabtree, 1647. [A.]

He d. (7) 1649. Inv. taken 12 (8) 1649. Admin. gr. to John R. [Reg. VII, 176.]

John, yeoman, planter, Sudbury, propr. 1640, frm. May 13, 1640. He and his horse took Capt. Leverett to the Manhatos in 1653-4. [Col. Rec.] He was one of the com. to convey lands at Whip Sufferage in 1657. He deposed 4 (8) 1664, ae. about 55 years. [Mdx. Files.] Rem. to Marlborough.

Will dated Jan. 28, prob. March 15, 1692-3, beq. to wife Rebecca; kinsmen John and Joseph Banester, Samuel Andrew, Jr. and Abigail, wife of Josiah Jones, Jr.; to the town a black broadcloth burying cloth; to his minister, Mr. William Brinsmeade, a chest that had belonged to his bro. Alexander B.

RUGG, RUGS,
Margery, before Gen. Court 30 April, 1640.

RUGGLES, RUGGLE,
George, Boston, adm. to chh. (9) 1633; wife Elizabeth adm. chh. 2 (12) 1633; both dism. to chh. of Braintree 16 (12) 1639-40. Had house-plot in Bo. in 1636, and lands at Br. in 1639. Frm. March 4, 1633-4. Sold land at Br. to the Iron Works Co. in Sept. 29, 1645. Ch. Elizabeth bapt. 8 (10) 1633, (m. 24 (2) 1655, Wm. Browne,) Mary bapt. 3 (11) 1635, John bapt. 31 (10) 1637, George b. 5 (3) 1640, d. 1641, Rachel b. 15 (12) 1642, Samuel b. 3 (11) 1648, a dau. b. 16 (12) [....], Sarah b. 29 (7) [....], Mehetabel b. 16 (5) 1650.

RUGGLES, etc., cont.
His widow petitioned, July 27, 1669, that her youngest son Samuel might have one half of the house, as her husband desired. [Reg. XXXI, 321.]

Jeffery, Boston, came from Sudbury, Eng.; had help from Mr. John Rogers in time of famine.
He d. soon. [W.] Wife Margaret memb. chh. 1630.

John, Sen., Boston, frm. July 3, 1632; built at Deer Island before 1641. Herdsman, 1643. Wife Frances memb. chh. 1630. He was memb. chh. in 1631. Ch. ae. 11, d. in Jan. 1631. [Du.]

John, shoemaker, ae. 44, with wife Barbara, ae. 30, and child John, ae. 2, came in the Hopewell in April, 1635, from Nazing, co. Essex, Eng. Settled at Roxbury. Propr. His wife d. (11) 1636; he m. Margery Hammond, q. v.

He d. 15 (7) 1658. Will prob. 30 Jan. 1663-4, names wife Margery, son John, bro.-in-law Edward Bridge, and servant Samuel Perry. [Reg. XII, 343.]

Thomas, elder bro. to John; children of a godly father; one of the Nazeing christians; came in the yeare 1637; his firstborn son d. in Eng.; his second son John was brought over as a servant by Philip Eliot, and he brought two other children with him, Sarah and Samuel; Mary his wife approved herself a godly christian by a holy and blameless conversation. [E.] Settled at Roxbury. Propr.

He d. Nov. 15, 1644. Will, dated 9 (9) 1644, gave to wife, sons John and Samuel, and dau. Sarah. [Reg. III, 265.] His son John, Called John R., Jr., d. in 1658. [Reg. IX, 139.] See Lyon. His widow m. — Roote, and d. 14 (12) 1674-5, in her 89th year.

RUM,
George, ae. 25, came in the Abigail in July, 1635.

RUMBALL, RUMBOLL, ROMEBALL,
Daniel, Salem, propr. 1643. Named as cousin in the will of William Gilson of Scituate in 1639. Furnished the iron for the meeting house in 1647. Deposed in 1681, ae. four score years and odd. Sarah, his wife, had land in the right of George Norton.

RUMBALL, etc., cont.

He made a will 1 Oct. 1677; beq. to dau. Elizabeth Richards; to son William; to dau. Mary and her sons John and Ephraim Kempthon; to gr. ch. John R.; sons Richard Richards and Ephraim Kempthon. He made another will 10 May, 1681; beq. to the same in quite different proportions, which led the son William to oppose the prob. of this will. [Es. Files XXXVI, 111, etc.]

Thomas, ae. 22, came in the Truelove in Sept. 1635.

RUSH,

Jasper, Dorchester, 1643, propr.; frm. May 29, 1644. His wife Elizabeth and dau. Thankful d. (9) 1657; he m. 2, 24 (1) 1664, Judith —. Ch. Preserved b. 24 (7) 1651, Elizabeth b. 24 (8) 1653, Thankful bapt. 1 (9) 1657.

He d. 23 (12) 1668, ae. 58. Admin. gr. to his widow Juidith and son Preserved for herself and children. Preserved chose William Sumner as his guardian and Elizabeth chose Samuel Thatcher, 30 (2) 1669.

RUSCO, RUSKEW, [ROSCOE?]

William, husbandman, ae. 41, wife Rebecca, ae. 40, children Sarah, ae. 9, Marie, ae. 7, Samuel, ae. 5, and William, ae. 1, cert. from the parish of Billerica in Eng. came in the Increase in April, 1635. Settled at Cambridge. Com. of Gen. Court 1635-6. He m. Hester, widow of (Edward) Muste; with whom he sold land at C. March 24, 1635-6.

RUSS,

John, Newbury. Rem. to Andover. He deposed in 1661, ae. about 50 years. Ch. John b. 24 June, 1641, Mary b. 16 Feb. 1643.

Will dated 7 Jan. 1691-2, prob. March 29, 1692, beq. to son John; to dau. Mary Foster and her dau. Hannah Astinn.

RUSSELL,

Elizabeth, adm. chh. Charlestown 21 (12) 1634.

George, ae. 19, came in the Elizabeth April 9, 1635; settled at Hingham; propr. 1636. Rem. to Plymouth; a "midstead" granted him 3 April, 1637. Frm. Plym. Col. 3 June, 1657. Rem. to Scituate; atba. 1643. Was a miller. Ret. to Hingham. He m. Feb. 14, 1639, Jane, widow of [Philip] James; she d. Feb. 22, 1688, ae. about 83

RUSSELL, cont.

years. [Gr. St.] Ch. [George, Samuel,] Mary b. April 1, 1641, (m. John Jacob,) Elizabeth b. Feb. 12, 1642, Martha b. Oct. 9, 1645, Patience, (m. Pertha Macvarlo).

He d. 26 May, 1694, ae. 99 years. [Gr. St.]

Henry, Weymouth, son of Thomas R. of Chalfont St. Gyles, co. Bucks, yeoman, d. May 24, 1640; wife Jane; only child living, Elizabeth, ae. 10 years. Will dated 28 (11) 1639, was presented before Gov. Thomas Dudley Oct. 10, 1640; [L.] prob. 30 (10) 1643. Beq. to wife; dau. Elizabeth and indentured servant John Comstock.

Mr. John, Dorchester, propr. 1633. He d. Aug. 26, 1633. Admin. gr. by Gen. Court Sept. 3, 1633, to Wm. Gaylard and Wm. Rockwell. He gave half of his est. to the church of Dorch.; the rest to his bros. Henry R. and Thomas Hyatt; to his man he gave his time; mentioned goodman Caping as one of the olde Dorch. people.

John, planter, Marshfield, atba. 1643; frm. 5 June, 1644. Bought land in 1651.

John, Barnstable, served against the Narragansetts in 1645.

John, Dartmouth, (probably one or the other of the foregoing,) made will 19 Jan. 1687-8, prob. 2 April, 1695; beq. to sons John and Jonathan and to gr. son John, son of Joseph.

John, Cambridge, propr. 1635, frm. March 3, 1635-6. Town officer; clerk of the writs. Rem. to Woburn; propr. 1640. His wife Elizabeth d. Dec. 16, 1644; he m. May 13, 1645, Elizabeth Baker. Ch. Samuel d. Dec. 1, 1667. He deposed 5 (2) 1671, ae. about 55 years. [Mdx. Files.] John R., "the Anabaptist," d. 1 (4) 1676. [Mdx. Rec.] [See Mass. Hist. Coll. 4-8.]

Will dated 27 (3) 1676, beq. to wife Elizabeth, son John and dau. Mary Brooks. The widow d. Jan. 17, 1689-90. Final settlement of the estates by gr. son John.

Nicholas, Lynn, living at the house of Thomas Pynion [Pinson,] in court, 1647.

Ralph, Lynn, a witness in court, 1647.

Richard, merchant, woolen-draper, Charlestown, with wife Maud adm. chh. 22 (3) 1641; frm. June 2, 1641; town officer. He bought cattle, etc. 1643; purchased property

RUSSELL, cont.
at Pemaquid and other points along the coast. Had a "quantity of glass" consigned to him about 1641. [A.] His wife Maud d. about 1652; and he m. Mary, widow of Leonard Chester, who was adm. chh. 21 (12) 1655; her dau. Prudence loaned money on mortg. to B. Barnard July 11, 1667. Ch. Katharine, (m. 29 (9) 1654, William Boswell,) James b. 1 (8) 1640, bapt. 30 (3) 1641, Elizabeth b. 12 (8) 1644, Daniel.

He d. 14 (3) 1676. Will dated 29 (1) 1674, prob. 18 (3) 1676, beq. to wife Mary and her children, (see Chester;) to sons James and Daniel Russell; daus. Katharine, wife of Wm. Roswell, and Elizabeth, wife of Nathaniel Graives; to sisters Elizabeth Corbett and Sarah Russell, widow, now living at Bristol; to sister Mary Newell, widow, and her sons John and Joseph N.; to James Carey; to the ch. of these persons; to Harvard College; the church and town of Charlestown; several ministers; house servants, etc. The widow d. Nov. 30, 1688, ae. about 80.

William, carpenter, Cambridge, about 1636; propr. 1645. Wife Martha memb. chh.; ch. Joseph b. in England; about 10 years old when his mother joined here; [Mi.] Benjamin, John b. 11 (7) 1645, Martha, Philip, William, Jason, Joyce bapt. May 13, 1660. Joseph deposed 30 (7) 1651, ae. 25 years. [Mdx. Files.]

He d. Feb. 14, 1661. The widow m. before 1665 Humphrey Bredsha; she signed the Billerica deed on behalf of her former husband W. R.

RUST,
Henry, glover, Boston. Rem. to Hingham; propr. 1635; frm. March, 1637-8; town clerk 1645. [Col. Rec.] He res. in Bo. again, and bought house and land of widow Awdrey Palmer March 11, 1652.

RUTH, see Druse,
Vincent, residence not stated, frm. May, 1645.

RUTTER, [RUTOR?]
John, ae. 22, servant of Peter Noyce, came in the Confidence April 24, 1638. Settled at Sudbury; propr. 1640. He contracted with the selectmen Feb. 17, 1642, to "sett, sawe, hew & frame" a house; [for the use of

RUTTER, cont.
the minister?] He m. Nov. 1, 1641, Elizabeth Plimton; ch. Elizabeth b. 6 (8) 1642, John b. Feb. 9, 1645, Rebecca b. 28 (12) 1647. In 1675 Baptist Smedley had a gr. ch. Jabish (Jabez) Rutor.

RYDEAT, see Rediat.

SABINE, SABIN,
William, miller, Rehoboth, 1643, frm. 3 June, 1657. First wife —; he m. 2, Dec. 22, 1663, Martha Allen of Medfield; ch. Samuel, Elizabeth, Joseph b. 24 (4) 1645, Benjamin b. 3 (5) 1646, Nehemiah b. 28 (3) 1647, Experience b. 8 (6) 1648, (m. Aug. 20, 1672, Samuel Ballins,) [Bullen?] Mary b. 23 (5) 1652, (m. April, 1674, Nathaniel Allen,) Abigail b. 8 (9) 1653, Hannah b. 22 (10) 1654, (m. Nov. 10, 1673, Joseph Allen,) Patience b. last of 12 mo. 1655, Jeremiah b. 24 (1) 1657, Sarah b. 27 (7) 1660, (m. July 1, 1686, John Kingsley,) James b. Jan. 1, 1664, John b. 27 (8) 1666, Hezekiah b. April 3, 1669, Noah b. March 4, 1671, Mehitabel b. May 16, 1673, Mary b. Sept. 8, 1675, Sarah b. Feb. 16, 1677, Margaret b. April 30, 1680.

He was bur. Feb. 9, 1686-7. Will dated June 4, 1685, prob. Suff. July 17, 1687, beq. to wife; to children Samuel, Joseph, Benjamin, James, John, Hesekia, Noah, Experience, Abigail, Hannah, Elizabeth, Patience, Mehetabel, Mary, Sarah and Margaret. [Genealogy. Reg. XXVI, 52.]

SACKETT,
Simon, Cambridge, propr. 1633.
He d. before Nov. 3, 1635, when admin. of his est. was gr. by the Gen. Court to his widow Isabel, who was a householder in February following.

SADLER,
Anthony, ae. 9, [19?] came as a servant with Stephen Kent in the Confidence, April, 1638. Shoemaker. Res. at Newbury until the settlement of Salisbury, where he settled. He m. Martha, dau. of John Cheney of N.; ch. Abiel b. 2 Nov. 1650.

He was drowned 23 (2) 1650. The widow m. 2, Thomas Burkby of Ipswich; was buried Jan. 24, 1658.

John, Plymouth, propr. frm. 2 March, 1640-1; rem. to Gloucester. Frm. May 19, 1642. Constable, and authorized to train men; selectman.

SADLER, cont.
Mr. Richard, Lynn, propr. 1638; frm. March 14, 1638-9. Clerk of writs, 1641. Rem. to Reading; propr. 1644.

SAFFIN, SAFFINE,
Mr. John, merchant, Boston, propr., town officer. Timothy Hatherly and James Cudworth testified 25 (10) 1657, that he lived in Scituate from the time he was 12 years old till about 1653; and was of good character during that time. [Midlsx. Files. Reg. XXI, 115.] He m. 2 Dec. 1658, Martha, dau. of Thomas Willett; ch. John d. Dec. 11, 1661, John b. April 14, 1662, Thomas b. March 18, 1664, Simon b. April 14, 1666, Josiah b. Jan. 31, 1667, Joseph b. Feb. 2, 1669, Benjamin b. June 15, 1672, Joseph b. Jan. 24, 1676, bapt. 12 (1) 1677. He deposed to the will of John Stebbin in 1681, ae. about 47 years. He m. 2, Elizabeth, widow of Peter Lidgett, whose will, dated 10 Feb. 1685-6, beqeathing to her son Charles Lidgett and dau. Usher, met with considerable opposition in 1687. He left a Diary, which is in the possession of a descendant.

SAFFORD,
Thomas, husbandman, Ipswich, propr. 1641. Bought farm of Henry Kingsbury 8 Feb. 1648.
His will dated 20 Feb. 1666, prob. 26 March, 1667, gave his farm, etc. to son Joseph, on condition of his care of the father and mother and paying certain amounts to daus. Elizabeth, Mary and Abigail. Joseph deposed March 29, 1692, ae. about 59 or 60 years, as to what he heard in Ips. 40 years before. One of the daus. had m. — "Killum."

SALE, SEAL, SEALE, SAYLE, SEALES, SEARL, see also Searl,
Edward, Marblehead, his wife Margaret before Gen. Court in 1637.

Edward, Weymouth, frm. Nov. 2, 1637; rem. to Rehoboth; propr. 1643-6. Returned to Wey. Ch. Ephraim bapt. at Hingham in May, 1638, Obediah b. at Wey. 26 (5) 1640, Nathaniel, Rebecca, (m. at Bo. 28 May, 1642, Jarrett Ingraham,) Marian, (m. at Reh. 10 (12) 1663, Wm. Carpenter. The wife, —, d. at Reh. July 13, 1664.
He d. at Wey. Inv. taken April 13, 1693. [See will of son Ephraim, prob. Jan. 29, 1690-1, beq. to "aged father Mr. Edward Sale" and bros. and sisters; account of admin. gives names.]

SALE, etc., cont.
John, Charlestown, inhabitant, memb. chh. 1630. Was punished for theft April 1, 1633; was bound over to Mr. Coxeshall for 3 years, and his dau. Phebe was also bound to Mr. C. for 14 years. Ran away to the Indians, but came back Jan. 30, 1634-5. [Col. Rec. and W.]

SALLOWES, SALLES,
Michael, Salem, propr. 1635.
Will dated 14 (9), prob. 31 (10) 1646. Sons Thomas, Robert, John, Samuel and Michael; dau. Martha; son-in-law Edward Wilson. See Wolf. The inv. of the est. of Grace S. was taken June 29, 1664.

SALINOVAS, SCILLA NOVA, DESALLENOVA, DESALLENOBA, De SALINOVAS,
Peter, Weymouth, consulted by the Gen. Court in Sept. 1635, about an expedition against the French. [W.] His lands referred to in deed of Waltham Dec. 12, 1637; made agreement with Mr. Waltham about a mill 27 (4) 1638. [L.]

SALLY, SOLLY,
Manus or Manes, Charlestown, adn.. chh. 3 (3) 1647, frm. May 26, 1647; town officer. Mary adm. chh. 9 (5) 1648. He m. Sarah Hepburn, [Wyman.] Ch. Rebecca b. 20 (8) 1646.
He d. 4 (3) 1650. [Mdx. Files.]

SALMON, SAMON, SAMMON,
Daniel, Salem; lawsuits in 1639. Was one of the creditors of the Iron Works Co. in 1654. He deposed in 1660, ae. about 50 years; had been a servant of the I. W. under Mr. Gifford. His wife Margery a legatee in will of widow Axey in 1670.

Thomas, a witness to deed in Boston in 1650. Admin. of his est. gr. at Northampton March 29, 1676, to his widow Mary.

SALTER,
Sampson, of Caversham, [Faversham?] Eng. fisherman, came in the James in April, 1635.

Theophilus, Ipswich, resident, 1648. Wife Martha. [Es. Files, 1650.]

William, fisherman, Boston, propr. 1635. Acted for Aug. Clement in sale of property in 1638. [L.] He deposed in 1655, ae. about 48 years. [Es. Files.] Wife Mary; ch. Peleg b. 15 (1) 1635, Elizabeth bapt. 26

SALTER, cont.

(2) 1640, Mary b. 10 (6) 1642, Jabez bapt. 17 (6) 1646, ae. about 8 days, Jabez b. (7) 1647, Mehetabel bapt. 30 (2) 1648, ae. about 4 days, John bapt. 8 (4) 1651, Elisha b. 7 March, 1654, d. 14 (7) 1655, Lydia b. 24 March, 1657, Ann bapt. 22 (1) 1657. Hannah m. in Bo. 4 (10) 1651, Nicholas Philips.

Goodman Salter d. 25 March, 1698. His will dated 11 May, prob. 23 Nov. 1675, beq. to wife; to son Jabez, dau. Beck, dau. Mehitable, son Jno. Inventory shows goods in shop, etc.

SALTONSTALL,

Sir Richard, knight, of Huntwick, Eng., came in the Arbella with Gov. Winthrop in 1630. Had been a stockholder and Assistant in the Mass. Bay Co. in Eng. since 1628. Was also one of the pattentees of Dover and Swampscott. He res. at Watertown. Was a signer of the church covenant at its organization; frm. May 18, 1631. He took an important share in the plans and movements of the colony. Deputy. Wrote a book, adverse to the Council, which was brought into court in 1642. Took high ground against the capture and murder of negroes in Guinea by Capt. Smith and Mr. Kesar in 1645. [W.] He returned to England and died there, Wife Grace, dau. of Robert Kaye, of Woodsome, Esq., d. before he came to N. E.; ch. Richard, Robert, Samuel, Henry, Rosamond, Grace came to N. E. The sons were active and influential citizens; the daus. returned to England. Second and third wives and other children recorded in Eng. See Genealogy.

SAMOND, see Simmons,

William, ae. 19, came in the Elizabeth and Ann in April, 1635.

SAMS, SAMMES, SAMENS,

John, Roxbury, bought lands about (8) 1640 which passed into possession of Gov. Thomas Dudley in 1642.

Thomas, Salem, Marblehead, 1638. Prosecuted for speaking to a maid servant and contracting marriage with her without leave of her master or mistress. [Es. Court Rec.]

SAMSON, SAMPSON,

Abraham, Duxbury, in court 4 Dec. 1638; propr. 1640; atba. 1643; town officer; frm. 6 June, 1654.

SAMSON, etc., cont.

Henry, cousin of Edward Tillie and his wife, came in the Mayflower to Plymouth. Propr.; frm. Jan. 5, 1635-6; volunteer for the Pequot war in 1637; com. of Court. He rem. to Duxbury.

Will dated 24 (10) 1684, prob. 5 March, 1684-5, beq. to sons Stephen, John, James and Caleb, daus. Elizabeth, wife of Robert Sprout, Hannah, wife of Josias Holmes, dau. now the wife of John Hanmore, Mary, wife of John Summers, Dorcas, wife of Thomas Bony.

John, Marblehead. He was appr. with Richard Chadwell, shipwright, June, 1635, by Francis Toby of Rotherhith, Surrey, Eng. [L.] Attachment against the est. of John Saunders gr. to him by the Court 2 (1) 1640-1. He d. and admin. was gr. 28 (7) 1654, to William Samson. [Reg. VIII, 356.]

Richard, tailor, ae. 28, came in the Elizabeth and Ann in May, 1635.

Robert, a cousin of Gov. John Winthrop, embarked with him for N. E. in 1630.

SANBROOKE, SANDBROOKE, SANDBROCK, SANDERBANT,

John, an only son, bro. to "Sarah, your sister Feake's maid;" had lived a year or two with an attorney; desired to spend his days in New Eng., and came from London to Gov. Winthrop in 1633, apprenticed for 5 years; mentioned by Edward Howes in letter to J. Winthrop, Jr. [Mass. Hist. Coll. 4-6.]

Thomas, Boston.

Will dated 16 (3), prob. 6 (12) 1649. Beq. to wife Elinor; to bro. William S., sister Alice S. and cosen Samuel S.; to the poor members of the chh. of Bo.; to Jonathan Shrimpton; residue to cosen Mr. William Pynson. [Reg. VII, 227.] William Pynson of Woolverhampton, co. Stafford, gent., sent power of attorney 20 Dec. 1658, for the collection of this legacy. [Suff. De. III, 244.]

SANDERS, SAUNDERS, SANDEN, SANDIN, SANDYN,

Arthur, Salem, 1638; Marblehead. Lic. to keep an ordinary in 1640. He and his son witnesses in court in 1645.

Admin. of his est. 25 (4) 1667. The widow Margaret made will Aug. 20, 1667, prob. 23 (5) 1675. To children of dec. son John,

SANDERS, etc., cont.

viz. Samuel and Ephraim; to ch. of Nicholas Merritt by her dau. Mary, being 8 sons and a daughter.

Edward, Watertown, sick at Piscataqua when called to appear before Gen. Court at Boston, 5 (1) 1638-9. Punished 19 Oct. 1654.

Edward, Scituate, served against the Narragansetts in 1645, may be the same.

Daniel, Cambridge, d. Feb. 27, 1639-40.

John, husbandman, ae. 25, from Lanford, Wilts, Eng., with wife Sarah and servants Roger Easman, Wm. Cottle and Robert [Ring,] came in the Confidence April 11, 1638. Was one of those allowed to begin the plantation at "Merrimack," Salisbury, 6 (7) 1638. Frm. May 13, 1640. Rem. to Newbury; town officer. Ret to Weeks in the parish of Downton, Wilts, England, 1655; appointed his kinsman Richard Dole his attorney for business in N. E. 9 May, 1674. He m. [2?] Hester, dau. of John Rolfe; ch. Hester b. Sept. 5, 1639, John b. and d. 1641, Ruth b. Dec. 16, 1642, John b. Dec. 10, 1644, Sarah b. Aug. 20, 1646, Mary b. June 12, 1649, Abigail b. April 12, 1651, Joseph b. 1653, d 1654, Elizabeth b. 26 Jan. 1654.

John, Salem, propr., frm. May 25, 1636. Of Marblehead in 1639. Deputy 1642. "Elizabeth Sanders, i. e. Kitchen," adm. chh. 10 (3) 1640. Ch. John bapt. 1 (9) 1640.

Will Oct. 28, 1643; son John, under age; father Joseph Grafton; wife.

John, Ipswich, propr. 1635; sold before 1639.

John, chief of Mr. Weston's plantation at Weymouth in Feb., 1622-3. [B.]

Marie, ae. 15, came in the Planter April 6, 1635.

Martin, currier, ae. 40, wife Rachel, ae. 40, children Lea, ae. 10, Judith, ae. 8, and Martin, ae. 4, with servants Marie Fuller, ae. 17, Richard Smith, ae. 14, and Richard Ridley, ae. 16, came in the Planter April 6, 1635. Settled at Braintree. Wife Rachel adm. chh. Boston 8 (9) 1635, dism. to chh. of Br. 16 (2) 1639. He deeded lands to his son John when about to marry Mary Monjoy; acknowledged 13 (6) 1657. His wife d. Sept. 15, 1651; he m. Elizabeth, widow of Roger Bancroft.

SANDERS, etc., cont.

He d. Aug. 4, 1658. The widow m. 3, John Bridge. An agreement, made between Elizabeth, John and Martin Saunders, and Francis Eliot, all of Br., the widow and ch. of Martin S., late of Br., was signed 28 (7), and endorsed by Elizabeth Bridge, late widow of M. S., 7 (2) 1659.

Robert, Cambridge, propr. 1639; town officer; frm. May 23, 1639. In partnership with H. Usher 10 (10) 1645. [A.]

Will dated 1 March, prob. 3 May, 1683, beq. to Christian Pelton for the care of him in his old age, and to his sons John, Hopestill and Samuel.

Sylvester, book-binder, Boston, 1637.

Tobiah, Lynn, in court in 1650.

Tobias, Taunton, atba. 1643.

William, carpenter, indebted to Mr. Bellingham and Mr. Gibbins, contracted to serve them 3 years 19 (10) 1636. [W.] One of the founders of Hampton 6 (7) 1638.

SANDERSON, SAUNDERSON,

Edward, Watertown, m. Oct. 15, 1645, Mary Eggleston; ch. Jonathan b. 15 (7) 1646.

Henry, Sandwich, atba. 1643.

Robert, goldsmith, silversmith, Hampton, 1638. Rem. to Watertown; deacon. Sold Hamp. lands in 1650. Rem. to Boston; partner of John Hull, the mint-master. Wife Lydia; second wife Mary, widow of John Cross. Ch. Mary bapt. Oct. 29, 1639, (m. James Peniman,) Joseph b. 1 (11) 1641, Benjamin bapt. 29 (5) 1649, Sarah bapt. 18 (11) 1651, Robert bapt. 22 (8) 1652, John d. Sept. 18, 1658. His wife Mary d. June 21, 1681, ae. 74 years. [Gr. St.] He m. 3, Elizabeth —, who d. Oct. 15, 1695, ae. about 78 years. [Gr. St.]

He d. 7 Oct. 1693. Will prob. 20 Oct. beq. to wife Elizabeth; son Robert S. and dau. Anne West; gr. ch. Robert Darby, Mary Caswell, Joseph Jones, the ch. of Robert and Anna and of James Peniman; gr. gr. dau. Abia Beard; son-in-law Richard West; brother Edward S.; Joseph, son of William S.; refers to house and land at Wat., had by former wife; kinsman Wm. Shattuck of Wat.

The widow's will prob. 21 Nov. 1694, beq. to daus. Ann Beckford and Anna West; to

SANDERSON, etc., cont.
Alice Beard, Mary Caswell, niece Alice Carlile and her dau. Elizabeth, cousin Francis Carlile, Jr.; to Mehitable and Mary, dau. of Thomas Lincoln, Joseph, Richard and Benjamin West; Mary and Lydia, daus. of Wm. Saunderson; gr. dau. Mary Caswell and others. [Reg. LII, 23.]

SANDS, SANDIS, SANDYES,
Mr. Henry, Boston, dism. to the gathering of a church at Rowley 24 (9) 1639; frm. Oct. 6, 1640. Ret. to Bo. Gave letter of attorney 5 (2) 1646. [A.] Assigned ¼ of ship Welcome 3 (11) 1648. Wife Sibil adm. chh. with him 30 (10) 1638; ch. Deliverance bapt. 6 (11) 1638, John b. 28 (6) 1646, Deliverance b. (6) 1644, Mary d. 14 (8) 1654, Samuel b. 20 (4) 1640, d. 20 Feb. 1658, Mercy b. 24 (1) 1640.

He d. in 1651; admin. gr. 30 (11) 1651; many names of creditors given in the papers. [Reg. VII, 336.] The widow's servant, Hannah, dau. of — Ireson of Lynn, d. 5 (9) 1654.

SANFORD, SANDFORD, SAMFORD, SAMFOARD,
John, Boston, memb. chh. 1630, frm. April 3, 1632. Cannonier at the fort, 1634. Memb. of bridge committee, 1633. Wife —; ch. John bapt. 26 (4) 1633, Eliphal, dau. bapt. 10 (10) 1637. Rem. to Rhode Island and was one of the signers of the constitution of that plantation 7 (1) 1637-8.

Richard, laborer, planter, Boston, adm. chh. 30 (11) 1640, frm. June 2, 1641. Placed his son John apprentice with Joseph Armitage, tailor, 14 (11) 1640. [L.] John became a schoolmaster; d. in 1676; beq. to his bro. Robert S. and the ch. of Edward Turner. Wife Margery d. in 1640. Dau. Mary m. 25 (8) 1656, Edward Turner. Son Thomas made will 10 Sept. 1681, inv. filed 7 Aug. 1683.

Thomas, Dorchester, 1634, propr., frm. March 9, 1636-7.

SANKEY,
Robert, ae. 30, "sent away by Robert Cordell, goldsmith, Lombard street, London," came in the Increase April 14, 1635.

SANTLEY, SANCLEY,
John, ae. 34, came in the Abigail in July, 1635. Settled at Cambridge; propr. 1635; sold before 1638.

SANGER, SANGAR,
Richard, ae. 18, came as servant of Edmund Goodenow in the Confidence, April, 1638. Res. at Sudbury; propr. 1639; rem. to Watertown in 1649. Was a blacksmith. Wife Mary; ch. Mary b. 26 (7) 1650, Nathaniel b. Feb. 14, 1651, John b. Sept. 6, 1657, Sarah b. March 31, 1663, Richard b. Feb. 22, 1666-7, Elizabeth b. July 23, 1669, David b. Dec. 21, 1671.

He d. Aug. 20, 1691. He and his sons Nathaniel and John guarded the mill at Wat. during King Philip's War. [Bond.]

SAPE,
Mary, ae. 12, came with the family of Thomas Oliver of Norwich, Eng. May 13, 1637.

SARELL, see Sale and Searl.

SARGENT, SARGEANT, SERGEANT,
Mary, servant to Thomas Matson, d. in Braintree (8) 1641.

William, late of Northampton, haberdasher of hats, now of Charlestown in N. E. planter, and Sarah, his wife, late the wife of William Minshall of Whitchurch, Salop, Eng.; a certificate of their health was made Nov. 14, 1639. [L.] Adm. chh. Char. 10 and 17 (1) 1638-9. Rem. to Malden, where he was an active citizen, deacon and lay-preacher in the church. [J.] Rem. to Barnstable. Wife Sarah; ch. Elizabeth, Hannah, John bapt. 8 (10) 1639, Ruth b. 25 (8) 1642, Samuel b. 3 (1) 1644.

He d. Dec. 16, 1682. Will dated 9 March, 1679-80, prob. March 3, 1682-3, beq. to wife Sarah his house at Mal.; to sons John and Samuel and daus. Hannah Felch and Ruth Bourn; to gr. son Samuel Bill. The widow d. Jan. 12, 1688-9.

Mr. William, seaman, one of the first to plant at "Agawam," or Ipswich, April 1, 1633. [Col. Rec.] Frm. May 2, 1638. Also one of the first proprs. of Hampton, 6 (7) 1638. Propr. and res. of Salisbury, 1639-1650; res. at Newbury in 1652. Ret. to Salis.; one of the founders of Amesbury. Made gift-deeds to sons Thomas and William in 1669. Theophilus Shatswell calls him brother. [He m. Elizabeth, dau. of John Perkins;] he m. Sept. 18, 1670, Joanna, wid-

SARGENT, etc., cont.
ow of Valentine Rowell, who survived him and m. Oct. 26, 1676, Richard Currier. Ch. Lydia, Mary, (m. Philip Challis,) Elizabeth d. Sept. 14, 1641, Thomas b. June 11, 1643, William b. Jan. 2, 1645, Elizabeth b. Nov. 22, 1648, (m. Samuel Colby,) Sarah b. Feb. 29, 1651, (m. Orlando Bagley). His will dated March 24, 1670-1, prob. April 13, 1675, beq. to ch. Thomas, William, Mary, Elizabeth and Sarah; gr. ch. William, Elizabeth, Lydia, Mary and Philip Watson Challis; Dorothy and Elizabeth Colby and William Sargent. Thomas and Sarah execs.; bro.-in-law Thomas Bradbury and friend Maj. Robert Pike overseers.

William, Gloucester, propr. 1645. He signed the mill agreement in 1664, and deposed regarding it in 1694, ae. about 71 years. Wife Abigail; ch. William b. Aug. 16, 1658, Samuel b. May 22, 1661, Nathaniel b. and d. 1663, Abigail b. May 8, 1665, Nathaniel b. 28 (3) 1671, Joseph b. 27 (1) 1675, Mary b. 24 (9) 1678. Inv. of his est. taken 25 May, 1711; admin. gr. to Daniel Sargent.

SATCHWELL, see Shatswell.

SARY,
Ralph, [Roxbury?] had leave from Gen. Court 22 May, 1639, to reside where his house was,—though above half a mile from the meeting-house.

SAVAGE,
Thomas, tailor, ae. 27, cert. from the parish of St. Albons, Eng., came in the Planter April 2, 1635; settled at Boston; adm. chh. 3 (11) 1635, frm. May 25, 1636. Became captain in militia. Rem. to R. I. in 1637, and was one of the signers of the constitution and purchasers of the land from the Indians. Sold property 12 (6) 1639; [L.] ret. to Boston, in a short time. Signed inv. of Wm. Joice in 1648. Did a large business as a merchant. He deposed 26 (9) 1664, ae. about 57 years. [Es. Files X, 59.] He m. 1, Faith, dau. of William Hutchinson; ch. Abijah b. 1 (6) 1638, Thomas b. 28 (3) 1640, Hannah b. 28 (4) 1643, (m. Oct. 26, 1660, Benjamin Gillam,) Ephraim b. 2 (5) 1645, Mary bapt. 6 (4) 1647, Dorithea bapt. 30 (10) 1649, Perez b. 17 (12) 1651. Faith d. 20 (12) 1651. He m. 2, 15 (7) 1652, Mary, dau. of Zachariah

SAVAGE, cont.
Symmes, pastor of Charlestown; ch. Sarah b. June 25, 1653, Richard bapt. 27 (6) 1654, d. 23 (7) 1655, Samuel b. Nov. 16, 1655, Samuel b. Aug. 22, d. 22 (6) 1657, Zachariah bapt. 4 (5) 1658, Ebenezer b. May 22, 1660, John b. Aug. 15, 1661, Benjamin bapt. 12 (8) 1662, Arthur b. Feb. 26, 1663, Elizabeth b. Nov. 8, 1667.

Will prob. 23 Feb. 1681, devised to wife Mary; daus. Hannah Gillam, Mary Thatcher, — Higginson, H. Dinnice; sons Thomas, Ephraim, Ebenezer, Benjamin and Perez; to the widow Hannah and son Thomas of dec. son Habia; to the four ch. of Mary Thatcher, and to Mary, dau. of dau. Higginson.

SAVEL, SAVILL,
William, joiner, Cambridge; account of work for Nathl. Eaton, 1641. [L.] Rem. to Braintree. Wife Hanna; ch. John b. 22 (2) 1642, Samuel b. 30 (8) 1643, Benjamin b. 28 (8) 1645, Hannah b. 11 (1) 1647, (m. (3) 1669, John Needam,) William b. 17 (5) 1650. His wife Hanna d. 14 (6) 1650; he m. 2, 6 (9) 1655, Sarah Gannitt; ch. Sarah b. 1 (8) 1654.

He d. 6 (2) 1669. Will 19 Feb. 1668-9. Wife Sarah; sons John, Samuel, Benjamin and William; daus. Hannah and Sarah. Agreement made 14 June, 1669, between widow and sons; she to have all she brought their father. [Reg. XLVIII, 323.]

SAVORY,
Anthony, Plymouth, frm. 1633.

John, a servant of Walter Merry, shipwright, Boston, in 1640. [L.]

Thomas, came in the Mary and John March 24, 1633-4; settled at Plymouth; one of the party at Kennebec, in the Hocking affair in 1634. In Plym. Court 5 Oct. 1636. Marshall, 1652. Before Gen. Court at Boston in 1638 and 1640. Sold a house about 16 Sept. 1641. Suit for a canoe, Plym. Court, 1646. He rec'd beq. from Timothy Hatherly, his employer, in 1644. He placed his son Thomas, ae. 5 years, apprentice to Thomas Lettice, carpenter, 2 Aug. 1653, and Benjamin, ae. 9 years, with John Shaw 3 Nov. 1653. Ch. Moses b. 22 Jan. 1649, d. 9 June, 1050, Samuel b. 4 June, 1651, Jonathan b. 4 March, 1652, Mara b. 7 April, 1654. Wife Annis.

SAVORY, cont.
Will dated April, 1674, prob. 7 March, 1676, beq. all to wife Anne, she to consider son Aaron at her decease. She deeded in 1677-8 to sons Anthony and Aaron, land her husband obtained of their bro.-in-law Samuel Eddy. [Genealogy, Reg. XLI, 369.]

William, came in the Mary and John March 24, 1633.

SAWEN, SAWIN, SAWING,
John, cordwinder, Watertown, frm. May 26, 1652. A son of Robert Sawin, late of Boxford, co. of Suff. Eng. He sold Oct. 12, 1651, to Samuel Groome of Langham, Essex, [Eng.] shipwright, his house and garden in Boxford; reserving the rights of his bro.'s wife, promising to give in addition a deed from his wife if desired. Legatee of Edward Skinner of Cambridge in 1641. Wife Abigail, [dau. of George Munning;] ch. Munning b. 14 (2) 1655, Thomas b. Sept. 27, 1657.
Inv. taken 1 Oct. 1690; admin. gr. to his sons John and Munning S.

SAWKYNN,
William, ae. 25, came in the Defense in July, 1635.

SAWFORD,
Elizabeth, Charlestown, adm. chh. 28 (11) 1641.

SAWTELL, SARETELL, SATELL,
Richard, Watertown, propr. 1636. Wife Elizabeth; ch. Elizabeth b. 1 (3) 1640, Jonathan b. 24 (6) 1639, Mary b. 19 (9) 1640, Hannah b. 10 (10) 1642, Zechariah b. 26 (5) 1643. Rem. to Groton; town clerk.
He d. Aug. 2, 1694. His wife d. Oct. 18 1694.

Thomas, Boston, one of our Teacher's servants, adm. chh. 17 (2) 1647; frm. May 2, 1649.
Will, written by Mr. John Wilson, prob. 18 (9) 1651. To Mary Wilson, dau. of the minister; to his bro. Richard Sattell and to Richard's eldest son; to his bro. and sister Kenricke at Muddy River. Admin. gr. to Richard Sautell. [Reg. IV, 286, and XXX, 204.]

SAYER, SAYERS, SAYRE, SAYRES, SAY, SAYS, SEGARS,
Elizabeth, and Mary came from Hingham, Eng., in 1638, and settled in Hingham.

James, tailor, of Northbourn, Eng., came in the Hercules of Sandwich, in March, 1634.

Job, Lynn, propr. in 1638 of 60 acres at Rumney Marsh. [Suff. De. I, 55.] Rem. to Southampton, L. I. Deposed 16 May, 1641, ae. 28 yrs.; b. in Bretfortshier, [Bedfordshire.]

Thomas, Lynn, propr., frm. May 22, 1638. Rem. to Southampton, L. I. in 1640.

SAWYER, SAYER, SAYERS, SAIER, SAWER, SAYWARD,
Edmund, Ipswich, propr. 1635.

Edward, Rowley, propr. before 1645; deposed in 1668, ae. about 60 years. Wife Mary; ch. Sarah b. and d. 1645, John b. 17 (7) 1647.
He was bur. 9 March, 1673; nunc. will prob. 31 March, 1674.

Henry, millwright, Salisbury, propr., recd. grant of land with Abraham Morrill for a corn mill in 1641.

Thomas, yeoman, Lancaster, propr. 1648; town officer, 1652. He m. [in 1648] Mary [Prescott.] Ch. Thomas b. 2 (5) 1649, Ephraim b. 16 (1) 1650, Marie b. 4 (11) 1652, Joshua b. 13 (1) 1655, James b. 22 (1) 1657, Caleb b. 22 (2) 1659.
Will dated 6 March, 1705-6, prob. April 12, 1720, beq. to wife Mary, sons Thomas, Joshua, James, Caleb and Nathaniel, and dau. Mary Wilder. The latter testified that she had her father and mother during 8 or 9 months while her bro. Thomas was in captivity.

William, Salem, propr. 1642. Rem. to Newbury. Sold house and lot March 24, 1648. Wife Ruth; ch. John b. 24 Aug. 1645, Samuel b. 22 Nov. 1646, Ruth b. 16 Sept. 1648, Mary b. 7 Feb. 1649, d. June 24, 1659, Hannah b. and d. 1659, Frances b. 1658, d. 1659, Mary b. 29 July, 1660, Stephen b. 25 April, 1663, Hannah b. 11 Jan. 1664, d. Aug. 1, 1683, Francis b. 3 Nov. 1670.

SAXTON, see Sexton,
Thomas, miller, inn-holder, Boston, 1644. Wife Luce; ch. Mary b. 2 (11) 1644, John b. 29 June, 1647. He m. 2, 10 (1) 1651, Ann Atwood, widow; ch. Samuel b. 8 Oct. 1653, Joseph bapt. 11 (3) 1656, Nathaniel b. Nov. 29, 1658, Elizabeth b. June 8, 1661, (m. at Chelmsford May 8, 1678, Josiah, son of Capt. James Parker). The wife Ann d. 23 June, 1661. Third wife Mary; ch. Benjamin b. May 18, 1664, Mary b. Jan. 9, 1665, Moses b. May 31, 1669. With wife Mary he mortg. land in 1674.

Will of Thomas Saxton, Sen. of Boston, inn-holder, dated 11 May, 1676, prob. 2 Dec. 1686, beq. to wife Mary and children. Inv. mentions money to his son Thomas S.'s relict.

SCADDING,
William, Scituate, witness and appraiser to will of John Bryant, 1638.

SCALES, SCAILS,
William, Rowley, prop. frm. May 13, 1640. [John, James, Susanna, were they his children?]
He was bur. July 10, 1682.

SCARBARROW, SCARBROW, SCARBOROUGH,
John, Roxbury, frm. May 13, 1640; his wife Mary adm. chh. about the same time. Ch. John b. and d. in 1642, Hannah bapt. Dec. 3, 1643, Samuel b. Jan. 20, 1645.

He was slaine by charging a great gunne, June 9, 1646. Inv. filed 17 (12) 1656. [Reg. VIII, 56.] His widow m. 2, Oct. 1, 1647, Philip Torrey. [Court Rec. 4 (9) 1646.]

SCARLET,
Anne, widow, Salem, member chh. and propr. 1636; d. 28 (12) 1639; will prob. (11) 1642. Bro. Samuel Scarlet in old Eng.; her three ch. Mary, Margaret and Joseph; sister Dennice; bro. James [Hindes] and his wife; bro. Joseph Grafton. Margaret adm. chh. 27 (12) 1642.

Jane, widow, mother of Edward Bendall, adm. chh. Boston, 6 (10) 1635.

John, mariner, Boston, 1640. Occupied a house and brew-house of Edward Bendall's in 1653. Bought land April 24, 1658. Wife Thomasine adm. chh. 2 (2) 1654; ch. Mary and Jane b. Sept. 21, 1653.

SCARLET, cont.
Will dated Feb. 16, prob. 21 March, 1687-8. To wife; to dau. Thomasine Taylor; to gr. son James Fryer.

Robert, servant of Benjamin Felton, in Court in 1635 and 1636.

Samuel, Boston, mariner, a witness in 1645 to James Smith's sale; deposed July 30, 1663, ae. about 43 years. His wife Mary (Ellis) Scarlet had house in Boston from her uncle, Maj. Gen. Edward Gibbons, in 1645. [Suff. De. II, 172.]

His will dated April 22, prob. 16 May, 1675, beq. his very large property to his wife; to ffreegrace Bendall; Love Proute and her heirs; Jerusha Rae and her heirs; to Hopefor and Ephraim Bendall; Mary, Thomasine, Betty and Jane Scarlett; to his brother's 3 daughters; to John Feake, Jr.; to the second church in Boston; to Harvard College; and to the poor of the town of Kersy in Suffolk in old England, the place of his nativity. Final division made by the trustees 30 Jan. 1679.

SCHOFIELD, SCOFIELD,
Richard, ae. 23, came in the Susan and Ellen in April, 1635; settled at Ipswich; leather-dresser; bought house and land in 1640. Sold 2 (5) 1643. Wife Mary.

SCHOULER,
William, Merrimack, near Newbury, a vintner, from London. For murder of Mary Sholy, sentenced to be hung 19 (7) 1637.

SCOBELL,
John, carpenter, Boston, brought suit against John Holland for work done, 10 (1) 1640. [L.]

SCOLLARD, SCULLARD, SKULLARD,
Samuel, Newbury, 1637. One of the original grantees of Hampton, 1638; but did not go to reside. He m. Rebecca, [dau. of Richard Kent.] Ch. Mary b. 9 Jan. 1641, Rebekah b. 4 Feb. d. 6 March, 1643, Sarah b. 18 June, 1645, Martha d. 6 March, 1645.

He d. in April, 1647. Will dated 27 (1) prob. 28 (7) 1647; beq. to wife and daus. Mary and Sarah; provision for expected son. The widow m. John Bishop.

SCOATES, see Scott and Scotto.
Thomas, of Sarum, came in the James April 5, 1635.

SCOTT,
Benjamin, Cambridge. Wife Mary; ch. Joseph b. 14 (15) 1644, Benjamin b. 5 (5) 1645. Wife Margaret; ch. John b. 2 (5) 1648. Is Benjamin of Rowley, 1662, the same? Will dated June 6, prob. Sept. 26, 1671. His widow Margaret was executed for witchcraft in Salem 22 Sept. 1693.

Benjamin, Braintree, 1643. Wife Hannah; ch. Hannah, (m. Christopher Webb 18 (11) 1654,) John b. 25 (10) 1640, Peter b. 6 March, 1643, Benjamin, (d. 1683; beq to Benjamin, son of his bro. Peter S., and to the ch. of his bro. Chr. Webb).

He d., and the widow Hannah m. 21 (7) 1647, John Harbor, who gave bonds for the payments of the children's portions.

John, Charlestown, adm. chh. 17 (2) 1642, frm. May 22, 1639. Constable, 1658; deposed, ae. about 50 years. [Mdx. Files.] Will dated 9 Nov. 1681, prob. April 4, 1682, beq. to William Wilson and his wife Remember, their son William; to the ch. of Edward Wilson.

John, servant to Lawrence Southwick, of Salem; his time extended by Gen. Court 10 May, 1648.

Richard, shoemaker, Boston, adm. chh. 28 (6) 1634. [See Newport records.] Is he the man who m. a sister of Mrs. Hutchinson and was re-bapt. by Williams, the wife by Holyman, in 1638? [W.] He recd. beq. from his bro. George Scott, of London, merchant, in will dated 9 Sept. 1640, prob. 22 April, 1642; in which reference is made to their father Edward Scott, of Glemsford, co. Suffolk, clothier. [Reg. LI, 254.]

Robert, late servant to John Sampford, was adm. chh. Boston 15 (10) 1633; merchant, haberdasher, 1639, [L.] frm. May 10, 1643. Bought ½ of the bark Bride 18 (9) 1648. Was a partner of Robert Harding at one time. His wife Elizabeth was adm. chh. 10 (12) 1638. She deposed 4 Dec. 1663, ae. about 47, that she knew Robert Smith about 26 years ago. [See Smith.] Ch. Nathaniel bapt. 19 (6) 1638, Elizabeth b. 10 (10) 1640, Mary b. 28 (12) 1642, Mary bapt. 5 (1) 1643, ae. about 6 days, John b. and d. 1645, John bapt. 16

SCOTT, cont.
(6) 1646, ae. about 20 days, Samuel bapt. 1 (6) 1647, ae. about 4 days, John bapt. 6 (3) 1649, ae. about 15 days, Joseph bapt. 9 (4) 1650, Redemption b. March 2, 1653, *Deliverance* bapt. 6 (1) 1653, Eleazer b. 18 July, 1654.

Admin. gr. to widow Elizabeth March 24, 1653. [Reg. VIII, 276.] She m. 2, John Sweete.

Roger, before Es. grand jury 14 (10) 1642.

Thomas, ae. 40, with wife Elizabeth, ae. 40, and ch. Thomas, ae. 11, and Elizabeth, ae. 9, came in the Elizabeth of Ipswich April 30, 1635. Martha Scott, ae. 60, came in the same ship. He settled at Cambridge; propr. 1633, frm. March 4, 1634-5. Rem. to Ipswich; propr. 1635; town officer, 1653. He was a son of Henry Skott of Rattlesden, Suffolk, yeoman, and his wife Martha; the father d. in 1624, and the widow came as above; her dau. Ursula, wife of Richard Kembold or Kimball, came in the same ship. [Reg. LII, 248.]

Will dated 8 March, 1653-4, prob. 28 (1) 1654, beq. to son Thomas; daus. Elizabeth, Abigail, Hannah, Sarah and Mary. Bros. Richard Kimball, Thomas Rowlinson, Sen. and Edmund Bridges, execs. His son Thomas S., of Stamford, Conn. sold land in Ips. by his agent Rich. K. 31 Jan. 1654. He paid legacy of his father to his sister Hannah, wife of Edmund Lockwood, of Stamford, 15 March, [1667.] After his death, in 1683, his sisters Abigail, wife of Haniel Bosworth, and Elizabeth Spofford, with Thomas Patch, petitioned for re-admin. of the est. of their father. [Es. Files 41, 71.] The widow m. Mr. Ezekiel Rogers; made will at Boston, June 22, 1678, prob. 2 (6) 1678, beq. to son and dau. Snelling's children and dau. Martha R.

SCOTTO, SCOTTON, [see Cobbett,]
Joshua, merchant, Boston, adm. chh. 19 (3) 1639, with his bro. Thomas; reference to their mother, "our sister Thomasine Scottoe." Propr., ensign. Sold house and land at B. to Robert Windsor Jan. 2, 1656. He deposed 7 (2) 1657, ae. about 40 years. [Mdx. Files.] Wife Lydia adm. chh. 23 (3) 1641; ch. Joshua b. and d. 1641, Joshua b. 12 (6) 1643, Lydia b. 30 (4) 1645, Elizabeth bapt. 1 (6) 1647, ae. about 2 days, Rebecca b. 10

SCOTTO, etc., cont.

Oct. 1652, Mary b. 11 May, 1656, Thomas b. 30 June, 1659.

He d. Jan. 2, 1697-8, ae. 83 years. [Gr. St.] Will dated 23 June, 1696, prob. 3 March, 1697-8, beq. to wife Lydia; ch. Thomas, Elizabeth Savage, Rebecca Blackman, Mary Checkley and Sarah Walker; sons-in-law Maj. Thomas Savage and Capt. Samuel Checkley.

Thomas, joiner, Boston, frm. May 22, 1638, adm. chh. 19 (3) 1639. The town gave leave March 6, 1637-8, to Thomas Scottoe, the son of our sister Thomasine Scottoe, to build an house on his mother's ground. Thomas and wife Joan had ch. Thomas bapt. 8 (10) 1639, Thomas b. and d. (4) 1641, Thomas b. and d. 1642, John b. 2 (3) 1644, Thomas b. 3 (1) 1646-7, d. 11 (9) 1657, Mehetabel bapt. 11 (12) 1648, ae. about 4 days, Joshua (of Thomas and Sarah) b. 23 Dec. 1655, Sarah b. 27 Sept. 1657, Thomasine b. 4, d. 26 Aug. 1659, Thomasine b. Aug. 18, 1660. Sarah adm. chh. 26 (3) 1661.

Will prob. Dec. 18, 1661; wife Sarah, son John; other children; bro. Joshua Scotto, aged mother Sanford. [Reg. X, 362.]

Thomasine, widow, adm. chh. Boston 7 (7) 1634. She had sons Thomas and Joshua.

SCRAGGS, SCRUGGS,

Thomas, Salem, propr., frm. and deputy, Sept. 2, 1635. Town officer. Comr. of first Quarterly Court held at Salem, 27 (4) 1636. Wife Margery. His dau. Rachel Raiment adm. to full communion in chh. 22 (11) 1661.

Inv. filed 24 (4) 1654. The widow sold her rights of dower to her son-in-law John Rayment same month.

SCUDDER, SKUDDER,

John, ae. 16, came in the James in June, 1635. Settled at Salem; currier. Propr. 1642-6. His wife memb. chh. 21 (1) 1647; ch. Mary bapt. 11 (4) 1648, Hannah bapt. 19 (6) 1649. He rem. to Southold, L. I.; sold Salem land in 1665.

John, Barnstable, atba. 1643; frm. June 6, 1654. Elizabeth, Gamaliel Wayte's maid adm. chh. of Boston 28 (5) 1644; dism. to chh. of Barnstable 10 (8) 1644; she m. Nov. 28, 1644, Samuel, son of Mr. John Lothrop.

SCUDDER, etc., cont.

He d. and she m. John Scudder. Ch. John, (of Elizabeth, formerly Lothrop, now wife of J. S.,) bapt. in Boston 7 (10) 1645, Elizabeth and Sarah bapt. at Barnstable May 10, 1646, Mary bur. Dec. 3, 1649, Hannah bapt. Oct. 5, 1651. Goody Scudder was a sister of the wife of Abraham Pierce. [Sci. and Bar. Chh. Rec., Reg. IX and X.]

Thomas, Sen. Salem, propr. 1638-1649. [Wife] Elizabeth adm. chh. 21 (4) 1640; ch. Eliza. bapt. 18 (1) 1649, Rachel, not described,) adm. chh. 4 (1) 1649.

His will dated 30 Sept. 1657, prob. 29 June, 1658, beq. to wife Elizabeth; ch. John, Thomas, Henry, Elizabeth Bartholomew; to Thomas, son of dec. son William. The inv. of widow Elizabeth was filed 29 (9) 1666.

SEABERRY, SEABURY,

John, planter, seaman, Boston, bought house 25 (9) 1639, and was adm. inhabitant. Rem. to Barbadoes. [Depos. of Chr. Clarke in Arch. 15 B.] Wife Grace adm. chh. 15 (3) 1642; ch. Samuel b. 10 (10) 1640, bapt. 22 (3) 1642. She went to her husband at Bardoes, and after his death, but before Feb. 1650, m. Anthonie Lane. She approved 14 Oct. 1651, of the sale of a house of her husband's by John Milam. [Gen. Court Rec.] Sons Samuel of Duxbury and John of Barbadoes, laid claim to certain lands formerly belonging to their father, April 16, 1662.

SEAGAR, SEAGER, SEGAR,

Jacob, Watertown, propr. 1642.

Lawrence, a youth of about 17 yrs., from Hampton, Eng., came in the James April 5, 1635.

Thomas, Newbury, 1637.

William, Watertown, his lands referred to in a deed of Simon Onge in 1646.

SEALIS, SILLIS, SYLICE, SYLLIS,

Richard, planter, Scituate, joined the chh. Dec. 24, 1637. Deacon, 1653. He m. Dec. 15, 1637, Eglin Handford, Mr. Hatherly's sister, who had joined the chh. Nov. 21, 1635. Frm. Sept. 4, 1638. Edward Foster, in his will, 1643, calls him father.

Will 17 (11) 1653; wife Egline, daus. Hannah, wife of John Winchester, and Hester, wife of Samuel Jackson. [Reg. V, 335.]

SEABORNE,
John, tailor, Boston, 1639. Wife Mary adm. chh. 20 (6) 1644.

SEARL, SEARLE, SERLE, SALE, see also Sale,
John, Springfield, lot-measurer, 1637; propr., taxed in 1638. He m. 19 (1) 1638-9, Sarah Bauldwin. Ch. John b. 30 (3) 1641. He was bur. 6 (7) 1641. His widow had additional lands granted.

Philip, Sen., Roxbury, sold his share in Nipmung lands in 1639. [Sons] Philip and John had families. [Rox. rec.]

Richard, servant to Elias Parkman of Dorchester, prosecuted for resisting punishment 3 (3) 1637. [W.]

SEARCH,
John, weaver, Boston, adm. chh. 19 (7) 1641, frm. May 18, 1642. Wife Katharine adm. chh. 29 (11) 1641. Bought house and land in B. which they had occupied some time Oct. 7, 1661.

SEARS, SEARES, SARES, SAYER, SAYERS, SEERS, SEIR,
John, Charlestown, adm. chh. 28 (1) 1641; deposed in 1663, ae. about 50. [Arch. 106.] Frm. June 2, 1641. Rem. to Woburn, 1640; town officer. Licensed to keep a house of common entertainment in 1653. Wife Susanna adm. chh. 2 (12) 1639; she d. Aug. 29, 1677. He m. 2, Hester, widow of Henry Mason, q. v. She d. Aug. 14, 1680; he m. 3, Nov. 2, 1680, Ann Farrar. Hester's will, dated 2 March, 1679-80, prob. at Boston July 12, 1680, beq. to Joseph, son of Joseph and Mary Ellitt; to my sister Deborah Sketton, sister Curtice, bros. Isaac, Israel and Abraham How and their ch.; cousin Mary Grandee's ch.; to Sarah and Hester Parker; to her husband John S.
He d. Oct. 5, 1697.

Richard, Plymouth, taxed in 1632. Taxed at Marblehead in 1637. Rem. to Yarmouth; propr. 1638; atba. 1643; frm. 7 June, 1653. Comrs. app. 26 Oct. 1647, to meet at his house on Indian affairs.
Will, dated 10 (3) 1667, cod. dated 3 Feb. 1675, prob. 15 Nov. 1676, by widow Dorothy and eldest son Paul; beq. to youngest son Sylas; to son-in-law Zachery Paddock and his wife Deborah; to eldest son Paull; to

SEARS, etc., cont.
wife Dorothy; brother Thacher; to Ichabod Paddock. [Reg. XL, 261.]
[The pedigree stated in Sears' Genealogy shown to be mythical, in Reg. XL, 261.]

Thomas, Newbury, propr. 1638; bought house and lot of Wm. Sawyer in 1648. He m. 11 Dec. 1656, Mary Hilton alias Downer; ch. Mary b. 30 Oct. 1657, Rebecca b. 15 Nov. 1661.
He d. 16 May, 1661, inv. pres. 26 (9) 1661.

SEAVER, SEVER,
Robert, Roxbury, came in the Mary and John March 24, 1633-4; frm. April 18, 1637. He m. Dec. 10, 1634, Elizabeth Allard; she d. June 6, 1657. He m. 2, Elizabeth Ballard, who d. 18 (10) 1669; he d. May 13, 1683, ae. about 74. Ch. Shuball b. Jan. 31, 1639, Caleb and Joshua b. Aug. 30, 1641, Elizabeth b. 19 (9) 1643, Nathaniel bapt. Jan. 8, 1645, Hannah b. Feb. 14, 1647, d. 3 (4) 1648, Hannah b. Oct. 13, 1650, d. 3 (12) 1653. [Reg. IX, 287.]
His will, dated 16 Jan. 1681, prob. 5 July, 1683, beq. to his wife; to sons Shubael, Joshua and Caleb; to son Samuel Crafts and gr. son John Seavers. Signed Robert Seaver.

SEDGWICK,
John, ae. 24, came in the Truelove in Sept. 1635.

Robert, captain, merchant, deputy and frm. March 9, 1636-7, Charlestown. With wife Joanna adm. chh. 27 (12) 1636. Bought part of a house in Boston Sept. 1, 1638. [L.] One of the founders of the Artillery company in 1638. As Major General he had command of all the ships sailing from New England in 1654. [Suff. De. II, 185.] He recd. from the government 6 June, 1655, £ 1793 for naval services. John Sedgwicke, brewer, of St. Saviour's, Southwark, Eng. in his will, dated 27 Nov. 1638, speaks of Woburn Bedfs. where he was born; beq. to his bro. Robert Sedgwicke of Charlestown in N. E.; mentions his mother Elizabeth Sedgwick of W., widow He was a son of William S. of London, gent. [Reg. XXXVIII, 206.] Ch. Samuel bapt. 31 (1) 1639, Hannah bapt. 14 (1) 1641, William, Robert.
He d. in Jamaica, May 24, 1656. Admin. gr. in London to his widow Johanna 30 Sept. 1656. She afterward m. Rev. Thomas Allen, formerly of Char.

SEDLEY,
James, Wessaguscus, (Weymouth,) paid by Mr. Pynchon for killing a wolf in 1632.

SEELEY, SELY,
Robert, Watertown, 1630; frm. May 18, 1631. Sold to his servant, Philip Swadden the balance of his service, 14 June, 1631. App. to lay out and measure lots Sept. 13, 1634. Rem. to Wethersfield, Conn. Was second in command under Capt. Mason in the Pequot War; one of the founders of New Haven.

SELLECK, ZELLECK, ZELLESH, ZULLESH,
David, soap-boiler, Dorchester, frm. May 18, 1642. Bought house and land in Dorch. 24 (4) 1639, [L.] and in Boston 24 (12) 1641, and rem. thither. He did a large amount of trading and commerce along the coast. Wife Susan adm. chh. Boston 25 (1) 1643. He was rec'd from Dorch. chh. 23 (1) 1644. Ch. David b. 11 (10) 1638, Jonathan b. 20 (3) 1641, John b. 21 (2) 1643, Nathaniel bapt. 27 (5) 1645, ae. about 9 days, Johanna bapt. 13 (12) 1647, ae. about 2 days, Elizabeth b. 1 (12) 1651, Susanna d. 10 (9) 1653.
He d. about Oct. 1, 1654, in Virginia. Admin. by William Brenton 18 (12) 1654-5. [Reg. IX, 58, and 141, and XVI, 49.]

SELLEN,
Joan, ae. 52, and Ann, ae. 7, came in the Elizabeth April 17, 1635.

John, allowed to plant at Agawam, (Ipswich,) May 29, 1633. [Court Rec.]

Thomas, Boston, 1638, Braintree, d. 3 (10) 1642.
[Is this the "Solling" who was expected to go with his wife to John Winthrop, Jr., at Hartford in 1636? [W.]]

SEMOND, see Simmons.

SENDALL, SINDALL,
Samuel, cooper, Newbury, Boston; frm. May, 1645. Wife Joanna; they sold land in B. Nov. 16, 1663. Ch. Joanna bapt. in B. 21 (7) 1651, Mary b. March 13, 1652, d. 23 (5) 1654, Ann bapt. 26 (2) 1657. He deposed 30 Oct., 1667, ae. about 50 yrs.
Will prob. 8 Oct. 1684, beq. to his "singular comfortable and good wife," to whom he made deed of gift before marriage, dated 4 Oct. 1681; to her dau. Abigail Warren; to his dau. Johanna Hunloke; to cousins Mary, wife of John Cotta, and Johanna Wing; to son-in-law John Hunloke and his ch. John, Jonathan, Johanna, Sarah and Mary. Certain lands in co. with Maj. Robert Pike.

SENNETT, SINNOTT,
Nicholas, ae. 13, came in the Elizabeth and Ann in April, 1635.

Walter, Waters, fisherman, Boston. Wife Mary adm. chh. 23 (3) 1647; ch. Mary b. 19 (9) 1640, (m. 26 Nov. 1661, John Sparke,) Elizabeth b. 23 (4) 1642, John b. 10 (5) 1643, Stephen b. 12 (9) 1645, d. 14 (7) 1657; all but Elizabeth bapt. 30 (3) 1647; Joseph bapt. 12 (1) 1648, Sarah bapt. 28 (2) 1650, Thomas bapt. 28 (1) 1652, Isaac b. and d. 1654.
He d. intestate. Order for division of his est. Nov. 20, 1667; and land sold by John for all the heirs Feb. 11, folg.

SENSION,
Matthias, Dorchester, frm. Sept. 3, 1634. Rem. to Windsor, Conn.

SEPHEN,
Henry, Sandwich, atba. 1643.

SEWALL, SEWELL, SEWILL, SHEWELL,
Henry, of Coventry, Eng., gent., "son of Henry Sewall or Shewell of C., alderman, dec.," gave an outfit of servants and cattle to his son Henry, who came in the Elizabeth and Dorcas in 1634; wintered at Ipswich, and in spring of 1635 rem. to Newbury. He also gave 500 acres of land in N. and valuable property in Coventry to Henry upon his marriage with Jane, dau. of Stephen Dummer March 25, 1646. [A.] He and his wife Ellen arranged before Gen. Court 6 Oct., 1635, with reference to residence and support. Called to court in 1650. [See will of his mother Margaret, ae. 72 years, 7 May, 1628. [Reg. LII, 250.]
He d. in Rowley in March, 1656-7, in his 81st year.
The son Henry, frm. May 17, 1637, was an important citizen of Newbury. He returned to England and resided some years; several of his children were born there. He came back before 1648. He d. May 16, 1700, ae. 86. His widow d. 13 Jan. folg. ae. 74. Of their ch. the most distinguished was Sam-

SEWALL, etc., cont.
uel, known in history as "Judge Sewall." His inter-leaved almanacs, which have come down to us, contain many very valuable notes upon personages of the colonial period. [See Hist. Col.; Hist. Newbury; Reg. VII, 46, 205.]

Nathaniel, one of the 20 ch. sent over from Eng. in the Seabridge in 1643; d. in 1644 through exposure and ill-use of his master William Franklin.

Thomas, (also called Sowell,) Springfield, 1648. Ch. — b. and d. in 1648, Abigail b. 14 (1) 1649.

SEWARD, see Sawyer,
William, Taunton, atba. 1643. Rem. to Conn. [Reg. LII, 323.]

SEVERANCE, SEVERANS,
John, victualler, vintner, Ipswich, propr. 1637. Rem. to Salisbury; propr. 1639. Wife Abigail d. June 17, 1658; he m. Oct. 2, 1663, Susanna, widow of Henry Ambrose. Ch. Samuel b. 19 (7) 1637, Ebenezer b. 7 (1) 1637, Abigail b. and d. 1641, Abigail b. 25 (3) 1643, (m. John Church,) Mary b. 5 (6) 1645, (m. James Coffin,) John b. 24 (9) 1647, Joseph b. 14 (12) 1649, Elizabeth b. 8 (2) 1652, d. 23 (4) 1658, Benjamin b. Jan., 1654, Ephraim b. April 8, 1656, Elizabeth b. June 17, 1658, d. Feb. 5, 1662-3.

He d. April 9, 1682. Will dated April 7, prob. May 9, 1682, beq. to wife Susanna; sons John, Ephraim and others; gr. ch. Jonathan Church; son-in-law James Coffin.

SEVERN, SEAVERN, SEVERNE, SEBBORNE, SYVERENS, see Seaborn,
John, tailor, Boston, frm. May 17, 1637. Having served 3 yrs. in town, was adm. inhab. 12 (6) 1639. Wife Mary; ch. Elizabeth b. 21 (8) 1642, Mary b. 15 (7) 1644, Deborah b. and d. 1645.

SEXTON, SAXTON, see Saxton,
[Rev.] Giles, [Charlestown,] memb. jury at Bratcher inquest Sept., 1630; frm. May, 1631. He appears to be the minister, a Yorkshire man, studious and learned, who resided at Scituate and Boston, and afterward returned to England—to Leeds. [C. M.] [L., P. D.]

Richard, ae. 24, came in the Blessing in July, 1635.

SHAFLIN, SHAFFLIN,
Michael, tailor, came in the James April 5, 1635; settled at Charlestown; propr. 1635. Rem. to Salem; propr. 1636; frm. May 18, 1642. He deposed July 1, 1685, ae. about 80 years, as to the contract between Wm. King, Jr. and his dau. Katharine about 1652. Her sister Sarah m. Robert Stone. [Es. Court Files, in Es. Inst. Coll. XVI.] Elizabeth memb. chh. 1639.

He d. 12 Dec. 1686. Will dated 5 April, 1686, prob. 19 May, 1687, beq. to wife Alice, daus. Katharine and Sarah Stone.

SHAPLEIGH, see Treworgy,
Nicholas, of Kingsweare, Devon, merchant, bought of James Treworgy now resident in New England, for 1500 li., all his lands, houses, fish, fishing coast, etc., in N. E. April 2, 1641. [York Deeds.] He res. some time at Strawberry Bank and elsewhere in the Piscataqua region, where his father, Mr. Alexander Shapleigh, was early an agent of Gorges. He sold S. B. property and bought house and land in Boston 22 (3) 1645. Rem. to Charlestown and bought lands there 8 (8) 1648. Called Captain in depos. 24 (9) 1651. Wife Anne; ch. Joseph; Benjamin b. in Boston (7) 1645.

He d. in 1661-2. Will dated 21 (11) 1661-2, beq. to "Nicholas"; to sons Joseph and Benjamin. The widow Anne and son Joseph execs. [Mdx. Files, 1666.]

SHARPE, SHARP,
Alice, maid servant of Wm. Ting, Boston, adm. chh. 9 (8) 1642; "now wife of one Peter Aspinwall of Dorchester," dism. to that chh. 30 (1) 1645.

Robert, ae. 20, came in the Abigail in July, 1635; settled at Braintree, rem. to Rehoboth in 1643. Propr., town officer; prop. for frm. 4 June, 1650. Rem. to Muddy River, Roxbury. First wife Mary; 2d wife Abigail; ch. John b. at Braintree 12 (1) 1642, Abigail b. 1647, Mary bapt. at Rox. Dec. 5, 1652.

He d. in July, 1653 or 1654; admin. 19 (11) 1654; his widow Abigail requested that Thomas Meekins and Peter Aspinwall be app. trustees of his est. and that the son be placed under care of the former and the 2 daus. Abigail and Mary be under that of the latter. In 1665 John was reported 22

SHARPE, etc., cont.
yrs. old, Abigail 17, and Mary 12. John gave bonds for payment of his sisters' portions. The widow m. 2, Nicholas Clap of Dorch. about 1656. [Reg. VIII, 276, X, 84, and XXXI, 103.]

Mr. Samuel, master gunner of ordinance, app. a memb. of Gov. Endecott's Council for 3 yrs. 3 March, 1628; came with him to Salem; appl. frm. Oct. 19, 1630, adm. frm. July 3, 1632. Propr. 1635; elder of the chh.; town officer. Wife Alice memb. chh. before 1636. The town voted 1 (10) for the relief of Mrs. S. for the year ensuing, 17 (12) 1657. Ch. a dau., who d. 3 Jan. 1631, [Du.] Elias bapt. 1 (11) 1636, Edward bapt. 14 (2) 1639, Mary bapt. 29 (4) 1640, Experience bapt. 19 (7) 1641, Nathaniel bapt. 10 (9) 1644, Hannah bapt. 31 (11) 1646. Admin. of his est. 27 (6) 1666; division made to his ch. Nathaniel and Hannah Sharpe, Thomas Jeggells, Christopher Phelps and John Morton, Nov. 29, 1667.

Mr. Thomas, one of the Assts. of the Mass. Company, came to Boston probably with Gov. Winthrop; memb. chh. 1630. His dau. d. 3 Jan. 1630-1; his house burned March 16, 1630-1. [W.] He went away (to Eng.) 29 March, folg. [Reg. XXXV, 233.]

SHATSWELL, SATCHELL, SATCHWELL, SATSWELL,
John, Ipswich, with his wife 1633. [Court Rec.] Propr. 1634.

His will dated 11 Feb. 1646, prob. 30 March, 1647; wife Johan, son Richard, about to marry Rebecca Tuttle; my brothers and sisters children that are here in N. E.; bro. Theophilus S., bro. Curwin and sister Webster. The widow Joanna d. 17 April, 1648.

Richard, Ipswich, rented lands of John Tuttle; renewed lease in 1654. Propr. 1648. Ch. Mary d. Sept. 1657, Richard d. 28 Jan. 1662, Sarah b. 19 Aug. 1658, Ann b. 21 Feb. 1664, Richard, (m. at Newbury 17 Dec. 1696, Eleanor Cheney).

He d. July 13, 1694.

Theophilus, husbandman, Ipswich, recd. pay from the town in 1643 for service against the Indians. Propr. 1648. Rem. to Haverhill; town officer and propr., 1649 and onward. Deposed concerning the lease of

SHATSWELL, etc., cont.
Tuttle lands in 1662, ae. about 45 years. Mentioned kinsman Richard S. He m. Susanna, [Bosworth, says Hav. Town Rec.] Ch. Mary, Lydia, (m. Sept. 17, 1663, John Griffin,) Hannah, (m. Richard Mercer).

He d. Aug. 17, 1663. He signed his will 20 (4) 1663, prob. 13 (8) folg.; beq. to wife; to daus. Mary, Lydia and Hannah; to Haniel Clark; kinsmen Philip Challis and brother William Sargent overseers. Wife Susanna and dau. Hannah Mercer execs. After their death Haniel Bosworth petitioned the court, 10 April, 1683, that his ward Abiall Mercier might be appointed admin.; which was done 19 June, 1704. Susanna, "spinster widow" of Theophilus, deeded land 3 Jan. 1670, to her son-in-law Richard M. [Ips. De.] The inv. of her est. was pres. 23 May, 1672, by Haniel Bosworth and John Griffin.

SHATTUCK, SHATTOCK, SHATOK,
Samuel, feltmaker, Salem, adm. chh. 2 (5) 1641, son of widow Damaris, who was adm. chh. 15 (3) 1642, m. 2, Thomas Gardner. He deposed 27 (4) 1674, ae. about 58 years. He was a propr.; a leading Quaker of the town; was banished, as such, in 1657. Went to England and obtained concessions for the sect. Came back to Salem. [Es. Inst. Col. III.] Wife Grace; ch. Samuel b. 7 (8) 1649, Hannah b. 28 (6) 1651, Damaris b. 1 (9) 1653, Priscilla b. 1 (3) 1659, Return b. 16 (6) 1662, Retire b. 28 (1) 1664, Patience b. 18 (9) 1666.

He d. 6 June, 1689. Will dated April 6, previous, beq. to wife Hannah, sons Samuel and Retire, and six daus. Division made Nov. 1, 1701.

William, shoemaker, Watertown, propr. 1642. He deposed 3 (2) 1660, ae. about 38 years. [Mdx. Files.] Wife Susanna; ch. Mary b. 25 (6) 1645, John b. 11 (12) 1646. He res. at Boston, 1652-4. Ret. to Wat.

He died Aug. 14, 1672, ae. 50. In his will he gave to son Samuel Church; to sons John, Philip, William, Benjamin and Samuel; "to my ten younger children that are married;" to wife Susanna and to each gr. child. The widow m. 2, Mr. Richard Norcross. She d. Dec. 11, 1686. Philip, William and Samuel Shattuck, Jonathan Brown, Fay and Abigail Morse, all children, natural or by marriage, receipted for their portions of the estate 29 March, 1687. See Genealogy.

SHAW, SHAWE, SHAUE, SHAWS, SHASE,

Abraham, called in his will, "sometime of Halifax in co. York, clothier, then of Dedham, N. E., planter," frm. March 9, 1636-7. Came first to Watertown, propr., 1636. His house was burnt in Oct. 1636, and he rem. to Dedham. Constable 6 (7) 1638. Rem. to Cambridge; town officer 1640. Had grant of coal or iron stone which may be found in any common ground at this country's disposing 2 Nov., 1637. Had liberty to erect a corn mill Feb. 12, 1636-7. Mary, [his wife?] adm. chh. Charlestown, 1 (5) 1645. Will made about Nov., 1638, prob. in 1638; ch. eldest son Joseph; ch. Mary, John and Martha, the 2 latter being infants; Joseph and John to have his lot at Dedham. Mr. Edward Allen admin. [Reg. II, 180.] Nicholas Biram was his son-in-law. Coal mines at Halifax, Eng., to be sold. [L.]

Edward, sawyer, Duxbury, 1632; in Court 2 Oct. 1637. Hired Dec. 1, 1638, for 1 year, with Robert Bartlett.

James, Plymouth, atba. 1643. frm. 6 June, 1654.

John, Sen., planter, Plymouth, one of the "purchasers or old-comers," had share in the division of cattle in 1627, frm. 1632-3. One of those who undertook to cut a passage from Green's harbor to the Bay before July 1, 1633. Had additional lands in 1636; juryman, 1648. John [Sen. or Jr.?] served 17 days against the Narragansetts in 1645. The son John sold land to his bro.-in-law Stephen Bryant in 1651. Wife Alice was bur. March 6, 1654-5.

John, butcher, Boston, 1649. Wife Elizabeth bought land in B. Nov. 9, 1654.

Robert, in Court Sept. 4, 1632.

Roger, Cambridge, propr. 1636, frm. March 14, 1638-9; town officer. Rem. to Hampton; deputy 1651. Wife Anne; ch. Mary d. 26 (11) 1639, Esther b. (4) 1638, Mary b. 29 (7) 1645.

Thomas, "Shase," "Chase," planter, Hingham, 1639. [L.]

Thomas, Barnstable, atba. 1643. Town officer 1646; in Court 1647.

Will dated June 25, prob. July 1, 1672;

SHAW, etc., cont.
kinsman, Robert Parker, etc. [Reg. VII, 236.]

Thomas, Charlestown. Ch. John b. 4 (1) 1647.

SHEAFE,

Mr. Jacob, merchant, Roxbury, [perhaps son of Mrs. S., widow, memb. chh. and propr. at Rox. about 1637.] He rem. to Boston. Sold house and yard in Rox. about 22 (7) 1643. Town officer, wealthy man. He m. about 1643 Margaret, dau. of Henry Webb; she was adm. chh. 15 (3) 1647; ch. Elizabeth b. 1 (8) 1644, (m. Sept. 7, 1660, Robert Gibbs,) Samuel bapt. 9 (2) 1648, Mary bapt. 19 (3) 1650, Sarah b. Sept. 14, 1652, Ebenezer b. Feb. 4, 1653-4, Marcye bapt. 29 (5) 1655, Mehitabel b. May 28, 1658, (m. Sampson Sheafe; see Suff. De. III and VI,) Jacob, (posthumous), b. July 23, 1659.

He d. March 22, 1659. Admin. by widow Margaret 23 (9) 1659. Large est.; a quarter part of 3 mills at Rox.; house and ground at Boston; sugar at Barbadoes and Eng.; ¼ of the ketch Tryall and her cargo, acct. of sales of provisions at Newfoundland by Mr. Croad, etc. [Reg. X, 83.] The widow m. 2, Rev. Thomas Thatcher of Boston.

SHED,

Daniel, Braintree. He rem. to Billerica. Wife Mary; ch. Mary b. 1 (8) 1647, Daniel b. 30 (6) 1649, Hannah b. 7 (7) 1651, John b. 1 (2) 1654, Elizabeth and Zachariah b. 17 (4) 1656.

SHEFFIELD, SHEAFFIELD,

Deliverance, "now wife of Mr. Hugh Peters, pastor of the chh. of Salem," dism. to that chh. from Boston 2 (11) 1639.

Edmund, Roxbury, frm. May 29, 1644. Rem. to Braintree. He m. April 17, 1644, Mary, dau. of Richard Woodie; she d. 30 (1) 1662. He m. 5 (7) 1662, Sarah, dau. of John Beal, and widow of Thomas Marsh, of Hingham; who d. Nov. 9, 1710, ae. about 84 yrs. Ch. John b. March 6, 1644-5, Edmund b. 15 (10) 1646, Anne b. 1 (2) 1649, Isaac b. 15 (1) 1651, Mary b. 14 (4) 1653, Matthew b. 26 (3) 1655, Samuel b. 26 (9) 1657, Mary b. 20 (4) 1663, Nathaniel b. 16 (1) 1665, a dau. b. 23 (4) 1667. He admin. on the est. of his son Edmund 27 June, 1679.

He d. 13 Oct. 1705, ae. about 90 yrs.

SHELDON, SHELTON,
Sampson, Boston, 1636.

SHELLEY, SHELLY, SHEELE,
Robert, embarked for N. E. June 22, 1632; settled at Boston; propr. He was probably the husband of "widow Shelley," whose house is referred to in the bounds of land, 25 (9) 1637. Her "son" had land grant in Captaines Plaines at Mount Woolystone, 27 (11) 1639. Anne, maid servant to John Coggeshall of Roxbury, afterward wife of Richard Foxwell of Scituate, Robert, (following,) and Margaret, maid servant to Wm. Coddington, adm. chh. Boston 19 (4) 1636, seem to the writer to be children of Robert and this woman.

Robert, Scituate, 1636; adm. chh. May 14, 1637. Rem. to Barnstable. He m. at Sci. Sept. 20, 1636, Judith —; she was rec'd to chh. of Barn. in 1644 by letter from the chh. of Boston. He was adm. frm. June 6, 1654. Ch. Hannah bapt. July 2, (m. March 9, 1652, David Lynnett,) Mary bapt. Nov. 23, 1639, John bapt. July 31, 1642.

He d. 6 Sept. 1692. Will dated 11 March, 1688-9, prob. 19 Oct. 1692, gave all to wife Susanna for the support of herself and "them that I leave with her." Refers to son John.

SHEPARD, SHEPHERD, SHEPHEARD,
Edward, mariner, Cambridge, bought house and lands of James Herring; deed recorded in 1639. Was adm. chh. with "his first wife, Violet;" their children that were in minority when he joyned are Abigail now living at Dedham, Deborah now also at Dedham, Sarah now dwelling at Braintree; the eldest of these aged 12 years, the 2d, 10; the 3d, 7 yeer, being all baptised in England." [Mi. in 1658.] The wife Violet d. Jan. 9, 1648-9; Capt. Shepard m. 2, Mary, widow of Robert Pond, of Dorchester, about 1650. Ch. John adm. chh. Camb. before 1658; Elizabeth, Abigail, (m. Daniel Pond of Dedham; d. 4 (5) 1661;) Deborah, Sarah, (m. Samuel Tompson, of Braintree.

His will dated 1 Oct. 1674, "having arrived unto old age;" prob. Aug. 20, 1680, beq. to wife Mary; to ch. John, Elizabeth, Deborah, Sarah, and to their ch. in case of their own decease before himself; also to

SHEPARD, etc., cont.
the ch. of his dec. dau. Abigail, formerly wife of Daniel Pond. The son John, in a receipt, mentions his "loving unkel Gregory Winterton." [Conn. Col. Rec. I, 360.]

George, Boston, 1639.

Humphrey, husbandman, ae. 32, embarked from Weymouth, Eng., before March 20, 1635.

John, husbandman, ae. 36, with [wife] Margaret, ae. 31, and [son] Thomas, ae. 3 months, came in the Defense in July, 1635. [Settled at Braintree;] frm. May 10, 1643. Ch. Samuel d. 29 (6) 1641.

Admin. of his estate 22 (7) 1650; widow Margaret and ch. [Reg. VIII, 58.] The widow Margaret made nunc. will at Medfield, testified to 16 (12) 1675; beq. to John, the son, and Elizabeth the dau. of John Warfield, her grandchildren; to her gr. ch. the dau. of goodman Hollbrook, and to her son Samuel.

Ralph, ae. 29, with wife Thankes, ae. 23, and dau. Sarah, ae. 2, came in the Abigail in July, 1635; a tailor, settled in Charlestown. Pioneer at Dedham, 1636. Rem. to Weymouth; town officer, 1645. Rem. to Malden; rem. to Concord after 1653. Ch. Isaac b. 20 (4) 1639, Tryall b. 19 (10) 1641, Thanks b. Feb. 10, 1651-2, (m. at Chelmsford 13 (10) 1669, Peter Dill,) Jacob b. June, 1653.

Mr. Samuel, Cambridge, frm. March 13, 1635-6; propr. and town officer 1638; deputy 1638-9; major. Settled with Robert Keayne on behalf of the execs. of Robert Barrington, Esq. (of Eng.) Oct. 11, 1647. He and his wife were living in Ireland in 1658, though still members of Camb. chh.; their dau. Jane was then in C. under care of Mr. Edw. Collins. Wife Hannah; ch. Thomas b. 5 (9) 1638, d. 9 (12) 1649, Samuel b. (12) 1639, bur. 16 (1) 1644-5, Hannah b. 20 (4) 1642, Jane b. 16 (3) 1645.

Admin. gr. to Edward Collins Sept. 15, 1673.

Rev. Thomas, first pastor of the church at Cambridge, b. at Towcester, Northamptonshire, Eng. Nov. 5, 1605; grad. at Emanuel Coll. Cambridge; ministered at Earl's Coln, Towcester and Heddon. [C. M.] [See Hist. First Church of Camb.]

SHEPARD, etc., cont.

He came to Boston 6 (8) 1635; frm. March 3, 1635-6. He m. 1, in 1632, in Eng., Margaret Touteville, who d. early in 1636. He m. 2, 1637, Joanna, dau. of Rev. Thomas Hooker, who d. April 28, 1646. He m. 3, Sept. 8, 1647, Margaret Boradile or Boradel; ch. Thomas who d., Thomas, (adm. chh. March 28, 1656; dismissed to the chh. of Charlestown to become teacher;) a son b. and d. 1638, Samuel, (ord. pastor at Rowley, Nov. 15, 1665,) John b. 2 (..) 1646, John, Jeremiah b. 11 (6) 1648.

He d. Aug. 28, 1649. His widow Margaret m. 2, Mr. Jonathan Mitchell.

William, Dorchester, servant to Wm. Sumner, in Court 5 April, 1636. May be the following.

William, Taunton, before Plymouth Court 1650, for fault to his mother-in-law. Inv. of his est. left at the house of Thomas Jones of Tau. taken 27 Feb. 1664; many of the articles suggest a shop; also household goods.

SHEOPARDSON, SHEPARDSON,

Daniel, blacksmith, Charlestown, adm. chh. 3 (4) 1633; lived in Malden. He m. Joanna —, who sold land in 1646. She m. 2, Thomas Call. Ch. Lydia bapt. 24 (5) 1637, Daniel bapt. 14 (4) 1640, Joanna bapt. 13 (1) 1642.

He d. 25 (5) 1644. Will, dated 16 (5) 1644; wife, daus. Lydia and Joanna; son Daniel to be brought up to the trade of a smith. He made his master Nowell and bros. Heborne and Cutler overseers of the will. [Reg. VII, 32, and XXX, 81.] The Court divided the est. 26 May, 1647.

SHEPLEY, SHIPLEY, see Shapleigh,

John, Salem, land grant to him and his wife in 1636. Rem. to Wenham. Wife adm. chh. 29 (8) 1648, and ch. John, Nathaniel and Lydia bapt. He deposed 29 (1) 1673, ae. about 86 years; desired to be excused from training. [Mdx. Files.]

SHERBONE, SHERBOLE,

Mrs. Elizabeth, Cambridge, resident and propr., 1639-1648.

SHEPPE, SHEPPY,

—, Charlestown, before Gen. Court 5 (9) 1639.

Elizabeth, adm. chh. Charlestown 12 (2) 1650.

Thomas, [Char.] deposed 3 (2) 1640, ae. about 40 years. [Mdx. Files.]

SHERMAN, SHEARMAN,

Edmund, clothier, Watertown, town officer in 1635; frm. May 25, 1636. Ret. to Eng., and made his bro. John pastor of the chh. of Wat., his attorney April 8, 1663, to collect payment for broadcloth shipped to Thomas Hammond of Wat. in 1648. [Mdx. Files.]

Rev. John, b. at Dedham, Eng. Dec. 26, 1613, studied at Trinity Coll., Cambridge, but did not graduate because he had Puritan scruples against the subscription required. [C. M.] Came to Watertown in 1635. [E.] Rem. to New Haven, Conn. Ret. to Wat. and became minister of the church after the death of Mr. Philips. Was a famous preacher. He m. 1, a wife, name not found, by whom he had children; he m. 2, (Mary,), dau. of Mr. Launce, a wealthy Puritan gentleman, member of Parliament; her mother was dau. to Lord Darcy, earl of Rivers; she had many children; was living in 1698. [C. M.] Ch. rec. at New Haven: Samuel b. April 14, 1644; rec. at Wat.: Abigail b. 1 (12) 1647, Johanna b. Sept. 3, 1652, Mary b. March 5, 1656, Grace b. March 10, 1658, John b. March 17, 1660.

He d. Aug. 8, 1685. Will dated 6 Aug., prob. 6 Oct. 1685, beq. to wife Mary; to each unmarried child; to son-in-law Samuel Willard for his ch. by my dau. Abigail; to the ch. of dec. son Bezaleel; to ch. Daniel, Samuel, Mary Allen, Mary Barron, James, John, Abiah, Elizabeth, Hester, Grace and Mercy.

John, ae. 20, came in the Elizabeth of Ipswich April 30, 1634. Settled at Watertown; town officer; deputy, captain; frm. May 17, 1637. Clerk of writs, 1645; steward of Harvard College, 1662. Signed inv. of Henry Kemball in 1648. Wife Martha, dau. of William Palmer, of Newbury and Hampton, to whose son Joseph they sold their share of estate, 3 (8) 1661. She was also a legatee of Grace, widow of Roger Porter, in 1662. Ch. John b. 2 (9) 1638, Martha b.

SHERMAN, etc., cont.
21 (12) 1640, Mary b. 25 (1) 1643, Sarah b. 17 (11) 1647, Elishaba, [Elizabeth?] d. 15 (1) 1648, Joseph b. 14 (3) 1650, Grace b. 20 (10) 1653, d. Feb. 21, 1654.

He d. Jan. 25, 1690-1, and his widow d. Feb. 7, 1700-1. Admin. of his est. was gr. Feb. 13, 1690-1, to his son Joseph. [Reg. LI, 309.]

Philip, came into the land in the year 1623 [1633,] a single man, and after married Sarah Odding, the dau. of Margaret, wife of John Porter by a former husband. [E.] Settled at Roxbury; bought land in Boston in 1637. Rem. to Rhode Island; was one of the trustees of the Sanford children in 1657.

Richard, merchant, planter, Boston, 1635; adm. chh. 21 (3) 1654. Ch. Elizabeth b. 1 (10) 1635. "Ould Richard Sherman of New England" named in the will of Simon Whiting, of Dedham, Essex, Eng. dated 17 April, 1637. [Reg. XXXI, 413, and L.] He conveyed house, lands, etc., July 10, 1649. Deed of gift April 1, 1658, to wife Elizabeth, for daus. Ann and Priscilla in Eng.; dau. Martha Brown of Dorchester, dau. Abigail Damen of Reading; and to his gr. ch. in Boston, Mary and Elizabeth, daus. of Thomas Spaule, Aug. 25, 1658.

He d. 30 May, 1660. Will dated 7 April, prob. July 31, 1660; wife Elizabeth, daus. Ann Shearman and Priscilla, wife of Martin Garett, Martha Browne, and Abigail Damine; gr. daus. Mary and Elizabeth Spaule; cousin Mr. Anger of Camb.; kinsman, John Lovermore of Wat. [Reg. IX, 227.] The widow deeded land in B. to her nephew, John Greenleafe of B. 6 March, 1662. She m. 2, Thomas Robinson. She made will 21 Aug. 1666, prob. 16 Nov. 1667: John, son of Edmund Browne of Dorchester; Samuel, son of John Deamon of Redding; Elizabeth and Mary, daus. of Thomas Spaule of Boston; sister Bridget Locks children of Faucett in England; kinsman John Greenleafe and his sister Mary; 50 li. due from the est. of her husband Thomas Robinson as by covenant upon marriage. [Reg. XVIII, 156.]

Samuel, husbandman, Ipswich, propr. 1636; Boston, 1637; adm. chh. 1 (1) 1640, frm. May 13, 1640; propr. of land at Watertown. Was of Ipswich when disarmed for

SHERMAN, etc., cont.
favoring the Hutchinson cause in 1637. He hailed from Aquithneck Island 9 (5) 1643. Wife Grace adm. chh. 29 (6) 1641; ch. Philip b. Dec. 31, 1637, d. 12 (10) 1652, Martha b. 5 (7) 1639, Nathaniel, ae. about 12 days, bapt. 19 (10) 1642, Jonathan, ae. about 3 days, bapt. 11 (12) 1643.

He and his wife both d. in 1644, and admin. was gr. 2 (1) 1644, and July 28, 1652, to Valentine Hill and others; one of the ch. Philip had d.; remaining heirs Samuel, Martha, and Mary. [Reg. IX, 226.]

Thomas, Ipswch, propr. 1636.

William, Duxbury, yeoman, planter, taxed in 1652, propr. 1637, atba. 1643. He m. Jan. 23, 1638, Prudence Hill. Rem. to Marshfield; adm. inhabitant 13 Nov. 1644. Town officer. He deeded lands to his sons; to Samuel June 9, 1673, to John Feb. 5, 1673, to William Aug. 15, 1676.

He d. Oct. 25, 1679. Inv. taken 30 Dec. 1680.

SHERIN, SHERRIN,
Robert, ae. 32, came in the Elizabeth of Ipswich April 30, 1634.

SHERRATT, SHERROTT,
Hugh, Ipswich, propr. 1635; frm. March 4, 1634. Rem. to Haverhill; propr. 1644. Lic. to sell wines 26 May, 1647. His wife Elizabeth d. May 20, 1662; and he m. Feb. 10, 1662-3, Elizabeth, widow of Humphrey Griffin. He secured to her the sum of £ 42 by mortg. deed of house and lands April 27, 1665. She made will July 30, prob. Oct. 10, 1670; beq. to sons John, Nathaniel and Samuel G.; to daus. Lydia G. and Elizabeth Deare; to her son John's 3 ch. and her son Deare's 4 ch.

SHERWOOD,
Thomas, ae. 48, with wife Alice, ae. 47, and ch. Anna, ae. 14, Rose, ae. 11, Thomas, ae. 10, and Rebecca, ae. 9, came in the Francis of Ipswich April 30, 1634.

SHILLINGSWORTH, see Chillingsworth.

SHOLY,
Mary, a poor maid, Newbury, murdered in 1637. [W.]

SHIRTLEY, SHETLE, SHERCLIFFE, SHERTCLIFFE, SHURTLEFF,
William, Plymouth, apprentice to Thomas Clarke for 11 yrs. from 16 May, 1634; atba. 1643; attack made upon him 2 Oct. 1650. He rem. to Marshfield. Propr.; town officer. He m. 18 Oct. 1655, Elizabeth, dau. of Thomas Lettice.
He was killed by lightning; was bur. June 24, 1666. His widow admin. 3 July, 1666. She m. Nov. 18, 1669, Jacob Cooke. She was living at the date of her father's will, 1678. Son William had suit at law with Thomas Clarke in 1680.

SHORE, SHOREBORNE,
Samson, tailor, Boston, townsman 29 (9); adm. chh. 29 (11) 1641; frm. May 18, 1642. Wife Abigail adm. chh. 31 (3) 1646; ch. Jonathan b. 12 (4) 1643, Jonathan b. and bur. (3) 1644, Samson bapt. 26 (11) 1644, ae. about 14 days, Abigail bapt. 14 (1) 1647, ae. about 7 days, Jonathan bapt. 29 (2) 1649, ae. about 6 days, James bapt. 2 (12) 1650, Abigail b. 6 Dec. 1653, Elizabeth b. and d 1657, Susanna b. May 28, 1660, d. 22 June, 1661, Ann b. Aug. 16, 1663, d. June 26, 1664. He admin. on the est. of his son Sampson, Jr., 3 Feb. 1678-9.

SHORT,
Anthony, Ipswich, propr. 1634; rem. to Newbury; propr., town officer.
He d. 4 April, 1671.

Henry, came in the Mary and John, March 26, 1634; settled at Ipswich; court deputy in 1634-5. Frm. Sept. 3, 1634. Rem. to Newbury before 1637; propr., town officer. Wife Elizabeth d. 22 March, 1647. He m. 9 Oct. 1648, Sarah Glover. Ch. Sarah b. 18 Dec. 1649, d. March 12, 1650, Henry b. 11 March, 1652, John b. and d. 1653, Sarah b. 28 Jan. 1659.
He d. 5 May, 1673. Will dated Feb. 13, 1672, prob. 19 June, 1673, beq. to wife Sarah, son Henry and dau. Sarah; to cousin Samuel Holt, Robert Long's children and Nathan Parker, Jr.

SHORTHOSE, SHORTHUS, SHORTAS,
Robert, of Charlestown, 1634. In Gen. Court 1636. Wife Katharine; ch. John b. 13 (7) 1637, Elizabeth b. 7 (7) 1640. Suit brought against against him by Wm. Tuttle in 1637. [W.] The widow m. in 1645 Baptist Smedley.

SHOTTON,
Samson, planter, Mt. Wollaston, (Braintree,) sold to his bro. Anthony of Cropston, Leicester, Eng., his share in the est. of their late father, Thomas Shotton; Oct. 22, 1638.

SHOVE,
Rev. George, gent., minister, Taunton, was the son of Margery and — Shove; the mother was adm. to chh. of Boston, as a widow, 30 (10) 1638; rem. to Rowley; was a propr.; sold her land and rem. to Roxbury, where she m. Richard Peacock in 1654. She was bur. at Taunton 17 April, 1680, with note that she was "mother of Mr. George Shove." [Plym. Col. Rec.]
He m. 14 July, 1664, Hopestill, dau. of Rev. Samuel Newman; she d., and he m. Feb. 17, 1674-5, Mrs. Hannah Walley; she d. Sept., 1685, and he m. Dec. 8, 1686, Mrs. Sarah Farwell. Ch. Edward b. and d. 1665, Elizabeth b. Aug. 10, 1666, Seth b. Dec. 10, 1667, Nathaniel b. Jan. 29, 1668, Samuel b. June 16, 1670, Sarah b. July 30, 1671, Mary b. Aug. 11, 1676, Johanna b. Sept. 28, 1678, Edward b. Oct., 1680, Mercy b. 7 Nov. 1682.
He d. April 21, 1687. Will dated 4 (2) prob. 21 (7) 1687, beq. to wife Sarah estate that was hers before marriage, etc.; to ch. Seth, Nathaniel, Samuel, Elizabeth, Sara, Mary, Johanna and "Yet Mary." [See Bacon.]

SHREVE, SHEREVE, SHERIVE,
Thomas, Plymouth, atba. 1643; propr. 1646; in court, 1650. Ch. Thomas b. 2 Sept. 1649.

SHRIMPTON,
Edward, merchant, of Bednal Green, Eng., trading for N. E., bro. of Henry Shrimpton of Boston.
His will prob. in Eng. and copy brought here for record Sept. 6, 1662; son Jonathan. [Reg. XI, 170, XXXI, 413.] [Suff. De. IV, 169, V, 505, and 507.]

Henry, brazier and merchant, Boston, adm. chh. 15 (7) 1639. Wife Eleanor; ch. Elizabeth bapt. 3 (8) 1641, d. Aug. 12, 1659, Samuel bapt. 25 (4) 1643, Mary bapt. 10 (6) 1645, John, [record says "of Robert,"] bapt. 28 (3) 1648, Henry b. April 26, 1654, Jonathan b. Nov. 18, 1656, d. 22 (5) 1657, Abigail b. Jan. 3, 1657, Mehetabel d. 29 (5) 1657, Bethia

SHRIMPTON, cont.
b. Jan. 30, 1658, Elizabeth b. April 11, 1660; Sarah, ae. 11 yrs., and Abigail, Bethia and Elizabeth, were bapt. 15 (2) 1660. He m. 2, Mrs. Mary Fenn, widow, Feb. 27, 1661.

Will, dated 17 (5), prob. 6 (12) 1666. To the wife of his late bro. Edward, and their ch. Jonathan, Mary, Ebenezer, Epafras, Silas, Elizabeth and Lydia; to his wife Mary 40 li. per an. for life and all the est. she brought; to his daus. Sarah, Abigail, Bethiah and Elizabeth 1000 li. and a house lot apiece; son Samuel residuary legatee and executor. Desired to be bur. in tomb where his wife Elinor was bur. Mentioned his bro. Edward Fletcher and sister Fletcher, his wife; sister Blanchett. [Reg. XV.]

SIBLEY, SEBLEY, SYBLEY,
John, Charlestown, adm. chh. with wife Sarah 21 (12) 1634. Frm. Sept. 3, 1634; propr.

He d. Nov. 30, 1649.

John, Salem, propr., juryman, 1636; memb. chh.; frm. May 6, 1635. Constable. Ch. Sarah bapt. 18 (7) 1642, Mary bapt. 8 (7) 1644, Rachel bapt. 3 (3) 1646, John bapt. 14 (3) 1648, Hannah bapt. 22 (4) 1651, William bapt. 8 (7) 1653, Samuel bapt. 12 (2) 1657, Abigail bapt. 3 (5) 1659.

Admin. gr. to widow Rachel June 24, 1661; 9 ch., 5 boys, and 4 girls; eldest dau. 19, next 17, third 15, a son 12, etc.

SILL, SCILL, SELL,
John, Cambridge, propr., frm. May 2, 1638. While in Northumberland heard Mr. Shepard preach. [Rel.] Wife Joanna; ch. Joseph, (3 years old at his mother's joining Camb. chh.,) Elizabeth, (2 years old at her mother's joining; m. — Hicks. [Mi.]

He d. before 1658. His widow Joanna had a grant of land in 1665. She was made attorney for Susann Blackiston of Newcastle upon Tyne, widow, Aug. 27, 1653, to recover debts; from Anne Errington, widow, a debt, due from 1637; Andrew Stevenson, cobbler, debt. 1637; John Trumble, cooper, 1637; Thomas Chesholme, tailor, 1635; all formerly of Newcastle upon Tyne, and now of N. E. [Mdx. De. I, 87.]

SILLIS, see Sealis.

SILSBY, SILLSBY,
Henry, shoemaker, Salem, 1638. Mr. Sharpe's man; inhabitant and propr. 1639. Rem. to Ipswich; propr. 1647. Bought house in Lynn in 1653 and in 1670. Wife Dorothy d. 27 Sept. 1676. He m. 18 Nov. 1680, Grace Eaton.

Will signed 17 March, 1698-9, prob. 16 Dec. 1700. [Genealogy. Es. Inst. Col. XVII.]

SKOFIELD, see Scholfield.

SILVER, see Gilven,
Thomas, Ipswich, propr. 1637. Thomas, Newbury, m. 1, 8 Aug. 1649, Katharine —. She d. 30 July, 1665. He deposed in 1674, ae. about 50 years. Ch. [Mary,] Elizabeth and Martha b. 14 March, 1651, Thomas b. 26 March, 1653, d. 3 March, 1655, Hannah and Sarah b. 18 Oct. 1655, Thomas b. 26 March, 1658, John b. 24 Aug. 1660, Samuel b. 16 Feb. 1662, a dau. b. July 19, 1665.

He d. 6 Sept. 1682. His est was divided 26 Sept. 1682, between Thomas, John and Samuel Silver, Mary Robeson, Martha Willett, Hannah Akers and Sarah Ashley.

SIMES,
Sarah, ae. 30, came in the Defence in July, 1635, as a servant of Roger Harlakenden.

SIMMONS, SEMOND, see Symonds,
William, Boston. Wife Anne; ch. Hannah b. (7) 1640, bapt. 30 (2) 1643, (her mother now Porter).

He d. in 1642. The widow m. Abel Porter.

SIMONSON, SYMONSON, SYMONS, SIMONS,
Moses, came in the Fortune in 1621. One of the "purchasers," and being a ch. of one that was in communion with the Dutch chh. at Leyden was adm. chh. at Plymouth, N. E., his children also to baptism. [W.] Frm. 1634; juryman 1637; had additional land grant in 1638.

Will (of Moses Symons) dated 17 Dec. 1676, prob. 7 March, 1676-7, beq. to wife; sons Moses, Aaron, John and Job; to daughters. The widow Patience deposed.

SIMKINS, SIMPKINS, SYMPKINS,
Nicholas, gent., tailor, draper, Boston; rem. to Dorchester, then to Cambridge, where he bought land Nov. 20, 1637. Was first commander of the fort on Castle Island, Boston Harbor. [Capt. Roger Clap.] He deposed before Gen. Court in 1645 as to gun he took to the castle in 1635. Was of Yarmouth 1638-1640. Rem. to Barnstable; sold land there in 1645. Of Scituate, sold house and land there 1 March, 1648. He deposed June 1, 1654, ae. about 54 yrs., and Isabel deposed at the same time, ae. 44 yrs.
Admin. of his est. was gr. to the widow Isabel 30 (8) 1656, for herself and ch. [Reg. IX, 226.] Admin. of her est. was gr. to her son Pilgrim S. 11 Sept. 1669.

SIMPSON, SIMSON,
Mr. John, propr. Watertown before 1634; brought suit in Court. Perhaps he ret. to Eng. and was the John, ae. 30, who came in the Truelove in Sept. 1635. A deed (with Latin preamble in due form,) made and attested by him 25 Nov. 1639, indicates that he was an educated man. [Mdx. De. IV, original.] A "Mr. Simson of London" was persecuted with other Puritan ministers in 1633. [Letter of Francis Kirby to John Winthrop, Jr., in Mass. Hist. Coll. 4-7.] Wife Susanna; ch. Sarah b. 28 (3) 1634, Hannah b. 25 (5) 1636, Jonathan b. Dec. 17, 1640, (m. Wait, dau. of Capt. Roger Clap,) Elizabeth b. 3 (1) 1642.
He was bur. June 10, 1643; admin. April 24, 1645. The widow m. 2, George Parkhurst of Wat. who sold land formerly Mr. Simson's, 21 (9) 1644. The Gen. Court authorized them 23 May, 1655, to sell certain other lands reserving two thirds of the price with Mr. Browne for the use of her 2 eldest sons when they become 21 yrs. old.

SIMS, *alias* **Ford,**
Peter, Salem, 1643; in court in 1646.

SINGLETARY,
Richard, Salem, propr. 1637. Rem. to Newbury; propr. 1638. Rem. to Salisbury; propr. 1639. Rem. to Haverhill; propr. 1651. Town officer. He deposed 22 Nov. 1662, ae. about 67 years; again, 24 (1) 1662-3, ae. about 70. Goodwife Singletery d. at Newbury about 1639. He m. Susanna Cooke, who deposed in 1662, ae. about 46 years. Ch. Jonathan b. Jan. 17, 1639, Eunice b. Jan.

SINGLETARY, cont.
7, 1641, (m. Thomas Eaton,) Nathaniel b. Oct. 28, 1644, Lydia b. April 30, 1648, (m. Daniel Ladd, Jr.,) Amos b. April, 1651, Benjamin b. April 4, 1656. The wife Susanna d. April 11, 1682.
He d. Oct. 25, 1687, ["ae. 102," says Hav. record.]

SIRKMAN,
Henry, m. at Plymouth 30 Sept. 1641, Bridget Fuller.

SKILLING, SKILLIN, SKILLINGS, SKELLING,
Thomas, Salem, 1642, propr. Wife Deborah deposed in 1657, ae. about 34 years. Ch. Thomas b. Nov. 1643. [Es. Files.] He rem. to Wenham. Thomas Prince, Jr., of Gloc. calls Thomas brother-in-law, 1687.
He d. Dec. 30, 1676; admin. gr. to his widow Mary, March 14, 1676-7.

SKELTON,
Mr. Samuel, minister, rector at Sempringham, Lincolnshire, from about 1618, came under the appointment of the Mass. Bay Co. in the George Bonaventure to Salem, sailing May 4, 1629; welcomed Winthrop's party the next year. Frm. May 18, 1631. He m. 27 April, 1619, Susanna Travis; she d. 15 March, 1630-1. [Du.] Ch. Sarah bapt. and bur. 1621, Samuel bapt. at Tattershall 8 Jan. 1622, Susanna bapt. 3 April, 1626, Mary bapt. June 28, 1628, Elizabeth b. (in Salem,) about 1631, (m. Robert Sanford of Boston, N. E.).
He d. Aug. 2, 1634. [W.] With consent of Mrs. Baggerly the division of the est. was ordered to be made in June, 1638, his 3 eldest ch. to receive personal effects. [Reg. LII, and LIII.] The house in which he lived passed to the ownership of Nathl. Felton, who sold it in 1643 to Wm. Browne, Sen. [Es. Inst. Col.] His farm was bought by John Porter; final deed by the son Samuel 30 March, 1663.

SKERRY,
Francis, husbandman, malster, Salem, 1636; frm. May 17, 1637; propr.
Will dated June 25, prob. Aug. 30, 1684, beq. to wife; bro. Henry; bro. Robert in England, and his son Thomas; cousin Henry and his ch.; cousin Elizabeth, wife of Benj. Fitch of Reading, and her 3 daus.; cousin

SKERRY, cont.

Elizabeth, wife of John Williams; cousin Mary Nelson; Abigail, wife of John Smith; Isaac Whittaker, Deliverance Coary, Mary Holman, Elizabeth Smith and Matthew Price's widow. His widow d. 10 Aug. 1692.

Henry, cordwainer, ae. 31, of Great Yarmouth, Eng. with wife Elizabeth, ae. 25, ch. Henry, and apprentice Edmund Towne, passed exam. to go to N. E. April 11, 1637. Came to Salem, frm. March, 1637-8. Constable, 1646. [Es. Court.] Propr. He deposed in 1663, ae. 50 years. Ch. Henry, Eliza bapt. 4 (1) 1638, Mary bapt. 8 (7) 1640, Ephraim bapt. 26 (1) 1643, John bapt. 3 (4) 1649.

He d. Dec. 30, 1691. The widow Elizabeth d. 6 March, 1692.

SKIFFE, SKEFFE, SKIFF,

James, yeoman, Plymouth, rec'd 5 acres of land for services done to Isaac Allerton; and bought 5 more acres of Peter Talbot, Aug. 22, 1636. Sold house and land 1 Jan. 1637, and rem. to Sandwich. Lands granted 1641. Frm. 5 June, 1644. Town officer, deputy. He deeded lands to son Nathaniel 27 Feb. 1671. Ch. James b. Sept. 12, 1638, Stephen b. April 14, 1641, Nathaniel b. March 20, 1645, Sarah b. Oct. 12, 1646, Bathshuah b. 21 April, 1648, Mary b. 24 March, 1650, Marienne b. March 25, 1652, Benjamin b. Nov. 15, 1655, Nathan b. May 16, 1658, Patience b. March 25, 1653, (m. Elisha Bourne 26 Oct. 1675). His wife Mary d. Sept. 21, 1673.

SKIPPER, SKEPPAR,

Mr. William, [Lynn,] had writings made 14 (3) 1640 for his 4 children. [L.] He d. and admin. was gr. to Mr. Cotton and Mr. Cobbett by Gen. Court 16 Oct. 1650, at request of Zachary Phillips and his wife who was a daughter. Perhaps Theophilus, an apprentice to Benjamin Keayne, Jr., of Lynn, whose rights were guarded by Gen. Court 4 Nov. 1646, and Jane, spinster, Boston, a creditor of Valentine Hill, 18 (11) 1651, were also children of William.

SKOULING,

Robert, came from Hingham, Eng., or there about with Thomas Cooper in 1638, and settled at Hingham.

SKIDMORE, SCIDMORE, SCUDAMORE,

John, before Boston court 1 (4) 1641.

Thomas, blacksmith, of Westerley, co. Gloc., Eng. came to Cambridge about 1639; propr. Petitioner for Nashaway plantation but not a resident. Wife Ellen; son Thomas; [L.] son John b. April 11, 1643. He selected some cattle to be sent to John Winthrop, Jr. in Conn., May, 1636. [W.]

SKINNER,

Edward, Cambridge, owned a house and 6 acres of land.

Will 25 (10) 1641; to Mr. Robert Ibbitt of Cambridge, Eng.; to Thomas Parish, his wife, and Marie [Hanner] their servant; several other persons; things to stand as they are in Eng. Thomas Parish executor. [Reg. II, 103.]

Thomas, victualer, Malden, 1645, frm. May 18, 1653. Ch. Thomas b. "in Subdeanerie parish, Chichester," July 25, 1645, Abram bapt. "in Pallant parish, chh." Sept. 29, 1649, Mary, "wife of Thomas," d. April 9, 1671. [Malden and Mdx. Court Rec.]

SLADE,

Robert, Sudbury, propr. 1639.

SLAWSON,

George, Sandwich, cultivated a piece of land in 1638; propr. 1640.

SLEEPER,

Thomas, of Hampton, bought land at Boston 15 (5) 1645. No further record of him found in Massachusetts.

SLOCUM, SLOCUME, SLOCOMB,

Anthony, Taunton, atba. 1643; juror, 1650. Frm. 3 June, 1657; juryman, town officer. Had family of six persons in 1659. [Tau. Rec.] His son John, 9 years old, lost and died in the woods Feb. 25, 1651-2.

Edward, Taunton, town officer, 1647. [Compare Genealogy in Reg. XXXIV, 391.]

SMALL,

John, servant to Edmund Batter, malter, came in the James April 5, 1635. Settled at Salem; propr. 1642.

SMALLEDGE,
William, fisherman, Ipswich, bought house and land 21 (8) 1650.

SMALLEY, SMALLY,
John, tailor, embarked for N. E. March 7, 1631; came to Plymouth. Had land grant 5 Feb. 1637-8, atba. 1643. Rem. to Eastham; propr. Took Samuel Godbertson apprentice 31 Aug. 1639. Juryman, 1641. He m. 29 Nov. 1638, Ann Walden; ch. Hannah b. 14 June, 1641, John b. 8 Sept. 1644, Isaac and Mary b. 11 Dec., bapt. at Barnstable 27 Feb. 1647.

SMART,
John, Hingham, propr. 1636.

SMEAD, SMEADE,
Judith, Dorchester, memb. chh. before 1639. She was a widow at the time of her death; her bro. Mr. Israel Stoughton was app. admin. of her est. 22 (3) 1639, and filed an inv., taken 18 (3) 1639. After her children became of age appraisers divided the est. as per Mr. S.'s books: to John Denman, Mary Denman, wife of Clement Maxfield, and to William Smead who had been an apprentice of John Pope, weaver; at his indenture £32 was paid. See Lawrence, Thomas. [Reg. IX, 344, and XXX, 79.]

SMEDLY, SMEADLEY, SMEEDLY,
Baptist, Concord, frm. May 29, 1644. He m. 27 (1) 1645, Katharine, widow of Robert Shorthose; ch. Samuel b. 27 (1) 1646, Mary b. 7 (4) 1648.
He d. Aug. 16, 1675. Inv. mentions his gr. ch. Jabish Rutor.

John, Concord, frm. May 27, 1644. Wife Anne; ch. John b. 31 (8) 1646.

SMITH, SMYTH,
Caution. After long study of this surname,—I will not say this family,—the following paragraphs have been prepared. There are, perhaps, some errors of combination, as the assignment of children to the wrong parent; the affixing of the date of freemanship among the various persons of the same christian name; the connection of two records as parts of one life, when they relate to different men, etc. Yet the reader may be fairly confident that these pages contain the elements of the solution of the

SMITH, etc., cont.
problems, if not all wrought out with absolute accuracy.

Abraham, Cambridge, resident in 1646; bought land at Charlestown, next to Camb., in 1651. Alice, ae. 40, with John, ae. 13, came in the Planter, April 10, 1635, cert. from Sidbury, Eng.

Alice, widow, d., apparently in Boston; admin. of her est. was gr. 14 (8) 1663, to her kinsman Joseph Bayley and two of her sons, Samuel and Abraham Smith. Daniel of Watertown, calls Abraham bro.

Abraham d. in Bo. March 26, 1696; admin. gr. to widow Mary. She d. Aug. 23, leaving a will, dated 13 May, prob. Aug. 27; beq. to gr. dau. Elizabeth Mullegan; gave freedom to negro servants "Sew" and "Marea;" rest of her est. to be divided between her five ch., John Wilmot, Elizabeth Newland, Hannah Adams, Abigail Adams and Ann Allen. Bonds of admin. were signed by Nathaniel Adams of Char. blockmaker, and James Smith, shop-keeper.

Benjamin, yeoman, Dedham, propr., 10 (5) 1642, adm. chh. 28 (3) 1641, frm. June 2, 1641. Rem. to Boston; was attorney for Henry Willis of St. Bury Edmunds, felmonger, Martha Hues, widow, Ann Langhorne, widow, and Mary Biggs, of London, in 1650-1, for collection of their shares in the est. of his uncle Nicholas Willis and Ann, his wife. Suit in Es. court in 1662. He m. at Ded. 10 (6) 1641, Mary Clarke; ch. Mary d. 24 (10) 1642, Benjamin b. 24 (8) 1646.

Christopher, Dedham, propr. 1640, adm. chh. Oct. 1642, frm. May 10, 1643. He m. Mary, dau. of Jonathan Fairbank and widow of Michael Metcalf. Ch. John b. 19 (9) 1655.
He d. 7 (9) 1676. His widow d. 4 (4) 1684. Her will dated 30 May, prob. 3 July, 1684, beq. to son John Smith; to ch. Michael, Hannah, Melatia, and Eleazer Metcalf, and Sarah and Robert Wares; brother John Fairbank.

Daniel, planter, Watertown, son of Alice, above. Wife Elizabeth, dau. of Roger Porter; ch. Daniel b. 27 (7) 1642. Bought land 23 (8) 1645.

SMITH, etc., cont.

He d. July 14, 1660. Will dated July 14, prob. Oct. 1660, beq. to wife Elizabeth, son Daniel; to Abigail Sherman; mentions bro. Abraham Smith.

Dorothy, ae. 45, with dau. Mary, ae. 15, and John, ae. 12, the last cert. from the parish of St. Saviour's, Southwark, came in the Elizabeth in April, 1635. [See Henry, from Norfolk co., below.]

Mr. Edward, Weymouth; his servant Thomas Rocke d. 15 (5) 1642. Ch. Phebe b. 15 (9) 1642. Rem. to Rehoboth, 1643, town clerk, propr., frm. 4 June, 1645. Was called before Plymouth Court in 1650 for "attending private meetings."

Edward, gunsmith, Boston, [may be the foregoing.] Will dated 13 Oct. 1686, prob. 2 June, 1687, bound on a voyage to sea; beq. to wife, and daus. Sarah and Mary. Bro. Daniel Smith exec. A house and land in Leicester, Eng. and est. in N. E.

Ellen, widow, Boston, adm. chh. 21 (1) 1641.

Francis, cord-maker, cord-winder, card-maker, Roxbury, memb. chh., came in 1630. [E.] Juryman 1630. Frm. May 18, 1631. Rem. to Boston about 1646. Propr. at Bo. and owner of property at Lynn, and of a share in a bark. His [first] wife d. at Rox.; was bur. March 15, 1639. He m. 2, Ch. Andrew bur. March 15, 1639, Elizabeth, (3) 1646; she d. 13 (3) 1667, ae. about 84. Elizabeth —, who was adm. chh. of Bo. 31 (m. 1, in Bo. in 1656, James Sanford; m. 2, George Hunniborne, m. 3, — Burges;) John b. 30 (6) 1644, Joseph b. 24 (6) 1646, Nathaniel bapt. 18 (12) 1648, ae. about 5 days, Mercy bapt. 9 (1) 1651, d. 4 (7) 1652, James bapt. 8 (6) 1653, Sarah b. at Rox. May 6, 1655, Benjamin b. April 10, 1658, Francis bapt. Nov. 18, 1660, Mary b. July 18, 1663, bapt. 26 July, 1663. He and his wife mortg. house and land 6 May, 1664, to George Hunniborne and his wife Elizabeth, their dau.; release was given June 10, 1664, and Elizabeth Burges, sometime wife to Geo. Hunniborne, acknowledged the act 9 Jan. 1666. John and Joseph Smith witnessed the release.

SMITH, etc., cont.

Francis, tailor, came in the James April 5, 1635; probably one of the two following.

Francis, Watertown, propr. 1636. Frm. April 17, 1637. Rem. to Reading; memb. chh.; propr. 1644; town officer. "Son John" propr. and town officer also. Son Benjamin b. at Wat., (rec. in Reading,) Oct. 10, 1637, Leift. Smith and wife membs. chh. before 1648.

He d. March 20, 1649-50. [Es. Files.]

Francis, Hingham, propr. 1635; res. in 1646. [See petition to Gen. Court.] Frm. May 13, 1640. Rem. to Taunton. Wife Agnes joined him in deed of land at Weymouth 8 (7) 1651. [Wey. Town Rec.] Ch. bapt. at Hing.: Samuel, Oct. 1639.

Will made Feb. 22, 1679, ae. about 60 years; beq. to wife Sarah, eldest son Samuel and his ch. Hannah, Samuel and Susanna; youngest son John and his dau. Elizabeth.

George, Salem, propr. 1635. Admin. gr. to widow (4) 1663; inv. taken 9 March, 1663.

George, Ipswich, res. 1648, propr. 1659.

Hannah, ae. 30, and Marie, ae. 21, were enrolled as passengers in the Susan and Ellen in April, 1635. Hannah, ae. 18, and Marie, ae. 18, were enrolled in the Planter in April, 1635.

Henry, a very early settler of Dorchester; frm. May 18, 1631; propr. 1634. First recorder of births, etc.; prominent citizen. His mother, Mrs. Frances (Smith) Sanford, became the wife of Mr. William Pynchon, and he rem. with them to Springfield. Was paid £8 for building the chimneys and plastering the plantation-house. Signed the compact May 16, 1636. [Reg. XIII, 297.] Sergeant, 1639. Deputy, magistrate. Ch. Martha b. 31 (5) 1641, Mary b. 15 (9) 1641, [some error in record or copy here;] Mary b. 7 (1) 1642-3, Elizabeth b. 22 (8) 1644, Margaret b. 26 (2) 1646, Sarah b. 8 (6) 1647, Marguret 1 (9) 1648, Rebecca b. 1 (2) 1650, Samuel b. 23 (4) 1651, Abigail b. 10 (12) 1652.

Henry, of New Bucknam, Eng. hus-

SMITH, etc., cont.
bandman, ae. 30, with wife Elizabeth, ae. 34, and children John and Sethe, passed exam. April 12, 1637, to go to N. E. Settled at Dedham; propr. 28 (9) 1637, adm. chh. 22 (7) 1639, frm. May 13, 1640. His house was burned in 1641. He rem. to Medfield. Wife Elizabeth adm. chh. 1639; ch. Daniel b. 13 (8) 1639, d. 1 (1) 1641, Samuel b. 13 (8) 1641, Joseph b. 15 (6) 1643.

Will dated 2 Aug. 1683, prob. 3 March, 1686, beq. to son John and his ch. John and Lydia; to son Seth and his 4 ch.; to son Samuel and his ch.

Henry, with wife, 3 sons, 2 daus. 3 men-servants and 2 maid-servants, came from Ha..en Hall in Norfolk, Eng. Settled first at Charlestown, I think; as Henry and Dorothy were adm. chh. there 10 (5) 1637. Rem. to Hingham. Frm. March 13, 1638-9. Deacon, deputy. Rem. to Rehoboth; prop. frm. of Plym. Col. 4 June, 1645.

Will dated the day of his death, 3 Nov. 1647, prob. 4 June, 1651; wife; bro. Thomas Cooper; sons Henry and Daniel; dau. Judith. Son Henry may think of going to old England. The widow Judith's will was prob. 14 (10) 1650; sons Henry and Daniel, and dau. Judith, son and dau. Hunt. [Reg. IV, 319 and 320.]

Bequests to the family (by names) in will of Mr. Nicholas Stanton of Ipswich, Eng. in 1648. [E. and W.]

Henry, Rowley, propr. 1649. Inv. rendered 25 (1) 1656.

Hugh, Rowley, propr., frm. May 18, 1642; town officer. Wife Mary survived him, and m. 2, Dec. 2, 1657, Jeremiah Ellsworth. Ch. John, (m. 24 Feb. 1657, Faith Parrat,) Mary b. 17 (1) 1642, (m. Daniel Wickam,) Sarah b. and d. 1643, Martha b. 5 (12) 1648, (m. May 6, 1669, Caleb Burbank,) Edward b. 1 (4) 1654, John and Jonathan b. and d. 1659, Samuel, (of whom D. Wickam was guardian,) Hannah, (whose guardian was Leonard Harriman).

Will dated 19 (9) 1655, prob. 20 (1) 1655-6, beq. to wife Mary; est. to be divided to children at her death or marriage.

Jacob, residence not stated, before Gen. Court in 1637.

SMITH, etc., cont.
propr. at Marblehead in 1648; propr. at Gloucester before 1649; frm. May 3, 1654. Before Court for receiving too high wages 27 (7) 1636. He and his son James in Court in 1640. [Wife] Mary adm. chh. of Salem 14 (2) 1650. James, Marblehead, gives to his only son, James Smith, living at Bristol, Eng. land at Salem, called Castlehill, June 13, 1656. [Suff. De.]

His will prob. 27 (4) 1661, beq. to wife Mary, son James, dau. Katharine Eborne and her six children, and to dau. Mary, wife of Richard Rowland, and her son Samuel and her three other children. The widow's will dated 28 March, 1663, prob. 16 April, 1662, gave to the same persons.

James, Sen. Weymouth, 1639; propr.; lands referred to in deed of Margery Staple in 1658. Ch. James, Joshua, Nathaniel b. 8 (4) 1639, Hannah, (m. 1, John Snell, m. 2, — Parramore).

Will dated 19 June, 1673, prob. 22 June, 1676; beq. to wife Joane; sons James and Nathaniel; dau. Hannah Parramore; gr. son James, son of dec. son Joshua.

Mr. James, a shipmaster, Boston, sold house and land before 1645; adm. chh. Boston 12 (8) 1644. Sold ship Rainbowe to Thomas Fowle and Robert Hardinge 7 Feb. 1645. [A.] Went to Guinea to trade for negroes in 1645; had trouble with his mate, Keysar. Both were tried for kidnapping two negroes and causing the death of others. [W.] He may be the

James, who d. at Seaconk; admin. gr. Sept. 7, 1653, to Amos Richardson of Boston.

John, "a boy," apprenticed July 3, 1632, to Mr. John Wilson of Boston for 5 years; goods that came with him to remain in Mr. W.'s hands, who should be accountable to those that sent them. Smyth also bound himself to be accountable for his company's goods now inventoried and remaining in his hands. [Col. Rec.] Rev. Stephen Bachiler claimed part of the goods. Statement by "Mrs. Smith" of Wat. that the boy's father and uncle adventured £ 10 with him. [Mass. Hist. Col. 4-7.] He may be the son of the wife of Jeremiah Nor-

SMITH, etc., cont.
cross, whose acounts are given in Col Rec. 1 (10) 1640; mentioned in his will in 1657 with wife Mary.

John, tailor, Boston, adm. chh. 6 (12) 1638. Frm. May 22, 1639. Had lot at Muddy River for 3 heads 29 (5) 1639. Wife Mercie adm. chh. 14 (2) 1644. Dau. Rachel, (m. 1, Robert Woodward, m. 2, 7 (5) 1654, Thomas Harwood). Will dated 23 (7) 1673, prob. 13 June, 1674, beq. to dau. Rachel, wife of Thomas Harwood.

John, residence not stated, frm. March 4, 1632-3. He was banished by Gen. Court 3 Sept. 1635, "for dangerous opinions." Rem. to Rhode Island.

John, Weymouth. He sympathized with Mr. Lenthall and combined with others to hinder the orderly gathering of the church, and trying to set up another there; was fined by the Court 13 (1) 1638-9. See Silvester. [W. and Col Rec.]

Rev. John, yeoman, minister, Barnstable, atba. 1643. Adm. chh. Oct. 6, 1644; prop. frm. 6 June, 1649, frm. 5 June, 1651. Juryman; deputy. App. to attend meetings of the Quakers and hear their defense. Reported in their favor. Withdrew from the communion of the church for conscientious reasons; was "declared noe member for that reason only," but restored later. Preached occasionally at Bar. In Sept. 1661, he led in organizing a church which a council refused to approve. [MS. in Mass. Hist. Coll., quoted by Felt.] Was called to be pastor at Sandwich. Accepted, and served them from 1673 till 1689. Res. at Sand. in 1694. Sold house and lands in Bar. 21 Oct. 1667, for £150. He m. about June 13, 1643, Susanna, dau. of Samuel Hinckley; ch. Samuel bapt. Oct. 20, 1644, Sarah bapt. May 11, 1645, Ebenezer b. and d. 1646, Mary bapt. Nov. 21, 1649, Dorcas bapt. Aug. 18, 1650, John b. and d. 1651, Shubael bapt. March 16, 1652-3, John b. Sept. 1656, Benjamin b. Jan. 7, 1658, Ichabod b. Jan. 7, 1660, Elizabeth b. Feb. 1662, Thomas b. Feb. 1664, Joseph b. Dec. 6, 1667.

John, a parishioner of Mr. Richard Mather at Toxteth, [Prince,] came with Mr.

SMITH, etc., cont.
M. in the James from Bristol, May 23, 1635. His wife and Mary also mentioned by Mr. M. as being on board. Settled at Dorchester. Frm. May 25, 1636. Herdsman, propr.; made repairs on the meeting-house in 1653; chosen Quarter Master of the troop of Suffolk regiment; confirmed by the Court 19 Oct. 1652. He m. in Roxbury, Aug. 1, 1647, Katharine, dau. of Isaac Morrel. Ch. Mary, (m. 1, Nathaniel Glover, 2, Mr. Thomas, afterward Gov. Thomas Hinckley, and d. July 29, 1703, "ae. 73;") Elizabeth bapt. 19 (10) 1647, Anna bapt. 7 (7) 1651, Mary bapt. 17 (4) 1655, (m. 16 (5) 1673, Samuel Pelton,) John bapt. 12 (8) 1656, Waitstill b. 11 (10) 1658, [1657?] Samuel b. 18 (1) 1658-9, Deliverance b. 21 (11) 1660, Samuel b. 26 (10) 1662, Sarah b. 9 (2) 1665, Abigail b. 31 (6) 1668, Joseph b. 30 (3) 1671, d. about a month after.

He d. April 29, 1678. Will dated Dec. 10, 1676, prob. July 25, 1678. Beq. to wife Katharine, dau. Mary Pelton, son John, and other children not named. Refers to the portion given to his dau. Mrs. Mary Hinckley at her marriage with Nathaniel Glover, and her receipt dated 1 (9) 1660, and gives her nothing at this time. Dau. Mary Pelton had received a part of her portion. Inv. filed by the widow 3 Aug. 1678; another inventory filed after her death by Samuel Bayley, son-in-law, 1 Nov. 1710. [Reg. XXXVII, 344.]

John, Lynn, juror, 1636; frm. April 17. 1637; had land grant in 1638. Rem. to Reading. Ch. Mary b. 15 (9) 1648, John b. 4 (8) 1651. See Jeremiah Norcross.

John, planter, Salem; propr. 1642. Perhaps the J. S., frm. May 26, 1647. Rem. to Marblehead. Sold land adjoining his father Goodell in 1658 and 1667. He m. Elizabeth, dau. of Robert Goodell; 3 children. Inv. of his est. taken Sept. 8, 1688, returned by the widow.

John, Medford, before Gen. Court 5 June, 1638.

John, Hampton, about 1640; rem. to Nantucket. Mentioned in H. records as J. S. of Nantucket. His son John remained in H. and m. Deborah —; had dau. Deborah,

SMITH, etc., cont.
who became the wife of Nathaniel Bacheller. See Dalton.

John, Plymouth, apprenticed for 7 years July 25, 1633, to John Jenny; time shortened to 5 years. He m. 7 Dec. 1638, Bennett Moorecock. He was a planter; had suit in court 5 March, 1643. Ch. Jeremiah b. about 1645, appr. to Thomas Whitney and wife Jan. 30, 1649; Joseph b. 16 April, 1652.

Mr. John, from Dublin, Ireland, partner with Samuel Cooke, March 10; 1639. [L.] His wife Hannah was recd. as an inhabitant at Dedham (lately arrived from Ireland,) 23 (4) 1640, and adm. chh. Boston 21 (12) 1640-1. Though proposed for a propr. at Ded. with Cooke and Bacon, he settled at Boston. Propr.; the rate of John Smith, gent., was remitted 30 (11) 1642, on account of his great losses in Ireland.

John, Sen., Watertown, propr. 1636. Frm. Dec. 7, 1636. His land adjacent to that of John Benjamin in 1645. Wife Isabel was bur. 12 (8) 1639, ae. 60. Note
John, Sudbury, perhaps son of this "Senior;" he m. 13 (8) 1647, Sarah Hunt; ch. John b. 7 (11) 1648, Robert b. 11 May, 1654. See also.
John, Lancaster. His will dated 12 (2) 1665, prob. 27 (7) 1669, beq. to sons John and Richard; daus. Ann More and Ales.

John, Dedham. Wife Margaret; ch. John b. 5 (5) 1644, d. 14 (6) 1645.

John, Taunton, prop. frm. 3 Sept. 1639.

John, Charlestown, ship-carpenter, inhabitant 1644. Wife Sarah; ch. Benoni, d. 15 (4) 1646.
He d. 26 (1) 1673. Will dated 8 March, prob. 17 (4) 1673; "Senior" beq. to wife Sarah and ch. 2,000 acres of land at Lancaster, given him by the Indians; to sons John, James and Josiah, and daus. Elizabeth, Sarah and Mary, property at Char. etc. The widow, an aged woman, d. Nov. 12, 1687.

Judith, maid-servant to Edward Hutchinson, Boston, adm. chh. 2 (8) 1634.

Lawrence, Dorchester, propr., frm. May 10, 1643. Bought house and lands in

SMITH, etc., cont.
1650. Wife Mary; ch. Mary bapt. 5 (4) 1642, Mary b. 28 (12) 1642-3, Rebecca bapt. 22 (12) 1644-5, (m. John Nash of Boston.) [Suff. De. IX.] The Clap Memorial asserts that there was another dau., Elizabeth, who m. 31 Oct. 1668, Nathaniel Clap. [See children attributed to John Smith of Dorch., ante.]
He d. 3 (8) 1665. Nunc. will prob. Jan. 31, 1665-6. Wife exec. Est. to be divided between her and their children. [Reg. XIII, 337.] The widow d. June 11, 1683.

Lucy, apprenticed to Mr. Ludlow of Dorchester for 7 years, July 5, 1631. Perhaps dau. of Mrs. Frances [Smith] Sandford, and sister of Henry.

Martin, servant to John Byrt, witnessed a bond in Boston 9 (8) 1645.

Matthew, shoemaker, embarked at Sandwich, co. Kent, Eng., for N. E. before June 9, 1635. Brought wife Jane and 4 children. Res. at Charlestown in 1637. The wife was adm. chh. 22 (10) 1639; he was adm. chh. 1 (5) 1640. Propr. at Salem, 1637, but no evidence of residence. Frm. May, 1645.

Matthew, Dorchester, bought house of Wm. Barber Oct. 3, 1639. [Town rec.] Perhaps he is Matthew of Braintree, who had a grant of land for 5 heads 24 (12) 1639-40.

Michael or Mighill, Charlestown, propr., adm. chh. 1 (5) 1645, frm. May 26, 1647. Lived at Malden. Wife Jane; ch. Michael, Samuel b. 19 (5) 1648, Pelatiah, John, Nathaniel, Sarah bapt. 4 (6) 1661.

Nathaniel, "died in New England," perhaps at Ipswich.
His will dated 1 Jan. 1648, and 19 Feb. 1650, prob. at London 20 March, 1650, prob. also at Ipswich 30 Sept. 1651, copy filed also in Mass. Court, [Arch. 15 B.] beq. money and goods in N. E. and elsewhere, some in Mr. George Corwin's hands. Kinsman Thomas Edwards; cousin Nathaniel Edwards; uncle John Smith; sister Hanna Mellowes and cousin Hannah M. in N. E.; bro. Samuel Wandley; bro. Samuel Fisher; sisters Wandley and Halford. Mr. John Niccols, flaxman, bro. Andrew Halford and his son William H. Another will was offered by Mr. Joseph Hills. [Reg. XXVIII, 418.] [Mdx. Files.]

Nehemiah, Marshfield, prop. frm. 6 March, 1638-9. Com. on the allotment of

SMITH, etc., cont.
meadows 5 May, 1640. He m. 21 Jan. 1639, Ann, dau. of Mr. Thomas Bourne.

Rev. Ralph, a Puritan of an independant type, asked permission to come to New England with the colony of the Mass. Bay Co.; they consented to his application, and allowed him to come to N. E. in one of their ships in 1628, expresing doubts as to the probability of his independent views harmonizing with the standards held by the company. He was, therefore, taken on the condition that he would submit to such orders as should be established, and that he would not exercise the ministry within the limits of their patent.

He stayed awhile, with his wife and family at Nantasket; requested passage with some Plymouth people to that plantation in 1629, and was soon engaged by the church to be their pastor, and duly ordained to the office. Resigned in 1637, but continued to reside there for some years, [B. and Col. Recs.] Frm. 1632. Appointed on important matters.

Was invited by the people of Jeffrey's Creek, (Manchester,) to be their minister, and sold his house at Plym. and rem. thither about 1645. Was adm. to chh. of Salem 14 (9) 1647.

He d. at Boston, March 1, 1660-1. Admin. of his est. was gr. April 18, 1661, to Nathaniel Masterson, his late wife's son. The inv. taken by Wm. Cotton and Wm. English, shows books of some value, appraised by the bookseller, Hezekiah Usher, etc.

Ralph, came from Hingham, Eng., in 1633, and settled at Charlestown; rem. about 1636 to Hingham. Propr. 1637. Rem. to Eastham in 1653. Ch. "child" bur. Feb. 15, 1640, Samuel bapt. July 11, 1641, John bapt. July 7, 1644, Daniel bapt. March 2, 1646-7, Elizabeth bapt. Sept. 1648. (Thomas; see Reg. XXVI, 438;) Deborah b. at Eastham 8 March, 1654.

Ralph Smith d. at Eastham, and admin. was gr. Oct. 27, 1685, to his widow Grace and son Samuel. [Plym. Col. Rec.] A perplexing question in this connection is, who was the Ralph Smith who d. at Roxbury 7 (6) 1672, ae. 95?

Richard, Cohannet, (Taunton,) took oath of allegiance 3 Dec. 1638, prop. frm. 3

SMITH, etc., cont.
Sept. 1639. He m. 27 March, 1646, Ruth Bonum; ch. Thomas b. 23 April, 1647, d. in 1648, Hannah, (twin,) b. 23 April, 1647.

Inv. of his est. and that of his wife Ruth filed 28 Oct. 1684.

Richard, Ipswich, propr. 1641. His dau. m. Edward Gilman, Jr., who bought land of him at Ips. 9 Oct. 1647; this land he mortg. 25 (10) 1648, to his father Edward Gilman, Sen., who sold it 2 Oct. 1651, to *his brother* Richard Smith, of Shroppum, co. Norfolk, Eng., evidently the same man.

Richard, Sudbury, m. 6 Oct. 1647, Mary Kerley; ch. Hannah b. 21 (7) 1651. The wife with infant, d. 27 (3) 1654. He rem. to Lancaster. He m. 2, 2 (6) 1654, in Boston, widow Joanna Quarlis; ch. John b. 20 (11) 1655, Frances b. 26 (6) 1657.

Will dated 14 June, 1680, ae. about 55 years; son of Antony Smith of Burvild [Burghfield?] in Berkshire, Eng.; lived 14 years at Watertown; served Jeremiah Norcross; rem. to Sudbury; lived with cousin Thomas Read, Sen.; refers to marriage and death of wife and child at Boston, and residence at various places at the East; returned to Sud. and was cared for by Read, to whom he beq. all his est.

Robert, wine cooper, London, came about 1637 to N. E., bringing with him his wife and sister Mary Smith; had sent over his sister Anne Smith the year before. He and his wife ret. to Eng., leaving his sisters here; Anne m. John Kenrick of Boston about 1638, and had several children by him; Mary m. Philip Torrey and had children and was living in Bo. 4 Dec. 1663, when Elizabeth, widow of Robert Scott, deposed to the foregoing statement. [See Scarbarrow.] [Reg. XL, 63.]

Samuel, ae. 32, with wife Elizabeth, ae. 32, and children Samuel, ae. 9, Elizabeth, ae. 7, Mary, ae. 4, and Philip, ae. 1, came in the Elizabeth of Ipswich April 30, 1634. Settled at Salem; frm. Sept. 3, 1634; propr. 1638. Rem. to Enon, (Wenham.)

Will dated 5 Oct., prob. 27 (10) 1642. Wife Sarah; refers to promise made to her at marriage; son William Browne with his sons William and John; son Thomas Smith, dau. Mary.

SMITH, etc., cont.

Thomas, Salem, frm. June 11, 1633; deputy, 1635. Had leave to accompany those who set out the bounds of Boston and Saugus, July 8, 1635. Rem. to Gloucester. Com. to end small causes, 1644. Wife Grace testified for Mr. Blinman in 1647. [Wenham chh. rec.] Ch. Benjamin bapt. 17 (12) 1636, Nathaniel bapt. 24 (1) 1639.

He and his son George were drowned 5 (12) 1661. Admin. of his est. 28 (9) 1662, for the widow and children.

Thomas, weaver, from Romsey, Eng., came in the James, April 15, 1635. Settled at Ipswich. Propr. early. Rem. to Newbury. Frm. May 17, 1637. Ch. [Richard, John,] Thomas, (drowned Dec. 6, 1646), [Ips. De. 1,] Rebecca b. 20 Feb. 1639, James b. 10 Sept. 1645, John b. March 9, 1647, Mathias b. 27 Oct. 1652, Thomas d. 1652, Thomas b. 7 July, 1654, d. 1676.

He d. 26 April, 1666. The widow m. 2, Thomas Howlett; d. 1 Nov. 1680, and her est. was given to her sons James and John Smith.

Thomas, carpenter, Watertown, propr. 1636. Sold land in 1651. He m. Mary, [dau. of William] Knapp. Ch. James b. 18 (7) 1637, John bur. 26 (8) 1639, ae. 3 days, Thomas b. 26 (6) 1640, John b. 10 (10) 1641, Joseph b. 10 (4) 1643.

He d. 10 March, 1693. Will dated March 16, 1687-8, prob. May 8, 1693, beq. to wife Mary; sons Thomas, John, Ephraim, Jonathan and Joseph; dau. Mary and the ch. of dec. dau. Sarah; gr. ch. James Smith of Piscataqua.

William, Weymouth, frm. Sept. 2, 1635, deputy 1636; appointed by the Court to act for the magistrates in certain cases 6 (7) 1638. Propr. 1640. Complaint made against him in 1640, as one of the frm. and proprs. of the town, by one who had not had due proportion of land, as he claimed. [L.] Ch. Ruth b. 1639, d. 1640, Nehemiah b. Oct. 2, 1641.

William, tailor, Charlestown, inhabitant in 1637, adm. chh. 8 (5) 1643, frm. May 29, 1644. Wife Hannah or Anne, adm. chh. 23 (7) 1640; ch. Hannah or Anna b. and bapt. 27 (7) 1644, Nathaniel b. 25 (11), bapt. 3 (11)

SMITH, etc., cont.

1640, Mary b. 20 (10) 1642, Hephzibah b. 28 (12) 1644.

Inventory, dated 1 (2) 1654, of the est. of William Smith of Charlestown and of his wife, both deceased.

William, Rehoboth, propr. 1643; prop. for frm. 4 June, 1645; constable 1647; highway surveyor 1651.

Note. John Smith of London, citizen and merchant tailor, beq. to the children of his cousin William Smith in New Eng., and to Mary, his now or late wife, in will prob. 17 Dec. 1655. [Reg. XVI, 75, and XXXVIII, 71.]

SNELL,

John, Salem, 1637. He may be the following or the father of this man.

John, shipwright, Boston. Wife Philippee died, and he m. Hannah, dau. of James Smith of Weymouth. Ch. Susanna b. 21 June, 1659, Anna b. Jan. 2, 1661, John b. Oct. 9, 1663, Phillippe d. Oct. 10, 1663, Simon b. Aug. 22, 1667, of John and Hannah.

He d. 27 Nov. 1668. Will prob. 27 Jan. folg. Beq. to wife Hannah and four children; son John to be brought up by his father-in-law James Smith and mo.-in-law Jone S.; Susanna and youngest dau. Jane by wife; Hannah by his master and Mrs. Timothy Prout, Sen.; money to be sent to his bro. Symon S. of London, Eng.

Mary, adm. chh. Charlestown 12 (6) 1633.

SNELLING,

William, physician, son of Thomas S., Esq., and Johan, his wife, of Chaddlewood, in Plympton St. Mary in Devon, m. at Boston 5 July, 1648, Margaret, dau. of Gyles Stagge, gent., and Anne, his wife, of Southwark, Eng. [Newbury town rec.] Came to Newbury; res. there some time; rem. to Boston. Bought house and land Oct. 13, 1654, and sold same with wife Margaret in 1657. Ch. William b. 24 June 1649, Anne b. 2 March, 1652, Anne b. at Boston 7 May, 1654. Wife Margaret d. 18 June, 1667, ae. 46 years. [Copps Hill Epitaph.]

He d. in Nov. 1674; will dated 7 May, prob. Nov. 12, 1674; stricken in years; beq. to son William and dau. Anne. [Genealogy in Reg. LII, 342.]

SNOW,

Anthony, feltmaker, Plymouth, 1639. Res. at Marshfield, atba. 1643. He m. 8 Nov. 1639, Abigail, dau. of Richard Warren. Ch. (rec. at Marshfield) son b. 25 March, 1655, Ales b. 18 [Jan.] 1657.

Will dated 20 Dec. 1685, prob. Jan. 3, 1692-3, beq. to wife Abigail, son Josiah, daus. Lydia, Sarah and Alice and the children of dau. Abigail; gr. ch. James, Hannah and Abigail Foord. Bro. Joseph Warren one of the overseers.

Nicholas, Plymouth, came in 1623; taxed in 1632, frm. 1633; atba. 1643. Rem. to Eastham. He m. before 1627, Constance, dau. of Stephen Hopkins. Ch. Mark b. May 9, 1628.

He d. Nov. 16, 1676. He made will 14 Nov. 1676. Beq. to ch. Mark, Joseph, Stephen, John and Jabez; to wife Constant; to the church of E. The widow d. Oct. 1677.

Richard, Woburn, propr. 1645. Ch. Daniel b. Feb. 4, 1644-5, d. July 18, 1646, Samuel b. May 28, 1647, Zachariah b. March 29, 1649.

He d. 5 May, 1677. Will dated 30 (11) 1676, prob. 19 June, 1677, beq. to wife Anis and sons John, James, Samuel and Zachary. Genealogy in Reg. XLVII, 81.

Thomas, barber, Boston, adm. chh. 5 (7) 1644, frm. May 18, 1642. Wife Milcah adm. chh. 18 (4) 1643. They mortg. their house, to which the sign of the dove was fixed, 16 Dec. 1667. Ch. Melatiah b. (8) 1638, bapt. 12 (7) 1641, ae. about 3 years, Hannah bapt. 21 (2) 1644, Samuel bapt. 6 (3) 1649, Abigail b. 10 (1), bapt. 14 (1) 1651, Mehetabel b. 8 Feb. 1654, Milcha, (m. 22 March, 1659, Samuel Fisher.)

He d. in 1668-9. Will dated 10 Nov. 1688, prob. April 28, 1669. Wife Milcha to dispose of the est. at her discretion among his children. [Reg. XX, 240.]

William, ae. 18, came in the Susan and Ellen in April, 1635, as a servant of Mr. Richard Derby to Plymouth. Was transferred 31 Aug. 1630, to Edward Dotey, to serve 7 years longer.

SOMERBY,

Anthony, son of Richard, son of Henry, of Little Bythum in Lincolnshire, [his own statement in Newb. rec.] came in the Jonathan in 1639, as he deposed in the Blanchard case in 1652. [Es. Files 2, 32.] Settled at Newbury. Kept the school one year. The Gen. Court app. him clerk of writs and recorder of births, etc., 27 Oct. 1647, Frm. May 18, 1642. Propr., town officer. He deposed April 3, 1680, ae. 70 years. Wife Abigail d. 3 June, 1673; only child Abiel b. 8 Sept. 1641.

He d. 31 July, 1686. Beq. his est. to grand children Henry, Abiel and Anthony S. and Elizabeth Moody (and her son Daniel,) to gr. daus. Abigail and Rebecca; to Elizabeth Morse; dau.-in-law has had allowance out of her husband's estate, and £60 is in her bro. John Kelly's hands; bro. Tristam Coffin and cousin Nathaniel Clark overseers.

Henry, bro. of Anthony, Newbury, frm. May 18, 1642. Propr. He m. Judith, dau. of Edmund Greenleaf; ch. Sarah b. Feb. 10, 1645, Elizabeth b. Nov. 1646, John b. Dec. 24, 1648, d. in 1650, Daniel b. Nov. 18, 1650, d. 1676.

He d. Oct. 2, 1652; widow pres. inv. and petitioned Es. Court that her ch. Daniel, Sara and Elizabeth might have his est., 18 (9) 1652. She m. 2, March 2, 1653, Tristam Coffin.

SOMES, SOAMES, SOOMS, SOMNES,

Morris, Gloucester, in court in 1647; propr. 1649. He m. 2, June 26, 1647, Elizabeth Kendall. Ch. Mary b. March 1, 1641-2, (m. John Hammond,) Sarah b. June 15, 1643, (m. Henry Witham,) Timothy, John b. April 22, 1648, Lydia b. Oct. 3, 1649, Nathaniel, Patience, Joseph, Abigail, Hannah b. Sept. 3, 1658. He deposed in 1658, ae. about 58 years.

He d. Jan. 16, 1689. Admin. gr. Dec. 28, 1692.

SOULE,

George, servant to Edward Winslow, came in the Mayflower to Plymouth. Frm. 1633; volunteer for the Pequot War in 1637; res. at Duxbury. Com. of Court, 1640; deputy, 1642. His wife Mary and son Zachariah had shares of cattle with him in 1627. He had 8 children living in 1650. [B.]

He made will 11 Aug. 1677, aged and weak; prob. 5 March, 1679-80; sons John, Nathaniel and George, daus. Elizabeth, Patience, Susannah, Mary.

SOUTH,
Thomas, Lynn, propr. 1638; excused from training in regard of his age, in Salem Court, 29 (10) 1640.

William, residence not stated, banished by the Gen. Court 4 (7) 1638.

SOUTHCOAT, SOUTHCOTE,
Captain, came in the Mary and John with the church-colony that founded Dorchester in 1629-30. Had been a Low Country soldier; led the exploring party that went up Charles River in search of a place for the colony. [Cl.]

Mr. Richard and Mr. Thomas appl. frm. Oct. 19, 1630; "Captain" was adm. frm. May 18, 1631. Propr. Dorch. until Dec. 2, 1633. Both removed soon. See Hist. Windsor and other Conn. histories.

SOUTHER, SOWTHER,
Nathaniel, Plymouth, frm. Oct. 4, 1635; clerk Plym. Court Jan. 3, 1636-7. Rem. to Boston. Adm. townsman in 1649; frm. Mass. May 18, 1653. Was a notary. He deposed Oct. 19, 1654, ae. about 62 years. Wife Alice d. 27 (7) 1651; he m. 5 (11) 1653, Sarah Hill, widow; same day his dau. Mary m. Joseph Shaw, (afterward m. John Blake;) a dau., Mrs. Hannah Johnson, is referred to in Plym. Col rec. in 1659; Joseph and John Souther in Bo. 1657-1660.

He d. 27 (4) 1655. Admin. gr. July 31, 1655, to his widow; goods she brought with her were allowed to her. [Reg. IX, 135.]

SOUTHERLAND,
Matthew, Plymouth, in Court 1 Oct. 1638.

SOUTHMEADE, SOUTHMAYDE,
William, mariner, Gloucester. He m. 28 Nov. 1642, Millicent, dau. of William Addis; ch. William b. Sept. 12, 1643, John b. and d. 1645, John b. 31 (10) 1646.

Admin. of his est. 20 (12) 1648. His sons William and John rem. to New London, Conn.; the widow m. 2, William Ash; deeded land to him (4) 1650, which was to go at his death to her sons. She m. 3, Thomas Beebe, and joined with them June 12, 1668, in deed of land at Boston. [Petition in Arch. 15 B.]

SOUTHWICK, SOUTHICK, SETHICK,
John, Salem. He m. Sarah, widow of Samuel Tid; ch. Sarah b. June, 1644, Mary b. 10 (8) 1646, Samuel b. 19 (12) 1658. [Salem rec.]

Lawrence, glassman, Salem, propr., frm. Sept. 6, 1639. [See Conckling and Holmes.] His wife Cassandra memb. chh. 1639. They were Quakers. Elizabeth adm. chh. 1 (7) 1650. Ch. Provided bapt. 6 (10) 1639, Provided b. (10) 1641. [Es. Files.]

Will dated 10 (5) 1659, at the house of Nathaniel Silvester at Shelter Island; prob. Ess. Court 29 (9) 1660. Sons Daniel S. and John Burnell; daus. Provided S. and Mary, wife of Henry Traske; to Deborah and Josiah S.; to Ann Potter; to Henry Traske's ch. Mary, Sarah and Hannah; Samuel and Sarah, ch. of John S.

SOUTHWORTH, SOUTHWOOD,
Constant, son of the second wife of Gov. Bradford, came early to Plymouth. Lands granted to William Bradford for Constant and Thomas S. on North side of Eel River, (Duxbury,) Oct. 6, 1636. He m. 2 Nov. 1637, Elizabeth Collier.

Will dated 27 Feb. 1678, inv. taken 15 March, 1678-9; beq. to wife Elizabeth, sons Edward, Nathaniel and William, daus. Mercye Freeman, Alice Church, Mary Alden, Elizabeth and Priscilla S.; to cozen Elizabeth Howland; to gr. son Constant Freeman.

Thomas, Plymouth, bro. of Constant, Duxbury; captain. He m. 1 Sept. 1641, Elizabeth, [dau. of Mr. John] Reyner.

He d. Dec. 8, 1669, "a great and good man;" will prob. March 1, 1669-70. To dau. Elizabeth, wife of Joseph Howland; bro. Constant S. to join with them in care of his wife in her poor condition; to Thomas Faunce and Wm. Churchill. [Reg. VII, 179.]

SPARROW,
Richard, Plymouth, taxed in 1633, constable 1639-40. Rem. to Eastham, townsman 1655.

Will dated 19 (9) 1660; wife Pandora, son Jonathan, grandchildren John, Priscilla and Rebecca S.; to the church of E. [Reg. V, 388.]

SPARHAWK, SPARROWHAWK,

Mr. Nathaniel, Cambridge, propr. 1636, frm. May 23, 1639. Deacon. He was a son of Samuel S. of Dedham, Eng., b. Feb. 16, 1597-8; m. Mary, dau. of John Angier of same place. [Rel.] [Reg. L, 400, 415, etc.] He gave a letter of attorney 20 (10) 1644, to Thomas Adams of London, to recover a debt of 16 li. 2 s. 10 d. of Mr. Owen Roe of L. for clothes, dyet, bookes and other necessaries for his son. [A.] Deputy, deacon. Wife Mary d. Jan. 25, 1643-4. Wife Katharine d. July 5, 1647. Ch. Nathaniel, Anne, (m. John Cooper,) Mary, Esther, (living in 1658 with Thomas Cheesholme,) [Mi.] Samuel b. 27 (8) 1638, d. 13 (8) 1639, John d. 21 (7) 1644, Ruth b. and d. 1645.

He d. June 27, 1647. Admin. of his est. in 1649; long list of debtors and creditors; reference to Wm. S.'s est.; to Easter S.; John S. at Copell in Eng. [Reg. VII, 175.]

SPAULE, SPALLE, SPOWELL,

Thomas, Boston, propr. before 1649. Wife Alice, dau. of Richard Sherman, died. He m. 18 (6) 1653, Mary Gutteridge. Ch. Mary b. (7) 1644, Elizabeth b. 29 (7) 1646. Will dated 23 Feb. 1670, prob. 29 (2) 1671. Inv. taken 22 (2) 1671. Beq. to wife Mary, dau. Mary Knight and her husband Joseph Knight; kinswoman Elizabeth, dau. of Edmund Browne of Dorchester.

SPALDING, SPAULDING, SPALDEN, SPOLDEN,

Edward, Braintree, propr. 1640; frm. 13 May, 1640. Rem. to Wenham. One of the witnesses of Christopher Young's will 9 (1) 1647. Juryman, 1648. Sold house and lands in 1654, wife Rachel consenting. Was one of the founders of Chelmsford in 1655. Town officer. Wife [Margaret d. in 1640;] he m. 2, Rachel —; ch. Grace bur. (3) 1641, Benjamin b. 7 (2) 1643, Edward, John, Josiah, (ae. 21 years in 1670, [Mdx. Files,] Dinah, (m. at Chelms. Feb. 9, 1674, Eleazer Brown).

He d. Feb. 26, 1670. Will dated 13 Feb. 1666, prob. 5 (2) 1670, beq. to wife Rachel; sons Edward, John and Andrew; dau. Dinah. The widow Rachel d. soon after, and admin. on both estates was gr. to sons John and Edward.

SPEAR,

George, [Braintree?] frm. May 29, 1644.

George Speare m. at Braintree 27 (2) 1675, Mary Dearing.

SPENCER, SPENSER,

Edward, Lynn, propr. 1638.

Garrett or Jarrett, Cambridge, propr. 1634, frm. March 9, 1636-7. The Court granted him leave to keep the ferry at Lynn 13 March, 1638-9. A witness in Ess. Court in 1641.

Mr. John, gent. came in the Mary and John, March 26, 1633-4. Frm. Sept. 3, 1634. Settled at Ipswich. Had liberty to build a mill and weir, Nov. 1634. Deputy. Authorized by the Court 3 March, 1635-6, to have a house built for the plantation to be settled at Wenicunnett. Res. at Newbury, and was a propr. in 1635. Testimony regarding his business, Ips. De. I, 38. He ret. to England and d. about 1650. His will, dated 1 (6) 1637, recorded in Ips. De. I, 55; beq. all his lands and goods in N. E. to his nephew John Spenser, who is to pay £10 to his reverent instructor in Christ Mr. Cotton after three years; to every child of bro. Thomas Spenser; in case John die the est. to go to bro. T. S. and his ch.; or if they die, then to the ch. of bro. Nicholas and sister Rachel Kidwell; to cosen Gardner's ch. The nephew John sold some of the N. lands 28 Aug. 1650.

Michael, Cambridge, propr. 1635, frm. March, 1637-8. Propr. at Lynn in 1638. Lawsuit, 1641. Made draft Jan. 19, 1648, upon his cousin, Daniel Spencer, grocer, in Friday street, London, payable to Thomas Ruck, haberdasher, at London bridge, for 30 li. part of a legacy from his uncle Richard Spencer. [Ess. Court Files, XVII, 75.]

Thomas, Cambridge, propr. 1633, frm. May 14, 1634.

William, Cambridge, frm. March 4, 1632; propr. 1633; town officer and deputy 1634. Perhaps he returned to England, and was the William who came in the Mary and John in March, 1633-4.

SPIGHT,
James, Charlestown. Ch. James b. 1 (11) 1646.

SPILSBERRIE, SPILSBERY,
William, Newbury, bought land of Samuel Hall 18 July, 1657. [See Pilsbury.]

SPOFARD, SPOFFORD, SPAFFORD, SPAFORD,
John, Rowley, propr. before 1643. He deposed to Bellingham matters in 1662, ae. about 50 years. He m. Elizabeth, dau. of Thomas Scott, q. v. Ch. Elizabeth b. 14 (12) 1646, John b. 24 (10) 1648, Thomas b. 4 (11) 1650, Samuel b. Jan. 31, 1652, Hannah b. 1654, Mary b. 1 (9) 1656, Sarah b. 15 Jan. 1658, bur. Feb. 15, 1660, Sarah b. 22 March, 1661, Francis b. Sept. 24 1665.
Will prob. 6 (9) 1678. Wife Elizabeth; sons Francis, John, Thomas and Samuel; daus. Elizabeth, Hannah, Mary and Sarah. Genealogy.

SPOONER,
Thomas, linen weaver, Salem, frm. March, 1637-8; propr., town officer. Clerk of the market, 1656. Amy memb. chh. 1637. Admin. of his est. gr. to his widow Elizabeth 29 (9) 1664. She d. 31 (10) 1676. Her will prob. 26 (1) 1677. Cousins Margaret Rucke at Boston and Thomas Clarke at Cambridge; children of her son Rucke and his wife her dau., Hannah Spooner; other grandchildren John, Jr., and Elizabeth Osborne; widow Elizabeth Owen. Son-in-law John Rucke exec.

William, of Colchester, Eng. apprenticed himself, 27 March, 1637, to John Holmes of New Plymouth, in America, gent.; was transferred 1 July, 1637, to John Coombs of Plym., gent. [Plym. Col. Rec.] Settled at Plymouth. Frm. June 6, 1654. Was ordered to pay the debts of his master, Mr. Coombs, and to take care of his children, Aug. 1, 1648. Rem. to Dartmouth in 1660. Wife Elizabeth d. 28 April, 1648; he m. 2, 18 March, 1651, Hannah Pratt; ch. John, Sarah b. 5 Oct. 1653, (m. John Sherman,) Samuel b. 14 Jan. 1655, Martha, (m. John Wing,) William, Isaac, Hannah, Ebenezer, Mercy.
He d. in March, 1683-4. Will dated March 8, inv. taken 14th. Aged; beq. to the children named above and to Joshua, son of his dau. Hannah. [Genealogy.]

SPOWELL, see Spaule.

SPRAGUE, SPRAGE,
Francis, came to Plymouth in 1623; taxed in 1632; in court July 1, 1634, etc., frm. 7 Feb. 1636-7. Of Duxbury, 1643. Sold land at D. April 1, 1644, to son-in-law Wm. Laurence. Anna and Mercy had shares in cattle with him in 1627.

Ralph, husbandman, fuller, son of Edward, of Upway, Dorset, fuller, "sometimes of Fordington, co. of Dorset," came with his bro. Richard to Salem in 1628. They made their way through the woods to Charlestown in the spring of 1629, and were there when the party arrived to build the Great House and make other preparations for the coming of Gov. Winthrop and his party. He appl. frm. Oct. 19, 1630, was adm. frm. May 18, 1631. Lieut. The court app. him constable of Watertown in 1630. Deputy 1635 and afterward. He rem. to the part of Char. which became Malden.

He m. Joane, dau. of Richard Warren of Fordington, yeoman, who left legacy to her and her children John, Jonathan, Richard, Samuel, Mary and Phinehas; she empowered John Holland of Tinckleton, Dorset, fuller, to collect this for her, 29 (6) 1640. [L.] She was adm. to the chh. with her husband in 1630, and joined with him in the organization of the Charlestown chh. in Nov. 1632, and in that of Malden in 1649. His father-in-law, John Corbin, wrote him from Upway, Dorset, March 25, 1651. [Reg. IV, 289, and LI, 105.] Ch. Samuel bapt. at Bo. 3 (4) 1632, Mary bapt. at Char. 14 (7) 1634, (m. Daniel Edmunds,) Phinehas bapt. 31 (5) 1637, Jonathan d. Dec. 1650.

He d. (9) 1650. Distribution of his est. was made 6 (11) 1650, to widow Joanna and ch. John, Richard, Samuel, Mary and Phinehas. The widow m. 2, Edward Converse, q. v.

Richard, bro. of Ralph, [see letter of Corbin, above said, and will of their father Edward, in Reg. XLIX, 264.], Charlestown 1629. Frm. May 18, 1631. Town officer. One of the appraisers of Thompson's Island in 1657. Lieut. His wife Mary was memb. chh. Boston with him in 1630, and in that of Char. at its organization in 1632.

He d. Nov. 25, 1668, ae. 63. Will dated 17 (7) prob. 11 Dec. 1668, beq. to wife Mary; to Nathaniel Rand; cousins Richard and John

SPRAGUE, etc., cont.

S.; Mary, wife of Daniel Edmunds; bro. William S. of Hingham; Margery, wife of Lawrence Dowse; Alice, wife of Thomas Lord; to Harvard College; a liberal amount to the church of Char. His widow deeded to the chh. 1 March, 1671, her shop and chamber over it adjoining the meeting house, fronting on the market-place, adjoining land of John Long.

William, bro. of Ralph and Richard, planter, Charlestown, rem. to Hingham. Propr. 1636. Town officer. Wife Millicent adm. chh. Char. 3 (2) 1635; ch. Antony bapt. 23 (3) 1636, John bapt. at Hing. April, 1638, Samuel bapt. May 24, 1640, Jonathan bapt. March 20, 1641-2, d. 4 July, 1647, Persis b. Nov. 12, 1643, (m. John Doggett,) Joanna b. Dec. 1645, (m. Caleb Church,) Jonathan b. May 28, 1648, William b. July 2, 1650, Mary b. April 5, 1652, (m. Thomas King,) Hannah b. Feb. 25, 1654, d. 31 March, 1659. He d. 26 Oct. 1675. Will dated 19 Oct. 1675. To wife Millicent; ch. Anthony, Samuel, William, John, Jonathan, Persis, wife of John Doggett, Johanna, wife of Caleb Church, and Mary, wife of Thomas King. To Anthony the sword that was his bro. Richard Sprague's. The widow d. 8 Feb. 1695-6.

SPRING,

John, ae. 45, with wife Elinor, ae. 46, and children Mary, ae. 11, Henry, ae. 6, John, ae. 4, and William, ae. 9 months, came in the Elizabeth of Ipswich, April 30, 1634. Settled at Watertown; planter; propr. 1636. Took oath of fidelity, 1652. Made deed of gift to his son Henry, March 21, 1656-7, with reserve for his lifetime. His [second] wife, Grace, formerly widow of Thomas Hatch of Scituate, res. at Sci. in 1659. [Plym. Col. Rec.] See Hatch.

SPUR, SPURR, SPOOER,

John, husbandman, late of Clapton in Somersetshire, with his bro. John Mattocke, cooper, had grant of land in Boston, 1638. Frm. May 22, 1638-9. Wife Elizabeth adm. chh. with him 14 (2) 1639; ch. Mary b. 20 (1) 1637, Mary bapt. 21 (2) 1639, Ebenezer b. 3 (3) 1642, Elizabeth bapt. 30 (1) 1645, ae. about 6 days, Martha b. and d. 1648, John b. 16 (4) 1650.

SPRALL,

Mary, ae. 20, came in the Blessing in July, 1635.

SPURKS,

Edward, ae. 22, servant of Thomas Page, came in April, 1635.

SQUIRE,

George, Concord; his son — b. 11 (1) 1643.

Samuel, Salem, adm. chh. 30 (2) 1648.

Thomas, planter, Charlestown, one of the membs. chh. at local re-organization, Nov. 2, 1632; frm. May 14, 1634. Town officer, 1646. Res. at Malden in 1653. Res. at Boston, and sold land in 1659, Wife Bridget; they were m. about 1633. [Mdx. Files, 1653.]

STACKHOUSE, STAGHOUSE,

Richard, Salem, propr. 1636. Rem. to Beverly. Kept the ferry toward Ipswich from June 30, 1653. With wife Susan sold land in S. in 1658. He deposed in 1690, ae. about 78 years. Ch. Jonathan, Hannah and Abigail bapt. 14 (3) 1648, Ruth bapt. 8 (5) 1649, Samuel bapt. 13 (12) 1652, Mary bapt. 25 (4) 1654.

Admin. of his est. was gr. 1 Jan. 1704, to eldest dau. Hannah Harris, of Boston; John Harris and Isaac Perkins of Ipswich signed her bond.

STACY, STACEY,

Hugh, Salem, 1639; rem. to Dedham. Propr. 28 (9) 1640; frm. Feb. 28, 1642-3. Ret. to Salem; with wife Margaret dism. to chh. of Sal. Nov. 1641. Ch. Hannah b. 17 (12) 1640, John bapt. Sal. 9 (8) 1642, Deborah bapt. 30 (9) 1643, John bapt. 29 (1) 1646.

John, Salem, witness in court, 1646; propr. at Marblehead in 1648; deposed in 1654, ae. 60 years; referred to his son Henry, John, Jr., before Court 4 (4) 1639.

Admin. Ess. court 27 (4) 1672, gr. to widow Eleanor.

Nicholas, Salem, a witness in 1643.

Richard, Taunton, atba. 1643, town officer 1648, juror 1651.

Admin. of his est. gr. 7 Dec. 1687, to Thomas Lincoln.

Simon, Ipswich, propr. 1637; town officer. Simon, Jr. deposed March 29, 1692, ae. about 50 years. Capt. Simon d. Oct. 27, 1699.

STACY, etc., cont.

Thomas, miller, Ipswich, 1648. Rem. to Salem. He m. 4 (8) 1653, Susanna Wooster; ch. Thomas b. July 6, 1654, William b. April 21, 1656, Rebecca b. Dec. 7, 1657, Elizabeth b. April 16, 1659, Joseph b. June 27, 1660, Mary b. Nov. 7, 1661. [Es. Court Files.] He and his wife and 9 ch. were recd. to Salem chh. from that of Ips. April 20, 1676.

He d. 23 July, 1690. Will dated 9 Feb. 1689-90, prob. 25 Nov. 1690, beq. to wife Susannah, ch. Thomas, William, Joseph, Simon, John, Elizabeth, Mary and Susannah.

STANBURY, STANBOROUGH,

Josiah, planter, Lynn, propr. 1638. Rem. to Southampton, L. I. Wife, Frances, dau. of Henry Cransden or Gransden, of Tunbridge, Eng., sued his widow for her patrimony 27 (7) 1639. [L.] He gave letter of attorney 15 (9) 1647, to Hez. Usher of Boston regarding a house at Banbury, Eng. beq. to him by his father William Stanborough, late of Cannons Ashbie, Northamptonshire. [A.]

Thomas, laborer, yeoman, Boston, townsman 25 (11) 1640. Wife Martha adm. chh. 29 (9) 1645; ch. Thomas b. 15 (8) 1642, John b. 15 (7) 1645, Nathan b. 25 (10) 1646, Martha bapt. 11 (1) 1649, ae. about 6 days, Sarah bapt. 1 (4) 1651, [of William?]

He d. 26 (7) 1652. Admin. gr. after many years, 26 Nov. 1697, to eldest son Thomas.

STANDISH, STANDISHE, STANDIGE,
see Stanley,

James, Salem, propr., 1636; frm. May 13, 1640. Juryman, 1641. Sarah, memb. chh. 1637.

The inv. of his est. was filed 27 (9) 1679, by his widow Sarah.

Captain Myles, came in the Mayflower; signed the **Compact; res. first** at Plymouth, then at Duxbury. Frm. 1633; Asst.; chief officer of the militia of the Colony; com. of the United Colonies; a partner in the Trading Company. A brave, tireless worker for public weal, a sagacious magistrate and worthy character. He m. 1, Rose —, who came with him, and d. Jan. 29, 1620-1; he m. 2, Barbara —, before 1627, when she and his children, Alexander, Charles and John, had shares of cattle with him.

His will, dated March 7, 1655, prob. May, 1657; desired to be buried near his dec. dau.

STANDISH, etc., cont.

Lora and dau.-in-law Mary; beq. to wife Barbara; eldest son Alexander; sons Myles, Charles and Josias; to "Marrye Robenson whome I tenderly love for her Grandfathers sake;" to servant John Swift, Jr.; to son and heir apparent, Alexander, lands in Ormsticke, Borsconge, Wrightington, Maralsley, Wooburrow, Crawston and the Isle of Man, which were detained from him; his great-grandfather being a younger brother from the house of Standish of Standish.

STANDLAKE, STANDLECK, STANDLY, STANDLEY,

Daniel, Scituate.

He was bur. May 7, 1638. -Will prob. 3 March, 1639-40. Beq. to wife and two children. [Reg. IV, 36.] His youngest child, a girl, was bur. April 19, 1639. Joane, who m. Thomas Pinson, may have been of this family.

STANDY,

Robert, ae. 22, came in the Elizabeth and Ann in May, 1635.

Thomas, interpreter for the Mass. troops in the Pequot war. [B.]

STANESBY,

John, Cambridge, propr. and chh. memb. about 1638. Remained with his father in England till 11 years of age. [Rel.]

STANLEY, STANDLY, STANLECK, STANDISH, STANDIGE,

Christopher, tailor, ae. 32, with wife Susanna, ae. 31, came in the Elizabeth and Ann in April, 1635. Settled at Boston; frm. June 2, 1641. Wife Susanna adm. chh. 23 (4) 1639; ch. Rebecca, (m. Robert Lord,) Martha, (m. Richard Thurston).

He d. 27 (1) 1646; will dated 27 (1) 1646, prob. 19 (1) 1649, beq. a house and certain lands to Richard and George Benet; to Sarah, dau. of Rev. John Cotton, and Mary, dau. of Rev. John Wilson; to the church and Free School of Boston; to each of the teaching elders of Boston and their wives a pair of gloves; residue to wife Susan. The widow m. William Phillips.

John, d. intestate on the way to New England; the Court ordered, 3 March, 1634-5, that his bro. Thomas S. should have part of the est. in trust, and bring up the son

STANLEY, etc., cont.
John; his bro. Timothy S. should have the remainder, and bring up the dau. Ruth. A third child d. soon after the father. [Col. Rec.]

Thomas, Saugus, deputy 1635. Constable at Es. court 27 (4) 1636. Rem. to Hartford, Conn., and later to Hadley. He d. Jan. 31, 1663. Will dated 29 Jan. 1659, beq. to wife Bennett; son Nathaniel and his three daus. These are said to have been Hannah, (m. Samuel Porter,) Mary, (m. John Porter,) Sarah, (m. John Wadsworth). [Hist. Hadley.]

Timothy, Cambridge, propr. 1635. Rem. to Hartford, Conn.

STANYON, STANION,
Anthony, glover, planter, ae. 24. came in the Planter, April 6, 1635. Settled at Boston. Rem. to Exeter, and afterward rem. to Hampton, N. H. He deposed 13 April, 1675, ae. about 68 years. Wife Mary; ch. John b. in Bo. 16 (5) 1642.

STANTON,
Margaret, Rowley, propr. 1643; she was bur. 15 (2) 1646.

STAPLES, STAPLE,
Jeffrey, Weymouth, propr. Ch. Martha bur. 17 (12) 1639.
He d. in 1646-7. Inv. taken by Edward Bates and John Upham (1) 1647. Margery, widow, [of Jeffrey?] sold land in Wey. 10 Jan. 1658; she was not able to go to Court for the record of the deed by reason of age and weakness. Lieut. John Holbrook acted for her in the case.

John, Sen., Weymouth, frm. May 10, 1648, propr. He and his son gave testimony in town matter in 1654. Ch. Rebecca b. 27 (9) 1639, Joseph b. 19 (12) 1641.
He d. at Dorchester. Inv. taken 13 July, 1683. Will dated 18 March, 1681-2, prob. 2 Aug. 1683; beq. to sons John, Abraham, Joseph, and to daus. Rebecca, wife of Samuel Sumner, and Sarah, wife of Increase Sumner.

Samuel, Braintree, propr. He m. Mary Cole, 1644; m. Mary Boles 30 (6) 1652. Ch. Mary b. 24 (7) 1655, Rachel b. 31 (8) 1657, Sarah b. 5 (10) 1660.

STARCY,
John, Dorchester, propr. 1638.

STARK, STARKE,
Robert, [Concord.]

Admin. of his est. gr. 31 (8) 1646, to Capt. Willard, Joseph Wheeler and Richard Lettin. [Reg. VIII, 57.]

STARKWEATHER,
Robert, husbandman, Roxbury, propr.; rem. about 1650 to Ipswich. Sold house and land in Rox. given him by his father John Roberts, Dec. 18, 1651. Wife Janet; ch. Elizabeth bapt. July 23, 1643, Lydia b. June 23, 1644, John bapt. 2 (6) 1646, Deborah bapt. 27 (6) 1648.

STARR, STARES,
Mr. Comfort, chirurgion, of Ashford, Eng., came in the Hercules in March, 1634, with 3 children and 3 servants. Settled at Cambridge; propr. 1635; rem. to Duxbury; had land grant 7 Aug. 1638; frm. 4 June, 1639; his servant William Godden in court 3 Aug. 1640. His sister Constant, memb. chh. Dorchester before 1639, m. John Morley. He was remembered in the will of his bro. Jehoshaphat Starr of Ashford, Feb. 2, 1659. Rem. to Boston. Wife — d. June 25, 1658, ae. 63.
He d. Jan. 2, 1659. Will prob. Feb. 3, folg., beq. to Samuel S.; to the 5 ch. of dec. dau. Maynard; to the ch. of dec. son Thomas S., and to his widow Hannah, in Eng.; to gr. son Simon Eire for his education; to son John S.; to dau. Elizabeth Ferniside; to bros.-in-law John Morley and Faithful Rouse; property in Boston and at Eshitisford in Kent, in old England. [Reg. IX, 223.]

Robert, mariner, Salem, m. 24 (9) 1650, Susanna, dau. of [Richard] Hollingsworth; she d. 17 May, 1665. He m. 30 (10) 1669, Mary Conkling, widow, deeding a house, etc. to her, as a marriage portion. [Es. Files.] Ch. Susanna b. and d. 1652, Robert b. and d. 1653, Robert b. 8 (2) 1655, Susanna b. 31 (10) 1661, Mary b. 9 (8) 1670, Sarah and Hannah b. 22 June, 1673.
He deeded in March, 1671-2, to Richard Moore and Philip Cromwell certain property for the benefit of his ch. Robert, Richard and Susanna.
The inv. of his est. was taken 24 (4) 1679;

STARR, etc., cont.
widow Mary to have all for the maintenance of herself and the children.

Thomas, yeoman, of Canterbury, Eng. ae. 31, with wife Sarah and one child, Susan Johnson, ae. 12, took passage from Sandwich, Eng. March 11, 1634. Settled at Dorchester; taxed in 1640. Wife Susanna memb. chh. about 1639.
He died, and the widow Susanna was appointed admin. of his est. 2 (1) 1641. "Sister Starr of the Dorchester church" was noted as communing with the chh. of Wenham 17 (9) 1644.

STATIE,
Hugh, came in the Fortune in 1621; had lands assigned in Plymouth in 1623. Compare with Stacy.

STEADMAN, STEDMAN, STIDMAN,
Isaac, ae. 30, with Elizabeth, ae. 26, Nathaniel, ae. 5, and Isaac, ae. 1, came in the Elizabeth April 8, 1635. Settled at Scituate; adm. chh. July 17, 1630. Constable and frm. 7 June, 1648. Ch. Elizabeth bapt. Nov. 24, 1637. Rem. to Boston. Isaac, of Muddy River, Boston, yeoman, bought the Stanford Farm of the heirs of Mrs. Anne Hibbens Dec. 28, 1657.
Will dated 2 (8) prob. 19 (10) 1678, beq. to sons Nathaniel and Thomas; wife to have the estate she brought; daus. Elizabeth [Hanum,] Hannah Hide and Sara French. Inv. states his age about 70 years.

John, merchant, Cambridge, propr., town officer, frm. May 13, 1640. The Gen. Court app. him ensign 1 Oct. 1645. He made marriage contract for his dau. Martha with Joseph, son of Joseph Cooke, formerly of Camb. 29 Oct. 1665. [Mdx. De. III, 436.] Wife Alice; she went to London, before coming to this country, to get spiritual help from some minister. [Rel.] Ch. Elizabeth, [Mi.] Sarah b. 11 (11) 1643, Martha b. 3 (4) 1646, (m. — Bracket,) [Mi.]
He d. Dec. 16, 1693, ae. 92. His wife d. March 6, 1689-90, ae. about 80.

Robert, Cambridge, frm. March 14, 1638-9. He deposed 25 (6) 1659, ae. about 58 years. His dau. Elizabeth, ae. about 18, and maid Elizabeth Willinton, ae. about 24 years, also deposed. [Mdx. Files.] Ch. born

STEADMAN, etc., cont.
and bapt. at Camb.: John, Mary and Thomas; the latter d. April 2, 1659. [Mi.]
He d. about 20 Jan. 1666. Inv. on file.

STEBBINS, STEBBING, STEBBEN, STIBBINS,
Edward, Cambridge, propr. 1633, frm. May 14, 1634. Memb. of a com. of Gen. Court in 1635. Rem. to Hartford.

John, biscuit maker, Roxbury, 1644. He m. April 17, 1644, Anne Munke. She was bur. 4 (2) 1680. He sold land 29 Dec. 1666. He m. 2, June 4, 1680, Rebecca Hawkins of Boston. [See depositions with his will.]
He d. 4, was bur. 7 (10) 1681, ae. 70 years. His will, dated 23 Jan. 1677, prob. 15 Dec. 1681, beq. to wife Anne, cousins John and Jane Keene and Mehitabel Eldridge. He said before witnesses that his second wife should have exactly what he had devised to the first.

John, Watertown, propr. 1644. Wife Margaret; ch. John b. 25 (1) 1640, Mary b. 6 (8) 1641.

Martin, gardiner, Roxbury, signed an obligation to pay money in semi-annual instalments 17 (8) 1639. [L.] He rem. to Boston about 1647, where he was a brewer; sold Rox. property in 1648. He m. Dec. 25, 1639, Jane Greene; she d. in Bo. 24 July, 1659. Ch. Hannah b. Oct. 23, 1640, Mary b. Feb. 1, 1642, Nathaniel bapt. March 22, 1644.
He d. about (8) 1659. Admin. gr. to John S. 23 (9) 1659. Many names of debtors given in prob. papers. [Reg. XXXII, 317.]

Rowland, ae. 40, with wife Sarah, ae. 43, and children Thomas, ae. 14, Sarah, ae. 11, John, ae. 8, and Elizabeth, ae. 6, and Mary Winche, ae. 15, came in the Francis of Ipswich April 30, 1634. He res. at Springfield soon after its settlement; propr. 1641. Rem. to Northampton after some years. His wife Sarah d. in Spr.; was bur. 4 (8) 1649.
He d. at North. Dec. 14, 1671. Will dated 1 (1) 1669; beq. to son Thomas and his seven children; to son John and nine ch.; to dau. Elizabeth, wife of John Clarke, and her three ch.; to son-in-law Merrick's three daus.; to Mary Munde; friend John Pynchon and bro. Robert Bartlett overseers. [Reg. V, 71.]

STEBBINS, etc., cont.
William, gent. Boston, purchased the reversion of the Glover est. 21 (4) 1641. [L.]

STEELE, STEEL,
George, Cambridge, propr. 1633; frm. May 14, 1634; town officer, 1634. Rem. to Hartford.

John, Cambridge, propr. 1633, frm. May 14, 1634. Rem. to Hartford, Conn.

STEMSON, see Stephenson.

STEPHENS, STEVENS,
Francis, [Salem Court,] testified concerning an agreement of goodman James and Mr. Hill, 1 (5) 1649.

Henry, stone-mason, ae. 24, came in the Defence in July, 1635; Alice, his wife, came in the Abigail in July, 1635. Was in the employ of John Humphrey in 1640. [Es. Court Rec.] [Col. Rec.] Settled at Boston. Adm. chh. 8 (12) 1651, frm. May 26, 1652. Bought land at Muddy River 22 (9) 1644; sold Feb. 27, 1661. He deposed 2 (1) 1673, ae. 60. Wife Alice adm. chh. 18 (4) 1643; [second] wife Mary adm. chh. 15 (12) 1651. Ch. John b. 10 (7) 1637, James b. 10 (2) 1640, Joseph b. 1 (7) 1642, all these bapt. 18 (4) 1643; Deborah b. 25 (2) 1645, Deliverance bapt. 15 (2) 1650, ae. about 4 days, Joanna b. May 28, 1652, Henry b. July 20, 1656, Thomas bapt. 11 (5) 1658, Joshua b. and d. 1659, Henry b. May 25, 1663, *John* bapt. 19 (5) 1663, Samuel b. Sept. 24, 1665, Silence b. July 26, 1668.
Henry Stevens d. June 11, 1690.

John, tailor, Boston, custodian of articles of Thomas Watson in 1639. [L.] Frm. June 2, 1641.

John, husbandman, ae. 31, from Gonsham, Oxfordshire, came in the Confidence in April, 1638. Settled at Newbury. Frm. May 18, 1642. Propr. Rem. to Andover. Ch. John b. June 20, 1639, Timothy b. 22 Sept. 1641, Nathan, Ephraim, Elizabeth, (m. Joshua Woodman,) Mary, (m. John Barker,) Joseph b. 15 May, 1654, Benjamin b. 24 June, 1656.
He d. 11 April, 1662. Admin. gr. 24 (4) 1662, to widow Elizabeth. She testified 16 (4) 1673, ae. 60 years, concerning Samuel, son of her brother Joseph Parker, of An-

STEPHENS, etc., cont.
dover. [Mdx. Files.] She d. 1 May, 1694, "ae. 81 years." Her will, signed Oct. 21, 1687, codicil added Sept. 7, 1691, beq. to ch. John, Timothy, Nathan, Ephraim, Joseph, Benjamin, Elizabeth Woodman, Mary Barker, and their children. Prob. Sept. 25, 1694.

John, husbandman, sergeant, Salisbury, propr. 1640-1654. He deposed in 1667, ae. about 56. Wife Katharine; ch. John b. Nov. 2, 1639, Elizabeth b. and d. 1641, Elizabeth b. Feb. 4, 1642, (m. Morris Tucker,) Nathaniel, Mary, (m. 1, John Osgood, 2, Nathaniel Whittier,) Benjamin.
He d. Feb. 1688-9; will dated April 12, 1686, prob. Nov. 26, 1689, beq. to sons John, Benjamin and Nathaniel; dau. Mary Osgood; to gr. ch. Benoni Tucker a "kiverlet of goodman Buswell's weaving," etc.

Robert, sawyer, ae. 22, cert. from Stepney parish, Eng., came in the Planter March 22, 1634. Res. at Braintree; land grant 24 (12) 1639, for 3 heads. Propr., town officer; living in 1672. Widow Mary d. 22 Jan. 1691-2, ae. about 90 years. Ch. Sarah b. 31 (3) 1641.

Thomas, ae. 12, came in the Abigail in May, 1635; res. at Boston; frm. May 3, 1665. Rem. to Sudbury. Iron monger; bought land in 1665. Wife Sarah; ch. John b. May 15, 1648, Thomas b. Dec. 28, 1651, Jonas b. Oct. 27, 1653, Aaron b. Feb. 28, 1654, Sarah b. Aug. 31, 1657, d. June 29, 1658, Thomas b. May 20, 1658, Moses b. April 22, 1659, Joseph b. April 17, 1661, Sarah b. Dec. 8, 1663.

Mr. William, shipwright, Salem, propr. 1636-7; taxed at Marblehead in 1637; frm. May 13, 1640. Rem. to Gloucester. Built a vessel for Mr. Griffin in 1633, and one for John Brown of Salem and Nicholas and John Bulhack, of Jersey, merchants, in 1661-2; contract in Es. Co. Files; printed in Es. Inst. Coll. XIII. A prominent citizen Ch. Isaac and Mary bapt. at Salem 2 (11) 1639, Ruth bapt. 7 (1) 1640-1, Joshua, of sister S. bapt. 21 (5) 1666. Deeded land to wife Phillip and sons James and Isaac in 1667. Was charged with treason to Charles II in 1667 and fined; the wife Philip petitioned for relief on ground of their old age, etc. Granted Oct. 9, 1667. [Arch. 106.]

STEPHENS, etc., cont.

William, husbandman, ae. 21, from Gonsham, Oxon, Eng., with his mother Alice and his wife Elizabeth, and servants. came in the Confidence April 24, 1638. Settled at Newbury; frm. May 18, 1642. Propr.; yeoman. He m. 19 May, 1645, Elizabeth —. Ch. Bitfield b. 16 March, d. July 23, 1649, John b. 19 Nov. 1650, Samuel b. 18 Nov. 1652. Ann [Alice?] widow, d. at Newbury July 17, 1652.

He d. 19 May, 1653. Will signed, prob. 30 (4) 1653. Wife Elizabeth, sons John and Samuel. His widow m. March 3, 1653-4, Wm. Titcomb.

STEPHENSON, STEVENSON, STEMSON, STIMSON,

Ambrose, residence not given, frm. May 10, 1643.

Andrew, shoemaker, cobbler, formerly of Newcastle, Eng., [see Sill,] res. at Cambridge; propr. before 1648. His house was bought by the town for a house of Correction, and he was hired for service therewith Jan. 17, 1655. [Mdx. Files.] Wife Joane; ch. Deborah bapt. in Eng. and about 6 years old when her parents joined here, [Mi.] (m. Robert Wilson;) Sarah, Rebecca b. 20 (11) 1642, John b. 29 (10) 1644, Mary, Lydia b. 2 (6) 1648, Andrew, Hannah. He deposed in 1672, ae. 60 years.

His will dated May 3, 1681, prob. Oct. 1, 1683, beq. to wife Jane, eldest son Andrew, dau. Sarah and her ch. Joseph and Mary Lowden; and other children.

John, cobbler, Boston, adm. chh. 23 (1) 1644; frm. May, 1645. Wife Sarah; ch. Onesimus b. 26 (10) 1643, John b. (7) 1645, Paul bapt. 21 (8) 1647, ae. about 3 days, Joseph bapt. 23 (1) d. 10 (7) 1651, James b. Oct. 1, 1653, Sarah b. Feb. 6, 1655.

He d. (date not known,) and the widow, called in record "Stephson," m. 4 July, 1659, Rev. William Blackston. After his death Plymouth Court granted to her son John 55 acres of land in fulfilment of a marriage contract.

STERNE, STERNES, STEARNS,

Charles, Watertown, frm. May 6, 1646. Wife Rebecca, dau. of John and Rebecca Gibson of Cambridge. Ch. Samuel b. June 27, 1650, Shubael, Charles, John, Isaac, Samuel, Rebecca, (Sternes alias Traine,) Mar-

STERNE, etc., cont.

tha Hutchinson. [The son] Charles died at Salem; admin. gr. to his bro. Shubael Sept. 9, 1696, and division made to the above-named bros. and sisters.

Isaac, sometime of Stoke Nayland, co. Suffolk, Eng. tailor, came early to Watertown. Planter, propr.; frm. May 18, 1631. Town officer. His wife was a dau. of John Barker of S. N., clothier, and her mother m. 2, — Munnings of Gaynes Colne, Essex, Eng.; letter of attorney Aug. 24, 1640. [L.] Ch. Isaac b. 6 (11) 1632, Sarah b. 22 (7) 1635, Samuel b. 2 (2) 1638. Other ch. known: Mary, (m. Isaac Lerned July 9, 1646,) Hannah, (m. Dec. 25, 1650, Henry Freeman,) John, Elizabeth, (m. Samuel Manning,) Abigail, (m. John Morse).

He d. June 19, 1671; will prob. in Oct. folg., beq. to wife Mary; to ch. Isaac, John, Samuel, the ch. of dec. dau. Mary Lernet; daus. Sarah Stone, Elizabeth Manning and Abigail Morse; to kinsman Charles Sternes; to several grand children. The widow d. April 23, 1677.

Mr. Nathaniel, Dedham, adm. chh. 15 (6) 1647, frm. May 2, 1649. Lieut. Wife Mary; ch. Mary b. 22 (6) 1661, Samuel b. 25 (9) 1666, Nathaniel b. 4 Dec. 1668, Isaac b. 15 (6) 1672, d. 13 (6) 1676. The wife Mary d. Dec. 10, 1683.

STERTE, STERRT,

Thomas, ae. 15, came in the Truelove in Sept. 1635.

William, Boston, d. in 1644 or 1645. No record of him. His widow Jane was adm. chh. 4 (8) 1645; ch. Sarah, ae. about 1 year, 6 weeks, bapt. 5 (8) 1645.

STETSON, STUDSON, STEEDSON, STITSON,

Robert, carpenter, Duxbury, constable 7 March, 1642-3; frm. and deputy 7 June, 1653; cornet of the troop of horse 6 Oct. 1659. Ch. bapt. at the second church of Scituate: Joseph b. June, 1639, Benjamin b. Aug. 1641, Thomas b. 11 Dec. 1643, Samuel b. June, 1646, John b. April, 1648, Eunice b. 28 April, 1650, Lois b. Feb. 1652, Robert b. 29 Jan. 1653.

He made will 4 Sept. 1702, being aged; prob. 5 March, 1702-3; beq. to wife Mary; sons Joseph, Benjamin, Samuel and Robert;

STETSON, etc., cont.

dau. Eunice Rogers; Abigail, widow of dec. son John.

William, yeoman, Boston, propr. 1637; rem. to Charlestown before 1640; propr. next to Winnisimmet bounds. Deacon. Had accounts with persons in Bristol, Eng. Jan. 25, 1640. [Suff. De. I, 1.] He m. 1, widow Elizabeth Harris; he m. 2, Mary, widow of Zechariah Hill, whose ch. Thomas, Daniel and Ann are called cousins by Richard Eels in 1639.

His will dated 12 April, 1668, prob. 21 Nov. 1692, beq. to John, Thomas, William and Daniel Harris and Anna, wife of Elias Maverick, ch. of his first wife; to Sarah Norton, dau. of his late wife Mary; to Deborah, wife of Matthew Griffen, and Zechariah and Abraham, sons of her former husband, Zech. Hill; to kinsmen Elias Hill and Abigail his wife; to Sarah Johnson who now dwells with me; negro Sambo shall have his freedom.

STIBBINS, see Stebbins.

STICHE,

Henry, Lynn, before the court in 1647; Richard S. a witness in the case.

STICKLAND, see Strickland.

STICKNEY,

William, husbandman, Boston, with wife Elizabeth adm. chh. 6 (11) 1638. Frm. Oct. 7, 1640. He was dism. to the gathering of a chh. at Rowley 24 (9) 1643. With wife Elizabeth sold land in R. 27 May, 1662. Ch. Amos, (names bros. Andrew and Samuel in his will Aug. 27, 1678;) Samuel, Mary, (m. May 10, 1667, James Barker, Jr.,) John b. 14 (1) 1640, Faith b. 4 (12) 1641, Andrew b. 11 (3) 1644, Thomas and Elizabeth b. 3 (1) 1646, Mercy and Adding (daus.) b. 14 (11) 1648, Elizabeth bur. 4 Dec. 1659.

He was bur. 25 Jan. 1664.

STILEMAN, STILLMAN,

Elias, Sen. Salem, frm. July 3, 1632, propr. 1636. Elias, Jr. a father in 1639. Hannah adm. chh. 27 (2) 1651. Rem. to New Hampshire; was recorder of deeds, etc., a man of affairs.

Admin. of his est. 26 (9) 1663.

STILEMAN, etc., cont.

Richard, scrivener, Cambridge, 1644. Rem. to Salem; sold house and land in S. 9 Aug. 1647. Wife Hannah; ch. Samuel b. 23 (3) 1644, Samuel bapt. at Salem 20 (5) 1651. He m. at Andover 4 Oct. 1660, Elizabeth Fry.

STILSON, STILLSON,

William, yeoman, Charlestown, adm. chh. with wife Elizabeth 22 (1) 1633; frm. June 11, 1633; propr. 1635; deputy; town officer. Ord. deacon 16 (8) 1659. Owned land at Winnisimmet from about 1641; sold it 8 (2) 1662. He deposed 28 (10) 1658, ae. about 58 years. [Mdx. Files.] Wife Elizabeth d. Feb. 16, 1669-70. He m. Aug. 22, 1670, Mary Norton.

He d. April 11, 1691, ae. 90. Will.

STIMSON, see Stephenson.

STOCKBRIDGE,

John, wheelwright, ae. 27, came in the Blessing in July, 1635, with wife Ann, ae. 21, and son Charles, ae. 1. Settled at Scituate. Wife joined the chh. July 16, 1637. He carried on a water-mill. Took oath of allegiance 1 Feb. 1638. Town officer. Rem. to Boston about 1650. Wife Anna d. and he m. 9 Oct. 1643, Elizabeth Sone, of Scituate. She d., and he m. Mary —. Ch. rec.: Hannah, bapt at Sci. by Mr. Lothrop Oct. 8, 1637, (m. 29 (8) 1656, William Ticknor;) Elizabeth b. at Sci. about (7) 1639, taken to Bo. for baptism 10 (5) 1642, to avoid her being immersed, as Mr. Chauncey insisted must be done;) Sarah bapt. by Mr. Wetherell at Sci. March 15, 1645-6, Hesther bapt. July 11, 1647, John b. at Bo. 19 July, 1657.

He d. 13 (8) 1657. Will dated 4 (7) 1657, prob. 8 April, 1658. To wife Mary house and household goods at Bo., etc.; to eldest son Charles the mill at Sci. with connected house and land, he paying 10 li. to his sister Elizabeth; youngest son John to have a house at Sci. where Gilbert Brocks lived, and pay 10 li. to his sister Mary; to dau. Esther the house at Sci. where Wm. Ticknor lived, etc.; to dau. Hannah H. 40 s. out of money in her husband's hands; to dau. Sarah 10 li. [Reg. VII, 352.] The widow m. 8 April, 1660, Daniel Henricke.

STINNINGS,
Richard, Plymouth, apprenticed to Robert Bartlett in 1635; executed with two others in 1635 for complicity in the robbery and murder of an Indian.

STOCKER,
Thomas, Boston, an agreement with John Cogan referred to 2 (12) 1640. [L.] Res. at Rumney Marsh in 1651, when James Browne of Bo. beq. to his children.

STOCKMAN,
Isaac, Scituate, town officer, 1647.

STODDARD, STODDAR, STODDER, STODER,
Anthony, linen draper, Boston, adm. chh. 28 (7) 1639, frm. May 13, 1640. Deputy 1650; town officer. He m. 1, Mary, whom the Stoddard Genealogy states to have been the dau. of Mr. Emanuel Downing; (she may be the person, "kinswoman to Gov. John Winthrop, who was adm. chh. Boston (9) 1633.) He m. 2, about 24 (6) 1647, (date of marriage contract,) Barbara, dau. of Nicholas Clap of Venn Ottery, Eng., widow of Joseph Weld of Rox.; she was recd. to chh. of Bo. from that of Rox. 25 (10) 1647; she d. 15 (2) 1655, and he m. Christian —. Ch. Benjamin bapt. 23 (6) 1640, ae. about 11 days, Solomon bapt. 1 (8) 1643, ae. about 4 days, Samson b. 3 (10) 1645, Grace bapt. 16 (5) 1648, ae. about 2 days, Samuel bapt. 20 (11) 1649, ae. about 6 days, Simeon bapt. 25 (3) 1651, Sarah b. Oct. 21, 1652, Stephen bapt. 8 (11) 1653, Anthony b. June 16, 1656, Christian b. March 22, 1658, Lydia b. March 27, 1660, Joseph b. and d. Dec. 1661, John b. April 22, 1663, Ebenezer b. July 1, 1664, Dorothy b. Nov. 24, 1665, Mary b. March 25, 1668, Jane b. July 29, 1669.

He d. March 16, 1686-7. [S.] Will dated 29 Dec. 1684, prob. 19 May, 1687, beq. to wife what is due according to contract before marriage; to dau. Grace; rest to other eight children, Solomon, Samson, Anthony, Christion, Lydia, Dorothy, Mary and Jane.

John, Hingham, propr. 1638; frm. May 18, 1642. One of the first proprs. at Hull; but ret. to Hing.

He d. 19 Dec. 1661. Will prob. Jan. 31 folg..; sons John, Daniel and Samuel.; dau. Hannah, wife of Gershom Wheelock; gr. ch. John and Elizabeth Low. [Reg. XI, 35. See also V, 21.]

STOCKIN,
George, Cambridge, propr., 1634., frm. May 6, 1635. Rem. to Hartford, Conn. [Genealogy, Reg. L, 171.]

STOKES,
Grace, ae. 20, came in the Hopewell in Sept. 1635.

James, Boston, sold house to George Brown before 1642.

STONE, STON,
Gregory, Watertown, 1636, rem. to Cambridge; propr. 1637; frm. May 25, 1636. Deacon. Deputy. He deposed 18 (7) 1658, ae. about 67 years. [Es. Files.]

He d. Nov. 30, 1672, ae. 82. Will prob. 14 (10) 1672. Wife Lydia and her children by former husband, John Cooper and Lydia Fiske; sons Daniel, David, John and Samuel; daus. Elizabeth, (wife of — Potter, living at Ipswich in 1658;) [Mi.] and Sarah, (wife of Joseph Miriam;) gr. son John, son of David S. [Reg. VIII, 69.] The widow d. June 24, 1674.

John, ae. 40, came in the Elizabeth April 9, 1635.

John, Salem, propr. 1636. Maintained a ferry to Cape Ann side. Adm. chh. 13 (6) 1654; Ellen adm. chh. 6 (1) 1653. Wife Abigail; ch. John b. 25 (9) 1654, Samuel b. 15 (9) 1658. Elizabeth, bro. Dixey's dau., was adm. chh. 20 (6) 1665, and had ch. John, William, Samuel and Abigail bapt. Nathaniel S. had Nathaniel, Samuel and Elizabeth bapt. 29 (7) 1666. Was he a son of John?

John, fisherman, Lynn; a meadow named for him; rem. before 1648, [Mass. Hist. Coll. 6.4,] to Hull; had leave from Plymouth Colony govt. to fish for bass at Cape Cod divers years; permission recalled 2 Oct. 1650, to accommodate Plym. persons. Had additional grant of land, 1657.

He d. Dec. 23, 1663; will dated 5 May, 1659, prob. Jan. 27, 1663-4, all to wife Joane except 60 ll. to bro. Simon Stone's 3 children who lived sometime at Cousingstone, Somersetshire, Eng. [Reg. XII, 273.]

John, householder, "an old Kentish man," Roxbury, was bur. Oct. 25 or 26, 1643. [Chh. and town recs.] The land of his heirs was noted in proprs.' list. Perhaps Thomas,

STONE, etc., cont.
who m. Dec. 4, 1639, Mary Cragg, was one of these.

Robert, Weymouth, propr. before 1651.

Rev. Samuel, b. at Hartford, Eng.; grad. of Emanuel Coll. Cambridge; was a lecturer at Towcester; [C. M.] came as an assistant to Mr. Hooker Sept. 4, 1633. Settled at Cambridge; propr. 1633. Frm. May 14, 1634. He rem. to Hartford, Conn., in 1636. Mrs. Elizabeth, lately called Mrs. Elizabeth Allen but now wife of Mr. Samuel Stone, teacher of the church at Hartford, was dism. from the chh. of Boston to Hartford chh. 25 (5) 1641.

Simon, husbandman, ae. 50, with wife Joan, ae. 38, and children Frances, ae. 16, Ann, ae. 11, Simon, ae. 4, Marie, ae. 3, and John, ae. 5 weeks, came in the Increase April 15, 1635. Settled at Watertwn; frm. May 25, 1636; town officer, deacon. Ch. rec. at Wat.: John b. or bapt. 15 (6) 1635, Elizabeth b. 5 (2) 1639. His wife d., and he m. Sarah, widow of Richard Lumpkin of Ipswich; her will prob. Oct. 6, 1663.

He d. Sept. 22, 1665. Will prob. Oct. 3, 1665, by his bro. Gregory Stone and Stephen Day. Sons Simon and John; daus. Frances and Mary; Johanna and Nathaniel Green, ch. of Frances and her husband Thomas Greene; kinsmen John and Daniel Warner and Thomas Wells. [Reg. II, 128, and III, 182.]

STONHARD, STONEHARD, STONNARD, STONIARD, STANNARD,
John, Roxbury, propr. 1645.

He d. 13 (6) 1649; inv. taken a week later; the Court allowed the widow Margaret to sell house and land for payment of his debts and for her support, Oct. 17, 1649.

STORER,
Richard, son to Elizabeth, wife of Robert Hull, was adm. inhabitant of Boston and had a great lot at the Mount, (Braintree,) for 3 heads, 25 (9) 1639.

STORY, STOREY, STORYE, STORYN,
Andrew, Ipswich, propr. 1635; served in the Pequot War; was before Gen. Court 1635; had grant of land from the town in 1639.

STORY, etc., cont.
Elias, servant to Edward Winslow, came in the Mayflower to Plymouth; d. soon after arrival. [B.]

Elizabeth, Boston, dau. of Mrs. John Cotton, adm. chh. 24 (1) 1639. She m. Wentworth Day.

George, a young merchant of London, had a lawsuit at Salem in 1641; kept in the house of Mrs. Sherman in Boston; was the chief mover in the controversy of Mrs. S. against Mr. Keayne in 1642. [W.]

William, ae. 23, servant to Samuel Dix, joiner, of Norwich, Eng., passed exam. to go to Boston in N. E. to reside, April 8, 1637. Probably he is

William, carpenter, Ipswich, propr. 1642; recd. mortg. of land as security for a debt Oct. 21, 1650. [His wife] Sarah deposed in 1668, ae. about 48 years.

STOTT, error in record for Scott.

STOUGHTON,
Mr. Israel, came early to Dorchester; propr., deputy, Asst.; frm. Nov. 5, 1633. Did important service in the Pequot War in 1637; see letter in W. He ret. to England in 1644; was a lieut. col. in the Parliamentary army.

He d. in the service. Will prob. in 1650. Wife Elizabeth. He beq. 300 acres of land to Harvard Coll. [Reg. VII, 333.] Inv. taken 2 (2) 1650. The dau. Hannah m. James Minot; he joined the widow in the sale of house, mill, etc., to Thomas Meakins, Nov. 14, 1655. Ch. rec. in Dorch.: William b. 30 (7) 1631, Hannah b. (2) 1637, John bapt. 1 (10) 1638, Rebecca bapt. 29 (6) 1641, (m. William Taylor 25 (6) 1664,) Thomas bapt. 30 (5) 1644. Eldest son Israel. The widow Judith Smead was his sister, and in the inv. of her est. he mentions "my brother Clarke."

Thomas, "ancient," i. e. ensign, Dorchester, came in the first company; constable 28 Sept. 1630; frm. May 18, 1631; propr., town officer. He took it upon him to join Clement Briggs and Joane Allen in marriage; for which the Gen. Court fined him 1 March, 1630-1. Rem. to Windsor, Conn.

He d. 25 March, 1661.

STOW, STOWE,

John, Roxbury, arrived in N. E. 17th of 3d month, 1634; brought with him his wife and 6 children, Thomas, Elizabeth, John, Nathaniel, Samuel and Thankful. His wife Elizabeth, a very godly woman, was bur. Aug. 24, 1638. [E.] She was a dau. of Mrs. Rachel Biggs, who came in 1635 to Dorchester, with her dau. Foster; and the Foster and Stow children recd. valuable legacies from their uncles John and Smalhope Biggs of Cranbrook and Maidstone, Kent. He was adm. frm. Sept. 3, 1634; propr.; deputy. Rem. to Concord; sold Rox. property 20 (4) 1648. Signed inv. of John Levens in 1648. Dau. Elizabeth m. Henry Archer of Ipswich. The son Nathaniel of Ips. deposed in 1670, ae. 48 years. Thankful m. John Pierpoint of Roxbury. [Es. Files. XVI, 68.]

STOWELL,

Samuel, Hingham, propr. He m. Oct. 25, 1649, Mary, dau. of John Farrow; ch. Mary b. Oct. 16, 1653, (m. John Garnet,) Samuel b. July 8, 1655, John b. March 15, 1657, David b. April 8, 1660, Remember b. April 22, 1662, (m. Thomas Remington,) a child b. and d. 1664, William b. Jan. 23, 1665, Israel b. 1668, d. 1669, Israel b. Aug. 10, 1670, Elizabeth b. June 7, 1673, (m. George Lane,) Benjamin b. June 3, 1676.

He d. 9 Nov. 1683. Will prob. 30 Jan. 1683-4. Wife Mary and sons Samuel and David. Other ch. to share with them after the mother's death. The widow m. Oct. 10, 1689, Joshua Beal.

STOWER, STOWERS,

John, planter, Watertown, frm. May 25, 1636; selectman.

John Stowers, Sen., of Parham, co. Suffolk, Eng., his father is referred to in a deed of land 4 Oct. 1650. Wife Jane; second wife Phebe, who joined him in a deed of land in 1650. Ch. Elizabeth bur. 10 (10) 1635, ae. 8 months, Elizabeth b. 14 (2) 1637, Sarah b. 8 (1) 1641-2. He. rem. to Newport, R. I.

Nicholas, memb. chh. Boston 1630, but res. at Charlestown; one of the founders of Char. chh. in 1632. Frm. May 18, 1631. Wife Amy; ch. Richard, adm. chh. 12 (2) 1650, Joanna adm. chh. 14 (1) 1652, Sarah, Joseph bapt. 23 (12) 1632, Abigail bapt. 28 (4) 1636, John d. 15 (6) 1638.

STOWER, etc., cont.

He d. 17 (3) 1646. Will dated 16 (3) 1646, beq. to ch. Joseph, Richard, Jone, Abigail, and dau. Farr; John Burrage and John Knight joined with Richard and Joseph 16 (1) 1668, in asking that their bro. Samuel Hayward be app. admin. To wife Amy house and ground in Charlestown, and a hay lot on Mistick side near the North spring, next our sister Rands, etc.; to sons Richard and Joseph; to daus Abigail and Jone Stower and dau. Farre. [Reg. III, 179.] The inv. taken 1 (5) 1646, is entitled "Inventory of Lands, etc.," of Amy Stower, widdowe of Nicholas Stower late deceased." [Suff. Prob.] The widow d. Feb. 2, 1667-8. The son Richard, with his wife Hannah, dau. of Henry Frost, of Ipswich, co. Suffolk, Eng., mariner, gave power of attorney 15 (8) 1647, for collection of rents of a house and garden near the tower church in I., the inheritance of said Henry. [A.]

STRANGE, STRANG,

George, gent., Dorchester, propr. 1634; frm. May 6, 1635. Rem. to Hingham. Took advice about searching in England for his wife's lands, 18 (8) 1638. [L.] Recd. deed 4 Dec. 1638, of property in Northam, co. Devon, Eng. Suit was brought against him in 1640 by his servant Dermondt Matthew. His nephew William James and Thomas Foster made him their attorney for collections in Eng. in 1640. Ch. Nathaniel bapt. at Hing. Feb. 1637, bur. 29 Nov. 1642, Elizabeth bapt. 2 May, 1641.

John, Boston, propr. 1649. Wife Sarah; ch. Sarah b. 18 (8) 1651. "Goody" adm. chh. 9 (2) 1654.

He d. about 1657; admin. gr. Oct. 15, 1657, to Richard Curtis. [Reg. IX, 230.]

STRAIGHT, STRAIT, STRAITE, STREIT,

Capt. Thomas, Watertown, bought house and land in 1646. Took oath of fidelity, 1652. He deposed in 1666, ae. 47 years. He m. Elizabeth, dau. of Henry Kimball; ch. Susanna, (m. John Wellington,) Thomas b. Feb. 19, 1659, Elizabeth, m. June 6, 1684, Joseph Wellington.

He d. Nov. 22, 1681. Will prob. 20 (10) 1681, beq. to wife; daus. Elizabeth S. and Susanna Wellington, and son Thomas.

STRAINE,

Richard, brewer, Boston, sold land April 1, 1648. Residing at Westminster, Eng., he and wife Anne sold other Boston land April 9, 1659.

STRATTON, STRETTON, STREATON,

Ann, widow, plaintiff in suit against Wm. Pester at Ipswich in 1642.

Elizabeth, ae. 19, came in the Increase April 15, 1635.

John, gent., merchant, came to Salem about 1631; frm. May 21, 1663. A fine, levied upon him by the Gen. Court, was ordered to be remitted 19 Sept. 1637, if he go to Merrimack. Charlestown, propr. 1638. He was a son of John Stratton, of Shotley, Eng., gent., b. about 1606; his mother was a dau. of Mrs. Mary Dearhaugh of Barringham, co. Suffolk, Eng. His bro. William S. was ready to come to N. E. in 1628, but was left behind by his uncle Joseph, who settled at James City, Va.; so he deposed in a lawsuit in 1640. Sister Elizabeth, wife of John Thorndike, sister Dorothy, spinster, and his mother, were all of Salem. [L.]

Mr. Samuel, Watertown, surveyor of town lots in 1647. He deposed in 1672, ae. 80 years; his son John ae. 39 years. [Mdx. Files.] His wife d., and he. m. in Boston 27 (6) 1657, Margaret Parker, widow, who survived him and d. Dec. 7, 1676, ae. 81.

He d. Dec. 18, 1672, leaving maintenance to his wife, and beq. to sons Samuel and John, and to Samuel, son of dec. son Richard.

William, Salem, bought land in 1649.

STREAM, STREEM, STREME, STROMYE, STRONYE,

John, Hingham, propr. 1635. Propr. also at Weymouth. Wife Elizabeth; ch. Benjamin d. 27 (3) 1663, Thomas d. July 1, 1662.

He died, and the widow m. 2, John Otis. After his death she is referred to in Weymouth records as Widow Oates in connection with town lots in the first and second divisions which had belonged to her former husband.

STREET,

Alice, ae. 28, came in the Susan and Ellen in April, 1635.

Rev. Nicholas, came to Taunton about 1637, when he was ordained assistant pastor. [L., P. D.] Enrolled as atba. 1643. Rem. to New Haven in 1659. Genealogy.

STREETER,

Stephen, shoemaker, Gloucester, propr. 1642 or earlier; [may be the Ste. Streete, frm. May 29, 1644.] Rem. to Charlestown; adm. to chh. with wife Ursula 14 (1) 1652. Ch. Stephen, Samuel, John, Sarah, Hannah b. at Char. 10 (9) 1654, Rebecca.

His will dated 10 (4), prob. 24 (5) 1652, beq. to wife Ursula and these children, committing the two latter, respectively, to Richard Sprague and Charles Chadwick. The widow m. 13 Oct. 1657, Samuel Hosier of Watertown. [Reg. XXXVI, 161.]

STRICKLAND, STICKLAND, STICKLING,

John, Charlestown, 1629-30; rem. to Watertown, 1630; juryman; frm. May 18, 1631. Rem. to Wethersfield, Conn.

Thwaites or Thweights, Dedham, propr. 27 (8) 1640. Wife Elizabeth adm. chh. 3 (3) 1650; ch. Elizabeth b. 12 (2) 1647, John b. 17 (12) 1648, Rebecca bapt. 19 (11) 1650, Joseph b. 22 (11) 1654, Jonathan b. 23 (4) 1657.

STRONG,

John, tanner, Dorchester, a member of the original church-colony that came in the Mary and John in 1629-30. Frm. March 9, 1636-7. Rem. to Taunton; was constable 4 Dec. 1638, juryman in 1640. Rem. to Windsor, Conn. He rem. to Northampton about 1659. Was ruling elder of that church. He m. Abigail, dau. of Thomas Ford, of both Dorchesters, and of Windsor. Ch. John, Return, Thomas, Jedidiah bapt. at Dorch. by communion of churches 14 (2) 1639, Josiah, Ebenezer, Abigail, Elizabeth b. 24 Feb. 1647, Experience b. 4 Aug. 1650, Samuel b. 5 Aug. 1652, Joseph, Mary b. 25 Oct. 1654, Sarah, Hannah b. 30 May, 1659, Esther or Hester b. 7 June, 1661, Thankful b. 25 July, 1663, Jerijah b. 12 Dec. 1665. [Reg. VIII, 180.]

He d. 14 April, 1699, [ae. 94?] He beq. to ch. and gr. ch. Sons Samuel and Jerijah execs. Genealogy.

STRINGER,
John, servant to Mrs. Knight, whipped for miscarriages toward his mistress and Mrs. Stoughton, 21 (8) 1637. [W.]

STROUD, STROWDE,
John, ae. 15, came in the Abigail in July, 1635.

STUBBS, STUBS, STABBS,
Joshua, Watertown, frm. May 2, 1649. He m. Abigail, dau. of John and Abigail Benjamin; ch. Samuel b. 3 (6) 1646, Mary, (m. March 24, 1674-5, John Traine,) Elizabeth, (m. Jonathan Stimson.) He rem. to Charlestown, and sold in 1654 his homestall in Wat., his wife's mother consenting.
He d. soon after, and his widow m. John Woodward. She was adm. to Char. chh. 9 (1) 1656.

Richard, Hull, one of the first planters, noted by Gen. Court May 20, 1642. He m. [1?] in Boston, March 3, 1659, Margaret Read. He m. Elizabeth, who survived him. Ch. Richard and others.
Will dated 22 May, prob. June 21, 1677, beq. est. to wife for life or until she marry; children to have portions when they come of age.

STUDLEY, STUTLY, STOODLY,
John, Gloucester, lawsuit brought against him by his master in 1643. A witness in court in 1647; propr. 1650. Mortg. his house and land in 1651. Referred to in letter of Tristram Dalliber.

John, Boston. Wife Elizabeth; ch. Jonathan b. 8 Dec. 1659, Benjamin b. May 23, 1661.

STURGES, see Turges,
Edward, yeoman, Charlestown, 1634. Rem. to Yarmouth; atba 1643. Town officer; frm. June 5, 1651. Kept an ordinary. Ch. Mary bapt. at Barnstable June 1, 1646, Elizabeth b. at Y. 20 April, 1648, Joseph, (a child?) bur. 16 April, 1650.
Inv. of his est. taken 12 Oct. 1695; widow Mary, son Thomas. The marriage contract he made with Mary, widow of Zephaniah Rider of Yarmouth 20 April, 1692, is in Barnstable Prob. rec. vol. 2 folio 14.

William, Charlestown, propr. 1635.

STUBBIN,
John, Watertown, soldier on two occasions, petitioned for land and support for wife and child 13 (3) 1640. Wife Margaret, ae. 30. [L.]

STURTEVANT, STERTEVANT, STURDIVANT,
Samuel, Plymouth, planted land on shares in 1641; atba. 1643; bought land 1647; town officer. Ch. Ann b. 4 June, 1647, (m. 7 Dec. 1665, John Waterman,) John b. and d. 1650, Mary b. 7 Dec. 1651, Samuel b. 19 April, 1654, Hannah b. 4 Sept. 1656, John b. 6 Sept. 1658, Lydia b. 18 Dec. 1660, James b. 11 Feb. 1663, Joseph b. 19 July, 1666.
Will dated Aug. 1, prob. Oct. 29, 1669; beq. to wife to son-in-law John Waterman; to sons Samuel, James, John, Joseph; child expected. [Reg. VII, 180.]

STUTSON, see Stetson.

STUTTIN,
Joan, Boston, adm. chh. 21 (9) 1634.

STYTH,
Margaret, memb. chh. Dorchester before 1639.

SUCKLIN,
Thomas, a servant of Francis James, came from Hingham, Eng., to Hingham, N. E., in 1638.

SUMNER, SOMNER, SUMER, SOMERS,
Henry, ae. 15, and Elizabeth, ae. 18, came in the Abigail July 4, 1635, cert. from Northampton, Eng. Res. at Woburn in 1663; wife then in Barnstable. She d. at the house of her mother Elizabeth Worden before Sept. 28, 1668. He m. 2, Mabel, widow of William Read, a sister of Francis Kendall, and mother of Francis and John Wyman. [See Mdx. Files 13.]
His will dated 14 Oct., prob. 23 Nov. 1675, beq. to son Henry Somers and wife Mabel and her children. Henry opposed the probating of the will, giving reasons which were duly answered. [Suff. Prob., file 750.] Prob. 23 (10) 1684. The widow made will 22 Jan. 1689-90, prob. June 17 folg.; beq. to son George Read and his wife and her other children.

Thomas, Rowley, propr. and purchaser

SUMNER, etc., cont.

before 1643. "The goods of Abigail, the late wife of Thomas Sumer deceased," were appraised 31 (8) 1643. The widow filed the inv. stating that she owed £1, 18. [Suff. Prob.] She m. 2, Thomas Ellithorp. His dau. Jane, b. about 1641, m. Robert Coates, Sen., of Lynn; deposed to these facts and petitioned for admin. on the est. of her bro. Thomas.

William, Sen., Dorchester, b. at Bicester, Oxfordshire, Eng., bapt. 27 Jan. 1604-5, son of Roger and Joan [Franklin] Sumner; m. 22 Oct. 1625, Mary West. Ch. William, Roger bapt. 8 Aug. 1632, George bapt. 1 March, 1633-4, Samuel b. in Dorch. 18 (3) 1638, Increase b. 23 (12) 1642, Joan, (m. — Way,) Abigail d. 19 Feb. 1657. He and his wife "Marie" were membs. chh. in 1636; he was adm. frm. May 17, 1637. Deputy, town officer, com. to try small causes. His wife d. June 7, 1676.

He d. Dec. 9, 1688. Will dated 23 June, 1681, prob. 24 March, 1691-2, beq. to the 9 children of his dec. son William; to sons Roger, George, Samuel and Increase, and to dau. Joane Way. Beq. to servants Rebecca Adams and Anthony Hancocke. [Genealogy in Reg. VIII, 128 a, and IX, 297.]

SUNDERLAND, SINDERLAND, SYNDERLAND, SYNDERLING,

John, parchment maker, Boston, 1640; adm. chh. 9 (2) 1643. Bought and sold land in 1644. His servant, Clement Critchet, d. 29 (3) 1653. Wife Dorothy; ch. John b. (10) 1640, Mary b. 12 (1) 1642, (m. 29 (9) 1656, Jonathan Ransford,) Hannah b. (8) 1643, James b. 18 (1) 1646, James bapt. 6 (6) 1648, Benjamin bapt. 26 (5) 1652. The wife d. Jan. 29, 1663. He m. Thomasin —, who joined him in a deed June 29, 1664. Matthew Armstrong calls him father-in-law. [Suff. De. V, 51.]

SUTTON,

Ambrose, carpenter, Charlestown, b. 1612, at Westwell, near Burford, Eng.; went to Aquidnet in 1638. [L.]

Elizabeth, spinster, Charlestown, dau. of John Sutton, late citizen and draper of London, dec., and of Elizabeth, sometime his wife, gave letter of attorney 23 (5) 1641, to Francis Lisle of Boston and Walter Blackborne of London, haberdasher.

SUTTON, cont.

George, planter, Scituate, prop. frm. 5 March, 1638-9; atba. 1643. Town officer. He m. March 13, 1636, Sarah, dau. of Nathaniel Tilden. Ch. Lydia bapt. Sept. 13, 1646, Sarah bapt. Sept. 15, 1650, Elizabeth bapt. Aug. 28, 1653.

John and his wife came from Attleburg, Eng., in 1638, and settled at Hingham. Propr. [Ch.] Hannah d. Oct. 1642.

He made will 12 Nov. 1691, ae. about 70 years; beq. to wife Elizabeth and ch. John, Nathaniel, Nathan, Elizabeth, Mary, Sarah and Hester.

Lambert, Charlestown, adm. chh. 4 (2) 1641, frm. May 29, 1644. Rem. to Woburn; taxed, 1645.
He d Nov. 27, 1649. Will dated 8 (9) 1649, rec. Mdx. Deeds I, 13; wife Elizabeth; John Russell, Jr., and Mary Russell.

Richard, Roxbury, propr. before 1650. Wife Sarah d. 12 (9) 1672.

SWAIN, SWAYNE, SWAINE, [SWAN,]

Henry, Charlestown, propr. 1638.

Jeremiah, Charlestown, propr. 1642; rem. to Reading. Propr. 1647. Town officer. Wife Mary memb. chh. of Reading. Ch. Jeremie bapt. 1 (1) 1643, John b. 30 (11) 1644, Mary b. at Reading 15 (2) 1647, Thomas b. 6 (8) 1649, Elizabeth b. 8 (12) 1651.

He d. April 2, 1658. Inv. filed 25 (4) 1658, and admin. gr. to the widow Mary.

John, Watertown, propr. 1642. Rem. to Cambridge. He m. Feb. 1, 1650, Rebecca Palfrey; she d. July 12, 1654. He m. 2, March 2, 1655, Mary Pratt, who d. 11 Feb. 1702, in her 70th year.

He d. June 5, 1708, in his 88th year. [Gr. st.]

Richard, planter, Hampton, 6 (7) 1638; frm. March 13, 1638-9. He owned a house and land at Exeter before 1650. Gave part of his house-lot in Hamp. to his dau. Grace and her husband, Nathaniel Boulter, Sept. 4, 1660; another tract, 12 (5) 1663, to Hezekiah, eldest son of his son William, dec.; the widow Prudence to have the use of it till Hez. is 21 years old. He deposed 10 (7) 1662, ae. about 67 years. He rem. to Nantucket, and sold his remaining estate to his son-in-law Boulter 6 July, 1663. Martha, widow of

SWAIN, etc., cont.

his son Francis, m. 2, Caleb Leverich of Middleborough, Long Island; confirmed a gift of lands he had made to his sister Elizabeth, wife of Nathaniel Weare of Hampton. He m. Jane, widow of George Bunker of Topsfield, with whom he sold land at T. July 5, 1660.

William, ae. 50, and Elizabeth, ae. 16, came in the Elizabeth and Ann; Elizabeth, ae. 20, came in the Planter, and William, ae. 16, and Francis, ae. 11, came in the Rebecca in April, 1635.

William settled at Watertown; frm. and deputy March 3, 1635-6. Was appointed by the Gen. Court one of the com. to govern the people at Connecticut. His dau. Mary lived at Roxbury, but rem. to Conn. with him, and married at New Haven. [E.]

SWAN, [SWAIN,]

Henry, Charlestown, propr. 1638, Salem, propr. 1639; frm. May 22, 1639. Ch. Thomas bapt. 26 (12) 1642, Eliza bapt. 8 (12) 1645.

He d. before 23 (10) 1651, when Sarah, child of Henry, dec. and Joan d. in Boston. [See Halsey.]

Richard, husbandman, Boston, adm. chh. 6 (11) 1638, frm. May 13, 1640. He was dismissed to the gathering of a ch. at Rowley 24 (9) 1639. His first wife Ann was bur. April 4, 1658; and he m. March 1, 1658-9, Ann, widow of John Trumble. She deposed 30 March, 1675, ae. about 60 years. Ch. John bapt. at Bo. 13 (11) 1638, Robert, (deposed in 1662, ae. 36 years,) Mercy b. 4 (5) 1640, Faith b. 30 (1) 1644, Sarah, (name written and crossed out in 1647.)

He was bur. May 14, 1678. Will dated 25 April, prob. 23 May, 1678, beq. to wife Ann, as by mar. contract; to son Robert and his son Richard; to son-in-law Joseph Boynton, his wife Sarah and ch. Elizabeth, Samuel and Sarah B.; to daus. Frances Quilter, Jane Wilson, Dorothy Chapman and Mercy Warener. The widow Ann made will 4 July, prob. 24 Sept. 1678; beq. to daus. Abigail Bayley and Mary Kilborne; to son Caleb Hopkinson a chest that father Gott made; to sons John and Jonathan Hopkinson; one book to John Trumble.

SWANSON,

Anna, Boston, memb. chh. 1632. May be for Swan. See Richard above.

SWEET, SWEETE, SWETT,

Benjamin, Newbury. Confirmed as ensign by Gen. Court 14 Oct. 1651; captain. He m. 1 (9) 1647, Hester, dau. of Nathaniel Weare; ch. Hester b. 17 June, 1648, Sarah b. 7 Nov. 1650, Mary b. 7 Jan. 1651, Mary b. 2 May, 1654, Benjamin b. 5 Aug. 1656, Joseph b. 21 Jan. 1659, Moses b. 16 Sept. 1661.

He was slain by the Indians at Black Point 29 June, 1677. Inv. filed 17 (8) 1679. [Norf. Court Rec.] His widow m. 31 March, 1679, Stephen Greenleaf. She d. 16 Jan. 1718, ae. 89.

John, Salem, propr. 1636. Frm. May 18, 1642. Fined 5 li., 6 June, 1637, for shooting a wolf dog of Col. Endecot's in the Col.'s back yard.

John, caulker, ship-carpenter, merchant, Boston, adm. chh. 10 (12) 1640, frm. June 2, 1641. Propr. Charlestown, 1650. Wife Temperance adm. chh. 10 (12) 1638, d. (11) 1645. Second wife Susanna adm. chh. 22 (3) 1647, d. July 16, 1666, ae. 44 years. [Copps Hill Ep.] Third wife Elizabeth, widow of Robert Scott, joined him in a deed of Scott's lands 16 Dec. 1668. [See Upshall.] Ch. Susanna b. 3 (2) 1647, Temperance bapt. 5 (6) 1649, d. 28 (9) 1661, John b. 8 Sept. 1651, Mary b. and d. 1654, Abigail b. and d. 1656, Mehetabel b. 1657, d. 1658, Mehetabel b. 8 Dec. 1659.

He d. April 25, 1685, ae. 82 years. [Copps Hill Ep.] Will dated 18 Oct. 1677, prob. 14 May, 1685, beq. to son John Oliver and dau. Susanna; to son Edwards and dau. Mary; to their children; to the college at Cambridge; to Wm. Browne; to his bros. three children in England.

Phebe, widow, d. at Newbury May 6, 1665.

Stephen, cordwainer, Newbury, 1647. He deposed in 1664, ae. about 40 years. He m. 24 May, 1647, Hannah, dau. of John Merrill; she d. 4 April, 1662. He m. 4 Aug. 1663, Rebecca Smith, who d. 1 March, 1670. Ch. John b. 20 Oct. 1648, d. 13 Jan. 1652, Stephen b. and d. 1650, Hannah b. 7 Oct. 1651, Stephen b. 28 Jan. 1654, Elizabeth b. 16 Jan. 1656, Joseph b. 28 Nov. 1657, Mary b.

SWEET, etc., cont.
April 25, 1660, Mary b. 17 March, 1662, Benjamin b. 20 May, 1664, Rebecca b. 4 Dec. 1665, d. 31 May, 1666, Rebecca b. 27 Feb. 1670.

Thomas, came in the Mary and John March 24, 1633-4.

SWETMAN, SWEETMAN, SWATMAN,
Thomas, weaver, Cambridge, propr. frm. May 2, 1638. Wife Isabel; ch. Elizabeth b. 16 (11) 1645, Rebecca b. 7 (2) 1649, Mehetabel, Sarah, [Thomas?] Ruhamah, Samuel bapt. May 22, 1659, Bethia bapt. July 7, 1661, [Mi.] [Hephzibah?]

He d. Jan. 8, 1682-3, ae. 73. Inv. of his est. was filed by widow Isabel.

SWEETSER, SWITSIR, SWITZER,
Seth, shoemaker, Charlestown, adm. chh. 8 (11) 1638, frm. March 14, 1638-9. A letter to him from his cousin Daniel Field, dated at Tring, Herts, Eng. May 10, 1642, mentions his cousin Crane, father Lake, Aunt Hoten, his brothers, and his sister Elis. He was to receive a butt of leather, for which he was to pay 10 li. to Thomas Welch or goodman ffowler; love to Wm. Philips and his wife. [A.] He made a deed of gift to his son Benjamin in 1660. Wife Bethia; second wife Elizabeth Oakes, m. at Cambridge April, 1661. Ch. Benjamin, Sarah, Mary, (m. 3 (11) 1654, Samuel Blanchard,) Hannah bapt. 12 (11) 1638, Elizabeth b. 27 (11) 1642.

He d. May 27, 1662, ae. 56. Will signed 24 May, prob. June 17, 1662, beq. to wife Elizabeth, dau. Sarah, son Samuel Blancher and his wife Mary, dau. Hanna Fitch, and to his wife's three children. Son Benjamin and Edward Drinker execs.; Mr. Richard Russell and my brother Thomas Gold overseers.

SWIFT, SWYFT,
Margaret, brought suit for damage against Robert Cotta in Salem Quarterly Court 27 (4) 1636; decision in her favor; rest of the stuff to be restored to her.

Thomas, Dorchester, propr. 1634. frm. May 6, 1635. Town officer. Wife Elizabeth; ch. Joan, (m. in Boston 5 (9) 1657, John Baker,) Thomas b. 17 (4) 1635, Obediah b. 16 (5) 1638, Elizabeth bapt. 24 (11) 1640, Ruth bapt. 16 (5) 1643, (m. 10 Oct. 1660, Wm.

SWIFT, etc., cont.
Greenow,) Mary bapt. 21 (7) 1645, (m. 11 (11) 1663, John White,) Anna bapt. 14 (9) 1647, James bapt. 10 (1) 1649, Hannah b. March 11, 1651, *Susanna* bapt. 15 (12) 1651, (m. 18 (2) 1672, Hopestill Clap,) Ephraim b. June 7, 1656.

He d. May 4, 1675, ae. 75. Will dated 20 April, prob. 30 July, 1675, beq. to wife Elizabeth; sons Thomas and Obediah; to daus. not specified; to the town for the maintaining an able ministry; to former servants, Henry Merryfield and Anne, wife of Robert Spurr. Bros.-in-law William Sumner and John Capen overseers. His widow d. Jan. 26, 1677, ae. 67. [See Upsall.]

William, Watertown, propr. 1636; rem. to Sudbury; propr. 1642. Rem. to Sandwich. Lawsuit at Salem in 1638. His son Edward was apprenticed to George Andrews, butcher, in Eastchepe, London. He sold a house and land at Sud. 28 (4) 1641. [Suff. De. and Col. Rec. vol. I.]

He d. at Sandwich; inv. taken 29 Jan. 1642. Wife Joane admin., and Daniel Wing gave bonds with her; a house at Sudbury was mortg. to Mr. Burton. The widow's will was prob. 12 (8) 1662. Beq. to Daniel Wing's two sons, Samuel and John; grand children Hannah Swift and Experience Allen; to Mary Darby; to Hannah Wing the elder, and her daus.; to Zebadiah Allin; son William exec. [Reg. IV, 173, and VI, 96.]

SWINDON,
William, ae. 20, came in the Elizabeth and Ann in May, 1635. Settled at Ipswich; propr. 1636. Soldier in the Pequot war; had grant from the town in 1639.

SWINNERTON,
Job, planter, Salem, propr. 1637. frm. Sept. 6, 1639. [Wife] Elizabeth, Salem, memb. chh. 1639. He m. 19 (5) 1658, Ruth Symons; she d. 22 May, 1670. He m. 2 (7) 1673, Hester Baker. Ch. Jasper b. 4 (4) 1659, Joseph b. 8 (12) 1660, Eliza b. 26 (12) 1662, Ruth b. 22 March, 1664, Mary b. 17 May, 1670.

Job Swinnerton, yeoman, made will 14 March, 1699-1700, prob. May 6, 1700; beq. to wife Easter, sons Jasper, Joseph, Benjamin, Joshua and James, (two last under 21 years,) daus. Mary, Easter, Abigail Hannah, and the children of dau. Elizabeth Hutchinson.

SWINFORTH,
John, ship-carpenter, partner of Thomas Robinson of Boston, died, and the account of partnership in the bark Speedwell was filed 29 (5) 1640. [L.]

SYDLEY, SIDLEY,
Thomas, ae. 22, came in the Susan and Ellen in April, 1635.

SYKES, SIKES,
Richard, Dorchester, adm. chh. 4 (9) 1639, frm. May 13, 1640. Wife Phebe adm. chh. 9 (4) 1640; ch. Rebecca bapt. 9 (3) 1641; "went to Springfield." [Note in Dorch. chh. rec.] Propr. Jan. 5, 1641-2; town officer 1642. Covenanted Feb. 10, 1653, to ring the bell and care for the meeting house. Ch. Experience b. 5 (9) 1642, Encrease [Increase] b. 6 (6) 1644, Nathaniel b. 30 (8) 1646, Victory b. 3 (1) 1648-9, James b. 11 (4) 1651.

He made will Feb. 24, 1676, and beq. to wife Phebe, sons Nathaniel, Encrease, Victory and James; some land next to brother Burt's. The widow Phebe d. Jan. 2, 1687.

SYLVESTER, SILVESTER,
Richard, Dorchester, propr.; appl. frm. 19 Oct. 1630. Rem. to Weymouth. Was fined 2 li. and disfranchised 13 (1) 1638-9, for joining in an attempt at organizing a church which was not authorized by the authorities. [See Smith, John.] Sold house and lot 23 (7) 1640. Rem. to Marshfield. Town officer. Wife Naomi; ch. Lydia b. 8 (10) 1633, (m. at Scituate Sept. 4, 1652, Nathaniel Rawlings,) John b. 14 (1) 1634, Peter bur. Aug. 30, 1642, Joseph b. 12 (2) 1642, Elizabeth b. 23 (11) 1643, (m. at Sci. Jan. 24, 1658, John Lowell,) Naomi bapt. April 14, 1650, Hesther bapt. March 26, 1654, Benjamin bapt. May 17, 1657.

He made will which was prob. Sept. 24, 1663. Beq. to wife Naomi; sons John, Joseph, Israel, Richard and Benjamin; daus. Lydia, Dinah, Elizabeth, Naomi and Hester. The widow's est. was admin. Nov. 26, 1666. [Reg. VI, 95, and VII, 178.]

SYMMES, SIMMS, SIMS, SEMMES,
Rev. Zechariah, son of Rev. William, b. at Canterbury, Eng. April 5, 1599, grad. at Cambridge univ.; was rector at Dunstable, Eng., from Sept. 1625, till 1633. Came to Boston in 1634. Was adm. chh. 5 (8) 1634.

SYMMES, etc., cont.
Was invited to become teacher of the chh. of Charlestown, adm. chh. Dec. 6, 1634, and ordained Dec. 22. On the resignation of Rev. Thomas James from the office of pastor, he was called to that position, which he filled from 1636 till his death in 1670. A man of high character, a strong upholder of the truth, very serviceable to the parish and the colony. [See Cudworth.] He m. Sarah —, "whose goodness exceeded her stature;" [Johnson.] Ch. William bapt. at Dunstable Jan. 10, 1626, Marie bapt. April 16, 1628, (m. Thomas Savage,) Elizabeth bapt. Jan. 1, 1629, (m. Hezekiah Usher,) Huldah bapt. March 18, 1630, (m. William Davis,) Hannah bapt. Aug. 22, 1632, Rebecca bapt. Feb. 12, 1633; Ruth b. at Char. Oct. 25, 1635, (m. Edward Willice,) Zachary b. 9 Jan. 1638, Timothy b. 7 May, 1640, Deborah b. Aug. 28, 1642.

He d. Feb. 4, 1670. [S.] Will dated 20 (11) 1664, prob. 31 (1) 1671, had given marriage portions to son William and daus. Sarah, Mary, Elizabeth, Huldah, Rebecca and Deborah, and something to daus. Brock and Savage; set aside a portion for dau. Ruth; son Zechary had a library and some household stuff when he went to Rehoboth; beq. to son Timothy, brother Mr. William Symmes; rest to wife, through whom most of his property came; a large English Bible that was her mother's specified; referring to his papers, said he never intended or prepared anything to be put in print. Gave a token to each of his sons-in-law and grandchildren.

The widow Sarah d. June 10, 1673. Her will, prob. Dec. 28, 1676, beq. to son Zachary; gr. dau. Margaret Prout; son Timothy; gr. ch. Margaret and Hannah Davies; son William; sons Zachary, Timothy and William; sons John Breke and his wife, Thomas Savage and his wife, Humphrey Both, Edward Willice and his wife. Ruth Willise and Deborah Prout testified to the will.

SYMONDS, SIMONDS, SYMONS, SIMONS, see Simonson,
Mr. Henry, merchant, Boston, adm. townsman 30 (11) 1643; frm. May 10, 1643. Land granted to him and his partners to erect one or more corn mills upon. Liberty was given them or their successors to alter the draw-bridge. He was one of the first

SYMONDS, etc., cont.
to trade and plant at Lancaster. His ch. Rich-Grace was bapt. at Bo. 21 (2) 1644.

He was bur. 14 (7) 1643. His widow Susanna m. 2, Isaac Walker, and confirmed a sale of land May 14, 1645. [Col. Rec.]

John, Salem, propr., 1636; frm. March, 1637-8. [Wife] Mary memb. chh., 1638. Ch. Samuel bapt. 4 (9) 1638. Elizabeth before the court in 1648.

Will prob. 19 (7) 1671, beq. to wife Elizabeth; sons James and Samuel; refers to dec. dau. Ruth Swinnerton; servant John Pease.

Mark, Ipswich, propr. 1636; frm. May 2, 1638; constable, 1639; held other town offices.

Samuel, gent., Ipswich, propr., frm. March, 1637-8, deputy and Asst. 6 June, 1638; deputy governor. A man of large ability and excellent record as a citizen and public official. Mentions cousins Gallop, Waite and Harris in a letter to J. Winthrop, Jr. in 1652. In a letter in 1662, mentions his only brother, who dwells at Much Yeldham, Essex.

He m. 1, Dorothy Harlakenden; m. 2, Martha, dau. of Edmund Reade and widow of Daniel Epps, Sen.; m. 3, Rebecca, widow of John Hall of Salisbury. Ch. Samuel, (d. in 1654; will on file;) John, (in England in 1653;) Harlakenden, William, Martha, Ruth, Priscilla, Dorothy, (m. Thomas Harrison of the parish of Dunstans in the East, London; they sent power of attorney 10 Feb. 1053, to her bros. Samuel and William S., for the collection of anything due them).

His will dated 16 Feb. 1673, and Jan. 8, 1677, prob. Nov. 6, 1678, beq. to wife Rebecca all that belonged to her in Eng. before marriage with him; also ample provision at his farm in Ipswich called Argilla, or elsewhere, if she prefer; to sons Harlakenden and William; to son and dau. Epps; she to have the "damaske sute which was the lady Cheynies if she desire"; to dau. Martha and her husband John Denison; to son and dau. Emerson; to daus. Baker and Dunkin; to son Chute; to gr. dau. Sarah Symonds; to wife's gr. dau. Rebecca Stace; son John Hale one of the overseers; refers to brother Mr. Richard Fitz Symonds, from whom a legacy is expected for son Harlakenden. The widow Rebecca d. July 21, 1695. Her inv. showed articles marked W.

SYMONDS, etc., cont.
R. and others marked R. H.; son and dau. Hall mentioned. Mrs. Martyn is one of the ch. to whom Mr. Symond's estate was divided 15 Oct. 1679.

Thomas, carpenter, Braintree, had land grant for a family of 10 persons in 1639. Ch. Joan b. 8 (9) 1638, Abigail b. 8 (9) 1640, d. 20 (3) 1642, Anne d. (4) 1640, Thomas, (whether a child or the father, the record does not show).

Thomas, Boston, in old age, made will 28 Nov. 1681, prob. 10 Aug. 1682; beq. to Abraham Bushey's wife and Samuel Perce, cooper.

William, planter, Ipswich, propr., 1635. Had charge of the herd of cattle. Sold land in 1654. Rem. to Haverhill. With wife Elizabeth sold land 4 Sept. 1658.

William, Concord, his wife Sarah was bur. 3 (2) 1641. Rem. to Woburn. Taxed in 1645. Town officer. He m. Jan. 18, 1643, Judith, widow of James Hayward. He deposed in Dec. 1658, ae. about 47 years. Ch. Sarah b. July 28, 1644, Judith b. March 3, 1045, Mary b. Dec. 9, 1647, Caleb b. Aug. 11, 1649, William b. April 15, 1651, Joseph b. Oct. 18, 1652, Benjamin b. March 18, 1653-4, Tabitha b. Aug. 20, 1655, James b. Nov. 1, 1658, Bethiah b. May 9, 1659, Huldah b. Nov. 20, 1660.

He d. June 17, 1672. Admin. gr. to widow Judith and sons Caleb and William. The latter died in 1672, and his est. was divided between his ten bros. and sisters and a gr. ch. of widow Judith Simons; Joseph, Benjamin and James S. were minors, and their guardians acted for them. [Mdx. Files.] The widow d. Jan. 3, 1689.

TABOR,
John, Sir Richard Saltonstall's "man," witnessed a deed of his March 2, 1629. [Mass. Arch. 100, 1.]

Philip, Watertown, contributed plank to the building of the fort at Boston, April 1, 1634, frm. May 14, 1634. He was one of the proprs. of Yarmouth, 7 Jan. 1638-9. Lydia T. was one of the daus. of John Masters, to whom he beq. in 1639.

Timothy, of Batcome, Eng. tailor, ae. 35, with wife Jane, ae. 35, children, Jane,

TABOR, cont.
ae. 10, Anne, ae. 8, Sarah, ae. 5, and servant, William Fever, embarked for N. E. from Weymouth, Eng. before March 20, 1635.

TAINTOR, TAYNTOR,
Joseph, ae. 25, servant of Nicholas Guy, carpenter, from Upton Gray, co. Southampton, came in the Confidence April 11, 1638. Settled at Watertown; propr., town officer. Propr. at Sudbury, 1639. He m. —, dau. of Nicholas Guy, whose widow beq. to his children. Ch. Anne b. 2 (7) 1644. Joseph b. 2 (7) 1645, Rebecca b. 18 (6; 1647, Benjamin b. 22 (11) 1650, Jonathan b. 10 (8) 1654, Sarah b. Nov. 20, 1657, Simon b. 30 (7) 1660, Dorothy b. Aug. 13, 1663. He deposed 2 (8) 1663, ae. about 49 years. [Mdx. Files.]

He d. Feb. 20, 1689-90. Will beq. to wife Mary; sons Joseph, Benjamin, Jonathan and Simon T.; sons-in-law Elnathan Beers and John Tailer; dau. Mary Pollard; gr. ch. John Tailer and others.

TALBIE, TALBY,
John, Salem, propr. 1636. Wife Dorothy; ch. Difficulty bapt. 25 (10) 1636. Dorothy, in court for violent actions toward him in 1637, was executed 6 (10) 1639, for the murder of her child Difficult. [W.]

Inv. of his est. rendered (11) 1644. John [his son?] was apprenticed to Henry Cooke 29 (11) 1655.

TALBOT, TALBUT,
Moses, Plymouth, one of the crew of John Howland at Kennebec River in April, 1634, was shot by Hocking.

Peter, Plymouth, having been in the employ of Edward Dotey, and having a claim on land for his service, sold his claim Aug. 22, 1636. Peter, who m. at Dorchester, Jan. 12, 1667, Mary Waddell, may be the same person.

Ralph, Salem, a witness, 1643. [Ess. Court Files.]

TALCOTT,
John, embarked for N. E. June 22, 1632, settled at Cambridge; frm. Nov. 6, 1632; deputy, propr. Sold May 1, 1636. Rem. to Hartford, Conn. We note the following:
Admin. of the est. of Lieut. Col. J. T. of Hartford was gr. at Boston 12 Nov. 1688, to

TALCOTT, etc., cont.
his bro. Samuel T., gent., and his son-in-law Joseph Wadsworth, gent., both of Hartford.

TALMADGE, TALMAGE, TALMIGE,
Thomas, Lynn, juryman, Es. Quarterly Court, 27 (4) 1636. He and Thomas, Jr. had lands in 1638. Elizabeth d. 20 (10) 1660.

William, carpenter, Boston, memb. chh. 1630, frm. May 14, 1634. Res. at Roxbury some time and rem. to Lynn, where his wife died. [E.] Rem. to Boston before Aug. 8, 1640, when he and his bros. Thomas and Robert Talmage and their deceased sister Jane's husband, Richard Walker, gave letter of attorney for the receiving of money due them from the estate of their father, John T. husbandman, late of Newton Stacey, co. Hants. He had grant of land in Bo. 1635. Wife Elizabeth; ch. Elizabeth b. Sept. 2°, 1666, Mary b. Jan. 13, 1668.

TAPLEY, TOPLEY, see Topliff.

TAPP, see Topper.

TAPPAN, see Toppan.

TARBELL, TARBALL, TARBOL,
Thomas, Watertown, propr. 1647. He deposed in 1656, ae. about 38 years. Rem. to Groton in 1662; had liberty to erect a mill. Wife Mary; ch. Thomas, adult in 1662, perhaps Abigail, (m. Sept. 30, 1672, Joshua Whitney,) Elizabeth b. Jan. 5, 1656, William b. 26 (12) 1658. Mary T. d. 29 (2) 1674, ae. 54.

He d. at Charlestown, of small pox 11 June, 1678. Inv. of his est. taken 25 (7) 1678. [L. H.]

TARBOX,
John, Lynn, lawsuit in 1639. One of the creditors of the Iron Works Co. in 1655. [Suff. De. I.]. Ch. Jonathan d. 16 (4) 1654. He d. 26 May, 1674. Will dated 25 (9) 1673, prob. 2 (5) 1674. Wife; sons John and Samuel. Samuel deposed 30 (4) 1669, ae. about 22 years.

TARLING,
Christopher, ran away from his master; in Court Nov. 5, 1633.

TARNE, TERNE,
Miles, leather-dresser, Boston, appl. for a lot for 5 heads 28 (10) 1640; adm. chh. 8 (8) 1642; frm. May 10, 1643. Wife Sarah adm. chh. 14 (2) 1639; d. before 23 Oct. 1652, when he and his second wife (probably widow of Robert Rice,) sold land for the use of her two small children by former husband, their names not given. [Col. Rec.] Ch. Hannah b. (8) 1638, bapt. 21 (2) 1639, Deliverance b. 30 (7) 1641, Sarah, (m. 7 (7) 1654, Edward Bobbett). The dau. Deliverance recd. legacy from Charity White Feb. 5, 1660. Inv. of his est. filed by his widow Elizabeth July 27, 1676; "the house and land where he lived, the reversion whereof at the death of his wife being the inheritance of Joshua Rice as by covenant the 15 : 12 : 60."

TART, TARTE,
Edward, Scituate, atba. 1643. Servant of Nathaniel Tilden in 1641.

Thomas, planter, Scituate; juryman, 1640; with wife Elizabeth joined chh. in 1641. Dau. Elizabeth m. Thomas Williams; her portion to be paid out of goods in hands of Wm. Brackenbury, 3 May, 1641. [Plym. Col. Rec.] Ch. Jonathan and Eunice bapt. at Boston 11 (2) 1641.

TATMAN, see Totman.

TAUSLEY,
Thomas, servant to Joshua Hewes, Roxbury, was bur. 23 (10) 1641.

TAYLOR, TAILOR,
Dennys, widow, one of the family of Mr. John Wilson, Boston, adm. chh. 8 (9) 1635. Is most probably the Dionis, ae. 48, who came in the Susan and Ellen in April, 1635, with Elizabeth, ae. 10.

Edward, Reading, propr. 1647; with wife memb. chh. in 1648. Town officer. Wife Christian d. about 1673. Wife Elizabeth d. Jan. 22, 1686. [See Bridges, John.]

—, of Haverhill, Eng., came to N. E. in 1630; his wife died soon. [W.] No clue yet found to his identity.

George, ae. 31, came in the Truelove in Sept. 1635; settled at Lynn; propr. 1638. Frm. May 2, 1638. Constable 31 (16) 1647. Opposed infant baptism. [Es. Files.] Deposed in 1654 to the bringing of beaver from

TAYLOR, etc., cont.
Saco to Boston for Francis Johnson about 1636.
He d. 28 (10) 1667.

Gregory, Boston, memb. chh. 1630-1. Rem. to Watertown. Frm. May 14, 1634. He sold land to Simon Eire prior to 1644. Constable 1642. Wife Alice; ch. Samuel bur. 6 (2) 1632, ae. 3 days.

Henry, Barnstable. He m. Dec. 19, 1650, Lydia Hatch; ch. Lydia b. 21 June, 1655, Jonathan b. 20 April, 1658.

Henry, chirurgeon, Boston, mentioned in 1667. [Arch. 100, 116.]

Mr. Henry, Boston, wife Mary; ch Hannah b. July 7, 1665. They sold warehouse, land, etc. in Bo. May 6, 1667. Other ch. later.

James, Concord. He m. 19 (8) 1641, Isabel Tomkins; ch. Henry b. and d. 1648. Wife Elizabeth; ch. Samuel b. June 21, 1656, Thomas b. and d. 1659. He deposed 19 (11) 1671, ae. about 64 years. [Mdx. Files.] Isabel deposed 11 (3) 1675, ae. about 60 years, to the will of Sarah Parker.

John, residence not stated, frm. May 18, 1631. May be the " — Taylor, of Haverhill, Eng." who came in 1630, and whose "wife d." soon after. [W.] Witness to a document in Boston in 1645. [A.] Frm. May 7, 1651. He may be the

John, Cambridge, with wife Katharine, membs. chh. in 1658; ch. Joseph b. and bapt. in Camb. [Mi.]

He d. 7 (7) 1683, ae. 73. [Mdx. Rec.] [Gr. St.] Beq. all to wife Katharine, who beq. 21 Sept. 1685, to her gr. ch. John and Joseph T., ch. of dec. son Joseph, late of Long Island, and to several female friends in Camb.; dau.-in-law Mrs. Mary T.

Jonathan, Springfield. Ch. Mary b. 1 (6) 1649.

Philip, residence unknown, frm. May 18, 1642.

Richard, Boston, frm. May 18, 1642. Wife Mary; ch. John bapt. 6 (12) 1646.

Richard, Watertown, made will 6 May, prob. Oct. 4, 1659; beq. to wife Ann and dau. Frances Adams.

Richard, Yarmouth, atba. 1643; town officer, juror. He was lic. to marry Ruth,

TAYLOR, etc., cont.

dau. of Gabriel Whelding, 27 Oct. 1646; ch. Ruth b. 29 July, 1647, bur. 1648, Ann b. 2 Dec. 1648, bur. 29 March, 1650, Ruth b. 11 April, 1649, Martha b. 18 Dec. 1650.

Admin. of his est. gr. 4 March, 1673-4, to John T., John Gorum and John Thatcher; division made to two sons and five daus. Note made of articles he had given to ch. John, Martha, Joseph, [Mary.]

Samuel, Ipswich, resident 1648; keeper of one of the herds of cattle. Memb. town committee. Deposed in 1658, ae. about 40 years.

Thomas, Salem, 1636.

Thomas, planter, Watertown, gave a bond 7 (1) 1640. [L.] Propr. 1642. Rem. to Reading; sold land at Wat. in 1660. Wife Elizabeth; ch. Seabred b. 11 (1) 1642; the wife Elizabeth and child Benoni d. Feb. 18, 1650.

Old Thomas T. d. at Ipswich April 15, 1686.

Tobias, had lawsuit vs. John Shaw of Plymouth in 1646.

William, son of William of Boddington, in Cornwall, carpenter, covenant servant of Mr. John Atwood of Plymouth, was transferred March 12, 1638-9, to Thomas Little for 7 years.

William, Concord, 1649. Wife Mary; ch. Mary b. 19 (12) 1649, Samuel b. and d. 1655, John b. 19 Oct. 1656, Abraham b. 14 Nov. 1656 [7?] Isaac b. 5 March, 1659, Jacob b. 8 May, 1662, Joseph b. 7 April, 1664.

TEAD, TEED, TEDD, TIDD, TYDD,

John, tailor, came early. Settled at Charlestown, propr. 1637. Rem. to Woburn, 1640. Sold land in 1652. Town officer. Petitioned Gen. Court regarding land in 1648. Ch. John, Jr., propr. also in 1646; John, ae. 19, servant to Samuel Greenfield, weaver, who came from Norwich, Eng. May 12, 1637, I think; Samuel, Mary, (m. Dec. 24, 1644, Francis Wyman,) Elizabeth, (m. Jan. 13, 1643, Thomas Fuller). Wife Margaret d. 1651. He d. April 24, 1656.

Will dated 9 (2) prob. 10 (9) 1656, beq. to wife Alice, son John, daus. Mary and Elizabeth; to son Savell's ch. Benjamin, Hannah, John and Samuel; to son Samuel's daus.; to gr. ch. Thomas Fuller and John Kendall.

TEAD, etc., cont.

Joshua, Charlestown, adm. chh. 10 (1) 1639; frm. 22 May, 1639. Rem. to Salem. Had large estate. Owned and commanded a vessel named the Swallow, and traded along the Eastern shore. John Richards and others of Kennebeck, captured the bark and a freight of beaver, etc. in May, 1656. Testimony given in suit of J. T. against Richard Callicot in Mdx. court, 18 (4) 1657. [Gen. Adv. I, 90.] Wife Sarah adm. chh. 9 (7) 1639. She d. 15 Oct. 1677, ae. 71 years. He m. 2. Rhoda, [whom the writer believes to have been successively wife of John Gore, John Remington, and Edward Porter. She d. at Roxbury Aug. 22, 1693, ae. 86 years.] Ch. John b. at Char. 15 (4) 1641, Joseph b. 15 (10) 1643, Sarah, (m. 24 Sept. 1656, Zechariah Long, dau. (m. Samuel Lord).

His will dated 12 April, 1675, prob. 30 Oct. 1678, beq. to wife Sarah; dau. Lord and her children; gr. ch. Marie Long; rest to be divided between his gr. ch. Admin. of the estate was gr. to widow Rhoda and Samuel Lord; the widow declined the trust and L. gave bonds Nov. 1, 1678.

TEAL, see Theal.

TEFFE, TEFT, TIFF, TIFTE,

William, tailor, Boston, adm. inhabitant 24 (10) 1638; with wife Anne adm. chh. 2 (6) 1640. Frm. June 2, 1641. Will dated 1 (3) 1646, prob. 2 (8) 1648; testified to and recorded Nov. 23, 1672. Beq. to dau. Lydia £ 7 recd. for her in England as a legacy from Robert Elving; she is not to marry without her mother-in-law's consent; to the eldest child of his bro. John T.; rest to wife Anne, whom he made exec. [Original in Arch. B.] The widow m. Henry Allen, q. v.

TEMPLAR, TEMPLER, TEMPLE,

Richard, husbandman, Yarmouth, constable 4 June, 1645, propr., town officer 1650. Ch. Abigail b. at Charlestown 15 (5) 1647. His wife, dau. of Richard Pritchet, adm. chh. Charlestown 29 (5) 1660. Ch. Richard bapt. at Char. 5 (5) 1663.

TENCH,

William, Plymouth, came in the Fortune in 1621; had lands assigned in 1623; deeded land with John Carman before 1630.

TEMPLE,
Abraham, Salem, propr. 1636; lawsuit 1638.

Dorothy, Plymouth, servant to Stephen Hopkins; she and her child bound, 8 Feb. 1638 ,to John Holmes.

Richard, Salem, propr. 1644. Ch. Richard b. at Char. 15 Oct. 1654. Richard of Concord bought land at C. 3 (11) 1660.

TERRE, TERRY, TERREY,
John, ae. 32, came in the Abigail in July, 1635.

Robert, ae. 25, and Richard, ae. 17, came in the James in July, 1635.

Mr. Stephen, came in the Mary and John in 1629-30 to Dorchester. [Bl.] Frm. May 18, 1631. Constable, 1635. [Col. Rec.] Rem. to Windsor, Conn.; thence to Hadley. His [first] wife was bur. June 5, 1647. He m. [second] Elizabeth —. Ch. Mary b. 31 Dec. 1631, (m. Richard Goodman,) John b. 6 March, 1637, Elizabeth b. 9 Jan. 1641, (m. Philip Russell,) Abigail b. 21 Sept. 1646.

His widow d. at Hadley. Her nunc. will prob. March 25, 1684, beq. to daus. Goodman and Kellogg; admin. gr. to son-in-law, Mr. Joseph Kellogg.

Thomas, ae. 28, came in the James in July, 1635. Before Gen. Court 4 (10) 1638.

TENNEY, TENNY,
Thomas, Rowley, propr. 1643. Rem. to Bradford. He deposed 4 May, 1680, ae. about 66 years. Wife Ann was bur. 26 (7) 1657. Ch. John b. 14 (10) 1640, Hannah b. 15 (1) 1642, Mercy b. 17 (4) 1644, Thomas b. 16 (5) 1648, James b. 15 (6) 1650, Sarah b. 15 (2) 1652, d. 10 April, 1653, Daniel b. 16 (5) 1653. He d. 20 Feb. 1699.

William, Rowley, propr. 1643; deacon. Wife Katharine; ch. Elizabeth b. 9 (2) 1643, Mary b. 24 (7) 1646, Samuel b. 6 (2) 1650, bur. Aug. 5, 1660, Ruth b. 16 March, 1653, Sarah b. 20 (7) 1656.

He d. 5 Aug. 1685; inv. ret. by widow Katharine 29 Sept. 1691.

TEY, [TAY,]
John, Boston, made will in presence of Jacob Eliot, prob. 7 (10) 1641. Son Allin to have books when he is of age, to be given to him when he comes over; his trees to be given to persons named; beq. to his cousin Jackson of Watterton, to goodwife Wormwoode, to Mr. Raynsford, Mr. Offley, goodwife Search, Mr. Rainsford's man John; the rest to be divided between John Whight and John Wylie, his kinsmen.

THATCHER, THACHER,
Mr. Anthony, of Sarum, tailor, came with his wife in the James in April, 1635; they were the sole survivors of a wreck at Cape Ann Aug. 16, 1635; the Gen. Court apptd. him adminr. of the est. of Mr. Joseph Avery Sept. 1, 1635; gave him the island on which the wreck occurred 9 March, 1636-7. He was taxed as a propr. at Marblehead 1 (11) 1637. Rem. to Yarmouth; took oath of allegiance to Plym. Col. 7 Jan. 1638-9. Deputy; had lic. to marry persons; magistrate. Richard Sears called him brother.

Admin. of his est. was gr. to John T. 30 Oct. 1667, and to his widow Mary 5 March, 1667-8.

Samuel, husbandman, Watertown, deacon, selectman; frm. May 18, 1642. Deputy. Member of chh. of Cambridge. He signed the inv. of Wm. Goodrich in 1647. Wife Hannah; ch. Hannah b. 9 (8) 1645, (m. John Holmes,) Samuel b. 20 (10) 1648.

He d. 30 (9) 1669. The widow's will names son and dau. John and Hannah Holmes; son Samuel and his dau. Mary; sister Cheevers; the widow of Jonathan Mitchell; Elizabeth Rush; Nathaniel and Joseph, sons of Jonas Clarke; Samuel Prentice.

Rev. Thomas, son of Rev. Peter, of Sarum, Eng. and a nephew of Anthony, above, [C. M.] b. May 1, 1620, came in 1635 to Boston. Frm. May, 1645. Was not a university grad. but studied with Rev. Charles Chauncey. Became highly educated; was skilled in medicine, and very ingenius in mechanical matters. [C. M.] He was ordained pastor of the chh. at Weymouth Jan. 2, 1644. After a long term of useful service there, he was called to be pastor of the South chh. of Boston, Feb. 16, 1669. He m. May 11, 1643, Elizabeth, dau. of Rev. Ralph Partridge, minister at Duxbury; she d. June 2, 1664. He m. 2, Margaret, dau. of Henry Webb, and widow of Jacob Sheafe, who survived him, and d. Feb. 23, 1693. Ch. Peter bapt. at Salem 20 (5) 1651, Ralph, Thomas, Patience, Elizabeth.

He d. Oct. 15, 1678. [Reg. XXXVII.]

THAXTER, THACKSTER,
Thomas, linen-weaver, Hingham,propr. 1638, frm. 18 May, 1642; deacon. Thomas, son of Mr. John Thaxter, parson of Bridgham, co. Norfolk, Eng. and Anne, his wife, was bapt. Feb. 1, 1595; admin. on the est. of his bro. Daniel, minister of Kirkby, 5 Oct. 1625; recd. property at K. and at Bramerton; his name does not appear later in Norf. co. records. May be believed to be the Hingham man. Wife Elizabeth; ch. John, b. about 1626, Elizabeth, Sarah, (m. Thomas Thurston,) Thomas d. 6 Jan. 1646, Daniel d. 22 April, 1663, Samuel b. May 19, 1641, Samuel bapt. March 27, 1642.

He d. Feb. 4, 1653-4. Inv. taken Feb. 20. Agreement of the heirs regarding the est. April 20, 1654. The widow m. 29 (7) 1654, William Ripley, who d. 20 (5) 1656. She m. at Dedham 20 (11) 1657, John Dwight. She d. July 17, 1660, "drowned in a well." [Hob.] [Reg. VIII, 128 w.]

THAYLER,
Faithful, Springfield, a witness to the Indian deed in 1636.

THAYER, TAYER, TARE,
Richard, [shoemaker,] probably bro. of Thomas, folg., and bapt. at Thornbury, Eng. April, 1601. He came in 1641, bringing 8 children. [Depos. of son Richard.] Settled at Braintree. Sold land to son Richard in 1648. Rem. to Boston. He m. at Thornbury 5 April, 1624, Dorothy Mortimore; ch. Richard bapt. Feb. 10, 1624-5, Cornelius, Deborah bapt. Feb. 1629-30, (m. 11 April, 1653, Thomas Faxon,) Jael, (m. 17 March, 1654, John Harbour, Jr.) Sarah, (m. 20 July, 1651, Samuel Davis,) Hannah, (m. 28 May, 1664, Samuel Hayden,) Zachariah, (d. 29 July, 1693, and est. admin. by bro. Richard,) Nathaniel, [Abigail d. 6 Aug. 1717, ae. 66 years.] He m. 2, Jane, widow of John Parker; joined her in conveyance of land to her Parker children in 1652.

He d. before 1668. [Suff. De. V, 446.]

Thomas, shoemaker, Braintree, b. at Thornbury, Eng., came before 1639; when he had a grant of land for 9 heads and 40 acres more, 76 acres in all. He m. at Thornbury April 13, 1618, Margerie Wheeler; ch. Thomas bapt. at T. 15 Sept. 1622, Ferdinando bapt. April 18, 1625, Shadrach, (Sydrick,)

THAYER, etc., cont.
bapt. May 10, 1629, [Sarah, (m. Jonathan Hayward.)]

He d. 2 (4) 1665. Will dated 24 June, 1664, prob. Sept. 13, 1665. Beq. to wife and sons mentioned above. The widow d. 11 (12) 1672. [Reg. XIII, 335, and XXXVII, 84.]

THEAL, THELE, [TEAL,]
Nicholas, Watertown, in court 6 March, 1637-8. Sold house and lands 23 (7) 1645. Wife Elizabeth; ch. Joseph b. 24 (8) 1640, Elizabeth b. 5 (4) 1643.

THICKSTON,
Katharine, m. in 1639 William Hurst of Sandwich.

THING,
Jonathan, before the Gen. Court 1 (4) 1641. In the service of Henry Ambrose, [Charlestown,] as per Court Rec. 29 May, 1644. Rem. to Exeter. He deposed in 1667, ae. about 46 years. [Es. Files.] Inv. of his est. taken 29 April, 1674; agreement made between Johanna and Jonathan T. to manage the est. jointly, bring up and educate the children, and pay Samuel, Elizabeth and Mary their portions when they come of age.

THIRBER, see Thurber.

THOMAS,
Evan, vintner, Boston, a Welchman, with wife and children, had grant of land from Gen. Court 1 Sept. 1640. Adm. chh. 4 (2) 1641; frm. June 2, 1641. Town officer. Wife Jane adm. chh. 7 (1) 1646; he had grant of land for 6 heads 25 (11) 1640; ch. rec. at Bo.: Jane b. 16 (3) 1641, (m. 14 (9) 1657, John Jackson,) Dorcas b. and d. 1642, Elinor, b. before 1654 Lyonel Whitley, (Wheatley,) and conveyed land with him in 1667 which had belonged to her father). His wife d., and he m. about Nov. 8, 1659, Alice, widow of Philip Catland (Kirtland,) of Lynn.

He d. Aug. 25, 1661. Admin. gr. to widow Alice Oct. 30, 1661. [Reg. XI, 38.]

Hugh, Roxbury, propr., adm. chh. 1650, frm. May 7, 1651. He and his wife were legatees of his nephew John Roberts of Roxbury, in will prob. July 28, 1676.

He d. May 6, 1683, ae. about 76 years. His widow Clement d. Sept. 24, 1683.

James, Salem, propr. 1649.

THOMAS, cont.

John, ae. 14, came in the Hopewell in Sept., 1635.

John, Marshfield, atba. 1643. He m. Dec. 21, 1648, Sarah, dau. of James Pitney; ch. John b. Nov. 16, 1649, Elizabeth b. Sept. 12, 1652, Samuel b. Nov. 6, 1655, Daniel b. Nov. 20, 1659, Sarah b. Sept. 1661, James b. Nov. 1663, Ephraim b. [1667.] Admin. gr. Aug. 7, 1699, to widow Sarah.

Mary, Roxbury, servant to Hugh Pritchard, d. 10 (4) 1643.

Rowland, Springfield, propr., town officer. He m. 14 (2) 1647, Sarah Chapin; she d. Aug. 5, 1684. Ch. Joseph bur. 12 (4) 1648, Samuel bur. 5 (1) 1649, Mary b. and d. 1650.

William, a very early settler at Marshfield, one of the "purchasers or old comers," frm. 4 Dec. 1638. Son Nathaniel, who acted for him in taking an apprentice 2 Nov. 1636, d. 13 Feb. 1674, ae. about 68 years. [Gr. St.] He d. in Aug. 1651, ae. about 78 years. Will dated July 9, 1651; beq. to son Nathaniel, his wife, and children Nathaniel, Mary, Elizabeth and Dorothy. To Marshfield church "a table-cloth of nine foot long;" gifts to James Petney, William Collier, Edward Bulkley and Edward Bumpas. [Reg. IV, 319.]

William, ae. 26, husbandman, from Great Comberton, Worcester, Eng., passed exam. to go to N. E. May 10, 1637.

THOMPSON, THOMSON, see also Tompson,

Archibald, Marblehead, propr.; lawsuit, 1637. He was drowned in 1641. [W.]

Mr. David, fishmonger, from London, came over about 1623 to begin a plantation at Piscataqua River. [Hub.] Took possession in 1626 of the island called Trevour's in Boston harbour, afterward called by his name, and erected a habitation there; died soon after. These facts shown to the Gen. Court, they granted the island (which had been included in Dorchester) to his son John Thompson, 10 May, 1648. [See also Reg. IX, 248.]

Edmund or Edward, Salem, propr., memb. chh. 1638. He and his wife were

THOMPSON, etc., cont.

witnesses in court in 1643. Propr. at Wenham, 1643. Ch. Thomas bapt. 12 (12) 1642-3, Anna bapt. 4 (5) 1647.

Edward, servant to William White, came in the Mayflower to Plymouth. Died soon after arrival. [B.]

James, Charlestown, adm. chh. with wife, 31 (6) 1633; frm. May 14, 1634; propr. 1635. Rem. to Woburn in 1640; propr., town officer. He deposed in 1658, ae. about 65 years. His wife Elizabeth d. Nov. 8, 1643; he m. Feb. 14, 1643-4, Susanna Blodgett; she d. Feb. 10, 1660-1. Ch. Simon, James, (d. Jan. 24, 1646,) [Olive, (m. Sept. 3, 1650, John Cutler,)] perhaps others.

John, Watertown, propr., frm. May 6, 1635. Wife Margaret; ch. John bur. 10 (2) 1636, ae. 3 months, [Samuel bur. 28 (1) 1642.] He was bur. 28 (12) 1638, ae. 30 years.

John, Weymouth, town officer, 1645.

John, Plymouth, atba. 1643. Served against the Narragansetts 17 days from 15 Aug. 1645. In court 3 March, 1644-5. Town officer; juryman. Did he rem. to Barnstable? He m. at Plym. 26 Dec. 1645, Mary Cooke; ch. John d. 11 Feb. 1648, John b. 24 Nov. 1649. Ch. of John of Barnstable: Hester b. 28 July, 1652, Elizabeth b. 28 Jan. 1654, Sarah b. 4 April, 1657, Lydia b. Oct. 5, 1659, Jude b. 24 April, 1662, Thomas b. 19 Oct. 1664. Will dated 23 April, 1696, "weak through infirmities of age;" prob. 8 July, 1696.

Simon (Tompson,) rope-maker, Ipswich, propr. 1636; frm. June 2, 1641. Bought house and land in 1648. Rem. to Chelmsford. Was active in securing the removal of Wenham people to Chem. in 1654-5. Ret. to Ipswich. He deposed April 4, 1668, ae. about 60 years. [Ips. De. II, 61.] He m. a sister of Henry Short, as the latter deposed in 1665.

His will, dated 25 June, 1675, prob. 28 March, 1676, beq. to wife Rachel what she brought at marriage, etc.; to son-in-law Abraham Fitts; to gr. ch. Symon, Samuel, William, Thomas, Tompson, Mary and Joannah Wood; gr. ch. Abraham and Sarah Fitts; dau. Wood and son-in-law Isaiah Wood.

Thomas, ae. 18, came in the Abigail in July, 1635; settled at Springfield; propr. 1636.

THORN, THORNE,

John, carpenter, Lynn, propr. 1638. Nunc. will testified to 27 July, prob. 4 (6) 1646. A gift to James Thomas; best hat to John Jackson, Jr.; residue to Ann Paulsgrave.

John, cooper, Cambridge, probably not a "pioneer," made will 20 Dec. 1681, prob. 14 April, which is here given on account of its important statements. He beq. to son John land at South Molton, co. Devon, Eng.; to Nathaniel, Hannah and Anna, ch. of his "predecessor" Nathaniel Merrick a tenement in Barnstable, Eng.; to sister Ann T. of Bar.; kinsmen Joseph Prout of Boston and Wm. Barratt of Cambridge; to wife Ann and son Symon T.

Peter, ae. 20, came in the Elizabeth in April, 1635.

Sarah, distracted, placed by the Court under care of Alexander Beck of Boston, 22 May, 1646.

William, laborer, res. at Muddy River, Boston, memb. chh. Roxbury; frm. May 2, 1638. [William, residence not given, a juryman at Essex Court in 1641, may be the same.] Adm. chh. Boston 17 (2) 1647. Wife —, memb. chh. of Bo.; ch. Desire-truth bapt. at Rox. 22 March, 1644, Hannah bapt. 9 (3) 1647, Israel bapt. in Bo. 14 (5) 1650, Mary bapt. 5 (6) 1655.

THORNDIKE, THORNEDICKE,

Mr. John, gent., Salem, 1635. One of the first to plant at Agawam, i. e. Ipswich, April 1, 1633. [Col. Rec.] He m. Elizabeth, dau. of John and Ann Stratton, gent. of Shotley, Eng. who came to Salem in 1635; she was ae. about 26 years in 1640. [See Stratton.]

Will dated July 29, 1668, prob. 2 (10) 1670, inv. June 29, 1671. Purposing to go this year to England. Eldest dau. Anne; son Paul; daus. Mary, Martha, and Alice; sons-in-law John Proctor and John Low. Anne in melancholy state; provision for her; Martha and Alice to go with him to Eng. [See wills of Francis T. of Scamelsby, co. Lincoln, and Herbert T., prebent of Westminster, in Reg. LI, 129.]

THOROUGHGOOD,

Thomas, a witness in Boston 24 Aug. 1648. [Gen. Court.] Signed as witness of a Roxbury deed 25 (4) 1651.

THORNTON, THORNETON,

John, Ipswich, propr. before 1637. He d. and his widow Joane m. about 1639 Mathias Button, who sold the house and land he had owned.

Peter, Boston. Wife Mary; ch. Joseph b. 5 (2) 1647.

His nunc. will prob. Feb. 9, 1651; beq. to wife and children. [Reg. VIII, 57.]

Robert, ae. 11, came in the Elizabeth in April, 1635. Settled at Dorchester; propr. 1646. At some time owned land at Taunton, which he sold to Elizabeth Poole; see her will. Rem. to Boston. Premises referred to in deed of Ambrose Leach in 1663. He m. 13 (9) 1657, Mary, widow of Walter Merry; ch. Experience b. and. d. 1658, Rebecca b. Sept. 1, 1663.

Thomas, husbandman, Dorchester, frm. Sept. 3, 1634. Propr. to 1636. Rem. to Windsor, Conn. Tanner.

Walter, husbandman, ae. 36, with Joanna, ae. 44, came in the Susan and Ellen in April, 1635.

THORP, THORPE,

Elizabeth, Boston, recd. legacy from Elizabeth, wife of Mr. George Thompson of London, merchant, July 26, 1641. [L.]

Henry, Watertown, propr.; some land on Cambridge side of the line, sold about 1642; frm. May 6, 1646. He married Anne, widow of Robert Bullard. He gave bonds 25 Nov. 1639, that he would not alienate any of the estate then in her possession, and consented to a deed she had made to her son Benjamin B. and his sisters. The bond was made before John Simpson and witnessed by William Bullard.

He d. May 21, 1672, and her children inherited his estate.

John, carpenter, Plymouth; taxed in 1632; in court 1632.

He d. before Aug. 15, 1633. Inv. taken Nov. 15, admin. Nov. 25, 1633. His widow

THORP, etc., cont.
Alice deposed. [Plym. Col. Rec. and Reg. IV, 34.]

Robert, before Gen. Court 5 (1) 1638-9.

THRESHER, THRASHER,
Christopher, Taunton, atba. 1643. Ch. Israel b. 16 Sept. 1648.
Will dated July 13, 1678, prob. 3 June, 1679, beq. to eldest son Israel, youngest son John, son Samuel, daus. Hannah and Sarah, and wife Katharine.

THROCKMORTON, THROGMORTON,
Mr. George, gent., arrived in the Lyon at Salem, 5 Feb. 1630. Frm. May 18, 1631. Rem. to Providence.

Mr. John, gent. made contract to deliver goats, etc. at Boston, June 11, 1641. [L.] Suit in Plymouth court, 1641, settled by arbitration.

THRODINGHAM, see Frothingham.

THORLA, THORLO, THURLEY, THURLOW,
Richard, planter, Rowley, propr. Rem. to Newbury. Wife Jane; ch. Lydia b. 1 (2) 1640. Having built a bridge at his own cost over Newbury river, the Gen. Court fixed a rate of toll for animals only, 3 May, 1654. He gave part of his farm to his son Thomas, 27 Jan. 1669, in case of his death to son Francis; the wife joined in the deed.

THURBER,
John, Salem, 1643.

THURSTON, THRUSTON,
Benjamin, weaver, Boston, frm. May, 1645.
Admin. of his est. gr. 11 Dec. 1678, to his widow Elishua, and again 5 Dec. 1684, to dau. Mehetabel.

Charles, Plymouth, servant to Wm. Hanbury, atba. 1643; in court 5 June, 1644; his time of service extended to July 25, 1648.

Daniel, Newbury, propr. 1638; juryman. His wife d. 25 May, 1648. He m. 29 Aug. 1648, Anne Lightfoot. D. T. m. Oct. 20, 1655, Anna Bell.
He d. 16 Feb. 1666, leaving estate to his

THURSTON, etc., cont.
kinsman Daniel T. of Newbury. His widow Anne d. Feb. 17, 1673.

John, carpenter, ae. 30, with wife Margaret, ae. 32, and children Thomas and John, from Wrentom, co. Suffolk, Eng., passed exam. May 10, 1637, to go to N. E. [May be the J. T. who was propr. at Salem in 1639, and witness at Ipswich court in 1641.] Settled at Dedham; adm. chh. 28 (3) 1641, propr. 10 (5) 1642. Frm. May 10, 1643. He rem. to Medfield. Wife adm. chh. 28 (6) 1640; she d. May 9, 1662. Ch. rec. at Ded.: Benjamin b. 8 (5) 1640, Joseph bapt. 15 (7) 1640, Mary b. 8 (1) 1643, Daniel b. 5 (5) 1646, Judith b. 17 (3) 1648, Hannah b. 28 (2) 1650.
He d. Nov. 1, 1685. Will dated 13 June, 1683, prob. 21 Oct. 1686, beq. to sons Thomas, John, Joseph and Daniel; to the widow of dec. son Benjamin; to dau. Mary Smith; to sons-in-law Jonathan Treadway and Joseph Cheny.

Richard, carpenter, Salem, propr. 1637.

Capt. **Richard,** merchant, Boston, propr. 1650. Partner of William Brenton and others 1651. [Suff. De. I.] Wife Martha, dau. of Christopher Stanley; ch. Samuel b. 11 July, 1652, Elizabeth b. Sept. 29, 1664, Elizabeth (of Capt. Richard and Mary) b. May 26, 1666, Hannah, who m. 23 (7) 1652, Thomas Love, and Benjamin, who m. 12 Dec. 1660, Elishua, dau. of Robert Walker, may have been ch. of Capt. Richard.

THWAYTE,
Alexander, [Concord,] the Gen. Court granted his corn to Mr. Peter Bulkley 2 (4) 1640.

THWING,
Benjamin, ae. 16, came in the Susan and Ellen in April, 1635. Settled at Boston; joiner. Townsman 28 (1) 1642; adm. chh. 17 (12) 1643; frm. May, 1645. Wife Deborah adm. chh. 9 (8) 1642; ch. Deborah b. and d. 1642, John b. 21 (9) 1644, Benjamin bapt. 18 (5) 1647, ae. about 4 days, Rachel bapt. 17 (1) 1650, ae. about 5 days, Edward b. 14 Nov. 1652, William bapt. 28 (10) 1656, Deborah b. 13 Jan. 1659.
Admin. gr. to his widow Deborah and son John 8 Jan. 1673.

TIBBALDES,
Thomas, ae. 20, came in the Truelove in Sept. 1635.

TIBBET, TIBBETTS, TIBBOT, TIBBOTTS, TYBBOTT, TYPIT,
Henry, shoemaker, ae. 39, with Elizabeth, ae. 39, and children Jeremy, ae. 4, Samuel, ae. 2, and Remembrance, ae. 28, came in the James in July, 1635. Rem. to Dover.

Joane, before Es. Court in 1648.

Walter, came with Rev. Richard Blinman and others to Marshfield; and was prop. frm. 2 March, 1640-1, but did not remain. Settled at Gloucester. Frm. May 19, 1642. Selectman and constable 1643. [Ess. Court.] Licensed to sell wine 26 May, 1647.

He d. 14 (6) 1651. Will signed 5 (4), prob. 19 Oct. 1651. Beq. to his wife for her life and then to grand son Richard Dicke; to dau. Mary, her husband, Wm. Haskell, and their children; to son-in-law Edward Clarke, and to John and Joseph C.; to Elizabeth Dick, Elnor Bapsone, wife of James Bapsome, and to Zebulon Hill. Inv. filed in Ipswich court 1 (7) 1651. The widow m. John Harding, q. v.

TICKNALL,
Henry, ae. 15, came in the Hopewell in Sept. 1635.

TIDD, TYDD, see Tead.

TIFF, see Teff.

TIKE,
Robert, Salem, 1643.

TILDEN,
John, Scituate, atba. 1643. Perhaps a son of Nathaniel.

Nathaniel, yeoman, from Tenterden, Eng. came in the Hercules of Sandwich in March, 1634, bringing wife Lydia, 7 children and 7 servants. Settled at Scituate, where his house was noted by Parson Lothrop in Sept. 1634. Town officer, ruling elder. Dau. Mary m. March 13, 1636, Thomas Lapham; dau. Sarah m. same day George Sutton; Judith m. Abraham Preble.

His will, dated May 25, prob. July 31, 1641, beq. to wife, sons Joseph, Thomas and Ste-

TILDEN, cont.
phen, daus. Judith, Mary, Sarah and Lydia; to servants Edward Ginkins and Edward Tarte. Wife to have a house at Tenterden. The son Thomas, b. in 1621, deposed at prob. of R. Chapman's will; son Joseph was made exec. of the will of his father's bro. Joseph Tilden, citizen and girdler of London, Feb. 1, 1642. The widow Lydia and her daus. Mary and Sarah were legatees. The dau. Lydia afterward m. Richard Garrett. [Plym. Col. Rec. XII; Reg. IV, 173, and XXXVIII, 322.]

Thomas, came to Plymouth in 1623; had 3 lots assigned him.

TILER, see Tyler,
Job, a criminal at Mt. Wollaston in 1637. [W.]

TILESTON, TILSTON, TILESTONE,
Thomas, Dorchester, propr. 1634, frm. March 9, 1636-7. Juryman 1640; town officer. Wife Elizabeth; ch. Timothy, Elizabeth bapt. 3 (6) 1639, Ruth bapt. 3 (8) 1641, (m. 1, Richard Denton, 2, Timothy Foster,) Cornelius bapt. 17 (3) 1646, d. 20 (5) 1659, Naomi bapt. 7 (3) 1648, Bathshuba bapt. 16 (7) 1649, (m. John Payson,) Onesiphorus bapt. 19 (8) 1651.

He d. June 24, 1694, ae. 83 years. Will dated 19 Feb. prob. July 12, 1694, beq. to sons Timothy and Onesiphorus, and to the children of daus. Ruth Foster and Bathsheba Pason, dec.

TILL, TYLL, TYLLS,
James, Scituate, servant to John Emerson, 1637-9, and to Mr. Hatherly in 1643. Res. at or near New Haven in 1646. [A.]

Peter, servant of John Clois; the Court ordered his master to use him well and teach him the trade of a seaman or else discharge him, 31 (8) 1639. Peter, Boston, m. 26 (12) 1650, Elizabeth Nick. Bought land in 1662. The widow d. Nov. 26, 1690. Admin. of her est. gr. Aug. 25, 1691, to Thomas Downe.

TILLIE, TILLEY, TILLY, TELEY,
Mr. Edward, came in the Mayflower; signed the Compact; res. at Plymouth. Both he and his wife Ann who came with him died in the spring of 1621. They brought with them cousins Henry Samson and Humility Cooper. The former remained here;

TILLIE, etc., cont.

the latter was sent for into England, and died there. [B.]

John, came in the Mayflower; signed the Compact; res. at Plymouth. Took part in the explorations, and died from the exposure and hardships in the spring of 1621. He brought his wife and daughter Elizabeth. The wife d. about the same time as he; the dau. m. John Howland. [B. and Wins.]

Note. Among the marriages at Leyden, Holland, we find that of "Jan Telly, and Prijntgen van der Velde," 3 March, 1615, at Pieterskirk, (opposite the house of Mr. John Robinson). His trade was that of "saeijwercker," or say-weaver; he was accompanied by his father, Paulus Tellij, and the bride by her mother Maeijcken Tay, whose marriage is on record to Abraham van der Velde, 27 June, 1591. Many circumstances point to this as the John Tillie of the Mayflower; yet the date is late for the time of the birth of the eldest child of Elizabeth Howland; nor does it correspond to the age asserted for her at her death. It may be that this is a second marriage of J. T., and Elizabeth his child by a former wife; or that this Dutch wife died, and that Tillie m. a second wife, whose child by *her* former husband was the bride of John Howland.

Mr. John, Dorchester, came in the first company in 1629-30. [Bl.] Frm. March 4, 1634-5. Had a lot granted him July 5, 1636, as the great lot to his brother's home lot. Seems to have died soon; the house which had been his was ordered to be repaired. Mrs. Tilly's land mentioned in 1637 and 1660. She was a midwife in Boston, and for some reason was imprisoned; petitions of Bo. and Dorch. people for release were denied by the Gen. Court 23 May, 1650.

Nathaniel, ae. 32, came in the Abigail in May, 1635.

Thomas, Plymouth, court case 1636, atba. 1643.

William, ae. 28, cert. from the parish of Little Minories, Eng. came in the Abigail in June, 1635. William, Barnstable, atba. 1643. William, with wife Alice, sold dwelling-house at Boston 26 (4) 1649; by his authority Hugh Gunnison guaranteed the sale. His dau. Sarah m. 1, Henry Linn, 2. Hugh Gunnison, 3, — Mitchell. See H. G.

TILLOTSON, TILLISON,

John, Rowley, propr. about 1645; rem. to Newbury. Before the court in 1650. [Es. Files.] He m. 14 July, 1648, Dorcas Coleman; she d. 1 Jan. 1654. He m. 24 May, 1655, Jane Evans. Ch. a ch. b. and bur. in 1648, Mary b. 13 Feb. 1649, John b. 21 Feb. 1650, James b. 19 Dec. 1652, Philadelphia b. 28 Dec. 1656, Joseph b. 11 Jan. 1657, Jonathan b. 6 July, 1659.

TILLY *als.* **HILLIER,**

Hugh, came in the Lyon's Whelp to Salem in 1629, appointed to help in setting up a saw-mill. Rem. to Yarmouth. One of the witnesses to the will of Peter Werden in 1638; atba. 1643. Wife Rose; ch. Deborah b. 30 Oct. 1643, Samuel b. July, 1646.

Widow Tillye m. at Nocett Nov. 3, 1648, Thomas Higgins. [Scituate Chh. Rec.]

TILSON, TILLSON,

Edmond or Edward, Plymouth, had land grant 3 Sept. 1638; frm. 1 March, 1641-2. Juryman.

Admin. of his est. and allowance gr. to his widow Joane 5 March, 1660-1. [Reg. V, 338.]

TILTON,

John, Salem, 1641. The wife of his son John presented to the Court for opposing Infant Baptism in 1641.

TING, see Tyng.

TINKER, TINCKER,

John, planter, agent for Augustine Clement 27 (4) 1638. [L.] Res. at Boston; adm. chh. 5 (12) 1653; frm. May 3, 1654. He m. Sarah, divorced wife of William Barnes, q. v., and undertook to bring up the younger child, 13 (10) 1648, according to her will. He m. Alice —, who was adm. chh. 19 (4) 1653; ch. Sarah b. and d. 1651, Mary b. July 2, 1653, John bapt. 30 (7) 1655, Amos bapt. 16 (3) 1658.

John T., of Lancaster, trader, had dealings with Nomanacomak Nov. 9, 1659. [Suff. De. III, 307.]

Thomas, came in the Mayflower to Plymouth, with wife and a son; all died in the first sickness. [B.]

TINGLEY, TINGLE,
Palmer, miller, ae. 21, came in the Planter in April, 1635. Settled at Ipswich. Recd. land in 1639 for service in the Pequot war; sold before 1643.

TINKHAM, TINCUM,
Ephraim, servant to Timothy Hatherly; transferred in 1634 to John Winslow. Propr. 2 Aug. 1642. Ch. Ephraim b. 5 Aug. 1649, Ebenezer b. 30 Sept. 1651, Peter b. 25 Dec. 1653, Hezekiah b. 8 Feb. 1655, John b. 7 June, 1658, Mary b. 5 Aug. 1661, John b. 15 Nov. 1663, Isaac b. 11 April, 1666. He made will 17 Jan. 1683, prob. 5 June, 1685; beq. to wife Mary, ch. Ephraim, Ebenezer, Peter, Elkiah, John, Isaac, Mary Tomson.

TISDALE,
John, yeoman, Duxbury, brought suit in court 7 June, 1636; planter and propr. 5 Nov. 1638, atba. 1643, constable 1645. Of Taunton, Dec. 26, 1651, bought land at Dux. of Wm. Brett.

John, Sen., was killed by the Indians 27 June, 1675. His wife Sarah d. Dec., 1676. His will prob. 2 Nov. 1676, beq. to sons John, James, Joshua and Joseph; gave to daus. Elizabeth, Sarah, Mary and Abigail. The Court made note that the two younger had endangered their lives in protecting the property. [Plym. Col. Rec.] An agreement was made 4 June, 1677, between these four sons and the three sons-in-law, John Smith, James Dean and Nathaniel French.

TITCOMB,
William, yeoman, Newbury, frm. June 22, 1642. Deputy 1655. Town officer. He m. Joanna, dau. of Richard Bartlett; she d. June 28, 1653; he m. 3 March, 1654, Elizabeth, widow of William Stephens; ch. Sarah b. Feb. 17, 1640, Hannah b. 8 Jan. 1641, Mary b. 17 Feb. 1643, Milla (Millicent) b. 7 June, 1646, d. 20 Jan. 1664, William b. 18 March, 1648, d. 2 June, 1659, Penuel b. 16 Dec. 1650, Benajah b. 28 June, 1653, Elizabeth b. 12 Dec. 1654, Rebecca b. 1 April, 1656, Tirza b. 21 Feb. 1657, William b. 14 Aug. 1659, Thomas b. 11 Oct. 1661, Lydia b. 13 June, 1663, "Millesent" d. Feb. 8, 1663, John b. 17 Sept. 1664, Ann b. 7 July, 1666. Will dated 18 Sept. 1676, prob. at Ipswich 8 days later; beq. to daus. Sarah, Mary, Elizabeth Bartlett, Rebecca, Tersa, Lydia

TITCOMB, cont.
and Anne; to sons Bennia, William, Peniel, Thomas and John. Peniell heir and exec.

TITUS, TYTUS,
Robert, husbandman, ae. 35, with wife Hannah, ae. 21, and children John, ae. 8, and Edmond, ae. 5, came in the Hopewell in April, 1635. Settled at Boston. Had land adjoining Mr. Blackstone 14 (10) 1635. Frm. May 13, 1640. Rem. to Weymouth. Rem. about 1644 to Rehoboth. Frm. Plymouth Colony 7 June, 1650. Ch. rec. at Weymouth: Abiel b. 17 (1) 1640, Content b. 28 (1) 1643.

TOBEY, TOBY,
Francis, in court 7 July, 1635.

Thomas, Scituate; rem. to Sandwich; was a member of the chh. in 1694. He m. at Sandwich, 18 Nov. 1650, Martha Knott. Ch. Thomas b. Dec. 8, 1651.

TODD, TOD, TOOD,
John, clothier, merchant, Rowley, propr. early; taxed in 1650; juryman, 1651, town officer. Kept the ordinary. He deposed in 1672, ae. about 50 years. Wife Susanna; ch. Mehitabel b. 10 (11) 1649, John b. and d. 1645, Mary b. June 10, 1659, Susanna b. Sept. 5, 1664, Thomas b. 3 (10) 1665, Timothy b. May 2, 1668, James b. Feb. 8, 1671.

He d. 14 Feb. 1689; will prob. 25 March, 1690.

TOLLER,
Marie, ae. 16, came in the Increase April 15, 1635.

TOLMAN, TOULMAN, TOULEMAN, TOLEMAN,
Thomas, wheelwright, Dorchester, res. 1639, propr., frm. May 13, 1640. Town officer. Wife Sarah; ch. Sarah, (m. 18 (1) 1658-9, Henry Leadbetter,) Hannah bapt. 2 (6) 1639, Hannah b. 27 (5) 1642, *John* bapt. 31 (5) 1642, Ruth bapt. 7 (10) 1644. His wife Katharine d. Nov. 7, 1677.

He d. June 18, 1690. Will dated Oct. 29, 1688, in his 80th year, prob. 5 (12) 1691. Eldest son Thomas; daus. Sarah Leadbetter, Rebecca Tucker, Ruth Ryall, Hannah Lyon and Mary Collins; son John Tolman; James Tucker, husband of Rebecca, to pay a certain sum to Isaac Ryall's two eldest daus. Ruth and Mary. [Reg. XV.]

TOMLIN, TOMLINE, TOMLYN, THOMLINS, TOMLINS, TOMLYNS,

Mr. Edward, Lynn, propr., frm. May 18, 1631. Ordered by Gen. Court Sept. 3, 1634, to impress men for the manufacture of military supplies. Deputy 1634. Foreman of jury, 1636.

Edward, ae. 30, and Benjamin, ae. 18, came in the Susan and Ellen in April, 1635. Propr. at Lynn, 1638; constable 31 (1) 1641. [Es. Court.] He and Timothy T. and Mr. Hansard Knowles and others, warned from claims on Long Island 28 (7) 1641. Capt. Ed. Tomlins, of London, gent. bought land of Jos. Rednape of Lynn Feb. 1, 1648.

Mr. Timothy, Cambridge, propr. 1635; frm. March 4, 1632; rem. to Lynn; propr. 1638. Licensed to keep house of entertainment at Saugus 8 Sept. 1636. Deputy.

TOMPKINS, TOMKIN, TOMKINS,

John, Salem, 1636, frm. May 18, 1642. Wife Margaret; ch. Hannah bapt. 10 (12) 1638, Elizabeth bapt. 19 (3) 1639, Hannah bapt. 21 (12) 1640, Sarah bapt. 1 (11) 1642, (m. 1 (6) 1663, John Waters,) Elizabeth b. 29 (9) bapt. 17 (11) 1646, Mary bapt. 29 (2) 1649, Deborah bapt. 8 (4) 1651. Wife Margaret d. 18 (5) 1672. He m. Sept. 1673, Mary Read.

He d. 23 June, 1681.

John, Concord. Ch. Ruth b. 1 (4) 1640, John b. 25 (7) 1642.

Ralph, husbandman, ae. 50, with wife Katharine, ae. 58, and ch. Samuel, ae. 22, Elizabeth, ae. 18, and Marie, ae. 14, came in the Truelove in Sept. 1635. Res. at Dorchester in 1637 and later. Frm. May 2, 1638. Rem. to Salem. Planter. Sold house, lands and common rights 2 (4) 1648, to John Farnham of Dorch. Wife Katharine adm. chh. 3 (2) 1642; Martha, (m. John Foster,) John bapt. 16 (12) 1644, (he deposed in 1670, ae. about 25 years). He expressed his mind about disposing of his estate to his bro. Samuel Eborne and Nathaniel Felton just after the burial of his wife, before he removed to Bridgewater to his son Samuel. Would carry out agreement made with his wife at marriage; would talk with his son Foster.

Admin. gr. 12 (9) 1666, to son John, who had the land; rest to Mary, dau. of John Foster.

TOMPSON, see also Thompson,

Rev. William, curate of the church of Winwick, Lancashire, some time; there his son Eliezer was bapt. Oct. 21, 1635. He came to New England in 1636 or 1637; joined the chh. of Dorchester, of which his life-long friend Mr. Richard Mather was pastor. Preached a while at Accomenticus, (Kittery;) then came to Braintree, where he was installed pastor, with Mr. Henry Flint as teacher, Nov. 19, 1639. He was "a very gracious, sincere man,—an instrument of much good,—a man of much faith." [W.] He was selected as the leader of the party of ministers sent by the Mass. Bay government to Virginia in 1643 to present to that colony the distinctive principles of the churches and government of New England. He wrote, in conjunction with Mr. Mather, a book entitled "An Answer to Mr. Charles Herle," reviewing the history of affairs in Lancashire in which they had taken part. He was adm. frm. May 13, 1640. He m. in England Abigail —, who d. Jan. 1, 1642-3. He m. 2, Annah, widow of Simon Crosby, who survived him. She is called "An Tomson" in Cambridge records in 1646. Ch. Samuel b. Feb. 16, 1630, William, Eliezer, Mary, Elinor, Joseph b. 1 (3) 1640, Benjamin b. 14 (5) 1642.

He d. 10 (10) 1666, "in the 69th year of his age." [D.] His widow d. 11 (8) 1675.

TOOGOOD, TWOGOOD,

John, sent 1 (10) 1640, by the Gen. Court to the wife of Thomas Marshfield of Conn., to whom his father Robert Fen had appr. him.

TOOKIE, see Tucky.

TOOTHAKER,

Roger, ae. 23, with Margaret, ae. 28, and child Roger, ae. 1, came in the Hopewell in Sept. 1635. Settled at Plymouth.

He d. soon; lands granted to his widow Margaret 5 Feb. 1637-8. She m. 21 Dec. 1638, Ralph Hill.

TOPPER, TAPP,

Thomas, had beq. of 5 li. from Dennis Geere of Lynn 10 Dec. 1635. Joan, Lynn, sued persons for defamation in 1639.

TOPPAN, TAPPAN, TOPPING, TAPPING,

Abraham, cooper, of Yarmouth, Eng. ae. 31, Susanna his wife, ae. 30, children Peter and Elizabeth, and servant Anne Goodin, passed exam. May 10, 1637, to go to N. E. Came to Newbury, where he had lands and house; was town officer. Elizabeth m. Samuel Mighill. Other ch. Isaac, Abraham, Jacob b. Dec. 24, 1644, Susanna b. 13 June, 1649, a child d. Feb. 12, 1649, John b. 23 April, 1651.

He d. Nov. 5, 1672. Will dated 7 June, 1670, prob. 25 March, 1673; beq. to wife Susan; sons Peter, Jacob, (about to marry Hannah Sewall,) Abraham, Isaac and John; to son-in-law Samuel Mighill. The widow Susanna who had deposed 9 Dec. 1670, ae. 66 years, d. March 20, 1689. Genealogy; [Reg. XXXIII and XXXIV.]

George, Charlestown, d. 14 (..) 1650. [Mdx. Rec.]

Richard, draper, Boston, adm. chh. with wife Judith (9) 1633, frm. March 4, 1633-4. He sold to Thomas Robinson of Scituate, Aug. 29, 1654, all houses and lands in Boston, his wife Alice co-signing. His wife Judith d. in 1635; he m. 2, Alice —, who was adm. chh. 17 (2) 1647. Ch. Timothy b. and d. 1633, Joseph b. and d. 1645, Joseph bapt. 11 (4) 1648, ae. about 15 days, Benjamin bapt. 21 (5) 1650.

TOPLIFF, TOPLEY, TAPLEY, TOPLIF,

Clement, Dorchester, propr. about 1637; adm. chh. 4 (12) 1639, frm. May 13, 1640. Herdsman, 1653. One of the signers to the Thompson's Island agreement 7 (12) 1641. Wife Sarah adm. chh. about 1638; ch. Jonathan b. (2) 1637, Sarah bapt. 26 (3) 1639, Obedience bapt. 2 (8) 1642, (m. 20 Feb. 1659, David Cope,) Samuel bapt. 10 (3) 1646, Patience, (m. 27 (1) 1667, Nathaniel Homes).

He d. Dec. 24, 1672, ae. 69 years. Will dated 26 Jan. 1666, prob. 31 Jan. 1672. Beq. to wife Sarah; ch. Samuel Toplif, David Jones, David Cope, Patience Toplif. The widow Sarah d. July 29, 1693, ae. 88 years.

TORREY, TORY,

James, Scituate, lieut., frm. 8 June, 1655. He deposed in 1657, ae. 44 years. He m. 2 Nov. 1643, Ann, dau. of William Hatch; ch. James b. 3 Sept. 1644, William b. March 15, 1646, Joseph b. March 18, 1648, Damaris b. 26 Oct. 1651, Jonathan b. 20 Sept. 1654, Mary b. 14 Feb. 1656, Josiah b. 28 Jan. 1658, Sarah b. 9 Feb. 1660, Joanna b. 4 May, 1663, Bethiah b. July 19, 1665.

He d. July 6, 1665, and inv. was pres. by his widow Ann Oct. 11, 1665. [Reg. V, 338, and VI, 187.]

Joseph, one of the purchasers at Rehoboth, 1643; juryman 1646, frm. 7 June, 1648; in court 1650.

Philip, yeoman, from Combe St. Nicholas, co. Somerset, Eng., came in 1640 to Roxbury. Frm. May 18, 1642. He deposed 5 March, 1673-4, as to his history; was ae. about 59 years; testified to his acquaintance with William Torrey and his son Samuel, who came with him from the same place, and whom he had known ever since. Statements confirmed by George Fry. [Suff. De. VIII, 392, and Arch. XV, A, 11.] [Reg. XL, 62.] He m. Oct. 1, 1647, Mary, dau. of Robert Smith, and widow of John Scarbarow; ch. Joseph b. and d. 1649, Jonathan bapt. 22 (4) 1651, Mary bapt. 9 (2) 1654.

He was bur. 16 (3) 1686.

William, from Combe St. Nicholas, Somerset, came in 1640, and settled at Weymouth. Captain, commissioner, town officer, deputy. A good penman and skilled in the Latin tongue, usually clerk of the deputies. [J.] His son Samuel, who came with him, became pastor of the chh. of Weymouth in 1664. He had life-lease of ground in Bristol, called The Torreys, in possession of John Hollister, whose will refers to it Sept. 12, 1690. [Reg. XL, 62.] Ch. Naomi b. 3 (10) 1641, [13 (10) 1640,] Mary b. 3 (10) 1642. [Aug. 4, 1642.] Mycajah b. 12 (8) 1643, [12 (10) 1643,] Angel b. June 4, 1657.

Will dated 15 May, 1686, prob. July 2, 1691, beq. to sons Samuel, William, Micajah; to wife and her sons Josiah and Angel; to gr. dau. Hayward.

TOTMAN, TATMAN,

John, embarked for New Eng. June 2, 1632; came to Roxbury. Frm. May 2, 1638. Propr. Wife Joannah d. Sept. 29, 1668. Ch. Jabez b. Nov. 19, 1641.

He d. Oct. 28, 1670; will dated 30 (7) prob. 13 (9) 1670, beq. all to his only son Jabez.

TOSE,
John, planter, Hingham, defendant in a lawsuit, 1639. [L.]

TOTTINGHAM,
Henry, yeoman, Woburn, propr. 1640. He deposed in 1658, ae. about 50 years. His wife Anna d. Feb. 23, 1653-4; he m. July 13, 1654, Alice Eager. [Mdx. Court Rec.] Will dated 16 (7) 1678, prob. April 1, 1679, beq. to son Nehemiah and to children he may have; to son Elijah; a token to the minister, Rev. Thomas Carter.

TOWER, TOWERS,
John, planter, Hingham, propr. 1637; frm. 13 March, 1638-9. Before Gen. Court 1640 and 1645. He deposed 9 Jan. 1676, ae. about 69 years. [To. Rec.] He m. Feb. 13, 1638, Margaret, dau. of Richard Ibrook; she d. 15 May, 1700. Ch. John b. Dec. 13, 1639, Jonathan b. Aug. 1, 1641, Ibrook b. Feb. 1643, Jeremiah b. March 9, 1645-6, Elizabeth b. June 4, 1648, (m. Wm. Roberts,) Sarah b. July 16, 1650, Hannah b. July 17, 1652, (m. David Whipple,) Benjamin b. Nov. 5, 1654, Jemina b. April 25, 1659, Samuel b. Jan. 26, 1661.
He d. 13 Feb. 1701-2.

TOWLE, TOLL,
John, Sudbury, propr. 1644, frm. May, 1645, town officer, 1647. Wife Katharine; ch. John b. 20 (9) 1641, d. 31 (11) 1642, Mary b. 8 (10) 1643, Rebecca b. 5 (3) 1646, John b. 28 (12) 1647.

Roger, Boston, servant to Henry Webb in 1639. [L.] Frm. May 29, 1644.

TOWN, TOWNE,
Edmund, apprentice to Henry Skerry, came in 1637 to Salem. Sergeant. Rem. to Topsfield. Wife Mary; ch. Sarah b. 26 April, 1657, d. in 1661 and — d. in 1662-3. His est. was divided 27 (4) 1678, as his widow declared he had wished, to herself, 4 sons and 5 daus. Distribution in 1682 to ch. Edmund, Jacob, Joseph, Rebecca, wife of Francis Nurse, and Sarah Bridges.

John, Springfield, a witness to the Indian deed in 1636.

William, planter, Cambridge, propr. 1635. Wife Martha; ch. Peter bapt. in Eng-

TOWN, etc., cont.
land, and about 3 years old when his parents joined Camb. chh.; [Mi.] Mary b. (7) 1637. His wife d. Jan. 20, 1673-4.
He d. March 30, 1685, ae. 80. Inv. taken 26 May, 1685.

William, gardiner, Salem, frm. April 18, 1637. Rem. to Topsfield. With wife Joanna deeded land to son Joseph in 1663, when he was about to marry Phebe, dau. of Thomas Perkins. Joanna was recd. from Sal. chh. to that of Tops. 19 (4) 1664. She deposed in 1670, ae. 70 years; he deposed in 1660, ae. about 60 years.

TOWNSEND, TOWNSHEND,
Thomas, Lynn, propr. 1638, frm. March 14, 1638-9. He deposed in 1661, ae. about 60 years. He was a bro.-in-law of John Newgate of Boston, who made a beq. to him in 1665.
He d. 22 (10) 1677.

Christopher, scrivener, witnessed a bond in Boston 9 (8) 1645.

William, baker, husbandman, Boston, servant to Nicholas Willys, adm. chh. 3 (6) 1634, frm. May 25, 1636. Sold land in 1651. He deposed 17 (7) 1668, ae. about 67 years. Wife Hannah, sister of elder James Penn; ch. Eleazer bapt. 12 (4) 1636, Patience bapt. 28 (3) 1637, Hannah b. 4 (2) 1641, (m. 1, 3 April, 1657, Thomas Hull 2, Hope Allen, 3, Richard Knight, 4, Richard Way,) Peter b. 26 (8) 1642, Mary bapt. 24 (9) 1644, ae. about 7 days, d. 29 Nov. 1658, James b. 15 (11) 1646, Isaiah bapt. 5 (9) 1648, ae. about 3 days, Deborah bapt. 25 (6) 1650, (m. Nathl. Thayer,) Penn b. 20 (10) 1651, John b. 3 Sept. 1653, d. 17 (6) 1654.
He d. in 1669; inv. taken 27 (7) 1669; admin. gr. to widow Hannah 29 Oct.; division made 20 Oct. 1669, between Nathaniel Thayer, husband of Deborah, Hannah (then Knight,) and James, Peter and Penn T. The widow taught school in 1691; she d. Jan. 17, 1699-1700, in her 93d year. [S.] Inv. rendered by son Penn T. 26 March folg.

TOY,
William, laborer, husbandman, distiller of strong water, Boston, adm. chh. 8 (8) 1642, frm. May 27, 1663. Rem. to Billerica, whence he sold lands in Bo. Oct. 5, 1663. He m. Sept. 14, 1644, Grace, dau. of Abraham

TOY, cont.
Newell; ch. Grace b. 23 (6) 1645, John bapt. 21 (9) 1647, ae. about 5 days, Isaiah bapt. 10 (1) 1650, ae. about 7 days, Abiel b. 21 Jan. 1652, Nathaniel b. 23 Feb. 1654, *Peter* bapt. 25 (12) 1654, Jeremiah b. 18 July, 1657, Elizabeth b. June 25, 1660.

The widow Grace d. at Roxbury 11 April, 1712, in her 91st year.

TRACY, TRACE,
Thomas, ship-carpenter, Watertown, rem. to Salem in 1636. [Sal. Town Rec.]

Stephen, say-maker, youngman, from England, accompanied by Anthony Clemens, married at Leyden, Holland, Dec. 18, 1621, Trifose Le —, maid, of England. He came to Plymouth in 1623. Frm. 1633. Res. at Duxbury. Town officer 1638-9. His wife Triphosa and ch. Sarah and Rebecca had shares in cattle in 1627. Ret. to England; was at Great Yarmouth 20 March, 1654-5; gave power of attorney to John Winslow to divide his lands and chattels at D. between his son John, dau. Ruth and the rest of his five ch. living in N. E. [Ply. Deeds, II.]

William, came in the Mary and John March 24, 1633-4.

TRAIN, TRAINE, TRANE,
John, ae. 25, came in the Susan and Ellen in April, 1635. Settled at Watertown; propr. 1636; husbandman; took oath of fidelity 1652. He deposed 20 (10) 1664, ae. about 50 years. [Mdx. Files.] He m. Margaret —, who d. 18 (10) 1660, ae. about 44 years. He m. Oct. 12, 1675, Abigail Bent, who d. Aug. 17, 1691. Ch. Elizabeth b. 30 (7) 1640, Mary b. 10 (8) 1642, Rebecca, (m. Michael Barstow,) Sarah b. 3 (11) 1646, Abigail b. 31 (11) 1648, John b. May 25, 1651, Thomas, Hannah b. Sept. 7, 1657.

He d. Jan. 29, 1680-1. Will prob. April 4, 1681, beq. to wife Abigail; sons John and Thomas; daus. Elizabeth Stratton, Rebecca Basto, Sarah Cole, Abigail Towning and Hannah Child, and their ch.; to dau. Mary Memory's ch. John, Samuel, Joseph and Mary.

TRASK, TRASKE,
Osman, Osmund, planter, Salem, propr. before 1649. Rem. to Beverly; constable. He deposed in 1665, ae. about 38 years. He m. 1 (11) 1649, Mary —; she d. 2 Jan. 1661,

TRASK, etc., cont.
and he m. 2, May 22, 1663, Eliza Galley. Ch. Sarah b. (7) 1650, Edward b. 6 (4) 1652, Mary b. (3) 1657, John b. 15 (6) 1658, William b. and d. 1660.

He d. about 1676. Inv. of his est. taken 5 March, 1676, filed by widow Elizabeth in Ipswich court 27 March, 1677. One of the items is 2 pounds due from John Traske his brother's son. The court made the widow admin. and placed the rest in her hands; she to give the eldest son 40 acres of land with house upon it; the other 8 children, Sarah, Mary, Samuel, Benjamin, Joseph, Elizabeth, William and Jonathan, to have 50 pounds apiece; the same for the expected child. The widow deeded land to her five sons, Samuel, Benjamin, Joseph, William and Edward T. 27 March, 1679, to be delivered after she had paid the legacies due to daus. Sarah, Mary and Elizabeth. [Ips. De. IV, 242.]

Mr. William, a very early resident of Salem, certainly by 1628; memb. chh. Aug. 6, 1629, appl. frm. Oct. 19, 1630. Com. of Gen. Court in 1632; deputy. Captain of the East regiment, and muster master. Commanded a company in the Pequot war in 1637. Had large tracts of land for his services. Set up a water-mill for grinding corn and a fulling mill before 1640. [Es. Court Files.] He deposed in the Dexter case, 22 (2) 1657, ae. about 69 years; depos. also 29 Nov. 1664, ae. 77 years, that he was one of the lot-layers of the town about 34 years ago. This age corresponds with a deposition made by William Trask in London, Jan. 15, 1623, ae. 34, when about to go to Delft, Holland. Wife Sarah; ch. Mary bapt. 1 (11) 1636, Susanna bapt. 10 (4) 1638, (m. 19 (12) 1663, Samuel Eborne,) William bapt. 19 (7) 1640, John bapt. 18 (7) 1642, Eliza bapt. 21 (7) 1645, Mary bapt. 2 (8) 1652, Anna (dau. of Mary,) bapt. 18 (4) 1654, Sarah (of sister T.) bapt. 14 (7) 1656. [Henry, adult in Salem in 1652; no token of relationship in records. The mention of John T., his brother's son, in inv. of Osman T., seems to prove him a brother of William.]

He d. May 15, 1666. Will dated May 15, prob. June 24, 1666. Beq. to wife Sarah provision for her life; to sons William and John; to daus. Sarah, Susan and Mary; to grand children. Inv. taken May 15, 1666. [See Genealogy in Reg. XI, 257, and LIII, 43.]

TRAVELL, TREVELL, TREBLE,
Henry, Marblehead, a witness in 1646.

John, accused by Jane Moulton in 1640. [L.]

Nathaniel, before Gen. Court 30 (2) 1640.

TRAVERS,
Henry, came in the Mary and John March 24, 1633-4. Settled at Newbury; propr. 1637. Wife Bridget; ch. Sarah, James b. 28 April, 1645.

He made will July 26, 1648. Ret. to England and d. there. The widow m. March 30, 1659, Richard Windorr or Window of Gloucester, with whom she sold land in 1659.

TREADWAY,
Nathaniel, Sudbury, propr. 1639; rem. to Watertown. Town officer. Wife Sufferana or Sufrany d. July 22, 1682; ch. Jonathan b. Nov. 11, 1640, Mary b. Aug. 1, 1642, Elizabeth b. 3 (2) 1646, Deborah b. 2 (6) 1657, Lydia, (m. Oct. 2, 1667, Josiah Jones,) James, Josiah.

He d. July 20, 1689. Will names sons Jonathan, James and Josiah; dau. Mary Hawkins' children, Jonathan Fisher and Mary H.; children of dau. Haward by her husbands Hapgood and Haward; sons-in-law Josiah Jones and Joseph Goddard; kinsman John Jacuas.

TREADWELL, TREDWELL,
Edward, Ipswich, had a lot granted to him by the Gen. Court 2 Nov. 1637, and other lots by the town later.

Thomas, smith, ae. 30, with wife Mary, ae. 30, and child Thomas, ae. 1, came in the Hopewell in July, 1635. Settled at Dorchester. Propr. 1636-7. Suit against him in Gen. Court 29 (6) 1036. Sold all est. 20 June, 1638. Rem. to Ipswich; propr. 1635. Purchased house and lands 27 (4) 1638. [Ips. Rec.] Ch. Mary b. 29 Sept. 1636, Nathaniel b. 13 (March) 1640, [H....] b. 21 March, 1643, Martha b. 16 March, 1643. [Es. Files VII, 48.]

His will dated 1 June, prob. 26 Sept. 1671, beq. to wife; sons Thomas and Nathaniel; daus. Mary, [Ester] and Martha. "My sister Bachellor" is mentioned. The widow Mary filed the inv. 26 (7) 1671.

TRENTUM,
Thomas, ae. 14, came in the Blessing in July, 1635.

TRESCOTT,
William, husbandman, Dorchester, frm. May 10, 1643. He m. Elizabeth, dau. of George Dyer. With wife Elizabeth sold land in D. 27 March, 1665. She d. July 31, 1699. He admin. March 20, 1654-5, on the est. of his bro. Thomas, mariner, of Boston. He d. Sept. 11, 1699, ae. 84 years, 8 months. Made will 9 Aug. 1699, prob. 25 Oct. 1699; beq. to sons Samuel and John; to dau. Martha Adams and her ch. Mercy, Mary and Martha Huens; to dau. Abigail and her ch. Amiel and George Weeks; to dau. Sarah Modesly; to gr. ch. Joseph Trescott. Bequests made to his wife Elizabeth by her father Dyer, late of Dorch. are to be given as he directed in his will.

TREBLE,
John, accused of crime in 1640. [L.]

TRERICE, TRERISE, TREROISE, TRARICE,
Nicholas, mariner, master of the ship Planter, 1635-9, settled at Charlestown. Propr. also at Woburn in 1640. He mortg. all his lands in Char., Linefield and Mistickfield to Joshua Foote, ironmonger, of London, 10 (10) 1644. Rem. to Woburn. Wife Elizabeth adm. chh. 12 (3) 1639; ch. John b. 26 (3) bapt. 3 (4) 1639, Samuel b. 7 (3) 1643. He m. second wife Rebecca, who deposed 2 (2) 1662, ae. 56 years; acknowledged the sale of land formerly her husband's to Edward Johnson, and filed copy of the admin. papers gr. by the court at Boston on the estate of Nicholas Trerise, dated 6 (7) 1653. Mary Lock witnessed her deed, and William Lock testified with her. [Mdx. Files.] The widow Rebecca m. 22 (2) 1655, Thomas Genner [Jenner.]

TREVORE, TREVOUR, TREVOYRE,
William, a seaman, came in Mayflower; was hired to stay a year in this country; when his time was out he returned to England. [B.] He testified in 1650 before Increase Nowell, probably at Charlestown, that he was here in 1619 and took possession of "the island of Trevour" for David Thompson. [Reg. IX, 248.] See Thompson, David.

TRESLER, TRUSLER, TRUSLOE,
Thomas, Salem, propr., 1639; frm. Dec. 27, 1642. Constable 4 (7) 1643. [Es. Court.] Clerk of the Market; refuted charges brought against him before Gen. Court in 1650. Wife Eleanor memb. chh. 1639.
He d. March 5, 1653-4. Inv. on file. The will of his widow Eleanor dated 15 Feb. 1654, prob. 26 (4) 1655, beq. to sons Henry, Nicholas and Edward; two daus; gr. ch. John Phelps and others; a legacy left by her late husband to a dau. in Eng. [Reg. XXXI, 103.] The inv. mentions son-in-law Edward Phelps.

TROTT, TROT,
Thomas, Dorchester, propr., town officer; frm. May 29, 1644. Wife Sarah; ch. Preserved bapt. 19 (1) 1646, (m. 11 (5) 1667, John Baker,) Sarah bapt. 12 (1) 1654, (m. June 2, 1675, Bernard Capen,) Mary b. 26 (11) 1656, Samuel b. 27 (6) 1660, John b. 24 (9) 1664, Thankful bapt. 5 (11) 1667, ae. about 6 weeks, James b. 2 (4) 1671, Thomas, Jr. a father in 1682.
He d. July 28, 1696, ae. about 82 years. Will prob. Sept. 10, 1696, beq. to son Thomas' children Thomas and Mary, and his widow; to sons John, James and Samuel, and daus. Preserved Baker, Sarah Capen and Thankful Kinsley; and to wife Sarah.

TROWBRIDGE, TROBRIDGE,
Mr. Thomas, merchant, gent. Dorchester, propr. before 1637, rem. to Boston; res. 20 (7) 1639, and was of New Haven before 12 (8) 1647. [A.] Wife memb. chh. about 1637; ch. James bapt. in 1637-8, (m. 30 (10) 1659, Margaret, dau. of Maj. Humphrey Atherton, and rem. to Newton).

TRUANT, TROUANT,
Morris, Dorchester, 1630, [Col. Rec.] Duxbury, atba. 1643; town officer. Rem. to Marshfield about 1647; constable 1650. He m. 16 Oct. 1639, Jane —.
He d. April 21, 1685. Will dated 31 Dec. 1678, prob. Oct. 20, 1685, beq. to wife Jane; ch. John, Joseph, Mary, Elizabeth, Mehetabel and Hannah.

TROTMAN,
John, bought house and land in Boston; ret. to London, and sent power of attorney 16 (12) 1644, to his wife Katharine in Bo. by virtue of which she sold it 28 (4) 1645.

TRUE, TREW,
Henry, Salem, propr. before 1646. [Es. Files.] Rem. to Salisbury; bought house and lot in 1657. He m. Israel, dau. of John Pike, Sen.; she survived him, and m. 2, June 18, 1660, Joseph Fletcher. Ch. John bapt. 13 (5) 1645, Henry b. 8 (1) 1646, bapt. 14 (1) 1647, Lydia bapt. 4 (12) 1648, Joseph bapt. 8 (12) 1651, Benjamin bapt. 19 (12) 1653, Jemima bapt. 26 (2) 1657.
His est. was settled upon his son John by Salis. court 10 (2) 1660. [Norf. co. De. III, 85.]

TREWORGY, TRUEWORTHY,
John, Newbury, son of James and Katharine (Shapleigh) T., m. 15 Jan. 1646, Mrs. Penuel Spencer, [perhaps dau. of John S.] Ch. John b. 12 Aug. 1649. [See Reg. V, 345.] His mother m. 2, Edward Hilton. [Will in Norf. De. III, pt. 3, 115.] *
*Mrs. Katharine Hilton, dau. of Alexander Shapleigh, wife, first of James Treworthy, second of Edward Hilton, made nunc. will, attested at Hampton Court 30 May, 1676. Beq. to James, son of John Treworthy, a silver beaker, to be kept in the hands of her dau. Elizabeth Gilman till he comes of age; to James, son of John T.; to Edward Hilton, Jr.; to gr. ch. Samuel and Mary G. and Joanna Merideth; to Mr. Samuel Dudley; to daus. Joanna M. and Elizabeth G.; to Abigail, wife of Edward G.; to Betty, Katharine, Sarah and Lydia G.; to Mrs. Lucie Wells, goodwife Robinson and Jane H. Son-in-law Capt. John Gilman exec. Mr. Wells to be paid. Rest to be divided among all her gr. ch.

TRUESDALE, TRUESDELL,
Richard, Boston, servant to Mr. John Cotton, adm. chh. 27 (5) 1634; frm. March 4, 1634-5. Became a butcher. Deacon. He deposed 28 Jan. 1670, ae. about 64 years.
His will dated 9 Sept. 1669, verbally amended before his death, was proved in Jan. 1671-2. Beq. to wife Mary; cousins Samuel, Rebecca, Thomas and Richard T.; kinsman William Gilbert; Mr. Cotton's 3 children, Seaborn, John and Maria Mather. The widow, in her will prob. Nov. 26, 1674, beq. to these persons, mentioning Rebecca wife of her cousin Wm. Gilbert, and her son W. G. Jr.; to cousin Wm. Emblin; bro. John Hood's 2 children; to Mr. Thos. Thatcher; to the first and third churches of Boston.

TRUMBULL, TRUMBLE, TRUMLE, TRUMMELL,
John, ship-master, mariner, Charlestown, in Court 7 March, 1636-7; propr.; frm. May 13, 1640. Res. at Cambridge 1638-1643; was living in 1655, ae. 80. [Wyman.] Went to London to hear Mr. Sedgwick preach before coming to N. E.; and made notes of the sermon. [Rel.] Wife Elizabeth adm. chh. Char. 27 (9) 1652; ch. Elizabeth b. (4) 1638, John b. 4 (6) 1641, Hannah b. 10 (10) 1642, Mary b. at Char. 9 (12) 1644, James b. 7 (10) 1647.
The widow Elizabeth d. in 1696, ae. 86.

John, Roxbury, propr. and memb. chh. about 1640. Agreed to division of the Thousand acre tract 20 (11) 1657.

John, Rowley, propr. about 1643; selectman, 1650; kept the book. Land given for keeping school, confirmed to his son John. He m. (6) 1650, Ann, widow of Michael Hopkinson. Ch. Abigail, (m. — Baily,) Mary, (m. — Kilburne,) and John.
He was bur. 18 (5) 1657. Inv. ret. by widow Ann 29 (7) 1657. She m. afterward Richard Swan, q. v. [Reg. XXXI, 115.]

Ralph, Marshfield, atba. 1643.

TROWTON,
Thomas, witness of a deed of Watertown property, 19 (12) 1645.

TUBBS,
William, Plymouth, Duxbury, atba. 1643. Brought suit in 1635 against John Barnes. Frm. 7 Feb. 1636-7. Volunteer in the Pequot war in 1637. He m. 9 Nov. 1637, Mercy Sprague. She went to Rhode Island, and he obtained a divorce from her 7 July, 1668.
He d. 2 (3) 1688; will dated Feb. 20, 1677, prob. June 13, 1688. Wife Dorothy; ch. Samuel, William, Bethiah, Benjamin and Joseph. [Gen. Adv. I, 19.]

TUCK,
Robert, vintner, Watertown, propr. 1636; a pioneer at Hampton (7) 1638. Frm. Sept. 7, 1639.
He. d. at Hampton; inv. taken 17 Nov. 1664. His widow Johannah d. 14 Feb. 1673; double inv. rend. in April, 1674. John Samborne, the adminr., and John Sherbourn, part heir to the est., made an agreement

TUCK, cont.
with William, son of Robert Tuck, of Gorlston, near Yarmouth, Eng., a son of the above, 25 (12) 1674. John Tuck of Hampton, carpenter, gr. son of R. T. Sen., recd. a share 26 (12) 1673.

Thomas, blacksmith, Salem, propr. 1636. Made the iron work for the carriages of the "peeces" [guns] in 1644. He deposed in 1667, ae. 55 years.

TUCKER,
George, Marblehead, in court (10) 1647.

John, yeoman, Watertown, propr. before 1636; rem. to Hingham. Propr. 1635-6. Admin. 25 (11) 1659, upon est. of Marg. Johnson, who beq. to his dau. Mary. Wife — d. 23 May, 1644; he m. 2, June 11, 1649, Ann, widow of William Nolton or Knowlton; ch. John, Joseph bur. 5 Dec. 1642, Mary bapt. Oct. 8, 1640, (m. Dec. 30, 1660, Joseph Church).
He d. Aug. 5, 1661; nunc. will prob. Aug. 15; wife Anne; son John; dau. Mary; goodwife Jacob who hath been a mother to me and mine; goodwife Beal; Mr. Hubbard, *et als*. The widow d. Oct. 8, 1675; will prob. 26 (8) 1675. Beq. to her gr. ch. Paul Gifford and his sister Susanna Jewell. [Reg. X, 269, and XXXI, 178.]

John, Salem, 1644. Sawed the boards for the meeting house in 1644.

Robert, Weymouth, town officer, 1643. Ch. Sarah b. 17 (1) 1639. Rem. to Gloucester; town officer, 1650. Wife Elizabeth; ch. Ebenezer d. 1652, Experience b. and d. 1652, Ephraim b. 27 (6) 1653. Rem. to Milton; selectman, 1677.
Will dated 7 March, prob. 30 March, 1681-2, beq. to sons James, Joseph, Manasseh, Ephraim, Benjamin; daus. Rebecca Feno, Elizabeth Clap, Mary Jones, and Wife Elizabeth; bro.-in-law Dea. Henry Allen, of Boston.

TUCKY, TOOKIE,
John, Charlestown, adm. chh. 12 (2) 1650.
He made will Aug. 16, 1665, prob. March 2, 1667; beq. to his master William Bachelder and his dame Bridget Wines, widow.

TUFTS,
John, came in 1638 from Hingham, Eng., to our Hingham, as a servant to Thomas Cooper.

Peter, yeoman, planter, Charlestown, propr., ferryman in 1646 with his brother-in-law William Bridges. Rem. to Malden. Frm. 3 May, 1665. He m. Mary Pierce; ch. Peter, James, John b. 7 (3) 1653, Mary b. 10 (4) 1655, Jonathan b. 1657, d. 1658, Jonathan b. 3 (1) 1660, Elizabeth, Mercy, Sarah.

He d. May 13, 1700, ae. 83. Will dated 1 March, 1693, codicil dated July 8, 1695, prob. June 10, 1700, beq. to wife Mary; sons Peter, Jonathan and John; daus. Mary, widow of John Eades; Elizabeth, wife of Joseph Lynde; Mercy, widow of Joseph Waite, called Mercy Jenkins in codicil; and Sarah, wife of Thomas Oakes; to gr. ch. James Tufts, the 3 sons of Peter, and all other gr. ch. The widow d. Jan. 10, 1702-3, ae. 75. [Genealogy in Reg. LI, 299.]

TUPPER,
Thomas, shoemaker, Lynn, propr. April 3, 1637. Ch. — b. Jan. 16, 1638. Rem. to Sandwich; atba. 1643. In Court March 1, 1641. Thomas who had ch. b. 1675, may be his son.

Thomas, Sen., d. 28 March, 1676, in 98th year and 2d month. Anne, [his widow,] d. 4 June, 1676, in 90th year.

TURBALL,
Thomas, Watertown, had land adj. that of Thomas Streit in 1648.

TURGES, see Sturges,
Mr., Cambridge, propr. 1642.

TURLAND,
Ann, Salem, dau. of Jarvis Garfoard, propr. 1635.

TURNER,
Charles, Salem, in Court in 1639.

Daniel, Duxbury, atba. 1643. Daniel, Springfield, 1645, escaped from prison. [Pynchon.]

Elizabeth, ae. 20, came in the Hopewell in April, 1635. Elizabeth, Salem, memb. chh. 1637.

Humphrey, tanner, [Col. Rec. 1643,] Plymouth; frm. 1632-3. Rem. to Scituate;

TURNER, cont.
memb. chh. 1634. Town officer. Ch. Mary bapt. Jan. 25, 1634-5, (m. Nov. 13, 1651, William Parker,) Joseph bapt. Jan. 1, 1636, Nathaniel bapt. March 10, 1638, Lydia, (m. James Doughty).

Will dated 28 Feb. 1669, prob. 5 June, 1673. Eldest son John, other ch. Joseph, Daniel, Nathaniel, Mary Parker, Lydia Doughty; gr. ch. Humphrey T.; gr. ch. Jonathan and Joseph, sons of his eldest son; gr. ch. Abigail T., dau. of son Nathaniel; gr. ch. Mary Doughty.

Jeffrey, husbandman, Dorchester, propr. Ch. Praise-ever, son, bapt. 24 (3) 1640, Increase bapt. 15 (8) 1642, Patience bapt. 10 (9) 1644.

He d. (2) or (3) 1654. Will prob. 25 (3) 1654. Wife Isabel; sons Praise-ever and Increase. The widow d. 12 (10) 1660; admin. of her est. 5 days later. [Reg. V, 305, VIII, 354, X, 266, and XXXI, 178.]

John, came in the Mayflower to Plymouth from Leyden, Holland. Signed the Compact. Brought two sons. All died in the spring of 1621. Another child, a daughter, came some years after to Salem and married there; was living in 1650. [B.]

John, Scituate, served against the Narragansetts in 1645. Ch. Jonathan b 30 Sept. 1646, Joseph b. and d. 1647, Joseph b. 12 Jan. 1649, Ezekiel b. 7 Jan. 1650, Lydia b. 24 Jan. 1652, John b. 30 Oct. 1654, Elisha b. 8 March, 1656, Mary b. Dec. 10, 1658, Benjamin b. March 5, 1660, Ruth bapt. May 17, 1663.

Inv. of his est. taken by John Chipman and John Ottis 31 May, 1667. [Reg. VII, 177.]

John, merchant, Roxbury, frm. May 2, 1649. Some John Turner bought ¼ of the pinnace St. John Jan. 29, 1640. [Suff. De. I, 50.] Wife Elizabeth d. Oct. 2, 1647. He m. ...... Ch. Elizabeth b. Sept. 27, 1647, Deborah bapt. 14 (11) 1648, John bapt. 8 (4) 1651. John, son of John Turner of Walton, co. Suffolk, yeoman, with consent of his aunts Susan and Sarah Boyton of Walton, placed himself an apprentice with Edward Bendall of Boston in N. E. and the West Indies, April 20, 1647. Was transferred 7 (5) 1648, to Mr. Richard Parker of Bo.; and March 10, 1657-8, to John Saffin, merchant, who engaged to teach him to write and cipher if he be capable. [Suff. De. III, 130 a.]

TURNER, cont.

Lawrence, Lynn. Wife Sarah in Court in 1650. L. T. of Rhode Island deposed in 1653, ae. about 32 years. [Es. Files.]

Margery, Cohannet, (Taunton,) m. 8 Nov. 1638, Richard Paul.

Michael, Sandwich, bought suit in court, 1637, against John Davis, who brought goods for him from Weymouth; constable 1641; atba. 1643.

Mr. Nathaniel, Saugus, appl. frm. Oct. 19, 1630; frm. July 3, 1632. Captain; deputy. One of the force sent by the Mass. Bay government 25 (3) 1636, to avenge the death of Mr. Oldham. His house and goods accidentally burned in 1636. [W.] A commissioner of the Essex Quarterly Court at its first session, 27 (4) 1636.

One Turner of Charlestown, a man about 50 years of age, drowned himself in 1641. Left a wife. [W.]

Richard, planter, Boston, adm. chh. 1632; rem. to Providence. Arrangements for collection of money in 1640. [L.]

Robert, Boston, Edward Bendall's manservant, adm. chh. 8 (7) 1633. Vintner, innholder at the sign of the Anchor, propr.; frm. March 4, 1633-4. Wife Penelope; ch. Ephraim b. 13 (10) 1639, Sarah b. 11 (1) 1640, (m. Nov. 15, 1660, John Fairweather,) John b. 1 (10) 1642, Joseph b. 7 (7) 1644, Benjamin b. 6 (1) 1646, Daniel b. 26 (9) 1650, d. 4 (2) 1651.

He d. in 1664. Will dated 9 (5), prob. 24 (6) 1664; beq. to wife; to ch. Ephraim, John, Joseph and dau. Fairweather; to the first and new chhs. of Boston and that of Cambridge; to Capt. Oliver's company and the other three cos.; to Mr. Stalham of Tarling in Essex. Land and minerals at Chelmsford, land at Centry Hill, Boston, etc. [Reg. XIII, 11.]

Robert, shoemaker, Boston, a res. in 1640; [L.] adm. chh. 17 (12) 1643. Wife Elizabeth adm. chh. 7 (1) 1646; ch. John b. and d. 1643, John bapt. 15 (7) 1644, ae. about 7 days, Habbakuk b. 18 (2) 1647, Elizabeth bapt. 18 (4) 1648, Frances bapt. 26 (4) 1650, ae. about 6 days, Robert b. and d. 1652.

He d. in 1651. Will dated 14 Aug., prob. 3 Dec. 1651, beq. to wife and ch. John, Habbakuk and Elizabeth; in case of their de-

TURNER, cont.

cease the est. was to go to Abigail Death, dau. of his bro. Peter Turner, and to Hanna Hill, dau. of his wife's sister Frances H. Beq. to John Spurr's wife. [Reg. IV, 285.]

Thomas, ae. 42, came in the Hopewell in Sept. 1635. Settled at Hingham. Sold house and land in 1646. Mortg. ¼ of his bark Nov. 1, 1648. Rem. to Scituate. He m. 6 Jan. 1651, Sarah Hiland; ch. Nathaniel b. 1 March, 1654, Elizabeth b. July, 1656, Mary b. Sept. 15, 1658, Eunice b. April 10, 1662, Grace b. 1665, Ephraim b. June, 1668.

He and his wife Sarah both d. Nov. 1688. Will dated Dec. 4, 1688, prob. March 13, 1688-9. Beq. to dau. Grace T.; to eldest son Nathan T., to son Thomas T. loom and the tackling; to all his children 5 li. apiece. [Gen. Adv. I, 42.]

Widow ...., Salem, 1636.

William, tailor, Dorchester, adm. chh. 16 (11) 1642; propr. before 1646. Frm. May 10, 1643; bailiff 1661. Rem. to Boston. A prominent member of the First Baptist church of Charlestown and Boston, and suffered great persecution in consequence. Was imprisoned a long time. Afterward did remarkable service as a soldier and Captain in the war aginst King Philip and his Indians.

He m. Frances, mother of his child Prudence, b. at Bo. Oct. 12, 1665. She d.; he m. Mary, widow of John Pratt; she d. about 167⅔, and he m. Mary, widow of Key Alsop. A son William was with him in the Indian war; Thomas, an other soldier in his company, is believed to have been the father of the William, who, as "grandson of William," had a grant of land in 1736. [See Bodge's King Philip's War; Reg. XI.]

He was killed at Hadley May 18, 1676. "Turner's Falls" is his memorial. Will dated 16 Feb. 1675-6, "about to go forth in the service of this country against the heathen our barbarous enemies," beq. to wife Mary property left to her by her former husband, Key Alsop, and other property; his children to inherit the latter after her death. The church of Dorchester took a collection for his family 10 (6) 1679.

TUSOLIE,

Elizabeth, ae. 55, came in the Abigail in June, 1635.

TURNEY,
Benjamin, Concord, frm. June 2, 1641. Ch. Rebecca b. 16 (12) 1639, Sarah b. 11 (10) 1641, Ruth b. 28 (11) 1643.

TURRELL, TURRILL, TERRILL, TURAND, TURIN, TARANT,
Daniel, blacksmith, anchor smith, captain, Boston, propr. before 1649. Wife Lydia adm. chh. 29 (6) 1647, d. June 23, 1659. He m. 2, Mary Barrell, widow, dau. of Elder Wm. Coleborne. She d. Jan. 23, 1697. Ch. Daniel b. 16 (6) 1646, John bapt. 4 (1) 1649, Joseph b. Dec. 27, 1653, d. 10 (3) 1654, Joseph b. March 25, 1655, Rebecca b. Dec. 26, 1655, Anna b. Aug. 20, 1657, d. Aug. 8, 1658, Samuel b. June 14, 1659, Lydia b. Nov. 30, 1660, Coleborne b. Dec. 4, 1662, Sarah and Elizabeth b. and d. 1663, Benjamin b. June 21, 1665, Humphrey b. Sept. 10, 1669, Mary b. April 4, 1672.
He made will 12 July, 1688, prob. Aug. 3, 1693; beq. to wife Mary, sons Daniel, Colborn and Samuel; Humphrey and Sarah, ch. of son Joseph; Sarah and Lydia Foster, ch. of dec. dau. Lydia; to kinswoman Elizabeth Gording.

TUTTELL, TUTTLE,
Henry, Hingham, propr. 1635; frm. March, 1637-8; constable 1640.

John, mercer, ae. 39, with Joan, ae. 42, John Lawrence, ae. 17, William Lawrence, ae. 12, Marie Lawrence, ae. 9, Abigail Tuttell, ae. 6, Symon Tuttell, ae. 4, Sara Tuttell, ae. 2, and John Tuttell, ae. 1, cert. from the parish of St. Albons, Herts, Eng. came in the Planter in April, 1635. Settled at Ipswich; propr. 1635; frm. March 13, 1638-9; deputy 1643. Shipped goods to Barbadoes in 1650, in account with London parties; his wife Joanna signing invoices. [Suff. De. I.] During his absence in Ireland in 1654, she renewed a lease of land to Richard Shatswell. She went to Carrick Fergus, Ireland, where the husband d. Dec. 30, 1656, as she wrote 6 April folg.; she refers to his will and to her Lawrence and Tuttell children. Hanna married there. [Letters in Es. Files 5, 29, 31.] Depositions in Essex Court in 1662.

Richard, husbandman, ae. 42, with Ann, ae. 41, and children Anna, ae. 12, John, ae. 10, Rebecca, ae. 6, and Isbel, ae. 70, (sic). came in the Planter in April, 1635. Settled

TUTTELL, etc., cont.
at Boston. Adm. chh. with wife Anne 27 (10) 1635; frm. March 3, 1635-6. He was a bro. of John, above. [Es. Files 5, 28.] His servant John Goordley d. (10) 1638.
He d. 8 (3) 1640. His dau. Hannah was adm. chh. 25 (10) 1647; dism. 8 (5) 1649, to chh. of Hartford, now wife of one John Pantry.

William, husbandman, ae. 26, with Elizabeth, ae. 23, and children John, ae. 3½, Ann, ae. 2½, and Thomas, ae. 3 months, came in the Planter in April, 1635. Settled at Boston. Wife Elizabeth adm. chh. 14 (6) 1636. Had liberty to build a windmill at Charlestown in 1635; propr. 1636. He brought suit about a mare in 1637. [W.] Ch. Jonathan bapt. 2 (5) 1637, David bapt. 7 (2) 1639. The wife was dism. 8 (7) 1639, to the church of [Ipswich.]

TWINING, TWYNING,
William, Yarmouth, atba. 1643; served against the Narragansetts in 1645. Frm. 3 June, 1652. He rem. to Eastham; townsman, 1655. Ch. Stephen b. 6 Feb. 1659, William. He (William, Senior,) d. at E. 15 April, 1659.

TWISDEN,
John, planter, Scituate, prop. frm. 5 March, 1638-9. Juryman, 1641. An infant child was bur. Aug. 9, 1638. Ellice T. [his widow,] m. Nov. 20, 1649, Joseph Tilden.

TWITCHELL, TUCHELL, TUCHINE,
Francis, Dorchester, propr. 1634.

Joseph, Dorchester, Nov. 1633, [Col. Rec.] frm. May 14, 1634; propr. Deed of land May 24, 1656.
He d. 13 (7) 1657. Inv. of his est. pres. 26 (9) 1657, by Timothy Wales and Benjamin Twitchell.

Joshua, Dorchester, propr. 1635. Clerical error for Joseph, probably.

TYBBOTT, see Tibbets.

TYLER, TILER,
Abraham, Haverhill, propr. 1644. He m. Dec. 26, 1650, Hannah or Johannah Farnum; ch. Abraham b. June 4, 1652, d. Dec.

TYLER, etc., cont.

2, 1654, Hannah b. Dec. 16, 1655, d. June 8, 1662, Abraham b. May 21, 1659, d. Nov. 23, 1668.

He d. May 6, 1673. Will dated 5 May, prob. 14 Oct. 1673; beq. to wife and to Robert, son of Robert Clements. The widow was recd. to the chh. of Salem from that of Haverhill Feb. 1679; m. 2, Edward Brumidge, who d. June 10, 1699.

Job, husbandman, at Mt. Wollaston in 1637; [W.] settled at Andover, gave mortg. of house, etc. as security for a payment of money, 5 March, 1650. He deposed in 1661, ae. about 40 years. Wife Mary same age. Ch. John d. 28 Sept. 1652, John b. 16 April, 1653, Samuel b. 24 May, 1654.

Joseph, witnessed a deed at Salem in 1645, and at Boston in 1649.

Nathaniel, husbandman, Lynn, with wife Jane, 1640; witnessed deed at Salem in 1645. Sold land in 1652, and sailed for England. Son Joseph T., living at Shrewsbury; sister Jane, wife of Edward Sanford of London. [Ess. De. I, and Suff. De I.] [Reg. XIII, 33.]

TYNG, TING, TINGE,

Edward, upholsterer, merchant, from London, came to Boston before 13 (7) 1636, when he bought house-plot and garden. Brother of William. Adm. chh. 30 (11) 1640; frm. 2 June, 1641. He deposed Oct. 6, 1657, ae. about 46 years. [Mdx. Files.] Town officer; his dial-post mentioned in 1643. Owned large farm at Braintree, wharf, etc. in Bo. Gave land in 1652 to his cousin John Francklin. [Book of Pos.] Wife Mary adm. chh. 5 (7) 1640; ch. Hannah b. 7 (1) 1640, (m. May 8, 1661, Habiah Savage,) Mary b. 17 (2) 1641, Jonathan bapt. 14 (10) 1642, ae. about 4 days, Deliverance b. 6 (6) 1645, Rebecca b. 23 (1) 1646, d. 16 (1) 1649, Edward bapt. 1 (2) 1649, Rebecca b. 13 (5) 1651, William b. March 3, 1652, Eunice b. March 8, 1655, Joseph b. July 12, 1657, d. July 30, 1658. Deliverance m. Col. Daniel Searle, Esq., gov. of Barbadoes.

He d. Sept. 28, 1681, ae. 81 years. [S.] Will dated 25 Aug. 1677, prob. Sept. 19, 1681, beq. to son Edward; dau. Eunice, (m. Samuel Willard,) son-in-law Joseph Dudley; to gr. ch. Thomas, Hannah and Mary Savage, Thomas, Edward, Joseph and Paul Dudley, Samuel Searle and John Tyng. Rest to wife

TYNG, etc., cont.

Mary. Edward T., Esq. d. at Dunstable Dec. 27, 1681.

William, merchant, captain, Boston, propr. 8 (8) 1638; adm. chh. 3 (1) 1639; frm. and deputy; much in office in town and colony. Treasurer. Wife Elizabeth, dau. of Rowland and Katharine Coytmore of Wapping, Eng. She d. and he m. Jane —, who d. (3) 8 1652. Ch. Elizabeth b. 6 (12) 1637, (m. Capt. Thomas Brattle,) Anna b. 6 (11) 1639, adm. chh. of Charlestown 9 (6) 1656, (m. Mr. Thomas Shepard, Jr.) Bethiah b. 17 (3) 1641, (m. Richard Wharton,) Mercy b. 13 (11) 1642, (m. Samuel Bradstreet).

He d. 18 (11) 1652. Inv. of his est. 25 (3) 1653. [Reg. VIII, 62; Suff. De. III, 294.] Suits at Ess. Court in 1654 by Capt. Edward Bridge.

TYNKLER,

Sarah, ae. 15, came in the Blessing in July, 1635.

TYPIT, see Tibbet.

UDALL,

Philip, Gloucester, plaintiff in an action in Essex Court 26 (9) 1642. Propr. 1650.

UFFORD, UFFOTT,

Thomas, embarked June 22, 1632; frm. March 4, 1632-3. One of the founders of Springfield in 1636. [Reg. XIII, 297.]

UNDERHILL,

Capt. John, Boston, adm. chh. 1630; frm. May 18, 1631. Deputy 1634. Became governor of Piscataqua plantation; and there made utterances which gave offence to Mass. Bay authorities. For this and other charges he was summoned to Boston; came 29 (11) 1639, and apologized to the church. Was restored to fellowship 3 (7) 1640. Wife Helena, a Dutch woman, adm. chh. Bo. 15 (10) 1633; dism. to chh. of Exeter 22 (6) 1641; ch. Elizabeth bapt. 14 (12) 1635, John bapt. 24 (2) 1642, ae. about 13 days.

He rem. to the Dutch settlement, (New York) in 1642. [W.]

UNDERWOOD,
James, baker, Salem, 1637. Lawsuit, 1639. Mr. Thomas Oliver depos. 6 (3) 1654, to having visited U.'s wife in Norwich, Eng. recently, and tried in vain to persuade her to come to him in Salem. [Arch. Dom. 9.] He deposed in 1661, ae. about 50 years. Sold land in 1651. Was owner of the ketch Dolphin in 1658.

Joseph, Hingham, 1637; rem. to Watertown. Frm. May 16, 1645. Wife Mary; ch. Thomas b. 11 (8) 1658. The mother d. 4 months later. He m. 2, in Dorchester, 26 (2) 1665, Mary How.
He d. 16 (12) 1676, ae. about 62. Admin. papers name his ch. Joseph, Sarah, Hannah, Elizabeth, Thomas and Margaret. [Genealogy, Reg. XXXVIII, 400.]

Martin, ae. 38, with wife Martha, ae. 31, came in the Elizabeth of Ipswich April 30, 1634. Settled at Watertown. Frm. Sept. 3, 1634. The wife wrote a letter to Mr. John Fiske in 1645, concerning her cousin Phinehas Fiske. [See Wenham Chh. Rec.] Martha d. 6 (3) 1684, ae. 83 years.

Peter, husbandman, ae. 22, came in the Rebecca in April, 1635.

Thomas, gentleman, Hingham, propr. 1636, frm. March 9, 1636-7; deputy. Rem. to Dorchester; later to Watertown, where he bought house and land 3 (1) 1651-2. Will dated 19 July, 1679, prob. 2 (8) 1680, beq. to wife Magdalen the est. she brought and the rest of his est. unless son Thomas, now in England, should come within two years to claim his portion. The widow Magdalen d. at Cambridge village April 10, 1687, ae. about 80; est. appraised next day. Will prob. 20 April; beq. to kinsmen, John and Hannah Gibson, Thomas Underwood, Richard Child, his wife Mehitabel Demake (Dimock), and their children.

William, Concord, frm. May 22, 1650. Rem. to Chelmsford; town officer. Wife Sarah; ch. Remembrance b. 27 (12) 1639, Sarah b. 25 (7) 1641, (m. Daniel Blogget, and at his death in 1672, requested that her father W. U. be made adminr. of his est.;) Priscilla b. 16 (12) 1646, Aquilla b. 3 (5) 1647, Rebecca d. 6 (2) 1650, [Deborah, Samuel.] The wife Sarah d. 5 Nov. 1684.

UPHAM, UPPAM,
John, husbandman, ae. 35, with [wife]

UPHAM, etc., cont.
Elizabeth, ae. 32, [children] John, ae. 7, Nathaniel, ae. 5, and Elizabeth, ae. 3, and Sarah Upham, ae. 26, embarked from Weymouth, Eng. before 20 March, 1635. Settled at Weymouth. Yeoman, deputy, deacon. Frm. Sept. 2, 1635. Rem. to Malden. [L.] Made gifts of land in 1662 to Elizabeth, widow of son Nathaniel; to son Thomas in 1664, and to son Phineas 2 (12) 1670. He m. 2, Katharine, widow of Angel Hollard, renouncing claim to the est. she recd. from Hollard 14 (6) 1671. His son John bur. at Wey. 5 (4) 1640. Robert Martin calls him brother.
He d. Feb. 25, 1681, ae. 84. [Reg. XXXIl, 41.] Genealogy.

UPSALL, UPSHALL, UPSELL,
John, Salem, wrote a deposition in a case in Essex Court in 1643.

Nicholas, inn-keeper, Dorchester, juryman 1630, frm. May 18, 1631. Rem. to Boston. With wife Dorothy recd. from Dorch. chh. 28 (5) 1644. Kept the Red Lion tavern. He was prosecuted in 1651 for speaking reproachfully of the Court's judgment against Quakers, and was imprisoned and banished for his fellowship with them. His wife suffered much with him, and the family had many hardships. Ch. Anna b. (12) 1635, d. 7 (9) 1651, Elizabeth b. (12) 1637, (m. July 4, 1652, William Greenow,) Susanna b. 7 (12) 1639, (m. Joseph Cocke,) Experience b. 19 (1) 1640, d. Aug. 2, 1659, Ruth bapt. 15 (8) 1642.

He d. in Aug. 1666, ae. about 70. His wife d. Sept. 18, 1675, ae. about 73. Will prob. Oct. 31, 1666, gave to his wife Dorothy, to his dau. Elizabeth, wife of Wm. Greenow, his dau. Susanna, wife of Joseph Cock, gr. ch. Elizabeth Greenow and Elizabeth Cock. The furnishings of a chamber and his books and papers to the Society of Quakers. [Reg. XXXIV, 21, and XV, 250.] The widow made will 30 Aug. 1673, prob. 17 Jan. 1675; beq. to her ch. and gr. ch. of the Cocke and Greenow families; to her bro. John Capen and sisters Elizabeth Swift and Honour Hannam.

UPSON,
Stephen, a lawyer, ae. 23, came in the Increase April 15, 1635. See Wright, Edward.

UPTON,
John, servant of Edward Winslow of Salisbury, in 1640. [L.]

John, sometime of Hammersmith [Lynn,] rem. to Salem; bought land in S. in 1662.

USHER,
Hezekiah, book-seller, Cambridge, 1645, frm. March 14, 1638-9; propr., town officer. Rem. to Boston in 1644 or 1645. Engaged in trade with Barbadoes, etc. Wife Frances d. 25 (2) 1652; he m. 2 (9) 1652, Elizabeth, dau. of Rev. Zechariah Symmes; they were adm. chh. Boston from chhs. of Camb. and Char. 14 (12) 1646. He m. 3, Mary, dau. of William Alford, widow of Peter Butler. Ch. Hezekiah b. (4) 1639, John b. 11 (7) 1643, bur. (10) 1645, Elizabeth b. 1 (12) 1645, John b. 17 (2) 1648, Sarah bapt. 17 (9) 1650, Hannah b. Dec. 29, 1653, d. 24 (5) 1654, Zechariah b. Dec. 26, 1654, d. 23 (6) 1656, Rebecca, (m. 1 May, 1660, Abraham Browne).

He d. May 13 or 14, 1676. Will dated 11 May, prob. 19 May, 1676, beq. to wife Mary: sons Hezekiah and John; dau. Sarah Tyng and her ch. John and Mary; gr. ch. Hezekiah and Elizabeth Browne; to wife's ch. Hannah, Mary, Peter and Samuel Butler; bro. Samuel Usher in England; Robert and Elizabeth U.; son-in-law Samuel Shrimpton; Elizabeth the wife and Elizabeth the dau. of son John; bro. John Harwood and sister Elizabeth, Elizabeth Sedgwick and the rest of their children; Hannah Scottow; Rachel, wife of Thomas Harwood and her ch.; mother Sarah Symmes and several of her children; Harvard College; the poor of Boston and those of the Third church; church of Cambridge; bros. Thomas and Robert Rolph and their families; bro. Robert Alfery of Mayfield; Mr. Thomas and Mr. Peter Thatcher; Moses Payne, Sen.; Maudit Ings, and Rebecca Myrick.

UTTON, UTTING,
Anne, Roxbury, adm. chh. 11 (10) 1640; d. (11) 1641. Will recorded; beq. to George Berber, to Anne, wife of Henry Philips, to John and Elizabeth Brock, to Elizabeth, wife of Henry Brock.

UTLEY, see Otley,
Samuel, Scituate, m. 6 Dec. 1648, Hannah Hatch; ch. Lydia b. 28 Dec. 1659.
Admin. of his est. was gr. 3 June, 1662, to his widow.

VALE,
Jeremiah, Salem, witness in court in 1639; propr. 1647. Bought land in 1648. Sold house and land in 1651 and removed out of this plantation and jurisdiction. [Es. De. I, 11.] Katharine adm. chh. 6 (2) 1645; ch. Abigail bapt. 18 (3) 1645, Sarah bapt. 21 (1) 1646-7, Jeremiah bapt. 30 (10) 1649.

Nathaniel, Concord, 1647. Wife Mary; ch. John b. 27 (5) 1647, Nathaniel b. 23 (9) 1649. [Mdx. De.]

VAINE, see Fane.

VANE,
Sir Henry, Esquire, son and heir to Sir Henry Vane, comptroller of the King's house, [W.] b. about 1612, educated at Magdalen College, Oxford; travelled in France and Geneva; adopted Puritan views. He came to Boston in the Defence, arriving in Oct. 1635. He was adm. chh. Boston 1 (9) 1635; chosen governor May 25, 1636.

He was not re-elected the following spring, owing to a strong opposition from the party of Mr. Winthrop, who was again chosen. He returned to England Aug. 3, 1637. There he entered unto public life, and became treasurer of the realm. On the breaking out of the struggle between King Charles and the Parliament he took the side of the people. His subsequent history is well known. New England has great cause to be proud of having had a share in the manly, humane work of this noble statesman. See Winthrop, *et als*. [Reg. II, 121.]

VARNHAM, VARNUM,
George, Ipswich, propr. 1635.
Will dated 21 (2) prob. 12 (8) 1649. Wife; son Samuel, dau. Hannah. The son, Samuel, ae. 64, deposed Sept. 25, 1683, concerning his father's ownership of certain lands. Thomas, ae. about 25 years, deposed in Ips. in 1657.

VARNEY,
William, Ipswich. One of the appraisers of the est. of Thos. Cook (7) 1650. Inv. taken 1 (1), filed 30 (1) 1654.

VASSALL, VASSELL,
Mr. William, Esquire, came first in 1628, as one of the Assistants of the Mass. Bay Co. to Salem. Ret to England with his family in the Lyon in 1630. [Du.] He came again in the Blessing, in July, 1635, ae. 42, with wife Ann, ae. 42, and ch. Judith, ae. 16, Francis, ae. 12, John, ae. 10, Ann, ae. 6, Margaret, ae. 2, and Mary, ae. 1. Settled at Roxbury. His wife joined the chh. in 1635. [E.] Rem. to Scituate. Adm. chh. Nov. 28, 1636. Took oath of allegiance to Plym. Col. Feb. 1, 1638-9. Town officer. His surveying instruments referred to in Plym. Col Rec. in 1642. Rem. to Marshfield; propr. 1643; town officer. Was not in sympathy with the attitude of Mass. Bay and Plymouth governments toward persons who differed from the received opinions in politics and religion; and used his influence for greater charity toward Quakers, etc. The elders expressed their disapproval of his utterances; the church of Plymouth sent him a message by John Cook, which is recorded in the book of the Second Church, Scituate, dated Apr. 14, 1645; hoping he would desist from proceedings intended, but questioning whether they would commune with him if he went on. He went to England in 1646. with a petition to Parliament for the liberty of English subjects.

He rem. to Barbadoes; died in 1655-6. Will dated 13 July, 1655, gave property to his son John; daus. Judith, (who m. April 8, 1640, Resolved White,) Frances, (m. July 16, 1640, James Adams,) Anna m. Nicholas Ware. Margaret and Mary. Part of these heirs sold their shares in certain lands 18 July, 1657. [Suff. De. III, 34.] [Reg. LI, 286.]

VAUGHAN, VAUGHN, VAUHAN, VAHAN,
John, Watertown, 1633, propr. 1636. Sold land before 1642.

William, Springfield, propr.; leased his ground Jan. 10, 1644, to Rise Burdondon for 6 years.

VEAZIE, VEASIE, VEZAY, VESEY, VEZA, PHESE, FACY, FEASY,
Robert, Watertown, propr. 1636, died before 1642 when his widow Mary, having m. 2, George Parkhurst, sold land to William Parker. [Mdx. De. II, 58.] Robert [called fface] who d. in 1656-7, and beq. to friend John Founell, may have been a child of his.

William, Braintree, frm. May 10, 1643. Bought house and land of James Covey in 1651. Wife Ellinor; ch. Hannah b. 18 (1) 1644, (m. 26 (7) 1665, John Greenleaf,) William b. 6 (8) 1647, Solomon b. 3 (11) 1650, Elizabeth b. 13 (8) 1653, Samuel b. 24 (6) 1656, Ellen b. 4 (3) 1659, (m. Feb. 20, 1680, Stephen Paine,) Mehetabel b. 17 (12) 1665, Mercy b. 20 (11) 1669, (m. 24 April, 1690, John Ruggles).

He d. June 16, 1681, ae. 65. [Gr. St.] The widow contracted marriage with John French 8 July, 1683. His will dated 30 June, prob. 27 July, 1681, beq. to wife Elen; sons William, Solomon, Samuel; to daus. Hannah Grenleafe, Abigail tayr, [Thayer,] Elen, Mehetabel and Mercy Veazy; to Christian Alison.

VENN,
Thomas, residence not mentioned, but probably in or near Boston. The Gen. Court promised May 29, 1644, to give him land in proportion to the stock taken in the Company by his father, Mr. John Venn, if he should show an order from his father therefor.

VENNER, VENNOR, VINOR,
Rebecca, Dorchester, memb. chh. about 1637.

Thomas, cooper, Salem, frm. March, 1637-8. Rem. to Boston. Ret. in 1651 to London, and sold Boston lands, house and warehouses in 1656. Wife Alice; ch. Thomas bapt. 16 (3) 1641, Hannah bapt. at Bo. 2 (12) 1644, Samuel bapt. 3 (12) 1649. He was leader of the "Fifth Monarchy Riot," in London, and was executed Jan. 19, 1661. [Reg. XLVII, 437.]

VERY, VEREY, [see Giles,]
Thomas, Gloucester, propr. 1649. With wife Hannah sold land in 1661. [To. Rec.]

VEREN, VEREING,
Joshua, called a "repr", came in the James April 5, 1635. Settled at Salem; he and his wife Jane were adm. chh. 21 (4) 1640. Dorcas memb. chh. before 1636. She sold her farm in 1650. Hilliard adm. chh. 1 (9) 1648, Mary adm. chh. 21 (1) 1647. Hilliard deposed in 1658, ae. about 37 years.

Philip, "roopr," came in the James April 5, 1635. Settled at Salem; wheelwright; constable 10 (12) 1637; [Es. Court.] lawsuit in 1639. Wife Dorcas memb. chh. 1636. Rem. to Providence. [W.] Probably the "Verin" of whom W. narrates that he was punished because he would not allow his wife to attend Mr. Williams' meetings as often as she wished. Philip with wife Johanna sold land in 1661. Philip, Jr. adm. chh. 3 (4) 1640.

VERMAIS, VERMASE, see Fermaes.

VIALL, VYALL,
John, laborer, weaver, webster, Boston, 1639, adm. chh. 2 (3), frm. June 2, 1641. He sold house and land about 1659. Wife Mary adm. chh. 11 (5) 1641; ch. Hopestill, dau. b. 14 (6) 1639, (m. 1 July, 1659, William Shutt,) Mary b. 30 (9) 1641, (m. 26 Jan. 1658, John Sunderland,) John bapt. 2 (4) 1644, ae. about 5 days, Nathaniel bapt. 26 (5) 1646, ae. about 3 days, Marie bapt. 18 (1) 1649, ae. about 7 days, Sarah b. 14 March, 1651-2, Joseph b. 4 June, 1654, Abigail b. 21 Oct. 1656.

He rem. to Swansey; d. 26 Feb. 1685; inv. filed 6 June, 1687, by widow Elizabeth. Will devised to wife Elizabeth; to his children by her and to the six ch. of his first wife, viz. sons John and Nathaniel, and daus. Hopestill Pitts, Mary Burroughs, Sarah Moore, and Abigail [Magick.] John had the Ship tavern in Boston. Benj. was blind.

Jellyan, maidservant to Thomas Grubb, Boston, adm. chh. 13 (4) 1640.

VICKARY, VICKARS, VICKERY, VECKARE,
George, Salem, 1636. He rem. to Hull; propr. 1657. He m. Rebecca, dau. of David Phippen.
Admin. of his est. was gr. to his widow Rebecca, and son Jonathan "Vickary"; son George "Vickare" also signed admin. bond.

VERNAM,
Margaret, widow, one of Thomas Leverett's family, adm. chh. Boston 28 (12) 1635.

VINAL,
Stephen, Scituate, prop. frm. 5 March, 1638-9. Anna, spinster, [his widow?] recd. deed of land with other proprs. in 1648. She d Oct. 6, 1664; admin. of her est. gr. to Stephen and John V. [Reg. VI, 186.] Stephen m. Feb. 26, 1662, Mary Baker, Martha m. April, 1646, Isaac Chittenden.

VINCENT, VINSON, VINCETT,
Adrian, came in the Mary and John March 24, 1633-4.

Humphrey, Cambridge, propr. 1634. Rem. to Ipswich. Propr. 1637.
He d. Dec. 5, 1664. Will dated 1 (11) 1660, prob. 28 March, 1665; growing aged; beq. to Mr. Samuel Symonds and his dau. Martha, and to Thomas Harris.

Mr. John, Sandwich, had land grant 20 March, 1636-7. Frm. Oct. 1637.

Mary, Sandwich, m. 8 Nov. 1648, (man's name wanting), [Plym. Col. Rec.]

William, pot-maker, Saugus; applied for land at Salem (Marblehead,) in 1636; a tract laid out to him, his mother and his cosen Anthony Bucstone. Frm. May 10, 1643. Keeper of the ordinary; selectman. Wife Sarah adm. chh. with him 23 (11) 1650; testified, ae. about 40 years, in the case of Mr. Blinman vs. George Norton in 1660. [Wenham Chh. Rec.] He deposed in 1663, ae. about 53 years. Ch. Elizabeth b. May 16, 1644, John b. May 15, 1648, William b. Sept. 9, 1651, d. 1675, Richard d. 24 July, 1652, Jacob bapt. 11 (2) 1658, Richard b. Sept. 1, 1658, Thomas b. April 1, 1662, Abigail b. May 21, 1668, (m. Jacob Elwell.) He sold land in 1684 to son-in-law Hugh Row.

He d. 17 Sept. 1690. The widow Rachel d. Feb. 15, 1707. His will dated 19 March, 1684, prob. 25 (9) 1690, beq. to wife Rachel, son John, dau. Abigail, dau. Sarah Parsons, the children of dec. daus. Gardner and Ellery; gr. son John, son of John Cooke.

William, witness at Plymouth 1 Oct. 1638. May be the foregoing.

William, yeoman, of Bromfield, Essex, gave a bond, dated Aug. 25, 1636, in favor of

VINCENT, etc., cont.
Abraham Page of Great Baddow, Essex, tailor, for £20. [Suff. De. 1.] Whether this is the above-named person or not is an interesting question. One wonders why this document should have been recorded in Suff. De. if not relating to persons here resident.

VINES,
Edward, servant to Robert Darrill, Sudbury, was bur. 1 (1) 1640.

VIXON, VICKSON, see Wickson.

VOBES, see Fobes.

VOYSEY,
Simon, a witness to a deed of Robert Nash Sept. 24, 1642.

VINTON,
John, Salem or vicinity. Children of John and Anna recorded: Elnor b. (3) 1648, John b. 2 (1) 1650, William b. 30 (2) 1652, Blaze b. 22 (2) 1654, Ann b. 4 (2) 1656, Elizabeth b. (11) 1657, Sara b. 16 (7) 1662.

WADE, WAYDE,
Jonathan, embarked June 22, 1632; came to Charlestown; propr. 1632. Wife Susanna adm. chh. 25 (3) 1633; frm. May 14, 1634. Rem. to Ipswich; propr. 1635. Engaged in business with William Paine and others. [Suff. De. III, 357.] Ch. Jonathan, Nathaniel, (ae. 36 in 1684,) Thomas, Mary bapt. 2 (8) 1633, Elizabeth. Wife Susanna d. Nov. 29, 1678.
He d. 13 June, 1683. Will dated 17 June, 1657, and another dated 22 (3) 1669, were presented in court 25 (1) 1684, and the second approved. Beq. to sons Jonathan, Nathaniel and Thomas; wife Susanna; son Anthony Crosby, dau. Prudence C. and their ch. Thomas, Nathaniel and Jonathan C.; son William Symonds and his dau. Susanna; son Elihu Wardell and his wife Elizabeth. Mentions land in England; debt due to Sir William Peak. Many details. [Es. Inst. Coll. IV, 23.]

Nicholas, Scituate, took oath of allegiance 1 Feb. 1638.
Will made 7 Feb. 1683, beq. to sons John, Thomas, Nicholas, and Nathaniel; dau. Susannah White had her portion in her former

WADE, etc., cont.
husband Wilcom's days; he beq. to his ch. Nicholas, Nathaniel, Elizabeth and Hannah.

Richard, cooper, from Simstuly, ae. 60, with wife Elizabeth, ae. [5] 6, dau. Dinah, ae. 22, and servants Henry Lush, ae. 17, and Andrew Hallett, ae. 28, embarked from Weymouth, Eng. before March 20, 1635. Settled at Dorchester; propr. Rem. to Sandwich; propr. 1640.

Samuel, Lynn, propr. His servant, Richard Wilson, before the Court in 1639. Rem. and gave power of attorney for disposing of his lands, 20 (8) 1641.

Thomas, bro. of Jonathan, had accounts in Court June 2, 1635.
Col. Thomas d. in Ipswich Oct. 4, 1696; bro. or son of Jonathan?

WADFIELD,
John, Scituate, atba. 1643.

WADILOUE,
Nicholas, Yarmouth, atba. 1643.

WADSWORTH,
Christopher, Duxbury, taxed in 1632; frm. 1633. Constable for the section between Jones' river and Green's Harbour Jan. 1, 1633-4, and in 1638.
He was slain by the Indians 18 (2) 1676. [S.] His widow Grace made will, dated Jan. 1687-8, in old age and infirmities, prob. June 13, 1688. Son John, exec.; son Joseph and his wife; children of dec. son Samuel; dau. Mary Andrewes, widow; gr. ch. John, Mary and Abigail W. [Gen. Adv. I, 20.]

William, embarked June 22, 1632; settled at Cambridge. Frm. Nov. 6, 1632; propr. 1633. Town officer. Sold Camb. property in 1637 and rem. to Hartford.

WAFFE,
John, Charlestown. Katharine adm. chh. 1 (5) 1645; ch. John b. 22 (7) 1645, Thomas b. 29 (9) 1646.

WAINWRIGHT, WAINMAN, WANERITES,
Francis, Ipswich, merchant, propr.; had land for service in the Pequot war in 1637. He and his wife Philip, made William Norton their attorney 23 (9) 1647, to re-

WAINWRIGHT, etc., cont.
cover property left Philip by her father, George Sewall, of Hasted, co. Essex, Eng.; another letter to John Tuttle. [A.] Was paid by the town for service against the Indians in 1643. He and his company had suit to recover fish that had been lost in 1648. [Es. Files.] Bought land at Haverhill in 1685. Promised to give eldest son John a portion on his marriage with Elizabeth, dau. of Mr. Wm. Norton of Ipswich, March 10, 1674; and deeded land to him April 4, 1691, his wife Hannah consenting. He d. at Salem May 19, 1692.

WAIT, WAITE, WAYTE, WEIGHT, see also Wade,

Alexander, before Gen. Court 17 May, 1637.

Gamaliel, planter, Boston, servant to John Sampford, adm. chh. 15 (10) 1633; frm. March 4, 1634-5. Conveyed house and land to his wife Grace Sept. 26, 1666. Ch. Moses b. (4) 1637, d. (1) 1638, Grace b. 10 (11) 1638, (m. 6 May, 1662, Richard Price,) Moses bapt. 23 (6) 1640, Samuel bapt. 7 (9) 1641, ae. about 7 days, Deborah bapt. 21 (11) 1643, ae. about 4 days, John bapt. 16 (9) 1645, ae. about 3 days, Elizabeth bapt. 16 (11) 1647, ae. about 5 days, Gamaliel bapt. 17 (9) 1650.

He d. suddenly Dec. 9, 1685, ae. about 87. The widow was bur. June 3, 1687. [S.] Admin. of his est. was gr. to widow Grace 12 Jan. 1685.

John, Charlestown, adm. chh. 15 (11) 1646; frm. May 26, 1647. Rem. to Malden. He deposed in 1663, ae. about 45 years. Ch. Samuel, (called in record "of Samuel,") b. Oct. 11, 1650, Mary b. Aug. 31, 1653, Hannah b. 9 (7) 1656, Mehetabel b. 15 (7) 1658, Thomas b. 1 (7) 1660, Rebecca b. Nov. 22, 1662, Nathaniel b. May 27, 1667.

Capt. John d. Sept. 2, 1693, ae. 75 years. [Gr. St.] [See will of Joseph Waite, clerk, of Sproughton, co. Suffolk, Eng., 7 June, 1670. Reg. XXXI, 160.]

Richard, tailor, Boston, adm. chh. 28 (6) 1634; frm. 9 (1) 1636-7. Had garden plot toward the new mylne 25 (7) 1637; a lot at Braintree Jan. 11, 1637-8; had liberty to set up a porch before his house 31 (3) 1652. He deposed 24 (1) 1650, ae. about 50 years. [Es. Files.] Wife Elizabeth, member of the chh. of Newbury in 1639, recd. Bo. chh. 4 (8) 1645;

WAIT, etc., cont.
ch. Isaac b. and d. 1638, Returne, son, bapt. 14 (5) 1639, Hannah b. 14 (7) 1641, Nathaniel bapt. 5 (9) 1643, ae. about 11 days, Mary b. 15 (12) 1645, Samuel bapt. 9 (5) 1648, ae. about 20 days, Elizabeth bapt. 17 (9) 1650, Joseph, ae. 14 years, d. 20 (9) 1651, Elizabeth bapt. 18 (2) 1652, John (of Richard and Rebecca) b. 1 Nov. 1653, d. 5 Nov. 1658, Abigail bapt. 15 (4) 1656, Richard b. Dec. 16, 1658, John b. Feb. 9, 1660, Rebecca b. Jan. 3, 1663, Sarah b. June 23, 1665, Heiborne bapt. 23 (7) 1667. His servant Mary Fitch d. 24 (8) 1644.

Richard Waite of Boston, marshall, made will 6 Jan. 1671, prob. 9 Nov. 1680. Wife Rebecca; ch. Return, Richard, John, Abigail (Jones). Bro. Gamaliel W. and bros. son John W. execs.

Richard, Watertown, 1637. Wife Mary; ch. Stephen bur. 8 (1) 1638, ae. 9 days, John b. 6 (3) 1639, Thomas b. 3 (1) 1641.

He d. Jan. 16, 1668, ae. about 60 years. Admin. gr. to widow Mary Feb. 16 folg. on request of her three sons John, Thomas and Joseph. The widow d. Jan. 21, 1678-9, ae. 72 years. Admin. gr. to eldest son John April 2, 1679.

WAKEFIELD,

John, Salem, Marblehead, propr. 1637. Was witness to a document at Martin's Vineyard Oct. 14, 1647. He rem. to Boston. His dau. Elizabeth m. Aug. 20, 1660, Jasper Frost.

Admin. of his est. was gr. at Boston, 18 July, 1667, to his widow Anne.

William, ae. 22, and Anne, ae. 20, came in the Bevis in May, 1638. Settled at Hampton. Frm. March 13, 1638-9. Clerk of writs 1641. Witnessed a bond at Newbury in 1646.

WAKELY, WAKELIE,

Henry, Springfield, propr. 1649. He m. 4 (7) 1649, Sarah Gregory.

Thomas, husbandman, Hingham, propr. 1635, frm. March 3, 1635-6. Sold land Sept., 1647. Ch. Thomas bapt. June 14, 1640, Sarah b. and d. 1641.

Thomas, Gloucester, town officer, 1646. He with wife Elizabeth and John with *his* wife Elizabeth sold land in 1661.

WAKE,
William, Salem, 1637. Lawsuit in Es. and Gen. Court 1 (7) 1640. Will prob. 22 (4) 1654. Dau. Katharine W. in Eng., if living. Bro. John W. in Eng.

WAKEMAN, WACKMAN,
Samuel, came to N. E. with wife Elizabeth (9) 1631. [E.] Settled at Roxbury. Frm. Aug. 7, 1632. Rem. to Cambridge. Propr. 1635. Deputy. One of the undertakers of the ships Charles and Hopewell in 1640. [L.] Rem. to Hartford, and was killed with other colonists, in attempting to land at Providence in the West Indies, in 1641. [W.]

WALDEN,
Anne, memb. chh. Boston, 1632. She m. at Plymouth 29 Nov. 1638, John Smaley.

WALDO,
Cornelius, suit in Ipswich Court in 1646. Before the Court at Salem 6 (5) 1647, as security for his bro. Thomas W. He m. Hannah, dau. of Jonn Coggswell of Ipswich, and recd. from him a deed of house and land Jan. 2, 1651-2. Rem. to Chelmsford. Ch. Elizabeth, (m. Josiah Brackett.) John, Cornelius, Daniel b. Aug. 19, 1657, Martha b. Feb. 27, 1658, twin sons b. and d. 1659, Deborah b. Jan. 28, 1662, (m. Edward Emerson,) Judith b. July 12, 1664, Mary b. and d. 1665, Jonathan.
He d. Jan. 3, 1700, ae. 75. His widow d. Dec. 25, 1704, ae. 80. Genealogy. [Reg. LII, 213.]

WALES,
Nathaniel, weaver or webster, came with Mr. Richard Mather from England in 1635. Settled at Dorchester; propr., memb. chh., frm. Nov. 2, 1637. He rem. to Boston; was recd. to chh. with wife Susan 3 (1) 1651. She was a dau. of John Greenaway; q. v.
He d. Dec. 4, 1661. Will prob. Feb. 1 folg.; beq. to wife Susan; sons Timothy, John and Nathaniel; bro.-in-law Humphrey Atherton. [Reg. XI, 37, and XXXII, 321.]

WALFORD,
Thomas, blacksmith, came to Charlestown before 1628, and was living in a thatched and palisadoed house on the arrival of the Spragues. In some unexplained way he incurred the displeasure of the authorities, and was ordered to leave the province with his wife and to pay a fine of XL

WALFORD, cont.
shillings, "for contempt of authority and for confronting officers," Oct. 20, 1631. He paid the fine by killing a wolf. His goods were sequestrated for debts Sept. 3, 1633.
Thomas Walford d. in New Hampshire. Depositions made in N. H. court 27 June, 1667, by his widow Jane, ae. 69, son Jeremiah W., gr. son John Homes, ae. 26, Mary Brooken, ae. 32, and Martha Westbrook, ae. 22, respecting his estate.

WALGRAVE,
Thomas, Sudbury, propr. 1643.

WALKER, WAKER, WOAKER,
Augustine, mariner, Charlestown, adm. chh. 23 (7) 1640, frm. June 2, 1641. Wife Hannah; ch. Hannah b. 12 (7) 1640, Samuel b. 11 (8) 1642, Augustine b. 14 (10) 1646, James b. 25 (5) 1647.
He d. before 8 (6) 1654, when the inv. of his est. was taken; admin. was gr. to George Bunker and Edward Burt; whose sale of certain lands was confirmed by the Gen. Court 22 May, 1656.
Captain W., a very aged planter, bur. at Lynn May 16, 1687. [E.]
Henry, Ipswich, 1644; worked on the bridge, made pipe-staves, &c. Rem. to Gloucester; propr. 1647. Sold land on South side of Chebacco river 29 (7) 1653.
He d. Aug. 30, 1693. Will dated 29 Aug. 1690, prob. 20 Oct. 1693, beq. to the children of his sons William Haskell and Abraham Robinson, and to Nathaniel Coyt who lived with him.
Isaiah, residence not stated, frm. May 6, 1646.
Isaac, Sen. shop-keeper, res. at Salem. One of the petitioners for privilege of planting at Nashaway in 1645. Rem. to Boston; adm. chh. 2 (3) 1646. Signed inv. of John Hill in 1646. He bought Long Island in Casco Bay June 4, 1655. Wife Susanna, widow of Henry Simmons, d. after 14 May, 1645. He m. 2, Margaret —. Ch. Isaac b. and d. 1645, Susanna b. and d. 1646, Isaac b. 11 (8) 1647, Experience bapt. 20 (8) 1649, d. Feb. 11, 1657, Nicholas b. 1 (10) 1651, Stephen b. and d. 1656.
Will dated 8 Sept. 1672, prob. 17 (7) 1674, beq. to son Isaac, Nicholas and Stephen; to dau. Susanna and her husband Thomas Stanbury; to nevew Thomas Stanbury, Jr.; residue to wife, Susanna. Refers to his bro.

474

WALKER, etc., cont.
Nicholas Cowling. Admin. on the est. of N. C. late of Bristol, Eng. was gr. to his sister Susanna W. and her husband I. W. 7 Aug. 1669.

James, ae. 15, apprentice to John Browne, baker, came in the Elizabeth in April, 1635. Sarah, ae. 17, servant to William Bracey, linen draper, Cheapside, London, came in the same. He settled at Taunton; atba. 1643; juryman, 1643; frm. 4 June, 1650. James, (Walker,) lately married, had letter from Gov. Winslow of Plym. Col. to Gov. Winthrop, as he went to admin. on the est. of his wife's kinsman Samuel Crum, 4 (4) 1646. James W., Jr., m. at Taunton 23 Dec. 1647, Barsheba —. James W., Sen.; his wife Elizabeth d. 30 July, 1678; he m. 4 Nov. 1678, Sarah Rew. He performed a marriage in 1680. [Plym. Col. Rec.]

John, Roxbury, memb. chh. 1633; frm. May 14, 1634. His wife memb. chh. 1633-4. Dorcas W. was bur. April 17, 1640.

John, Hingham, propr. 1636; rem. to Marshfield, atba. 1643; son-in-law of Arthur Howland; called into Court 6 June, 1643. He m. 20 Oct. 1654, Lydia Reid; ch. Lydia b. Sept. 30, 1655, John b. Oct. 26, 1657. Admin. Dec. 28, 1663; wife Lydia, daus. Lydia, Martha and Mary, under age. [Reg. VI, 187.]

Richard, shoemaker, from Marlborough, Eng., came in the James April 5, 1635.

Richard, ae. 24, came in the Elizabeth April 15, 1635.

Richard, Salem, propr., frm. March 4, 1633-4. Prescis, [Persis or Priscilla,] Salem, memb. chh. 1639; ch. Abraham and Sarah bapt. 6 (10) 1639.

Richard, residence not stated, deposed in the Burnap case in 1653, ae. about 41 years. [Arch. 38 B.]

Richard, Boston, propr., allotment vacated 21 (1) 1636. His wife, Anne, formerly wife of Robert Houlton, was in Court for intemperance 30 (2) 1638.

Richard, gent., Lynn, juryman, 1636, propr. 1638; captain; deputy; planter; surety for Howes of Mattacheeset, 1638. Rem. to Reading; propr. 1644; town officer. Lent money on mortgage to Sir Richard Temple

WALKER, etc., cont.
in 1669, and cancelled the bond in 1670. He deposed in 1676, ae. about 65 years. Ch. Tabitha b. 1647. [Mdx. De. I.]

He, (residence not stated,) joined in 1639 with William, Thomas and Robert Talmage, bros. of his late wife Jane, in a letter of attorney for the collection of moneys from the overseers of the will of John Talmage of Newton Stacey in the co. of Southampton, husbandman, the bro. of their father, Thomas Talmage, and from the execs. of the will of their bro. Symon Talmage. [L.]

Capt. Richard W. bur. 16 May, 1687. Admin. of his est. gr. 19 June, 1688, to widow Sarah.

Robert, linen webster, Boston, memb. chh. 1631-2, frm. May 14, 1634; propr.; cow-keeper 1638. Shop-keeper. He deposed April 10, 1679, ae. about 72 years, that he resided with his father in Manchester, co. of Lancaster, Eng. in the year 1623; that he there knew Mr. Henry Sewall and his son Henry who came to Newbury, N. E., they being his overthwart neighbors. [Ess. Court Rec.] Wife Sarah; ch. Elishua b. 14 (12) 1635, (m. Dec. 12, 1660, Benjamin Thurston,) Zacharias b. 15 (7) 1637, John b. 22 (7) 1639, Sarah b. 15 (9) 1641, bur. 19 (10) 1643, Jacob b. 21 (1) 1644, Joseph b. (5) 1646, Thomas and Mary bapt. 22 (2) 1649, ae. about 10 days, Eliakim b. 3 (5) 1652, d. 30 (7) 1654, John d. 22 (5) 1652, Mary b. 1 (9) 1654.

He d. May 29, 1687. Admin. of his est. gr. 17 Aug. 1687, to widow Sarah. The widow d. Dec. 21, 1695. [S.]

Robert, probably error for Augustine, in bapt. rec. of Hannah in Charlestown 27 (7) 1640.

Samuel, Reading, propr. 1643. Rem. to Woburn. With wife adm. chh. about 1650. Town officer. Deposed April 2, 1661, ae. about 44 years. Licensed to sell strong waters in April, 1662. Ch. Samuel b. 28 (7) 1643, Joseph b. 10 (1) 1645, Hannah b. 11 (2) 1647, d. 28 (2) 1648, Israel and Hannah b. 28 (4) 1648, John b. 14 (12) 1649, Benjamin b. June 4, 1652, d. 26 April, 1653.

He d. Nov. 6, 1684. Admin. of his est. was gr. to sons Samuel and Joseph.

N. B. The Samuel of Woburn who m. Ann, widow of Arthur Alger, and had several children, whose widow deeded land in 1702 to sons Isaac and Ezekiel, seems to the writ-

WALKER, etc., cont.
er to have been the person who was b. in 1643.

Thomas, brick-maker, Boston, 1650. Wife Anne; ch. Thomas, Elizabeth b. 18 (6) 1650, John b. March 15, 1652, Anne b. 1654, d. 1655, Samuel b. June 26, 1656, Anne b. and d. 1659.

He d. in 1659. Admin. Sept. 1, 1659, gr. to widow Anne and son Thomas. [Reg. IX, 347.]

William, ae. 15, came in the Elizabeth April 15, 1635.

William, servant of John Gedney of Norwich, Eng. came to reside at Salem, N. E. May 11, 1637.

WALL,
Joan, ae. 19, came in the Abigail in July, 1635.

WALLEN,
Ralph, came in the Anne to Plymouth. Taxed in 1632, frm. 1633. Sold part of his land in 1633. His wife Joyce had share of cattle with him in 1627. She, as widow, sold land 7 Sept. 1643.

WALLER,
Christopher, tray-maker, Salem, propr. 1649. He deposed in 1661, ae. about 41 years. Mortg. house and land to James Browne, glazier 16 June, 1664. [Es. Files XIX, 115.]
Will dated 7 Oct. 1676, prob. 30 (9) 1676. Wife Margaret; Joseph Woodrow, living with her.

Matthew, Salem, propr. 1636. Lawsuit about finishing a house in 1641.

William, Salem, propr. 1644; town officer.

WALLINGTON, WALLINGFORD, see Wellington,
Nicholas, ae. 9, a poor boy, servant of Stephen Kent, came in the Confidence, April 24, 1638. Resided at Newbury. Bought the Henry Travers farm of Richard and Bridget Windorr Oct. 1, 1659. Rem. to Bradford. Gave an acre of land to the town toward the settlement of an able and faithful ministry,

WALLINGTON, etc., cont.
Feb. 7, 1677. He m. 30 Aug. 1654, Sarah Travers. Ch. John b. and d. 1655, Nicholas b. 2 Jan. 1656, John b. 7 April, 1659, Sarah b. 20 May, 1661, (m. Nov. 25, 1679, Caleb Hopkinson,) Mary b. 22 Aug. 1663, James b. 6 Oct. 1665, Hannah b. 27 Nov. 1667, William b. 7 Feb. 1670, Joseph b. April 20, 1672, Elizabeth b. June 23, 1674, Esther b. June 8, 1676, Benjamin b. June 27, 1678, Abigail b. June 24, 1680.

He was taken captive at sea, and never came home. He d. 10 May, 1682. Inv. of his est. taken 22 Sept. folg.; est. left in the widow's hands for the bringing up of the young child and the lame child, Nicholas. [Es. Files 38, 49.] Final division made Aug. 1, 1703, to James, Joseph, Elizabeth, Esther, Benjamin, Abigail and Nicholas W., Caleb Hopkinson, Daniel Russell and Joseph Poor.

WALLIS, WALLACE,
Henry, Duxbury, made a covenant with John Irish that which ever of them out-lived the other should inherit his 5 acre lot.
He d. before April 2, 1641, when the Court gave the land to Irish.

Ralph, husbandman, ae. 40, with George, ae. 15, came in the Abigail in June, 1635.
George, gent. now residing in N. E., recd. mortg. of farm-house and lands at Rumney Marsh, Boston, called Rumly Hall, Dec. 3, 1656; discharged April 2, 1657. He and his son and two men were there 5 months.

Robert, Ipswich, propr. 1638. He and [son?] Nicholas W. bought land in 1661. Nicholas deposed March 29, 1692, ae. about 58 years.

Thomas, merchant, Plymouth, bought land 1639; made contract to buy sturgeon of Henry Watts, fishmonger, of Black Point, Prov. of Maine, 1639. [L.] Frm. Mass. Bay Col. May 10, 1643.

William, Charlestown, adm. chh. 30 (9) 1642.

WALSTON,
Jane, ae. 19, came in the Truelove in Sept. 1635.

WALSBY,
David, Braintree, 1650; frm. May 7, 1651. He m. Hannah, dau. of William Manning, who beq. to his gr. son Samuel W.; she d. 2 (12) 1655, and he m. 24 (7) 1656, Ruth Bass. Ch. Samuel b. 9 (2) 1651, d. March, 1679, David b. 29 (7) 1655, Ruth b. 22 (7) 1659, Abigail b. 15 (4) 1667, Mary b. 15 (11) 1673.

WALTHAM, WALTUM, WALTON,
Henry, merchant, Weymouth; memb. of Fishing company allowed by Gen. Court 1635; deputy 1636. Arranged about mill 27 (4) 1633. [L.] Sold house and land granted him by the town to Mr. Thomas Thatcher, pastor of the church, 5 (6) 1656. His son William was bur. Nov. 3, 1640, leaving est. to bros. Thomas and Henry, and sisters Anne and Phillyne. [Reg. II, 103.] His widow Ann petitioned concerning the estate in 1659. [Arch. 15 B.]

James, Plymouth, case in court, 1636.

Jonathan, Weymouth, witnessed deed of Francis Williams in Boston in 1645. Town officer, 1651.

WALTER,
Lieut. Lynn, rem. before 1643. [Mass. Arch.]

WALTON, see Waltham,
George, before Gen. Court 4 (10) 1638.

Mr. Henry, Lynn, propr. 1638. Rem. to Boston. Salem court rec. mentions his servant Mary —, a witness in 1641, and himself in 1643. He rem. to Portsmouth, R. I., whence he gave a letter of attorney 11 May, 1646, to Richard Bulgar of Bo. [A.] Wife Mary; ch. Job b. at Bo. 27 (7) 1639, Adam b. 8 (3) 1643, William b. 29 (7) 1645.

Rev. William, of Seaton, co. Devon, Eng., came to N. E. about 1636. [J.] Settled at Hingham; propr. 1635; frm. 3 March, 1635-6. Rem. to Weymouth; thence to Marblehead; taxed in 1637. Was one of those to whom the Court gave leave to plant at Jeffrey's Creek or Manchester in 1640, but remained as minister at Marblehead. Wife Elizabeth; children as certified by himself in Es. Files: John b. at Seaton in Devon 6 (2) 1627, Elizabeth b. at same 27 (8) 1629, Martha b. at same 26 (2) 1632, Nathaniel b. at Hingham 3 (1) 1636, Samuel b. at Mar-

WALTON, cont.
blehead 5 (4) 1639, Josiah b. 20 (10) 1641, Marie b. 14 May, 1644, (m. Robert Bartlett). He d. at Marblehead "of an appoplexie;" was bur. 9 (9) 1668. [Rox. Chh. Rec.] Admin. was gr. to his widow Elizabeth 27 (9) 1668. In the will of his son Josiah, 27 (9) 1673, we learn the names of the married daus.: Martha Munjoy, Elizabeth Conant and Mary Bartlett. Final agreement for division made 29 March, 1685, after the death of the widow and Josiah; Elizabeth is called Mansfield. [Es. Files XLV, 12.]

WALUER,
Abraham, mentioned in the inv. of Nathl. Sparhawk of Cambridge in 1647.

WARD,
Andrew, Watertown, propr., frm. May 14, 1634. Rem. to Wethersfield, Conn.

Benjamin, ship-carpenter, Boston, propr. 1635 and 1637; adm. chh. with wife Mary 6 (4) 1640; frm. June 2, 1641.

He d., and admin. of his est. was gr. 26 Dec. to his widow Mary. She deposed that she had a son Stephen Butler by a former husband; that she had lived abut 45 years with her husband, Ward. She made will 4 July, prob. 21 July, 1667; son Stephen Butler exec.; beq. to her three gr. ch. Mary Holloway whom she and her husband had brought up, and William and Benjamin H., their father, William H. to have care of their portions; to other individuals, and to the poor. [Reg. XVIII, 154.]

Esther, maid servant to Mr. Atherton Haulgh, adm. chh. Boston 26 (11) 1633; Hester, now wife of Richard Kettle of Charlestown, she was dism. to the chh. of Char. 17 (5) 1642.

John, Salem, propr. 1641; memb. chh. 1639. Alice was adm. chh. 7 (12) 1640. One Ward, an honest young man of Salem, was drowned in 1641. [W.]

The will of Alice, widow, dated 28 Dec. 1652, was prob. 27 (1) 1655; inv. taken 23 (11) 1654. She desired that her dau.-in-law Sarah Ward should be brought up by John Baker and Elizabeth, his wife.

John, chirurgeon, Ipswich, frm. May 3, 1649. Sold house and land in 1648. Had

WARD, cont.
mortg. of property in Boston from John Low Oct. 9, 1652.

His will dated 28 Dec. 1652, prob. 25 (1) 1656; beq. to cousin Nathaniel, son of uncle Nathaniel Ward, house and lands at East Mersey in Essex, Eng., given to him by his father in his will, of which Edmund Sharman of Dedham had been agent; to two sons of cousin Ward of Wethersfield; to cousin John Barker's eldest dau., Anne, and son Samuel, of Boxstead in Essex; to mother's poor relations; to the youngest sons of cousin Samuel Sharman who died some time since in Boston, N. E.; to cousin Philip Sharman in Rhode Island; conditional bequest to Harvard College; books and chirurgery chest to Thomas Andrews of Ipswich.

Miles, mariner, Salem, frm. June 2, 1641. A sea-captain, who made voyages coastwise. Was made attorney of Thomas Painter, 5 (11) 1647, to collect money of Wm. Withington of Rhode Island. [A.] Margaret, [his wife?] was adm. chh. Salem 21 (9) 1640. Ch. — bapt. 25 (2) 1641, John bapt. 26 (10) 1641, Lydia bapt. 31 (11) 1646, Martha bapt. 1 (1) 1648-9.

He made an oral (nuncupative) will in Virginia 3 (1) 1650; it was prob. here (7) 1650; beq. all his est. to his wife and four children. A legacy of £40 is expected from his father in Eng.; to be paid by his brother.

Rev. Nathaniel, was grad. at Emanuel coll., Cambridge, Eng. 1603, adm. Lincoln's Inn May 15, 1607, and nominated as a barrister 17 Oct. 1615. [Reg. XLIII, 326.] Was ordained; rector of Stondon Massey; came to New Eng. about 1634. Settled at Ipswich. Pastor of the church. The Gen. Court gave him a farm of 600 acres near Andover; this he gave to Harvard College Dec. 10, 1646. He returned to Eng.; settled at Sherfield, near Brentwood. He was a very original and valuable writer; his chief work is The Simple Cobbler of Agawam. His children, (as given in the Candler Pedigree,) were John, who came here, was first minister of Haverhill; Susan, who m. Giles Firmin, q. v.; and James. See Memoir by John Ward Dean.

Samuel, yeoman, Hingham, propr. 3 April, 1636; frm. March 9, 1636-7. Deputy. Had lawsuit in 1640 about land which he had rec'd in payment for cloth sold. The

WARD, cont.
town granted permission 12 June, 1643, to Anthony Eames, Samuel Ward and Bozoun Allen to set up a common Corne Mill for the town; Gowen Wilson had been miller of the town; in future either Thomas Lincoln or John Pogger was to be miller. [uning. town rec., quoted in Arch. 59, 8.] Rem. to Hull before 1655. [Mdx. De. I, 119.] Rem. to Charlestown. Sold land at Hingham March 30, 1665. Owned large tracts of land at Hingham, Hull, Charlestown. His wife — died at Hing. Nov. 28, 1638; he m. 2, Frances —, [See Recroft.] They were adm. to chh. of Char. 9 (6) 1656. Ch. Samuel bapt. Nov. 18, 1638, Henry bur. 15 May, 1642, Mary, (m. Ambrose Gould,) Martha, (m. Isaac Lobdell).

He d. Aug. 30, 1682, ae. 89. Will signed March 6, 1681-2, prob. Oct. 3, 1682; beq. to wife Frances all that she brought when they were married and life-use of house and lands which were to be inherited by son Samuel at her death; other property to Samuel; to the daus. of his son Samuel and son-in-law Isaac Lobdell a house he had built at Char.; to dau. Mary and her husband Ambrose Gool land at Hull; to Harvard College the island lying betwixt Hing. and Hull, called "Bomkin Iland," which he wished to have called Ward's Island. Man Rogers to serve 3 years longer. The est. at Hull was appraised at the request of dau. Martha Lobdell. The widow Frances d. in Boston June 10, 1690.

See will of John Ward of Stratford, Suffolk, clothier, dated 19 Oct. 1629, prob. 18 May, 1631, in which is a bequest to son Samewell. [Reg. L, 113.]

Thomas, juryman, Gen. Court 28 Sept. 1630. Dedham, prop. for propr. 1638.

William, Sudbury, 1639; frm. May 10, 1643. Deputy, town officer, com. to end small causes. He deposed 4 (8) 1664, ae. about 61 years. [Mdx. Files.] Rem. to Marlborough. Wife Elizabeth; ch. William b. 22 (11) 1640, Samuel b. 24 Sept. 1641, Elizabeth b. 14 (2) 1642, Increase b. 22 (11) 1644, dau. Hopestill b. 24 (11) 1646, William b. 22 (12) 1648.

He d. Aug. 10, 1687. Will dated 6 April, 1686, beq. to wife Elizabeth; ch. John, Increase; the ch. of sons Richard and Eleazer, dec.; son-in-law Abraham Williams; to all his ch. by former wife and present wife.

WARD, cont.

The widow d. Dec. 9, 1700, in 87th year. [Gr. St.] Genealogy.

WARDALL, WARDELL, WODDELL, WADDELL, WARDWELL, see Wattell,

Thomas, shoemaker, Boston, adm. chh. 9 (9) 1634, frm. March 4, 1634-5; propr. Jan. 1635-6. Dism. to Paschataqua with Wheelwright adherents 6 (11) 1638, but returned. Wife Elizabeth; ch. Eliakim bapt. 23 (9) 1634, Martha b. (6) 1637, Samuel b. 16 (3) 1643.

He d. in Boston Dec. 10, 1646. "Mis. Wardel, an antient wido," d. 22 Feb. 1697.

Thomas, Ipswich, propr. 1648.

William, servant to Edmund Quinsey, adm. chh. Boston 9 (12) 1633. He was dism. to the chh. of Pashcataqua with Wheelwright party 6 (11) 1638. Rem. to Rhode Island, whence he was brought for trial in 1643 with Gorton and others, on accusation of heresy, etc.; confined at Watertown. Wife Alice d.; he m. Dec. 5, 1657, Elizabeth, widow of John Gillitt, (Jellett,) with whom he contracted to bring up her dau. Hannah, then 2 years old, in consideration of living in the widow's house. [Reg. XII, 275.] Ch. Meribah bapt. 25 (4) 1637, Usal, son, b. 7 (2) 1639, Elihu bapt. 5 (10) 1641, Elihu b. (9) 1642, Mary b. (2) 1644, Leah b. 7 (10) 1646, Abigail b. April 24, 1660, d. 23 Aug. 1661.

His will, prob. 18 April, 1670, beq. to wife Elizabeth one half of house in Boston for life; to her daus. Hannah and Deborah Gillett; to his eldest son Uzall and son Elihu; to daus. Leah, wife to William Tower, Meribah, wife to Francis Littlefield of Wells, and Mary, wife to Nathaniel Rust. [Reg. XLVIII, 458.]

WARDEN,

Jane, Plymouth, sued — Weeks for money lent 5 Jan. 1635.

WARE, WEAR, WARES, WEARE, WARRE, WAR,

Nicholas, [Scituate,] m. Anna, dau. of William Vassall.

Robert, Dedham, propr. Nov. 25, 1642, adm. chh. 2 (8) 1646; frm. May 26, 1647. He m. 24 (1) 1645, Margaret Hunting; she d. 26

WARE, etc., cont.

(6) 1670; he m. 3 (3) 1676, Hannah Jones; she d. 20 April, 1721, ae. 84. Ch. John b. 6 (8) 1646, Nathaniel b. 7 (8) 1648, Margaret b. 14 (12) 1650, d. 22 July, 1664, Robert b. 1 (6) 1653, Esther b. 28 (7) 1655, (m. Samuel Man,) Samuel b. 30 (7) 1657, Ephraim b. 5 (9) 1659, Elizabeth b. 19 (9) 1661, Joseph b. and d. 1663, Ebenezer b. 28 Oct. 1667.

He, "the aged," d. April 19, 1699. Will dated Feb. 25, 1698, prob. May 11, 1699, gave his large est. to wife Hannah, sons John, Robert, Samuel, Ephraim, Ebenezer and other children. [Reg. XLI, 21.]

William, shoemaker, Dorchester, adm. chh. 17 (2) 1643; one of the ruling elders in 1640, according to Lechford; an arbitrator in a lawsuit. Rem. to Boston.

He d. Feb. 11, 1657. Will dated March 26, 1656, prob. 1 April, 1658. Wife Elizabeth; dau. Sarah; gr. ch. Obediah and Elizabeth Gill; lands and house in Bo. and Dorch. John Gill, mariner, and Edward Grant, ship-carpenter, husbands, respectively, of Elizabeth and Sarah, confirmed a deed of land at Dorch. made by the widow July 9, 1661. [Reg. VIII, 353.]

WARHAM, WAREHAM,

Rev. John, ordained by the bishop of Exeter at Silferton, Devon, May 23, 1619. Preached also at Exeter. [Dorch. Pope Family, p. 11.] One of the two ministers of the Dorchester Colony, chosen to office at Plymouth in March, 1629, came in the Mary and John; arrived at Nantasket May 30, 1630, and settled at Mattapan, soon called Dorchester. Frm. May 18, 1631. Rem. to Windsor, Conn. with about half of the church during 1635 and 1636. He was a man of great strength of character, and deserves much praise for his consecration and service in laying the foundations of two commonwealths. His wife d. in the autumn of 1634. [W.] He m. 2, Jane, widow of Thomas Newberry, who d. 23 April, 1645. He m. 3, 9 Oct. 1662, Abigail, widow of John Branker.

He d. 1 April, 1670. Ch. Samuel d. 1647; Abigail bapt. 27 May, 1638, (m. Thomas Allyn,) Hephzibah bapt. 9 Aug. 1640, d. 1647, Sarah b. 28 Aug. 1642, (m. Return Strong,) Hester b. 8 Dec. 1644, (m. 1, Rev. Eleazer Mather, 2, Rev. Solomon Stoddard, and was grandmother of Rev. Jonathan Edwards).

WARNER, WERNER,
Andrew, Cambridge, propr. 1633; frm. May 14, 1634; propr., town officer. He sold in 1636, and rem. to Hartford, Conn. He rem. to Hadley about 1659.
He d. Dec. 18, 1684. Will dated 18 June, 1681, prob. March 31, 1685, beq. to wife Eastor, sons Jacob, Daniel, Isaac, Andrew, Robert, John; daus. Ruth, — Pratt, and — Hills; to Mary, wife of John Taylor.

Daniel, Ipswich, propr. adjoining John Wyate in 1639; frm. June 2, 1641. He m. about 1660 Faith, widow of Edmund Browne; her will dated 25 June, 1669, prob. 30 March, 1680, made her husband D. exec.; beq. to sons Joseph and John and dau. Lydia B.; eldest daughter has received her portion.
He d. Sept. 9, 1688. [Believed by Hoyt to be a son of William, below.]

John, ae. 20, came in the Increase April 15, 1635. Settled at Watertown; propr. 1636. Rem. to Rhode Island. He was arrested in 1643 and brought to Boston; tried and imprisoned for alleged religious errors. Permitted to ship himself and family for England at some Mass. port, 27 May, 1642. [Col. Rec.]

Thomas, before Gen. Court 3 (7) 1639.
Thomas, wife Katharine, had ch. b. at Boston Dec. 24, 1658.
Thomas, of Boston, fisherman, admin. of his est. by Mr. Richard Russell April 24, 1660. [Reg. IX, 348.]

William, Ipswich, propr. 1635; propr. 1639; frm. May 2, 1638.

WARR, see Hooper,
Abraham, Ipswich, res. 1648.
His will dated 22 (3) 1654, beq. to wife and dau. Sarah, asking the former to care for S. as if she were her own.

WARREN, WARRIN,
Abraham, Salem, 1635. In Es. Court in 1638. Bought land adjoining some he owned in 1661.

Arthur, Weymouth, before Gen. Court 6 (1) 1637-8. Ch. Arthur b. 17 (9) 1639, Abigail b. 27 (8) 1640, Jacob b. 26 (8) 1642.
Inv. of his estate "which he bequeathed to his wife for the maintenance of his children," taken by Will Vessie, John Rogers

WARREN, etc., cont.
and Thomas Dyer. Lands, house and furnishings; musket given to his eldest son. Not dated. [Suff. Prob.]

John, Watertown, came [probably] in 1630. Frm. May 18, 1631. Town officer. Sympathized with Quakers. In court concerning baptism, (8) 1651. [Mdx. Files.] Wife Margaret d. Nov. 6, 1662. Ch. John, Mary, (m. John Bigelow,) Daniel, Elizabeth, (m. James Knapp).
He d. 13 (10) 1667, [ae. 82.] He made will 30 Nov. prob. 16 Dec. 1667, being aged; beq. to ch. Daniel, John, Mary Begelow and Elizabeth Knope; to gr. ch. Mary B.; to Michell, dau. to Richard Bloyce, dec.; to each gr. ch.

Ralph, Salem, Marblehead, taxed in 1638; before Gen. Court in 1639.

Richard, of London, came in the Mayflower; signed the Compact; settled at Plymouth; "an useful instrument; bore a deep share in the difficulties and troubles of the settlement." [Mor.] His wife and children came in the Anne in 1623. In the division of cattle in 1627 shares were given to him, to his wife Elizabeth, and to ch. Nathaniel, Joseph, Mary, Anna, Sarah, Elizabeth and Abigail.
He d. before 1628. His widow Elizabeth d. Oct. 2, 1673, ae. about 90. Mary m. Robert Bartlett, Elizabeth m. Richard Church, Ann m. Thomas Little, Sarah m. John Cooke, Jr., and Abigail m. Anthony Snow. [See Reg. VII, 177, and Plym. Col. Recs.]

WARRINER, WARRENER,
William, Springfield, frm. May 2, 1638. Propr.; town officer. Signature in town records, 1649. He m. 31 (5) 1639, Johanna Scant. Ch. James b. 21 (11) 1640, Hannah b. 17 (6) 1643, Joseph b. 6 (12) 1644.
Division of his estate was made by agreement Sept. 27, 1676, between the widow Elizabeth and her ch. James and Joseph W. and Thomas Noble.

WASHBURN,
John, tailor, Duxbury, taxed 1632; bought house and land March, 1634-5. Atba. 1643; frm. June 2, 1646. Rem. to Bridgewater. His wife Margery, ae. 49, with sons, John, ae. 14, and Philip, ae. 11, came in the Elizabeth and Ann April 13, 1635, cert. from

WASHBURN, cont.
Eversham, co. Worcester, Eng. John, Jr., and Philip also atba. in 1643. John, the younger, mentioned in Plym. Rec. 4 Dec. 1638; served against the Narragansetts in 1645; he m. Dec. 6, 1645, Elizabeth Mitchell.

WASON,
Phebe, widow, Boston, adm. chh. 16 (4) 1639.

WATERBURY,
John, Watertown, sold house and land, (cellar to be completed,) 15 (8) 1646.

William, Boston, with wife Alice, memb. chh. 1630-1.

WATERHOUSE,
Mr. Thomas, schoolmaster, Dorchester, 1639; frm. May 13, 1640. "Mrs." W., also memb. church.

WATERMAN,
John, passenger on the Jonathan in 1639, in care of Peter Noyes. [Reg. XXXII, 410.] Settled at Sudbury; propr. 1639.

Richard, sent over by the Mass. Bay Company in 1629 to Salem; his chief employment to be to get venison for the government. [Suff. De. I, x.] Paid by treasurer Pynchon in 1632 for killing a wolf. Propr. and town officer, 1636. He was banished for sympathy with the Hutchinson party in 1638. Brought from Rhode Island in 1643, with Gorton and others, and tried for alleged heresy; some of his property confiscated for charges, and he bound over for later appearance. [W.] Ch. Nathaniel bapt. 20 (6) 1637, two ch. bapt. 8 (5) 1638.

Robert, yeoman, Plymouth, bought land 7 May, 1639. Rem. to Marshfield, frm. 7 March, 1642; propr. 1643; deputy 1646; town officer. He m. 11 Dec. 1638, Elizabeth, dau. of Thomas Bourne; ch. John b. April 19, 1642, Thomas b. 30 Nov. 1644.

He d. Dec. 10, 1652. Admin. gr. to widow Elizabeth March 1, 1652-3. [Reg. V, 259.]

Thomas, Roxbury, his wife Ann (Hannah,) d. June 5, 1641. He d. Jan. 22, 1675, "aged." Beq. to son Thomas, Mr. John Eliot, Nicholas Williams and to his wife. His [second] wife Margaret, with his consent made her will 19 May, 1670, prob. 27 (12) 1682. Beq. to son Thomas W., Jr.; to sister

WATERMAN, cont.
Ann Burnett of Redding; to cousin Ann Bullard, her eldest dau. Abigail Wight, and her bro. Thomas Burnett; to cousin John Bowles' 3 children; to the Indian church at Nonantum; to Mess. Eliot and Danforth; to Sarah Southricke; cousin Robert Burnett and Isaac Bullard execs. As the execs. had d. before her, the Court gr. admin. to Anne Bullard; Richard Ellice and James Thorpe, bondsmen.

WATERS, WATTERS,
Anthony, Marshfield, atba. 1643, propr. 1645.

John, Boston or Charlestown, memb. chh. with wife Francis, in 1630. Both d. before Nov. 29, 1630. "My servant, old Waters of Neyland." [W.] Mary, [a dau.?] adm. chh. Bo. 1632-3.

Lawrence, carpenter, Watertown, propr. 1636-7. Planted the intervale between Penacook and Still rivers before 1647; a region then included in Lancaster. Son-in-law of Richard Linton. [Suff. De. I, 79 and 85.] Rem. in 1675 to Charlestown, where his son Stephen resided. Wife Anna; ch. Lawrence b. 14 Feb. 1634, Sarah b. Dec. 7, 1636, Mary b. Jan. 27, 1637-8, Rebecca b. 1639, d. 1640, Daniel b. 6 (12) 1641, Stephen b. Jan. 24, 1642, Joseph b. at Lancaster 29 (2) 1647, Jacob and Rachel b. 1 (1) 1649, Rachel d. 31 (1) 1649, Samuel b. 14 (11) 1651, Johannah b. 26 (1) 1652, d. 21 (2) 1654, Ephraim b. 27 (11) 1655, d. 17 (4) 1659, Rebecca, (m. at Lancaster 4 (11) 1664, Josiah Whetcombe).

He d. Dec. 9, 1687, ae. near 85 years. [Mdx. Rec.]

Richard, bapt. at St. Botolph Aldersgate, London, Eng., March 3, 1604, son of James Waters, citizen and ironmonger, and his wife. Phebe, dau. of Mr. George Manning, gent. of Downe, Kent. James W. was bur. Feb. 2, 1617, and the widow m. 2, Feb. 23, 1618, William Plasse, gunmaker; they came to Salem, N. E. where Richard had his home from about 1636. He was a gunsmith. Frm. 22 May, 1639. Propr. He deeded land to dau. Mary and her husband, Clement English, in 1673. His wife Joyce, was adm. chh. 23 (3) 1641. Ch. rec. here, a dau. bapt. 27 (9) 1640, Eliza bapt. 26 (12) 1642, d. 4 (12) 1662, Abigail bapt. 18 (3) 1645, (m. 26 Oct. 1669, Wm. Punchard,) Ezekiel bapt. 9 (2) 1647,

WATERS, etc., cont.
Susanna bapt. 1 (2) 1649, (m. — Pulsifer,) Hannah bapt. 30 (11) 1652, (m. — Striker,) Sarah, [a dau.?] (m. 26 Feb. 1651, Joshua Ray,) Phebe, [a dau.?] (m. 11 (8) 1658, Thomas West; she d. 16 April, 1674;) Mary, (m. 27 Aug. 1667, Clement English,) Martha, William, John and James also named in will. He signed his will 16 July, 1676; it was prob. 28 (9) 1677; he beq. to wife Joyce and ch. William, Ezekiel, John, James, Martha, Abigail Punchard, Mary English, Susanna Pulsifer and Hannah Striker.

WATHEN, WATHIN, WARREN,
— Wathen, propr. at Lynn in 1638.

George, Salem, propr. 1640; adm. chh. 23 (3) 1641.

Margaret, widow, [Salem,] admin. gr. 3 (11) 1644, to Dea. Charles Gott and John Horne.

Thomas, Gloucester, son of Edmund W., 1648; [Salem Court Files.] went to the war in Eng. and died with Prince Rupert. Rebecca Joy, a little related to him, asked for the appointment of William Sergent of Gloc., who was his father's sister's son, as admin. of his est. 27 (7) 1652. Inv. ret. (4) 1653. Another inv. ret. by kinsman Ezekiel W. June 30, 1658. [Essex Inst. Coll.; Reg. XXXII, 341.]

John, Salem, servant of Walter Price, d. in 1641; admin. by Price, who had paid his passage, etc., for which he had the estate.

WATLIN,
Richard, ae. 28, came in the Francis of Ipswich April 30, 1634.

WATTELS, see Wardall,
Richard, Ipswich, propr. 1637.

WATSON, see Challis,
Elizabeth, widow, Plymouth, assigned her servant, Henry Blage, Nov. 8, 1638, to Thomas Watson.

George, yeoman, Plymouth, frm. 1633, bondsman 1639, juror 1646. Wife Phebe d. 22 May, 1663. Ch. Samuel b. 18 Jan. 1647, d. 20 Aug. 1649, Elizabeth b. 18 Jan. 1647, Jonathan b. 9 March, 1651, Elkanah b. 25 Feb. 1655-6.
Inv. of his est. taken Feb. 2, 1688-9; his

WATSON, cont.
son Elkanah deposed March 13, 1688-9. [Gen. Adv. I, 43.]

John, embarked June 22, 1632; came to Roxbury; frm. Nov. 5, 1633. Propr. He m. April 3, 1634, Alice, widow of Valentine Prentiss; ch. John b. Jan. 1634-5, Joshua b. Aug. 1637, d. 30 (2) 1649, Dorcas b. Sept. 20, 1639, Caleb b. June 29, 1641, Mary b. May 2, 1644.
He d. 5 (11) 1671. Will prob. 5 (12) 1671, beq. to his 4 children, John, Caleb, dau. Darkell [Dorcas] and dau. Mary. Wife Alice to have life use.

John, yeoman, Cambridge. He gave power of attorney 11 (8) 1647, to George Hutchins for collection of legacy from the will of Richard Walters, late of Whickamin, co. of Durham, Eng., smith. [A.] Will of John Watson, Sen. prob. Mdx. Court 5 (9) 1672. John Watson, Jr., and Rebecca Watson, Sen. mentioned. He or his son John m. Rebecca Errington, who d. Nov. 11, 1690, ae. 65.
He d. May 20, 1711, ae. 92.

Thomas, tailor, Salem, 1636; frm. May 13, 1640. Wife Johane, memb. chh. before 1636, joined him in a deed in 1672.
He d. 1 March, 1672-3; the widow d. (10) 1674.

Thomas, planter, Duxbury, made statement of accounts and will 28 (7) 1639, when about to embark for England. Certain moneys to go, in case of his death, to his niece Anna W., dau. of John W., dec.; she dwells with her mother-in-law Elizabeth, wife of John Grey, dwelling near Quinapeage. [L.]

WAY, WAYE,
Aaron, Dorchester, propr. 1640, frm. May 7, 1651. Bought a farm at Rumley Marsh, jointly with Wm. Ireland, 19 Feb. 1651, and rem. to Boston. Gave bonds for his bro. Richard Way in 1657. Was dism. to the New chh. Bo. with his wife and W. I. 3 (12) 1660. Ch. Mary bapt. 14 (11) 1648, Aaron bapt. 6 (8) 1650, William bapt. 30 (11) 1652, Susanna bapt. 1 (2) 1660, Joanna (of Aaron and Joan, in Bo.) March 5, 1663, John b. May 8, 1666, Elizabeth b. June 23, 1667, Moses b. June 13, 1672.
Will dated 25 Aug. prob. 26 Sept. 1695, beq. to wife; to ch. Mary, Susanna, Moses, Aaron,

WAY, etc., cont.

William, Joanna. Bros. George and Increase Sumner and cousin Wm. Ireland overseers.

George, mentioned in Dorchester Records 2 Jan. 1637-8, as having had a grant of land formerly, but no proof that he came.

George, Boston, deposed 27 (5) 1652, ae. about 33 years. [Arch. 38 B.] Wife Elizabeth; ch. Elizabeth b. 19 (1) 1651.

Mr. Henry, Dorchester, one of the first company; [Bl.] carried on fishing business. His boat saved three shipwrecked men off the coast, 26 July, 1631. Two other boats of his were lost, 5 men killed by the Indians and 2 drowned, in 1632. [W.] Adm. chh. 5 (3) 1643. His wife Elizabeth d. 23 (4) 1665, ae. 84.

He d. 24 (3) 1667, ae. 84.

Richard, cooper, lieut. Dorchester, adm. chh. 5 (3), frm. 10 (3) 1643; propr. 1648. Rem. to Salem, but ret. before 1655. Rem. to Boston; adm. townsman 27 (2) 1657. Deposed in 1666, ae. about 42 years. Ch. Henry bapt. at Sal. 23 (10) 1651, Eliza bapt. 8 (7) 1653. Wife Hester adm. chh. Dorch. 14 (8) 1655; joined in deed of land at Sal. in 1659. Ch. Richard bapt. 17 (4) 1655, Jonathan bapt. 3 (11) 1657, d. 6 (9) 1658, Hannah b. in Bo. May 23, 1662, Hannah (of Richard and Bethiah) b. July 13, 1677. Richard Way m. Hannah Knight Aug. 13, 1689. His son Henry made will Dec. 2, 1674, prob. Nov. 15, 1675. Beq. to sister Elizabeth and bro. Richard Way, Jr. His father Richard and uncle Aaron Way overseers.

He d. 23 June, 1697. Will dated 2 Jan. 1696-7, prob. Oct. 8, 1697, beq. all to wife Hannah, believing that none of his own children were surviving.

Robert, Dorchester, under the care of "Mr. Way" and Mr. Ludlow up to Aug. 5, 1634, was then placed by the Court in charge of Edward Burton.

Widow, Dorchester, her land mentioned in a list of proprs. of great lots, 23 (12) 1646.

WEAVER,

James, stationer, cert. from St. Albons, Herts., Eng. ae. 23, came in the Planter April 3, 1635.

WEAVER, cont.

Clement, before Gen. Court 2 (4) 1640.

Edmund, husbandman, ae. 28, from Anckstrey, Herts. came in the Planter April 3, 1635, with wife Margaret, ae. 30.

WEBB, WEB, WEBBE, see Audey and Everard,

Christopher, Braintree, frm. May, 1645. Propr. 1656.

He d. June, 1671. Will prob. 2 (9) 1671, beq. to son Christopher, wife Humility, daus. Mary Sheffield and Sarah Buckmaster. The son Christopher d. 30 May, 1694, ae. 64 years. The widow Humility d. Nov. 1687, ae. 99.

Mr. Henry, merchant, from Salisbury, Eng., came to Boston about 1637; had leave to buy the house where he dwelt 25 (7) 1637; adm. chh. 6 (12) 1638, frm. March 13, 1638-9. Had great lot at the Mount for 10 heads Jan. 11, 1637-8, and grant of a farm of 200 acres 28 (7) 1640. Bought one seventh of the ship Seabright 9 (8) 1642. [A.] Town officer; allowed to trade with the Indians. [Letter to Iron Works co. in 1653 in Es. Files 4.] Wife Dowsabel adm. chh. 10 (12) 1638, d. Feb. 28, 1659. Dau. Margaret b. in Salisbury Sept. 25, 1625, m. 1, Jacob Sheafe, 2, Mr. Thomas Thatcher.

He d. Sept. 7, 1660. Will dated 5 April, prob. 13 Sept. 1660. Only dau. Margaret, late wife of Jacob Sheafe, and her dau. Elizabeth and Mehitabel principal heirs; beq. to sister Jane, wife of dec. bro. John Webb of Titherly in Hampshire; to his cousin Elizabeth, wife of John Blackleach, and her dau. Elizabeth; to cousin Francis Grunn and her ch. Elizabeth and Jone; to late sister Elizabeth Sanford's sons, John and Samuel Sanford; to wife's sister Barbara, wife of Reinold Sewall, of Salisbury, joiner; to David and Elizabeth Sewall, his late wife's cousins; to Harvard College; to the town of Boston; to several individuals. [Reg. X, 177, and XL, 259.]

John, yeoman, brasier, Roxbury, set free from his master, William Parks, June 11, 1633. Rem. to Boston; adm. chh., singleman, 9 (12) 1633; frm. Dec. 7, 1636. Owned house and land at Braintree, which he sold 19 (2) 1648. Adm. inhabitant of Boston in 1651. Town officer. Wife Anna; ch. Susan d. 17 (10) and Richard d. 30 (10) 1651.

Richard, Cambridge; wife Elizabeth

WEBB, etc., cont.
adm. chh. Boston, 1631. Frm. Nov. 2, 1632; propr. 1633; sold in 1635. Rem. to Hartford, Conn.

Richard, shoemaker, Weymouth, propr. 1640. Rem. to Boston. Adm. chh. 28 (10) 1644. Propr.; town officer; sealer of leather 1649. Wife Mary adm. chh. 22 (1) 1645; ch. Joseph, ae. about 4 years, and Nehemiah, ae. about 3 years, bapt. 12 (11) 1644-5; He d. July 2; will prob. July 21, 1659. Divided his house and yard between his eldest son Joseph and his youngest son Nehemiah; beq. other things to Nehemiah, to dau.-in-law Ester Pearce and her ch. Moses and Ester; rest to Joseph, whom he appoints exec. Dea. Upham of Malden and Lieut. Roger Clap of Dorchester, overseers and advisers of the children. Joseph chose his uncle Upham, Lieut. Clap and Dea. Clap to be his guardian. [Reg. IX, 138.] Joseph m. at Scituate 16 April, 1666, Grace Dipple. [See Baker, Nicholas.] He was clerk of courts, 1689-1698. [Suff. De. X, Introduction.]

William, Roxbury, frm. May 25, 1636. Rem. to Boston. Wife Rebecca followed the business of baking. [E.] Both recd. to Bo. chh. 31 (1) 1644.
He d. (10) 1644. The widow sold Rox. lands April 21, 1653. Her will, Dec. 10, 1654, gave est. to grand. dau. Rebecca, dau. of Godfrey Armitage. [Reg. V, 303, VIII, 356, XXXI, 104; and E.]

WEBBER,
Thomas, mariner, Roxbury, rem. to Boston about 1643; recd. from that chh. to Bo. chh. 31 (1) 1644. Master of the ship Mayflower, made contract Oct. 7, 1652, then residing in Eng. [Suff. De. III, 66.] Wife Sarah; ch. Sarah, b. 1643, Bathsheba bapt. 24 (7) 1648, ae. about 3 days, Thomas bapt. 2 (12) 1650, Mehitabel b. and d. 1652.

WEBSTER,
John, Ipswich, propr. 1634; frm. March 4, 1634-5; clerk of the bonds, 1642. He seems to be the John Webster, baker, who was admitted an inhabitant of Salem in 1637 and had a grant of land; who was a witness in Ess. court in 1639, and applied for land at the Creek in 1642. His wife, Mary, was a sister of John Shatswell, who mentioned her in his will.

WEBSTER, cont.
He d. before Nov. 4, 1646, when the Court gave admin. to the widow Mary. At her desire division was made to the 8 minor children thus: to the eldest son, John, the farm, he paying to the youngest son Nathan 5 li. or a quarter of the value of the farm; Mary, Stephen and Hannah to have equal shares in the island bought of widow Andrews; Elizabeth, Abigail and Israel to have 20 nobles apiece; all at 21 years of age. The widow m. 29 (8) 1650, John Emery. He and his son John Emery were appointed guardians of Israel, ae. 18, and Nathan, ae. 16, at their request, 26 (9) 1662. The family rem. to Newbury. Mary m. Oct. 2, 1648, John Emery, Jr.; John m. June 13, 1653, Anne, dau. of Nicholas Batt; Hannah m. April 1, 1657, Michael Emerson, (and had dau. Hannah who m. Thomas Duston, and was the heroine of the Indian captivity;) Abigail m. Abraham Merrill; Stephen m. 1, Hannah Ayer, 2, Judith Broad; Elizabeth m. Samuel Simmons; Israel m. 1, Elizabeth Browne, 2, Elizabeth Lunt; Nathan m. Mary Haseltine. See the mother's will under Emery.

Thomas, frm. May 29, 1644; see Hampton, N. H. records.

WEDGEWOOD,
John, Ipswich, propr. 1637; before Gen. Court 3 (7) 1639. Rem. to Hampton.

WEED, WEEDE,
Jonas, Watertown, frm. May 18, 1631. Was dism. from the chh. to that of Wethersfield, Conn., May 29, 1635.

John, planter, Salisbury, propr. 1650-1664. Lieut.; he deposed at Salis. court 8 (2) 1662, ae. about 35 years. He m. Nov. 14, 1650, Deborah, dau. of Samuel Winsley; ch. Samuel b. Feb. 15, 1651, Mary b. Sept. 5, 1653, John b. Nov. 1, 1655, Ann b. July 26, 1657, (m. Edward Hunt,) Deborah b. June 15, 1659, (m. Christopher Bartlett,) George b. May 25, 1661, Nathaniel, Ephraim b. Feb. 24, 1666, Joseph b. July 9, 1671, Thomas b. July 17, 1674.
He d. March 15, 1688-9; inv. of his est. taken March 21, admin. gr. June 24, 1690. The widow Deborah d. April 20, 1695.

WEEDEN,

Edward, carpenter, ae. 22, came in the Susan and Ellen April, 1635. Settled at Lynn; res. 1639; rem. to Boston about 1641. Wife Elizabeth; ch. Samuel b. (6) 1644, Elizabeth, Sarah, Mary, Ann and Edward bapt. 17 (4) 1667.

Admin. on his est. was gr. 18 Dec. 1679, to his widow Elizabeth. She,—Elizabeth Weeden, the midwife,—d. June 11, 1696.

WEEKS, WICKS,

George, Dorchester, frm. May 18, 1640, propr. Town officer. Signed inv. of John Pope, 1646. He m. in Eng. Jane, dau. of William Clap of Salcombe Regis; she and her son Thomas were named in the will of her bro. William C. in 1636; she was adm. to chh. of Dorch. with her husband 21 (10) 1639.

He d. Dec. 28, 1650; admin. 22 (11) 1650. The widow m. 2, Jonas Humphreys of Dorch.; she d. 2 (6) 1668. Will dated 29 (11) 1666, prob. 19 Nov. 1668, gave to sons Amiel and William and their wives; to son Joseph, dau. Jane; to gr. ch. Amiell, Ebenezer, Thankful, Elizabeth and Jane; to son-in-law Benjamin Bates; sisters Jone and Susanna Clap and cousin Hannah Clap; to Mary Atherton. [Reg. VII, 334, and Genealogy.]

John, tanner, ae. 26, with Marie, ae. 28, and Anna, ae. 1, came in the Hopewell in Sept. 1635. May be the following.

Mr. John, planter, Plymouth, frm. 3 Jan. 1636. Res. near John Alden. Was expelled from the church with his wife for opinions considered very wrong, about 1637. [Mass. Hist. Coll. 4.] Rem. to Aquidneck or Rhode Island; had a bro. Thomas at Staines, Middlesex, Eng. in 1639. [L.] Was captured with Gorton and others; tried at Boston, and imprisoned at Ipswich in 1643 for alleged religious errors. [W.]

Thomas, turner, inhabitant Charlestown 1636. Rem. to Salem 1638. William Plasse d. at his house in 1646. [See George, above.] He sold land in 1652. Wife Alice adm. chh. Char. 12 (12) 1636; to chh. Salem 1639. Ch. Bethiah bapt. 27 (12) 1641, Hannah bapt. 5 (11) 1644.

Will dated 9 (7) 1655, prob. Ess. Court (4) 1656. Wife Alice; daus. Bethiah and Hannah; cousin Robert Gray.

WEIGHTMAN, WIGHTMAN,

John, Charlestown, adm. chh. 31 (5) 1641.

He d. 24 (7) 1684, ae. 80 years. [Mdx. Rec.] His will dated 12 Oct. 1681, prob. 21 (8) 1684, beq. to three cousins Sarah Ran[d], Hannah Cleesby and Rebecca Edington; to sister Elizabeth Skiffe, and after her decease to her dau. Rebecca Edington; shop to Thomas Rand and Thomas Beard. John Cleesby of Boston, exec.

WEILLUST,

Joist, chosen by the Gen. Court, 1 March, 1630-1, surveyor of ordinance and cannonneer. Had leave to go to his own country as he desired July 3, 1632.

WELBIE, WELBY, WILBY,

George, ae. 16, came in the Susan and Ellen in April, 1635. Settled at Lynn; propr. 1638. Brought suit at Ipswich court in 1641. Rem. to Southampton, Long Island. Deposed May 16, 1641, at New York; b. at Northamptonshire, ae. about 25 years.

WELCH, WELSH,

Jacob, husbandman, ae. 32, came in the Rebecca April 9, 1635.

Thomas, yeoman, Charlestown: Seth Sweetser was to pay him money in 1642. Mentioned at Cambridge in 1646. Adm. chh. Char. 12 (2) 1650; frm. May 22, 1650. Wife Elizabeth adm. chh. 9 (6) 1656. Ch. Thomas b. 7 July, 1655, Jonathan bapt. 9 (8) 1659, Jonathan bapt. 8 (4) 1660, Nathaniel bapt. 10 (7) 1665, Jonathan bapt. 16 (7) 1666.

Will dated 15 Feb. 1700, prob. May 26, 1701, beq. to wife Elizabeth; ch. Thomas, Elkanah, Jonathan, and Dorcas Eaglestone, and gr. son Thomas, son of Thomas. Priscilla Croswell testified that she had often heard her bro. Thomas Welsh speak of his son Elkanah's fidelity.

WELD, WELDE, WELLS,

Daniel, Braintree, frm. June 2, 1641. He rem. to Roxbury March 23, 1651. Wife Alse was bur. 18 (2) 1647; he m. 30 (5) 1647, Ann Hide.

He d. 22 (5) 1666, ae. 80 or 81. Will prob. Nov. 3, 1666. Wife Ann; son Daniel in England; ch. of himself and wife, namely: Joseph and Bethiah Weld, Timothy Hide; dau.

WELD, etc., cont.
Mary Hide hath had her portion already, but her son may have something at Ann's death.

Joseph, Roxbury, captain, householder, propr., town officer, deputy. Wife Elizabeth d. Oct. 1638. He m. April 30, 1639, Barbara, dau. of Nicholas Clap of Venn Ottery, Eng. Ch. Edmund b. July 14, 1636, Sarah bapt. Dec. 21, 1640, Daniel b. Sept. 18, 1642, Joseph bapt. 9 (12) 1644, d. 7 (10) 1645, Marah b. Aug. 2, 1646.

He was bur. Oct. 7, 1646. See accounts in A. Will dated at Ipswich, 2 (4) 1646, prob. 10 (8) 1646, beq. to wife Barbara and her children Daniel, Sarah and Mara; to his ch. by first wife, John, Thomas, Edmund, Mary and Hannah; to dau. Dennison; to the college at Cambridge; annuity to Mr. Cuddington; to the poor of the church; refers to Mr. Hooker. [Reg. VII, 33.] Mary m. Daniel Harris; Sarah m. John Franck; Marah m. Comfort Starr. Mortg. discharged 4 July, 1666. The widow m. 2, Anthony Stoddard.

Rev. Thomas, vicar at Terling, co. Essex, Eng. from 1624 to 1632; was noted by archbishop Laud as "uncomfortable" Nov. 25, 1630; fined 16 Nov. 1631. Came to Roxbury with his family, arriving June 5, 1632. Was minister alone some months, and then ordained pastor, in company with Mr. John Eliot, teacher, Nov., 1632. Was in full sympathy with the Winthrop party against Mrs. Hutchinson and Mr. Wheelwright in 1637. Wrote preface to second edition of Winthrop's Antinomians and Familists Condemned in 1643. Wrote The Bay Psalm Book, jointly with Richard Mather and John Eliot in 1639. Wrote other books. Was sent by the government to England with Mr. Hugh Peter and Mr. William Hibbens in 1641, and accomplished much in advancing the interests of the colony during the period of the Revolution. After much public service, he became vicar of Gateshead parish, at Newcastle, Eng. about 1649.

He d. in London March 23, 1660. [D.] Wife Margaret; ch. rec. at Terling: John bapt. 6 June, 1625, Thomas bapt. 26 July, 1626, Samuel bapt. 8 Oct. 1629, Edmund bapt. 8 July, 1631. Joseph, who also came to Roxbury, was his brother. [Reg. XXXVI, 36, 62 and 405.] Margaret, widow of Thomas Weld late of Gate side by Newcastle, clerk, made will 20 March, 1664, prob. 16 Nov. 1671.

WELD, etc., cont.
Beq. to bro. Mr. William Doget and her sister Anna, his wife; to sister Elizabeth Wade, dec. and their children; to kinsman John Jeffreson. [Reg. LII, 249.]

WELDIN, WELDEN,
Robert, Charlestown, chosen captain of 100 foot. [Du.] He d. of consumption Feb. 16, 1630-1; bur. in Boston with a military funeral 18th. Elizabeth, memb. chh. Boston 1630-1, rec. by early clerk as "gone to Watertown." See Wheldon.

WELLINGTON, WILLINGTON, see Wallington,
Roger, planter, Watertown, 1636. Suit in court in 1651. He deposed Dec. 1673, ae. about 64 years. [Mdx. Files.] He m. Mary, dau. of Dr. Richard Palsgrave; ch. John b. 25 (5) 1638, Mary b. 10 (12) 1640, Joseph b. 9 (8) 1643, Benjamin, Oliver b. Nov. 23, 1648, Palsgrave.

He d. March 11, 1697-8. Will dated 17 Dec. 1697, prob. April 11, 1698; "feeble by reason of age;" beq. to sons John, Joseph, Benjamin, Oliver and Palsgrave; gr. ch. John Mattocks, Roger W., and Mary Livermore.

WELLMAN, WILLMAN,
William, Gloucester, propr. 1649.

WELLS, WELLES, see Weld,
Isaac, Scituate, took oath of allegiance 1 Feb. 1638. Rem. to Barnstable. Juryman 1642. Adm. chh. May 27, 1643. His will dated 5 June, prob. 5 March, 1673, beq. all to wife. His widow Margaret died. Admin. gr. 27 Oct. 1675, to Mr. John Miller and Isaac Chapman, nearly related to her; they were to be residuary legatees.

Joseph, residence not stated, frm. March 3, 1635-6. Deputy 1636.

Richard, Lynn, propr. 1638. Frm. March 14, 1638-9.

Richard, glover, Salisbury, propr. 1640-1654. Deacon. He deposed 11 (2) 1671, ae. about 64 years.

He d. July 12, 1672; admin. Oct. folg. He m. Elizabeth Rowlandson, who survived him and made will Aug. 26, 1677, prob. April 11, 1683. Beq. to her bros. Thomas and Joseph R., her sister Martha Eaton, and some of their children.

WELLS, etc., cont.

Thomas, ae. 30, and Ann, ae. 20, came in the Susan and Ellen in April, 1635. Ann, ae. 15, was also enrolled in the Planter in April, 1635. Settled at Ipswich. Propr. 1635; additional in 1651. Frm. May 17, 1637. Husbandman. He m. Abigail Warner. Ch. Nathaniel, John, Sarah, Abigail, Thomas b. Jan. 11, 1646, Elizabeth, (m. John Burnham,) Hannah, Lydia.

He d. Oct. 26, will prob. Nov. 15, 1666. Widow Abigail d. July 22, will prob. Sept. 26, 1671.

Thomas, Cambridge, householder, 1635-6.

William, before Gen. Court Sept. 7, 1641.

WEN, WENBANE, see Winbourne.

WENDALL,

Thomas, before Gen. Court Sept. 7, 1643. Referred to Ipswich; his master to pay charges of the trial, and extend his time of service to make it up.

WEST,

Edmond, creditor of Wm. Launders of Marshfield in 1648.

Francis, carpenter, Duxbury, in Court 2 Nov. 1640. Marshfield, constable March 1, 1641-2. Bought house and land Aug. 4, 1642. Atba. 1643. Frm. 8 June, 1655. He m. Margery — about 1640.

Isabel, inv. of her est. pres. in Ess. Court 2 (11) 1644.

John, ae. 11, came in the Abigail July, 1635. Settled at Ipswich, propr. Brought suit in court in 1642. Sold house and lot 28 June, 1649. He deposed in 1673, ae. about 58 years. John, Beverly, m. Mary, widow of Henry Ley. Inv. of his est. gr. 13 Nov. 1683, to Thos. West.

Launslet, a witness in a Lynn case at Es. Court in 1639.

Matthew, Lynn, frm. March 9, 1636-7; propr. 1638. Witness in Gen. Court, 1645. Opposed to Infant baptism in 1646. [Es. Files.]

Susan, Salem, called to Court 3 (4) 1645.

WEST, cont.

Thomas, came in the Mary and John March 24, 1633-4. Res. at Salem. Henry and Thomas seem to be his sons. Henry deposed 31 May, 1686, ae. about 57 years. Henry and Elizabeth, his wife, and Thomas adm. chh. 4 (11) 1665; their ch. Elizabeth bapt. 25 (1) 1666. Thomas m. 11 (8) 1658, Phebe, dau. of Richard Waters; removing to Bradford, had a letter of dismission to the chh. at Haverhill Dec. 3, 1677. His ch. Samuel, Joseph and Benjamin bapt. at Sal. 25 (1) 1666, and John bapt. 20 (1) 1667, Samuel, of H., bapt. 10 (12) 1666.

Twiford, Plymouth, servant to Edward Winslow for 7 years from Feb. 22, 1635-6. Marshfield, atba. 1643. Served against the Narragansetts in 1645. Bought house and land at Ipswich in 1657.

WESTCOTT, WASKOTE,

Marie, Marblehead, witness in Court in 1646.

Stuckley, Salem, 1636. Banished in 1638 for sympathy with the Hutchinson party.

WESTGATE,

John, singleman, Boston, adm. chh. 12 (7) 1640. Dism. 26 (7) 1647, to the church of Pulham Mary, in Norfolk in England.

WESTON,

Edmund, planter, Duxbury, servant to John Winslow, transferred 2 Nov. 1636, to William Thomas. Land grant 1 June, 1640. Town officer. Atba. 1643.

He d. in 1686 in his 80th year. Will dated Feb. 18, 1685-6, prob. June 3, 1686. Genealogy. [Reg. XLI, 285.]

Francis, Plymouth, taxed in 1632, frm. 1633. He m. 27 Feb. 1639-40, Margery Reeves.

Francis, Duxborough, admin. of his est. gr. April 4, 1693, to his son Peter.

Francis, Salem. [See Margaret and John Pease.] Frm. Nov. 5, 1633. Deputy 1635. Town officer 1636. He and Margaret sued for defamation 26 (10) 1637. Banished for adherence to Mrs. Hutchinson in 1638. Brought from Rhode Island with Gorton

WESTON, cont.
and others in 1643; tried and imprisoned. [W.]

John, Salem, adm. chh. 13 (6) 1648. He deposed in 1685, ae. about 63 years. [See King, Wm.] Ch. Sarah bapt. 10 (3) 1657, John bapt. 29 (6) 1661, Elizabeth bapt. 28 (8) 1663.

Matthew, sued in Salem court in 1636.

Mr. Thomas, citizen and iron-monger of London, was at first an associate, but afterwards a rival of the colonists of Plymouth. Sent over a colony of his own to Wessaguscus (Weymouth) in 1622, consisting of about 60 men and 19 women. The settlement was a miserable failure; and was entirely abandoned at the end of about a year. [Mor.] He came to N. E. in 1623. After some stay on this coast he went to Virginia, whence he returned to England. He died at Bristol at the time of the wars, of the sickness at that place. [B.] [See Moore, Richard.] His only dau. Elizabeth m. at the house of Moses Maverick, Roger Conant, of Marblehead. [Depos. in Maryland Archives. See Reg. L, 202.]

Thomas, took Joshua Harris as an apprentice before Gen. Court Nov. 5, 1633.

WESTWOOD,
William, ae. 28, with wife Bridget, ae. 32, and John Lea, ae. 13, came in the Francis of Ipswich April 30, 1634. Settled at Cambridge; propr.; frm. March 4, 1634-5. He rem. to Hartford in 1636, and to Hadley about 1659. Comm. of the court.

He d. at H. April 9, 1669, ae. about 63. Will dated 27 Dec. 1665, prob. Sept. 29, 1669, beq. to wife Bridget, son Aaron and dau. Sarah Cooke. The widow d. May 12, 1676, ae. about 74; will made 20 Dec. 1670, prob. Sept. 22, 1676, beq. to dau. Sarah and her husband Aaron Cooke, with their ch. Westwood, Aaron, Sarah and Joanna; to the church of Hadley; and to individuals.

WETHERELL, WITHERELL, WITHRILL, WEATHERALL, WETHERILL,
John, Sudbury, propr. 1639. Rem. to Watertown; propr.; frm. May 13, 1642. In a petition to the Gen. Court in 1663, he mentions his bro. Stephen Fosdick. Wife Grace deposed in 1654, ae. about 60 years.

WETHERELL, etc., cont.
She d. Dec. 16, 1670. Dau. Mary was bur. 20 (2) 1655, ae. about 20 years.

He d. Jan. 23, 1672, ae. about 78 years. He beq. to Mr. Sherman; to kinswoman Mary Webb of Charlestown; to kinsmen Ralph Day and James Thorp of Dedham; to Wm. Priest of Wat.

Rev. William, M.A., of Maidstone, Eng. schoolmaster, with wife Mary, 3 children and 1 servant, came in the Hercules of Sandwich March 14, 1634-5. He had grad. from Corpus Christi Coll., Cambridge, July 3, 1619, from co. York; took degrees of B.A. and M.A.; was licensed, as of Maidstone, ba., about 25, to marry Mary Fisher, maiden, dau. of Joan Martin alias Fisher, now wife of John Martin, yeoman, March 26, 1627. [Gen. Adv. I, 21.] Settled at Charlestown; taught the Grammar school; his salary for the year 1636 adjusted by a com. Rem. to Cambridge, where he stayed till 1638, when he rem. to Duxbury. Propr. 31 Aug. 1640. Was called to be pastor of the second church at Scituate in Sept. 1644, and filled the position the rest of his life. [Records extant.] Frm. Ply. Col. 1 June, 1658. Ch. Samuel, John, Mary, (m. Nov. 20, 1656, Thomas Oldam,) Elizabeth, (m. Dec. 22, 1657, John Bryant,) Theophilus, Daniel, Sarah b. Feb. 10, 1644, bapt. Sept. 7, 1645, Hannah b. 20, bapt. 28 Feb. 1646.

He d. April 9, 1684, ae. 84. Will dated 29 March, prob. 4 June, 1684, beq. to gr. ch. Samuel, Joshua and Hannah, the ch. of his eldest son Samuel, dec. and to his widow Isabel; to sons John, Theophilus and Daniel; to dau. Mary Oldam.

WEYBORNE, see Wyborn.

WHALE,
Philemon, weaver, Sudbury, bought land in 1643; frm. May 10, 1648. His wife Elizabeth d. 20 (4) 1647. He m. 7 Nov. 1649, Sarah, widow of Thomas Cakebread. She d. Dec. 165[.]. He m. 3, Elizabeth —, who d. Nov. 8, 1688.

He d. 22 Feb. 1675. Will dated 19 Jan. 1675, prob. 4 (2) 1676, beq. to wife Elizabeth; to William, Jacob, Joseph and Benjamin, ch. of his dau. Elizabeth Moores. See will of John W. of Colchester, Eng. 1609; bro. Philemon. [Reg. LIII, 303.]

WEYLEY,
John, Reading. Ch. Elizabeth b. 4 (1) 1649. [Mdx. De.]

WEYMOUTH, WEIMOUTH,
Jonathan, seaman, residence not given, brought suit in court at Boston against Edward Hale and Arthur Browne 5 Nov. 1639. [L.] Made will 19 Nov. 1639, prob. 24 (5) 1643; beq. to John Sweete, shipwright, of Bo.

WHARTON,
Edward, Salem; propr.; recd. additional land, near his house 16 (4) 1651, showing prior residence.

He d. 12 (1) 1677-8. Nunc. will, testified to 27 (4) 1678; 2 bros. in England and a bro. and sister by the mother's side; sister's son Edward Winditt, whom he brought out of Eng.; to Mary, wife of Henry Trask, Hannah Sibley, widow, and Sarah Mills and her children.

WHEAT,
Jane, servant of Peter Palfrey of Salem, in court in 1637.

Joshua, ae. 17, cert. from St. Saviour's, Southwark, Eng., came in the Elizabeth in April, 1635.

Moses, Concord, frm. May 18, 1642. Wife Thomasin deposed 15 July, 1660, ae. about 45 years. Ch. Samuel b. 25 (8) 1640, Moses bur. 28 (4) 1641, Hannah b. 15 (11) 1643, Rebecca b. 16 (4) 1644, Jane d. 13 (8) 1648, John b. 19 (9) 1649, Aaron d. 13 June, 1658.

He d. May 5, 1700; will dated 19 Sept. 1691, prob. June 11, 1700, beq. to ch. Samuel, John, Moses, Rebecca, Joshua, Hannah, (wife of Samuel) Stratton, and Sarah Hill.

WHEATLEY,
Gabriel, Watertown.
Will prob. 13 (5) 1647; placed his estate in the hands of Bryan Pendleton, who was to pay himself what was his due and give the rest to his (W.'s) daughter. [Reg. III, 79.]

John, residence not given, frm. May 10, 1643.

WHEATON,
Robert, Rehoboth, propr. 1643.

WHEELDON, WEELDEN, WHEILDON, WHEILDEN, WELDING,
Gabriel, had permit from Plymouth Court to dwell at Mattacheese (Yarmouth,) 3 Sept. 1638. Town officer 1641-2. Rem. to Lynn, then to Malden. He and his youngest son John W. sold to Wm. Crofts 21 Oct. 1653, lands in Arnold and elsewhere in Nottinghamshire, Eng. [Es. De. I, 24.] Ch. Ruth, about to marry Richard Taylor, 27 Oct. 1646. Sarah, (parentage not stated,) b. 21 June, 1650.

He d. Jan. 1653-4. He made his will 11 (12) 1653, prob. 4 (2) 1654. Gave 10 shillings to the church; rest of est. and money due him from Wm. Crofts of Lynn to wife Margaret. [Reg. XVI, 75.] Sons Henry and John brought suit for their portions in 1655. [Mdx. Files.]

Henry, Yarmouth, atba. 1643. Served against the Narragansetts in 1645.

Katharine, wrote a letter to John Shanvat of Nottingham, 29 (4) 1639, concerning the death of Martha Weelden of Dedham, drowned about 12 days before. [L.] Katharine m. at Plymouth 9 Oct. 1639, Giles Hopkins.

Ralph, [Yarmouth,] called to Court with his dau. 7 July, 1648.

WHEELER, WHELLER,
Isaac, tailor, Charlestown, 1639; adm. chh. 30 (9) 1642, frm. May 10, 1643. Town officer, 1646. Wife Frances adm. chh. 1 (5) 1645; ch. Isaac, Thomas, Elizabeth b. 8 (5) 1641, Sarah b. 13 (1) 1643.

He d. before 1650; the widow m. 2, Richard Cooke of Malden. She deposed in 1652, ae. 44 years, that she came in the Jonathan in 1639 with the Blanchards. Joined in a deed of land in 1657. Her ch. mentioned in the will of Mr. Cooke.

John, came in the Mary and John March 24, 1663-4. Settled at Salisbury; barber; propr. 1639-1652. Rem. to Newbury. Wife Anne d. Aug. 15, 1662. Ch. David, (who came in the Confidence in April, 1638, ae. 11,) George, of Concord, and others named in will.

He d. in 1670; his will dated March 28, 1668, prob. Oct. 11, 1670, beq. to son David; sons John and Adam of Salisbury, Eng.; to son William, if he come over into this coun-

WHEELER, etc., cont.
try; to daus. Mercy, Elizabeth Button and Ann Chase; to Susanna, wife of his son George, and to his ch. Ephraim and Samuel; to son Roger's ch. Mary and Joseph; to dau. Elizabeth's ch. Thomas, Mary and Elizabeth; to dau.-in-law Susanna the land formerly given to her husband George, on which he built. Son Henry exec. and residuary legatee. [Norf. De.]

Joseph, Concord, frm. May 13, 1640. Wife Sarah was bur. 19 (5) 1642. Second wife Elizabeth; ch. Joseph b. 1641, d. 1642, Mary b. 20 (7) 1643, Rebecca b. 6 (7) 1645. He deposed to the will of Thomas W. 17 (1) 1678, ae. about 68 years.

Obediah, Concord, frm. June 2, 1641. Wife Susanna d. 24 (1) 1649. Ch. John b. 27 (11) 1640, Ruth b. 23 (2) 1642, a son b. and d. 1643, Samuel b. 22 (12) 1644, Susanna b. 17 (1) 16[..]

He d. Oct. 27, 1671. He made will 6 (8) 1671, ae. about 63 years; beq. to his six children, Joshua, Obediah, Samuel, John, Josiah and Susannah. Admin. was gr. Dec. 19, 1671, to kinsman Thomas W. and son John.

Richard, Dedham, propr. 1644. He m. 4 (3) 1644, Elizabeth Turner; ch. Sarah b. 4 (12) 1645, Mary b. 5 (8) 1646, John b. 18 (8) 1648, d. 17 (12) 1661, Samuel b. 4 (11) 1650, Hannah b. 30 (6) 1653, Joseph b. 5 (12) 1655, Abraham b. 7 (10) 1659; Elizabeth, Samuel and Sarah d. in 1656. He m. at Lancaster 2 (6) 1658, Sarah, dau. of John Prescott; ch. rec. at L.: Jacob b. and d. 1663, Zebadiah b. 2 (11) 1664, Sarah b. 1 (12) 1666, Elizabeth b. May 22, 1669, Samuel b. 29 (2) 1671.

He was slain by the Indians Feb. 10, 1676. Inv. of his est. taken 21 (6) 1676, mentions goods at Dedham as well as land and goods at Lancaster.

Thomas, miller, yeoman, Salem, worked on the bridge in 1646; propr. 1647. Rem. to Lynn. He deposed in 1653, ae. about 50 years. With wife Mary sold land in L. in 1657; she was adm. chh. 1 (9) 1648. Ch. Isaac and Zipporah bapt. 19 (9) 1648.

Thomas, captain, Concord, frm. May 18, 1642. Wife Ruth, dau. of William Wood; ch. Joseph, (deposed at Probate of the will of [his bro.] Thomas Wheeler 17 (10) 1678,

WHEELER, etc., cont.
ae. about 68 years,) Ephraim, (ae. about 21 years in 1639,) [L.] Deliverance, Thomas, Nathaniel d. 6 Jan. 1676.

Capt. Thomas, husband of Ruth, d. Dec. 10, 1676.

Thomas, servant to Austin Clement, painter, came in the James April 17, 1635. Afterward called tailor. Settled at Boston; adm. chh. 11 (7) 1636; propr.; frm. April 17, 1637. He deposed 2 (2) 1652, ae. about 48 years. [Arch. 38 B.] Wife Rebecca; ch. Jonathan b. 20 (8) 1637, Joseph b. 15 (3) 1640, Rebecca b. 17 (4) 1653.

He d. 16 (3), and his will was prob. 25 (5) 1654. Beq. to wife Rebecca, son Joseph and dau. Rebecca. [Reg. V, 305.] The widow m. 2, 10 (6) 1654, John Peirce.

Timothy, captain, Watertown, propr. 1642; rem. to Concord; frm. May 13, 1640. Signed inv. of Robert Miller 26 (12) 1646. He sold land at Charlestown 9 (7) 1657. Wife Jane d. 12 (12) 1642; he m. 2, Mary —. Ch. Elizabeth b. 6 Oct. 1661.

He d. July 30, 1687, ae. about 86 years. [Gr. St.] Will prob. Sept. 6, 1687. Mentions Joseph, Ephraim and Deliverance, sons of his bro. Thomas W. [Reg. XXXVIII, 34.]

William, Salem, called to court 30 (10) 1645.

WHEELOCK, WHEELOCKE,
Ralph, [believed, though without absolute evidence, to be the Rev. Ralph Wheelock, who was an alumnus of Clare Coll., Cambridge, Eng., A.B. in 1626, and A.M. in 1631, and was ordained in the church of England;] appears here first at Watertown; thence rem. to Dedham, of which church and town he was one of the most valuable founders, learned, devout, unselfish, and practical. He was propr. 14 (7) 1637; frm. March 13, 1638-9; selectman; schoolmaster; deputy to the Gen. Court; com. to end small causes; appointed to join persons in marriage. He rem. to Medfield, continuing his prominence and usefulness. Wife Rebecca was with him from the first at Dedham; ch. Rebecca, (m. in Roxbury 7 (4) 1654, John Crafts,) Gershom, Eliezer, Benjamin b. 8 (11) 1639, Samuel b. 22 (7) 1642, Record b. 15 (10) 1643, Experience b. 1648.

He signed his will 3 (3) 1681; inv. taken 31 Jan. 1683; prob. 1 May, 1684; beq. to eld-

WHEELOCK, etc., cont.
est son Gershom and other sons Benjamin, Eliezer and Samuel; sons-in-law Increase Ward and Joseph Warren; gr. ch. Rebecca Craft; refers to deceased wife; brother George Barbur one of the overseers of the will.

WHEELWRIGHT,
Rev. John, grad. Cambridge univ. 1614; vicar of Bilsby, co. Lincoln, Eng. 1623-1631. He came to Boston with wife and family in 1636. Recd. to chh. 12 (4) 1636. Preached at Braintree and often at Boston. Joined with his sister-in-law, Mrs. Ann Hutchinson, in advancing views which were regarded erroneous and seditious by most of the clergy and rulers; after much controversy was banished 2 (9) 1637. Rem. to Exeter, N. H., and later to Wells, Maine. His sentence of banishment was revoked by the Gen. Court in 1644, upon his making an apology for "inconsiderate" words at the time of the controversy. He was pastor at Hampton, 1647-1658; at Salisbury from Dec. 9, 1662, till his death. He was conceded to be upright, earnest and efficient for good; and rendered valuable service in laying foundations for three states. He deeded, 22 Oct. 1677, to his dau. Sarah Crispe, of Boston, land and tenement at Mawthorp in the parish of Willoughby, co. Lincoln, Eng., referring to Belleaw, same co. as his former residence.

He m. 1, Nov. 8, 1621, Marie Storre, who d. in Eng.; he m. 2, Mary, dau. of Mr. Edward Hutchinson, mercer, of Alford, Eng. and his wife Susanna; ch. [John,] Samuel, Susanna, Katharine, (m. 1, Robert Nanney, m. 2, Edward Naylor,) Mary b. and bapt. at Boston 25 (4) 1637, (m. 1, Dec. 4, 1660, Edward Lloyd, m. 2, — Lyde, m. 3, Theodore Atkinson,) Elizabeth, (m. George Person,) Rebecca, (m. Samuel Maverick, Jr., m. 2, Wm. Bradbury,) Hannah, (m. — Checkley,) Sarah, (m. Richard Crispe,) Thomas. The son Thomas and six daus. are mentioned in the will of their uncle Samuel Hutchinson of Boston in 1667.

He d. Nov. 15, 1679; made will May 25, 1675, "aged;" prob. 26 Nov. 1679. Beq. to gr. son Edward Lyde est. in Mumby, Langham and Minge, Lincolnshire, Eng., to be paid to his mother, Mary Atkinson; to gr. dau. Mary Mavericke other lands in Eng.; to son-in-law Edward Rishworth and his

WHEELWRIGHT, cont.
dau. Mary White; to gr. ch. Thomas and Jacob Bradbury; to son Samuel lands at Craft near Waneflitt, Eng. and at Wells, N. E. together with clothing, books, etc. To his latter wife's children all his plate.

WHIPPLE,
John, carpenter, Dorchester, in employ of Mr. Stoughton in 1632; rem. to Ipswich; propr. 1638; ret. to Dorch.; frm. and deputy May 13, 1640. One of the Court's com. of valuation in 1640. Engaged in trade with William Paine and others in 1647. Cornet, town officer. [Suff. De. III, 357.] Sold land and buildings at Dorch. and rem. to Providence in 1658. Ret. to Ipswich. Sold land May 31, 1673. Wife Sarah adm. chh. 29 (8) 1641; ch. John bapt. 1 (9) 1641, Sarah bapt. 6 (12) 1641, Samuel bapt. 17 (1) 1644, Eliezer bapt. 8 (1) 1646, Mary bapt. 9 (2) 1648, William bapt. 16 (3) 1652, Benjamin bapt. 4 (4) 1654, David bapt. 28 (7) 1656, Joseph, Jonathan and Abigail b. at Providence.

He d. 16 May, 1685, ae. about 68 years. [Gr. St.] Genealogy, [Reg. XXXII, 403.]

Matthew, bro. of John, Ipswich, propr. 1638. See Nevill.

Will dated 7 (3) 1645, altered after marriage 13 (9) 1646, was prob. 28 (7) 1647. Beq. to ch. John, Matthew, Joseph, Mary, Anna and Elizabeth; to wife Rose the est. she had before marriage to him, and £10; to the elders Nathaniel Rogers and John Norton; bro. John Whipple to be one of the overseers. A large estate.

WHISTON, WHISTONS, WHETSTONE,
John, planter, embarked March 6, 1631; settled at Scituate. Before the Court with others 7 Dec. 1641, concerning goods found after a shipwreck. Ch. Increase bapt. Aug. 10, 1656, Bathsheba bapt. July 1, 1660.

He d. intestate; his heir apparent, Joseph, yielded up a considerable portion of the est. to his mother Susanna and his small bros. and sisters, 4 Oct. 1664. Joseph was assisted by his father-in-law William Brookes and his uncle Edward Jenkins in settling some of the lands in 1666. He d. in Boston in 1666; and his bro. John, ae. 18, had his uncle Jenkins app. guardian 31 Oct. 1666.

WHITAKER, see Whittier.

WHITCOMB, WHITCOMBE, WHITECOMBE, WHETCOMB,
John, planter, may be the Mr. W. who was to see the leather discharged at Salem in 1629. [Suff. De. I, xix.] Dorchester, planter; propr. 1636-9; rem. to Scituate; suit in court, 1639; atba. 1643; frm. 3 June, 1652. He res. at Lancaster about 1652. He petitioned 28 (10) 1658, being weak and aged, to be excused from paying Stephen Gates for swine killed by three of his sons. [Mdx. Files.]

He d. April 6, 1683. Inv. of his est. was taken 26 April, 1683.

WHITE,
Anthony, Watertown, propr. at Sudbury, 1639. He m. at Wat. 8 (7) 1645, Grace Hall; ch. Abigail b. 21 (4) 1646, John b. Feb. 25, 1648-9, Mary b. March 1, 1650, (m. Jacob Willard).

He d. March, 1686.

Charity, singlewoman, Boston, adm. chh. 13 (4) 1641; propr. 1648. She d. 28 Jan. 1660. Admin. Feb. 1, 1660. Beq. house and lands to the church; rest of her est. to Deliverance, dau. of Miles Tarne. [Reg. X, 265, and XXXI, 178.]

Edward, husbandman, ae. 42, with wife Martha, ae. 39, and daus. Martha, ae. 10, and Mary, ae. 8, came in the Abigail, June 22, 1635, cert. from the parish of Craibroke, (Cranbrook,) co. Kent, Eng. Settled at Dorchester; frm. May 26, 1647. Propr. Ch. rec. at Dorch.: James b. Jan. 1, 1637, John bapt. 16 (10) 1639.

Edward, Roxbury, propr. Ch. Zechariah b. Aug. 5, 1642, Samuel b. Feb. 27, 1644, Eliezer b. 12 (10) 1646.

Edward, Charlestown, d. Jan. 13, 1648; inv. of his est. taken by George Hepburne and Samuel Adams.

Edmund, Watertown, propr. 1637.

Emanuel, Watertown, propr. 1636; rem. to Yarmouth; atba. 1643. Frm. 7 June, 1642; town officer. Wife Katharine; they adopted Alice Benfield, an orphan 3 years old Nov. 10, 1636, for the term of 15 years. [W.]

Francis, ae. 24, came in the Elizabeth April 17, **1635.**

WHITE, cont.
Goyen, Gowen, or Going, planter, Scituate, propr.; town officer 1644. He m. Oct. 15, 1638, Elizabeth Ward, servant to Mr. Hatherly. Sold land 9 Dec. 1654.

Inv. taken Dec. 8, 1664, and pres. on the oaths of Timothy and Joseph White 8 Dec. 1664.

James, Marblehead, 1633. [Col. Rec.]

John, embarked for New Eng. June 22, 1632. Settled at Cambridge. Frm. March 4, 1632-3. Propr. 1633; town officer 1634; sold lands Oct. 20, 1635; rem. "to the Newe Towne uppo Quinetucquet river," i. e. Hartford, Conn. One of the first settlers of Hadley; deputy. Ret. to Hartford; elder in chh. Wife Mary; ch. Mary, (m. Jonathan Gilbert,) Nathaniel, John, Daniel, Sarah, (m. 1, Stephen Taylor, 2, Barnabas Hinsdale, 3, Walter Hickson,) Jacob.

He d. at Hartford, Conn. about Dec. 17, 1683.

John, yeoman, Lynn, propr. 1638. Salem, recd. inhabitant and granted 60 acres of land 8 (6) 1639. Propr. at Wenham (Enon) in 1642. Rem. to Lancaster. Wife Joane adm. chh. 26 (12) 1642, dism. to Wenham chh. 10 (2) 1645. Ch. Sarah bapt. 9 (2) 1643, Josiah bapt. 4 (4) 1643, Ruth bapt. 8 (7) 1644.

Will prob. 27 (4) 1673. Son Josiah; Ruth, widow of dec. son Thomas, her son Thomas and other ch.; daus. Joane, Elizabeth, Marie and Sara, already married; youngest dau. Hannah who has lived with him.

John, merchant, Watertown, before Gen. Court, 1636; [W.] propr. 1642; bought land on the South side of Charles river 4 (1) 1646. Rem. to Boston; with wife Frances sold land at Wat. 4 (8) 1653. Ch. John, Joseph, Benjamin, Mary, of sister White of Watertown, bapt. at Roxbury 6 (4) 1652; Mary, ch. of John W., bur. at Rox. 26 (3) 1669. His son Joseph was apprenticed May 22, 1646, for 7 years, to Samson Shore, tailor, of Boston. [Col. Rec.]

He d. April 15, 1691. Will, dated 2 days earlier, beq. to wife Frances and three sons, viz. John, Joseph and Benjamin, and to gr. ch. John, Benjamin, Mary, (dau. of Joseph,) and Mary, (dau. of John). [Genealogy in Reg. LII, 421.]

Nicholas, Weymouth, propr. 1643, frm.

WHITE, cont.
May 10, 1643. Res. at Dorchester, 1653; propr.

Richard, carpenter, ae. 30, came in the Elizabeth and Ann in May, 1635. Settled at Charlestown; propr. and res. 3 (11) 1636-7. Rem. to Sudbury; propr. 1639. Admin. of his est. gr. in Essex Court 30 (4) 1663, to widow Smith.

Robert, admin. of his est. gr. by the Gen. Court 4 Aug. 1635, to William Stitson of Charlestown.

Thomas, yeoman, Cambridge, frm. March 3, 1635-6; Watertown, propr.; sold in 1640 a house he had bought of William Swift. Bought land at Sudbury; rem. thither; propr. 1640; town officer, 1642. Deputy, 1637. Rem. to Charlestown. Sold land at Sud. in 1654. Wife Margaret d. at Sud. 17 Nov. 1649.

He d. 6 (3) 1664. Widow Susanna d. March 6, 1686-7, ae. 89. Will prob. March 29, 1687; children Thomas, John, Mary, Sarah.

Thomas, Weymouth, propr. 1643; deposed to the will of Anne Looman 21 (8) 1659, ae. about 60 years. [Reg. IX, 142.]

Will dated 5 July, prob. 28 Aug. 1679, beq. to sons Joseph, Samuel, Thomas, Ebenezer and dau. Hannah; gr. ch. Lydia, Mary and Ebenezer White, and Hannah Baxter; pastor Samuel Torrey and elder Edward Bate.

Mr. William, wool-carder, young man, from England, married at Leyden, Holland, Jan. 27, 1612, Anna Fuller, maid, of England. Her full name was Susanna. They came in the Mayflower to Plymouth. They brought one child, Resolved, and had a second son, Peregrine, born on board the Mayflower in Cape Cod harbour, in Dec. 1620. They also brought 2 servants, William Holbeck and Edward Thomson, who d. soon after the landing.

He d. Feb. 21, 1621-2. His widow m. 2, Gov. Edward Winslow. The son Resolved, ae. about 63 years, deposed relative to an occurrence at Salem, in 1678. [Es. Files XXXI, 113.]

William, husbandman, came in the Mary and John in March, 1633-4. Settled at Ipswich; propr. 1634; frm. June 22, 1642. Rem. to Haverhill about 1642. Propr., town officer. Wife Mary d. Feb. 22, 1681;

WHITE, cont.
he m. Sept. 21, 1682, Sarah Foster. She ret. to Ips. after his death and d. there. His son John's will was prob. 13 (2) 1669. He d. Sept. 28, 1690, ae. about 80 years.

William, ae. 14, came in the Increase April 15, 1635.

William, bricklayer, Boston, 1646. Witnessed Maverick's deed in 1649. Wife Elizabeth; she d., and he m. 4 (6) 1653, Phillip Wood, who d. 5 (5) 1654; ch. Cornelius b. 7 (11) 1646, Dorcas b. 19 April, 1654, d. 30 (7) 1655.

Will dated at Boston 13 Oct. prob. 31 (11) 1673, beq. to wife; to sons Isaac and Cornelius his salt-works, soap-works, mills, stone-cutter's tools, soddering tools, etc.; to dau. Susanna, wife of Thos. Waggett; to son William; to daus. Elizabeth, wife of Benjamin Harnden, Margaret, wife of Thomas Wallen and Ursula, wife of John Bennet.

WHITLE,
John, before Gen. Court in 1636.

WHITFIELD,
Edward, [Reading,] estated a tract of land at R. upon Sarah, dau. of Ralph Root; this she and her father sold to Thomas Taylor; deed confirmed by Gen. Court 17 Oct. 1649.

WHITEHAIR, see Whittier.

WHITEHAND,
George, Charlestown, propr., adm. chh. 7 (6) 1633. Rem. to Woburn; propr. 1641. Wife Alice; ch. Loyis bapt. 31 (6) 1633, Anna bapt. 13 (10) 1636.

WHITEHEAD,
Samuel, Cambridge, propr. 1634.

WHITEMORE, WHITTEMORE, WHITAMORE, WHETEMORE, WHITMORE,
Lawrence, husbandman, ae. 63. with wife Elizabeth, ae. 57, came in the Hopewell in April, 1635. Settled at Roxbury. Adm. chh. 1635; frm. April 18, 1637. Propr. His wife d. Feb. 18, 1642; he was bur. 24 (9) 1644, ae. 80. [Rox. Rec.]

Thomas, Charlestown. Rem. to Mystic side, (Malden;) signed petition with neighbors for better privileges in 1640. [L.]

WHITTEMORE, etc., cont.

Bought land of Mr. John Cotton in 1645. His name mentioned in an indenture of R. Bellingham in 1652. Wife Hannah deposed [Dec. 16, 1662,] ae. about 50 years. Sons Nathaniel, ae. 28, and Abraham, ae. 17 years, with Daniel and Samuel, deposed 4 (8) 1670. [Mdx. Files.]

He d. May 25, 1661. Will prob. June 25 folg. beq. to wife Hannah; ch. Daniel, Nathaniel, John, Elizabeth, Benjamin, Thomas, Samuel, Pelatiah and Abraham; eldest son Thomas, now in England, had rec'd a bequest there.

WHITMORE,

Francis, tailor, Cambridge, propr. 1648; frm. May 3, 1654. He deposed 18 (10) 1660, ae. about 35 years. [Mdx. Files.] He m. about 1648, Isabel, dau. of Thomas Parks. [Mdx. Files, 1672.] She d. March 31, 1665. He m. 2, Margaret Harty; ch. Elizabeth b. 2 (3) 1649, Francis, John, Samuel, Abigail bapt. July 3, 1659, Sarah bapt. March 30, 1662, Margery bapt. March 27, 1664, Hannah (by second wife) bapt. Feb. 15, 1667. [Mi.]

He d. Oct. 12, 1685, [Town Rec.] ae. 62. [Gr. St.] Will dated 8 (8) 1685, beq. to wife; eldest son Francis; two youngest sons Thomas and Joseph; other children; the ch. of his dau. Elizabeth and her husband Daniel Markham; son Samuel has had his portion already. Friends William Locke and Francis Moore execs. The widow Margaret d. March 1, 1685-6. Admin. on both estates was gr. June 17, 1690, to son John and son-in-law William Locke, Jr.; sons-in-law Thomas Carter and Jonathan Thompson united in the petition.

WHITING, WHYTING, WHITINGE,

Nathaniel, miller, propr. at Lynn, 1638; rem. to Dedham. Propr. 1640, adm. chh. 30 (5) 1641; frm. May 18, 1642. He m. 4 (9) 1643, Hannah, dau. of John Dwight; ch. Nathaniel b. 26 (7) 1644, John b. 28 (7) 1646, d. 1647, Samuel b. 20 (10) 1649, Hannah b. 17 (12) 1651, Timothy b. 5 (11) 1653, John and Mary b. and d. 1656, Mary b. 12 (8) 1658, Abigail b. June 7, 1663.

He d. 15 (11) 1682. Will dated 15 (3) 1677, prob. 19 April, 1683, gave whole estate to wife Hannah to distribute at her discretion. The widow d. Nov. 4, 1714, ae. 89.

WHITING, etc., cont.

Rev. Samuel, b. in Boston, Lincolnshire ,Eng. 20 Nov. 1570, son of John Whiting, Esquire, sometime mayor of Boston; grad. at Emanuel Coll. Camb.; was chaplain to Sirs Nathaniel Bacon and Roger Townsend 3 years, then colleague to Rev. Mr. Price 3 more. [C. M.] He was rector of the parish of Skirbeck, adjoining Boston till 1635, when he came to N. E. Became pastor of the chh. at Lynn, where he spent the rest of his life. Scholarly, devoted, popular, he had a strong hold on the regard of his people and was esteemed very highly by the leaders of the state. Frm. Dec., 1636. Had large estate. He m. 1, —, by whom he had two sons that d. in Eng. and a dau. that m. Mr. Thomas Weld in another land. [C. M.] He m. 2, Aug. 6, 1629, Elizabeth, dau. of Right Hon. Oliver St. John and his wife Sarah Bulkley. Her bro. Hon. Oliver St. John, was lord chief justice of England under Cromwell. [See account of Mrs. Whiting's pedigree, with its strains of royal blood, in the Whiting Memorial. See wills of her father, brother and other relatives in Reg. LII, 255.] Children, Samuel b. in Skirbeck March 25, 1633, (became minister of the chh. at Billerica,) Joseph, (also resided here,) John, Dorothy, (m. 4 June, 1650, Thomas Weld of Roxbury,) Elizabeth, (m. Rev. Jeremiah Hubbard). The wife d. 3 March, 1676-7, in her 73d year. [C. M.]

He d. Dec. 11, 1679. Will dated 25 Feb. 1678, prob. 30 March, 1680, beq. to son Samuel, living at Billerica; John, living at Leverton, Lincolnshire, Eng.; Joseph, at Lynn; dau., wife of Jeremiah Hubbard, of Topsfield.

WHITMAN, WHITEMAN, WHYTMAN, see Wightman,

John, Weymouth, deacon, frm. March 13, 1638-9; town officer 1643; com. to end small causes, and ensign of the military company 14 May, 1645. (Some J. W. was propr. at Charlestown in 1647.) Sold land at Braintree March 19, 1648, acknowledged Nov. 26, 1656. Ch. Hannah b. 24 (6) 1641.

Will dated 9 March, 1685, prob. 16 March, 1692-3, beq. to sons John, Abijah and Zechariah; daus. Sarah Joanes, Mary Pratt, Judah, wife of Philip King, and Elizabeth Green; gr. ch. Joseph and Elizabeth Green and the ch. of dec. dau. Hannah French.

WHITMAN, etc., cont.

Richard, Lynn, witness at court, 1647.

Robert, ae. 20, from the parish of Little Minories, Eng., came in the Abigail in June, 1635. Settled at Ipswich; propr., goatkeeper, husbandman, 1644. Had land, formerly belonging to Susan Manning in 1639, and all Thomas Manning's right in house and land in 1647.

Zechariah, ae. 40, with Sarah, ae. 25, and child Zechariah, ae. 2½, came in the Elizabeth April 11, 1635.

WHITMARK, WHITMARCK, WHITMARKE,

John, ae. 39, with wife Alce, ae. 35, and children John, ae. 11, Jane, ae. 7, Ouseph, (sic) ae. 2, came from Weymouth, Eng. before March 20, 1635.

WHITNEY,

Jeremiah, Plymouth, atba. 1643.

John, ae. 35, with Ellen, ae. 30, Richard, ae. 9, Nathaniel, ae. 8, Thomas, ae. 6, and Jonathan, ae. 1, came in the Elizabeth and Ann in April, 1635. Settled at Watertown; frm. March 3, 1635-6. Tailor; propr., town officer. Bought land 6 (2) 1653. His wife Elinor d. May 11, 1659; he m. 2, Sept. 29, 1659, Judah (Judith) Clement. Ch. rec. in Wat.: Joshua b. 15 (5) 1635, Caleb bur. 12 (5) 1640, Benjamin b. 6 (4) 1643.

He d. a widower, June 1, 1673, ae. about 84. Will dated April 3, 1673, prob. 17 (4) beq. to sons John, Richard, Thomas, Jonathan, Joshua and Benjamin. [See Genealogy.]

Thomas, Plymouth, in Court, 1636. Took oath of fidelity Jan. 6, 1636-7; bought house and land 30 Aug. 1644. Wife Winnifred d. 23 July, 1660.

His will dated .... 1673, prob. in March, 1673-4, beq. to son Jeremiah, gr. ch. Thomas, wife Patience.

WHITON, WHITTON, WITON, WYTON,

James, Hingham, farmer, propr., mariner, gave letter of attorney 6 (8) 1647, to Richard Betscomb of Hing. to collect a legacy due him from Thomas Wyton of Hooke Norton, Oxfordshire, yeoman, deceased. [A.] Frm. May 30, 1660. He m. Dec. 30, 1647, Mary, dau. of John Beal; she d. 12 Dec. 1696, ae. 74 years. Ch. James b. 10 (2) 1649, d. 11

WHITON, etc., cont.

(9) 1650, James b. July 15, 1651, Matthew b. Oct. 30, 1653, John b. Dec. 2, 1655, David and Jonathan b. and d. 1658, Enoch b. March 8, 1659-60, Thomas b. May 18, 1662, Mary b. April 29 1664, (m. 1, Isaac Wilder, 2, Barak Jordan, 3, Thomas Sayer).

He d. 26 April, 1710. Will dated 29 Sept. 1708; beq. his extensive property to three sons and one dau. then living, and to the seven children of his dec. son Thomas.

Thomas, ae. 36, with Audrey, ae. 45, Jeremy, ae. 8, came in the Elizabeth and Ann in May, 1635. We may surmise that he is

Thomas, of Plymouth, propr. 1638. His dau.-in-law, Mary Morecock, was appr. to Richard Sparrow and Pandora his wife for 9 years, 24 June, 1639. [See also Bennett and Nicholas Morecock.] He m. 22 Nov. 1639, Winnyfride Harding.

WHITTIER, WHITEHAIR, WHITEYEARE, WHITYEAR, WHITAKER,

Abraham, (Whitaker, generally,) carpenter, Salem, taxed as a res. of Marblehead, 1637; one of the parties to a law-suit, 1637; rem. to Manchester. He deposed in 1666, ae. about 40 years.

He made an oral will 6 (6), prob. 26 (9) 1674; beq. to son Edward one half the land; the other half to wife for the bringing up of the children he had by her; 5 shillings apiece to the two ch. of the first wife; 5 li. debt due to son John above his share of the est., to be paid him when 21 years of age. The son Edward, of Beverly, sold his share of the land 2 (11) 1674.

John, Ipswich, propr., 1635; sold property before 1639.

He d. at sea Feb. 20, 1678-9; nunc. will, beq. to John and Abiel Kelly.

Thomas, (perhaps the Thomas Whittle, who came in the Confidence in 1638, servant of John Rolfe,) Salisbury, res. in 1644; had liberty to make tar in 1649. Rem. to Haverhill; propr. from 1649; frm. 23 May, 1666. He m. Ruth Green, [Hav. Rec.]; ch. Mary b. Oct. 9, 1647, (m. Sept. 21, 1666, Benjamin Page,) John b. Dec. 23, 1649, Ruth b. Aug. 9, 1651, (m. April 20, 1675, Joseph True,) Thomas b. Jan. 12, 1653, Susanna b. March 27, 1656, (m. July 15, 1674, Jacob Morrill,) Nathaniel b. Aug. 11, 1658, Hannah b. Sept.

WHITTIER, etc., cont.
10, 1660, (m. May 30, 1683, Edward Young,) Richard b. June 27, 1663, Elizabeth b. Nov. 21, 1666, (m. June 22, 1669, James Sanders, Jr.,) Joseph b. May 8, 1669.

He d. Nov. 28, 1696. Admin. on his est. gr. Feb. 1, folg.; division of est. May, 1699. The widow d. July, 1710; admin. of her est. Sept. 19, folg. See will of John Rolfe.

WHITRIDGE, WHITERIDGE, WHITERED,
William, carpenter, ae. 36, with wife Elizabeth, ae. 30, and son Thomas, ae. 10, came in the Elizabeth April 11, 1635. Settled at Ipswich; propr. 1636. Served in the Pequot war and had grant of land from the town in 1639. [Samuel, and William (b. March 31, 1658,) are believed to have been sons.] He m. 2, Susanna, widow of Anthony Colby.

He d. Dec. 9, 1668. Estate settled July 2, 1669, by son Thomas, and in 1699 by gr. son Thomas.

WHITTINGHAM,
John, gent., came from Boston, Lincolnshire, in 1638, bringing with him servants Haniel Bosworth, Richard and Matthew Coye, John Anniball, Robert Smith, and perhaps others. [Depos. in Es. Files 3, 4.] Settled at Ipswich; partner of William Paine and Co. [Suff. De. 111, 367.] He m. a dau. of Mr. William Hubbard; dau. Martha m. Dr. John Clarke. [Reg. XXXIII, 226, and XXXIX, 170.]

His will was prob. 27 (1) 1649; beq. to wife Martha; to youngest sons Richard and William certain lands at Southerton near Boston, co. Lincoln; other lands to eldest son John; to three daus. Martha, Elizabeth and Judith, money, stock in Ipswich Trading Co., and rents of land in Eng.; father-in-law Mr. Wm. Hubbard, bro. Mr. Samuel Haugh, and wife execs.; beq. also to Mrs. Smith and Haniel Bosworth.

WIBORNE, see Wyborne.

WICKAM, WICCOM, WICOME, WYCOME,
Richard, Rowley, propr. 1643. Deeded lands to son Daniel 26 Jan. 1661, mentioning son John. Wife Ann bur. Aug. 25, 1674.

He was bur. Jan. 27, 1663.

WICKS, see Weeks.

WICKSON, WIXAM, WIXON, VIXON,
Robert, Plymouth ,servant of William Edge, transferred 8 Nov. 1638, to Thomas Prence. Atba. 1643. In Court 3 March, 1644-5. Town officer, 1646. Frm. 5 June, 1651. Rem. to Eastham.

Will dated 1 Oct., prob. 18 Oct. 1686; beq. to wife Alice, dau. Jemimah, sons Titus and Barnabas, gr. ch. Nathaniel Mayo.

WIER, WYER,
Robert, Boston. Wife Mary; ch. John b. 1 (9) 1646.

Nathaniel, Haverhill, propr. 1645.

WIFE, WIFFE, see Wise.

WIGGINS, WIGGIN,
Thomas, Lynn, 1649. Worked for the Iron Works Co.; carted coal, helped build the finery chimney, etc. He m. at Reading 27 (6) 1649, Sarah —. Rem. to Rustport, N. Y.; deposition, 1660. [Es. Files.]

Distinguish carefully from Capt. Thomas Wiggin, the eminent pioneer of New Hampshire.

WIGGLESWORTH,
Edward, Charlestown, 1638. Rem. to New Haven. His son Michael came to Harvard College, from which he was graduated in 1651, and became the eminent preacher of the church of Malden, author of the striking poem, The Day of Doom.

Edward d. at New Haven Oct. 1, 1653.

WIGHT,
Henry, Dedham, frm. May 26, 1647. Wife Jane; ch. John b. 13 (10) 1652, Joseph b. 11 (3) 1654, Daniel b. 24 (9) 1656, Benjamin b. 18 (4) 1659, Jonathan b. 2 July, 1662.

Admin. of his est. was gr. 28 April, 1681, to the widow Jane and son Joseph. Inv. showed land and buildings at Dedham and land at Wrentham.

Thomas, bro. of Henry, Dedham, propr. 18 (5) 1637, adm. chh. with wife Alice 6 (7) 1640; frm. Oct. 8, 1640; selectman. Rem. to Medfield. Ch. Samuel b. 5 (12) 1639, Ephraim b. 27 (11) 1645.

Will prob. 24 (2) 1674; mentions agreement made with his present wife before their marriage which is in the hands of Mr. John Eliot, her brother; beq. to sons Henry, Thom-

WIGHT, cont.

as, Samuel and Ephraim, dau. Mary, wife of Thomas Ellis, and her dau. Juda. The widow Lydia made will 20 Dec. 1673, prob. July 27, 1676; beq. to the children of her former husband James Peniman, Samuel, Mary, Lydia Adams, Bethiah Allin, Hannah Hall, Abigail Carie. Cousin Jacob Eliot and Theophilus Frary overseers; son Samuel P. exec. Ephraim Wight was indebted to the estate when inv. was taken, a sum beq. in his father's will.

WIGHTMAN, see Weightman.

WIGNALL,

Mr. Alexander, juryman May 3, 1631; frm. May 18, 1631.

John, built a house and resided in Charlestown 1630.

WILBOARE, WILBORE, WILBORNE,

Samuel, merchant, with wife Ann, adm. chh. Boston 1 (10) 1633. Frm. March 4, 1633-4. Was one of the incorporators of Providence Plantation in 1637, but returned to Boston. He m. about 1645 Elizabeth, widow of Thomas Lechford, the famous notary.

He d. 29 (7) 1656. Will dated April 30, prob. Oct. 23, 1656. Beq. to wife Elizabeth sons Samuel, Joseph, Shadrack; to his man John Macklist, a Scotchman. [Reg. V, 385, VI, 290, and XXX, 201.] The widow m. 3, Feb. 20, 1656, Henry Bishop.

WILCOCKS, WILCOX,

William, Cambridge, propr.; town officer; frm. May 25, 1636. He m. 22 (11) 1650, Mary Powell.

He d. Nov. 28, 1653. Will prob. 3 (11) 1653. Legacies to "loving brethren that are of my family meeting," Roger Bancroft, John Hastings, Thos. Fox, Wm. Patton and Francis Whitmore; to pastor, Mr. Mitchell, and elder Frost; to honored bro. Richard Francis; to cousin John Woods; to sister, the widow Hall, and to her son William and dau. Susan; residue to wife and to the children of his sister Christian Boyden in England. [Reg. XVI, 76.]

WILCOCKSON, WILCOXON,

William, linen weaver, ae. 34, with Margaret, ae. 24, and son John, ae. 2, cert. from St. Albons, Herts, Eng. came in the Planter April 2, 1635. Residence unknown. Frm. Dec. 7, 1636.

WILD, WILDE, WILDES,

George, ae. 37, husbandman, came in the Elizabeth and Ann in May, 1635.

Joseph, m. at Roxbury Dec. 3, 1641, Mary Tompson.

William, ae. 30, Alice, ae. 40, and John, ae. 17, came in the Elizabeth in April, 1635. Settled at Ipswich; propr. 1635. Rem. to Rowley; carpenter. With wife Elizabeth sold land to James Barker 1 (3) 1649; deed made 16 (4) 1652.

Will dated 6 May, prob. 30 Sept. 1662, beq. to wife Elizabeth and kinsman John Wild and his son John.

WILDER, WYLDER,

Edward, husbandman, Hingham, propr. 1637, frm. May 29, 1644. Town officer. He served in King Philip's war. He m. Elizabeth, dau. of Anthony Eames of Medfield. [Hist. Hing.] She d. 9 June, 1652. Ch. Elizabeth, (m. Israel Fearing,) John, Ephraim, Isaac, Jabez, Abiah, (m. William Clark of Plymouth,) Mehitabel, (m. Joseph Warren of Plym.) Abigail, Anna or Hannah b. March 16, 1665-6, Mary b. April 5, 1668, (m. Francis Le Baron, and second Return Wait).

His estate was admin. June 26, 1691, by widow Elizabeth and son Jabez; division made 2 July, 1694, to son John, to Isaac's son Thomas, to son Jabez, daus. Elizabeth, Abia, Mehetabel, Anna, Abigail, Mary.

Martha, widow, spinster, from Shiplock, Oxfordshire, Eng., with dau. Mary Wilder, came in the Confidence April 11, 1638. Settled at Hingham. Propr. 1638. She d. 20 April, 1652.

Roger, servant to John Carver, came in the Mayflower to Plymouth; d. in 1621.

Thomas, husbandman, Charlestown, propr. 1638. Frm. June 2, 1641. Bought land in Char. 27 (8) 1643; town officer. Rem. to Lancaster, 1659. Wife Anna adm. chh. 7 (3) 1650. Signed inv. of Philip Drinker in 1647. Ch. Mary bapt. 3 (5) 1642, Thomas b.

WILDER, etc., cont.

4 (7) 1644. He deposed 17 (4) 1654, ae. 33 [35] years. [Mdx. Files.]

He d. Oct. 23, 1667. Will dated 22 (11) 1667, prob. March 4, 1667-8, beq. to wife Ann and ch. Marie, Thomas, John, Nathaniel, Elizabeth and Ebenezer.

WILEY, WILLY,

John, Reading, gave bonds for John White before Gen. Court 30 July, 1640. Propr. 1648. Wife Elizabeth memb. chh. 1648, d. Aug. 3, 1662. Ch. Elizabeth b. March 4, 1649, Timothy b. April 24, 1653, Susanna b. July 16, 1655, Sarah b. Feb. 4, 1658.

WILKES,

Mr. Samuel, Boston, propr., town officer 1634. One of the richer inhabitants who contributed to the free school in 1636.

William, Boston, propr. 1636. Wife Joan adm. chh. 9 (12) 1633. Dism. to church [of Ipswich?] 8 (7) 1639.

WILKINS, WILKINSON, WILKENS,

Bray, husbandman, Dorchester, propr., frm. May 14, 1634. Licensed to keep a ferry over Neponsett river 6 (7) 1638. (See Gingine.) With Henry Way and Richard Leeds had land granted in 1639 at Thompson's Island, provided they set forward fishing, etc. Either he or a son Brave was adm. to the re-organized church 9 (4) 1640. He and John Gingine bought a large tract of land at Salem to which they rem.; they mortg. two thirds of the tract March 31, 1673. [Reg. XL, 256.] He deposed 30 (4) 1680, ae. about 68 years. Wife Hannah adm. chh. before 1639; adm. chh. of Salem 24 (6) 1654; ch. Samuel bapt. 5 (11) 1639, John bapt. 22 (3) 1642, Lydia bapt. 25 (9) 1644, Thomas bapt. 16 (3) 1647, Margaret bapt. 10 (12) 1648-9, Henry bapt. 7 (1) 1651.

He d. Jan. 1, 1702, in his 92d year. [Diary of Joseph Green.]

WILKINSON, WILKERSON,

Ann, ae. 94, d. at Billerica 2 (3) 1684. [Mdx. Rec.]

Isabel, widow, Cambridge, propr. 1637-8. She d. Feb. 23, 1655. Edward Winship and Edward Goffe m. her daughters.

Henry, tallow-chandler, ae. 25, came in

WILKINSON, etc., cont.

the Elizabeth and Ann in April, 1635. Settled at Ipswich; propr. 1635; sold house and land 30 Aug. 1638. [Ipsw. Rec.]

Prudence, widow, Charlestown, propr.; rem. to Mystic Side before 1640. [L.]

In her will dated 9 (11) 1655, she names her son John, and her dau. Elizabeth Felt. "Sister Joane, wife of John Wilkinson, now in N. E." was a legatee in the will of Mary Skilton of London in 1655. [E. and W.]

WILLARD,

George, planter, Scituate, took oath of allegiance 1 Feb. 1638. In court 1 June, 1641. Ch. Deborah and Daniel bapt. Sept. 14, 1645, Joshua bapt. Nov. 2, 1645. [Second Chh. Rec.]

Simon, Cambridge, propr. 1634. Rem. to Concord. Sergeant; appointed to exercise the military company 13 (8) 1636. [W.] "A Kentish soldier;" [J.] Was either deputy or Assistant for about 40 years. Major. Had a patent, with associates, in 1641, for trading with the Indians and collecting tribute from them. [L.] Rem. to Lancaster. Signature in inv. of Thomas Atkinson in 1646. A man of unusual energy, sagacity and character. He m. Mary, sister of Rev. Henry Dunster, q. v. Ch. [Mary, (m. Joshua Edmunds,) Elizabeth, (m. Robert Blood,) Josiah, Samuel,] Simon b. 31 (11) 1639, Sarah b. 24 (5) or 27 (4) 1642, [m. Nathaniel Howard,] Above-hope b. 30 (8) 1646, d. at Lanc. Dec. 23, 1663, Simon b. 23 (9) 1649, Mary b. 7 (7) 1653, [m. Cyprian Stevens,] Henry b. 4 June, 1655, John b. 30 June, 1657, Daniel b. 26 Dec. 1658, Joseph b. at Lanc. 4 (11) 1660, Benjamin, Hannah b. 6 (8) 1666, (m. Capt. Thomas Brintnall,) Jonathan b. Dec. 14, 1669.

He was bur. 27 (2) 1676. [S.] Inv. of his est. filed 6 (1) 1676-7, by Mrs. Willard. She petitioned the Court in 1681, (having meantime married Joseph Noyes,) for further settlement of the estate, especially as to lands due him from the Indians, for the benefit of the six younger children, some of whom were "very young."

The Willard Memoir states that at Horsemonden, Kent, Eng., there lived a Richard Willard, who had son Simon bapt. 8 April, 1605, and George bapt. 4 Dec. 1614, to whom he made beq. in his will, dated 12 Feb. 1616, prob. 9 March folg. It is believed that these are the above-mentioned pioneers.

WILLETT, WILLET, WILLETTS,
Mrs. Isabel, residence not stated, sold a share in the Piscataqua patents. [Suff. De. I, 90.]

Thomas, merchant, Plymouth. Frm. 1633. Agent for Plymouth Colony at Kennebec, 1635. Lands confirmed to him, 1638. Partner in building a bark in 1641. Captain, 1647. Partner in the Kennebec trade, 1649. Assistant, 1651. He m. July 6, 1636, Mary, dau. of Mr. John Browne; she d. Jan. 8, 1699. Ch. Martha, (m. John Saffin,) Esther b. 6 July, 1647, Hezekiah b. and d. 1651; Rebecca, [his child?] d. 2 April, 1652.

He d. at Seakonk Aug. 3, 1674, in 64th year. [Plym. Col. Rec., Reg. X, 181.] Will dated 26 April, 1671, prob. 12 Aug. 1674. Beq. to sons James, Hezekiah, Andrew and Samuel; sons-in-law John Saffin and Samuel Hooker; bro.-in-law James Browne; gr. ch. Samuel Hooker's six sons, John Saffin's four sons by my dau. Martha; dau. Esther Willett; gr. ch. Sarah Eliot; to the church of Rehoboth and to Rev. John Myles; to dau. Mary Hooker. Mr. John Saffin, merchant, of Boston, deposed to the inv. 25 Nov. 1674. [See MS. notebook of John Saffin.]

Toby, embarked June 22, 1632, for N. E.

WILLEY,
Allen, husbandman, Boston, adm. chh. 2 (9) 1634. Wife Alice adm. chh. 9 (9) 1634. Alice, [dau. or widow,] m. in Bo. 5 Dec. 1659, John Garretson. Frances m. in Bo. 16 (5) 1652, Joseph Howe.

Isaac, Boston. Wife Johanna; ch. Isaac bapt. 2 (6) 1640, Hannah bapt. 6 (1) 1642, Sarah b. 19 (4) 1644. He m. in Bo. 8 June, 1660, Frances, dau. of Edward Burcham of Lynn.

WILLIAMS,
Alexander, servant to Mr. William Thomas, Marshfield, 1641; atba. 1643.

Ann, ae. 10, came in the Abigail in July, 1635. Ann, memb. chh. of Salem in 1639.

Edward, Scituate, atba. 1643.
Admin. of his est. gr. to Ensign John W. 29 Oct. 1671.

Eleazer, Salem, memb. chh. 1637. [Wife] Elizabeth, Salem, deposed in 1690, ae. about 80 years, regarding the family of R. Hollingworth, Sen.

WILLIAMS, cont.
George, Salem, frm. May 14, 1634; juryman 1636. Ch. Jon. bapt. 25 (10) 1636, Samuel bapt. 12 (6) 1638, Joseph bapt. 10 (3) 1640, Bethiah bapt. 13 (9) 1642, George bapt. 1 (7) 1644.

Will dated 23 (7) prob. 18 (8) 1654. Wife Marie; eldest son John; dau. Marie Bishop and her 2 children; sons Samuel, Joseph and George; daus. Sarah and Bethia. The widow Marie's will dated 1 (8) was prob. 17 (9) 1654.

Hugh, feltmaker, Boston, a singleman, adm. chh. 1 (11) 1641. Frm. May 18, 1642. With wife Sarah he sold land in Bo. Jan. 8, 1657. Sold land in Bo. and at Block Island June 17, 1663, to his bro. John W., of Barnabe st., London, feltmaker. Rem. to Block Island. Wife Sarah adm. chh. 23 (1) 1644. Servant Elizabeth Rose d. 20 (11) 1655.

John, the confessed murderer of John Hobby, was sentenced by Gen. Court 19 Sept. 1637.

John, Sen., Scituate, farmer, frm. 3 Dec. 1639; deputy 1640.

Will, dec.19, 1667; beq. to dau. Mary Dodson, son John, Ann, wife of John Pratt, Deborah, wife of Wm. Burden, Mary Barker, and his two gr. ch. John and Abraham B.; Nicholas Baker of Scituate. [Reg. VII, 178.]

John, Roxbury, his dau. Elizabeth memb. chh. about 1644. [E.]

John, Newbury, husbandman, bought land in 1642. Rem. to Haverhill in 1647. He m. Jane, who d. Nov. 21, 1680. Ch. John, Sarah, (m. John Ayer, Jr.) Mary b. 20 Sept. 1641, (m. Daniel Bradley,) Lydia b. 15 March, 1642, Joseph b. April 18, 1649.

He d. Feb. 10, 1673. Will dated Dec. 9, 1670, prob. March 18, 1673-4. Sons John and Joseph; daus. Mary, Lydia and Sarah; gr. ch. Sarah Eyers. Inv. of the widow's est. was pres. by son Joseph 29 March, 1681.

Nathaniel, laborer, glover, sergeant, Boston, adm. chh. 26 (3) 1639; frm. May 13, 1640. Wife Mary adm. chh. 4 (5) 1640; ch. Ruth b. 1638, Elizabeth b. 21 (8) 1640, Nathaniel b. 16 (7) 1642, John bapt. 18 (6) 1644, ae. about 3 days, Mary b. 30 (9) 1646, Hannah bapt. 7 (11) 1648, ae. about 9 days.

Will dated 22 (2) 1661, prob. 10 (7) 1662. Wife Mary; dau. Belknap and her two chil-

WILLIAMS, cont.
dren; the rest of his children. Inv. taken 7 (3) 1661. [Reg. X, 270, and Reg. XXXI, 178.] The widow m. Peter Brackett.

Matthew, lawsuit in Salem Court in 1641. See Thomas Carter.

Richard, tanner, Dorchester, 1633. [Col. Rec.] His wife Frances and [sister] Elizabeth were membs. chh. of Dorch. before 1639. Rem. to Taunton; sold land and privileges at Dorch. 20 (8) 1646. Made his bro. Samuel, of Essington, Gloucestershire, Eng. his attorney 21 (8) 1646, to sell his share of a tucke mill at Sinwell, adjoining Essington. [A.] He and his sister Elizabeth, now in New Eng., were legatees in the will of his sister Jane W. of Whetenhurste, co. Gloc. dated 31 May, 1650, prob. 30 June, 1655. Frm. Plym. Col. 5 June, 1644; deacon, deputy, town officer. Ret. to Dorchester; town officer 1658.

He d. 13 July, 1688. Elizabeth was drowned 13 Oct. 1688. He made will 5 May, 1686, aged about 80; prob. 10 Oct. 1693; beq. to sons Samuel, Nathaniel, Joseph, Thomas and Benjamin; daus. Elizabeth and Hannah; wife Frances. The widow, being of great age, made will 20 Oct. 1703, prob. March 7, 1705-6; beq. to son Parmiter; to the widows of sons Nathaniel, Joseph and Benjamin; to son Thomas and dau. Elizabeth Bird of Dorchester. [See wills, etc. in Reg. XXXVII, XLV and LI.]

Robert, laborer, Boston, adm. chh. 10 (2) 1642; townsman 1642; frm. May 10, 1643. Ch. Joseph b. (5) 1641, bapt. 17 (2) 1642, Phebe b. (rec. "of Richard,") (6) 1643, bapt. 3 (7) 1643, ae. about 8 days, Benjamin b. (rec. "of Richard,") (6) 1645, John bapt. 7 (7) 1645.

Will dated 12 Dec. Prob. 30 Jan. 1677, beq. to ch. Joseph and Benjamin Williams and Phebe Eglon. Inv. presented in court Feb. 28, 1677-8, by son Joseph.

Robert, Roxbury, frm. May 2, 1638. Wife Elizabeth adm. chh. 1637; she was bur. 27 (5) 1674, ae. 80. Ch. Isaac b. Sept. 1, 1638, Stephen b. Nov. 8, 1640, John, (d. 6 Oct. 1658,) Samuel, (ae. between 15 and 16 years, adm. chh. in 1647-8. [Town Rec.] Wife Elizabeth d. July 28, 1674. Did he marry Nov. 3, 1675, Margaret, widow of John Fearing of Hingham? And did he marry later Martha Strong, who d. Dec. 22, 1704, ae. 91 years? Did he die at Rox. Sept. 1693? His

WILLIAMS, cont.
wife d. at Rox. 22 Dec. 1690. [Genealogy in Reg. XXXIV, 69.]

Mr. Roger,—not the minister,—one of the founders of Dorchester, 1630. [Bl.] Frm. May 18, 1631. Propr.; town officer. Had rem. to Windsor, Conn. before 1639. Rem. to Boston; deeded 2 acres of land in Dorch. conditionally, 7 (8) 1650. Made reference to the kindred of Lydia Buck. [Suff. De. I, 127.] His wife is stated by his son, (as quoted in note in Dorch. Church Rec.,) to have been Lydia Bates. Son Ebenezer b. in Jan. 1649.

Rev. Roger, b. according to a deposition he made, about 1601, may be quite confidently stated to have been the son of James Williams, citizen and merchant tailor of London, and his wife Alice; their wills, prob. respectively in 1621 and 1634, mention sons Roger, Robert and Sydrach, and dau. Katharine, wife, successively, of Ralph Wightman and John Davies; Alice specifies that Roger is "beyond the seas." [See the very full study of this matter by Mr. Henry F. Waters in Reg. XLII.] He refers in letters to a bro. Robert, schoolmaster at Newport, and a bro. who was a Turkish merchant.

He arrived at Boston, with his wife, Mary, Feb. 5, 1630. Became discontented and rem. to Plymouth. Was rec'd to the chh. after a time, and chosen assistant minister with Rev. Ralph Smith. [Mor.] Rem. to Salem in 1633 and became minister of that chh. Composed a treatise, in which he maintained that it was wrong for the Colony to depend upon the King's patent as a ground of claiming the country; that the churches of England were unchristian. He sent a copy of this writing to the governor 27 Dec. 1633; was rebuked, and promised to refrain from teaching such things publicly; but broke the truce. He further taught that a magistrate ought not to tender the oath of fidelity to an unregenerate man, and that no christian ought to pray with such a person, though it were his wife or child; that a man ought not to give thanks after the Sacrament or after a meal; etc. He wrote a letter to his church in August, 1635, protesting that he would not commune with the churches at The Bay, who held with the magistrates, nor with them unless they would refuse all such communion; and for this reason refused to pray with his own wife. Kept a

WILLIAMS, cont.

meeting at his house for those who agreed with him. [Mor.] After much discussion he was sentenced, 3 Sept. 1635, to depart out of the jurisdiction within six weeks. Rem. to Providence.

After removing he adopted views antagonistic to the baptism of infants and in favor of immersion of adults; but his condemnation by Mass. Bay Colony was on wholly different grounds.

He rendered most valuable service to all New England by his wise influence over the Indians, averting several threatened conflicts. He went to Eng. about 1644; brought back a charter for Providence plantation and letters of commendation from persons of high station, which favorably impressed Mass. Bay authorities. [See W., B., Mass. and Plym. Col. Rec., and letters to Winthrop, father and son, in Mass. Hist. Coll.]

Children: Mary b. at Plym. Aug. 1633, Freeborne b. at Salem Oct. 1635, Providence b. at Prov. Sept. 1638, Mercy b. about 15 Sept. 1640, Daniel b. 15 Feb. 1641, Joseph b. (10) 1643. [Prov. Town Rec.; Es. Inst. Coll. II, 48.]

He died about April, 1683. [Reg. LIII, 60.]

Ruth, Boston, maid servant to Mrs. Messenger, adm. chh. 17 (2) 1647.

Samuel, Yarmouth, atba. 1643. He may be

Samuel, cooper, Salem, bought land of John Williams of Sal. 14 Dec. 1658.

Thomas, came in the Mayflower to Plymouth; died soon after arrival. [B.]

Thomas, Plymouth, servant to Widow Warren, in court 1635. Volunteer for the Pequot war in 1637. Rem. to Eastham about 1649; townsman, 1655. He m. 30 Nov. 1638, Elizabeth, dau. of Thomas Tarte, of Scituate; ch. Nathaniel b. 24 April, 1655.

"Having lived to old age," he made will 10 May, 1692, prob. Oct. 22, 1696. Beq. to gr. ch. John Smith and William, son of John Nickerson; to daus. Sarah Nickerson, Marcy Nickerson, Elizabeth and Mary Hopkins, and the ch. of dau. Hannah Mulford. These ch., except Hannah, signed an agreement 12 Oct. 1696, and with them signed two William Nickersons, Rich Col (Cole,) John Smith, Joshua Higgins and Joseph Smith, as heirs.

WILLIAMS, cont.

Thomas, Charlestown, set up a ferry between Char. and Winnissimmet, (now Chelsea,) 18 May, 1631. From his occupation we may judge him to be the

Thomas, of Salem, servant to Mr. Holgrave, who made will 25 (2) 1646, prob. 5 (9) folg. Beq. to John Spoor of Boston his share in the boat and certain money, due. Inv. taken 1 (3) 1646.

Thomas, Boston, either he or his wife had been members of the chh. of Exeter. Wife Elizabeth d. April 30, 1658; he m. 2, Anne —. Ch. Mary bapt. 11 (6) 1650, Mary b. July 30, 1652, Thomas b. March 29, 1661, Charles b. Sept. 20, 1662, Thomas b. April 9, 1664, Elizabeth b. Feb. 6, 1667, Susanna b. June 1, 1669.

William, of Great Yarmouth, Eng. ae. 40, with wife Alice, ae. 38, and 2 children, and Elizabeth W. of the same place, singlewoman, ae. 31, passed exam. to go to N. E. April 11, 1637. [For Elizabeth see Richard W.] He settled at Watertown. Propr. 1642. Probably his son Abraham is the person who was notified concerning swine Feb. 26, 1655-6, for himself, his mother, his brother and his bro.'s wife.

William, Lynn, in the employ of Mr. John Humphrey in 1641. [Es. Court Rec.]

WILLIAMSON,

Ann, ae. 18, came in the Hopewell in Sept. 1635.

Michael, ae. 30, servant to George Giddings, came in the Defence in July, 1635. Settled at Ipswich; propr. 1635. Michael W., locksmith, of Rhode Island, and Anne, his wife, gave letter of attorney 2 (8) 1639, for the collection of a legacy bequeathed to her by Dennis Geere late of Saugus, given to her under the name of Anne Panckhurst. Gave release 1 Sept. 1640. [L.]

Paul, Ipswich, propr. 1635.

Timothy, Marshfield, frm. Plym. Col. 3 June, 1637. Perhaps the "Mr. Williamson," who, with Capt. Standish, met Massasoit in conference March, 1621. [Mou.] He m. June, 1653, Mary Howland. Ch. Mary b. July 7, 1654, Timothy b. Feb. 15, 1655-6, Joanna b. Nov. 21, 1657, Martha b. May 1, 1670, Abigail b. Aug. 10, 1672, George b. May 2, 1675.

WILLIAMSON, cont.
He was bur. Aug. 6, 1676. Will prob. 20 June folg. beq. to son Timothy; rest to wife for the bringing up of the children.

WILLIS, WILLICE, WILLYES, WILLIES, WILLISE, WILLOIS, WILLOWS,
Elizabeth, servant to Mr. Increase Nowell of Charlestown, d. 16 (10) 1635.

George, Cambridge, propr. 1636; frm. May 2, 1638. Desired to be excused from training about 1662, ae. 61 years. [Mdx. Files.] He m. widow Jane Palfrey, who had children John and Elizabeth Palfrey. [Mi.] On joining the chh. in 1640 she spoke of being formerly in Newcastle and Heddon, Eng. [Rel.] Ch. Thomas b. 28 (10) 1638, Stephen b. 14 (8) 1644.

He d. in 1690; surviving wife Sarah.

Henry, Plymouth colony, volunteer for the Pequot war in 1637.

Henry, Boston, wife Mary; ch. John d. S (1) 1653, Mary b. 26 July, 1655, Henry b. 2 Aug. 1657.

Jeremiah, Duxbury, before Plym. Court 4 Dec. 1638. Jeremiah, Lynn, before Salem Court 28 (1) 1637; owed for a "shorthand book" in 1639. [L.]

John, Duxbury; he m. Elizabeth, widow of Wm. Palmer, [Jr.?] and was one of the appraisers of the est. of Wm. Palmer, Sen., 1637. See his accounts in Plym. Col. Rec. and in L. Had land grant in 1640; atba. 1643; frm. 3 June, 1652. His dau.-in-law Rebecca Palmer was servant of Mr. John Mayo in 1651. John, [Sen. or Jr.?] m. at Boston 11 (11) 1654, Hannah Elsse.

Will dated 15 (4) 1692, prob. 20 Sept. 1693, beq. to sons Nathaniel, Jonathan, John, Joseph and Comfort; daus. Hannah Hayward and Elizabeth Harvey.

Mr. John, Boston, adm. chh. with [wife] Jane in 1632; frm. Nov. 6, 1632; deputy 1634.

He was drowned 21 Nov. 1634. [W.]

Lawrence, Sandwich, atba. 1643. Served against the Narragansetts in 1645. Probably the same as
Lawrence, of Bridgewater, who m. at Boston 5 (7) 1657, Mary, dau. of Thomas Makepeace, of Bo.

WILLIS, etc., cont.
He died intestate; admin. gr. 14 May, 1703, to the nearest kinsman, his nephew Elkanah W.

Michael, cutler, Dorchester, frm. May 2, 1638; propr. Rem. to Boston. Adm. inhabitant in 1647. Wife Joane adm. chh. Dorch. with him about 1637. Second wife Mildred; ch. rec. in Bo.: Michael b. 11 Nov. 1652, dau. Addingstill d. Sept. 6, 1658.

Will 21 June, 1669. Wife Mildred; sons Experience and Michael to have shop and tools; dau. Temperance; grandchild Joseph Philips; married daughters and gr. ch.; cousin Jabesh Salmon of Roxbury.

Nathaniel, Boston, propr. at Spectacle Island, before 1640.
Nathaniel, Sen., Sandwich, constable 1640-1; atba. 1643. Rem. to Bridgewater. Ch. b. at Sandwich: Elkanan b. May 20, 1639, Judith b. June 14, 1641, Mary and Nathaniel b. April 14, 1648.

He d., leaving widow, dau. Bethiah and son Elkanan. Inv. of his est. taken 9 (7) 1686; his son admin. with the aid of his uncle John W. [Gen. Adv. I, 17.]

Nicholas, mercer, Boston, adm. chh. 27 (5) 1634, frm. Sept. 3, 1634. Wife Ann adm. chh. 3 (6) 1634.

He d. leaving a will; inv. taken 20 (4) 1650; [Reg. VII, 234.] 24 Feb. 1650-1, Henry Willis of Bury St. Edmunds, felmonger, Martha Hues, Mary Biggs and Ann Langhorne, widows, of London, app. Benjamin Smith of Boston, N. E. their attorney for collection of their shares in this est. Smith calls Willis his uncle. [Suff. De. I, 158.]

Richard, planter, Plymouth, servant to John Barnes, transferred to Thomas Prence in 1634. Propr. 1638. He m. 11 Oct. 1639, Amey Glasse. He d., and his widow m. Edward Holman. His son Richard, about 7 years old, was appr. Jan. 24, 1648, to Giles Rickard, weaver.

Robert, Boston. Wife Sarah; ch. Sarah b. 10 (11) 1642, Mary b. 18 July, 1653.

Mr. Thomas, Lynn, propr. 1638; memb. Salem Particular Court 6 June, 1639. His land referred to in a deed of Timothy Tomlins June 14, 1641.

WILLIX, WILLIP,

Belshazzar, Salisbury, propr. 1648. He m Mary, widow of Thomas Hawksworth; he d. Jan. 23, 1650-1. Widow Mary admin. on the est. of both husbands in 1651. Robert Tuck was paid for diet of two children of B. W. She d. July, 1675.

WILLS,

William, Scituate, frm. 5 June, 1651. He m. at Plymouth, 4 or 5 Sept. 1638, Luce —. [Scituate Chh. Rec.] Ch. Samuel b. May, 1640, Lydia b. April, 1645.

He d. Oct. 1688. Will made Feb. 26, 1683, in his 85th year; prob. Dec. 12, 1688. Beq. to wife Luce; son Samuel, his wife Rebecca and his children. [Gen. Adv. I, 42.] The widow d. June 21, 1697.

WILLOUGHBY,

Mr. Francis, merchant, Charlestown, adm. propr. 1638; adm. chh. with wife Mary 3 (10) 1639, frm. May 13, 1640. Gave bond in trade concerning tobacco in 1640. [L.] Deputy in 1642 and afterward. Town officer, 1646. Magistrate.

He rendered important service to the colonies as a member of Parliament from Portsmouth, Eng. in 1647, and again in 1657-8. He ret. to Charlestown from his second absence about 1662. The Court gave him 1000 acres of land in token of his services 15 Oct. 1669.

His wife Mary died, and he m. 2, in Eng. Mrs. Margaret Taylor, dau. of William Locke and widow of Mr. Daniel Taylor; she was adm. chh. Char. 13 (8) 1667; ch. Sarah bapt. 13 (4) 1641, Hannah b. and d. 1643, Nehemiah b. 18 (4) 1644, Jeremiah b. 29 (5) 1647, Francis bapt. at St. Olaves in London 29 Feb. 1659-60, Susanna, dau. of the Worshipful Francis Willoughby bapt. at Char. 21 (6) 1664. The two last ch. had bequests from their mother's sister Jane Locke, in 1669. [L., A., Reg. XXX, XXXV, and XL.]

His will dated 4 June, 1670, prob. April 10, 1671; refers to his mother's payment of legacies from his father to his children; beq. to eldest son Jonathan and each of his children; to his wife the estate which she shall testify to having brought at her marriage and a share of his other property; to sons Nehemiah, William and Francis, and dau. Susannah; to dau. Campfield, who had previously recd. her portion; to aunt Hammond if alive, and to cousin Laur. H.; to his pas-

WILLOUGHBY, cont.

tor and teacher; to cousin March during her widowhood free use of the house where she dwells; to the school in Charlestown 300 acres of land given him by the town but never laid out, lying beyond Woburn; to Laur. Dowse and Edward Wilson, and to his man, Richard Waldron.

WILLOWES, see Willis.

WILMOT,

Ralph, residence not mentioned, set free from his master by order of Gen. Court 7 Oct. 1641.

Thomas, Braintree, witness of a document 27 (9) 1645. [A.] Wife Elizabeth; ch. Elizabeth b. 4 (2) 1647.

WILLY, see Wiley.

WILSON, WILLSON,

Benjamin, Taunton, atba. 1643. Compare with

Benjamin, Charlestown, inhabitant, 1657; his wife memb. chh. and their son Benjamin bapt. 1 (3) 1664.

He d. at sea; inv. of his est taken 9 Jan. 1666.

Edward, Salem, made will April 19, 1638. Prob. at Boston. Beq. his est. to bros. Thomas and William; all to Thomas in case William do not come over to New Eng. Witness, Robert Hawkins. [Reg. VII, 30.]

Henry, Dedham, propr. 23 (4) 1640, frm. June 2, 1641. He m. 24 (9) 1642, Mary, dau. of Michael Metcalf. She deposed 11 Nov. 1669, to will of Hezekiah Gay, her age being about 54. [Reg. XLVIII, 324.] Ch. Michael b. 7 (6) 1644, Sarah b. 24 (4) 1650, Mary b. 7 (9) 1652, Elizabeth b. 4 (11) 1653, Ephraim b. 2 (4) 1656.

He d. Feb. 8, 1686.

Jacob, sawyer, Braintree, 1638; frm. June 3, 1641. Ch. Isaac b. 28 (11) 1640, Sarah b. 28 (11) 1641.

Jacob, Taunton, in Plymouth Court 20 Aug. 1644.

Lambert, chirurgeon, was engaged by the Mass. Bay Co. in Eng. in 1629 to remain with the Salem people three years if he will, to practise his profession, learn reme-

WILSON, etc., cont.

dies of the Indians, and teach one or more youths his art. Winthrop says that Mr. Wilson, our chief surgeon, was with the soldiers in the Pequot war in 1637. [Col. Rec. and B.]

Rev. John, son of Rev. William Wilson, canon of St. George's chapel, Windsor, Eng., was b. in 1588, grad. from Christ's coll., Cambridge, was ordained and entered upon the work of the ministry in England, chiefly at Sudbury.

He was engaged by the Mass. Bay Co. to come to N. E., and came in the fleet with Winthrop. Began to preach at Charlestown 10 July, 1630; joined in organizing the first church July 30, and was ordained its teacher Aug. 27, 1630. Continued in office after the chh. rem. to Boston, and till the close of his life. Was a good preacher, an ardent advocate of what he believed and and vigorous in opposing measures or persons when he thought them opposed to the Word of God. Took a leading part in all the great movements of his day, and stood for orthodoxy and conservatism, even when that involved intense persecution of opponents. Yet was reputed kind and liberal in personal dealings.

He m. Elizabeth, dau. of Sir John Mansfield, a sister of the wife of Benjamin Keayne. She did not come over with him at first; was adm. chh. 20 (1) 1636; she d. before 1661. Ch. John adm. chh. Boston 3 (1) 1644, became minister at Dorchester and afterward at Medfield; Mary b. in Boston 12, bapt. 15 (7) 1633, adm. chh. 19 (9) 1648, (m. Mr. Samuel Danforth, long minister at Roxbury,) Elizabeth adm. chh. 19 (9) 1648.

He d. Aug. 7, 1667, ae. about 78 years and a half. [D.] Will dated 31 May, prob. 21 Aug. 1667. Beq. to John Wilson, Jr., son of his dec. son Edmund W., Doctor of Physic, late of the city of London, and to Bridget, wife of Nicholas Prideaux, merchant, of Barbadoes, dau. of the same; to his son John W., pastor of the church of Medfield, and to Sarah, Elizabeth, John and Susanna, his children; to his dau. Mary, wife of Mr. Samuel Danforth, pastor of the church of Roxbury, and to their children John, Mary, Elizabeth and Samuel; to his cousin Edward Rawson; to his kinswoman Mrs. Anna Page; to his bro. John Mansfield, his wife and children; to cousin, Mrs. Sarah Higginson; to his friends Gaudy and Ann James a testi-

WILSON, etc., cont.

monial for their love and service to him; to fellow officers in the church and several brethren in the ministry. [Reg. XVII, 343, and XXXVIII, 306.]

Joseph, Dorchester, frm. May 2, 1638. He gave letter of attorney 21 (2) 1646, to William Harvee to receive his part of the goods of his bro. Benjamin, deceased. Residing at Boston, 19 (9) 1646, he was attorney for John Crabtree of Barbadoes. [A.]

Nathaniel, planter, Roxbury, Muddy River. He made John Wilson of Halifax in Yorkshire, cloth-worker, his attorney 19 (*) 1647, to collect legacy left him by Nathaniel Holgate of Halifax, dec. [A.] He sold house at Rox. Feb. 16, 1652. He m. April 2, 1645, Hannah, dau. of Griffin Crafts; ch. Hannah bapt. 2 May, 1647, Nathaniel bapt. April 30 or 8 (3) 1653, Joseph and Benjamin bapt. Jan. 31 or 17 (12) 1655, Isaac b. Aug. 24, 1658, Mary b. May 2, 1661, (rec. in Boston,) Abigail bapt. 10 (2) 1664, Samuel b. June 10, 1666.

Richard, servant of Samuel Wade of Lynn, was before the Gen. Court 3 (7) 1639. Richard, servant of Mr. Thomas Cheesholme, before Court 29 April, 1641. Richard, tanner, bricklayer, Cambridge, propr. 1636. Bought a house at Charlestown, which he sold 8 (8) 1647. [Town Rec.] He sold Camb. land and house March 16, 1651, and rem. to Boston. He had ch. John bapt. 1 (4) 1651. He m. 2, 7 (2) 1654, Sarah Hurst.

He d. about 1654. Will dated Aug. 19, 1654; beq. all his est. to wife Sarah. List of debts mentions something due to her sister Elizabeth if she be alive, and refers to her mother; attested by his widow Sarah, now wife of John Benham. [Reg. V, 305, and VIII, 277.]

Theophilus, Ipswich, propr. 1637; sold land 28 (12) 1641; bought land 20 (10) 1642. Dorchester, propr., frm. March 13, 1638-9. His land passed to Thomas Tredwell. With [wife] Elizabeth witnessed the will of his sister Margery Knowlton in 1654. He deposed in 1680, ae. about 79 years.

Thomas, miller, Roxbury, bro. of Edward and William, arrived in N. E. (4) 1633. [E.] Frm. May 14, 1634. Was before the Court 4 (10) 1638, for taking too much toll. See Edward, *ante*. He was dism. 12 (4)

WILSON, etc., cont.
1642, to the chh. of Hampton; rem. thence to Exeter. Wife Ann; ch. Humphrey, Samuel, Joshua, Deborah b. at Rox. (6) 1634, Lydia b. (9) 1636.
Will dated 9 (11) 1642, prob. Suff. and Ipswich 9 (11) 1642; beq. to wife and children. [Reg. II, 384.] The widow m. John Legat of Ex. who made over to Anthony Stanian certain cattle for the benefit of her dau. Deborah W. 5 (12) 1644.

William, joiner, planter, Boston, bro. of Edward and Thomas, adm. chh. with wife Patience 6 (7) 1635; frm. May 25, 1636. Rem. to Braintree. Leased, 22 (8) 1638, land in Dunnington, Lincolnshire, Eng., adjoining his bro. Thomas and his father William W.; his mother Alice may come over. [L.] He was keeper of the prison at Boston in 1645. Ch. Shoreborne b. 6 (6) 1635, Mary b. 11 (11) 1637, John bapt. 9 (12) 1639, Joseph bapt. 13 (9) 1642, ae. about 5 days, Joseph b. 10 (9) 1643, [1642?] Newgrace b. and d. 1645. He d. before 18 May, 1653, when his widow brought suit against Thomas Faxon about her son Joseph; the Court freed the boy, and permitted her to appr. him to a new master. She d., and her est. was divided to her children, (no names mentioned,) April 30, 1663. [Reg. XII, 53.]

WILTON,
David, Dorchester, paid Mr. Pynchon for beaver in 1632; propr. 1633, frm. June 11, 1633. Rem. to Windsor, Conn. Lieut. Rem. to Northampton.
He d. Feb. 5, and was bur. at Windsor Feb. 6, 1677-8. His widow m. goodman Hosmer of Hartford. Dau. Mary m. Capt. Samuel Marshall of W.

WINBOURNE, WIMBOURNE, WENBORNE, WENBANE,
William, husbandman, Boston, before Gen. Court in 1645; adm. chh. with wife Elizabeth 9 (1) 1650; frm. May, 1645. He bought a house and lot 14 (12) 1644; sold Aug. 11, 1662. [Is he the William Wen who, with wife Elizabeth, had son John b. in Bo. 2? (9) 1635?] Son John b. 21 (7) 1638.

WINCALL, WINCHELL, WINCHILL,
John, yeoman, Watertown, propr. 1636, frm. May 6, 1646; chosen surveyor in 1647. Rem. to Piscataqua. Engaged in 1659 to

WINCALL, etc., cont.
build a sawmill upon the salmon falls of great Newickawannock river for Walter Price and Richard Cooke. Deposed 6 July, 1671, relative to contracts he had made for the sale of lumber; referred to his bro. Thomas Broughton.

Robert, Dorchester, propr. 1635, frm. May 6, 1635.

Thomas, yeoman, before Gen. Court March 4, 1632-3; propr. at Cambridge; sold lands before 1638. Rem. to Watertown; propr. 1642. Sergt. Elizabeth, who came in the Rebecca April 9, 1635, ae. 52, may have been his wife, and John, ae. 13, who came at the same time, his son. His [second?] wife Beatrix d. June 11, 1655, ae. about 80 years.
He d. June 10, 1657, ae. about 70 years. Son John filed inv. of the est. Oct. 6, 1657.

WINCHESTER,
Alexander, Boston, servant to Mr. Henry Vane, adm. chh. 8 (9) 1635. Propr.; rem. to Braintree, having his dismission to that chh. 12 (5) 1640. Frm. Dec. 7, 1636; deputy 1641. Rem. to Rehoboth; prop. frm. Plymouth Col. 4 June, 1645. Ch. Marie bapt. 19 (9) 1637, Elizabeth b. 28 (1) 1640, Hannah b. 10 (10) 1642.
He d. July 16, 1647. Will prob. June 8, 1648. Wife, children under 15 years of age. [Reg. IV, 283.] Account presented 6 March, 1648-9. Portion in the est. confirmed 3 June, 1657, to Mr. Nicholas Peck, who had married Mary, the eldest dau. [Plym. Col. Rec.]

John, Roxbury, frm. March 9, 1636-7. Rem. to Hingham; propr. 1636; rem. to Muddy River, Boston, and bought Ronton Farm of the heirs of Mrs. Ann Hibbens Dec. 28, 1657. He m. in Scituate, Oct. 15, 1638, Hannah, dau. of Richard Syllice; she d. 18 Sept. 1697; ch. John bapt. at Hing. June 2, 1644, Mary bapt. March 26, 1648, Josiah b. March 27, 1655, rec. at Rox.
He made will 17 June, 1691, ae. fourscore years and upward; prob. 14 June, 1694; beq. to wife Hannah; ch. John, Josiah, Mary Drew; Mary, dau. of dec. son Jonathan.

WINDOWE, WINDOE, WINDOR, WINDE,
Richard, Gloucester, in court (10) 1647; was living away from his wife. Town offi-

WINDOWE, etc, cont.
cer, 1654. He m. March 30, 1659, Bridget, widow of Henry Travers.

Will dated 2 May, prob. 7 (4) 1665, beq. to wife Bridget and her son James Travers; dau. Ann; son-in-law Anthony, committing him to the care of his uncle Bennett; dau.-in-law Elizabeth Bennett a Bible that was her father's; Richard Goding. Inv. of the est. of the widow was taken 9 Oct. 1673.

WINDSOR, WINSOR, WINSWORTH,
John, Scituate. He m. Oct. 15, 1638, Hannah Syllice.

The inv. of his est., taken by John Andrews, John Blowar and Bernard Harris, was filed at Boston 15 Feb. 1666, and admin. gr. to James Neighbor.

Joseph, Sandwich, 1638, atba. 1643.

Robert, turner, Boston. His wife Rebecca adm. chh. 12 (8) 1644; approved to keep a cooks shop 29 (2) 1672. She d. "an antient wido," Jan. 28, 1697. Ch. John b. 10 (12) 1644, Joshua bapt. 13 (4) 1647, ae. about 7 days, Mary bapt. 30 (10) 1649, ae. about 11 days, Thomas b. Sept. 30, 1652, Rebecca b. Dec. 20, 1654, Constance b. May 7, 1657, Thomas b. Oct. 1, 1659, Sarah b. May 7, 1662, Samuel b. Sept. 18, 1664, *William* bapt. Sept. 25, 1664, Lydia b. Aug. 1, 1666, John b. April 22, 1669.

WINES, WIND, WINDS, WINDES,
Barnabas, Watertown, propr., frm. May 6, 1635. He sold planting ground in 1642. Rem. to Conn., thence to Southold, L. I. before 1662.

Faintnot, flax-dresser, Charlestown, inhabitant and propr. 1635, frm. May 29, 1644. He d. Feb. 25, 1664. Will dated 1 Sept. 1663, prob. 20 (4) 1665, beq. to wife Bridget; to the children of my cousin Nicholas which he had by cousin Hester W.; to the ch. of cousin Elizabeth Harsnett, now wife to [Ephraim] Pope, namely John Bacon, Ephraim and Elizabeth P.; to bro. Daniel W.; to cousin Peter Churchman's children.

WING,
Deborah, dau. of Rev. Stephen Bachiler, m. Rev. John Wing. He resided at Sandwich, Eng., then at Hanbury. Rem. to Flushing, Zealand, where he was pastor of the Puritan church; then resided at the Hague where he d. about 1629. The widow came to New Eng. bringing three sons, Daniel, John and Stephen, leaving son Matthew in Eng. Settled at Sandwich.

Daniel, Sandwich, atba. 1643. Ch. Hannah b. July 28, 1642, Lydia b. May 23, 1647, Samuel b. Aug. 28, 1652, Hephsibah b. Nov. 7, 1654, John b. Nov. 14, 1656, Beulah b. Nov. 16, 1658.

He d., and inv. of his small estate was presented May 3, 1659, by his bros. John and Stephen; est. confirmed to his children. [Reg. V, 387, XXXVIII, 376, XXXIX, 192, and XL, 325.]

John, bro. of Daniel, Sandwich, creditor of Thos. Hampton, 1637; propr. 1640; rem. to Yarmouth. Ch. Ephraim b. 30 May, 1648, drowned in the snow 11 Dec. 1648; Joseph b. 2 Sept. 1650. John Wing that married one of the daughters of James Davis is mentioned in the probate papers of Davis. [Reg. XI, 340.] He deposed in case of Francis Dent, before Gen. Court, in 1638-9.

He made will 2 May, 1696, grown aged; prob. Aug. 10, 1699. Beq. to wife Meriam, sons Joseph and Annanias, gr. ch. John and Elnathan W. and Elizabeth Turner; daus. Susanna Parslow and Oseah Turner. The widow Miriam's will dated at Harwich, May 24, 1701, was prob. Jan. 8, 1702-3; kinsman Deane Smith, son of her kinswoman Bethia S. of Manamoiet.

Robert, ae. 60, with wife Judith, ae. 43, came in the Francis of Ipswich April 30, 1634. Settled at Boston; laborer, adm. chh. 8 (8) 1642. Sent a message July 26, 1641, to his cousin Wing of Lomford, dwelling in Ladyes place, by Dedham, Eng. [L.] He was before the Court 11 Nov. 1647; was discharged as being a poor man with 4 small children and nothing to live upon, and 80 years of age. Wife Johanna; ch. John b. 22 (5) 1637, Hannah b. 14 (12) 1639, Jacob b. 31 (5) 1642, Elizabeth b. (6) 1644, (m. April 3, 1661, John Walley,) Joseph b. 13 (4) 1646, Benjamin b. 11 (12) 1648.

He d. 24 (9) 1651; nunc. will prob. 3 (10) 1651. All to wife Johanna, praying her to be good to his children. The Court ordered that she should be responsible to the four children she had by him. [Reg. IV, 54.]

Stephen, bro. of Daniel, Sandwich, 1640. Wife "Osith" d. April 29, 1654. He

WING, cont.
m. 2, 7 (11) 1654, Sarah Briggs. Ch. Deborah b. 10 Oct. 1648, Ephraim b. 2 April, 1649, Mercy or Mary b. 13 Nov. 1650, Stephen b. Sept. 2, 1656, Sarah b. Feb. 5, 1658, John b. Sept. 25, 1656, Sarah b. Feb. 5, 1658, John b. Sept. 25, 1661, Abigail b. May 1, 1664, Ebenezer b. 11 (5) 1671, Matthew b. 1 (1) 1673.

WINN, WINNE, WYNN,
Edward, carpenter, hired at Broughton, Eng. and brought over to N. E. by Barnabas Davis with his family about 1639. [L.] Settled at Woburn. Propr. 1640. Frm. 5 (10) 1643. His wife Joanna or Jane d. March 8, 1648-9. He deposed 17 June, 1670, ae. about 71 years. He m. Aug. 10, 1649, Sarah Beal. She deposed 7 (8) 1668, ae. about 60 years. [Mdx. Files.] Ch. Ann, (m. Sept. 26, 1648, Moses Cleveland,) Elizabeth, (m. May 21, 1649, George Polly,) Increase b. 5 (10) 1641. She d. March 15, 1679-80. He d. Sept. 5, 1682.

Mr., at Marshfield; his "man" enrolled as atba. 1643.

WINSHIP, WINSHEP, WINDSHIP, WINCHIP,
Edward, Cambridge, propr. 1635. Serg. 1643. Deputy; town officer. Sold his share in the Billerica lands, including one share that "was his father Parks." Wife Elizabeth memb. with him in 1658; ch. by first wife Jane, also a memb. Camb. chh. Sarah, Mary, Ephraim and Joanna; ch. by Elizabeth: Edward, Abigail, Samuel, Joseph bapt. Aug. 25, 1661, Margery bapt. Feb. 5, 1664, Mehitabel bapt. Nov. 17, 1667; all b. and bapt. in Camb. [Mi.]

He d. Dec. 2, 1688, in his 76th year; his widow Elizabeth d. 19 Sept. 1690, in her 58th year. [Gr. St.] His will dated Sept. 16, 1685, prob. Oct. 1, 1689, beq. to sons Ephraim, Edward, Samuel, Joseph, daus. Mary, Elizabeth, Abigail, Margery, Joannah and Mehitabel and wife. Bros. Samuel Stone and John Grene overseers. The widow, Oct. 18, 1689, beq. to her 3 sons Edward, Samuel and Joseph; and to her 4 daus. Elizabeth, Abigail, Margery and Mehetabel; also to Mary Brown and her sister Joanna. [See Goffe and Witchfield.]

WINSLEY, WENSLEY, WINSLOW,
Mr. Samuel, planter, Salisbury, 6 (7) 1638. [Col. Rec.] Frm. May 22, 1638. Surveyor of the arms, 1 Sept. 1640; seller of strong waters, 1654; deputy. His wife Elizabeth d. June 2, 1649; he m. 2, Ann —, who d. March 21, 1676-7. Ch. Deborah, (m. John Weed,) Samuel, Nathaniel, (see North,) Ephraim b. April 15, 1641, Elisha b. May 30, 1646.

He d. June 2, 1663. Inv. and admin. of his est. by son Samuel in Oct. folg. The inv. of the est. of the widow mentions a bill of Wm. Buswell for 4 years, 5 months diet. [Es. Inst. Col. VII.]

WINSLOW,
Edward, printer, son of Edward Winslow, Esquire, b. at Droitwich, Eng. Oct. 19, 1595; res. at London. Rem. to Leyden, Holland. There he married, May 6, 1614, Elizabeth Barker of Chatsun, Eng. He came in the Mayflower; signed the Compact; settled at Plymouth. Was one of the Trading co.; agent of the Colony; magistrate, Assistant, and in 1644 was chosen Governor. He wrote Hypocrisy Unmasked, Good News from New England, and numerous important letters. Was a man of large powers and deep devotion to the interests of the Colony. He brought with him his wife; two men-servants, George Sowle and Elias Story, and a little girl who had been placed in his care, Ellen More; she d. in 1621. His wife d. soon after coming, and he m. 2, May 12, 1621, Susanna, widow of Mr. William White; she survived him, and d. Oct. 1, 1680.

He d. at sea May 8, 1655. Ch. Edward, John, Josiah, Elizabeth.

Gilbert, bro. of Edward, bapt. Oct. 29, 1600, came in the Mayflower; signed the Compact; drew lots in Plymouth in 1623. Ret. after a few years to Eng. and d. there.

John, bro. of Edward, yeoman, bapt. April 18, 1597, came to Plymouth in the Fortune in 1621. He rem. to Boston in 1655. Bought the mansion of the late Antipas Boice 19 Sept. 1671. Wife Mary came with him to Plymouth, and drew share in cattle in 1627. Ch. Sarah, (m. in Bo. 19 July, 1660, Myles Standish, Jr.,) Benjamin b. at Plym. 12 Aug. 1653.

Will dated 12 March, 1673, prob. 21 May, 1674. Beq. to wife Mary; sons Benjamin, Edward, and John; to William Payne, son

WINSLOW, cont.
of his dau. Sarah Meddlecott; to Parnell, dau. of his son Isaac; to the children of his dau. Latham; to son Edward's children; to son Edward Grey's children which he had by my dau. Mary; to son Joseph's two children; to gr. ch. Mary Harris' two children; to kinsman Josiah Winslow, governor of New Plymouth; to bro. Josiah; to kinswoman Eleanor Baker, dau. of my bro. Kenelm; to Mr. Paddy's widow; to negro girl Jane her freedom after 20 years.

Josiah, bro. of Edward, bapt. Feb. 16, 1605-6; was sent over as an accountant to Mr. Shirley in 1631 to Plymouth. Settled at Marshfield; frm. 1633; deputy 1643. Ch. Elizabeth b. Sept. 24, 1637, Jonathan b. Aug. 8, 1638, Margaret b. July 15, 1640, Rebecca b. July 15, 1643, Hannah b. 30 Nov. 1644.

He was bur. Dec. 1, 1674, in his 69th year. Will prob. 1 March, 1674-5, beq. to his four daus.; to gr. ch. Hannah Miller, living with his wife; to Mr. Samuel Arnold, the teacher. The will was declared void in regard to his bequeathing house and lands at Marshfield after having previously given them to his son Josiah; otherwise the will was declared in force. Widow Margaret exec.

Kenelm, bro. of Edward, joiner, bapt. May 3, 1599. Came to Marshfield; frm. 1633. He m. in June, 1634, Ellen or Eleanor, widow of John Adams.

He d. at Salem Sept. 13, 1672; his widow Ellen was bur. Dec. 5, 1682, ae. 83 years. His will dated 8 Aug.; testified before Wm. Hawthorne, was prob. at Plymouth 5 June, 1673. Certain estate, formerly given to son Kenelme; wife Ellinor's est. to go to son Nathaniel after her decease; son Job; dau. Ellinor; gr. ch. Kenelme Baker, Mary Adams and others not specified.

WINSOR, see Windsor.

WINTER,
Christopher, planter, Plymouth and Scituate, atba. 1643. He m. about 4 Sept. 1638, Mrs. Jane Cooper. [See Church and Court Records.]

Christopher, Marshfield, made will 6 (7) 1680, prob. 5 March, 1683-4. Daus. Mary Read, Naomy Turner, Annah Badson, Martha Huett; gr. ch. Mary and John Read; Solomon, Bridget and Elizabeth Huett; kins-

WINTER, cont.
man Christopher, son of Timothy Winter of Braintree.

John, Scituate, prop. frm. 5 Nov. 1638-9; atba. 1643. His son John bapt. April 1, 1638. [His wife] Katharine d. 19 Dec. 1653.

John, tanner, Watertown, propr. 1636. He d. 14 (2) 1662, ae. about 90 years. Will mentions sons Richard and Thomas, late of London; son John of Wat.; dau. Alice Lachman of London.

William, Lynn. He deposed in 1657, ae. about 73 years, respecting Thomas Dexter's buying Nahant of the Indian called Blacke Will or Duke William for a suit of clothes. He was presented to the Court in 1641 for speaking against Baptism of Infants, etc. He and his son Josias Hale and his dau. Emma Hale, were legatees in the will of Hugh Churchman in 1640.

WINTHROP,
John, Esquire, son of Adam Winthrop of Groton, co. Suffolk, Eng., was born Jan. 12, 1587-8.

He was elected governor of the Mass. Bay Company in London, Oct. 20, 1629; the Co. having voted to combine in one person the two offices previously existing, the moderator of the Company's deliberations and the executive officer of the plantation. He sailed from the Cowes Easter Monday, March 29, 1630, in the Arbella, and arrived at Cape Ann June 12, 1630, at "Mattachusetts" June 17. His letters to his wife and others, (preserved in his History of New England,) describe the arrival of other vessels at "Charleton" July 1; he dated letters at that point up to Aug. 14; first dates at Boston Nov. 29, 1630. He received the reins of government from Gov. Endecott, whose term had expired; and entered at once upon a wonderful career of office and influence. His History of New England is the most complete mirror of the life and spirit of that day; referred to in this work as W.

He married 1, April 16, 1605, Mary, dau. of John Forth, who was bur. June 26, 1615; he m. 2, Dec. 6, 1615, Thomasine, dau. of William Clopton, who d. Dec. 8, 1616; he m. 3, April 29, 1619, Margaret, dau. of Sir John Tindall, knight, b. about 1590, who came to Boston a year after him, and d. June 14, 1647; he m. 4, Dec. 4, 1647, Martha, dau. of

WINTHROP, cont.
Capt. William Rainsborough, and widow of Capt. Thomas Coytmore of Charlestown; she survived him, and m. John Cogan. Children: John, (became governor of Conn.,) Henry, Forth, Mary, Anna, Stephen, Adam, Deane, Nathaniel, Samuel, William bapt. in Boston 26 (6) 1631, Sarah, Joshua bapt. 17 (10) 1648, d. 11 (11) 1651.
He died March 26, 1649. [E.]

WISE, WISSE, (sometimes incorrectly written Wife and Wiffe,) see Wyeth,
Elizabeth, a widow, memb. chh. Roxbury about 1634. [E.]

Jane, widow, Roxbury, bur. April, 1637.

Humphrey, husbandman, Ipswich, propr. 1635; d. in 1638. Ipswich Court considered his estate 26 March, 1639. The widow Susan had m. Samuel Greenfield, formerly of Salem; the Court allowed them to admin., to sell the house, lands and goods; G. gave bonds to bring up the five children, Benjamin, Joseph, Em, Sarah and Ann, and pay them their portions at age. Benj. was apprenticed to Abraham Perkins for 7 years.

John, Cambridge, d. 9 (7) 1644.

Joseph, Roxbury, propr. about 1640. Mortg. house, malthouse and kiln 25 (6) 1647. Wife Mary memb. chh.; ch. Joseph bapt. April 1, 1643, Joseph and Jeremiah bapt. 3 (3) 1646, Sarah bapt. 26 (10) 1647, (m. June 30, 1669, Caleb Lamb,) Mary bapt. 3 (12) 1649, John bapt. Aug. 15, 1652, Henry bapt. 4 (1) 1654, Bethia bapt. 19 (2) 1657, Katharine bapt. 10 (8) 1658, Benjamin b. and d. 1660, William bapt. 9 (1) 1661, Benjamin b. and d. 1664, Abigail bapt. 24 (4) 1666.
He d. Sept. 12, 1684. Admin. was gr. 15 Sept. 1684, to his widow and son John, of Chebacto, co. of Essex, minister. His widow Mary d. Aug. 4, 1693.

WISEWALL, WISWELL, WISWALL,
John, iron-monger, Dorchester, propr.; frm. March 14, 1638-9. Deacon, deputy; chosen ruling elder, but declined; afterward accepted the office in Boston, to which he removed about 1669. Mortg. land in Dorch. 7 Nov. 1668. Wife Margaret adm. chh. with him about 1636. See letter to them from her parents, Thomas and Ann Smith in Eng. dated May 11, 1660, referring to their relatives, either Wiswall or Smith. [Mass. Arch.,

WISEWALL, etc., cont.
printed in Reg. VII, 273.] Ch. John, [Suff. De.] Rebecca b. 3 (6) 1639, Deborah bapt. 30 (3) 1641, (m. Wm. Cheney, Jr.,) Sarah b. 19 (12) bapt. 26 (12) 1642-3, Lydia bapt. 13 (2) 1645, Mary, (m. Mahaleel Munnings,) Benjamin bapt. 16 (2) 1649, Martha b. 23 (12) 1651, about 11 o'clock at night & bapt. 14 (1) 1652.
Will dated 9 July, prob. 24 Aug. 1687, beq. to son John, dau. Hannah Overman, dau. Fisher and her ch., son and dau. Cutter, son Matthew and dau. Johnson, dau. Lydia Ballard's ch., dau. Mary Emans, son [Henry] and dau. Mountfort. The inv. filed 14 Feb. 1687: iron ware; lands in Bo. and Dorch., etc.; refers to gr. ch. Benjamin Cheney and Jacob and Samuel Royal.

Thomas, Dorchester, propr., memb. chh. about 1636 with wife Elizabeth. He deeded houses and lands at Dorch. 25 (9) 1657, to his son Enoch, who was about to marry Elizabeth, dau. of Mr. John Oliver. His dau. Hester m. "Captin Johnson's son" and was dism. 24 (1) 1661-2 to the chh. of Woburn. He was dism. 5 (4) 1664, for the beginning of a chh. at Cambridge Village, and was there chosen ruling elder. [Dorch. Chh. Rec.] Ch. Enoch, Noah bapt. 30 (10) 1638, Ebenezer b. 8 (12) 1641, bapt. 9 (4) 1650, Hester, (m. — Johnson).

WISEMAN,
James, Braintree, had grant of land for 3 heads 24 (12) 1639. Ch. James b. 8 (8) 1640, Mercie b. 28 (1) 1643.
Will, dated 7 Feb. 1680, prob. 3 May, 1681, beq. to son James; dau. Martha Vearin and her 5 ch. John, Thomas, James, Joseph and Ebenezer; to youngest dau. Sarah.

WITCHFIELD,
John, embarked for N E. June 22, 1632; settled at Dorchester; propr.; frm. June 11, 1633. Rem. to Windsor, Conn. Ruling elder. His wife d. 26 April, [1657,] and he m. Margaret, widow of Edward Goffe of Cambridge.
Margaret, of Windsor upon Canoeticoate River, d. at Cambridge about the end of the 4th month, 1667; made will 21 April, 1663, prob. 5 (8) 1668; beq. to her husband; to her daus. Hannah and Abia Goffe; to the children of dec. sister Jane Winship; to Edward and Deborah, ch. of Samuel G.; to dau.-in-law Elizabeth Hayward, and others.

WITHERDEN, WETHERDEN, WYTH-ERDEN, WITHERNDEN,
John, miller, millwright, Scituate, atba. 1643. Sold land in 1645. Rem. to Boston. Sold ¼ of the wind-mill on the common, near to Fox Hill Feb. 12, 1654. Bought another tract in 1661, which he and his wife Mary sold same year.

WITHERELL, see Wetherell.

WITHERIDGE, WYTHERIDGE,
Edward, mariner, Boston, adm. chh. 24 (12) 1643, frm. May 20, 1644. Had accounts with Sedgwick, Hill and Mills 23 (3) 1648. [A.]

John, Watertown, (perhaps same as Witherell,) mentioned in Col. Rec. 1 (4) 1641.
Admin. gr. Nov. 5, 1672, to widow Mary; dau. Mary recd. balance of est. 24 Dec. 1680.

WITHERLEY,
Thomas, before Gen. Court 6 June, 1639.

WITH, WITHIE, WITHE, see Wyeth,
Robert, ae. 20, "Marg." ae. 60, and Susan, ae. 16, came in the Hopewell in Sept. 1635.

WITHINGTON,
Henry, Dorchester, is believed to have come about the same time as Mr. Richard Mather, in 1635; one of the seven signers of the church covenant at the re-organizing, 23 Aug. 1636. Selectman 2 Oct. 1636; propr. Ruling elder; "a man that excelled in wisdom, meekness and goodness." [D.] By first wife Elizabeth who d. 6 (12) 1660, he had ch. Richard, Mary, (m. Thomas Danforth,) Ann, (m. James Bates, Jr.,) Faith, (m. Richard Baker). He m. widow Margarie Paul, (formerly Turner,) of Taunton; she survived him and d. May 20, 1676.

He d. Feb. 2, 1666, ae. 79. Will dated 8 (11) 1664, ae. about 76 or upon 77 years of age; son Richard to perform contract made at marriage with wife Margarie, and pay her 10 li. extra; beq. to Richard, to Faith Baker, Mary Danforth and Anna Batte; to John Baker, Samuel Danforth, Samuel Batte and Samuel Paull; to all his grandchildren except Mary Robinson; to Messrs. Mather and Tompson; to the church; to Richard's four sons John, Ebenezer, Henry and Philip. Prob. 15 Feb. 1666-7. [Reg. XVI, 52.]

WITHMAN,
John, place of residence not given, frm. May 18, 1642.

WITTER,
William, Lynn, lawsuit, 1639. Called to Court for antagonizing Infant Baptism 22 May, 1646.
Will dated 5 (6) 1652, inv. taken Nov. 15, 1659, prob. 24 (4) 1661; wife Annis; son Josiah; dau. Hannah, wife of Robert Burdin.

WOAKER, see Walker.

WOLLASTON,
Captain, Mr., founder of the Colony of Mt. Wollaston about 1623; a man of pretie parts. When the colony failed he took part of his servants to Virginia and sold them there. [B.] Had a conditional grant of land at Scituate in 1640. Was before the Gen. Court 7 Sept. 1641. Compare with next name.

WOLLENSTON,
Edward, gent., sued for debt in Plymouth Court and swine attached by George Allen of Sandwich, 1641.

WOOD, WOODS,
Constant, ae. 12, came in the Abigail in June, 1635.

Daniel, Ipswich, paid for service against the Indians in 1643; propr. 1644. Inv. of his est. taken 23 March, 1648.

Edmond, Springfield, one of the original proprietors in 1636. [See Reg. XIII, 297.] Jonas also appears as a propr., and John, a father in 1658.

Edward, baker, Charlestown, bought half of a house Nov. 1, 1639. [L.] Adm. chh. 30 (1) 1640, frm. May 13, 1640. His wife Ruth adm. chh. 24 (3) 1640, d. 29 (6) 1642; ch. Tabitha bapt. 30 (3) 1641. Edward Wood, "the elder of that name," died 27 (9) 1642. Admin. gr. 4 (10) 1642. [Reg. III, 81.]

Edward, mariner, would seem to be the younger of the name, referred to above; his wife Elizabeth seems to be the person, ae. 38, who came in the Increase April 15, 1635, with [son] Nathaniel, ae. 12. Edward bought land at Boston Jan. 12, 1655; which his wife Elizabeth, acting in his absence, mortg. July 21, 1659. Elizabeth adm. chh.

WOOD, etc., cont.

Char. 10 (4) 1644; Joanna adm. chh. Char. 31 (5) 1644.

Admin. of the est. of Capt. Wood was gr. 11 Feb. 1674, to his widow Elizabeth; John Sandys and Joseph Webb witnesses.

Henry, Plymouth, sometimes called "Wood *alias* Atwood," propr. 16 Sept. 1641; atba. 1643. Rem. to Middleborough. He m. 25 April, 1644, Abigail, dau. of John Jenney; ch. Samuel b. 25 May, 1647, Jonathan b. 1 Jan. 1649, David b. 17 Oct. 1651.

He d. before 30 Sept. 1670, when inv. of his est. was taken. Admin. was gr. to his widow Abigail. His son John made nunc. will April 13, 1673, bequeathing to his two youngest bros., his sister Mary and his mother. The court ordered lands of his to be given over to Abiall and James, the two youngest bros., by Samuel, the eldest bro.

John, Salem, 1636; propr. at Lynn, 1638. Frm. May 13, 1640. We may note that a John Woods of Ipswich d. 13 Aug. 1684.

John, pin-maker, Sudbury, propr. 1639; frm. May 10, 1643; town officer. Rem. to Marlborough; sold S. land Sept. 29, 1663. Deposed 4 (8) 1664, ae. about 54. [Mdx. Files.] Wife Mary; ch. John b. 8 (3) 1641, Frances b. 10 (3) 1645, Isaac b. 14 July, 1655.

John, servant to Mr. Joseph Hull, came from Weymouth, Eng. before March 20, 1635.

John, Wood alias Atwood, Plymouth, propr. 1636; juryman 1638; atba. 1643. He m. Sara, dau. of Richard Masterson, q. v.; ch. John b. 4 March, 1649, Nathaniel b. 25 Feb. 1651, Isaac b. 27 Feb. 1653; other ch. Mary Holmes, Sarah Fallowell, Abigail Leanard, Mercy, Elizabeth and Hannah.

He d. and in his will, prob. 7 March, 1675, beq. all to widow Sarah, after her death to be divided to all his children. Admin. on est. of his son John, Jr., gr. same day to Nathaniel. Whole family mentioned. [Plym. Col. Rec.]

Jonas, Springfield, propr. in 1636.

Nicholas, Dorchester, propr. 1638; herdsman; frm. June 2, 1641. He was a member of the chh. of Braintree; he m. [Mary], dau. of Thomas Pidge, of Roxbury; their twin daus., Mary and Sarah were bapt.

WOOD, etc., cont.

at Rox. 25 (10) 1642. Ch. Jonathan b. Jan. 3, 1651. He rem. to Medfield.

Will dated 16 Jan. 1669-70, at his farm in Natick; beq. to Anna, his now wife; son Jonathan, not yet 21; son Eleazer; daus. Mary Thurston, Mehitabel and Abigail Wood, and 3 others; dec. dau. Hannah Harding's son Abraham; dau. Bethia to have houses and lands in Watertown he had by last wife, after her decease. [Reg. XLIII, 457.] His dau. Elizabeth m. Samuel Morse; Sarah Bass was also a dau.; John Thirston and Thomas Bass admin. on the est. 2 (2) 1670. [Mdx. Files.]

Obediah, biscuit maker, Ipswich, propr. 1649; sold land Dec. 4, 1671.

His will signed 26 Oct. 1694, prob. Dec. 3, folg., beq. to wife (called Hazelpena in Inventory;) ch. Obediah, James, Nathaniel, Josiah, Samuel, Elizabeth, Mary, Susanna and Margaret; to the ch. of dau. Ruth, dec.

William, husbandman, ae. 27, with Elizabeth, ae. 24, and John, ae. 46, [?] came in the Hopewell in Sept. 1635. Settled at Saugus; frm. May 18, 1631; deputy 1635. Rem. to Sandwich; propr. 3 April, 1637; town officer. Wife Jane called to testify in Court 20 Aug. 1644. Ch. (parentage not stated,) Miriam b. and d. in May, 1648, Mary b. 29 March, 1649.

We must note here the William who d. at Concord May 14, 1671. Will dated 15 Sept. 1670; ae. about 88 years; prob. 20 (4) 1672; beq. to dau. Ruth Wheeler and son Thomas W.; to gr. ch. Abigail Hosmer; to son Michael Wood.

WOODBERY, WOODBURY,

John, from Somersetshire, Eng. came to Cape Ann about 1624; ret. to Eng. after about 3 years, and remained six months; son Humphrey came back with him. See deposition of H. 16 (12) 1680, ae. about 72 years. [Ess. Files.] Settled at Salem; constable Sept. 28, 1630; deputy, 1635. Agnes memb. chh. 1636.

His will was prob. by his widow Ann 8 (12) 1643, but is not on file. [Ess. Files.] She sold house and land in 1660.

William, Salem, adm. chh. Dec. 29, 1639, frm. June 2, 1641. Elizabeth adm. chh. 21 (8) 1640. His dau. Hannah bapt. 25 (10) 1636, m. — Baker and was adm. to full com.

WOODBERY, etc., cont.
22 (11) 1661, Abigail bapt. 12 (9) 1637, Peter bapt. 19 (7) 1640.
He d. 29 (11) 1676, ae. about 88 years. Will dated 5 (4) 1663; prob. 26 (4) 1677. Wife Elizabeth, sons Nicholas, the eldest, William, Andrew, Hugh and Isaac, dau. Hannah Haskell.

WOODBRIDGE,
Rev. Benjamin, son of Rev. John, of Stanton, Wilts, and of his wife Dorothy, dau. of Rev. Thomas Parker, came to N. E. [with his brother John?] and settled at Newbury. Grad. Harvard College in the first class, 1642; returned to England and took orders. Had a long and useful ministry. Died at Newbury, Eng. Nov. 4, 1684.

Rev. John, bro. of the above, came to New Eng. in the Mary and John March 24, 1633-4. Resided at Ipswich, then at Newbury. Town clerk, deputy, surveyor of the arms May 17, 1636. Rem. to Boston, and was schoolmaster in 1643. Having been advised by his father-in-law, Gov. Thomas Dudley, in letter dated Nov. 8, 1642, to enter the ministry, he completed preparation, and was ordained pastor of the church at Andover at its organization, (8) 1645. [W.] Ret. to Eng. in 1647; was chaplain of the Parliamentary commissioners, treating with King Charles. Was minister at Andover, Hants, and at Barford, Wilts. Ret. to N. E. in 1663; res. at Newbury; colleague pastor with his kinsman Mr. Thomas Parker till 1670.

He m. Mercy, dau. of Thomas Dudley, Esq. Ch. Sarah b. June 7, 1640, Lucia b. 13 March, 1641-2, (m. Mr. Simon Bradstreet, and 2, Mr. Daniel Epps,) John, Benjamin, Thomas, Dorothy, Mary, Anne, Timothy, Joseph, Martha.

Will dated Sept. 12, 1691, prob. March 27, 1695, beq. to dau. Sarah and her 5 ch., daus. Lucy Eps, Dorothy Fryer, Martha Ruggles, Mary Appleton and Anne W.; sons John, Benjamin, Joseph, Thomas, Timothy; and to several of their children. Bro. Benjamin. Gr. son Richard Broccas afterward receipted. [Reg. XXXII, 292, 337, 342, XXXVII, 241, and The Woodbridge Record.]

WOODCOCK, WOODCOCKE,
John, came from Weymouth, Eng. before March 20, 1635. Res. at Roxbury. Sold house and land 6 (4) 1651.

WOODCOCK, etc., cont.
John, Springfield, propr., taxed in 1638.

WOODFIELD,
John, planter, Scituate, propr., bought land in 1648.
Will prob. June 18, 1669. Wife Hester exec. She made will May 27, 1672, beq. to various persons, with no indication of relationship. [Reg. VII, 236.]

WOODFORD,
Thomas, steward, embarked March 7, 1631-2, for N. E. Settled at Roxbury in 1632. [E.] He m. Mary, dau. of Robert Blott, who names her and her ch. in his will. Rem. to Hartford, Conn. Thence to Springfield, where he is mentioned in the Compact of settlers in 1636. Rem. to Northampton.

He made will April 26, 1665, prob. March 26, 1667. Beq. to dau. Mary and her children; to daus. Hannah and Sarah; to sons-in-law Isaac Sheldin and Nehemiah Allen.

WOODHAM, WOODAM,
John, bricklayer, Ipswich, 1647; propr. 1649. With wife Mary sold land in 1653. She d. Feb. 12, 1682.
He d. May 29, 1678; inv. of his est. July 1 folg.

WOODIE, WOODES, WOODS, WOODIES, WOODHOUSE,
Henry, husbandman, Concord, probably before 1650. Bought land in C. in 1660. Wife Elenor d. Sept. 4, 1693; ch. John b. Nov. 17, 1651, d. Feb. 2, 1666, Mary b. Sept. 7, 1653, (m. Nov. 27, 1678, Joseph Lee,) Hannah b. March 11, 1656, (m. Sept. 24, 1684, Thomas Cheney,) Millicent b. April 4, 1660, (m. Dec. 31, 1689, Joseph Estabrooke,) Sarah b. Feb. 29, 1663. He m. 2, Sarah —, who survived him and d. Jan. 19, 1717. He d. June 16, 1700. [See notes in "John Leigh of Agawam."]

Richard, Roxbury, frm. May 13, 1642; propr. His wife Anna was bur. April 4, 1656; he m. 2, —.
He d. "old," Dec. 6, 1658. Will prob. Dec. 16 folg. Sons Richard and Isaac; dau. Mary Sheffield; wife to have what she brought with her; he also made beq. to her and her two children. [Reg. IX, 346.] The probate papers of his son John who d. in 1650, show

WOODIE, etc., cont.
relationships. Mary married Edmund Sheffield of Braintree, and d. before (8) 1657.

Richard, fisherman, Boston, frm. May 29, 1644. Wife Mary adm. chh. 7 (3) 1643; second wife Sarah; ch. Mary b. and d. 1637, Mary b. 14 (11) 1638, (m. in 1659, George Pearse; her father gave land to their son George 30 Oct. 1668;) John b. 9 (2) 1641, Hannah b. 15 (1) 1643, Jonathan b. about 16 (2) 1647, [Thomas, ch. of Richard and Sarah, b. at Cambridge 22 (8) 1649,] Hopestill bapt. 2 (4) 1650, Francis and Hopestill b. March 8, 1661.

His est. was admin. upon by the widow Sarah Oct. 31, 1676. Inv. of house, land and moveables filed Nov. 3, 1676.

WOODLAND,
John, Dorchester, and Braintree. Ch. Thankful bapt. at Dorch. 9 (6) 1646, Martha bapt. do. 3 (7) 1648, John bapt. do. 12 (6) 1649; John b. at Br. 25 (1) 1651.

WOODLEY,
Edward, in Gen. Court 6 Sept. 1636. Edmund, may be the same, in Es. Court in 1641.

WOODMAN,
Archelaus, mercer, Newbury, 1637; frm. May 17, 1637, town officer, lieut. His wife Elizabeth d. 17 Dec. 1677. He m. 13 Nov. 1678, Dorothy Chapman. Ch. Sarah, (m. John Brocklebank).

He d. 7 Oct. 1702.

Edward, mercer, merchant, of Malford, Eng. came in the James April 5, 1635; settled at Newbury: frm. May 25, 1636. Licensed to sell wine and strong water 12 March, 1637. App. to aid the magistrates in execution of court decrees 6 (7) 1638. Deputy, town officer; active in church agitation. Wife Joanna. Either he or son Edward arranged with John Hull of Newbury for payment of an annuity. [Es. Files.] Ch. Edward, John, Joshua, Mary, (m. John Brown,) Sarah b. 12 Jan. 1641, (m. John Kent, Jr.,) Jonathan b. 5 Nov. 1643, Ruth b. 28 March, 1646, (m. Benjamin Lowell).

Richard, ae. 9, came in the Abigail in July, 1635. Res. at Lynn.

Will prob. 1 (10) 1647; beq. to the elders of the church; to his master, John Gillow, Joseph Redknape and Richard Moore.

WOODMANSEY,
Robert, schoolmaster, Ipswich, propr. 1635; rem. to Boston, 1644; 50 li. appropriated for his salary 11 (1) 1650; lived in the town's house in 1652. Mr. Daniel Henchman was engaged to assist him in the grammar school March 26, 1666. Gave land in Ips. to Joseph Emerson as a marriage portion with his dau. Elizabeth, which they sold 14 Sept. 1652. He sold rest of his farm at Ips. 18 (10) 1655. Wife Margaret; ch. Seth b. 26 (1) 1644, Joseph bapt. 1 (2) 1649, ae. about 4 days, (his father being a member of the chh. of Ipswich,) Bethiah bapt. 15 (10) 1650, Sarah d. 10 (9) 1653, Mary, (m. 20 (6) 1654, John Tappin).

He d. 13 Aug. 1667. [Es. Files XV, 138.] Will dated 5 July, inv. taken Sept. 13, prob. Nov. 15, 1667. Estate left to wife Margaret and two daus. Martha and Bethia; refers to written inventory and directions there given.

WOODROW, see Canterbury.

WOODWARD, WOODWORTH, WOODARD, WOODWORD,
Ezekiel, carpenter, Boston, m. about 1650 Anne, dau. of William Beamsley, and had deeds of house and orchard in Bo. in 1651 and 1658. Rem. to Ipswich, from which he sold Bo. lands in 1662. He deposed at Salem 30 (9) 1680, ae. about 58 years; had m. Elizabeth, widow of John Solart, Sen. of Wenham in 1672. Ch. Anne b. Aug. 10, 1651, Sarah b. Jan. 21, 1653, Sarah b. 14 July, 1653, (sic), Margaret b. Feb. 24, 1655, Elizabeth b. Oct. 22, 1657, Prudence b. April, 1660. [Reg. XXXII, 75.]

George, fishmonger, ae. 35, cert. from St. Botolphs, Billingsgate, London, shipped in the Hopewell and the Rebecca in April, 1635.

George, soap-boiler, Boston, res. in 1637; frm. May 6, 1646. Nothing further has been found regarding him, but the folg. may relate to a son of the same name. Admin. of the est. of George Woodward of Boston was gr. 1 May, 1697, to widow Lydia. Final division made 2 April, 1711, to eldest son Abraham, bros. George, Nathaniel and Ichabod, sister Lydia ,wife of Robert Harris, and to the widow Lydia.

Henry, husbandman, Dorchester,

WOODWARD, etc., cont.
memb. chh. 1639, frm. May 10, 1643; propr. With wife Elizabeth sold land 10 (9) 1659. [Reg. IX, 301.]

James, Watertown, servant to Mr. Saltonstall, called to Gen. Court 8 March, 1630-1.

Nathaniel, carpenter, Boston, servant to Mr. Coddington, adm. chh. 8 (10) 1633, frm. April 17, 1637. He was "mathematition" of the party that took observation for the most southerly parts of the patent, as reported to Gen. Court 10 (3) 1638. His wife Mary who was adm. chh. 23 (11) 1640, had beq. from her bro. Samuel Jackson of Boston, Eng. in his will, dated 7 Aug. 1642. He and his wife were dism. to Taunton 8 (8) 1648, and had letters of recommendation to that chh. 15 (6) 1653. Ch. John, Robert and Nathaniel had house-plots at Bo. Dec. 18, 1637; son Elisha d. 21 (2) 1644; Prudence, (dau. of Nathaniel W. of Bo.) m. in 1661 Christopher Mosse.]Genealogy in Reg. LI, 169.[

Peter, Dedham, propr. 28 (7) 1640, adm. chh. 7 (11) 1641, frm. May 18, 1642. Town officer. His wife was adm. chh. 7 (2) 1643. He deposed to the will of Edw. Richards in 1684, ae. about 80 years; his son Peter, also, ae. about 46 years. His dau. was killed by her horse 11 Aug. 1683. [Rox. Rec.]
Peter W., Sen., d. 9 (3) 1685.

Ralph, merchant, of Dublin, Ireland, leased ground in 1632; formed partnership with William Bladen and Fisher in 1637 for investments in New England. He came to Hingham. James Ridway was to work for him in the interest of Bladen, and Thomas Benson for Fisher. He accounted to his partners in 1658, and sold his interests in Dublin. Propr. at Hing. 1636-7; frm. March, 1637-8. Deacon, commissioner of Court. He m. Feb. 12, 1639, Mary —, who d. 4 Feb. 1660. His only dau. Sarah m. May 8, 1645, John Smith, of Hing.
He d. 5 Jan. 1662. Admin. of his est. gr. April 11, 1663, to John Smith. [Suff. De. III, 175; Reg. XII, 52.]

Richard, ae. 45, with wife Rose, ae. 50, and children George and John, ae. 13, came in the Elizabeth of Ipswich April 30, 1635. Settled at Watertown; miller; frm. Sept. 2, 1635. Bought a windmill in Boston

WOODWARD, etc., cont.
and sold (or mortgaged) the same in 1648. His wife Rose d. Oct. 6, 1662, ae. 80; he m. (settlement dated April 18, 1663,) Ann, widof Stephen Gates of Cambridge. She deposed 12 (4) 1673, ae. about 70 years. [Mdx. Files.]
He d. Feb. 16, 1664-5. Inv. of his est. filed April 4, 1665. His widow d. in Stow Feb. 5, 1682-3. See Gates. His son Amos, ae. 38 years, made will Oct. 9, prob. 5 Nov. 1679. He beq. to his bros. Thomas and Nathaniel Patten; to Sarah, dau. of his sister Griggs; to bros. Daniel and John W.; to sister Mary Wayte, Sarah Gates and Rebecca Fisher.

Walter, Scituate, taxed in 1633; frm. 2 March, 1640-1; atba. 1643; town officer 1645.

WOLCOTT, WOOLCOTT, WOOLCOOT,
Henry, b. at or near Tolland, Somersetshire, Eng. about 1578, came to Dorchester in the first company; appl. frm. Oct. 19, 1630, adm. frm. April 1, 1634; propr., selectman. Rem. in 1636-7 to Windsor, Conn. Was one of the undertakers of the ship Hopewell in 1640. [L.] Wife Elizabeth; ch. John, (d. in Eng.) Anna, (m. Matthew Griswold,) Henry, George, Christopher, Mary, (m. Job Drake,) and Simon.
He d. May 30, 1655. [Reg. I, 251.] His widow d. 5 July, 1655.

John, planter, yeoman, from Glaston, Eng., came to Watertown; frm. March 4, 1634-5. Householder at Cambridge, 1635-6. Rem. to Salem. Sold the Higginson-Williams house to Wm. Lord 23 (9) 1635. His wife Mary died, and he m. Winnifred. He died before 17 (5) 1638, when the inv. of his est. was taken. Nov. 26, 1638, his daus. Elizabeth and Mary, minors, applied for the appointment of their uncles Richard Vayle of Glaston, yeoman, and Christopher Atkins, mercer, as their guardians, to attend to their lands in Glaston, etc. Elizabeth m. David Offley, and gave letter of attorney on this business in 1639. The widow sold her Wat. lands to Edmund White 31 May, 1641.

William, Salem, 1636. A bill of his was underwritten 24 (3) 1643, by Aspinwall. [A.]

WOLF, WOOLF, WOOLFF,
Peter, yeoman, Salem, frm. May 14, 1634; juryman, 1639. Martha memb. chh. 1636. Dau. Freeborn Sallowe recd. to chh. March 27, 1644. Rem. to Beverly. He d. 20 (10) 1675. Will dated 20 Dec. prob. next day, beq. to wife Martha; gr. ch. Mary and Sarah Solace; son John Black exec.

WOLHOUSTON,
Marie, ae. 30, came in the Planter in April, 1635.

WOOLRIDGE, WOOLRICH, WOLRICH, WOOLRYCH,
Mr. John, Charlestown, appl. frm. Oct. 19, 1630; adm. frm. March 4, 1633-4. Traded with the Indians. Town officer. Wife Sarah memb. chh. Boston 1630; she survived him and m. 2, William Ayre. [Town Rec.] She was adm. chh. Char. with him 15 (1) 1633.

WOOLSTONE,
Elizabeth, Boston, maid servant of Nicholas Willis, adm. chh. 28 (10) 1634..

WOORY, WORY,
Ralph, white tanner of leather, Charlestown, propr. 1640; petitioned for regulation of the business 2 (4) 1641. [L.] Allowed by Gen. Court to export goat skins in 1645. He mortg. his house, warehouse and yard to Thomas Bell of London 8 (4) 1651. Adm. chh. 4 (9) 1643. Town officer, 1646. Was "of London" in 1646. [Mdx. Files.] Wife Margaret; ch. John b. 13 (4) 1641, Abel b. 13 (9) 1642, Hannah b. 8 (1) 1643-4.

WORCESTER, WOOSTER,
Rev. William, first minister of Salisbury; [J.] propr. 1639; frm. May 13, 1640. He m. 1, Sarah —, who d. April 23, 1650; he m. 2, July 22, 1650, Rebecca, widow, successively, of Henry Biley and John Hall. Ch. Susanna, (m. Oct. 4, 1653, Thomas Stacey,) Samuel, William, Sarah b. and d. 1641, Timothy, Moses, Sarah b. 1646, d. 1649, Elizabeth b. 1648, d. 1649, Elizabeth b. Jan. 9, 1649-50.
He d. Oct. 28, will prob. Dec. 2, 1662; he beq. to wife Rebecca; sons Samuel, William, Timothy and Moses; daus. Susanna Stacey and Rebecca Bylie; gr. ch. Rebecca Stacey and William Worcester. The widow m. 4, Deputy gov. Samuel Symonds.

WOOLLY,
Christopher, Concord. He m. 26 (12) 1646, Ursula Woddell; she d. June 13, 1674; ch. Hannah b. 24 (11) 1647, d. 21 (12) 1648, Sarah b. 8 (3) 1648-9.

WORDE,
Thomas, residence unknown, frm. May 18, 1642.

WORDEN, WERDEN,
Isaac, came in the Increase April 15, 1635.

Peter, Sen., Yarmouth. Will dated Feb. 9, 1638, prob. 5 March, 1638-9; beq. all to only son Peter and his son John, save a goat to John Lewis. [Reg. IV, 36.] Lands, tenements and goods at Claton, Lancashire, Eng.

Way, Marblehead, propr. 1648.

WORMALL, WORMWOOD, WORNAM,
James, Boston, owned house and wharf in 1649.

Joseph, carpenter, Concord. Rem. to Boston in 1648. He sold to the Iron Works Co. his house and land and interest in wharves, etc. Jan. 11, 1651. Rem. to Scituate. Frm. Plym. Col. June 3, 1657. Wife Miriam; ch. Josiah b. at Rowley (8) 1642, Mark bur. at Rowl. 6 (11) 1653, Hester bapt. at Bo. 21 (3) 1648, (he a memb. of chh. of Concord).

His will, dated Feb. 4, 1661, prob. June 24, 1662, beq. to wife Miriam; son Josias; daus. Sarah and Hester. [Reg. VI, 94.]

William, Boston. Wife Christian adm. chh. 4 (2) 1646. It may be inferred from several circumstances that he d. not long after this date, and that the widow m. Edward Belcher. His son Edward and her dau. Mary m. 8 (11) 1665.

WRAST,
Marie, ae. 24, cert. from St. Albons, Herts., came in the Planter April 2, 1635.

WRAY, see Ray.

WRIGHT, WRITE, RIGHT, RITE,

Anthony, Sandwich, propr. 1640, atba. 1643; town officer, 1645.

Dorothie, widow, Sudbury, m. 10 March, 1642, John Blandford. In his will he mentions "son-in-law" Edward Wright.

Edward, Sudbury, evidently came to New England with Dorothy above-mentioned; but whether his father also came or not can not be known from present data. He was propr. about 1656; captain of militia.
He sold to John Hoare March 4, 1671-2, all his right and title to an estate in "Castell Bromwick," (Castle Bromwich,) in the co. of Warwick, Eng., which fell to him as only son and heir of Francis Wright of same place; which was given to Francis 27 June, 10 James, on his marriage to Mary, dau. of John Wiggins, of Aldredge, co. Stafford, by his father Edward Wright of Castell Bromwich, whose heir apparent he was. He refers to having been in England a year before the date of this sale. He rec'd in part payment a house in Concord, of which John and Alice Hoar made full deed 1 Aug. 1682.
He m. in Boston, 27 (3) 1657, Mary Powell. He m. at Sudbury, June 18, 1659, Hannah Axtell, (as recorded in town book,) or Hannah Upson, (as given in the transcript at Cambridge). Ch. Hannah b. Jan. 10, 1660, Dorothy b. Oct. 20, 1662, Sarah b. Jan. 17, 1664, Mary b. Jan. 2, 1666-7, (m. July 28, 1690, Noah Clap,) Elizabeth b. March 6, 1668, Samuel b. April 9, 1670, Edward b. March 18, 1677, Martha b. 25 (10) 1681.
He deeded lands 26 Jan. 1683, his (third) wife Elizabeth joining, to his sons Samuel and Edward, they to pay certain sums to their three sisters; conditions included life income for himself and wife. He also gave land Dec. 31, 1683, to his son Peter, on the occasion of his marriage to Elizabeth, dau. of widow Elizabeth Lambson. An agreement was signed by all the heirs at a later day, Robert Blood joining in it. Peter agreed to pay a certain sum to his sister Sarah. [Mdx. De.]
He d. intestate 7 Aug. 1703; admin. of his est. gr. 6 Sept. 1703, to wife Elizabeth and eldest son Samuel.

George, Salem, 1636. [Es. Court and Town Rec.] Propr.; kept the ferry between Butt point and Darby fort. Elizabeth adm. chh. 21 (1) 1640-1.

George, planter, captain, Rehoboth, summoned to Plymouth Court in 1646.

Henry, Dorchester, propr. Nov. 2, 1634; frm. May 6, 1635. Wife Elizabeth; ch. Mary b. 1 (2) 1635, Samuel b. 14 (12) 1636.

John, Charlestown, 1640; one of the founders of Woburn; frm. May 10, 1643; deputy, town officer, deacon. Wife Priscilla; ch. John b. 27 (7) 1646, Joseph, Ruth, (m. Jonathan Knight,) Deborah b. Jan. 21, 1648-9, Sarah b. Feb. 16, 1652-3, (m. Joshua Sawyer). [Reg. XXXVIII, 76.]
He d. June 21, 1688; wife Priscilla d. April 10, 1687.

John, Newbury, had ch. John b. 7 Dec. 1650, Ruth b. 31 May, 1652. Admin. of his est. 30 (10) 1658, gr. to Edward Bragg.

Nicholas, Sandwich, had ch. b. at Sandwich: Sarah b. 8 Dec. 1648, Mordecai b. 30 Oct. 1649, bur. March 20, 1649-50, Mary b. June 4, 1651.

Richard, planter, Boston, memb. chh. with [wife] Margaret in 1630-1; frm. May 14, 1634. Was probably the com. of Gen. Court at Saugus in 1632. Leased lands at Neponset of Mrs. Warham 1 (3) 1639. [L.] Was dism. to chh. of Braintree 16 (12) 1639. Sold lands and a water mill at Br. 30 (8) 1640.

Richard, Plymouth, propr. 1636; atba. 1643; frm. June 5, 1644. He m. 6 Nov. 1644, Hester Cooke; ch. Esther b. 1649, Isaac b. and d. 1652. His son John went into military service, leaving a will which was prob. 7 June, 1676; his other sons Adam and Isaac, and dau. Esther, and the father were legatees.
In his will, dated 8 June, prob. 24 June, 1691, he beq. his est. to his three children, Adam, Esther and Mary, the last a widow.

Robert, Boston. Wife Mary; ch. John bur. (1) 1645, Robert b. 16 June, 1653, Joseph b. 14 Nov. 1655.

Samuel, Springfield, propr. 1641; rem. to Northampton. Frm. April 13, 1648; deacon. Was employed by the town to conduct divine service part of the time in 1656 and 1657, in absence of a minister. Wife Mar-

WRIGHT, etc., cont.
garet; ch. Samuel, (a father in 1654,) James, Mary, Hannah, (m. Nov. 1645, Thomas Stebbins,) Margaret, (m. 8 (10) 1653, Thomas Bancroft,) Hester, (m. Samuel Marshfield,) Lydia, (m. 1, Ltwrence Bliss, 2, John Norton, 3, John Lamb, 4, George Colton,) Judah b. 10 (3) 1642, Helped b. 15 (7) 1644.

His will dated 10 (9) 1663, prob. March 27, 1666, beq. to wife Margaret, sons James and Judah, with remainder to son Samuel; to daus. Mary, Margaret, Hester and Lydia. [Reg. IV, 335, and XL, 280.]

William, came in the Fortune in 1621; settled at Plymouth; had lands assigned in 1623; frm. 1633. Samuel Fuller, in his will, calls him brother.

Will Sept. 16, 1633; its prelude is a pretty full creed; beq. all to wife Priscilla except a ewe lamb to Plymouth church and certain articles to friend elder Brewster; refers to friend and brother Wm. Bradford, gent. [Reg. IV, 35.]

William, Sandwich, bur. May 2, 1648.

WYAT, WIAT, WIET,
Edward, Dorchester, frm. May, 1645. He brought suit against Robert Corbin, master of the Speedwell 15 (6) 1637. [W.] His wife Mary was a famous midwife; she had a record of 1100 and odd births which she had attended; she d. Feb. 6, 1705.

He d. Feb. 14, 1680. Will dated 9 (12) prob. 28 April, 1681. Inv. says he d. Feb. 13, 1680. Beq. to wife Mary, son Nathaniel, dau. Waitstill Vose.

James, Taunton, atba. 1643; constable 1644; frm. 1648; lieut. 7 Oct. 1651; juryman. He d. suddenly July 5, 1664. Admin. gr. to widow Mary; inv. taken July 27, 1664. [Reg. VI, 185.]

John, Ipswich, propr. 1639; record of lands in Ips. De. I, 151. Luke Heard's children were his grandchildren.

WYBERT,
Elizabeth, Boston, maid servant to Mr. John Winthrop, adm. chh. 22 (10) 1633.

WYBORNE, WEYBORNE, WYBURN, WIBORN,
Thomas, saddler, came from Tenterden, Kent, before June, 1638. [See Peter Branch.]

WYBORNE, etc., cont.
Settled at Duxbury, propr. 1638. Rem. to Scituate, 1643. Rem. to Boston. Sold land in 1652. Wife Elizabeth; ch. John, Jonathan d. 10 (10) 1653, Nathaniel b. March 12, 1655, Elizabeth, (m. 3 (2) 1655, John Merrick,) James d. March 7, 1658.

Will prob. Oct. 28, 1656; wife Elizabeth; son John; dau. Mary. [Reg. VI, 289.]

WYETH, WYTH, WIETH, WITH, WITHE,
Nicholas, mason, Cambridge, propr. 1645. He m. in England and had dau. Sarah bapt. in Eng. who came here; was about 13 years of age when he joined Camb. chh.; m. — Fisk of Watertown. Second wife Rebecca, widow of Thomas Andrews; ch. bapt. in Camb.: Mary b. 18 (11) 1648, Nicholas b. 20 (7) 1649, Martha, John and William. [Mi.] Joined chh. Jan. 7, 1644; said he was an apprentice when 16 years old; lived on 12 years; the Lord brought Mr. Banckes to a place 16 miles away; being able-bodied he often went to hear him. Came to N. E. in spite of the opposition of relatives. Had friends at Long Island, but did not wish to settle there. The Lord raised up his wife. [Rel.] Sold land in 1660.

WYTON, see Whiton.

WYMAN, WEYMAN,
Francis, tanner, Charlestown, 1640; rem. in 1640 to Woburn; frm. May 6, 1657. Propr. He m. 1, 30 (10) 1644, Judith Peirce; he m. 2, Oct. 2, 1650, Abigail, dau. of William Read. Ch. Judith b. and d. 1652, Francis, William, Abigail, Timothy b. Sept. 15, 1661, Joseph b. Nov. 9, 1663, Nathaniel b. Nov. 25, 1665, Samuel b. Nov. 29, 1667, Thomas b. April 1, 1671, Benjamin b. Aug. 25, 1674, Stephen b. and d. 1676, Judith b. Jan. 15, 1679.

He d. Nov. 28, 1699, ae. about 82 years. [Gr. St.] Will dated 5 Sept. 1698, prob. 11 Dec. 1699, beq. to wife Abigail, ch. William, Timothy, Benjamin, Joseph, Nathaniel, Samuel, Thomas, Abigail, Judah [Judith;] to the two elders of the Baptist church in Boston.

John, tanner, Charlestown, 1640; rem. to Woburn in 1640; propr. Frm. 26 May, 1647; lieut. He deposed 18 (10) 1660, ae. about 39 years. [Mdx. Files.] He m. Nov. 5, 1644, Sarah, dau. of Miles Nutt, who sur-

WYMAN, etc., cont.
vived him and m. 2, Thomas Fuller; ch. Samuel b. and d. 1646, John b. March 28, 1648, Sarah b. April 15, 1650, (m. Joseph Walker,) Solomon b. Feb. 26, 1652, David b. April 7, 1654, Elizabeth b. Jan. 18, 1656, d. Nov. 21, 1658, Bathsheba b. Oct. 6, 1658, (m. Nathaniel Tay or Fay,) Jonathan b. July 13, 1661, Seth b. Aug. 3, 1663, Jacob. The son John d. in 1676; inv. mentions housing and lands given by his gr. father Nutt.

He d. May 9, 1684. [Genealogy by T. B. Wyman in Reg. III, 33.]

YALE,
David, merchant, of London, one of the assignees of John Sampson 21 (4) 1641. [L.] Bought a house and land in Boston in 1645, which his agents sold in 1651. One of the petitioners for the extension of the privileges of freemanship to those who were not church-members in 1645. Was a brother of the wife of Gov. Hopkins of New Haven; [W.] Mrs. Eaton's son. [R. Williams; Mass. Hist. Coll. 4-6.] Wife Ursula; ch. Elizabeth b. and. d. 1644, David b. 18 (7) 1645.

YATES,
John, Duxbury. Child John b. 15 Aug. 1650. He rem. to Eastham, and there died. Admin. gr. June 8, 1651, to his widow Mary. She m. 2, Richard Higgins. [Plym. Col. Rec.]

William, ae. 14, came in the Abigail in July, 1635.

YEO, YEW,
Allen, seaman, Boston, mortg. two thirds of a shallop 28 (5) 1640. [L.] Suit in Salem Court, 1640.

Thomas, fisherman, mariner, Boston, witnessed a deed in 1638. [L.] Mortg. furniture, boats, tackling, salt, and debts due him at the Eastward, for the security of certain debts Dec. 17, 1651. With wife Sarah sold house and lands Dec. 16, 1653.

YEOMANS,
Edward, Charlestown, petitioned Gen. Court 16 Oct. 1650. He m. in Boston June

YEOMANS, cont.
12, 1652, Elizabeth, dau. of Thomas Joslin, of Hingham. He deposed in 1662, ae. about 32 years. He m. in Haverhill Dec. 2. 1652, Mary Button; ch. Mary b. Jan. 4, 1653. Samuel b. Sept. 1, 1655, Thomas b. Dec. 6, 1657, Elizabeth b. Jan. 10, 1659, Mehetabel b. Oct. 11, 1661, Edward b. Feb. 6, 1663.

YOUDALL, see Udall.

YOUNG, YOUNGE, YEONGE,
Christopher, son of Mr. Christopher Y., minister, of Southwold, Eng., came to Salem about 1636. He rem. to Wenham; propr. 1644. Ch. Sarah b. latter end of tenth month, 1639, Mary b. 8 (12) 1640, Christopher b. middle of 7 month, 1642, d. (11) 1643-4, Christopher b. 2 (12) 1644.

His will dated 19 (4) 1647, directed that his 3 children be sent back to Great Yarmouth in Norfolk, Eng.; the two daus. to his mother-in-law, the wife of Richard Elvin, to be brought up; mentions dau. Sarah, his sisters, the wife of Joseph Y. and the wife of Thomas Moore of Salem. Gen. Court, 2 May, 1649, ordered the execs. to put the boy forth in this country, as Mr. John Philips had declined to receive him; the two daus. also, unless Mr. Elvin should prove willing to receive them.

John, bro. of Christopher, Salem, 1636. He m. Mary, dau. of Thomas Warren of Southwold, Eng., merchant, who beq. to her two ch. Mary Gardiner and Benjamin Y. in his will dated 4 March, 1641, prob. Sept. 13, 1645. See also wills of the father Christopher and mother Margaret Y. in 1626 and 1630. [Reg. LII, 245.] His apprentice Edward Gell [Giles?] was in court in 1640.

John, Plymouth, atba. 1643. He m. 13 Dec. 1648, [name of bride wanting.] Ch. Joseph b. and d. 1651, Joseph b. Dec. 1654, Nathaniel b. April, 1656, Mary b. April 28, 1658, Abigail b. Oct. 1660, David b. April 17, 1662, Lydia b. 1664, Robert b. Aug. 1667, Henry b. 1669, d. 1670, Henry b. March 17, 1672.

He d. Jan. 28, 1690. Will dated 19 Jan. 1688, prob. April 21, 1691, beq. to wife Abigail; ch. John, Joseph, Nathaniel, David,

YOUNG, etc., cont.
Robert, Henry, and three daus. The widow d. April 7, 1692. Her est. was divided April 19, 1692.

Joseph, mariner, Salem, 1638. He took a freight of beaver to Eng. for the Plymouth Company in 1638, in the Mary and Ann. [B.] Sold land at Sal. in 1649.

Paul, Suffolk co., the Court ordered the constables to gather up and settle his estate 1 June, 1641. Perhaps he was the husband of the "widow Young" of Cambridge, to whom a grant of land was made Oct. 1638.

YOUNGLOVE,
Samuel, ae. 30, with Margaret, ae. 28, and child Samuel, ae. 1, came in the Hopewell in Sept. 1635. Settled at Ipswich. Butcher. Propr. 1635. Deposed as witness to an assault Nov. 23, 1668, ae. about 62 years. [Reg. XVI, 49.] Sold land in 1658.

Inv. of his est. Oct. 24; admin. gr. Nov. 26, 1689, to son Joseph with consent of son Samuel. His gr. son Samuel Griffin admin. on remainder Feb. 7, 1722-3. Mary Y. recd. beq. from her father Gerhard Haddon in 1690.

ZELLECK, ZULLESH, see Selleck.

AUTHORITIES QUOTED.

Aspinwall, William, His Notarial Record.	A.
Blake, James, Annals of Dorchester.	Bl.
Bradford, Gov. William, History of Plymouth Plantation.	B.
Clap, Capt. Roger, Autobiography.	C.
Records of Mass. Bay Colony or The General Court.	Col. Rec.
Cushing, Matthew, Record of Hingham Settlers.	Cu.
Danforth, Rev. Samuel, Journal, in Roxbury Church Records.	D.
Dudley, Gov. Thomas, Letter to Countess of Lincoln, in Mass. Hist. Coll. 8.	Du.
Eliot, Rev. John, in Roxbury Church Records	E.
Emmerton and Waters, Gleanings in English Wills, etc.	Em. and W.
Essex Antiquarian, The.	Es. Ant.
Essex Institute, Collections.	Es. Inst. Coll.
Founders of New England, (passengers from England), Samuel Gardner Drake.	
Genealogical Advertiser, The.	Gen. Ad.
Hammond, Lawrence, His Diary, in Mass Hist. Coll. Sec. Ser. vii.	L. H.
Register, The N. E. Historical-Genealogical.	Reg.
Hobart, Rev. Peter, Records of Hingham Church, Diary.	Hob.
Hubbard, Rev. William, History of New England.	Hub.
Johnson, Mr. Edward, Wonder-Working Providence.	J.
Lechford, Thomas, Note Book (legal memoranda).	L.
" " Plain Dealing.	L., P. D.
Massachusetts Historical Society, Collections.	Mass. Hiss. Coll.
Mather, Rev. Cotton, Magnalia.	C. M.
Mather, Rev. Richard, Autobiography and Sketch.	R. M.
Mitchell, Rev. Jonathan's, Record of Cambridge Church.	Mi.
Morton, Nathaniel, New England's Memorial.	Mor.
Mourt's Relation, Mass. Hist. Coll. 8.	Mou.
Original Lists, The, (passengers from England,) John Camden Hotten.	
Plymouth Colony Records.	Plym. Col. Rec.
Relations or narratives of persons joining the Church in Cambridge.	Rel.
Sewall, Judge Samuel, Diary.	S.
Winslow, Gov. Edward, "Hypocrisy Unmasked" and "Good News From N. E."	Wins.
Winthrop, Gov. John, History of Massachusetts.	W.

N.B. While the abstracts of Massachusetts wills and administrations in this book have been made by the compiler from the original papers or the earliest official copies at Boston, Cambridge, Salem, Plymouth, Taunton, Barnstable and Northampton, he has also referred to the "Genealogical Register," where the reader may find copies or abstracts of a portion of these, made by William Blake Trask, A.M., the late Justin Winsor, L.L.D., and others; and to the same periodical for the "Genealogical Gleanings in England," by Henry F. Waters, A.M., Mr. J. Henry Lea and others, from which a large number of Notes of Eng. wills and admins. have been taken. All these are credited to "Reg.", without specifying the individuals whose work is enshrined within the pages of that inestimable quarterly.

Ancient documents, printed in the valuable collections of the Mass. Historical Society and Essex Institute, have been acknowledged in detail when practicable, but more often in a general way. Genealogies in magazines or separately published are mentioned where special circumstances have made such reference seem desirable; but the statements in this volume are made upon entirely independent examination of original sources; and, in some cases, present facts not known to the writers of those genealogies.

ABBREVIATIONS.

Acct.	Account.	Exec.	Executor, executrix.
Ae.	Aged.	Folg.	Following.
Atba.	Able to bear arms.	Frm.	Freeman, (citizen).
Adm.	Admitted.	Gen.	General.
Admin.	Administer, administration	Gent.	Gentleman.
App.	Appointed.	Gov.	Governor.
Appr.	Apprentice, apprenticed.	Grad.	Graduated.
Appl.	Applied, applied for.	Gr. ch.	Grand-child.
Arch.	Archives, or official documents.	Gr. gr. ch.	Great-grand-child.
Asst.	Assistant, magistrate.	Gr.	Granted.
Bapt.	Baptized.	Gr. st.	Grave-stone.
Beq.	Bequeathed, bequests.	Inv.	Inventory.
b.	Born.	Mag.	Magistrate.
Bro.	Brother.	m.	Married.
bur.	Buried.	Mdx.	Middlesex, (county).
Cert.	Certified.	Memb. chh.	Member of church.
Ch.	Child, children.	Norf.	Norfolk, (county).
Chh.	Church.	Nunc.	Nuncupative, i. e., oral.
Col.	Colony, colonial.	Ord.	Ordained.
Co.	Company, County.	Org.	Organized.
Conn.	Connecticut.	Plym.	Plymouth.
Dau., daus.	Daughter, daughters.	Prob.	Probate, probated.
Dec.	Deceased.	Prop.	Proposed.
De.	Deeds.	Propr.	Proprietor.
Def.	Defendant.	Q. V.	Quod vide, (which see).
Depos.	Deposed or deposition.	Recd.	Received.
Dep.	Deputy, representative.	Rec.	Records.
d.	Died.	Ref.	Referred.
Dism.	Dismissed.	Rem.	Remained, Removed.
Eng.	England.	Res.	Resided, Residence.
Es.	Essex, (the county of).	Ret.	Returned.
Est.	Estate.	Suff.	Suffolk, (county).
Exam.	Examination.		

Brackets, [ ], are used in two ways.
1. They enclose the authority or source of a statement, or a reference to some book or document which may well be read in the connection.
2. They are also used to enclose words or statements which are believed to be correct, but for which the writer has not found absolute, documentary evidence.

THE PIONEER TOWNS.

SETTLED 1620 — 1650.

TOWNS.	PRIMITIVE NAMES.	DATE OF PLANTING.	ABBREVIATIONS.
Andover	Cochichewack	1634	And.
Barnstable	Seppecan	1638	Bar.
Boston	Shawmut	1630	Bo.
Braintree	Mt. Wollaston	1635	Br.
Cambridge	Newe Towne	1632	Camb
Charlestown	Charltowne	1629	Char.
Concord	Musketaquid	1635	Conc.
Dedham		1636	Ded.
Dorchester	Mattapan	1630	Dorch.
Eastham	Nawsett	1644	Easth.
Duxbury		1632	Dux.
Gloucester	Cape Ann	1642	Gloc.
Haverhill	Pentucket	1641	Hav.
Hingham	Bear or Bare Cove	1634	Hing.
Hull	Nantasket	1630	Hu.
Ipswich	Agawam	1633-4	Ipsw.
Lynn	Saugus	1632	Ln.
Lancaster	Nashaway	1643	Lan.
Malden	Mystic Side	1649	Mal.
Manchester	Jeffrey's Creek	1645	Man.
Marblehead	(included first in Salem.)	1630	Marb.
Marshfield	Rexhame	1632	Mars.
Medfield	Boggestowe	1650	Medfi.
Medford	Meadford	1630	Medfo.
Newbury		1635	Newb.
Northampton	Nonotuck	1653	North.
Plymouth		1620	Plym.
Reading	Lynn Village	1642	Red.
Rehoboth	Seekonk	1645	Reh.
Rowley		1639	Rowl.
Roxbury		1630	Rox.
Salem	Naumkeake	1626	Sal.
Salisbury	Colchester	1640	Salis.
Sandwich		1638	Sand.
Scituate		1633	Sci.
Springfield	Agawam	1636	Spr.
Sudbury		1639	Sud.
Taunton	Cohannet	1638	Tau.
Topsfield		1648	Tops.
Watertown		1630	Wat.
Wenham	Enon	1643	Wen.
Weymouth	Wessaguscus	1635	Wey.
Woburn	Charlestown Village	1647	Wob.
Yarmouth	Mattacheeset	1639	Yar.

OCCUPATIONS, TRADES, ETC.

As Specified in Original Documents.

Apprentices,	14	Glaziers,	5
Apothecaries,	4	Glovers,	15
Armourers,	3	Goldsmith,	1
Artist, (surveyor,)	1	Grocers,	2
Bakers,	19	Gunsmiths,	8
Barbers, barber surgeons,	7	Haberdashers,	5
Beehive maker,	1	Hatters, feltmakers,	8
Blacksmiths,	39	Innholders, vintners, ordinary keepers,	30
Boatmen, ferrymen or lightermen,	13	Ironmongers,	5
Bookbinder,	1	Lawyers,	5
Bookseller,	1	Limeburner,	1
Braziers, pewterers,	4	Locksmiths,	4
Brewers,	6	Mariners, sea captains,	75
Bricklayers, brickmakers,	23	Masons, plasterers,	11
Butchers,	14	Malsters,	9
Calinder,	1	Merchants, Mercers,	103
Cannonier,	1	Millers,	28
Carpenters, joiners, housewrights,	168	Millwrights,	13
Chandlers,	6	Ministers,	91
Chimney sweeper,	1	Nailers, (nail-makers,)	2
Clapboard ryver,	1	Notaries,	2
Clothiers, cloth-workers,	20	Oatmeal maker,	1
Collar-maker,	1	Ostler,	1
Collier,	1	Painters,	3
Confectioner, comfit maker,	1	Parchment maker,	1
Coopers,	54	Physicians, surgeons, chirurgeons,	21
Cow-leech,	1	Pin maker,	1
Cutlers,	5	Pipe-stave makers,	2
Dish-turners,	2	Planters, farmers, husbandmen,	323
Distiller,	1	Plow-wright,	1
Drapers,	10	Potters,	2
Dyer,	1	Printers,	2
Farrier,	1	Rope makers, cord makers,	11
Felmongers,	2	Sadlers,	2
Fineryman,	1	Sailors,	12
Fishermen,	34	Sail makers,	3
Fishmongers,	3	Salters, saltmakers,	5
Flax dressers, flaxmen,	2	Sawyers,	18
Fullers,	2	Scriveners,	5
Gardiners,	3	Sieve maker,	1
Girdler,	1	Schoolmasters,	16
Glassmen,	3	Skinners,	3

Ship carpenters, shipwrights,	52
Shoemakers, cordwainers,	81
Slaters,	2
Soap-boilers,	4
Starch makers,	3
Stationer,	1
Tailors, (limb-dressers,)	115
Tanners, curriers.	41
Thacker,	1
Tray makers,	2
Turners,	6
Upholsterer,	1
Weavers, say-makers, websters,	62
Wheelwrights,	16
Wool-carders,	3

The total number of "Pioneers" on record is about 6,000. Of these the occupations of only 1,725 were mentioned; 323 being called tillers of the soil, (including both wealthy landholders and humble plowmen,) 210 house and ship carpenters, 115 tailors, 103 merchants, 91 ministers, 81 shoemakers, 75 sea-captains, 62 weavers, and so on. We have further some 471 cases in which the records specify the settlers'

SOCIAL POSITION.

Gentlemen, Ladies, Esquires, Knights,	117
Yeomen,	122
Servants, Laborers,	240

NOTE.

Let it be remembered that the figures given above do not include all those who belonged to the classes mentioned, because the occupation and rank of the majority of the pioneers was not designated.

Besides, persons sometimes changed employment, and "servants" became "masters," or proved to be "gentlemen." Any employee or person under the control of another might be called "servant," whatever his family connections.

INDEX TO OTHER NAMES
AND
CROSS-INDEX TO PIONEERS.

Allow for great variety in Spelling.

ABBOT, ... 162, 346
ABDA, ... 383
ACOURT, ... 55
ADAMS, 29, 39, 48, 72, 122, 128, 139, 148, 167, 174, 196, 322, 339, 363, 369, 381, 418, 427, 441, 447, 461, 470, 492, 497, 508
ADDINGTON, ... 60, 83, 284
ADDIS 426
AEALY, ... 363
AGAR, ... 87, 153
AKERS, ... 273, 415
ALBEE, ... 10, 72
ALBESON, ... 328
ALCOCK, ... 19, 43, 140, 177, 239, 327, 341
ALDEN, ... 209, 322, 323, 358, 426, 485
ALDIS, ALDOWS, ... 154, 166, 167
ALDBURGH, ... 10, 175
ALDRIDGE, ... 109, 223, 264
ALEXANDER, ... 262
ALFERY, ... 469
ALFORD, ... 326, 469
ALGER, ... 475
ALLARD, ... 406
ALLEN, ALLIN, ALLEYNE, ALLYN, 17, 20, 28, 35, 64, 68, 78, 85, 87, 98, 138, 139, 145, 154, 171, 191, 195, 200, 201, 202, 206, 216, 231, 236, 241, 244, 251, 253, 259, 260, 276, 288, 294, 296, 320, 327, 328, 330, 342, 353, 366, 376, 386, 396, 406, 410, 412, 418, 437, 443, 448, 459, 463, 478, 479, 497, 510, 512
ALLERTON, 67, 76, 189, 239, 307, 374, 390
ALLEY, ... 112
ALLING, ... 264
ALLIS, ... 155, 325
ALLISON, ... 470
ALMOND, ALMY, ... 23, 294
ALSOPP, ... 186, 465
ALWARD, ALWOOD, ... 39, 196
ALXARSON, ... 28
AMBROSE, ... 129, 408, 450
AMEE, ... 259
AMES, ... 19, 53, 223
AMSDEN, ... 235

ANDERSON, ... 134, 234, 329
ANDREW, ANDREWS, 81, 92, 99, 102, 112, 119, 122, 130, 142, 163, 175, 201, 226, 238, 242, 247, 253, 255, 364, 394, 443, 472, 478, 506, 517
ANDROS, ... 163, 169
ANGIER, ... 17, 22, 38, 96, 120, 413, 427
ANNABALL, ... 15, 57, 100, 159, 496
ANNIS, ... 95
ANSELL, ... 292
ANTER, ... 217
ANTRUM, ANDRAM, ... 28, 39, 74
APPLETON, 139, 143, 185, 189, 255, 340, 512
APSLEY, ... 164
ARCHER, ... 249, 337, 438
ARMITAGE, ... 367, 400, 484
ARMSTRONG, ... 441
ARNOLD, ARNELL, 60, 126, 129, 161, 339, 345, 508
ARRES. see AYERS, ... 28
ARRINGTON, see ERRINGTON, ... 127
ASH, ... 426
ASHBY, ... 231, 234, 250, 268
ASHLEY, ... 240, 347, 415
ASPINWALL, 102, 243, 341, 344, 358, 408, 514
ASTWOOD, ... 190
ATHERTON, 19, 165, 203, 462, 474, 485, 498
ATKINS, ... 159, 514
ATKINSON, 13, 71, 77, 128, 223, 230, 306, 327, 491
ATWOOD, 26, 31, 103, 109, 118, 125, 215, 275, 280, 282, 289, 387, 403, 448, 511
AUDLEY, see ODLIN,
AUGER, ... 338
AUSTIN, ASTING, ... 26, 230, 280, 395
AVERILL, AVERY, ... 27, 231, 273
AWARDS, see HAYWARD,
AWKLEY, ... 345
AXEY, ... 397
AXTELL, ... 308, 516
AYER, AYERES, etc., 17, 21, 118, 159, 209, 242, 249, 277, 341, 484, 499, 515
AYLETT, ... 222, 341, 449

525

OTHER NAMES AND CROSS INDEX.

BABBAGE, ... 88
BABSON, ... 128, 454
BACHILER, BATCHELDER, etc., 23, 109, 129, 249, 420, 422, 461, 463
BACON, 31, 174, 245, 261, 293, 309, 338, 367, 384, 414, 422, 494, 506
BADCOCK 126, 130
BADGER, ... 74, 199
BADSON, ... 508
BAGG, ... 82
BAGLEY, BAGERLEY, 109, 374, 401, 416
BAKER, 17, 25, 28, 39, 46, 59, 89, 132, 173, 219, 220, 257, 262, 277, 278, 337, 355, 360, 387, 395, 443, 445, 462, 477, 484, 499, 508, 510, 511
BALCH, ... 128, 182
BALDEN, ... 29, 64
BALDUCKE, ... 184
BALDWIN, ... 66, 384, 385, 406
BALE, ... 188
BALL, ... 30, 38, 322, 323, 360
BALLANTINE, ... 96, 235
BALLARD, ... 43, 261, 274, 406, 509
William d. 10 July, 1689.
BALLINS, ... 396
BALSTON, ... 93, 300, 391
BANCROFT, 26, 55, 67, 152, 239, 313, 399, 497, 517
BAND, ... 53
BANESTER, ... 394
BANGS, ... 232
BANKS, ... 6, 220, 517
BARACHEW, ... 136
BARBER, BARBUR, 13, 70, 95, 287, 351, 422, 491
BARKER, 19, 27, 32, 54, 55, 186, 243, 246, 248, 259, 261, 266, 269, 270, 276, 356, 372, 389, 433, 434, 435, 478, 497, 499, 507
BARLOW, ... 47, 352
BARNARD, 70, 102, 113, 128, 169, 190, 223, 244, 270, 271, 288, 295, 325, 342, 351, 357
BARNES, 27, 54, 88, 152, 168, 188, 210, 226, 248, 261, 315, 364, 392, 455, 463, 502
BARNEY, ... 36, 116
BARRELL, ... 109, 466
BARRETT, 35, 85, 96, 172, 221, 294, 361, 367, 370, 375, 452
BARRON, ... 221, 412
BARRY, ... 94
BARSTOW, 209, 245, 286, 287, 296, 300, 355, 357, 374, 378, 460
BARTHOLOMEW, 116, 160, 291, 315, 329, 366, 405

BARSHAM, ... 58
BARTLETT, 13, 57, 173, 213, 221, 244, 258, 368, 385, 410, 432, 436, 456, 477, 480, 484
BARTON, ... 329
BARTROM, ... 85
BASS, ... 12, 52, 88, 243, 301, 477, 511
BASSETT, ... 37, 80, 82, 236
BATE, BATES, 49, 76, 162, 170, 173, 231, 280, 282, 266, 296, 348, 431, 485, 493, 500, 510
BATT, ... 19, 155, 484
BATTEN, ... 125, 200
BATTERLY, ... 296
BATTER, ... 19, 20, 193, 356, 417
BATTLE, ... 167
BAUDROCK, ... 24
BAXTER, ... 136, 255, 304, 493
BAYLEY, 49, 89, 123, 156, 165, 188, 248, 260, 331, 340, 345, 369, 374, 418, 421, 442, 463
BEACHAM, ... 107, 175, 338
BEADLE, ... 193, 283

BEAL, 41, 47. 64, 157, 161, 187, 245, 253, 255, 264, 410, 438, 463, 495, 507
BEAMAN, ... 130
BEAMSLEY, ... 513
BEANE, ... 77
BEARE, BEERS, ... 69, 98, 214, 446
BEARD, ... 239, 399, 485
BEASLEY, ... 73
BEAUFORD, ... 225
BECK, ... 65, 232, 262, 398, 452
BEDWELL, ... 186
BECKFORD, ... 399
BEEBE, ... 426
BEGGARLY, ... 130
BELCHER, 43, 27, 44, 50, 130, 186, 187, 340, 377, 515
BELCONGER, ... 265
BELKNAP, ... 162, 251, 262, 499
BELL, ... 254, 309, 453, 515
BELLINGHAM, 57, 62, 108, 124, 139, 144, 204, 233, 259, 326, 331, 351, 377, 399, 428, 494
BEMIS, ... 49
BENDALL, ... 288, 403, 464, 465
BENDIGHT, ... 21
BENDISH, ... 366
BENFIELD, ... 492
BENHAM, ... 504
BENJAMIN, ... 104, 191, 295, 359, 422, 440
BENNETT, 45, 46, 83, 107, 133, 155, 156, 159, 191, 257, 287, 354, 358, 430, 493, 506

OTHER NAMES AND CROSS INDEX.

BENSON, ... 514
BENT, ... 34, 40, 47, 54, 60, 460
BERBER, ... 469
BERNARD, ... 33, 350
BERRY, ... 122, 218, 265, 293
BEESBEECH, BISBY, ... 47, 51, 59, 75, 271
BESSEY, ... 32, 33
BETT, BETTS, ... 320
BETSCOMBE, ... 495
BEWFORD, ... 204
BIBBLE, ... 333
BICKNELL, ... 369
BICKNER, ... 300
BICKWELL, ... 272
BIDDLECOME, ... 206
BIGELOW, ... 169, 480
BIGGS, ... 172, 418, 438, 502
BIGSBY, ... 225
BILL, ... 157, 203, 400
BILLING, ... 50, 187, 200, 218, 371
BILLINGTON, ... 327
BINKS, ... 260
BINGLEY, ... 85
BIRAM, BYRAM, ... 410
BIRBIN, ... 195
BIRCHALL, etc., ... 115
BIRD, ... 22, 174, 185, 257, 500
BIRDLEY, ... 234
BISCOE, ... 58, 218
BIRTHS, ... 257
BISHOP, 51, 101, 159, 162, 165, 183, 237,
      239, 282, 285, 307, 357, 403, 497, 499
BISSELL, ... 101
BITFIELD, ... 123
BITNAR, ... 251
BLACK, ... 67, 297, 515
BLACKBOURNE, ... 97, 441
BLACKFORD, ... 226
BLACKLEACH, ... 61, 143, 300, 334, 483
BLACKLEY, ... 310
BLACKMAN, ... 366, 405
BLACKMORE, ... 111
BLACKISTON, ... 415
BLACKSTONE, ... 167, 256, 334, 434, 456
BLADEN, ... 514
BLAGE, ... 482
BLAKE, 41, 66, 100, 129, 159, 281, 368, 426
BLAKELEY, ... 58
BLANCHARD, 34, 46, 63, 116, 141, 230,
   292, 299, 300, 333, 364, 391, 415, 425,
                                      443, 489
BLAND, ... 54
BLANDFIELD, ... 12
BLANDFORD, ... 206, 290, 516

BLANER, ... 270
BLANTON, ... 54, 256
BLASDELL, ... 92, 205, 215
BLIGH, ... 51
BLINMAN, ... 288, 424, 454, 471
BLISH, BLUSH, ... 32, 130
BLISS, ... 82, 113, 251, 284, 302, 346, 517
BLODGET, BLOGHEAD, ... 110, 451, 468
BLOIS, ... 480
BLOOD, ... 498, 516
BLOOMFIELD, ... 340
BLOSSE, ... 31
BLOSSOM, ... 169, 393
BLOT, ... 293, 376, 512
BLOWER, ... 43, 506
BLUNT, ... 30
BOARDMAN, ... 19, 32, 135, 250
BLY, ... 183
BOBBETT, ... 447
BODFISH, ... 33, 231
BOFFE, ... 214
BOLTER, ... 441
BOND, ... 51, 98, 178, 218, 254, 306
BONHAM, BONUM, ... 368
BONNER, ... 102, 307
BONNEY, ...104, 398
BONYTHON, ... 53
BORADEL, ... 412
BOREMAN, ... 293
BOSWELL, ... 396
BOSWORTH, 79, 244, 270, 289, 404, 409, 496
BOUCIER, ... 72
BOULE, ... 28
BOURNE, 47, 125, 209, 279, 366, 377, 385,
                392, 400, 417, 423, 481
BOTH, ... 444
BOWEN, ... 137, 140, 248, 266, 301
BOWES, ... 55
BOUTWELL, ... 61, 266
BOWDITCH, ... 176
BOWER, ... 147, 275
BOWLES, BOLES, ... 225, 261, 431, 481
BOWSTREET, ... 61, 248
BOYDEN, ... 276, 497
BOYEN, ... 186
BOYLSTON, ... 167
BOYNTON, ... 213, 259, 352, 442
BOYES, BOYERS, 27, 231, 309, 323, 379, 507
BOYSON, ... 62
BOYTON, ... 464
BRACEY, ... 475
BRADFORD, 4, 5, 6, 56, 60, 63, 112, 117,
   164, 178, 189, 194, 230, 355, 379, 381,
                                 384, 426, 517

527

OTHER NAMES AND CROSS INDEX.

BRACKETT, 10, 62, 176, 354, 432, 474, 500
BRADBURY, ... 202, 308, 319, 354, 401, 491
BRADLEY, ... 29, 142, 283, 374, 499
BRADSTARE, ... 183
BRADSTREET, 145, 146, 236, 238, 355, 373, 390, 467, 512
BRADWICKE, ... 42
BRAGG, ... 375, 516
BRAINES, ... 184
BRAKENBURY, 15, 17, 29, 274, 330, 341, 447
BRAMPTON, ... 342
BRANCH, ... 517
BRAND, ... 225
BRANKER, ... 479
BRATCHER, ... 174, 342, 408
BRATTLE, ... 467
BREAME, ... 34
BRECK, ... 166, 222, 229, 348, 444
BREDSHA, ... 396
BREED, ... 180, 274
BREEDING, ... 388
BRENTON, ... 83, 329, 380, 407
BRETT, ...186, 347, 456
BREWER, ... 50, 271, 277, 290, 319, 369
BREWSTER, 16, 79, 84, 112, 127, 179, 205, 279, 290, 308, 316, 317, 320, 335, 517
BRIDGE, BRIDGES, 9, 47, 55, 112, 124, 215, 277, 314, 361, 370, 388, 394, 399, 404, 447, 459, 464, 467
BRIDGHAM, ... 85, 212
BRIDGMAN, ... 24
BRIGHAM, ... 383
BRIGGS, ...69, 126, 221, 232, 437, 507
BRIGHT, ... 35, 36, 73, 190, 343
BRIGNALL, ... 313
BRIMBLECOMBE, ... 132
BRIMSMEADE, ... 90, 394
BRINTNALL, ... 498
BRISCOE, ... 70, 71, 113, 150
BROAD, ... 484
BROCCAS, ... 512
BROCK, BROCKS, 31, 70, 134, 195, 357, 435, 444, 469
BROCKLEBANK, ... 141, 291, 513
BROMSON, ... 16
BROWN, BROWNE, 10, 25, 27, 30, 31, 35, 38, 41, 47, 48, 54, 81, 84, 128, 136, 137, 150, 151, 158, 163, 173, 178, 183, 192, 193, 196, 199, 212, 224, 236, 244, 246, 249, 254, 285, 293, 298, 303, 306, 307, 318, 328, 333, 337, 340, 349, 370, 375, 387, 394, 409, 413, 416, 423, 427, 433, 436, 442, 469, 475, 476, 480, 484, 489, 499, 507, 513

BROOK, BROOKS, 23, 47, 51, 60, 75, 119, 126, 174, 201, 219, 226, 238, 287, 322, 370, 384, 395, 491
BROOKEN, ... 474
BROUGHTON, ... 37, 51, 152, 505
BROWNING, ... 25
BRUCE, ... 214
BRUEN, ... 55, 355
BRUMIDGE, ... 467
BRUSH, ... 104
BRYANT, 39, 76, 226, 266, 285, 403, 410, 488
BUBIER, ... 45, 107
BUCK, ... 300, 318, 322
BUCKLAND, ... 59, 364
BUCKMASTER, ... 104, 175, 182, 483
BUCKNAM, ... 33, 274
BUCKNELL, ... 51
BUCKNER, ... 248
BUFFAM, ... 12, 27, 230, 322, 368
BUDD, ... 72
BUGBEE, ... 345
BULGAR, ... 477
BULL, ... 39, 139, 140, 363
BULHACKE, ... 433
BULKLEY, ... 170, 230, 262, 451, 453, 494
BULLARD, 80, 138, 202, 207, 313, 360, 383, 452, 481
BULLEN, ... 320, 396
BULLOCK, ... 170
BUMPASS, ... 451
BUMSTEAD, ... 314, 334
BUNDY, ... 316, 363
BUNKER, 65, 195, 242, 296, 297, 442, 474
BURBANK, ... 205, 312, 420
BURCHAM, ... 13, 53, 499
BURDEN, ... 51, 112, 133, 144, 499, 510
BURDENDON, ... 470
BURG, ... 97, 204, 258
BURGESS, ... 37, 184, 201, 236, 256, 419
BURKBEE, ... 97, 248, 265, 396
BURMAN, ... 59
BURNELL, ... 319, 426
BURNAP, ... 20, 80, 350, 475
BURNETT, ... 225, 481
BURNHAM, ... 18, 99, 362, 487
BURR, ... 146, 279
BURRAGE, ... 438
BURRELL, ... 83, 123, 363
BURROUGHS, ... 99, 167, 471
BURSLEY, ... 244
BURT, 30, 37, 41, 82, 100, 217, 306, 422, 444, 474
BURTON, ... 205, 337, 345, 443, 483
BUSBY, ... 202, 329
BUSCOTT, ... 225

528

OTHER NAMES AND CROSS INDEX.

BUSH, ... 98, 150
BUSHELL, ... 42
BUSHEY, ... 445
BUSSARD, ... 268
BUSSE, ... 63
BUSWELL, ... 180, 433, 507
BUTLER, ... 13, 469, 477
BUTMAN, ... 359
BUTT, ... 240
BUTTERFIELD, ... 30
BUTTALL, ... 23, 68, 105, 391
BUTTERICK, ... 38, 56, 85, 218
BUTTOLPH, ... 39, 50, 117, 212
BUTTERY, ... 273
BUTTON, .. 180, 211, 257, 294, 452, 490, 518
BUXTON, BUCSTONE, ... 86, 238, 471
BYLES, ... 65
BYRT, ... 422
BYLEY, ... 208, 382, 515
CADE, ... 264
CADMAN, ... 219
CADY, ... 273
CAINE, CANE, ... 329
CAKEBREAD, ... 488
CALKIN, ... 55, 241
CALL, ... 268, 412
CALLEM, see KILHAM.
CALEY, ... 139
CAMPFIELD, ... 503
CANADY, ... 115
CANNON, ... 268
CANTLEBURY, ... 364
CAPEN, 35, 37, 90, 100, 196, 349, 376,
                            389, 443, 462, 468
CARDER, ... 464
CARLE, ... 87, 150
CARLETON, ... 259
CARLILE, ... 399, 400
CARMAN, ... 448
CARPENTER, ... 64, 71, 178, 321, 381, 397
CARR, ... 106, 110, 310
CARRIE, ... 497
CARRINGTON, ... 49, 245
CARTER, 48, 70, 89, 92, 120, 129, 151, 186,
                    199, 274, 322, 350, 459, 494, 500
CARVER, 169, 172, 184, 244, 279, 316, 317, 497
CARY, ... 189, 258, 396
CASH, ... 359
CASSELL, ... 104, 366
CASWELL, ... 399, 400
CATLAND, see KIRTLAND, ... 51, 450
CAVE, ... 329
CHADWELL, ... 23, 132, 372, 398
CHADWICK, ... 174, 330, 439

CHAFFEE, ... 303
CHALLIS, ... 191, 401, 409, 482
CHAMBERLAIN, ... 77, 263, 344, 373
CHAMBERS, ... 306
CHAMPNEY, ... 96, 245, 317
CHANDLER, 9, 12 , 129, 132, 137, 152,
                            174, 229, 287, 291, 346
CHAPIN, ... 55, 116, 302, 451
CHAPLIN, ... 103
CHAPMAN, 25, 172, 228, 254, 288, 442,
                                   454, 486, 513
CHARLES, ... 95
CHASE, ... 28, 58, 92, 347, 357, 490
CHAUNCEY, ... 53, 147, 449
CHECKLEY, ... 153, 405, 491
CHEELCRAFT, ... 27
CHEESEBOROUGH, ... 332
CHEESEHOLM, ... 47, 150, 415, 427, 504
CHEEVER, .. 47, 49, 162, 224, 292, 346, 449
CHENERY, ... 62
CHENEY, 52, 80, 204, 218, 251, 280, 333,
                344, 364, 396, 409, 445, 453, 509, 512
CHESTER, ... 396
CHICHESTER, ... 294
CHICKEN, ... 292
CHICKERING, ... 14, 157, 167
CHILD, CHILDS, 60, 132, 176, 254, 460, 468
CHILLINGWORTH, ... 141
CHING, ... 297
CHINGLETON, ... 127
CHIPMAN, ... 82, 130, 244, 464
CHISAM, see CHEESEHOLM,
CHITTENDEN, ... 28, 471
CHITWOOD, ... 78
CHUBBOCK, ... 41
CHURCH, .. 29, 408, 409, 426, 429, 463, 480
CHURCHILL, ... 100, 101, 366, 426
CHURCHMAN, ... 390, 506, 508
CHUTE, ... 445
CILLEY, ... 105
CLAP, 12, 19, 88, 106, 113, 138, 155, 167,
    172, 187, 247, 282, 283, 303, 365, 368,
    378, 409, 416, 422, 436, 443, 463, 484,
                                422, 485, 486, 516
CLARK, 14, 15, 18, 28, 46, 49, 51, 61, 62,
    74, 78, 81, 94, 100, 102, 103, 108, 115,
    120, 132, 152, 158, 168, 198, 202, 218,
    243, 286, 289, 307, 326, 340, 352, 372,
    379, 405, 409, 414, 418, 425, 428, 432,
                            437, 449, 454, 496, 497
CLADDIS, ... 324
CLAUDIUS, ... 164
CLEASBY, ... 192, 485
CLEAVES, ... 93, 346

OTHER NAMES AND CROSS INDEX.

CLEMENT, 25, 146, 157, 162, 204, 306, 319, 337, 341, 362, 388, 455, 460, 467, 490, 495
[Mr. Robert, Andover, 1642.]
CLEVELAND, ... 179, 507
CLIFFORD, ... 229, 281
CLIFT, ... 111
CLIFTON, ... 85, 105, 164
CLOOKE, CLOCKE, ... 87
CLOPTON, ... 508
CLOUGH, ... 75, 203, 339
CLOYCE, ... 454
COATS, ... 441
COBB, .. 122, 130, 231, 234, 249, 326, 327
COBBET, .. 12, 106, 206, 285, 340, 389, 417
COBLECH, ... 17
COCKERELL, ... 100
COCK, ... 213, 257, 367, 468
COCCREY, ... 89
COCKRAINE, ... 251
CODDINGTON, COTTINGTON, 102, 119, 137, 181, 194, 338, 377, 411, 486, 514
CODNER, ... 45, 347
COE, COOE, ... 228
COFFYN, ... 199, 408, 425
COGAN, 19, 121, 122, 165, 207, 388, 436, 509
COGGESHALL, ...174, 181, 303, 397, 411
COGSWELL, ...221, 474
COIT, ... 474
COKE, ... 112
COKER, ...220, 261
COKING, ... 370
COLBORN, 72, 73, 78, 103, 109, 163, 252, 364, 466
COLBY, ... 244, 337, 401, 496
COLCORD, ... 339
COLDHAM, ... 360
COLÆ, COLES, 12, 55, 70, 92, 112, 143, 174, 181, 197, 198, 243, 253, 265, 293, 299, 303, 308, 338, 363, 393, 431, 460, 501
COLEMAN, ... 240, 259, 295, 337, 455
COLLAMORE, ... 40, 111, 212
COLLAR, ... 127
COLLICOT, ... 144, 237, 448
COLLIER, 29, 104, 110, 196, 262, 320, 372, 426, 451
COLLINS, 16, 27, 106, 108, 112, 122, 144, 174, 189, 201, 261, 272, 281, 342, 411, 456
COLLISHAWE, ... 320
COLQUIT, ... 109
COLTON, ... 347, 517
COMER, ... 186
COMSTOCK, ... 395
CONANT, ... 6, 182, 296, 363, 477, 488
CONCKLING, ... 431

CONY, ... 120
CONNELL, ... 30
CONNER, ... 191
CONNETT, ... 181
CONVERSE, ... 93, 112, 178, 290, 428
COOK, 26, 34, 67, 77, 86, 117, 133, 136, 150, 157, 169, 172, 179, 192, 199, 213, 219, 233, 240, 284, 366, 414, 416, 422, 432, 446, 451, 470, 471, 480, 488, 489, 505, 516
COOKERY, ... 290
COMBE, COOMBS, ... 189, 279, 428
COOLIDGE, 35, 58, 69, 121, 273, 289, 364
COOP, ... 458
COOPER, 11, 59, 82, 138, 163, 248, 269, 271, 298, 321, 417, 420, 427, 436, 454, 464, 508
COPP, ... 330
COPPER, ... 43
CORBER, ... 277
CORBET, ... 396
CORBIN, ... 77, 273, 344, 428, 517
CORDELL, ... 18, 324, 400
CORLIS, ... 133
COREY, COARY, ... 417
CORLET, ... 127, 128
CORLY, ... 118
CORNING, ...25, 118, 268
CORNISH,, ... 125, 313, 392
CORWIN, ... 71, 302, 409, 422
CORWITHEN, ... 12, 126, 161
COSTONE, ... 119
COTTA, ... 317, 407, 443
COTTLE, ... 386, 391, 399
COTTON, 5, 21, 22, 52, 58, 65, 80, 81, 94, 126, 135, 202, 233, 236, 239, 241, 305, 376, 417, 423, 427, 430, 437, 462, 494
COURSER, ... 120
COUSINS, ... 106
COVELL, ... 329
COVEY, ... 470
COWDALL, ... 134
COWDREY, ... 25
COWELL, ... 225
COWEN, ... 298
COWES, ... 209, 270
COWLES, ... 178, 179
COWLING, ... 475
COX, see COCK, ...9, 302, 304
COY, ... 206, 276, 496
COYTMORE, ... 332, 467, 509
CRABB, ... 156
CRABTREE, 181, 199, 228, 285, 387, 394, 504
CRACKBONE, ... 386

530

OTHER NAMES AND CROSS INDEX.

CRADOCK, 18, 50, 134, 155, 157, 174, 230, 261, 335, 377
CRAFT, ... 56, 406, 490, 491, 504
CRAG, CRAGG, ... 437
CRAINE, CRANE, ... 272, 390, 443
CRANNIWELL, ... 300
CRANSDEN, ... 430
CRAPO, ... 270
CRESSEY, ... 25
CRISMAS, ... 38
CRISP, ... 272, 491
CRITCHET, ... 441
CRITCHLEY, ... 139
CROADE, ... 227, 373
CROCKER, ... 57, 188, 384
CROFT, ... 239, 489
CROMWELL, ... 26, 61, 261, 267, 274, 431
CROOK, ... 181, 203, 381
CROSBY, ... 63, 176, 290, 362, 457, 472
CROSMAN, ... 71, 271
CROSS, ... 91, 97, 210, 299, 399
CROSWELL, ... 485
CROUCH, ... 322
CROW, ... 23
CROWLEY, ... 270
CROWN, ... 38, 48
CRUM, ... 475
CRUMP, ... 93
CUBBY, ... 328
CUE, ... 381
CUDWORTH, ... 244, 397, 444
CULLICK, ... 125, 164
CUMBERBACK, ... 312
CUMMINS, ... 62, 118, 244
CURRIER, ... 126, 212, 401
CURTIS, 12, 20, 53, 93, 119, 126, 202, 204, 255, 262, 264, 337, 365, 406, 438
CUSHING, ... 69, 187, 221, 255, 381
CUSHMAN, ... 16, 234, 244
CUTLER, ... 158, 187, 228, 271, 285, 317, 412, 451
CUTTER, ... 118, 209, 244, 509
CUTTING, ... 73, 128, 269, 333
DABE, ... 364
DABYN, ... 247
DACKES, ... 48
DALLIBER, 128, 137, 155, 156, 308, 349, 440
DALTON, ... 129, 281, 341, 422
DAMON, ... 150, 188, 243, 312, 364, 413
DAMPIER, ... 389
DANE, ... 93, 251, 346, 367
DANFORD, ... 186
DANFORTH, 43, 50, 283, 320, 344, 367, 481, 504, 510

DANIEL, ... 19, 43, 177, 200, 374
DARBY, DERBY, 55, 98, 130, 234, 399, 425, 443
DARCY, ... 412
DARLING, see Dorlon.
DARRELL, ... 472
DASSET, ... 170
DAVENPORT, ... 11, 69, 83, 204, 218, 375
DAVIS, DAVIES, 34, 49, 52, 82, 90, 93, 111, 113, 118, 121, 123, 133, 134, 141, 150, 152, 192, 200, 201, 238, 271, 287, 289, 319, 330, 338, 351, 366, 380, 444, 450, 465, 500, 506, 507
DAVISON, .. 17, 18, 88, 121, 267, 293, 314
DAWSE, ... 79, 315, 389
DAY, 51, 71, 119, 120, 152, 160, 179, 305, 311, 362, 437, 488
DAYTON, ... 366
DEACON, ... 359
DEANE, 38, 40, 75, 81, 109, 115, 179, 386, 456, 478
DEARE, ... 201, 362, 413
DEARHAUGH, ... 439
DEARING, ... 39, 327, 427
DEATH, ... 465
DEIGHTON, ... 145, 206
DELANOY, etc., ... 12, 188, 324
DELENE, ... 382
DELBRIDGE, ... 15
DELL, DILL, ... 69, 136, 160, 211, 411
DENMAN, ... 418
DENNIS, 12, 42, 95, 244, 288, 298, 401, 403
DENISON, 57 145, 146, 201, 221, 346, 379, 387, 445, 486
DENNY, ... 73, 240
DENSLOW, ... 114
DENT, ... 506
DENTON, ... 454
DESBOROUGH, ... 162
DEVEL, ... 267
DEWEY, ... 101, 221, 245
DEWSBERY, ... 136
DEXTER, 133, 145, 161, 176, 178, 209, 287, 508
DIAPER, ... 159
DIBBLE, ... 14
DIBBS, ... 319
DICK, ... 454
DICKERSON, ... 68, 117, 244, 278
DICKSON, DIXON, ... 325, 342, 359
DIKE, see DIX, ... 259, 363
DILL, see Dell.
DILLINGHAM, ... 163
DIMMOCK, ... 468

OTHER NAMES AND CROSS INDEX.

DIMOND, ... 34, 330
DINELY, ... 122, 369
DINGLEY, ... 328
DINSDALE, ... 159, 299
DIPPLE, ... 28, 372
DIRKEE, ... 124
DIX, DEIKE, DIKE, 128, 140, 287, 437, 454
DIXEY, ... 149, 436
DIXER, ... 140
DOBSON, ... 280, 305
DODD, ... 206, 324
DOE, ... 148
DODGE, ... 113, 218, 347, 375
DODSON, ... 51, 499
DOGGETT, DAGGETT, 98 166, 177, 221,
                 335, 371, 429, 486
DOLE, ... 103, 185, 391, 399
DOLING, ... 312
DONE, ... 74, 150, 215
DONSTALL, ... 51, 77, 138
DOOLITTLE, ... 48, 333
DORCHESTER, ... 346
DORLON, ... 200, 221
DORE, ... 367
DOTEN, DOTEY, 111, 207, 317, 358, 385,
                 425, 446, 464
DOTTERIS, ... 18
DOUGHTY, ... 103
DOUNARD, ... 241
DOUGLASS, ... 144, 171
DOVE, ... 125, 143
DOW, .. 92, 110, 150, 269, 271, 297, 333, 339
DOWDEN, ... 338
DOWELL, ... 349
DOWNE, ... 454
DOWNER, ... 406
DOWNING, 45, 62, 65, 107, 144, 331, 373, 436
DOWSE, ... 259, 314, 381, 429, 503
DRAKE, ... 143, 144, 234, 332, 514
DRAPER, ... 62, 205, 389
DRESSER, ... 283
DREW, DRUSE, ... 102, 145, 385
DRINKER, ... 190, 443, 497
DRURY, ... 51
DRUSE, see DREW, ... 210
DRYDEN, ... 250
DUDLEY, 14, 65, 86, 180, 206, 245, 259,
             338, 398, 462, 467, 512
DUDENY, ... 113
DUMMER, ... 81, 128, 326, 407
DUNBAR, ... 13, 181
DUNCAN, DUNKIN, ... 157, 266, 288, 445
DUNCKLEY, ... 176
DUNELL, ... 144

DUNHAM, ... 41, 161, 249, 274
DUNNING, ... 191
DUNTON, ... 257
DUNSTER, ... 189, 230, 498
DURDAL, ... 288
DUREING, ... 223
DUSTON, ... 86, 118, 484
DUTCH, DOOCH, ... 128, 309, 314, 391
DWIGHT, ... 353, 357, 370, 386, 450, 494
DYER, 24, 88, 117 148, 175, 212, 380, 461, 480
EAGER, ... 459
EAGLESFIELD, ... 10
EALE, EELS, ... 15, 148, 214, 435
EAMES, see also AMES, 53, 360, 478, 497
EAST, ... 357
EASTON, ... 43, 225, 362
EASTMAN, ... 33, 62, 115, 118, 363, 399
EASTWICK, ... 158, 164
EATON, 72, 96, 197, 241, 266, 309, 315,
     352, 364, 375, 378, 393, 401, 415, 486, 518
EBREW, ... 336
EBORNE, ... 186, 457, 460
ECCLES, ... 115, 254
EDEN, ... 74
EDDENDEN, ... 196, 202, 325
EDDINGTON, ... 29, 485
EDDY, ... 29, 45, 76, 141, 151, 309, 402
EDGE, ... 496
EEDES, ... 464
EDMUNDS, ... 319, 370, 392, 428, 429, 498
EDSALL, ... 349
EDSON, ... 86
EDWARDS, 120, 182, 221, 322, 327, 367,
                 422, 442, 479
EGGLESTONE, ... 399, 485
EGLON, ... 500
EIRE, EYRES, 39, 95, 96, 275, 319, 340,
                 431, 447, 499
ELDERKIN, ... 272
ELDRED, ELDREDGE, 153, 295, 329, 432
ELIOT, 12, 61, 73, 104, 126, 130, 153, 193,
     203, 205, 207, 230, 239, 240, 278, 304,
     320, 327, 352, 354, 355, 394, 399, 449,
            481, 486, 496, 497, 499
ELKIN, ... 281
ELLETSON, ... 216, 352
ELLEN, ... 14, 366
ELLERY, ... 471
ELLETT, ... 303, 304, 406
ELLIS, 56, 97, 100, 170, 175, 403, 443, 481, 497
ELLSWORTH, ... 420
ELITHORP, ... 39, 441
ELSE, ... 502
ELVIN, ELVING, ... 448, 518

532

OTHER NAMES AND CROSS INDEX.

ELWELL, ... 37, 128, 147, 315, 471
ELY, ... 125, 363
EMBLIN, ... 462
EMBSDEN, ... 127
EMERSON, 156, 196, 287, 292, 445, 454, 474, 484, 513
EMERY, ... 40, 158, 192, 336, 484
EMMETT, ... 82
EMMONS, ... 264, 509
EIMONS, ... 156
ENDECOTT, 65, 73, 74, 75, 117, 138, 197, 203, 241, 274, 341, 348, 367, 409, 442, 508
ENGLAND, ... 367
ENGLISH, ... 49, 87, 157, 423, 469, 482
ENSIGN, ... 48
EPPS, ... 31, 445, 512
ERRINGTON, ... 415, 482
ESTABROOK, ... 512
EUSTACE, ... 254
EVANS, ... 155, 208, 309, 362, 455
EVERED, EVERETT, ... 20, 326, 354
EVERILL, ... 54, 224, 297, 353, 358
EWELL, ... 19
EWER, ... 56, 258, 292
EWETT, ... 82
FACE, ... 470
FAIRBANK, ... 135, 293, 306, 418
FAIRFIELD, ... 95, 341
FALLOWELL, ... 41, 368, 511
FANNING, ... 130
FARMER, ... 3, 4, 134, 319
FARMISE, ... 319
FARNHAM, ... 65, 251, 367, 394, 457, 466
Ralph, came in July, 1635. Son Ralph m. Elizabeth Holt. R. F. d. 8 Jan. 1692-3; inv. filed March 29, 1693.

FARNWORTH, ... 277, 351
FARR, ... 161, 186, 438
FARRAR, ... 223, 406
FARRELL, ... 51
FARRINGTON, ... 123, 227, 274, 328
FARROW, ... 178, 181, 231, 438
FARWELL, ... 168, 414
FAUCET, ... 413
FAUNCE, ... 213, 426
FAWER, ... 186, 260, 280, 326, 373
FAUNE, ... 105
FAXON, ... 450, 505
FAY, ... 518
FAYERWEATHER, ... 159, 192, 465
FEAKE, ... 152, 342, 398, 403
FEARING, ... 221, 497, 500
FELCH, FELT, ... 400, 498
FELLOW, FELLOWS, ... 33, 59, 277, 319
FELMINGHAM, ... 117

FELTON, 12, 27, 240, 291, 301, 393, 403, 416, 421, 457
FEN, ... 222, 415, 457
FENNO, ... 463
FENWICK, ... 125
FERGUSON, ... 308
FERMAES, ... 64, 338
FERNSIDE, ... 127, 392, 431
FEVER, ... 446
FEVERYEAR, ... 363
FIELD, ... 152, 358, 387, 443
FIFIELD, ... 129
FILLEBROWN, ... 390
FILER, ... 367
FINCH, ... 196
FINNEY, ... 40, 59, 108, 160, 161
FIRMIN, ... 152, 478
FISHER, 39, 62, 66, 78, 159, 179, 225, 248, 311, 315, 319, 351, 422, 425, 461, 488, 509, 514
FISKE, 24, 135, 170, 177, 292, 314, 340, 381, 436, 468, 517
FITCH, 99, 108, 167, 284, 312, 416, 443, 473
FITCHER, ... 321
FFITLING, ... 363
FITTS, ... 99, 451
FITZ RANDOLPH, ... 236
FITZ SYMONDS, ... 455
FLAGG, ... 49, 91, 180, 284
FLANDERS, ... 90, 337
FLETCHER, ... 353, 415, 462
FLINDERS, ... 217
FLINT, 148, 173, 215, 217, 232, 233, 311, 457
FLOOD, ... 61
FLOWER, ... 179
FLOYD, ... 155
FOBES, FORBES, ... 170
FOGG, ... 339, 366
FOLLETT, ... 52, 324
FOLSAM, see FOULSHAM, ... 187
FONES, ... 163
FOOT, ... 126, 228, 281, 461
FOOTMAN, ... 225
FORD, 100, 140, 196, 271, 293, 326, 425, 439
FORTH, ... 508
FOSDIKE, ... 35, 127, 488
FOSKITT, ... 281
FOSTER, 35, 36, 49, 55, 65, 77, 186, 219, 255, 265, 270, 278, 345, 348, 395, 405, 438, 454, 457, 466, 493
FOUNELL, ... 470
FOULSHAM, ... 161, 363
FOWLE, ... 52, 70, 71, 107, 370, 420
FOWLER, ... 269, 337
FOX, ... 70, 181, 196, 199, 497
FOXWELL, ... 411

OTHER NAMES AND CROSS INDEX.

FRANCIS, ... 135, 497
FRANK, ... 486
FRANKLIN, ... 18, 297, 324, 408, 441, 467
FRARY, ... 85, 148, 153, 212, 497
FREE, ... 33
FREEBORN, ... 13
FREEMAN, ... 338, 372, 426, 434
FRENCH, 42, 72, 81, 93, 130, 149, 155,
  177, 180, 191, 211, 213, 222, 244, 247,
    271, 301, 311, 333, 350, 432, 456, 494
FRENCHAM, ... 41, 276
FRICK, ... 293
FRIEND, ... 138, 321
FRISSELL, ... 104, 165, 223, 225
FROST, 19, 85, 130, 147, 265, 438, 473, 497
FROTHINGHAM, ... 123
FRY, ... 141, 214, 248, 310, 370, 435, 458
FRYER, ... 384, 403, 512
FULLER, 51, 150, 156, 162, 178, 253, 255,
  262, 271, 281, 292, 333, 356, 393, 399,
    416, 448, 493, 517, 518
FURNELL, ... 276
FYNES, ... 260
GAGE, ... 274, 275, 331
GAINES, ... 222
GALE, ... 141, 168, 283
GALLOP, ... 264, 445
GALLOWAY, ... 210
GAMBLIN, ... 180
GEYNER, ... 22
GANNETT, ... 401
GARDNER, 29, 61, 73, 113, 119, 128, 144,
  156, 192, 196, 230, 240, 266, 297, 368,
    369, 391, 409, 427, 471
GARFIELD, ... 35, 77, 180
GARFOARD, ... 464
GARLIK, ... 54
GARNET, ... 438
GARNESEY, ... 18
GARRETT, 11, 72, 152, 161, 219, 222,
  323, 413, 454
GARRETSON, ... 499
GARY, ... 11, 225
GATES, ... 279, 492, 514
GATLIFFE, ... 234
GAULT, ... 51
GAUNT, ... 123
GAWDREN, ... 253
GAY, ... 29, 67, 221, 303, 383, 503
GAYLORD, ... 99, 307, 326, 389, 395
GEARE, 66, 95, 133, 200, 279, 334, 457, 501
GEARING, ... 36
GEDNEY, ... 236, 360, 370, 476
GEE, ... 297

GELL, ... 518
GENNER, see JENNER.
GENCKS, see JENKS.
GEORGE, ... 34, 190, 214, 352, 490
GERRISH, ... 191, 294, 321, 335, 373
GIBBONS, GIBBENS, 77, 122, 155, 161,
  212, 316, 342, 399, 403
GIBBS, ... 64, 171, 245, 410
GIBSON, ... 88, 157, 224, 372, 468
GIDDINGS, ... 320, 375
GIFFORD, ... 217, 371, 397, 463
GILBERT, 43, 55, 76, 94, 225, 302, 552,
  462, 492
GILES, ... 180, 337, 518
GILL, ... 49, 84, 106, 186, 309, 479
GILLAM, ... 205, 358, 401
GILLAWAY, ... 187, 268
GILLETT, ... 221, 355, 479
GILLOW, ... 513
GILMAN, ... 171, 227, 282, 423, 462
GILSON, ... 61, 74, 394
GINGEN, ... 498
GINKINS, ... 454
GINNINGS, ... 189
GLASIER, ... 185
GLASS, ... 136, 237, 279, 366, 385, 502
GLASSCOCK, ... 178
GLOVER, 27, 112, 121, 135, 147, 208, 322,
  347, 371, 384, 414, 421, 433
GODBERTSON, 16, 93, 116, 189, 229, 371, 418
GODDEN, ... 263, 431, 406
GODFREY, ... 22, 74
GODSOE, GODSON, ... 71, 291
GOFFE, ... 72, 128, 313, 353, 498, 507, 509
GOLDSMITH, ... 9, 95, 145, 214, 248
GOLDSTONE, ... 69, 184, 228
GOLDTHWAIGHT, ... 96
GOLDWYER, ... 198, 322
GOOCH, ... 235, 351
GOODALE, 15, 40, 185, 220, 293, 294,
  305, 335, 421
GOODENOW, ... 25, 85, 400
GOODERSON, see GUTTERSON, ... 326
GOODHUE, ... 196, 292
GOODMAN, ... 449
GOODRICH, ... 11, 14, 44, 218, 449
GOODSPEED, ... 133, 283
GOODWIN, ... 231, 266, 458
GOODYEAR, ... 276
GOOKIN, ... 39, 41, 93, 193
GOORDLEY, ... 466
GOOSE, ... 91, 164, 263
GORDING, ... 466
GORE, ... 11, 369, 382, 448

OTHER NAMES AND CROSS INDEX.

GORGES, ... 53, 319
GORHAM, ... 47, 244, 448
GORTON, ... 88, 350, 370, 371
GOSSE, ... 329
GOSMER, ... 90
GOTT, ... 292, 299, 380, 442, 482
GOUER, ... 157
GOULD, GOLD, 29, 124, 256, 329, 354,
381, 443, 478
    Samuel, Haverhill, propr. 1650.
GOULDER, ... 151
GOURD, ... 206
GOVE, ... 168, 299, 322
GOWING, ... 70
GRAFTON, ... 182, 291, 292, 399, 403
GRANDEE, ... 304, 406
GRANGER, ... 11
GRANT, 88, 101, 116, 159, 186, 196, 202,
224, 268, 389, 479
GRAVES, 16, 41, 42, 92, 113, 121, 138, 150,
224, 233, 308, 370, 396
GRAY, 121, 197, 284, 295, 332, 482, 485, 508
GREELEY, ... 72, 191, 322
GREEN, GREENE, 30, 43, 56, 72, 90, 102,
110, 116, 174, 201, 211, 230, 241, 266,
281, 290, 319, 322, 350, 367, 393, 432,
217, 437, 494, 495, 498, 507
GREENFIELD, ... 448, 509
GREENLEAF, 27, 107, 185, 231, 413, 425,
442, 470
GREENLAND, ... 149, 185
GREENOUGH, ... 338, 349, 377, 443, 468
GREENSLADE, ... 24
GREGORY, ... 158, 473
GRENAWAY, ... 39, 64, 130, 315, 361, 474
GREENWOOD, ... 15
GRENVILL, ... 184
GRIDLEY, ... 56, 125, 142, 170
GRIFFIN, 18, 54, 127, 138, 290, 386, 409,
413, 433, 435, 519
GRIFFITH, ... 112
GRICE, GRIST, ... 133, 338
GRIGGS, 29, 133, 218, 258, 269, 348, 356,
378, 514
GRISWALD, ... 78, 267, 514
GROOM, ... 402
GROSSE, ... 110
GROUT, ... 83
GROVER, ... 23, 35, 49, 218
GROW, ... 291
GRUBB, ... 295, 471
GRUNN, ... 483
GUILD, GILE, ... 14, 132
GUILLE, ... 270
GULLIVER, ... 272

GULLY, ... 87
GUN, ... 365
GUNISON, ... 287, 455
GURDON, ... 388
GURGEFIELD, ... 46
GURNEY, ... 79, 258, 269, 279
GUTTERIDGE, ... 427
GUY, ... 270, 446
GYPSON, ... 181

GWIN, ... 187
HABGOOD, see HAPGOOD
HACK, ... 286
HACKER, ... 309
HACKETT, ... 33, 205
HACKNEY, ... 83
HADBOURNE, HEBOURNE, 58, 263,
281, 412, 420
HADAWAY, ... 209
HADDEN, ... 519
HADLEY, ... 303, 375
HADLOCK, ... 144, 250, 303
HAFFIELD, ... 106, 251
HAGBOURNE, ... 14, 145
HAGER, ... 87
HAGGITT, ... 95
HAINES, HAYNES, 33, 48, 49, 54, 175,
213, 252, 277, 333, 382
HAIT. 143, 395
HALE, 49, 86, 100, 119, 121, 173, 207, 250,
251, 255, 278, 325, 327, 331, 386, 392,
445, 489
HALFORD, ... 422
HALL, 12, 31, 78, 86, 111, 235, 247, 428,
445, 492, 497, 515
HALLETT, ... 33, 103, 472
HALSALL, HALSEY, ... 442
HALSTEAD, ... 40, 223
HAM, ... 53
HAMMENT, ... 340
HAMLET, ... 245
HAMLIN, ... 59
HAMMOND, 124, 145, 212, 219, 329, 359,
394, 412, 425, 503
HAMPTON, ... 34, 180, 267, 272, 394
HANBURY, ... 102, 246, 260, 453
HANCHET, ... 277
HANCOCK, ... 372, 441
HANDS, ... 211
HANMORE, ... 398
HANNER, ... 417
HANNIFORD, HANDFORTH, 136, 172,
219, 285, 387, 405
HANNUM, ... 277, 432, 468
HANSON, ... 62, 63

OTHER NAMES AND CROSS INDEX.

HAPGOOD, ... 333, 461
HARADEN, ... 299, 375
HARBITTLE, ... 220, 276
HARBOUR, ... 404, 450
HARDING, 73, 76, 85, 115, 148, 210, 297, 404, 420, 454, 495, 511
HARDMAN, ... 271
HARDY, ... 210, 217
HARLAKENDEN, ... 115, 415, 445
HARLOW, ... 36, 69, 210
HARMAN, ... 55, 142
HARNDEN, ... 493
HARRIMAN, ... 420
HARRINGTON, ... 49
HARRIS, 148, 149, 177, 190, 224, 227, 241, 307, 300, 429, 435, 445, 471, 486, 488, 506, 508
HARRISON, ... 68, 234, 271, 316, 386, 445
HARROD, ... 17, 201
HARSEY, ... 86
HARSNET, ... 506
HART, 41, 73, 91 109, 215, 221, 325, 365, 392
HARTOPP, ... 389
HARTSHORNE, ... 277, 392
HARVARD, ... 15
HARVEY, ... 34, 75, 118, 186, 240, 502, 504
HARWOOD, ... 96, 227, 325, 421, 469
HASELTINE, ... 19, 259, 484,
HASEY, ... 209
HASKELL, ... 212, 454, 474, 512
HASKETT, ... 277
HASSELL, ... 38
HASTINGS, ... 36, 69, 85, 97, 309
HATCH, 19, 219, 220, 228, 229, 234, 270, 429, 447, 458, 469
HATHAWAY, ... 221, 368
HATHERLY, 53, 196, 211, 252, 287, 387, 397, 401, 405, 456, 492
HAUSEN, ... 366
HAVEN, ... 328, 335
HAWES, ... 138, 142, 160, 184, 193, 221
HAWKINS, 35, 47, 64, 87, 109, 121, 145, 164, 182, 198, 238, 272, 315, 329, 432, 461, 503
HAWKS, ... 13, 91, 163, 205, 286, 308, 314
HAWKSWORTH, ... 503
HAYDEN, ... 17, 325, 392, 450
HAYLET, see AYLETT.
HAYMAN, ... 14, 17
HAYWARD, HEYWOOD, etc., 13, 17, 23, 33, 85, 124, 152, 195, 201, 249, 264, 313, 334, 361, 370, 438, 445, 450, 458, 461, 502, 509
HAZARD, ... 49

HAZEN, ... 72
HEALD, ... 130, 284
HEALY, ... 253, 300
HEARD, ... 49, 225, 517
HEATH, ... 52, 65, 225, 248, 355
HEATON, see EATON, ... 315
HEBBERT, etc., ... 125
HEDGE, ... 18, 329
HELWYDE, HELWYS, ... 220
HEMENWAY, ... 234
HENCHMAN, ... 367, 513
HENDRICK, HENRICK, ... 435
HEPBURN, ... 294, 397, 492
HERBERT, ... 119, 314
HERFIELD, ... 196
HERLE, ... 305, 457
HERRICK, ... 99, 141, 278, 281, 381
HERRING, ... 361, 411
HERSEY, ... 99, 163, 383
HEWES, 16, 97, 121, 190, 193, 226, 447, 502
HIBBENS, ... 432, 486
HIGGINS, ... 31, 189, 390, 455, 501, 518
HIGGINSON, 69, 75, 194, 291, 369, 401, 504, 514
HILAND, ... 278, 465
HILDRETH, ... 375
HILER, HILLIER, see HILLIARD.
HILL, HILLS, 14, 24, 25, 40, 56, 77, 84, 103, 137, 144, 147, 152, 182, 189, 199, 208, 216, 245, 247, 282, 290, 295, 301, 318, 323, 331, 369, 376, 413, 417, 422, 426, 433, 435, 454, 457, 465, 474, 480, 489, 510
HILLIARD, 129, 221, 246, 311, 312, 319, 320, 365, 455
HILTON, ... 199, 406, 462
HINCKLEY, 57, 106, 133, 329, 368, 384, 421
HINCKSMAN, ... 156, 159, 173, 357
HINDS, HINES, ... 42, 234, 308, 349, 403
HINSDALE, ... 221, 492
HITCHCOCK, ... 94
HITT, see HAIT.
HIX, HEEKES, HICKES, 69, 142, 179, 184, 210, 244, 415
HIXON, ... 492
HOAG, ... 156
HOAR, ... 170, 180, 516
HOBART, see HUBBARD.
HOBSON, ... 331, 379
HOCKING, ... 112, 446
HODGES, ... 17, 72, 134, 215, 297, 363
HODGKINS, ... 147, 242
HODSDEN, ... 234
HOGG, ... 196

536

OTHER NAMES AND CROSS INDEX.

HOLBECK, ... 493
HOLBROOK, 226, 271, 337, 361, 363, 411, 431
HOLDEN, ... 172
HOLGATE, ... 504
HOLGRAVE, ... 69, 343, 501
HOLIMAN, ... 404
HOLLAND, ... 5, 51, 403, 428
HOLLARD, ... 181, 277, 468
HOLLEY, ... 169, 253, 266
HOLLICE, ... 374
HOLLINGSWORTH, 29, 307, 318, 370, 431, 499
HOLLISTER, ... 458
HOLLOWAY, ... 327, 358
HOLMAN, ... 19, 140, 166, 363, 417, 502
HOLMES, HOMES, 21, 85, 95, 100, 294, 307, 320, 326, 392, 398, 438, 449, 458, 474, 511
HOLT, ... 30, 64, 161, 305, 373, 414
 Nicholas, dish-turner, with wife Martha, sold land to his second son Henry 15 Dec. 1681. Henry m. Feb. 24, 1669, Sarah, dau. of William Ballard.
HOLTON, HOULTON, ... 166, 475
HOLYOKE, ... 376
HOMER, ... 144
HONOR, ... 374
HOOD, ... 328, 343, 462
HOOK, ... 130, 138, 308
HOOKER, 12, 46, 176, 371, 412, 437, 486, 499
HOOPER, ... 170, 221
HOPCOTT, ... 297
HOPKINS, 18, 109, 142, 218, 289, 386, 425, 449, 489, 501, 518
HOPKINSON, ... 103, 442, 463, 476
HOPPEN, HOPPER, ... 87, 298, 368
HORNE, ... 12, 27, 101, 105, 482
HORROCKS, ... 119
HORTON, ... 21, 95
HOSIER, ... 111, 334, 388, 439
HOSKINS, ... 98, 234
HOSMER, ... 143, 203, 505, 511
HOUGH, HAUGH, etc., 40, 94, 121, 268, 352, 377, 477, 496
HOUGHTON, ... 167, 331, 334, 443
HOULDSWORTH, ... 186
HOUSE, see also HOW, ... 210, 340
HOVEY, ... 18, 499
HOW, HOWES, 31, 46, 66, 79, 117, 129, 254, 255, 282, 301, 304, 306, 307, 309, 316, 334, 340, 343, 370, 372, 398, 406, 468, 475, 499
HOWARD, ... 222
HOWELL, ... 218
HOWLAND, 64, 91, 98, 129, 171, 177, 193, 202, 215, 282, 310, 324, 383, 426, 446, 455, 475, 501

HOWLETT, ... 101, 176, 370, 387, 424
HOYT, ... 34, 75, 92
HUBBARD, HOBART, 13, 16, 36, 41, 65, 99, 107, 145, 185, 191, 194, 209, 228, 251, 253, 266, 296, 302, 311, 320, 351, 390, 463, 494, 496
HUCKINS, ... 118, 309, 368
HUDSON, ... 13, 199, 269, 377, 390
HUGHES, see HEWES, ... 32, 413
HUGHSON, ... 145
HUIT, ... 94, 127, 508
HULL, 82, 128, 175, 192, 259, 319, 332, 353, 399, 437, 459, 511, 513
HUMPHREY, HUMPHREYE, 16, 22, 24, 44, 109, 132, 147, 177, 246, 251, 283, 328, 338, 379, 433, 485, 501
HUN, ... 357
HUNGERFOOT, ... 282
HUNLOKE, ... 407
HUNNIBORNE, ... 419
HUNT, 27, 34, 47, 120, 133, 172, 270, 318, 384, 420, 422, 484
HUNTER, ... 33, 124, 236
HUNTING, ... 14, 340, 357, 383, 479
HUNTINGTON, ... 205, 389
HURST, ... 203, 450, 504
HUSSEY, ... 26, 109
HUTCHINS, ... 152, 206, 269, 482
HUTCHINSON, 29, 45, 58, 86, 113, 121, 136, 164, 176, 184, 203, 210, 212, 221, 225, 250, 272, 274, 276, 301, 313, 324, 376, 384, 392, 401, 404, 422, 434, 443, 491
HYDE, .. 55, 103, 105, 142, 178, 432, 485, 486
INGERSOLL, ... 350, 356
IBBITT, ... 417
IBROOK, ... 107, 459
IDE, ... 55
ILES, ... 301
ILSLEY, ... 133, 206
INGALLS, ... 147, 150, 251, 283, 337
ING, INGS, INGLE, see English.
INGIONE, ... 340
INGRAHAM, ... 144, 186, 397
INGULDEN, ... 309
IRELAND, ... 200, 203, 253, 307, 483
IRESON, ... 281, 400
IRISH, ... 99, 476
ISAAC, ... 133
IVES, ... 224
IVEY, ... 36
IVORY, ... 123
INGLEDEN, ... 65
JACUAS, see JAQUES, ... 461
JANSEN, ... 368
JACKLING, ... 350
JACKMAN, ... 333

OTHER NAMES AND CROSS INDEX.

JACKSON, 29, 41, 74, 90, 94, 105, 110, 112, 124, 192, 291, 327, 388, 405, 449, 450, 452, 514
JAMESON, ... 303
JACOB, ... 20, 26, 41, 149, 207, 395, 463
JAMES, 19, 39, 216, 226, 255, 280, 313, 395, 433, 440, 444, 504
JANES, ... 37, 438
JAQUES, ... 70, 86, 263
JARRETT, JARRARD, ... 298
JAY, ... 363
JEFFRESON, ... 486
JEFFREY, ... 48
JEFFS, ... 361
JEGGLES, ... 409
JENKS, ... 30, 203
JENKINS, ... 48, 116, 219, 454, 464, 491
JENNER, ... 188, 296, 461
JENNEY, ... 229, 368, 422, 511
JENNINGS, ... 124
JEWELL, ... 201, 463
JEWETT, ... 13, 49, 62, 88, 125, 291
JINGINE, ... 498
JOCELYN, ... 267, 329, 376, 518
JOHNSON, 6 17, 34, 44, 52, 70, 76, 78, 87, 97, 98, 111, 140, 162, 175, 180, 181, 199, 210, 225, 226, 238, 271, 290, 292, 294, 307, 310, 315, 326, 328, 331, 335, 341, 354, 357, 368, 369, 370, 426, 432, 435, 447, 461, 509
JOLLIFFE, ... 123, 274
JONES, 35, 39, 48, 81, 84, 125, 133, 136, 155, 178, 185, 186, 201, 243, 288, 331, 333, 337, 363, 370, 385, 394, 399, 412, 458, 461, 463, 473, 479, 494
JORDAN, 51, 108, 146, 205, 256, 296, 312, 495
JOY, ... 75, 180, 190, 363, 374, 482
JOYCE, ... 401
JUDKIN, ... 141, 223, 282
JUDSON, ... 13, 223
JUPE, ... 265
KAYE, ... 398
KADE, see CADE.
KEAYNE, KEENE, etc., 28, 68, 75, 94, 109, 110, 131, 140, 145, 148, 194, 208, 214, 264, 299, 338, 348, 352, 378, 411, 417, 432, 437, 504
KEBED, ... 115
KELLY, ... 80, 425, 495
KELLOGG, ... 449
KELSEY, KELSOE, ... 394
KEMBY, ... 311
KEMP, ... 166, 265
KEMPTHORN, ... 290

KEMPTON, ... 188, 379, 395
KENDALL, ...236, 425, 440, 448
KENDRICK, ... 97, 254, 321, 423
KENNEY, ... 162
KENNINGE, ... 370
KENNISTON, ... 123
KENT, 17, 18, 49, 99, 134, 196, 211, 403, 476, 513
KERBY, ... 89, 207, 279, 416
KERLY, ... 264, 393, 423
KERRIDGE, ... 345
KETTELL, ... 293, 477
KEYLEY, ... 47
KEY, KEYES, ... 190, 196
KEYSER, KEZAR, ... 238, 398, 420
KIBBEE, ... 201, 204, 258
KIBBEN, ... 11
KIDDER, ... 317
KIDWELL, ... 427
KILBOURNE, ...32, 159, 442, 463
KILHAM, CALLEM, ... 77, 191, 359, 397
KILIN, ... 117
KIMBALL, KEMBALL, 9, 36, 53, 68, 404, 412, 438
KING, 33, 40, 51, 66, 101, 127, 133, 161, 171, 172, 190, 201, 219, 260, 267, 374, 380, 385, 408, 429, 488, 494
KINGMAN, ... 49, 102, 133
KINGSBURY, ... 86, 118, 124, 223, 397
KINGSLEY, KINGLEY, 130, 277, 389, 396, 462
KINGSTON, ... 323
KINSMAN, ... 386
KIRK, ... 57
KIRTLAND, CATLAND, etc., ... 450
KITCHEN, ... 48, 196, 399
KITCHERILL, ... 142
KITSON, ... 383
KLINE, ... 65
KNAPP, ... 11, 87, 202, 352, 424, 480
KNELAND, ... 87
KNIGHT, 38, 66, 68, 103, 123, 188, 237, 252, 256, 261, 271, 283, 288, 368, 369, 427, 438, 440, 459, 483, 516
KNORE, KNOWER, ... 145
KNOTT, ... 456
KNOWLES, KNOLLYS, 45, 49, 242, 256, 457
KNOWLTON, ... 463, 504
LACHMAN, ... 508
LADD, ...118, 416
LAKE, ... 31, 181, 214, 262, 276, 370, 443
LAMB, ... 15, 38, 113, 176, 220, 509, 517
LAMBERT, ... 32, 156, 179, 331, 389
LAMBSON, ... 25, 115, 516

538

OTHER NAMES AND CROSS INDEX.

LANCASTER, ... 90, 151
LANE, 82, 186, 187, 243, 286, 366, 379, 385, 405, 438
LANGDON, LANCTON, 164, 288, 326, 374
LANGEMORE, ... 302
LANGER, ... 286
LANGLEY, ... 122, 187, 248, 298
LANGOME, ... 284
LAPHAM, ... 219, 454
LARKIN, LASKIN, ... 72, 227, 354
LASSELL, ... 41, 183, 282, 286
LATHAM, ... 69, 91, 305, 508
LATTIMORE, ... 201, 363
LAUGHTON, ... 44, 326
LAUNCE, ... 412
LAUNDER, ... 184 487
LAWRENCE, 26, 37, 44, 61, 122, 182, 190, 314, 357, 418, 428, 466
LAWS, ... 97, 325
LAWSON, ... 141, 265
LEECH, .. 86, 113, 156, 178, 190, 352, 452
LEADBETTER, ... 456
LEADER, ... 257
LEAGER, ... 54, 199
LEARNED, ... 49, 434
LEASON, ... 339
LEATHERBEE, LEATHERLAND, LERABY, .. 142, 163, 282, 326, 347, 393
LEAVITT, ... 187, 289
LE BARON, ... 497
LECROFT, ... 309
LECHFORD, ... 4, 225, 497
LEDGARD, ... 164
LEE, LEA, .. 23, 79, 87, 178, 282, 488, 512
LEAVER, ... 40, 179
LEEDS, ... 498
LEGAT, ... 504
LEGG, ... 349
LEIGHTON, ... 61, 192
LEMON, ... 122, 204, 278
LENNER, ... 77
LENTHAL, ... 70, 277, 421
LEPPINGWELL, ... 322
LEONARD, ... 203, 346, 511
LESSIE, ... 380
LESTOR, ... 70
LETTICE, ... 197, 401, 414
LETTIN, ... 431
LEVENS, ... 343, 438
LEVERETT, 11, 13, 37, 83, 205, 210, 212, 245, 246, 306, 377, 384, 394, 471
LEVERICH, ... 60, 442
LEWIS, 43, 51, 53, 72, 96, 131, 277, 286, 306, 346, 387, 515

LEY, ... 487
LIDGETT, ... 13, 397
LIGHT, ... 37
LIGHTFOOT, ... 453
LILY, LILLE, ... 37, 350
LINCOLN, 99, 221, 255, 261, 277, 278, 280, 400, 429, 478
LINDEN, ... 195
LINDSEY, ... 16, 140
LINN, LYNNE, ... 204, 455
LINNELL, LINNETT, LYNNETT, 98, 133, 292, 411
LINTON, ... 481
LISCOM, ... 260
LISHAM, ... 155
LITHERMORE, ... 124
LITCHFIELD, ... 14, 28, 136, 350
LITTLE, ... 448, 480
LITTLEFIELD, ... 230, 479
LIVERMORE, ... 202, 486
LLOYD, ... 491
LOBDELL, ... 282, 478
LOCKE, .. 104, 133, 364, 413, 461, 494, 503
LOCKER, ... 77
LOCKWOOD, ... 43, 305, 330, 404
LOKER, ... 133
LONG, 161, 229, 230, 277, 304, 331, 343, 429, 448
LONGHORNE, ... 124, 329, 418, 502
LORD, 135, 168, 207, 229, 358, 429, 430, 448
LORING, ... 28, 221, 255, 282, 374
LOOMAN, ... 316, 493
LOSON, ... 188
LOTHROP, 53, 96, 156, 159, 174, 178, 194, 210, 285, 287, 373, 379, 405, 435, 454
LOUGIE, ... 18
LOVE, ... 453
LOVEJOY, ... 244, 337
LOVELL, ... 97, 219
LOVERMORE, ... 413
LOVETT, ... 56, 268
LOW, 59, 243, 264, 293, 369, 436, 452, 478
LOWDEN, ... 110, 434
LOWELL, ... 191, 294, 317, 444, 513
LUDKIN, ... 227, 294
LUDLOW, ... 157, 273, 282, 422
LUGG, ... 206
LULLABY, see LERABY.
LUMBARD, ... 111, 155, 221, 287
LUMPKIN, ... 29, 153,437
LUND, ... 152
LUNT, ... 108, 230, 484
LUSE, ... 350
LUSH, ... 472

OTHER NAMES AND CROSS INDEX.

LUSHER, 97
LUXFORD, 96
LYDE, 23, 491
LYFORD, 245, 334
LYMAN, 37, 172, 231
LYNDE, 248, 249, 327, 464
LYON, 98, 314, 365, 394, 456
LYDDS, 165
LISLE, LYLE, 52, 68, 233, 288, 441
MACHAROY, 159
MACKARTEY, 260
MACKERWITHY, 159
MACKINTOSH, 313
MACKWORTH, 163
MACLIST, 497
MACNAB, 391
MACUMBER, 123
MACVARLO, 395
MACY, 239, 297, 330
MADDOX, 341, 379
MAHEW, 42, 73, 189, 340
MAINER, 392
MAKEPEACE, 102, 124, 310, 502
MAN, 69, 167, 479
MANLE, 71
MANNERING, 379
MANNING, 124, 143, 159, 181, 185, 344, 364, 434, 481, 495
MANSFIELD, 161, 186, 195, 238, 265, 325, 477, 504
MANSON, 37
MAPLEHEAD, 78
MARBLE, 384
MARBURY, 250
MARCH, 262, 503
MARCY, 372
MARGIN, 235
MARKHAM, 494
MARRETT, 35, 45, 122
MARSH, MARSE, MASH, 41, 43, 50, 61, 96, 171, 172, 227, 275, 286, 287, 372, 410
MARSHALL, 12, 33, 34, 51, 81, 178, 239, 299, 347, 352, 505
MARSHFIELD, 94, 164, 517
MARSTON, 231, 321, 339, 359
MARTIN, 101, 152, 184, 201, 238, 241, 268, 278, 331, 389, 445, 468, 488
MASON, 12, 26, 60, 79, 85, 113, 150, 204, 221, 242, 272, 273, 312, 351, 354, 383, 406, 407
MASSALL, 5
MASTERS, 49, 279, 423, 445
MASTERSON, 359
MATHER, 18, 20, 22, 100, 114, 120, 186, 266, 271, 276, 279, 302, 313, 421, 457, 462, 474, 479, 486, 510
MATOSIUS, 389
MATTHEW, 89, 178, 226, 138
MATSON, 20, 23, 120, 380, 381, 400
MATTOCKS, 160, 429, 436
MAUDE, 58
MAUDESLEY, MOSELY, 11, 280, 461
MAVERICK, 16, 41, 63, 99, 148, 182, 372, 387, 435, 488, 491, 493
MAXFIELD, 186, 418
MAY, 161, 166, 175
MAYNARD, 25, 54, 183, 392
MAYO, 165, 180, 186, 209, 340, 372, 386, 496, 502
MEACHAM, 76, 147
MEAD, 80, 196
MAY, 64, 189
MEAKINS, 44, 408, 437
MEANE, 218
MEARE, MEARS, 288
MECARTER, 309
MEDDLECOTT, 508
MEEKE, 279
MEGGS, 177
MELLOWS, 52, 79, 111, 120, 230, 298, 422
MEMORY, 460
MENDALL, 358
MENDAM, 243
MENDON, 317
MERCER, 26, 59, 159, 290, 409
MERIAM, MIRIAM, 66, 151, 190, 257, 436
MERICK, 31, 432, 452, 469, 517
MERIDITH, 462
MERKANT, 106
MERRABLE, 274
MERRIFIELD, 325, 443
MERRILL, 95, 105, 156, 263, 319, 484
MERRITT, 129, 398
MERRY, 63, 129, 387, 401, 452
MESSENGER, 87, 243, 304, 312, 510
METCALF, 5, 31, 160, 179, 266, 336, 360, 418, 503
MICHELL, MITCHELL, 23, 70, 93, 147, 171, 204, 239, 255, 265, 313, 321, 322, 368, 412, 449, 455, 481, 497
MIGHILL, 39, 458
MILES, 111, 121, 144, 332, 499
MILDMAY, 297
MILLARD, 84, 120, 254, 276, 294, 314, 360
MILLER, 18, 79, 128, 134, 166, 234, 344, 368, 486, 490, 508
MILLETT, 39, 200, 262
MILLS, 50, 489, 510

OTHER NAMES AND CROSS INDEX.

MINOR, ... 225, 255, 319, 342, 353
MINOT, ... 131, 142, 243, 437
MINSHALL, ... 400
MINSON, ... 349
MIXER, ... 116, 176, 182
MOLEFORD, ... 112
MONKE, ... 137
MODESLEY, see MAUDESLEY.
MONTAGUE, ... 291
MOODY, ... 63, 108, 137, 178, 275, 360, 425
MOON, ... 199
MOORE, MOORES, etc., 67, 90, 93, 118,
  151, 165, 177, 208, 214, 222, 228, 236,
  251, 278, 308, 317, 422, 431, 471, 488,
                    494, 507, 513, 518
  John, Mendon, signed a statement concerning a cow and provisions delivered to Capt. Henchman, May 1, 1676, ae. about 95 years. [Arch. 70.]
MOORECOCK, ... 75, 422, 495
MOREFIELD, ... 76
MORFREY, ... 298
MORGAN, ... 102, 116, 141, 231
MOREY, ... 31, 225, 260, 297, 317, 362
MORRELL, 34, 64, 104, 187, 203, 402, 421, 495
MORLEY, ... 392, 431
MOURT, ... 321
MORRICKE, ... 113
MORRIS, ... 16, 211, 225, 238, 309, 318
MORRISON, ... 186
MORTIMORE, ... 450
MORSE, MOSSE, 14, 33, 59, 61, 78, 100,
  102, 109, 130, 166, 265, 357, 360, 409,
                    425, 434, 511, 514
MORTON, ... 53, 117, 166, 168, 256, 386, 409
MOULD, ... 268
MOULTON, .. 44, 115, 265, 302, 313, 339, 461
MOUNTFORT, ... 509
MOUSALL, ... 70, 195, 220, 385
MOXAM, ... 328
MOYCE, ... 191, 225
MUDD, ... 110
MULFORD, ... 121, 501
MULLIGAN, ... 418
MULLINS, ... 12, 44, 90, 283
MUMFORD, ... 154
MUN, ... 30, 346
MUNDAY, MUNDE, ... 432
MUNJOY, ... 164, 357, 399
MUNNINGS, ... 368, 402, 434, 509
MUNSELL, ... 3
MUNSON, ... 323
MUNT, ... 222
MUSSELWHITE, MUSSILLOWAY, 95, 290
MURFORD, ... 75
MUSSEL, MUSSEY, ... 289, 393

MUST, ... 382, 395
MYLAM, ... 95, 193, 289, 325, 405
MYNATE, ... 315
NANNEY, ... 491
NASH, ... 84, 95, 114, 369, 422, 472
NAYLOR, ... 324, 491
NEAL, .. 77, 115, 169, 185, 215, 280, 354, 371
NEAVE, ... 139
NEFF, ... 118, 133
NEEDHAM, ... 27, 58, 91, 270, 300, 401
NEGOOSE, 14, 162, 164, 260, 325, 326, 357
NELSON, 124, 146, 159, 172, 174, 237, 259,
                    276, 294, 331, 389, 417
NEIGHBOR, ... 506
NELAND, ... 312
NEVILL, ... 491
NEWBERRY, ... 388, 479
NEWCOMB, ... 128, 136
NEWCOMIN, ... 130
NEWELL, .. 45, 186, 199, 225, 327, 370, 396
NEWGATE, ... 204, 253, 294, 327, 459
NEWLAND, ... 236, 327, 418
NEWHALL, ... 74, 169, 220, 230
NEWMAN, 51, 61, 170, 192, 233, 237, 320,
                                 322, 414
NEWMARCH, ... 195
NEWTON, ... 13, 90, 133
NICHOLS, 103, 118, 145, 163, 188, 194,
                    264, 266, 286, 422
NICHOLSON, ... 83, 130, 153, 365, 501
NICK, ... 454
NEVINSON, ... 58
NIXON, ... 90, 217
NOBLE, ... 480
NORCROSS, ... 91, 186, 409, 421, 423
NORCUT, ... 9
NORDEN, ... 113, 118, 369
NORE, see KNOWER.
NORMAN, ... 289, 308, 319, 392
NORRICE, ... 12, 260
NORTH, ... 152, 303, 507
NORTHCOATE, ... 367
NORTHEND, ... 40
NORTHEY, ... 159
NORTHROP, ... 354
NORTON, 25, 174, 183, 239, 304, 373, 394,
                    435, 471, 472, 473, 491, 517
NOURSE, ... 459
NOWELL, .. 84, 121, 254, 278, 412, 461, 502
NOYES, 73, 128, 131, 133, 206, 331, 345,
                    360, 364, 481, 498
NUDD, ... 143
NUTT, ... 48, 517, 518
NUTTER, ... 110
NUTTING, ... 122, 278
NYE, ... 6, 184

541

OTHER NAMES AND CROSS INDEX.

OAK, ... 96, 224, 443, 464
OAKLEY, ... 72
ODDING, ... 369, 413
ODLIN, ... 24, 69, 137, 163
OFFLEY, ... 449, 514
OLBON, ... 12
OLDHAM, ... 37, 53, 68, 75, 256, 465, 488
OLIVER, 47, 89, 134, 138, 141, 166, 185, 191, 253, 260, 299, 327, 376, 388, 400, 442, 465, 468, 509
ONGE, ... 405
ONION, ... 313
ORCHYARD, ... 55
ORDWAY, ... 156, 168
ORMSBY, ... 302, 303
ORTON, ... 151
OSBORN, ... 83, 310, 322, 428
OSGOOD, ... 174, 291, 292, 393, 433
OTIS, OATES, ... 83, 187, 255, 439, 464
OVERMAN, ... 509
OWEN, ... 201, 428
PACK, PAKES, ... 265
PACY, ... 145, 146
PADDOCK, ... 48, 110, 387, 406
PADDY, ... 107, 175, 349, 508
PAGE, 42, 105, 111, 130, 132, 203, 222, 301, 319, 429, 472, 495, 504
PAINE, PAYNE, 10, 20, 33, 40, 53, 89, 97, 109, 135, 143, 146, 153, 240, 243, 248, 272, 298, 344, 345, 354, 367, 370, 377, 391, 469, 470, 472, 491, 496, 507
PAINTER, ... 340, 478
PALFREY, 21, 87, 160, 259, 384, 441, 489, 502
PALGRAVE, PALSGRAVE, 117, 128, 308, 452, 486
PALMER, 66, 96, 119, 163, 186, 202, 246, 260, 310, 315, 328, 338, 364, 393, 396, 412, 502
PANKHURST, ... 184, 501
PANTRY, ... 466
PARAMORE, ... 26, 420
PARCYFULL, PERCIVAL, ... 76, 377
PARDON, ... 366
PARIS, ... 253, 513
PARISH, ... 417
PARK, PARKS, 52, 69, 127, 140, 201, 232, 266, 322, 337, 344, 349, 361, 483, 494
PARKER, 9, 48, 77, 85, 92, 97, 98, 105, 120, 126, 136, 160, 168, 185, 216, 220, 231, 239, 257, 289, 290, 304, 332, 333, 344, 379, 390, 403, 406, 410, 412, 414, 433, 439, 447, 450, 464, 470, 512
PARKHURST, 21, 72, 129, 182, 339, 416, 470
PARKMAN, ... 80, 158, 346, 406
PARMENTER, ... 93, 127
PARRATT, ... 314, 389, 420
PARRISE, ... 258, 277
PARSLOW, ... 506
PARSONS, ... 55, 322, 365, 367, 471
PARTRIDGE, ... 108, 249, 282, 449
PATCH, ... 65, 375, 404
PATRICK, ... 258
PATTESHALL, ... 256
PATTEN, ... 18, 201, 340, 514
PATTERSON, ... 92, 341
PAUL, ... 76, 166, 203, 257, 366, 465, 510
PAULMORE, ... 366
PAYBODY, PEABODY, .. 12, 164, 173, 392
PAYSON, ... 454
PEACH, ... 45
PEACOCK, ... 246, 414
PEAKE, ... 176, 288, 472
PEARL, ... 237
PEARSON, ... 24, 33, 91, 224, 266, 289, 491
PEASE, ... 31, 252, 253, 350, 445, 487
PEASELEY, ... 33, 186
PEAVIE, ... 128
PECK, ... 13, 100, 161, 248, 304, 505
PEDDINGTON, ... 101
PIERCE, PEARCE, PEIRCE, 11, 28, 51, 68, 109, 110, 112, 114, 149, 177, 200, 202, 227, 260, 266, 273, 298, 304, 314, 320, 368, 382, 405, 445, 464, 484, 490, 513, 517
PIERPOINT, ... 221, 297, 438
PELHAM, PEELHAM, 44, 90, 119, 190, 213, 273, 351, 365
PELL, ... 225, 285, 392
PELLET, ... 130
PELTON, ... 186, 399
PEMBERTON, ... 102, 301
PEN, ... 41, 459
PENDLETON, ... 357, 489
PENMAN, ... 148
PENNIMAN, 49, 50, 300, 346, 388, 399, 497
PENNY, ... 381
PENTICUS, ... 249
PEPPER, ... 11
PERCYVALL, see PARCYFULL.
PERKINS, 41, 63, 68, 224, 400, 429, 459, 509
PERLY, ... 244
PERNE, ... 379
PERRY, 36, 53, 80, 115, 153, 175, 211, 335, 370, 394
PESTER, ... 34, 224, 363, 439
PETER, PETERS, 94, 164, 228, 262, 366, 410, 486
PETTINGILL, ... 252, 333

OTHER NAMES AND CROSS INDEX.

PETTIFORD, ... 29
PEYTON, ... 200
PHELPS, ... 11, 18, 188, 378, 409, 462
PHETY, ... 44
PHILBERT, ... 357
PHILBRICK, ... 176, 273
PHILLIPS, 18, 20, 51, 70, 142, 148, 159,
174, 223, 236, 242, 275, 300, 323, 338,
340, 344, 345, 387, 389, 397, 417, 430,
443, 469, 502, 518
PHILPOT, ... 247
PHIPPEN, ... 471
PHIPPS, ... 110
PICKERING, ... 12, 135, 170, 373
PICKARD, ... 290
PICKETT, ... 331
PICKMAN, ... 140, 259, 341
PICKWORTH, ... 155
PIDCOCK, ... 385
PIDGE, ... 78, 313, 511
PIKE, 110, 167, 191, 226, 303, 336, 348,
401, 407, 462
PILKINTON, ... 253
PILSBURY, ... 428
PIN, PINNEY, ... 366
PINDAR, ... 126
PINGREE, ... 104, 135
PINSON, ... 138, 386, 395, 398, 430
PITCHER, ... 126, 189, 362
PITNEY, ... 451
PITTS, ... 57, 113, 226, 255, 471
PLACE, PLASSE, ... 481, 485
PLATTS, ... 40, 254
PLIMPTON, ... 12, 61, 72, 150, 333, 396
PLUMER, ... 33, 48, 97
PODGER, POGGER, ... 478
POFFER, PUFFER, ... 159, 161, 328
POLLEY, ... 152, 253, 507
POLLARD, ... 231, 288, 365, 446
POMEROY, ... 288
POND, ... 148, 154, 221, 411
PONTUS, ... 99, 136, 188
POOLE, 13, 25, 37, 60, 67, 76, 112, 116,
136, 334, 342, 348, 393, 452
POOR, ... 81, 255, 340, 476
POPE, 28, 77, 137, 215, 240, 241, 258, 311,
314, 325, 418, 506
PORMORT, ... 202
PORTER, 12, 193, 220, 274, 380, 382, 412,
413, 415, 416, 418, 431, 448
POST, ... 41
POTTER, 27, 35, 75, 123, 145, 152, 165,
174, 184, 266, 274, 277, 351, 376, 426, 436
POWELL, 106, 136, 148, 181, 318, 497, 516

PRATT, 32, 74, 79, 104, 109, 147, 189,
276, 278, 389, 428, 441, 465, 480, 494, 499
POULTEN, ... 92, 153, 344
PRAY, ... 325
PRENCE, .. 67, 112, 150, 153, 392, 496, 502
PREBLE, ... 219
PRENAM, ... 238
PRENTICE, ... 186, 253, 259, 449, 482
PRESBURY, ... 91
PRESCOTT, ... 176, 223, 233, 381, 402, 490
PRESSIE, ... 139
PRESTON, ... 186, 238, 254, 279, 380
PRICE, 123, 261, 392, 417, 473, 482, 494, 505
PRICHARD, PRITCHET, 38, 55, 277,
295, 448, 451
PRIDEAUX, ... 504
PRIEST, ... 186, 374, 488
PRINCE, 35, 36, 63, 64, 213, 291, 376, 388, 416
PRIOR, ... 219, 347
PRISSE, ... 204
PROCTOR, ... 92, 215, 452
PROUT, .. 34, 134, 240, 403, 424, 444, 452
PROWER, ... 302
PULSIFER, ... 482
PUNCHARD, ... 481, 482
PURCHASE, ... 88, 148, 163, 335, 340, 355
PUTNAM, ... 89, 184, 249, 250
PUTNEY, ... 115
PYLDRIM, ... 146
PYNCHON, 45 77, 134, 180, 293, 308, 346,
377, 385, 407, 419, 432, 464, 481, 505
QUARLES, ... 423
QUICK, ... 115
QUILTER, ... 278, 390, 442
QUIMBY, ... 337
QUINNEY, ... 247
QUINSEY, ... 232, 233, 309, 339, 376, 479
RAGHTELLIAGH, ... 159
RAINHILL, ... 189
RAINSBOROW, ... 60, 121, 246, 284, 509
RAINSFORD, RANSFORD, .. 14, 183, 449
RAMSDEN, ... 91, 234, 355
RAND, ... 122, 278, 428, 438, 485
RANDALL, .. 13, 35, 36, 176, 269, 338, 345
RANDOLPH, ... 169
RANE, ... 389
RANGER, ... 178
RANKIN, ... 146
RASDELL, ... 168
RASER, ... 52
RASHLEY, ... 11
RASH, ... 134
RAWLINGS, 177, 201, 205, 266, 290, 306,
345, 346, 444

543

OTHER NAMES AND CROSS INDEX.

RAWSON, ... 362, 504
RAY, ... 136, 185, 292, 403, 482
RAYMOND, RAYMENT, ... 405
RAYNER, REINER, 24, 101, 208, 217, 233, 261, 277, 347, 426
READ, 10, 31, 72, 115, 131, 157, 177, 236, 258, 266, 356, 360, 366, 423, 440, 445, 457, 475, 508, 517
RECROFT, ... 126, 309, 478
REDFORD, ... 75, 308
REDDING, REDDEN, ... 270
REDDINGTON, ... 195
REDNAPE, ... 457, 513
REEVE, ... 86, 160, 487
REIFE, ... 234
REMINGTON, ... 27, 43, 193, 369, 438, 448
RESKEW, ... 324
REW, ... 475
REYNOLDS, ... 9, 62, 148, 234
RHODES, ROAD, ... 60, 109, 255, 392
RICE, ... 42, 44, 46, 47, 145, 317, 361, 447
RICHARD, RICHARDS, 33 37, 178, 246, 330, 346, 369, 448, 514
RICHARDSON, 29, 93, 177, 179, 222, 263, 275, 420
RICKARD, ... 100, 188, 270, 359, 502
RIDER, ... 36, 277, 293, 440
RIDDETT, ... 206
RIDDINGS, ... 353
RIDGWAY, ... 65
RIDLEY, ... 399
RIDWAY, ... 514
RIGBY, ... 166, 185
RIGGS, ... 315, 391
RILEY, ... 155
RING, ... 135, 240, 391, 399
RIPLEY, ... 148, 161, 279, 450
RISHWORTH, ... 281, 491
RIVERS, ... 412
RIX, ... 132
ROBIE, ... 118
ROBBINS, ... 121
ROBERTS, ROBESON, 27, 121, 285, 308, 338, 389, 415, 431, 450, 459
ROBINSON, 29, 40, 42, 56, 75, 84, 108, 141, 162, 172, 219, 237, 240, 304, 326, 413, 430, 444, 458, 462, 474, 510
ROCKE, ... 108, 388
ROCKETT, ... 48, 155, 389
ROCKWELL, ... 88, 184, 196, 307, 395
ROGERS, 15, 20, 32, 38, 53, 76, 99, 112, 125, 134, 149, 193, 206, 214, 216, 242, 271, 276, 339, 357, 371, 388, 394, 404, 435, 480, 491

ROCKWOOD, ... 389
RODWELL, ... 127
ROKESBY, ... 276
ROLFE, 58, 64, 119, 141, 174, 238, 399, 469, 495
ROOE, ... 290
ROOME, ... 329
ROOS, ... 386
ROOT, ... 21, 112, 394, 493
ROOTFLOWER, ... 164
ROPER, ... 129
ROSE, ... 390, 499
ROSS, ... 35, 180, 337
ROSSITER, ... 215
ROUSE, ... 270, 319, 348, 358, 431
ROW, ROE, ROWES, 139, 185, 214, 282, 375, 381, 382, 391, 427, 471
ROWELL, ... 34, 126, 319, 337, 401
ROSWELL, ... 396
ROWLAND, ... 420
ROWLANDSON, ... 267, 324, 404, 486
ROWLEY, ... 56, 178, 218, 219, 342
ROWNEING, ... 185
ROY, ... 359
ROYAL, ... 110, 456, 509
RUCK, ... 37, 221, 302, 373, 427, 428
RUDDOCK, ... 193
RUGG, RUGE, ... 372
RUGGLES, 69, 135, 138, 173, 186, 297, 358, 470, 512
RUMBALL, ... 188
RUSH, ... 362, 449
RUSS, ... 337
RUSSELL, 20, 27, 29, 96, 97, 113, 119, 127, 147, 184, 255, 368, 390, 441, 443, 449, 476, 480
RUST, ... 236, 374, 390, 479
RYEECE, ... 20, 210
SABINE, ... 14, 365
RUTTRIFF, ... 169
SADLER, ... 55, 80, 216, 280
SAFFIN, ... 73, 464, 499
SAFFORD, ... 293
SAFFORY, ... 303
SALE, ... 173
SALLOWES, ... 283, 515
SALLY, ... 227
SALMON, ... 135, 502
SALTER, ... 152, 203, 358
SALTONSTALL, 75, 86, 111, 139, 141, 165, 238, 260, 301, 445
SAMBO, ... 435
SAMS, ... 52
SAMSON, ... 33, 133, 324, 364, 454, 518

544

OTHER NAMES AND CROSS INDEX.

SANBORN, SAMBORNE, 26, 321, 339, 463
SANDERS, SAUNDERS, 67, 90, 149, 188, 211, 323, 339, 363, 369, 391, 398, 496
SANDERSON, ... 124
SANDIS, ... 194, 511
SANDS, ... 244
SANDY, ... 37, 67, 185
SANFORD, 67, 234, 358, 376, 404, 405, 413, 416, 419, 422, 467, 473, 483
SANGER, ... 191
SAPE, ... 335
SARGENT, 34, 92, 109, 126, 242, 246, 264, 354, 357, 409, 482
SAVAGE, 3, 4, 134, 193, 250, 264, 331, 405, 444, 467
  Henry, Haverhill, propr. 1644.
SAVORY, ... 83, 220, 284, 378
SAWYER, ... 121, 313, 351, 372, 406, 516
SAYER, ... 82, 374, 495
SAYES, ... 75
SAXTON, ... 276
SAYWELL, ... 85
SCADLOCK, ... 267
SCANT, ... 480
SCARBARROW, ... 423, 458
SCARLET, ... 45, 155
SCOBELL, ... 156
SCOLLARD, ... 51, 267
SCOLLAY, ... 35
SCOTT, 16, 59, 76, 172, 212, 237, 269, 325, 327, 423, 428, 442
SCOTTO, ... 469
SCRADDING, ... 76
SCUDDER, ... 292, 360, 405
SEABORNE, ... 248
SEALE, ... 186
SEALIS, SILLICE, 172, 211, 254, 505, 506
SEARL, ... 176, 186, 345, 467
SEARCH, ... 449
SEARS, ... 242, 249, 304, 449
SEAVER, ... 240, 406
SEDGWICK, .. 15, 248, 406, 463, 469, 510
SELLECK, ... 186, 289, 353
SENTER, ... 235
SEWALL, 59, 146, 165, 175, 387, 458, 473, 475, 483
SEVERANCE, ... 80, 129, 270, 319
SEVERN, ... 196
SHAFLIN, ... 271
SHAPLEIGH, ... 195, 468, 462
SHARPE, 21, 100, 176, 187, 241, 257, 388, 409, 415
SHATSWELL, ... 59, 119, 400, 466, 484
SHAW, 50, 53, 76, 86, 179, 238, 281, 313, 401, 426, 448

SHATTUCK, ... 122, 182, 368, 399
SHEAFE, ... 449, 483
SHEARE, ... 202
SHED, ... 92
SHELDON, ... 512
SHEFFIELD, ... 41, 356, 483, 512, 513
SHELLEY, 92, 108, 174, 181, 213, 284, 287, 353
SHEPARD, 149, 157, 208, 213, 262, 276, 281, 313, 319, 339, 467
SHEOPARDSON, ... 87
SHERBORNE, ... 249, 463
SHERMAN, 77, 123, 124, 141, 260, 276, 335, 340, 342, 366, 369, 388, 419, 427, 428, 437, 478, 488
SHERIN, ... 291
SHERRATT, ... 201
SHERWOOD, ... 79
SHIRLEY, ... 112, 508
SHIRTLEY, ... 284
SHOLY, ... 403
SHOOTER, ... 321
SHORE, ... 46, 115, 220, 492
SHORT, ... 11, 146, 290, 323, 344, 451
SHORTHOSE, ... 418
SHOVE, ... 328, 349
SHRIMPTON, ... 145, 164, 398, 414
SHROPSHIRE, ... 391
SHURT, ... 181, 274
SHUTT, ... 471
SIBLEY, ... 88, 97, 105, 190, 359, 489
SILL, ... 43
SILPIN, ... 234
SILSBY, ... 37
SILVER, ... 188
SIMKINS, ... 153, 348
SIMMONS, 36, 62, 76, 85, 223, 369, 474, 484
SIMS, ... 171
SIMSON, SIMPSON, 74, 76, 101, 254, 263, 345, 452
SINGLETARY, ... 115
SINDERLAND, see SUNDERLAND.
SIRKMAN, ... 179
SISSON, ... 219
SKATHE, ... 311, 319, 320
SKELTON, ... 43, 69, 194, 304, 498
SKERRY, ... 25, 459
SKETTON, ... 406
SKIFFE, ... 198, 485
SKIPPE, ... 251
SKINNER, 31, 60, 139, 174, 195, 308, 310, 402
SLAMPE, ... 113
SMALL, ... 86, 88
SMEAD, ... 368, 418, 437

OTHER NAMES AND CROSS INDEX.

SMEADLEY, ... 396, 414
SMITH, 26, 29, 44, 49, 51, 53, 60, 61, 64,
  75, 77, 82, 95, 97, 108, 110, 114, 116,
  120, 122, 129, 140, 151, 152, 154, 160,
  177, 180, 181, 191, 196, 203, 231, 240,
  243, 244, 248, 255, 257, 265, 267, 268,
  273, 275, 280, 281, 293, 300, 305, 307,
  308, 318, 319, 320, 327, 330, 332, 336,
  338, 341, 343, 344, 347, 367, 369, 381,
  384, 398, 399, 403, 404, 417, 442, 453,
  456, 458, 493, 496, 500, 501, 506, 509, 514
SNELL, ... 214, 420
SNELLING, ... 186, 226, 404
SNOW, ... 32, 240, 372, 480
SOLACE, see SALLOWES.
SOLART, ... 513
SOULSBY, ... 80
SOMERBY, ... 199, 312
SONE, ... 435
SOPER, ... 12
SOULE, ... 507
SOUTER, ... 380
SOUTHCOATE, ... 13
SOUTHER, ... 160, 210
SOUTHMEADE, ... 21
SOUTHRICKE, ... 481
SOUTHWICK, ... 62, 81, 147, 404
SOUTHWORTH, ... 64, 112, 197
SPALDING, ... 30, 162, 257, 325
SPARHAWK, 66, 77, 96, 117, 149, 163,
  277, 297, 345, 390, 477
SPARKS, ... 391, 407
SPARROW, ... 31, 495
SPAULE, ... 77, 123, 182, 413
SPEAR, ... 136, 225
SPENCER, ... 30, 137, 189, 462
SPICER, ... 256
SPITTY, ... 258
SPOFARD, ... 404
SPOONER, ... 20, 116, 125, 371
SPOOR, ... 501
SPOWELL, see SPAULE.
SPRAGUE, 15, 18, 36, 49, 89, 97, 114,
  190, 220, 280, 329, 439, 463, 474
SPRING, ... 35, 128, 219
SPRINGFIELD, ... 298, 310
SPROUT, ... 398
SPUR, ... 443, 465, 501
SPURKS, ... 339
ST. JOHN, ... 78, 494
STACY, ... 445, 515
STAGGE, ... 424
STALHAM, ... 465
STANBURY, ... 474

STANDERWICK, ... 332, 366
STANDISH, ... 12, 15, 249, 501, 507
STANDLAKE, ... 35
STANFORD, ... 432
STANLEY, ... 40, 291, 358, 362, 453
STANTON, ... 309, 322, 420
STANYON, STANIAN, ... 63, 261, 505
STAPLES, ... 378, 420
STARBUCK, ... 107
STARKWEATHER, ... 362
STARR, ... 189, 296, 308, 319, 392, 486
STEADMAN, ... 47, 151, 189, 210, 382
STEBBINS, 30, 102, 311, 323, 346, 397, 517
STEPHENS, 33, 48, 70, 77, 95, 107, 113,
  133, 172, 189, 346, 304, 456, 498
STEPHENSON, ... 53, 375, 415
STERLING, ... 54
STERNE, STEARNS, etc., 49, 92, 176,
  186, 240, 316
STETSON, ... 221, 226, 246, 307, 377, 493
STEWART, ... 38, 210, 373
STICKNEY, ... 196, 283, 320, 331
STILEMAN, ... 388
STILES, ... 292, 321
STIMSON, ... 440
STOCKBRIDGE, ... 226
STOCK, ... 326
STOCKER, ... 73
STODDARD, 88, 187, 264, 293, 340, 479, 486
STOKES, ... 71
STONE, 13, 17, 42, 49, 117, 122, 140, 141,
  159, 239, 242, 262, 277, 295, 359, 364,
  389, 408, 434, 507
STONHARD, ... 352
STORER, ... 247
STORRE, ... 491
STORY, ... 119, 135, 140, 173, 187, 366, 507
STOUGHTON, 63, 68, 92, 103, 125, 131,
  277, 316, 325, 377, 418, 440, 491
STOW, ... 49, 52, 116, 172, 313
STOWELL, ... 161, 187
STOWER, STOWERS, 54, 81, 246, 257, 300
STRANGE, ... 126, 256, 298
STRAIGHT, ... 269, 464
STRATTON, 56, 171, 338, 351, 452, 460, 489
STREAM, ... 337
STREET, ... 286, 464
STREETER, ... 95, 240, 322, 388
STRIKER, ... 482
STRONG, ... 48, 100, 172, 479, 500
STROUD, ... 210
STUBBS, ... 45, 359
STUDLEY, ... 128
STURGES, ... 226

546

OTHER NAMES AND CROSS INDEX.

SUCKLIN, ... 255
SUGTHWICK, ... 27
SUMNER, SUMMERS, 155, 264, 344, 380, 395, 398, 431, 443, 483
SUMPNER, ... 260
SUNDERLAND, ... 295, 306, 471
SUTTON, ... 52, 60, 141, 219, 242, 369, 454
SWADDEN, ... 407
SWAIN, ... 86, 122
SWAN, ... 9, 52, 209, 240, 394, 463
SWANTON, ... 226
SWEAT, SWEET, 39, 69, 186, 312, 392, 489
SWEETSER, ... 174, 358
SWIFT, ...22, 53, 91, 200, 347, 430, 468, 493
SWINNERTON, ... 445
SYLVESTER, ... 238, 366, 421, 426
SYMMES, 121, 125, 134, 216, 217, 297, 331, 401, 469
SYMONDS, 42, 65, 67, 86, 94, 109, 115, 157, 179, 208, 344, 356, 471, 472, 515
TABOR, ... 305
TAINTON, ... 253
TAINTOR, ... 204, 340
TALBIE, ... 364
TALBOT, ... 18, 417
TALL, ... 340
TALMADGE, ... 475
TAPPON, see TOPPAN.
TARBELL, ... 278
TARBOX, ... 20, 220, 443
TARNE, ... 57, 335, 383, 492
TART, ... 454, 501
TAUKE, ... 232
TAY, ... 455, 518
TAYLOR, 67, 142, 200, 214, 276, 328, 339, 373, 383, 389, 392, 403, 437, 446, 447, 480, 489, 493, 503
TEAD, ... 179, 199, 266, 270
TEFFE, TIFT, ... 14
TEMPLAR, ... 373
TEMPLE, ... 276, 475
TENNER, ... 208
TENCH, ... 88
TENNEY, ... 225, 284, 314, 389
TERREY, ... 116, 162, 192, 318
TEWXBERY, ... 118, 217
THACHER, THATCHER, 12, 192, 229, 262, 314, 328, 347, 395, 401, 406, 410, 448, 462, 469, 477, 483
THACKSON, ... 54
THAXTER, ... 99, 148, 255, 286, 386
THAYER, TARE, 224, 325, 344, 350, 371, 374, 459, 470
THOMAS, 94, 125, 254, 255, 272, 279, 307, 363, 452, 487, 499

THICKSTON, ... 249
THOMPSON, see TOMPSON, 54, 114, 123, 168, 181 ,206, 308, 322, 325, 346, 387, 388, 452 461, 493, 494, 497
THORN, ... 156, 227
THORNDIKE, ... 10, 439
THORNTON, ... 86, 312
THORP, ... 32, 78, 214, 314, 360, 481, 488
THREADNEEDLE, ... 222
TRESHER, ... 71, 124
THORLA, THURLOW, ... 320
THRUMBLE, ... 255
THURSTON, 184, 281, 291, 358, 430, 450, 475, 511
THURTON, ... 178
THWING, ... 94, 96
TIBBETTS, ... 55, 212, 218
TICKNOR, ... 226, 435
TIDGE, ... 347
TILDEN, 60, 101, 219, 220, 257, 278, 372, 441, 447, 466
TILER, see TYLER.
TILESTON, ... 50, 68
TILL, ... 282
TILLIE, ... 117, 204, 229, 244, 311, 398
TILLY alias HILLIER, ... 246
TILSON, ... 122, 385
TILLISON, ... 23
TILTON, ... 238
TINDALL, ... 508
TINGLE, TINGLEY, ... 35, 87
TINKER, ... 34, 104
TINWELL, ... 10
TISDALE, ... 24
TITCOMB, ... 48, 119, 434
TITUS, ... 39, 89
TOBEY, ... 398
TOKER, ... 270
TOLLIOT, ... 352
TOLMAN, ... 261
TOMLIN, TOMLINS, ... 502
TOMPKINS, ... 173, 447
TOMPSON, 50, 63, 124, 193, 256, 275, 279, 305, 322, 328, 411. 510
TOPPAN, ...38, 191, 192, 294, 513
TOOGOOD, ... 164
TOOTHAKER, ... 230
TOPPER, ... 154
TORREY, .. 51, 148, 177, 219, 403, 423, 493
TOSIER, ... 56
TOTMAN, ... 345
TOUTERVILLE, ... 412
TOWER, ... 88, 251, 479
TOWLE, TOLL, ... 72
TOWN, ... 76, 164

OTHER NAMES AND CROSS INDEX.

TOWNING, ... 460
TOWNSEND, 11, 44, 57, 133, 143, 168, 289, 327, 350, 353, 494
TOY, ... 327
TRACEY, ... 342, 372, 373
TRAIN, ... 434, 440
TRASK, 5, 131, 157, 180, 215, 386, 426, 489
TRAVERS, TRAVIS, ... 168, 416, 476, 506
TREADWAY, ... 242, 307, 453
TREADWELL, ... 504
TRESCOTT, ... 148, 461
TREWORGY, TRUEWORTHY, .. 276, 408
TRERICE, ... 181, 289, 296, 297, 299
TROTT, ... 111
TROWBRIDGE, ... 22, 146, 254
TRUE, ... 63, 495
TRUESDALE, ... 243, 254, 315, 377, 383
TRUMBULL, ... 17, 240, 415, 442
TRUSSELL, ... 386,
TUCK, ... 329, 357, 463, 503
TUCKER, 187, 203, 261, 275, 332, 349, 362, 433, 456
TUDER, ... 235
TUESLEY, ... 184
TUFTS, ... 68, 464
TUMBERS, ... 267
TUPPER, ... 334
TURBIFIELD, ... 374
TURIN,, etc., ... 56, 109
TURLAND, ... 182
TURNER, 17, 47, 92, 133, 143, 166, 226, 246, 257, 279, 282, 289, 301, 308, 319, 345, 348, 371, 378, 384, 400, 496, 506, 508, 510
TURRELL, ... 132
TUTTELL, 81, 186, 193, 199, 238, 280, 336, 342, 409, 473
TWELVES, ... 62
TWINING, ... 115
TWISDEN, ... 127
TWITCHELL, ... 386
TYBBOTT, see TIBBOT.
TYDD, see TEAD.
TYLER, ... 53, 293, 365, 369
TYNG, ... 121, 174, 280, 380, 469
TYTHERLY, ... 323
UNDERHILL, ... 232, 320
UNDERWOOD, ... 91, 157, 168
UPHAM, ... 236, 303, 431, 484
UPSALL, ... 200, 442, 443
UPSON, ... 516
USLEBY, ... 159
USHER, 13, 134, 233, 242, 397, 399, 423, 430, 444

VALE, ... 221, 514
VAN der VELDE, ... 455
VANE, ... 65, 73, 120, 242, 505
VARNEY, ... 212, 375
VASSELL, ... 71, 479
VEAZIE, ... 176, 480
VEREN, ... 20, 113, 204, 373, 509
VERMASE, see FERMAES.
VICARS, ... 358
VICKARY, ... 246
VINAL, ... 28
VINCENT, ... 86, 128, 158, 338, 374
VINES, ... 214
VINING, ... 380
VOLT, ... 382
VORE, ... 346
VOSE, ... 27, 517
WADDELL, WODDELL, WARDWELL, ... 315, 386, 446, 472, 515
WADE, WAD, 65, 209, 226, 257, 295, 339, 486
WADLAND, ... 55
WADSWORTH, ... 431, 446
WAGGETT, ... 493
WAINWRIGHT, ... 51, 332
WAIT, 127, 191, 294, 405, 445, 464, 497, 514
WAKELEY, ... 107
WAKELIN, ... 366
WALDEN, ... 418
WALDO, ... 108, 351
WALDRON, ... 503
WALES, ... 22, 50, 133, 200, 466
WALKER, 71, 72, 112, 125, 141, 152, 175, 184, 232, 243, 279, 281, 313, 344, 345, 358, 405, 445, 446, 453, 518
WALLEN, ... 493
WALLEY, ... 414, 506
WALLIDGE, ... 316
WALLINGTON, see WELLINGTON.
WALLIS, ... 64, 252
WALSBY, ... 299
WALTER, ... 298, 482
WALTHAM, ... 117, 122, 315, 384, 397
WALTON, ... 307
WANDLEY, ... 422
WAMPOS, ... 175
WARD, 42, 102, 104, 110, 139, 161, 170, 173, 192, 214, 239, 243, 253, 264, 268, 289, 308, 332, 381, 491, 492
WARE, ... 184, 186, 248, 418, 442, 470
WARFIELD, ... 378, 411
WARHAM, ... 5, 11, 184, 307, 326, 388, 516
WARNER, ... 62, 72, 437, 487
WARREN, 35, 36, 48, 99, 258, 288, 374, 407, 425, 428, 491, 497, 501, 518

548

OTHER NAMES AND CROSS INDEX.

WARRENER, ... 316, 442
WARWICK, ... 53
WASHBURN, ... 68, 338
WATERMAN, ... 60, 225, 279, 286, 440
WATERS, 5, 12, 93, 216, 287, 349, 364, 457, 487, 500
WATHEN, ... 231, 303
WATKINS, ... 27, 373
WATSON, 32, 53, 72, 92, 158, 192, 232, 272, 433
WATTS, ... 159, 276, 369, 476
WAY, .. 82, 203, 263, 307, 387, 441, 459, 498
WEBB, 23, 28, 93, 114, 159, 172, 238, 273, 404, 410, 449, 459, 488, 511
WEBSTER, ... 25, 39, 156, 190, 409
WEDGEWOOD, ... 281
WEED, ... 507
WEEDEN, ... 110, 375
WEEKS, WICKS, 219, 247, 262, 297, 364, 461, 479
WEIGHTMAN, WIGHTMAN, ... 500
WELCH, ... 103, 443
WELD, 52, 60, 137, 138, 228, 250, 260, 436, 494
WELLINGTON, ... 58, 193, 341, 432, 438
WELLMAN, ... 108
WELLS, ... 111, 191, 246, 386, 393, 437, 462
WELSTEAD, ... 91
WEN, ... 505
WARDEN, see WORDEN.
WESSON, ... 168
WEST, ... 44, 309, 399, 400, 441, 482
WESTBROOK, ... 223, 474
WESTGATE, ... 5, 241
WESTON, 37, 88, 214, 243, 317, 318, 350, 351, 382, 399
WETHERELL, 51, 127, 172, 335, 362, 435
WHALE, ... 87, 317
WHALLEY, ... 313
WHARTON, ... 467
WHEATLEY, ... 306, 346, 450
WHEATON, ... 17, 374
WHEELDON, ... 235, 448
WHEELER, 16, 42, 71, 84, 86, 91, 116, 179, 223, 311, 360, 450, 511
WHEELOCK, ... 31, 78, 176, 436
WHEELWRIGHT, 158, 202, 241, 249, 250, 281, 324, 479
WHETSTONE, ... 257
WHITE, 14, 28, 29, 37, 45, 48, 61, 81, 90, 107, 119, 128, 140, 148, 175, 176, 234, 248, 249, 291, 316, 330, 335, 375, 389, 443, 447, 449, 451, 470, 472, 491, 507, 514

WHIPPLE, ... 326, 379, 459
WHITAKER, see also WHITTIER, 417, 492
WHITCOMB, ... 72, 125, 155, 188, 481
WHITTLE, ... 391, 495
WHITEHEAD, ... 12
WHITEMORE, ... 85, 95
WHITEWAY, ... 88
WHITFIELD, ... 391
WHITING, 12, 33, 50, 92, 97, 106, 112, 148, 285, 299, 392, 413
WHITLOCK, ... 343
WHITMAN, ... 29, 86
WHITMORE, ... 161, 181, 497
WHITNEY, 109, 220, 234, 262, 383, 422, 446
WHITON, ... 41, 212, 318, 363
WHITRIDGE, ... 109, 315
WHITTIER, ... 391, 433, 492
WHITTINGHAM, ... 19, 59, 121, 153
WICKAM, ... 72, 224, 420
WICKSON, ... 226
WIGEER, ... 306
WIGGIN, WIGGINS, 65, 71, 245, 284, 516
WIGHT, ... 97, 109, 191, 354, 481
WIGGLESWORTH, ... 65, 379
WIGNALL, ... 368
WILBOARE, ... 282
WILBORN, ... 41, 42
WILCOCKS, ... 117
WILCOM, ... 472
WILDER, ... 141, 157, 310, 402, 495
WILDING, ... 214
WILEY, ... 449
WILKES, ... 336
WILKINS, ... 179, 188, 329
WILKINSON, ... 77, 190
WILLARD, 23, 56, 65, 147, 170, 237, 261, 311, 325, 412, 431, 467, 492
WILLETT, 64, 73, 193, 246, 248, 338, 397, 415
WILLINGTON, see WELLINGTON.
WILLIAMS, 53, 55, 58, 62, 67, 76, 109, 121, 186, 208, 233, 245, 248, 274, 291, 297, 332, 343, 356, 373, 404, 417, 447, 471, 477, 478, 481, 514
WILLIAMSON, ... 186, 243
WILLIS, WILLICE, 16, 64, 134, 153, 188, 229, 237, 286, 298, 341, 342, 349, 418, 444, 459
WILLISTON, ... 347
WILLIX, ... 129, 222
WILSON, 33, 45, 50, 54, 66, 77, 80, 101, 107, 122, 154, 179, 207, 227, 253, 262, 263, 265, 275, 289, 291, 313, 337, 340, 379, 389, 397, 402, 404, 420, 430, 434, 442, 447, 472, 503

OTHER NAMES AND CROSS INDEX.

WILLS, ... 25, 57, 86, 94, 360
WILLOUGHBY, ... 59
WILMOT, ... 418
WINBOURNE, ... 215
WINCALL, ... 140
WINCH, ... 158, 432
WINCHESTER, ... 328, 405
WINCHCORN, ... 214
WINDITT, ... 489
WINDOWE, WINDORR, ... 461, 476
WINDSOR, ... 156, 157, 252
WINES, ... 45, 173, 463
WING, .. 26, 41, 105, 132, 219, 407, 428, 443
WINN, ... 365
WINSHIP, ... 35, 190, 214, 343, 498, 509
WINSLEY, ... 191, 198, 263, 303, 331, 484
WINSLOW, 10, 21, 60, 93, 98, 119, 125,
 144, 181, 197, 202, 263, 317, 323, 331,
 352, 359, 372, 425, 437, 456, 460, 469,
 475, 487, 493
WINTER, ... 100, 127
WINTERTON, ... 411
WINTHROP, 4, 5, 46, 53, 73, 75, 89, 101,
 106, 108, 116, 121, 125, 144, 145, 157,
 163, 166, 167, 176, 180, 181, 182, 184,
 185, 197, 207, 245, 246, 256, 270, 323,
 335, 340, 343, 350, 356, 365, 376, 377,
 379, 382, 388, 398, 407, 409, 416, 417,
 189, 428, 436, 445, 469, 475, 501, 504, 517
WINTON, ... 230
WISE, ... 12, 197, 346, 383
WISEMAN, ... 39, 123
WISEWALL, 29, 253, 254, 277, 279, 349, 381
WISTON, ... 71
WITCHFIELD, ... 96, 190, 507
WITHAM, ... 326, 425
WITHERBY, ... 243
WITHERIDGE, ... 215
WITHERLEY, ... 57, 162, 327, 388
WITHINGTON, ... 28, 154, 186, 340, 348
WITT, ... 34
WOLCOTT, ... 119, 252, 291, 326, 334
WOLF, ... 397
WOLLASTON, ... 321
WOODBERY, ... 128, 141, 347

WOOD, see ATWOOD, 49, 106, 130, 146,
 152, 168, 170, 213, 224, 247, 258, 261,
 290, 301, 305, 322, 332, 338, 346, 360,
 387, 451, 490, 493
WOODBRIDGE, ... 145, 146, 345
WOODCOCK, ... 68, 71, 116, 131, 223
WOODFALL, ... 335
WOODFIELD, ... 159
WOODFORD, ... 56
WOODHAM, ... 326
WOODIE, ... 43, 108, 159, 368, 388, 410
WOODMAN, ... 70, 192, 308, 353, 433
WOODMANSEY, ... 89
WOODROW, ... 88, 476
WOODWARD, 41, 42, 124, 183, 202, 210,
 368, 421, 440, 513
WOOLLY, ... 201
WOOLRIDGE, ... 268
WOOLSON, ... 190
WOOLSTONE, ... 251
WOORY, ... 322
WOOTON, ... 355
WORCESTER, WOOSTER, 86, 208, 430, 515
WORDEN, ... 236, 440, 455
WORMWOOD, ... 43, 449
WORTH, ... 297
WORNAM, see WORMWOOD.
WORSELEY, ... 305
WORTHINGTON, ... 61
WREN, ... 376
WRIGHT, 25, 54, 102, 113, 117, 142, 178,
 227, 302, 317, 326, 468
WYAT, ... 32, 225, 480
WYBORNE, ... 65, 163, 311
WYETH, ... 18, 174, 199
WYMAN, ... 134, 179, 333, 360, 440, 448
YEALE, ... 177
YATES, ... 229
YEARWOOD, ... 216
YEO, ... 358, 370
YEOMANS, ... 85, 264
YOUNG, 109, 185, 187, 244, 332, 347, 362,
 427, 496
YOUNGLOVE, ... 205

INDEX TO PLACES OUTSIDE OF THE STATE.

[The references to A, B, C, etc., are to divisions of the Additions and Corrections; A extends to Brasier, B to Cook, C to Eliot, D to Lyon, E to Rix, F to Shaw, G to Veazie, H to Yeomans.]

Abbotsason, . . . 376	Bishopstocke, . 24, 146	Cape Porpoise, Porpus,	Dinder, ... 262
Abbotsham, . . . 323	Bishops Stortford, 129,	258, 316, F.	Dorchester, 76, 88, 172,
Abutley, ... 22	137	Carrick Fergus, . 469	182, 334, 389
Acadia, ... 292	Biteswell, ... 139	Casco Bay, 110, 163, 393,	Dover, 6, 25, 231, 304,307,
Agamenticus, Accomen-	Blaby (home of Chester),	474, F.	320, 324, 337, 366, 371,
ticus, 239, 321, 390, 457	97	Castle Bromwich, . 516	379, 398, 454
Agmondsham, . . 248	Black Point, . . . 476	Caston, ... 187	Downe, ... 481
Alderman Bury, 125, 293	Blackwall, . . . 122	Cavendish, . . . 201	Downs, The, . . 197
Aldredge, ... 516	Block Island, 333, 335,	Caversham, . . . 397	Downton, . . 126, 399
Alford, 166, 176, 249, 250	499	Chaddlewood, . . 424	Droitwich, . . . 507
Amesbury, . . 89, 208	Blyborough, . . . 380	Chalfont St. Giles, . 395	Dublin, 27, 293, 422, 514
Anckstrey, . . . 483	Boddington, . . . 448	Channington, . . 61	Duffil, ... 351
Andover, . 333, 512, F.	Boram, Boreham, 68, 202,	Chatham, . . . 246	Dunhead, ... 191
Appley, ... 82	211	Chatsum, ... 507	Dunnington, . . . 505
Aquidneck, 143, 413, 485	Borsconge, . . . 430	Chelmsford, . . . 239	Dunstable, 290, 296, 444
Arnold, ... 489	Boston, 6, 19, 59, 67, 82,	Chester, ... 22	Dunstall, ... 265
Ashford, . . 88, 431	107, 119, 120, 241, 284,	Chesthunt, . . . 319	Durand, ... 189
Ashmore, ... 267	285, 494, 514	Chew Magna, . . 110	Earls' Coln, . .213, 411
Ashton Clinton, . . 66	Bow, . . . 69, 214	Chichester, . . . 417	Easthampton, 255, 256
Assington, . 225, 390	Boxford. 402	Chicknell, ... 146	East Mersey, . . 478
Attlebury, . . . 441	Boxstead, ... 242	Chidcocke, . . . F.	Eastward, 259, 291, 304,
Austerfield, . . . 63	Braddenham, . . . 34	Childesmone, . . . E.	316, 376
Axmouth, ... 367	Brauktry, ... 301	Chittington, . . . 93	Eastwell, ... 84
Aylesford, . . . 224	Bramton, . 117, 138, 269	Cholderton, . . . 332	Eaton Bray, . . . 241
Badgden, ... 170	Brenzet, ... G.	Cincenshier, . . . 212	Eckton, ... 256
Baddow, 73, 136, 215, 276	Braunton, ... 15	Clapton, ... 429	Edinburgh, . . . 112
Badlam, ... E.	Bray, . . . 131, 220	Claton, ... 515	Egerton, ... 292
Bahama, ... 279	Bredport, ... 237	Claybrooke, . . . 229	Ell-Tisley, . . . 137
Ballsbery, . . . A, G.	Brencsley, ... 270	Claxton, ... D.	Elsing, ... 263
Banbury, ... 430	Brentwood, . . . 109	Clement's Inn, . . 282	England, 6, 10, 13, 23, 24,
Bannestock, . . . 323	Bridgend, ... 158	Clifford's Inn, . . 321	27, 40, 41, 43, 44, 46, 47,
Barbadoes, 17, 42, 46, 82,	Bridgham, ... 450	Clisdon, ... 252	49, 51, 53, 60, 62, 63, 69,
101, 113, 134, 183, 211,	Bridhemson, . . . 184	Coggeshall, . . . 329	73, 78, 80-2, 90, 93, 95,
263, 302, 317, 324, 341,	Bridport, 48, 130, 147, 165	Colby, ... 14	98, 101, 103, 106, 107,
342, 349, 375, 405, 467,	Brinspittal, . . . 98	Colchester, 111, 258, 428,	109, 111, 113, 115, 116,
469, 470, 504, D.	Bristol, 20, 55, 79, 111,	E.	125, 131, 137, 139, 141,
Barford, ... 512	138, 142, 162, 231, 239,	Cold Norton, . . G.	142, 148, 168, 169, 177,
Barkham, ... B.	266, 274, 275, 305, 307,	Colliton (Colyton), 328	189, 190, 193-6, 204,
Barnstable, Barnstaple,	313, 335, 368, 396, 420,	Combe St. Nicholas, 177,	206, 210, 218, 219, 221,
15, 148, 171, 306, 452	421, 458, 475, 486, F.	458	222, 227, 223, 233, 236,
Barnestone, . . . 135	Brixham, ... 107	Comberton, . . . 295	237, 238, 240, 243, 245,
Barringham, . . . 439	Broadway, 234, 332, 366	Connecticut, 15, 131, 156,	246, 249, 257, 261, 263,
Barrow, ... 273	Bromfield, ... 471	165, 181, 296, 389	265, 267, 271, 274, 275,
Barrow Upton, . . 39	Bromley, ... 93	Cork, ... 6	279, 282, 287, 288, 292,
Barwick, ... 237	Broughton, . . . 506	Cotherstock, . . . 111	293-9, 300, 303, 310,311,
Basing, ... 177	Buckintun, . . . 12	Cousingstone, . . 486	313, 316, 317, 321, 323,
Barkhamstead, . . C.	Budleigh, ... 113	Coventry, 27, 59, 125, 131,	325, 326, 330, 332, 335,
Batly, ... F.	Buers St. Mary, . 273	407, B.	339, 348-350, 356, 357,
Batcome, Badcombe, 10,	Burchen Lane, . . 254	Cowes, ... 508	358, 365, 371, 372, 375,
33, 350, 380, 445	Burdport, Bridport, 165	Craft, ... 491	376, 377, 384, 386, 388,
Beaconsfield. . 248, 270	Bures Isle, . . . 278	Cranbrook, 49, 151, 172,	392, 396, 398, 403, 407,
Beauworthy, . . E.	Burford, ... 441	438, 492	409, 410, 411, 414, 423,
Beckingshall, . . 81	Burnley, ... 161	Crawston, ... 430	438, 442, 452, 455, 460,
Bedfordshire, 223, 252	Burrough Green, . 324	Crewkerne, . . . 37	469, 470, 474, 478, 480,
Bednal Green, . . 414	Burvild, [Burghfield?]	Cropston, ... 414	482, 486, 489, 490, 493,
Belcham, ... 365	423	Croyden, ... 178	494, 497, 500, 501, 503,
Belleaw, ... 491	Bury, ... 305	Culliton, ... 113	509, 516, 517, D.
Benecar Hall, . . 98	Bury St. Edmunds, 23, 72,	Cumley, ... G.	Epperston, . . . 334
Rerkhamstead, . . 129	94, 327, 418, 502	Danes Halle, . . . 207	Erby, ... 276
Bermondsey, . . . 59	Calcot, ... G.	Darkin. 82	Erlescolne (see Earl's C).
Bermuda, 258, 353, 361	Cambridge, 14, 78, 119,	Dartmouth, . . . 89	Essex, ... 206
Bewers Hamlet (Buers),	131, 157, 163, 216, 221,	Dedham, 19, 33, 100. 112,	Essington, . . . 500
351	229, 239, 356, 357, 389,	171,339,412,413,427,506	Esstum, ... 111
Bicester, ... 441	390, 412, 417, 444, 488,	Delaware, . . . 22	Ewill, ... 242
Biddeford, Bythefoard,	490, 491, 494	Delft, ... 463	Exeter, 38, 57, 90, 108,
19, 87, 323	Canada, ... 81	Deptford, Dertford, 101.	146, 154, 166, 171, 187,
Billerica, . 302, 395	Cannons Ashby, . 430	356	199, 202, 261, 263, 299,
Bilsby, ... 491	Canterbury, 6, 26,127,165,	Derby, ... 119	307, 320, 321, 358, 378,
Birmingham, . 350, 353	208, 259, 432, 444, G.	Devises, . . . 39, 48	380, 430, 441, 479, 491,
Birtsmorton, . . B.	Cape Fear, . . 132, 143	Devon, ... 307	505, B, C, F.

PLACE INDEX.

Falmouth, . . 163, 323
Farmington, 21, 45, 285
Faversham, 68, 87, 397
Fayall, ... 181
Fenchurch, . . . 62
Filton, ... 280
Flotam, ... 68
Flushing, . . 26, 506
Fordington, . . . 428
Fowy, ... 356
Framlingham, 106, 130
France, ... 469
Freston, ... 285
Frisby, ... 278
Frittenden, . . 47, 75
Fulham Palace, . . 63
Galway, ... 222
Gamscolne, . . . 216
Geneva, ... 469
Gildersome, . 379, E.
Gillingham, . . . 379
Glaston, . . 335, 514
Gloucester, 170, 206, 232, 233
Goldington, . . . 78
Gonsham, 46, 433, 434
Gorgeana, . . 28, 225
Gorlstone, ... 463
Gravesend, . 197, 316
Great Baddow, 338, 472
Great Bowden, . . 319
Great Chart, . . . 391
Great Coggeshall, . 390
Great Comberton, . 451
Great Dunmow, . E.
Great Misenden, . 277
Great Ormesby, . 342
Great Yarmouth, 139, 283, 293, 325, 417, 460, 501, 518
Great Yeldham, . 115
Grey's Inn, . . . 258
Groton, . . 144, 508
Guilford, ... 392
Guilsburgh, . . . 43
Guinea, . 185, 268, 420
Hackney, ... 136
Haddam, . . 14, 16
Ha..en Hall, . . . 420
Hadley, . . 199, 282
Hadloe, ... 311
Hague, ... 430
Halifax, 23, 160, 313, 410, 504
Halstead, . 238, 239, 343
Ham, ... 197
Hammersmith, . . 182
Hampstead, . . 18, C.
Hampsworth, . . . 19
Hampton, 17, 25, 26, 57, 73, 84, 95, 101, 105, 107, 111, 121-4, 129, 143, 158, 165, 178, 179, 183, 190, 198, 199, 208, 226, 229, 243, 249, 302, 321, 322, 324, 333, 339, 342, 354, 357, 382, 399, 400, 403, 405, 417, 421, 430, 441, 463, 473, 491, C, F, G.
Hampton Court, . 382
Hanbury, ... 506
Harliston, ... 241
Hartford, 13, 20, 52, 77, 84, 107, 113, 125, 142, 192, 207, 231, 239, 247,

265, 285, 346, 407, 431, 437, 474, 480, 492, 512
Hartfordshire, . . 95
Harwich, 43, 121, 180, 332, C.
Hasted, ... 473
Haverhill, . . 390, 447
Heddon, . 208, 411. 502
Henborough, . . 208
Heron (Herrn) Hill, 14, 259
Hertford, ... 196
Hetcorne, . . 47, 75
Hinderclay, . . . 90
Hingham, 39, 41, 76, 99, 116, 117, 126. 161, 171, 185, 255, 286, 313, 318, 351, 363, 417, 464
Hobling, ... 64
Holden, ... 65
Holland, . . 31, 56, 131
Hooke Norton, . . 495
Horncastle, . . . 176
Horninger, . . . 81
Horningerth, . . 327
Horrell, ... 337
Horsemonden, . . 498
Hoxton, ... 367
Hull, ... 326
Hundon, ... 185
Huntington, . . . 18
Huntwick, . . . 398
Ipswich, 144, 173, 348, 438
Ireland, 12, 26, 33, 115, 281, 296, 411, 466
Islington, ... 208
Jamaica, . 186, 406, 433
Kennebeck, 14, 16, 64, 86, 111, 117, 338, 383, 401, 448, 499
Kennebunk. . . . F.
Kennebunkport, see Cape Porpoise, . . . 353
Kenninghall, . 132, E.
Kent, . 98, 193, 436, 498
Kenton, ... 362
Kersy, ... 403
Kikatat, ... 84
Kingscleare, . 162, D.
Kingslynne, . . 203
Kingston, ... 52
Kingsweare, . . . 408
Kinweston. . . . G.
Kirkby, ... 450
Kittery, . 371, 457, B, D.
Koningberg, . . . 112
Lancashire, . . . 457
Landen, ... 201
Lanford, Langford, 149, 208, 323, 399
Langenith, ... 60
Langham, ... 491
Lanham, ... 340
Lavenham, . 210, 335
Lawford, ... 353
Lee, ... 248
Leeds, ... 62
Leicester, ... 305
Leighton, ... 268
Lemington Priors, . 12
Leverton, ... 494
Lewes, ... 184
Leyden, 6, 8, 16, 37, 56, 63, 67, 73, 90, 127, 136, 178, 189, 258, 305, 321,

366, 387, 415, 455, 460, 464, 493
Lillford, ... 377
Lincoln, . . . 53, 79
Lincolnshire, 64, 212, 320
Line House, . . . 72
Little Baddow, . . 239
Little Bowden, . . 117
Little Bythum, . . 425
Little Haunden, . . 277
Little Minories, 455, 495
Little Waldingfield, 20, 388.
London, 6, 16, 18, 24, 31, 32, 36, 38, 42, 43, 44, 48, 50, 52, 54, 55, 57, 60, 62, 68, 69, 71, 82, 83, 89, 95, 102, 109, 112, 115, 116, 121, 122, 131, 142, 144, 146, 148, 150, 151, 157, 159, 160, 162, 163, 164, 170, 171, 174, 175, 176, 178, 184, 189, 190, 193, 194, 197, 198, 202, 207, 208, 213, 215, 216, 221, 232, 234, 239, 245, 249, 253, 256, 260, 264, 282, 295, 296. 298, 306, 309, 317, 321, 324, 325, 327, 328, 331, 332, 334, 338, 339, 340, 342, 344, 353, 354, 356, 364, 366, 367, 372, 374, 379, 393, 398, 403, 404, 404, 416, 418, 422, 423, 424, 427, 437, 438, 441, 443, 445, 448, 451, 457, 460, 461, 463, 466, 467, 470, 484, 486, 498, 499, 500, 502, 503, 504, 518, A, C, D, E.
Long Island, 18, 51, 316, 350, 457, 474, 517, G.
Long Sutton, . . 369
Lowton, ... 305
Lydd, ... 38
Lynn (Kingslynne), 13, 134
Machias, ... 16
Maidstone, 31, 71, 438, 488
Maine, . 258, 376, F.
Malaga, ... 11
Malden, Mauldon, 76, 230 389, 393
Malford, . . 74, 513
Manchester, . . 475
Mandifield, . . . 206
Manhatos, . . . 394
Mapersall, ... F.
Maralsley, . . . 430
Marfield, ... 239
Marlborough, . 84, 120, 133, 157, 159, 320, 321, 343, 363, 475
Marsh Gibbon, . . 243
Marston, ... 95
Mawlyn, ... 175
Mawthorp, . . . 491
Melchitt Parke, . . 391
Merrimack, . 259, 439
Mersey, ... 110
Middleborough, . . 442
Middlesex, . . . 204
Milcomb, ... 165
Mildenhall, . . . 345

Milford, . . 66, 70, 298
Milton, . . 125, 367, G.
Minge, ... 491
Monhegan, . . . 137
Monks Ely, . . . 20
Monksoon, . . . 258
Moulsham, . . . 389
Much Yeldham, . 445
Moreton Underhill, A.
Mumby 491
Nasing, Nazing, 126, 153, 196, 349, 354, 394, C.
Navestock, . . . 110
Nayland, Naylonde, 253, 343
Needham, Needam, 265
Needham Market, . 256
Nevis, ... 373
Newark, ... 350
New Bucknam, 391, 419
Newbury, 16, 106, 344, 512
Newcastle, 127, 128, 434, 486, 502
Newcastle on Tyne, 96, 158, 233, 415
Newfoundland, 87, 300, 410
New Hampshire, . 150, 435, F.
New Haven, 12, 16, 55, 61, 95, 131, 239, 256, 276, 289, 294, 302, 320, 348, 405, 412, 454, 462, 496, 512
New Jersey, . . . 169
New London, 55, 76, 315, 426
Newport, 67, 127, 113, 168, 284, 500
New Sarum, . . . 46
Newton Ferrers, . 297
Newton Stacy, 446, 475
New York, . . . 308
Norchurch, . . . 131
Norfolk, ... 357
Northam, ... 87
Northbourn, . . . 402
North Stoneham, . 146
Northampton, . 10, 119, 145, 150, 227, 234, 440
Northamptonshire, 485
Northumberland, . 237, 415
North Yarmouth, . 163, 393
Norwalk, ... 289
Norwich, . 6, 15, 17, 25, 28, 83, 140, 141, 184, 199, 258, 280, 294, 312, 329, 335, 400, 437, 468, 476
Nottingham, . 200, 489
Nottinghamshire, . 114, 169, 489
Odell, ... 78
Olney, 117, 162, 178, 347
Onge, ... 329
Orchyard, ... 330
Orentum, ... 18
Ormsby, . . 143, 321
Ormesticke, . . . 430
Oyster Bay, . 18, 288
Oyster River, . 81, 231
Oxford, 26, 54, 106, 305, 307, 333, 463

PLACE INDEX.

Parham, ... 438
Patcham, ... 216
Patuxet, . . . 17, 110
Pebmershe, . . . 157
Pemaquid, 108, 196, 274, 396
Penobscot, . . . 276
Penton, . 34, 40, 46, 54, 333
Pequot, ... 265
Philadelphia, . . 383
Piscataqua, Pescataquack etc., 14, 76, 77, 91, 109, 238, 246, 274, 280, 285, 324, 343, 373, 408. 451, 479, 499, D.H.
Pitminster, . . . 35
Platford, ... 392
Plimpton, St. Mary, 424
Plymouth, 100, 112, 185, 307
Portsmouth, (see also Strawberry Bank,) 23, 26, 68, 353, 477, 503, G.
Portugal, ... 175
Preston, ... 20
Providence, 9, 21, 22, 43, 66, 88, 171, 175, 260, 471, 474, 491, 497, 501, H.
Pulham, Mary, . 6, 487
Putnam, ... 66
Quampegon, . . . 71
Quinepiak, . . . 375
Quomscooke, see Squamscot, ... 245
Ragwell, ... 32
Rainhill, ... 189
Raleigh, ... 344
Ratchford Hundred, 76
Ratcliffe, ... 197
Rattlesden, . 269, 404
Rattliffe, ... 264
Rayleigh, ... 69
Raynham, . . . 357
Readding, Reading, Redding, 106, 262, 278, B.
Redgrave, ... 81
Reydon, ... 20
Rhode Island, 22, 40, 53, 59, 85, 108, 175, 194, 235, 247, 250, 340, 347, 370, 371, 421, 463, 465, 478, 479, 480, 481, 485, 487, 501
Rickmansworth, . . 277
Rotherhith, . . . 398
Rowley, ... 389
Romsey, . 48, 156, 238, 273, 424
Rotterdam, 16, 356, 389
Royston, ... 320
Ruddington, . . . 56
Rumsey, ... 344
Saco, . . 353, A, F.
St. Albans, St. Albons, 19, 28, 99, 163, 186, 199, 206, 320, 335, 348, 355, 401, 466, 497, 515
St. Botolph Aldgate, 196
St. James, . . . 167
St. Katherine's, . . 10
St. Lawrence, . . 78
St. Martins, . . . 42
St. Mary Whitechapel, 24

Saffron Waldon, . 316
Salcombe Regis, 100, 485
Salisbury, 38, 39, 143, 483, 489
Sally, ... 173
Sanderstead, . . . 23
Sandwich, 25, 26, 47, 58, 61, 87, 109, 111, 122, 127, 151, 159, 219, 263, 305, 337, 360, 422, 506, H.
Sarum, . . 38, 86, 449
Saybrook, . 231, 345
Scamelsby, . . . 452
Scarborough, . . B.
Scrooby, 6, 63, 67, 387
Seabrook, . . 351, 379
Seaside, ... 354
Seaton, ... 477
Segotea, Segoten . 353
Semley, ... 191
Sempringham, 260, 416
Shadwell, ... 48
Shasbury, . . . 191
Shaston, . . 207, 271
Shelter Island, . . 147
Sherfield, ... 478
Shiplock, ... 497
Shotley, . . 439, 452
Shrewsbury, . 76, 373
Shroppum, . . . 423
Sidbury, ... 418
Silferton, ... 479
Simborough, . . . 349
Simstuly, ... 209
Simwell, ... 500
Sittingbourne, . . G.
Skirbeck, . . 494. D.
Skratbey, ... 91
Slymbridge, . . . 191
Somerset, . . 247, 511
Somerton, ... G.
Southertowne, 201, 342, 343, 496
Southampton, 6, 12, 51, 117, 119, 162, 172, 193, 204, 272, 333, 350, 402, 430, 485
Southold, 106, 114, 119, 227, 232, 251, 405, 506
Southwark, Southworth, 68, 77, 94, 122, 126, 155, 216, 219, 232, 252, 315, 331, 388, 406, 419, 424, 489
Southwold, . . . 518
Sowerby, ... 160
Spain, . . . 222, 272
Sproughton, . . . 473
Staines, ... 485
Stamford, Stanford, 18, 348, 353, 404
Stannaway, . . . 115
Stanton, ... 512
Staple, ... 151
Stapleton, ... 208
Starford, Startford, 115, 331
Stebbin, ... E.
Stepney, 48, 110, 112, 173, 205, 223, 297, 341, 358, 433, G.
Stockingham, . . D.
Stoke Abbot, 128, 155, C.
Stoke Clare, . . . 365
Stoke Nayland, . . 434

Stondon Massey . 478
Stone, ... 189
Stonington, . . . 343
Stratford, 18, 102, 216, 478
Stratford at Bow . 389
Strawberry Bank (see also Portsmouth), 26, 83, 343, 404
Sturtle, ... 130
Strowde, ... 159
Sudbury, 117, 166, 201, 206, 222, 291, 394, 504
Surinam, ... 72
Sutton, . 104, 110, 121, 332, 347, D.
Sutton Mandifield, 206, 382
Sutton Mansfield, . 54
Swampscot, Swamscot, 181, 246, 272, 398
Swanzey, ... 18
Swyer, ... 237
Tarling, Terling, 211, 212, 465, 486
Taunton, ... 330
Tenterden, 24, 65, 226, 231, 278, 285, 454, 517, D.
Tewksbury, . . . 131
Thetford, ... 94
Thidingworth, . . F.
Thornbury, . . . 450
Thorsthorp, . . . 166
Tichmersh, . . . 261
Timby, ... 23
Tinckleten, . . . 428
Tinmouth Castle, . 164
Titenden, ... 248
Titherly, ... 483
Tiverton, ... 108
Tolland, ... 514
Topcraft, ... 178
Towcester, . 195, 411
Town Marroling, . 180
Toxteth, Toxteth Park, 22, 305, 421
Tring, . . . 358, 443
Truro, ... 358
Tunbridge, . . . 430
Upton Bishop, . . E.
Upton Gray, . 204, 446
Upton on Seavern, . 54
Upway, ... 428
Uxbridge, . . 270, 329
Venn Ottery, 100, 368, 436, 486
Virginia, 52, 73, 84, 118, 149, 150, 193, 215, 235, 256, 275, 289, 295, 296, 314, 325, 457, 478, 488, 510
Waldern, ... 226
Walderswick, . . 90
Wales, Welsh, 18, 55, F.
Wanefilitt, . . . 491
Wapping, 24, 43, 99, 121, 222, 303, 339, 384, 387, 467, A.
Ware, ... 95
Watford, . . 195, 375
Watton Underwood, 243
Waybread, . . . 106
Wayhill, ... 46
Wayneflete St. Mary, 278

Wedmore, ... —
Wellingborow, . . 261
Wells, 102, 191, 324, 479, 491, C.
Wendover, . . 247, 378
West Indies, . . . 474
Westerley, . . . 417
Western Hall, . . 118
Westminster, 60, 95, 112, 116, 136, 334, 439
Westmoreland, . . 128
Westwell, ... 441
Wethersfield, 9, 94, 97, 111, 112, 165, 171, 216, 277, 316, 389, 407, F.
Weymouth, 10, 14, 33, 48, 97, 128, 138, 165, 171, 182, 197, 209, 228, 233, 247, 259, 262, 271, 272, 292, 295, 303, 350, 358, 369, 380, 472, 495, 511, 512
Wherwell, ... 26
Whickamin, . . . 482
White Chapel, . . 60
Wilton, ... E.
Whitchurch, . . . 400
White Hill, The . 165
Whittlebury, . . 298
Wickford, . 157, 228
Widford, . . 153, 354
Widgethorpe, . . 377
Willoughby, . . . 491
Wiltshire, ... 24
Winchmore Hill, . 248
Windham, 286, 317, 338
Windsor, 37, 80, 117, 138, 142, 144, 148, 153, 165, 172, 184, 185, 187, 196, 200, 221, 234, 240, 244, 247, 295, 301, 304, 307, 318, 326, 345, 346, 356, 365, 388, 407, 426, 439, 500, 504, 509, 514
Winfarthing, . . . 255
Winwick, . 22, 305, 457
Woburn, Wooburn, 190, 406
Wockingham, . . 306
Wooburrow, . . . 400
Woodbridge, 56, 122, 267, 300
Woodhull, ... 78
Wolverhampton, . 398
Wolverstone, . . 129
Worcester, . . . 111
Word, ... 122
Wormingfold, . . 115
Worminghurst, . . 125
Wortwell, ... 179
Wotton at Stone, . 207
Wrentham, 14, 64, 178, 357
Wrentom, ... 453
Wrightington, . . 430
Yarmouth (see also Great Yarmouth), 17, 183, 192, 377, 458, 463
Yealing, ... 165
Yeldham (see Much Yeldham).
York, 295, 299, 321, 375, D.
Yorkshire, 326, 403, 488

"GENTLE" PIONEERS OF MASSACHUSETTS.

Residents to whom the titles, *Knight, Esquire, Gentleman, Armiger* or *Lady* were applied in legal documents or by trustworthy writers in the Pioneer Period, and those whose fathers in England were so designated officially.

Probably there were many others of whom the writer has not found evidence.

Allen, Edward,
    Thomas,
Appleton, Samuel,
Atwood, John,
Barnes, John,
Beesbeech, Thomas,
Bellingham, Richard,
    William,
Berry, William,
Bowen, Griffith,
Bowman, Nathaniel,
Bradstreet, Simon,
Brampton, William,
Brenton, William,
Bright, Thomas,
Brown, John,
    William,
    William,
Browning, Malachi,
Bulkley, Peter,
Chester, Leonard,
Child, Robert,
Coddington, William,
Cole, William,
Collins, Edward,
Combe, John,
Cook, George,
    Joseph,
    Samuel,
Cudworth, James,
Curtis, Henry,
Cutting, John,
Darby, John,
    Richard,
Day, Wentworth,
Doughty, Francis,
Dow, Francis,
Downing, Emanuel,
Dudley, Thomas,
Dummer, Richard,
    Stephen,
    Thomas,
Eaton, Nathaniel,
Epps, Daniel,

Faune, John,
Falconer, Edmond,
Fenwick, George,
Fogg, Ralph,
Fordham, Robert,
Fowle, Thomas,
Freeman, Samuel,
Gardiner, Christopher,
Gerrish, William,
Glover, John,
Graves, Thomas,
Greenleaf, Stephen,
Haines, John,
Hall, Samuel,
Harlakenden, Richard,
    Roger,
Harrison, John,
Hatherley, Timothy,
Hedge, William,
Hibbens, William,
Holman, John,
Hopkins, Stephen,
Hough, Atherton,
Howell, Edward,
Hull, Edmund,
Humphrey, John,
Jackson, Edward,
Jeffrey, William,
Johnson, Arbella,
    Francis,
    Isaac,
Keayne, Mrs. Benjamin,
King, Daniel,
Leader, Richard,
Lechford, Thomas,
Ludlow, George,
    Roger,
Makepeace, Thomas,
Mansfield, John,
Mayhew, Mahew, Thomas,
Michelson, Edward,
Monday, Henry,
Moody, Deborah,
Morton, Thomas,

Nelson, Thomas,
Newberry, Thomas,
Oddingsell, Thomas,
Offley, David,
Paine, Moses,
Patten, Nathaniel,
Pelham, Herbert,
Perkins, William,
Plaistow, Jozias,
Poole, Elizabeth,
    William,
Potter, Vincent,
Prence, Thomas,
Purchase, Oliver,
    Thomas,
Pynchon, William,
Rawson, Edward,
Robinson, Thomas,
Rossiter, Bray,
Saltonstall, Richard,
Sewall, Henry,
Shove, George,
Simpkins, Nicholas,
Smith, John,
Snelling, William,
Spencer, John,
Strange, George,
Stratton, John,
Symonds, Samuel,
Thorndike, John,
Throckmorton, George,
    John,
Underwood, Thomas,
Vane, Henry,
Vassal, William,
Walker, Richard,
Whiting, Samuel,
    Elizabeth (St. John),
Whittington, John,
Wilson, John,
    Elizabeth, (Mansfield)
Winthrop, John,
Wollenston, Edward,

ADDITIONS AND CORRECTIONS, 1902.

The work of Farmer, mentioned on page 3, was issued in 1829; that of Dr. Savage, was given to the public in 1862.

The first word of the quotation from Bradford on page 6 is "opprobriously."

ABBOT, etc., Edward, Taunton, atba. 1643; bound himself a covenant servant to Robert Nash, Boston, for 2 years, Jan. 15, 1650. [A.]

ADAMS, John of Concord [son of Henry, Sen., of Braintree?], had power of attorney 25(10)1649 for collection of rents for John Shepheard of Braintree due upon lands lately in occupation of Jonathan Adams, living near Ballsbery, co. Somerset, Eng. [A.]

Thomas, Chelmsford, d. July 20, 1688, æ. 76. [Mdx. rec.]

ADDIS, William, Gloucester; town officer, 1641. Ch. Millicent (m. William Southmeade), Anne, (m. at Boston 24(9)1652, Ambrose Dart).

ADFORD, Henry; June 29, 1651, is the date of baptism of the children.

ALBEE, Benjamin; add children Hannah, bapt. 16(6)1641, and Lydia, b. 14(2)1642.

ALCOCK, Thomas, last line, first column, change 1634 to 1639.

ALDEN; "Mr. John Alden, the antient magistrate of Plymouth, died Sept. 12, 1687." [S.]

ALLEY, Philip, Salem, called to court in 1645, Add: Philip, ship-master, was lost at sea; his widow m. —— Pitts. Her nephew John Bundy petitioned May 31, 1671, for possession of her house and land, claiming that she had promised the same to him when he married his present wife with the advice and consent of his aunt and Mr. Alley, her first husband. [Mass. Arch. B, 15, 31.]

AMEE, etc., John; By wife Martha he had in Boston ch. John b. March 12, 1653, Martha b. Nov. 10, 1655, William b. March 27, 1657, Martha b. Feb. 29, 1659, Mary b. Oct. 10, 1661, Remembrance (son), b. March 18, 1664, Ruth b. June 24, 1666, Joseph b. Feb. 10, 1668, Ruth b. March 1, 1670. John "Ame," shipwright, with wife "Anne," mortg. house and land 3 Dec. 1691 and gave deed of sale 13 Oct. 1693.

ANDREW, ANDREWS, Samuel, died before Aug. 1, 14 Charles, when his widow recd. deed of 100 acres of land on the West side of Saco river in Maine, on which her husband formerly built a house, etc.; confirmed by the selectmen of Saco 26(4)1654. [York Deeds.] She married Arthur Mackworth; in a deed of land to George Felt, Jr., (who had married her second husband's dau. Phillippe), she mentions her son James Andrews and her dau. Purchas. [Norf. co. Rec. IV, 75,] She died in Boston in 1676; beq. to daus. Purchas, Sarah, wife of Abraham Adams, Rebecca wife of Nathaniel Whorfe and William Rogers (in turn), and a fourth daughter, name not given.

ARMITAGE, Thomas, came with Richard Mather; settled at Plymouth; frm. 7 March, 1636-7. Rem. to Sandwich; deputy.

APPLETON, Samuel; note, his birth was in 1586.

ARNOLD, Richard, Winnisimmet; he died, and admin. of his est. was gr. Sept. 3, 1633, to William Stitson.

Thomas, "now supposed to be in New England," mentioned in the will of his kinsman Richard Arnold, of London, goldsmith, as the son of William A. [Reg. XLVIII, 374.]

ASEY, see Hasey.

BAKER, Nathaniel, mentions children of his brother *Nicholas*.

Nicholas: add child Elizabeth, b. Nov. 10, 1644, (m. John Vinal).

BALLARD, Mr. William, add children, Elizabeth, (m. at Chelmsford Nov. 11, 1668, William Blunt), Lydia, (m. 12 (2) 1674, Joseph Butterfield). He d. 10 July, 1689.

BALCH, John; his son Freeborn testified in Piscataqua court 19 Aug. 1657, aged 23 years.

BARROW, see Burroughs.

BATEMAN, etc. John, sawyer, Boston, resident, 1648. Wife Hannah adm. chh. 7 (3) 1648. Ch. John b. about (10) 1644, Hannah b. about (1) 1646, Elizabeth b. about (8) 1647, all bapt. 14 (3) 1648; Sarah bapt. 7 (8) 1649, æ. about 8 days, Sarah b. 6 (3) 1651 *Rachel* bapt. 1 (4) 1651, Mary b. 1652, d. 1654, William b. 8 March, 1655, Joseph b. 21 Aug. 1658, Mary b. Sept. 4, 1660.

(72—a)

☞ Read Introduction and Directions to Searchers.

Additions and Corrections, 1902.

John B., of Boston, now resident in Hingham, made will Nov. 10, 1689, "being aged," prob. Sept. 16, 1690. Beq. to eldest son William and son Joseph if they appear in N. E. to receive it; to four daus. Elizabeth Arnold, Sarah Eells, Rachel Holman and Mary Jones; to gr. ch. Samuel and Hannah Holman. Sons-in-law Samuel Eells of Hing. and Isaac Jones of Bo. execs.

BATE, BATES, George; Joane *Crocour* deposed.

BIBBLE, John; his wife Sibil, a dau. of John Tuicknell of Wedmore, co. Somerset, gave power of attorney 26 (7) 1650, to her bro. John T., of Wed., to collect legacy, left by her father. [A.]

BLACKLEACH, John; his wife was a dau. of Robert Bacon, who lived sometime in Wapping, afterward near Cree church in London; certificate of her health made 4 (5) 1649. [A.]

BRASIER, etc., Edward, his wife Magdalen was adm. chh. Char. 9 (6) 1656; he was adm. 29 (5) 1658. Ch. Thomas bapt. 29 (2) 1660, Abigail b. 18 Dec. 1664.

BROWN, BROWNE, Nicholas, mariner, sent power of attorney 24 (10) 1649 for collection of rents etc. at Moreton Underhill [Birtsmorton?] co. Worcester. [A.]

Thomas, husbandman, planter, Sudbury, one of the petitioners to whom the Gen. Court gave authority to begin that plantation 6 Sept. 1638. Rem. to Concord; bought land 20 (3) 1655, 9 June, 1661, 3 (2) 1671,—" of Concord." Dau. Mary m. first William Woodhead, of Chelmsford, whose conduct made it necessary for Mr. Browne to write two letters to the governor in Dec. 1670; he deposed at that time, aged about 61 years; his son Thomas, Jr , deposed at the same time, aged about 19 years. [Mdx. files.] Mary m. second, John Gove of Cambridge. Thomas B., Sen. was a member of a committee to divide certain Concord property 26 March, 1675; [Mdx. Deeds]; but 20 Nov. 1680,—" late of Concord, now of Cambridge," —he deeded his Concord lands to his son Thomas, Jr., and acknowledged the deed before Randolph Dec. 6, 1687. He filed on March 11, 1681-2, a list of lands which he had given to his son Boaz before the latter's marriage;

John Gove was one of the witnesses. The son Jabez, who remained in Sudbury until the founding of Stow, in which he joined with Boaz and others, deposed 6 (2)1669, aged about 25 years; he died in 1692; his widow and son Thomas had a letter from Gove, who called her "my sister Brown," and offered to sign their administration bond, Sept. 29, 1692.

Thomas B., Sen.'s death is not recorded. Only one person of the name is mentioned in Camb. town and church records for this period; fined for nominal offence with others 9 (12) 1656; town officer 1660, 1663 and 1668; adm. chh. May 18, 1666,—children bapt. as stated in text. Having given lands to his older children, he willed his remaining property to his second wife and their children.

BUNDY, John, see Alley.

BULLARD, William, appoints " Sonnes Nath^{ll} Bullard & Moses Colliar executo^{rs} " of his will.

BULLOCKE, Edward, was son of " Mr. William B., late of Barkham in Barkshire." [Deposition of Elizabeth Clements 26 (5) 1649. A.]

BURTON, Edward; the record given under Thomas B. belongs to Edward. Aug. 3, 1682, Samuel Johnson, glover, of Boston, for his wife Phœbe, second dau. of the late E. B. of Hingham, sold her portion in certain lands, referring to Hannah, her oldest sister, and Sarah the third dau. [Suff. De. VI, 323].

BUTLER, Stephen, Boston, proprietor 1648. Ch. of Stephen and Jane: Benjamin b. 2 Aug. 1653, Benjamin b. 10 Feb. 1658, Isaac, b. Oct. 9, 1661, Isaac b. May 29, 1664, James b. Aug. 2, 1665, Isaac b. Aug. 10, 1667; Stephen and Tabitha had Stephen b. April 22, 1681. Stephen, blacksmith, died in 1717; his " mother Tabitha Butler" had certain articles that were her particular property reserved at the admin. of his estate.

BUTTON, Mathias; erase from list of his children Thomas, Elizabeth, Mehetabel and Edward, who were transferred in the records from the family of his son-in-law Edward Yeomans. He sued John Godfrey 13 (2) 1659, for " the fireing of his chimney, which caused the burning of my house and the death of my wife." [Es. Court files.]

☞ Read Introduction and Directions to Searchers.

Additions and Corrections, 1902.

CARTER, Richard; insert "He" in second line, page 90, after 1641.

CHAMBERLAIN, etc., Thomas; his wife "Mary" sold land in 1658. [Mdx. Deeds.]
William, planter; his wife Rebecca joined him in a deed of land 26 Oct. 1668.

CHENEY, William; second column, first and second lines should read: 1679-80. She rem. to Boston; d. 2 or 3 (5) 1686; will prob. Sept. 23, 1686.

CHESTER, Leonard, "armiger," [gravestone]. "The Chester arms" mentioned in the will of his widow. See Russell below.

CLEMENT, etc., Mr. Robert, resident in Andover, 1642; his dau. "Mary Osgood alias Clemence," deposed 19 July, 1695, aged 58 years; was of Coventry, co. Warwick, before 1652. [Es. De. X, 190; Reg. XIII, 272.]

COBBET, Rev. Thomas, died Nov. 5, 1685. [S.]

COLBORN, William; change "George" to John "Barrell."

COLLIER, Thomas, with wife Jane, dau. of —Curtes, late of Reading, co. Berks., constituted her bro. John Curtes attorney 21 (10) 1649 for collection of legacy left by her grandmother, Jane Alexander, of R. [A.]

COLLINS, Christopher, perhaps identical with the "shoemaker" who bought land at Scarborough, Maine, 10 Jan. 1659. His son Timothy removed to Newbury, and Dec. 28, 1680, sold land at "Blew Point," *i. e.* Scarborough, derived from his father Christopher Collins.

COOK, Walter; children recorded: Ebenezer b. May 30, 1656, Walter b. Sept. 10, 1657, Nicholas b. Feb. 9, 1659; "a dau. of Walter and Experience Cook" b. Nov. 9, 1662. Hannah m. James Albee; Experience m. Peter Adams.

CURTIS, Richard; insert after Mary Badcock another daughter, mentioned in his will, namely "Martha Clarke."

DALLIBER, etc., Tristram; add: See also the will of Robert Dalyber of Stoke Abbott, yeoman, dated 20 March, 1632, prob. 27 May, 1633; he beq. to sons Robert, Tristram, Samuel and Joseph; daus. Mary, Sarah and Rebecca; sons in law Walter Burt and John Lesty; and to "wife." [Reg. XLVIII, 128.]

DANE, John; his son John wrote a narrative of his early life, which, with family pedigree, is given in Reg. VIII, 147-156.

DANFORTH, Nicholas; erase "Martha," etc. from list of children, as she *bought* land of Thomas Danforth which *he* had "inherited," etc.

DARBY, DERBY, Edward; add children Mary b. Dec. 29, 1660, Priscilla b. June 20, 1672; John and Sarah bapt. 8 (10) 1672. Is the testator the same as the foregoing? Date of will should be *1723.*

DARLOE, Penelope, specified as a maidservant to Robert Keaine when admitted to the Church.

DARVILL, DEVEL, Robert; "Robert Davoll, of Sudbury, N. E.," made Henry Rice of London his attorney 19 (8) 1650, to collect dues on lands called the Harrots in the parish of [Norchurch] alias Barkhamsted in Hertfordshire. [A.]

DAVIS, DAVIES, etc., James, Hampton; it was the *son James* who deposed 14 (2) 1663, æ. about 60 years.

William, Roxbury, propr. 1643. Wife Elizabeth adm. chh., and children John, Samuel and Joseph bapt 8 (11) 1649; she was buried May 4, 1658; he mar. Oct. 21, 1658, Alice Thorpe, (perhaps widow of John, of Plymouth); she was adm. chh. Rox. 7 (4) 1663; died 24 (12) 1667. He mar. third, Jane–, who was adm; chh. 8 (4) 1673; he was adm. chh. "to full communion," 20 (2) 1673. Children, John b. Oct. 1, 1643, Samuel b. Feb. 21, 1644, William and Elizabeth bapt. 14 (4) 1663, Mathew bapt: 24 (11) 1663, Jonathan b. Feb. 7, 1666, Mary, Jane, Rachel b. Aug. 26, 1672,—these three bapt. 18 (3) 1673; Benjamin bapt. 7 (4) 1674, Ichabod b. April 1, 1676, Ebenezer b. April 9, 1678, William b. Jan. 3, 1679-80, Sarah b. July 20, 1681, Isaac b. April 18, 1683, Rachel (m. Josiah Goddard).

He died 9 Dec. 1683; [Probate papers]; will dated Dec. 6, prob. Dec. 28, 1683; beq. to wife (called Jane in the papers); to his "three eldest sons, John, Samuel and Joseph"; to sons Matthew and Jonathan, when they come to age; to dau. Elizabeth a trunk that was her mother's and a bill of 12 pounds. His age is given as 66 years; land specified in Rox. and Boston.

(168—a)
☞ Read Introduction and Directions to Searchers.

Additions and Corrections, 1902.

DEACON, alias FRANCIS, John, of Lynn, had accounts with Gifford in 1653 etc. [Es. files]. Is probably the man who came in 1635; constable, juryman, sergeant.

DEACON, DEAKIN, etc. "One Dakin and his wife dwelling near Meadford coming from Cambridge where they had spent their Sabbath," she narrowly escaped drowning while fording the river; was saved by their dog. [W.] Richard Francis, Cambridge, lived in "Meadford" 20 Dec. 1665, when he and "Ales" his wife sold land. He d. at Camb. "an antient and goodman indeed,"—æ. 80 years." [S. and Mdx. Rec.]

DENNIS, William, in his will speaks of son in law "William *Peakes*" not Parker.

DUNCAN, Nathaniel, mar. at Exeter, Eng., Elizabeth Jordon; license dated Jan. 3, 1616-7.

DYER, George, his wife Abigail was a member of the church in earliest list—before 1639. Query: did she die and did he mar. as a second wife Martha, formerly wife of Edward White, and mother of James W. whom he calls in his will "son in law"?

EAGLESFIELD, Mary, her mother was Susanna, dau. of Thomas and Katharine (Myles) Grey, of Harwich, Eng. [L.] See Coytmore.

EATON, Francis; read "child Samuel, an infant," etc.

ELIOT, etc. "Philip Elliott, of Nasing, co. Essex, husbandman, bachelor, aged about 22, and Elizabeth Sybthorpe, spinster, maiden, aged about 23, daughter of Robert Sybthorpe, deceased," were licensed to marry by the bishop of London Oct. 20, 1624, her widowed mother consenting. [Printed Rec.]

FARNHAM, Ralph; came in the year 1635; *his son* Ralph mar. Elizabeth Holt. The father d. 8 Jan. 1692-3; inv. filed March 29, 1693.

FALCONER, FAULKNER, etc., Edmund; he made Wm. Twiss, of Andover, his attorney, 2 (6) 1650, to collect legacy from the estate of his father Richard Falconer, late of Kingscleare, co. Hampshire. [A.]

FITCH, Richard, see Reg. XVI., 367.

GETCHELL, Samuel, ch. Samuel b. 8 Feb· 1657.

GLOVER, Rev. Josse, came from Sutton, co. Essex, Eng.; his windmill at Lynn was sold by trustees for the benefit of his children 22 (3) 1645. [Suff. De. I, 77.]

GOOKIN, Daniel, at his death was "aged 75 years." [Co. rec.]

GOULD, Samuel, Haverhill, propr. 1650.

GREENOUGH, William, Boston, made will July 24, 1678; beq. to wife; to dau. Elizabeth land next that of "brother Cooke"; land where kinsman William Greenough lives; and land bounded by that of "couzen Sumner"; to dau. Mary G. and to "couzen William Greenough." Prob. 18 Feb. by Mrs. Elizabeth G., who, as "Prout, late Greenough," filed inv. 22 May, 1686; as such she also recd. property from the estate of "her father, Nicholas Upshall." It was the nephew William who mar. Ruth Swift and later mar. Elizabeth, dau. of elder Rainsford, whose records became intertwined with those of the pioneer. Children Mary, Anna, Luke, William, John, Samuel and Consider were of the younger man, who died Aug. 6, 1693.

HAIT, HETT, HITT, etc., Thomas, of Hull, late of Stockingham, co. Lincoln, Eng., sent power of attorney thither 10 (7) 1647, for collection of rents. [A.]

HALL, Edmund, should be HULL.

HASEY, HALSEY, ASEY, etc., William, add child Joseph, baptized as "of Wm. Asey's wife," 28(4)1657. William Hasey mar. second, Judith, widow of Jonathan Poole; she survived him and mar. afterwards Lieut. Robert Gould, of Hull, and there died in 1704. [See deed of Judith, in possession of heirs of the late Robert Gould.] The Judith mentioned in article on page 217 is the dau. of Richard Jacobs and wife of William H., Jr., on whose estate she admin. in 1695.

HARBOUR, John; see article on Benj. Scott for marriage of the widow,

HEARD, HERD, etc., Luke, may be the son of Edmund Herd, weaver, of Claxton, Eng., who beq. his best loom and other things to his eldest son Luke, at 21 years of age, in his will of Nov 20, 1626. [Reg. LI., 423.]

HILL, HILLS, Joseph; his wife Helen, not Rose, was sister of Mr. Henry Dunster.

Zebulon deposed Feb. 7, 1684-5, æ. about 64 years. [Es. De. IX, 8.]

HILTON, William, Junior, is the Newbury resident, we judge; not William, Senior, who made his home at Piscataqua river.

HOLT, Nicholas, "dish-turner," with wife Martha, sold land to his second son Henry 15 Dec. 1681. Henry m. Feb. 24, 1669, Sarah, dau. of William Ballard.

HULL, Rev. Joseph, removed to York, Me. and was settled as their minister in 1643. [W.] He and Roger Garde measured land for Mr. Godfrey 5 May, 1644; his wife Agnes witnessed a deed with him in 1645. [York Deeds.]

HUTCHINSON, Edward, not "William," was husband of Susanna and father of William.

☞ Read Introduction and Directions to Searchers.

Additions and Corrections, 1902.

INGALLS, see will of Robert Ingolls, of Skirbeck, co. Lincoln, Eng. in Reg. L., p. 72.

JACKSON, Richard; erase "Wm." in last line.

JOHNSON, Francis, seems to be the "Capt. Johnson," who died at Boston Feb. 2, 1690–1, "aged between 86 and 90." [S.]

KENDRICK, KENRICKE, John, Boston, had grant of land at Muddy River, Boston, for 4 heads, 30(10)1639. N.B. This was erroneously copied and printed in the Boston Record Commissioners' volume as "Remicke," and followed by the compiler in former statement.

KIMBALL. Richard, died 22 June, 1675.

KNIGHT, Alcxander, married shortly before 10 Oct., 1640, Anne, dau. of William Tutty, gent., of St. Stephens, Colman street, London, Eng., who beq. to her in his will, prob. 9 Jan. 1640. [Reg. XLVIII., 142.]

John, Newbury, m. 2, Ann, widow of R. Ingersoll. John Jr. d. in Feb. 1677–8.

LAW, William, erase statement that his first wife was "widow of Anthony Saddler," which applies to her sister.

LEWIS, John, of Tenterden and Scituate; the christian name of Mr. Bishop, former husband of Alice, is not Nathaniel, and is not known to the writer. The date of the deed is 1669.

LOBDELL, Nicholas, gave letter of attorney 28 (4) 1648 for settlement of an account with Nathaniel Peck, of Barbadoes; one bill dated 4 Feb. 1636. [A.]

LORD, p. 294, heading of first column, should be LOWELL.

LUXFORD; "goodwife Luxford was buried Sept. 1, 1691." [S.]

LYON, etc.; change "Freefrace" to Freegrace.

MANNING, William, father and son were often confused in records. Hannah, dau. of William, Senior, having a child recorded at Braintree as born in 1651, cannot be the child born at Cambridge in 1642. This Hannah and all the children registered at Camb. were of William, Jr.

MANSFIELD, John; see will of John Mansfield, Esq., dated 13, prob. 31 July, 1601, recorded in Woodhull, 47. [Reg. XLVI, 324.]

MARION, MERIAN, etc., John, page 300, removed from Watertown to Boston; children given on page 311 belong to this person, viz. John bapt. 22 (12) 1651, and Isaac b. Jan. 20, 1652. He constituted John Maryon, the elder, of Braintree [Eng.] his attorney 6 (12) 1648, to collect what was due him from the estate of his father, Issac M., late of Stebbin, co. Essex, Eng. [A.]

MAVERICK, Rev. John, was rector of Beaworthy Aug. 30, 1615; resigned; his successor was instituted March 24, 1629. [Reg. 44, 214.]

MAYHEW, see MAHEW.

MAYOW, Francis, of Charlestown, sent letter of attorney 22 (8) 1650, to Mr. John Smith, minister, of Great Dunmow in Essex, Eng., to collect legacy from the estate of John Chaire, late of London. [A.]

MERRITT, MERRICK, John, mar. 3 (2) 1665, Elizabeth, dau. of Thomas Wyborne, q. v.

MILLETT, Thomas; the surname was dropped out of the form; he therefore appears under Miller!

MOORE, John, Mendon, signed a statement concerning a cow and provisions delivered to Capt. Henchman May 1, 1676; was "about 95 years old." [Arch. 70].

William, of Ipswich; will dated 14 Aug., 1660, prob. 26 Sept., 1671, beq. to daus. Mary Powell, Elizabeth More and Ruth Robye and her eldest daughter; to sons Thomas, and (eldest) William.

NICHOLLS, not NICHOLAS, Elizabeth, came in 1635.

ODLIN, John, "one of the first inhabitants of Boston, the oldest save the governour;" [Sewall.] [Reg. VI, 727.]

ORMSBY, Richard, removed to Rehoboth.

PADLEFOOTE, Jonathan, Cambridge, mentioned in the inventory of Nath. Sparrowhawke in 1647; he bought land in Camb. of Edward Winship 30 (3) 1649; sold his share in Billerica lands in 1650; administration of his estate was granted 1 Oct. 1661, to his widow Mary for herself and 4 small children.

(312—a)

☞ Read Introduction and Directions to Searchers.

ADDITIONS AND CORRECTIONS. 1902.

PARKER, John, Woburn; *wife Mary* married third, Thomas Chamberlain.

Rev. Thomas, Newbury; Lechford says he was son of "Robert Parker, sometime of Wilton, co. Wilts, author of De Politeia Ecclesiastica." [L., P. D.]

PARTRICH, PARTRIDGE, George, tailor, Duxbury, juror 2 March, 1635-6; house-lot of 30 acres granted him. Oct. 6, 1636; mar. Sarah Tracy in Nov. 1638; bought land XV Aug. 1639; had grant of land with meadow "*by his father's*" 2 Nov. 1640; grant recorded previous was to Steven Tracy. N. B. this entry led the compiler to suppose that George was the son of the minister, Rev. Ralph Partrich; but later researches, made at the instance of Mrs. Edward C. Chatfield, lead to the conclusion that such was not the case, and leave the origin of George unknown.

Atha. 1643; frm. 2 June, 1646; constable; took oath of fidelity in 1657; excise officer June 3, 1662; mentioned in list of "ancient freemen and servants" to whom land had been granted, before 1662; juror Dec. 6, 1673. Will dated 29 June, 1682, prob. 16 Oct. 1695, and inv. filed same day. Beq. to wife Sarah; dau. Marcy to have as much as other daus. already married have had; gr. dau. Bethia Allen, eldest son John P. and son James P.. "In case any estate belonging to me, beyond sea should be brought over heither," his wife should dispose of it among the children.

PEAKE, William, in his will bequeaths to *grandchildren* Dependance and Remembrance Luce.

PERKINS, William, called "gent." in a deed of which abstract is given by Lechford.

PHILLIPS, William, Charlestown and Boston; lieutenant, captain, major. He made William Phillips, of Badiam, shoemaker, his attorney for collection of accounts in Eng. 10 (12) 1648. [A.] His *son John* died in Aug. 1657. Bought land at Saco, Me. and removed thither. Carried on a large amount of business in mills, trading and real estate. Returned to Bo. about 1676; died in 1682-3; will dated Feb., prob. 29 Sept. 1683, beq. to wife Bridget, (who was third, not second wife,) sons Samuel and William, and daus. Mary Feild and Elizabeth Alden.

PICKERING, John, made Thomas Potter, of Childesmone, Eng. his attorney 25 (8) 1650, to take possession of a house in Coventry in his name. [A.]

PINGREE, PENGRY, Aaron and Moses, of Ipswich, N. E., made Thomas Pengry, Sen., of Colchester, Eng., their attorney for collection of rents in Upton Bishop, co. Hereford, Eng. 15 (8) 1650.

POLE, POOLE, "widow Jane died at River House in Boston Sept. 9, 1690." [S.]

PRENCE, Thomas; insert comma after name of first daughter, Hannah. The following heirs, directly or through their attornies, sold land of his estate June 10, 1676; Susanna Prence, single woman, at Catherine Gate neare the Tower in London; Capt John Freeman in behalf of his wife Marcye; Jonathan Sparrow and his wife Hannah; Nicholas Snow and his wife Jane; Jeremiah Howes and Sarah his wife; John Tracy and Mary his wife; and the widow Mary Prence.

PRINCE, Thomas, Gloc., deposed 27 (7) 1664, æ. about 45 years.

QUINSEY, QUINCY, Mr. Edmund, lands bounded out in *1635*.

READ, etc., Robert, was lost in a vessel which sailed from Hampton, N. H., Oct. 20, 1657. Goods and lands appraised 29 (8) 1657 and 5 (1) 1657-8.

William, of Boston and Woburn, the reference concerning his will should read Reg. XLVIII, 381.

READING, REDDING, Thomas, removed to East Saco, Maine, and afterward to Casco Bay; took oath of allegiance to Mass. govt. 5 July, 1653. He died before 10 March, 1673, when his widow Elinor sold land, referring to a mortgage he had given in 1672. John R. of Weymouth, Joseph Donell, of Casco Bay, with Ruth his wife, and John Taylor, of Boston, conveyed their right in another tract which the widow sold in 1680. [York Deeds.]

REMICKE, John; error in copying and printing records of Boston for KENRICKE, q. v. .

REYNER, Rev. John, made will 19 April, 1659; prob. by widow Frances 30 June, 1669; beq. to wife land at Gildersome in the parish of Batly, co. of York, Eng., etc.; to children John, Elizabeth, Dorothie, Abigail and Judith; to son Jachim, of Rowly, and dau. Hannah, wife to Job Lane, "a cup I had with their mother," etc.

☞ Read Introduction and Directions to Searchers.

ADDITIONS AND CORRECTIONS, 1902.

REYNOLDS, William, removed to Cape Porpoise, Me.; took oath of allegiance 5 July 1653. Ferryman at Kennybuncke river, to have 3 pence a passenger. With wife Alice deeded land to son John April 12, 1675, conditional upon his care of the parents for their life-time.

RICHMOND, Mr. John, a sea-captain trading on the coast of Maine, sued in court at York Feb. 7, 1636, for wages due for labor performed by a servant he had let out. Compare with the following.

John, Senior, Taunton, died March 30, 1663-4, aged 70 years. Will dated 14 Dec. 1663; eldest son John and his son Thomas; younger son Edward and his son Edward; son in law William Paule and Mary his wife; son in law Edward Rew and Sarah his wife. [Reg. VII, 180.]

RIDDLESDEN, Marie; her age was 17, not 27, in ship list.

RING, widow Mary; insert in her will "daughter Susan."

RIX, RICKS, REX, William, weaver, planter, son of Robert, of Kenninghall, co. Norfolk, grocer, sold partimony 31 (6) 1640, to sister Elizabeth Waters, of K., widow. Contracted for the building of a house in Boston same day. [L.] Wife Grace adm. chh. 7 (1) 1646. Ch. Elisha b. 6 (6) 1645, bapt. 8 (1) 1646. Mary b. 4 (1) 1646, Ezekiel b. 30 Nov. 1656, d. 17 (12) 1658, John, (admin. on estates of bro. Elisha and sister Mary in May, 1672,) Thomas, (partner with John R. and Andrew Newcomb in a house and land in Bo.)

He d. 13 (9) 1657.

ROBERTS, Hugh, Roxbury, adm. chh. Oct. 20, 1650; child – bapt. 23 (8) 1650.

John, Roxbury; Eliot's record says: "John Roberts he came to New England in the yeare (1636) he brought with him his aiged mother, wife and seven children: Thomas & Edward sons Elizabeth, Margery, Jones, Alce, Lidea, Ruth, Deborah, daughters. he was one of the first fruits of Wales yt came to N. E. calle to Christ by the ministry of yt Revend & worthy instrumt Mr. Wroth."

The John Roberts who died in Boston and whose admin. is given on page 386 is a different person; the brother to whom reference is made is Samuel Robins of Salisbury, who died between 1665 and 1672, stating in his will that he was son of "John Robins of Thidingworth, Leicestershire, Eng."

We find no further particulars of the Roxbury man; the death of his mother is given on page 387.

ROBINSON, John, Haverhill, gave a letter of attorney 17 (8) 1650, for collection of legacy left by his father John Robinson, blacksmith, of Mapersall, co. Bedford. [A.] He removed to Exeter, N. H.; deposed 26 June, 1661, æ. about 45 years. [Pisc. court files.] died in 1675. Wife Elizabeth and son David survived.

ROPER, Walter, resided at Hampton sometime; propr. in 1641; selectman, 1644; child Mary bapt. Aug. 22, 1641; sold house in 1647 and rem. to Topsfield.

ROYAL, William; it was Margaret Greene who was "second wife of Samuel Cole, of Boston."

RUSSELL, John, Cambridge, clerk of writs, 1645. With John R. Jr. witnessed a deed of land 4 Nov. 1646. [Col. rec.] It is claimed by certain eminent historians that he is the man who resided at Wethersfield, Conn., and later at Hadley, Mass., where his son John (grad. Harv. Coll. 1645), was minister. If this be the case the Woburn man is a different person. The widow of the latter deposed 20 (8) 1680, æ. 66 years.

Richard, merchant, "formerly of Bristol, Eng." [A.] His widow Mary, widow of Leonard Chester, made will 20 Nov. 1688, prob. Oct. 1, 1689; beq. to ch. Capt. John and Stephen Chester, of Wethersfield, Conn.; to Dorcas, wife of Rev. S. Whiting, of Billerica; the ch. of dec. dau. Prudence Russell, viz. Thomas, Mary and Prudence R.; to Mary "my silver wine cup marked $_M{}^I{}_D$" "and to Prudence my silver plate with the Chesters arms on it"; to sons in law James Russell and Capt. Richard Sprague.

SALISBURY, SALSBERY, SALSBURY, SOLSBURY, William, Dorchester, 1648; one of the herdsmen of the town cattle; rem. to Milton; signed agreement of inhabitants about parsonage land 18 May, 1664. He deposed 12 (3) 1656, æ. about 34 years. [Arch. 38 B, p. 191-3.] 7 May, 1677, Susanna his widow was adm. to full com. in Dorch. chh.; she was dismissed to Milton chh. 18 (7) 1681. Ch. Wil-

Additions and Corrections, 1902.

liam b. 14 (6) 1659, Abigail, Elizabeth, Susanna b. 27 (2) 1662; these four owned the covenant 1 (5) 1677; Samuel, Cornelius, Hannah and Joseph were bapt. same day.

He died before 25 Aug. 1675, when administration was granted to the widow; she d. about 11 Nov. 1684, when her eldest son William "of Swansey" was made adm. of her estate and his father's. Signature to bond " William Salsbery."

SANKEY, Robert, rem. to Saco, Me.; died before 1642. [York Deeds.]

SAVAGE, SAVIDGE, Henry, Haverhill, propr. 1644 : rem. to Portsmouth, N. H.

SAUNDERS, Edward; one of his name was agent for Capt. Francis Champernowne in New Hampshire in 1644.

John, Ipswich, rem. to Hampton, N. H., afterwards to Wells, Me.

SEDGWICK, Robert, mar. a dau. of Mr. William and Dorothie Blake, of Andover, Eng.; recd. a legacy from Jane, widow of Richard Blake, and another from Mrs. Martha Blake, 6 (12) 1650; paid out of the latter 3 pounds to Mrs. Dorothie Smith. [A.]

SHAW, Abraham, town officer *before* 1640. propr. 1644; removed to Portsmouth, N. H.

SHEPARD, etc. John, carpenter, of Braintree, with wife Margaret, dau. of Henry Squire, late of Kinweston, near Somerton, in Somersetshire, gave letter of attorney 25 (10) 1649 to John Adams of Concord to receive dues for lands lately in occupation of Jonathan Adams, living near Ballsberry, co. Som. [A.]

SHERMAN, see wills of English relations in Reg. L. and LI.

SLEEPER, Thomas; the land which he bought of Lawson is proved by the bounds given to be at Hampton. [Suff. De. 1, 61.]

SMITH, John, of Hampton, afterward of Nantucket, made will 14 Feb. 1670; beq. to sons John and Samuel all his land on Nantucket, they to pay to their sisters Deborah and Abigail 5 pounds apiece; land at "Martins Vineyard" to son Philip not then in good health; wife Deborah executrix, and friends Mr. Thomas Mayhew and Thomas Macy overseers.

STEWARD, James, came in the Fortune to Plymouth in 1621; had land assigned in 1623.

STILEMAN, Elias, Sen. was licensed innkeeper at Salem 3 Sept. 1635. He transacted much business in lumber etc. at Piscataqua. See letters in Es. court files IX, 150-3. He d. before Nov. 7, 1662, when the inv. of his estate was filed; his widow Judith sued Rich. Hutchinson in Nov. 1663 for her thirds in certain land which had been sold. "Damaris Mansfield the daughter of our brother Stileman," was baptized at Salem March 30, 1663. [Reg. XXVIII, 206 and LI, 346.]

Richard, rem. to Portsmouth, N. H. about 1657; Jan. 1662, he deposed, æ. 51 years. [Es. files]. Ch. Mary b. Jan. 6, 1657 (m. Nathaniel Fox), Elizabeth b. May 8. [1658] (m. John Jordan), Richard b. March 20, 1667-8.

He d. Oct. 11, 1678.

STODDARD, Anthony, "the antientest shopkeeper in town." [S.]

STONE, John, fisherman, mariner, was from Chidcocke, Dorset, and certificate of his health and that of his wife Joan was taken 25(10) 1649. [A.]

SWAYNE, Elizabeth, (p. 442,) came in the "Susan and Ellen."

SYMONDS, SIMONS, Henry, was one of the members of "the church which was gathered at Lynn for Long Island." [L., P. D.]

TAYLOR, George, Lynn, made will Dec. 20, 1665, prob. 31 March, 1668; beq. to wife Elizabeth all except a legacy to servant Joseph Farr.

TILLIE, TILLY, the Boston midwife here mentioned was Alice, wife of William. [Col. Rec. 11 May, 1647, and 2 and 4 May, 1649.]

TINKHAM, TINCUM, Ephraim, had a land grant at Plymouth. Resided at Duxbury in 1647.

TUTTELL, TUTTLE, Richard; his widow m. 2d, Mr. Edward Holyoke, and sold property with him 8 Sept. 1648. [Suff. De. I, 142].

VASSALL, William, made his will 31 July, 1655, prob. 12 June, 1657. He was a son of John Vassall, gent., mariner, captain and owner of 2 ships in the fleet against the Armada, by his second wife, Anna Russell, and was born at Stepney, Mdx., 27 Aug. 1592. He m. Anna, dau. of George Kinge, of Cold Norton, co. Es.; mar. license June 9, 1613.

☞ Read Introduction and Directions to Searchers.

ADDITIONS AND CORRECTIONS, 1902.

VEAZIE, etc., William, Braintree, made Henry Newban, of Calcot in co. Rutland, and Elizabeth Veazie his attornies 3(11)1649 to take possession for him of a house in Cumley, co. Leic. now in possession of Edward Wallis. [A.]

WARD, Samuel, Hingham, sold one eighth of the bark Sea Flower 23 Aug. 1649. [A.]

WALKER, Robert, in mentioning his decease Sewall says—"a very good man."

WARE, WEARE, WEYR, Nathaniel, Haverhill, propr. 1645; dau. Hester m. 1 (9) 1647 Benjamin Sweet, of Newbury; Nathaniel [his son] b. about 1631, m. Dec. 3 or 30, 1656, Elizabeth, dau. of Richard Swain, of Hampton; John, [his son?] d. at Newb. Oct. 12, 1653.

WEBB, Richard, "of Milton, near Sittingbourne, co. Kent, cordwainer, bachelor, about 21, and Joan Ashfold, of Brenzet, maiden, about 18, daughter of Thomas Ashfold, late of the same parish, Jurat, deceased, now in the government of her mother Joan Ashfold, as is testified by her son Thomas Ashfield," had license from the bishop of Canterbury to marry, Nov. 13, 1627; to be at St. Mary Bredin's, Canterbury. Richard Webb and Mary Rowlett, of St. Martin's, Cant. had license to marry Dec. 28, 1633.

WHALE, Elizabeth, third wife of Philemon, was widow of Hugh Griffin, as stated in the will of John Moore, Sen., whose wife Elizabeth was evidently a dau. of Whale.

WHARTON, Edward, was sued in Piscataqua court in 1642 and 1644. Came to court 30 June, 1663, "to bear witness to the truth" as he said; the judges ordered him placed in the stocks, and told him there he was "a vagabond Quaker," and had him passed from constable to constable to Salem, "his habitation."

WHEELWRIGHT, Rev. John; his dau. Mary m. 1 Edward Lloyd or Lide, 2, Theodore Atkinson.

WHEELER, Joseph, Concord; Elizabeth was the first wife and Sarah the second.
Thomas, of Sandwich, co. Kent., Eng., bought land in Sandwich 30 March, 1647, of George Crispie, of Plimouth, planter. [A.]

WHITCOMB, John, Sen., died 24 (7) 1662. Agreement was made 2 Oct. 1662, between the heirs, namely the widow, Frances, and children John, Jonathan, Job, Josiah, Abigail and Mary. The widow died 17 (3) 1671. It was John, Jr., who died April 6, 1683.

WHIPPLE, elder John, Sen., deposed 28 March, 1665, æ. about 60 years. [Es. files.]

WHITE, John, of Muddy River, deposed 8 June, 1676, aged "Sixty od years." [Arch. 106, 211.]

WHITING, Rev. Samuel, was born 20 Nov. *1597.*

WHITTAKER, WHITHARE, etc., Abraham "Whithare," of Manchester, deposed 24 (9) 1663; was "about threescore years old"; his wife Mary also deposed, æ. about 30 years. A. "Whittiker," of Haverhill, with wife Elizabeth, æ. about 29 years, deposed 27 (4) 1664 about what John Godfrey said in his house; sold land 2 Sept. 1671, which he had bought of his father in law, William Simmons; wife Elizabeth consented.

WILLIAMS, Rev. Roger, was re-baptized at Providence by Holyman in 1637, after which he re-baptized Holyman and ten others. [W.]

WISWALL, John, "elder, died Aug. 16, 1687, æ. 86." [S.]

WOODBRIDGE, Rev. John, "died March 17, 1694-5, æ. 80." [S.]

WRIGHT, Edward, deposed in April, 1669, æ. about 34 years. [Mdx. files.]

WYBORNE, Thomas; in his will insert daughter Elizabeth Merritt and her dau. Deborah; sons Thomas and James W. executors.

YEOMANS, Edward, resident at Haverhill in 1652; child Edward b. 6 May, 1657. Elizabeth Yeomans, widow, mar. 9 May, 1662 [1663?], Edward Kilby. Children of Edward Yeomans b. in Haverhill, Mary b. 4 (11) 1653, Thomas b. 6 (9) 1657, Elizabeth b. 10 June, 1659, Edward b. 6 Feb. 1663. [Es. co. files.] Erroneously placed in list of Matthias Button's children in the text.

(474—a)

☞ Read Introduction and Directions to Searchers.

ADDITIONS AND CORRECTIONS TO POPE'S PIONEERS OF MASSACHUSETTS.

Second Series. November, 1904. N. B.—See First Series.

AMES, William; his dau. Hannah m. John Heiden, Jr. His widow m. (2) John Niles, and petitioned with him to Gen. Court June 12, 1663, to confirm sale of Ames estate. [Col. Rec.]

BASSETT, "William, ae. 9"; "William Bassett, son of Roger Bassett," was bapt. at Dorking, co. Surrey, 30 May, 1624; "Roger Bassett and Ann Holland" were m. at Dorking 27 April, 1623. Edward Burt, son of Hugh Burt, bapt. July 9, 1627. [C. H. P.]

BULKLEY, Rev. Peter, was b. Jan. 31, 1582.

COGSWELL, John, frm. March 3, 1635-6.

DANFORTH, Nicholas, erase from "Martha" to "1654."

FARR, George, was "sent over in addition to the six shipwrights formerly sent" by the Mass. Bay Company, from England, 26 May, 1629. [Col. Rec. I, 402.]

FAXON, Joanna, m. Sept. 7, 1647, Anthony Fisher, Jr. of Dedham.

GARDNER, Mr. Thomas, deposed 10(10)1661, aged about 69.

GULLIVER, Anthony, m. (1) Lydia, dau. of Stephen Kingsley, who joined him in deeds Feb. 27, 1656-7 and March 25, 1662, m. (2) Elinor——

HIGGINSON, Rev. Francis, was b. in 1587 or 1588; rec'd A.B. from Jesus Coll. 1609, A.M. from St. John's Coll. 1613.

HORNE, John, frm. May 18, 1631.

HULL, Robert, m. (2) Judith, widow successively of Edmund Quinsey and Moses Paine; she d. 29(1)1654.

HUTCHINSON, Susanna, was widow of *Edward*, not "William."

William, Jr., son of *Edward*, not William; his wife Anne (Marbury) was b. in 1591. Their dau. Bridget m. (1) John Sanford, (2) William Phillips.

JACOB, Nicholas, frm. 3 March, 1635-6.

KINSMAN, Robert, made will Jan. 25, 1664, prob. 28 March, 1665. Dau. Mary, wife of Usual Wardwell, and her children named Ringe; dau. Sarah, wife of Samuel Younglove, dau. Martha, wife of Jacob Foster; dau. Hannah (who later m. William Danford); dau. Tabitha; cousin Richard Nicholl; son Robert Kinsman.

MATHER, Rev. Richard, d. 23(2)1669.

MULLENS, William; his will, certified to by John Carver, Giles Heale and Christopher Joanes 2 April, 1621, was proved in London 23 July, 1621. Mullens is said in the Probate record to have been "lately of Dorking in co. Surrey." He beq. to wife Alice, sons William and Joseph, dau. Priscilla and "eldest daughter," who, as "Sara Blunden als. Mullens," was appointed to admin. the estate. [Waters' Gleanings, p. 254.] "Ruth Mullings, daughter of William Mullings,"

was bapt. at Dorking parish church 31 Oct. 1619; no other entry of this family found there.

NILES, John, m. (2) Hannah, widow of Wm. Ames. [See above.]

PAINE, Thomas, of Wrentham, etc.; insert in abstract of will "my three sons."

PAINE, Thomas, Yarmouth, frm. and deputy Plymouth Court 4 June, 1639.

PROUT, Timothy, son *Benjamin*, not "Ebenezer," d. 14 March, 1656.

QUINSEY, Mr. Edmund, widow Judith m. (2) Moses Paine, m. (3) Robert Hull. [See above.]

PRITCHARD, PRICHARD, PRITCHET, insert as a heading before "Capt. Hugh" in middle of page 373 and at top of page 374.

ROCKE, Joseph, his dau. Mary, not his "widow," m. William Clements.

ROCKWELL, William, change order of lines 3, 4 and 5.

ROSSITER, Bray, frm. May 18, 1631.

SHAW, Abraham, made will in 1640. Abraham Shawe mar. to Bridget Best at North Ouram (Halifax) Yorkshire, England, June 24, 1616. Their children baptized: Joseph, March 14, 1618; Grace, Aug. 15, 1621; Martha, Dec. 1, 1623; Maria (Mary) June 18, 1626; John, Feb. 16, 1628; John, May 23, 1630; Martha, Jan. 6, 1632. [R. K. Shaw, in Reg. xlviii, 346.]

SHERMAN, William, taxed in 1632.

SNOW, Nicholas, Genealogy in Reg. xlviii, 81.

STEPHENS, Francis, Inv. 1 April, 1669 (Rehoboth). [Plymouth Scrap-Book.]

TABOR, Philip, b. about 1605, as he deposed in 1669; deputy from Yarmouth, 1639, to Plymouth Court; m. (2) Jane ——, who survived him. Rem. to Martha's Vineyard, then to Portsmouth, R. I.; thence about 1662 to Providence, R. I.; commissioner, assessor, constable, etc. in Po. and Pr.; d. before 1682 when petition was made for yearly allowance to his widow. Ch.: Thomas, Philip, Lydia (m. Pardon Tillinghast), perhaps others.

THOMPSON, John, Plymouth, rem. to Middleborough; lieut.; d. June 16, 1696. Dau. Mary, b. 1650, m. Philip Tabor, Jr. [Gen.]

WHITMAN, John, insert in will "eldest son Thomas."

WHITMARSH, John, identical with "Whitmark." Res. at Weymouth.

WILLIS, John, add youngest son Benjamin and dau. Sarah Ames to children named in will.

WING, Daniel, m. (1) Hannah, dau. Wm. Swift, 9(5)1642; her father's inv. it was that was filed in 1659. He m. (2) 4 mo. 1666, Anne Ewer. He made will 10(3)1698; beq. to ch. Lydia Mott, David, John, Bachiler and Jashub Wing; mentions "wife."

www.ingramcontent.com/pod-product-compliance
Lightning Source LLC
Chambersburg PA
CBHW071430300426
44114CB00013B/1381